CONTENTS

FOREWORD BY THE EDITOR

Britain is endowed with a legacy of historic buildings that except in the Channel Islands no invading armies have devastated since the days of Oliver Cromwell over 300 years ago. During World War II many hotels became emergency accommodation for troops or sometimes for evacuees, but the damage was mostly confined to the removal of banisters and other wooden items for fuel during bitter war-time winters.

When war was over, hoteliers came home to be greeted by familiar ivy adorning outside walls untouched by the enemy. The old buildings still stood and the best of them still stand today. The story was sadly different in city areas flattened by the Blitz where fine new hotels have since risen from the ashes.

Today, fifty years on, there are hotels all over the British Isles that, not just in their history, but in the excellence of their hospitality rival those anywhere else in the world. The Johansens guide contains over four hundred such hotels:– ancient buildings and modern buildings, country hotels and city hotels. We have inspected all of them and we recommend them to you.

Rodney Exton, Editor

KEY TO SYMBOLS

13 rms Total number of rooms	Nombre de chambres	Anzahl der Zimmer
MasterCard accepted	MasterCard accepté	MasterCard akzeptiert
Visa accepted	Visa accepté	Visa akzeptiert
American Express accepted	American Express accepté	American Express akzeptiert
Diners Club accepted	Diners Club accepté	Diners Club akzeptiert
Quiet location	Un lieu tranquille	Ruhige Lage
Access for wheelchairs to at least one bedroom and public rooms	Accès handicapé	Zugang für Behinderte
Chef-patron	Chef-patron	Chef-patron
M 20 Meeting/conference facilities with maximum number of delegates	Salle de conférences – capacité maximale	Konferenzraum-Höchstkapazität
8 Children welcome, with minimum age where applicable	Enfants bienvenus	Kinder willkommen
Dogs accommodated in rooms or kennels	Chiens autorisés	Hunde erlaubt
At least one room has a four-poster bed	Lit à baldaquin	Himmelbett
Cable/satellite TV in all bedrooms	TV câblée/satellite dans les chambres	Satellit-und Kabelfernsehen in allen Zimmern
Direct-dial telephone in all bedrooms	Téléphone dans les chambres	Telefon in allen Zimmern
No-smoking rooms (at least one no-smoking bedroom)	Chambres non-fumeurs	Zimmer für Nichtraucher
Lift available for guests' use	Ascenseur	Fahrstuhl
Air Conditioning	Climatisée	Klimatisiert
Indoor swimming pool	Piscine couverte	Hallenbad
Outdoor swimming pool	Piscine de plein air	Freibad
Tennis court at hotel	Tennis à l'hôtel	Hoteleigener Tennisplatz
Croquet lawn at hotel	Croquet à l'hôtel	Krocketrasen
Fishing can be arranged	Pêche	Angeln
Golf course on site or nearby, which has an arrangement with hotel allowing guests to play	Golf	Golfplatz
Shooting can be arranged	Chasse	Jagd
Riding can be arranged	Équitation	Reitpferd
Hotel has a helicopter landing pad	Piste pour hélicoptère	Hubschrauberlandplatz
Licensed for wedding ceremonies	Cérémonies de noces	Konzession für Eheschliessungen

Published by
Johansens, 175-179 St John Street, London EC1V 4RP
Tel: 0171-490 3090 Fax: 0171-490 2538
Find Johansens on the Internet at: http://www.johansen.com
E-Mail: admin@johansen.u–net.com

Editor: Rodney Exton
Group Publishing Director: Andrew Warren
P.A. to Group Publishing Director: & regional editorial research: Angela Franks
Sales Director: Peter Hancock
Secretary to Sales Director: Carol Sweeney
Regional Inspectors: Christopher Bond, Geraldine Bromley, Julie Dunkley, Susan Harangozo, Joan Henderson, Marie Iversen, Pauline Mason, Nora Mitra, Mary O'Neill, Fiona Patrick, Brian Sandell
Production Manager: Daniel Barnett
Production Controller: Kevin Bradbrook
Designer: Michael Tompsett
Copywriters: Sally Sutton, Jill Wyatt, Norman Flack
Sales and Marketing Manager: Laurent Martinez
Marketing Executive: Rebecca Ford
Marketing Assistant: Samantha Lhoas

Chairman: Martin Morgan

Hobsons Publishing plc,
a subsidiary of the Daily Mail and General Trust plc

ISBN 1 86017 3381

Printed in England by St Ives plc
Colour origination by Graphic Facilities

Distributed in the UK and Europe by Biblios PDS Ltd, Partridge Green, West Sussex, RH13 8LD. In North America by general sales agent: ETL Group, New York, NY (direct sales) and The Cimino Publishing Group, INC. New York (bookstores). In Australia and New Zealand by Bookwise International, Findon, South Australia.

HOW TO USE THIS GUIDE

If you want to identify a Hotel whose name you already know, look for it in the regional indexes on pages 484–490.

If you want to find a Hotel in a particular area you can

- Turn to the Maps on page 12 and pages 477–483
- Search the Indexes by County on pages 484–490
- Look for the Town or Village where you wish to stay in the main body of the Guide. This is divided into Countries. Place names in each Country are in alphabetical order.

The Indexes list the Hotels by Counties, they also show those with facilities such as wheelchair access, conference centres, swimming, golf, etc. (Please note some recent Local Government Boundary changes).

The Maps cover all regions including London. Each Hotel symbol (a blue circle) relates to a Hotel in this guide situated in or near the location shown.

Red Triangles and Green Squares show the location of Johansens Recommended Inns and Johansens Recommended Country Houses & Small Hotels respectively. If you cannot find a suitable hotel near where you wish to stay, you may decide to choose one of these smaller establishments as an alternative. They are all listed by place names on pages 473–475.

On page 476 the names of Johansens Recommended Hotels in Europe are similarily shown in their separate countries, although as such they do not appear in this guide on any maps. All guides are obtainable from bookshops or by Johansens Freephone 0800 269397 or by using the order coupons on pages 491–496.

The Prices, in most cases, refer to the cost of one night's accommodation, with breakfast, for two people. Prices are also shown for single occupancy. These rates are correct at the time of going to press but always should be checked with the hotel.

JOHANSENS AWARDS FOR EXCELLENCE

The names of the winners of the 1997 Awards will be published in the 1998 editions of Johansens guides. The winners of the 1996 Awards are listed below. They were presented with their certificates at the Johansens Annual Awards dinner, held at The Dorchester on 30th October 1995, by Loyd Grossman.

WINNERS OF THE 1996 JOHANSENS AWARDS

Johansens Country Hotel Award for Excellence
Hambleton Hall, Oakham, Leicestershire

Johansens City Hotel Award for Excellence
42 The Calls, Leeds, West Yorkshire

Johansens Country House Award for Excellence
Penyclawdd Court, Abergavenny, Gwent

Johansens Inn Award for Excellence
The Hoste Arms, Burnham Market, Norfolk

Johansens London Hotel Award for Excellence
The Halcyon, Holland Park

Johansens Most Excellent Value for Money Award
The Steppes, Hereford, Herefordshire

Johansens Most Excellent Service Award
Kirroughtree Hotel, Newton Stewart, Wigtownshire

Johansens Most Excellent Resturant Award
The Leatherne Bottel, Goring-on-Thames, Berkshire

Candidates for awards derive from two main sources: from the thousands of Johansens guide users who send us guest survey reports commending hotels, inns and country houses in which they have stayed and from our team of twelve regional inspectors who regularly visit all properties in our guides. Guest survey report forms can be found on pages 491–496. They are a vital part of our continuous process of assessment and they are the decisive factor in choosing the value for money and the most excellent service awards.

The judges were invited from among the winners of previous years awards.

The Judges for the 1996 Awards were:-

Jonathan Slater, The Chester Grosvenor, Winner of the 1995 Johansens City Hotel Award
Martin Cummings, Amberley Castle, Winner of the 1995 Johansens Country Hotel Award
Richard de Wolf, The Lamb at Burford, Winner of the 1995 Johansens Inn Award
Brian O'Hara, Coopershill House, Winner of the 1995 Johansens Country House Award
June Slatter, Hotel Maes-Y-Neuadd, Winner of the 1995 Johansens Most Excellent Service Award

INTRODUCTION

From Hambleton Hall, Oakham, Leicestershire
Winner of the 1996 Johansens Country Hotel Award

Nowadays Johansens is indeed an impressive book. The hotels are better than ever and it's more than ever gratifying to be the 1996 Country Hotel of the Year. The increasing number of Country Hotels of quality in Britain leads me to wonder whether we might, one day, look back on 1996 as a golden age for hotel keeping.

Hoteliers are doing well because in some respcts we are bad Europeans. Our currency floated free of the Deutschmark and we do not subscribe to the "Social Chapter".

The current situation in Britain is not just good for hoteliers – it is good for their clients, as British hoteliers fight a rear guard action against the disapperance of elements of service taken for granted in former times. Help with luggage, evening turn down service, early morning tea, and room service are early casualties in the world of dwindling staff structures. In some industries one very productive, well trained or energetic person can take the place of two, but no amount of training, technology or energy can alter the fact that, if one of my receptionists is on the phone or showing a client to his or her room, I am going to need another one to handle the next arrival or phone call.

I am not comparing our situation to that elsewhere in order to gloat. I remember very well that it was the great country restaurants and hotels of France that inspired Hambleton and many others like us . I am just placing on record my satisfaction with the status quo in Britain in 1996 and my dread that those of the harmonising tendency believe that what we need in Britain is a dose of the medicine that has confined to the sick bed the hôtellerie in other parts of Europe.

Tim Hart
Owner

From 42 The Calls, Leeds, West Yorkshire
Winner of the 1996 Johansens City Hotel Award

I have genuinely tried to design and equip the sort of hotel that I would like to come across on my own travels. Design is, however, only part of the equation. The real difference between a run of the mill hotel and a special one is always to be found in the attitude of the staff. At '42' I am lucky enough to have a dedicated team who really enjoy looking after our visitors and take a genuine interest in their well-being. It is their enthusiasm and humour that have turned a building into a thriving, welcoming hotel with a character and style that is unique to '42'. It is they who have won the awards of the past five years.

These last few years have seen tremendous changes. In the first place guests nowadays are far more inclined to say what they expect of us, thereby reducing the risk of disappointment. In the second, the greater the impact of uniform and characterless chains, the greater the opportunity for individual properties, like those featured in this guide, to be recognised and appreciated.

42 The Calls has had a cracking twelve months. The Good Hotel Guide César Award 1995 was followed by the Hotel of the Year from the industry's leading journal and now being the 1996 Johansens City Hotel of the Year is the crowning glory.

Jonathan Wix
Owner

MasterCard

INTRODUCTION

From The Halcyon, Holland Park, London
Winner of the 1996 Johansens London Hotel Award.

London is a vibrant city perceived as a destination full of tradition and innovation. Those of us who work there appreciate the diversity. Londoners take pride in their city and The Halcyon today represents so much of what London offers. All of us who work at The Halcyon were thrilled to receive the Johansens London Hotel of the Year Award as we have tried to reflect the many aspects of change in this great capital city. The façade of the hotel was built in 1842 and is architecturally unique yet behind the walls we offer all the modern comforts associated with a 5 star hotel. An asset that appeals to our many regular guests is the informality. There are not many hotels in the world where you can truly feel so at ease and it is our belief that it is this environment that encourages our guests to return.

1996 was a boom year for London. MasterCard with whom Johansens is associated, sponsored the Euro '96 championship as football came home. London, like Wembley, blends the traditional with the modern. Our cultural and architectural heritage has stood the test of time to adapt to the requirements of today.

If you are planning to visit London, the Halcyon has the best of both past and present.

Robert Wauters
General Manager

From Kirroughtree House, Newton Stewart
Winner of the 1996 Johansens Most Excellent Service Award.

I am delighted to accept Johansens invitation to write this introduction to the 1997 Johansens Guide. Over my 15 years working with the McMillan family, first at Cally Palace and now at Kirroughtree, I have seen Johansens grow into one of the premier guides of its kind and it was therefore a great honour to be awarded one of its highest accolades. I would like to thank all of the guests who took the time and trouble to complete a survey report and send it to Johansens.

The visitor to Kirroughtree House soon discovers that South West Scotland is indeed a rare treasure – a quiet and peaceful place as yet relatively undiscovered, but with an excellent network of roads leading to wonderful golf courses, (including our

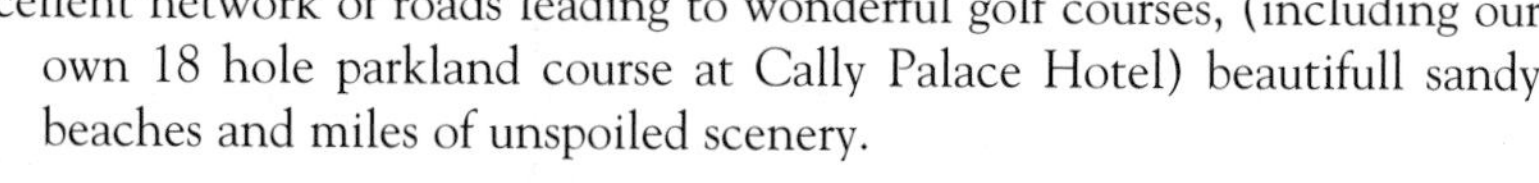

own 18 hole parkland course at Cally Palace Hotel) beautifull sandy beaches and miles of unspoiled scenery.

At Kirroughtree we are proud of our excellent food and wines, all served in beautiful surroundings in this magnificent historic house. McMillan hotels are strongly committed to giving every visitor a friendly welcome, excellent service and value for money and we are delighted that our guests should think so highly of us that they write to Johansens and praise us in sufficient numbers to merit this award.

I would like personally to thank the staff of Kirroughtree House who are so instrumental to the maintenance of such high standards. Our award belongs to them as much as to Kirroughtree House.

James Stirling
General Manager

BRUT IMPÉRIAL
MOËT & CHANDON
Turning nature into art
MOËT & CH

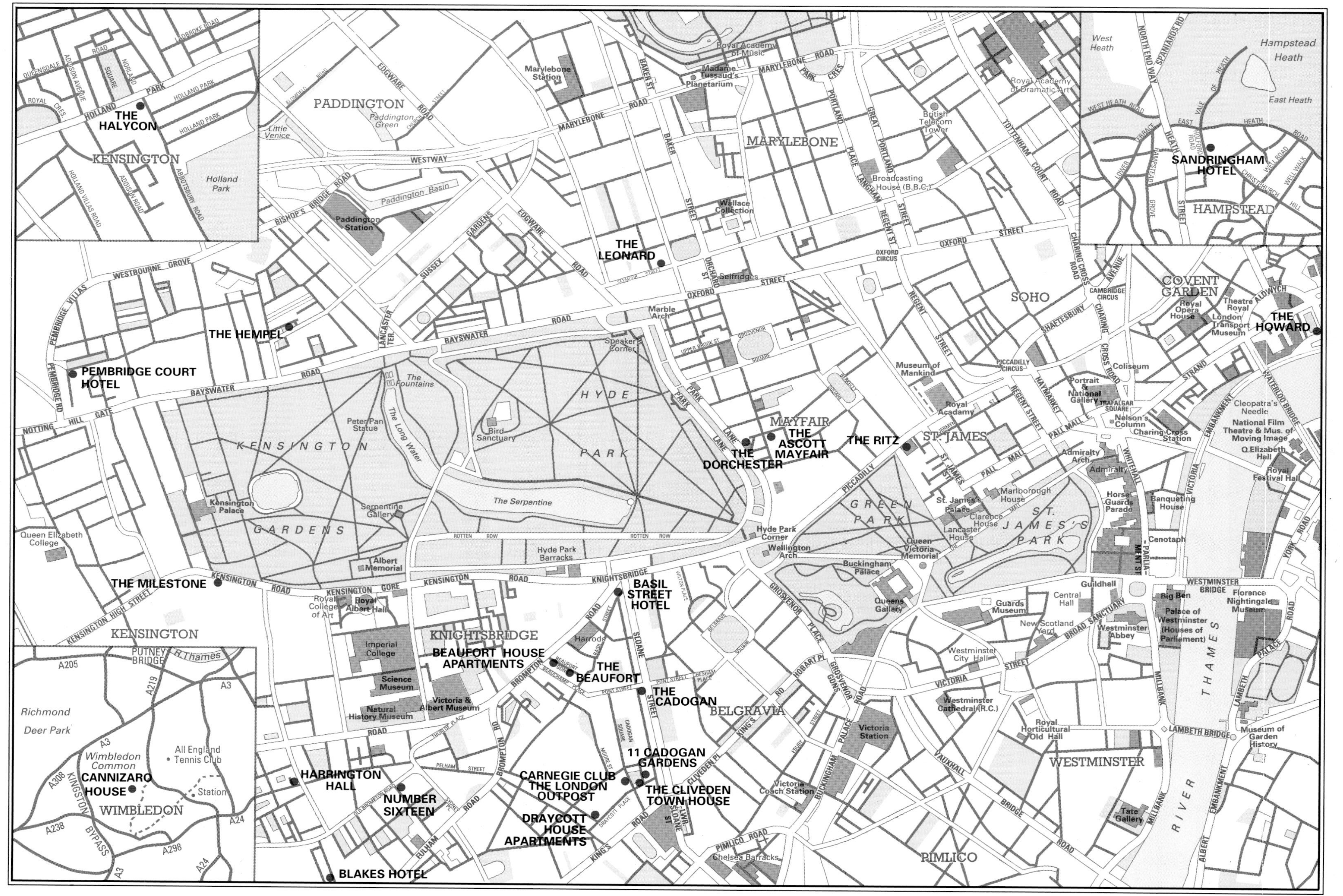

THE HALYCON
KENSINGTON
Holland Park
PADDINGTON
Paddington Station
MARYLEBONE
SANDRINGHAM HOTEL
HAMPSTEAD
Hampstead Heath
East Heath
West Heath
THE LEONARD
THE HEMPEL
PEMBRIDGE COURT HOTEL
SOHO
COVENT GARDEN
THE HOWARD
HYDE PARK
KENSINGTON GARDENS
The Serpentine
MAYFAIR
THE DORCHESTER
THE ASCOTT MAYFAIR
THE RITZ
ST. JAMES
GREEN PARK
ST. JAMES'S PARK
Buckingham Palace
THE MILESTONE
KENSINGTON
KNIGHTSBRIDGE
BASIL STREET HOTEL
BEAUFORT HOUSE APARTMENTS
THE BEAUFORT
THE CADOGAN
BELGRAVIA
11 CADOGAN GARDENS
CARNEGIE CLUB
THE LONDON OUTPOST
THE CLIVEDEN TOWN HOUSE
DRAYCOTT HOUSE APARTMENTS
HARRINGTON HALL
NUMBER SIXTEEN
BLAKES HOTEL
WESTMINSTER
PIMLICO
RIVER THAMES
Richmond Deer Park
Wimbledon Common
CANNIZARO HOUSE
WIMBLEDON
All England Tennis Club

Johansens Recommended Hotels & Apartments in London

London recommendations represent a fine selection of full service hotels, town house hotels and apartments, from the grand to the petite.

Our choice is based on location, reputation, value for money and excellence, above all else.

The Johansens guest can be comfortably accommodated within easy reach of the principal shopping areas, museums, galleries, restaurants, theatres and Wimbledon!

London is full of contrasts, a city brimming with history and pageantry and yet progressing in the fast lane to the 21st century, at the cutting edge of fashion, technology and entertainment.

At the 900-year old Tower of London, each evening the Chief Yeoman Warder in a long red coat and Tudor bonnet performs the 700-year Ceremony of the Keys*. Accompanied by an escort of Guards, he locks the main gate of the Tower of London. All along the route, the sentries and guards salute the Queen's Keys before the bugler sounds the Last Post.

Every day, hundreds of people crowd to see the changing of the guard at four royal palaces in some of the most impressive and historic ceremonies to be found anywhere in the world. At 11.00 a.m. (alternate days only in winter) the soldiers of the Household Division, usually accompanied by the regimental band, march via Birdcage Walk to Buckingham Palace, where they arrive at 11.30 a.m. to be handed the Palace Keys.

Meanwhile, only a short taxi ride away is the largest interactive attraction of its kind outside Japan. Segaworld is a £45 million futuristic indoor theme park and virtual reality centre, which opened in 1996 off Piccadilly Circus. Computer games and six high-tech rides (with a new one scheduled to be opened each year) are certain to keep youngsters white-knuckled and open-mouthed.

By contrast, travel to the Victoria & Albert Museum in South Kensington, where the Silver Galleries have re-opened with stunning displays of traditional craftsmanship. The Museum houses the National Collection of English Silver from 1300 to 1800, which includes a display of over 1500 objects illustrating the history, beauty and versatility of the material. While there, don't miss the stunning Glass Gallery with its glass staircase and glinting exhibits dating over 2,000 years of highly-skilled glassmaking.

Next-door, the New Earth Galleries at the Natural History Museum have been completely reworked – now you can tremble with fear in the Earthquake Experience, set in a recreated Japanese supermarket. Here the walls and floors shake and items fall from shelves, or you can take an escalator to a 'journey through the centre of the Earth' complete with pulsating sound and light effects. All this is a long way from looking at some fossils in a showcase.

The modern and the traditional is even evident among London's 5,000 restaurants. You can dine in style in 160 year-old Simpson's-in-the-Strand, where immaculate waiters serve from silver domed trollies. Alternatively, 'surf the net' in one of the Cyber cafes across the capital, or watch the latest stars of the big screen at Planet Hollywood, dedicated to the world of celluloid.

Nowhere are London's contrasts more striking than in the historic area of Docklands, where modern architecture has blossomed, new shops, driverless trains, state-of-the-art office blocks and the huge Canary Wharf building which dominates the East London skyline. But don't let this blind you to the Victorian pubs and 100-year old warehouses still nestling in its shadows – the real London is a combination of the two.

* This ceremony is open to members of the public – passes are essential and can be obtained by writing and enclosing a stamped addressed envelope or international reply coupon (giving as many alternative dates as possible) to:-

The Resident Governor
HM The Tower of London
EC3N 4AB

Segaworld
Trocadero
1 Piccadilly Circus
W1
Tel: 0171 734 2777

Victoria & Albert Museum
Cromwell Road
SW7
Tel: 0171 938 8500

Natural History Museum
Cromwell Road
SW7
Tel: 0171 938 9123

British Museum
Great Russell Street
WC1
Tel: 0171 636 1555

National Gallery
Trafalgar Square
WC2
Tel: 0171 839 3321

Tate Gallery
Millbank
SW1
Tel: 0171 887 8725

INFORMATION SUPPLIED BY:

London Tourist Board and Convention Bureau
26 Grosvenor Gardens
Victoria
London SW1W ODU

VISITORCALL

London Tourist Board operates a comprehensive range of recorded information services available 24 hours a day. **Visitorcall** is more than just a talking guidebook. It's updated daily to give you the lateset information on London's events, exhibitions, theatre, concerts, places to visit, sightseeing, pageantry and much more.

The **Visitorcall** service can be accessed via one general number 0839 123 456 which offers a selection of the most popular lines.

Please note that 0839 numbers are not accessible outside the UK.

THE ASCOTT MAYFAIR

49 HILL STREET, LONDON W1
TEL: 0171 499 6868 FAX: 0171 499 0705

This, the latest concept in city centre accommodation, offers all the benefits of a hotel and yet also privacy and space in what the brochure describes as "residences", with one, two or three bedrooms, in a spectacular art deco building. The apartments have a 24 hour concierge for security and assistance. A maid will be assigned to you for the full duration of your stay. There is no restaurant; however, a complimentary Continental breakfast is served on weekdays in The Terrace, overlooking the private gardens. There is an Honour Bar in The Club where guests can mingle or entertain. The Hothouse offers a gym, sauna, steamroom and solarium. The Business Service includes the use of a private boardroom. A marvellous kitchen is provided with everything necessary for entertaining in the versatile dining room. The study area has fax and computer links. The sitting room is extremely comfortable and beautifully decorated. It has satellite television, a music system and video. The luxurious bedrooms have amazing en suite bathrooms, full of soft white towels. The Ascott is in the heart of London – Mayfair being close to all the major shopping centres and best restaurants, theatre-land and sightseeing. **Directions:** Hill Street is off Berkeley Square, near Green Park Underground Station. Price guide: 1 bed from £149–£225 daily, £945–£1,420 weekly; 2 beds from £340 daily–£2,150 weekly.

56 apts MasterCard VISA AMERICAN EXPRESS M 30

For hotel location, see map on page 12

THE BEAUFORT

33 BEAUFORT GARDENS, KNIGHTSBRIDGE, LONDON SW3 1PP
TEL: 0171 584 5252 FAX: 0171 589 2834

The Beaufort offers the sophisticated traveller all the style and comfort of home – combining warm contempory colourings with the highest possible personal attention. The owner Diana Wallis (pictured below) believes that much of the success of the hotel is due to the charming, attentive staff – a feeling happily endorsed by guests. The Beaufort is situated in a quiet tree-lined square only 100 yards from Harrods and as guests arrive they are all greeted at the front door and given their own door key to come and go as they please. The closed front door gives added security and completes that feeling of home. All the bedrooms are individually decorated, with air conditioning and a great many extras such as shortbread, Swiss chocolates and brandy. The hotel owns a video and cassette library and is home to a magnificent collection of original English floral watercolours. Breakfast is brought to the bedroom – hot rolls and croissants, freshly squeezed orange juice and home-made preserves, tea and coffee. In the drawing room there is a 24-hour honour bar and between 4-5pm every day a free cream tea is served with complimentary champagne, scones, clotted cream and jam. The hotel is proud of its no tipping policy and is open all year. **Directions:** From the Harrods exit at Knightsbridge underground station take the third turning on the left. Price guide: Single £110; double/twin from £150; suites £240.

28 rms

For hotel location, see map on page 12

BASIL STREET HOTEL

BASIL STREET, LONDON SW3 1AH

TEL: 0171-581 3311 FAX: 0171-581 3693 – FROM USA CALL FREE: UTELL 1 800 448 8355

The Basil feels more like an English home than a hotel. Privately owned by the same family for three generations, this Edwardian hotel is situated in a quiet corner of Knightsbridge, on the threshold of London's most exclusive residential and shopping area. Harrods, Harvey Nichols and other famous stores are only minutes away. It is close to museums and theatres. The spacious public rooms are furnished with antiques, paintings, mirrors and *objets d'art*. The lounge, bar and dining room are on the first floor, reached by the distinctive staircase that dominates the front hall. Bedrooms, all individually furnished, vary in size, style and décor. The Hotel's Dining Room is an ideal venue either for unhurried, civilised lunch or dinner by candlelight with piano music. The Parrot Club, a lounge for the exclusive use of ladies, is a haven of rest in delightful surroundings. The Basil combines tradition and caring individual service with the comfort of a modern, cosmopolitan hotel. There is a discount scheme for regular guests, for weekends and stays of five nights or more. **Directions:** Close to Pavilion Road car park. Basil Street runs off Sloane Street in the direction of Harrods. Near Knightsbridge underground and bus routes. Price guide: Single £130–£140; double/twin £185–£195; family room £260–£270.

93 rms MasterCard VISA AMERICAN EXPRESS M 70

For hotel location, see map on page 12

BEAUFORT HOUSE APARTMENTS

45 BEAUFORT GARDENS, KNIGHTSBRIDGE, LONDON SW3 1PN
TEL: 0171 584 2600 FAX: 0171 584 6532 – USA CALL FREE: 1-800- 23-5463

Situated in Beaufort Gardens, a quiet tree-lined Regency cul-de-sac in the heart of Knightsbridge, 250 yards from Harrods, Beaufort House is an exclusive establishment comprising 22 self-contained fully serviced luxury apartments. All the comforts of a first-class hotel are combined with the privacy, discretion and the relaxed atmosphere of home. Accommodation ranges in size from an intimate one-bedroomed suite to a spacious, four-bedroomed apartment. Each apartment has been individually decorated in a contemporary style to a standard which is rigourously maintained. All apartments have satellite TV and video facilities. Most bedrooms benefit from en-suite bathrooms and several have west facing balconies. The fully fitted and equipped kitchens include washers/dryers; many have microwaves and dishwashers. A daily maid service is included at no additional charge. Full laundry/dry cleaning services are available. For your added security, a concierge is on call 24 hours a day, through whom taxis, theatre tickets, restaurant reservations and other services are also available. Executive support services are provided with confidentiality assured at all times. Complimentary membership to Champney's 'The London Club' is offered to all guests for the duration of their stay. **Directions:** Beaufort Gardens leads off Brompton road. Price Guide: From £121 per night.

For hotel location, see map on page 12

BLAKES HOTEL

33 ROLAND GARDENS, LONDON SW7 3PF
TEL: 0171 370 6701 FAX: 0171 373 0442 FROM USA CALL FREE: 1 800 926 3173

Anouska Hempel, the celebrated London hotelier and fashion designer, created Blakes to offer style and elegance to the travelled connoisseur – and convenience and efficiency to the international business man or woman. *Architectural Digest* described Blakes as 'bedrooms and suites, each a fantasy created with antiques, paintings, rare silks and velvets'. Blakes is just a 5-minute walk through the leafy streets of South Kensington to London's new centre of smart shops in Brompton Cross and a 5-minute taxi ride from Harrods. Its restaurant is one of the finest in London, open till midnight, providing 24-hour room service. If travelling on business, you can have a fax in your room, full secretarial facilities, courier service, CNN and other satellite television stations. *Architectural Digest* admiringly called Blakes 'Anouska Hempel's celebrated London refuge'. It is much more than that. It is a delight for all six senses. **Directions:** Roland Gardens is a turning off Old Brompton Road. South Kensington Underground is 5 minutes' walk. Price guide: Single £135; double/twin £175–£330; suite £520–£730.

50 rms MasterCard VISA AMERICAN EXPRESS M 22

For hotel location, see map on page 12

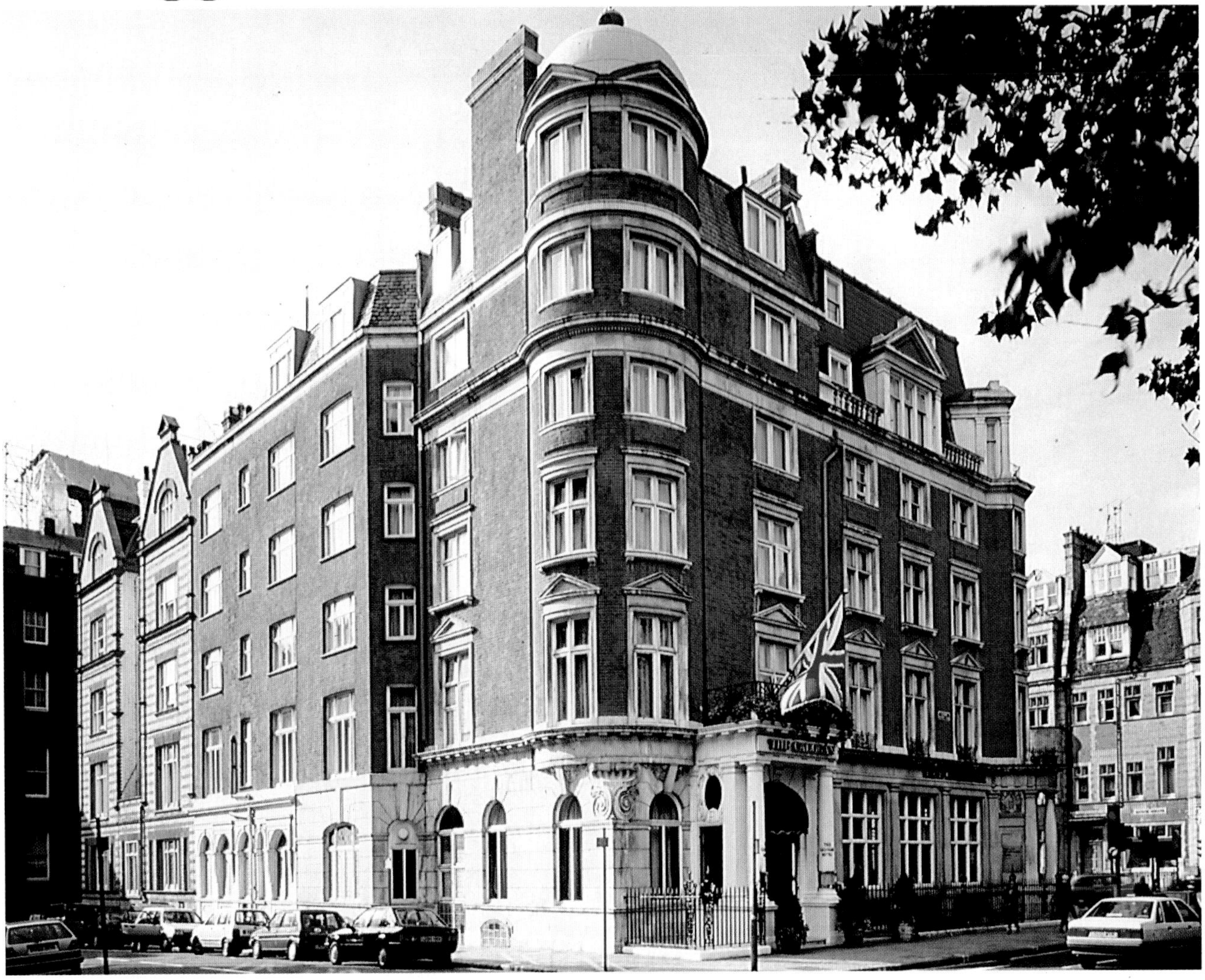

THE CADOGAN

SLOANE STREET, LONDON SW1X 9SG
TEL: 0171-235 7141 FAX: 0171-245 0994
FROM THE USA CALL TOLL FREE: Prima Hotels: 800 447 7462; Utell International 1800 44 UTELL

The Cadogan is an imposing late-Victorian building in warm terracotta brick situated in a most desirable location in Sloane Street, Knightsbridge. It is well known for its association with Lillie Langtry, the 'Jersey Lily', actress and friend of King Edward VII, and her house in Pont Street now forms part of the hotel. Playwright and wit Oscar Wilde was a regular guest at The Cadogan. The Cadogan's elegant drawing room is popular for afternoon tea and the meals served in the restaurant combine imaginatively prepared food with value for money. The hotel has 65 comfortable bedrooms and suites all equipped to the highest standards. The Langtry Rooms on the ground floor, once the famous actress's drawing room, make a delightful setting for private parties, wedding receptions and small meetings. The hotel is an excellent base for shopping trips being close to Harrods, Harvey Nichols and Peter Jones. Business visitors will find its central position and easy access make it a most acceptable place to stay when visiting London. **Directions:** The hotel is halfway along Sloane Street at the junction with Pont Street. Price guide: Single £135–£175; double/twin £165–£190; studios/suites £230–£275.

For hotel location, see map on page 12

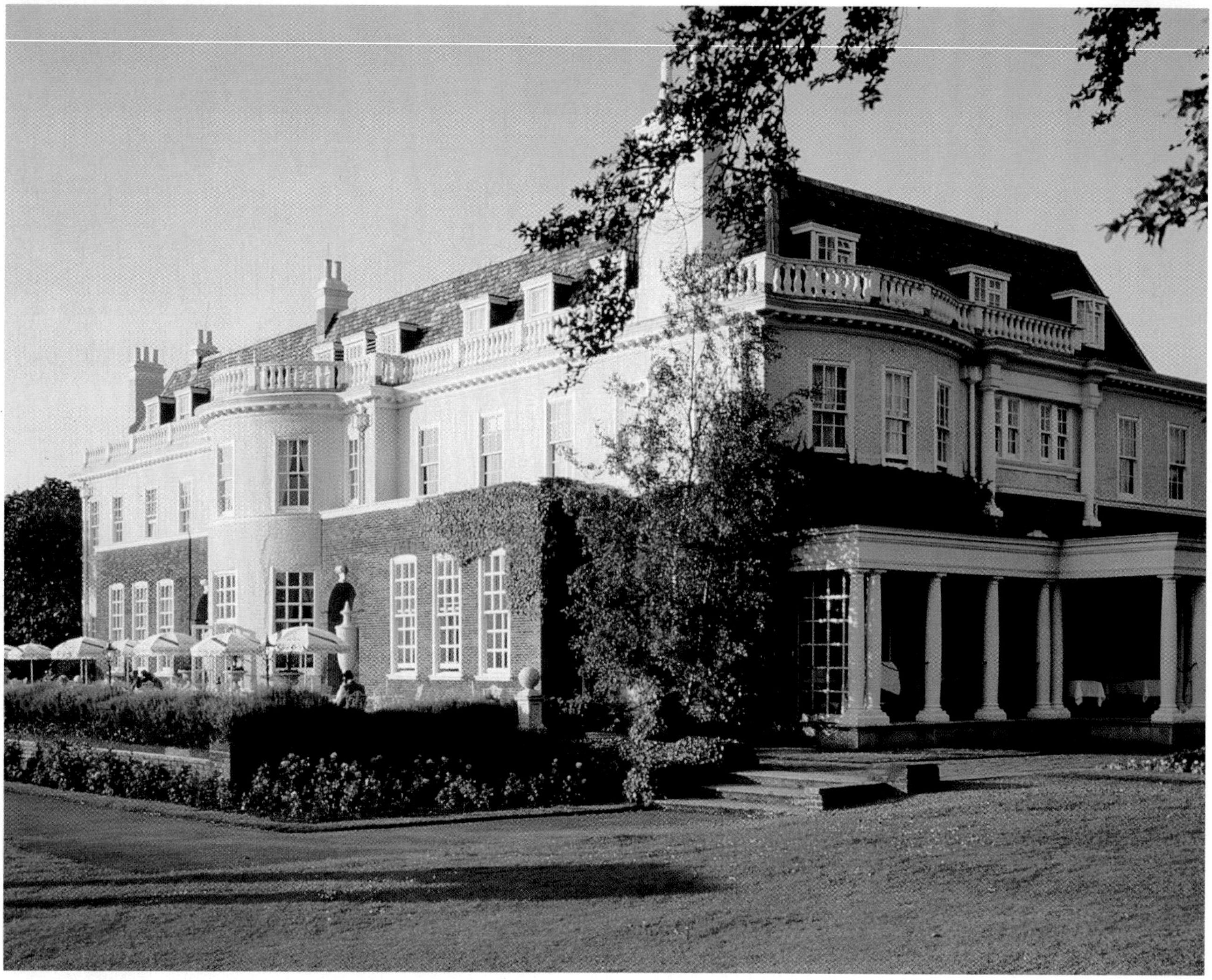

CANNIZARO HOUSE

WEST SIDE, WIMBLEDON COMMON, LONDON SW19 4UE
TEL: 0181 879 1464 FAX: 0181 879 7338

Cannizaro House, an elegant Georgian Country House, occupies a tranquil position on the edge of Wimbledon Common, yet is only 20 minutes by train from central London. Cannizaro House has, throughout its long and rich history, welcomed royalty and celebrities such as George III, Oscar Wilde and William Pitt, and is now restored as a hotel which offers the very highest standards of hospitality. The aura of the 18th century age is reflected in the ornate fireplaces and plaster mouldings, gilded mirrors and many antiques in the hotel. All of the hotel's 46 bedrooms are individually designed, with many overlooking beautiful Cannizaro Park. Several intimate rooms are available for meetings and private dining, including the elegant Queen Elizabeth Room – a popular venue for Wedding Ceremonies. The newly refurbished Viscount Melville Room offers air-conditioned comfort for up to 100 guests. Ray Slade, General Manager of Cannizaro House for many years, ensures the high standard of excellence for which the hotel is renowned, are consistently met. The award-winning kitchen produces the finest modern and classical cuisine, complemented by an impressive list of wines. **Directions:** The nearest tube and British Rail station is Wimbledon. Price guide: Single from £135; double/twin from £165; suite from £250. Special weekend rates available.

For hotel location, see map on page 12

THE LONDON OUTPOST OF THE CARNEGIE CLUB

69 CADOGAN GARDENS, LONDON SW3 2RB
TEL: 0171 589 7333 FAX: 0171 581 4958

The London Outpost of The Carnegie Club is ideally situated between Harrods and Kings Road, The Outpost was once an elegant private house and has been beautifully and sympathetically restored to its former greatness. All 11 en suite bedrooms of various sizes are fully air-conditioned and have every modern amenity. The atmosphere is relaxed and the ambience excellent. There are fine oil paintings and prints by 18th and 19th century English masters and the magnificently decorated rooms are furnished with period English antiques. Room service breakfast is served from 7am to 2pm and light meals and supper can also be enjoyed by guests in the privacy of their own rooms. Whilst only members of the Carnegie Club at Skibo Castle, the Country Club at Stapleford Park and the London Outpost itself have exclusive use of the library, snooker room and delightful conservatory, the relaxing surroundings of the drawing room are available to everyone. Guests have the use of the gymnasium and beauty rooms at nearby Number Eleven Cadogan Gardens and private access to the gardens opposite. The fashionable shops and first-class restaurants of Knightsbridge and Belgravia are within easy walking distance. Theatre tickets can be arranged. **Directions:** Nearest tube is Sloane Square. Price guide (excluding VAT): Single £150; suite £235.

For hotel location, see map on page 12

THE CLIVEDEN TOWN HOUSE

26 CADOGAN GARDENS, LONDON SW3 2RP
TEL: 0171 730 6466 FAX: 0171 730 0263 FROM USA TOLL FREE 1 800 747 4942

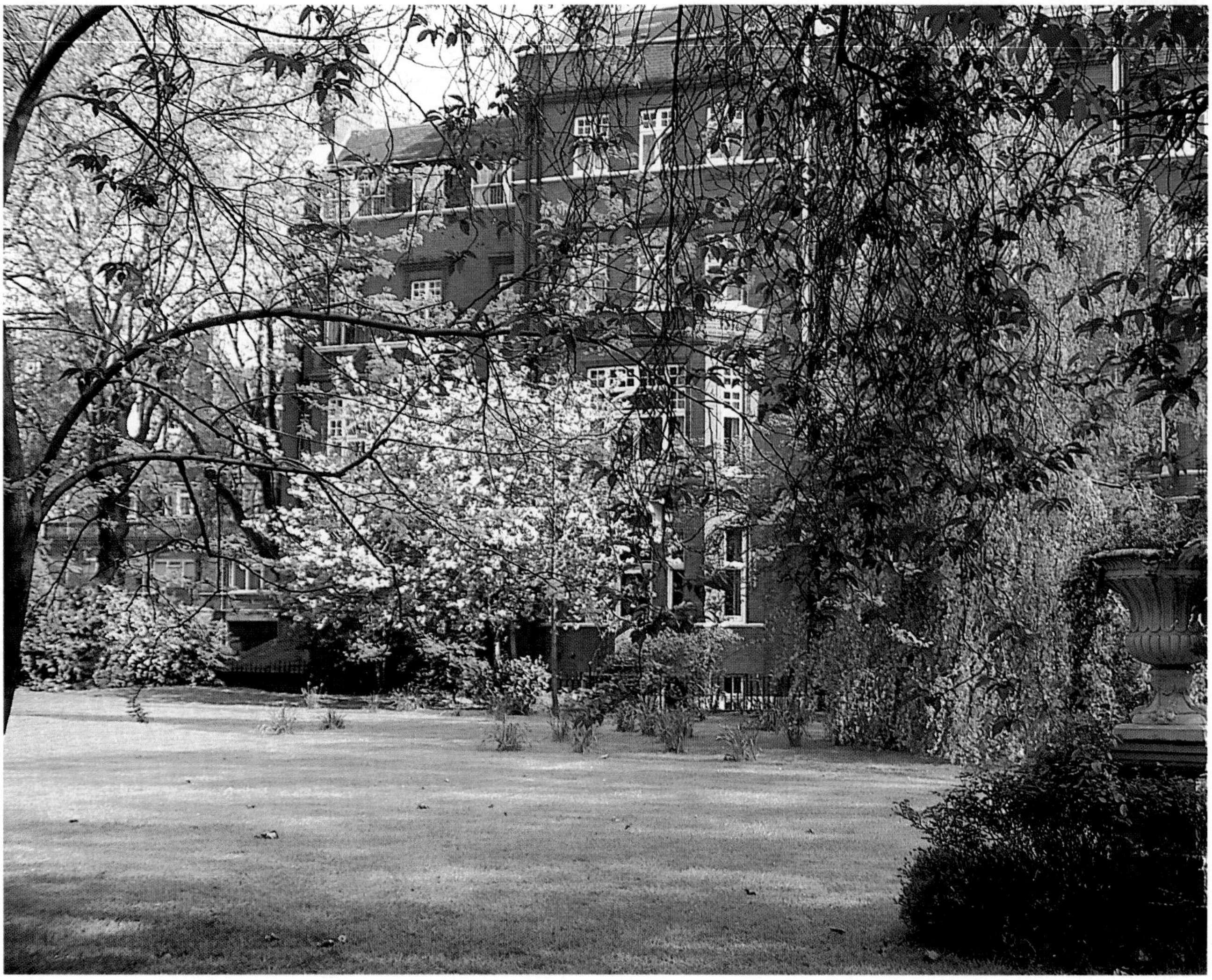

The Cliveden Town House overlooks one of London's most tranquil, tree-lined private garden squares between Harrods and Kings Road and is a paragon of good taste and elegance, offering the sophisticated traveller all the comfort, luxury and style of the grand private residence. It also reflects the gracious standards of its country cousin at Cliveden, one of England's most famous stately homes with its five Red AA stars. Recent renovation, refurbishment and redecoration were undertaken by the interior designers who successfully transformed Cliveden and the expertise of General Manager Michael Holiday, Butler and House Manager at Cliveden for 10 years, now creates the identical exclusive Cliveden atmosphere in The Cliveden Town House. Spacious rooms splendidly decorated, combine with the highest possible service and personal attention. The luxurious bedrooms and suites are beautifully and lavishly furnished in a variety of styles and all have air conditioning, satellite television, stereo video, CD players, dedicated fax lines and voice mail. A waiter, maid, valet or chauffeur come at the touch of a button and nanny and baby sitting services can be arranged. Knightsbridge is within walking distance, the West End within easy reach. **Directions:** Nearest tube is Sloane Square. Price guide: Single £110, double £195-£250; suite £310.

For hotel location, see map on page 12

THE DORCHESTER

PARK LANE, MAYFAIR W1A 2HJ
TEL: 0171 629 8888 FAX: 0171 409 0114 TELEX: 887704

The Dorchester first opened its doors in 1931, offering a unique experience which almost instantly became legendary. Its reopening in November 1990 after an extensive refurbishment marked the renaissance of one of the world's grand hotels. Its history has been consistently glamorous; from the early days a host of outstanding figures has been welcomed, including monarchs, statesmen and celebrities. The architectural features have been restored to their original splendour and remain at the heart of The Dorchester's heritage. The 192 bedrooms and 52 suites have been luxuriously designed in a variety of materials, furnishings and lay-outs. All bedrooms are fully air-conditioned and have spectacular Italian marble bathrooms. There are rooms for non-smokers and some equipped for the disabled. In addition to The Grill Room, there is The Oriental Restaurant where the accent is on Cantonese cuisine. Specialised health and beauty treatments are offered in The Dorchester Spa with its statues, Lalique-style glass and water fountain. A series of meeting rooms, with full supporting services, is available for business clientèle. As ever, personalised care is a pillar of The Dorchester's fine reputation. **Directions:** Toward the Hyde Park Corner/Piccadilly end of Park Lane. Price guide excluding VAT: Single £225–£250; double/twin £250–£280; suite £400–£1,600.

For hotel location, see map on page 12

DRAYCOTT HOUSE APARTMENTS

10 DRAYCOTT AVENUE, CHELSEA, LONDON SW3 3AA
TEL: 0171-584 4659 FAX: 0171-225 3694

Draycott House stands in a quiet, tree-lined avenue in the heart of Chelsea. Housed in an attractive period building, the apartments have been designed in individual styles to provide the ideal surroundings for a private or business visit, combining comfort, privacy and security with a convenient location. All are spacious, luxury, serviced apartments, with three, two or one bedrooms. Some have private balconies, a roof terrace and overlook the private courtyard garden. Each apartment is fully equipped with all home comforts; cable television, video, radio/cassette, a private direct line for telephone/fax/answer machine. Complimentary provisions on arrival, milk and newspapers delivered daily. Daily maid service Monday to Friday. In-house laundry room and covered garage parking. Additional services, laundry and dry cleaning services. On request cars, airport transfers, catering, travel and theatre arrangements, child minders and an introduction to an exclusive health club. The West End is within easy reach. Knightsbridge within walking distance. **Directions:** Draycott House is situated on the corner of Draycott Avenue and Draycott Place, close to Sloane Square. Price guide: from £988–£2402 +VAT per week: £156-£377 +VAT per night. Long term reservations may attract preferential terms.

For hotel location, see map on page 12

HARRINGTON HALL

5-25 HARRINGTON GARDENS, LONDON SW7 4JW
TEL: 0171 396 9696 FAX: 0171 396 9090

The original façade of late Victorian houses cleverly conceals a privately owned hotel of substantial proportions and contempory comfort. Harrington Hall offers 200 air-conditioned luxury bedrooms which have been most pleasantly furnished to the highest international standards and include an extensive array of facilities. A lovely marble fireplace is the focal point in the comfortable and relaxing Lounge Bar, where guests can enjoy a drink in elegant surroundings. The restaurant's mixture of classical decoration and dramatic colour creates a delightful setting for the appreciation of fine cuisine. A choice of buffet or à la carte menu is available, both offering a tempting selection of dishes. Ten fully air conditioned conference and banqueting suites, with walls panelled in rich lacewood and solid cherry, provide a sophisicated venue for conferences, exhibitions or corporate hospitality. Harrington Hall also has a Business Centre for the exclusive use of its guests, along with a private Fitness Centre with multigym, saunas and showers. **Directions:** Harrington Hall is situated in the Royal Borough of Kensington and Chelsea, in Harrington Gardens south of the Cromwell Road, close to Gloucester Road underground station, two stops from Knightsbridge and Harrods. Price guide: Single £140; double £140; suites £175 (including VAT & service).

200 rms

M 250

For hotel location, see map on page 12

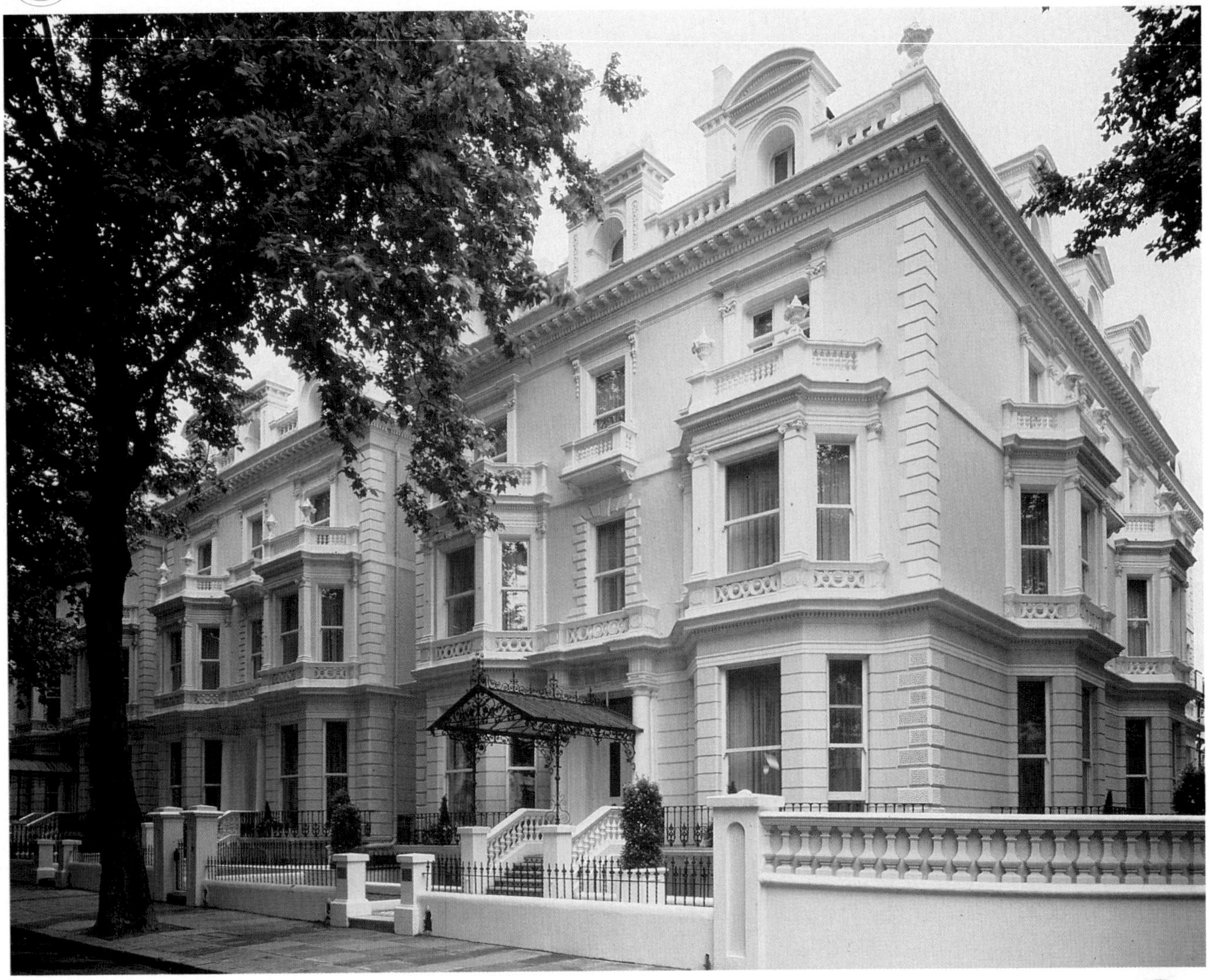

THE HALCYON

81 HOLLAND PARK, LONDON W11 3RZ
TEL: 0171 727 7288 FAX: 0171 229 8516 E-MAIL: 101712.2063@CompuServe.COM

This small, exclusive hotel in Holland Park, winner of Johansens Most Excellent London Hotel Award 1996, offers an exceptional standard of accommodation and service. Essentially a large Town House, its architecture has been meticulously restored to the splendour of the Belle Epoque to take its place amongst the many imposing residences in the area. The generous proportions of the rooms, along with the striking individuality of their furnishings, creates the atmosphere of a fine country house. Each of the bedrooms and suites has been beautifully furnished and has every modern amenity. All have marble bathrooms and several boast a Jacuzzi. A splendid restaurant, opening onto a ornamental garden and patio, serves distinctive international cuisine complemented by a well chosen wine list. The adjoining bar provides a relaxing environment to enjoy a cocktail and meet with friends. The Halcyon prides itself on offering a superb service and ensuring guests absolute comfort, privacy and security. Secretarial, Internet and fax facilities are all available. London's most fashionable shopping areas, restaurants and West End theatres are all easily accessible from The Halcyon. Directions: From Holland Park tube station, turn right. The Halcyon is on the left after the second set of traffic lights. Price guide: Single from £195; double/twin from £245; suite from £275.

For hotel location, see map on page 12

THE HEMPEL

HEMPEL GARDEN SQUARE, 31-35 CRAVEN HILL GARDENS, LONDON W2 3EA
TEL: 0171 298 9000; FAX: 0171 402 4666

The celebrated London hotelier and fashion designer Anouska Hempel has created The Hempel in a an elegant, modernistic style that will appeal to the connoisseur. Situated within easy reach of London's many attractions and with 50 delightful bedrooms and serviced apartments, the hotel with its Georgian facade is influenced by the stillness and the simplicity of the Orient, the grandeur of Italy and the best of the West's high-tech and comfort facilities. The Hempel is exotic, monochromatic and full of surprises – tapwater that is lit at night, an open fireplace that appears to float, a mix of light and shadow that can keep guests guessing and pondering on just how this can be real. The huge atrium within the lobby is breathtaking. A delicious mix of Italian-Thai and Japanese food, devised by Anouska Hempel is presented with style and flair in the I-Thai restaurant. Guests enjoying a pre-dinner drink in The Shadow Bar are surrounded by illusion and fantasy as The Hempel aims to take them out of this world and make their dreams a reality. **Directions:** The Hempel is situated in Bayswater within a short walk of Kensington Gardens and Hyde Park. Paddington railway station with Lancaster Gate and Queensway underground railway stations nearby. Price guide: Room from £205; suite from £411; apartment from £611.

50 rms

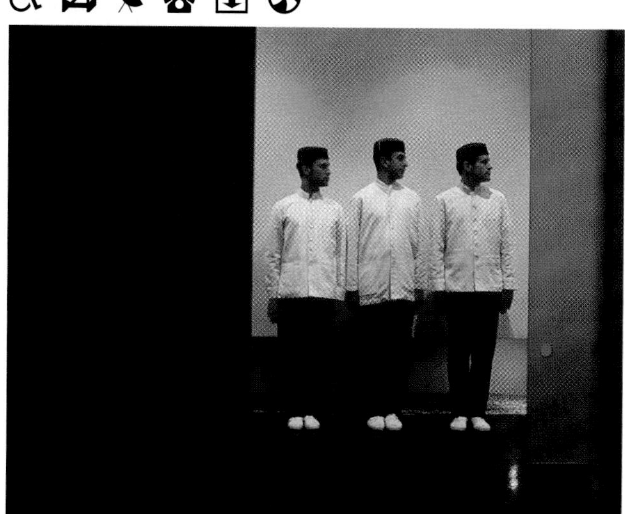

For hotel location, see map on page 12

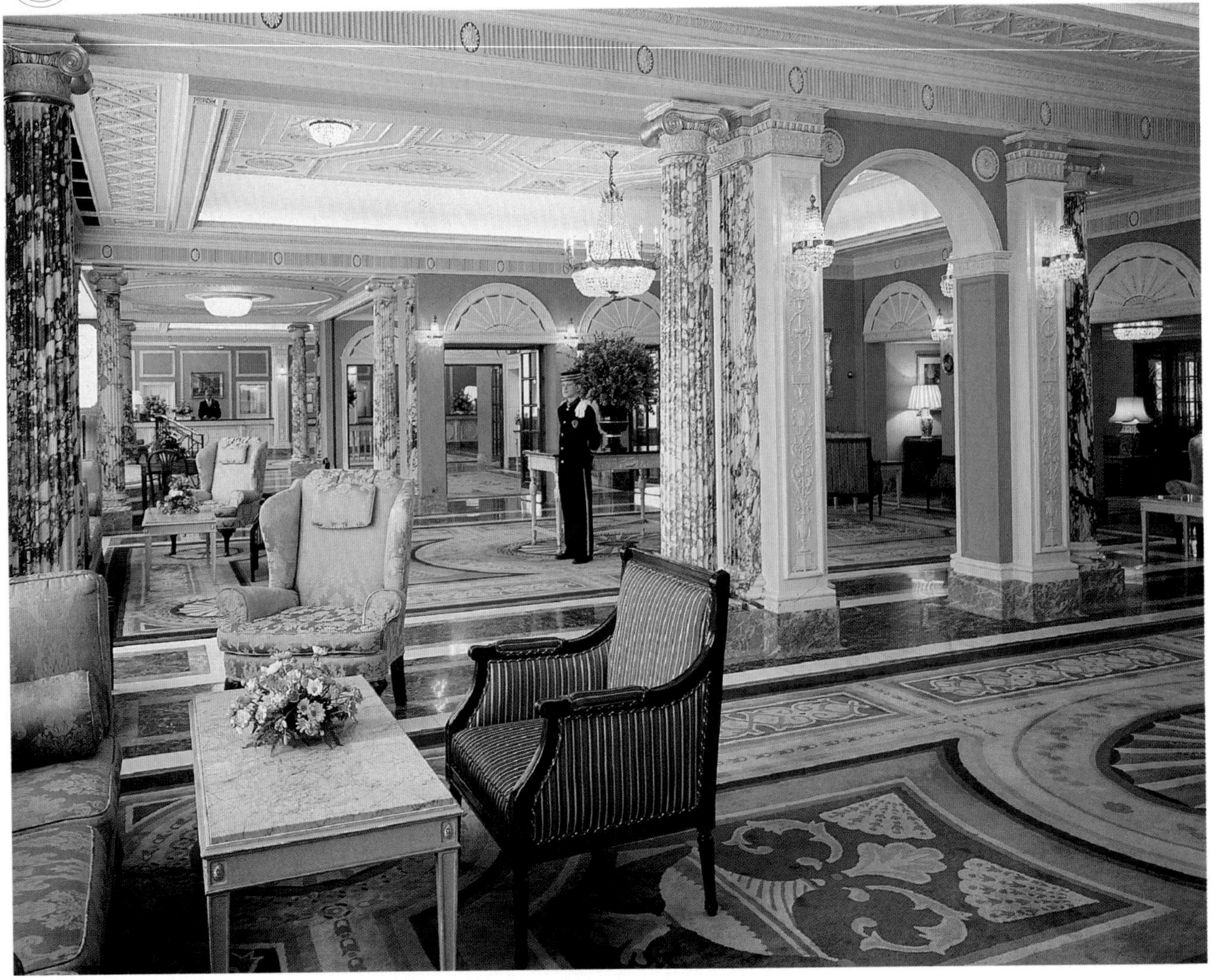

THE HOWARD

TEMPLE PLACE, THE STRAND, LONDON WC2R 2PR

TEL: 0171 836 3555 FAX: 0171 379 4547 FROM USA TOLL FREE: BTH Hotels 1 800 221 1074

Situated where the City meets the West End, The Howard Hotel is ideal for business and leisure. With décor that echoes the grace of yesteryear, the hotel's interiors are charmingly furnished. Guests can enjoy first-class accommodation, service and cuisine. The air-conditioned bedrooms, many of which have panoramic views across the River Thames, feature French marquetry furniture, marbled bathrooms, satellite television, a fridge-bar and 24-hour room service. One can relax with an aperitif in the elegant Temple Bar prior to savouring the superb International cuisine in the famous Quai d'Or Restaurant, with its domed ceiling and Renaissance decor. A variety of suites and conference rooms cater for up to 200 people. The rooms are equally suitable for dinner parties, luncheons, conferences and meetings. Full secretarial support services can be provided. The Howard's sister hotel, The Mirabeau in Monte Carlo, offers luxurious accommodation and is situated overlooking the sea. **Directions:** On the Embankment overlooking the River Thames, 14 miles from Heathrow, 1 mile from Charing Cross station. Temple underground opposite the hotel. Price guide: Single £230; double/twin £250; suite £275–£495.

For hotel location, see map on page 12

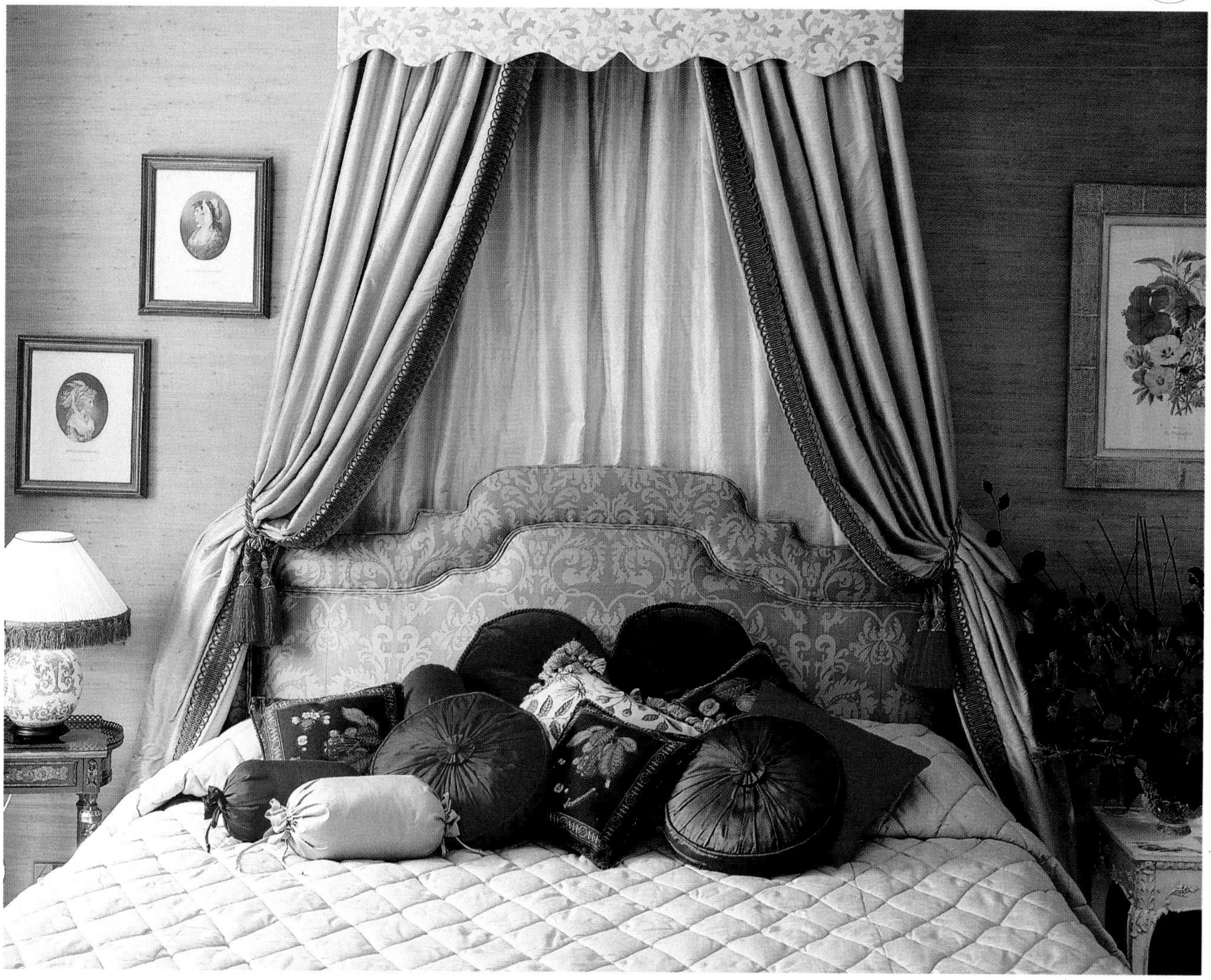

THE LEONARD

15 SEYMOUR STREET, LONDON W1H 5AA
TEL: 0171 935 2010 FAX: 0171 935 6700

Four late 18th century Georgian town houses set the character of this exciting new property which opened in 1995 and has already proved to be extremely popular with Johansens guests. Imaginative reconstruction created five rooms and twenty suites decorated individually to a very high standard. Wall coverings present striking colours, complemented by exquisite French furnishing fabrics creating a warm luxurious atmosphere. All rooms are fully air-conditioned and include a private safe, mini-bar, hi-fi system and provision for a PC/fax. Bathrooms are finished in marble and some of the larger suites have a butler's pantry or fully-equipped kitchen. For physical fitness and stress reductions there is an up-to-date exercise room. Experienced staff ensure that guests can enjoy the highest level of attention and service. Breakfast is available in the morning room and light meals are served throughout the day. 24-hour room service is also available. There are, of course, many good restaurants nearby. The Wallace Collection is just a short walk away and one of London's premier department stores, Selfridges, is round the corner in Oxford Street. **Directions:** The Leonard is on the south side of Seymour Street which is just north of Marble Arch and runs west off Portman Square. Car parking in Bryanston Street. Price guide: Double £140–£180; suites £200–£320.

For hotel location, see maps on page 12

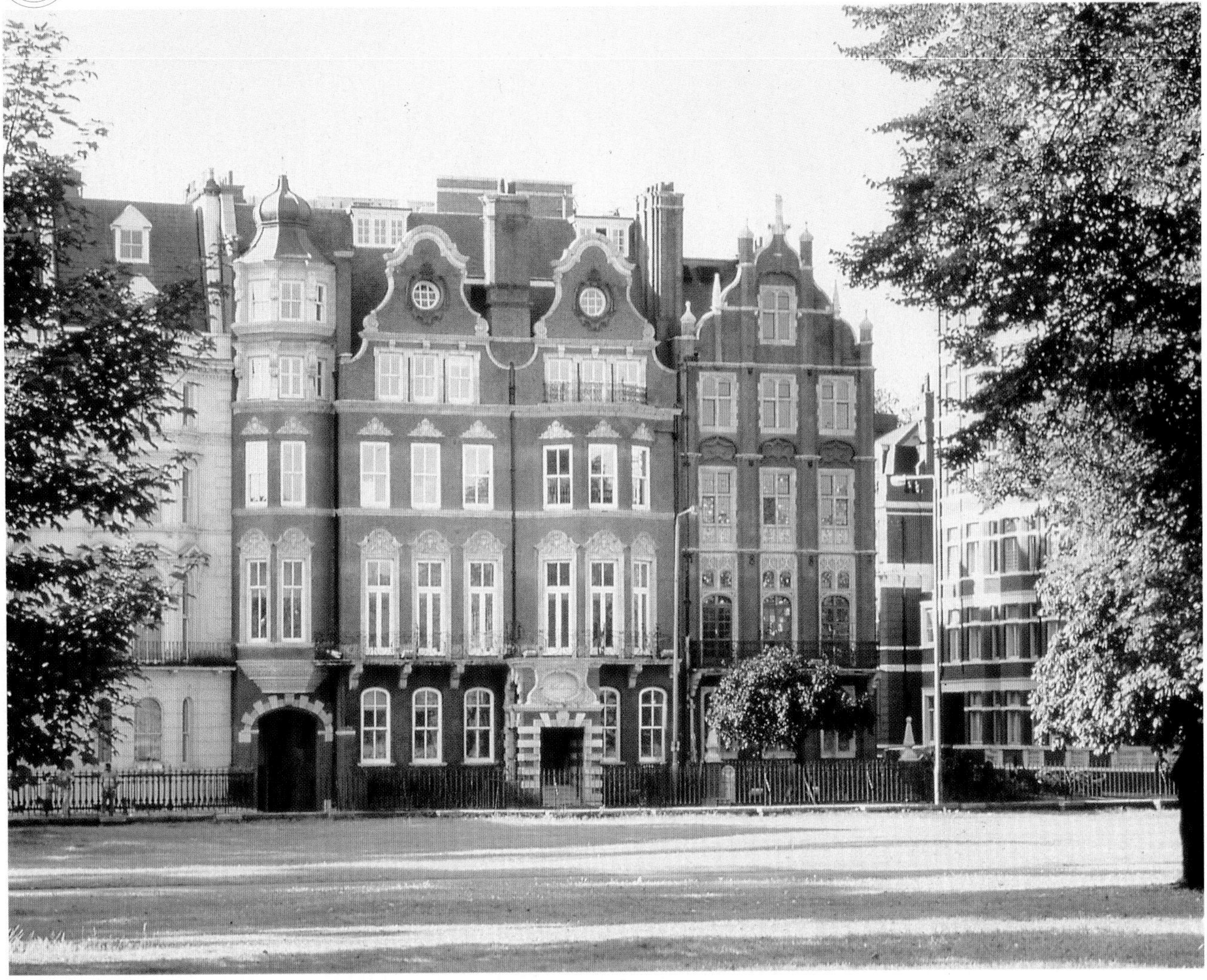

THE MILESTONE

1–2 KENSINGTON COURT, LONDON W8 5DL

TEL: 0171 917 1000 FAX: 0171 917 1010 FROM USA TOLL FREE 1 800 854 7092

The new and luxurious Milestone Hotel is situated opposite Kensington Palace. It enjoys uninterrupted views over Kensington Gardens and a remarkable vista of the royal parklands. A Victorian showpiece, this unique mansion has been meticulously restored to its original splendour while incorporating every modern facility. The 45 rooms and 12 suites are unusual in design, with antiques, elegant furnishings and private balconies. Guests may relax in the comfortable, panelled Park Lounge, which offers a 24-hour lounge service and menu. Cheneston's, the hotel's exceptional restaurant, has an elaborate carved ceiling, original fireplace, ornate windows, panelling and an oratory, which can be used for private dining. The exciting and innovative menu presents the latest in modern international cuisine. Stables Bar, fashioned after a traditional gentlemen's club, makes a convivial meeting place. The health and fitness centre offers guests the use of a solarium, spa bath, sauna and gymnasium. Some of London's finest shops and monuments are within walking distance. **Directions:** At the end of Kensington High Street, at the junction with Princes Gate. Price guide: Single from £220; double/twin £270; suites from £330–£450.

For hotel location, see map on page 12

NUMBER ELEVEN CADOGAN GARDENS

11 CADOGAN GARDENS, SLOANE SQUARE, KNIGHTSBRIDGE, LONDON SW3 2RJ
TEL: 0171-730 3426 FAX: 0171-730 5217

Number Eleven Cadogan Gardens was the first of the exclusive private town house hotels in London and now, with the addition of its own in-house gymnasium and beauty rooms it continues to take the lead. Number Eleven remains traditional; no reception desk, no endless signing of bills, total privacy and security. It also offers the services you have a right to expect in the 1990s: round-the-clock room service, a chauffeur-driven Mercedes for airport collection and sightseeing, and a private room which can accommodate 12 for a meeting. Another attraction is the Garden Suite, with a large double bedroom and a spacious drawing room overlooking the gardens. The hotel occupies four stately Victorian houses tucked away between Harrods and Kings Road in a quiet, tree-lined square. Wood-panelled rooms, hung with oil-paintings, are furnished with antiques and oriental rugs in a traditional understated style. The fashionable shops and first-class restaurants of Knightsbridge, Chelsea and Belgravia are within easy walking distance. Theatre tickets can be arranged. **Directions:** Off Sloane street. Nearest underground is Sloane Square. Price guide: Single from £100; double/twin from £155; suite from £250. (Excluding VAT)

60 rms · MasterCard · VISA · American Express · Diners · M 15

For hotel location, see map on page 12

NUMBER SIXTEEN

16 SUMNER PLACE, LONDON SW7 3EG
TEL: 0171 589 5232 FAX: 0171 584 8615

A passer-by may wonder what lies behind the immaculate pillared façade of Number Sixteen. Upon entering the hotel visitors will find themselves in an atmosphere of seclusion and comfort which has remained virtually unaltered in style since its early Victorian origins. The staff are friendly and attentive, regarding each visitor as a guest in a private home. The relaxed atmosphere of the lounge is the perfect place to pour a drink from the bar and meet friends or business associates. A fire blazing in the drawing room in cooler months creates an inviting warmth, whilst the conservatory opens on to a beautiful secluded walled garden which once again has won many accolades and awards for its floral displays. Each spacious bedroom is decorated with a discreet combination of antiques and traditional furnishings. The rooms are fully appointed with every facility that the discerning traveller would expect. A light breakfast is served in the privacy of guests' rooms and a tea and coffee service is available throughout the day. Although there is no dining room at Number Sixteen, some of London's finest restaurants are just round the corner. The hotel is close to the West End, Knightsbridge, Chelsea and Hyde Park. **Directions:** Sumner Place is off Old Brompton Road near Onslow Square. South Kensington Underground Station is 2 minutes' walk away. Price guide: Single £80–£105; double/twin £140–£170.

36 rms · MasterCard · VISA · AMERICAN EXPRESS · Diners · 12

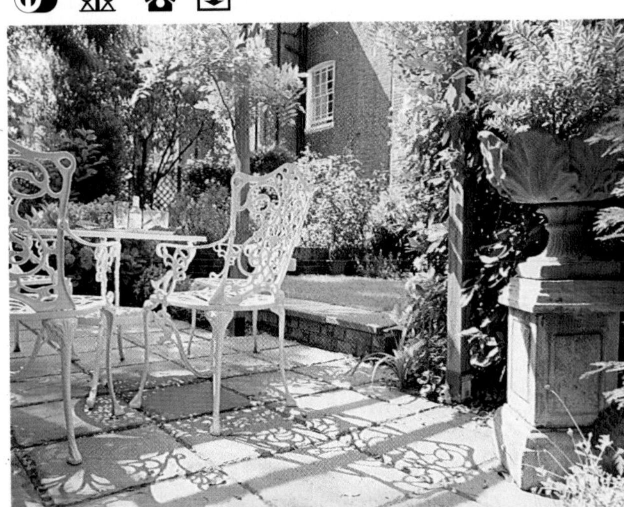

For hotel location, see map on page 12

PEMBRIDGE COURT HOTEL

34 PEMBRIDGE GARDENS, LONDON W2 4DX

TEL: 0171 229 9977 FAX: 0171 727 4982 – FROM USA TOLL FREE 1 800 709 9882

This gracious Victorian town house has been lovingly restored to its former glory whilst providing all the modern facilities demanded by today's discerning traveller. The 20 rooms are individually decorated with pretty fabrics and the walls adorned with an unusual collection of framed fans and Victoriana. The Pembridge Court is renowned for the devotion and humour with which it is run. Its long serving staff and its two famous cats "Spencer" and "Churchill" assure you of an immensely warm welcome and the very best in friendly, personal service. Over the years the hotel has built up a loyal following amongst its guests, many of whom regard it as their genuine 'home from home' in London. Winner of the 1994 RAC Award for Best Small Hotel in the South East of England, the Hotel is situated in quiet tree-lined gardens just off Notting Hill Gate, an area described by Travel & Leisure magazine as 'one of the liveliest, most prosperous corners of the city. "The Gate" as is affectionately known, is certainly lively, colourful and full of life with lots of great pubs and restaurants and the biggest antiques market in the world at nearby Portobello Road. **Directions:** Pembridge Gardens is a small turning off Notting Hill Gate/Bayswater Road, just 2 minutes from Portobello Road Antiques Market. Price guide: Single £100–£130; twin £125; deluxe double £150–£170

20 rms

For hotel location, see map on page 12

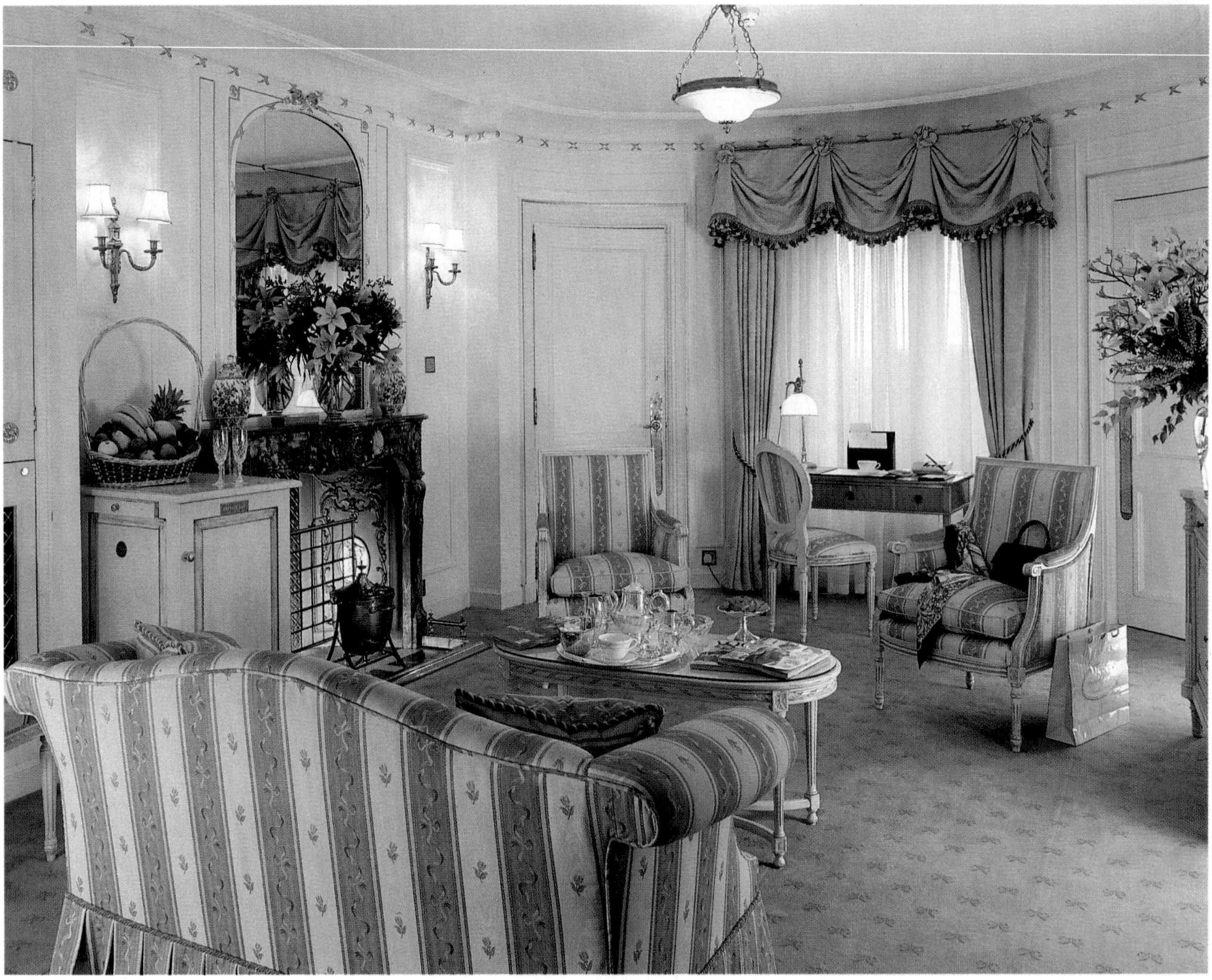

THE RITZ

150 PICCADILLY, LONDON W1V 9DG
TEL: 0171 493 8181 FAX: 0171 493 2687

The Ritz is one of the world's legendary hotels and over the past 90 years it has welcomed countless monarchs, statesmen and celebrities. It is sumptuously decorated throughout in the style of Louis XVI and, being situated in the heart of London's West End overlooking Green Park, offers easy access to exclusive shopping areas, galleries, auction houses, theatres and all the excitements and attractions of the capital. Guests are surrounded by comfort and elegance. The Long Gallery leads to a series of grand rooms in which to see and be seen. No two bedrooms or suites are alike. Each has been individually decorated and all offer levels of comfort befitting a world class hotel of character and glamour. Service is excellent and attentive. The chandeliered and magnificently draped Ritz Restaurant with its internationally famous cuisine is one of the prettiest dining rooms in Europe, the Palm Court a delightful place to have afternoon tea and there are three private suites in which to hold special luncheons, dinners, receptions and meetings. Each has its own butler. At the heart of the hotel is the desk in the rotunda where the famed porters provide a 24-hour source of knowledge and service for guests and can arrange tennis, riding, golf, fishing and shooting if required. Directions: The Ritz is situated between Piccadilly Circus and Hyde Park Corner. Price guide (excluding VAT): Rooms/suites £215- £695.

For hotel location, see map on page 12

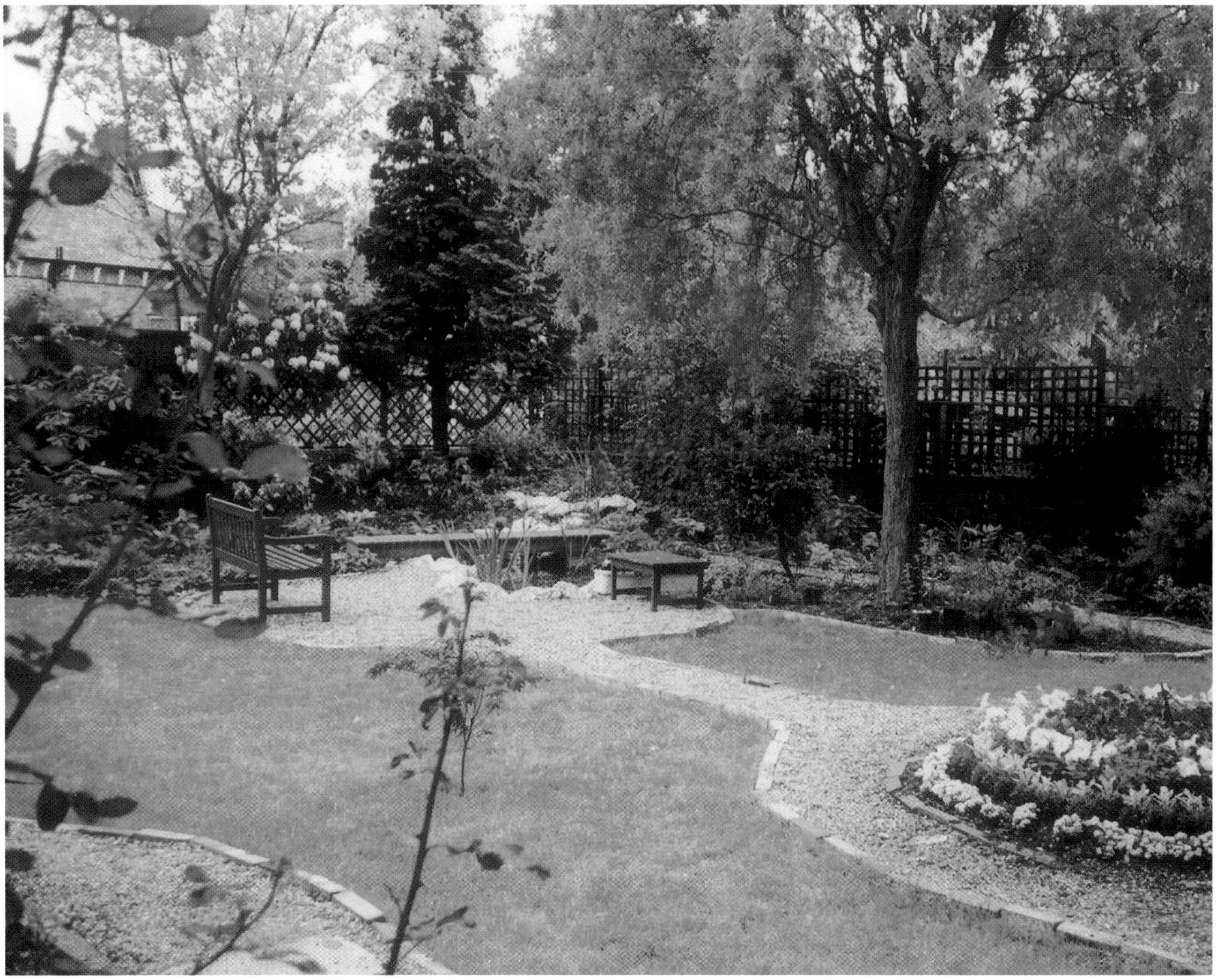

SANDRINGHAM HOTEL

3 HOLFORD ROAD, HAMPSTEAD VILLAGE, LONDON NW3 1AD
TEL: 0171 435 1569 FAX: 0171 431 5932

The Sandringham is a country house hotel in an elegant Victorian mansion situated in Hampstead Village only a short distance from London's busy West End and City. It is an oasis of serenity offering comfort and convenience to both the leisure and business visitor. The hotel's accent is on discreet and attentive service. All the bedrooms are individually designed with fine fabrics, furnishings and home comforts. Freshly squeezed orange juice revives guests each morning. There is a 24-hour room service and afternoon tea or an evening drink can be enjoyed in the privacy of a delightful walled garden. Sunday lunch is served in the intimate dining room. Business guests are particularly well catered for with thoughtful options such as 24 hour fax services, spare modems and a personalised limousine service. Boardroom, receptions, garden parties and other catering facilities are available. Numerous restaurants, antique shops, pubs, galleries and boutiques and Hampstead Heath's 950 acres are only 150 yards away from the front door for visitors who enjoy walking, jogging or just relaxing in a green environment. Restaurant and theatre bookings can be arranged. **Directions:** From Hampstead tube station turn uphill into Heath Street. The fourth turning on the right leads to Holford Road. Price guide: Single £80-£110; double/twin £130-£155; suite £165.

For hotel location, see map on page 12

The Grande Réserve of Cigars.
Some of life's great pleasures require both time and skill in their making.
The Dunhill Aged Cigar is one such example, a fine spirit such as Cognac another.
From manufacture to the appreciation of the intrinsic qualities of each, the Dunhill Aged Cigar and the finest Cognacs have much in common.
Both have roots in the soil culminating in the harvest of tobacco leaf or grape.
Both require the attentions of a Master Blender to ensure the end result consistently yields the highest standards of quality.
And both are aged and matured in wood to impart their unique and individual character.
A smoothness and mellowness of taste is also common to both, as is a subtlety of aroma.
Perhaps that's why, enjoyed together, they provide a perfect partnership.
And why the Dunhill Aged Cigar deserves to share Cognac's highest appellation – The Grande Réserve of Cigars.
HARVEST CROP
1994
HAND MADE
Dunhill
AGED CIGARS
25 DUNHILL AGED VALVERDES

Johansens Recommended Hotels in England

Castles, cathedrals, museums, great country houses and the opportunity to stay in areas of historical importance, England has much to offer. Whatever your leisure interests, there's a network of more than 560 Tourist Information Centres throughout England offering friendly, free advice on places to visit, entertainment, local facilities and travel information.

English Heritage
Keysign House
429 Oxford Street
London W1R 2HD
Tel: 0171-973 3396
Offers an unrivalled choice of properties to visit.

Historic Houses Association
2 Chester Street
London SW1X 7BB
Tel: 0171-259 5688
Ensures the survival of historic houses and gardens in private ownership in Great Britain.

The National Trust
36 Queen Anne's Gate
London SW1H 9AS
Tel: 0171-222 9251
Cares for more than 590,000 acres of countryside and over 400 historic buildings.

Regional Tourist Boards

The Heart of England

Here you have the essence of England, the country's very heart. From the thatched villages of Shakespeare Country, to some of the world's finest potteries in Stoke on Trent.

The Heart of England Tourist Board
PO Box 15
Worcester
Worcestershire WR5 1BR
Tel: 01905 763436

Cumbria

England's most beautiful lakes and tallest mountains reach out from the Lake District National Park to a landscape of spectacular coasts, hills and dales.

Cumbria Tourist Board
Ashleigh
Holly Road
Windermere
Cumbria LA23 2AQ
Tel: 015394 44444

Northumbria

The north east region of England is steeped in folklore and history and is celebrated as one of the most important centres of early English Christianity.

Northumbria Tourist Board
Aykley Heads
Durham
Co Durham DH1 5UX
Tel: 0191-384 6905

The North West

This region offers the very best in history and heritage, stunning countryside and vibrant towns and cities including Chester, Lancaster, Liverpool and Manchester.

The North West Tourist Board
Swan House
Swan Meadow Road
Wigan Pier
Wigan WN3 5BB
Tel: 01942 821222

Yorkshire & Humberside

Scenic coastline with lively resorts, and spectacular seascapes. Unspoilt natural grandeur in dales and moors. Historic cities, picturesque villages, impressive castles and stately homes.

Yorkshire & Humberside Tourist Board
312 Tadcaster Road
York
North Yorkshire YO2 2HF
Tel: 01904 707961

East Midlands

This region includes the coastal resorts of Lincolnshire, waterways such as the Grand Union Canal, the Trent & Mersey Canal and the Rivers Trent, Soar and Witham. Most of the Peak District National Park lies in Derbyshire.

East Midlands Tourist Board
Exchequergate
Lincoln
Lincolnshire LN2 1PZ
01522 531521

East Anglia

A place of farms and pine forests, quiet villages and thatched cottages, medieval towns and charming cities, lively seaside resorts and quaint villages.

East Anglia Tourist Board
Toppesfield Hall
Hadleigh
Suffolk IP7 5DN
Tel: 01473 822922

West Country

England's favourite holiday destination with a mild climate all year round and over 600 miles of contrasting coastline. Discover another world of legend, mystery and romance.

West Country Tourist Board
60 St Davids Hill
Exeter
Devon EX4 4SY
Tel: 01392 76351

Southern England

This area has connections with great literary figures. In the 19th century, Oxford was a centre for the pre-Raphaelite painters and many of their works can still be viewed in the city.

Southern Tourist Board
40 Chamberlayne Road
Eastleigh
Hampshire SO50 5JH
Tel: 01703 620006

South East

The region has 257 miles of coastline stretching from Gravesend, Kent, to the Witterings, West Sussex. The Channel Tunnel links this corner of England to mainland Europe.

South East England Tourist Board
The Old Brew House
Warwick Park
Royal Tunbridge Wells
Kent TN2 5TU
Tel: 01892 540766

London Tourist Board details appear on page 13.

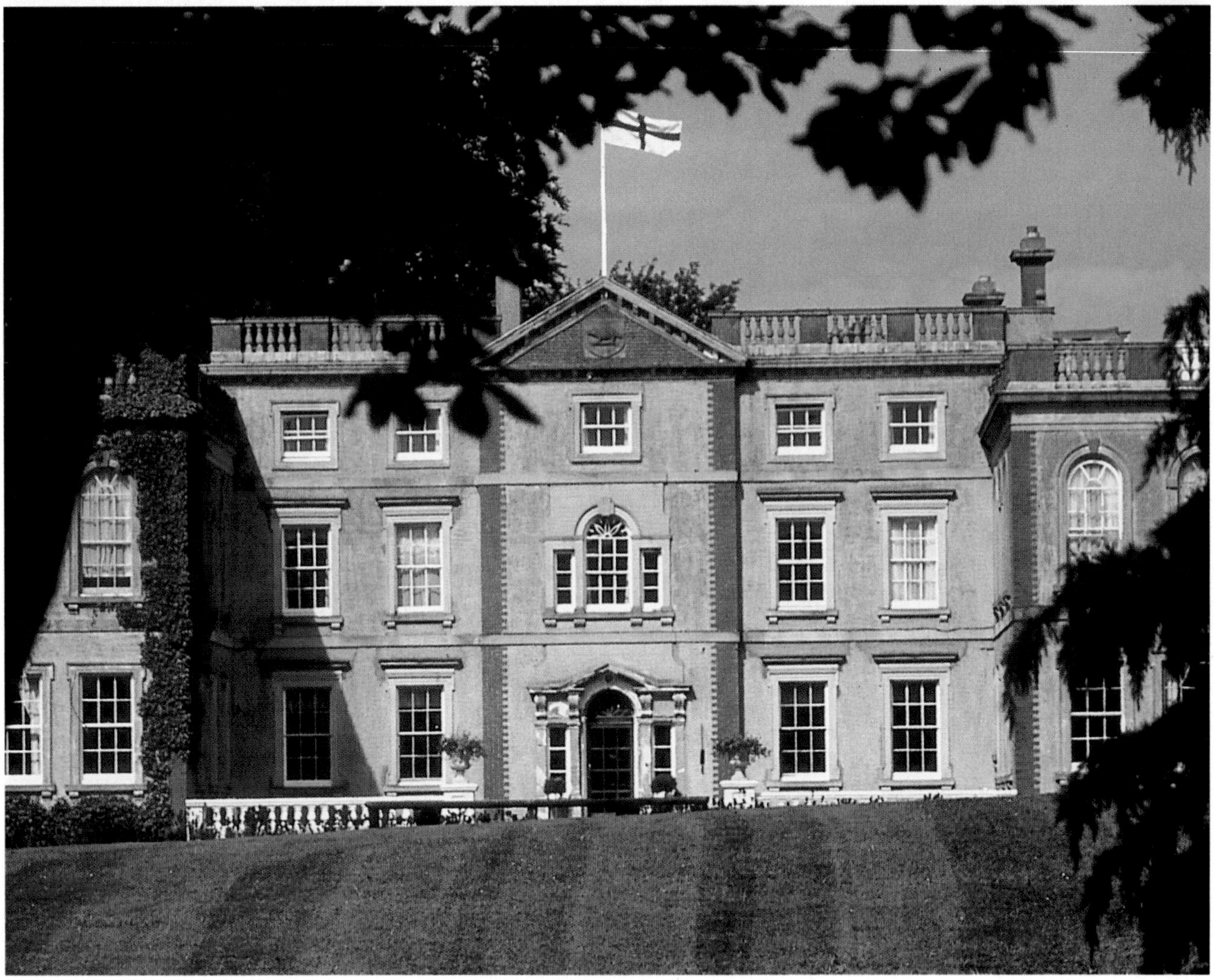

THE ELMS

ABBERLEY, WORCESTERSHIRE WR6 6AT
TEL: 01299 896666 FAX: 01299 896804

Built in 1710 by a pupil of Sir Christopher Wren and converted into a country house hotel in 1946, The Elms has achieved an international reputation for excellence spanning the past half century. Standing tall and impressively between Worcester and Tenbury Wells this fine Queen Anne mansion is surrounded by the beauties of the meadows, woodland, green hills, hop fields and orchards of cider apples and cherries of the Teme Valley whose river runs crimson when in flood from bankside soil tinged with red sandstone. Each of the hotel's 16 bedrooms has its own character, furnished with period antiques and having splendid views across the landscaped gardens and beyond to the beauty of the valley. There is a panelled bar and the elegant restaurant offers fine imaginative cuisine. The surrounding countryside offers opportunities for walking, fishing, shooting, golf and horseracing. Within easy reach are the attractions of the market town of Tenbury Wells, Witley Court, Bewdley and the ancient city of Worcester with its cathedral, county cricket ground and famous porcelain factory. **Directions:** From the M5, exit at junction 5 (Droitwich) or junction 6 (Worcester) then take the A443 towards Tenbury Wells. The Elms is two miles after Great Witley. Do not take the turning into Abberley village. Price guide: Single £75-£90; double/twin £110-£135.

For hotel location, see maps on pages 477-483

WENTWORTH HOTEL

WENTWORTH ROAD, ALDEBURGH, SUFFOLK IP15 5BD
TEL: 01728 452312 FAX: 01728 454343

The Wentworth Hotel is ideally situated opposite the beach at Aldeburgh on Suffolk's unspoilt coast. Aldeburgh has maritime traditions dating back to the 15th century which are still maintained today by the longshore fishermen who launch their boats from the shore. It has also become a centre for music lovers: every June the Aldeburgh International Festival of Music, founded by the late Benjamin Britten, is held at Snape Maltings. Privately owned by the Pritt family since 1920, the Wentworth has established a reputation for comfort and service, good food and wine, for which many guests return year after year. Relax in front of an open fire in one of the hotel lounges, or sample a pint of the famous local Adnam's ales in the bar, which also serves meals. Many of the 38 elegantly furnished en suite bedrooms have sea views. The restaurant offers an extensive menu for both lunch and dinner and there is a comprehensive wine list. The garden terrace is the perfect venue for a light lunch *alfresco*. Nearby, the Minsmere Bird Sanctuary will be of interest to nature enthusiasts, while for the keen golfer, two of Britain's most challenging courses are within easy reach of the hotel at Aldeburgh and Thorpeness. Closed from December 27 to early new year. **Directions:** Aldeburgh is on A1094 just 7 miles from the A12 between Ipswich and Lowestoft. Price guide: Single £55; double/twin £100.

For hotel location, see maps on pages 477-483

THE ALDERLEY EDGE HOTEL

MACCLESFIELD ROAD, ALDERLEY EDGE, CHESHIRE SK9 7BJ
TEL: 01625 583033 FAX: 01625 586343

This privately owned award-winning hotel has 21 executive rooms and 11 de luxe rooms, each with a whirlpool bath, offering a choice of traditional decor or cottage-style accomodation. The restaurant is in the sumptuous conservatory with exceptional views and attention is given to the highest standards of cooking; fresh produce, including fish delivered daily, is provided by local suppliers. Specialities include hot and cold seafood dishes, puddings served piping hot from the oven, and a daily selection of unusual and delicious breads, baked each morning in the hotel bakery. The wine list features 100 champagnes and 600 wines. Special wine and champagne dinners are held monthly. In addition to the main conference room there is a suite of meeting and private dining rooms. Secretarial services and fax machines are available. The famous Edge walks are nearby, as are Tatton and Lyme Parks, Quarry Bank Mill and Dunham Massey. Manchester's thriving city centre is 15 miles away and the airport is a 20-minute drive. **Directions:** Follow M6 to M56 Stockport. Exit junction 6, take A538 to Wilmslow. Follow signs 1¾ miles through Alderley Edge, turn left at Volvo garage and hotel is 200 yards on the right. From the M6 take junction 18 and follow signs for Holmes Chapel and Alderley Edge. Price guide: Single £95–£103; double/twin £116–£150.

For hotel location, see maps on pages 477-483

WHITE LODGE COUNTRY HOUSE HOTEL

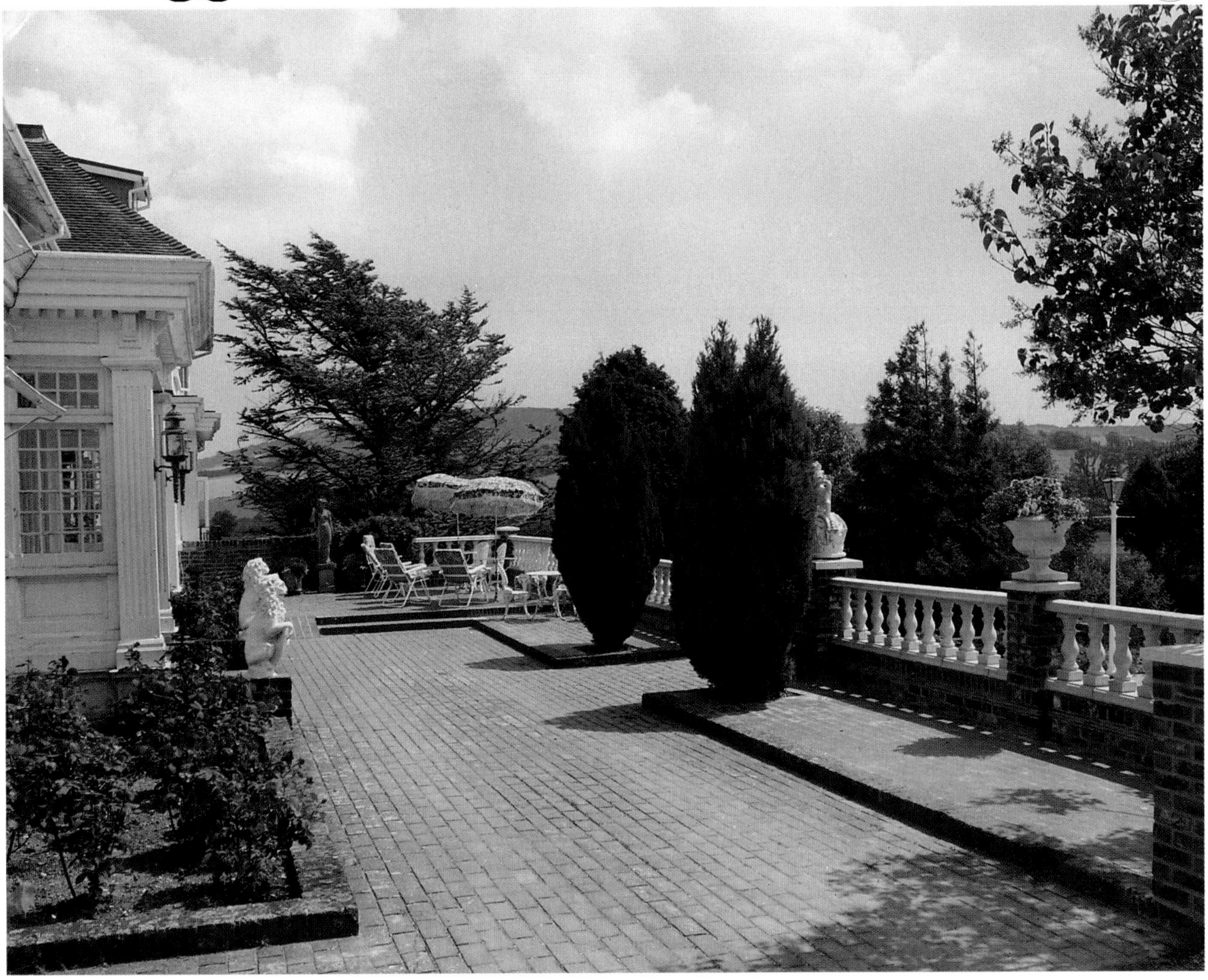

SLOE LANE, ALFRISTON, EAST SUSSEX BN26 5UR
TEL: 01323 870265 FAX: 01323 870284

The White Lodge Country House Hotel lies majestically on a rise within 5 acres of glorious Sussex downland in the undisturbed Cuckmere Valley, with picturesque views of the ancient village of Alfriston. The village church is known as the Cathedral of the Downs and the nearby clergy house was the first ever building owned by the National Trust. White Lodge is a setting in which to enjoy the style and luxury of a former age, with every comfort and facility of the present day. There are three comfortable lounges, all light and airy, where guests can relax. The cocktail bar is the ideal place to sip an apéritif in congenial surroundings prior to dinner. Whether dining in the attractive Orchid Restaurant or the more intimate Ruby dining room, a high standard of service and cuisine is assured. Each bedroom offers every amenity the discriminating guest would expect, with décor to match the quiet elegance which is the hotel's hallmark. White Lodge is only 10 minutes' drive from Glyndebourne, while Brighton, Eastbourne and the port of Newhaven are all within easy reach. The hotel is a romantic setting for wedding celebrations, while for business purposes small conferences and seminars can be catered for. **Directions:** Alfriston is on the B2108 between the A27/A259. Access from the market cross via West Street. Price guide: Single £50; double/twin £86–£120.

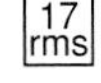           

For hotel location, see maps on pages 477-483

BREAMISH COUNTRY HOUSE HOTEL

POWBURN, ALNWICK, NORTHUMBERLAND NE66 4LL
TEL: 01665 578544/578266 FAX: 01665 578500

In the heart of Northumberland, close by the rambling Cheviot Hills, Breamish Country House Hotel is a fine Georgian-style building set in five acres of gardens and woodland, offering visitors a uniquely beautiful retreat from the pressures of the working week. The hotel was originally a 17th-century farmhouse converted in the 1800s into a hunting lodge. The owners, Alan and Doreen Johnson, have created an atmosphere of peace and hospitality for their many guests. There are 11 bedrooms, each sumptuously and individually furnished, and are double-glazed with modern conveniences and private facilities. Pre-dinner drinks can be enjoyed in the comfortable drawing room, beside a log fire on winter evenings. In the restaurant, cordon bleu cooks prepare gourmet English cuisine with flair and imagination. To complement the food, the fine cellar offers many wines of distinction at competitive prices. Smoking is not permitted in the dining room. Dogs by prior arrangement. Closed January to mid-February. Activities available locally include riding, golf, course and game fishing. Northumberland is one of Britain's least spoilt regions, with mile upon mile of remote and lovely coastline. The area is also rich in history. **Directions:** Powburn is midway between Morpeth and Coldstream on the A697. Price guide (including dinner): Single: £64–£80; double/twin: £103–£160.

For hotel location, see maps on pages 477-483

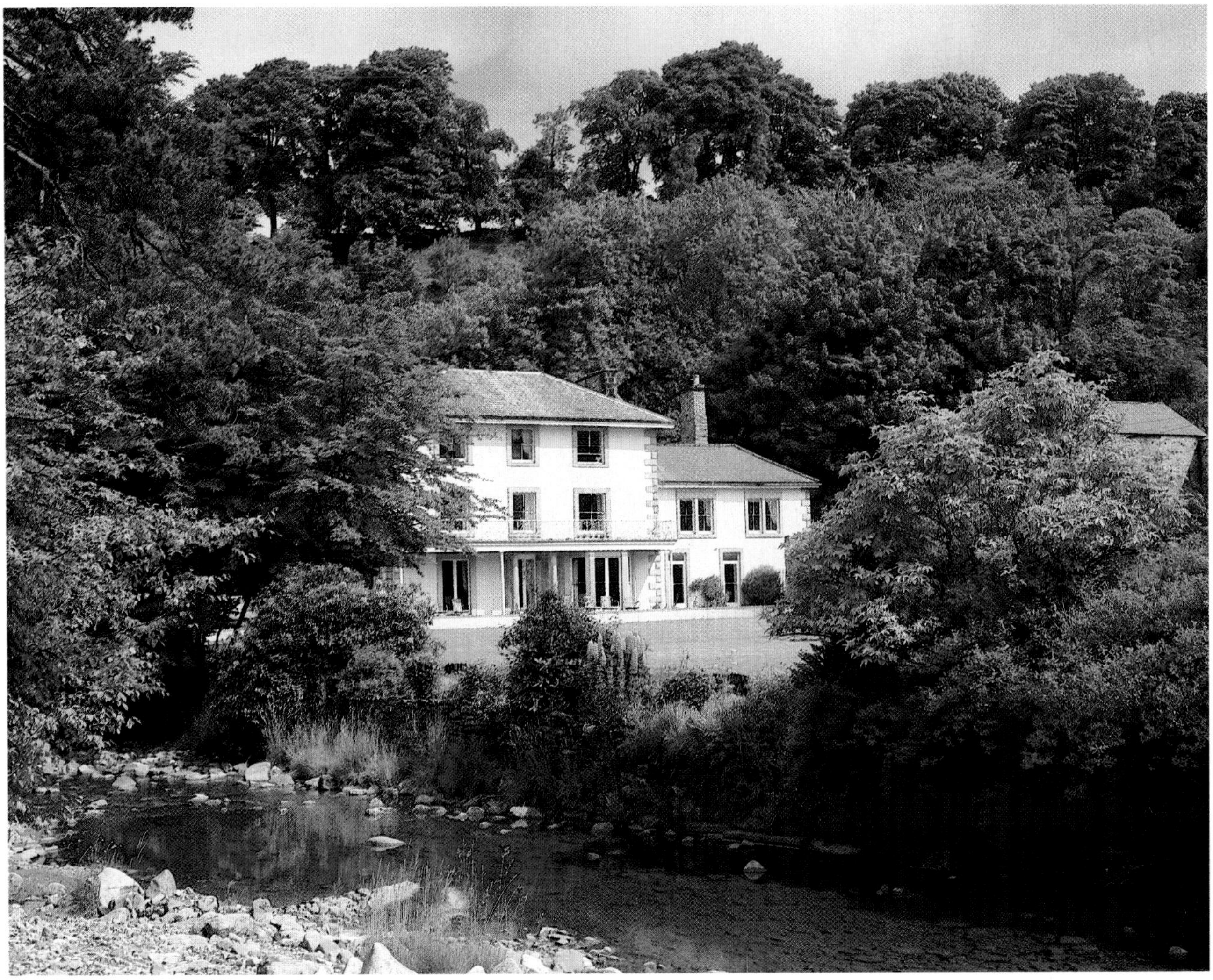

LOVELADY SHIELD COUNTRY HOUSE HOTEL

NENTHEAD ROAD, ALSTON, CUMBRIA CA9 3LF
TEL: 01434 381203 FAX: 01434 381515

Two-and-a-half miles from Alston, England's highest market town, Lovelady Shield nestles in three acres of secluded riverside gardens. Bright log fires in the library and drawing room enhance the hotel's welcoming atmosphere. Owners Kenneth and Margaret Lyons take great care to create a peaceful and tranquil haven where guests can relax. The five-course dinners created by chef Barrie Garton, rounded off by home-made puddings and a selection of English farmhouse cheeses, have won the hotel AA 2 Red Stars and 2 Rosettes for food. Lovelady Shield also boasts its own spring water. Many guests first discover Lovelady Shield en route for Scotland. They then return to explore this beautiful and unspoiled part of England and experience the comforts of the hotel. Golf, fishing, shooting, pony-trekking and riding can be arranged locally. The Pennine Way, Hadrian's Wall and the Lake District are within easy reach. Facilities for small conferences and boardroom meetings are available. Closed 3 January to 4th February. Special Christmas, New Year, winter and spring breaks are offered and special 3 day and weekly terms. **Directions:** The hotel's driveway is by the junction of the B6294 and the A689, 2¼ miles east of Alston, on the road between Durham and Carlisle. Price guide (including dinner): Single £75–£85; double/twin £145–£165.

For hotel location, see maps on pages 477-483

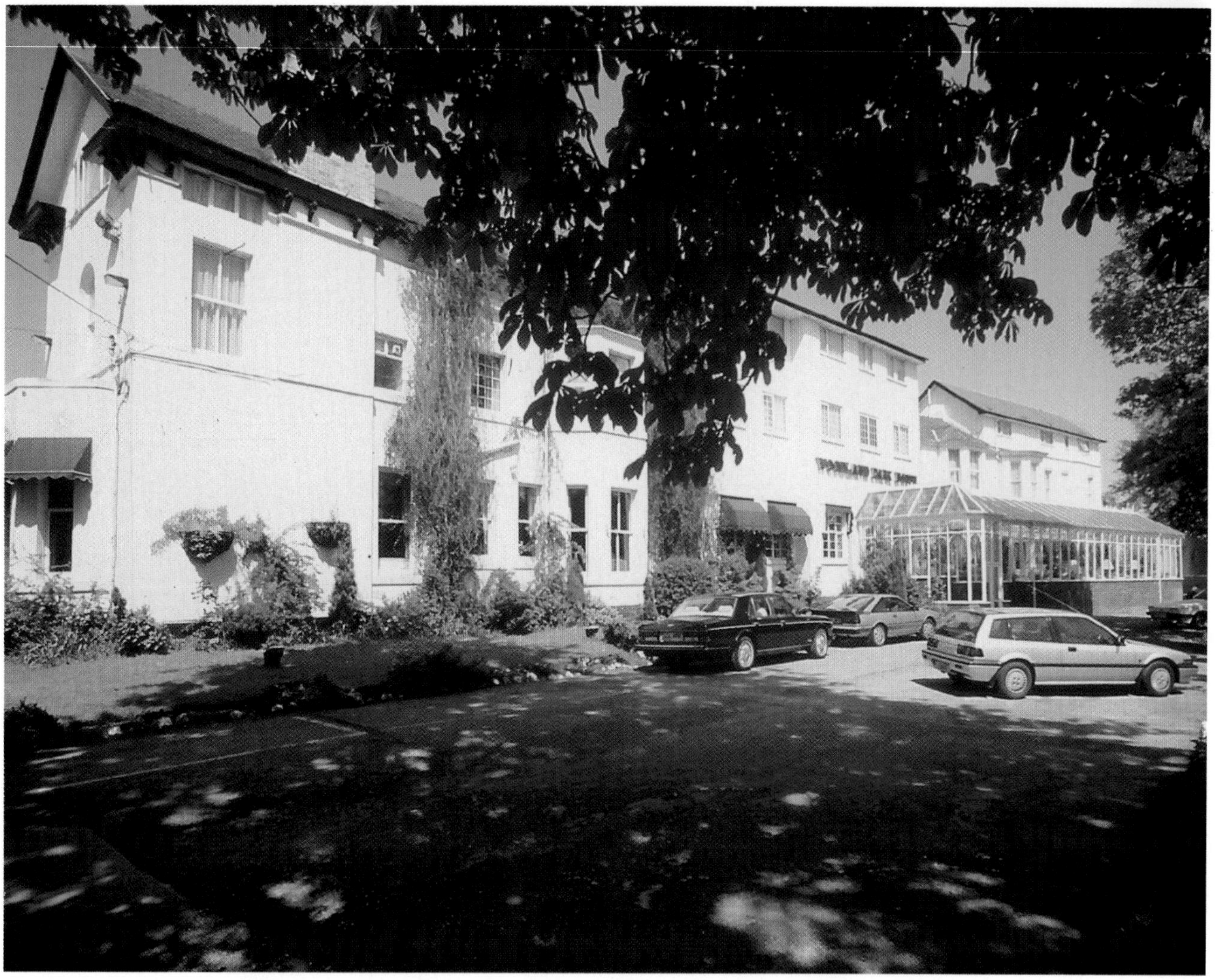

WOODLAND PARK HOTEL

WELLINGTON ROAD, TIMPERLEY, NR ALTRINCHAM, CHESHIRE WA15 7RG
TEL: 0161 928 8631 FAX: 0161 941 2821

The Woodland Park Hotel is a delightful family owned hotel in a secluded residential area. Brian and Shirley Walker offer their guests a warm and friendly welcome, working as a team with their staff to ensure the highest standards of comfort and service. All the bedrooms are individually designed and furnished and some offer the added luxury of an aero spa bath. Guests are invited either to relax in the two comfortable lounges one of which is non-smoking or to enjoy an apéritif in the elegant conservatory adjoining the Terrace Restaurant. The restaurant offers a choice of Brasserie style menu or table d'hôte. The hotel has extensive facilities for business meetings, conferences and weddings. Manchester City Centre is about eight miles away and offers wonderful theatre productions and the famous China Town. The hotel is also a convenient base for visiting Tatton Park, Dunham Park and Capesthorne Hall and the many historical places of interest in Chester. Manchester International Airport is just four miles away. **Directions:** Leave the M56 at Junction 3 and take the A560 towards Altrincham. Turn right onto Wellington Road. The hotel is signposted from the A560. Price guide: Single: £70–£85; double/twin £86–£105.

For hotel location, see maps on pages 477-483

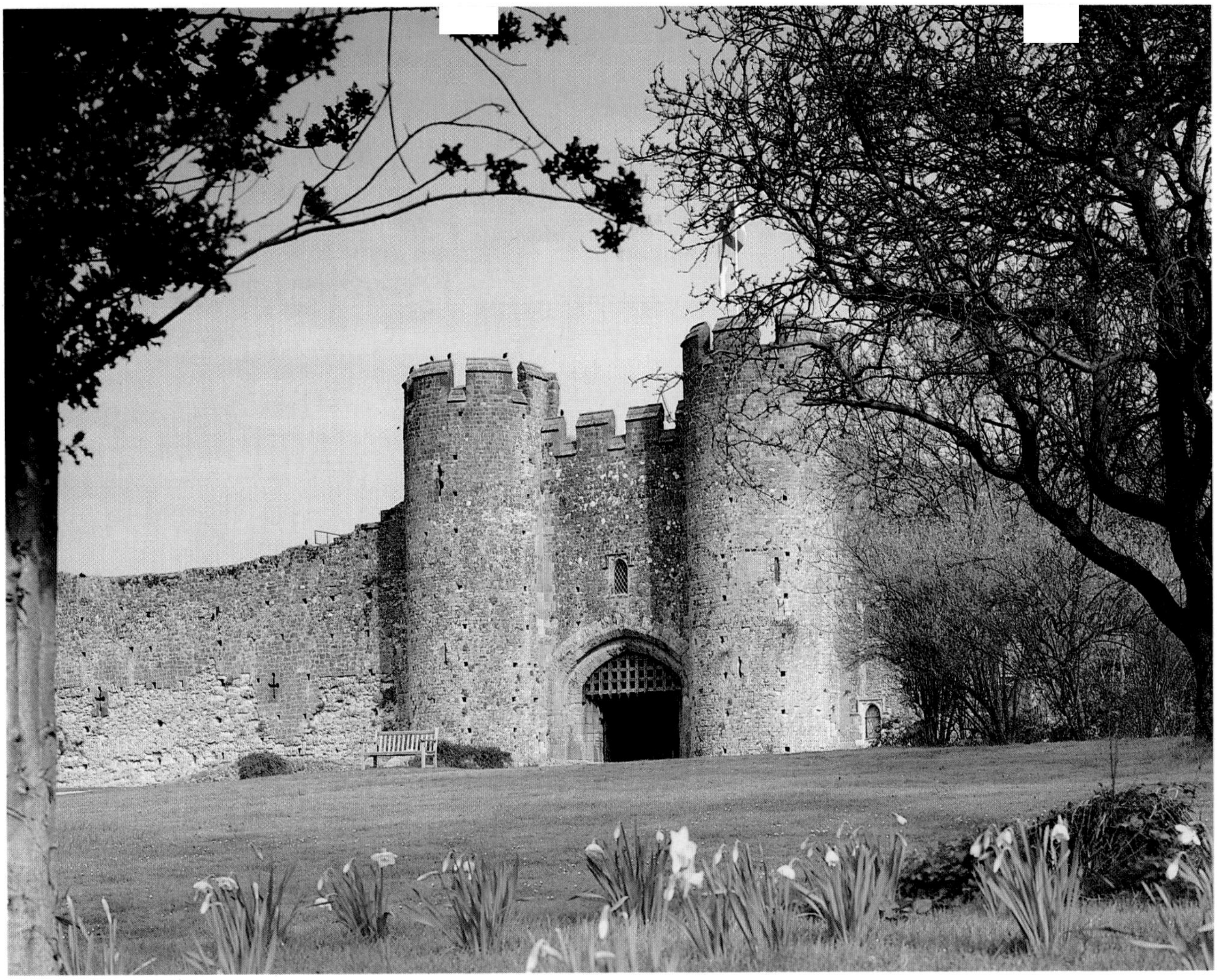

AMBERLEY CASTLE

AMBERLEY, NR ARUNDEL, WEST SUSSEX BN18 9ND
TEL: 01798 831992 FAX: 01798 831998

Winner of the Johansens 1995 Country Hotel Award, Amberley Castle is over 900 years old and is set between the rolling South Downs and the peaceful expanse of the Amberley Wildbrooks. Its towering battlements give breathtaking views while its massive, 14th-century curtain walls and mighty portcullis bear silent testimony to its fascinating history. Resident proprietors, Joy and Martin Cummings, have transformed this medieval fortress into a unique country castle hotel. They offer a warm, personal welcome and their hotel provides the ultimate in contemporary luxury, while retaining an atmosphere of timelessness. Guests can choose from four-poster, twin four-poster or brass double-bedded rooms. Each room is individually designed and has its own Jacuzzi bath. The exquisite 12th-century Queen's Room Restaurant is the perfect setting for the creative cuisine of new head chef Simon Thyer and his team. Amberley Castle is a natural first choice for romantic or cultural weekends, sporting breaks or confidential executive meetings. It is ideally situated for opera at Glyndebourne, theatre at Chichester and racing at Goodwood and Fontwell. It is easily accessible from London and the major air and channel ports. **Directions:** Amberley Castle is on the B2139, off the A29 between Fontwell and Bury. Price guide: Single £100; double/twin £130–£275.

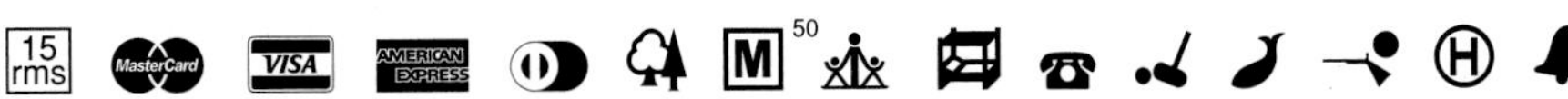

For hotel location, see maps on pages 477-483

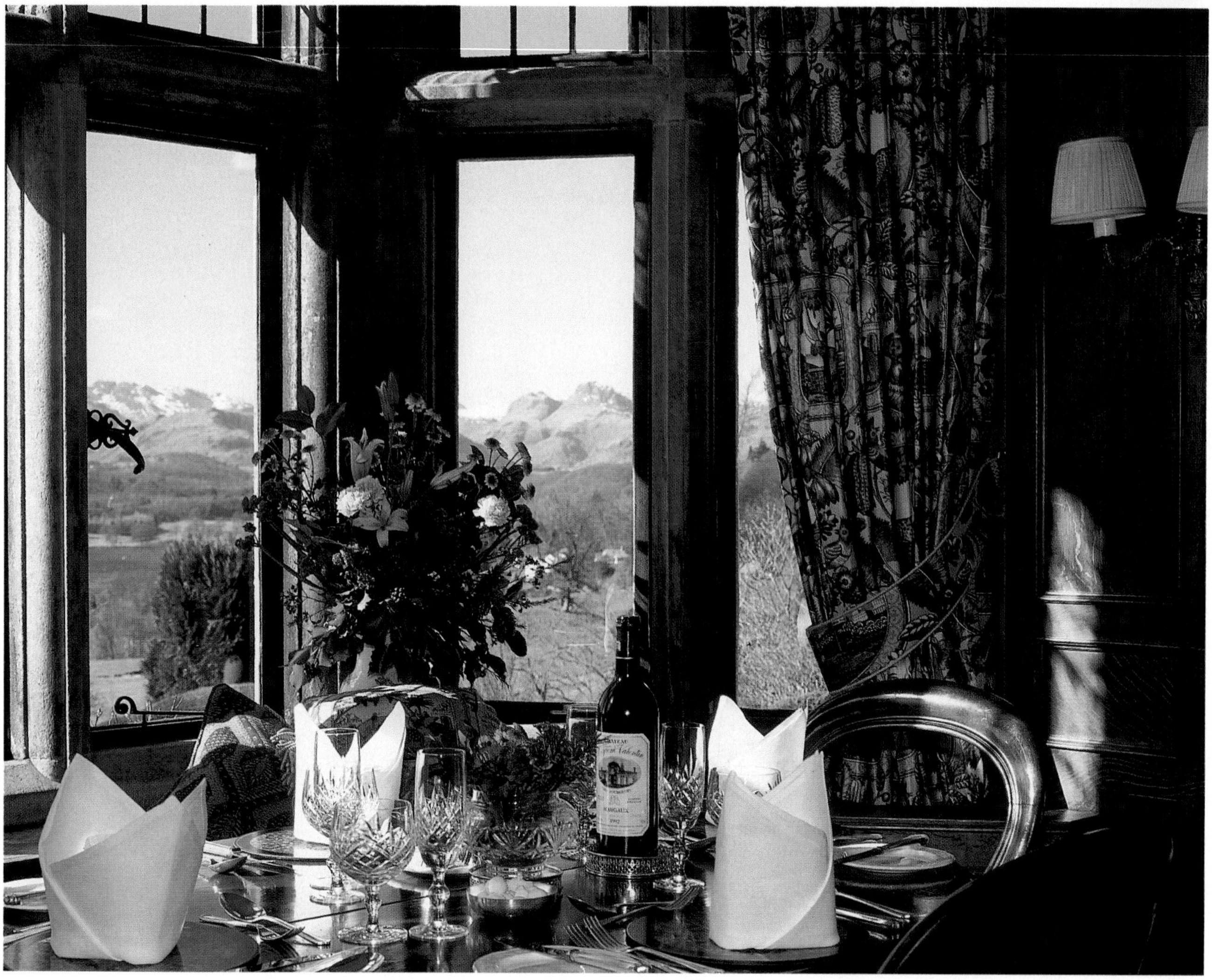

HOLBECK GHYLL COUNTRY HOUSE HOTEL

HOLBECK LANE, WINDERMERE, CUMBRIA LA23 1LU
TEL: 015394 32375 FAX: 015394 34743

The saying goes that all the best sites for building a house in England were taken long before the days of the motor car. Holbeck Ghyll has one such prime position. It was built in the early days of the 19th century and is superbly located overlooking Lake Windermere and the Langdale Fells. Today this luxury hotel has an outstanding reputation and is managed personally and expertly by its proprietors, David and Patricia Nicholson. As well as being awarded the RAC Blue Ribbon and AA Red Stars for six consecutive years, they are among an élite who have won an AA Courtesy and Care Award. The majority of bedrooms are large and have spectacular and breathtaking views. All are recently refurbished to a very high standard, are en suite and include decanters of sherry, fresh flowers, trouser presses, fluffy bathrobes and a lot more. The oak-panelled restaurant is a delightful setting for memorable dining and meals are classically prepared, with focus on flavours and presentation, while an extensive wine list reflects quality and variety. The hotel has an all-weather tennis court and a new health spa with gym, sauna, steam room and treatment facilities. **Directions:** From Windermere, pass Brockhole Visitors Centre, then after 1/2 mile turn right into Holbeck Lane (signed Troutbeck). Hotel is 1/2 mile on left. Price guide (including dinner): Single £85; double/twin £135–£190; suite £180–£240.

For hotel location, see maps on pages 477-483

ROTHAY MANOR

ROTHAY BRIDGE, AMBLESIDE, CUMBRIA LA22 0EH
TEL: 015394 33605 FAX: 015394 33607

Situated half a mile from Lake Windermere, this Georgian listed building stands in 1½ acres of grounds. The bedrooms include three beautifully furnished suites, two of which are in the lodge beside the manor and afford an unusual measure of space and privacy. One suite is equipped for five people and designed with particular attention to the comfort of guests with disabilities: it has a ramp leading to the garden and a spacious shower. Care and consideration are evident throughout. The menu is varied and meals are prepared with flair and imagination to high standards, complemented by an interesting wine list. For the actively inclined, residents have free use of the nearby Low Wood Leisure Club, with swimming pool, sauna, steam room, Jacuzzi, squash, sunbeds and a health and beauty salon. Permits are available for fishing, while locally guests can play golf, arrange to go riding, take a trip on a steam railway or visit Wordsworth's cottage. Small functions can be catered for with ease. Closed 4 January to 7 February. Represented in the USA by Josephine Barr: 800-323 5463. Each winter a full programme of special breaks with reduced rates is offered, as well as music, silver and antiques, walking and painting holidays. **Directions:** ¾ mile from Ambleside on A593, the road to Coniston. Price guide: Single £78; double/twin £118–£134; suite £165.

18 rms 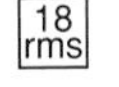       20 

For hotel location, see maps on pages 477-483

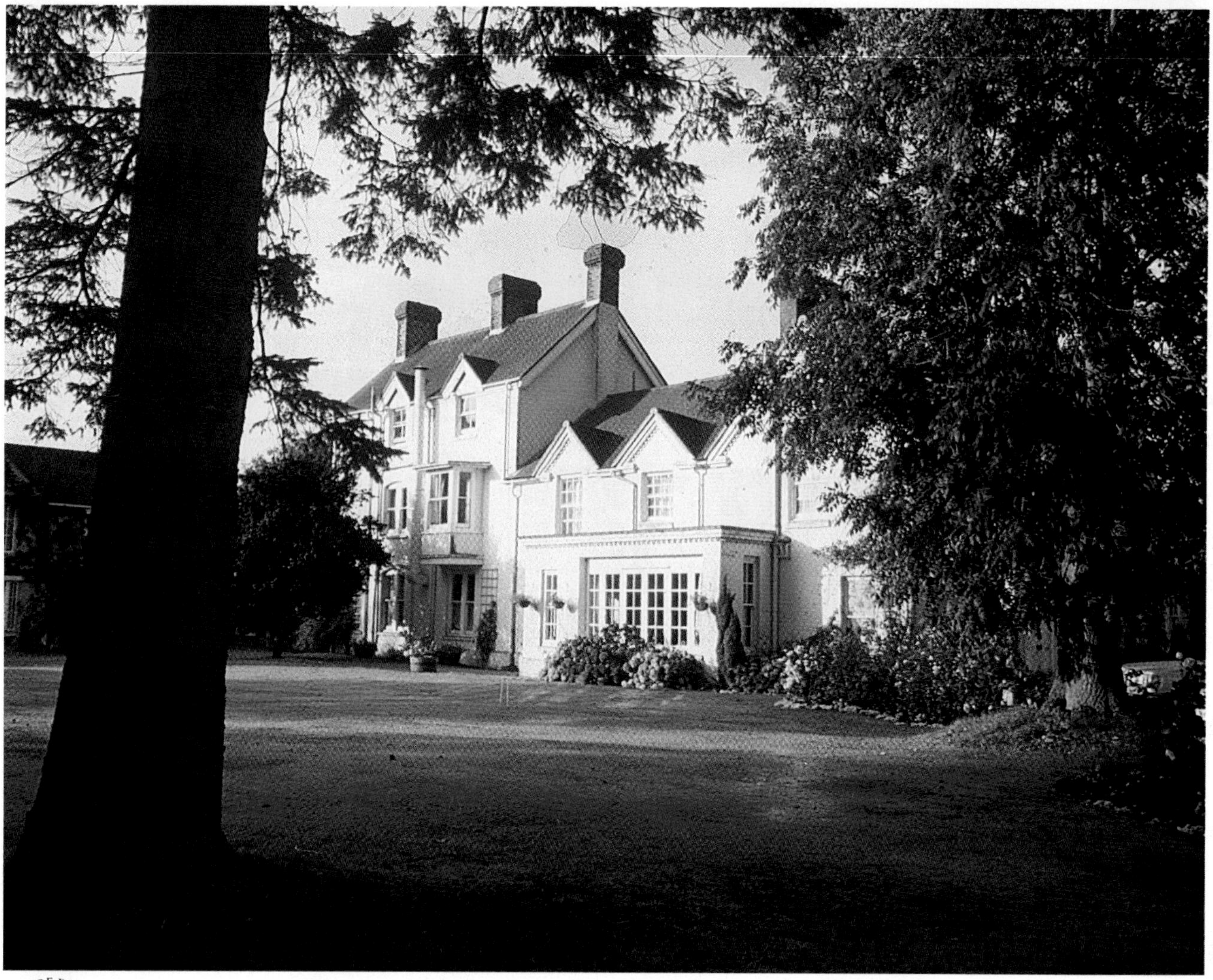

ESSEBORNE MANOR

HURSTBOURNE TARRANT, ANDOVER, HAMPSHIRE SP11 0ER

TEL: 01264 736444 FAX: 01264 736725

Esseborne Manor is small and unpretentious, yet stylish. The present house was built at the end of the 19th century and carries the name used to record details of the local village in the *Domesday Book*. It is set in a pleasing garden amid the rich farmland of the North Wessex Downs in a designated area of outstanding natural beauty. Ian and Lucilla Hamilton, who manage the house, have established the restful atmosphere of a private country home where guests can unwind and relax. There are just 10 comfortable bedrooms, some reached via a courtyard, each decorated and furnished to a high standard, with views of the gardens and surrounding countryside. During the winter, a log fire glows in the sitting room, where guests can enjoy an apéritif before dinner. The pretty dining room reflects the importance the owners place upon service and good food. Chef Nick Watson creates imaginative menus from carefully selected, fresh seasonal produce. In the grounds there is a herb garden, an all-weather tennis court, a croquet lawn and plenty of good walking beyond. Nearby Newbury racecourse has a busy programme of steeplechasing and flat racing. Places to visit include Highclere Castle, Stonehenge, Salisbury, Winchester and Oxford. **Directions:** Midway between Newbury and Andover on the A343, $1^1/_2$ miles north of Hurstbourne Tarrant. Price guide: Single £84–£95; double/twin £95–£135.

For hotel location, see maps on pages 477-483

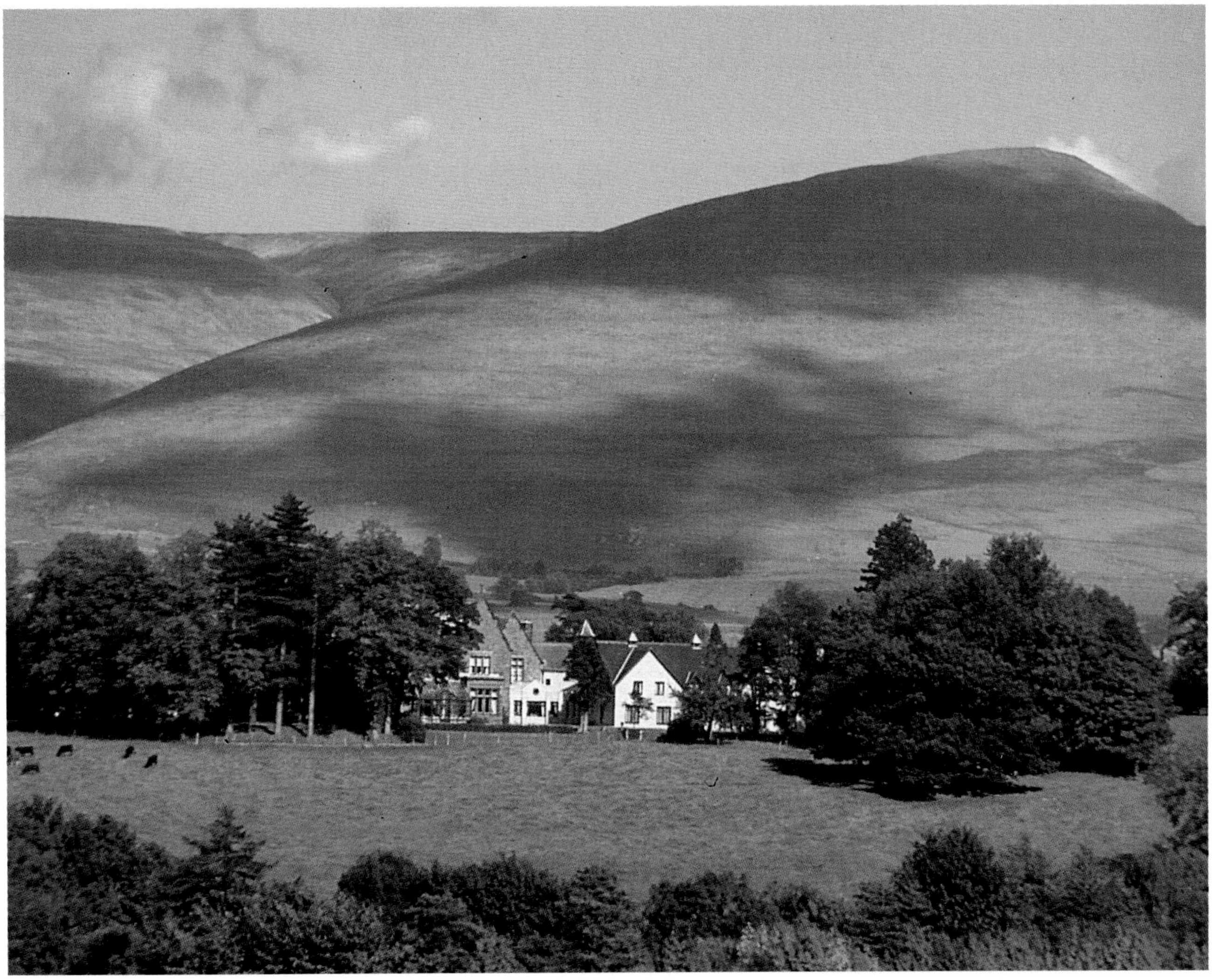

Appleby Manor Country House Hotel

ROMAN ROAD, APPLEBY-IN-WESTMORLAND, CUMBRIA CA16 6JB

TEL: 017683 51571 FAX: 017683 52888 E-MAIL: 100043.1561@compuserve.com

Surrounded by half a million acres of some of the most beautiful landscapes in England, sheltered by the mountains and fells of the Lake District, by the North Pennine Hills and Yorkshire Dales, in an area aptly known as Eden stands Appleby Manor, a friendly and relaxing hotel owned and run by the Swinscoe family. The high quality, spotlessly clean, bedrooms induce peaceful, undisturbed sleep. (Dogs are welcome only in The Coach House accommodation). The public areas are also restfully comfortable – the inviting lounges nicely warmed by log fires on cooler days, the cocktail bar luring guests with a choice of more than 70 malt whiskies and the restaurant offering an imaginative selection of tasty dishes and fine wines. The hotel pool, sauna, steam-room, Jacuzzi, solarium and games room keep indoor athletes happy. Locally there are outdoor sports: fishing, golf, riding, squash and, for the more venturesome, rambling on the fells. Appleby is an ideal base from which to visit the Lake District and an attractive stop-over on journeys north-south. **Directions:** From the South take junction 38 of the M6 and then the B6260 to Appleby (13 miles). Drive through the town to a T-junction, turn left, first right and follow road for two-thirds of a mile. Price guide: Single £61.50–£74; double/twin £88–£118.

For hotel location, see maps on pages 477-483

TUFTON ARMS HOTEL

MARKET SQUARE, APPLEBY-IN-WESTMORLAND, CUMBRIA CA16 6XA
TEL: 017683 51593 FAX: 017683 52761

This distinguished Victorian coaching inn, owned and run by the Milsom family, has been refurbished to provide a high standard of comfort. The bedrooms evoke the style of the 19th century, when the Tufton Arms became one of the premier hotels in Victorian England. The kitchen is run under the auspices of David Milsom, who spoils guests for choice with a gourmet dinner menu as well as a grill menu. The AA rosette and RAC Merit awarded restaurant is renowned for its fish dishes. Complementing the cuisine is an extensive wine list. There are conference and meeting rooms including the recently refurbished Hothfield Suite which can accommodate up to 100 people. 1995 RAC/Consort Hotel of the Year. RAC award for hospitality. Appleby, the historic county town of Westmorland, stands in splendid countryside and is ideal for touring the Lakes, Yorkshire Dales and Pennines. It is also a convenient stop-over en route to Scotland. Superb fishing for wild brown trout on a 24-mile stretch of the main River Eden, salmon fishing can be arranged on the lower reaches of the river. Shooting parties for grouse, duck and pheasant are a speciality. Appleby has an 18-hole moorland golf course. **Directions:** In centre of Appleby (bypassed by the A66), 38 miles west of Scotch Corner, 13 miles east of Penrith (M6 junction 40), 12 miles from M6 junction 38. Price guide: Single £55–£80; double/twin £90–£125; suite £130.

21 rms MasterCard VISA AMERICAN EXPRESS M 100

For hotel location, see maps on pages 477-483

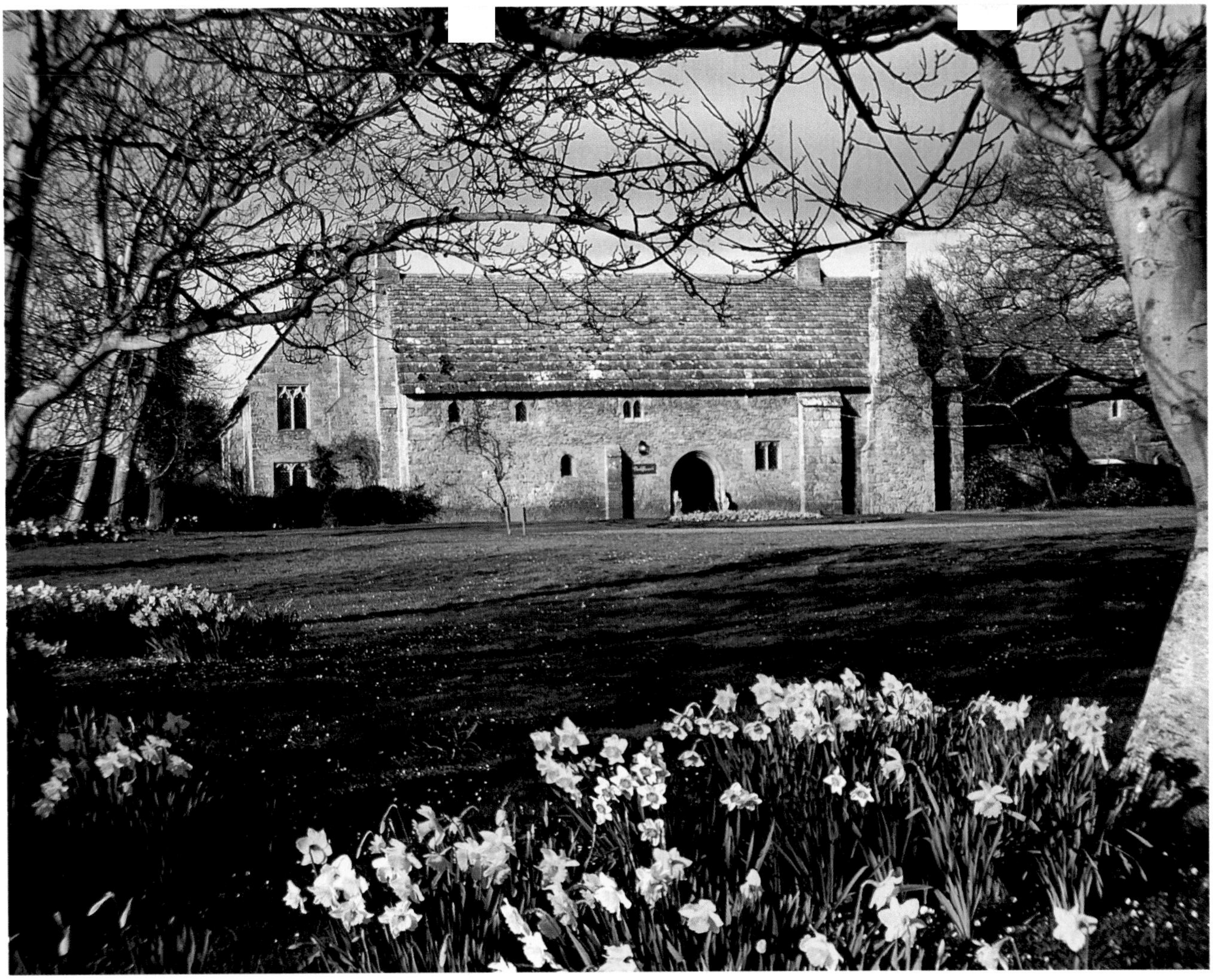

BAILIFFSCOURT

CLIMPING, WEST SUSSEX BN17 5RW
TEL: 01903 723511 FAX: 01903 723107

Bailiffscourt is a perfectly preserved "medieval" house, built in the 1930s using authentic material salvaged from historic old buildings. Gnarled 15th century beams and gothic mullioned windows combine to recreate a home from the Middle Ages. Set in 22 acres of beautiful pastures and walled gardens, it provides guests with a wonderful sanctuary in which to relax or work. The bedrooms are all individually decorated and luxuriously furnished, with many offering four poster beds, open log fires and beautiful views over the surrounding countryside. The restaurant offers a varied menu and summer lunches can be taken alfresco in a rose-clad courtyard or the walled garden. A good list of well-priced wines accompanies meals. Private dining rooms are available for weddings, conferences and meetings, and companies can hire the hotel as their 'country house' for 2 or 3 days. Bailiffscourt, which is AA three rosettes accredited, is surrounded by tranquil parkland with a golf practice area, outdoor pool and tennis courts. Climping Beach, 100 yards away, is ideal for windsurfing. Nearby are Arundel with its castle, Chichester and Goodwood. **Directions:** Three miles south of Arundel, off the A259. Price guide: Single £89; double from £125.

For hotel location, see maps on pages 477-483

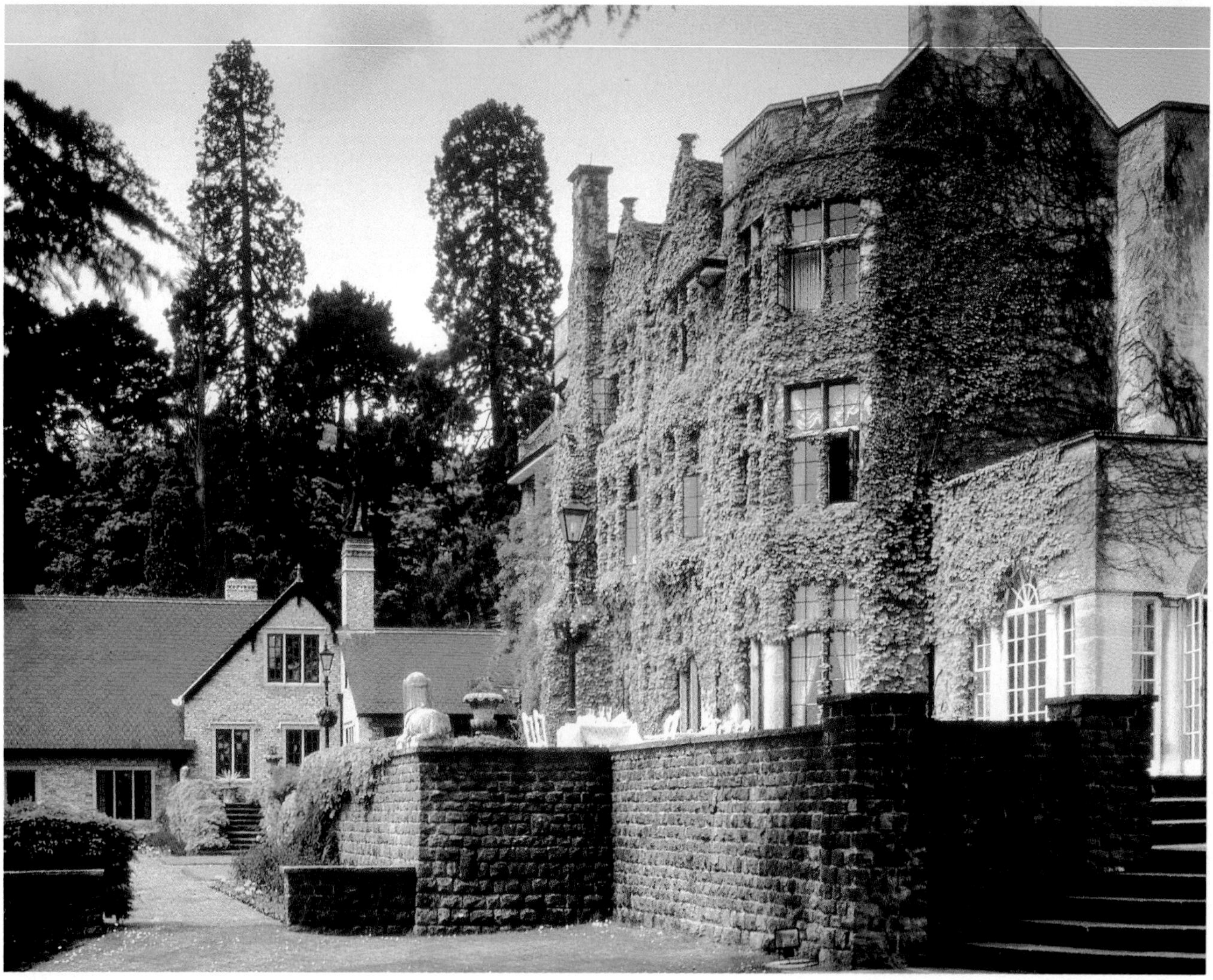

PENNYHILL PARK HOTEL AND COUNTRY CLUB

LONDON ROAD, BAGSHOT, SURREY GU19 5ET
TEL: 01276 471774 FAX: 01276 473217

Bagshot has been a centre of hospitality since the early Stuart sovereigns James I and Charles I had a hunting lodge there. Pennyhill Park Hotel continues to uphold that tradition. Built in 1849, this elegant mansion reflects its journey through Victorian and Edwardian times while providing every modern amenity. The bedrooms are outstanding: no two are identical, and infinite care has been invested in creating practical rooms with distinctive features. Impeccable service is to be expected, as staff are trained to classical, Edwardian standards. Cuisine is served in the welcoming setting of the Latymer Restaurant, accompanied by a wine list that includes many rare vintages. Pennyhill is continually introducing new facilities that never fail to delight. Recreational facilities are available within the grounds, which span 120 acres and include landscaped gardens, a 9-hole golf course, a swimming pool and a three acre lake. Pennyhill Park is conveniently located only 27 miles from central London and not far from Heathrow, Windsor Castle, Ascot, Wentworth and Sunningdale. **Directions:** From the M3, exit 3, take A322 towards Bracknell. Turn left on to A30 signposted to Camberley. 3/4 mile after Bagshot; turn right 50 yards past the Texaco garage. Price guide: Single from £135; double/twin £155–£210; suite from £285.

For hotel location, see maps on pages 477-483

THE ROYAL BERKSHIRE

LONDON ROAD, SUNNINGHILL, ASCOT, BERKSHIRE SL5 0PP
TEL: 01344 23322 FAX: 01344 27100/01344 874240

For over 100 years The Royal Berkshire was the home of the Churchill family. Now it is an elegant hotel, ideally located between Ascot racecourse and the Guards Polo Club. This Queen Anne mansion, built in 1705 by the Duke of Marlborough for his son, is set in 15 acres of gardens and woodlands. Guests have access to a wide range of leisure facilities including a putting green, indoor heated pool, squash court, whirlpool spa and sauna. The spacious interiors are smartly decorated in contemporary pastel shades, with the full-length windows bathing the rooms in light. Tea or drinks can be enjoyed in the drawing rooms or on the terrace with views across the lawns. The menu offers an eclectic choice of dishes to please connoisseurs of fine food. All meals are carefully prepared with meticulous attention to presentation. Some interesting vintages are included on the wine list. A series of well-equipped function rooms, combined with easy accessibility from Heathrow and central London, makes the Royal Berkshire a popular venue for business events. For golfers, Swinley, Sunningdale and Wentworth are all nearby. Royal Windsor and Eton are a short drive away. **Directions:** One mile from Ascot on the corner of A329 and B383. Nearest M25 exit is junction 13. Price guide: Single from £75; double/twin from £189 – weekend rate £116; weekend rate for suite from £220.

63 rms 65

For hotel location, see maps on pages 477-483

Callow Hall

MAPPLETON ROAD, ASHBOURNE, DERBYSHIRE DE6 2AA
TEL: 01335 343403 FAX: 01335 343624

The approach to Callow Hall is up a tree-lined drive through the 44-acre grounds. On arrival visitors can take in the splendid views from the hotel's elevated position, overlooking the valleys of Bentley Brook and the River Dove. The majestic building and Victorian gardens have been restored by resident proprietors, David, Dorothy and their son, Anthony Spencer, who represent the fifth and sixth generations of hoteliers in the Spencer family. The famous local Ashboure mineral water and home-made biscuits greet guests in the spacious period bedrooms. Fresh local produce is selected daily for use in the kitchen, where the term 'home-made' comes into its own. Home-cured bacon, sausages, fresh bread, traditional English puddings and melt-in-the-mouth pastries are among the items prepared on the premises. Visiting anglers can enjoy a rare opportunity to fish for trout and grayling along a mile-long private stretch of the Bentley Brook, which is mentioned in Izaak Walton's *The Compleat Angler*. Callow Hall is ideally located for some of Englands finest stately homes. Closed at Christmas. **Directions:** Take the A515 through Ashbourne towards Buxton. At the Bowling Green Inn on the brow of a steep hill, turn left, then take the first right, signposted Mappleton, and the hotel is over the bridge on the right. Price guide: Single £65–£85; double/twin £95–£120; suite £140.

For hotel location, see maps on pages 477-483

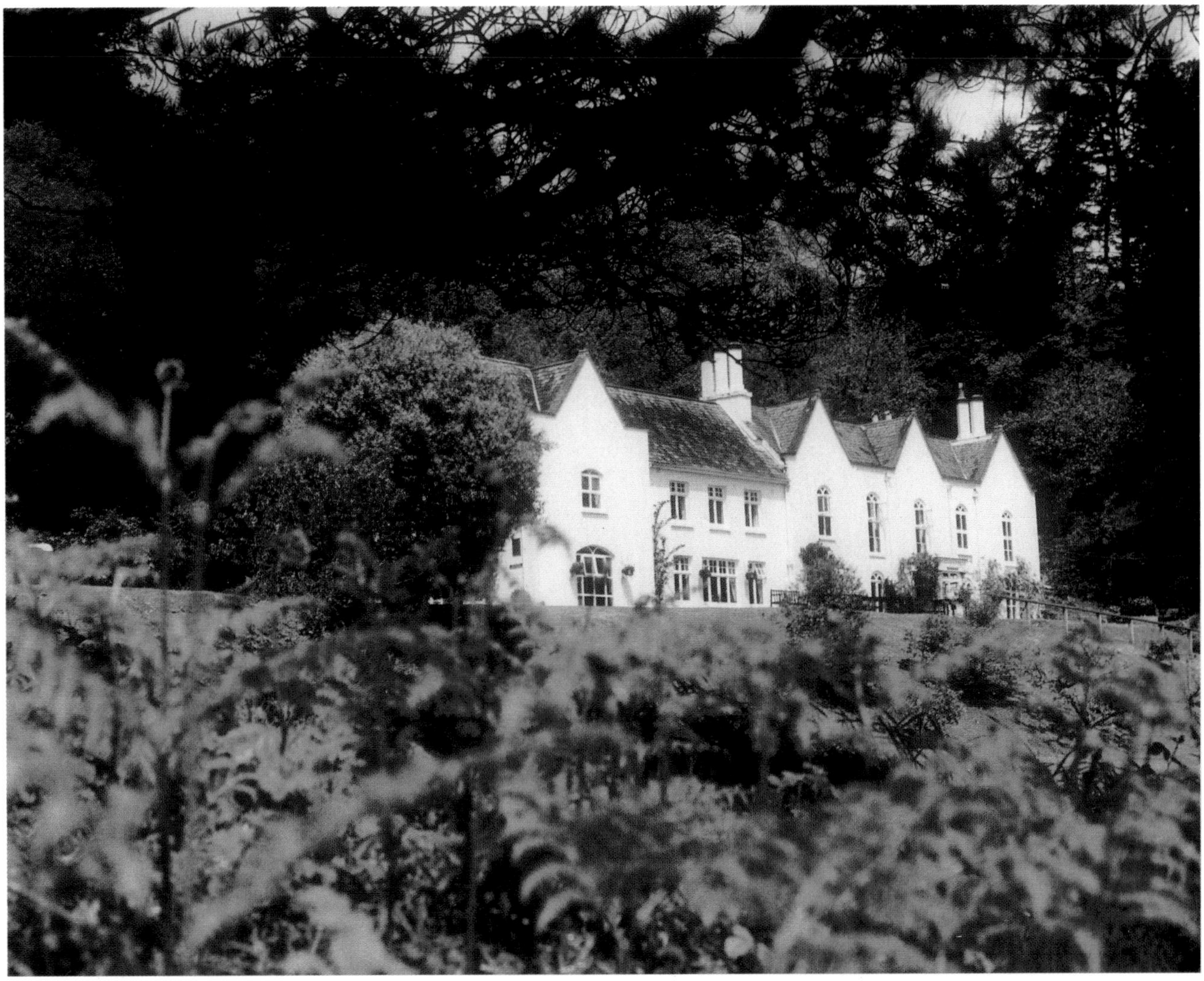

HOLNE CHASE HOTEL AND RESTAURANT

NR ASHBURTON, DEVON TQ13 7NS
TEL: 01364 631471 FAX: 01364 631453

With sweeping lawns, and an outstanding position in over 70 acres of park and woodland inside Dartmoor National Park, Holne Chase is dedicated to relaxation. Its previous role as a 11th-century hunting lodge has become the hotel's theme for attracting visitors to traditional pursuits in a break from the bustle of everyday life. Fly-fishermen can enjoy the hotel's mile-long beat on the River Dart and driven shoots can be arranged in season. The hotel's stables have been converted to provide "Sporting Lodges" with sitting room and fire downstairs and bedroom suite upstairs. All the hotel's en-suite bedrooms are individually furnished and many command spectacular views over the Dart Valley. A walled garden supplies the inviting restaurant, where chef Jonathan Bishop, formerly of Le Gavroche and Cliveden, provides imaginative cuisine. Holne Chase is a good base for exploring Dartmoor's open moorland and wooded valleys. Picturesque villages and sandy beaches are within reach while Exeter, Plymouth and the English Riviera are just a short drive away. Canoeing, golf and riding can all be arranged. **Directions:** Take the Ashburton turning off the A38 and follow the signs for Two Bridges. Holne Chase is on the right after the road crosses the River Dart. Price guide: Single £65; double/twin £110; suite £140.

For hotel location, see maps on pages 477-483

EASTWELL MANOR

BOUGHTON LEES, ASHFORD, KENT TN25 4HR
TEL: 01233 219955 FAX: 01233 635530

In the midst of a 3,000-acre estate, set in 62 acres of lovely grounds, lies Eastwell Manor. It was once the home of Queen Victoria's second son, Prince Alfred, and his wife. The Queen and her elder son, later to become Edward VII, were frequent visitors here. The elegant bedrooms are named after past owners, lords, ladies and gentlemen, bearing witness to the hotel's rich history. Each room is individually and gracefully furnished and offers every modern comfort. Huge open fireplaces with stone mantles, carved panelling, leather Chesterfield sofas and fine antique furniture are features of the lounges, billiard room and bar. Modern British cuisine is served in the handsome wood panelled dining room, matched by an excellent cellar of carefully chosen wines. Guests are invited to take advantage of the hotel's tennis court and croquet lawn, while a variety of other leisure pursuits are available locally. The Manor is conveniently located for visiting the historic cathedral city of Canterbury, Leeds Castle and a number of charming market towns. **Directions:** M20 junction 9. A28 towards Canterbury, then A251 signed Faversham. Hotel is three miles north of Ashford in the village of Boughton Lees. Price guide: Single £115–£150; double/twin £145–£190; suites £235–£255.

For hotel location, see maps on pages 477-483

RIVERSIDE COUNTRY HOUSE HOTEL

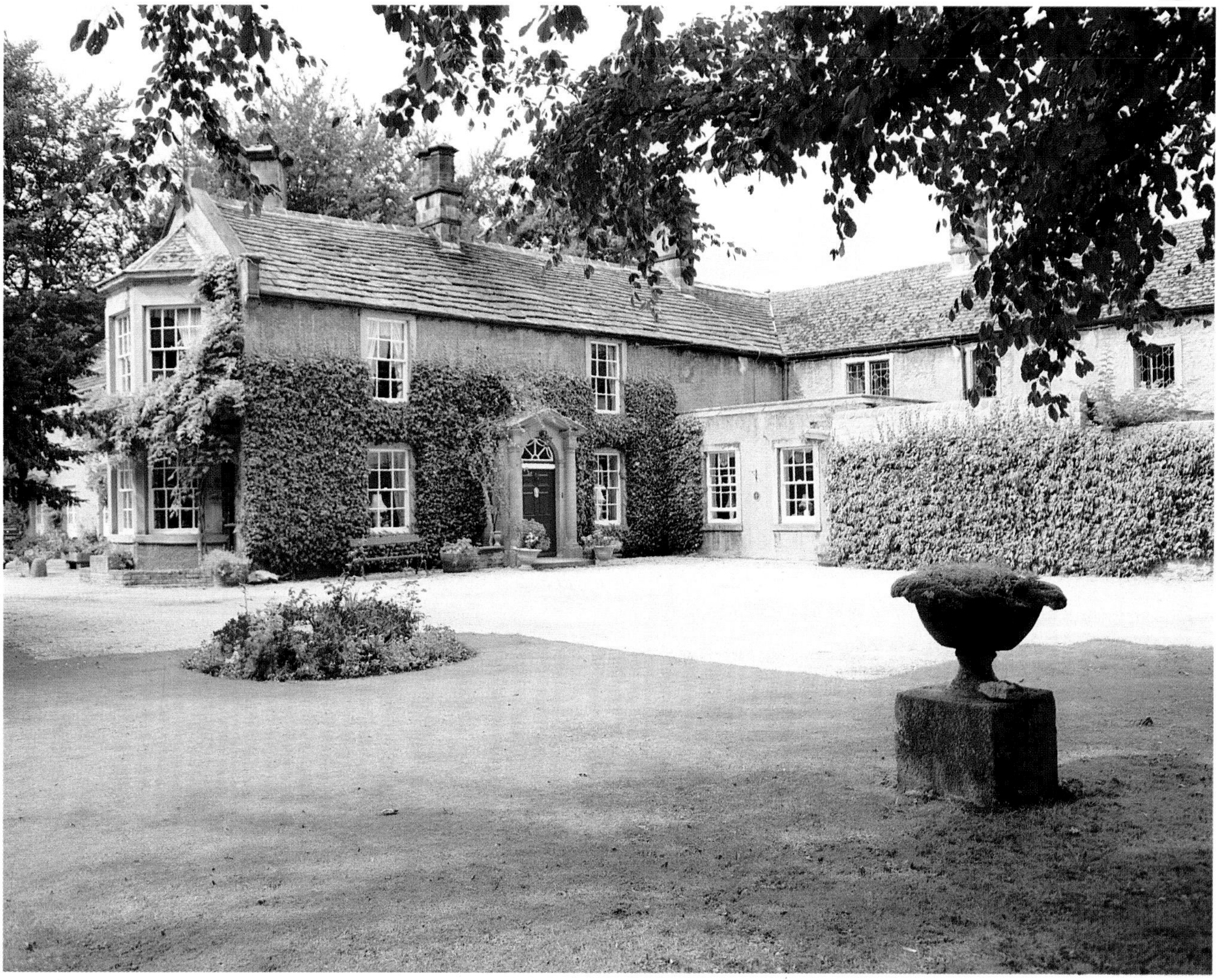

ASHFORD-IN-THE-WATER, NR BAKEWELL, DERBYSHIRE DE45 1QF
TEL: 01629 814275 FAX: 01629 812873

Ashford-in-the-Water lies in a limestone ravine of the River Wye in the Peak District National Park. This picture-postcard village of quaint, stone-built cottages in the centre stands the Riverside Country House, a small ivy-clad Georgian mansion in an acre of mature garden and river frontage. Oak panelling and inglenook fireplaces in the lounge create a sense of warmth – an ideal place to chat or curl up with a book. Using seasonally available game and freshly caught fish in the 2 red rosette restaurant, master chefs create a series of exciting dishes. Dinner and fine wines are served at antique tables set with gleaming silver, sparkling crystal and illuminated by candle-light. Lunch is always available and the Terrace Room buttery is open all day for light meals. All the prettily decorated bedrooms, with hand-made soft furnishings, have private facilities. 3 star AA hotel. Ideally situated for Chatsworth, Haddon Hall and Hardwick Hall, the hotel is also convenient for the Derbyshire Dales, Lathkill and Dovedale. Bargain breaks are offered for two to five-night stays. **Directions:** 1½ miles north of Bakewell on the A6 heading towards Buxton. Ashford-in-the-Water lies on the right side of the river. The hotel is at the end of the village main street next to the Sheepwash Bridge. Price guide: Single from £75; double from £99; twin £110.

For hotel location, see maps on pages 477-483

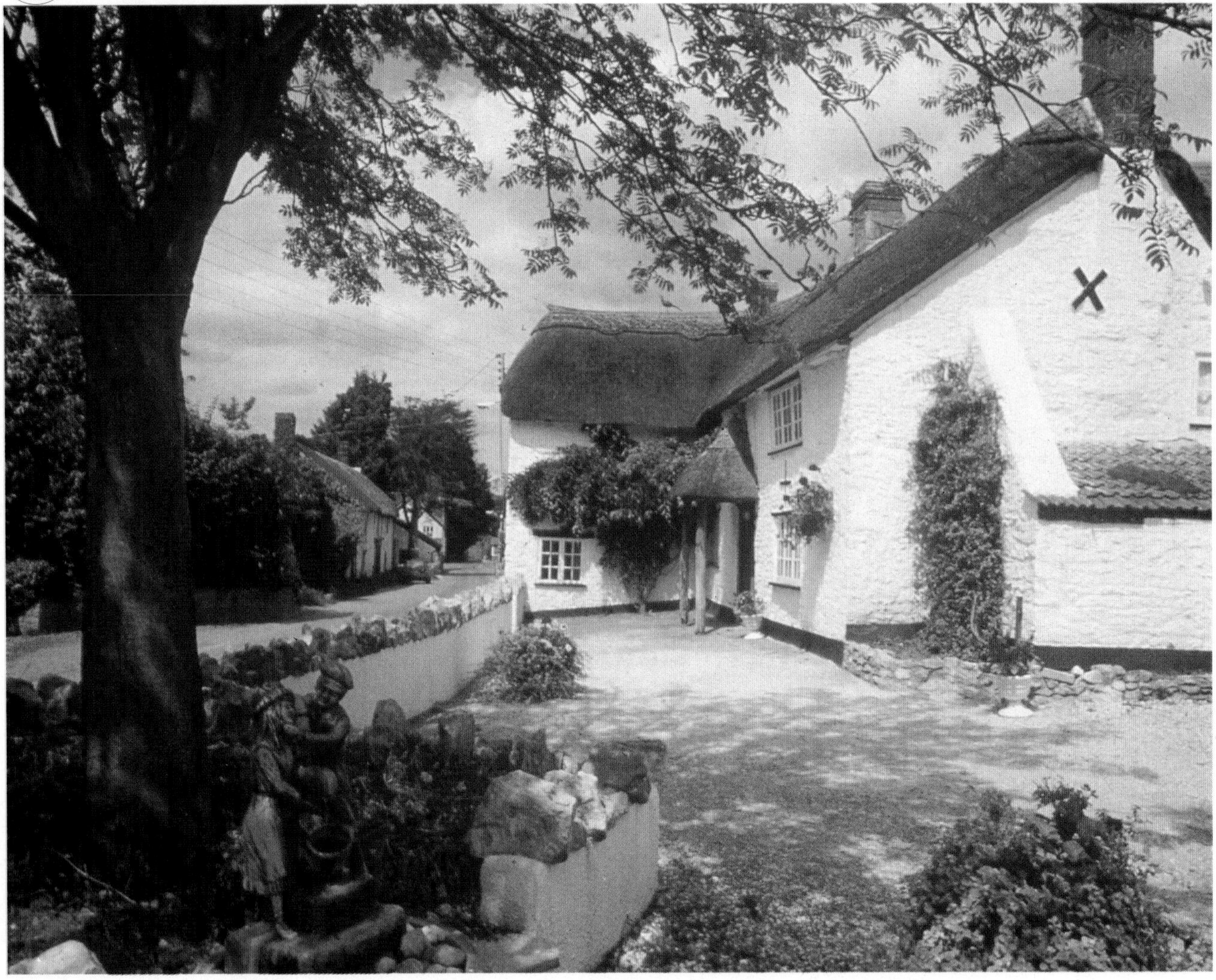

TYTHERLEIGH COT HOTEL

CHARDSTOCK, AXMINSTER, DEVON EX13 7BN
TEL: 01460 221170 FAX: 01460 221291

Originally the village cider house, this 14th-century Grade II listed building has been skilfully converted into a spacious modern hotel, idyllically situated in the secluded village of Chardstock on the Devon/Dorset/Somerset borders. The bedrooms, converted from former barns and outbuildings, are all individually designed, some with four-poster or half-tester beds and double Jacuzzis. The beautifully designed award winning restaurant is housed in a Victorian-style conservatory, overlooking an ornamental lily pond with cascading fountain and wrought-iron bridge. Special house parties are held at Christmas and New Year and bargain break weekends can be arranged. The hotel has an outdoor heated swimming pool, sauna, solarium and mini-gym. Riding, tennis, golf and clay pigeon shooting can be arranged locally. The hotel is ideally located for guests to explore the varied landscape of the South West with many historic houses and National Trust properties nearby. **Directions:** From Chard take A358 Axminster road; Chardstock signposted on right about 3 miles along. Price guide: Single £55; double/twin £98–£123.50.

For hotel location, see maps on pages 477-483

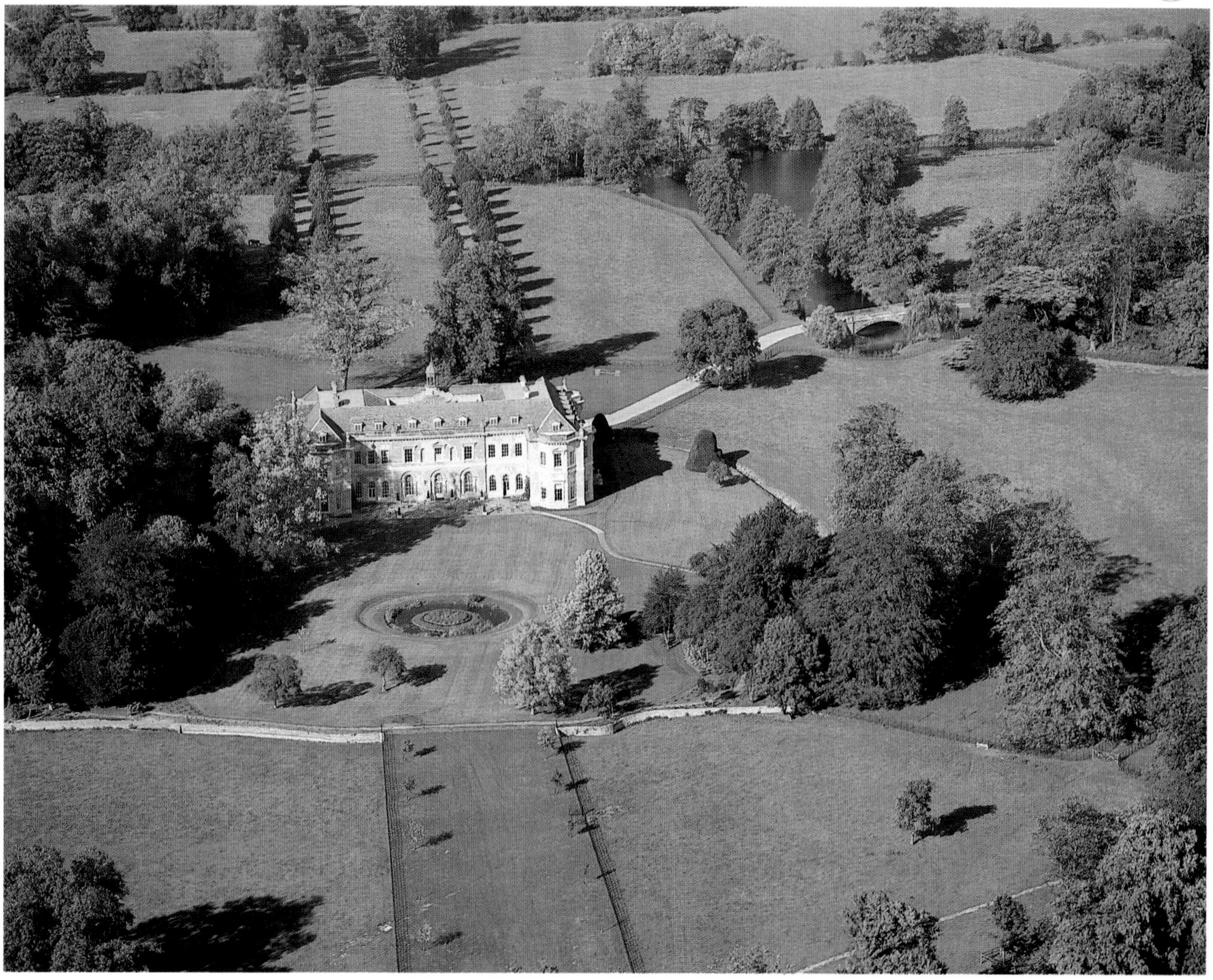

HARTWELL HOUSE

OXFORD ROAD, NR AYLESBURY, BUCKINGHAMSHIRE HP17 8NL
TEL: 01296 747444 FAX: 01296 747450 – FROM USA FAX FREE: 1 800 260 8338

Standing in 90 acres of gardens and parkland landscaped by a pupil of 'Capability' Brown, Hartwell House has both Jacobean and Georgian façades. This beautiful house, brilliantly restored by Historic House Hotels, was the residence in exile of King Louis XVIII of France from 1809 to 1814. The large ground floor reception rooms, with oak panelling and decorated ceilings, have antique furniture and fine paintings which evoke the elegance of the 18th century. There are 47 individually designed bedrooms and suites, some in the house and some in Hartwell Court, the restored 18th-century stables. The dining room at Hartwell is the setting for memorable meals produced by head chef Alan Maw. The Hartwell Spa adjacent to the hotel includes an indoor swimming pool, whirlpool spa bath, steam room, gymnasium, hairdressing and beauty salon. Situated in the Vale of Aylesbury, the hotel, which is a member of Relais & Chateaux, is only an hour from London and 20 miles from Oxford. Blenheim Palace, Waddesdon Manor and Woburn Abbey are nearby. Dogs are permitted only in the Hartwell Court bedrooms. **Directions:** On the A418 Oxford Road, 2 miles from Aylesbury. Price guide: Single £105; double/twin £160–£260; suites £220–£450.

For hotel location, see maps on pages 477-483

THE PRIORY HOTEL

HIGH STREET, WHITCHURCH, AYLESBURY, BUCKINGHAMSHIRE HP22 4JS
TEL: 01296 641239 FAX: 01296 641793

The Priory Hotel is a beautifully preserved, timber-framed house dating back to 1360. It is set in the picturesque conservation village of Whitchurch, which is about 5 miles north of Aylesbury. With its exposed timbers, leaded windows and open fires, it retains all its traditional character and charm – a refreshing alternative to the all-too-familiar chain hotels of today. All 11 bedrooms are individually furnished and many of them have four-poster beds. At the heart of the hotel is La Boiserie Restaurant, where classical French cuisine is served in intimate surroundings. An imaginative à la carte fixed-price menu is offered, including a range of seasonal dishes. Start, for example, with a rich terrine of partridge, wild mushrooms and pistachios, then perhaps choose marinated saddle of venison in Cognac butter sauce and garnished with truffles. Specialities include fresh lobster and flambé dishes. The self-contained conference suite can be used for private lunches, dinners and receptions. Among the places to visit locally are Waddesdon Manor, Claydon House, Stowe, Silverstone motor circuit and Oxford. Closed between Christmas and New Year's Eve; the restaurant also closes on Sunday evenings. **Directions:** Situated on the A413 4 miles north of Aylesbury. Price guide: Single £60–£80; double/twin £95–£110; suite from £102.

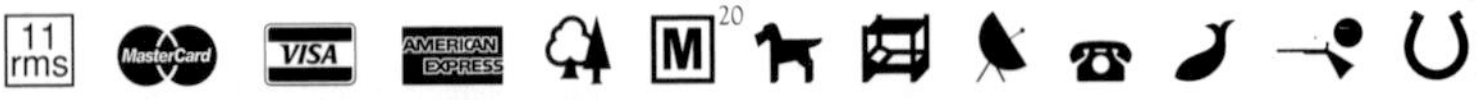

For hotel location, see maps on pages 477-483

HASSOP HALL

HASSOP, NR BAKEWELL, DERBYSHIRE DE45 1NS
TEL: 01629 640488 FAX: 01629 640577

The recorded history of Hassop Hall reaches back 900 years to the *Domesday Book*, to a time when the political scene in England was still dominated by the power struggle between the barons and the King, when the only sure access to that power was through possession of land. By 1643, when the Civil War was raging, the Hall was under the ownership of Rowland Eyre, who turned it into a Royalist garrison. It was the scene of several skirmishes before it was recaptured after the Parliamentary victory. Since purchasing Hassop Hall in 1975, Thomas Chapman has determinedly pursued the preservation of its outstanding heritage. Guests can enjoy the beautifully maintained gardens as well as the splendid countryside of the surrounding area. The bedrooms, some of which are particularly spacious, are well furnished and comfortable. A four-poster bedroom is available for romantic occasions. A comprehensive dinner menu offers a wide and varied selection of dishes, with catering for most tastes. As well as the glories of the Peak District, places to visit include Chatsworth House, Haddon Hall and Buxton Opera House. Christmas opening – details on application. **Directions:** From M1 exit 29 (Chesterfield), take A619 to Baslow, then A623 to Calver; left at lights to B6001. Hassop Hall is 2 miles on right. Price guide: Single £65–£89; double/twin £79–£99. Inclusive rates available on request.

For hotel location, see maps on pages 477-483

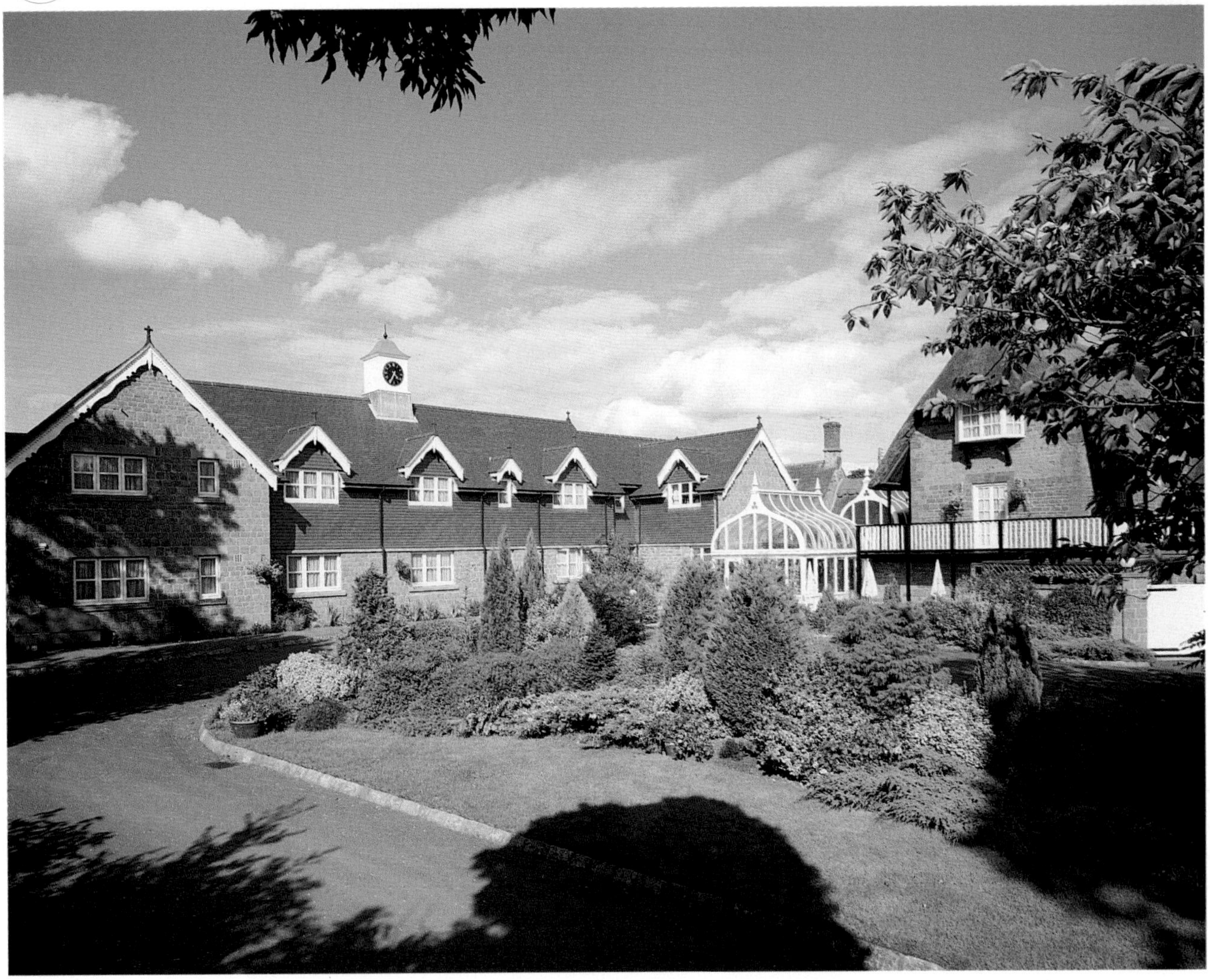

WROXTON HOUSE HOTEL

WROXTON ST MARY, NR BANBURY, OXFORDSHIRE OX15 6QB

TEL: 01295 730777 FAX: 01295 730800

Built of honeyed local stone, Wroxton House has undergone a sensitive restoration linking three village houses, dating from the 17th century, with a delightful clocktower wing and conservatory lounge. The relaxing character of the hotel is created by the carefully selected staff, who combine attentive service with friendliness and informality. The spacious and bright lounges contain thoughtfully chosen furnishings, comfortable armchairs and a profusion of flowers and plants. The 32 en suite bedrooms have been individually decorated and the original timbers preserved in many of the older rooms. The classic English styles complement the deeply polished woods of the furniture. Guests may dine by candlelight in the intimate restaurant, where a traditional Cotswold atmosphere is evoked by original beams, inglenooks, carved oak recesses, horse brasses and pewter. The expertly prepared menus display a personal interpretation of classic British dishes which make imaginative use of the freshest local produce. Wroxton House Hotel is a popular choice with businessmen, as it offers good meeting facilities in a quiet setting. Golf and riding can be arranged locally. **Directions:** Easily reached via M40, Wroxton is two miles outside Banbury on the A422 Stratford-upon-Avon road. Price guide: Single £75–£85; double/twin £95–£125.

For hotel location, see maps on pages 477-483

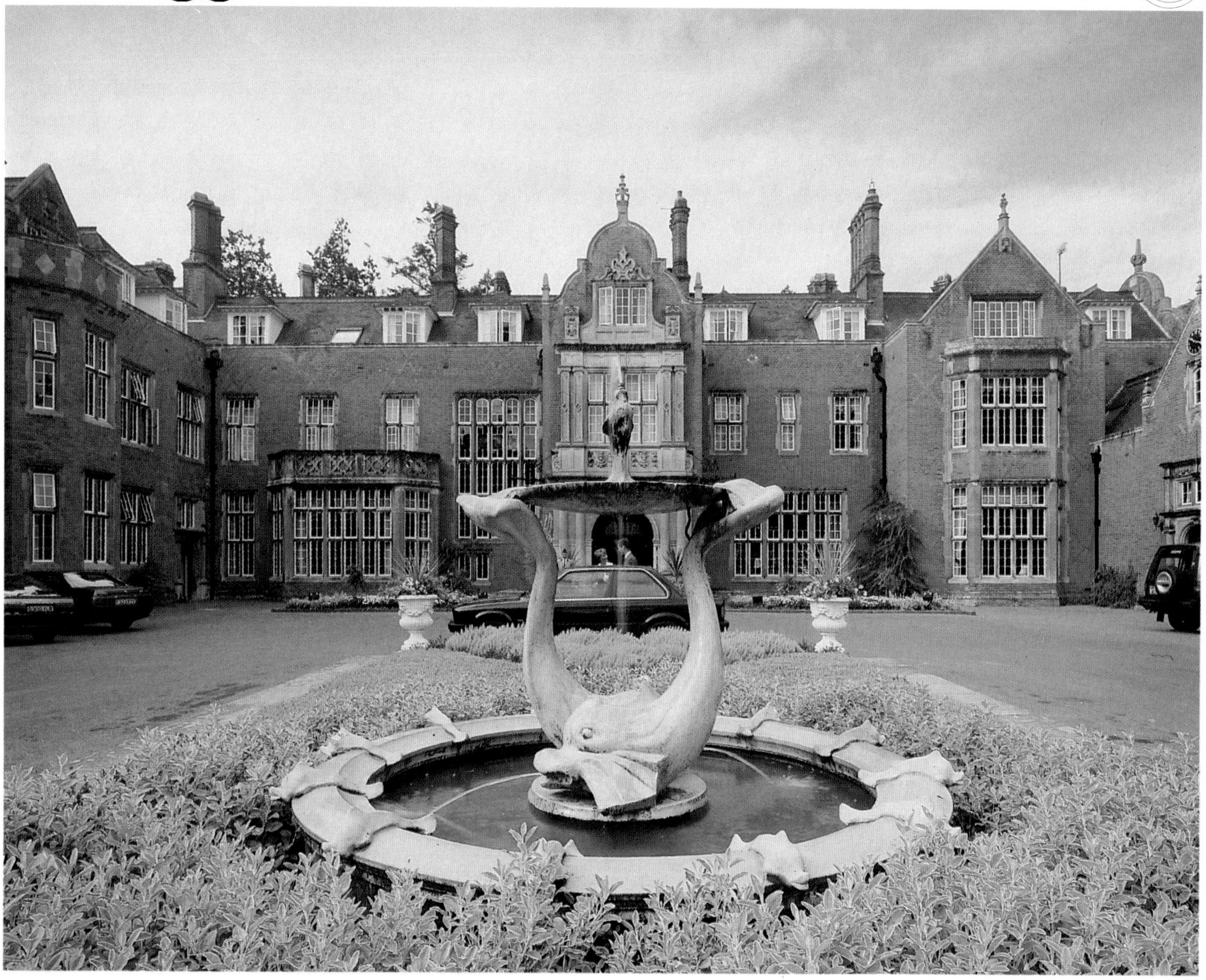

TYLNEY HALL

ROTHERWICK, NR HOOK, HAMPSHIRE RG27 9AZ
TEL: 01256 764881 FAX: 01256 768141

Arriving at this hotel in the evening, with its floodlit exterior and forecourt fountain, you can imagine that you are arriving for a party in a private stately home. Grade II listed and set in 66 acres of stunning gardens and parkland, Tylney Hall typifies the great houses of the past. Apéritifs are taken in the wood-panelled library bar; haute cuisine is served in the glass-domed Oak Room restaurant, complemented by conscientious service. The hotel was the 1990 winner of the AA Care and Courtesy Award and holds 2 AA Rosettes for food and also AA 4 Red Stars. Extensive leisure facilities include indoor and outdoor heated swimming pools, multi-gym, sauna, tennis, croquet and snooker, while hot-air ballooning, archery, clay pigeon shooting, golf and riding can be arranged. Surrounding the hotel are wooded trails ideal for rambling or jogging. Functions for up to a hundred are catered for in the Tylney Suite or Chestnut Suite, while more intimate gatherings are held in one of the other ten meeting rooms. The cathedral city of Winchester and Stratfield Saye House are all nearby. **Directions:** M4, junction 11, towards Hook and Rotherwick – follow signs to hotel. M3, junction 5, 3rd exit, A287 towards Newnham – over A30 into Old School Road. Left for Newnham and right onto Ridge Lane. Hotel is on the left after one mile. Price guide: Single from £104; double/twin from £124; suite from £214.

95 rms

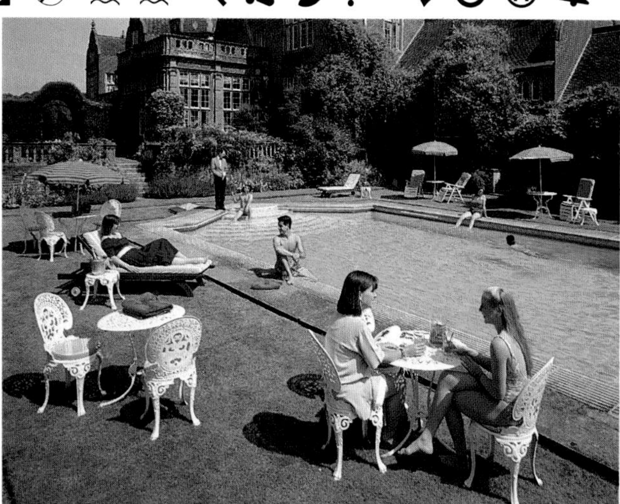

For hotel location, see maps on pages 477-483

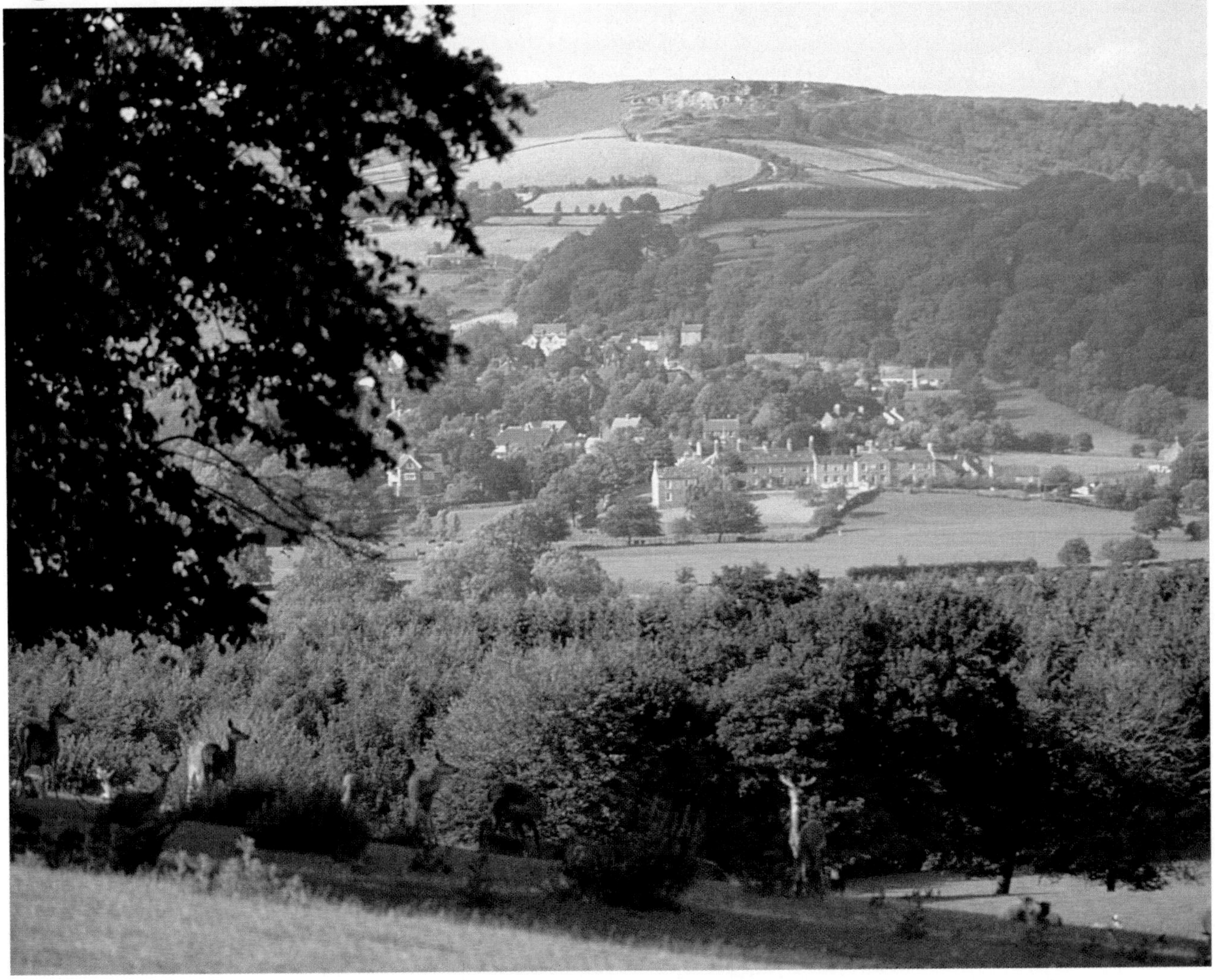

CAVENDISH HOTEL

BASLOW, DERBYSHIRE DE45 1SP
TEL: 01246 582311 FAX: 01246 582312

Dating from the late 18th century, the original Peacock Hotel has been considerably upgraded and was re-opened as the Cavendish in 1975. Set on the Duke and Duchess of Devonshire's estate at Chatsworth, the hotel occupies a unique position and makes a marvellous base for visitors who wish to explore this part of Derbyshire. A warm welcome is assured from proprietor Eric Marsh who greets guests personally. All the well-equipped bedrooms overlook the estate and have en suite facilities. The hotel has a relaxed, homely feel which is enhanced by crackling log fires in cooler weather. The tasteful furnishings include antiques and fine art from the Devonshire Collection. Meals are served throughout the day in the Garden Room Restaurant, where the informal atmosphere is in contrast to the other, more formal, dining room. Chef Nicholas Buckingham and his team have won many commendations for their creative cuisine. A footpath connects the hotel to the Chatsworth Estate where guests are welcome to stroll. Hardwick Hall, Haddon Hall, the Treak Cliff Cavern (the Blue John mine) and the Tramway Museum at Crich are all nearby. **Directions:** The hotel is on the A619 in Baslow, 9 miles west of Chesterfield; 15 miles from M1, junction 29. Price guide (excluding breakfast): Single £79; double/twin £99.

For hotel location, see maps on pages 477-483

FISCHER'S

BASLOW HALL, CALVER ROAD, BASLOW, DERBYSHIRE DE45 1RR
TEL: 01246 583259 FAX: 01246 583818

Situated on the edge of the magnificent Chatsworth Estate, Baslow Hall enjoys an enviable location surrounded by some of the country's finest stately homes and within easy reach of the Peak District's many cultural and historical attractions. Standing at the end of a winding chestnut tree-lined driveway, this fine Derbyshire manor house was tastefully converted by Max and Susan Fischer into an award winning country house hotel in 1989. Since opening Fischer's has consistently maintained its position as one of the finest establishments in the Derbyshire/ South Yorkshire regions earning the prestigious Egon Ronay 'Restaurant of the Year' award in 1995. Whether you are staying in the area for private or business reasons, it is a welcome change to find a place that feels less like a hotel and more like a home combining comfort and character with an eating experience which is a delight to the palate. Max presides in the kitchen. His Michelin starred cuisine can be savoured either in the more formal main dining room or in 'Café Max' – where the emphasis is on more informal eating and modern tastes. Baslow Hall offers facilities for small conferences or private functions. Baslow is within 12 miles of the M1 motorway, Chesterfield and Sheffield. Fischer's is on the A623 in Baslow. Price guide: Single £75–£90; double/twin £95–£120; suite £120.

6 rms MasterCard VISA AMERICAN EXPRESS M 10

For hotel location, see maps on pages 477-483

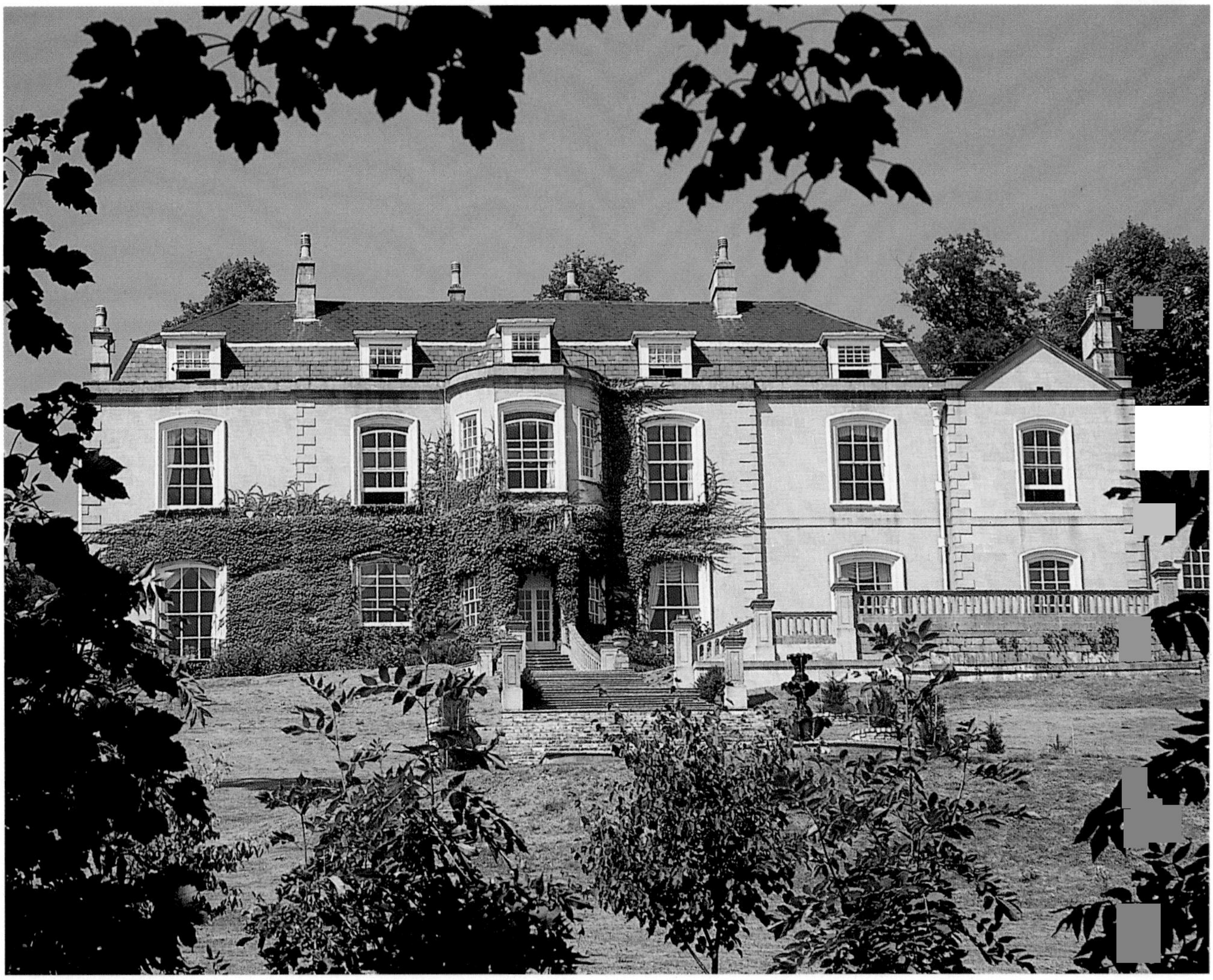

Combe Grove Manor Hotel & Country Club

BRASSKNOCKER HILL, MONKTON COMBE, BATH, AVON BA2 7HS
TEL: 01225 834644 FAX: 01225 834961

This is an exclusive 18th-century country house hotel situated two miles from the beautiful city of Bath. Built on the hillside site of a Roman settlement, Combe Grove Manor is set in 82 acres of formal gardens and woodland, with magnificent views over the Limpley Stoke Valley. In addition to the Georgian Restaurant, where superb food is served prepared by chef Paul Mingo-West, there is a private dining room, plus a wine bar and restaurant with a terrace garden. After dinner guests may relax with drinks in the elegant drawing room or library. The bedrooms are lavishly furnished, all individually designed with en suite facilities, two of which have Jacuzzi baths. Within the grounds are some of the finest leisure facilities in the South West, including indoor and outdoor heated pools, hydrospa beds and steam room, four all-weather tennis courts, a 5-hole par 3 golf course and a two-tiered driving range. Guests may use the Nautilus gym, aerobics studio, saunas and solaria or relax in the Clarins beauty rooms where a full range of treatments is offered. Separate from the Manor House is the Garden Lodge which provides 31 rooms, all with spectacular views and some have a private terrace. ETB 5 Crowns Highly Commended. AA 4 Stars. 2 Rosettes. **Directions:** Set south-east of Bath off the A36 near the University. Map can be supplied on request. Price guide: Single £98; double/twin from £98; suite from £195.

For hotel location, see maps on pages 477-483

HOMEWOOD PARK

HINTON CHARTERHOUSE, BATH, AVON BA3 6BB
TEL: 01225 723731 FAX: 01225 723820

Standing amid 10 acres of beautiful grounds and woodland on the edge of Limpley Stoke Valley, a designated area of natural beauty is Homewood Park, one of Britain's finest privately-owned smaller country house hotels. This lovely 19th century building has an elegant interior, adorned with beautiful fabrics, antiques, oriental rugs and original oil paintings. Lavishly furnished bedrooms offer the best in comfort, style and privacy. Each of them has a charm and character of its own and all have good views over the Victorian garden. The outstanding cuisine has won the hotel an excellent reputation. The à la carte menu uses wherever possible produce both from local suppliers and from Homewood itself. A range of carefully selected wines, stored in the hotel's original mediaeval cellars, lies patiently waiting to augment lunch and dinner. Before or after a meal guests can enjoy a drink in the comfortable bar or drawing rooms, both of which have a log fire during the cooler months. The hotel is well placed for guests to enjoy the varied attractions of the wonderful city of Bath with its unique hot springs, Roman remains, superb Georgian architecture and American Museum. Further afield but within reach are Stonehenge and Cheddar caves. **Directions:** On the A36 six miles from Bath towards Warminster. Price guide: Single £90; double/twin £98–£175; suite from £215.

19 rms 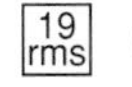        35 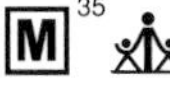       

For hotel location, see maps on pages 477-483

In association with MasterCard

HUNSTRETE HOUSE

HUNSTRETE, CHELWOOD, NR BRISTOL, B&NE SOMERSET BS18 4NS

TEL: 01761 490490 FAX: 01761 490732

In a classical English landscape on the edge of the Mendip Hills stands Hunstrete House. This Michelin Starred hotel, surrounded by lovely gardens, is largely 18th century, although the history of the estate goes back to 963AD. Each of the bedrooms is individually decorated and furnished to a high standard, combining the benefits of a hotel room with the atmosphere of a charming private country house. Many offer uninterrupted views over undulating fields and woodlands. The reception areas exhibit warmth and elegance and are liberally furnished with beautiful antiques. Log fires burn in the hall, library and drawing room through the winter and on cooler summer evenings. The Terrace dining room looks out on to an Italianate, flower filled courtyard. A highly skilled head chef offers light, elegant dishes using produce from the extensive garden, along with the best of English meat and fish. The menu changes regularly and the hotel has an excellent reputation for the quality and interest of its wine list. In a sheltered corner of the walled garden there is a heated swimming pool for guests to enjoy. For the energetic, the all weather tennis court provides another diversion and there are riding stables in Hunstrete village, a five minute walk away. **Directions:** From Bath take the A4 towards Bristol and then the A368 to Wells. Price guide: Single £115–£150; double/twin from £150; suite from £230.

For hotel location, see maps on pages 477-483

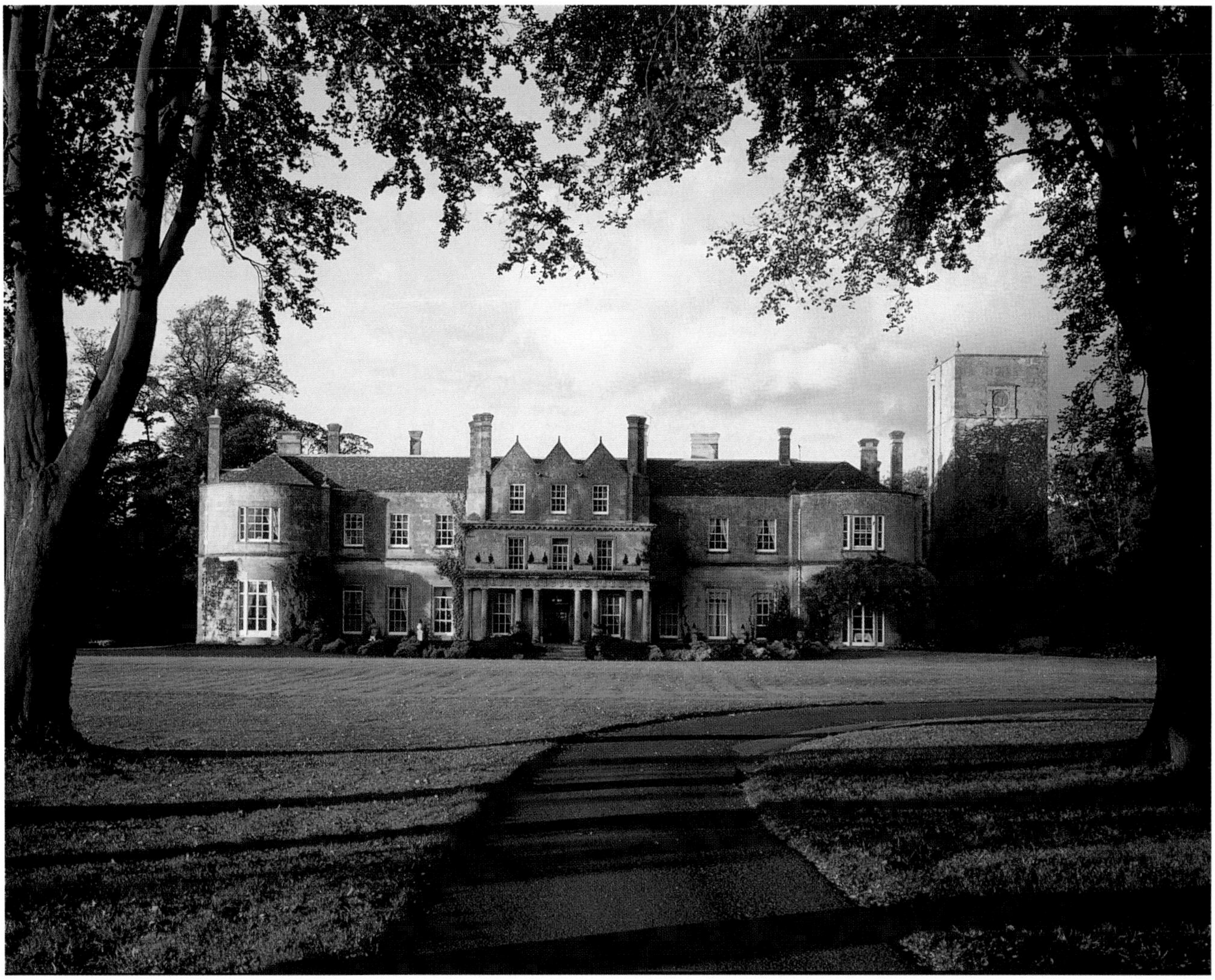

LUCKNAM PARK

COLERNE, NR BATH, WILTSHIRE SN14 8AZ
TEL: 01225 742777 FAX: 01225 743536

For over 250 years Lucknam Park has been a focus of fine society and aristocratic living, something guests will sense immediately upon their approach along the mile-long avenue lined with beech trees. Built in 1720, this magnificent Palladian mansion is situated just six miles from Bath on the southern edge of the Cotswolds. The delicate aura of historical context is reflected in fine art and antiques dating from the late Georgian and early Victorian periods. The Michelin-starred cuisine can be savoured in the elegant restaurant, at tables laid with exquisite porcelain, silver and glassware, accompanied with wines from an extensive cellar. Set within the walled gardens of the hotel is the Leisure Spa, comprising an indoor pool, sauna, solarium, steam room, whirlpool spa, gymnasium, beauty salon and snooker room. Numerous activities can be arranged on request, including hot-air ballooning, golf and archery. The Lucknam Park Equestrian Centre, which is situated on the estate, welcomes complete beginners and experienced riders, offers expert tuition from Heather Holgate and takes liverys. Bowood House, Corsham Court and Castle Combe are all nearby. **Directions:** Fifteen minutes from M4, junctions 17 and 18, located between A420 and A4 near the village of Colerne. Price guide: Single £120; double/twin £170; suite from £340.

For hotel location, see maps on pages 477-483

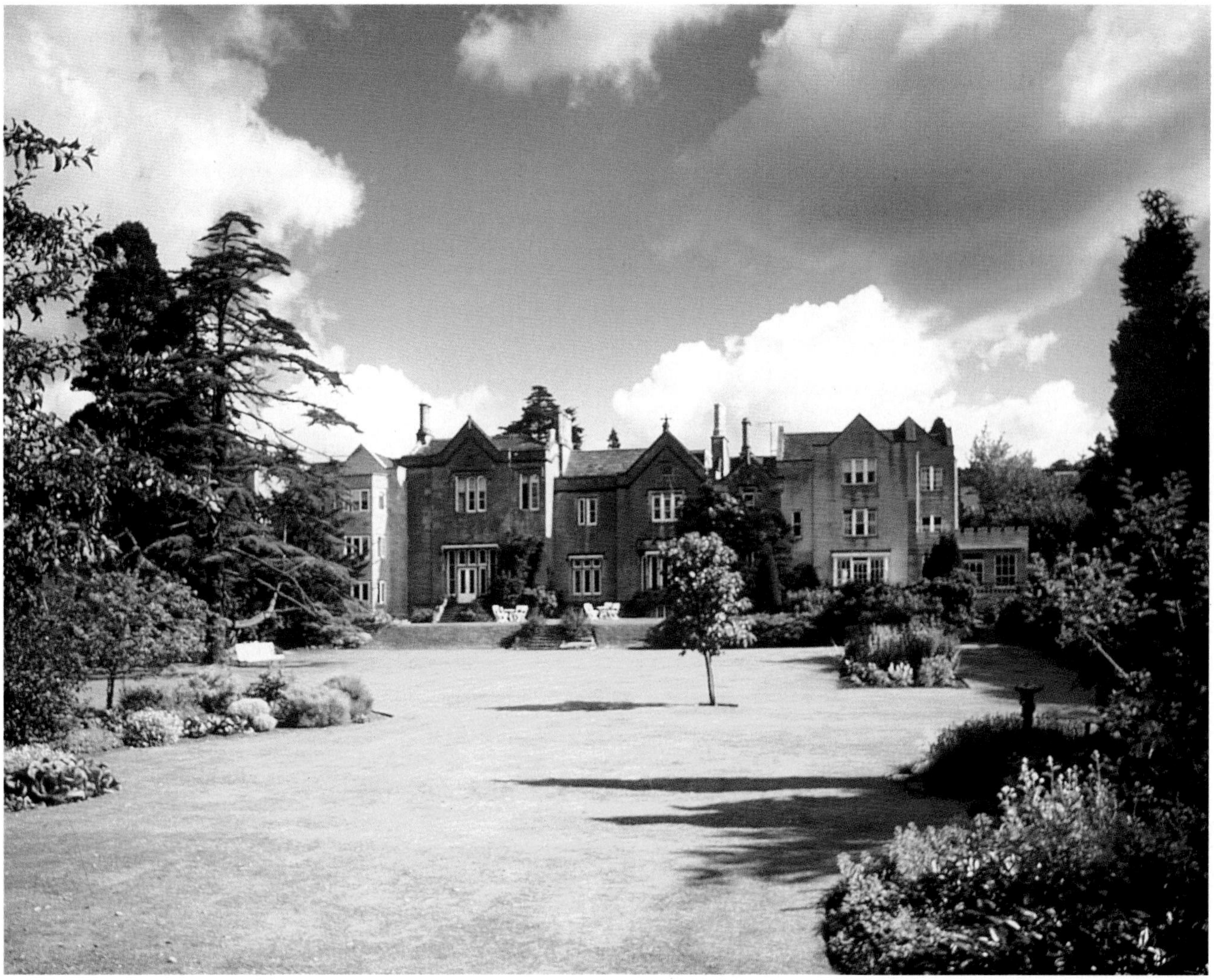

THE PRIORY

WESTON ROAD, BATH, SOMERSET BA1 2XT
TEL: 01225 331922 FAX: 01225 448276

Lying in the seclusion of landscaped grounds, The Priory Hotel is close to some of England's most famous and finest architecture. Within walking distance of Bath city centre, this Gothic-style mellow stone building dates from 1835, when it formed part of a row of fashionable residences on the west side of the city. Visitors will sense the luxury as they enter the hotel: antique furniture, plush rugs and *objets d'art* add interest to the two spacious reception rooms and the elegant drawing room. Well-defined colour schemes lend an uplifting brightness throughout, particularly in the tastefully appointed bedrooms. Chef Michael Collom's French classical style is the primary inspiration for the cuisine, served in three interconnecting dining rooms which overlook the garden. An especially good selection of wines can be recommended to accompany meals. Private functions can be accommodated both in the Drawing Room and the Orangery, with garden access an added bonus. The Roman Baths, Theatre Royal, Museum of Costume and a host of bijou shops offer plenty for visitors to see. **Directions:** Leave M4 at junction 18 to Bath on A46. Enter city on A4 London road and follow signs for Bristol. Turn right into Park Lane which runs through Royal Victoria Park. Then turn left into Weston Road. The hotel is on the left. Price guide: Single £115; double/twin £155–£195; suites £225.

For hotel location, see maps on pages 477-483

THE QUEENSBERRY

RUSSEL STREET, BATH, BATH & NE SOMERSET BA1 2QF
TEL: 01225 447928 FAX: 01225 446065

When the Marquis of Queensberry commissioned John Wood to build this house in Russel Street in 1772, little did he know that 200 years hence guests would still be being entertained in these elegant surroundings. An intimate town house hotel, The Queensberry is in a quiet residential street just a few minutes' walk from Wood's other splendours – the Royal Crescent, Circus and Assembly Rooms. Bath is one of England's most beautiful cities. Regency stucco ceilings, ornate cornices and panelling combined with enchanting interior décor complement the strong architectural style. However, the standards of hotel-keeping have far outpaced the traditional surroundings, with high-quality en suite bedrooms, room service and up-to-date office support for executives. The Olive Tree Restaurant is one of the leading restaurants in the Bath area. Proprietors Stephen and Penny Ross, who in the 1980's gained their admirable reputation at Homewood Park, are thoroughly versed in offering hospitality. Represented in America by Josephine Barr. The hotel is closed for one week at Christmas. **Directions:** From junction 18 of M4, enter Bath along A4 London Road. Turn sharp right up Lansdown Road, left into Bennett Street, then right into Russel Street opposite the Assembly Rooms. Price guide: Single £89; double/twin £110–£175.

For hotel location, see maps on pages 477-483

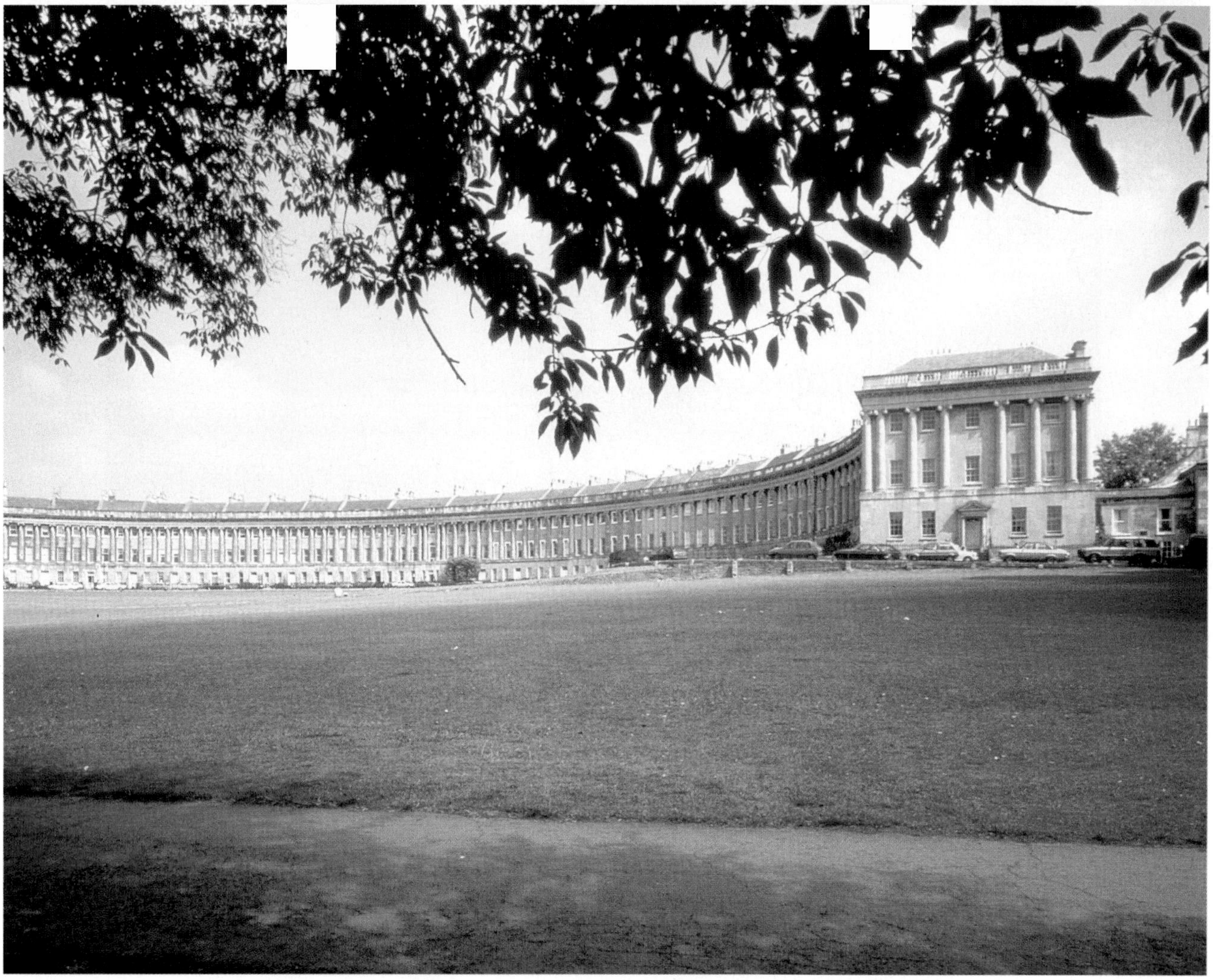

THE ROYAL CRESCENT

ROYAL CRESCENT, BATH, B&NE SOMERSET BA1 2LS
TEL: 01225 739955 FAX: 01225 339401

The Royal Crescent Hotel is part of the Royal Crescent itself a 500ft curve of 30 houses with identical façades. The Crescent was conceived in the latter part of the 18th century and is one of the greatest European architectural masterpieces. The hotel comprises the two central houses and within its beautiful gardens are The Pavilion, The Garden Villa and The Dower House. In the front hall of the hotel is a unique collection of original Bath landscapes and portraits of the famous people who have lived in the city. The bedrooms are individually decorated to suit every taste and each has its own character, while the suites are the last word in comfort. The Beau Nash suite, for example, has its own large spa pool room. Luxurious furnishings and tasteful décor are also a striking feature of the various reception rooms. Nestling in the gardens, the Dower House Restaurant offers a delicious table d'hôte menu which combines flair with imagination and originality. The restaurant has received three AA rosettes and an Egon Ronay Star. The hotel has peaceful conference facilities in The Royal Crescent Mews. Apart from the delights of Bath, there are innumerable local activities. These include motor racing at the Castle Combe Circuit and hot air ballooning. **Directions:** Detailed directions are available from the hotel on booking. Price guide Single: £105–£120; double/twin £165–£225; suites £295.

For hotel location, see maps on pages 477-483

STON EASTON PARK

STON EASTON, BATH, SOMERSET BA3 4DF

TEL: 01761 241631 FAX: 01761 241377 e-MAIL stoneaston@cityscape.co.uk

The internationally renowned hotel at Ston Easton Park is a Grade I Palladian mansion of notable distinction. A showpiece for some exceptional architectural and decorative features of its period, it dates from 1739 and has recently undergone extensive restoration, offering a unique opportunity to enjoy the opulent splendour of the 18th century. A high priority is given to the provision of friendly and unobtrusive service. The hotel has won innumerable awards for its décor, service and food. Jean Monro, an acknowledged expert on 18th century decoration, supervised the design and furnishing of the interiors, complementing the original features with choice antiques, paintings and *objets d'art.* Fresh, quality produce, delivered from all parts of Britain, is combined with herbs and vegetables from the Victorian kitchen garden to create English and French dishes. To accompany the meal, a wide selection of rare wines and old vintages is stocked in the house cellars. The grounds, landscaped by Humphry Repton in 1793, consist of romantic gardens and parkland. The 17th-century Gardener's Cottage, close to the main hotel on the wooded banks of the River Norr, provides private suite accommodation. A Relais et Châteaux member. **Directions:** Eleven miles south of Bath on the A37 between Bath and Wells. Price guide: Single from £125; double/twin £165–£360.

21 rms MasterCard VISA AMERICAN EXPRESS M 35 7

For hotel location, see maps on pages 477-483

In association with MasterCard

POWDERMILLS HOTEL

POWDERMILL LANE, BATTLE, EAST SUSSEX TN33 0SP
TEL: 01424 775511 FAX: 01424 774540

Situated outside the historic Sussex town famous for the 1066 battle, Powdermills is an 18th century listed country house which has been skilfully converted into an elegant hotel. Nestling in 150 acres of parks and woodland, the beautiful and tranquil grounds feature a 7-acre specimen fishing lake, as well as three smaller lakes stocked with trout for which guests may fish. Wild geese, swans, ducks, kingfishers and herons abound and a rare breed of Scottish sheep grazes nearby. Privately owned and run by Douglas and Julie Cowpland, the hotel has been carefully furnished with locally acquired antiques. On cooler days, log fires burn in the entrance hall and drawing room. The bedrooms – two with four-posters – are all individually furnished and decorated. The Orangery Restaurant has received many accolades and offers fine classical cooking by chef Paul Webbe. Guests may dine on the terrace in summer, looking out over the swimming pool and grounds. Light meals and snacks are available in the library. The location is ideal from which to explore the beautiful Sussex and Kent countryside and there are many villages and small towns in the area. **Directions:** From centre of Battle take the Hastings road south. After 1/4 mile turn right into Powdermill Lane. After sharp bend, entrance is on right; cross over bridge and lakes to reach hotel. Price guide: Single £55–£70; double/twin £80–£150.

For hotel location, see maps on pages 477-483

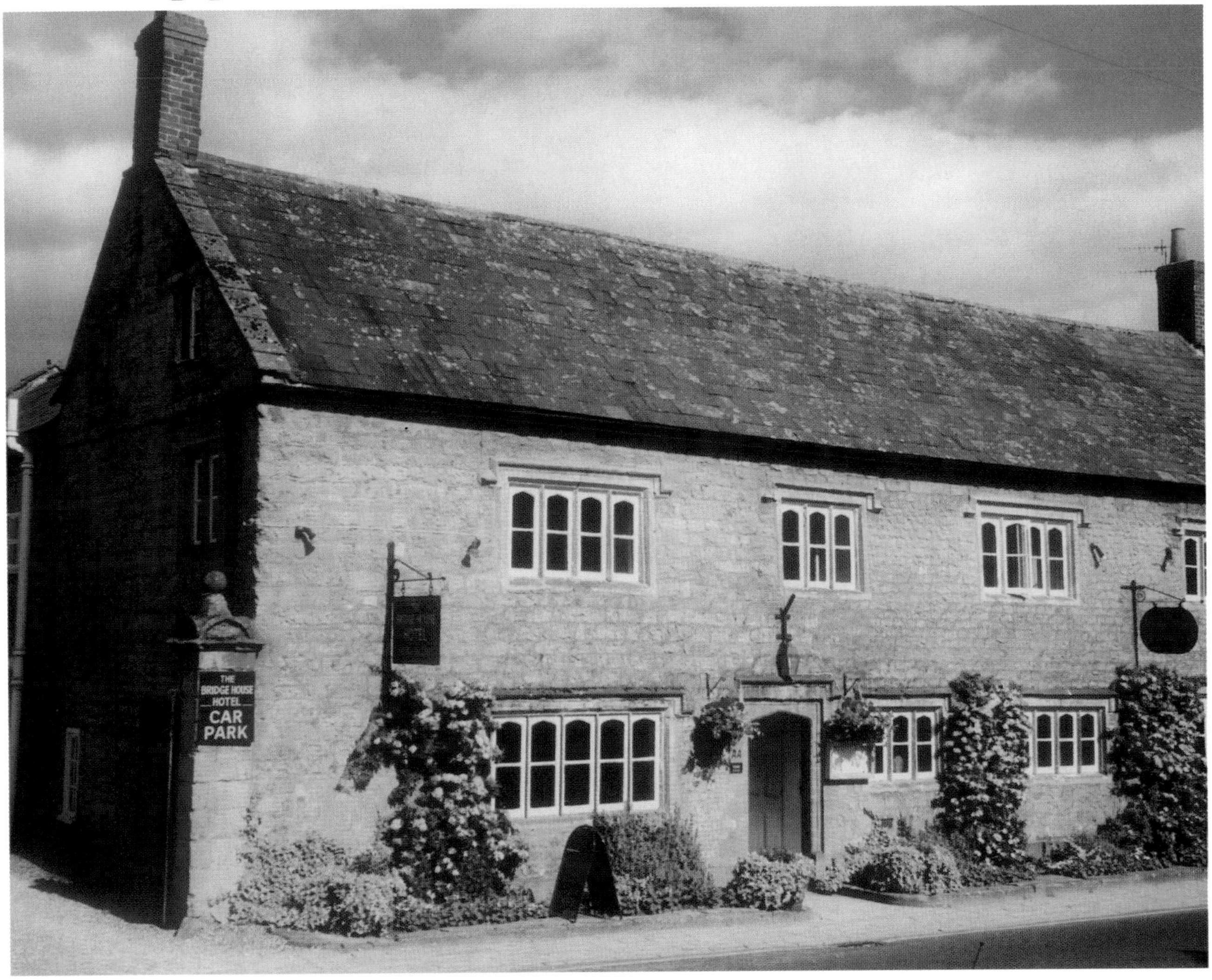

BRIDGE HOUSE HOTEL

BEAMINSTER, DORSET DT8 3AY

TEL: 01308 862200 FAX: 01308 863700

This country town hotel, built of mellow stone, was once a priest's house and dates back to the 13th century. It is set in the heart of Beaminster, an old market town. In this charming hotel, enclosed by a beautiful walled garden, emphasis is placed on creating a relaxing atmosphere for guests and providing them with the highest standards of comfort without sacrificing the character of the surroundings. The warm stone, beams and large fireplaces combine with every modern day amenity to provide a pleasant environment which visitors will remember. Attractively decorated and furnished bedrooms include a colour television and tea and coffee making facilities. Four of them are on the ground floor and offer easy access. The pride of the house is its food, where attention to detail is evident. In the candle-lit Georgian dining room an imaginative menu offers dishes that make use of fresh produce from the local farms and fishing ports. Beaminster is convenient for touring, walking and exploring the magnificent West Dorset countryside. Places of interest nearby include many fine houses and gardens. Several golf courses, fresh and salt water fishing, riding, sailing and sea bathing are all within reach. **Directions:** From M3 take A303 Crewkerne exit then A356 through Crewkerne, then A3066 to Beaminster. Hotel is 100 yds from town centre car park, on the left. Price guide Single £56-£70; twin/double £78-£99.

13 rms      

For hotel location, see maps on pages 477-483

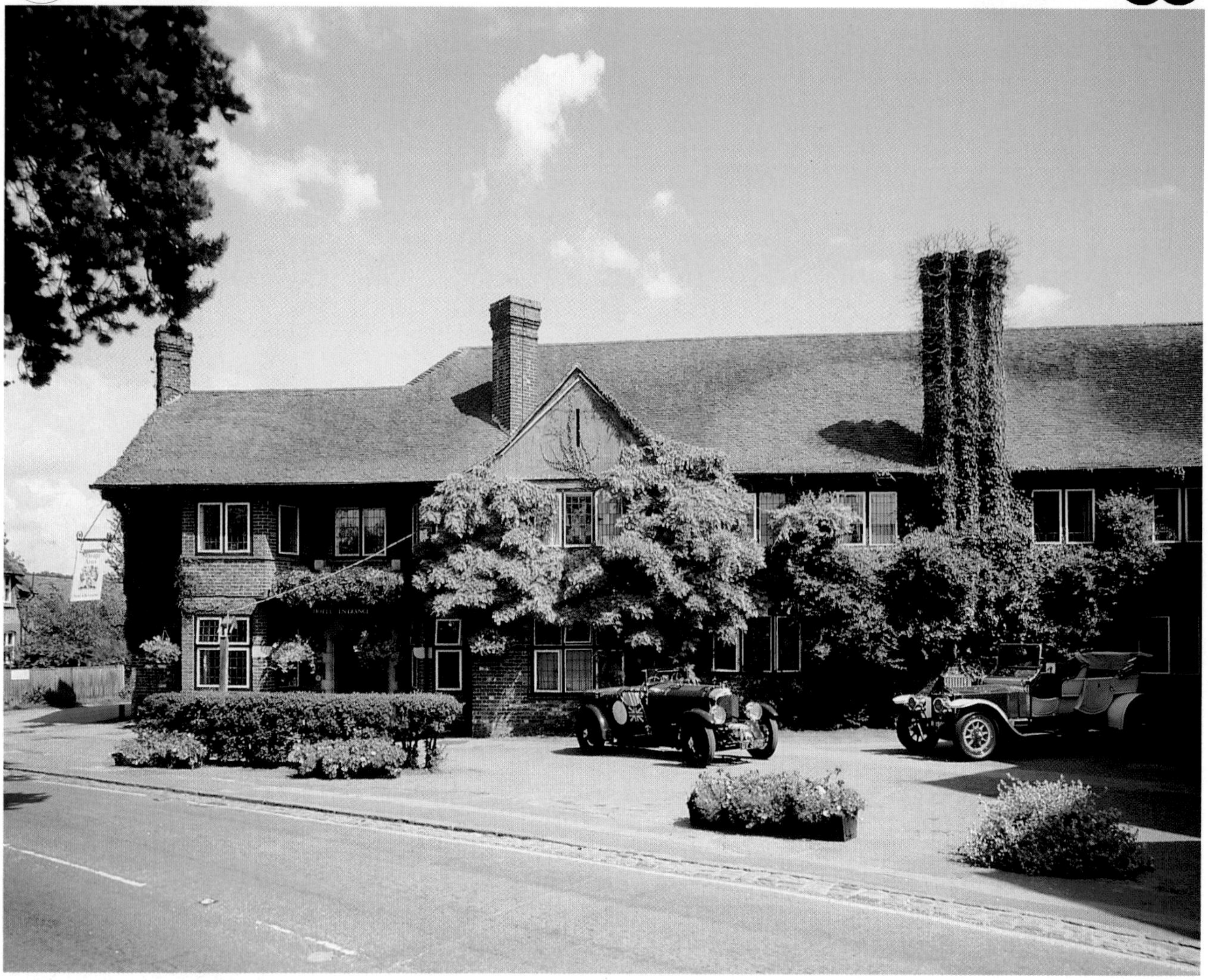

THE MONTAGU ARMS HOTEL

BEAULIEU, NEW FOREST, HAMPSHIRE S042 7ZL
TEL: 01590 612324 FAX: 01590 612188

Situated at the head of the River Beaulieu in the heart of the New Forest, The Montagu Arms Hotel carries on a tradition of hospitality started 700 years ago. As well as being a good place for a holiday, the hotel is an ideal venue for small conferences. Each of the 24 bedrooms has been individually styled and many are furnished with four-poster beds. Choose from sumptuous suites, luxurious junior suites, superior and standard accommodation. All rooms are equipped with colour television, direct-dial telephones, radio and a trouser press. Dine in the oak-panelled restaurant overlooking the garden, where you can enjoy cuisine prepared by award-winning chef Simon Fennell. The menu is supported by an outstanding wine list. The hotel offers complimentary membership of an exclusive health club 6 miles away. Facilities there include a supervised gymnasium, large indoor ozone pool, Jacuzzi, steam room, sauna and beauty therapist. With much to see and do around Beaulieu why not hire a mountain bike? Visit the National Motor Museum, Exbury Gardens or Bucklers Hard, or walk for miles through the beautiful New Forest. Special tariffs are available throughout the year. **Directions:** The village of Beaulieu is well signposted and the hotel commands an impressive position at the foot of the main street. Price guide: Single £69.90–£75.90; double/twin £98.90–£149.90; suite £175.90. Inclusive terms available

For hotel location, see maps on pages 477-483

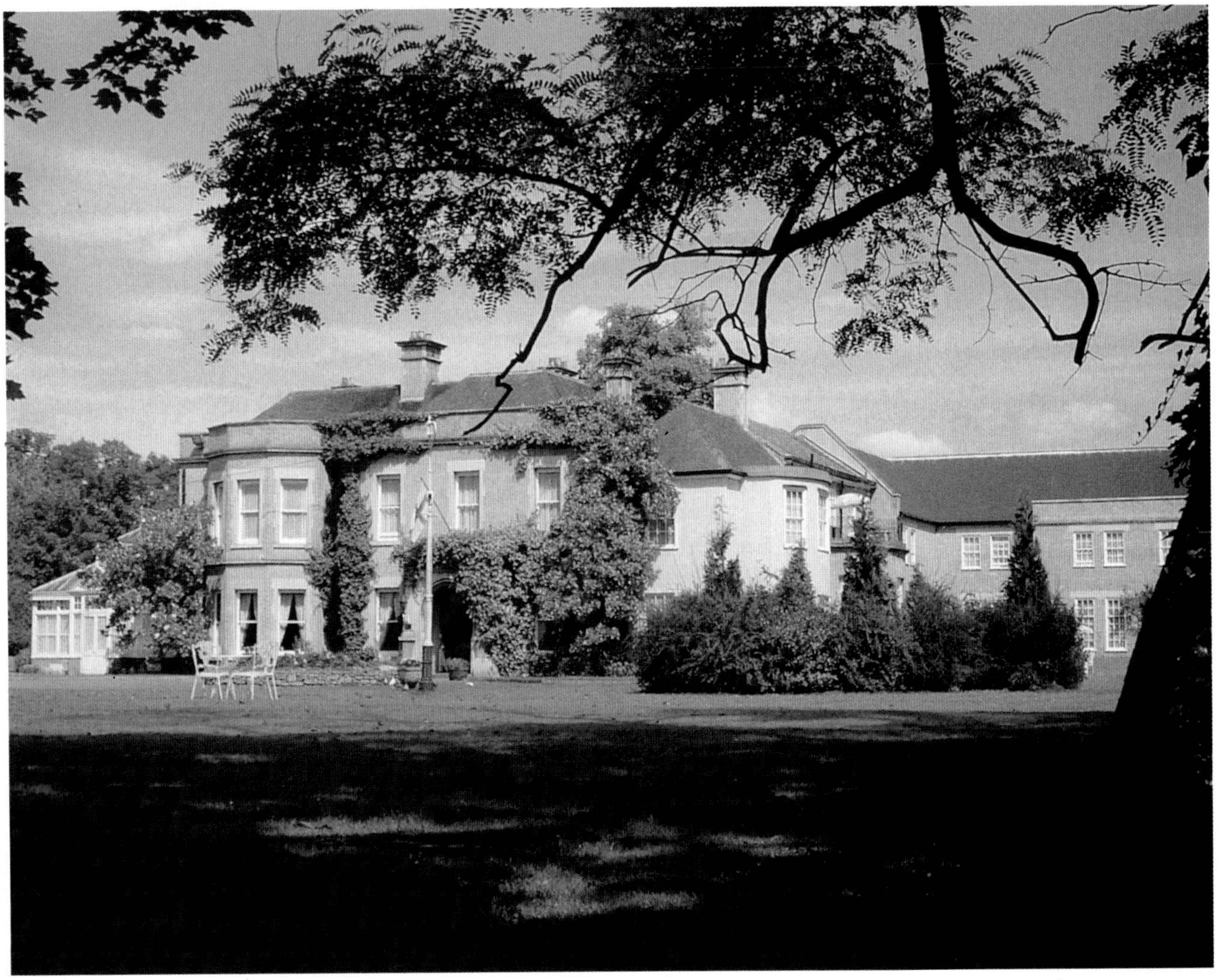

WOODLANDS MANOR

GREEN LANE, CLAPHAM, BEDFORD, BEDFORDSHIRE MK41 6EP
TEL: 01234 363281 FAX: 01234 272390

Woodlands Manor is a secluded period manor house, set in acres of wooded grounds and gardens, only two miles from the centre of Bedford. The hotel is privately owned and a personal welcome is assured. In the public rooms, stylish yet unpretentious furnishings preserve the feel of a country house, with open fires in winter. The en suite bedrooms are beautifully decorated and have extensive personal facilities. All have views of the gardens and surrounding countryside. The elegantly proportioned restaurant, once the house's main reception room, provides an agreeable venue for dining. The menus balance English tradition with the French flair for fresh, light flavours, complemented by wines from well-stocked cellars. The private library is well suited to business meetings and intimate dinner parties. Woodlands Manor is conveniently located for touring: the historic centres of Ely, Cambridge and Oxford, all within easy reach, and stately homes such as Woburn Abbey and Warwick Castle are not far away. The hotel is two miles from the county town of Bedford, with its riverside park and the Bunyan Museum. Other places of interest nearby include the RSPB at Sandy and the Shuttleworth Collection of aircraft at Biggleswade. **Directions:** Clapham village is two miles north of the centre of Bedford. Price guide: Single £62.50–£85; double/twin ££85–£97.50.

For hotel location, see maps on pages 477-483

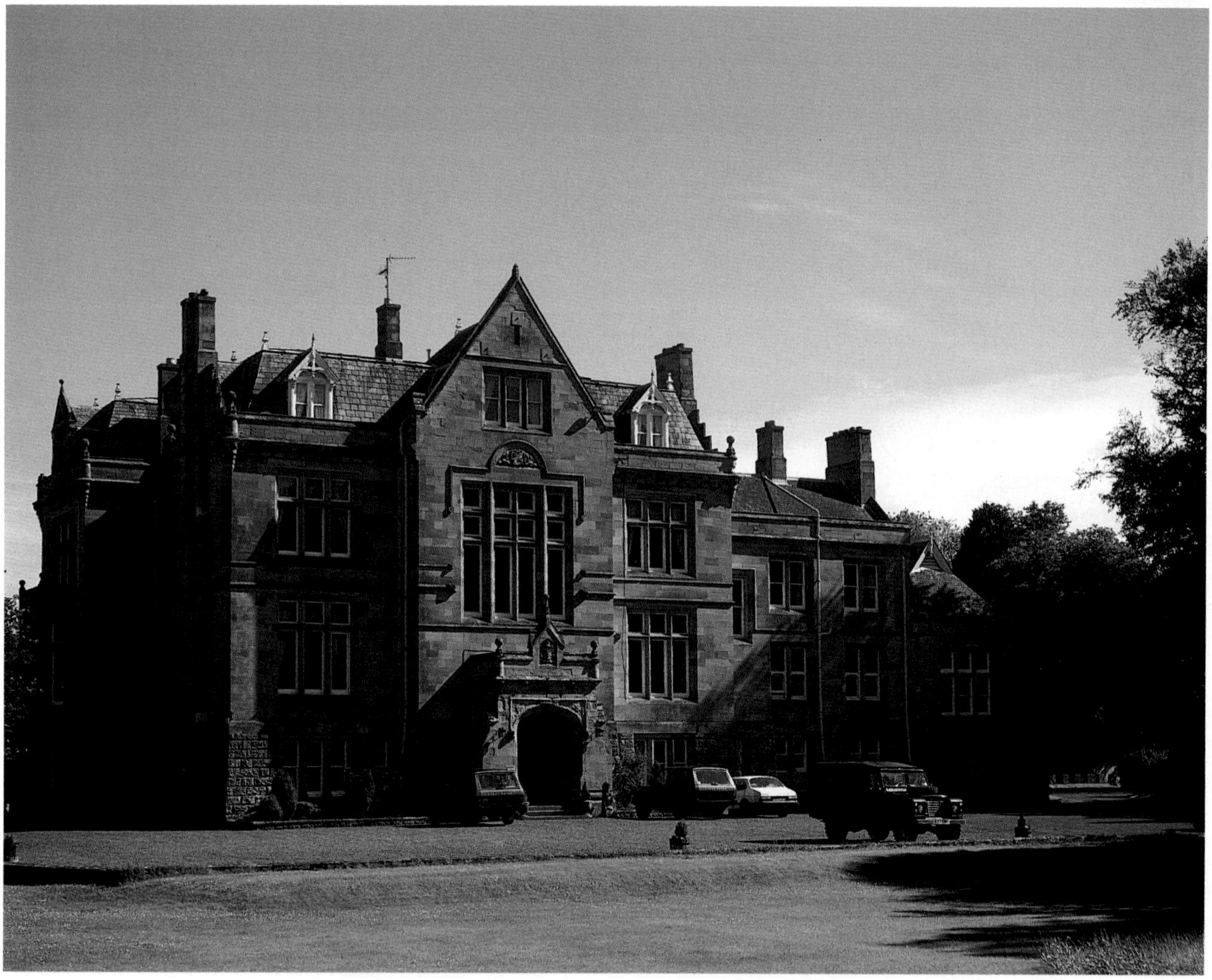

TILLMOUTH PARK

CORNHILL-ON-TWEED, NEAR BERWICK-UPON-TWEED, NORTHUMBERLAND TD12 4UU
TEL: 01890 882255 FAX: 01890 882540

Designed by Charles Barry, the son of the famous Victorian architect of the Houses of Parliament in Westminster, Tillmouth Park offers the same warm welcome today as it did when it was an exclusive private country house. It is situated in a rich countryside farmland of deciduous woodland and moor. The generously sized bedrooms have been recently refurbished in a distinctive old fashioned style with period furniture, although all offer modern day amenities. The kitchen prides itself on traditional country fare, with the chef using fresh local produce to create imaginative and well presented dishes. The restaurant serves a fine table d'hôte menu, while the Bistro is less formal. Fresh salmon and game are always available with 24 hours' notice. A well chosen wine list and a vast selection of malt whiskies complement the cuisine. Tillmouth Park is an ideal centre for country pursuits including field sports, fishing, hill walking, shooting, riding, birdwatching and golf. For the spectator there is rugby, curling and horse racing during the season. Places of interest nearby include stately homes such as Floors, Manderston and Paxton. Flodden Field, Lindisfarne and Holy Island are all within easy reach and the coast is just 15 minutes away. **Directions:** Tillmouth Park is on the A698 Cornhill-on-Tweed to Berwick-on-Tweed road. Price guide: Single £70–£90; twin/double £110–£145.

For hotel location, see maps on pages 477-483

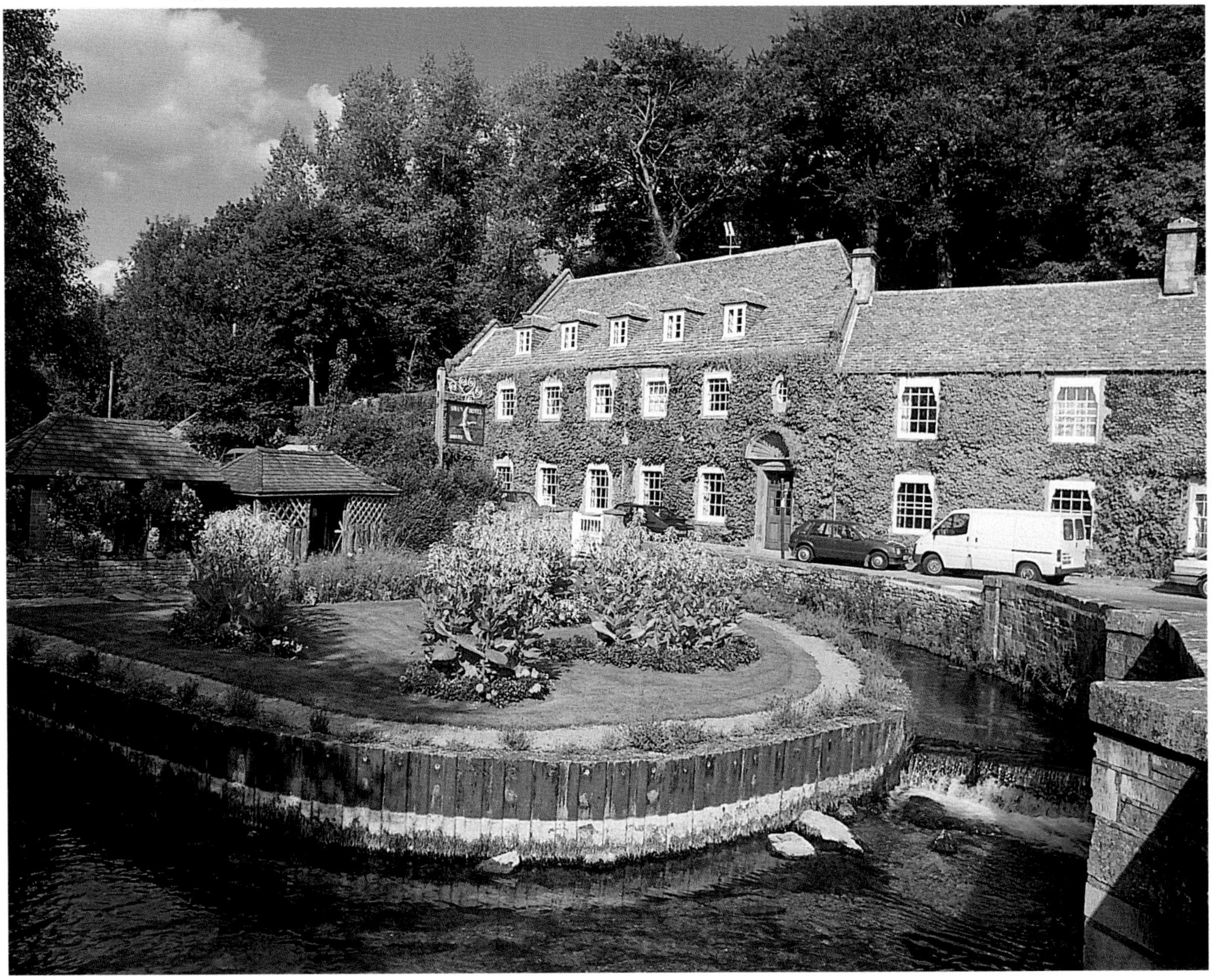

THE SWAN HOTEL AT BIBURY

BIBURY, GLOUCESTERSHIRE GL7 5NW

TEL: 01285 740695 FAX: 01285 740473

The Swan Hotel at Bibury in the South Cotswolds, a 17th century coaching inn, is a perfect base for both leisurely and active holidays which will appeal especially to motorists, fishermen and walkers. The hotel has its own fishing rights and a moated ornamental garden encircled by its own crystalline stream. Bibury itself is a delightful village, with its honey-coloured stonework, picturesque ponds, the trout filled River Coln and its utter lack of modern eyesores. The beautiful Arlington Row and its cottages are a vision of old England. When Liz and Alex Furtek acquired The Swan, they had the clear intention of creating a distinctive hotel in the English countryside which would acknowledge the needs of the sophisticated traveller of the 1990s. A programme of refurbishment and upgrading of the hotel and its services began with the accent on unpretentious comfort. Oak-panelling, plush carpets and sumptuous fabrics create the background for the fine paintings and antiques that grace the interiors. The 18 bedrooms are superbly appointed with luxury bathrooms and comfortable furnishings. Guests may dine in either the restaurant or the brasserie which serves meals all day. **Directions:** Bibury is signposted off A40 Oxford–Cheltenham road, on the left-hand side. Price guide: Single £86–£119; double/twin £115–£210.

For hotel location, see maps on pages 477-483

THE MILL HOUSE HOTEL AND LOMBARD ROOM RESTAURANT

180 LIFFORD LANE, KINGS NORTON, BIRMINGHAM B30 3NT
TEL: 0121 459 5800 FAX: 0121 459 8553

Situated just 15 minutes away from the city of Birmingham, the Mill House offers the latest up-to-date hospitality to both the leisure guest and business visitor. Owners Anthony Davis and Anthony Morgan pride themselves on providing the highest standards of efficiency and service. Standing in landscaped terraced gardens complete with a small indoor heated swimming pool, the hotel provides luxuriously appointed accommodation . Individually furnished bedrooms and suites offer every modern amenity. Each of the nine superb, beautifully decorated bedrooms has en suite marble bathrooms, colour television, mini bars, bath robes, mineral water and fresh fruit. Chef Anthony Morgan serves a tempting selection of English and continental specialities in the elegantly refurbished Lombard Room restaurant which is re-establishing its reputation as one of Birmingham's finest dining areas. Alternatively, guests can enjoy a light lunch or host a pre-dinner reception in the relaxing atmosphere of the spacious Victorian conservatory. Mill House also has excellent conference and exhibition facilities for up to 140 delegates. A purpose-built marquee is ideal for corporate hospitality or additional exhibition space. **Directions:** From M42, exit at junction 3 onto A435 to Kings Norton. Price guide: Single £85; double/twin £95; suite £125-£150.

For hotel location, see maps on pages 477-483

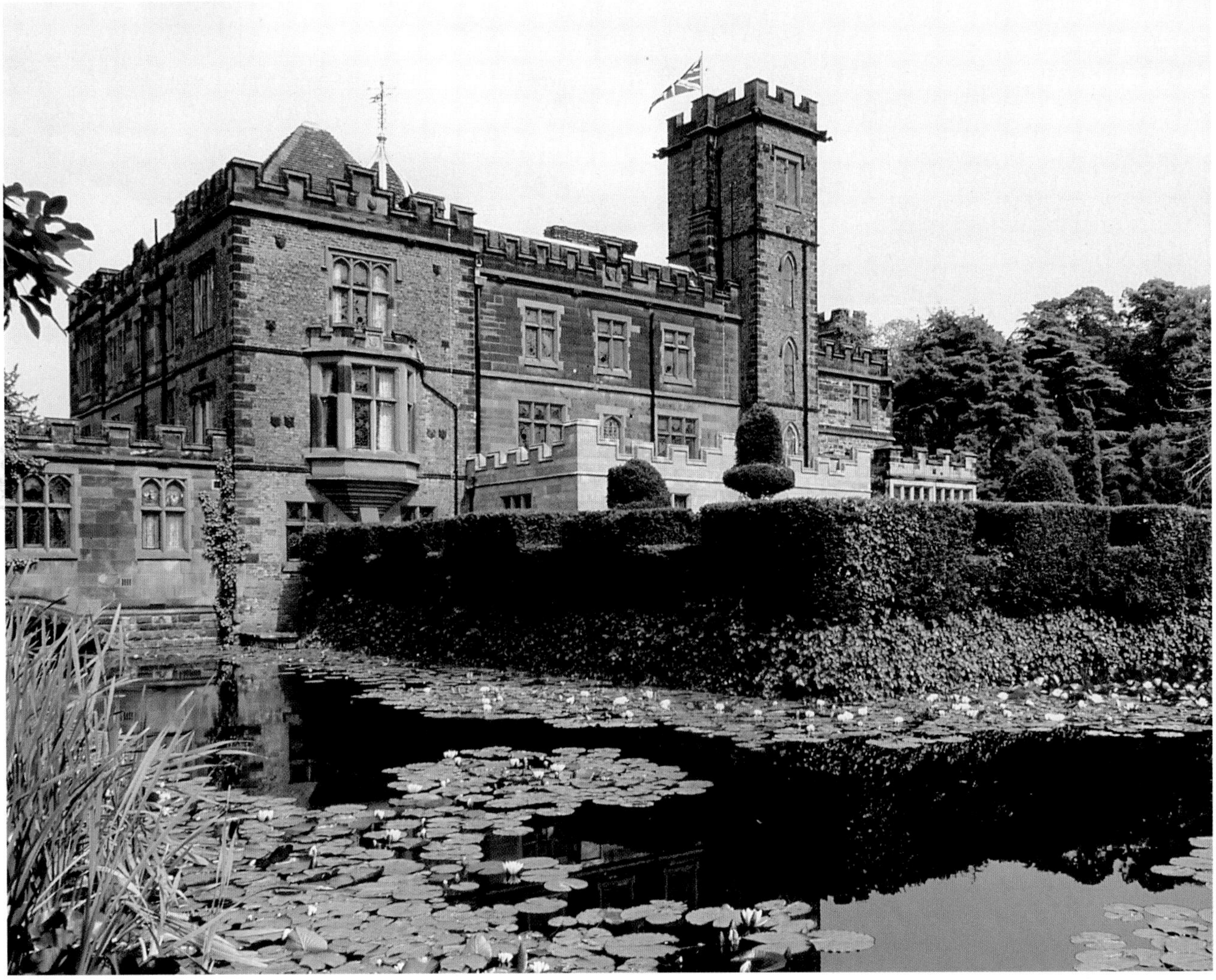

New Hall

WALMLEY ROAD, ROYAL SUTTON COLDFIELD, WEST MIDLANDS B76 1QX
TEL: 0121 378 2442 FAX: 0121 378 4637

Set in 26 acres of private gardens and surrounded by a lily-filled moat, New Hall dates from the 12th century and is reputedly the oldest fully moated manor house in England. This prestigious hotel offers a warm welcome to both the discriminating business visitor and leisure guest. Much acclaimed, New Hall proudly holds the coveted RAC Blue Ribbon Award, AA 4 Red stars and AA Inspectors' Hotel of the Year for England 1994. New Hall joins the elite band of Deluxe Hotels with an 80% rating, the highest in the West Midlands. The cocktail bar and adjoining drawing room overlook the terrace from which a bridge leads to the yew topiary, orchards and sunlit glades. Individually furnished bedrooms and suites offer every modern comfort and amenity with lovely views. A new 9-hole golf course is available for guests' use. Surrounded by a rich cultural heritage, New Hall is convenient for Lichfield Cathedral, Warwick Castle, Stratford-upon-Avon, the NEC and the ICC in Birmingham (only seven miles away). The Belfry Golf Centre is also nearby. Details of champagne weekend breaks, opera, ballet and other weekends are available on request. **Directions:** From exit 9 of M42, follow A4097 (ignoring signs to A38 Sutton Coldfield). At B4148 turn right at the traffic lights. New Hall is one mile on the left. Price guide: Single £105–£135; double/twin £120–£165; suite £175–£300.

For hotel location, see maps on pages 477-483

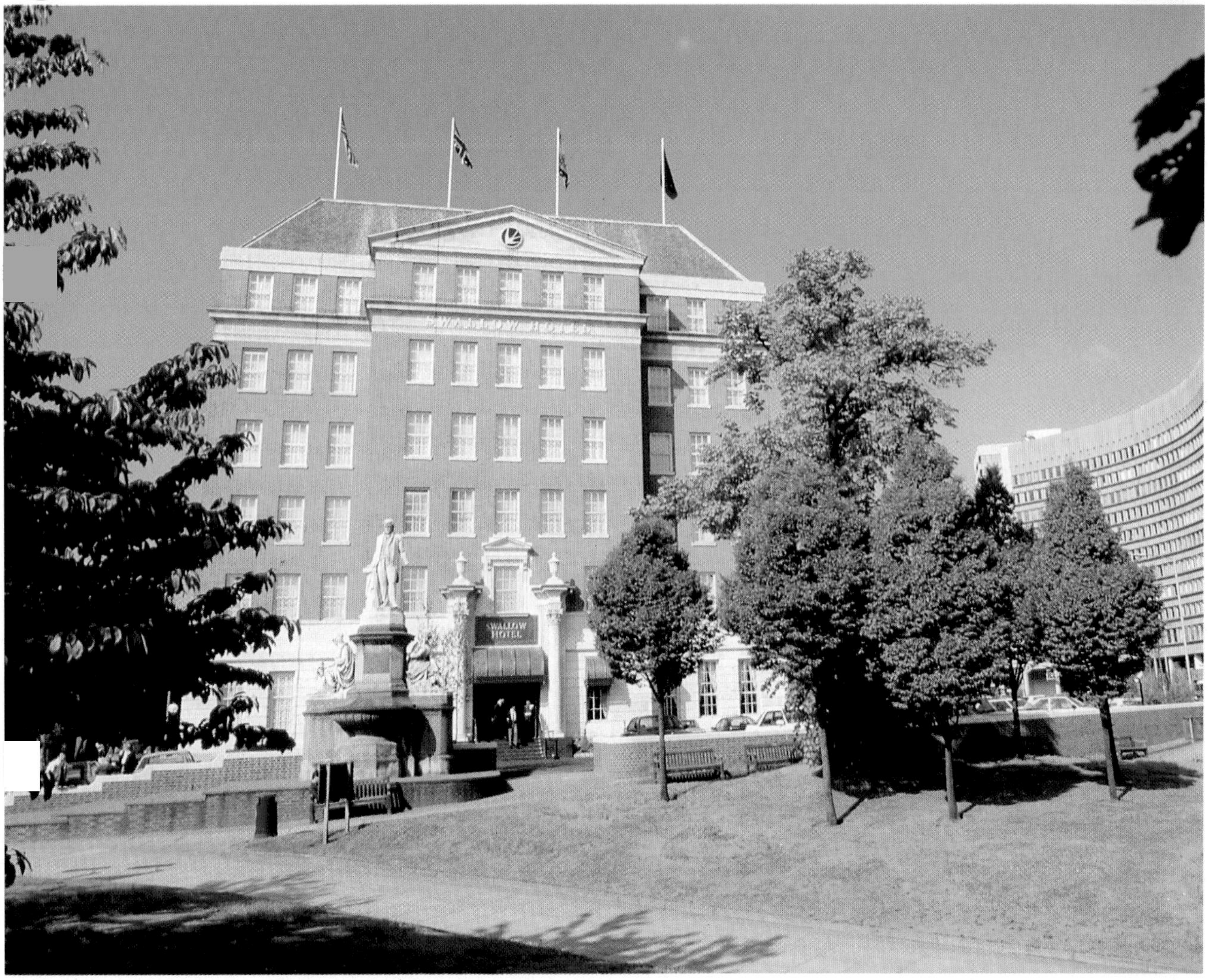

THE SWALLOW HOTEL

12 HAGLEY ROAD, FIVEWAYS, BIRMINGHAM B16 8SJ
TEL: 0121 452 1144 FAX: 0121 456 3442

As soon as it opened, this very special hotel became the first in the Midlands to achieve five stars and since then it has won innumerable awards. These include the Caterer and Hotelkeeper's 'Hotel of the Year 1992', AA Courtesy and Care award and five AA Stars. Two of the most highly regarded accolades have been given recently – English Tourist Board 'England for Excellence Award' 1993 (the Lanesborough in 1992 and the Chewton Glen in 1991) and Johansens 'City Hotel of the Year' 1994. Awards, however, do not give the whole picture. The Swallow Hotel offers business and leisure travellers an oasis of calm and warm hospitality in a fascinating and culturally diverse city. Service and surroundings are quite outstanding. Ninety eight luxuriously comfortable bedrooms and suites offer all one would expect from a hotel of this calibre. Dining is memorable whether in the Sir Edward Elgar Restaurant or in Langtry's which warrant an Egon Ronay 'Star' and three AA Rosettes: traditional afternoon tea in the Drawing Room is a favourite indulgence with all guests. Nowhere is luxury more apparent than in the Swallow Leisure Club with its theme of Ancient Egypt – including hieroglyphics. **Directions:** Fiveways roundabout – junction 1 (M5) 5 miles, junction 6 (M6) $5^1/_2$ miles. Price guide from: Single £130; double/twin £150; suite from £299.

For hotel location, see maps on pages 477-483

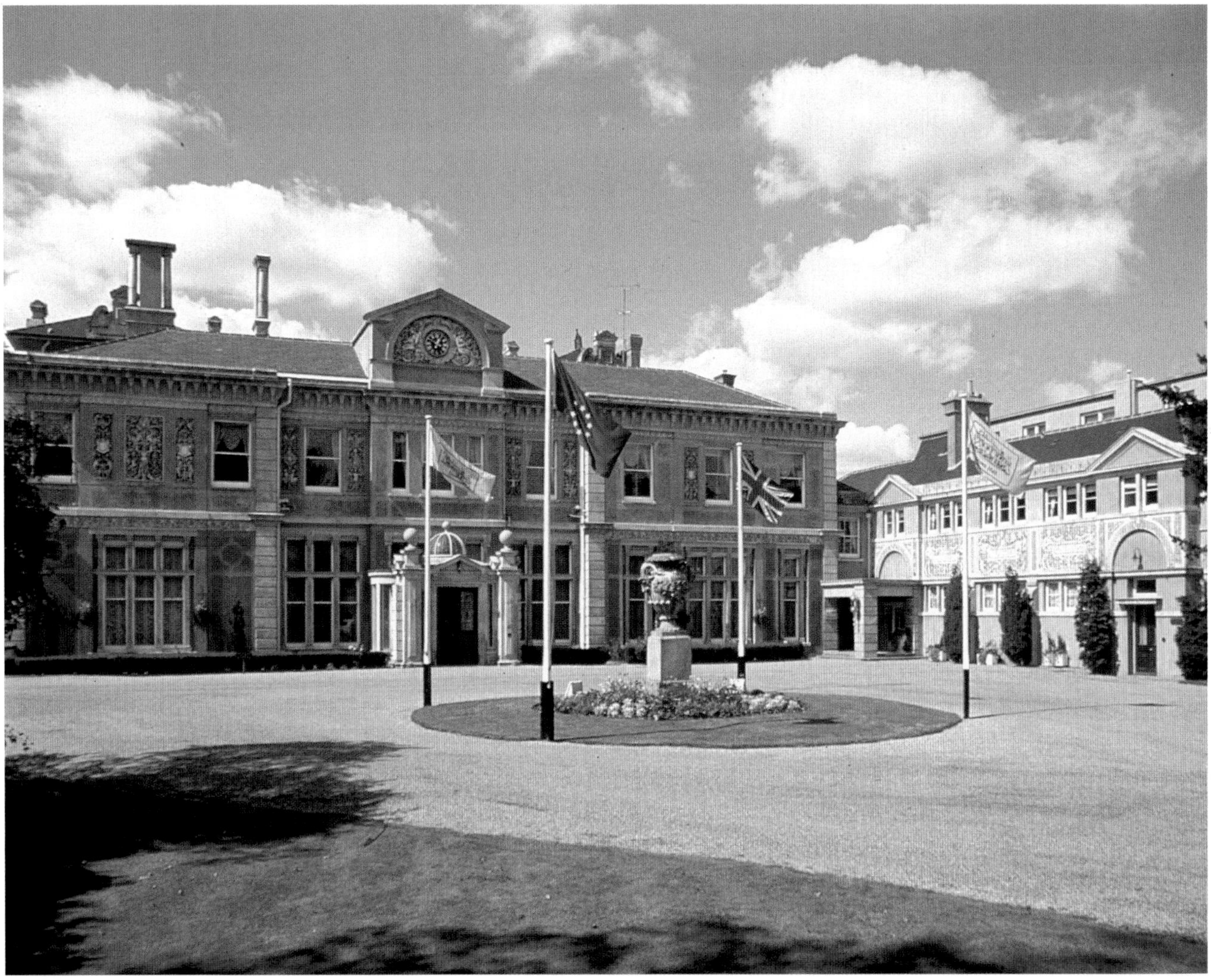

Down Hall Country House Hotel

HATFIELD HEATH, NR BISHOP'S STORTFORD, HERTFORDSHIRE CM22 7AS

TEL: 01279 731441 FAX: 01279 730416 E-MAIL: 101703.2450@COMPUSERVE.COM

Down Hall is an Italian-style mansion set in over 100 acres of woodland, park and landscaped gardens. The hotel is a splendid example of quality Victorian craftmanship, with many of the architectural details reproduced in the recently added West Wing. There is superb attention to detail throughout. The well-proportioned bedrooms have antique-style inlaid mahogany furniture and brass chandeliers. Italian granite is a feature of the luxurious en suite bathrooms. The hotel's public rooms offer comfort in the grand manner, with high ceilings, crystal chandeliers and paintings on the walls. There are two restaurants, offering English and international cuisine, with a wide selection of unusual dishes. For conferences, there are 26 meeting rooms, including 16 purpose-built syndicate rooms. Indoor and outdoor leisure facilities include a heated pool, whirlpool, sauna, croquet and putting lawns, giant chess, tennis courts and a fitness trail. Down Hall is within easy access of London and of Stansted Airport. For excursions, Cambridge, Constable country and the old timbered village of Thaxted are all within a few miles. **Directions:** Exit at junction 7 of M11. Follow the A414 towards Harlow. At the 4th roundabout follow the B183 to Hatfield Heath. Bear right towards Matching Green and the hotel is 1.3 miles on the right. Price guide: Single £90; double/twin £120.

For hotel location, see maps on pages 477-483

THE DEVONSHIRE ARMS COUNTRY HOUSE HOTEL

BOLTON ABBEY, SKIPTON, NORTH YORKSHIRE BD23 6AJ
TEL: 01756 710441 FAX: 01756 710564

The Devonshire reflects its charming setting in the Yorkshire Dales: a welcome escape from a busy and crowded world, peace and quiet, beauty, and the perfect place to relax. The hotel is owned by the Duke and Duchess of Devonshire and is set in 12 acres of parkland on their Bolton Abbey estate, in the Yorkshire Dales National Park. Many antiques and paintings from Chatsworth in the public rooms and bedrooms (several of which are themed) add to the country house atmosphere, which is complemented by excellent service and an award-winning restaurant. As well as a wide choice of outdoor activities and themed or activity breaks, The Devonshire Club is adjacent to the hotel and offers a full range of leisure, health and beauty therapy facilities including: heated indoor swimming pool, steam room, sauna, spa bath, cold water plunge pool, high-powered sunbed, fully equipped gymnasium, beauty therapy rooms – staffed by "Matis" trained therapists, health and relaxation treatments. In addition to the highest ETB rating (5 Crowns De Luxe), three AA Red Stars and two Rosettes the Devonshire is a member of 'Small Luxury Hotels of the World', was YHTB 'Hotel of the Year' for 1992, 1993 and 1994 and an English Tourist Board Silver Award Winner for 1993. **Directions:** Off the A59 Skipton–Harrogate road at junction with the B6160. Price guide: Single £100–£120; double/twin £140–£175; suite £225–£250.

41 rms MasterCard VISA AMERICAN EXPRESS M 150

For hotel location, see maps on pages 477-483

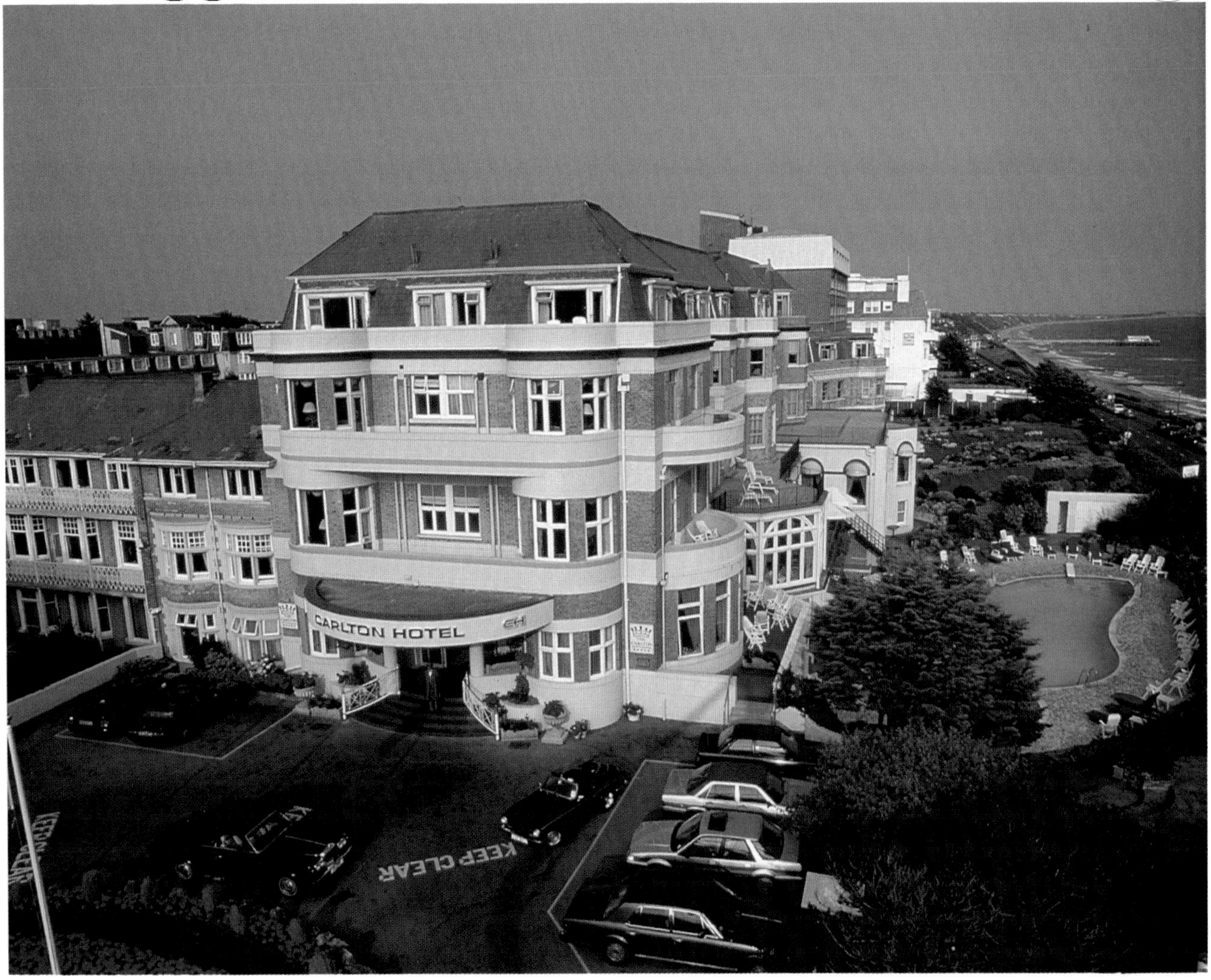

THE CARLTON HOTEL

EAST OVERCLIFF, BOURNEMOUTH, DORSET BH1 3DN
TEL: 01202 552011 FAX: 01202 299573

The Carlton, one of Bournemouth's premier hotels, has provided hospitality to royalty, heads of state and ministers of the Crown for generations. Perfectly positioned on the town's much favoured East Cliff, with miles of golden sands below, it creates a world of discreet luxury for its guests, offering impeccable service and unrivalled comfort. The interiors are a rich combination of classical furniture and contemporary decoration, creating an impression of space and opulence. The bedrooms are spacious, beautifully furnished and equipped with every modern facility, while the suites are unashamedly luxurious. Dining at the hotel is a memorable experience. In the beautifully decorated two-tier restaurant, guests are assured of international cuisine and fine wines. The versatile Meyrick Suite is suitable for banquets, wedding receptions, conferences or promotional events. For smaller functions, The Carlton offers its business suites, impressively furnished and featuring state-of-the-art equipment. Relaxation is provided by the facilities of the Health Club, with its sauna, solarium, Jacuzzi, gymnasium and heated indoor and outdoor pool. Luxury breaks, 2 nights or more from £59.50 per person including 4-course dinner. **Directions:** The Carlton is on the corner of East Overcliff Drive and Meyrick Road, on the sea front. Price guide: Single from £95; double/twin from £120; suites from £185.

70 rms 160

For hotel location, see maps on pages 477-483

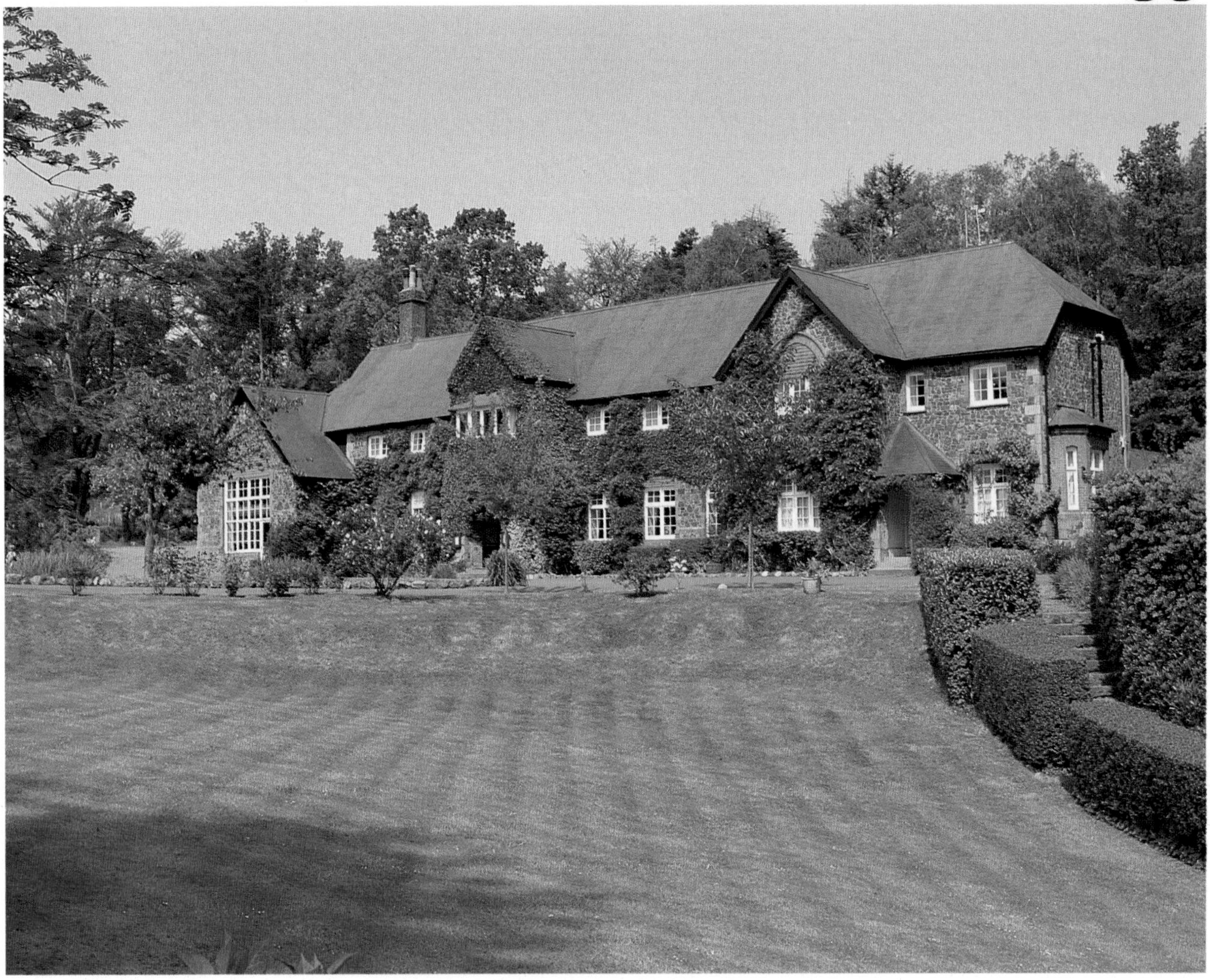

THE EDGEMOOR

HAYTOR ROAD, BOVEY TRACEY, SOUTH DEVON TQ13 9LE
TEL: 01626 832466 FAX: 01626 834760

Built in 1870, The Edgemoor Country House Hotel, owned and managed by Rod and Pat Day, stands in a peaceful location in two acres of grounds literally on the eastern boundary of the Dartmoor National Park. There are 12 charming bedrooms, two of which are on the ground floor. All have en suite bathrooms and some have four-poster beds. The public rooms look over the hotel grounds and provide comfortable and sophisticated surroundings in which guests enjoy their stay. In the restaurant, chef Edward Elliott prepares modern English and French cuisine using local produce whenever possible. The wine list offers an interesting and varied selection. Bar meals are available at lunch time and in the evenings. Children are welcome and a special high-tea is provided for them. With the hotel's close proximity to Dartmoor, walkers and naturalists are well catered for. Shooting, fishing and riding can be arranged locally. The Edgemoor is also a good touring base for the West Country. Worth a visit are Castle Drogo, Becky Falls and Haytor. **Directions:** On leaving the M5, join the A38 in the direction of Plymouth. At Drumbridges roundabout, take A382 towards Bovey Tracey. At the second roundabout turn left and, after approximately $^{1}/_{2}$ mile, fork left at the sign for Haytor. Price guide: Single £49.75; double/twin £75–£99

For hotel location, see maps on pages 477-483

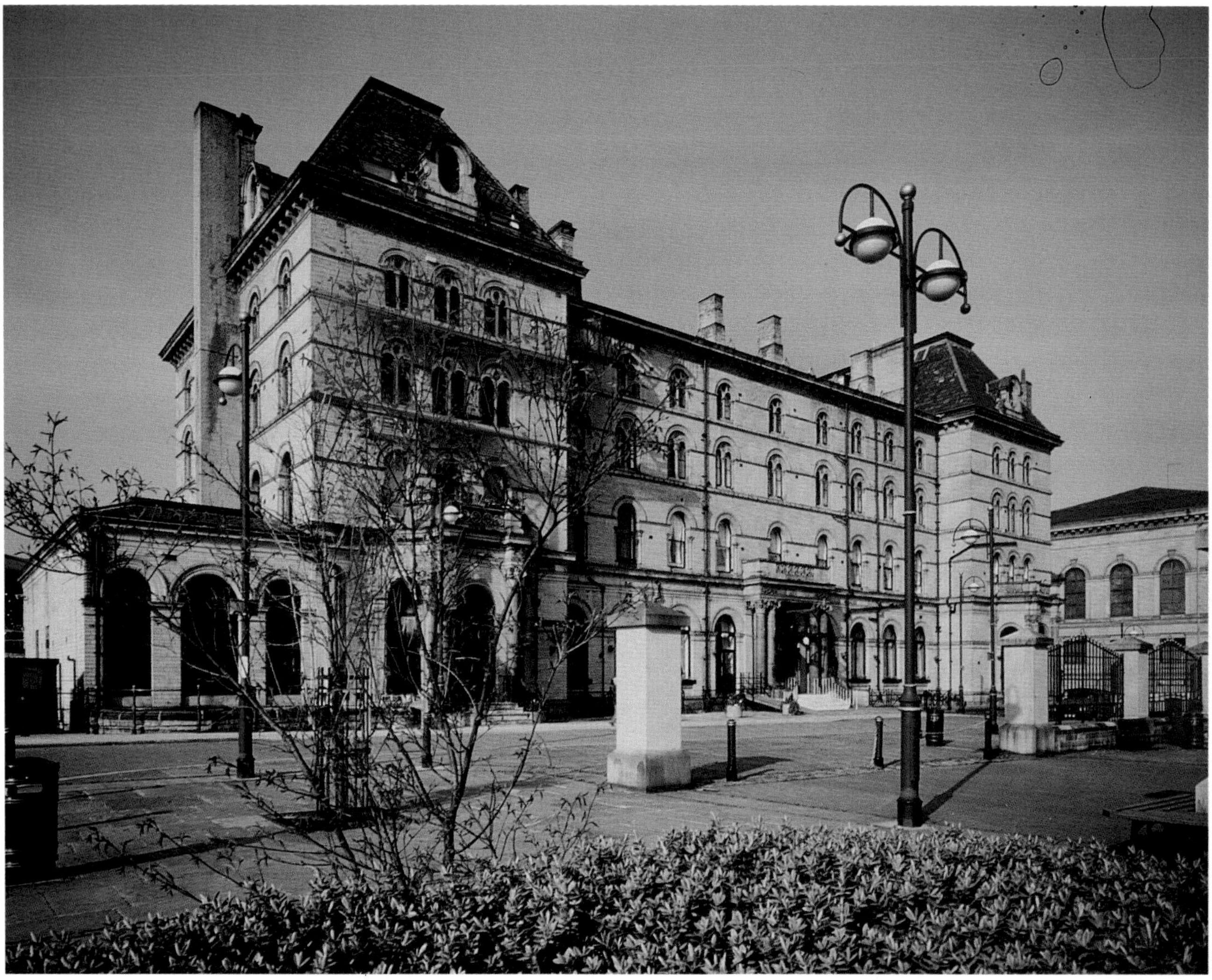

THE VICTORIA HOTEL

BRIDGE STREET, BRADFORD, WEST YORKSHIRE BD1 1JX
TEL: 01274 728706 FAX: 01274 736358

Built as the showpiece of the Lancashire and Yorkshire railway in 1875, The Victoria has been totally restored and refreshed since its purchase in January 1995 by the owners of the award-winning 42 The Calls in Leeds. Emphasis has been placed on producing an outstandingly comfortable hotel, but with service scaled down to keep room rates substantially below other hotels with comparable comforts. The bedrooms all have stereos, video players, trouser presses, hairdryers and superb bathrooms with power showers. Vic and Bert's Restaurant is a modern interpretation of a Parisian Brasserie with a selection of dishes prepared under the supervision of Bradford's only Michelin starred chef. The excellent facilities include a small gym and sauna, The Pie Eyed Parrot Pub and a beautiful banquetting room for special events. Bradford is a base from which to visit Herriot country and the Brontë parsonage, whilst the world-famous National Museum of Film, Photography and Television and the Alhambra Theatre are within walking distance. **Directions:** From M62 take junction 26 onto the M606, then the A6177 and A611. At end of dual carriageway take right exit at roundabout to Hall Ings. Turn right at traffic lights and the hotel is on the left. Price guide: Single £79–£99; double/twin £89–£109; suites £109–£119. Exceptional rates for week-ends and August.

For hotel location, see maps on pages 477-483

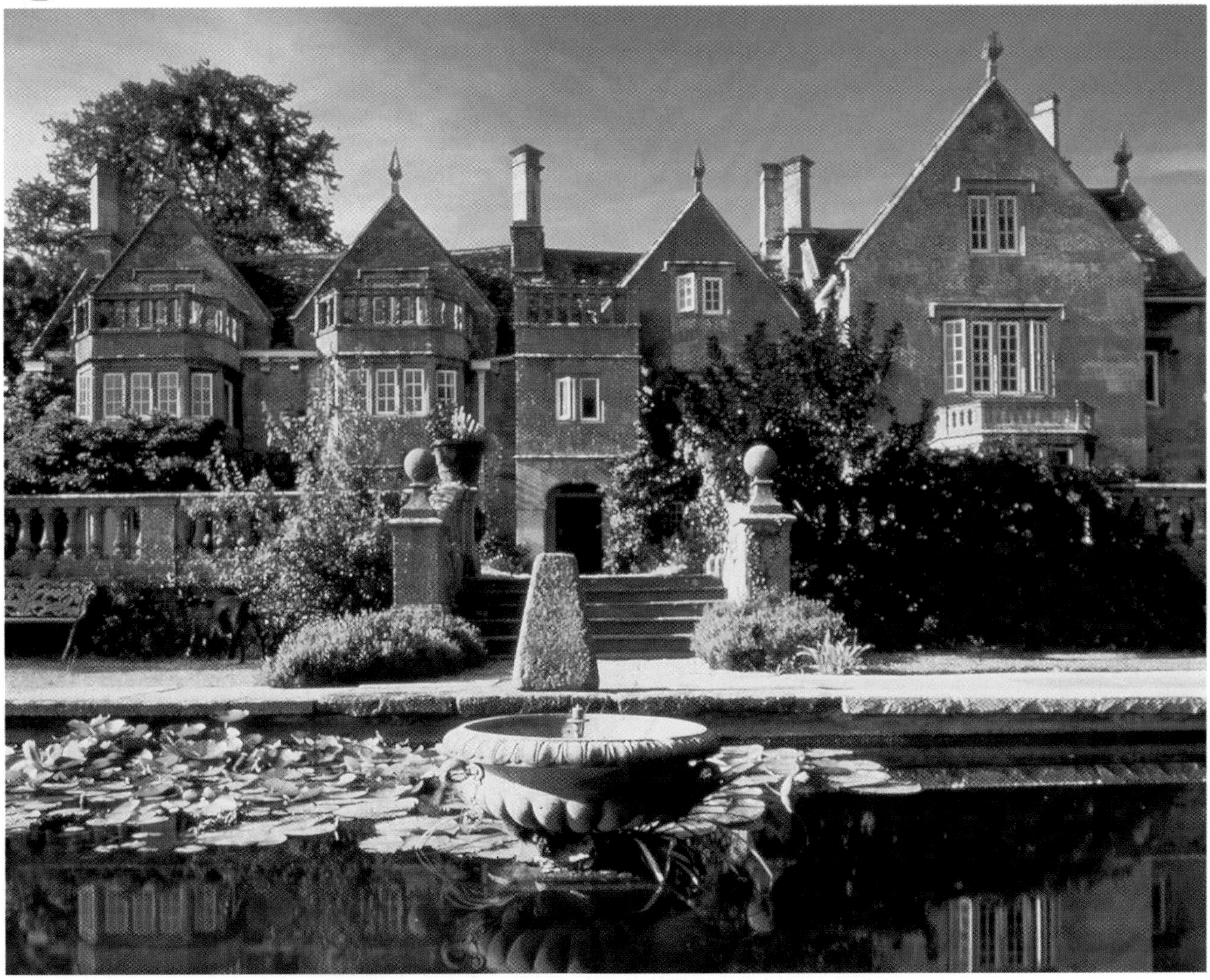

WOOLLEY GRANGE

WOOLLEY GRANGE, BRADFORD-ON-AVON, WILTSHIRE BA15 1TX
TEL: 01225 864705 FAX: 01225 864059 E-MAIL: Woolley@Cityscape.com.uk

Woolley Grange is a 17th century Jacobean stone manor house set in 14 acres of formal gardens and paddocks. Standing on high ground, it affords southerly views of the White Horse at Westbury and beyond. Furnished with flair and an air of eccentricity, the interior décor and paintings echo the taste of owners Nigel and Heather Chapman. Woolley Grange is gaining a reputation for outstanding cuisine and is highly rated in *The Good Food Guide*. Using local farm produce and organically grown fruit and vegetables from the Victorian kitchen gardens, the chef has created a sophisticated style of country house food which aims to revive the focus on flavours. Children are particularly welcome; the owners have four of their own and theu do not expect their young visitors to be 'seen but not heard'. In the Victorian coach house there is a huge games room and a well-equipped nursery with a full-time nanny available to look after guests' children 10am–6pm every day. A children's lunch and tea are provided daily. Nearby attractions include medieval Bradford-on-Avon, Georgian Bath, Longlear and prehistoric Stonehenge. Riding can be arranged. **Directions:** From Bath on A363, fork left at Frankleigh House after town sign. From Chippenham, A4 to Bath, fork left on B3109; turn left after town sign. Price guide: SIngle £89; double/twin £99–£145; Suite from £180

For hotel location, see maps on pages 477-483

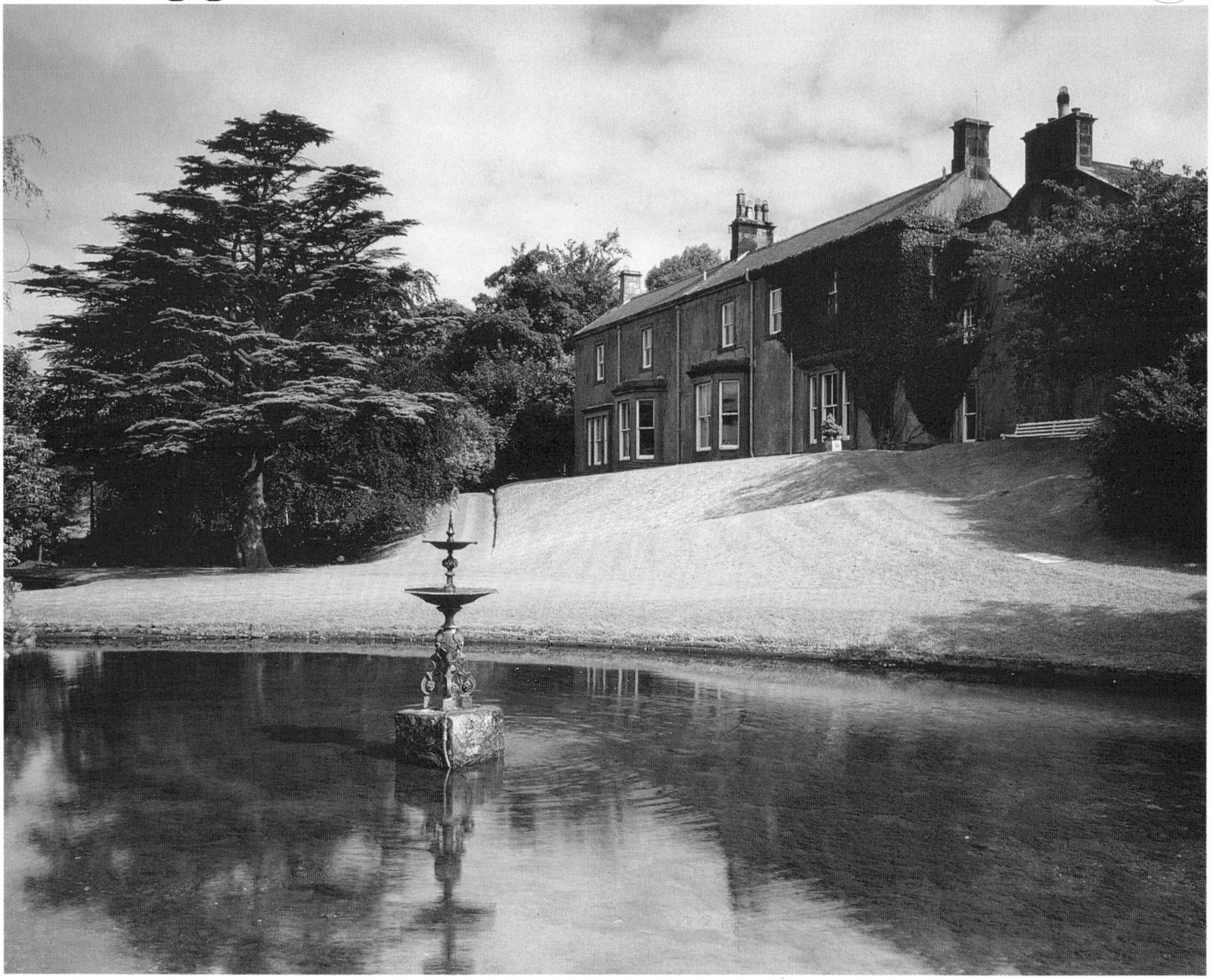

FARLAM HALL HOTEL

BRAMPTON, CUMBRIA CA8 2NG
TEL: 016977 46234 FAX: 016977 46683

Farlam Hall was opened in 1975 by the Quinion and Stevenson families who over the years have managed to achieve and maintain consistently high standards of food, service and comfort. These standards have been recognised and rewarded by all the major guides and membership of Relais et Châteaux. This old border house, dating in parts from the 17th century, is set in mature gardens which can be seen from the elegant lounges and dining room, creating a relaxing and pleasing environment. The fine silver and crystal in the dining room complement the quality of the English country house cooking produced by Barry Quinion and his team of chefs. There are 12 individually decorated bedrooms varying in size and shape, some having Jacuzzi baths, one an antique four-poster bed, and there are two ground floor bedrooms. This area offers many different attractions: miles of unspoiled countryside for walking, eight golf courses within 30 minutes of the hotel, Hadrian's Wall, Lanercost Priory and Carlisle with its castle, cathedral and museum. The Lake District, Scottish Borders and Yorkshire Dales each make an ideal day's touring. Winter and spring breaks are offered. Closed Christmas. **Directions:** Farlam Hall is 2½ miles east of Brampton on the A689, not in Farlam village. Price guide (including dinner): Single £110–£120; double/twin £190–£230.

For hotel location, see maps on pages 477-483

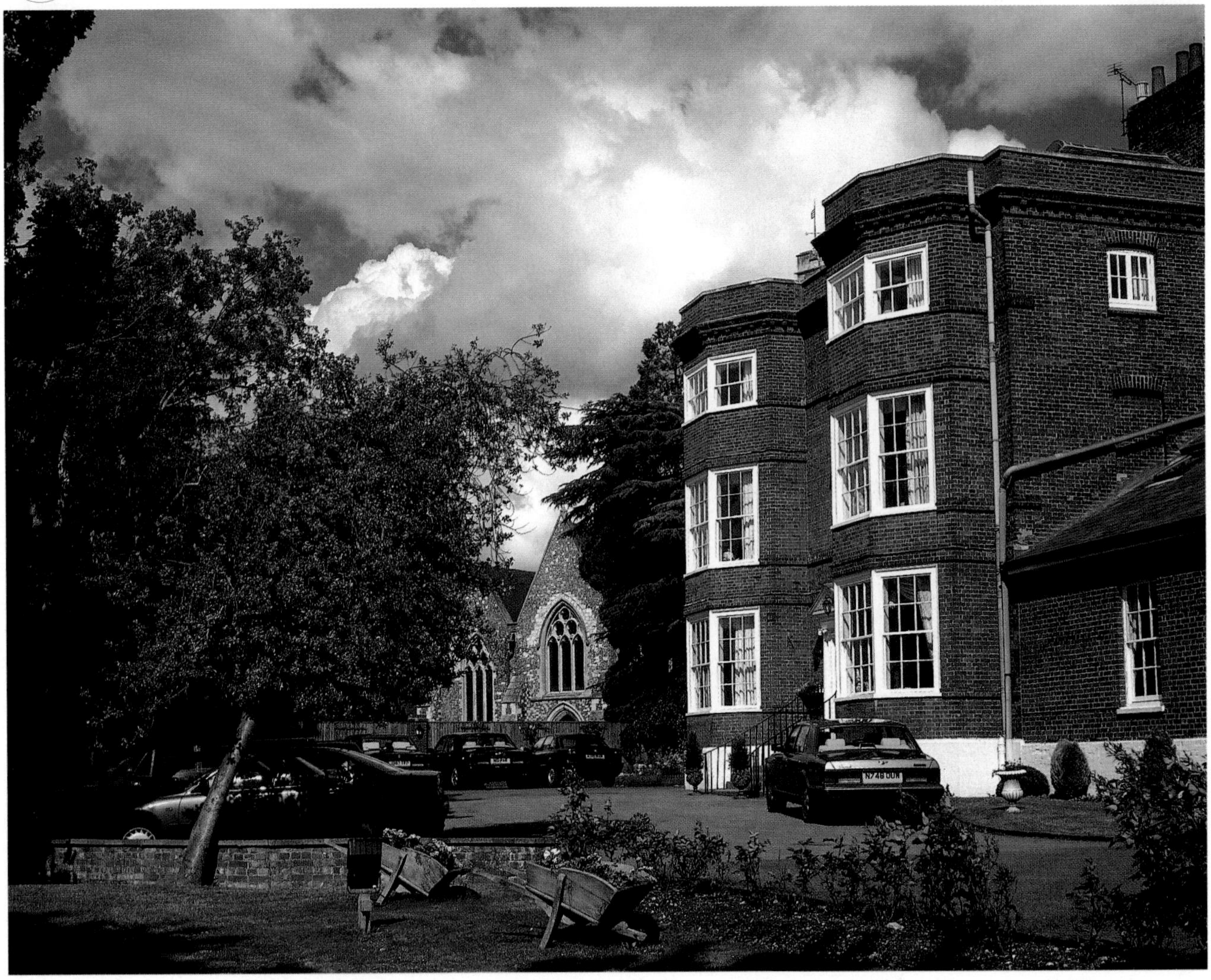

CHAUNTRY HOUSE HOTEL AND RESTAURANT

HIGH STREET, BRAY, BERKSHIRE SL6 2AB
TEL: 01628 73991 FAX: 01628 773089

Tucked between the local church and cricket club in the small, delightful Thames-side village of Bray, and a minutes walk to the famous Roux's Waterside Inn, Chauntry House is comfortable, friendly and has a plentiful supply of charm and character. With a spacious and secluded garden in which to lounge it is a fine example of an early 18th century country house: an ideal place to relax. The 15 en suite bedrooms are individually appointed in the best English designs and all have cable television, radio, direct dial telephones and tea and coffee making facilities. The public rooms offer comfort in the traditional country house manner and the welcoming drawing room, with an open fire for the winter months, is an ideal and comfortable environment in which to enjoy a pre-dinner aperitif. Modern English and Continental specialities with a distinctively oriental influence are served in the stylish restaurant. The hotel can accommodate conferences and meetings in an adjoining building for up to 30 delegates, boardroom style. Maidenhead, Royal Windsor, Eton, Henley, Ascot, Marlow, London and Heathrow Airport are within easy reach. Golf, fishing and riding can be arranged locally. **Directions:** From M4, exit at junction 8/9 and take A 308 (M) towards Maidenhead and Windsor. Then join B3028 to Bray village, just before M4 overhead bridge. Price guide: Single £80-£95; double/twin £105-£135.

For hotel location, see maps on pages 477-483

MONKEY ISLAND HOTEL

BRAY-ON-THAMES, MAIDENHEAD, BERKSHIRE SL6 2EE
TEL: 01628 23400 FAX: 01628 784732

The name Monkey Island derives from the medieval Monk's Eyot. Circa 1723 the island was purchased by Charles Spencer, the third Duke of Marlborough, who built the fishing lodge now known as the Pavilion, and the fishing temple, both of which are Grade I listed buildings. The Pavilion's Terrace Bar, overlooking acres of riverside lawn, is an ideal spot for a relaxing cocktail, and the Pavilion Restaurant, perched on the island's narrowest tip with fine views upstream, boasts fine English cuisine, an award-winning cellar and friendly service. The River Room is suitable for weddings or other large functions, while the Regency-style boardroom is perfect for smaller parties. It is even possible to arrange exclusive use of the whole island for a truly memorable occasion. The Temple houses not only the comfortable bedrooms and suites but also the Wedgwood Room, with its splendid ceiling in high-relief plaster, and the octagonal Temple Room below. Monkey Island is one mile downstream from Maidenhead, within easy reach of Royal Windsor, Eton, Henley and London. Closed from 26 December to mid-January. Weekend breaks from £75 p.p. **Directions:** Take A308 from Maidenhead towards Windsor; turn left following signposts to Bray. Entering Bray, go right along Old Mill Lane, which goes over M4; the hotel is on the left. Price guide: Single £80–£95; double/twin £90–£130; suites from £155.

For hotel location, see maps on pages 477-483

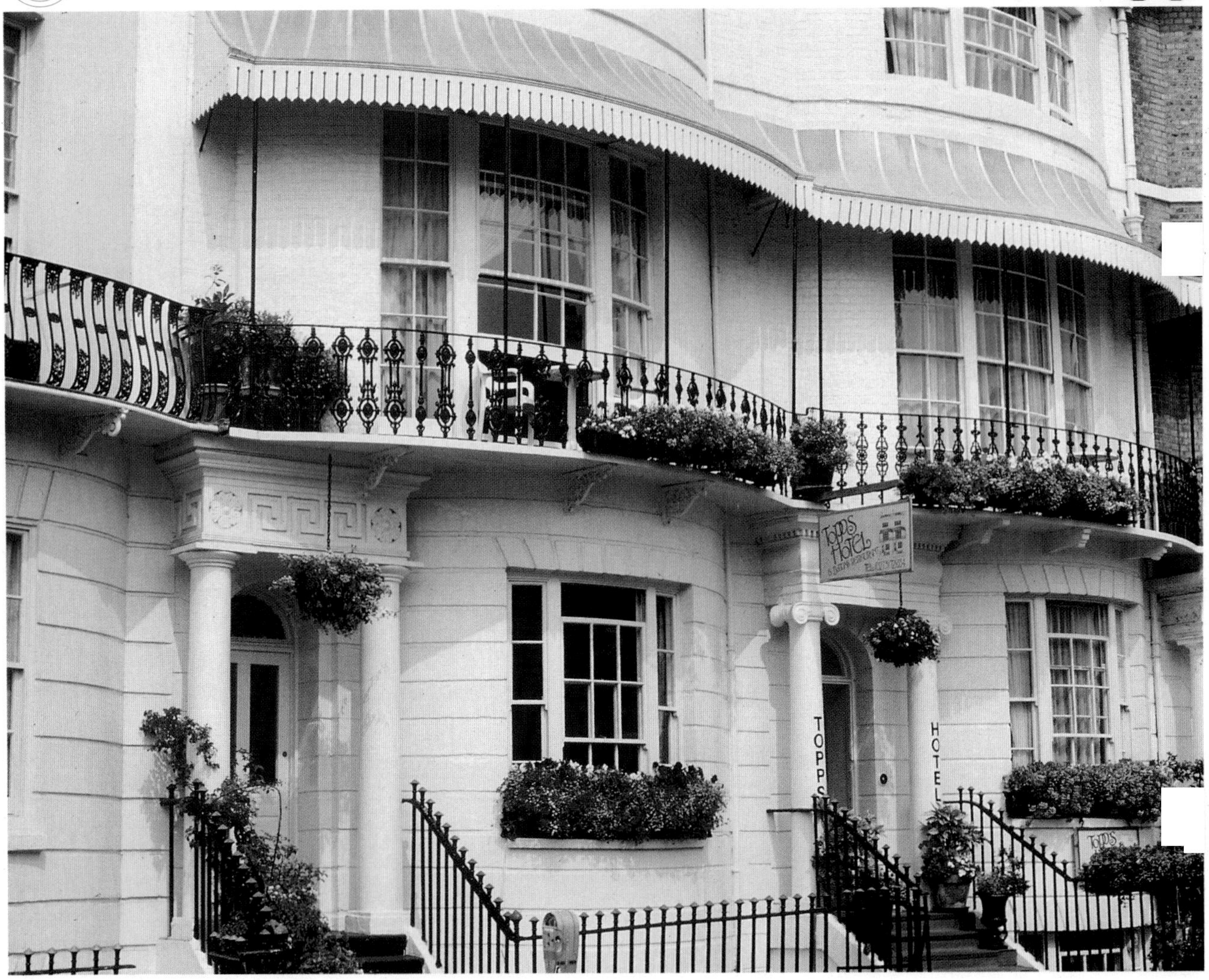

TOPPS HOTEL

17 REGENCY SQUARE, BRIGHTON, EAST SUSSEX BN1 2FG
TEL: 01273 729334 FAX: 01273 203679

Quietly situated in Regency Square at the heart of Brighton, the Topps Hotel is only 2 minutes' walk from the sea and the Metropole Conference Centre, with the Lanes and Royal Pavilion nearby. This charming hotel offers an attractive alternative to the more anonymous large establishments in the vicinity and is under the personal supervision of resident proprietors, Paul and Pauline Collins. With its friendly welcome and efficient service, the Topps Hotel is certainly deserving of its name. The bedrooms are all elegantly appointed and every need of the discerning visitor has been anticipated. The hotel has long featured in our recommendations and remains unchallenged for value in Brighton. There is underground car parking below Regency Square. Brighton is often described as 'London-by-the-sea' – its urbane atmosphere and wide range of shops, clubs and theatres make it a popular town for pleasure-seeking visitors following the Georgian examples of the Prince Regent. Glyndebourne, Arundel, Chichester and Lewes are within easy reach and London is only 52 minutes away by train. **Directions:** Regency Square is off King's Road (A259), opposite the West Pier. Price guide: Single from £45; double/twin £79–£109.

For hotel location, see maps on pages 477-483

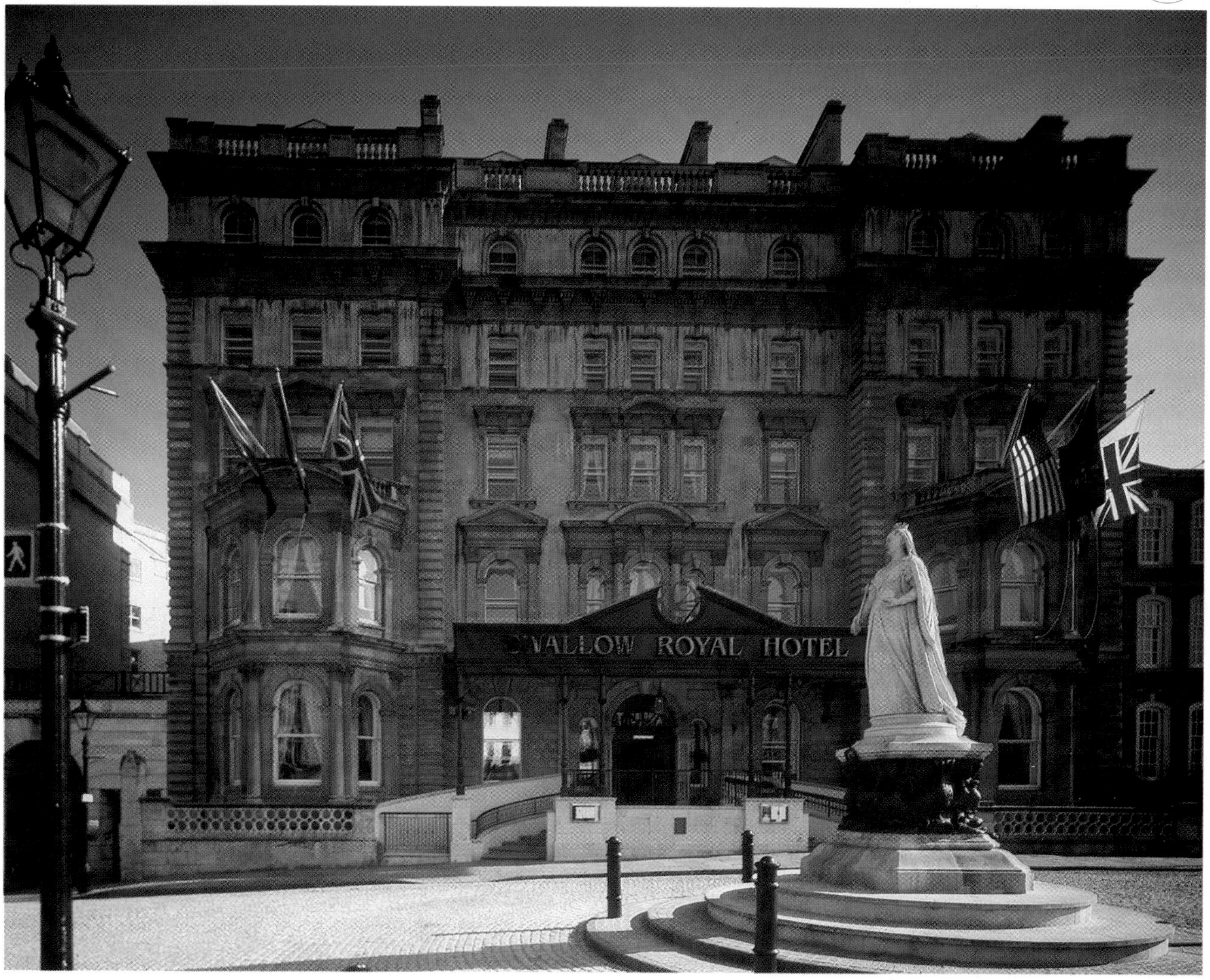

SWALLOW ROYAL HOTEL

COLLEGE GREEN, BRISTOL BS1 5TA
TEL: 0117 9255200 FAX: 0117 9251515

The Swallow Royal Hotel enjoys a central position next to Bristol Cathedral and overlooking College Green. It was much admired by Queen Victoria and Sir Winston Churchill and it survived Second World War bombs. Today it is restored to its former glory and is Bristol's leading luxury hotel. The warmest welcomes await guests, who are invited to savour the combined experience of Victorian elegance and modern day comfort. There are 242 rooms including 16 suites, all individually designed and furnished to the highest standards and many offer superb views over the city and harbour. There is a choice of two restaurants; the imposing Victorian Palm Court with its spectacular glass roof or the less formal Terrace Restaurant which overlooks Cathedral Square. Awarded 2 AA Rosettes. The Swallow Leisure Club, designed with Ancient Rome in mind, has handpainted murals, mosaics and Roman columns and offers an ideal environment for those seeking energetic pursuits or relaxation. Facilities include a heated indoor swimming pool, sauna, spa bath, steam room, sunbeds and fitness room. The hotel now has its own internal "pub" the Queen Vic where you can "surf the net" and watch sport on satellite TV. The hotel has its own car park. **Directions:** At the end of the M32 keep right and follow the signs for the City Centre. Price guide: Single from £110; double/twin from £125; suites £150–£300.

242 rms MasterCard VISA AMERICAN EXPRESS M 300

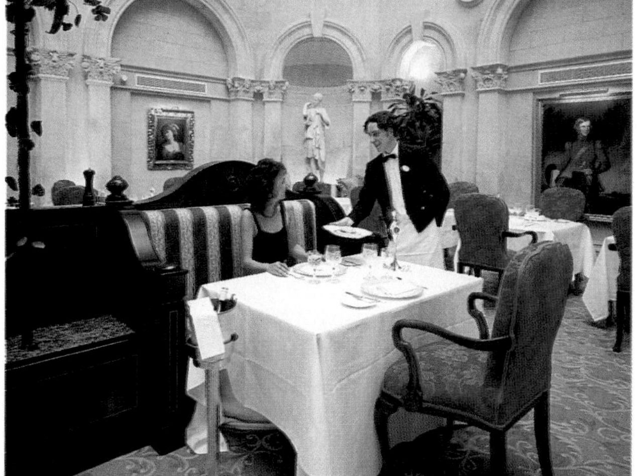

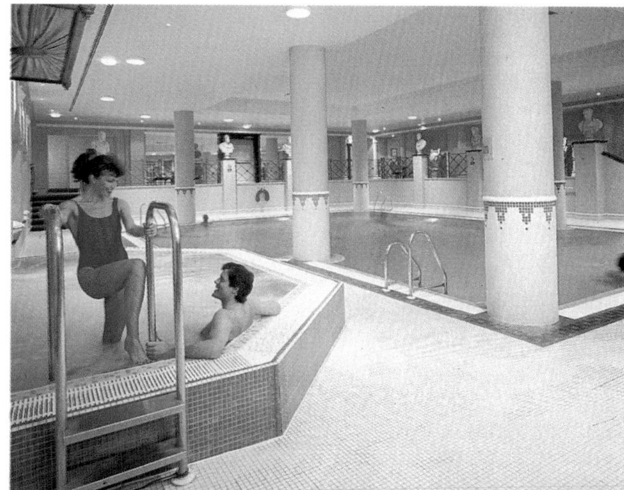

For hotel location, see maps on pages 477-483

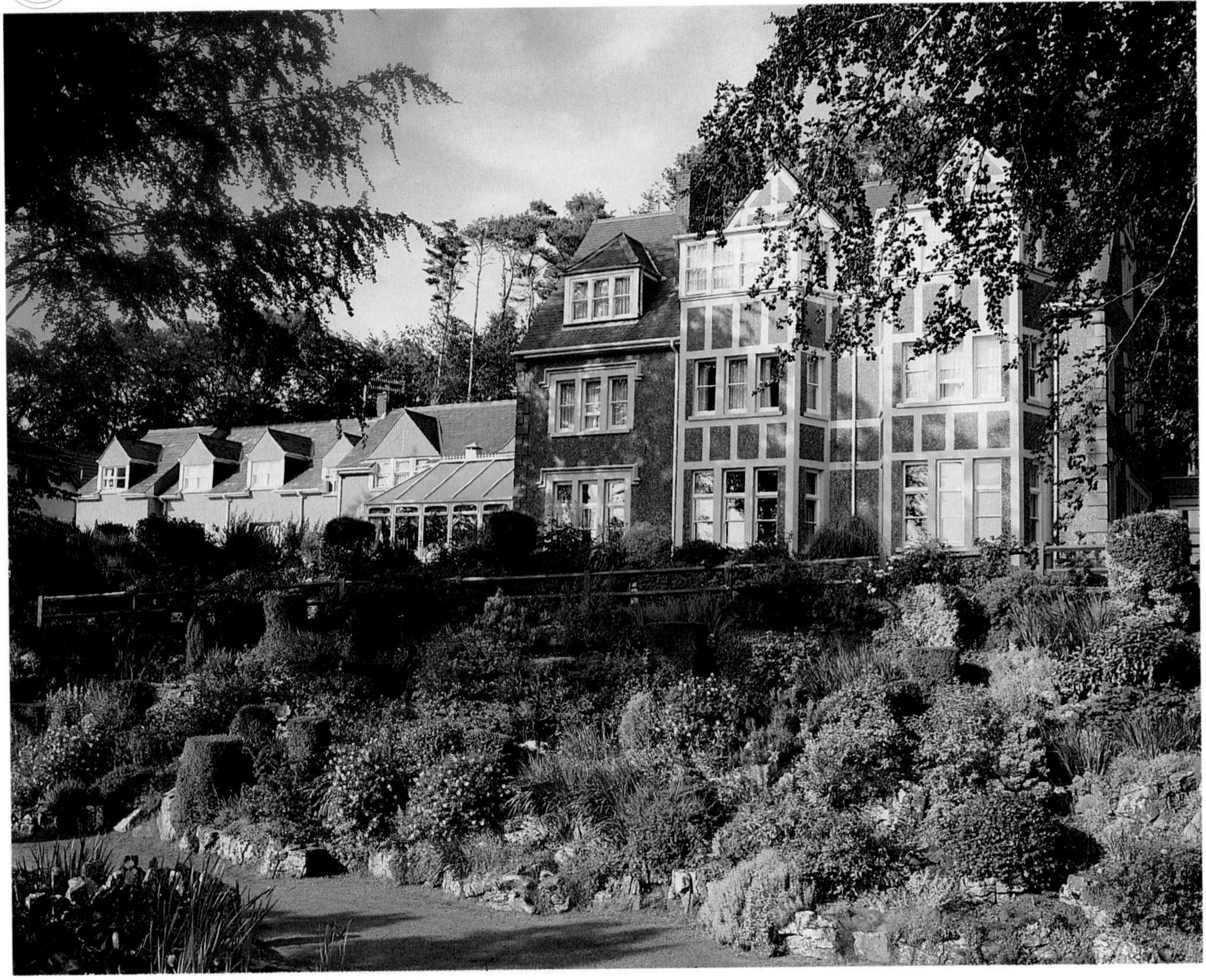

DANESWOOD HOUSE HOTEL

CUCK HILL, SHIPHAM, NR WINSCOMBE, SOMERSET BS25 1RD

TEL: 01934 843145 FAX: 01934 843824 E-MAIL: 101604.3531@COMPUSERVE.COM

A small country house hotel, Daneswood House overlooks a leafy valley in the heart of the Mendip Hills – on a clear day, the views stretch as far as Wales. It was built by the Edwardians as a homeopathic health hydro and under the enthusiastic ownership of David and Elise Hodges it has been transformed into a charming hotel. Each bedroom is well furnished and individually decorated with striking fabrics. The honeymoon suite, with its king-sized bed, frescoed ceiling and antiques, is particularly comfortable. First-class cooking places equal emphasis on presentation and taste. Each dish is carefully prepared in a style that combines traditional English and French cooking. During the summer, guests can dine alfresco and enjoy barbecued dishes such as Indonesian duck and baked sea bass with fennel and armagnac. There is a carefully selected wine list and a wide choice of liqueurs. The private conference lounge makes a quiet setting for meetings, while private functions can be catered for with ease. Awarded 2 AA Rosettes. Cheddar Gorge is 2 miles away, and Wells, Glastonbury, Bristol and Bath are nearby. Guide dogs accommodated only. **Directions:** Shipham is signposted from A38 Bristol–Bridgwater road. Go through village towards Cheddar; hotel drive is on left leaving village. Price guide: Single £57.50–£69.50; double/twin £69.50–£79.50; suite £112.

For hotel location, see maps on pages 477-483

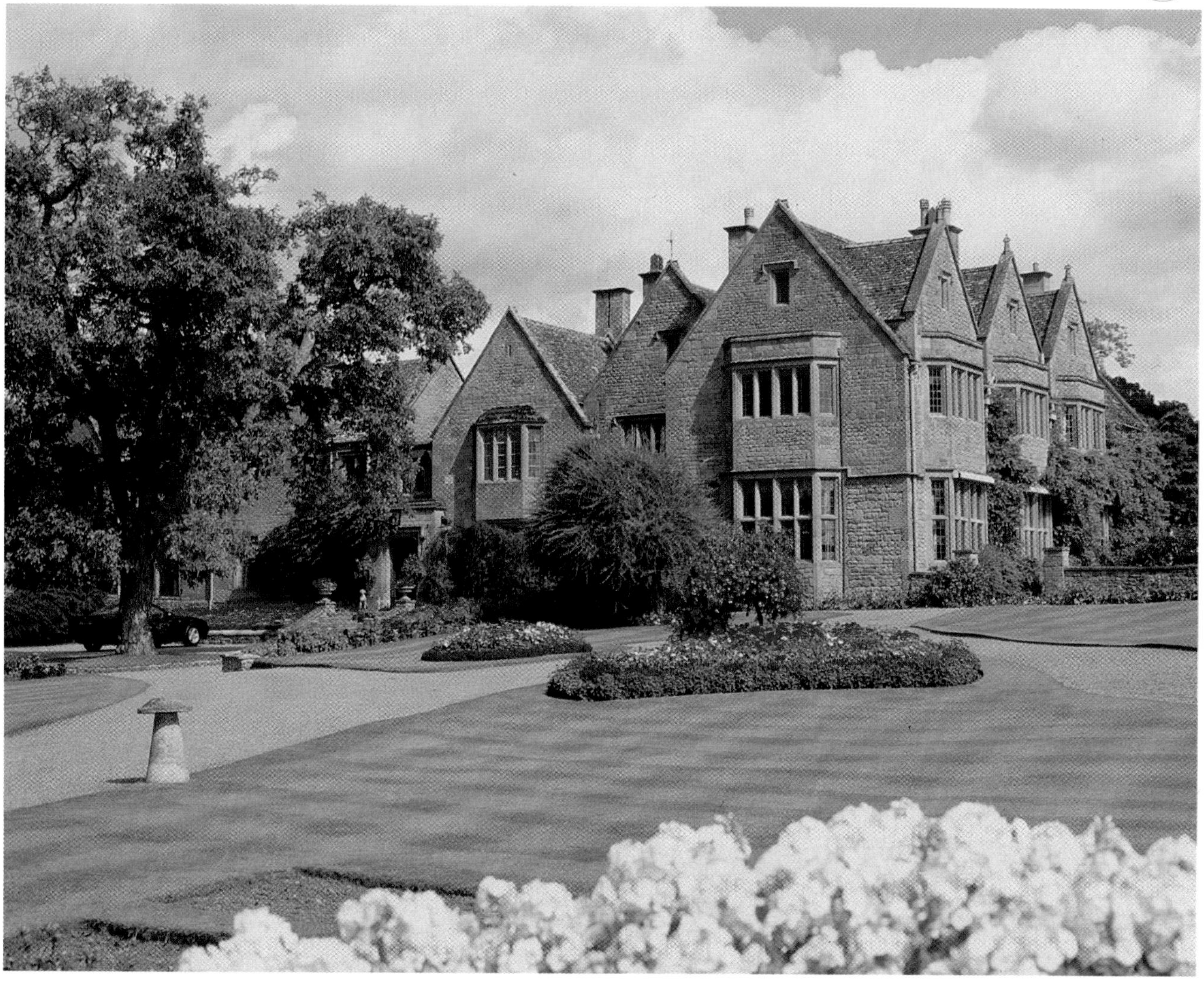

BUCKLAND MANOR

BUCKLAND, NR BROADWAY, GLOUCESTERSHIRE WR12 7LY
TEL: 01386 852626 FAX: 01386 853557

Set in an idyllic Cotswold valley, this fine gabled mansion house – parts of which date back to the 13th century – was tastefully converted in 1982 into an award-winning country house hotel. Privately owned by Roy and Daphne Vaughan. A member of Relais & Chateaux. The lounge, morning room and bedrooms are of the highest standard, exquisitely furnished, with luxury bathrooms fed from the Manor's own spring water. Downstairs, the lounge and reception rooms feature impressive fireplaces, burnished oak panelling, antiques and plentiful displays of fresh flowers. Buckland Manor's resident manager is Nigel Power, previously of The Savoy and Hôtel du Rhône, Geneva. The head chef, Martyn Pearn, trained at the Connaught and Claridge's in London and was previously head chef of La Réserve in Bordeaux. Given sufficient notice he will be happy to cook to order, and whatever the dish, only the best provisions are selected to meet the hotel's exacting standards. There are good recreational facilities at Buckland Manor in addition to the putting green and extensive gardens. Nearby attractions include Cheltenham and Stratford-upon-Avon. The 'Cotswold Way' which is behind the manor has magnificent views and is excellent for walking. **Directions:** Off the B4632, 2 miles south of Broadway. Price guide: Single £165–£315; double/twin £175–£325.

For hotel location, see maps on pages 477-483

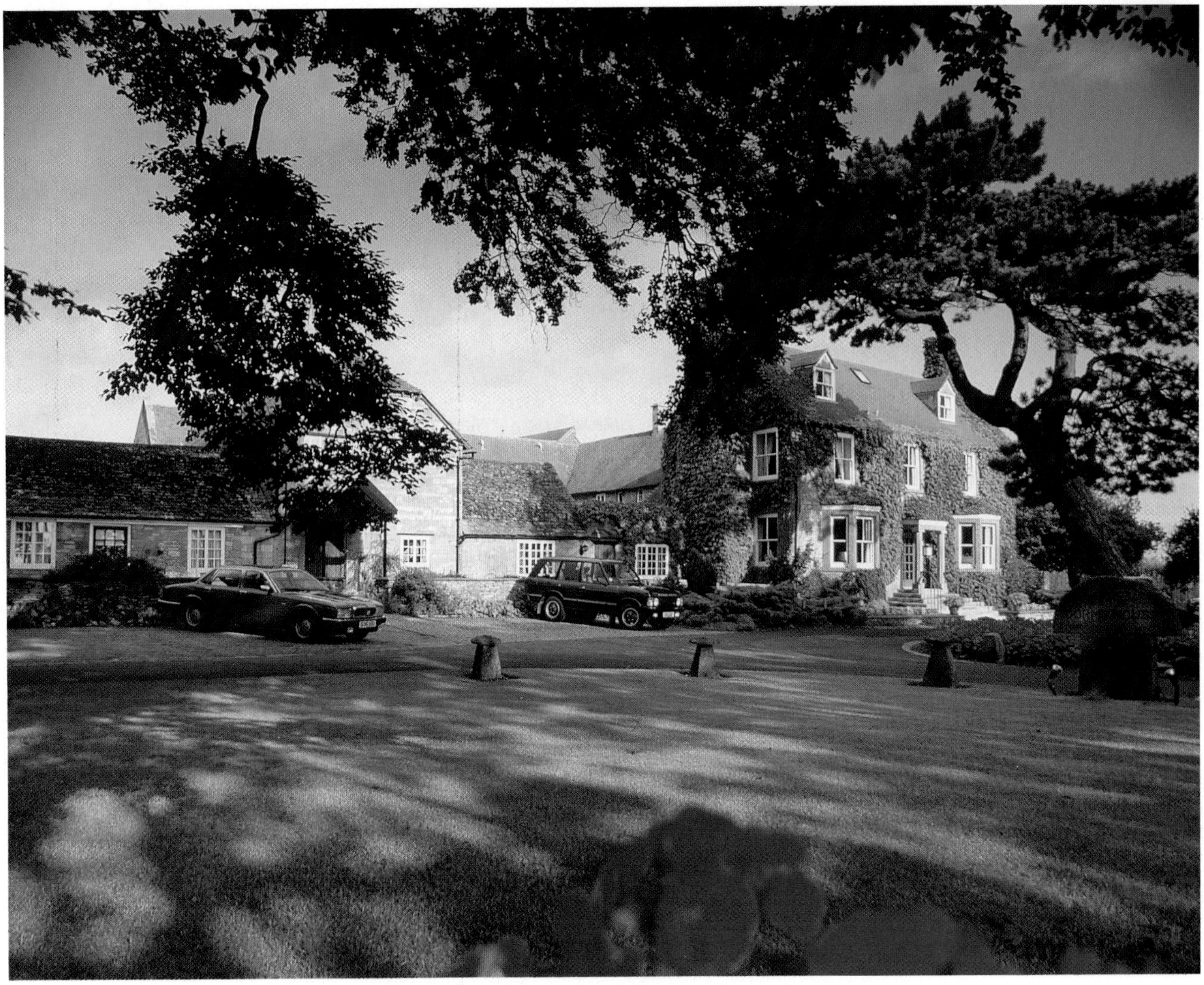

DORMY HOUSE

WILLERSEY HILL, BROADWAY, WORCESTERSHIRE WR12 7LF
TEL: 01386 852711 FAX: 01386 858636

This former 17th-century farmhouse has been beautifully converted into a delightful hotel which retains much of its original character. With its oak beams, stone-flagged floors and honey-coloured local stone walls it imparts warmth and tranquillity. Dormy House provides a wealth of comforts for the most discerning guest. Each bedroom is individually decorated – some are furnished with four-poster beds – and suites are available. Head Chef, Alan Cutler, prepares a superb choice of menus and Tapestries Restaurant, expertly managed by Saverio Buchicchio, offers an extensive wine list includes many half bottles. The versatile Dormy Suite is an ideal venue for conferences, meetings or private functions – professionally arranged to individual requirements. The hotel has its own leisure facilities which include a games room, gym, sauna/steam, room, croquet lawn and putting green. Mountain bikes are available for hire. Broadway Golf Club is adjacent. The locality is idyllic for walkers. Stratford-upon-Avon, Cheltenham Spa, Hidcote Manor Garden and Sudeley Castle are all within easy reach. USA representative: Josephine Barr, 1-800-323-5463. Closed 2 days at Christmas. **Directions:** Hotel is ½ mile off A44 between Moreton-in-Marsh and Broadway. Taking the turning signposted Saintbury, the hotel is first on left past picnic area. Price guide: Single £63–£84; double/twin £126–£152.

For hotel location, see maps on pages 477-483

THE LYGON ARMS

BROADWAY, WORCESTERSHIRE WR12 7DU
TEL: 01386 852255 FAX: 01386 858611

The Lygon Arms, a magnificent Tudor building with numerous historical associations, stands in Broadway, acclaimed by many as 'the prettiest village in England', in the heart of the Cotswolds. Over the years much restoration has been carried out, emphasising the outstanding period features, such as original 17th century oak panelling and an ancient hidden stairway. All the bedrooms are individually and tastefully furnished and offer guests every modern luxury, even telephone voice-mail, combined with the elegance of an earlier age. The Great Hall, complete with a 17th century minstrels' gallery, and the smaller private dining rooms provide a fine setting for a well-chosen and imaginative menu. Conference facilities including the state-of-the-art Torrington Room are available for up to 70 participants. Guests can enjoy a superb range of leisure amenities including all-weather tennis, indoor pool, gymnasium, billiard room, beauty salon, steam room, solarium, saunas and table tennis. Golf can be arranged locally. The many Cotswold villages; Stratford-upon-Avon, Oxford and Cheltenham are nearby, while Broadway itself is a paradise for the antique collector. **Directions:** Set on the right-hand side of Broadway High Street on the A44 in the direction of London to Worcester. Price guide: Single from £98; double/twin from £155 including Continental breakfast, excluding VAT.

For hotel location, see maps on pages 477-483

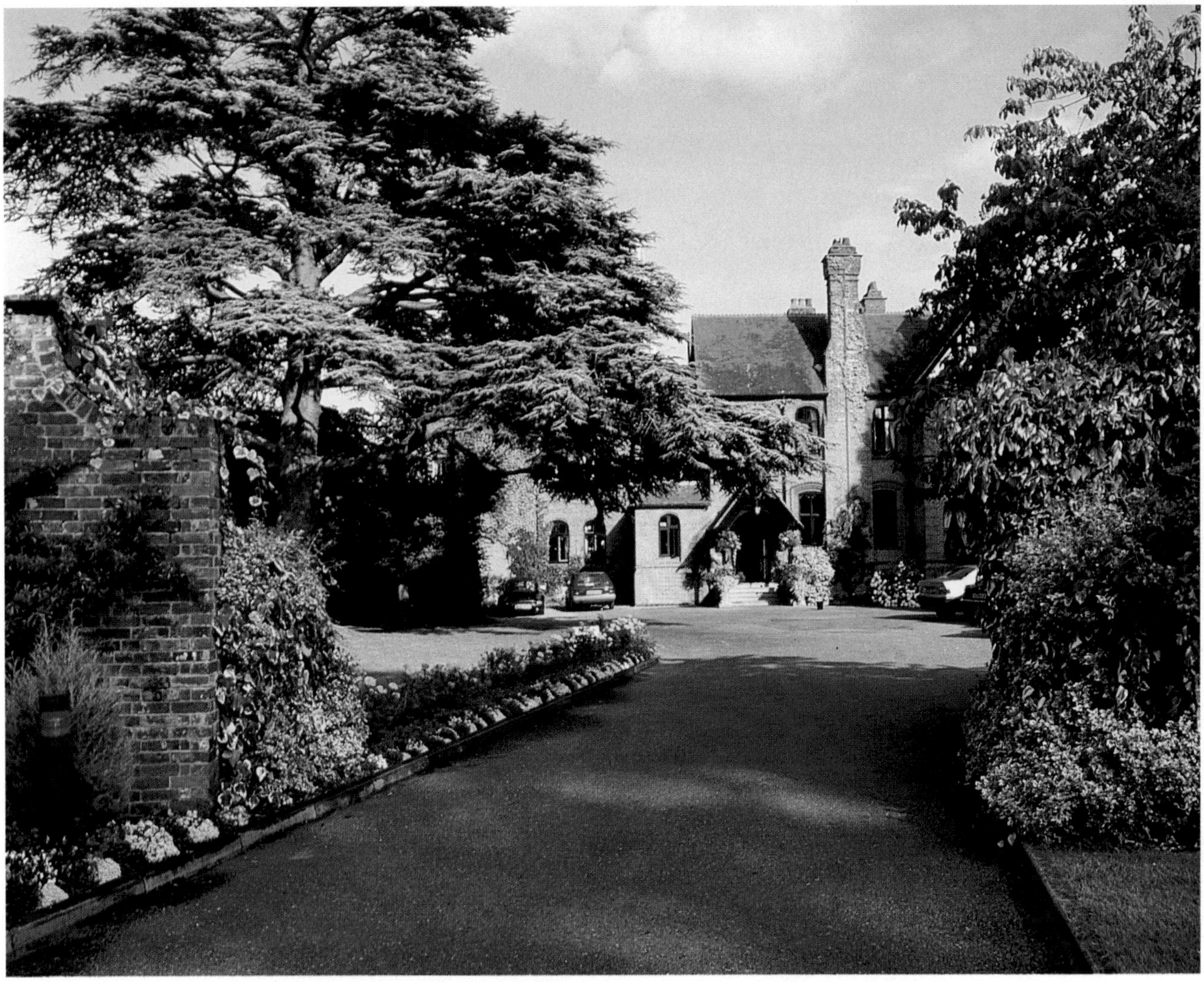

CAREYS MANOR HOTEL

BROCKENHURST, NEW FOREST, HAMPSHIRE SO42 7RH
TEL: 01590 623551 FAX: 01590 622799

Careys Manor, an elegant country house, dates from 1888 and is built on the site of a royal hunting lodge used by Charles II. Situated in 5 acres of landscaped grounds and surrounded by glorious New Forest countryside, the hotel is proud of the personal welcome and care it extends to its visitors. The comfortably furnished bedrooms are appointed to the highest standards. In the Garden Wing, there is a choice of luxury bedrooms, some opening directly onto the lawns and others with a balcony overlooking the pretty gardens. The restaurant offers fine English and French cuisine, prepared and presented to gourmet standards. A prestigious sports complex comprises a large indoor swimming pool with Jacuzzi, sauna, solarium and a Turkish steam room. In addition, guests can work out in the professionally supervised gymnasium, where there is also a room for massage, sports injury and beauty treatments. Wind-surfing, riding and sailing can all be enjoyed locally, while Stonehenge, Beaulieu, Broadlands, Salisbury and Winchester are a short distance away. Business interests can be catered for – there are comprehensive self-contained conference facilities. **Directions:** From M27 junction 1, follow A337 to Lymington. Careys Manor is on the left after 30 mph sign at Brockenhurst. Price guide from: Single £69–£79; double/twin £109–£129; suite £159.

For hotel location, see maps on pages 477-483

RHINEFIELD HOUSE HOTEL

RHINEFIELD ROAD, BROCKENHURST, HAMPSHIRE SO42 7QB
TEL: 01590 622922 FAX: 01590 622800

Known locally as the 'jewel in the forest', at first sight the sheer grandeur of Rhinefield House surpasses all expectaitions. A hint of Italian Renaissance sweeps across ornamental gardens, with canals reflecting the mellow stonework. Lovingly restored to their original 1890s design, over 5,000 yew trees form the maze and formal parterres where a grass ampitheatre has been carved out of the western slopes for summer evening concerts. The interiors are equally impressive, the journey through the rooms is a voyage of discovery. Authentically created in the style of a Moorish Palace, the Alhambra Room has Islamic inscriptions, onyx pillars and mosaic flooring. Fine cuisine is served in the elegant Armada Restaurant – so called after its splendid carving depicting the Spanish Armada. An airy sun-lit conservatory and attractive bedrooms appointed in accordance with the style of the house all add up to Rhinefield's appeal. The Grand Hall is a replica of Westminster Hall – an ideal setting for Balls, Society Weddings and stylish Banquets. A wide range of conference rooms and equipment is available for business events. Guests may unwind in the Atlantis Leisure Club with its plunge pool, solarium, sauna and gymnasium. Directions: A35 West from Lyndhurst, or along Rhinefield Road from Brockenhurst. Price guide: Single £90; double/twin £125; suite £155–£170.

34 rms MasterCard VISA AMERICAN EXPRESS M 150

For hotel location, see maps on pages 477-483

NEW PARK MANOR

LYNDHURST ROAD, BROCKENHURST, NEW FOREST, HAMPSHIRE SO42 7QH
TEL: 01590 623467 FAX: 01590 622268

Escape from the crowds to one of the New Forest's finest country house hotels. A former hunting lodge of Charles II, the building is grade II listed and dates back to the 16th century. It stands in a very fine position a good distance from the road to Lyndhurst, the "capital" of the New Forest, where "Alice in Wonderland's" grave, and Rufus Stone are curiosities to be visited. The en-suite bedrooms are all individually decorated, keeping in mind the style and grandeur of the old manor; most offer superb views over the surrounding parklands with its wandering ponies and deer. Enjoy a romantic evening with fine wines and French influenced cuisine in the Stag Head Restaurant or relax with a good book from the library in front of the open log fire in the historic Rufus Bar. The New Forest suite creates a wonderful setting for all types of functions – tailor made to suit your personal requirements. For the more energetic New Park Manor offers riding from its own equestrian centre with BHS trained stable crew, a tennis court and an outdoor heated swimming pool. There is something for everyone so why not get away from it all and escape to the peace and tranquility, topped with service par excellence, of the New Park Manor? **Directions:** New Park Manor is 1/2 mile off the A337 between Lyndhurst and Brockenhurst easily reached from M27 via Cadnam. Price guide: Single from £82.50; double/twin £110–£150.

24 rms MasterCard VISA AMERICAN EXPRESS M 80 7

For hotel location, see maps on pages 477-483

GRAFTON MANOR COUNTRY HOUSE HOTEL

GRAFTON LANE, BROMSGROVE, WORCESTERSHIRE B61 7HA
TEL: 01527 579007 FAX: 01527 575221

Closely associated with many of the leading events in English history, Grafton Manor's illustrious past can be traced back to Norman times. Commissioned in 1567, the present manor is set in several acres of gardens leading to a lake. Modern comfort and style are combined with the atmosphere of an earlier age. Pot-pourri from the hotel's 19th-century rose gardens scents the rooms and over 100 herbs are grown in a unique, chessboard-pattern garden. All the herbs are in regular use in the restaurant kitchen, where Simon Morris aims to 'produce only the best' for guests. Preserves made from estate produce are on sale. Meals are served in the 18th-century dining room, the focal point of Grafton Manor. Damask-rose petal and mulberry sorbets are indicative of the inspired culinary style. Indian cuisine is Simon's award winning hobby and Asian dishes often complement the traditional English cooking. The fully equipped bedrooms have been meticulously restored and furnished, some with open fires on cooler evenings. Grafton Manor is ideally placed for Birmingham, the NEC and the International Conference Centre. It is an equally good base from which to explore the Worcestershire countryside. **Directions:** From M5 junction 5 proceed via A38 towards Bromsgrove. Bear left at first roundabout; Grafton Lane is first left after 1/2 mile. Price guide: Single £85; double/twin £95; suite £150.

For hotel location, see maps on pages 477-483

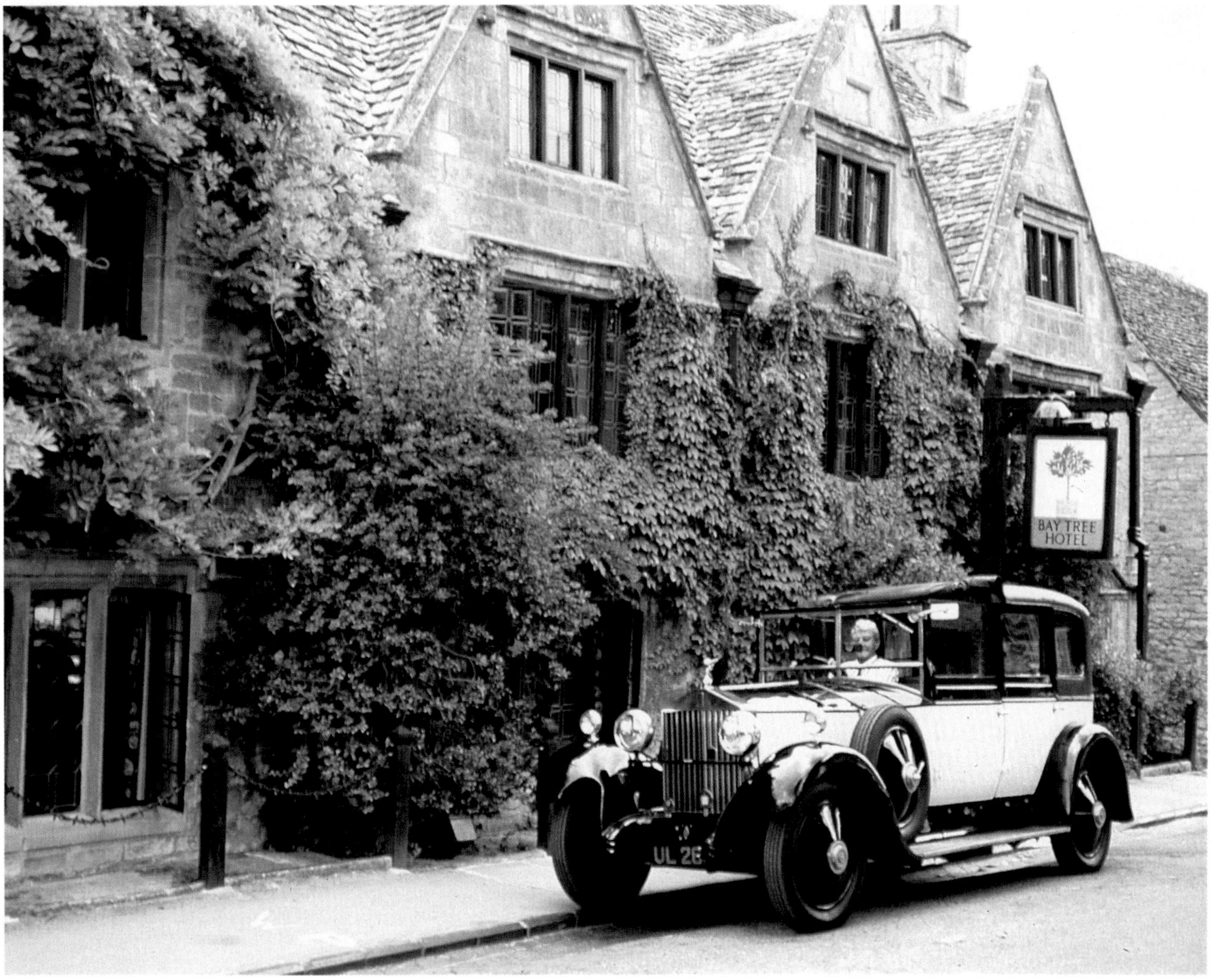

THE BAY TREE HOTEL AND RESTAURANT

SHEEP STREET, BURFORD, OXON OX18 4LW
TEL: 01993 822791 FAX: 01993 823008

The Bay Tree has been expertly refurbished so that it retains all its Tudor splendour while offering every modern facility. The oak-panelled rooms have huge stone fireplaces, and a galleried staircase leads upstairs from the raftered hall. All the bedrooms are en suite, three of them furnished with four-poster beds and two of the five suites have half-tester beds. In the summer, you can relax in the delightful walled gardens, featuring landscaped terraces of lawn and flower beds. A relaxing atmosphere is enhanced by the staff's attentive service in the flagstoned dining room where the head chef's creative cuisine is complemented by a comprehensive selection of fine wines. Light meals are served in a country-style bar, while the conservatory lounge is the place to unwind and enjoy the view over the grounds. Burford, often described as the gateway to the Cotswolds, is renowned for its assortment of antique shops and the Tolsey Museum of local history. The Bay Tree Hotel makes a convenient base for day trips to Stratford-upon-Avon, Stow-on-the-Wold and Blenheim Palace. Golf, clay pigeon shooting and riding can be arranged locally. **Directions:** Burford is on the A40 between Oxford and Cheltenham. Proceed halfway down the hill into Burford, turn left into Sheep Street and The Bay Tree Hotel is 30 yards on your right. Price guide: Single £60–£80; double/twin £110–£115.

For hotel location, see maps on pages 477-483

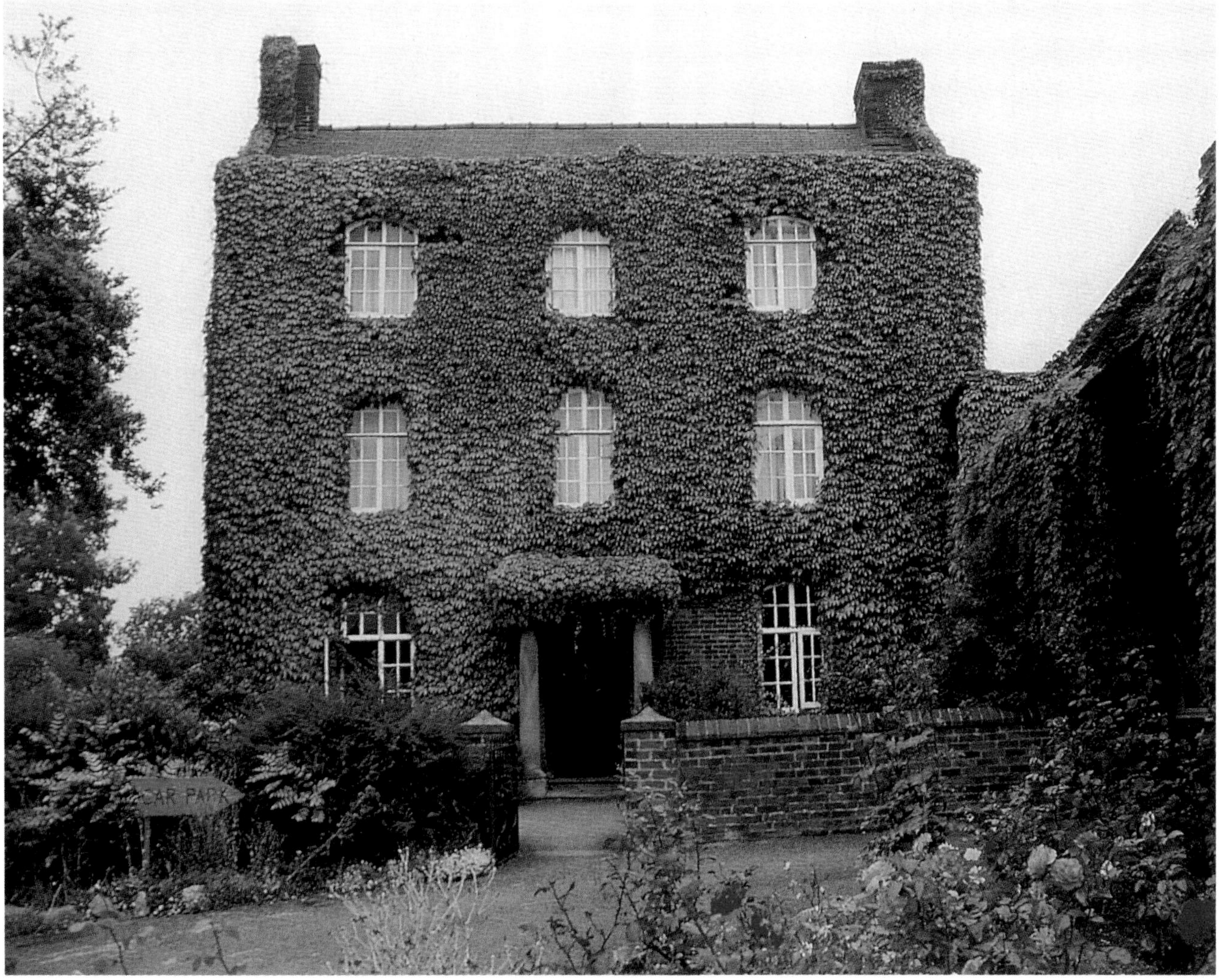

The Brookhouse

ROLLESTON-ON-DOVE, NR BURTON UPON TRENT, STAFFORDSHIRE DE13 9AA
TEL: 01283 814188 FAX: 01283 813644

Originally built as a farmhouse in 1694, this attractive, ivy-clad William and Mary house stands in a tranquil position beside a gently flowing brook and lush gardens. Grade II listed, the building was converted into a hotel in 1976, and since then it has earned a reputation for its friendly service and hospitality. Of particular interest are the pretty bedrooms, with four-poster, half-tester or Victorian brass beds. The bedding is trimmed with Nottingham lace. Downstairs, the décor and antique furniture are in keeping with the cosy cottage style. In the restaurant, soft wall-lighting and candles create an intimate atmosphere, while polished wooden tables are set with silver and crystal. The food is of a consistently high quality. An extensive menu presents a wide choice to suit all tastes. Small private functions can be catered for: fax, photo-copying and secretarial services can be arranged for business meetings. Serious hikers and ramblers alike will find plenty of good walking in the nearby Derbyshire Dales and Peak District. Notable local attractions include the Shugborough Estate, Calke Abbey, The Bass Museum of Brewing, Haddon and Kedleston Halls. **Directions:** Rolleston is just outside Burton upon Trent between the A50 to Stoke-on-Trent and the A38 to Derby. Price guide: Single £69–£79; double/twin £89–£99.

For hotel location, see maps on pages 477-483

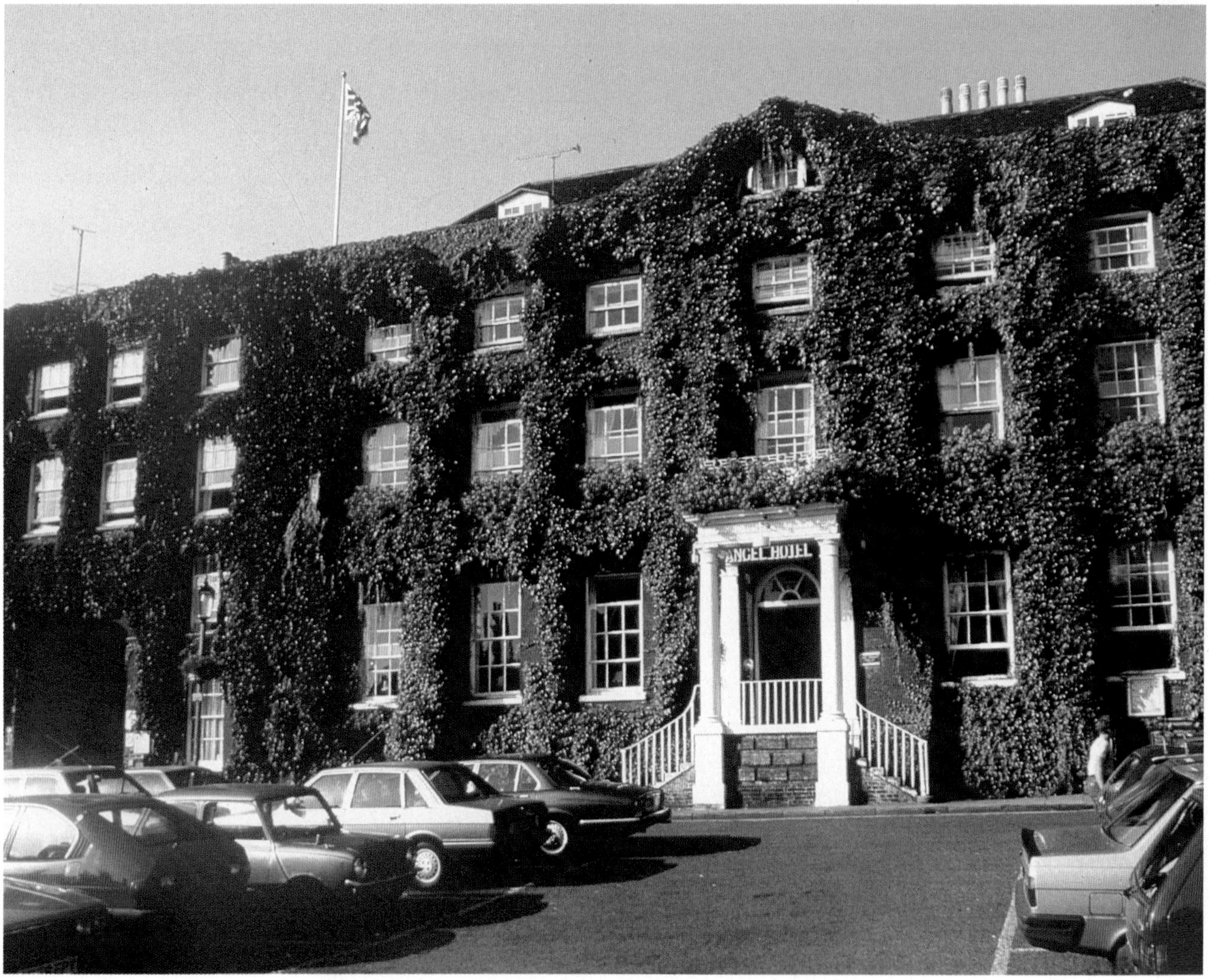

THE ANGEL HOTEL

BURY ST EDMUNDS, SUFFOLK IP33 1LT
TEL: 01284 753926 FAX: 01284 750092

Immortalised by Charles Dickens as the hostelry where Mr Pickwick enjoyed an excellent roast dinner, The Angel Hotel is renowned for its first-class service to travellers, continuing the tradition since first becoming an inn in 1452. Visitors have the immediate impression of a hotel that is loved and nurtured by its owners. In the public rooms, guests will appreciate the carefully chosen ornaments and pictures, fresh flowers and log fires. Bedrooms are individually furnished and decorated and all have en suite bathrooms. The elegant dining room has been awarded 2 rosettes by the AA for excellent food and service. Overlooking the ancient abbey, the restaurant serves classic English cuisine, including local speciality dishes and succulent roasts. The Angel can offer a wide range of quality conference and banqueting facilities catering for private dinners, meetings and weddings from 10–120 persons. The hotel is within an hour of east coast ferry ports and 45 minutes from Stansted Airport. Nearby there is racing at Newmarket and several golf courses within easy reach. Bury St Edmunds is an interesting and historic market town and an excellent centre for touring East Anglia. **Directions:** The hotel is situated in the centre of the town. Price guide: Single £59–£65; double/twin £69–£75; suite £95–£105. Weekend rates £35 per person bed and breakfast.

For hotel location, see maps on pages 477-483

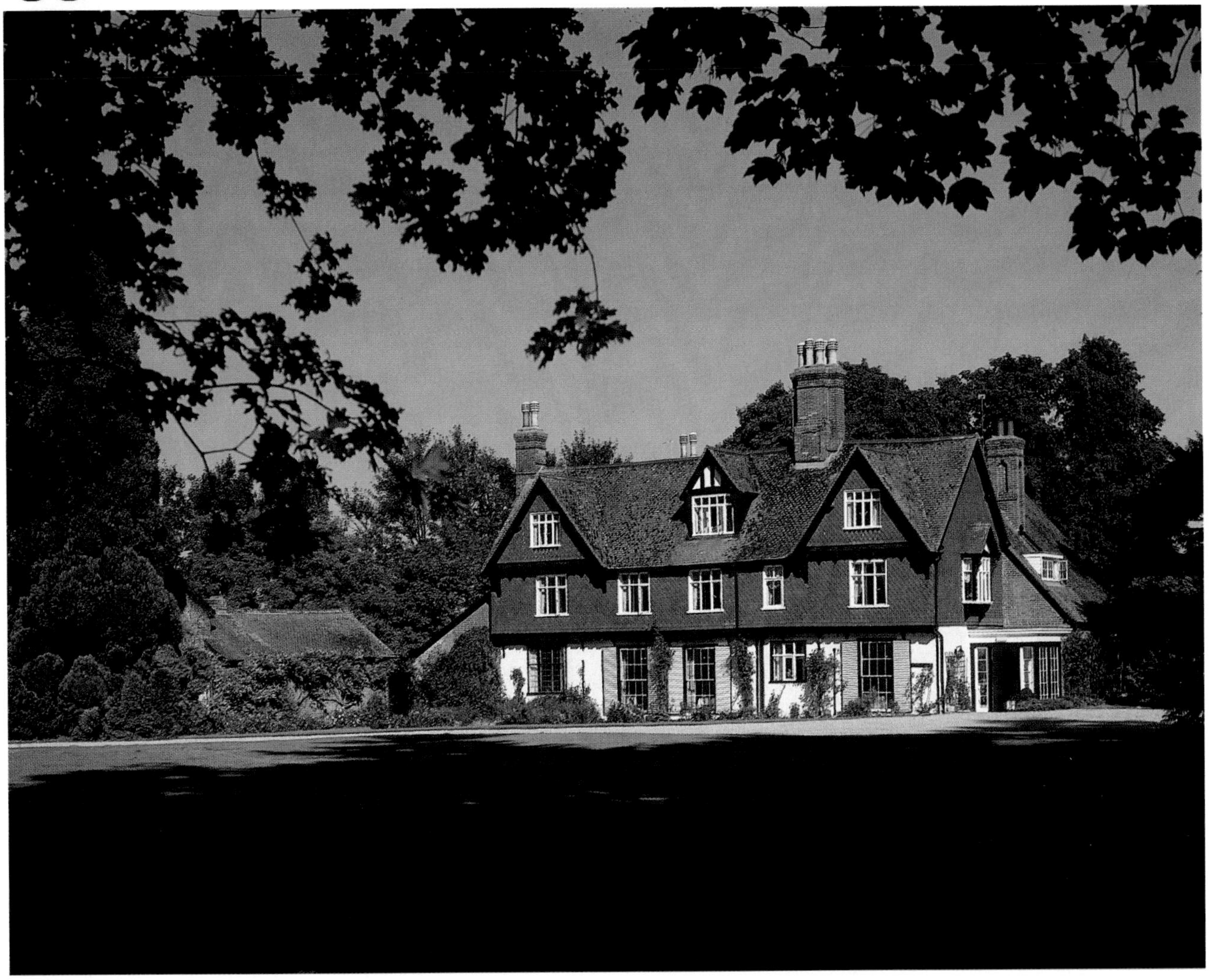

Ravenwood Hall

ROUGHAM, BURY ST EDMUNDS, SUFFOLK IP30 9JA
TEL: 01359 270345 FAX: 01359 270788

Nestling within 7 acres of lovely lawns and woodlands deep in the heart of Suffolk lies Ravenwood Hall. Now an excellent country house hotel, this fine Tudor building dates back to 1530 and retains many of its original features. The restaurant, still boasting the carved timbers and huge inglenook from Tudor times, creates a delightfully intimate atmosphere in which to enjoy imaginative cuisine. The menu is a combination of adventurous and classical dishes, featuring long forgotten English recipes. The Hall's extensive cellars are stocked with some of the finest vintages, along with a selection of rare ports and brandies. A cosy bar offers a less formal setting in which to enjoy some unusual snacks. Comfortable bedrooms are furnished with antiques, reflecting the historic tradition of the Hall, although each is equipped with every modern facility. A wide range of leisure facilities is available for guests, including a hard tennis court, a croquet lawn and heated swimming pool. There are golf courses and woodland walks to enjoy locally; hunting and shooting can be arranged. Places of interest nearby include the famous medieval wool towns of Lavenham and Long Melford; the historic cities of Norwich and Cambridge are within easy reach. **Directions:** 2 miles East of Bury St. Edmunds off the A14. Price guide: £59–£79; double/twin: £79–£109.

For hotel location, see maps on pages 477-483

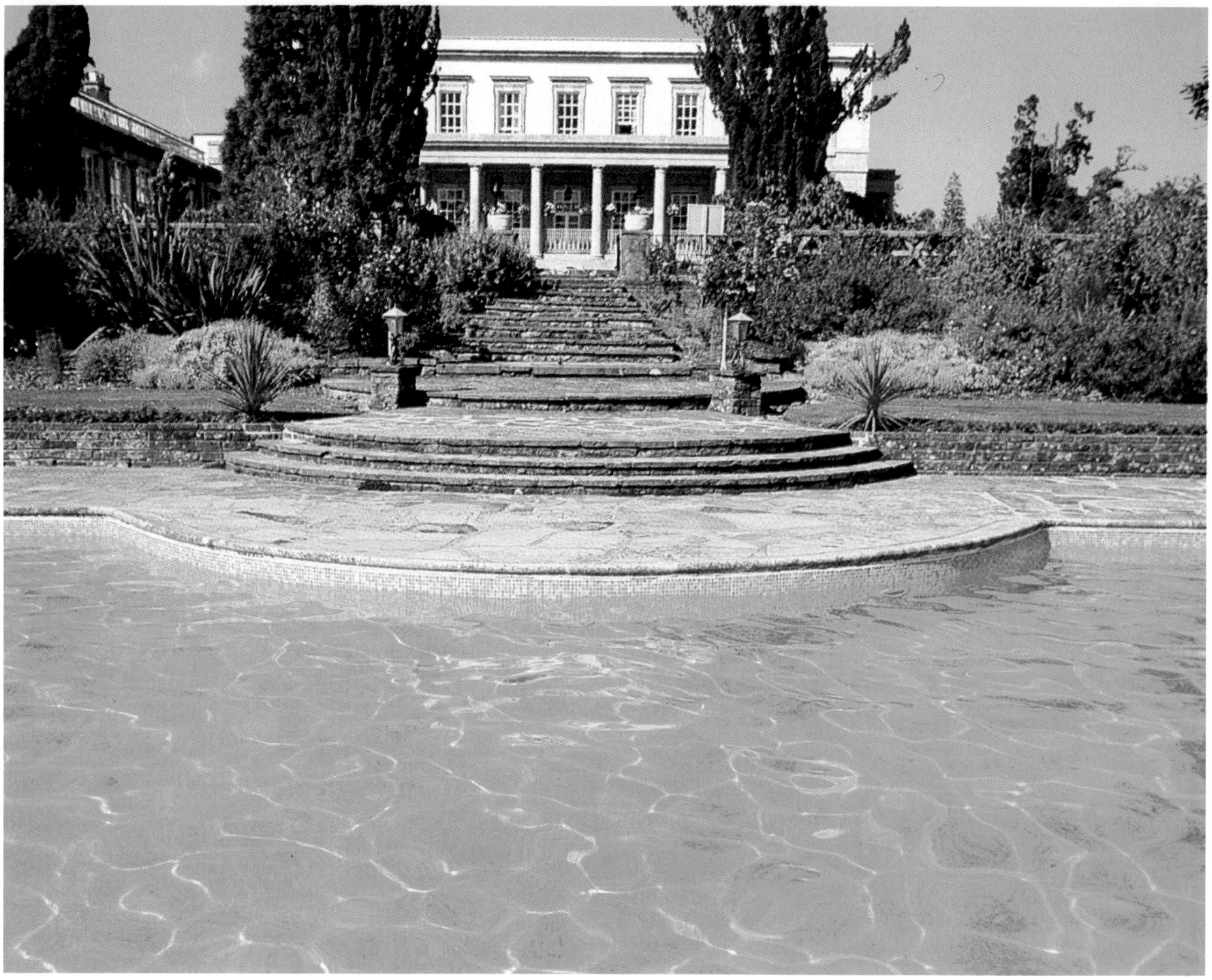

BUXTED PARK COUNTRY HOUSE HOTEL

BUXTED, UCKFIELD, EAST SUSSEX TN22 4AY
TEL: 01825 732711 FAX: 01825 732770

Buxted Park is set in over 312 acres of parkland, boasting a herd of deer and lakes stocked with rare species of ducks, swans and geese. The estate dates back to 1725. In 1940 the house was redesigned by Basil Ionides, interior designer of The Savoy and Claridge's. The hotel has recently been extensively renovated and refurbished, including the magnificent Victorian conservatory – now called The Orangery restaurant. Spacious and attractively decorated bedrooms offer every modern amenity, some have balconies and others direct access to the gardens. The restaurant provides elegant surroundings in which to enjoy excellent English cuisine, with an occasional Thai influence. A full range of fine wines is available to complement the meal. The stunning Coat of Arms drawing room and the Ballroom each provide an ideal venue for all types of social and corporate entertaining and there are a number of other drawing rooms for conferences. A state of the art 54 seater cinema is perfect for presentations. Full Health Club facilities are available, including a well equipped gym, sauna, outdoor heated swimming pool and snooker room. **Directions:** The hotel is on the A272, east of its junction with the A22. Price guide Single from £80; double/twin from £105; junior suites from £165. Two night leisure breaks to include 4 course dinner from £70 per person per night.

For hotel location, see maps on pages 477-483

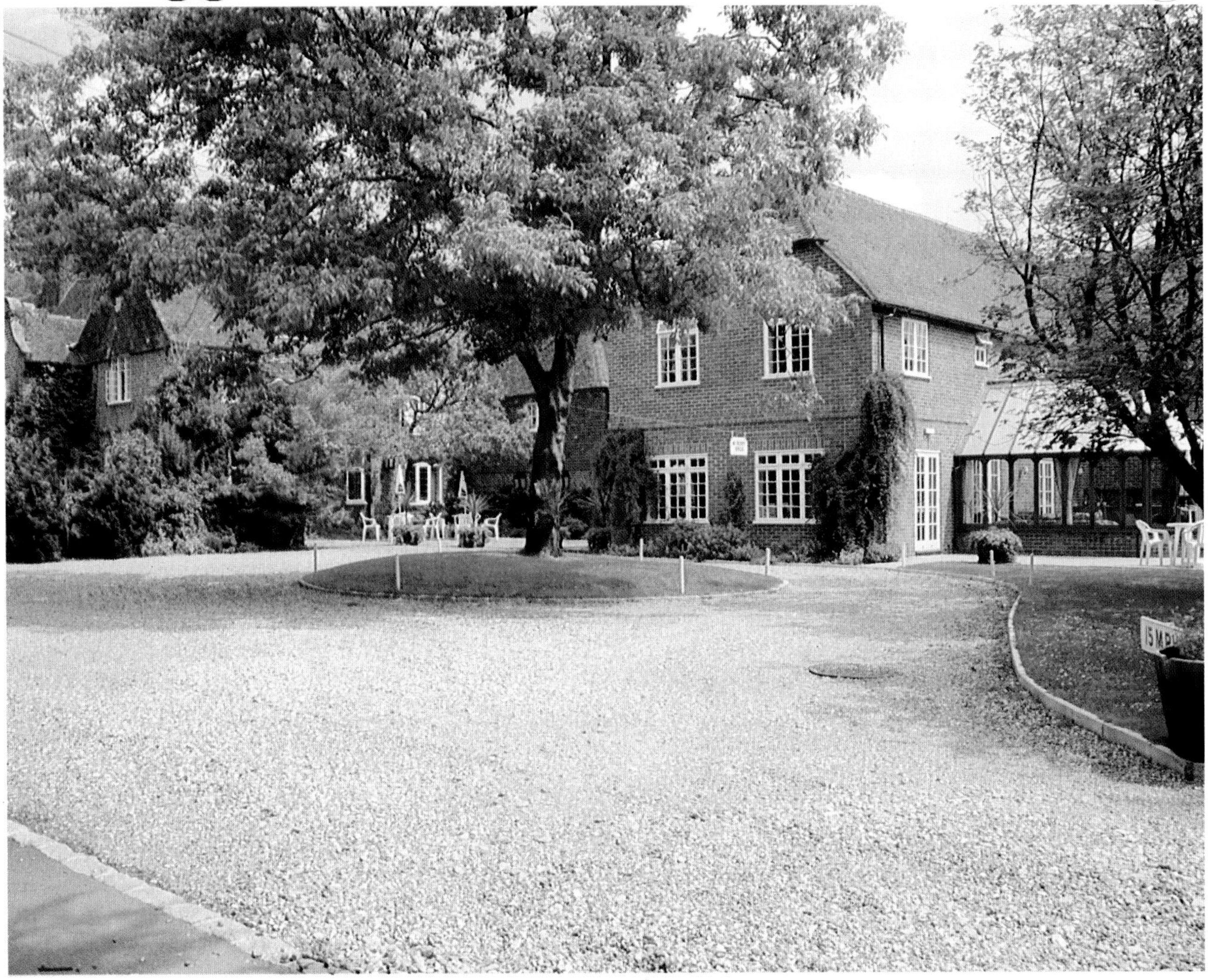

HOWFIELD MANOR

CHARTHAM HATCH, NR CANTERBURY, KENT CT4 7HQ

TEL: 01227 738294 FAX: 01227 731535

At Howfield Manor great care has been taken to preserve a long tradition of hospitality dating back to 1181, while discreetly providing modern comforts. Originally part of the Priory of St Gregory, this historic country house is set in 5 acres of secluded grounds with a formal English rose garden. The hotel has an authentic priest hole and, in the Priory Bar, striking *trompe l'oeil* murals. Illuminated under the floor of the Old Well Restaurant is the ferned ancient well, which was the main source of water for the monks who lived here 800 years ago. A selection of wines and other refreshments nourishes today's visitors. Guests have the choice of an extensive range of menus to cater for every occasion – from an intimate à la carte meal for two to a gourmet dinner party in the self-contained conference and banqueting suite. The well-furnished bedrooms have been thoughtfully equipped. Located only 2 miles from the cathedral city of Canterbury, Howfield Manor makes an ideal base for touring this area and as a stopping-off point to and from the continent. Special weekend breaks are also available. **Directions:** From A2 London–Dover road, follow signs for Chartham Hatch after the Gate Service Station, then follow straight on for 2¼ miles. Hotel is on left at junction with A28. Price guide: Single £67.50; double/twin £87.50–£95.

For hotel location, see maps on pages 477-483

THE MANOR HOUSE

CASTLE COMBE, CHIPPENHAM, WILTSHIRE SN14 7HR
TEL: 01249 782206 FAX: 01249 782159

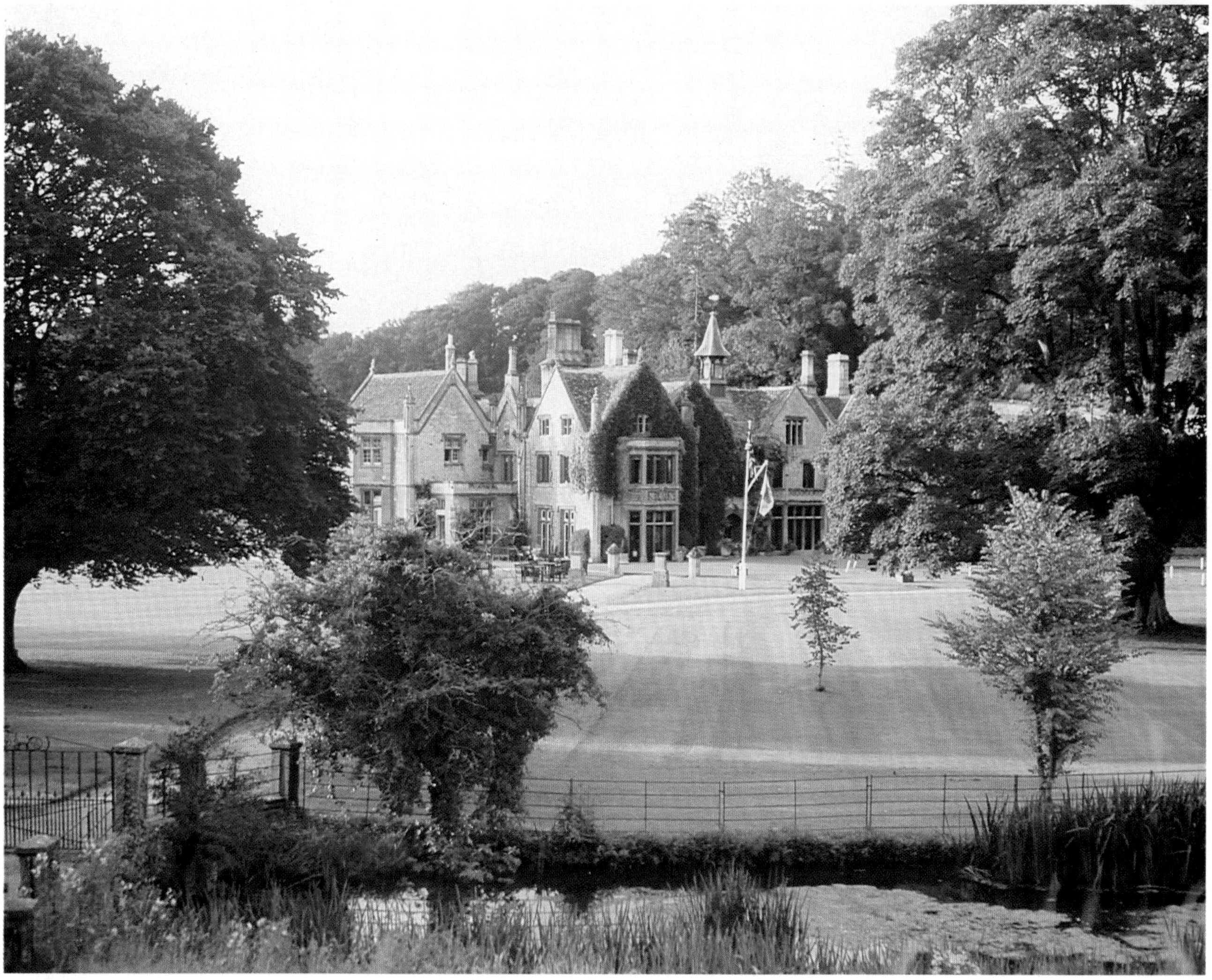

Nestling in the heart of one of England's prettiest villages deep in the Southern Cotswolds, the 14th century Manor House at Castle Combe is one of Britain's most architecturally beautiful and idyllically set country house hotels. Ivy clad stone walls and mullioned windows, oak panelling, log fires and antique furniture blend sympathetically with the individually designed bedrooms, many of which feature four poster beds, original beams and exposed walls. Designed by Peter Allis and Clive Clark and set in 200 acres of woodland valley and downland, the 6340 yard par 73, championship golf course is one of the most spectacular and challenging courses in the South of England. Delightful walks in the surrounding countryside or a stroll through Castle Combe, unchanged for almost 200 years, is a magical experience. 26 acres of gardens and parkland, a gently flowing trout stream and the romance of a terraced Italian garden, The Manor House provides tranquillity in enchanting surroundings, together with a friendly atmosphere and award winning cuisine and hospitality. **Directions:** 15 minutes' drive from junctions 17 & 18 of the M4, or 20 minutes from the M5/M4 intersection. 12 miles from the beautiful Georgian city of Bath and only 2 hours drive from central London. Approached directly from A420 and B4039. Price guide: Single/double/twin from £100; suite from £235.

For hotel location, see maps on pages 477-483

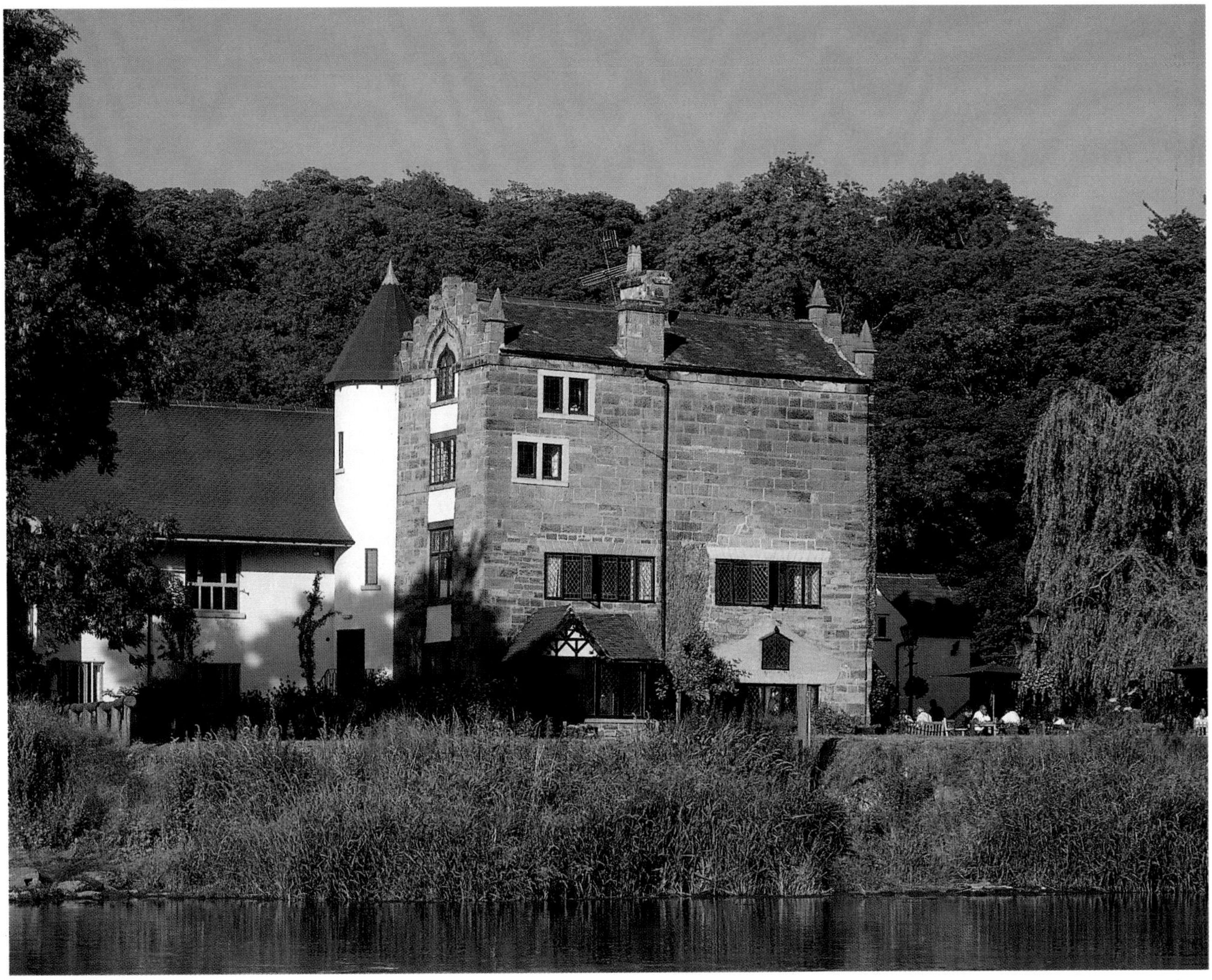

THE PRIEST HOUSE

ON THE RIVER, KINGS MILLS, CASTLE DONINGTON, LEICESTERSHIRE DE74 2RR
TEL: 01332 810649 FAX: 01332 811141

Magnificently situated on the banks of the River Trent, The Priest House is surrounded by 54 acres of mature unspoilt woodlands. Each of the bedrooms has been individually styled and the splendid Heron and Stocker suites are designed within the original Gothic Tower. Opening onto the private courtyard garden, the elegant library provides a perfect environment in which to read and relax. The traditional Mill Bar offers a selection of real ales and is a popular venue for guests and non-residents alike, along with the 'Malt Bar' which boasts over 50 different malt whiskies. The Mille Fleame Restaurant enjoys a growing reputation for the imaginative cuisine that it provides at both lunch and dinner, complemented by an excellent wine list. A number of spacious suites is available for banquets, receptions, weddings and private parties. A variety of leisure activities is available within the hotel, including clay pigeon shooting, coarse fishing and go-karting (all by arrangement). Places of interest nearby include Calke Abbey and Donington Park race circuit. **Directions:** From M1, junction 24, follow signs for Donington Park then Castle Donington. At Castle Donington go left at traffic lights and follow road marked Kings Mills to the Priest House. Price guide: Single from £79; double/twin from £99; four-poster from £125; suite from £145.

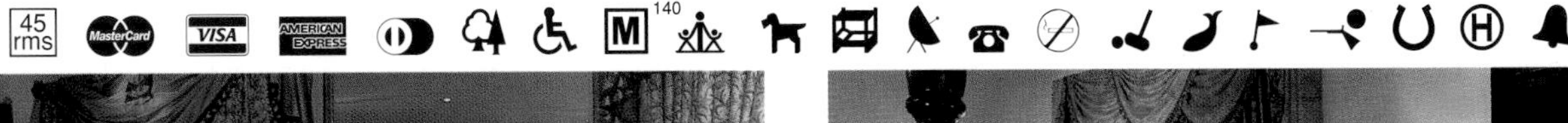

For hotel location, see maps on pages 477-483

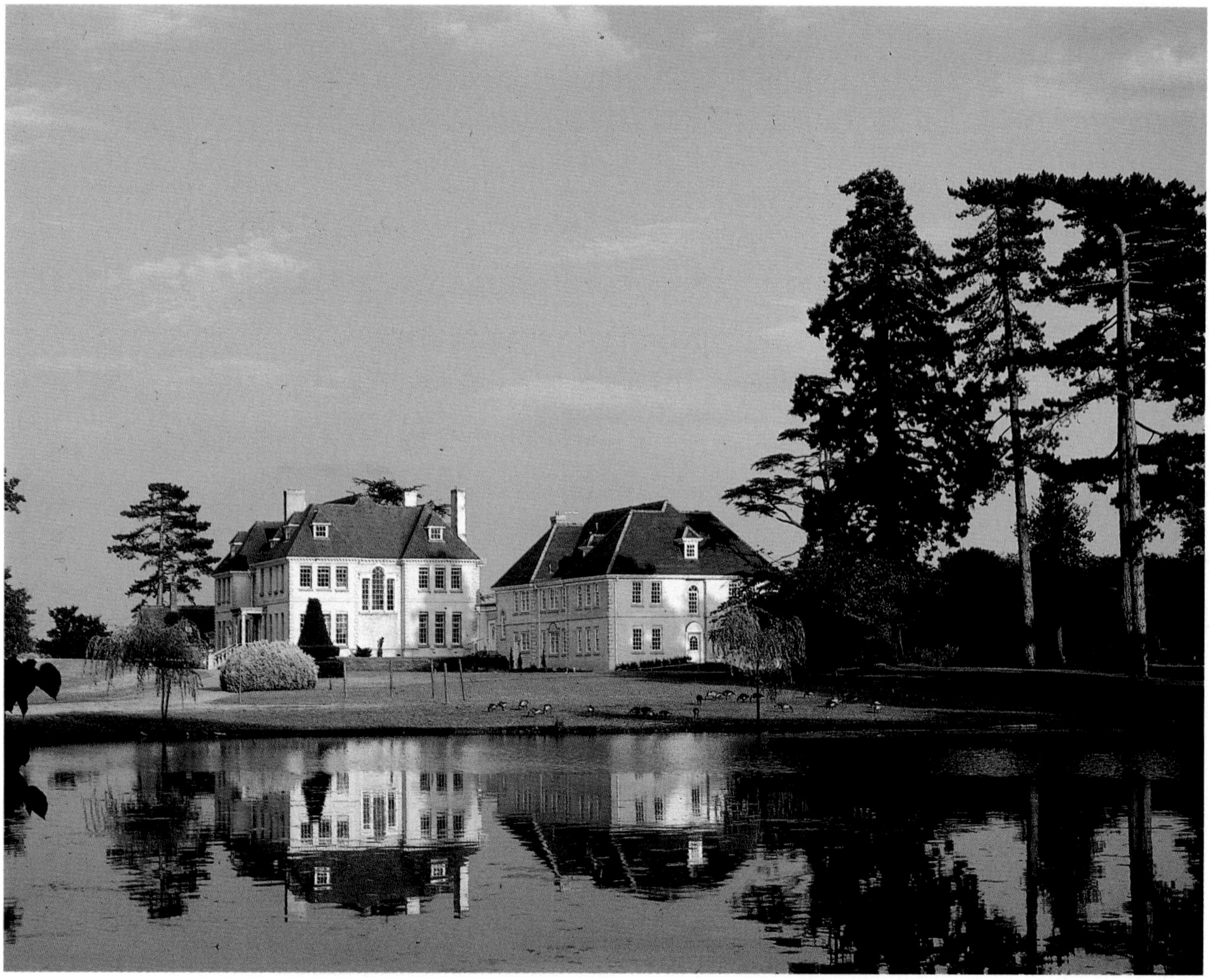

BROCKENCOTE HALL

CHADDESLEY CORBETT, NR KIDDERMINSTER, WORCESTERSHIRE DY10 4PY
TEL: 01562 777876 FAX: 01562 777872

The Brockencote estate consists of 70 acres of landscaped grounds surrounding a magnificent hall. There are a gatehouse, half-timbered dovecote, lake, some fine European and North American trees and an elegant conservatory. The estate dates back over three centuries and the style of the building reflects the changes which have taken place in fashion and taste over the years. At present, the interior combines classical architectural features with contemporary creature comforts. As in most country houses, each of the bedrooms is different: all have their own character, complemented by tasteful furnishings and décor. The friendly staff provide a splendid service under the supervision of owners Alison and Joseph Petitjean. Head chef, Didier Philipot specialises in traditional French cuisine with occasional regional and seasonal specialities. Brockencote Hall is an ideal setting for those seeking peace and quiet in an unspoiled corner of the English countryside. Located a few miles south of Birmingham, it is convenient for business people and sightseers alike – it makes a fine base for touring historic Worcestershire. English Tourist Board – Silver award Hotel of the Year '95. **Directions:** Exit 4 from M5 or exit 1 from M42. Brockencote Hall is set back from the A448 at Chaddesley Corbett between Bromsgrove and Kidderminster. Price guide: Single £85; double/twin £115–£140.

For hotel location, see maps on pages 477-483

GIDLEIGH PARK

CHAGFORD, DEVON TQ13 8HH

TEL: 01647 432367 FAX: 01647 432574 E-MAIL: gidleighpark@gidleigh.co.uk

Gidleigh Park enjoys an outstanding international reputation among connoisseurs for its comfort and gastronomy. It has collected a clutch of top culinary awards for its imaginative cuisine, and the Gidleigh Park wine list is one of the best in Britain. Service throughout the hotel is faultless. The en suite bedrooms – two of them in a converted chapel – are luxuriously furnished with antiques. The public rooms are elegantly appointed, and during the cooler months a fire burns merrily in the lounge's impressive fireplace. Set amid 45 secluded acres in the Teign Valley, Gidleigh Park is 1½ miles from the nearest public road. Two croquet lawns, an all-weather tennis court, a bowling lawn and a splendid water garden can be found in the grounds. A 250 yard long, par 27 putting course designed by Peter Alliss was opened in 1995. Guests can swim in the river or explore Dartmoor on foot or in the saddle. There are 14 miles of trout, sea trout and salmon fishing, as well as golf facilities nearby. Gidleigh Park is a Relais et Châteaux member. **Directions:** Approach from Chagford: go along Mill Street from Chagford Square. Fork right after 150 yards, cross into Holy Street at factory crossroads and follow lane for two miles. Price guide (including dinner): Single £200–£345; double/twin £325–£400.

For hotel location, see maps on pages 477-483

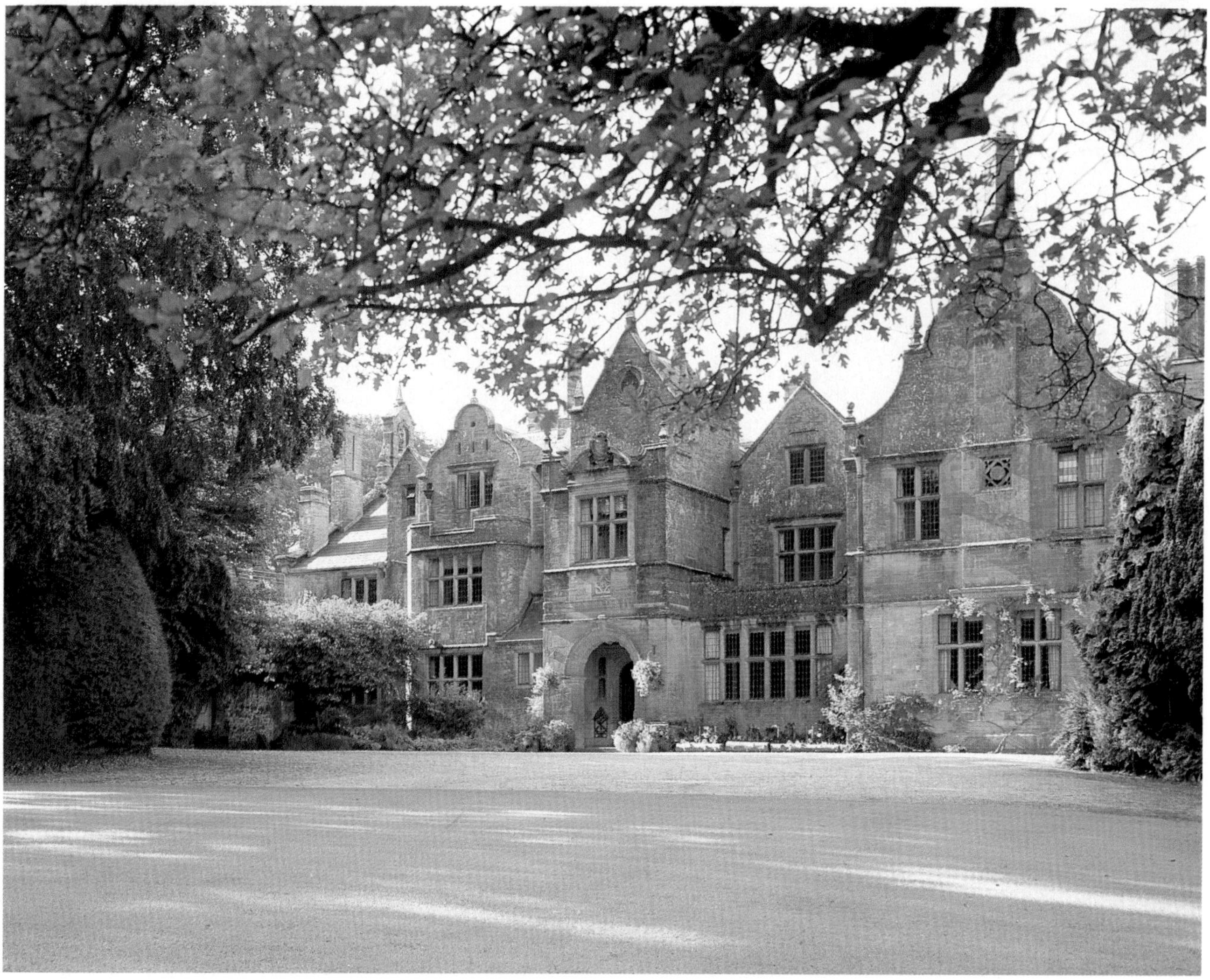

CHEDINGTON COURT

CHEDINGTON, NR BEAMINSTER, DORSET DT8 3HY
TEL: 01935 891265 FAX: 01935 891442

Situated in the Dorset Hills near the borders of Somerset and Devon, Chedington Court stands 600 feet above sea level and commands magnificent views over the surrounding countryside. This striking Jacobean-style mansion is set in 10 acres of grounds which contain ancient trees, a variety of shrubs, sweeping lawns, terraces and an ornamental water garden. Proprietors Philip and Hilary Chapman aim to provide a high standard of comfort, delicious food and a good selection of fine wines in beautiful surroundings. All ten bedrooms, some of which are huge, have antique furnishings and en suite bathrooms. The equally fine public rooms include a conservatory full of unusual plants. One mile from the hotel, and taking pride of place among the leisure facilities, is the par 72, 18 hole golf course, which attracts players of all abilities. There is also a billiard room, a croquet lawn and a putting green. In this part of the world there are numerous small unspoiled villages and charming towns to explore. Lulworth Cove, Lyme Regis, Dorchester, Weymouth and the splendid coastlines of Dorset and South Devon can be easily reached by car. **Directions:** Just off the A356, 4½ miles south-east of Crewkerne at Winyard's Gap. Price guide: (including dinner) Single £89–£105; double/twin £158–£190.

For hotel location, see maps on pages 477-483

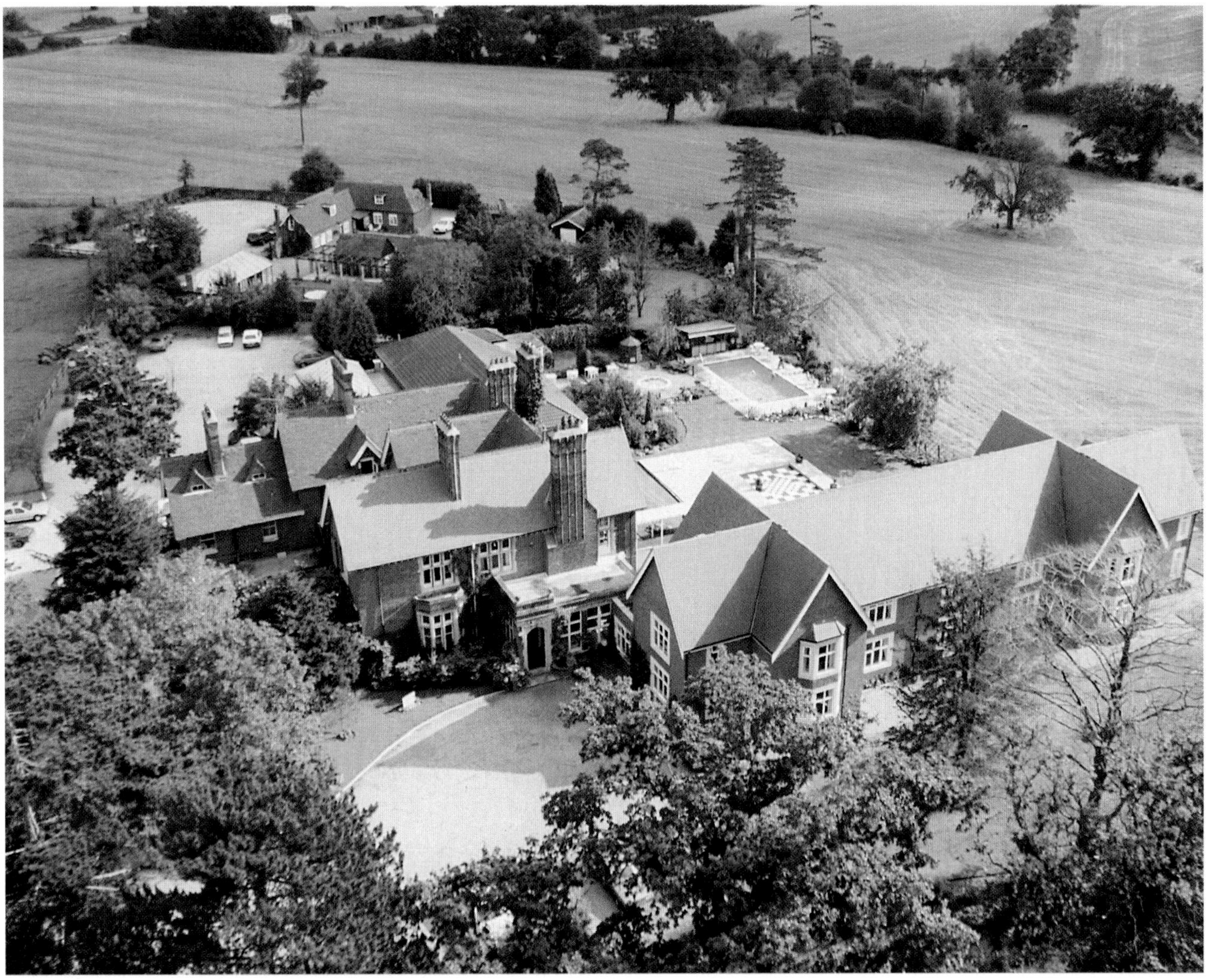

PONTLANDS PARK COUNTRY HOTEL & RESTAURANT

WEST HANNINGFIELD ROAD, GREAT BADDOW, NR CHELMSFORD, ESSEX CM2 8HR
TEL: 01245 476444 FAX: 01245 478393

Pontlands Park is a fine Victorian mansion, originally built for the Thomasin-Foster family in 1879. It became a hotel in 1981. The Victorian theme is still much in evidence, tempered with the best of contemporary interior styling. Immaculate public rooms – the conservatory-style Garden Room, the residents' lounge with its deep sofas and the relaxed ambience of the Victorian bar – are designed with guests' comfort in mind. Beautifully furnished bedrooms have co-ordinated fabrics and well-defined colour schemes. Diners are offered a selection of imaginative menus, with fine wines and attentive service. Within the grounds, Trimmers Leisure Centre has indoor and outdoor swimming pools, Jacuzzis, saunas and a solarium. The beauty salon offers many figure-toning, hairstyling and beauty treatments. Meetings and private dinners for from 2 to 100 guests can be accommodated, and functions for up to 200 guests can be held in the marquee. Closed 26 December to 4 January (but open for New Year's Eve). **Directions:** Pontlands Park is only about 30 miles from London. From A12 Chelmsford bypass take Great Baddow intersection (A130). Take first slip-road off A130 to Sandon/Great Baddow; bear left for Great Baddow, then first left for West Hanningfield Road. Price guide: Single £90; double/twin £120.

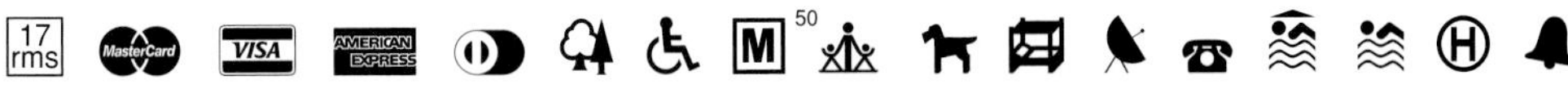

For hotel location, see maps on pages 477-483

THE CHELTENHAM PARK HOTEL

CIRENCESTER ROAD, CHARLTON KINGS, CHELTENHAM CL53 8EA
TEL: 01242 222021 FAX: 01242 226935

Nestling at the foot of the Cotswold Hills, just 2 miles south of the town centre, this splendid Georgian AA/RAC 4 Star hotel combines the character and style of its heritage with the comfort and efficiency of a modern luxury hotel. Colourful gardens, a natural lake and a gazebo enhance the atmosphere of elegance. All the bedrooms are en suite and comfortably furnished, many with scenic views. The Lakeside Restaurant with its imaginative selection of international cuisine, carefully chosen menus and extensive wine list ensure that a meal is a memorable experience. Overlooking the lake to the golf course beyond, The Lilly Brook Bar and Terrace provide an ideal setting to enjoy morning coffee or an afternoon cocktail. The splendid Leisure Club includes a 15 meter indoor swimming pool, spa bath, steam room, sauna, solarium and health suite with cardio vascular and resistance gymnasiums. There are 7 conference rooms including a suite which can accommodate up to 350 delegates and a 10 further syndicate or small meeting rooms. Special weekend rates are available. **Directions:** From M5, exit at junction 11a. Follow A417 towards Cirencester/Birdlip. Straight over roundabout direction A436 Oxford. At 'T' junction, turn left direction Cheltenham, the hotel is on the left hand side just past the golf course. Price guide: Single £85; double/twin £110; suite £175.

144 rms · 350

For hotel location, see maps on pages 477-483

THE GREENWAY

SHURDINGTON, CHELTENHAM, GLOUCESTERSHIRE GL51 5UG
TEL: 01242 862352 FAX: 01242 862780

Set amid gentle parkland with the rolling Cotswold hills beyond, The Greenway is an Elizabethan country house with a style that is uniquely its own – very individual and very special. Renowned for the warmth of its welcome, its friendly atmosphere and its immaculate personal service, The Greenway is the ideal place for total relaxation. The public rooms with their antique furniture and fresh flowers are elegant and spacious yet comfortable, with roaring log fires in winter and access to the formal gardens in summer. The 19 bedrooms all have private bathrooms and are individually decorated with co-ordinated colour schemes. Eleven of the rooms are located in the main house with a further eight rooms in the converted Georgian coach house immediately adjacent to the main building. The award winning conservatory dining room overlooks the sunken garden and lily pond, providing the perfect backdrop to superb cuisine of international appeal complemented by an outstanding selection of wines. Situated in one of Britain's most charming areas, The Greenway is well placed for visiting the spa town of Cheltenham, the Cotswold villages and Shakespeare country. **Directions:** On the outskirts of Cheltenham off the A46 Cheltenham–Stroud road, 2 1/2 miles from the city centre. Price guide: Single £87.50; double/twin £130–£195.

For hotel location, see maps on pages 477-483

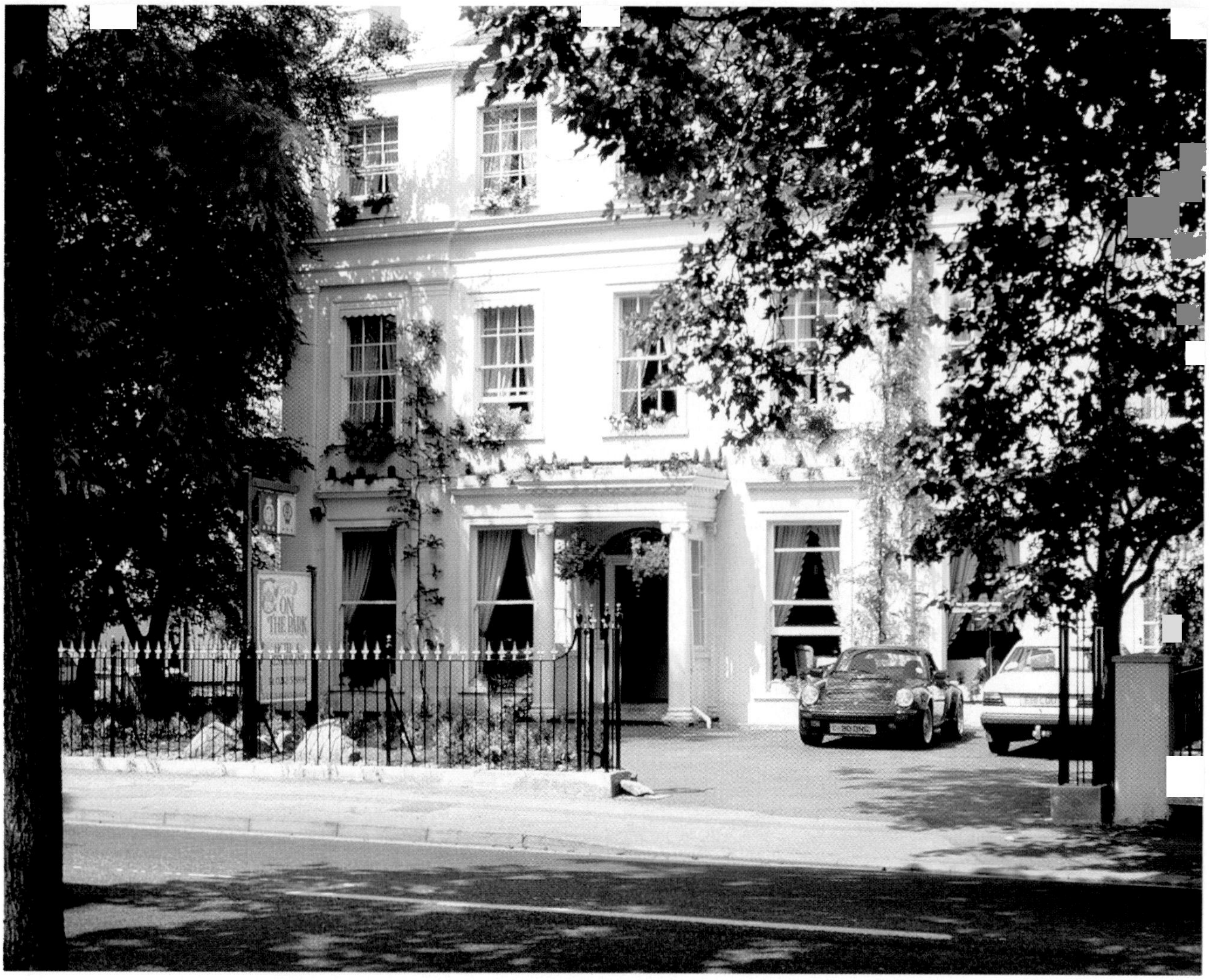

HOTEL ON THE PARK

EVESHAM ROAD, CHELTENHAM, GLOUCESTERSHIRE GL52 2AH
TEL: 01242 518898 FAX: 01242 511526

Hotel On The Park is an exclusive AA three red-starred Town House Hotel situated in the elegant spa town of Cheltenham. It enjoys an envied position overlooking the beautiful Pittville Park. A classic example of a Regency villa, the atmosphere inside is one of warmth and sophistication, akin to that of a traditional country house. The 12 intimate and restful bedrooms are individually styled and furnished with antiques, offering everything that one would expect to find in a small, luxury hotel. Each room has a private bathroom en suite, colour satellite television, direct-dial telephone, hairdryer and refreshments. A board meeting room for 18 people is available. Guests can enjoy some of the best modern cooking on offer today in The Restaurant, where fresh produce is meticulously prepared with imagination and flair to produce well-balanced menus. The wine list has been carefully selected to offer something for all tastes. Cheltenham, with its Regency architecture, attractive promenade and exclusive shops, has plenty to offer visitors and is set in the heart of the Cotswolds. Cheltenham racecourse has a busy National Hunt programme. For details of terms during Gold Cup week, apply well in advance. Dogs accommodated by prior arrangement. **Directions:** Opposite Pittville Park, 5 minutes' walk from town centre. Price guide: Single from £74.50; double/twin from £89.50; suites from £119.50. Room Only.

For hotel location, see maps on pages 477-483

BROXTON HALL COUNTRY HOUSE HOTEL

WHITCHURCH ROAD, BROXTON, CHESTER, CHESHIRE CH3 9JS
TEL: 01829 782321 FAX: 01829 782330

Built in 1671 by a local landowner, Broxton Hall is a black-and-white half-timbered building set in five acres of grounds and extensive gardens amid the rolling Cheshire countryside. The medieval city of Chester is eight miles away. The hotel provides every modern comfort while retaining the ambience of a bygone age. The reception area reflects the character of the entire hotel, with its magnificent Jacobean fireplace, plush furnishings, oak panelled walls and carved mahogany staircase. On cool evenings log fires are lit. The small but well-appointed bedrooms are furnished with antiques and have en suite bathrooms as well as every modern comfort. Overlooking the gardens, the restaurant receives constant praise from regular diners. French and English cuisine is served, using local game in season and freshly caught fish. There is an extensive wine list. Breakfast may be taken in the sunny conservatory overlooking the lawned gardens. The hotel is an ideal venue for business meetings and conferences. Broxton Hall is the perfect base from which to visit the North Wales coast and Snowdonia. There are a number of excellent golf courses nearby, and racecourses at Chester and Bangor-on-Dee. **Directions:** Broxton Hall is on the A41 Whitchurch–Chester road, eight miles between Whitchurch and Chester. Price guide: Single £60–£65; double/twin £70–£105.

12 rms MasterCard VISA AMERICAN EXPRESS M 30

For hotel location, see maps on pages 477-483

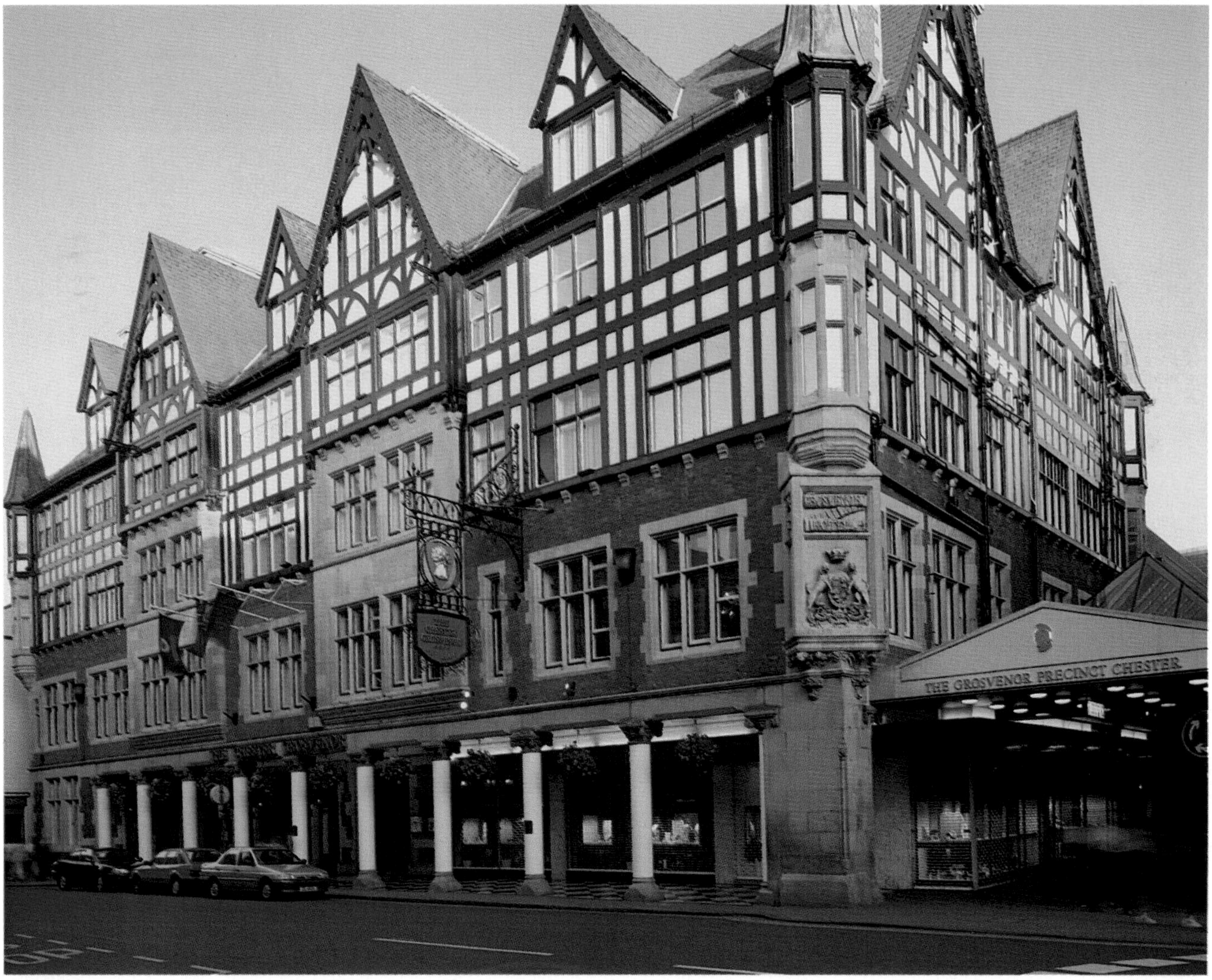

THE CHESTER GROSVENOR

EASTGATE, CHESTER CH1 1LT
TEL: 01244 324024 FAX: 01244 313246

The Chester Grosvenor is in the heart of the historic city of Chester beneath the famous Queen Victoria Clock. The hotel is owned by the Duke of Westminster's Grosvenor Estate. It is renowned for its fabulous cuisine and has two restaurants – the Arkle and La Brasserie. The Arkle is an award winning gourmet restaurant, named after the famous racehorse Arkle. La Brasserie is an informal Parisian style restaurant which is open all day every day. The Chester Grosvenor has an extensive cellar with over 600 bins of fine wine. There are 86 bedrooms of which 11 are suites. All are beautifully appointed, fully air-conditioned with 24 hour room service provided and each room is equipped with all the amenities expected in a deluxe hotel. The hotel has its own leisure suite with a multi-gymnasium, sauna and solarium and membership of an exclusive local country club which has indoor and outdoor swimming pools, tennis and squash. Adjacent are the famous Roman Walls and the Chester Rows with their boutiques and exclusive shops. A short stroll away is Chester Cathedral, Chester race course and the River Dee. **Directions:** In the centre of Chester on Eastgate. 24-hour NCP car parking – follow signs to Grosvenor Precinct Car Park. Price guide: Weekend break rate £140 per double room per night – bed, breakfast and VAT included. Single from £120; double/twin from £180; suites £300.

For hotel location, see maps on pages 477-483

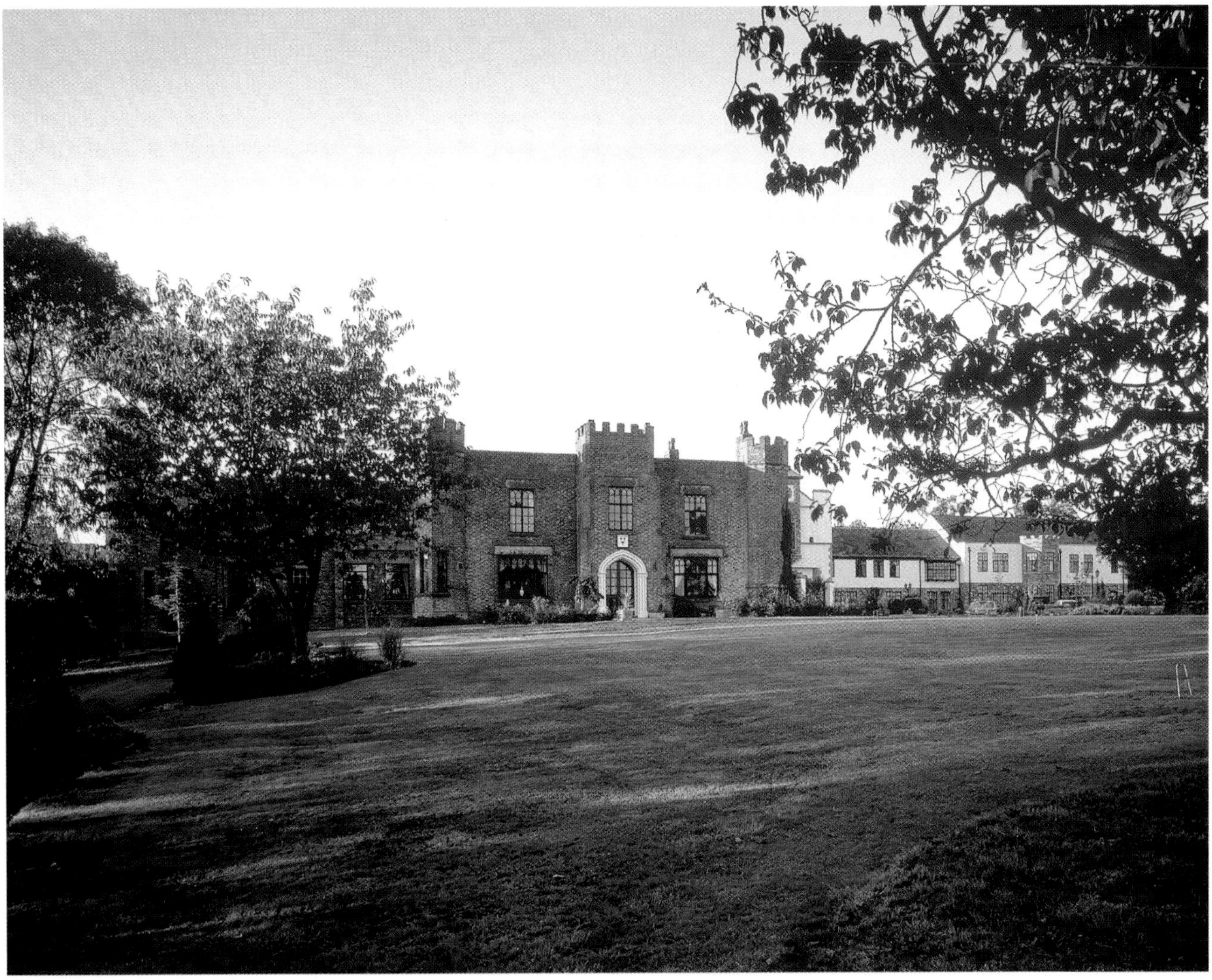

CRABWALL MANOR

PARKGATE ROAD, MOLLINGTON, CHESTER, CHESHIRE CH1 6NE
TEL: 01244 851666 FAX: 01244 851400 E-MAIL: SALES@CRABWALL.U-NET.COM

Crabwall Manor can be traced back to Saxon England, prior to the Norman Conquest. The present Grade II listed manor at the heart of the hotel is believed to have originated from a Tudor farmhouse. Set in 11 acres of wooded parkland on the outer reaches of Chester, the hotel has achieved a fine reputation under the ownership of Carl Lewis. A relaxed ambience is enhanced by staff who combine attentive service with friendliness and care. Bathrobes and sherry are among the many extras to be found in the bedrooms and luxury suites. Brightly printed drapes and pastel shades lend a freshness to the décor of the spacious lounge and reception areas, while a log fire crackling away in the inglenook fireplace adds warmth. Chef Michael Truelove, formerly of The Box Tree Restaurant in Ilkley, introduces a classic French influence to traditional English dishes. Manchester and Liverpool Airports are 30 minutes away by road. Chester, the Wirral and North Wales are all easily accessible. **Directions:** Go to end of M56, ignoring signs to Chester. Follow signs to Queensferry and North Wales, taking the A5117 to the next roundabout. Left onto the A540, towards Chester for 2 miles. Crabwall Manor is on the right. Price guide: Single £99; double/twin £140; suite £170. Weekend rates available. Internet: http://www.hotelnet.co.uk/crabwall

For hotel location, see maps on pages 477-483

NUNSMERE HALL

TARPORLEY ROAD, OAKMERE, NORTHWICH, CHESHIRE CW8 2ES
TEL: 01606 889100 FAX: 01606 889055

Set in peaceful Cheshire countryside and surrounded on three sides by a lake, Nunsmere Hall epitomises the elegant country manor where superior standards of hospitality still exist. Wood panelling, antique furniture, exclusive fabrics, Chinese lamps and magnificent chandeliers evoke an air of luxury. The 32 bedrooms, with spectacular views of the lake and gardens, are beautifully appointed with king-size beds, comfortable breakfast seating and marbled bathrooms containing soft bathrobes and toiletries. The Brocklebank, Delamere and Oakmere business suites are air-conditioned, soundproofed and offer excellent facilities for boardroom meetings, private dining and seminars. The Garden Restaurant has a reputation for fine food and uses only fresh seasonal produce. County Restaurant of the Year in the 1996 Good Food Guide. A snooker room is provided, while there are several golf courses. Oulton Park Racing Circuit is nearby and the Cheshire Polo Club is next door. Archery and golf practice nets are available in the grounds. Although secluded, Nunsmere is convenient for major towns and routes. AA 3 Red Star and RAC 4 Star, ETB 5 Crowns Deluxe. **Directions:** Leave M6 at junction 18 northbound or 19 southbound, take A556 to Chester (approximately 12 miles). Turn left onto A49. Hotel is 1 mile on left. Price guide: Single £110; double/twin £140–£180; suite £200.

For hotel location, see maps on pages 477-483

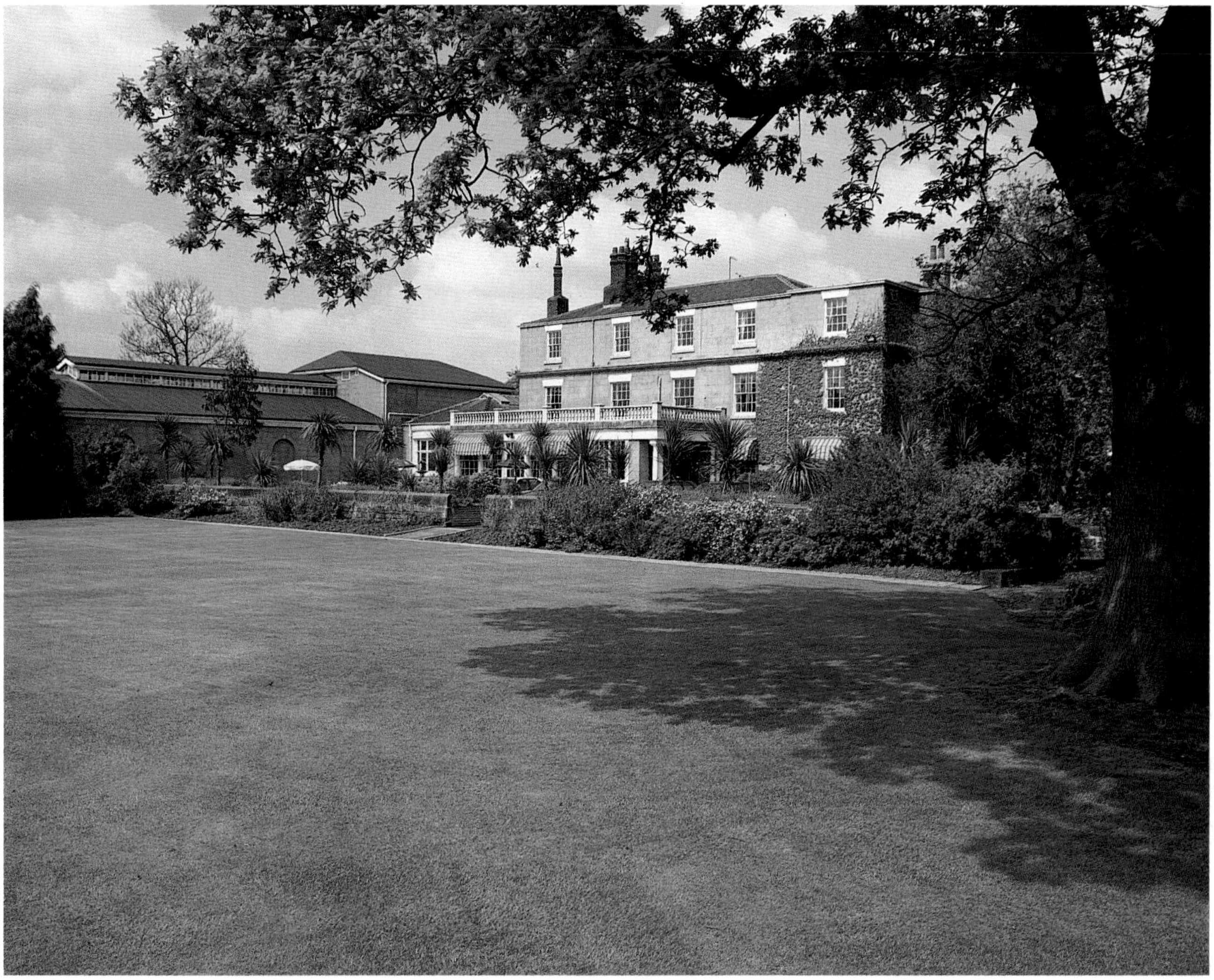

Rowton Hall Hotel

WHITCHURCH ROAD, ROWTON, CHESTER, CHESHIRE CH3 6AD
TEL: 01244 335262 FAX: 01244 335464

Standing in eight acres of gardens and pastureland on the outskirts of the city of Chester, Rowton Hall enjoys far-reaching views across the Cheshire Plains to the Welsh hills. Built as a private residence in 1779, the hall is renowned for the informal country-house atmosphere which welcomes all its guests. It retains many original features, including a Robert Adam fireplace and superb carved staircase. The conservatory-style Hamilton Lounge, overlooking the garden, is the perfect place to enjoy morning coffee, afternoon tea or cocktails, while the Cavalier Bar is ideal for a lunchtime snack. The bedrooms are furnished with chintzy fabrics and all have en suite bathrooms. In the Langdale Restaurant, which has earned a first-class reputation, chef Roger Price's à la carte and table d'hôte menus can be sampled in elegant and restful surroundings. Fresh vegetables and herbs are supplied by the hall's kitchen garden. Hotel guests have complimentary use of Hamiltons Leisure Club – facilities include a swimming pool, multi-gym, sauna and solarium. There are five conference/meeting rooms accommodating up to 200. The hotel offers special weekend rates. **Directions:** From the centre of Chester, take the A41 towards Whitchurch. After three miles, turn right to Rowton village. The hotel is in the centre of the village. Price guide: Single £72–£78; double/twin £88–£95; four poster suite £98.

For hotel location, see maps on pages 477-483

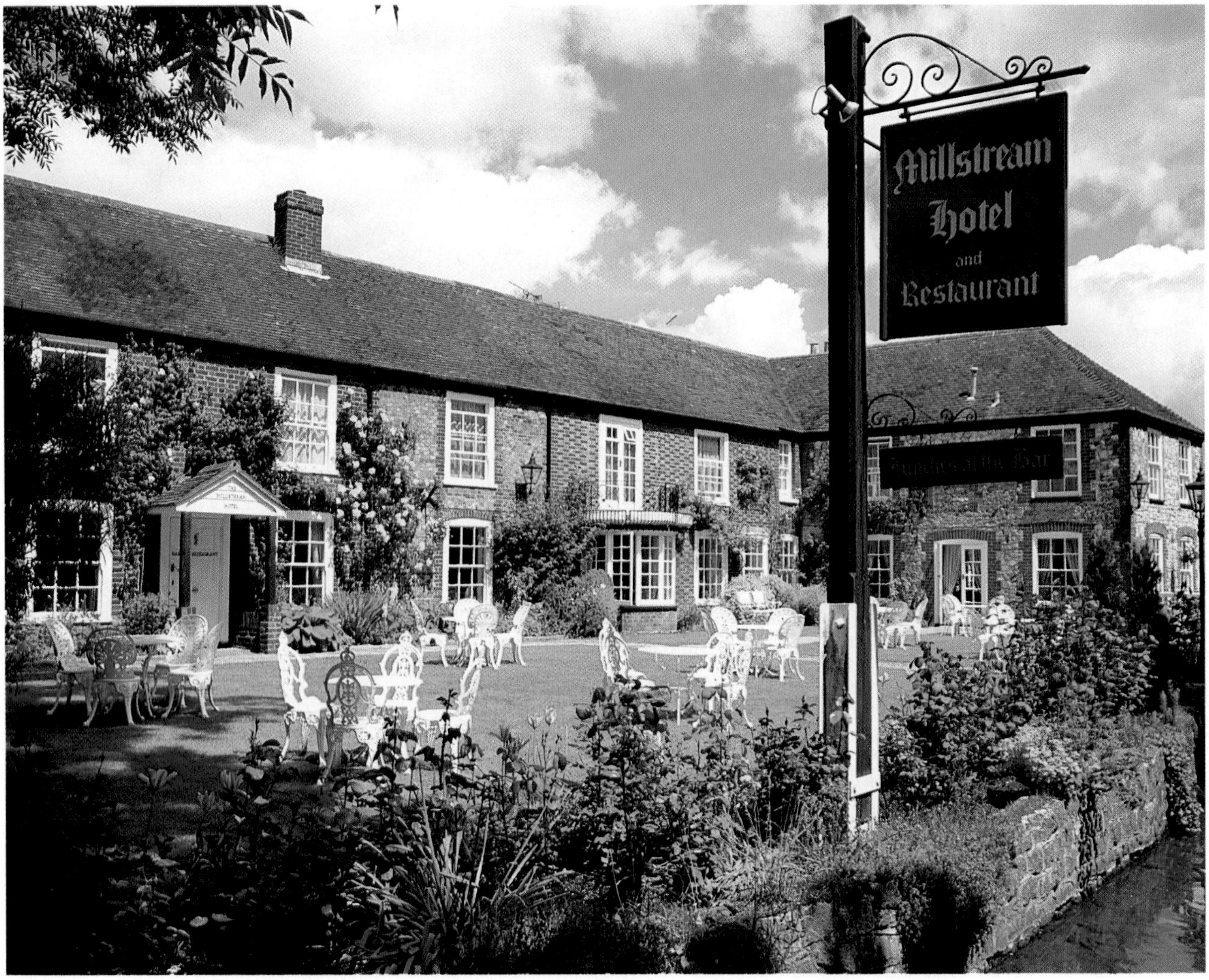

THE MILLSTREAM HOTEL

BOSHAM, NR CHICHESTER, WEST SUSSEX PO18 8HL
TEL: 01243 573234 FAX: 01243 573459

A village rich in heritage, Bosham is depicted in the Bayeux Tapestry and is associated with King Canute, whose daughter is buried in the local Saxon church. Moreover, sailors from the world over navigate their way to Bosham, which is a yachtsman's idyll on the banks of Chichester Harbour. The Millstream consists of a restored 18th-century malthouse and adjoining cottages linked to The Grange, a small English manor house. Individually furnished bedrooms are complemented by chintz fabrics and pastel décor. Period furniture, a grand piano and bowls of freshly cut flowers feature in the drawing room. A stream meanders past the front of the delightful gardens, where traditional herbs are grown for use by the *chef de cuisine*. Whatever the season, care is taken to ensure that the composition and presentation of the dishes reflect high standards. An appetising luncheon menu is offered and includes local seafood specialities such as: dressed Selsey crab, home cured and smoked salmon and freshly broiled lobster (seasonal). During the winter, good-value 'Hibernation Breaks' are available. **Directions:** From M27, junction 12, continue along A27. Bosham is signed just west of Chichester. Price guide: Single £65–£75; double/twin £105–£120.

29 rms MasterCard VISA AMERICAN EXPRESS M 40

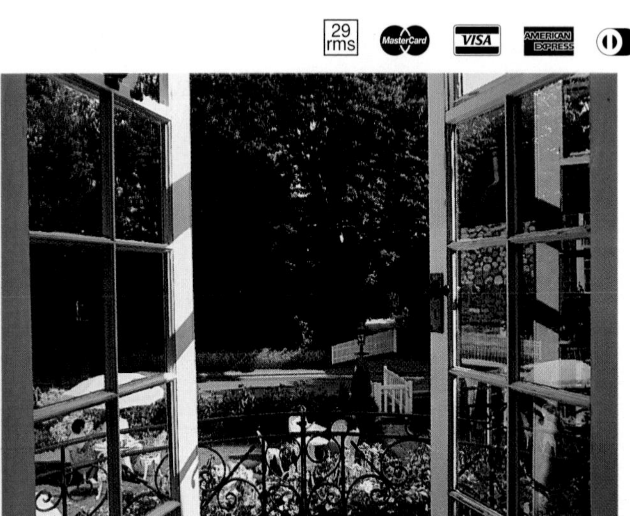

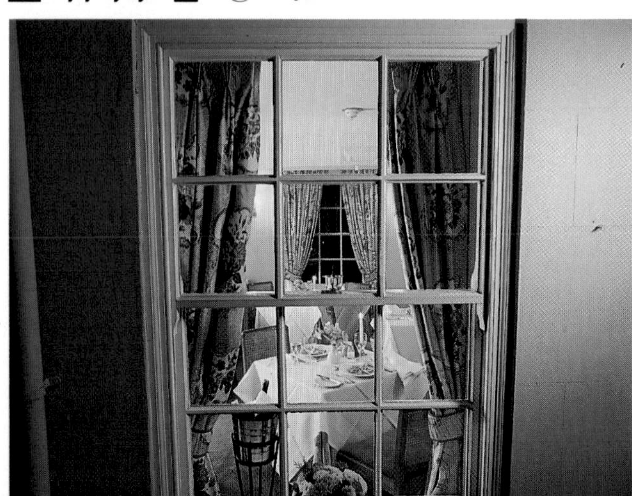

For hotel location, see maps on pages 477-483

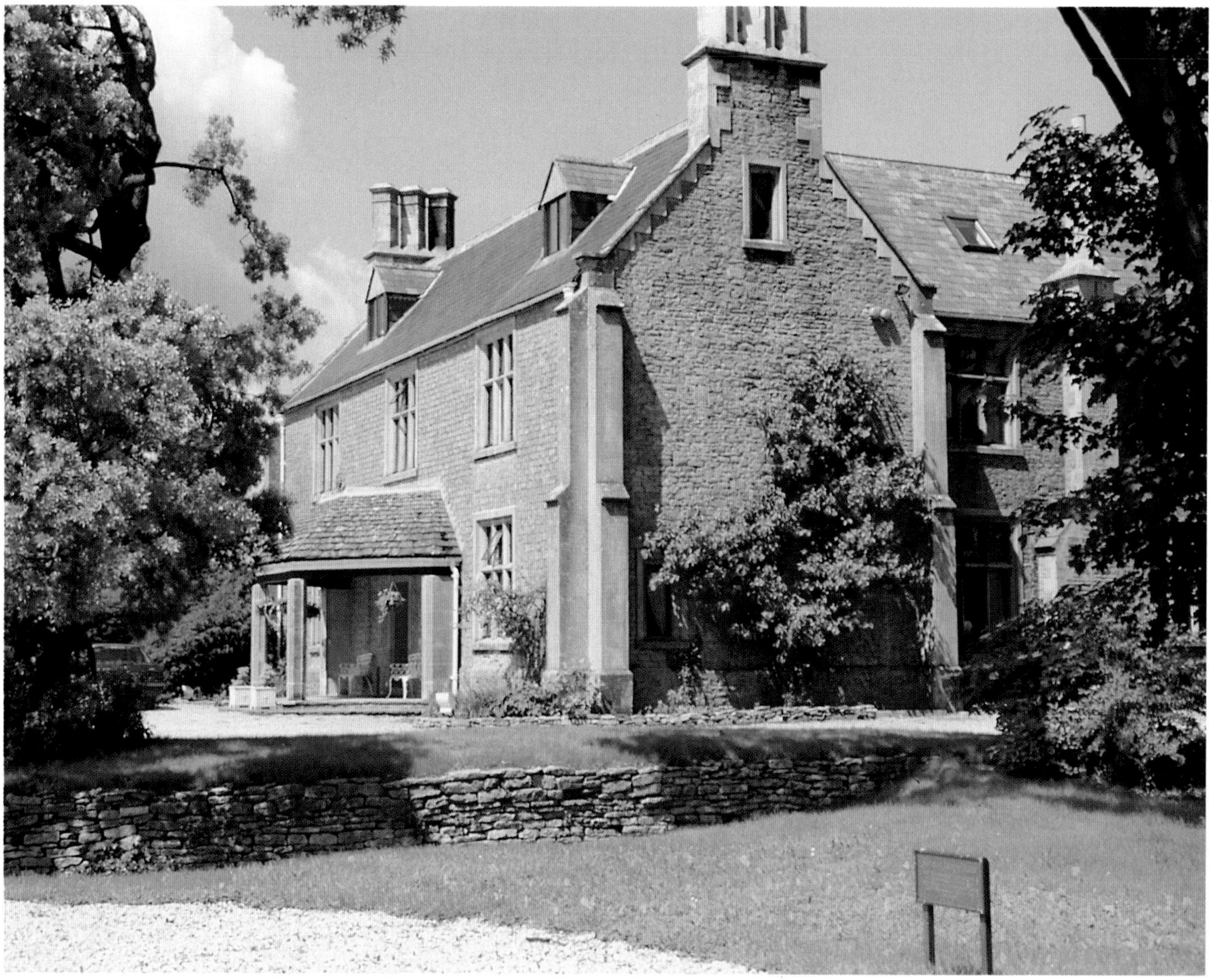

STANTON MANOR

STANTON SAINT QUINTIN, NR CHIPPENHAM, WILTSHIRE SN14 6DQ
TEL: 01666 837552 FAX: 01666 837022

Near to the M4 just off the beaten track in five acres of leafy gardens, there has been a habitation at Stanton Manor for over 900 years. The original house was listed in the *Domesday Book* and was later owned by Lord Burghley, Elizabeth I's chief minister. The Elizabethan dovecote in the garden bears witness to that period, although the present building dates largely from the 19th century. The bedrooms are furnished in a homely, country style and several offer views over Wiltshire farmland. Choices from the à la carte menu might include a starter of king prawns and mussels provençale or chicken liver parfait followed, for a main course, by saddle of spring lamb in a brandy, tomato and tarragon sauce. A variety of light meals is available in either the lounge or the bar. Proprietors Elizabeth and Philip Bullock are usually on hand to ensure that a friendly, personal service is extended to all their visitors. The Roman city of Cirencester, Chippenham, and a wealth of pretty villages all invite exploration. **Directions:** Leave the M4 at junction 17 and join the A429 towards Cirencester. After 200 yards, turn left to Stanton Saint Quintin; Stanton Manor is on the left in the village. Price guide: Single £68–£75; double/twin £82–£95.

For hotel location, see maps on pages 477-483

In association with MasterCard

Charingworth Manor

NR CHIPPING CAMPDEN, GLOUCESTERSHIRE GL55 6NS
TEL: 01386 593555 FAX: 01386 593353

The ancient manor of Charingworth lies amid the gently rolling Cotswold countryside, just a few miles from the historic towns of Chipping Campden and Broadway. Beautiful old stone buildings everywhere recall the flourishing wool trade that gave the area its wealth. The 14th-century manor house overlooks its own 50-acre grounds and offers peace and enthralling views. Inside, Charingworth is a historic patchwork of intimate public rooms with log fires burning during the colder months. There are 24 individually designed bedrooms, all furnished with antiques and fine fabrics. Outstanding cuisine is regarded as being of great importance and guests at Charingworth are assured of imaginative dishes. Great emphasis is placed on using only the finest produce and the AA has awarded the cuisine two Rosettes. There is an all-weather tennis court within the grounds, while inside, a beautiful swimming pool, sauna, steam room, solarium and billiard room are available, allowing guests to relax and unwind. Hidcote Manor Gardens, Batsford Arboretum, Stratford-upon-Avon, Oxford and Cheltenham are all within easy reach. Short-break rates are available on request. **Directions:** Charingworth Manor is on the B4035 between Chipping Campden and Shipston-on-Stour. Price guide: (including full breakfast) Single from £95; double/twin from £159.

For hotel location, see maps on pages 477-483

THE COTSWOLD HOUSE

HIGH STREET, CHIPPING CAMPDEN, GLOUCESTERSHIRE GL55 6AN
TEL: 01386 840330 FAX: 01386 840310

The Cotswold House takes pride of place on Chipping Campden's historic High Street, described by Trevelyan as 'the most beautiful street left in this island'. The beauty and harmony of this unique setting are reflected within the hotel, where antiques, choice fabrics, works of art and vast bowls of freshly cut flowers complement the elegant Regency architecture, creating a warm and welcoming atmosphere where friendly, efficient service is the hallmark. There are 15 very comfortable bedrooms, ranging from the whimsical Aunt Lizzie's Room to a wonderfully 'over the top' Four-Poster Room. In the Restaurant, menus combine fresh local produce with seasonal variety imparting a new meaning to the words 'English cooking'. The award to proprietors Christopher and Louise Forbes of AA Rosettes and Red Stars acknowledges exceptional all-round standards. A private room is available for small parties, weddings and conferences. The Cotswold House is perfectly located for visiting the many famous houses and gardens nearby such as Hidcote Manor and is just a short drive from Stratford-upon-Avon, Warwick, Oxford and Cheltenham Spa. Special short-stay breaks are available all year, except at Christmas when the hotel is closed. **Directions:** Chipping Campden lies 2 miles north-east of the A44 on the B4081. Price guide: Single from £70; double/twin from £100; four poster from £160.

15 rms MasterCard VISA AMERICAN EXPRESS M 30 6

For hotel location, see maps on pages 477-483

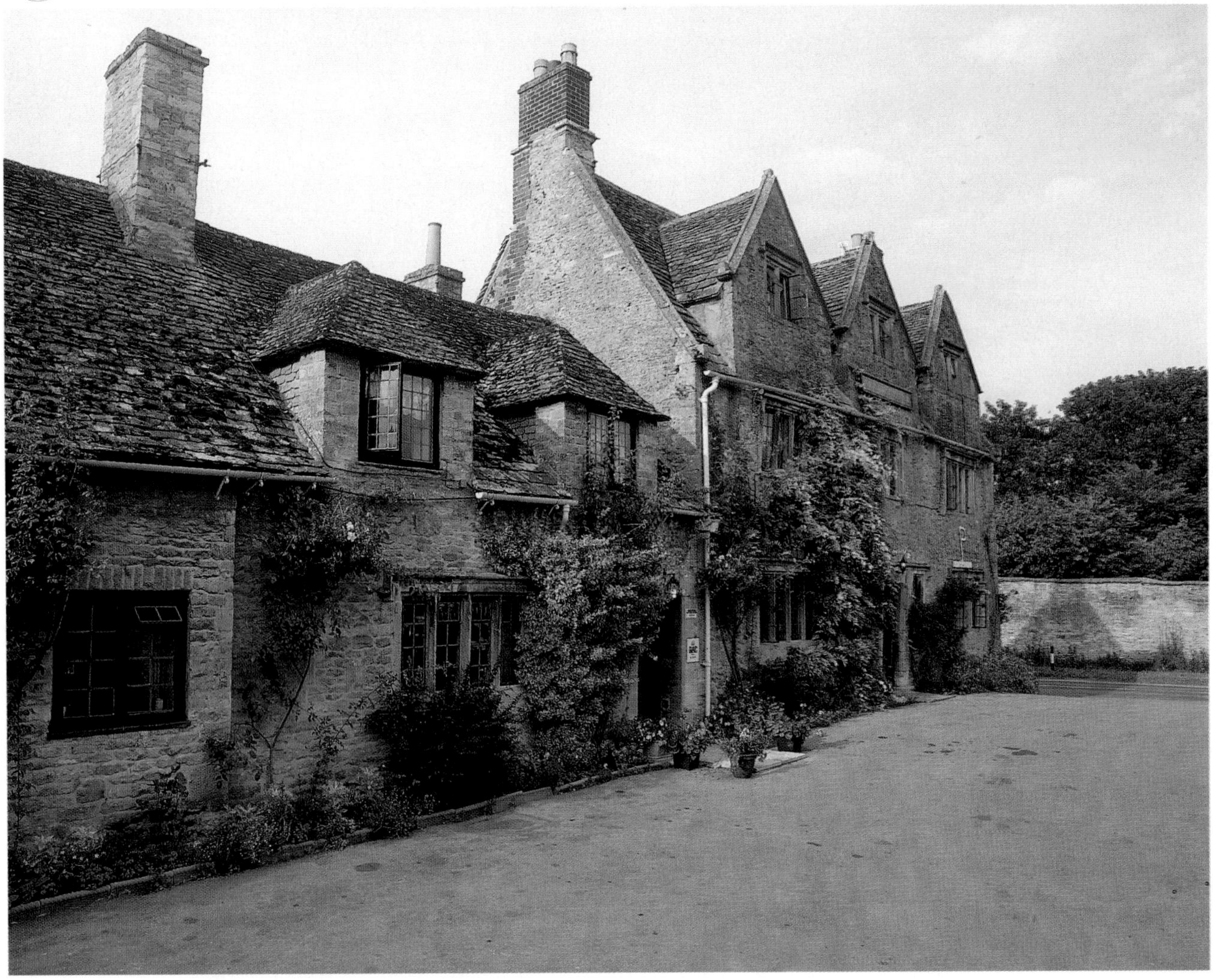

The Plough At Clanfield

BOURTON ROAD, CLANFIELD, OXFORDSHIRE OX18 2RB
TEL: 01367 810222 FAX: 01367 810596

The Plough at Clanfield is an idyllic hideaway for the romantic at heart. Set on the edge of the village of Clanfield in the heart of the Oxfordshire Cotswolds, The Plough dates from 1560 and is a fine example of well-preserved Elizabethan architecture. The hotel is owned and personally run by John and Rosemary Hodges, who have taken great care to preserve the charm and character of this historic building. Because there are only six bedrooms, guests can enjoy an intimate atmosphere and attentive, personal service. All the bedrooms are beautifully appointed to the highest standard and all have en suite bathrooms. At the heart of the hotel is the two AA Rosette Restaurant, regarded as one of the finest in the area. The cuisine is superbly prepared and impeccably served, with an interesting selection of wines. Two additional dining rooms are available for private entertaining. The hotel is an ideal base from which to explore the Cotswolds or the Thames Valley. There are many historic houses and gardens in the area, as well as racing at Newbury and Cheltenham. **Directions:** The hotel is located on the edge of the village of Clanfield, at the junction of the A4095 and B4020, between the towns of Witney and Faringdon, some 15 miles to the west of the city of Oxford. Price guide: Single £65; Double £90–£105.

6 rms MasterCard VISA AMERICAN EXPRESS 10 12

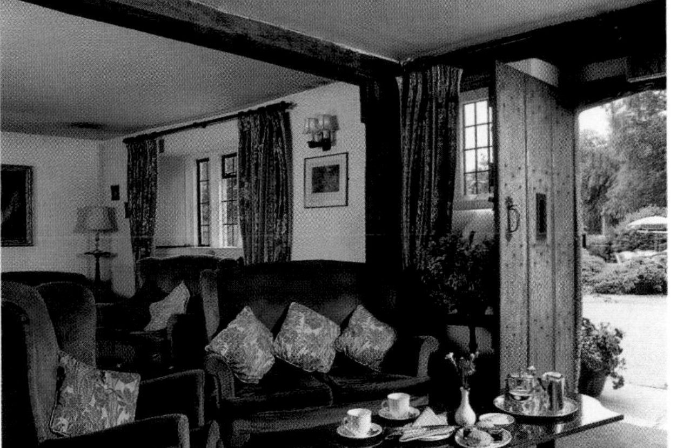

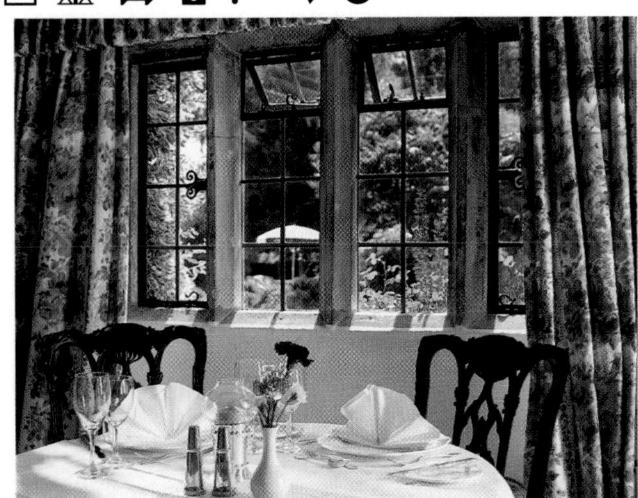

For hotel location, see maps on pages 477-483

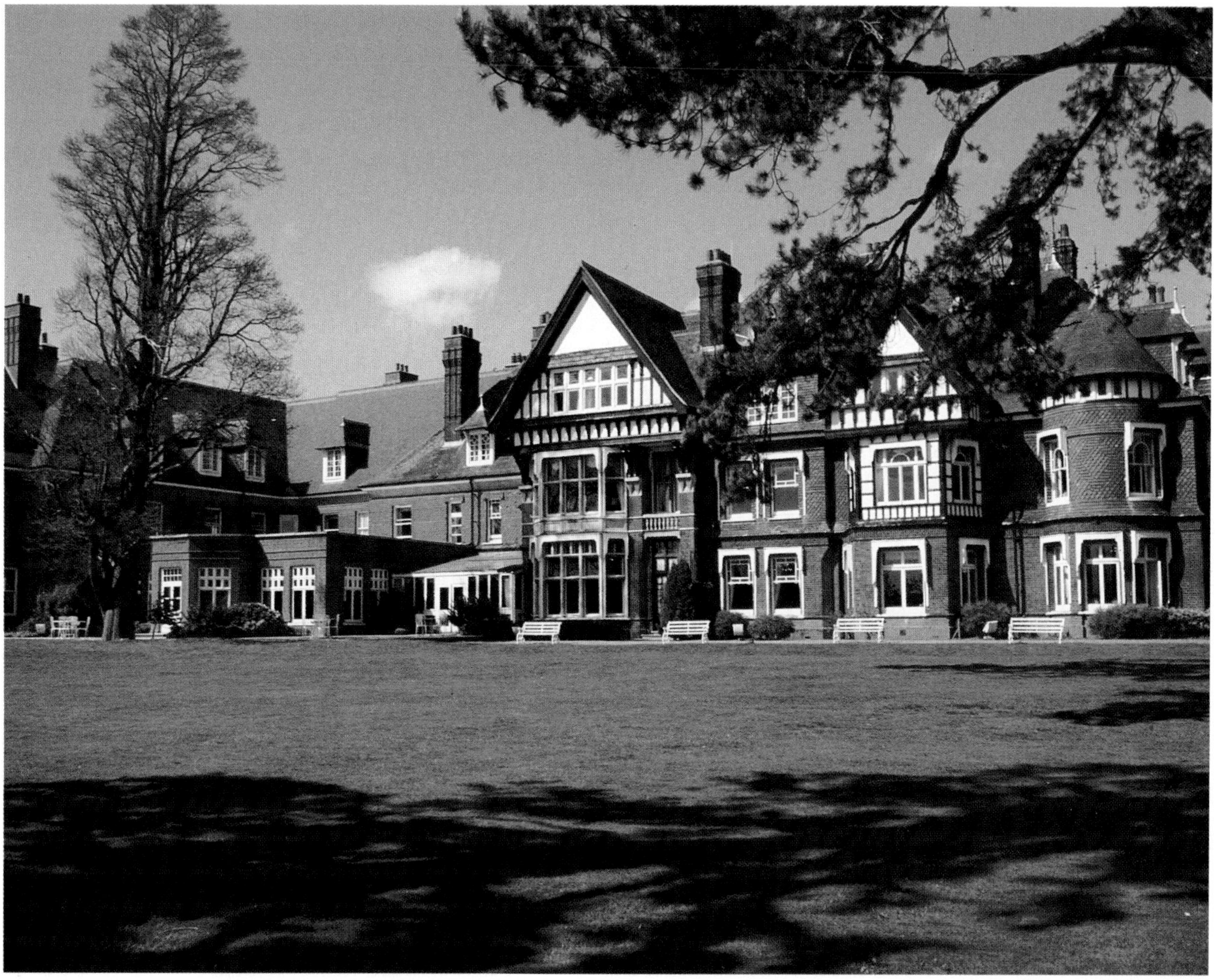

WOODLANDS PARK HOTEL

WOODLANDS LANE, STOKE D'ABERNON, COBHAM, SURREY KT11 3QB
TEL: 01372 843933 FAX: 01372 842704

Set in 10 acres of parkland, Woodlands Park Hotel is an ideal location for touring the surrounding Surrey and Berkshire countryside. At the turn of the century, the then Prince of Wales and the famous actress Lillie Langtry were frequent visitors to this splendid Victorian mansion. Well equipped en suite bedrooms retain an appealing Victorian theme and ambience, despite having been refurbished to the highest standards. Each offers its guests luxury, comfort and every modern amenity. The Oak Room Restaurant serves imaginative English and French cuisine in elegant surroundings, while Langtry's Bar and Brasserie, offering a daily blackboard menu and a wide selection of dishes from the speciality menu, is designed for those who prefer less formal dining. Small meeting rooms can be reached from the Grand Hall and can accommodate between 10 and 60 for private dinners or meetings, while the modern Prince of Wales Suite seats up to 300. Nearby are Wisley Gardens, Hampton Court and Brooklands Museum. Kempton Park and Sandown are within a short distance for those who enjoy racing. **Directions:** On the M25 take junction 9 or 10. The hotel is east of Cobham at Stoke d'Abernon on the A245. Price guide: Single £110; twin/double £140–£185; suites £215.

For hotel location, see maps on pages 477-483

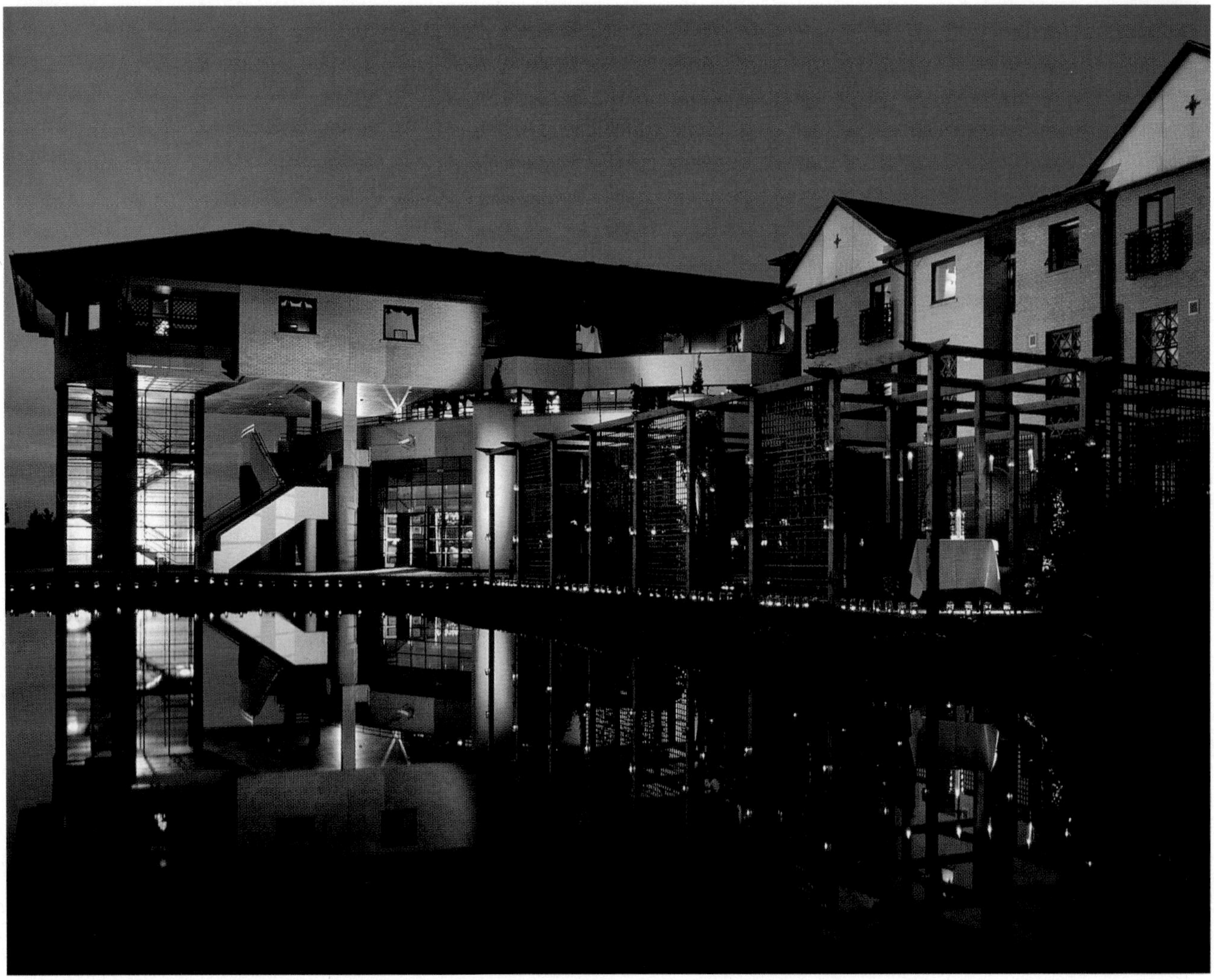

FIVE LAKES HOTEL, GOLF & COUNTRY CLUB

COLCHESTER ROAD, TOLLESHUNT KNIGHTS, MALDON, ESSEX CM9 8HX
TEL: 01621 868888 FAX: 01621 869696

Set in 320 acres , Five Lakes is a superb 21st century hotel which combines the latest in sporting, leisure and health activities with state-of-the-art conference, meeting and banqueting facilities. The 114 bedrooms are furnished to a high standard and offer every comfort and convenience. With its two 18-hole courses – the Lakes a PGA European Tour course – the hotel is already recognised as one of East Anglia's leading golf venues. Guests are also invited to take advantage of the Championship standard indoor tennis; outdoor tennis; squash; indoor pool with Jacuzzi, steam and sauna; gymnasium; jogging trail; snooker and an outstanding health spa. There is a choice of restaurants, where good food is complemented by excellent service. Lounges and cocktail bars provide a comfortable environment in which to relax and enjoy a drink. Extensive facilities for conferences, meetings, exhibitions and functions include 18 rooms and a 3,500 sqm exhibition arena, suitable for from four to over two thousand people. All rooms are air-conditioned or comfort-cooled, with 16 rooms having natural daylight. **Directions:** Approximately 40 minutes from junction 28 of the M25 follow A12 towards Colchester and take B1024 at Kelvedon. Price guide: Single £85; double/twin £115–£135; suites £165.

For hotel location, see maps on pages 477-483

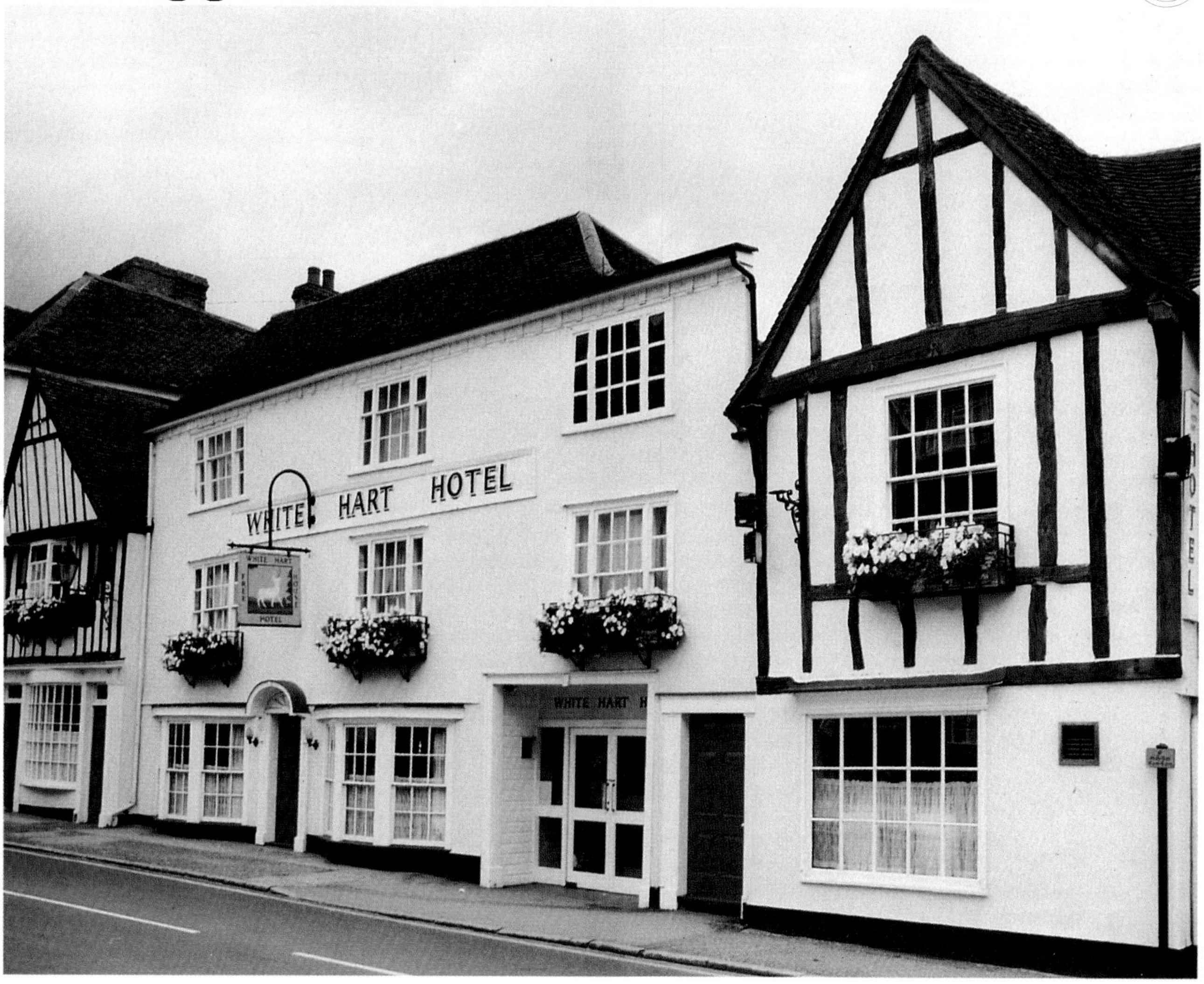

THE WHITE HART HOTEL & RESTAURANT

MARKET END, COGGESHALL, ESSEX CO6 1NH
TEL: 01376 561654 FAX: 01376 561789

A historic, family-run hotel, The White Hart is situated in the Essex town of Coggeshall, where it has played an integral part for many years. In 1489 The White Hart became the town's meeting place when most of the adjoining Guildhall was destroyed by fire. Part of that original Guildhall now forms the residents' lounge, and features magnificent roof timbers hewn from sweet chestnut. Sympathetically restored throughout, the hotel has been comfortably appointed with much attention to detail. All the en suite bedrooms have been decorated with bright fabrics to reflect the hotel's colourful character. Heavily timbered and spacious, the restaurant enjoys a good reputation locally. The table d'hôte and à la carte menus feature a choice of Italian dishes with a particular emphasis on seafood and shellfish. Pasta is freshly made, and aromatic sauces and tender cuts of meat figure prominently on the menu. The hotel has recently received merit awards from the RAC for comfort and its restaurant, which already holds 2 AA rosettes and an Egon Ronay recommendedation. Coggeshall is noted for its antiques shops. It is also convenient for Colchester and Chelmsford and the ferry ports of Felixstowe and Harwich. **Directions:** Coggeshall is just off the A120 between Colchester and Braintree. From the A12 follow signs through Kelvedon, then take B1024. Price guide: Single £61.50; double/twin £97.

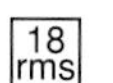

For hotel location, see maps on pages 477-483

COOMBE ABBEY

BRINKLOW ROAD, BINLEY, WARWICKSHIRE CV3 2AB
TEL: 01203 450450 FAX: 01203 635101

Coombe Abbey is approached by travelling along a lovely avenue of lime trees and chestnuts, crossing a moat and passing through a cloistered entrance. Originally a Cistercian Abbey dating back to the 11th century, this hotel lies in the heart of 500 acres of parkland and formal gardens. Deep colours, carefully selected fabrics and antique furnishing and lighting are all features of its restful bedrooms. Room designs, often eccentric or mischievous, include hidden bathrooms, four poster beds and the occasional hand painted Victorian bath in the centre of the room. Many bedrooms overlook the grounds with their splendid 80 acre lake. The restaurants and private dining rooms each have their individual charm and offer a variety of settings suitable for all occasions. Sophisticated and creative menus provide a good choice of delightful dishes and the service is attentive but never intrusive. The hotel is an ideal venue for conferences and weddings. Among the local attractions are Warwick Castle and Stratford and the surrounding area is excellent for walking and birdwatching. **Directions:** Leave the M40 at junction 15 and take the A46 towards Binley. Coombe Abbey is on the B4027. Price guide: Single £95–£105; twin/double £120–£295; suite £225.

63 rms MasterCard VISA AMERICAN EXPRESS M 120

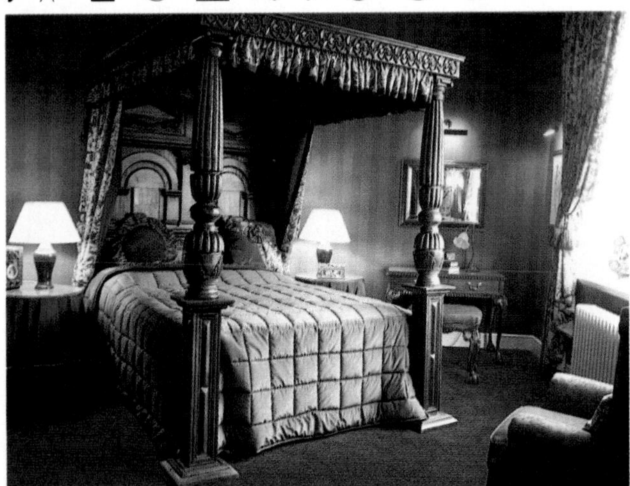

For hotel location, see maps on pages 477-483

NAILCOTE HALL

NAILCOTE LANE, BERKSWELL, NR COVENTRY, WARWICKSHIRE CV7 7DE
TEL: 01203 466174 FAX: 01203 470720

Nailcote Hall is a charming Elizabethan country house hotel set in 15 acres of gardens and surrounded by Warwickshire countryside. Built in 1640, the house was used by Cromwell during the Civil War and was damaged by his troops prior to the assault on Kenilworth Castle. Ideally located in the heart of England, Nailcote Hall is within 15 minutes' drive of the castle towns of Kenilworth and Warwick, Coventry Cathedral, Birmingham International Airport/Station and the NEC. Situated at the centre of the Midlands motorway network, Birmingham city centre, the ICC and Stratford-upon-Avon are less than 30 minutes away. Leisure facilities include indoor swimming pool, gymnasium, solarium and sauna. Outside are all-weather tennis courts, petanque, croquet, a 9-hole par-3 golf course and putting green. The hotel is associated with Stoneleigh Deer Park Golf Club. In the intimate Tudor surroundings of the Oak Room restaurant, the chef will delight you with superb cuisine, while the cellar boasts an extensive choice of international wines. Forty en suite bedrooms offer luxury accommodation, and elegant facilities are available for conferences, private dining and corporate hospitality. **Directions:** Situated 6 miles south of Birmingham International Airport/ NEC on the B4101 Balsall Common–Coventry road. Price guide: Single £120–£145; double/twin £130–£195.

40 rms MasterCard VISA AMERICAN EXPRESS 100

For hotel location, see maps on pages 477-483

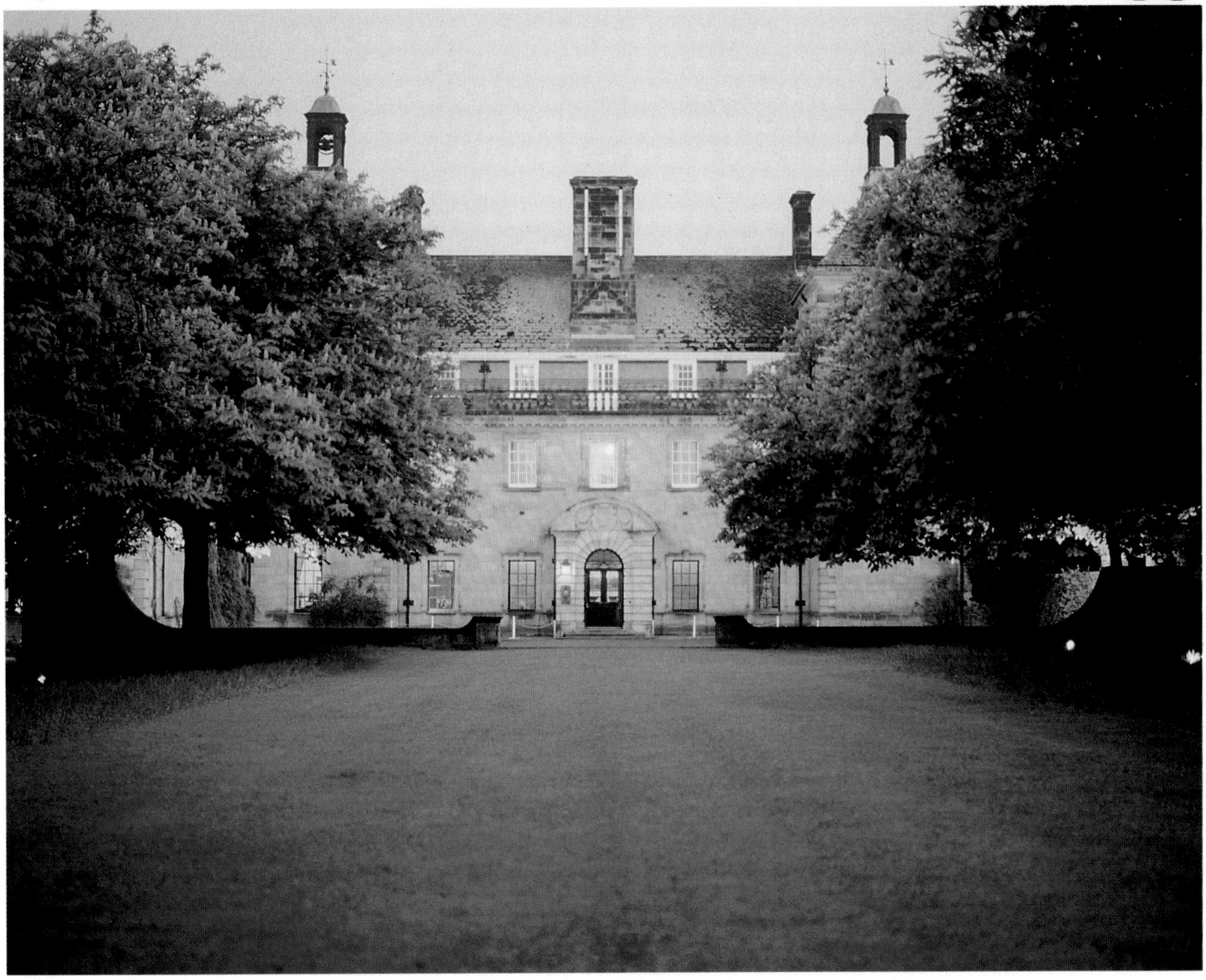

Crathorne Hall Hotel

CRATHORNE, NR YARM, NORTH YORKSHIRE TS15 0AR
TEL: 01642 700398 FAX: 01642 700814

Part of the Virgin group, Richard Branson's Crathorne Hall was the last great stately home built in the Edwardian era. Now a splendid country house hotel, it is set in 15 acres of woodland overlooking the River Leven and the Cleveland Hills. True to their original fashion, the interiors have elegant antique furnishings complementing the grand architectural style. There is no traffic to wake up to here: just the dawn chorus, all the comforts of a luxury hotel and, if desired, a champagne breakfast in bed. From a simple main course to a gastronomic dinner, the food is of the highest quality, complemented by a comprehensive wine list. Whether catering for conferences, product launches, wedding receptions or a quiet weekend for two, professional, courteous service is guaranteed. In the grounds guests can play croquet, follow the jogging trail or try clay pigeon shooting with a tutor on a layout designed to entertain the beginner and test the expert. Hot-air ballooning, fishing, archery and tennis can be arranged. The Yorkshire Dales, Durham and York are nearby. **Directions:** From A19 Thirsk–Teesside road, turn to Yarm and Crathorne. Follow signs to Crathorne village; hotel is on left. Teesside Airport and Darlington rail station are both seven miles; a courtesy collection service is available. Price guide: Single £104–£110; double/twin £140–£195.

For hotel location, see maps on pages 477-483

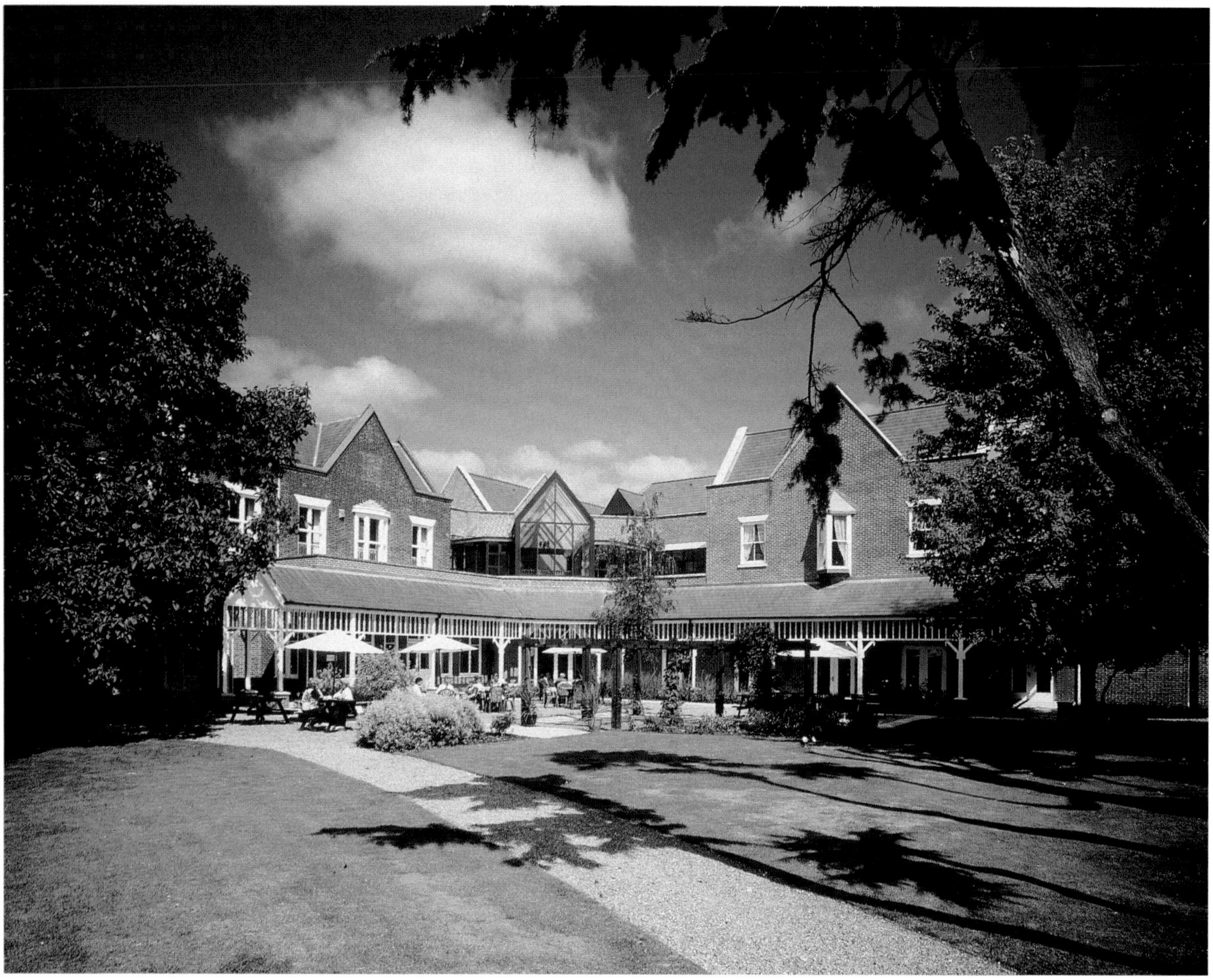

COULSDON MANOR HOTEL

COULSDON COURT ROAD, COULSDON, NR CROYDON, SURREY CR5 2LL

TEL: 0181 668 0414 FAX: 0181 668 3118

Coulsdon Manor enjoys a splendid location amid the peace and quiet of 140 acres of parkland, a large part of it laid down as a challenging 18-hole, par 70 golf course. Built in the 1850s the manor house has been faithfully restored and sympathetically extended. With fine furnishings, rich woodwork and impressive chandeliers Coulsdon Manor has a peaceful country house atmosphere and has been awarded 4 stars by the AA and RAC and two AA rosettes for its restaurant. Byrons Bar provides drinks and light meals throughout the day and guests can enjoy a pre-lunch or dinner drink in an elegant cocktail bar. All rooms have every modern facility. Many have views over the golf course. Business visitors are well catered for with five fully equipped conference rooms and six syndicate rooms. Coulsdon Manor has four all-weather tennis courts, four squash courts, racketball, a 1,000 sq ft gymnasium and sauna and steam rooms. 15 miles from Central London and within easy reach of Hever Castle and Chartwell. **Directions:** From M23/M25 junction 7 follow M23/A23 north and turn right after Coulsdon South Railway Station onto B2030 signposted Old Coulsdon and Caterham. After 1 mile turn left at the pond and continue until reaching Coulsdon Court Road on your right. Price guide: Single £65-£85; double/twin £75-£95.

For hotel location, see maps on pages 477-483

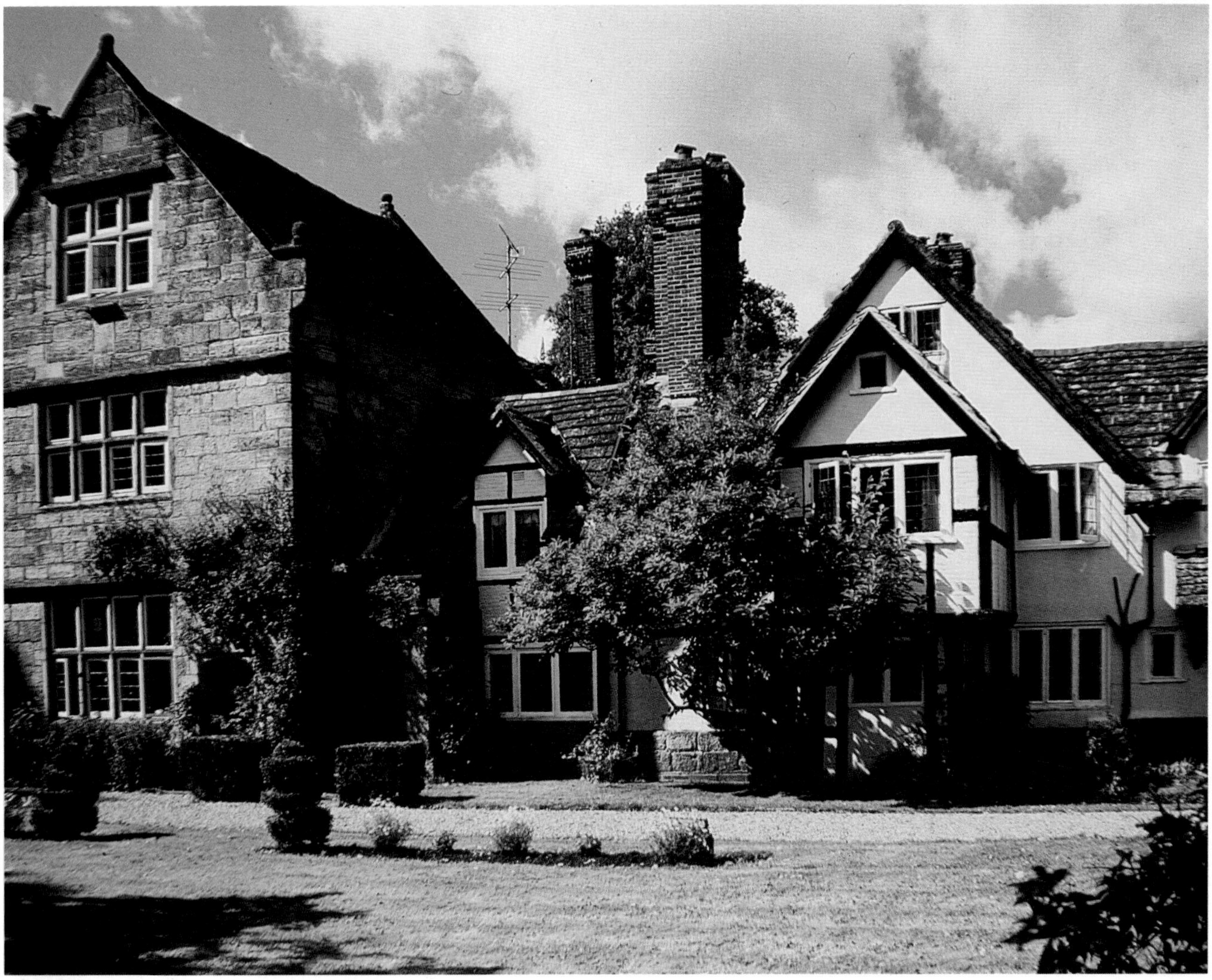

OCKENDEN MANOR

OCKENDEN LANE, CUCKFIELD, WEST SUSSEX RH17 5LD
TEL: 01444 416111 FAX: 01444 415549

Set in 9 acres of gardens in the centre of the Tudor village of Cuckfield on the Southern Forest Ridge, this hotel is an ideal base from which to discover Sussex and Kent, the Garden of England. First recorded in 1520, Ockenden Manor has become a hotel of great charm and character. The bedrooms all have their own individual identity: climb your private staircase to Thomas or Elizabeth, look out across the lovely Sussex countryside from Victoria's bay window or choose Charles, with its handsome four-poster bed. The restaurant, with its beautifully painted ceiling, is a dignified setting in which to enjoy acclaimed cuisine. 'Modern English' is how the chef describes his culinary style, offering an à la carte menu with a daily table d'hôte choice to include fresh seasonal produce and herbs from the hotel garden. An outstanding, extensive wine list offers, for example, a splendid choice of first-growth clarets. Spacious and elegantly furnished, the Ockenden Suite welcomes private lunch and dinner parties. A beautiful conservatory is attached to the Ockenden Suite, this opens on to the lawns, where marquees can be set up for summer celebrations. The gardens of Nymans, Wakehurst Place and Leonardslee are nearby, as is the opera at Glyndebourne. **Directions:** In the centre of Cuckfield on the A272. Less than 3 miles east of the A23. Price guide: Single from £85; double/twin from £98.

For hotel location, see maps on pages 477-483

HALL GARTH GOLF & COUNTRY CLUB HOTEL

COATHAM MUNDEVILLE, NR DARLINGTON, COUNTY DURHAM DL1 3LU
TEL: 01325 300400 FAX: 01325 310083

Hall Garth is a unique blend of style and the best of English tradition. Standing in 65 acres of lush parkland, it dates back to 1540 with Georgian and Victorian added gabled wings and features. It has its own 9-hole golf course. All the main rooms reflect the architecture and elegance of the period and are comfortably furnished with antiques and pictures. The 41 bedrooms in the hotel and Stables Wing, including five with four-poster beds and two suites, overlook the walled garden and surrounding countryside. Each has a bath or shower-room, satellite television, direct-dial telephone, trouser press, hair dryer and tea and coffee making facilities. There is a welcoming cocktail bar, a country pub in the grounds serving real ales and good food throughout the day, and three relaxing sitting rooms each with a cheerful log fire in winter, furnished with comfortable sofas and armchairs. Hugo's restaurant provides delicious dishes which have been recognised with an AA rosette. Hall Garth's leisure facilities include a tennis court, indoor swimming pool, spa bath, solarium and a gym with trainer-supervision. The conference and function facilities can cater for up to 300. **Directions:** From the A1(M) exit at junction 59 and take A167 towards Darlington. Turn left to Brafferton and Hall Garth is 200 yards on the left. Price guide: Single £50-£80; double/twin £60-

41 rms MasterCard VISA AMERICAN EXPRESS M 300

For hotel location, see maps on pages 477-483

HEADLAM HALL

HEADLAM, NR GAINFORD, DARLINGTON, COUNTY DURHAM DL2 3HA
TEL: 01325 730238 FAX: 01325 730790

This magnificent Jacobean mansion is set in three acres of formal gardens in the quiet countryside of rural Teesdale. Originally built in the 17th century, the hall was home for 150 years to the Brocket family and more recently to Lord Gainford. Since 1979 Headlam Hall has been owned and personally run by the Robinson family. The grounds include a small private trout water enclosed by ancient yew and beech hedges. The hotel has a tennis court, croquet lawn, a fine swimming pool, sauna and snooker room. All the bedrooms are individually furnished, and the restaurant provides the best of traditional English cuisine. The main hall features a magnificent carved oak fireplace and open staircase, while the Georgian drawing room opens onto a stepped terrace overlooking the lawns. There are four separate conference and meeting rooms including the Edwardian Suite holding up to 150 people. A free night's accommodation and champagne breakfast are provided for newly-weds holding their reception here. Fishing and golf can be enjoyed nearby and Barnard Castle and Durham are only a short drive away. Dogs by prior arrangement. **Directions:** Headlam is two miles north of Gainford off the A67 Darlington–Barnard Castle road. Price guide: Single £55–£75; double/twin £70–£85; suite £95.

For hotel location, see maps on pages 477-483

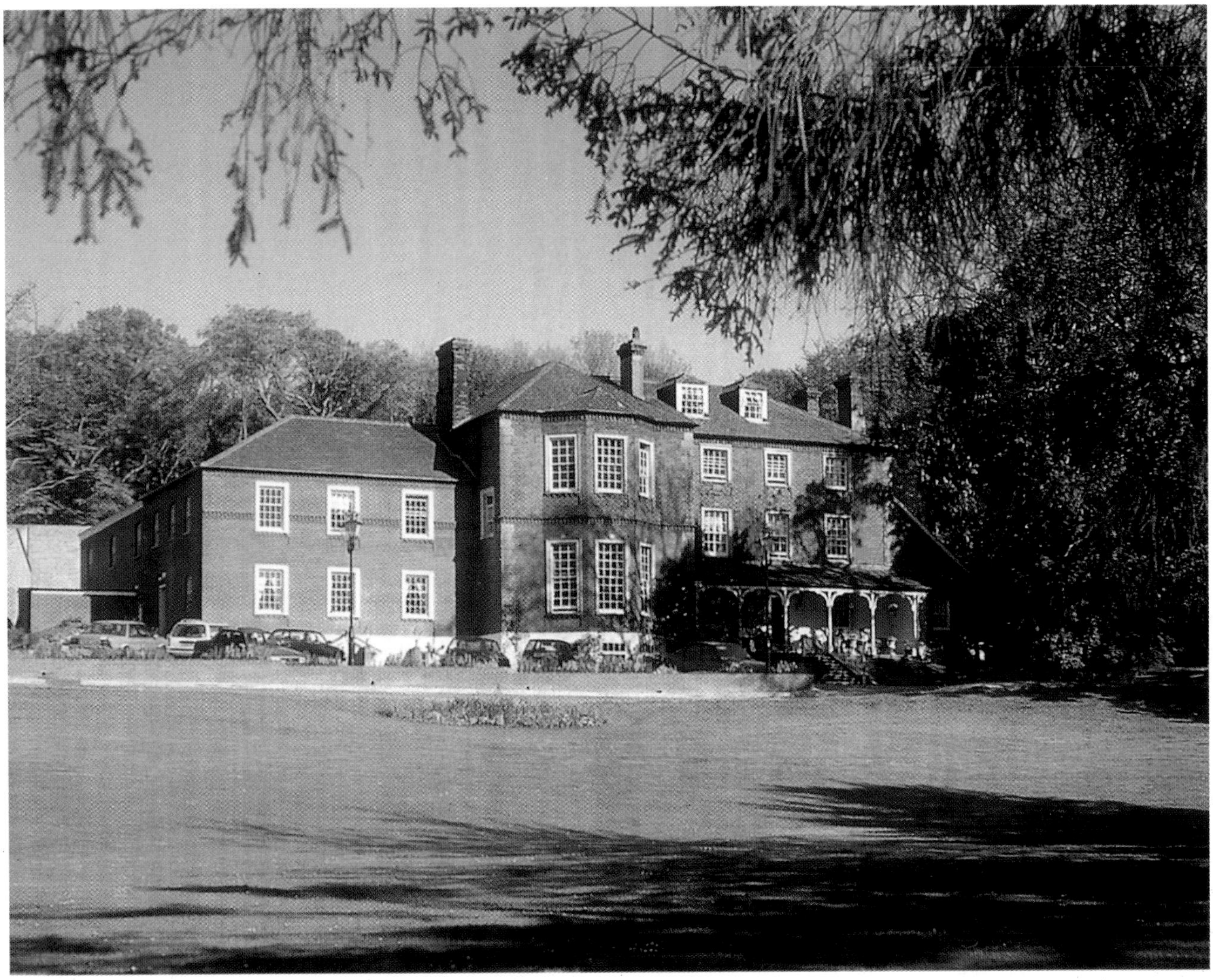

BRANDSHATCH PLACE HOTEL

FAWKHAM VALLEY ROAD, FAWKHAM, KENT DA3 8NQ
TEL: 01474 872239 FAX: 01474 879652

Set amidst 12 acres of private parkland and gardens, Brandshatch Place is a distinguished Georgian residence built in 1806. Approached along an impressive tree-lined drive, it offers a peaceful getaway from London, only 20 miles to the north. The hotel is being carefully renovated to include every modern amenity, from banqueting and conference rooms to a fully equipped leisure club. Bedrooms are pleasantly decorated, 12 of which are located in the recently converted mews. Dine in the award-winning Hatchwood Restaurant where chefs create dishes of originality using only the best produce available. After your meal enjoy a relaxing drink in the restful bar. You are always welcome to use Fredericks, the sports and leisure complex with its indoor pool, three squash courts, supervised gymnasium, dance studio, hair and beauty salon, sauna, steam room, two solariums, snooker room and tennis courts. Business and private functions are easily accommodated in the eight meeting rooms. **Directions:** From M25 junction 3 follow A20 south, then signs to Fawkham Green, hotel is on the right about ½ mile before Fawkham village. Price guide: Single: £79–£89; double/twin £98–£130.

For hotel location, see maps on pages 477-483

ROWHILL GRANGE

WILMINGTON, DARTFORD, KENT DA2 7QH
TEL: 01322 615136 FAX: 01322 615137

An unexpected find on the outer edge of London bordering on the Kent countryside, Rowhill Grange nestles in nine acres of woodlands and mature gardens descending to a picturesque lake. A combination of top service and friendliness makes Rowhill Grange the perfect venue for everything from weekend breaks to special occasions such as weddings and anniversaries. All the luxurious bedrooms are named after flowers and boast individual character and decoration, with a full range of facilities available to ensure maximum comfort and convenience for guests. The à la Carte Restaurant is now supplemented with the delightful new Topiary Brasserie. From late spring and through the summer months guests may take dinner on the terrace, sharing a scenic view with the swans and ducks. For special occasions, business meetings or dinners the private oak panelled dining room is available. The Clockhouse Suite is a self contained functions annexe with a dining/dancing area, comfortable lounge and a bar. The new Utopia Health and Leisure Spa is outstanding with all the latest equipment for women and for men including the UKs first therapy pool of its kind. **Directions:** M20 junction 1/M25 junction 3. Take the B2173 into Swanley and B258 north at Superstore roundabout. After Hextable Green the entrance is almost immediately on the left. Price guide: Double/twin £99–£145.

For hotel location, see maps on pages 477-483

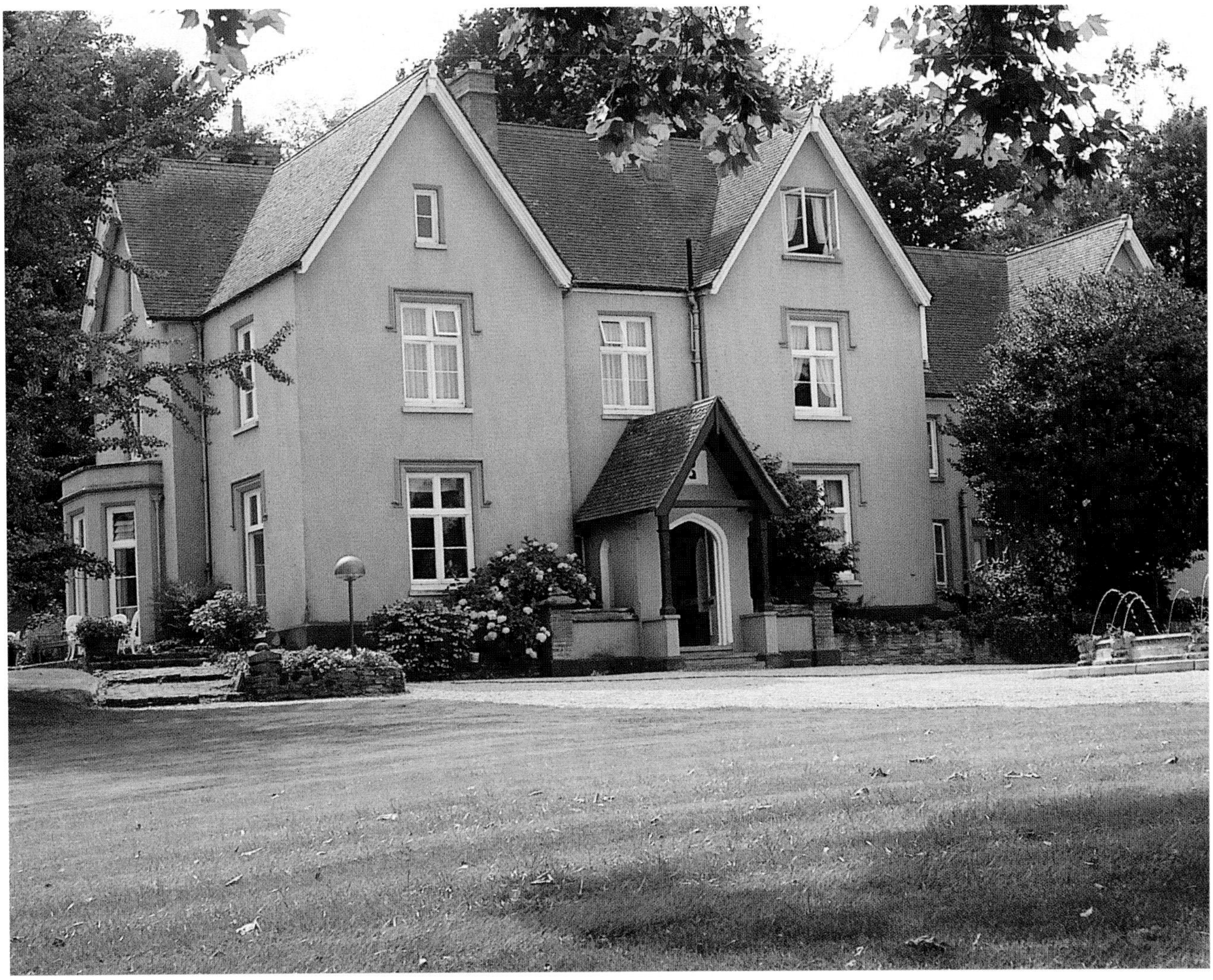

MAISON TALBOOTH

STRATFORD ROAD, DEDHAM, COLCHESTER, ESSEX CO7 6HN
TEL: 01206 322367 FAX: 01206 322752

In the north-east corner of Essex, where the River Stour borders with Suffolk, is the Vale of Dedham, an idyllic riverside setting immortalised in the early 19th century by the paintings of John Constable. One summer's day many years later, in 1952, the young Gerald Milsom enjoyed a 'cuppa' in the Talbooth tea room and soon afterwards took the helm at what would develop into Le Talbooth Restaurant. Business was soon booming and the restaurant built itself a reputation as one of the best in the country. By 1969 Gerald had branched out, and Maison Talbooth was created in a nearby Victorian rectory, to become, as it still is, a standard bearer for Britain's premier country house hotels. Indeed, in 1982 Gerald Milsom became the founder of the Pride of Britain group. With its atmosphere of opulence, Maison Talbooth has ten spacious guest suites which all have an air of quiet luxury. Every comfort has been provided. Breakfast is served in the suites. The original Le Talbooth Restaurant is about half a mile upstream on a riverside terrace reached by leisurely foot or courtsey car. It has recently been awarded the coveted Booker Sword of Excellence for quality,flair and renown. The hotel arranges special Constable tours. **Directions:** Dedham is about a mile from the A12 between Colchester and Ipswich. Price guide: Single £85–£120; double/twin £105–£160. Telephone for details of special short breaks. Exclusive use available.

For hotel location, see maps on pages 477-483

MAKENEY HALL COUNTRY HOUSE HOTEL

MAKENEY, MILFORD, DERBYSHIRE DE56 0RS
TEL: 01332 842999 FAX: 01332 842777

Set in a restful location on the River Derwent, Makeney Hall is surrounded by over 6 acres of beautifully landscaped gardens just 10 minutes' drive from Derby, a historic city famous for its china, its silk and Rolls Royce. Built originally by the Strutt family this capacious and restful hotel, with its mid-Victorian features, offers guests a warm, distinctive welcome. The carefully chosen décor imparts an air of bygone comfort. Bedrooms in the main house are spacious and individually appointed and many overlook the gardens. A splendid covered courtyard gives access to a further eighteen new rooms. Guests dine in Lavinia's AA rosetted restaurant, where expert cooking and fresh local produce create cuisine of the highest standard. The fare is British in flavour and a selection of fine wines is available. Conference and Banqueting suites accommodate wedding receptions and business meetings of up to 130 visitors. Places of interest locally include the Derwent Valley – an area of outstanding natural beauty – the Peak District, the stately homes of Chatsworth and Haddon Hall, and Alton Towers. **Directions:** From M1 (exits 25 or 28) head for Derby and A38 northbound. Follow A6 (signposted Matlock). Makeney is signposted at Milford, 6 miles NW of Derby. Price guide: Double-twin: from £75; suite: from £140.

For hotel location, see maps on pages 477-483

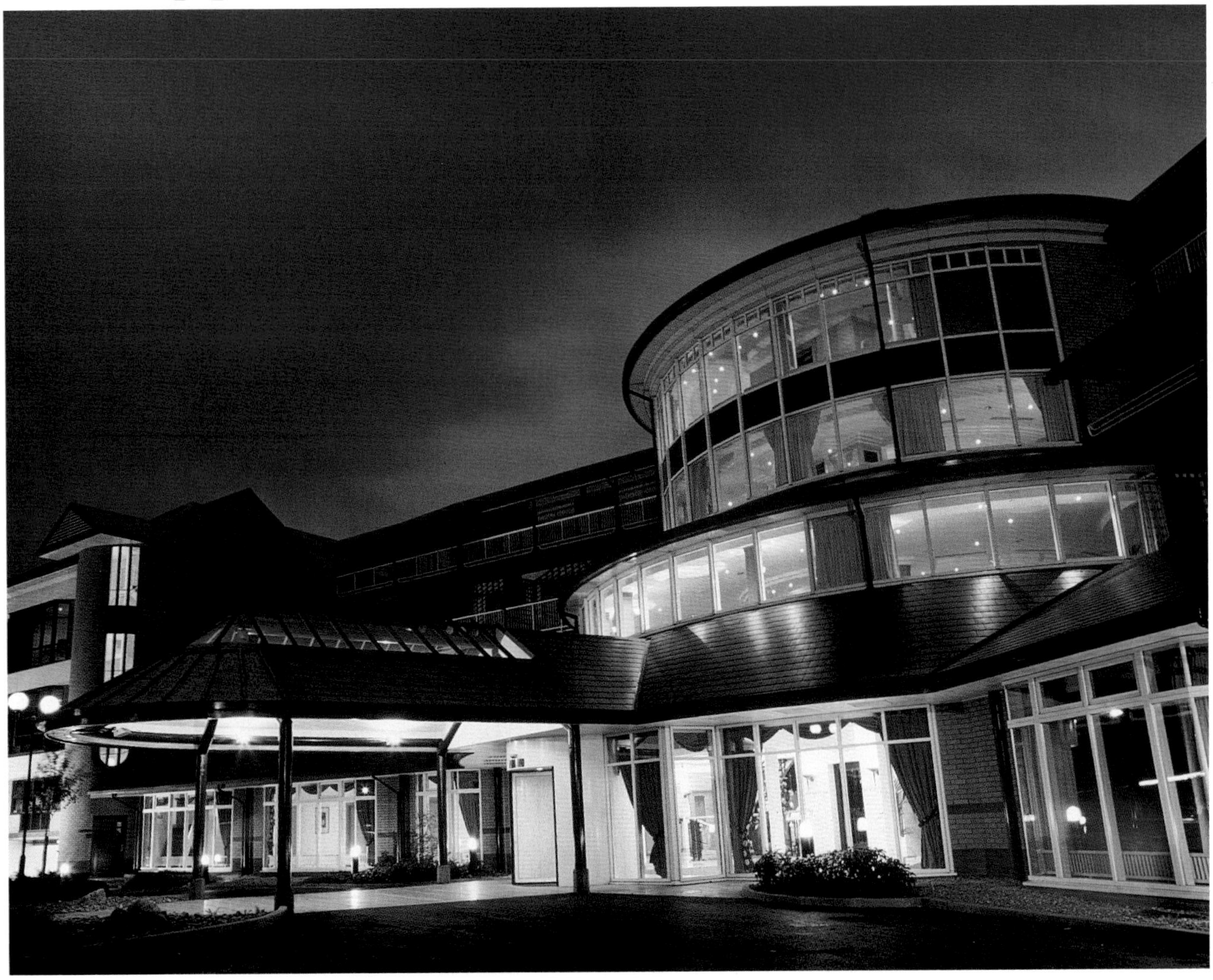

MICKLEOVER COURT

ETWALL ROAD, MICKLEOVER, DERBYSHIRE DE3 5XX
TEL: 01332 521234 FAX: 01332 521238

This luxurious modern hotel located in Derbyshire offers impressive bedrooms all pleasantly furnished with welcoming finishing touches such as fresh fruit, bathrobes, free 'in-house' movies and satellite television. Dining is an experience not to be missed, the award winning English Restaurant offers a delicious menu prepared with the finest and freshest local produce. The Italian Trattoria located in the atrium specialises in regional Italian dishes with a lively informal atmosphere. The Oasis Champagne Bar is the perfect place to enjoy a pre-dinner drink or perhaps just to relax with a night cap. Castaway Leisure Club has the latest state-of-the-art gymnasium equipment, a large tropical pool, steam room, sauna, a coffee shop serving an all day snack menu and the *'Castaways'* hair and beauty salon. The hotel's extensive conference and banqueting facilities are extremely versatile and can accommodate up to 200 people. Located around Derbyshire are a wide range of activities and country pursuits including golf, hot air ballooning, gliding, racing car tuition, clay pigeon shooting, water-skiing and riding. Places of interest nearby include Alton Towers, Uttoxeter Race Course and the Peak District. **Directions:** From M1 junction 28 follow signs to Derby. Ignore signs for city centre and take first exit for Micklover. The hotel is on the right before the round about. Price guide: Single from £95; double/twin from £105.

For hotel location, see maps on pages 477-483

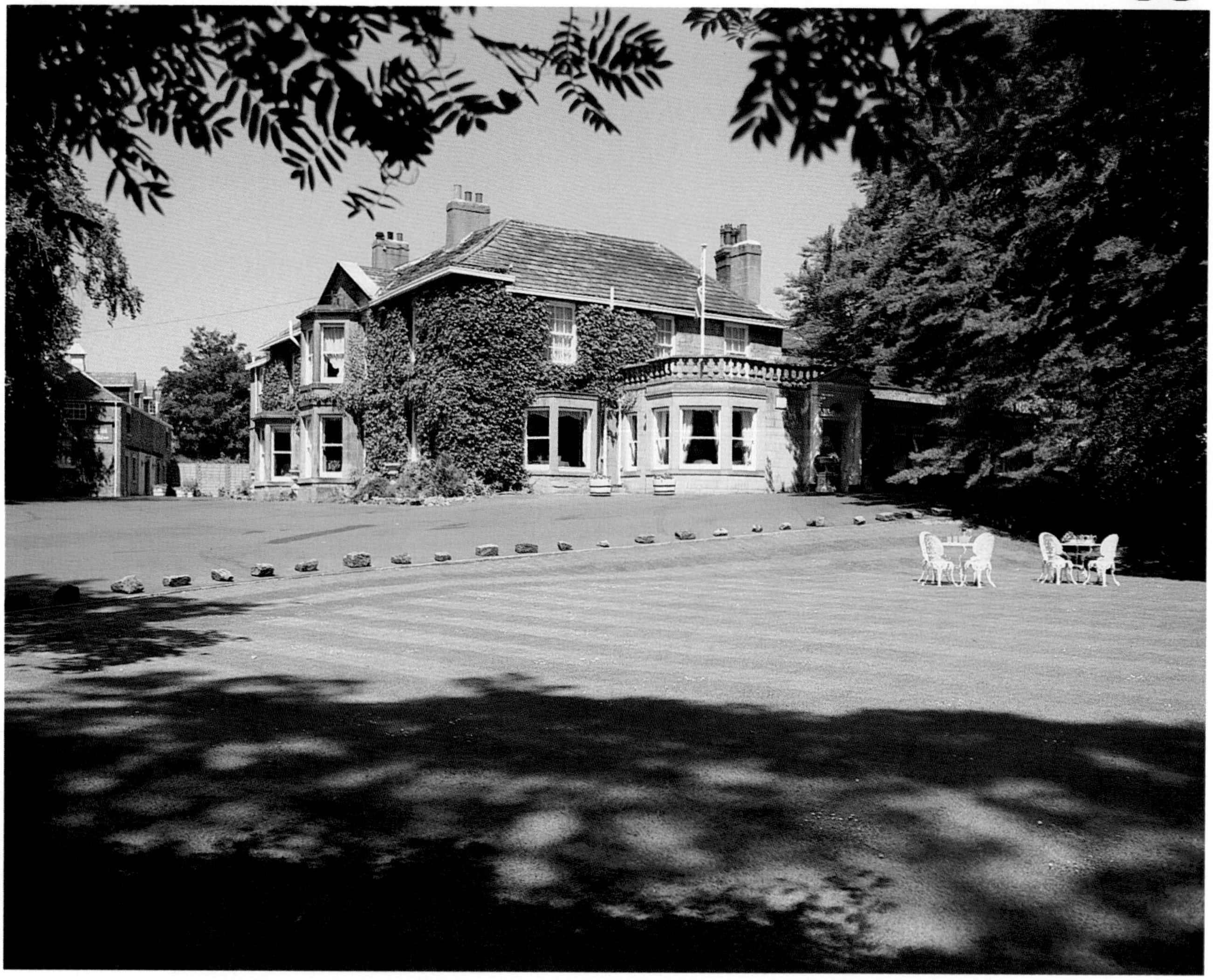

WENTBRIDGE HOUSE HOTEL

WENTBRIDGE, NR PONTEFRACT, WEST YORKSHIRE WF8 3JJ
TEL: 01977 620444 FAX: 01977 620148

Wentbridge House dates from 1700 and is set in 20 acres of grounds in the beautiful Went Valley. This fine building was once owned by the Bowes Lyon family and is renowned for its antiques and Thompson of Kilburn furniture. It is surrounded by superb lawns and trees and provides guests with a wonderful setting in which to enjoy a break. All the bedrooms are individually furnished and decorated to a high standard, including the spacious Oak Room with its four-poster bed, antiques and Persian rugs. The award-winning Fleur de Lys restaurant enjoys an excellent reputation for its cuisine and interesting selection of unusual and great wines. The hotel is ideal for executive meetings and conferences. The Leatham Suite can accommodate 40 delegates theatre style, while the elegant oak beamed and panelled Tudor Room offers an exceptional setting for an maximum of 20 people. the Crystal suite, which overlooks the courtyard, is eminently suitable for presentations, conferences and wedding receptions. Wentbridge House is recommended by Egon Ronay, Michelin and The Good Hotel Guide and has the English Tourist Board's 4 Crowns Highly Commended rating. Directions: Wentbridge is half a mile off the A1, four miles south of the M62/A1 interchange. Price guide £65–£90; double/twin £75–£99

For hotel location, see maps on pages 477-483

LUMLEY CASTLE HOTEL

CHESTER-LE-STREET, COUNTY DURHAM DH3 4NX

TEL: 0191 389 1111 FAX: 0191 389 1881/0191 387 1437

This magnificent 14th century castle offers an exciting blend of ancient history and modern convenience. The hotel has 62bedrooms each individually styled and appointed to a high standard. The King James Suite is Lumley's hallmark of taste and distinction. The public areas of the hotel, amply supported by medieval pillars, captivate the attention and imagination of all visitors. The subdued lighting and hidden corridors enhance the exciting atmosphere that pervades this amazing building. The Black Knight Restaurant will tease the most experienced palate. Lumley Castle's Medieval Memories weekend breaks offer a magnificent 'get-away' opportunity. These include an evening at the award-winning Elizabethan Banquet, full of fun, feasting (5-course meal) and merriment. The sharp wit and musical talent of the Castle's entertainers in their striking costumery offer a night to remember. There are 25 golf courses within 25 minutes drive. The Riverside Health Club offers 'full'facilities for Hotel guests at a discounted rate. For the more serious minded, Lumley has a number of conference and meeting rooms which provide an unusual setting for business matters. **Directions:** From A1(M) northbound take A693/A167 to Chester-le-Street and Durham. At the second roundabout take first left to Lumley Castle. Price guide: Single £83–£145; double/twin £115–£145; suite £180.

62 rms M 150

For hotel location, see maps on pages 477-483

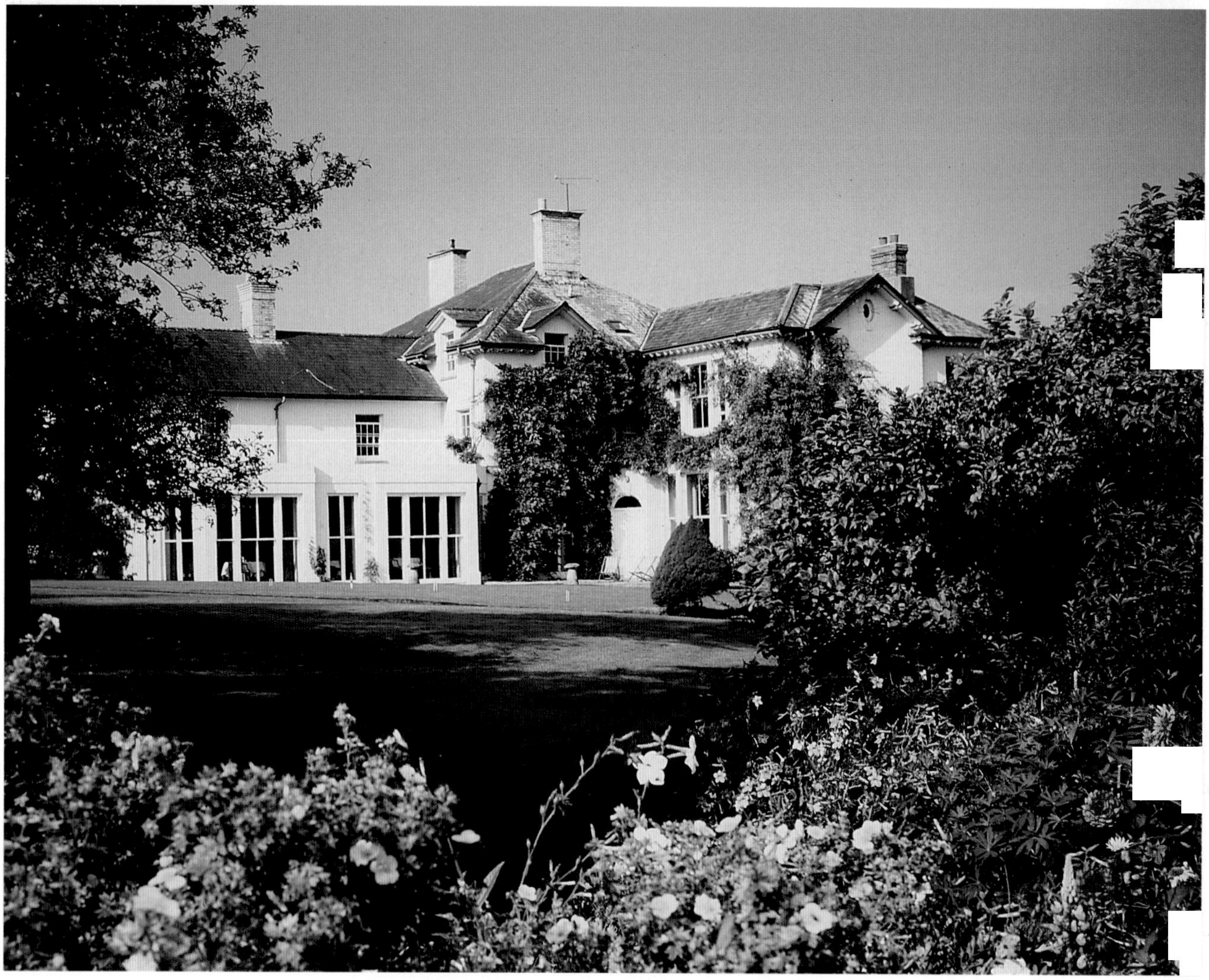

SUMMER LODGE

SUMMER LANE, EVERSHOT, DORSET DT2 0JR
TEL: 01935 83424 FAX: 01935 83005

A charming Georgian building, idyllically located in Hardy country, the Summer Lodge was formerly the dower house of the Earls of Ilchester. Now it is a luxurious hotel where owners Nigel and Margaret Corbett offer their visitors a genuinely friendly welcome, encouraging them to relax as if in their own home. The bedrooms have views over the 4-acre sheltered gardens or overlook the village rooftops across the meadowland. In the dining room, with its French windows that open on to the garden, the cuisine is highly regarded. Fresh local produce is combined with the culinary expertise of chef Tim Ford to create a distinctive brand of English cooking. The unspoiled Dorset countryside, and coastline 12 miles south, make for limitless exploration, and bring to life the setting of *Tess of the d'Urbevilles*, *The Mayor of Casterbridge*, *Far from the Madding Crowd* and the other Hardy novels. Many National Trust properties and gardens in the locality are open to the public. There are stables, golf courses and trout lakes nearby. Summer Lodge has earned the distinction of becoming a member of Relais et Châteaux. **Directions:** The turning to Evershot leaves the A37 halfway between Dorchester and Yeovil. Once in the village turn left into Summer Lane and the hotel entrance is 150 yards on the right. Price guide: Single £105; double/twin £135–£225.

17 rms       20      

For hotel location, see maps on pages 477-483

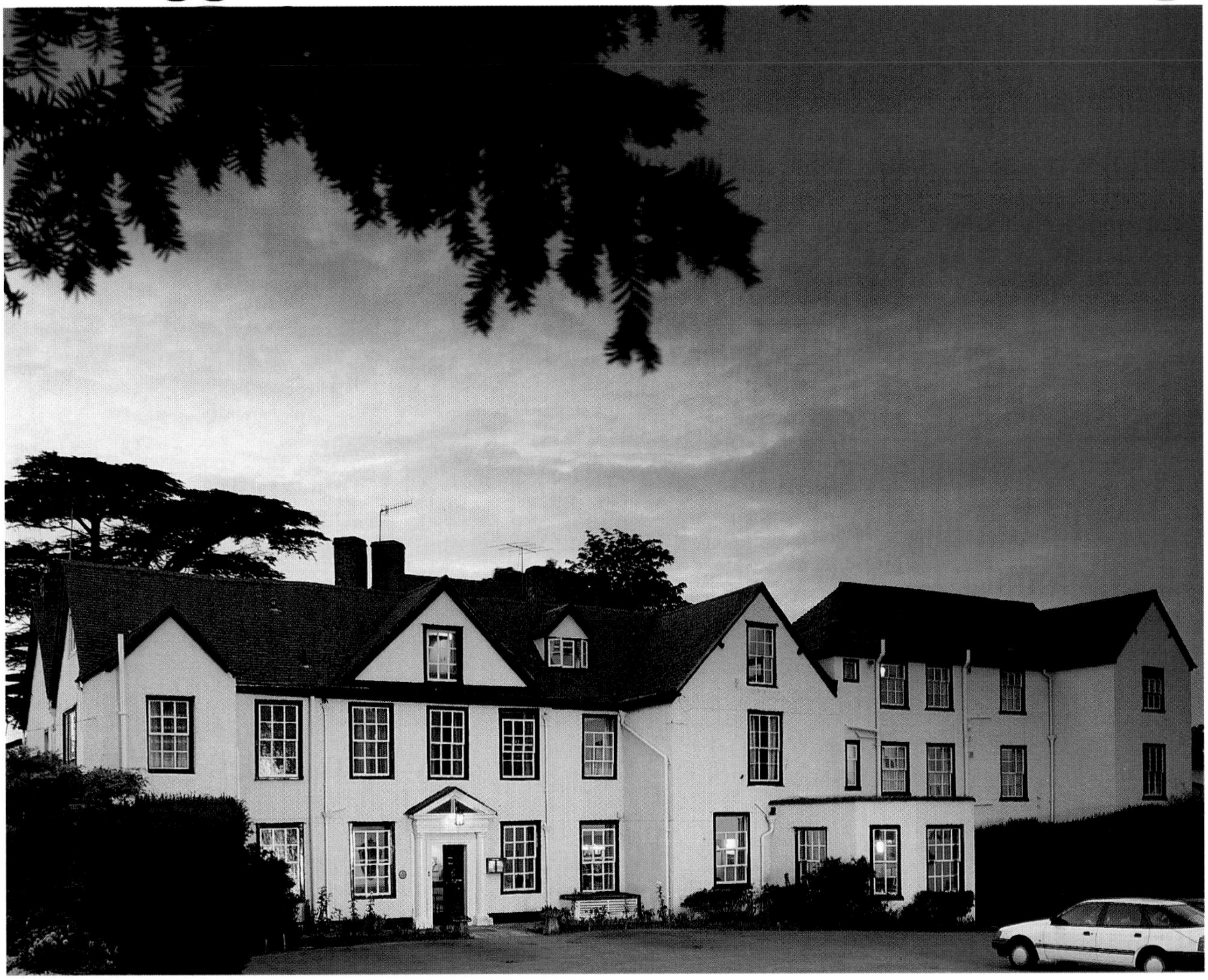

THE EVESHAM HOTEL

COOPERS LANE, OFF WATERSIDE, EVESHAM, WORCESTERSHIRE WR11 6DA
TEL: 01386 765566 RESERVATIONS: 0800 716969 FAX: 01386 765443

It is the atmosphere at the Evesham Hotel that stays in the memory. Not remotely stuffy, it is totally efficient but completely relaxing in a sometimes unconventional manner. Originally a Tudor farmhouse, the hotel was extended and converted into a Georgian mansion house in 1810. Privately owned and managed by the Jenkinson family since the mid-1970s, guests can be assured of prompt, friendly service and a relaxed atmosphere. Each of the 40 en suite bedrooms is furnished complete with a teddy bear and a toy duck for the bath. The restaurant offers delicious cuisine from a very imaginative and versatile menu, accompanied by a somewhat unique "Euro-sceptic" wine list (everything but French and German!). The drinks selection is an amazing myriad. The indoor swimming pool has a seaside theme, and guests have access to squash and tennis at a nearby sports club. The peace of the 2½-acre garden belies the hotel's proximity to the town – a 5-minute walk away. In the gardens are six 300 year-old mulberry trees and a magnificent cedar of Lebanon, planted in 1809. The hotel is a good base from which to explore the Cotswolds, Stratford-upon-Avon and the Severn Valley. Closed at Christmas. **Directions:** Coopers Lane lies just off Waterside (the River Avon). Price guide: Single £60–£68; double/twin £88–£98.

40 rms          

For hotel location, see maps on pages 477-483

Wood Norton Hall

WOOD NORTON, EVESHAM, WORCESTERSHIRE WR11 4YB
TEL: 01386 420007 FAX: 01386 420190

Wood Norton Hall is a glorious Grade 2 listed Victorian country house standing in 170 acres of beautiful Worcestershire countryside just a short drive from the historic market town of Evesham. French connections dating back to 1872 culminated in the wedding of the Princess Louise of Orleans and Prince Charles of Bourbon in 1907. The Hall's original character pervades the atmosphere. Rich interiors capture the Victorian splendour perfectly. Original fleur-de-lys carved oak panelling lines the walls. Grand fireplaces, elegant furniture and beautiful tapestries add comfort and colour. Each of the 45 en suite rooms is furnished to the very highest standards. The ground floor public rooms reflect the grandeur of the Victorian era with voluptuous window drapes framing magnificent views to the Vale of Evesham and the River Avon. The Duc's Restaurant, with its excellent but unobtrusive service, provides the perfect ambience to savour a fine culinary tradition and a small, intimate bar offers pre and post dining relaxation. Extensive leisure facilities include a swimming pool, billiard room, fitness suite, tennis, clay pigeon shooting and golf at a nearby championship course. **Directions:** Evesham is reached from M5 via junction 7 and then south east on A44, or via junction 9 and then north-east on A435. Price guide: Single from £99; double/twin from £158; suite from £134.

45 rms

For hotel location, see maps on pages 477-483

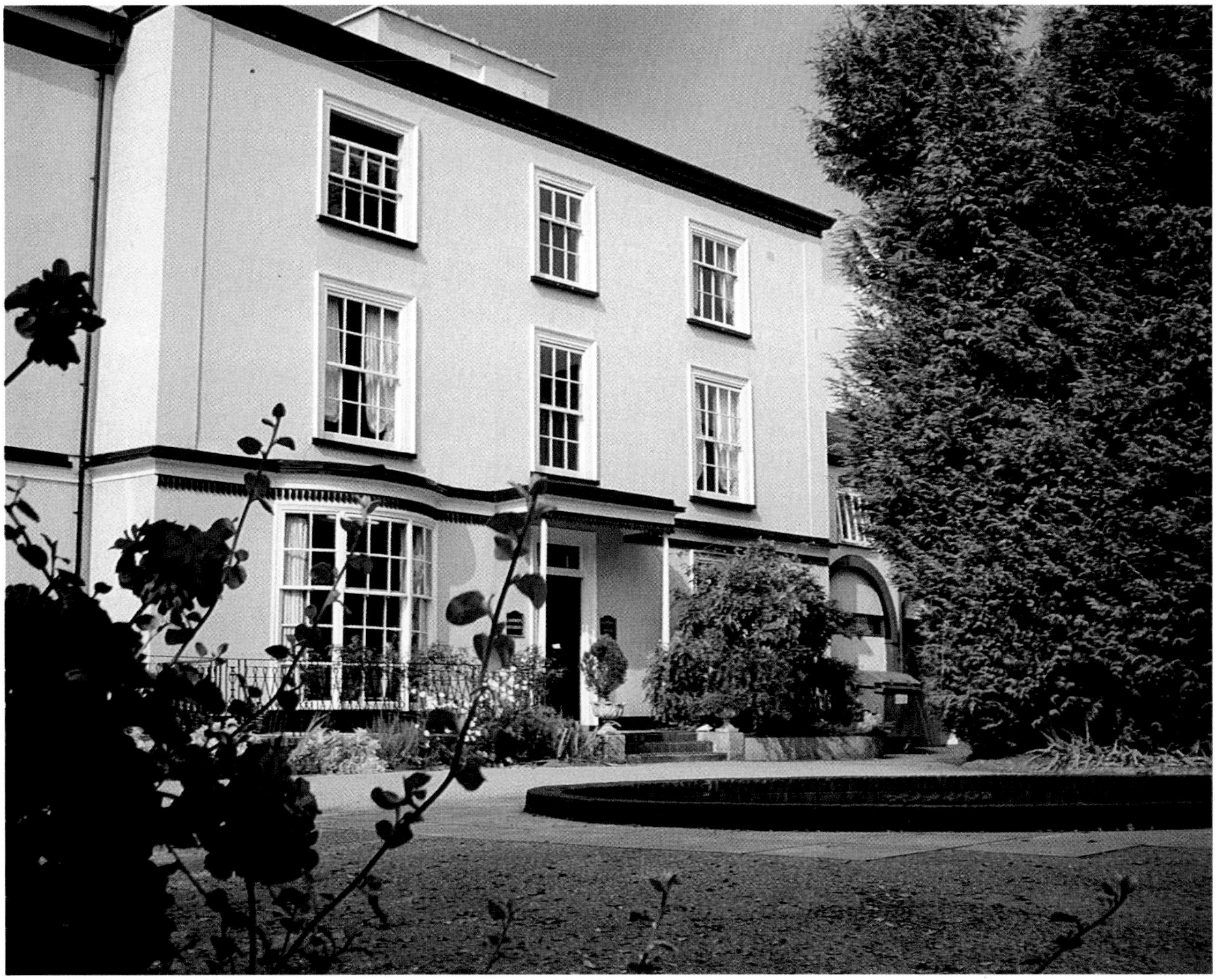

ST OLAVES COURT HOTEL

MARY ARCHES STREET, EXETER, DEVON EX4 3AZ
TEL: 01392 217736 FAX: 01392 413054

St Olaves Court, famous for its restaurant and home from home atmosphere, stands just 400 yards from Exeter Cathedral. It is a lovely Georgian building which is secluded in its own walled garden an oasis in the city centre. The rooms are very well cared for and range from single and twins to luxurious double bedrooms with Jacuzzi. The hotel has been discreetly furnished, partly with antiques, and the public rooms are spacious and comfortable. A particularly attractive cocktail bar overlooks the garden. The level of service provided is first rate and reassuringly old fashioned. Central to the enjoyment of St Olaves is the excellence of the cooking. The candle-lit restaurant one of the best in south west England is renowned for its outstanding cuisine. The Head Chef, winner of the young Irish Chef of the Year competition, achieves taste, texture and colour as well as excellence in presentation. The restaurant is featured in the Good Food Guide and has many other prestigious accolades. St Olaves Court Hotel is ideally placed for visiting famous National Trust gardens like Killerton and for exploring the City of Exeter as well as the South Devon coastline and the beauties of Dartmoor National Park. **Directions:** From Exeter city centre follow signs to 'Mary Arches P'. The hotel entrance is directly opposite. Price guide: Single £55–£80; double/twin £85–£100.

For hotel location, see maps on pages 477-483

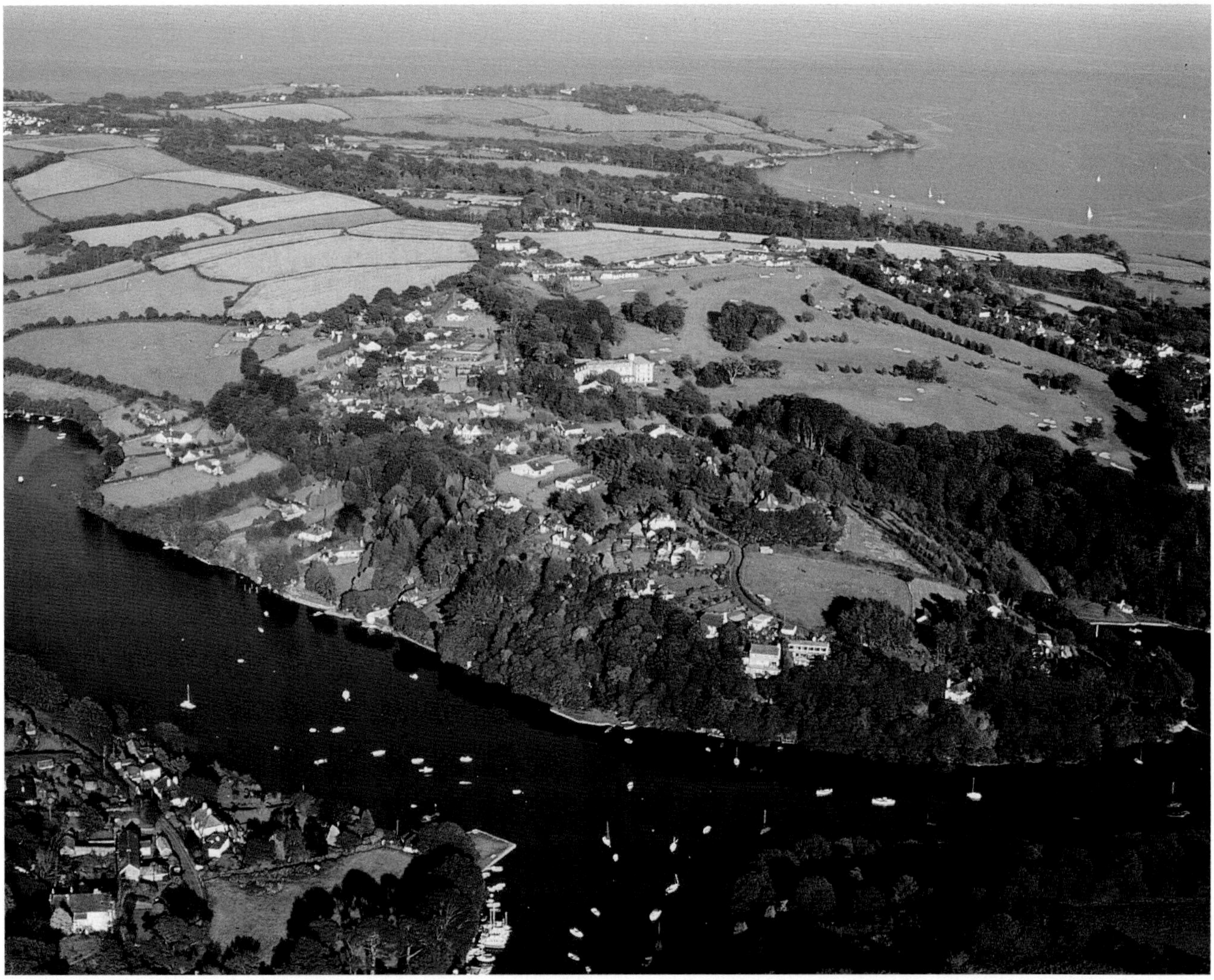

BUDOCK VEAN GOLF & COUNTRY HOUSE HOTEL

HELFORD RIVER, MAWNAN SMITH, FALMOUTH, CORNWALL TR11 5LG
TEL: 01326 250288 FAX: 01326 250892 RESERVATIONS: 01326 250230

The elegant Budock Vean Golf and Country House Hotel is set in 65 acres of beautiful gardens and parklands, with a private foreshore leading to the Helford and Frenchman's Creek immortalised by Daphne du Maurier. Most of the comfortably furnished bedrooms enjoy stunning views over the hotel's sub-tropical gardens, some have adjoining sitting rooms and all are well equipped with modern amenities. Keen appetites will be well satisfied by the variety of dishes offered on the hotel's excellent and original menus. Seafood, including local lobsters and oysters, is an obvious speciality. In addition to traditional food, there is a choice of dishes with an international flavour. The hotel has its own tennis courts, golf course and swimming pool and activities including watersports, horse riding, yachting, boating and fishing are all within easy reach of the hotel. Numerous places of interest nearby include the Seal Sanctuary at Gweek, several heritage sites, and many magnificent gardens and properties of the National Trust. **Directions:** Follow A39 to Falmouth, at Hillhead roundabout follow signs for Trebah Gardens and Mawnan Smith. Take the right at the Red Lion. Pass Trebah Gardens and the turning for Helford Passage – Budock Vean is on the left. Price guide (including dinner): Single £47–£80; double/twin/suites £94–£160.

For hotel location, see maps on pages 477-483

MEUDON HOTEL

MAWNAN SMITH, NR FALMOUTH, CORNWALL TR11 5HT
TEL: 01326 250541 FAX: 01326 250543

Set against a delightfully romantic backdrop of densely wooded countryside between the Fal and Helford Rivers, Meudon Hotel is a unique, superior retreat: a luxury, family-run establishment which has its origins in two humble 17th century coastguards' cottages. The French name comes from a nearby farmhouse built by Napoleonic prisoners of war and called after their eponymous home village in the environs of Paris. Set in nearly nine acres of fertile gardens – laid out by landscape gardener 'Capability' Brown, and now coaxed annually into early bloom by the mild Cornish climate – Meudon is safely surrounded by 200 acres of beautiful National Trust land and the sea. All bedrooms are en suite and enjoy spectacular views over sub-tropical gardens. Many a guest is enticed by the cuisine to return: in the restaurant (or the gardens during warm weather), fresh seafood and kitchen garden produce is served with wines from a judiciously compiled list. There are opportunities locally for fishing, sailing and walking. Golf is free. **Directions:** From Truro A39 to Hillhead roundabout turn right and the hotel is four miles on the left. Price guide (including dinner): Single £85–£100; double/twin £150–£176; suite £210–£240.

For hotel location, see maps on pages 477-483

NANSIDWELL COUNTRY HOUSE

MAWNAN, NR FALMOUTH, CORNWALL TR11 5HU
TEL: 01326 250340 FAX: 01326 250440 E-MAIL:BOMBEROB@aol.com

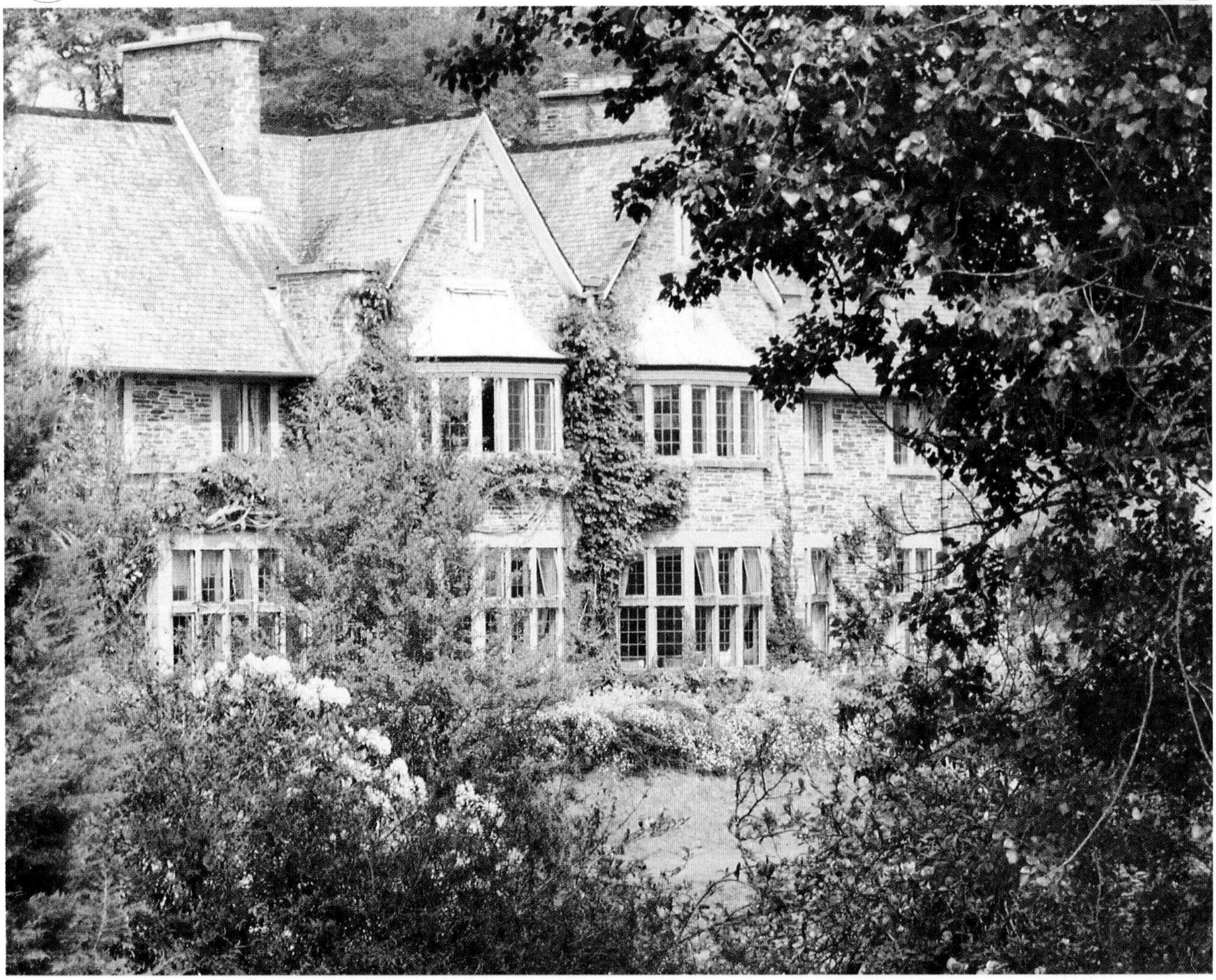

Lying at the head of a wooded farmland valley running down to the sea, Nansidwell Country House is bounded by several acres of grounds between National Trust coastland and the Helford River. The house has five acres of sub-tropical gardens with Camellias coming out in December and also extraordinary banana trees, sometimes bearing tiny fruit. The philosophy of proprietors Jamie and Felicity Robertson is that their guests should experience the atmosphere of an amiable, well-run country house. That so many guests return each year is a credit to the hotel. The bedrooms are prettily furnished and offer every comfort. Chef Anthony Allcott places an emphasis on fresh, local produce, particularly seafood such as lobster, mussels and oysters. For the sports enthusiast, there are five 18-hole golf courses within a short drive, as well as sea fishing and reservoir trout fishing and the hotel has a tennis court. Windsurfing, sailing, riding and bowls can all be enjoyed in the vicinity and there is the natural beauty of Falmouth's great harbour, the Helford River and Frenchman's Creek. Closed 2 January to 1 February. Internet: BOMBEROB@aol.com **Directions:** Follow signs from Truro to Falmouth. After approx. 8 miles follow signs to Trebah and Glendurgan Gardens to Mawnan Smith. Price guide Single from £110; double/twin from £145 to include dinner and continental breakfast. Bed and breakfast rates available.

For hotel location, see maps on pages 477-483

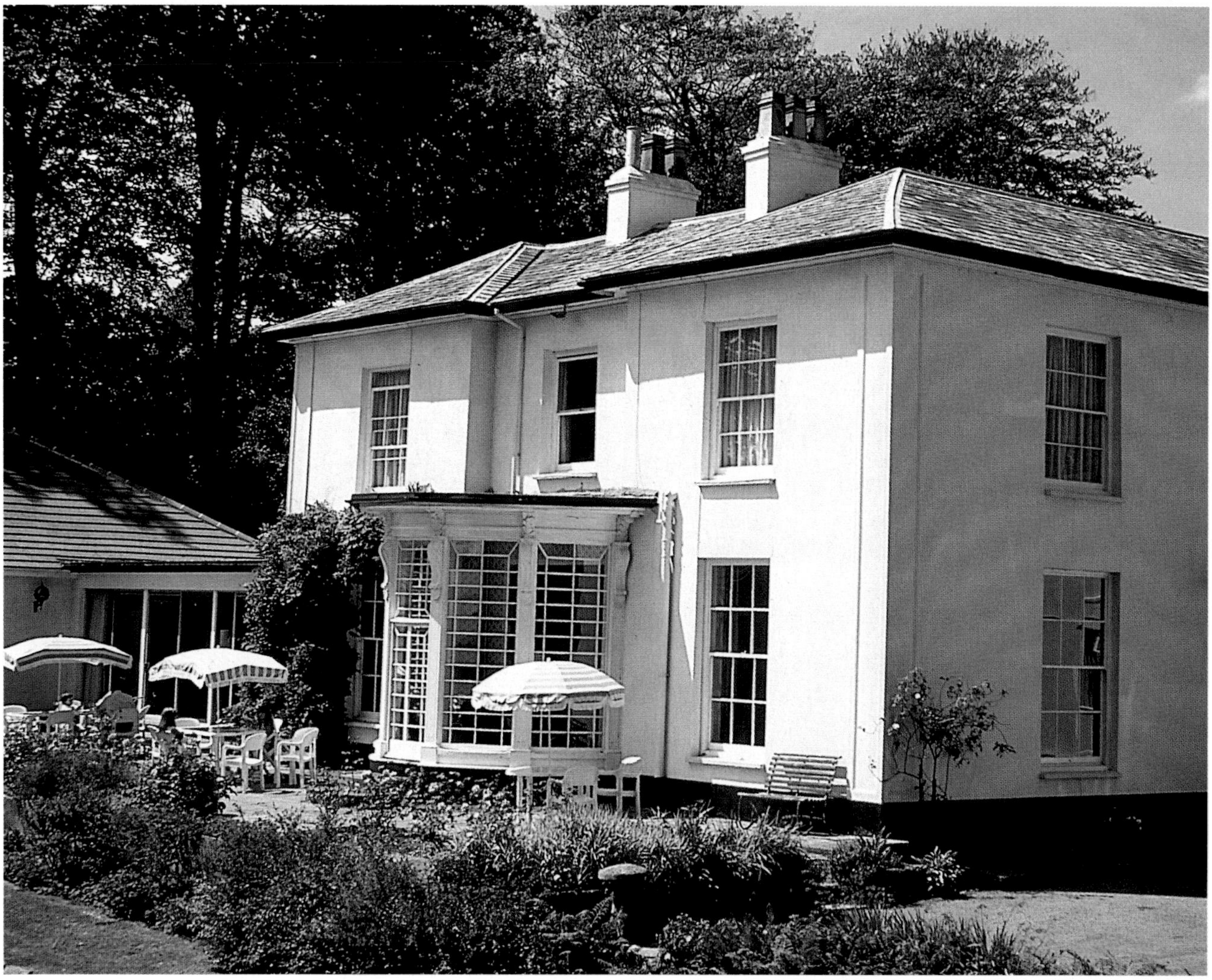

PENMERE MANOR

MONGLEATH ROAD, FALMOUTH, CORNWALL TR11 4PN
TEL: 01326 211411 FAX: 01326 317588

Set in five acres of sub-tropical gardens and woodlands, this elegant Georgian country house is an oasis of gracious living and fine food. From arrival to departure the Manor's attentive staff ensure that guests have everything they need to enjoy their stay. Bedrooms offer every comfort and are furnished to maintain the country house ambience. The spacious Garden rooms are delightful. Each is named after a famous Cornish garden and has either king or queen size beds and a lounge area. The restaurant serves excellent international cuisine that includes an extensive lobster speciality menu. Light snacks and substantial lunchtime dishes are also provided in the bar which overlooks the garden and terrace. There is a heated outdoor swimming pool in the old walled garden and a splendid indoor pool, together with Jacuzzi spa, sauna, solarium and gym. Golfers can make use of the hotel's practice net and benefit from reduced green fees at Falmouth Golf Course. Cornish gardens, National Trust and English Heritage properties are within reach. Flambards Theme Park, Poldark Mine and Gweek Seal Sanctuary are less than ten miles away. Directions: From Truro follow the A39 towards Falmouth. Turn right at Hillhead roundabout and after 1 mile turn left into Mongleath Road. Price guide: Single £57; double/twin £83-£105.

For hotel location, see maps on pages 477-483

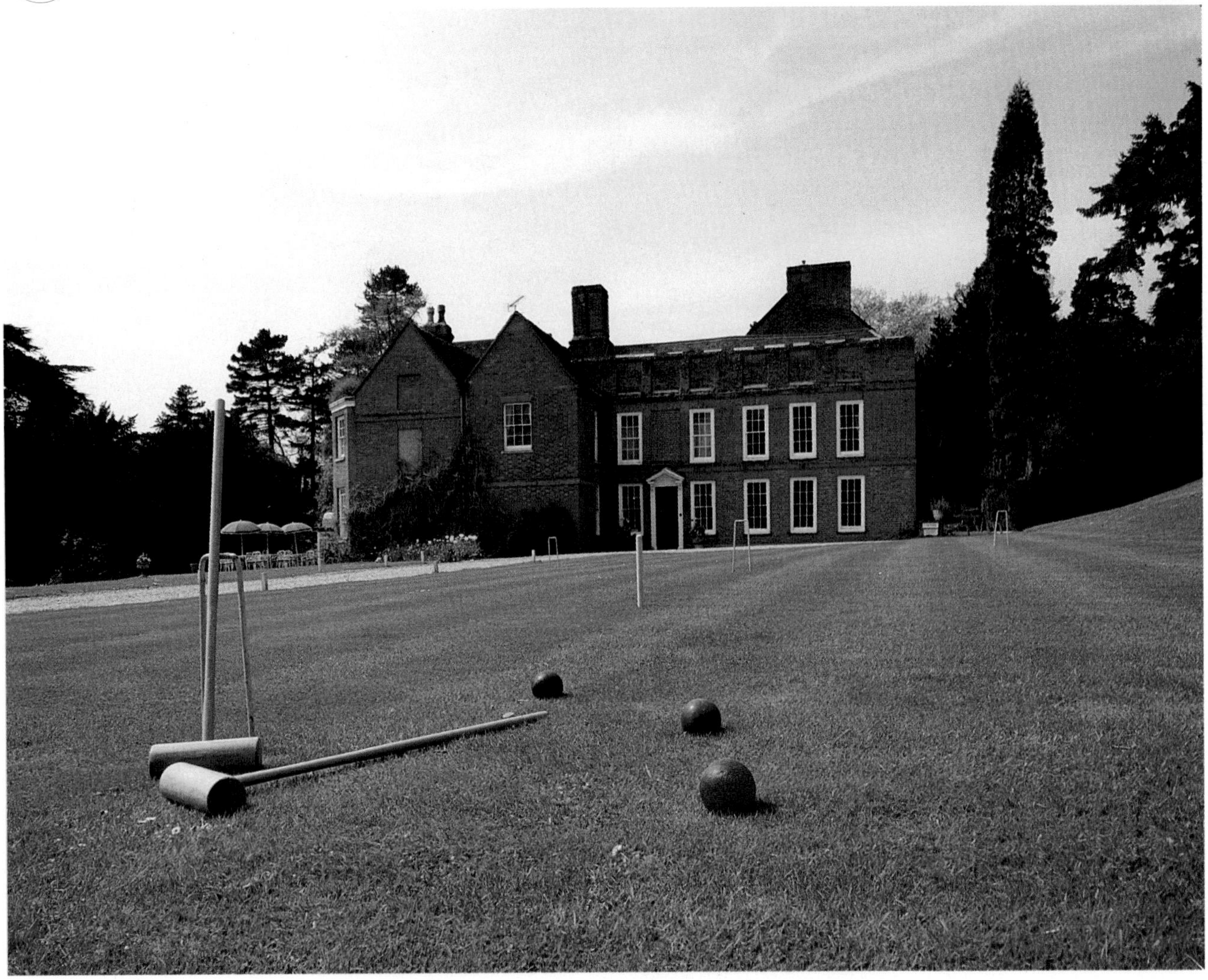

FLITWICK MANOR

CHURCH ROAD, FLITWICK, BEDFORDSHIRE MK45 1AE
TEL: 01525 712242 FAX: 01525 718753

Flitwick Manor is a Georgian gem, classical in style, elegant in décor, comfortable in appointment, a country house hotel that remains true to the traditions of country house hospitality. Nestling in acres of glorious rolling parkland complete with lake, grotto and church, the manor has the intimacy and warmth that makes it the ideal retreat for both pleasure and business. The fifteen bedrooms, with their distinctive characters and idiosyncrasies, add to the charm of the reception rooms: a soothing withdrawing room, a cosy library and pine panelled morning room, the latter two doubling up as both meeting and private dining rooms. Fine antiques and period pieces, easy chairs and inviting sofas, winter fires and summer flowers, they all blend effortlessly together to make a perfect whole. The restaurant is highly acclaimed by all the major food guides and indeed the AA, with its bestowal of three Rosettes, rated Flitwick Manor as the county's best and amongst the top one hundred establishments in the country. Outside pleasures are afforded by the all-weather tennis court, croquet lawns and putting green as well as a range of local attractions such as Woburn Abbey and Safari Park. **Directions:** Flitwick is on the A5120 just north of the M1 junction 12. Price guide: Single £90–£190; double/twin/suite £125–£225. Special weekend rates available.

For hotel location, see maps on pages 477-483

ASHDOWN PARK HOTEL

WYCH CROSS, FOREST ROW, ASHDOWN FOREST, EAST SUSSEX RH18 5JR
TEL: 01342 824988 FAX: 01342 826206

Ashdown Park is a grand, rambling 19th century mansion overlooking almost 200 acres of landscaped gardens to the forest beyond. Built in 1867, the hotel is situated within easy reach of Gatwick Airport, London and the South Coast, and provides the perfect backdrop for every occasion, from a weekend getaway to a honeymoon or business convention. The hotel is subtly furnished throughout to satisfy the needs of escapees from urban stress. The 95 en suite bedrooms are beautifully decorated – several with elegant four-poster beds, all with up-to-date amenities. The Anderida restaurant offers a thoughtfully compiled menu and wine list, complemented by discreetly attentive service in soigné surroundings. Guests seeking relaxation can retire to the indoor pool and sauna, pamper themselves with a massage, before using the solarium, or visiting the beauty salon. Alternatively, guests may prefer to amble through the gardens and nearby woodland paths; the more energetic can indulge in tennis, squash pitch and putt, croquet or use the Fitness Studio and Beauty Therapy. There is also an indoor driving range, a lounge/bar and a 9-hole par 3 golf course with an outdoor driving range. **Directions:** East of A22 at Wych Cross on road signposted to Hartfield. Price guide: Single from £99; double/twin from £124; suite from £164–£244.

95 rms MasterCard VISA AMERICAN EXPRESS M 150

For hotel location, see maps on pages 477-483

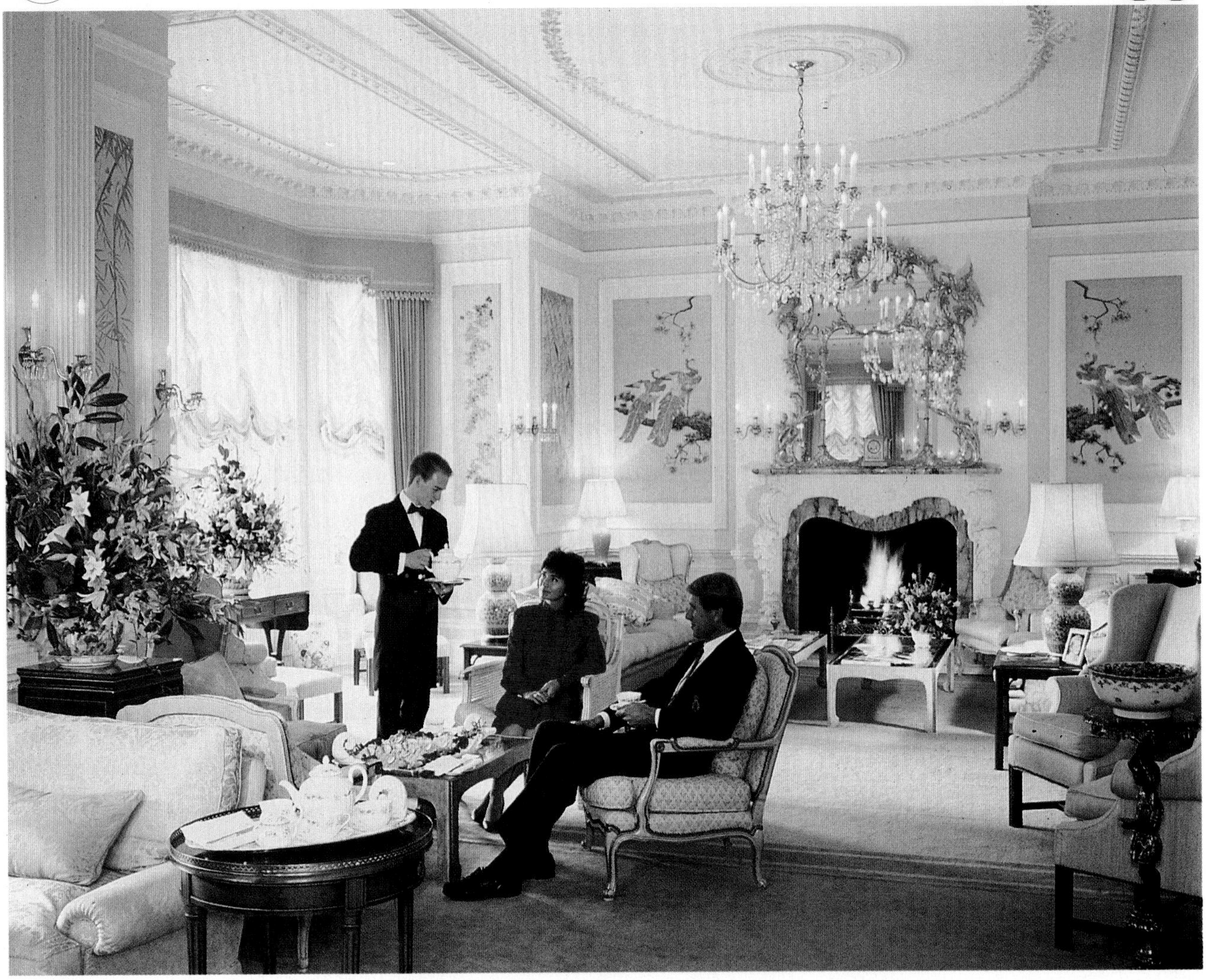

ALEXANDER HOUSE

TURNER'S HILL, WEST SUSSEX RH10 4QD
TEL: 01342 714914 FAX: 01342 717328

Alexander House is a magnificent mansion with its own secluded 135 acres of park, including a gently sloping valley which forms the head of the River Medway. Records trace the estate from 1332 when a certain John Atte Fen made it his home. Alexander House is now a modern paragon of good taste and excellence. Spacious rooms throughout this luxurious hotel are splendidly decorated to emphasise their many original features and the bedrooms are lavishly furnished to the highest standards of comfort. The House is renowned for its delicious classic English and French cuisine, rare wines and vintage liqueurs. Music recitals and garden parties are among the events held here and there are good conference facilities available. Guests are invited to take part in activities including clay pigeon shooting, croquet, snooker and tennis. There is also a new fitness room and solarium; there is in addition a resident beautician. A chauffeured Daimler can take guests to Gatwick Airport in under 15 minutes. Antique shops, National Trust properties, museums and the Royal Pavilion in Brighton are nearby. **Directions:** Alexander House lies on the B2110 road between Turner's Hill and East Grinstead, six miles from junction 10 of the M23 motorway. Price guide: Single £95–£150; double/twin £125; suites £150–£195.

For hotel location, see maps on pages 477-483

LANGSHOTT MANOR

LANGSHOTT, HORLEY, SURREY RH6 9LN
TEL: 01293 786680 FAX: 01293 783905

The peace and seclusion of this beautiful Manor House belies its close proximity to London's Gatwick Airport, 8 minutes away by taxi or Hotel car. Geoffrey, Patricia and Christopher Noble offer the kind of welcome and hospitality seldom found in the world of airports and travel. The Manor becomes the perfect beginning or end to your holiday in Britain or is a safe haven for your car if you are flying abroad. Free car parking (2 weeks) and luxury courtesy car to Gatwick Airport are offered. Although Langshott Manor is only 8 minutes drive away the airport, the house is tucked away down a quiet country lane amidst 3 acres of beautiful gardens and ponds and offers its guests peace and seclusion. The property is not under the flight path. Hever Castle, Chartwell, Knole Park, Brighton Pavilion and many other properties are all within 30 minutes' drive. Central London is 30 minutes away via the Gatwick/Victoria Express. **Directions:** From A23 in Horley take Ladbroke Road (Chequers Hotel roundabout) to Langshott. The manor is three quarters of a mile (one kilometer) on the right. Price guide: Single £95; double/twin £118–£165.

For hotel location, see maps on pages 477-483

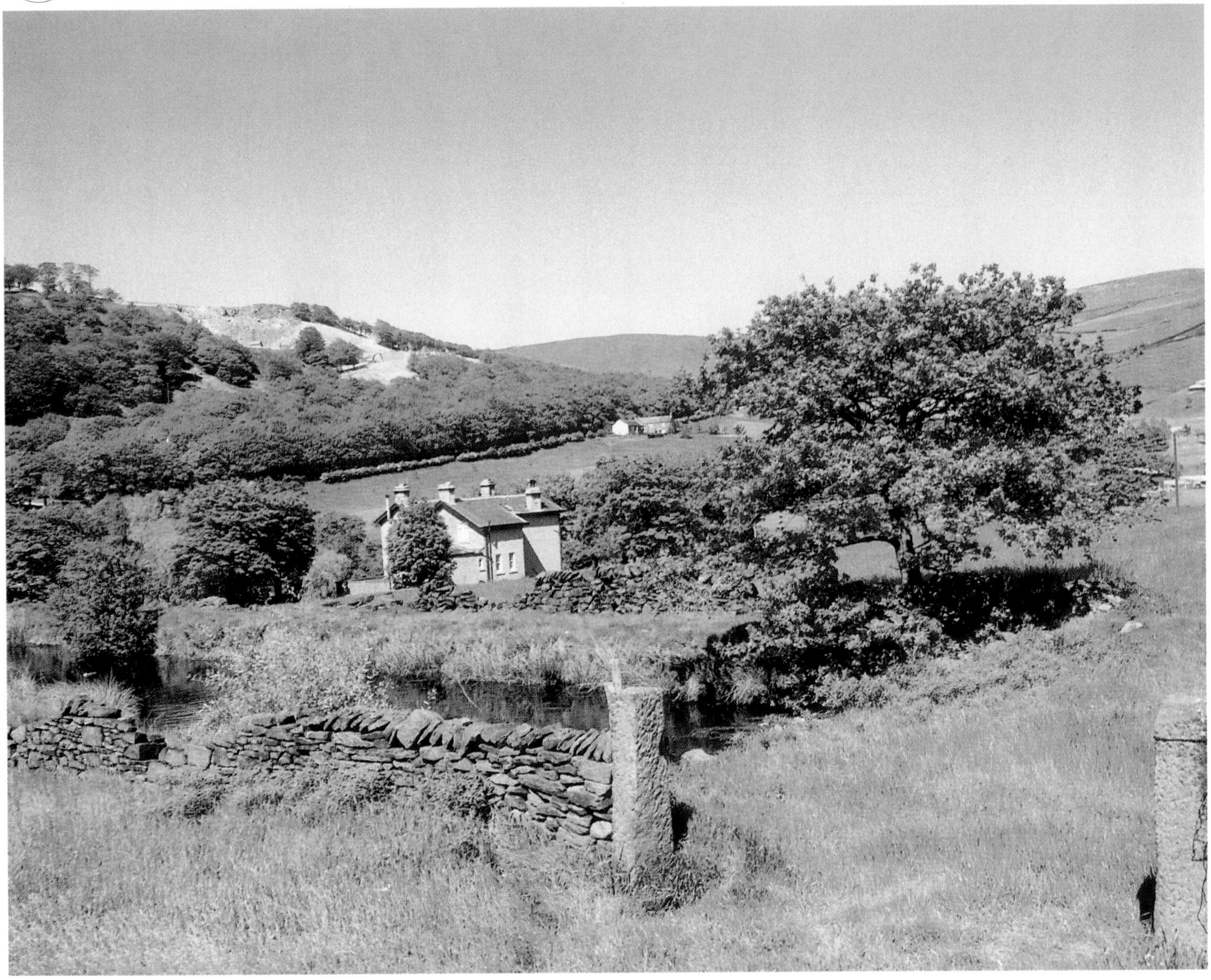

THE WIND IN THE WILLOWS

DERBYSHIRE LEVEL, GLOSSOP, DERBYSHIRE SK13 9PT
TEL: 01457 868001 FAX: 01457 853354

"Not so much a hotel, more a delightful experience"wrote a guest of this charming, small, family-run hotel on the edge of the Peak District. The Mother-and-Son team of Anne and Peter Marsh have added lavish care, attention to detail and a sincere courtesy to their recipe of antiques, Victorian bric-à-brac and delightful charm that is characteristic of The Wind in the Willows. If you don't know how it gets its name, stay there and read your bedside book! The marvellous scenery of the National Park is, literally, at the doorstep. All of the twelve, en-suite bedrooms enjoy superb views, and all are full of character, even the newer ones, opened in 1995, having their share of antique furniture and traditional decor that embellishes the whole house. There are some very special features, too – huge antique mahogany beds, a Victorian style bath and individual touches created by Anne in various rooms. Anne also supervises in the kitchen from where delicious home-cooking is served to both the private dining room and the purpose-built meeting room. Many activities can be arranged locally, including pot-holing, horse riding, gliding and para/hang gliding. **Directions:** One mile east of Glossop on the A57, 400 yards down the road opposite the Royal Oak. Price guide: Single £57–£75; double/twin £67–£95.

For hotel location, see maps on pages 477-483

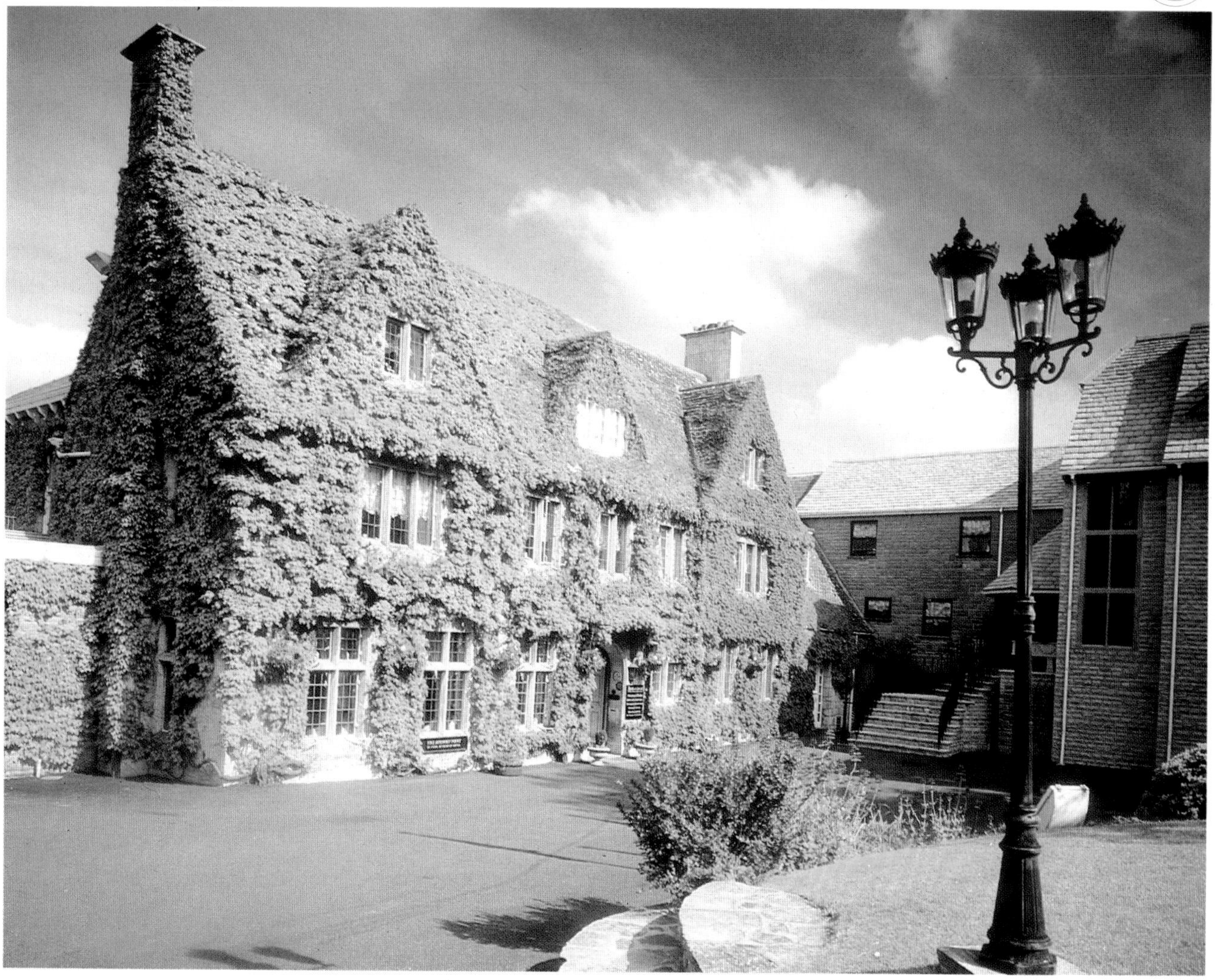

HATTON COURT HOTEL

UPTON HILL, UPTON ST LEONARDS, GLOUCESTERSHIRE GL4 8DE
TEL: 01452 617412 FAX: 01452 612945

This old ivy-clad Cotswold manor is set in seven acres of beautifully maintained gardens and 30 acres of green pastures. Nestling in the hills of Upton St Leonards, it enjoys stunning views over the Severn Valley towards the Malvern Hills. Extensive refurbishment of the manor has sought to combine modern comfort and sophistication with 17th century charm and character. Lavishly furnished bedrooms, many featuring Jacuzzis, offer a host of amenities and a number of personal extras including fresh fruit, mineral water, home-made cookies and bathrobes. Carrington's, Hatton Court's restaurant, has delightful decor, panoramic views and gastronomic delights. Classical traditional dishes and food cooked in the modern French style are complemented by wines from some 300 bins. Riding, golf and dry skiing are available just minutes from the hotel. Places to visit nearby include the elegant spa towns of Bath and Cheltenham, the Wildfowl and Wetlands Trust at Slimbridge, Prinknash Abbey, Berkeley Castle and Stratford-upon-Avon. Special breaks are available and details of these can be supplied on request. A member of Hatton Hotels. **Directions:** Hatton Court is located three miles south of Gloucester on the B4073 Gloucester–Painswick road, off the A46. Price guide: Single £88–£98; double/twin £100–£120; suite £135.

For hotel location, see maps on pages 477-483

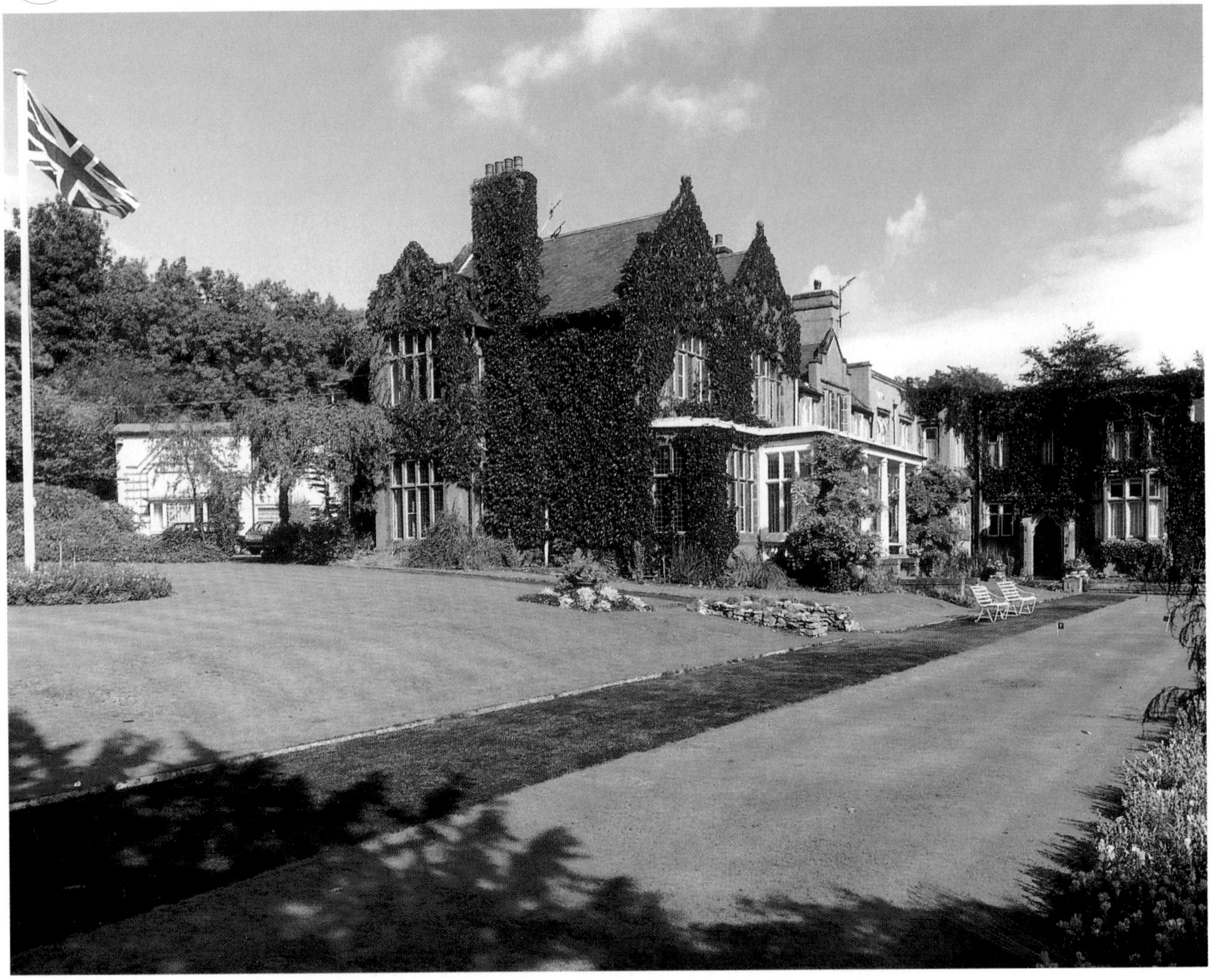

GRAYTHWAITE MANOR

FERNHILL ROAD, GRANGE-OVER-SANDS, CUMBRIA LA11 7JE
TEL: 015395 32001 FAX: 015395 35549

This beautifully furnished, traditionally run country house has been owned and run by the Blakemore family since 1937 and extends a warm welcome to its guests. It enjoys a superb setting in eight acres of private landscaped gardens and woodland on the hillside overlooking Morecambe Bay. Each bedroom is decorated and furnished in the best of taste and many offer superb views across the gardens and bay to the Pennines beyond. Elegant, spacious lounges with fresh flowers and antiques provide an exclusive setting and log fires are lit to add extra cheer on chillier nights. The Manor enjoys an excellent reputation for its cuisine and guests can look forward to a six course dinner comprising carefully prepared dishes complemented by the right wine from the extensive cellar. A few miles inland from Grange-over-Sands are Lake Windermere and Coniston Water and some of the most majestic scenery in the country. Nearby are the village of Cartmel, Holker Hall, Levens Hall and Sizergh Castle. The area abounds with historic buildings, gardens and museums. **Directions:** Take M6 to junction 36 and then the A65 towards Kendal, followed by the A590 towards Barrow. At roundabout take B5277 to Grange-over-Sands and go through town turning right opposite the fire station into Fernhill Road. The hotel is on the left. Price guide: Single £45–£55; double/twin £80–£98.

For hotel location, see maps on pages 477-483

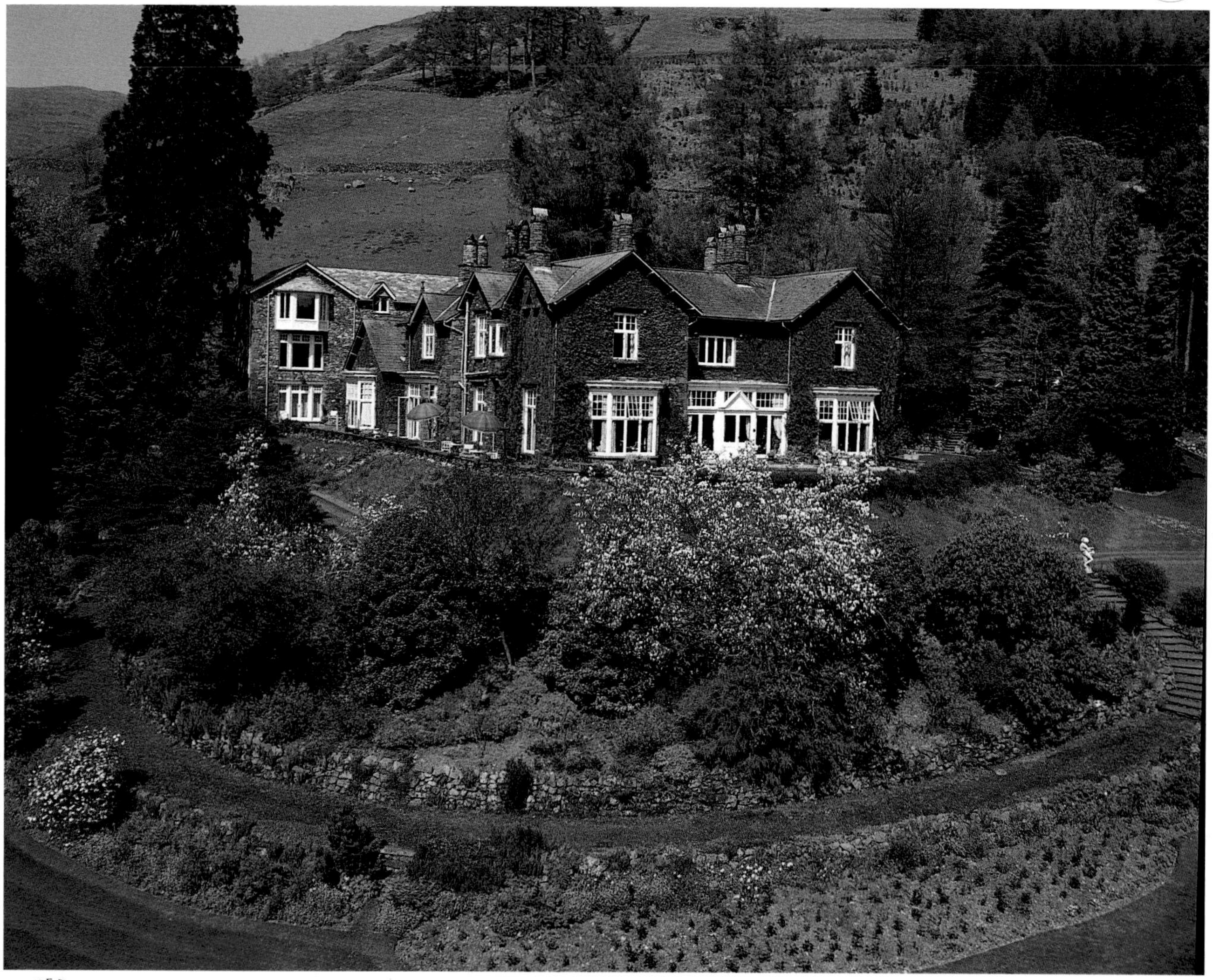

MICHAELS NOOK

GRASMERE, CUMBRIA LA22 9RP
TEL: 015394 35496 FAX: 015394 35645

Built in 1859 and named after Michael the eponymous shepherd of Wordsworth's poem, Michael's Nook has long been established as one of Britain's leading country house hotels. Opened as a hotel in 1969 by Reg and Elizabeth Gifford, it overlooks Grasmere Valley and is surrounded by gardens and trees. Reg is a respected antiques dealer, and the hotel's interior reflects his appreciation of English furniture, rugs, prints and porcelain. There are two suites, and twelve individually designed bedrooms, all with en suite bathrooms. In the acclaimed restaurant, polished tables are set with fine crystal and china. The best ingredients are used to create dishes memorable for their delicate flavours and artistic presentation. The panelled Oak Room, with its stone fireplace and gilt furnishings, can be booked for private parties and executive meetings. Leisure facilities at the nearby Wordsworth Hotel are available to guests, as is free golf at Keswick Golf Club, Monday–Friday. Michael's Nook is, first and foremost, a home where comfort is the watchword. **Directions:** Approaching Grasmere on the A591 from the south, ignore signs for Grasmere Village and continue to The Swan Hotel on the right. There turn sharp right and follow the lane uphill for 400 yds to Michael's Nook. Price guide (including dinner): Single from £120; double/twin £160–£290; suite £300–£350.

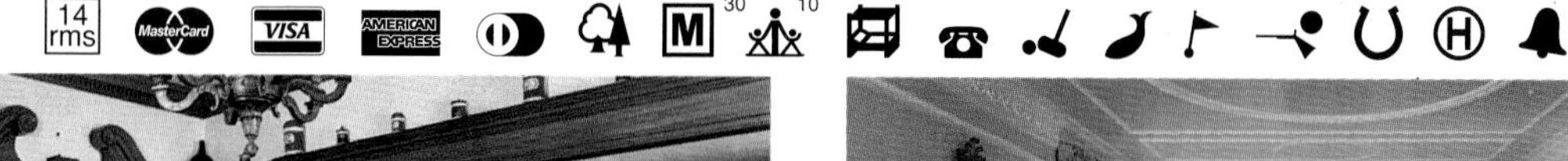

For hotel location, see maps on pages 477-483

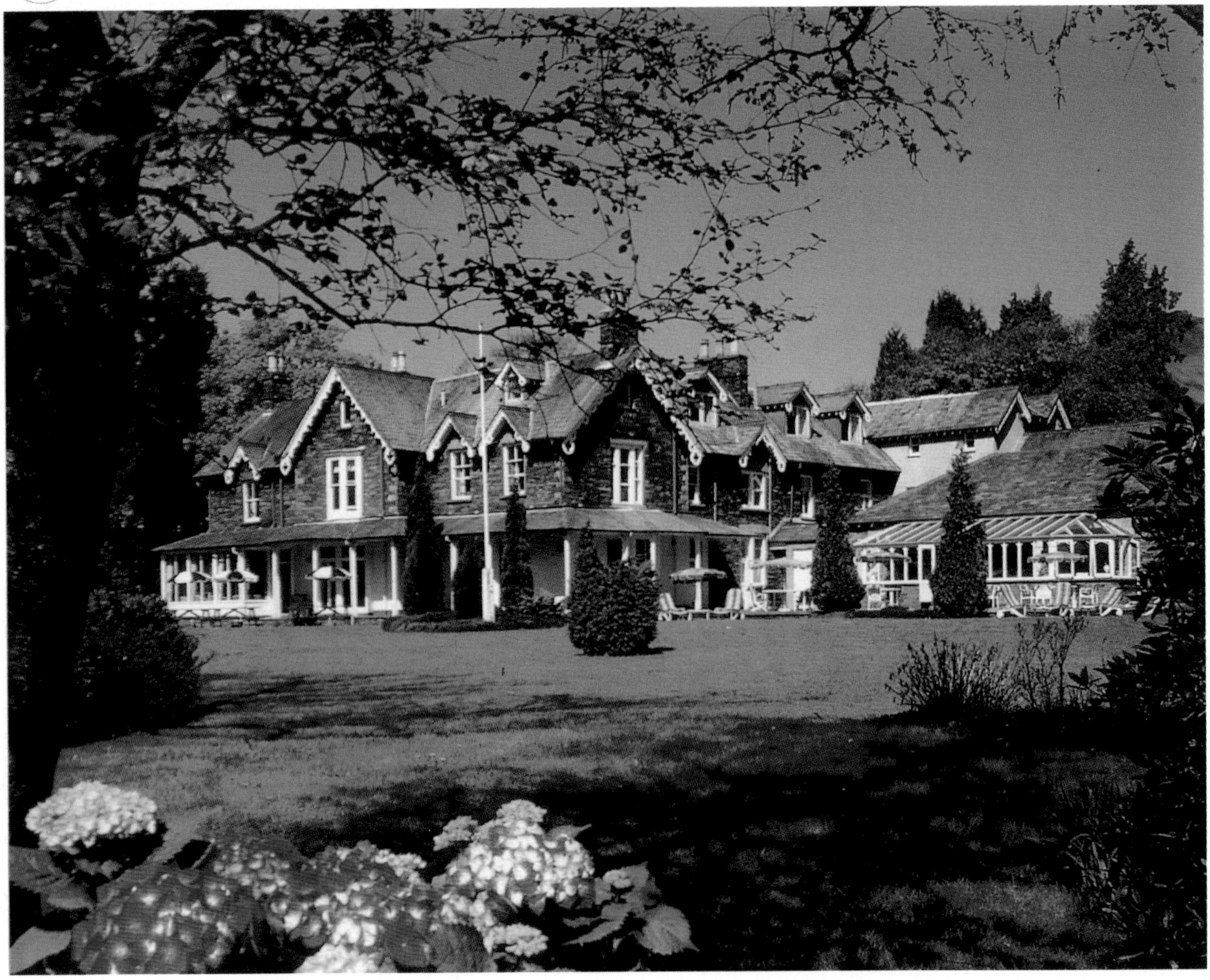

THE WORDSWORTH HOTEL

GRASMERE, NR AMBLESIDE, CUMBRIA LA22 9SW
TEL: 015394 35592 FAX: 015394 35765

In the very heart of the English Lakeland, The Wordsworth Hotel combines AA 4 Star standards with the magnificence of the surrounding fells. Set in its own grounds in the village of Grasmere, the hotel provides first-class, year-round facilities for both business and leisure travellers. It has a reputaion for the high quality of its food, accommodation and hospitality. The comfortable bedrooms have well-equipped bathrooms, and there are two suites with whirlpool baths. 24-hour room service is available for drinks and light refreshments. Peaceful lounges overlook landscaped gardens, and the heated indoor pool opens on to a sun-trap terrace. There is a Jacuzzi, mini-gym, sauna and solarium. As well as a Cocktail Bar, the hotel has its own pub, "The Dove and Olive Branch", which has received accolades from The Good Pub Guide. In "The Prelude Restaurant" menus offer a good choice of dishes, prepared with skill and imagination from the freshest produce. The Wordsworth Hotel is a perfect venue for conferences, incentive weekends and corporate entertaining. Three function rooms are available with highly professional back-up. Lakeland's principal places of interest are all within easy reach. **Directions:** The hotel is located next to Grasmere village church. Price guide: Single £64–£78; double/twin £128–£158; suite £200.

For hotel location, see maps on pages 477-483

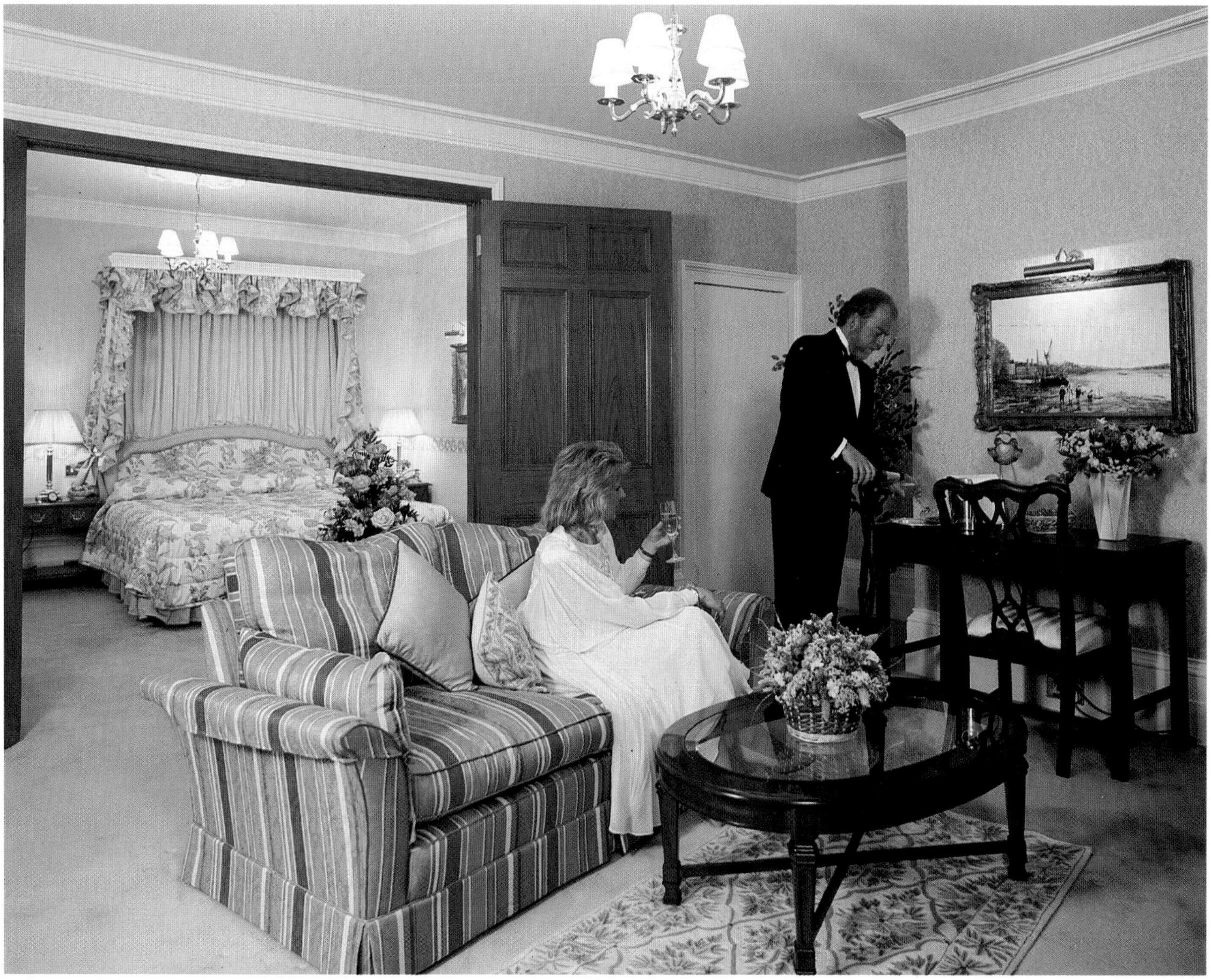

THE ANGEL POSTING HOUSE AND LIVERY

91 THE HIGH STREET, GUILDFORD, SURREY GU1 3DP
TEL: 01483 564555 FAX: 01483 33770 (from April 1997 – 533770)

The Angel, a delightful historic coaching inn on the old Portsmouth road, now a luxurious small hotel, has stood in Guildford High Street since the 16th century. This timber-framed building has welcomed many famous visitors, including Lord Nelson, Jane Austen and Charles Dickens. Today, with easy access to Gatwick, Heathrow, the M4, M3 and M25, The Angel is ideally placed for both business and pleasure. The galleried lounge with its oak-beamed Jacobean fireplace and 17th-century parliament clock is a welcome retreat from the bustle of the nearby shops. The Crypt Restaurant, with its vaulted ceiling and intimate atmosphere, serves a wide choice of superb English and Continental cuisine together with fine wines and impeccable service. The charming bedrooms and suites, decorated with soft furnishings and fabrics, are all unique. Excellent communications, presentation facilities and 24-hour service make this a good choice for business meetings. Private dinners, buffets, dances and wedding receptions can also be catered for. **Directions:** From M3 junction 3 take the A322; or from M25 junction 10 take the A3. The Angel is in the centre of Guildford, within the pedestrian priority area – guests should enquire about vehicle access when booking. Price guide (room only): Double/twin £135–£150; suite £180–£250.

For hotel location, see maps on pages 477-483

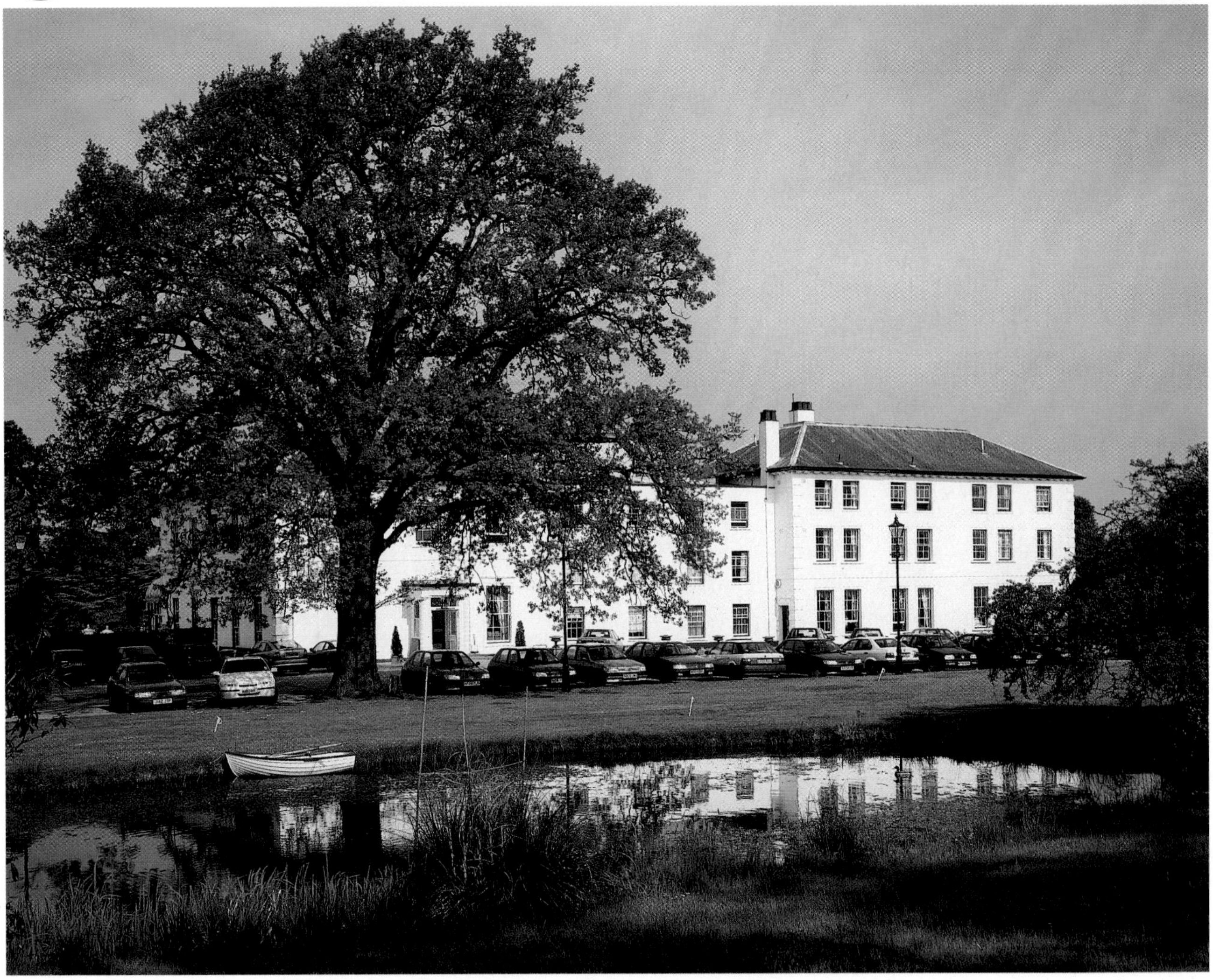

WEST LODGE PARK

COCKFOSTERS ROAD, HADLEY WOOD, BARNET, HERTFORDSHIRE EN4 0PY
TEL: 0181 440 8311 FAX: 0181 449 3698

West Lodge Park is a country house hotel which stands in 34 acres of Green Belt parklands and gardens. These include a lake and an arboretum with hundreds of mature trees. Despite the advantages of this idyllic setting, the hotel is only 1 mile from the M25 and within easy reach of London. Run by the Beale family for 50 years, West Lodge Park was originally a gentleman's country seat, rebuilt in 1838 on the site of an earlier keeper's lodge. In the public rooms, antiques, original paintings and period furnishings create a restful atmosphere, while a Regency style conservatory adds space and offers excellent views over the surrounding countryside. All the bright and individually furnished bedrooms, many of which enjoy country views, have a full range of modern amenities. Well presented cuisine is available in the elegant restaurant. Residents enjoy free membership and a free taxi to the nearby David Lloyd leisure centre, which has excellent facilities. Hatfield House and St Albans Abbey are 15 minutes' drive. The hotel is credited with AA 4 stars and rosette, RAC 4 stars plus 3 merit awards and was the 1995 County Hotel of the Year in the Which? Hotel Guide. **Directions:** The hotel is on A111 one mile north of Cockfosters underground station and one mile south of junction 24 on M25. Price guide: Single £77.50–£112.50; double/twin from £112.50; suites £140–176.50.

For hotel location, see maps on pages 477-483

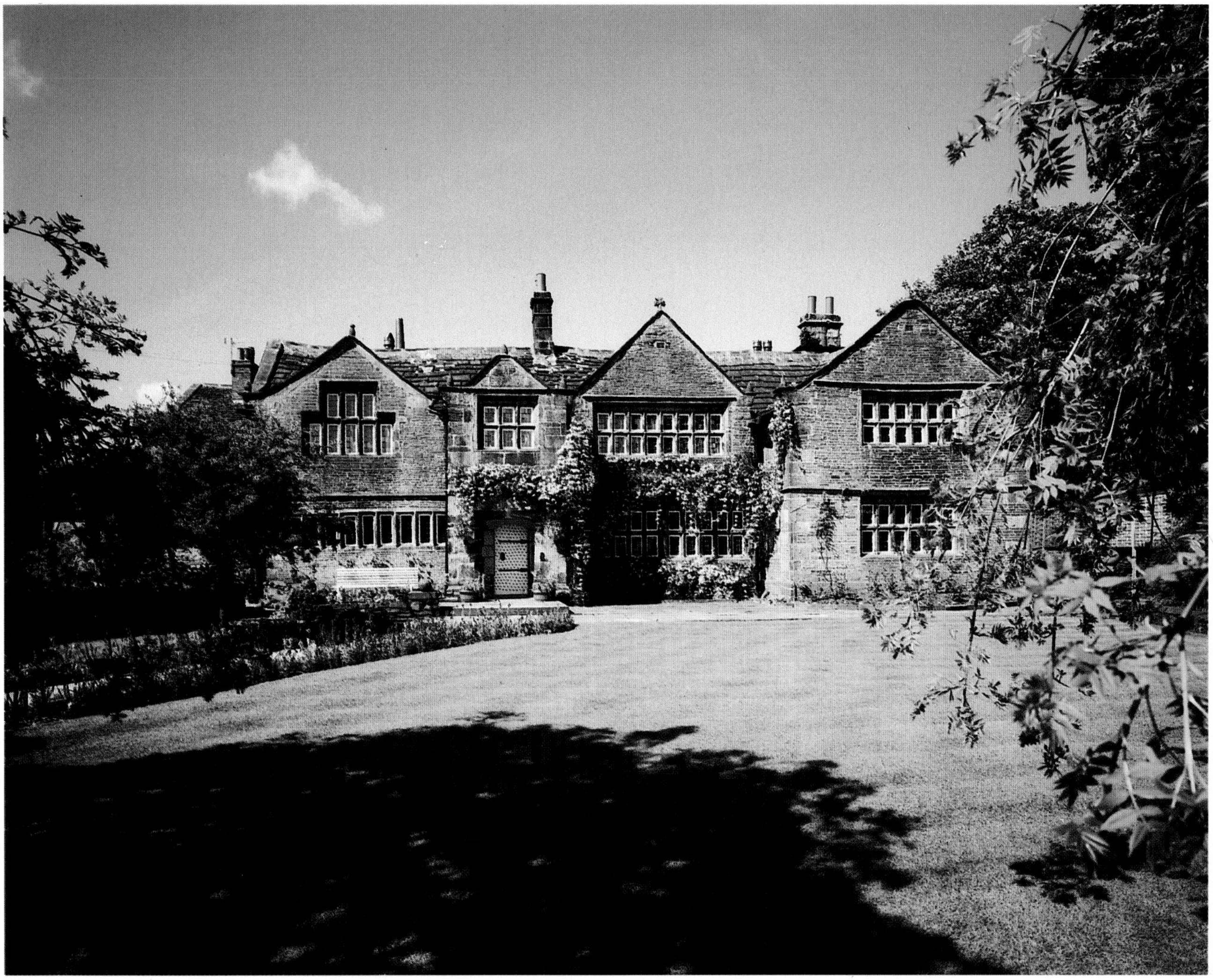

HOLDSWORTH HOUSE

HOLDSWORTH ROAD, HOLMFIELD, HALIFAX, WEST YORKSHIRE HX2 9TG
TEL: 01422 240024 FAX: 01422 245174

Holdsworth House is a retreat of quality and charm standing three miles north of Halifax in the heart of Yorkshire's West Riding. Built in 1633, it was acquired by the Pearson family over 30 years ago. With care, skill and professionalism they have created a hotel and restaurant of considerable repute. The interior of the house, with its polished panelling and open fireplaces, has been carefully preserved and embellished with fine antique furniture and ornaments. The comfortable lounge opens onto a pretty courtyard and overlooks the herb garden and gazebo. The restaurant comprises three beautifully furnished rooms, ideally arranged for private dinner parties. Exciting modern English and continental cuisine is meticulously prepared and presented by Eric Claveau, complemented by a thoughtfully compiled wine list. The restaurant now has two AA Rosettes. Each cosy bedroom has its own style – from the four split-level suites to the two single rooms designed for wheelchair access. This is the perfect base from which to explore the Pennines, the Yorkshire Dales and Haworth – the home of the Brontë family. Closed at Christmas. **Directions:** From M1 junction 42 take M62 westbound to junction 26. Follow A58 to Halifax (ignore signs to town centre). At Burdock Way roundabout take A629 to Keighley; after 1½ miles go right into Shay Lane; hotel is one mile, on right. Price guide: Single £72.50–£82; double/twin £90–£95; suite £110.

For hotel location, see maps on pages 477-483

In association with MasterCard 

THE BALMORAL HOTEL

FRANKLIN MOUNT, HARROGATE, NORTH YORKSHIRE HG1 5EJ
TEL: 01423 508208 FAX: 01423 530652

The Balmoral is a delightful privately owned individual hotel with an award winning garden, near the heart of the elegant spa town of Harrogate. All bedrooms are luxurious with individual decoration and furnishings offering the highest standards of comfort. Nine rooms have beautiful four-posters – each in a different style. For ultimate luxury, The Windsor Suite even boasts its own whirlpool bath. Guests enjoy the fascinating memorabilia on various themes throuhout the Hotel and they can relax in the exquisite Oriental Bar or enjoy a quiet drink in the cosy Snug before taking dinner in Henry's Restaurant. Henry's has a magical theme based on Houdini and enjoys a great reputation for conjuring up the finest modern English cuisine, complemented by an extensive list of predominantly New World wines. Guests can enjoy the use of the Academy – one of the finest Leisure, Health & Fitness Centres in the North, ten minutes from the Hotel. Special Spa Breaks throughout the year. Harrogate is famed for its antique and fashion shops, art galleries and Herriot country, and the many historic homes and castles in the area. **Directions:** From Harogate Conference Centre, follow the Kings Road up, and the hotel is 1/2 mile on the right. Price guide: Single £83.50–£95; double/twin £107–£117; suites £127–£167. Special Breaks available.

For hotel location, see maps on pages 477-483

THE BOAR'S HEAD HOTEL

THE RIPLEY CASTLE ESTATE, HARROGATE, NORTH YORKSHIRE HG3 3AY
TEL: 01423 771888 FAX: 01423 771509

Imagine relaxing in a four star hotel at the centre of a historic 1700 acre private country estate in England's incredibly beautiful North Country. The Ingilby family who have lived in Ripley Castle for 28 generations invite you to enjoy their hospitality at The Boar's Head Hotel. There are 25 luxury bedrooms, individually decorated and furnished, most with king-size beds. The restaurant menu is outstanding, presented by a creative and imaginative kitchen brigade, and complemented by a wide selection of reasonably priced, good quality wines. There is a welcoming bar serving traditional ales straight from the wood, and popular bar meal selections. When staying at The Boar's Head, guests can enjoy complimentary access to the delightful walled gardens and grounds of Ripley Castle, which include the lakes and a deer park. A conference at Ripley is a different experience – using the idyllic meeting facilities available in the castle, organisers and delegates alike will appreciate the peace and tranquility of the location which offers opportunities for all forms of leisure activity outside meeting hours. **Directions:** Ripley is very accessible, just 10 minutes from the conference town of Harrogate, 20 minutes from the motorway network, and Leeds/Bradford Airport, and 40 minutes from the City of York. Price guide: Single £80–£95; double/twin £95–£110.

For hotel location, see maps on pages 477-483

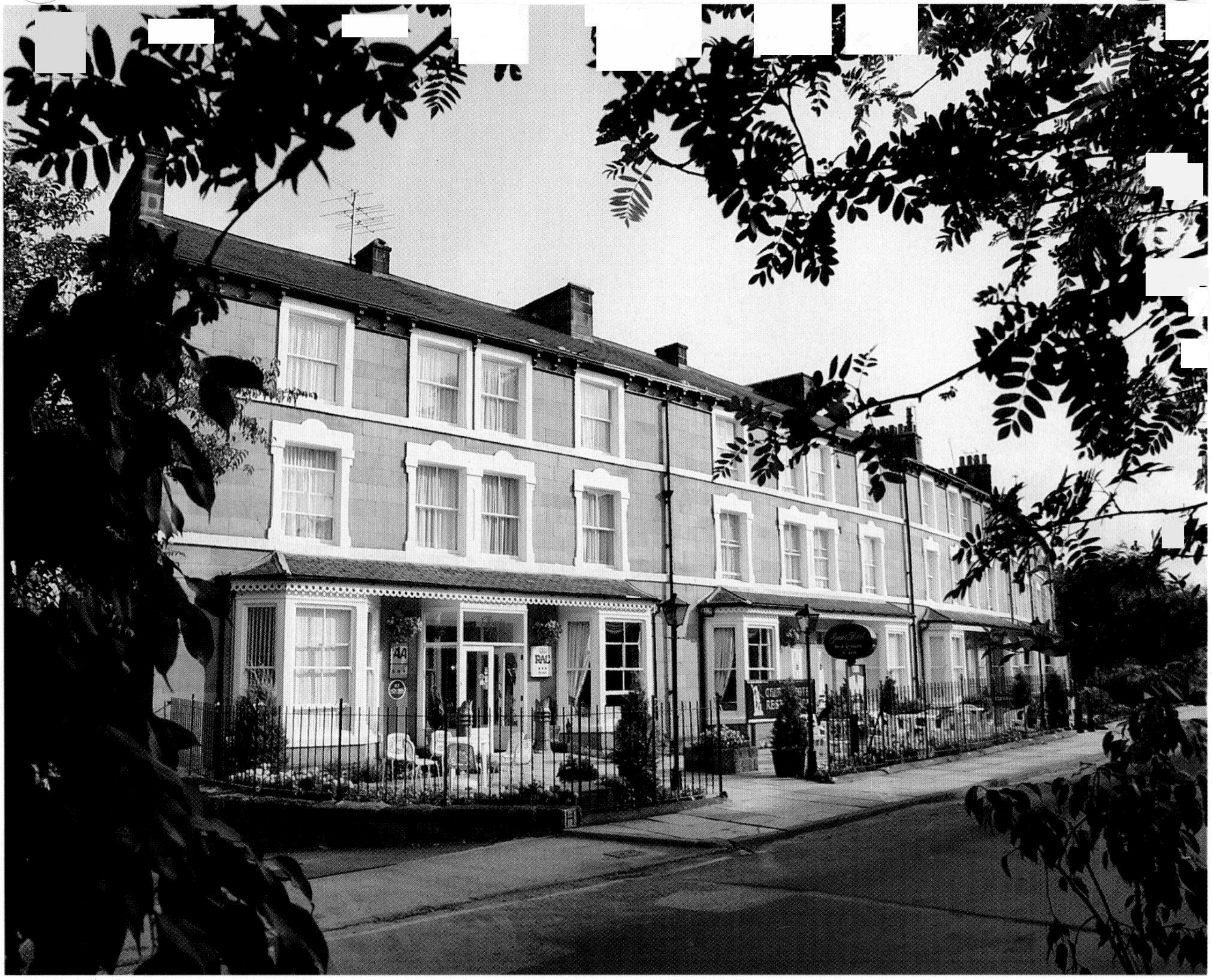

GRANTS HOTEL

SWAN ROAD, HARROGATE, NORTH YORKSHIRE HG1 2SS
TEL: 01423 560666 FAX: 01423 502550

Towards the end of the last century, Harrogate became fashionable among the affluent Victorian gentry, who came to 'take the waters' of the famous spa. Today's visitors have one advantage over their Victorian counterparts – they can enjoy the hospitality of Grants Hotel, the creation of Pam and Peter Grant. The friendly welcome, coupled with high standards of service, ensures a pleasurable stay. All the bedrooms are attractively decorated and have en suite bathrooms. Downstairs, guests can relax in the comfortable lounge or take refreshments out to the terrace gardens. Drinks and light meals are available at all times from the cocktail bar, whereas dinner is a more formal occasion in the air-conditioned Chimney Pots restaurant. Cooking is in the modern English style, with old favourites adapted to accommodate more contemporary tastes – a blend which meets with the approval of local gourmets. Located less than five minutes' walk from Harrogate's Conference and Exhibition Centre, Grants offers its own luxury suite of meeting and syndicate rooms, the Herriot Suite. The Royal Pump Room Museum and the Royal Baths Assembly Rooms are nearby. Guests have free use of "The Academy Health and Leisure Club". **Directions:** Swan Road is in the centre of Harrogate, off the A61 to Ripon. Price guide: Single £92–£99; double/twin £99–£145; suites £148

For hotel location, see maps on pages 477-483

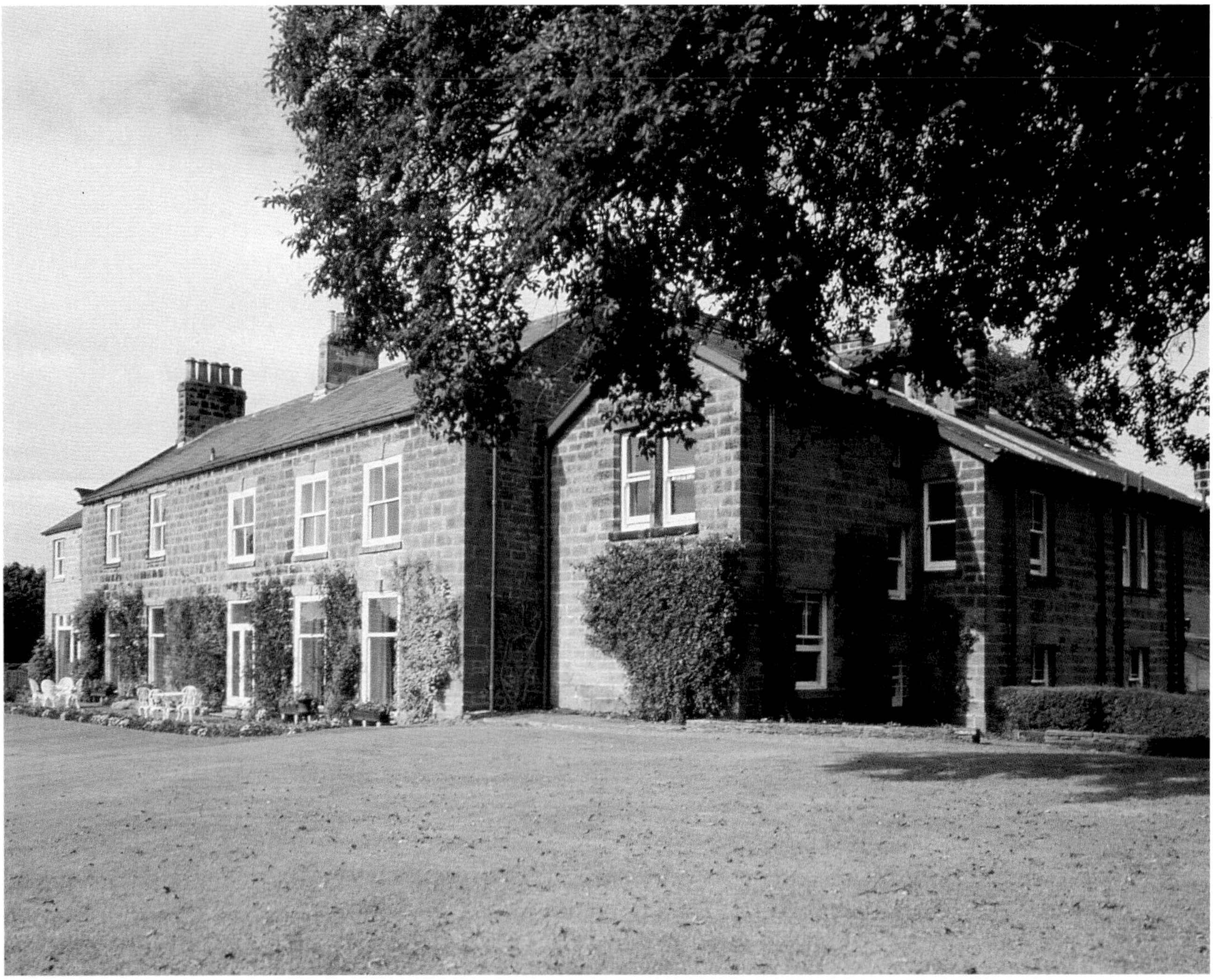

Hob Green Hotel And Restaurant

MARKINGTON, HARROGATE, NORTH YORKSHIRE HG3 3PJ
TEL: 01423 770031 FAX: 01423 771589

Hob Green is a small country house hotel set in 870 acres of farm and woodland. The gardens, which include a croquet lawn, have won awards regularly in the Harrogate District Best Kept Garden Competition. The hall and drawing room are furnished with a combination of antique and contemporary furniture, while glowing fires in the winter months create a warm and welcoming atmosphere. Overlooking manicured lawns, with views towards the ha-ha, fields and woodland, is the restaurant, where guests can enjoy interesting and varied cooking, incorporating fresh vegetables from the garden. The comfortably appointed bedrooms also have fine views. Markington is the perfect setting for equestrian enthusiasts, as the Yorkshire Riding Centre, run by two former Olympic dressage team members, is located in the village and offers some of the best riding facilities in Europe. Golf, fishing, cricket and horse-racing are all within easy reach of the hotel. Fountains Abbey, Markenfield Hall, Ripley Castle and the cathedral cities of York and Ripon are also nearby. **Directions:** Follow the A61 Harrogate–Ripon road for about four miles, then turn left to Markington at Wormald Green. Go through the village of Markington and the hotel is one mile on the left. Price guide: Single £70; double/twin £85–£95; suite £110.

For hotel location, see maps on pages 477-483

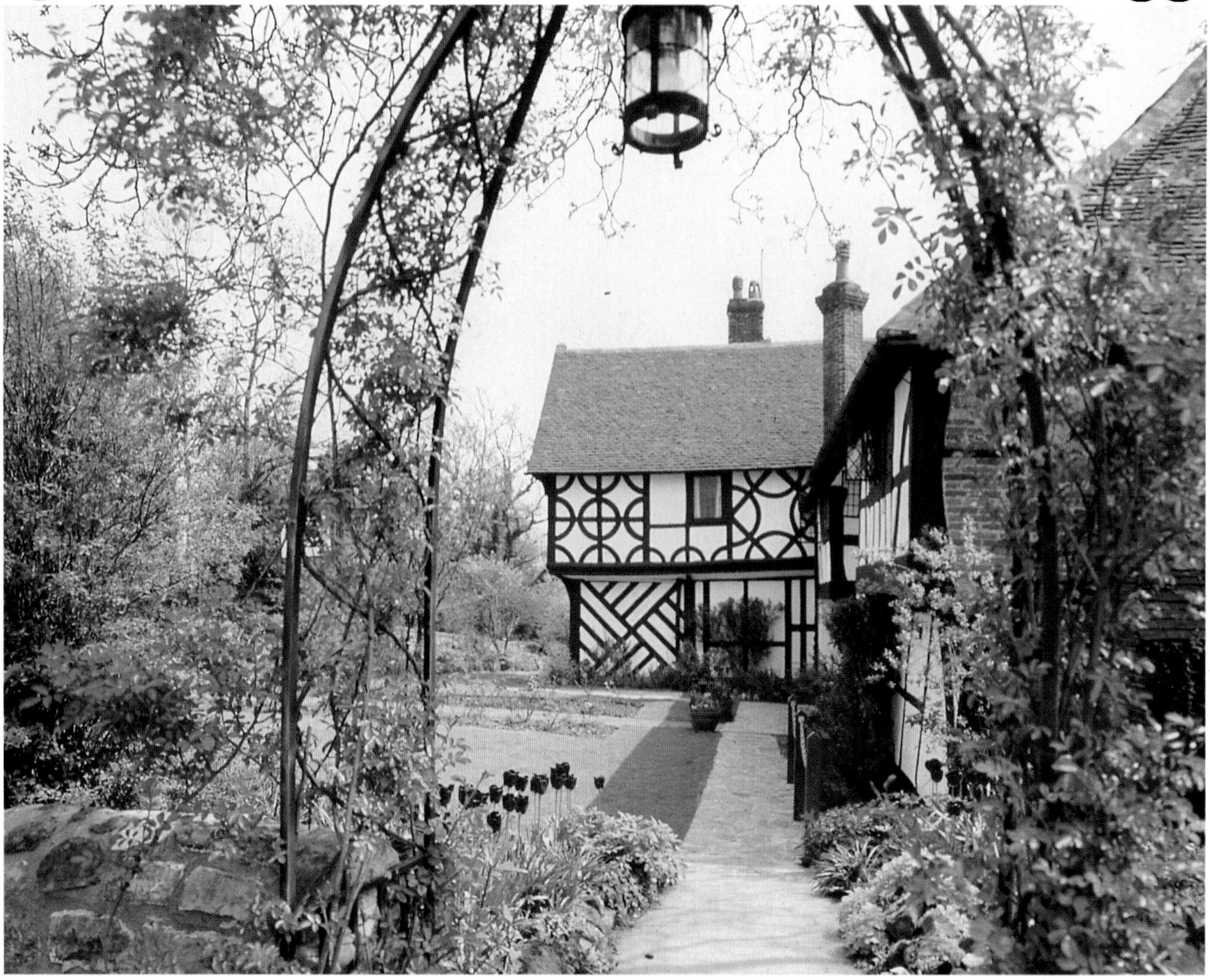

LYTHE HILL HOTEL

PETWORTH ROAD, HASLEMERE, SURREY GU27 3BQ
TEL: 01428 651251 FAX: 01428 644131

Cradled by the Surrey foothills in a tranquil setting is the enchanting Lythe Hill Hotel. It is an unusual cluster of ancient buildings – parts of which date from the 14th century. While most of the beautifully appointed accommodation is in the more recently converted part of the hotel, there are five charming bedrooms in the Tudor House, including the Henry VIII room with a four-poster bed dated 1614! There are two delightful restaurants, the Auberge de France offers classic French cuisine in the oak-panelled room which overlooks the lake and parklands, and the 'Dining Room' has the choice of imaginative English fayre. An exceptional wine list offers over 200 wines from more than a dozen countries. Its situation, easily accessible from London, Gatwick and Heathrow. An excellent train service at Haslemere makes both central London and Portsmouth less than one hour away. National Trust hillside adjoining the hotel grounds provides interesting walking and views over the surrounding countryside. The area is steeped in history, with the country houses of Petworth, Clandon and Uppark to visit as well as racing at Goodwood and polo at Cowdray Park. Brighton and the south coast are only a few miles away. **Directions:** Lythe Hill lies about $1\frac{1}{2}$ miles from the centre of Haslemere, east on the B2131. Price guide: Single from £84; double/twin from £95; suite from£135.

For hotel location, see maps on pages 477-483

Bel Alp House

HAYTOR, NR BOVEY TRACEY, SOUTH DEVON TQ13 9XX
TEL: 01364 661217 FAX: 01364 661292

Peace and seclusion are guaranteed at the Bel Alp House with its spectacular outlook from the edge of Dartmoor across a rolling patchwork of fields and woodland to the sea, 20 miles away. Built as an Edwardian country mansion and owned in the 1920s by millionairess Dame Violet Wills, Bel Alp has been lovingly restored and the proprietors' personal attention ensures their guests' enjoyment and comfort in the atmosphere of a private home. Sarah takes charge of the cooking and the set dinner is changed nightly. The set dinner is changed nightly, using only the best local produce, and the meals are accompanied by a well-chosen and comprehensive wine list. Of the nine en suite bedrooms, two still have their original Edwardian basins and baths mounted on marble plinths, and all have views over the gardens. An abundance of house plants, open log fires and restful colours complements the family antiques and pictures to create the perfect environment in which to relax. AA Rosette. Bel Alp is ideally situated for exploring Devon and parts of Cornwall: Plymouth, famed for Drake and the Pilgrim Fathers, Exeter with its Norman cathedral, and National Trust properties Castle Drogo and Cotehele Manor House are all within an hour's drive. **Directions:** Bel Alp is off the B3387 Haytor road, 2½ miles from Bovey Tracey. Price guide: Single £78–£87; double/twin £120–£156.

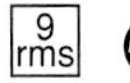

For hotel location, see maps on pages 477-483

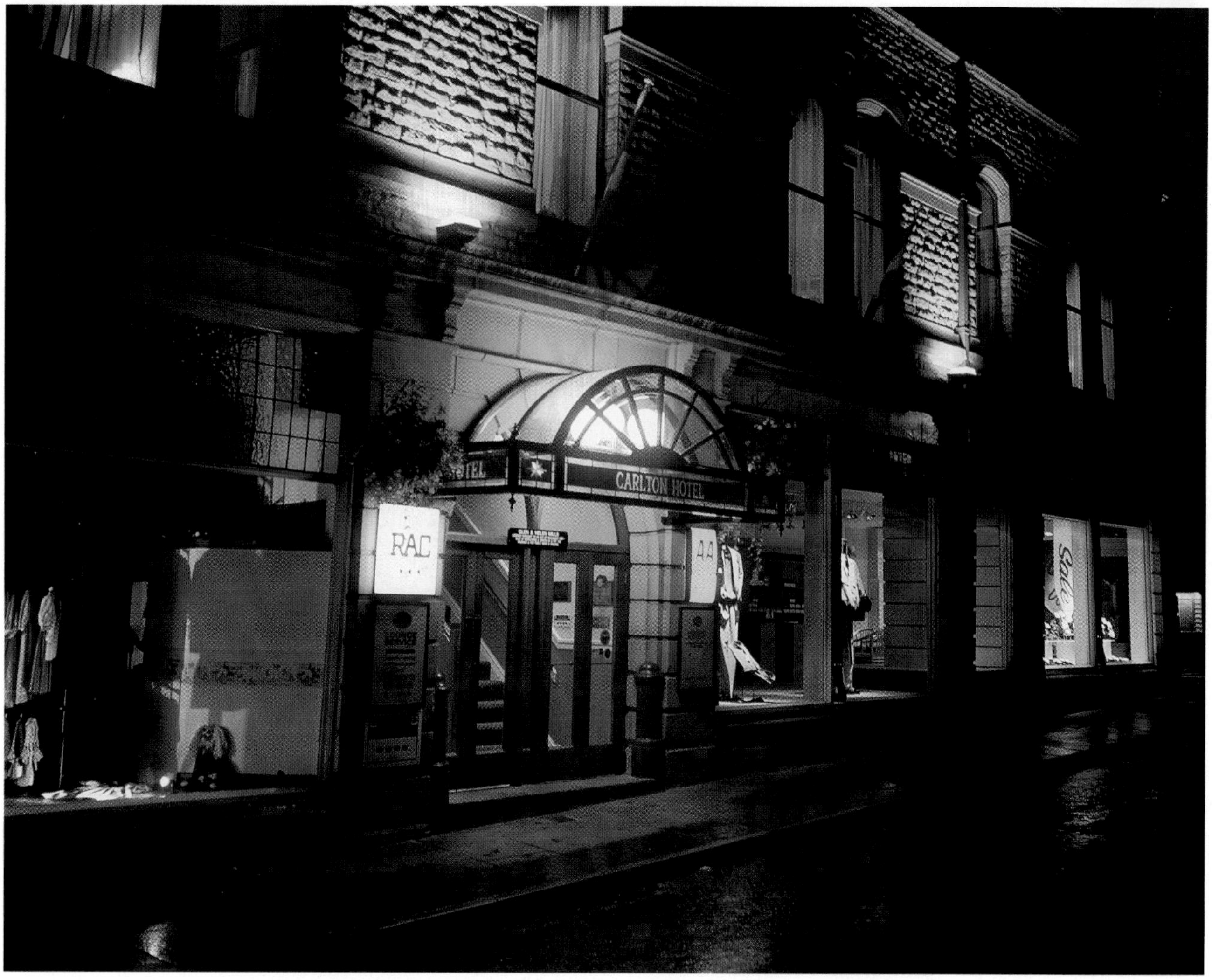

THE CARLTON HOTEL

ALBERT STREET, HEBDEN BRIDGE, WEST YORKSHIRE HX7 8ES
TEL: 01422 844400 FAX: 01422 843117

The Carlton is an unusual town house hotel, centrally situated on the first and second floors of the old Co-operative Society building, dating from 1867. Following a full refurbishment of this Victorian emporium, The Carlton Hotel was able to continue serving the local community, while also attracting a much wider, international clientèle. A lift takes visitors from the entrance hall up to the elegant reception area where a friendly welcome waits. The 18 en suite bedrooms are individually appointed with attractive furnishings, satellite T.V. and hospitality bars. In the Hawkstones Restaurant imaginative menus combining European and traditionally English food are prepared daily by the kitchen team under the direction of head chef Earl McIniess. As an alternative to the restaurant a fine selection of hearty bar snacks is available daily in the Wragley Bar. Conference parties and banquets can be accommodated in the Hardcastle Suite. Situated at the head of the Calder Valley, Hebden Bridge is a thriving mill town, with a motor car museum and many quaint antique and craft shops. The hotel is well placed for walkers to explore the Yorkshire Dales and nearby Howarth. Special weekend breaks available. **Directions:** Entering Hebden Bridge on the A646, turn down Hope Street, which runs into Albert Street. The hotel is on the left. Price guide: Single £49–£75; double/twin £69–£89.

For hotel location, see maps on pages 477-483

THE PHEASANT

HAROME, HELMSLEY, NORTH YORKSHIRE YO6 5JG
TEL: 01439 771241/770416 FAX:01439 771744

The Pheasant, rich in oak beams and open log fires, offers two types of accommodation, some in the hotel and some in a charming, 16th century thatched cottage. The Binks family, who built the hotel and now own and manage it, have created a friendly atmosphere which is part of the warm Yorkshire welcome all guests receive. The bedrooms and suites are brightly decorated in an attractive, cottage style and all are complete with en suite facilities. Traditional English cooking is the speciality of the restaurant, many of the dishes prepared using fresh fruit and vegetables grown in the hotel gardens. During the summer, guests may chat or relax on the terrace overlooking the pond. The opening of a new indoor heated swimming pool is an added attraction. Other sporting activities available locally include swimming, riding, golf and fishing. York is a short drive away, as are a host of historic landmarks including Byland and Rievaulx Abbeys and Castle Howard of *Brideshead Revisited* fame. Also nearby is the magnificent North York Moors National Park. Dogs by arrangement. Closed Christmas, January and February. **Directions:** From Helmsley, take the A170 towards Scarborough; after 1/4 mile turn right for Harome. Hotel is near the church in the village. Price guide: Single £55–£65; double/twin £110–£130. (Including five-course dinner).

For hotel location, see maps on pages 477-483

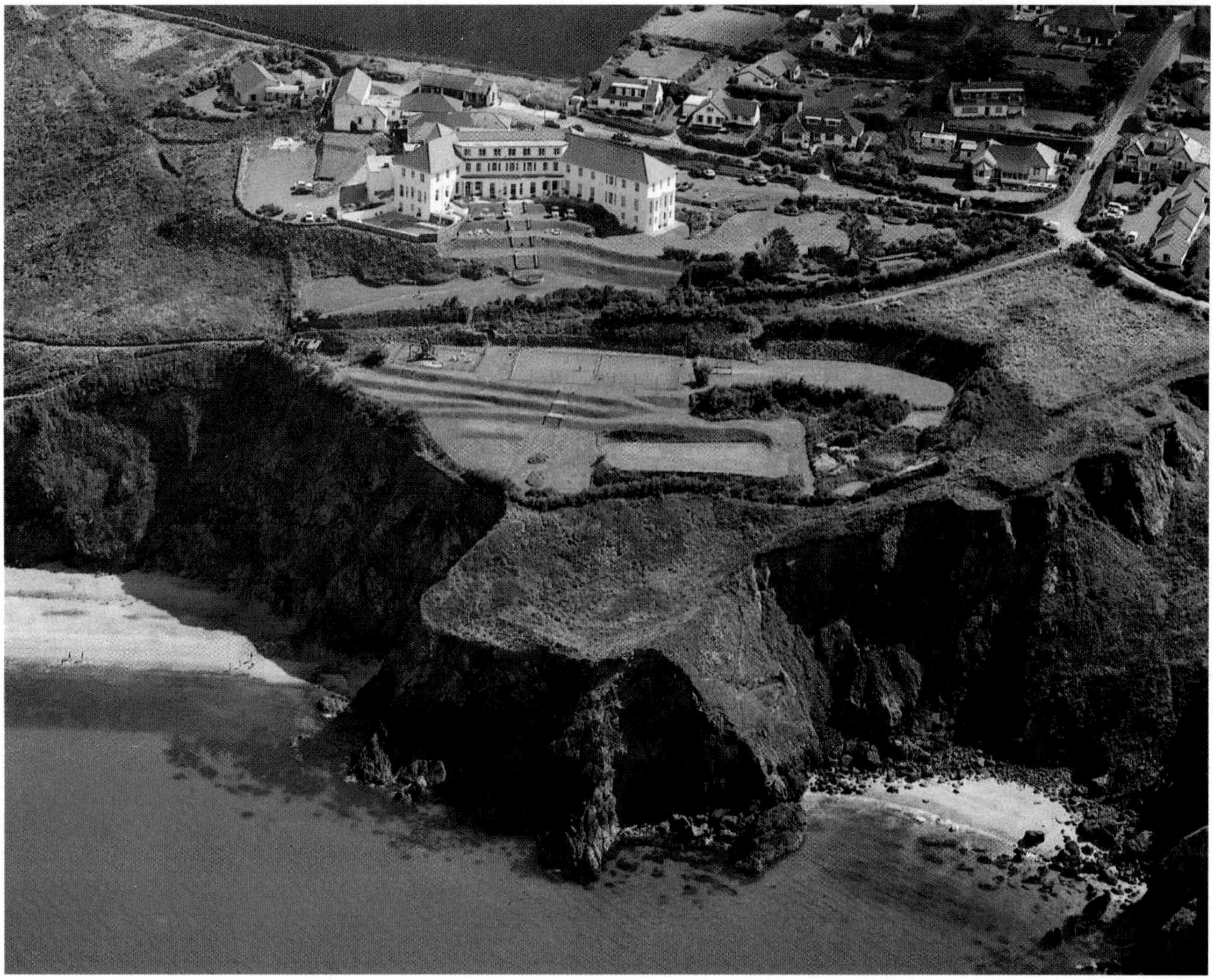

The Polurrian Hotel

MULLION, LIZARD PENINSULA, SOUTH CORNWALL TR12 7EN
TEL: 01326 240421 FAX: 01326 240083

The Polurrian Hotel, a building of splendid Edwardian elegance perched on 300 feet high cliffs, is set in beautiful landscaped gardens and surrounded by National Trust coastline. Comfort is the key and there are a host of modern amenities including a baby-listening device. Daily changing, four course menus offer excellent food, with fresh fish among the specialities. Guests are invited to take advantage of the luxurious Leisure Club where there is a heated pool, solarium, sauna and gym. Other activities within the hotel and its grounds include tennis, badminton, snooker, croquet and squash. The pleasures of the 18-hole Mullion golf course are just two miles away. Polurrian Hotel also offers a number of self-catering bungalows and apartments. Places of interest nearby include RNAS Culdrose, home of the Sea King helicopters, Goonhilly Earth Station, The Lizard, Gweek Seal Sanctuary, and Land's End. There are plenty of leisure activities available in the vicinity, such as fishing, sailing and spectacular coastal walks. **Directions:** From Helston follow A3083 towards the The Lizard. After six miles turn right onto the B3296 to Mullion. Price guide (including dinner): Single £42–£86; double/twin £84–£172; suites £116–£184.

For hotel location, see maps on pages 477-483

STOCKS

STOCKS ROAD, ALDBURY, NR TRING, HERTFORDSHIRE HP23 5RX
TEL: 01442 851 341 FAX: 01442 851 253

Set amidst 10,000 acres of National Trust property Stocks nestles in 182 acres of beautiful parkland on the edge of the Chiltern Hills. This Georgian Mansion, built in 1773, boasts 18 individually furnished bedrooms most of which offer excellent views. The Tapestry Restaurant, with its intricate plasterwork and tapestries, offers fine dining from the à la carte & table d'hôte menus, whilst the Orangery Restaurant provides a more informal dining atmosphere. Guests have access to an excellent combination of leisure activities, comprising an outdoor heated swimming pool (May to September), reputedly the largest Jacuzzi in England, gymnasium, four all weather tennis courts, sauna, steam room, solarium and full size snooker table. On-site Riding and Livery Stables offer equine persuits from show jumping lessons to hacking in Ashbridge Forest. Stocks Golf Club features a challenging parkland course (SSS 74) 7016 yards and a fully equipped pro-shop. A team of qualified PGA professionals will improve skill and add to pleasure. Local attractions include Woburn Safari Park, Whipsnade Zoo, Grand Union Canal and the Ridgeway Path. **Directions:** Leave M1 at J8 or M25 at J20 and head for Hemel Hempstead and Tring on A41. In Tring turn right towards Tring station. Aldbury is one mile past Tring station. Price guide: Single £60.00; double/twin £80-£100; suite £110

For hotel location, see maps on pages 477-483

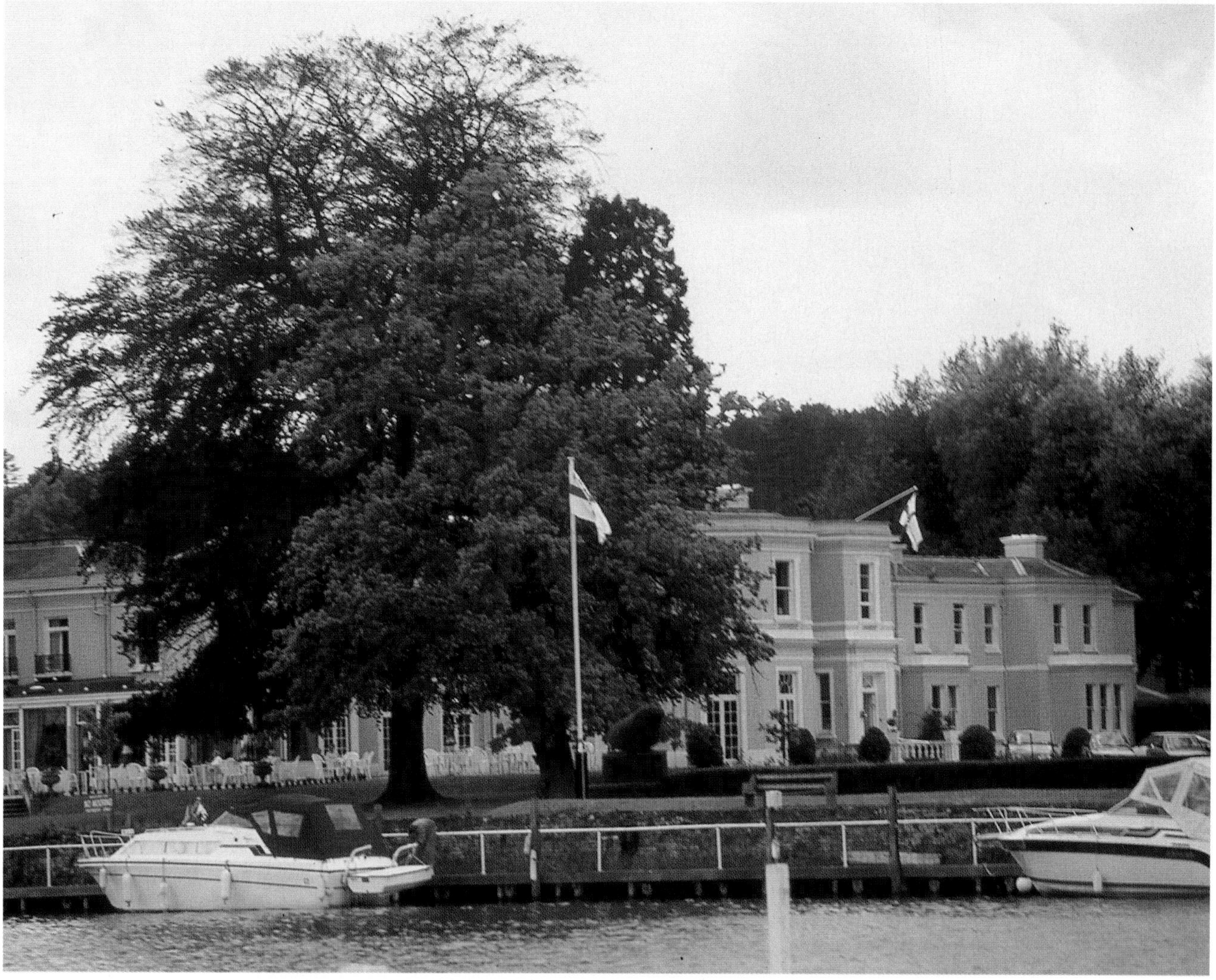

PHYLLIS COURT CLUB

MARLOW ROAD, HENLEY-ON-THAMES, OXFORDSHIRE RG9 2HT
TEL: 01491 574366 FAX: 01491 410725

Founded in 1906 by the owner of the house and a group of friends and London businessmen, the Club has an intriguing history spanning six centuries and involving royal patronage. Phyllis Court occupies an unrivalled position on the banks of the Thames, and overlooking the Henley Royal Regatta course. Phyllis Court prides itself on retaining the traditions of its illustrious past while guests today who now stay in this fine historic residence can in modern times enjoy the highest standards of up to date hospitality. Oliver Cromwell slept here and he built the embankment wall; and it was here that William II held his first Royal Court. Years later, when the name Henley became synonymous with rowing, there came as patrons of the Royal Regatta Prince Albert, King George V and Edward, Prince of Wales. The character of the place remains unaltered in its hallowed setting, but the comfortable bedrooms, the restaurant, the "cellar" and the entire complement of amenities are of the latest high quality. What is more, they are available for all. Likely to be fully booked far ahead during the season. Ideal for meetings, functions and wedding parties. **Directions:** M40 junction 4 to Marlow or M4 junction 8/9 then follow signposts to Henley-on-Thames. Price guide: Single £73; twin/double £85.

For hotel location, see maps on pages 477-483

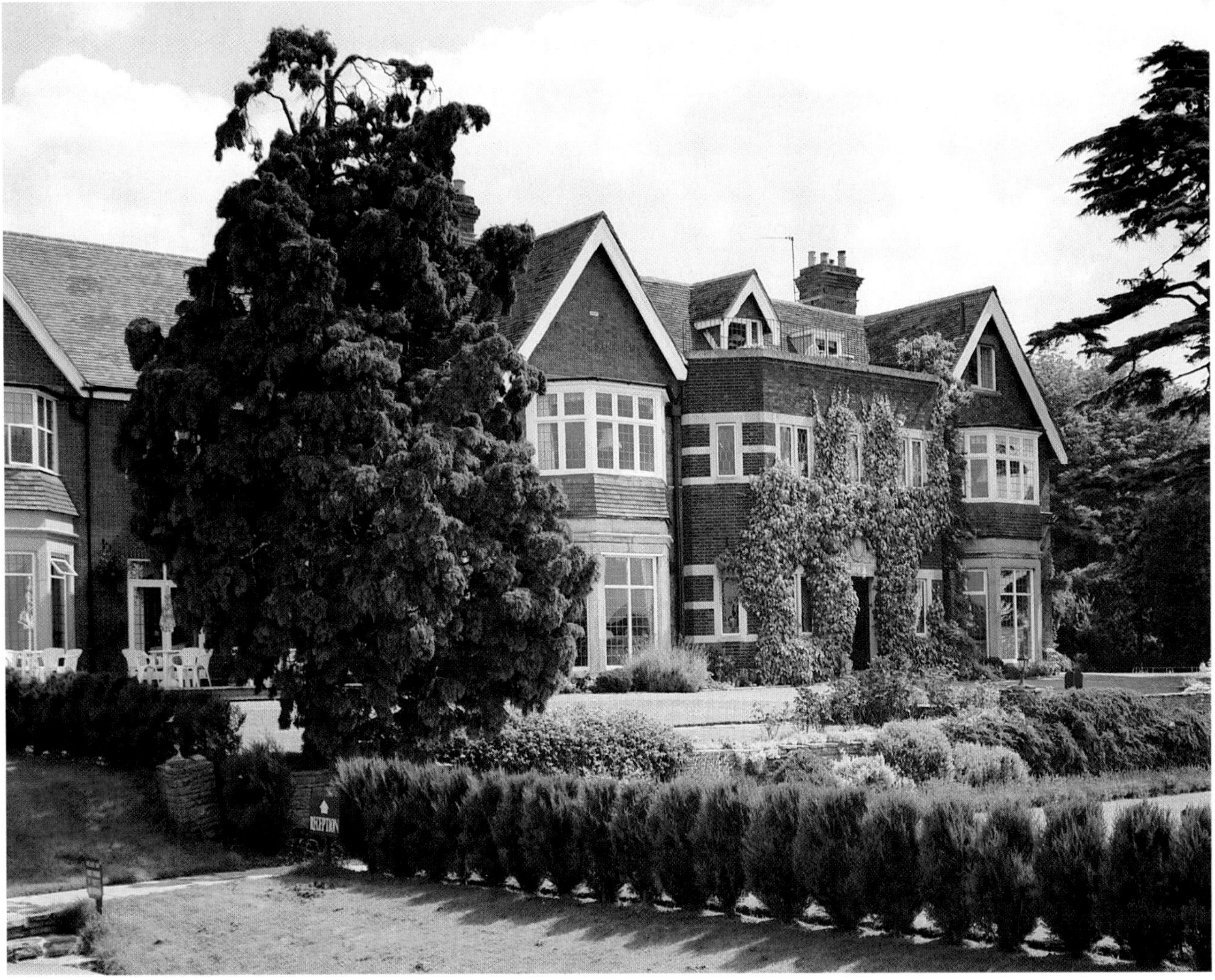

NUTHURST GRANGE

HOCKLEY HEATH, WARWICKSHIRE B94 5NL
TEL: 01564 783972 FAX: 01564 783919

The most memorable feature of this friendly country house hotel is its outstanding restaurant. Chef-patron David Randolph and his team have won many accolades for their imaginative menus, described as 'English, cooked in the light French style'. Diners can enjoy their superb cuisine in the three adjoining rooms which comprise the restaurant and form the heart of Nuthurst Grange. The rest of the house is no less charming – the spacious bedrooms have a country house atmosphere and are appointed with extra luxuries such as an exhilarating air-spa bath, a trouser press, hairdryer and a safe for valuables. For special occasions there is a room furnished with a four-poster bed and a marble bathroom. There are fine views across the 7½ acres of landscaped gardens. Executive meetings can be accommodated at Nuthurst Grange – within a 12-mile radius of the hotel lie Central Birmingham, the NEC, Stratford-upon-Avon, Coventry and Birmingham International Airport. Sporting activities available nearby include golf, canal boating and tennis. **Directions:** From M42 exit 4 take A3400 signposted Hockley Heath (2 miles, south). Entrance to Nuthurst Grange Lane is ¼ mile south of village. Also, M40 (exit 16 – southbound only), take first left, entrance 300 yards. Price guide: Single £95; double/twin £115–£130; suite £140.

For hotel location, see maps on pages 477-483

SOUTH LODGE HOTEL

LOWER BEEDING, NR HORSHAM, WEST SUSSEX RH13 6PS
TEL: 01403 891711 FAX: 01403 891766

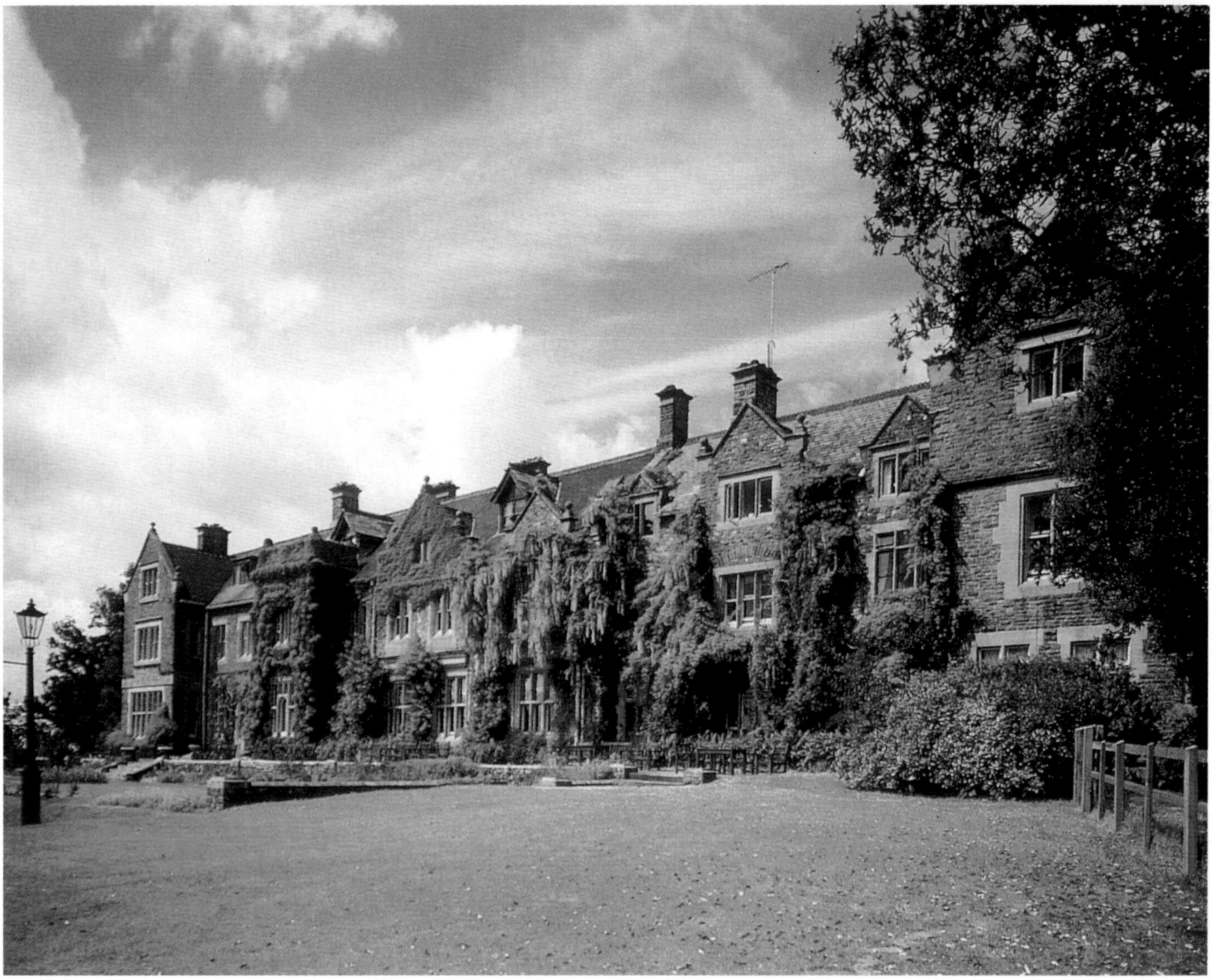

From its elevated position in the heart of West Sussex, South Lodge has commanding views over the rolling South Downs. The house was originally built as a family home by Frederick Ducane Godman, an eminent 19th-century botanist and explorer, and the hotel's 90-acre grounds are evidence of his abiding passion – many of the shrubs and trees were planted by him. The hotel prides itself on the warm welcome extended to guests, ensuring a memorable stay. Wood panelling and open fires in the reception rooms create an atmosphere of comfortable elegance and the luxuriously appointed bedrooms offer every modern amenity. From the south-facing dining room there are views over the rolling Sussex countryside, from where comes much of what features on the menu, perfectly complemented by a comprehensive yet carefully chosen wine list. Private and business functions can be catered for in one of the private rooms. South Lodge offers a wide variety of sporting and leisure facilities, including croquet, tennis and clay pigeon shooting, golf at Mannings Heath just minutes from the hotel, fishing and riding. Nearby attractions include Glyndebourne and Chartwell, Leonardslee gardens and racing at Goodwood, Plumpton and Brighton. **Directions:** South Lodge is situated on the A 281 at Lower Beeding, south of Horsham. Price guide: Single from £110; double/twin from £135; suite from £255.

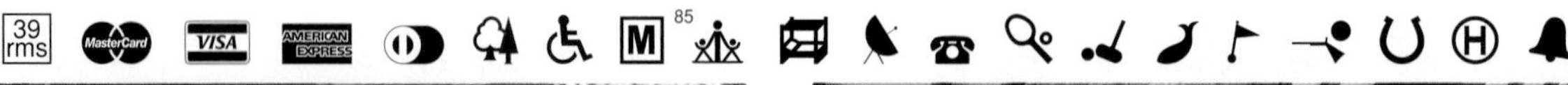

For hotel location, see maps on pages 477-483

THE WORSLEY ARMS HOTEL

HOVINGHAM, YORK, NORTH YORKSHIRE YO6 4LA
TEL: 01653 628234 FAX: 01653 628130

The Worsley Arms is an attractive stone-built Victorian coaching inn in the heart of Hovingham, a pleasant and unspoiled Yorkshire village with a history stretching back to Roman times. The hotel, which overlooks the village green and is set amid delightful gardens, was built in 1841 by the baronet Sir William Worsley and is now owned and personally run by Euan and Debbi Rodger. Hovingham Hall the Worsley family and childhood home of the Duchess of Kent is nearby. Elegant furnishings and open fires create a welcoming atmosphere. The spacious sitting rooms are an ideal place to relax over morning coffee or afternoon tea. The award-winning Wyvern Restaurant (2 AA Rosettes) offers creatively prepared dishes, including game from the estate, cooked and presented with flair. The Cricketers Bistro provides a more informal setting to enjoy modern cooking at its best. The en suite bedrooms range in size and are all prettily decorated with room service available. There is plenty to do nearby, including tennis, squash, jogging, golf and scenic walks along nature trails. Guests can explore the beauty of the Dales and the spectacular coastline or discover the historic abbeys, stately homes and castles nearby like Castle Howard just five miles away. **Directions:** Hovingham is on the B1257, eight miles from Malton and Helmsley. Price guide: (including dinner) Single £80; double/twin £120.

19 rms MasterCard VISA AMERICAN EXPRESS M 50

For hotel location, see maps on pages 477-483

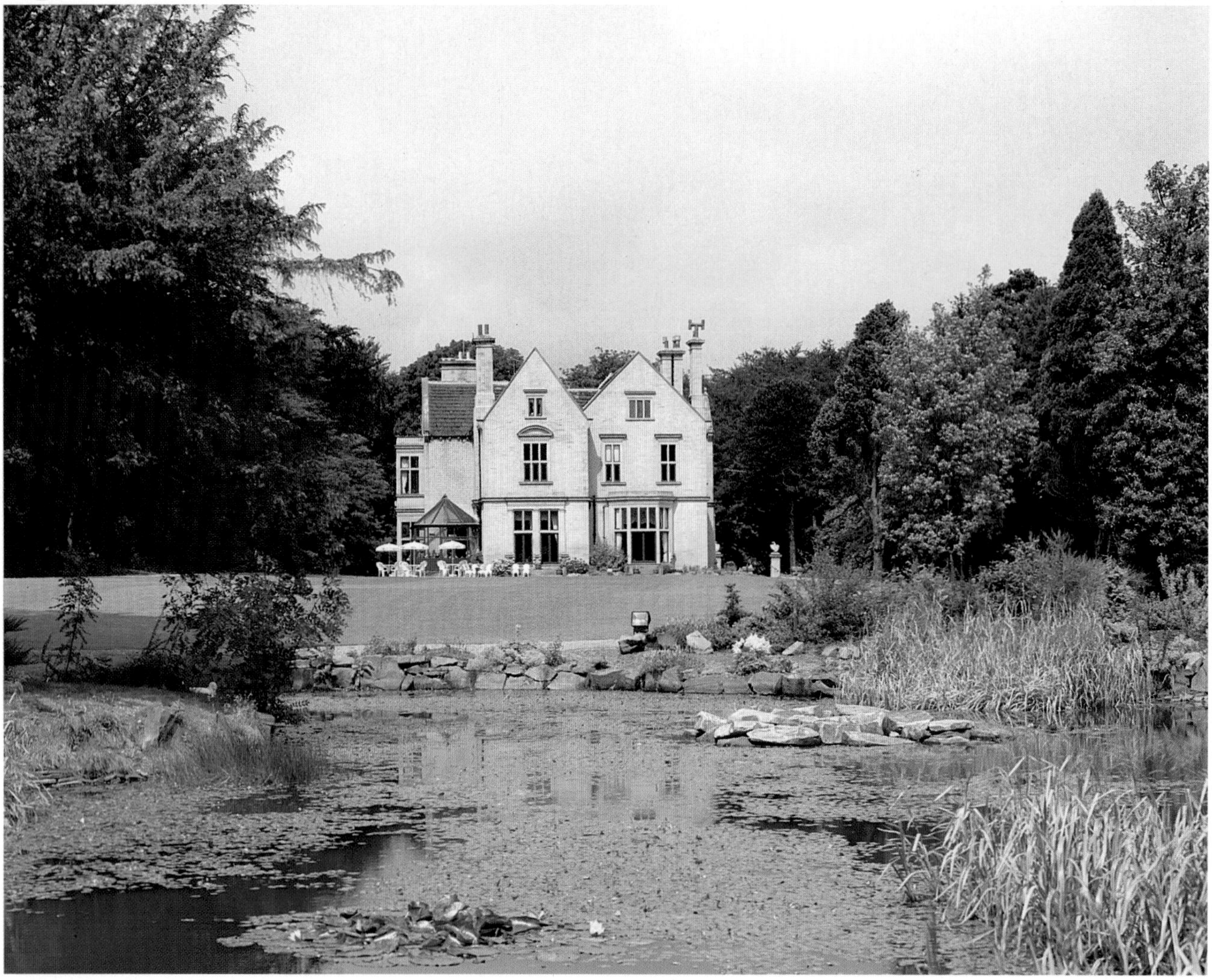

BAGDEN HALL HOTEL & GOLF COURSE

WAKEFIELD ROAD, SCISSETT, NR HUDDERSFIELD, WEST YORKSHIRE HD8 9LE
TEL: 01484 865330 FAX: 01484 861001

Bagden Hall is set in 40 acres of parkland, yet less than 10 minutes from the M1. It was built in the mid-19th century by local mill owner George Norton as a home for his family, whose portraits still hang in the foyer. Lovingly restored by current owners the Braithwaite family, Bagden has been transformed into an elegant hotel. The grounds comprise magnificent lawns, superb landscaped gardens, a lake and an 18th century boathouse. Inside, the hotel has recently undergone a major programme of renovation and now has all the facilities one would expect of a modern hotel while retaining its original character. Each of the 17 bedrooms – one with four-poster – has en suite facilities. The oak-panelled lounge bar and conservatory have views over the lawns to the lake, an ideal setting for a drink before moving on to the Glendale Restaurant. Here, traditional and modern English food with classical French influences is served amid tasteful surroundings. There is a fine wine list to complement the food. For golfers, there is a 9-hole par 3/4 golf course on site. Conference facilities are available. **Directions:** From south, leave M1 at junction 38, taking A637 towards Huddersfield. Take A636 to Denby Dale. From north, leave M1 at junction 39, taking A636 to Denby Dale. Hotel is 1/2 mile through Clayton West on left. Price guide: Single £60–£65; double/twin £80–£110.

For hotel location, see maps on pages 477-483

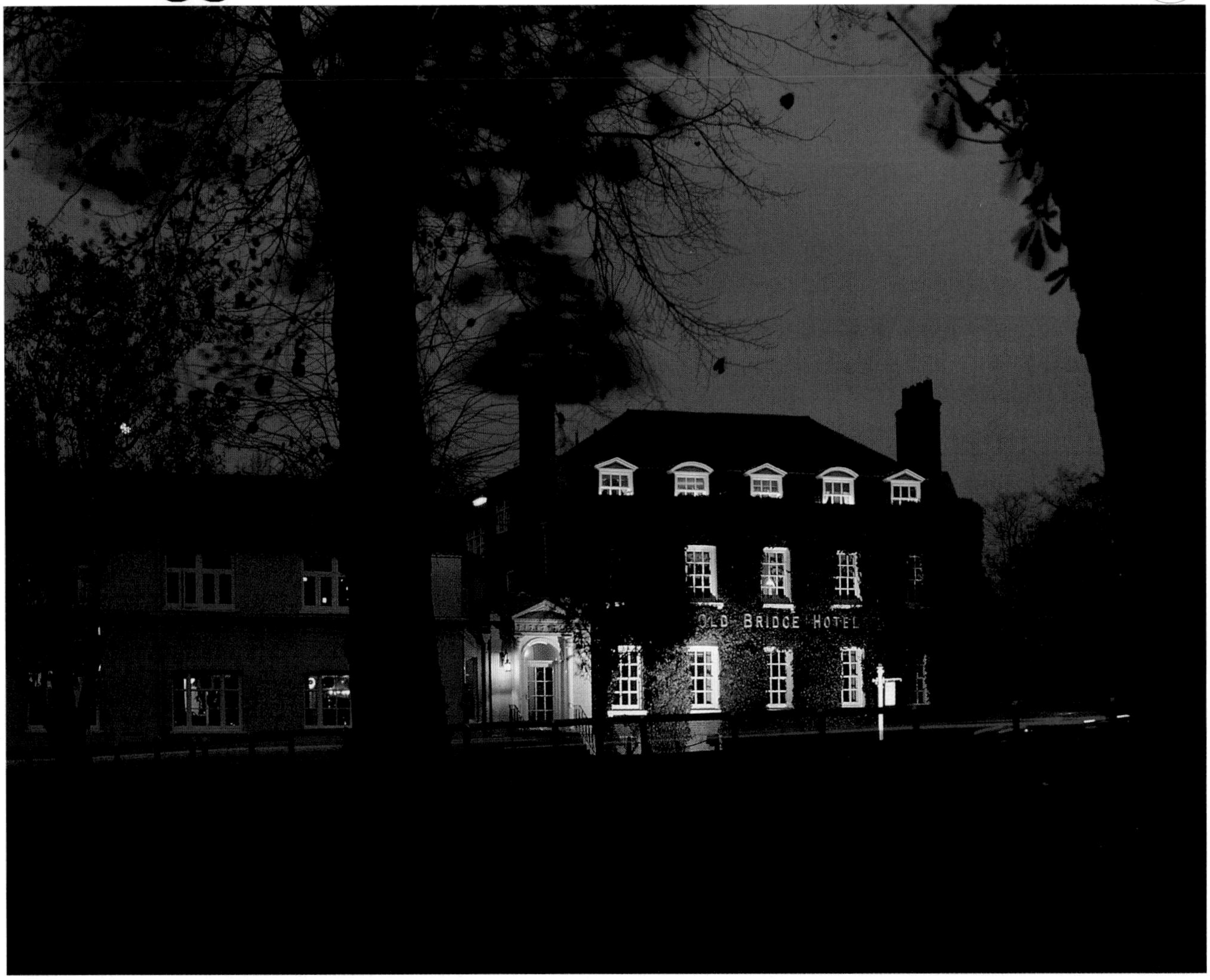

The Old Bridge Hotel

1 HIGH STREET, HUNTINGDON, CAMBRIDGESHIRE PE18 6TQ
TEL: 01480 452681 FAX: 01480 411017

The Old Bridge is a handsome, 18th-century edifice standing on the banks of the River Ouse close to the centre of Huntingdon, a thriving market town and the birthplace of Oliver Cromwell. The hotel has been decorated in keeping with its original character. In the panelled dining room and main lounge, sumptuous fabrics, quality prints and beautiful furnishings impart a sense of elegance. Each of the 26 guest rooms is unique in its style and décor – all have been luxuriously appointed with every attention to detail, and with a full complement of facilities. The menu exemplifies British cooking at its best – traditional dishes are interpreted with imagination and flair, and is balanced by an exceptional and award winning wine list. The restaurant menu is also offered in the more informal setting of The Terrace which has a delightful series of murals painted by Julia Rushbury. Private parties or business lunches can be accommodated in the Cromwell Room and a fully integrated business centre is available for executive meetings. Guests can enjoy boating trips from the private jetty or visit nearby Cambridge, Ely and Newmarket. **Directions:** Situated off the A1 where it joins both the A1–M1 link and the M11/A14. The hotel is just off the inner ring road. Price guide: Single £69.50; double/twin £85–£120.

For hotel location, see maps on pages 477-483

Ye Olde Bell

HIGH STREET, HURLEY, BERKSHIRE SL6 5LX
TEL: 01628 825881 FAX: 01628 825939

Built in 1135 as the guest house for a 12th century Benedictine Monastery, Ye Olde Bell is reputed to be the oldest inn in England. It prides itself on living up to the old monastic rule that visitors must be received with warmth and respect – the service is excellent. The bedrooms, which include three with four poster beds, have wooden beams, leaded windows and comfortable chairs. Despite a delightful ambience of days gone by, they nevertheless offer a full range of modern amenities such as remote control satellite TV, hairdryer, trouser press, mini bar and tea and coffee making facilities. 'No smoking' rooms are available and baby sitting can be arranged. In the bar guests can relax in front of an open fire and enjoy a quiet drink before moving into the restaurant. Here they can enjoy a full range of traditional and continental dishes which have won the award of an AA Rosette. Modern hi-tech telecommunications systems and their associated paraphernalia are discreetly hidden in oak timbers, knarled floors and rafters so that business meetings can take place in this charming old inn. Rowing along the river can be arranged and boat trips. A host of attractions nearby include Windsor, Henley-on-Thames, Marlow, Royal Ascot Racecourse and Cliveden. **Directions:** From M40 exit 4 follow signs to Henley-on-Thames. The hotel is in the village of Hurley. Price guide: Single £99; double/twin £115; suites £150.

41 rms

For hotel location, see maps on pages 477-483

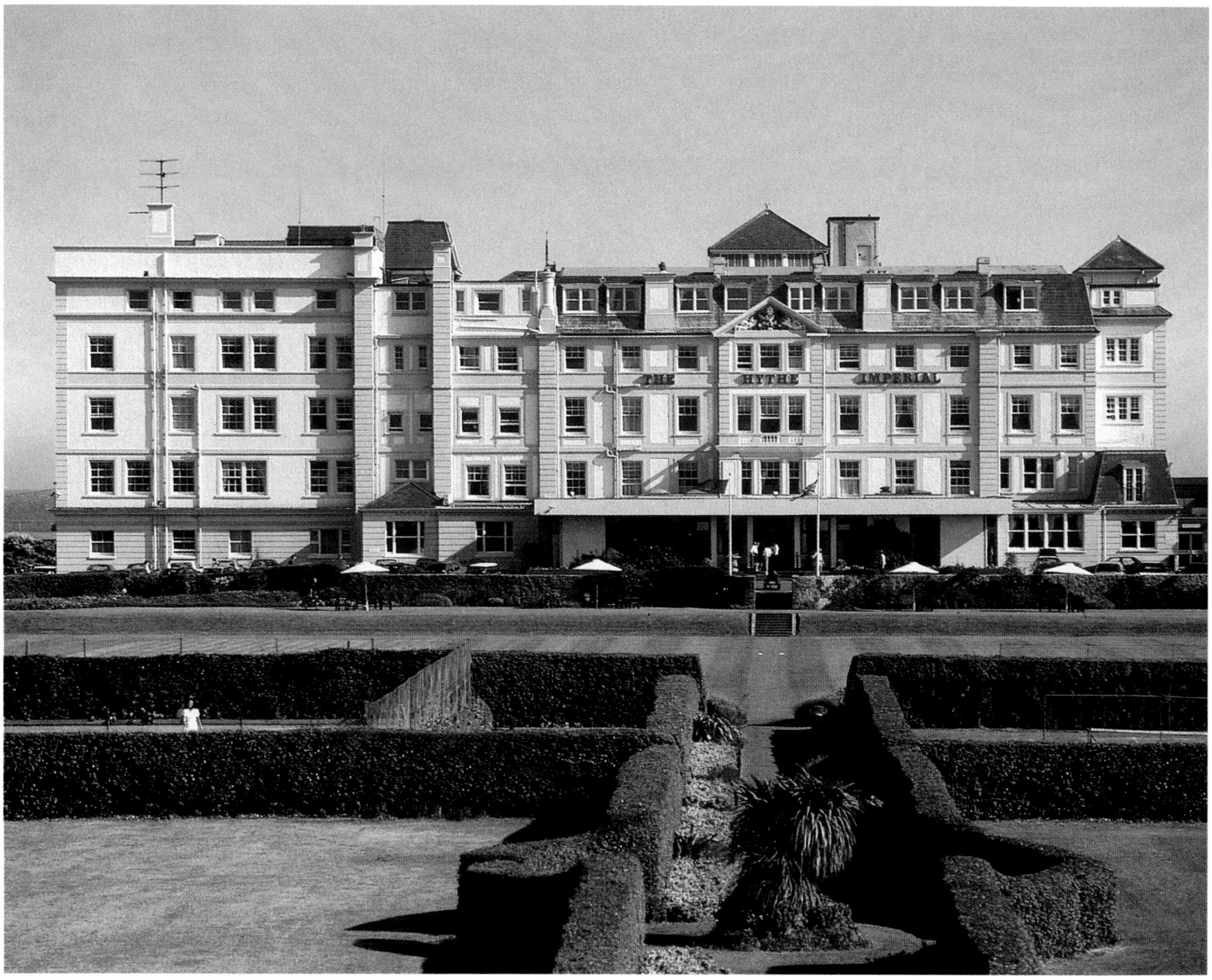

THE HYTHE IMPERIAL

PRINCE'S PARADE, HYTHE, KENT CT21 6AE
TEL: 01303 267441 FAX: 01303 264610

The imposing Hythe Imperial stands majestically on the seafront of the historic Cinque Port of Hythe. Built in 1880, the hotel embodies the elegance of the Victorian age, combined with all the amenities expected by today's discerning visitor. All 100 en-suite bedrooms, suites and family rooms – some with four poster beds, half testers and Jacuzzis – enjoy wonderful views. The restaurant has an enviable reputation and has been awarded an AA Rosette for its cuisine. The hotel's 9-hole 18 tee links course, bounded by the Royal Military Canal, is a challenging test. There is also an extensive newly refurbished leisure centre with a heated pool, gymnasium, spa bath, steam and sauna rooms, squash, snooker tables and a bar and bistro. Outside are all-weather floodlit tennis courts, putting, croquet and bowls. Twelve fully equipped conference rooms and six syndicate rooms are available. Proximity to the Le Shuttle terminal and Channel ports makes the hotel an ideal base for visiting France as well as exploring the beautiful Kent countryside. Sailing and fishing locally and horseracing at Folkestone. Directions: From M20, exit at junction 11 onto A261 to Hythe. When in the town follow signs towards Folkestone and turn right into Twiss Road, opposite the Bell Inn, towards the seafront. Price guide: Single £90-£100; double/twin £115-£135; Suite £155.

For hotel location, see maps on pages 477-483

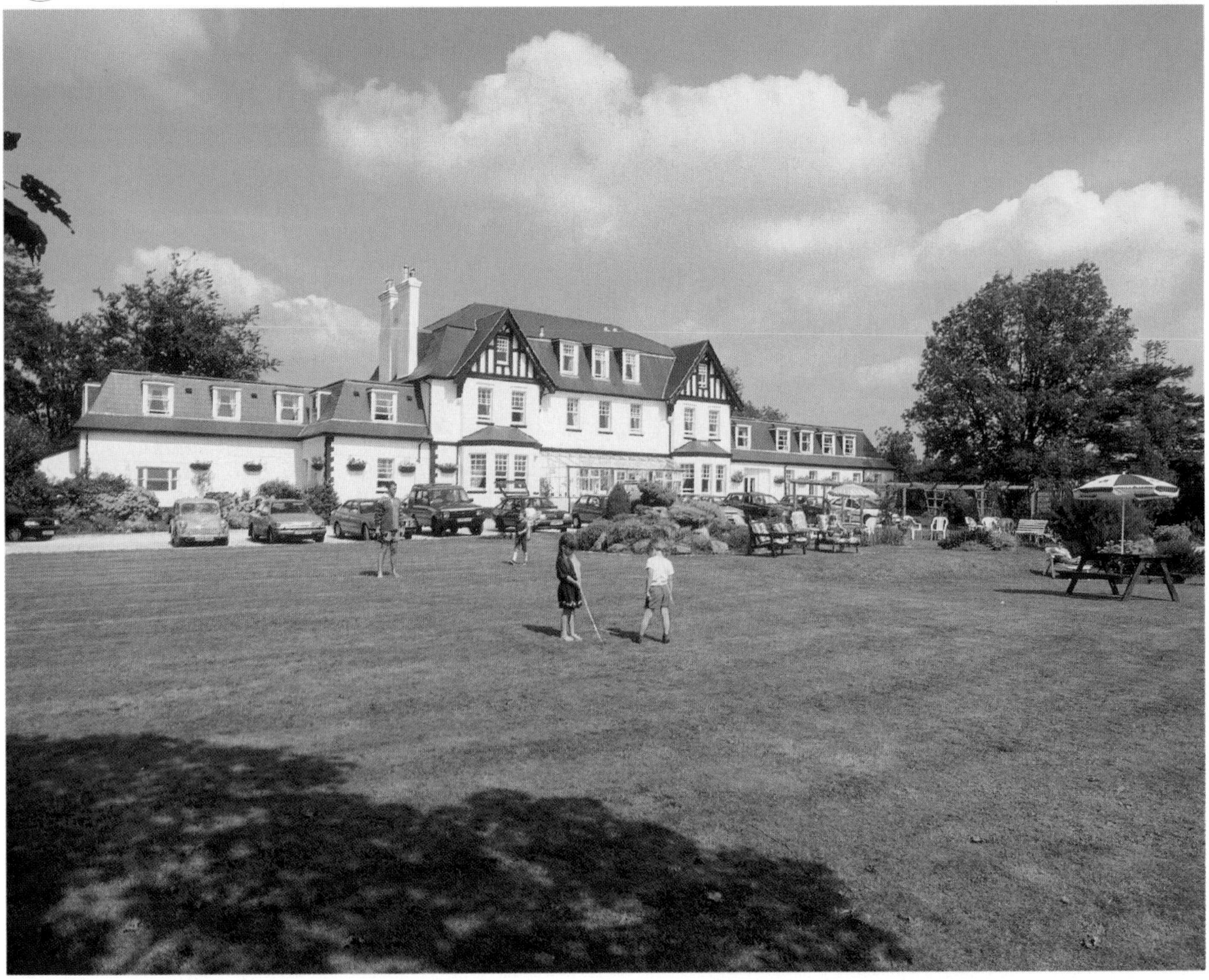

ILSINGTON COUNTRY HOTEL

ILSINGTON, NEWTON ABBOT, DEVON TQ13 9RR
TEL: 01364 661452 FAX: 01364 661307

The Ilsington Hotel stands in ten acres of beautiful private grounds within the Dartmoor National Park. Run by charming owners, Howard and Karen Astbury, the delightful furnishings and friendly ambience offer a most comfortable environment in which to relax. Stylish bedrooms and suites all boast outstanding views across the rolling pastoral countryside and every comfort and convenience to make guests feel at home, including English toiletries. The distinctive candle-lit dining room is perfect for savouring the superb cuisine created by talented chefs from fresh local produce. The library is ideal for an intimate dining party or celebration whilst the Victorian conservatory is the place for morning coffee or a Devon cream tea. There is a fully equipped purpose built gymnasium, heated indoor pool, sauna and spa – also experienced masseurs. Some of England's most idyllic and unspoilt scenery surrounds Ilsington, with the picturesque villages of Lustleigh, Widecombe-in-the-Moor and Manaton all closeby. Footpaths lead from the hotel on to Dartmoor. Riding, fishing and many other country pursuits can be arranged nearby. **Directions:** From M5 join A38 at Exeter following Plymouth signs. After approximately 12 miles exit for Moretonhampstead and Newton Abbot. At roundabout follow signs for Ilsington. Price guide: (including dinner) Single £70; double/twin £110.

For hotel location, see maps on pages 477-483

THE COMMODORE

MARINE PARADE, INSTOW, NORTH DEVON EX39 4JN
TEL: 01271 860347 FAX: 01271 861233

The Commodore Hotel is set in the charming waterside village of Instow and overlooks the sandy beach at the mouth of the Taw and Torridge Estuaries. Originally a Georgian Gentleman's residence, it has been sympathetically extended and converted and offers every modern comfort. The individually designed bedrooms are spacious, airy and tastefully decorated to a high standard. Sea facing rooms have the benefit of balconies and all rooms are provided with reclining sun loungers. Among a full range of modern amenities are thoughtful extras such as hairdryers and trouser presses. A spacious and inviting restaurant offers table d'hôte and à la carte seasonal menus with seafood specialities. A varied choice of bar meals is served in the lounge areas of the hotel, or during the summer months on the patio terrace. Instow is ideally situated for discovering Henry Williamson's "Tarka the Otter" country, set between the historic market towns of Bideford and Barnstaple and within easy reach of the Exmoor and Dartmoor National Parks. Places of interest nearby include a number of excellent museums and art galleries, while other recreational activities include sailing, windsurfing and water skiing. **Directions:** Exit M5 junction 27. Join A361 link road to Barnstaple, then A39. Sign for Instow is just before Torridge bridge. Price guide: Single £55–£70; double/twin: £90–£110, (including dinner).

20 rms MasterCard VISA AMERICAN EXPRESS M 250

For hotel location, see maps on pages 477-483

BELSTEAD BROOK MANOR HOTEL

BELSTEAD BROOK PARK, BELSTEAD ROAD, IPSWICH, SUFFOLK IP2 9HB
TEL: 01473 684241 FAX: 01473 681249

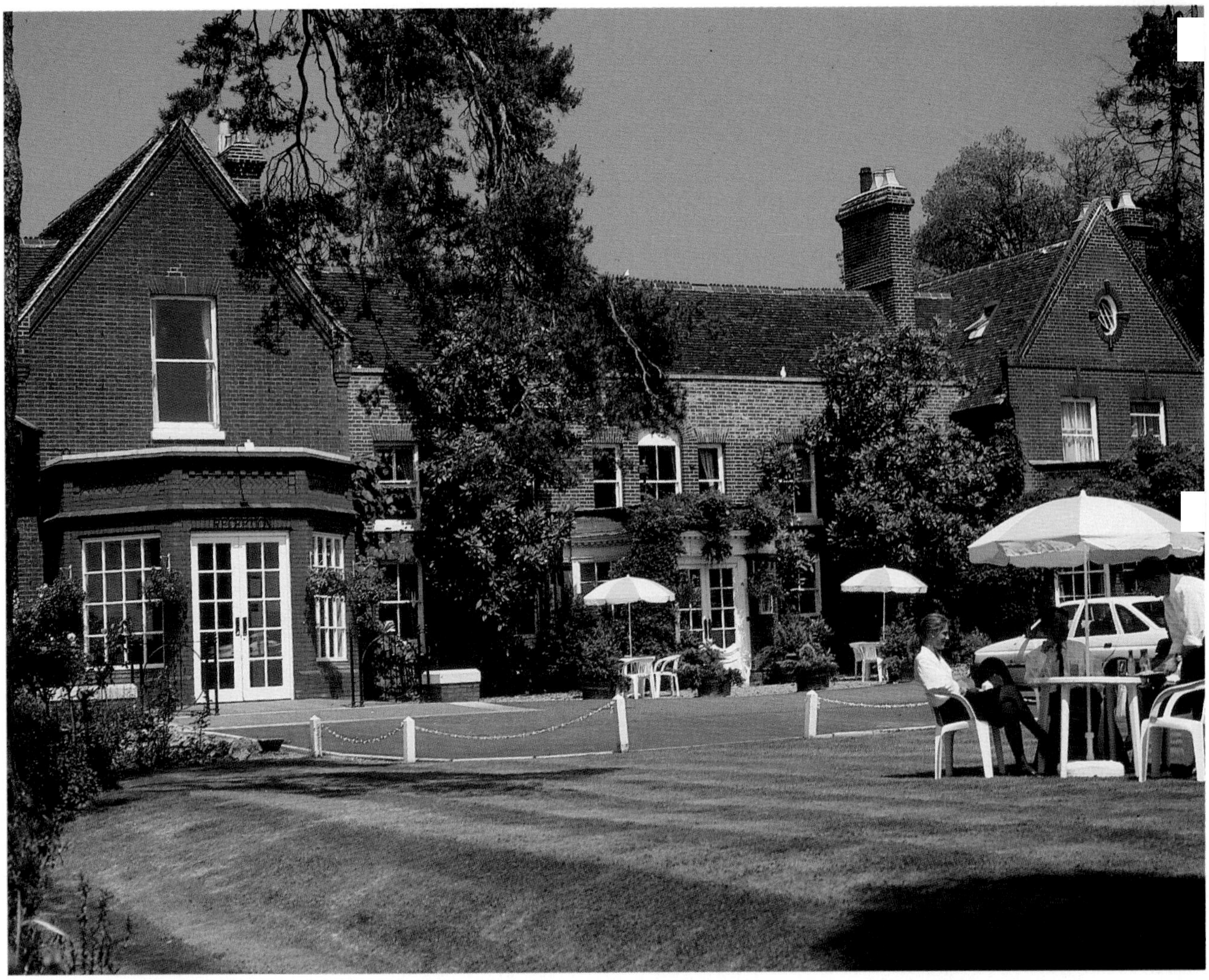

An oasis on the edge of Ipswich, Belstead Brook Manor Hotel is surrounded by eight acres of landscaped gardens and woodlands. It combines the charm and tranquillity of the original 16th century country house with every modern day comfort. Bedrooms are pleasantly furnished and many overlook the garden where resident peacocks stroll. New this year is a luxurious swimming pool with sauna, steam room, large jacuzzi, separate pool for children and a well equipped gymnasium. The award winning restaurant offers a choice of menus, complemented by a comprehensive cellar. For weddings, conferences or banquets, the hotel offers private dining rooms and a choice of purpose built meeting and syndicate rooms to accommodate up to 130 guests or delegates. The hotel is an ideal base from which to explore the delights of Suffolk; These include Southwold, Aldeburgh, Woodbridge, the estuaries of the Deben and the Orwell, the wool towns of Lavenham and Long Melford and the countryside of the Stour Valley made famous by John Constable. **Directions:** At the A12/A14 interchange roundabout take the A1214 Ipswich West exit. Follow signs to Belstead. At the T junction at the bottom of the hill take a small lane signposted to Belstead Brook. The hotel is visible through trees on your left. Price guide: Double/twin £72–£82; suites £115.

For hotel location, see maps on pages 477-483

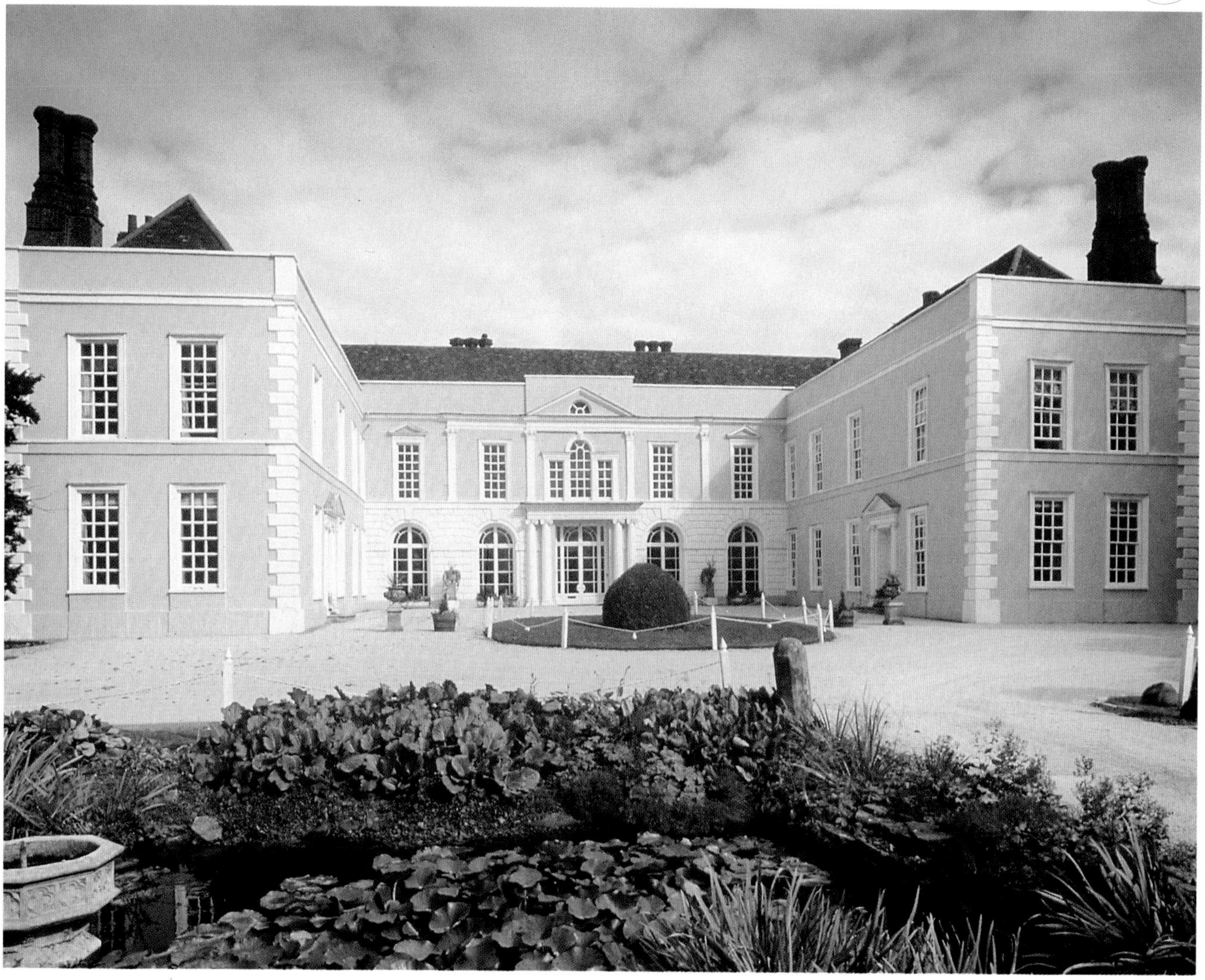

HINTLESHAM HALL

HINTLESHAM, IPSWICH, SUFFOLK IP8 3NS

TEL: 01473 652268 FAX: 01473 652463

The epitome of grandeur, Hintlesham Hall is a house of evolving styles: its splendid Georgian façade belies its 16th-century origins, to which the red-brick Tudor rear of the hall is a testament. The Stuart period also left its mark, in the form of a magnificent carved-oak staircase leading to the north wing of the hall. The combination of styles works extremely well, with the lofty proportions of the Georgian reception rooms contrasting with the timbered Tudor rooms. The décor throughout is superb – all rooms are individually appointed in a discriminating fashion. Iced mineral water, toiletries and towelling robes are to be found in each of the comfortable bedrooms. The herb garden supplies many of the flavours for the well-balanced menu which will appeal to the gourmet and the health-conscious alike, complemented by a 300-bin wine list. Bounded by 175 acres of rolling countryside, leisure facilities include the Hall's own 18-hole championship golf course, gymnasium, saunas, steam room, spa bath, tennis, croquet and snooker. Guests can also explore Suffolk's 16th-century wool merchants' villages, its pretty coast, 'Constable country' and Newmarket. **Directions:** Hintlesham Hall is 4 miles west of Ipswich on the A1071 Sudbury road. Price guide: Single £85; double/twin £110; suite £210.

For hotel location, see maps on pages 477-483

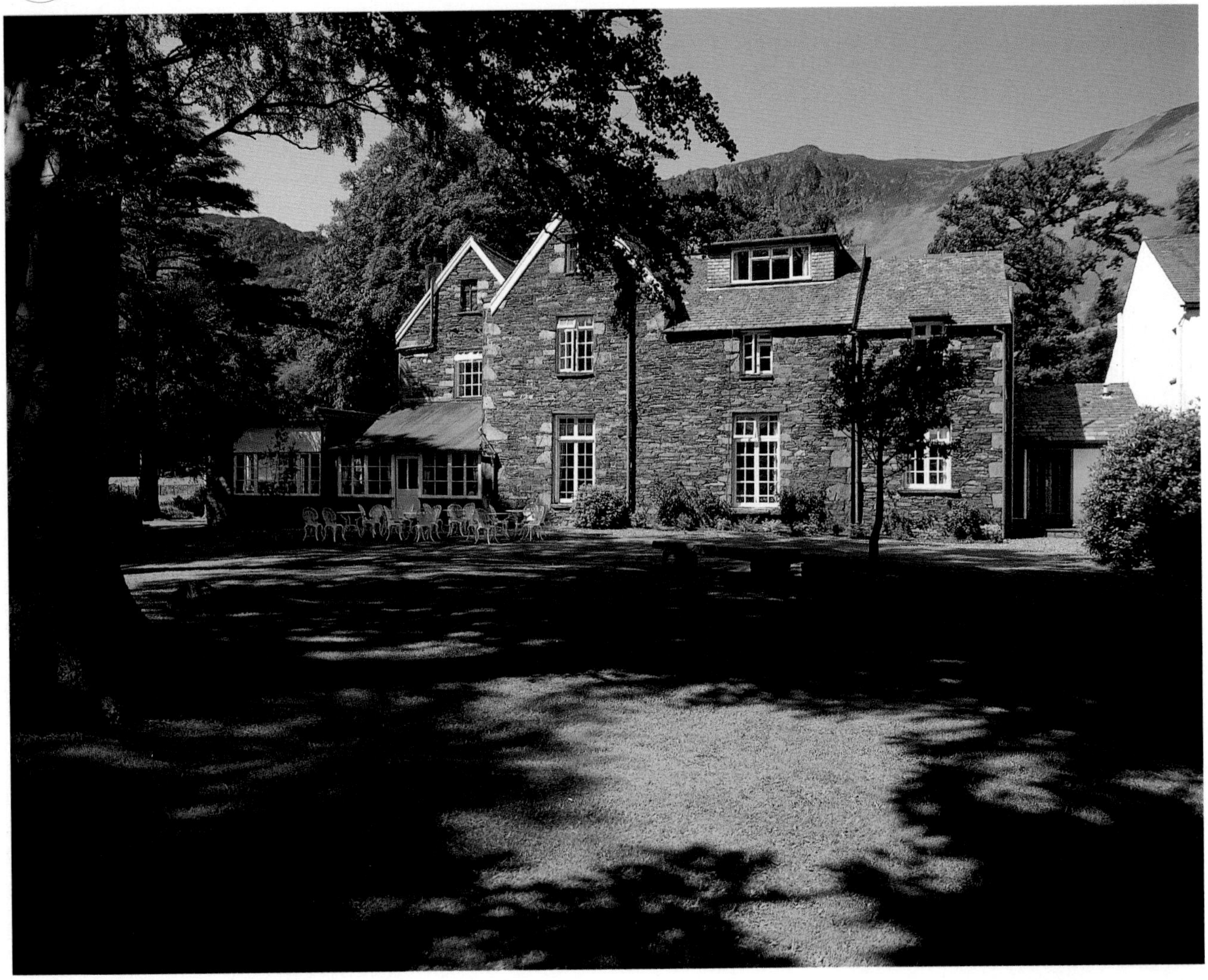

THE BORROWDALE GATES COUNTRY HOUSE HOTEL

GRANGE-IN-BORROWDALE, KESWICK, CUMBRIA CA12 5UQ
TEL: 01768 777204 FAX: 01768 777254

Built in 1860, Borrowdale Gates is surrounded on all sides by the rugged charm of the Lake District National Park. It affords panoramic views of the Borrowdale Valley and surrounding fells and nestles in two acres of wooded gardens on the edge of the ancient hamlet of Grange, close to the shores of Derwentwater. Tastefully decorated bedrooms offer every modern comfort and command picturesque views of the surrounding scenery. The comfortable lounges and bar, decorated with fine antiques and warmed by glowing log fires in cooler months, create the perfect setting in which to enjoy a drink and forget the bustle of everyday life. Fine food is served in the restaurant, with menus offering a wide and imaginative selection of dishes. The cuisine is complemented by a thoughtfully chosen wine list and excellent service. This Lakeland home is a haven of peace and tranquillity and is ideally located for walking, climbing and touring. There are also many places of literary and historical interest within easy reach, for example Wordsworth's birthplace in Cockermouth. The hotel is closed throughout January. **Directions:** M6 junction 40 A66 into Keswick. B5289 to Borrowdale. After four miles right into Grange over double hump back bridge. Price guide: Single £57–£75; double/twin £105–£142.50 (Including dinner). Special breaks available.

For hotel location, see maps on pages 477-483

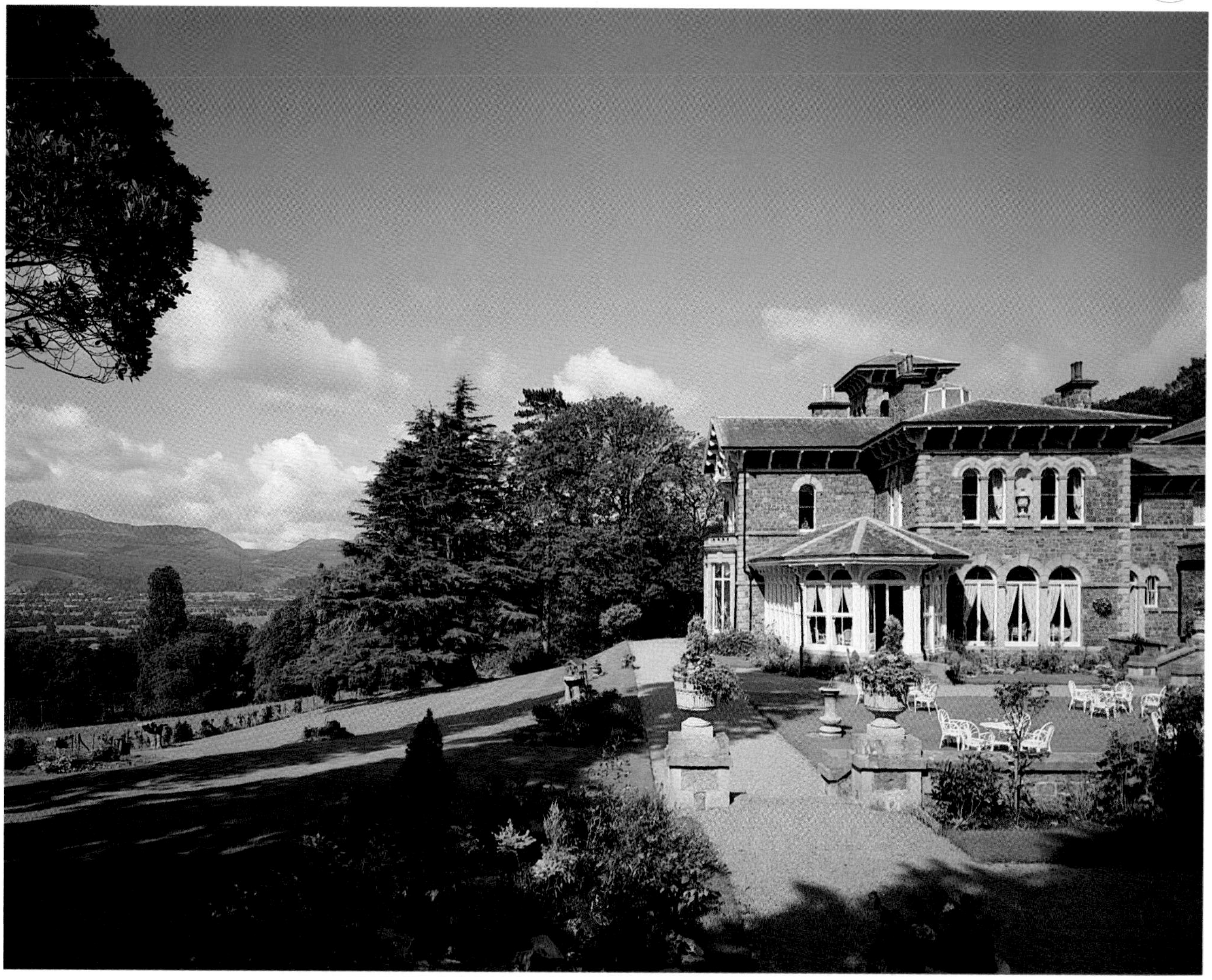

Underscar Manor

APPLETHWAITE, NEAR KESWICK, CUMBRIA CA12 4PH
TEL: 017687 75000 FAX: 017687 74904

This beautiful Italianate house, recently extensively refurbished, was built in Victorian times and enjoys an elevated position with panoramic views over Derwentwater and the mountains beyond. It is set in 40 acres of serene gardens and woodlands, home of roe deer and red squirrels. Individually created bedrooms offer ever-changing views over the lakes and mountains and the public rooms provide an ideal atmosphere in which to relax. The house is operated by Pauline and Derek Harrison with Pauline's brother Robert Thorton the Head Chef – for dinner, choose from a tantalising selection of dishes, including local Herdwick lamb cutlets, pan fried with home-made herb cake and served on a chive and tarragon sauce, and roast guinea fowl, served with chicken livers on an orange flavoured sauce. Excellent fishing is available on the local lakes and tarns, while golfers may chose from Keswick (four miles), Penrith, Silloth, Workington and Carlisle golf courses. There are regular horse races at Carlisle, Cartmel and Hexham. For walking, pony trekking, sailing, bird watching or paragliding opportunities, the Lakes can match and excel anywhere in Britain. **Directions:** From M6, junction 40, take A66 bypassing Keswick. At roundabout take A591 exit, then turn immediately right and Underscar Manor is a short distance. Price guide: Single £95; double/twin £150–£250 (including à la carte dinner).

For hotel location, see maps on pages 477-483

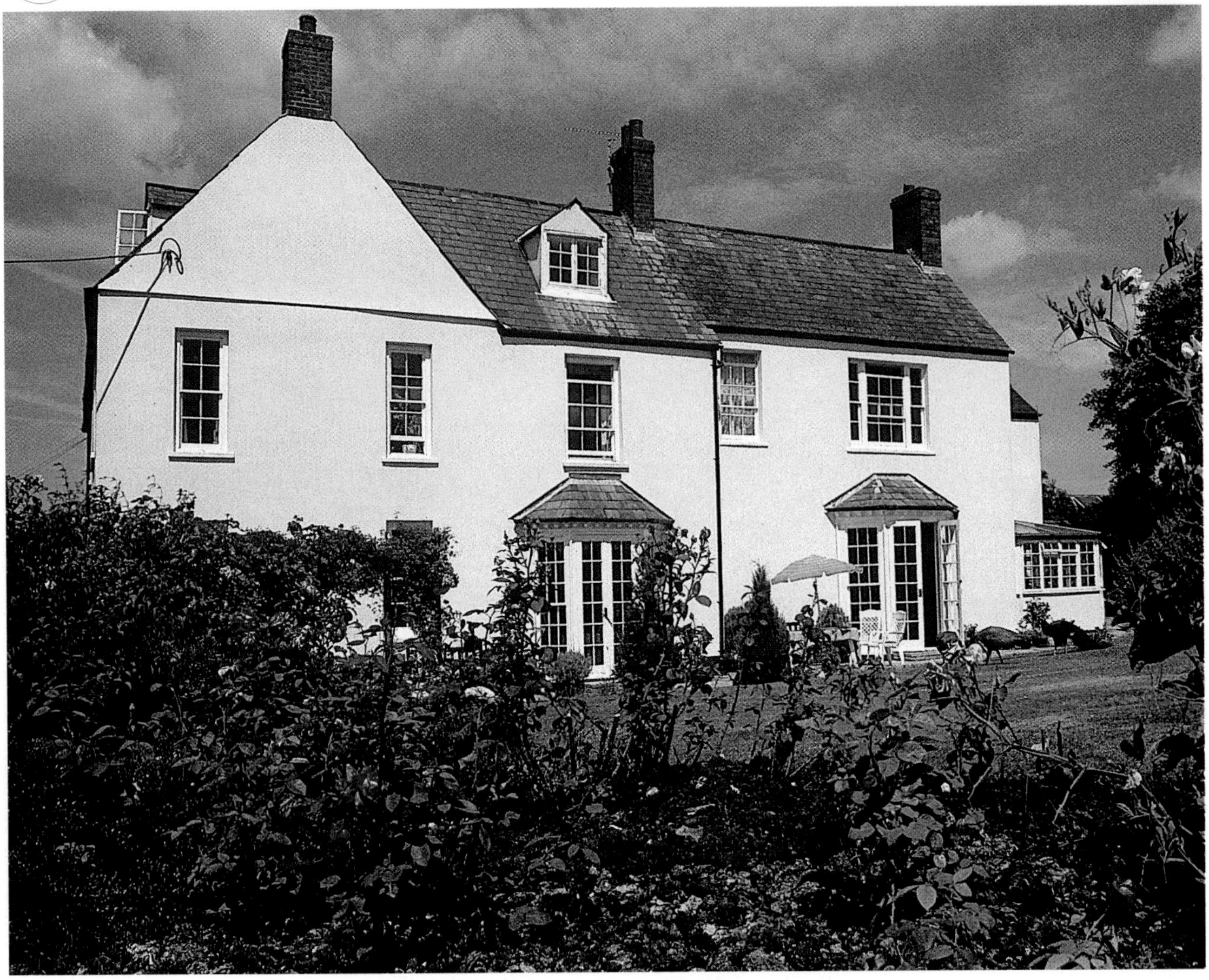

MEADOW HOUSE

SEA LANE, KILVE, SOMERSET TA5 1EG
TEL: 01278 741546 FAX: 01278 741663

With its origins dating from around 1600, Meadow House was enlarged in Georgian times to become a rectory. Standing in eight acres of grounds, the hotel is entirely surrounded by countryside with rolling meadows and woodland and has views encompassing the nearby Quantocks, Bristol Channel and Welsh coast. A stream feeds the hotel pond as it wends its way to the sea only a few minutes' walk away. Unspoiled Kilve Beach is renowned for its rock formations, fossils and spectacular cliff views. The spacious bedrooms are comfortably furnished and guests will find mineral water, fresh flowers and biscuits when they arrive. French windows open on to a large, south-facing terrace overlooking the garden, which is a profusion of colour during the summer. Antiques, curios and books abound in the drawing room and study, while log fires create a cosy atmosphere in winter. Guests may dine in the main restaurant or in the adjoining conservatory. The frequently changing menu pays particular attention to English recipes, using fruit and vegetables from the kitchen garden whenever possible. The wine list is exceptional. Dogs can be accommodated in some rooms. **Directions:** Leave M5 at junction 23. Join A39 at Bridgwater. Turn right at Kilve into Sea Lane; hotel is ½ mile on left. Price guide: Single from £55–£75; double/twin from £75–£110.

For hotel location, see maps on pages 477-483

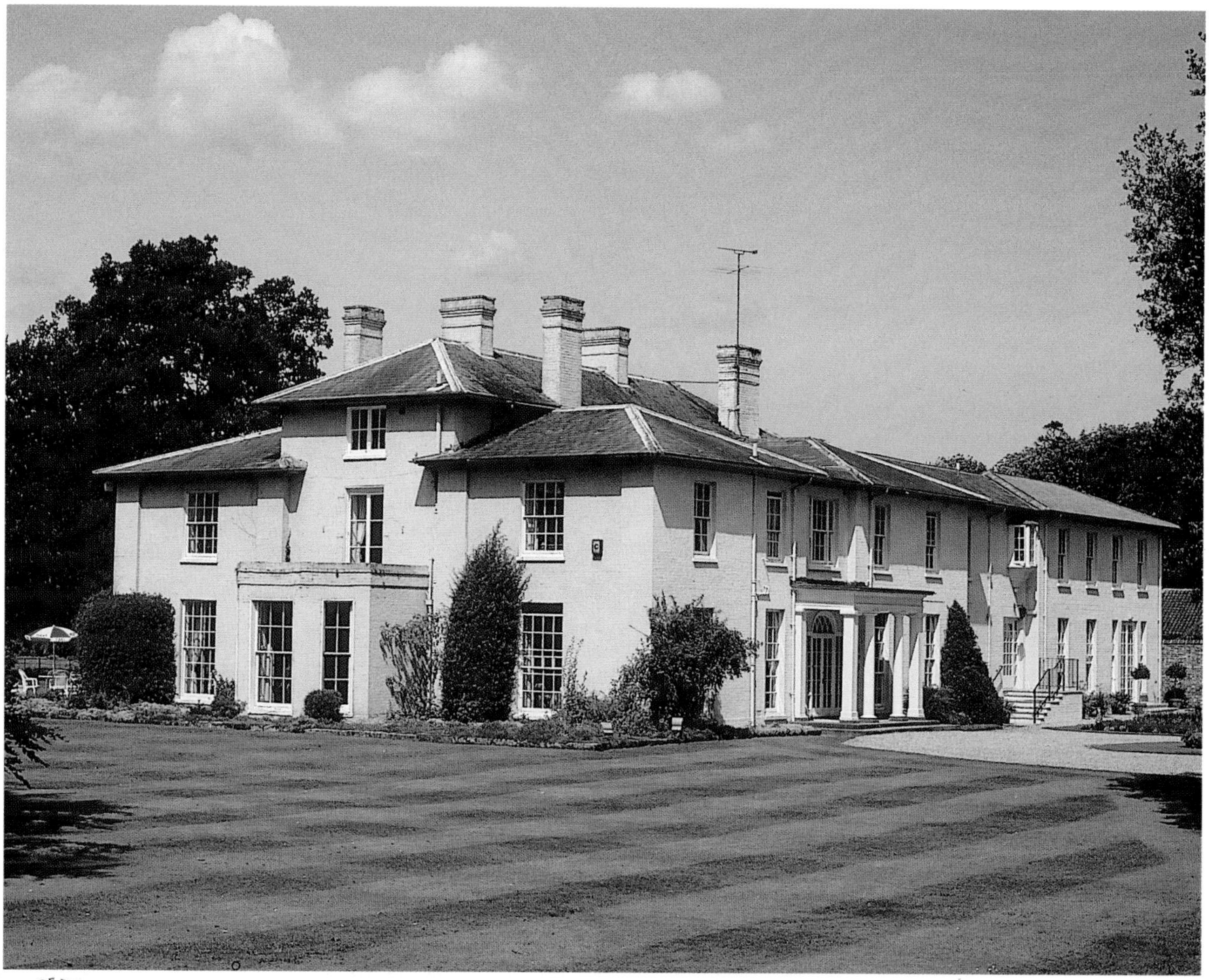

CONGHAM HALL

GRIMSTON, KING'S LYNN, NORFOLK PE32 1AH
TEL: 01485 600250 FAX: 01485 601191

Dating from the mid-18th century, this stately manor house is set in 40 acres of paddocks, orchards and gardens, including its own cricket pitch. The conversion from country house to luxury hotel in 1982 was executed with care to enhance the elegance of the classic interiors. Proprietors Christine and Trevor Forecast have, however, retained the atmosphere of a family home. Christine's particular forte is the herb garden and flower arranging, and her displays enliven the décor throughout, while the delicate fragrance of home-made pot-pourri perfumes the air. Winners of the Johansens Hotel Award for Excellence 1993. Light lunches available in the Bar, Lounge, Restaurant and Terrace. In the Orangery restaurant, guests can relish modern English cooking. The origin of many of the flavours is explained by the herb garden, with over 100 varieties for the chef's use. Even the most discerning palate will be delighted by the choice of wines. Congham Hall is an ideal base for touring the countryside of West Norfolk, as well as Sandringham, Fakenham races and the coastal nature reserves. **Directions:** Go to the A149/A148 interchange northeast of King's Lynn. Follow the A148 towards Sandringham/Fakenham/Cromer for 100 yards. Turn right to Grimston. The hotel is then $2^1/_2$ miles on the left. Price guide: Single £79–£89; double/twin £105–£135; suites from £170.

For hotel location, see maps on pages 477-483

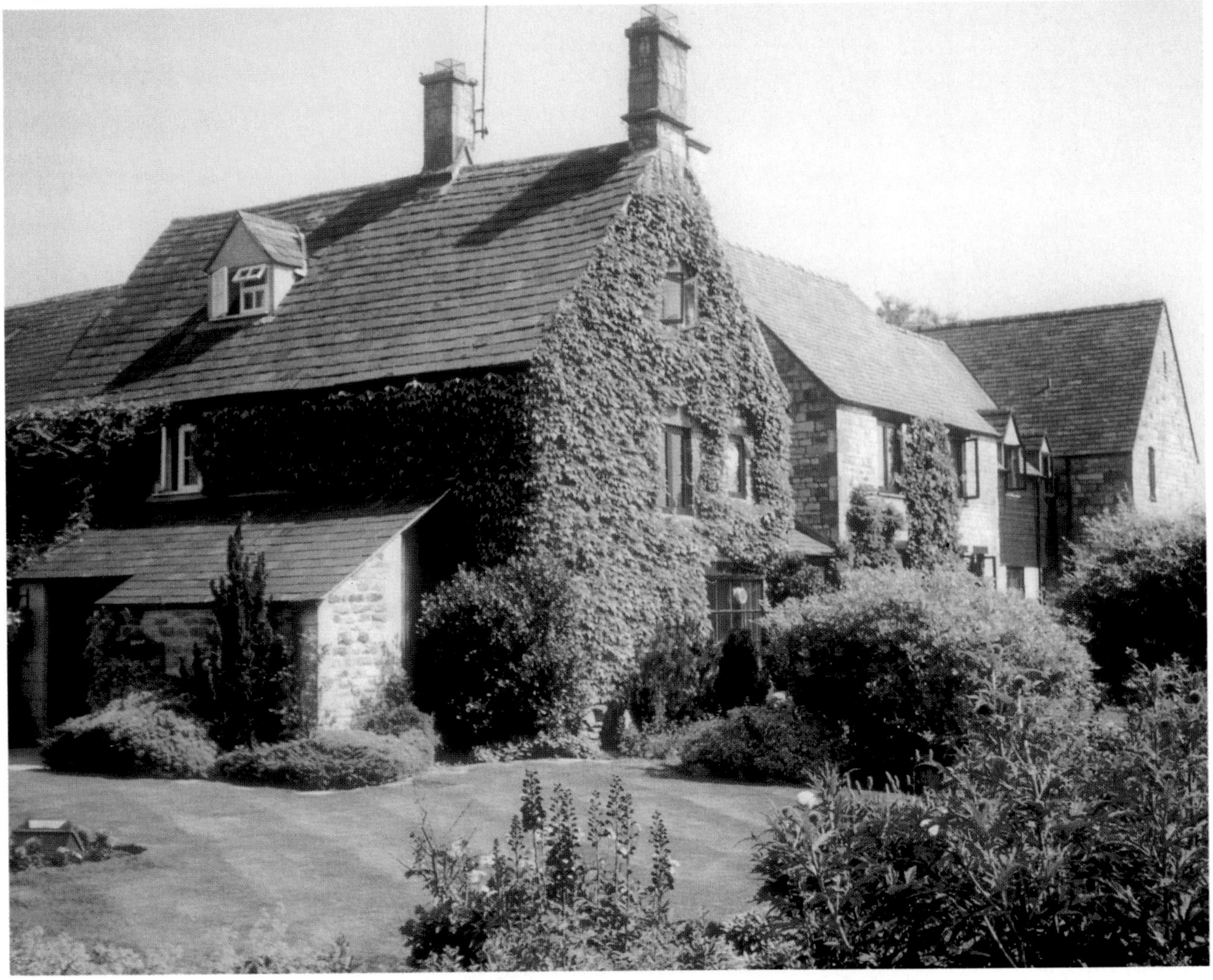

Mill House Hotel

KINGHAM, OXFORDSHIRE OX7 6UH
TEL: 01608 658188 FAX: 01608 658492

Superbly converted Cotswold stone Mill House listed in the *Domesday Book* and set in nine tranquil acres with its own trout stream in the heart of the Cotswolds between Burford, Chipping Norton and Stow-on-the-Wold. The 23 luxury en suite bedrooms are all elegantly appointed and overlook the surrounding Cotswold countryside. There is a comfortable lounge with deep armchairs and sofas, and the bar features the ancient beamed ceiling and orginal bread ovens of the landfall flour mill. Open log fires are a feature throughout the winter; in summer, all rooms are enhanced by beautiful flour arrangements and fragrant pot-pourri. The heart of the hotel is the Marionette Room restaurant which provides cuisine of the highest standards. The menus are changed daily to take advantage of the very best of fresh, seasonal produce. With the whole of the Cotswolds within easy reach, the Mill House is the ideal base from which to explore: Broadway, Chipping Campden, Moreton-in-Marsh, the Slaughters and Bourton-on-the-Water are all within 30 minutes drive. The Mill House has AA 3 Stars and 2 Rosettes for food; RAC 3 Stars withHospitality, Comfort and Restaurant Awards. **Directions:** South of Kingham village midway between Chipping Norton and Stow-on-the-Wold just off the B4450. Price guide: Single £55–£65; double/twin £90–£110.

For hotel location, see maps on pages 477-483

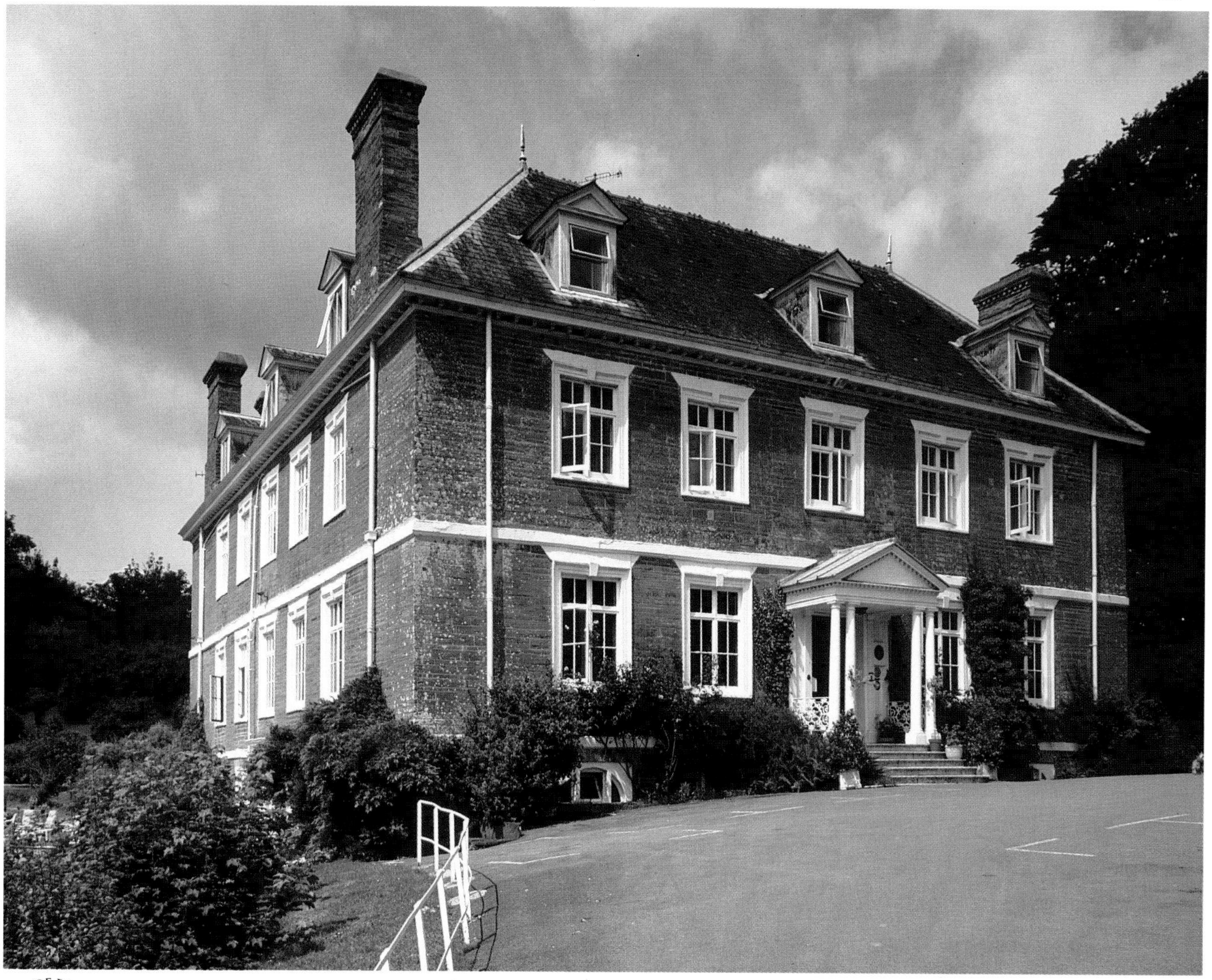

BUCKLAND-TOUT-SAINTS

GOVETON, KINGSBRIDGE, DEVON TQ7 2DS
TEL: 01548 853055 FAX: 01548 856261

Situated in rural South Devon, Buckland-Tout-Saints was built in 1690, when William, Prince of Orange, and Mary were on the throne of England. The hotel is in a beautiful and peaceful situation. It has 7 acres of lovely gardens. John and Tove Taylor, are here to care for you. They are continuing the tradition of country house entertaining, promoting the feeling of being a privileged guest in a private house. On the first floor, four de luxe rooms and three suites are decorated in harmony with the period setting. Six smaller rooms on the second floor have Provence-style shuttered windows and lovely views. In the pine-panelled Queen Anne Restaurant, simple, crisp linen, china and glassware provide elegant surroundings for dinner. 2 AA Rosettes. Chef Richard Cranfield prepares imaginative English and French dishes which are presented in the modern English style. An extensive range of wines provides something to enhance each meal. Kingsbridge, 2 miles away, is a bustling market town, while Dartmouth is further round the coast. The wilds of Dartmoor, Dartington Glassworks, numerous quaint fishing ports and several National Trust properties are nearby. Children and dogs by prior arrangement. Winter breaks available **Directions:** Signposted from the A381 between Totnes and Kingsbridge. Price guide: (including dinner) Single £80; double/twin £160–£180; suite £200.

For hotel location, see maps on pages 477-483

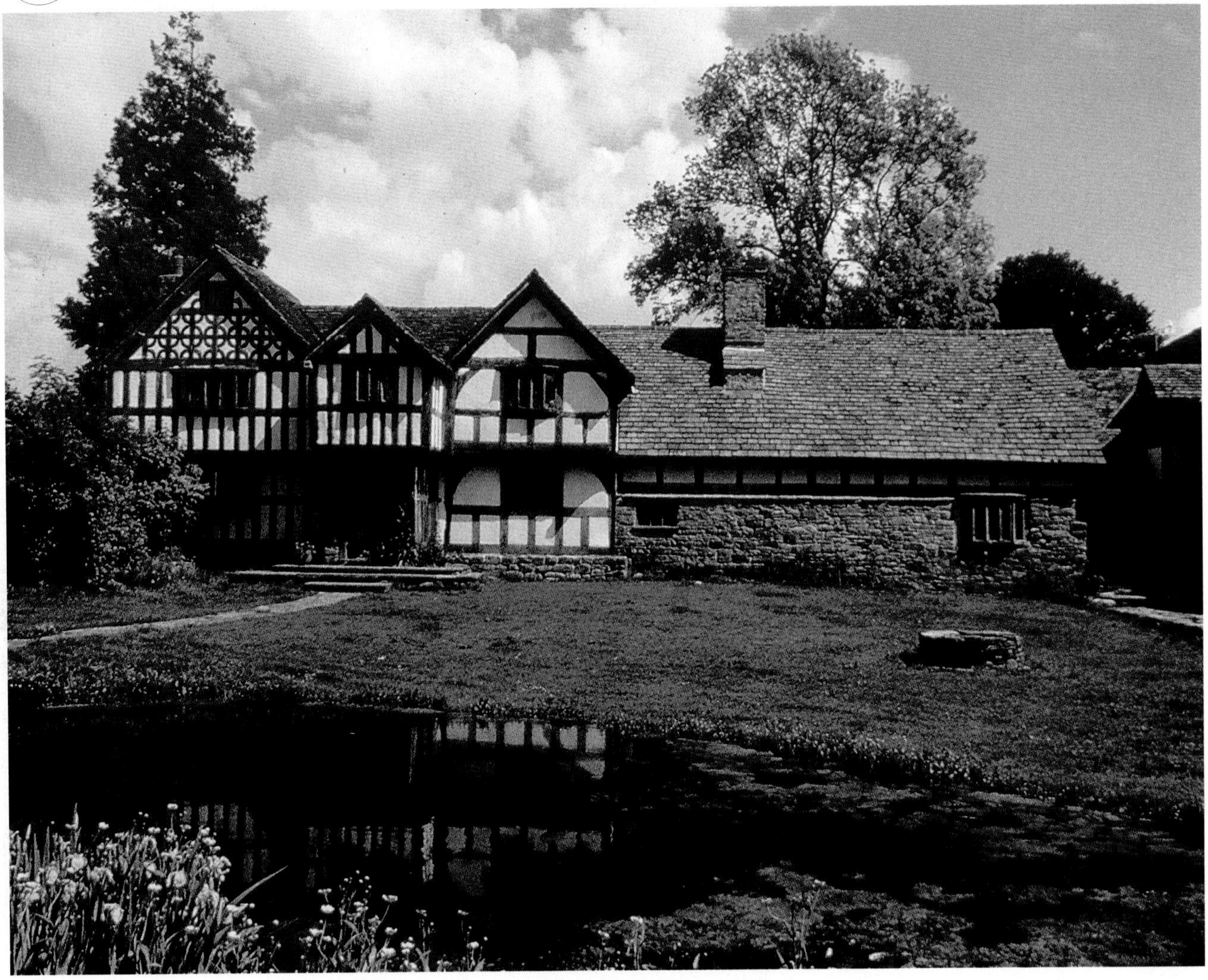

PENRHOS COURT

KINGTON, HEREFORDSHIRE HR5 3LH
TEL: 01544 230720 FAX: 01544 230754

Penrhos was built in 1280, the year when Edward I, King of England, took Kington away from the Welsh. This unique farm building is set in six acres of grounds and stands on the border of Herefordshire and Wales. Many years of devoted work by the owners have transformed Penrhos into a delightful small hotel, offering seclusion and high standards of comfort and service. Chef-patronne Daphne Lambert prepares the dishes served in the hotel's restaurant and over the years she has evolved her own style of cooking. She uses only fresh ingredients of the highest quality, preparing them in a way that does not mask the natural flavours nor strip the food of its nutritional value. The four-course meal, which changes every day, offers a choice for all tastes. Practically all food served is organic and many of the herbs, vegetables and fruit are grown in the garden next to the kitchen. Daphne's Cookery Courses run throughout the year and her project for The Penrhos School of Food & Health has been nominated for a Millennium Marque award. Penrhos is within easy reach of five golf courses and other activities available in the area include riding, hang-gliding, rally driving and go-carting. Also nearby are Hay-on-Wye, the Wye Valley and Hereford. **Directions:** Half mile south of Kington on the A44. Price guide: Single £50–£90; double/twin £80–£100; suites £120.

For hotel location, see maps on pages 477-483

RAMPSBECK COUNTRY HOUSE HOTEL

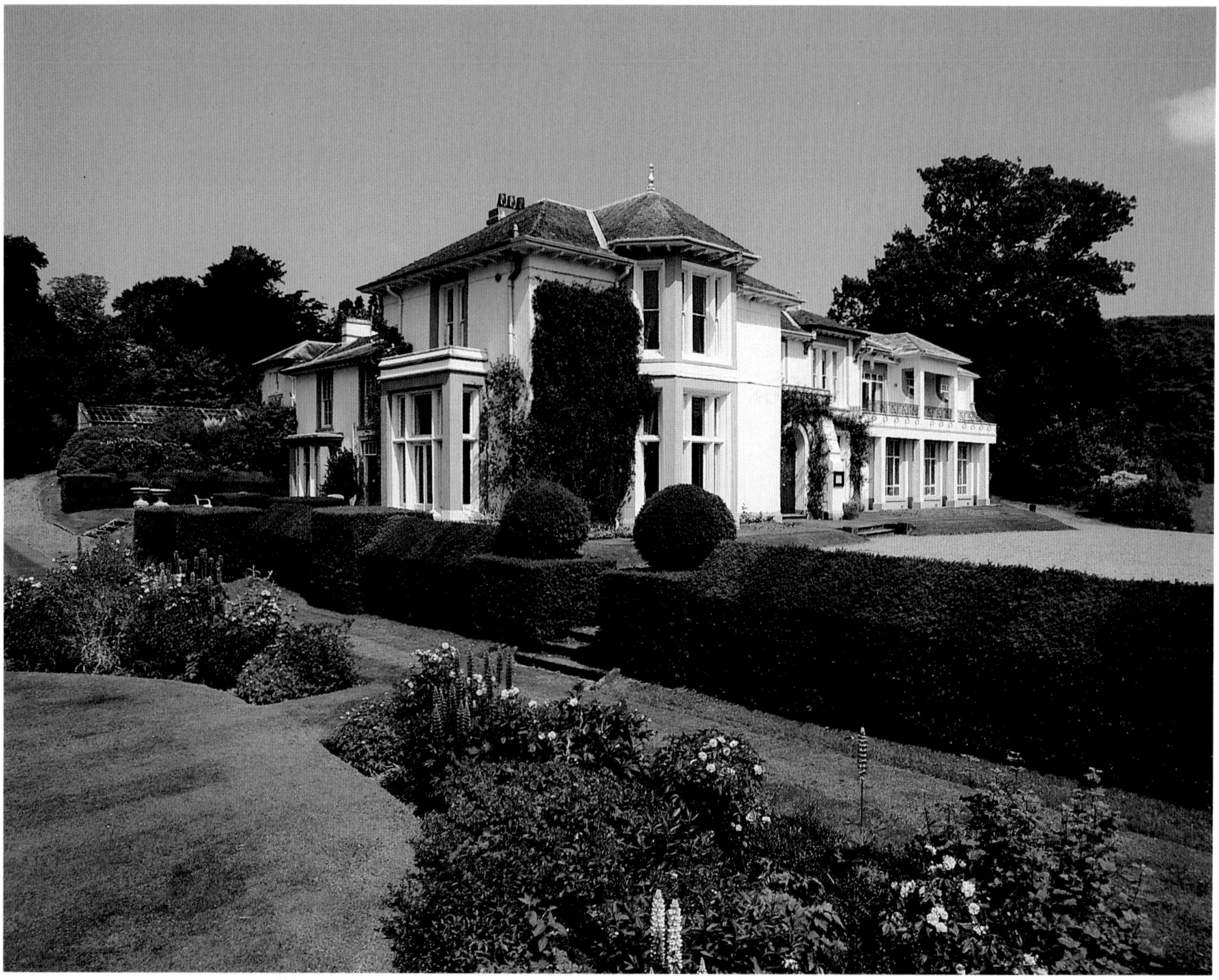

WATERMILLOCK, LAKE ULLSWATER, NR PENRITH, CUMBRIA CA11 0LP
TEL: 017684 86442 FAX: 017684 86688

A beautifully situated hotel, Rampsbeck Country House stands in 18 acres of landscaped gardens and meadows leading to the shores of Lake Ullswater. Built in 1714, it first became a hotel in 1947, before the present owners acquired it in 1983. Thomas and Marion Gibb, with the help of Marion's mother, Marguerite MacDowall, completely refurbished Rampsbeck with the aim of maintaining its character and adding only to its comfort. Most of the well-appointed bedrooms have lake and garden views. Three have a private balcony and the suite overlooks the lake. In the elegant drawing room, a log fire burns and French windows lead to the garden. Guests and non-residents are welcome to dine in the intimate candle-lit restaurant. Imaginative menus offer a choice of delicious dishes, carefully prepared by head chef Andrew McGeorge and his team. A good bar lunch menu offers light snacks as well as hot food. Guests can stroll through the gardens, play croquet or fish from the lake shore, around which there are designated walks. Lake steamer trips, riding, golf, sailing, windsurfing and fell-walking are available nearby. Closed from the first week in January to mid-February. Dogs by arrangement only. **Directions:** Leave M6 at junction 40, take A592 to Ullswater. At T-junction at lake turn right; hotel is 1½ miles on left. Price guide: Single £50–£95; double/twin £90–£170; suite £170.

For hotel location, see maps on pages 477-483

SHARROW BAY COUNTRY HOUSE HOTEL

HOWTOWN, LAKE ULLSWATER, PENRITH, CUMBRIA CA10 2LZ
TEL: 017684 86301/86483 FAX: 017684 86349

Now in its 49th year, Sharrow Bay is known to discerning travellers the world over, who return again and again to this magnificent lakeside hotel. It wasn't always so. Francis Coulson arrived in 1948. He was joined by Brian Sack in 1952 and the partnership flourished, to make Sharrow Bay what it is today. Recently they have been joined by Nigel Lawrence and Nigel Lightburn who carry on the tradition. All the bedrooms are elegantly furnished and guests are guaranteed the utmost comfort. In addition to the main hotel, there are four cottages nearby which offer similarly luxurious accommodation. All the reception rooms are delightfully decorated. Sharrow Bay is universally renowned for its wonderful cuisine. The team of chefs lead by Johnnie Martin and Colin Akrigg ensure that each meal is a special occasion, a mouthwatering adventure! With its private jetty and 12 acres of lakeside gardens Sharrow Bay offers guests boating, swimming, and fishing. Fell-walking is a challenge for the upwardly mobile. Sharrow Bay is the oldest British member of Relais et Châteaux. Closed in December and January. **Directions:** M6 junction 40, A592 to Lake Ullswater, into Pooley Bridge, then take Howtown road for 2 miles. Price guide: (including 7 course Dinner and full English Breakfast) Single £125–£250; double/twin £190–£320; suite £320.

For hotel location, see maps on pages 477-483

THE ARUNDELL ARMS

LIFTON, DEVON PL16 0AA
TEL: 01566 784666 FAX: 01566 784494

In a lovely valley close to the uplands of Dartmoor, the Arundell Arms is a former coaching inn which dates back to Saxon times. Its beautiful flagstone floors, cosy fires, paintings and antiques combine to create a haven of warmth and comfort in an atmosphere of old world charm. One of England's best-known sporting hotels for more than half a century, it boasts 20 miles of its own fishing on the Tamar and five of its tributaries. Guests also enjoy a host of other country activities, including hill walking and shooting. The hotel takes great pride in its elegant 3 AA Rosette restaurant, presided over by Master Chef Philip Burgess, formerly of L'Ecu de France in London. His exceptional cuisine, which includes traditional English and French dishes, is winning the restaurant an international reputation. A splendid base from which to enjoy the wonderful surfing beaches nearby, the Arundell Arms is also well placed for visits to Tintagel and the historic houses and gardens of Devon and Cornwall. Boats can be hired in the fishing villages of Boscastle and Port Isaac. Only 45 minutes' from Exeter and Plymouth, it is also ideal for the business executive, reached by fast roads from all directions. A spacious conference suite is available. **Directions:** Lifton is approximately 1/4 mile off A30 2 miles east of Launceston and the Cornish Border. Price guide: Single £61-£65; double/twin £97-£102.

For hotel location, see maps on pages 477-483

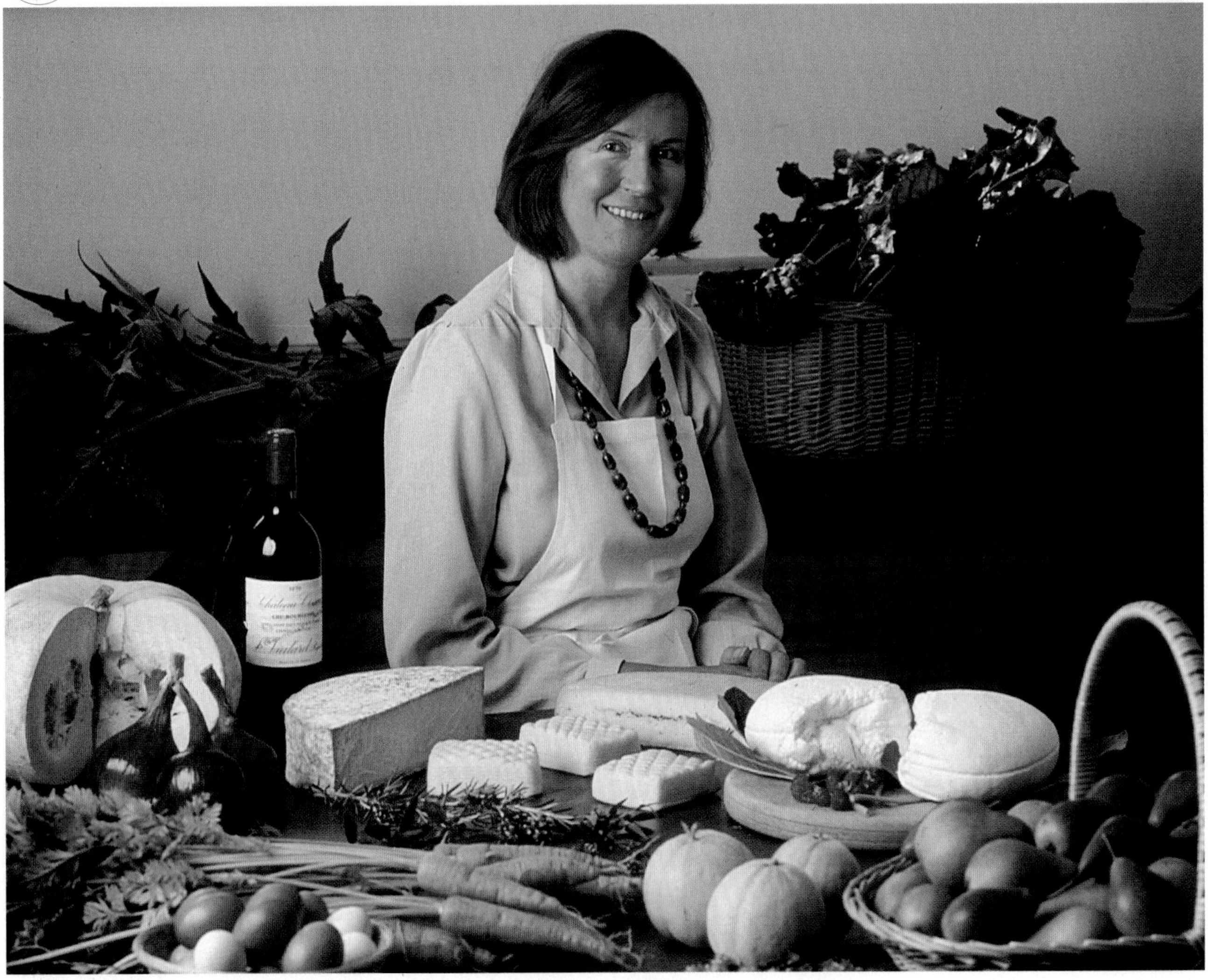

HOPE END HOTEL

HOPE END, LEDBURY, HEREFORDSHIRE HR8 1JQ
TEL: 01531 633613 FAX: 01531 636366

Hope End is a most romantic small hotel, set in 40 acres of restored 18th-century listed parkland. This very individual Georgian hotel provides total peace and an opportunity to enjoy an idle holiday amid rural surroundings. Formerly the childhood home of poet Elizabeth Barrett Browning, the building has been refurbished to offer discreet comfort. Eight en suite bedrooms are furnished with antiques and paintings, while the absence of TV ensures complete tranquillity. An extraordinary range of organic fruit, vegetables and herbs is grown in the walled kitchen garden. Free-range eggs, milk, yoghurt, local beef, lamb, fish and game in season are used in the kitchen. Fresh home-made bread is always available, along with a wide selection of farmhouse cheeses and the hotel's own spring water. Chef-patronne Patricia Hegarty prepares delicious dishes in the English country style to a high standard that has earned both national acclaim and 3 AA Rosettes. The wine list includes over 150 labels, with some rare vintages. Hope End is an ideal touring base as the Welsh Marches, Cotswolds and Malvern Hills are nearby. Ledbury itself is an interesting old market town with black and white houses. Closed from mid-December to early February. **Directions:** Two miles north of Ledbury, just beyond Wellington Heath. Price guide: Single £85; double/twin £120.

12

For hotel location, see maps on pages 477-483

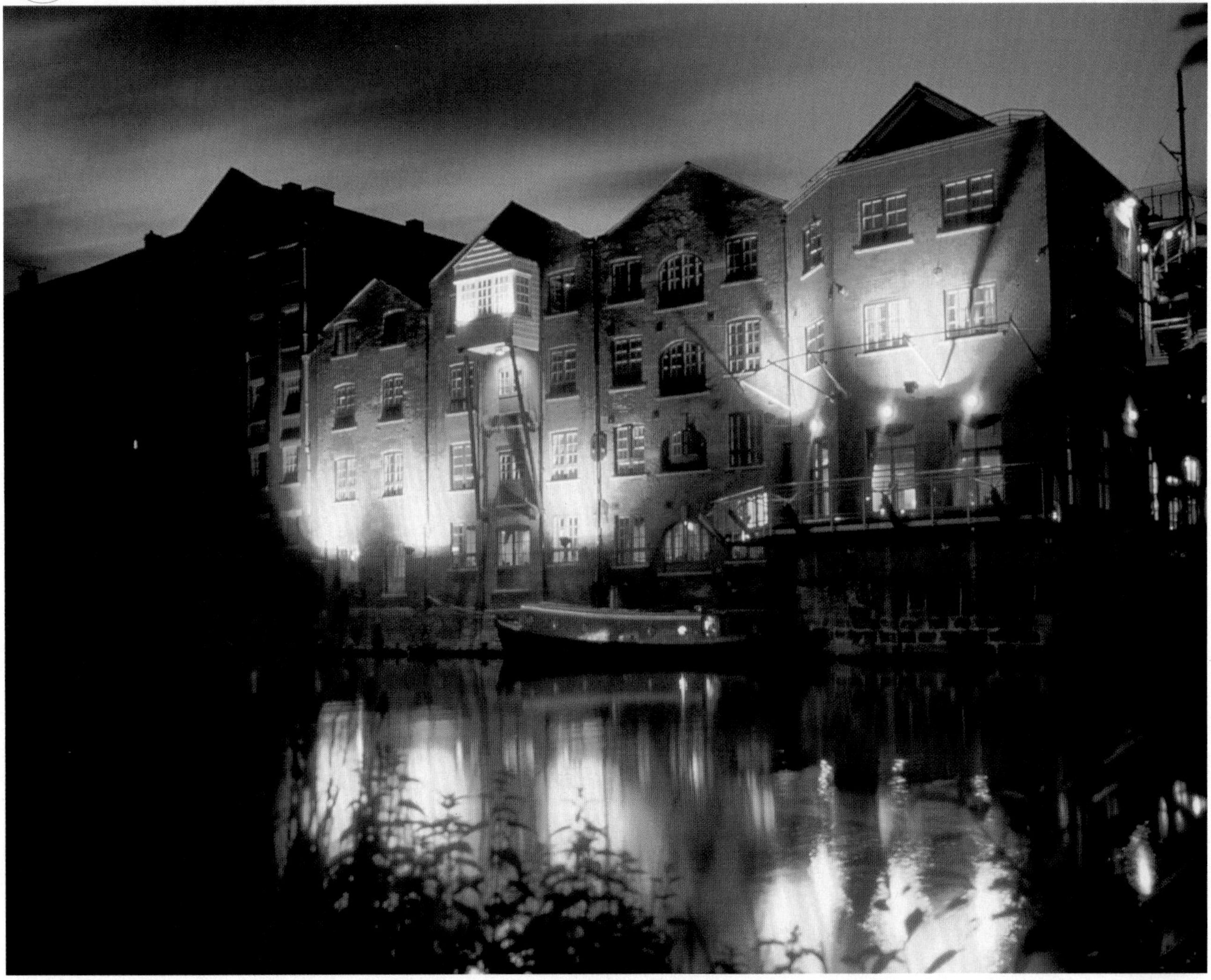

42 The Calls

42 THE CALLS, LEEDS, WEST YORKSHIRE LS2 7EW
TEL: 0113 244 0099 FAX: 0113 234 4100

This remarkable hotel is absolutely unique. Converted from an old riverside corn mill, it is run as a very personal and luxurious hotel by Jonathan Wix with General Manager Belinda Scott and a dedicated team of staff, in a peaceful location in the centre of Leeds. Shops, offices and theatres are within a few minutes' walk. The bedrooms have been individually decorated and furnished, taking full advantage of the many original features from small grain shutes to massive beams, girders and old machinery. Each room has 10 channel TV, a fresh filter coffee machine, complimentry sweets and cordials, luxury toiletries, trouser press and hair dryer. Stereo CD players are fitted in all the bedrooms and a library of disks is available to guests. Every comfort has been provided with full-size desks, handmade beds and armchairs, a liberal scattering of eastern rugs and beautiful bathrooms. Valet car parking and 24-hour room service are offered. Next door to the hotel is the simple but stylish Brasserie 44 and the superb Michelin Starred Pool Court at 42. **Directions:** M1 junction 46, follow signs to Harrogate, turn right by Tetley's Brewery. Go over Crown Point Bridge, then second left keeping the parish church on your left. Turn left again by Calls Landing and 42 will be directly in front of you. Price guide: Single £95–£135; double/twin £124–£140; suite £150–£220.

For hotel location, see maps on pages 477-483

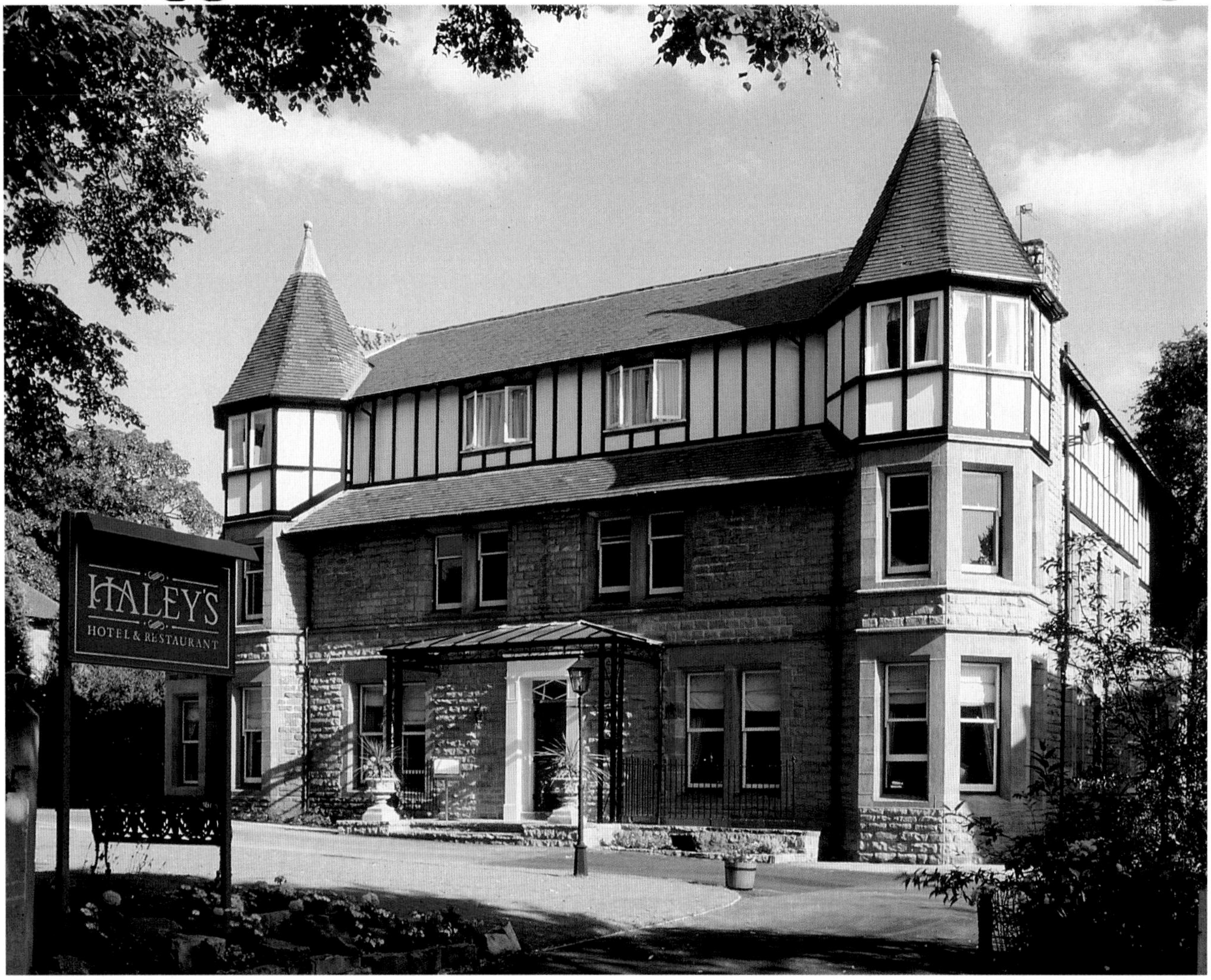

HALEY'S HOTEL & RESTAURANT

SHIRE OAK ROAD, HEADINGLEY, LEEDS, WEST YORKSHIRE LS6 2DE
TEL: 0113 278 4446 FAX: 0113 275 3342

Just two miles from Leeds City Centre, yet set in a quiet leafy lane in the Headingley conservation area close to the cricket ground and the university, Haley's is truly the Country House Hotel in the City. Each of the 22 guest rooms offers the highest levels of comfort, and is as individual as the fine antiques and rich furnishings which grace the hotel. The Bramley Room and Library are popular venues for private meetings, lunch or dinner parties. Haley's Restaurant has an enviable reputation, holding two AA rosettes, and was voted County Restaurant of the Year in the 1994 Good Food Guide. An imaginative menu of modern English cuisine is accompanied by a fine wine list. Numerous accolades even include winning the Loo of the Year Award five times! Leeds offers superb shopping in the Victorian arcades (including the newly opened Harvey Nichols), and is also home to the magnificent new Royal Armouries museum. Opera North and the theatres combine with Haley's superb food to offer relaxing weekends. Haley's superb food to offer relaxing weekends. Haley's is an independently owned member of Richard Branson's Virgin Hotel collection. **Directions:** Two miles north of Leeds City Centre off the main A660 Otley Road – the main route to Leeds/Bradford Airport, Ilkley and Wharfedale. Price guide: Single £95; double/twin £112; suite £185. Weekend tariff also available.

For hotel location, see maps on pages 477-483

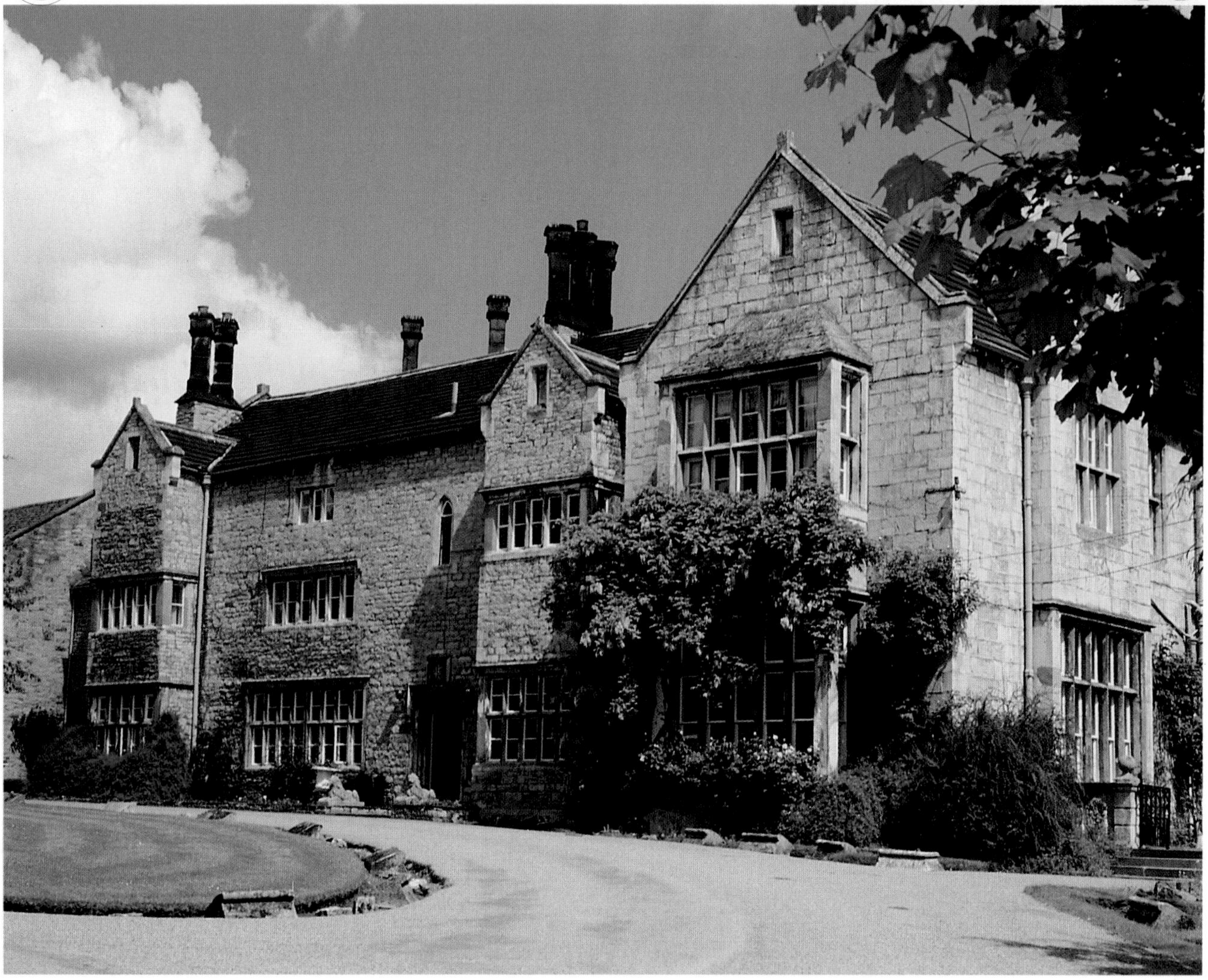

MONK FRYSTON HALL

MONK FRYSTON, LEEDS, NORTH YORKSHIRE LS25 5DU
TEL: 01977 682369 FAX: 01977 683544

This mellow old manor house, with origins dating back to the time of William the Conqueror, is of great architectural interest. The mullioned and transom windows, and the family coat of arms above the doorway, are reminiscent of Monk Fryston's fascinating past. In 1954 the hall was acquired by the Duke of Rutland, who has since created an elegant hotel for the 20th century, while successfully preserving the strong sense of heritage and tradition. The bedrooms, ranging from cosy, to airy and spacious, all have private en suite bathrooms and are appointed to a high standard. A comprehensive menu offers a wide choice of traditional English dishes with something to suit all tastes. From the hall, the terrace leads to landscaped Italian gardens which overlook an ornamental lake and are a delight to see at any time of year. Wedding receptions and dinner-dances are catered for in the oak-panelled Haddon Room with its splendid carved fireplace. The Rutland Room makes a good conference venue. Monk Fryston Hall is an ideal choice for business people, tourists or those seeking a relaxing break. York is 16 miles, Leeds 14 miles and Harrogate 18 miles away. **Directions:** Three miles off A1, on the A63 towards Selby in the centre of Monk Fryston. Price guide: Single £68–£72; double/twin £95–£110.

28 rms

For hotel location, see maps on pages 477-483

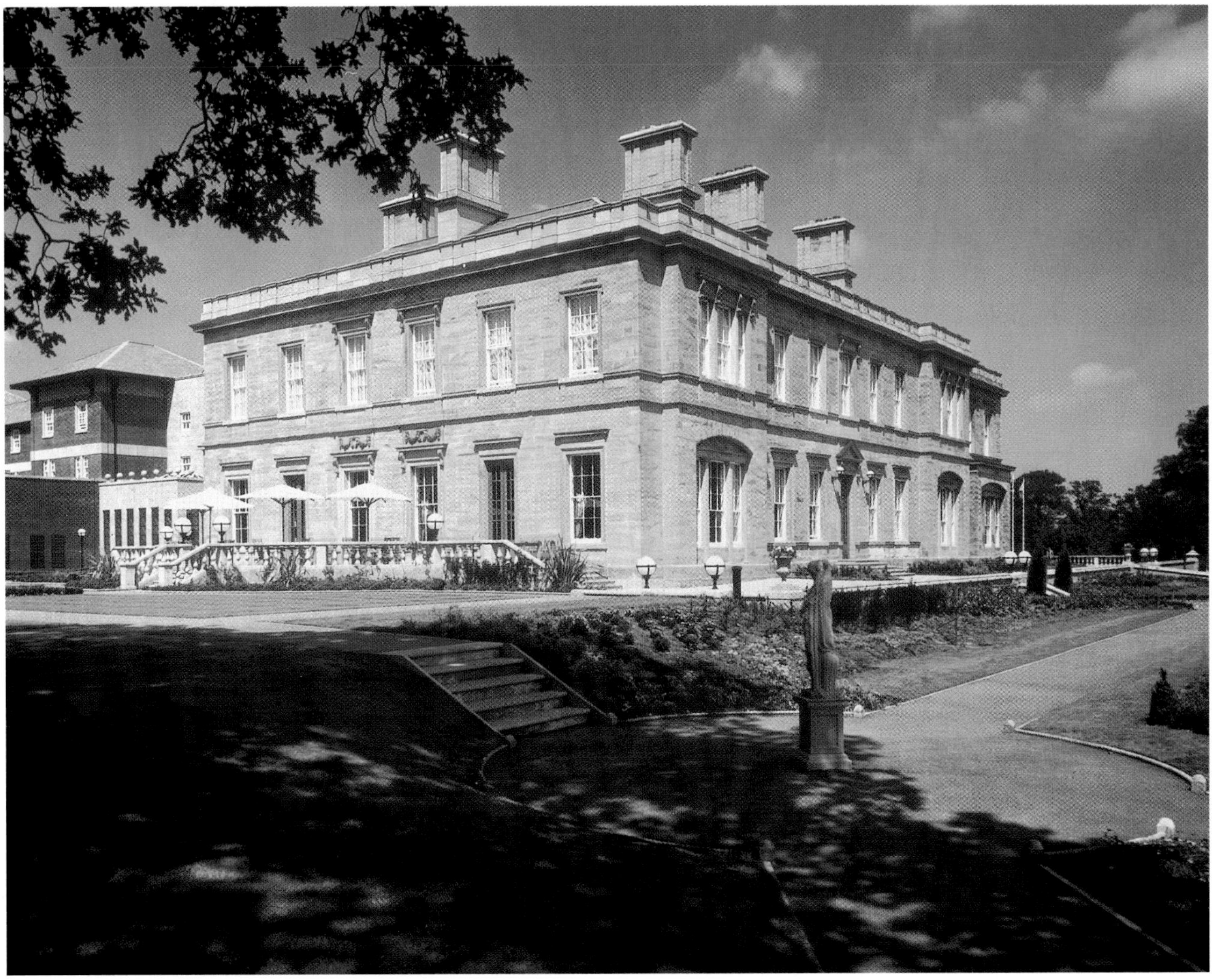

OULTON HALL

ROTHWELL LANE, OULTON, LEEDS, WEST YORKSHIRE LS26 8HN
TEL: 0113 2821000 FAX: 0113 2828066

Oulton Hall stands majestically amid acres of woodland and rolling Yorkshire dales. Its 19th century formal gardens are on the English Heritage Register of Historic Gardens. A Grade II listed building, the Hall has a long and fascinating history. In 1850 it was re-built in the neoclassical style. Restored and extended as a 5-Star hotel with traditional character and unique charm it combines today the elegance of a Victorian mansion with impeccable service and the most modern facilities for business and leisure. These include 152 superb, en suite bedrooms complemented by 7 deluxe suites above the Great Hall. Guests can enjoy excellent cuisine in the intimate Brontë Restaurant, which pays decorative tribute to the great literary sisters, or comfortably relax in the softly furnished lounges or the panelled library. The conference facilities have been carefully constructed to a demanding professional standard and can accommodate up to 300 delegates. There is a large indoor swimming pool, Jacuzzi, sauna, steam room, solarium and a squash court. Adjacent to the hotel are the 9-hole and 18-hole Oulton Park golf courses. Shooting, fishing and riding are nearby. Special leisure breaks available. Directions: From M62, exit at junction 30 and take A642 north. After 2 miles, turn left at roundabout onto Rothwell Lane and the hotel is on the left. Price guide: Single £115-£120; double/twin £125-£130; suite £165-£215.

For hotel location, see maps on pages 477-483

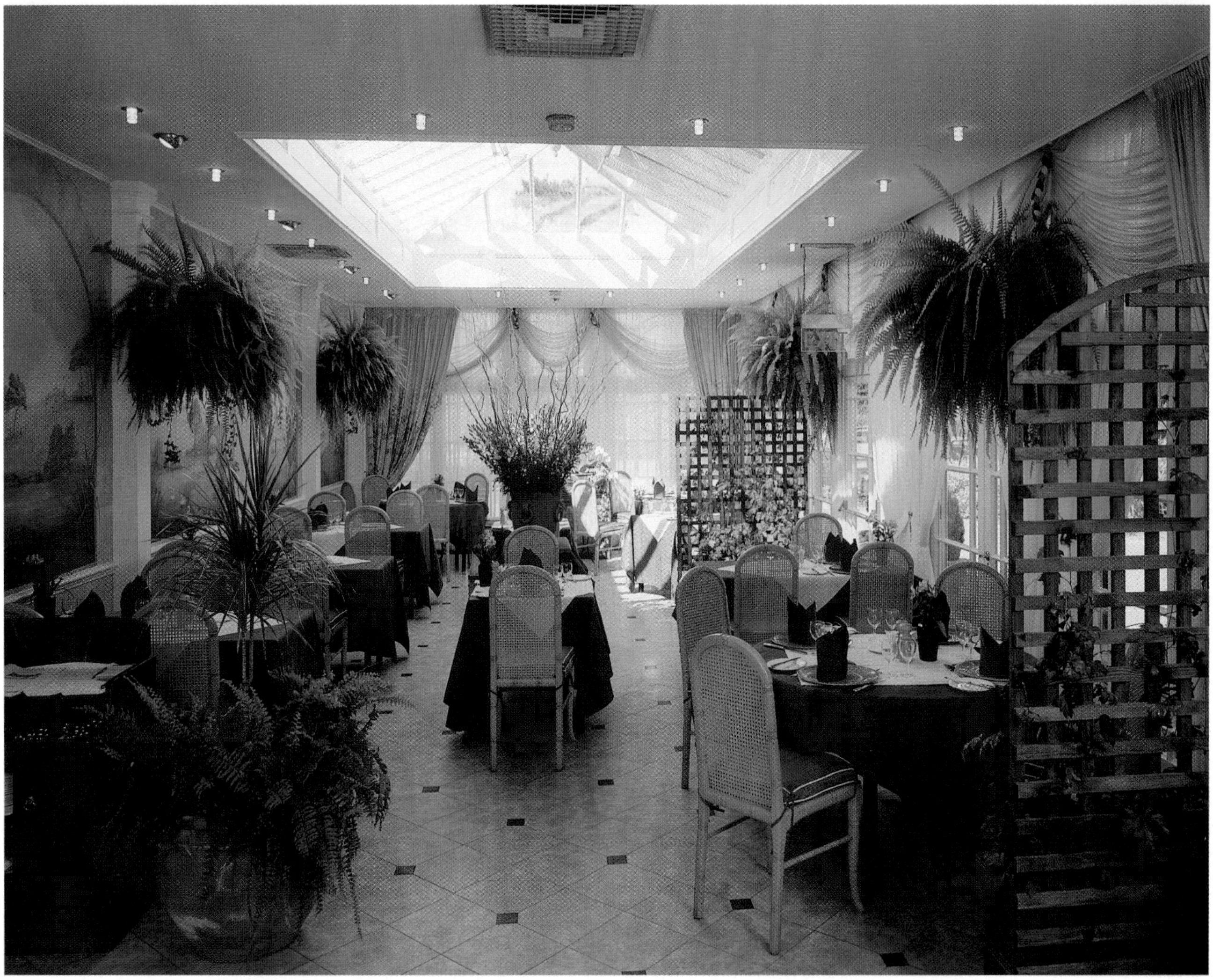

QUORN COUNTRY HOTEL

66 LEICESTER ROAD, QUORN, LEICESTERSHIRE LE12 8BB
TEL: 01509 415050 FAX: 01509 415557

Originally Leicestershire's most exclusive private club, created around the original 17th century listed building, this award winning hotel, set in four acres of landscaped gardens is the only non city centre hotel in Leicestershire to be awarded 4 stars by the AA. For the ninth consecutive year the hotel has received RAC merit awards for excellence in cuisine, hospitality and comfort and AA Rosette Award 1995. The bedrooms are equipped to the very highest standards with attention given to every detail for the businessman who needs an 'office in the bedroom' or for weekend guests seeking those extra 'touches' which help create the ideal peaceful retreat. Ladies travelling alone can feel reassured that their special needs are met and indeed exceeded. Particular emphasis is given to the enjoyment of food with a declared policy of using, whenever possible, the freshest local produce. Guests' stay will be enhanced by the choice of two different dining experiences. They can choose between the Shires Restaurant with its alcoves and low beamed ceiling and full à la carte service, or the light bright, airy atmosphere of the Orangery Brasserie. **Directions:** Situated just off the A6 Leicester to Nottingham main road, in the bypassed village of Quorn (Quorndon), five miles from junction 23 of the M1 from North, junction 21A from South, East and West. Price Guide: Single £84 ; double/twin £96 ; suite £125.

For hotel location, see maps on pages 477-483

LEWTRENCHARD MANOR

LEWDOWN, NR OKEHAMPTON, DEVON EX20 4PN
TEL: 01566 783 256 FAX: 01566 783 332

Nestling in the soft green Devon countryside just below Dartmoor, Lewtrenchard Manor is a beautiful 17th century grey stone manor house standing on the site of an earlier dwelling recorded in the Doomsday Book. Once the home of the Rev. Sabine Baring Gould, best remembered as a hymn writer and novelist, the Manor is rich in ornate ceilings, oak panelling, carvings and large open fireplaces. Personally run by owners James and Sue Murray the warm atmosphere of a large family house has been enhanced with the introduction of family antiques, fine paintings, warm colours and comfortable furniture. Nine spacious and light bedrooms have uninterrupted views through leaded windows over the peaceful countryside. The oak panelled dining room is the perfect setting in which to enjoy excellent dishes that combine superb flavour and delicacy with artistic presentation. There are lovely walks through the Lewtrenchard Estate, which also offers shooting and trout fishing nearby. Exeter, wild Dartmoor and quaint Devon villages are within easy reach and there are good facilities nearby for riding and golf. **Directions:** From Exeter and the M5 take A30 towards Okehampton and then join A386 for Tavistock. AT T-junction turn right and then left on to old A30 signposted to Bridestowe. Turn left at Lewdown for Lewtrenchard. Price guide: Single £75–£90; double/twin £100–£130; suite £140.

For hotel location, see maps on pages 477-483

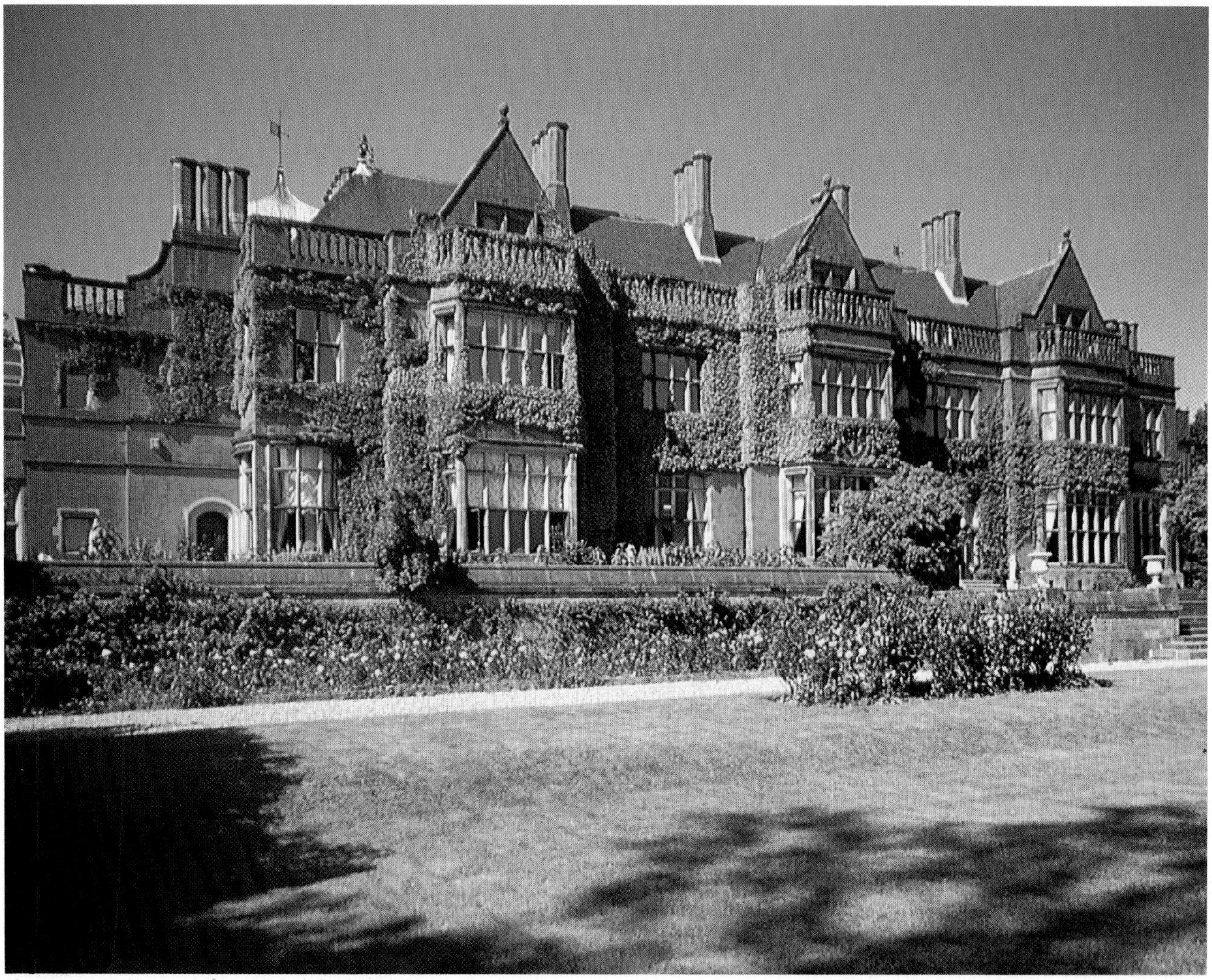

Hoar Cross Hall Health Spa Resort

HOAR CROSS, NR YOXALL, STAFFORDSHIRE DE13 8QS
TEL: 01283 575671 FAX: 01283 575652

Hoar Cross Hall is a health spa resort in a stately home hidden in the Staffordshire countryside with all the facilities of a 4 star hotel. Built in the 1860's it is a graceful listed residence. Today's guests want more than just to languish in beautiful surroundings they also wish to rejuvenate their mind and body. Water-based treatments are behind their successful philosophy; from hydro-therapy, baths and blitz jet douches, floatation therapy, saunas and steamrooms, to the superb hydrotherapy swimming pool, over 50 therapists pamper you with your choice of over 80 treatments. Peripheral activities are extensive. Partake of a full fitness assessment, a new hairstyle or venture into the 100 acres of woodlands and formal gardens. Play tennis, croquet and boules, or bicycle through the countryside. A Golf Academy with a PGA professional will teach you to play or improve your golf. Delight in the a la carte dining room where mouth watering dishes are served. Bedrooms and suites are exquisite with priceless views. Enjoy a day of relaxed luxury or a week of professional pampering. (minimum guest age is sixteen years). Price includes accommodation, breakfast, lunch, dinner, unlimited use of facilities and treatments according to length of stay. **Directions:** From Lichfield turn off A51 onto A515 towards Ashbourne. Go through Yoxall and turn left to Hoar Cross. Price guide (fully inclusive, see above): Single £105; double/twin £210.

For hotel location, see maps on pages 477-483

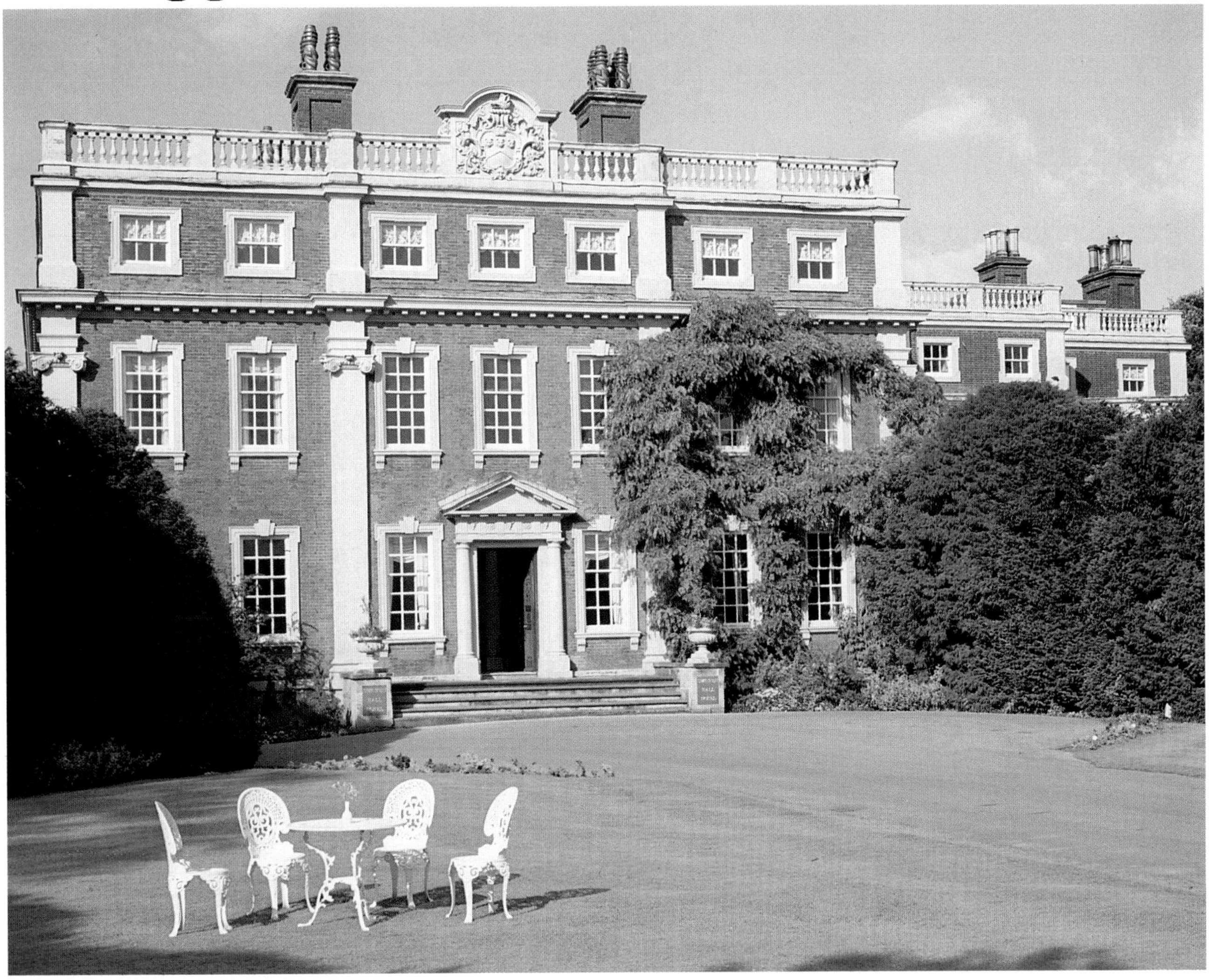

SWINFEN HALL

SWINFEN, NR LICHFIELD, STAFFORDSHIRE WS14 9RS
TEL: 01543 481494 FAX: 01543 480341

Swinfen Hall is a luxurious country house hotel built in the mid-18th century under the supervision of local architect Benjamin Wyatt. The money lavished on this dream residence is evident today in Swinfen Hall's balustraded Minstrels' Gallery and superb stucco ceilings crafted by Italian artisans. Elsewhere, fine architectural touches include the splendid carved-wood lobby ceiling, plus magnificent panelling and tiled fireplaces perfect in every detail. Owned by Helen and Victor Wiser, Swinfen is expertly managed by Paul Gilmore, who ensures a quality of service and hospitality befitting such a setting. In the restaurant and private dining room, guests can select from fresh fish, meat and local game (the breakfast menu is famed for its choice and value). A sun-filled banqueting hall with oak-panelled walls and magnificent Grinling Gibbons carvings is available for receptions and dinner dances. Bedrooms, decorated in pastel shades, are light, airy and comfortable, with period furnishings and modern conveniences including hospitality trays and hairdryers. Birmingham, and the International Airport are only 20 minutes away, and places to visit include Tamworth Castle and Lichfield Cathedral. **Directions:** Exit M42 at junctions A5. Lichfield is signposted off A5. Price guide: Single £65–£95; double/twin £90–£110; suite £120–£140.

For hotel location, see maps on pages 477-483

THE WOOLTON REDBOURNE HOTEL

ACREFIELD ROAD, WOOLTON, LIVERPOOL, MERSEYSIDE L25 5JN
TEL: 0151 421 1500/428 2152 FAX: 0151 421 1501

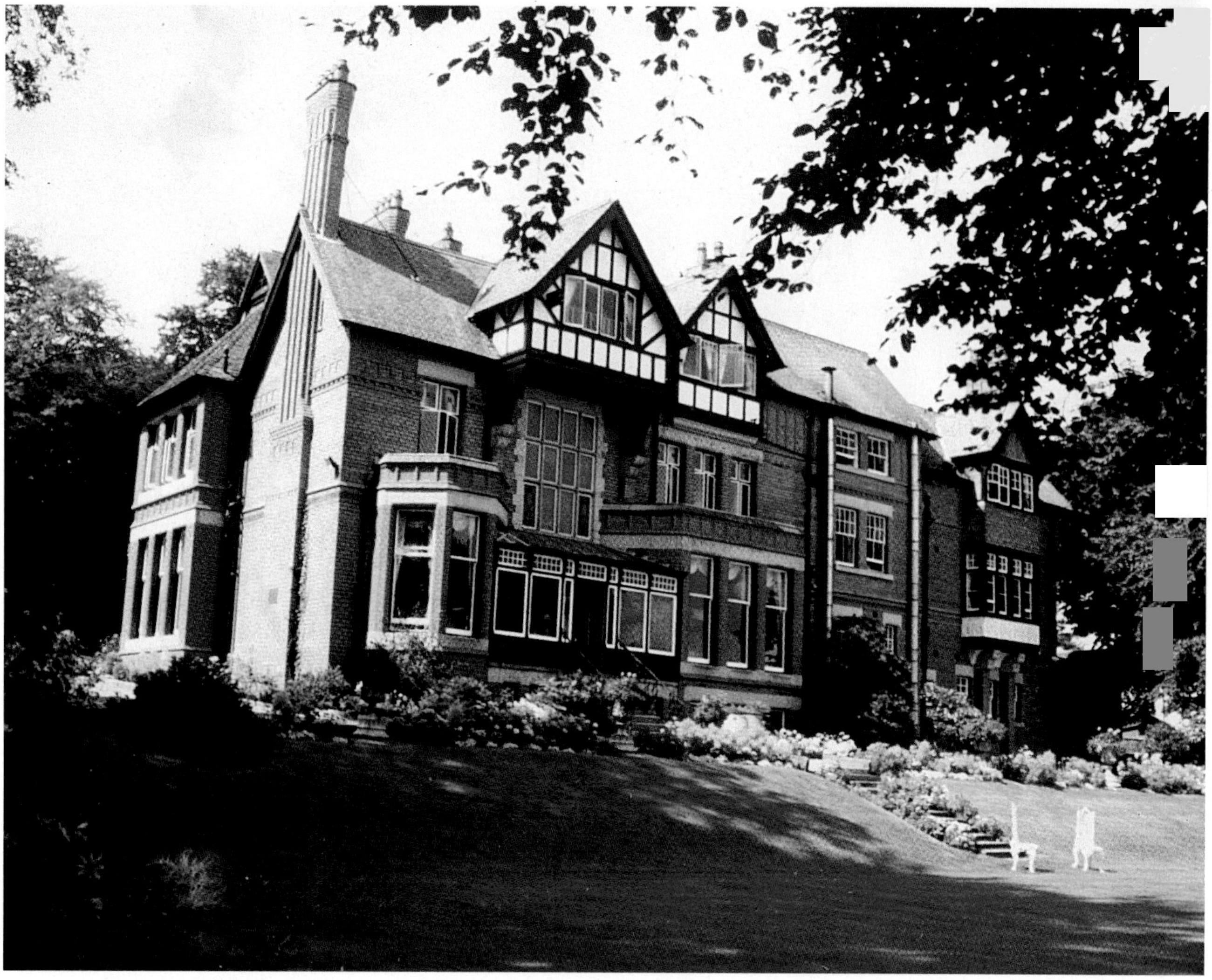

The Woolton Redbourne Hotel is a fine Grade II listed building which was built in the grand country house style by the great Victorian industrialist, Sir Henry Tate. Set amidst beautiful landscaped gardens and lawns, the hotel is a refuge of peace and tranquillity. Completely refurbished to original Victorian splendour by the Collins family, the Woolton Redbourne has quickly established itself as one of the region's foremost hotels. Whether for business or pleasure the hotel succeeds in creating a very homely atmosphere with highly personal and friendly service. The hotel is filled with intriguing Victorian antiques and each bedroom is delightfully decorated and furnished in period style. For those seeking the ultimate in comfort, the hotels seven suites are highly recommended. In the dining room an imaginative select table d'hôte is served. A meal at the Woolton Redbourne Hotel is an integral part of the experience and one which would have astounded the famous Lord Woolton who presided over food rationing in World War II. A full wine list is offered. The hotel caters for small business meetings and is just five miles from the city centre. **Directions:** At the end of the M62, junction 4, turn left onto the A5058. At third traffic lights turn left onto Woolton Road. The hotel is two miles on the left. Price guide: Single £60–£90; double/twin £86–£140; suite £150.

For hotel location, see maps on pages 477-483

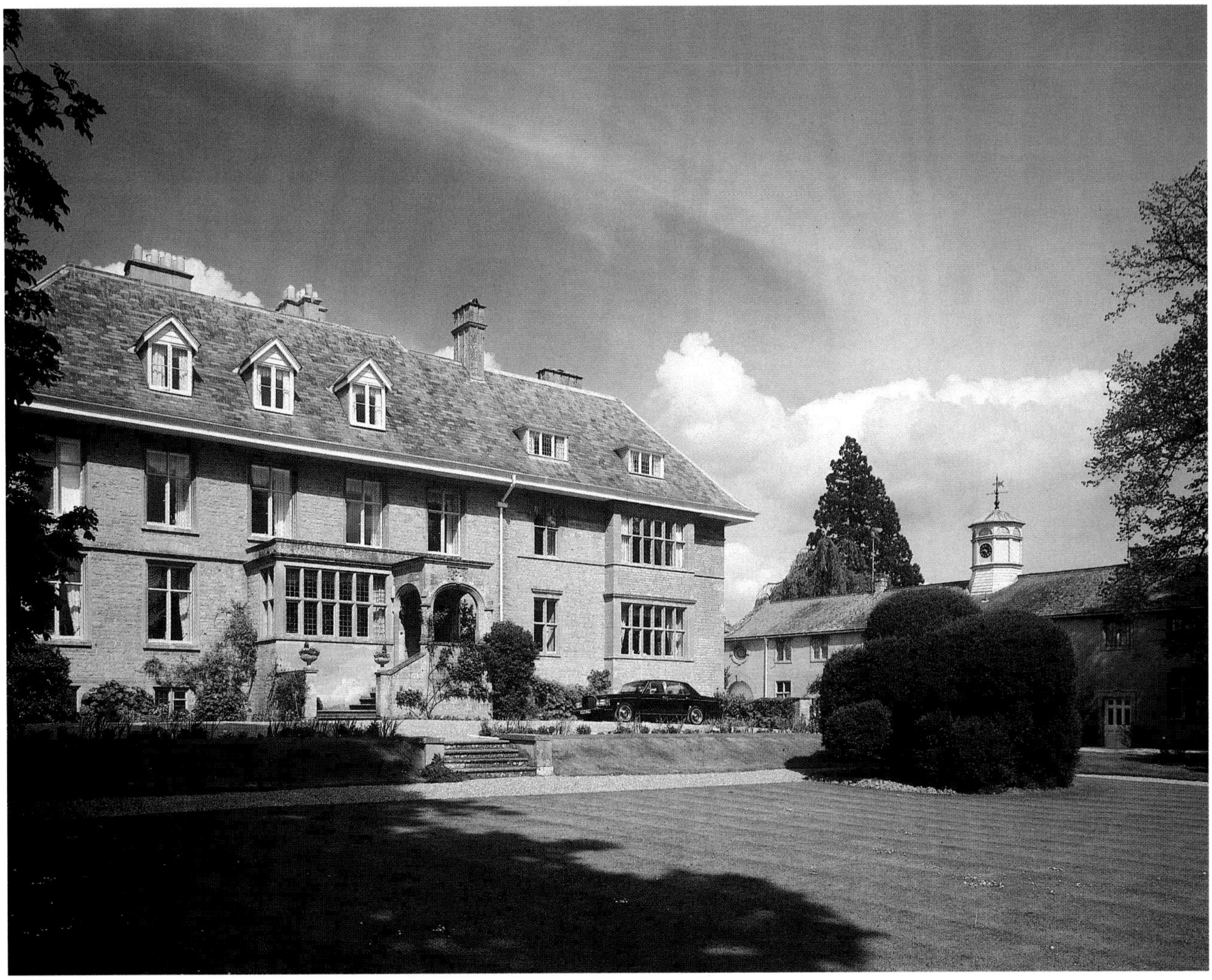

LOWER SLAUGHTER MANOR

LOWER SLAUGHTER, NR BOURTON-ON-THE-WATER, GLOUCESTERSHIRE GL54 2HP
TEL: 01451 820456 FAX: 01451 822150

One of the best kept secrets in the Cotswolds. In three years, this magnificent 17th century manor house has been transformed into one of the highest rated country house hotels in England. The Manor has been awarded the prestigious three Red Star rating and the Courtesy and Care Award from the AA. It is also the recipient of a Blue Ribbon Award from the RAC. Flowers abound in all the elegant public rooms where fine antiques, works of art and blazing log fires in the winter add to the very special atmosphere. Exceptionally spacious bedrooms look out onto the picturesque gardens. Alan Dann's cuisine has gained much praise from the guides including the award of 3 AA Rosettes. There is a fine range of wines from the old and new worlds and the Manor was awarded Egon Ronay's guides 'Californian Wine Cellar of the Year 1994'. The emphasis is on style, comfort and service. There is an indoor heated swimming pool, sauna, all-weather tennis court, croquet lawn and putting green. The Manor is ideally located as a base from which to tour the Cotswolds and as an excellent venue for discreet meetings in the private conference suite. **Directions:** From the A419, follow the signs to The Slaughters; the Manor is on the right entering the village. Price guide: All prices include English breakfast and dinner from the à la carte menu. Single £140–£195; double/twin £205–£275; suites £290.

For hotel location, see maps on pages 477-483

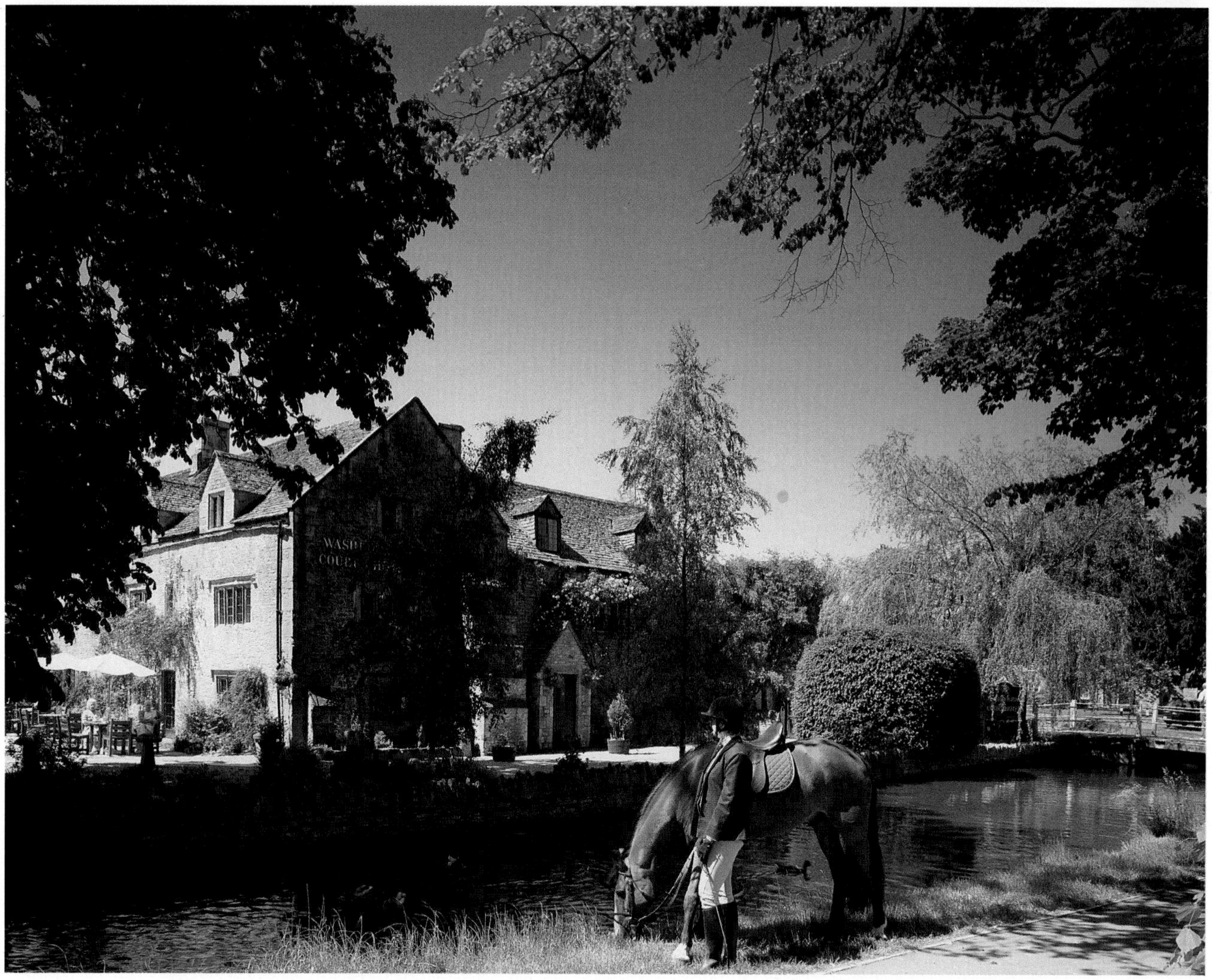

WASHBOURNE COURT HOTEL

LOWER SLAUGHTER, GLOUCESTERSHIRE GL54 2HS
TEL: 01451 822143 FAX: 01451 821045

Washbourne Court Hotel is a magnificent 17th Century building set in 4 acres of grounds alongside the river in Lower Slaughter, one of the Cotswolds most beautiful and unspoilt villages. Owned and managed by the Pender family the hotel prides itself on offering high quality accommodation and friendly personal service. The main house retains much of its original charm and character with beamed ceilings, flagstone floors and mullioned windows, whilst the new coachouse and cottage suites have been built in mellowed natural stone in keeping with the lovely surroundings. Guests can enjoy a drink or light lunch on the riverside terrace during the summer months or by the real log fire in winter. Modern English cuisine is served to a very high standard and the restaurant has been awarded 3 AA red rosettes. All bedrooms are individually furnished and have private facilities. There are a number of suites with private lounges and jacuzzi bathrooms. The surrounding area is renowned for its natural beauty with many gentle walks. **Directions:** The hotel is situated ½ a mile from the main A429 Fosseway between Stow-on-the-Wold and Bourton-on-the-Water (signed To the Slaughters). Price guide: Single £85; double/twin £95–£120; suite £150–£185. Breaks available throughout the year.

For hotel location, see maps on pages 477-483

DINHAM HALL

LUDLOW, SHROPSHIRE SY8 1EJ
TEL: 01584 876464 FAX: 01584 876019

Built in 1792 Dinham Hall is situated in the historic town of Ludlow. It lies only 40 metres from the Castle which, having played an important part in England's history, today hosts the Shakespearian productions which form the major part of the annual Ludlow Festival. Dinham's enviable location provides its guests with the combination of ready access to the town and picturesque views over the open Shropshire countryside. There is a magnificent fireplace in the sitting room, with log fires in the winter. In the restaurant flowers help to provide a subtle atmosphere in which to enjoy prize-winning cuisine while the Merchant Suite, with its 14th century timbers, is an ideal setting for private dinners and meetings. During the summer afternoon teas are served on the terrace overlooking the walled garden. The décor of the bedrooms is a harmony of modern facilities and period design, a number of rooms having four-poster beds. The restaurant and many bedrooms command views over the gardens and Teme Valley to wooded hills. Guests may also enjoy a visit to Ludlow races or spend a few hours browsing in the town's antique shops. South Shropshire is one of the most beautiful parts of the country with Ludlow itself being one of the finest market towns. **Directions:** In the centre of Ludlow overlooking the castle. Price guide: Single £68.50–£78.50; double/twin £90–£125.

14 rms MasterCard VISA AMERICAN EXPRESS M 20

For hotel location, see maps on pages 477-483

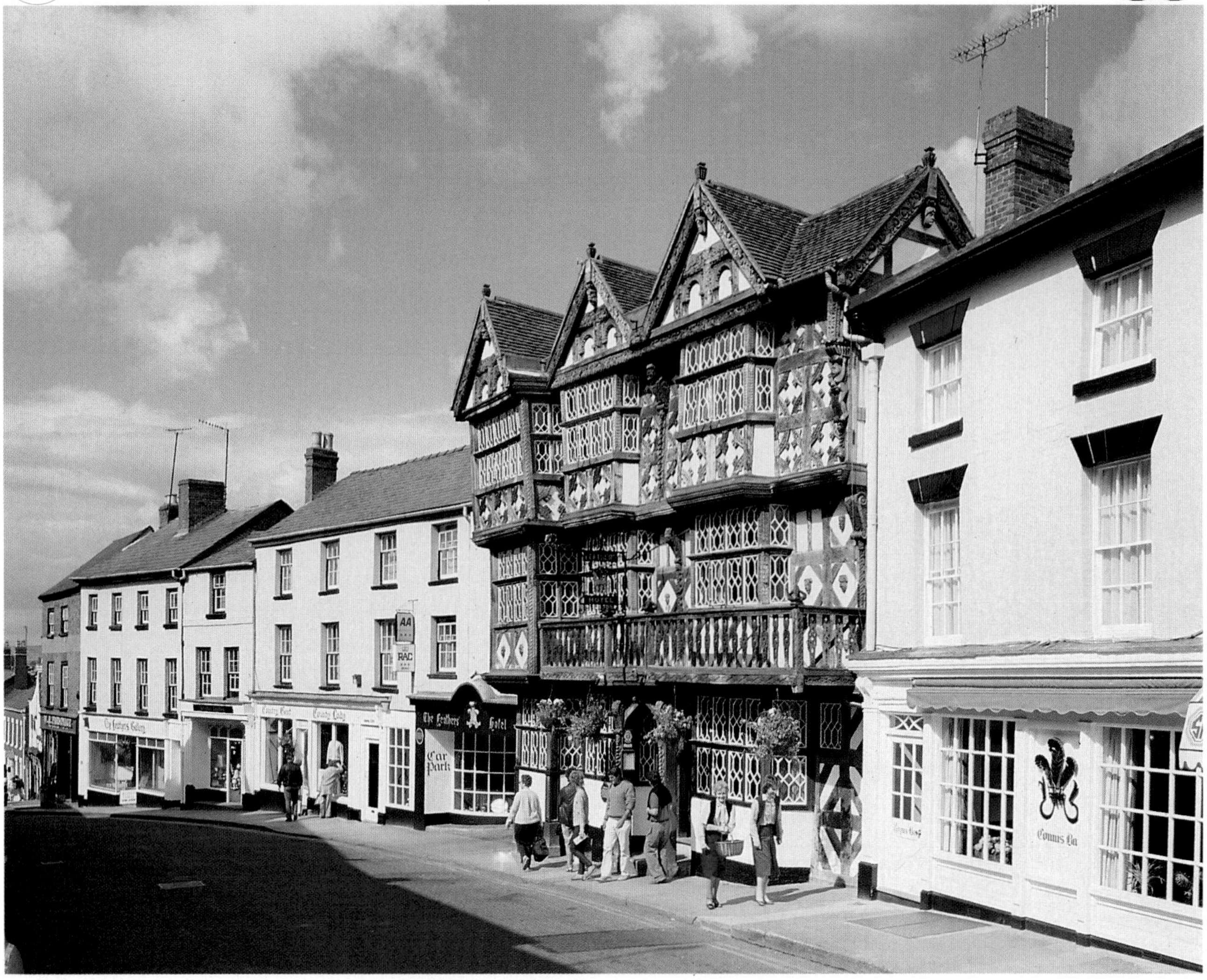

THE FEATHERS

BULL RING, LUDLOW, SHROPSHIRE SY8 1AA
TEL: 01584 875261 FAX: 01584 876030

The 11th-century Feathers hotel stands in white and black timber-framed splendour in the centre of Ludlow, just a short stroll from the historic town's massive 11th century sandstone castle and the cathedral-like grandeur of the 15th-century Church of St Lawrence. Brimful of atmosphere and character The Feathers has been described as one of the most handsome inns in the world. It abounds with heavy beams, oak panelling, intricate carvings, ornate plasterwork and hugh open hearths with log fires in the winter. Two bars and a spacious, deep carpeted lounge provide comfort and relaxation. The cosy Housman Restaurant, with its attractive courtyard summer extension, serves cuisine of the highest quality while a baronial hall, complete with banners, swords, shields and armour, is an ideal setting for special occasions. The decor of the bedrooms is a harmony of modern facilities and period design. Some have open fires and four-poster beds. The Feathers is an ideal base from which to explore South Shropshire and the Marches. Fishing, shooting and golf are nearby and there is horse racing at Ludlow itself. Directions: From M5, exit at junction 7 to Worcester and take the A44 towards Leominster. Turn right onto A49 Shrewsbury road and Ludlow is nine miles north. Price guide: Single £65; double/twin £88-£110; suite £130-£140.

For hotel location, see maps on pages 473–479

THE FERNIE LODGE HOTEL

BERRIDGES LANE, HUSBANDS BOSWORTH, LUTTERWORTH, LEICESTERSHIRE LE17 6LE
TEL: 01858 880551 FAX: 01858 880014

The Fernie Lodge is a long established Georgian country house hotel, set in the heart of the rolling Leicestershire landscape, where the charm of a bygone age combines with the very best of modern comfort and facilities. Each bedroom is individually decorated and possesses its own unique character. Dining at the hotel is always a pleasurable experience. Creative cuisine, skilfully prepared by chefs using only the finest fresh produce and highest quality ingredients, has won it an excellent culinary reputation. Enticing dishes are complemented by an extensive range of wines. A traditional conservatory, where the resident pianist regularly entertains in time honoured style, is a perfect place to relax after a meal. For business meetings, Fernie Lodge offers a wide choice of rooms sizes and lay outs and a full range of audio visual equipment is provided. The hotel prides itself on a friendly, cheerful and quietly professional service and nothing is ever too much trouble. Fernie Lodge is within easy driving distance of Northampton, Leicester and many smaller historic towns. Originally famous for hunting, the area now offers a wide range of equine pursuits, along with clay pigeon shooting, trout fishing, golfing, gliding and sailing. **Directions:** Take Junction 20 from M1. At Lutterworth take A427 to Husbands Bosworth. Price guide: Single £55; double/twin £67.

17 rms MasterCard VISA AMERICAN EXPRESS M 90

For hotel location, see maps on pages 477-483

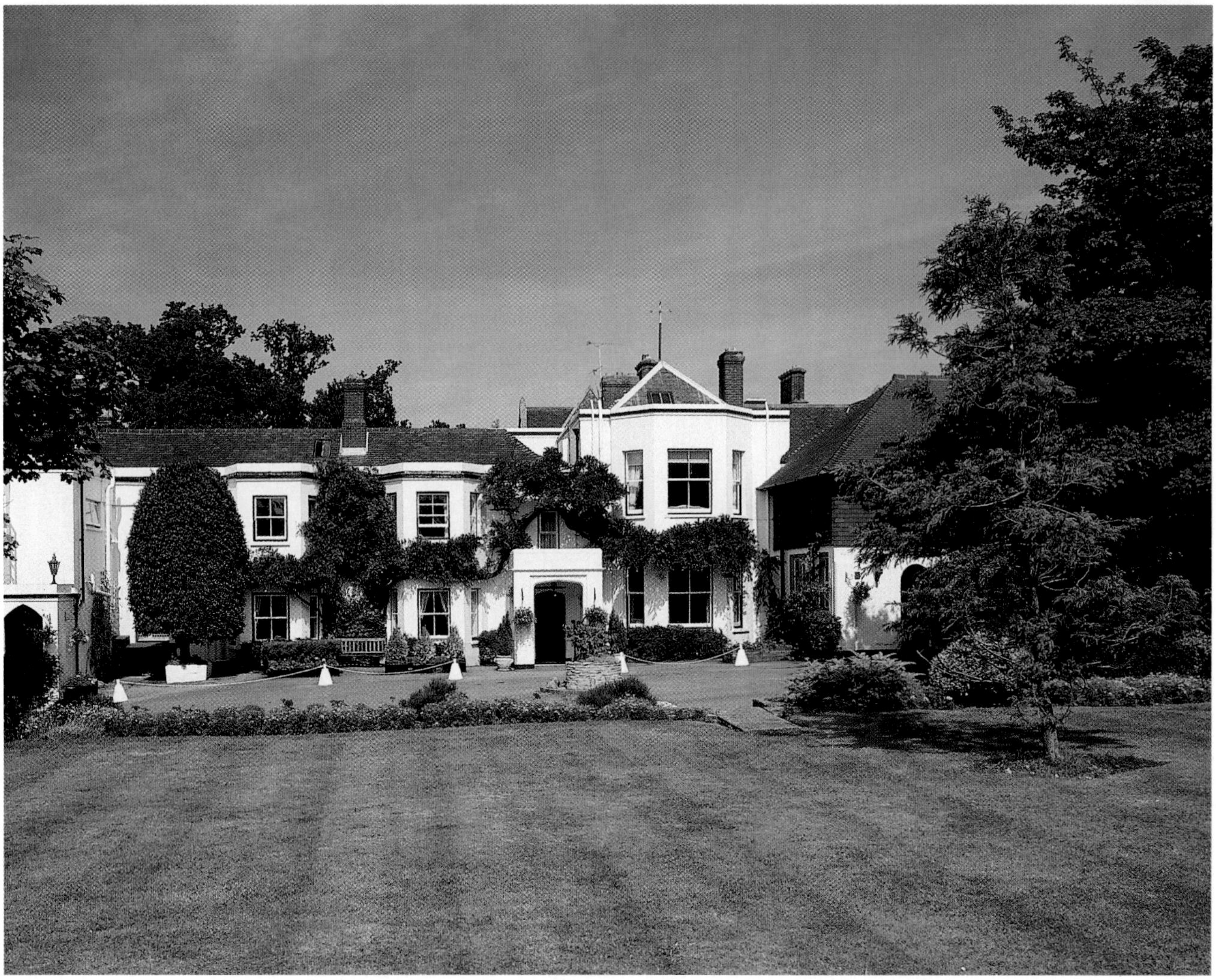

PASSFORD HOUSE HOTEL

MOUNT PLEASANT LANE, LYMINGTON, HAMPSHIRE SO41 8LS
TEL: 01590 682398 FAX: 01590 683494

Set in nine acres of picturesque gardens and rolling parkland, the Passford House Hotel lies midway between the charming New Forest village of Sway and the Georgian splendour of Lymington. Once the home of Lord Arthur Cecil, it is steeped in history and the traditions of leisurely country life. Pleasantly decorated bedrooms include a number of de luxe rooms, while comfort is the keynote in the four public lounges. The hotel prides itself on the standard and variety of cuisine served in its delightful restaurant and the extensive menu aims to give pleasure to the most discerning of palates. Meals are complemented by a speciality wine list. The hotel boasts a superb leisure centre, catering for all ages and activities. In addition to two heated swimming pools, there is a multi-gym, sauna, solarium, pool table, croquet lawn, petanque and tennis court. Just a short drive away are Beaulieu, the cathedral cities of Winchester and Salisbury and ferry ports to the Isle of Wight and France. The New Forest area has five golf courses and, for those interested in riding, there are many stables and trekking centres. Milford-on-Sea, four miles away, is the nearest beach. **Directions:** At Lymington leave the A337 at the Tollhouse Inn, then take the first turning right and the hotel is on the right. Price guide: £75: double/twin £110–£135.

50 rms MasterCard VISA AMERICAN EXPRESS M 100

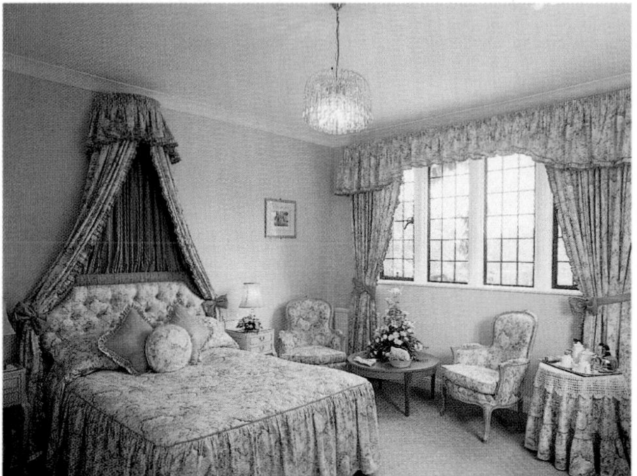

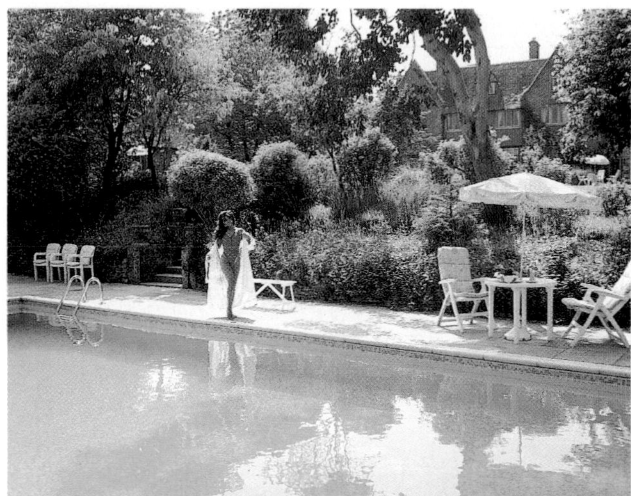

For hotel location, see maps on pages 477-483

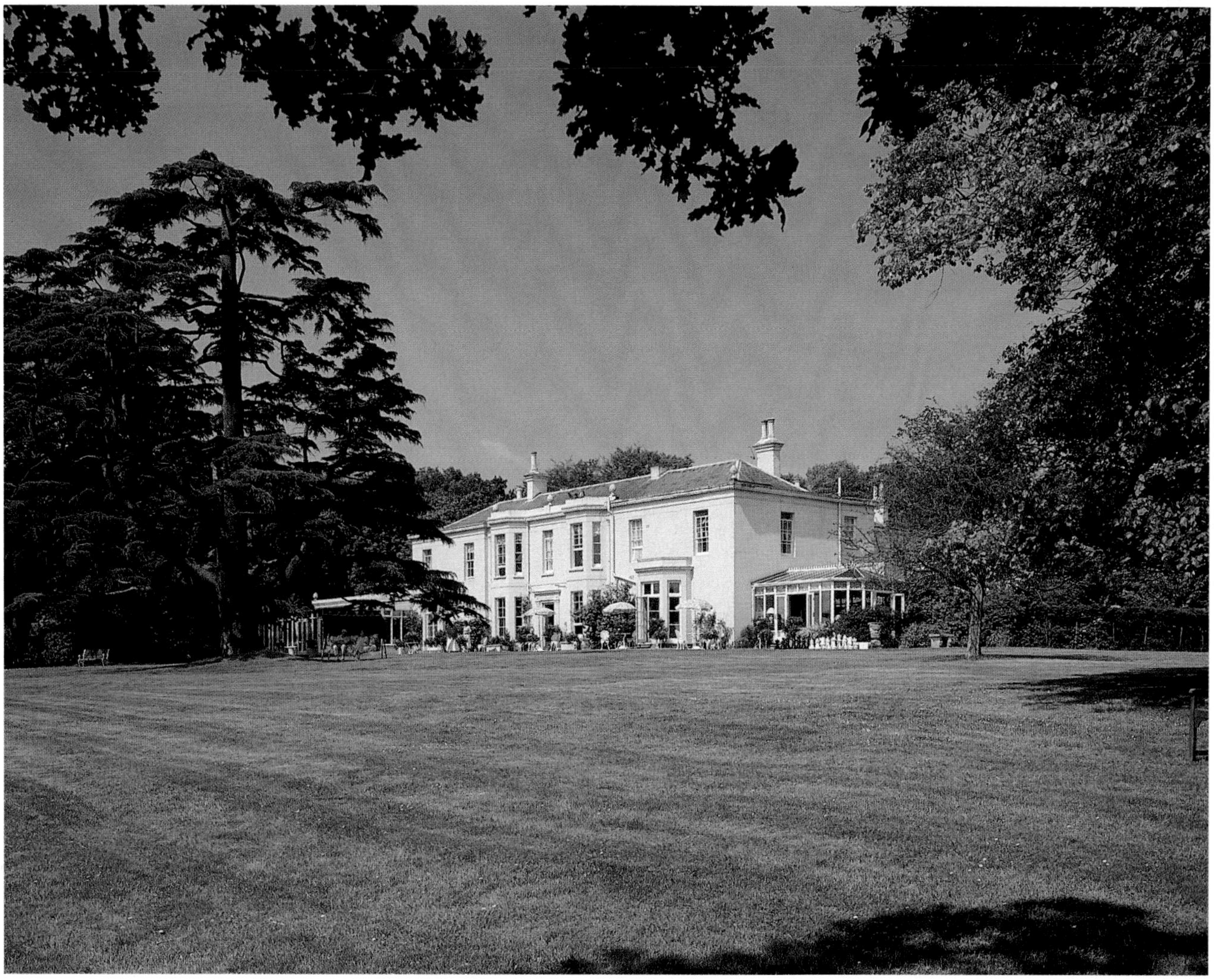

PARKHILL HOTEL

BEAULIEU ROAD, LYNDHURST, NEW FOREST, HAMPSHIRE SO43 7FZ
TEL: 01703 282944 FAX: 01703 283268

Reached by way of a winding drive through glorious parkland from the scenic route between Lyndhurst and Beaulieu, Parkhill, situated in an elevated position with superb views across open forest and heathland, is perfect for a restful break or holiday and makes the ideal venue for special business meetings and small conferences, offering a charming New Forest remoteness coupled with an excellence of standards and service. Dining at Parkhill is very much an integral part of your overall pleasure. The award winning restaurant offers a most tranquil setting with fine views across the lawns, where deer can frequently be seen grazing. Cuisine is a delicious blend of modern and classical English cooking, where local fresh produce is used to create appetising menus, balanced by a carefully chosen and well-stocked cellar. Parkhill is also an ideal base for touring not only the delightful surrounding areas, but also the many places of interest which are all within easy driving distance, including Exbury Gardens, home to one of the world's finest collections of rhododendrons and azaleas, Broadlands, the home of Lord Mountbatten, the *Mary Rose* in Portsmouth Dockyard, and the graceful cathedral cities of Salisbury and Winchester. **Directions:** From Lyndhurst take the B3056 toward Beaulieu; Parkhill is about 1 mile from Lyndhurst on your right. Price guide: Single £59.50–£76; double £99–£132.

For hotel location, see maps on pages 477-483

THE LYNTON COTTAGE HOTEL

NORTH WALK, LYNTON, NORTH DEVON EX35 6ED
TEL: 01598 752342 FAX: 01598 752597

Once the residence of a knight of the realm, The Lynton Cottage Hotel has a panoramic view of the Lyn Valley and Lynmouth Bay – a spectacular sight to greet visitors approaching along the winding drive. Dating back to the 17th century, the hotel combines period charm with modern comforts. The 16 en suite bedrooms and suites are individually decorated with taste and style and equipped to reflect the perfectionist approach of enthusiastic proprietors John and Maisie Jones. Under the auspices of chef Leon Balanche, innovative cuisine is prepared with flair, finesse and an influence of French culinary style. AA Rosette awarded. Gastronomic house parties have proved popular on regular weekends throughout the year, offering guests an opportunity to enjoy the finest gourmet cooking accompanied by wines carefully selected for the occasion. Other special breaks available include mystery whodunnit and champagne weekends. Riding, clay pigeon shooting, golf and salmon fishing are all available locally and the hotel is an ideal base from which to discover the rugged beauty of Exmoor and the Valley of Rocks. Closed January. **Directions:** From M5 take A39 to Porlock then on to Lynton, where the hotel is on the North Walk. Price guide (including dinner): Single £57–£75; double/twin £110–£150.

For hotel location, see maps on pages 477-483

CLIVEDEN

TAPLOW, BERKSHIRE SL6 0JF
TEL: 01628 668561 FAX: 01628 661837

Cliveden, Britain's only 5 Red AA star hotel that is also a stately home, is set in 376 acres of gardens and parkland, overlooking the Thames. As the former home of Frederick, Prince of Wales, three Dukes and the Astor family, Cliveden has been at the centre of Britain's social and political life for over 300 years. It is exquisitely furnished in a classically English style, with a multitude of oil paintings, antiques and *objets d'art*. The spacious guest rooms and suites are appointed to the most luxurious standards. The new Cliveden Town House in London is of a similar excellence. One of the greatest pleasures of eating at Cliveden is in the choice of dining rooms and the scope of the menus. The French Dining Room, with its original Madame de Pompadour rococo decoration, is the finest 18th-century *boiserie* outside France. Alternatively, relish the Michelin-starred cuisine of chef Ron Maxfield in Waldo's Restaurant. The Pavilion offers a full range of health and fitness facilities and beauty therapies. Guests can ride Cliveden's horses over the estate or enjoy a leisurely river cruise on an Edwardian launch. Comprehensively equipped, the two secure private boardrooms provide self-contained business meeting facilities. Exclusive use of the hotel can be arranged. **Directions:** Situated on B476, 2 miles north of Taplow. Price guide: Single £220; double/twin £245; suites from £398.

For hotel location, see maps on pages 477-483

FREDRICK'S HOTEL & RESTAURANT

SHOPPENHANGERS ROAD, MAIDENHEAD, BERKSHIRE SL6 2PZ
TEL: 01628 35934 FAX: 01628 771054

'Putting people first' is the guiding philosophy behind the running of this sumptuously equipped hotel and, indeed, is indicative of the uncompromising service guests can expect to receive. Set in two acres of grounds, Fredrick's overlooks the fairways and greens of Maidenhead Golf Club beyond. The immaculate reception rooms are distinctively styled to create something out of the ordinary. Minute attention to detail is evident in the 37 bedrooms, all immaculate with gleaming, marble-tiled bathrooms, while the suites have their own patio garden or balcony. A quiet drink can be enjoyed in the light, airy Wintergarden lounge before entering the air-conditioned restaurant. Amid the elegant décor of crystal chandeliers and crisp white linen, fine gourmet cuisine is served which has received recognition from leading guides for many years. Particularly suited to conferences, four private function rooms with full secretarial facilities are available. Helicopter landing can be arranged. Easily accessible from Windsor, Henley, Ascot, Heathrow and London. Closed 24-30 December. **Directions:** Leave M4 at exit 8/9, take A404(M) and leave at first turning signed Cox Green/White Waltham. Turn into Shoppenhangers Road; Fredrick's is on the right. Price guide: Single £148–£158; double/twin £178–£188; suite £250.

For hotel location, see maps on pages 477-483

Chilston Park Country House

SANDWAY, LENHAM, NR MAIDSTONE, KENT ME17 2BE

TEL: 01622 859803 FAX: 01622 858588

This magnificent Grade I listed mansion, one of England's most richly decorated hotels, was built in the 13th century and remodelled in the 18th century. Now sensitively refurbished, the hotel's ambience is enhanced by the lighting at dusk each day of over 200 candles. The drawing room and reading room offer guests an opportunity to relax and to admire the outstanding collection of antiques. The entire hotel is a treasure trove for the many interesting *objets d'art*. The opulently furnished bedrooms are fitted to a high standard and many have four-poster beds.

Good, fresh English cooking is offered in each of Chilston's five dining rooms, where outstanding menus are supported by an excellent wine list. In keeping with the traditions of a country house, a wide variety of sporting activities is available, golf and riding nearby, fishing in the natural spring lake and punting. **Directions:** Take junction 8 off the M20, then A20 to Lenham Station. Turn left into Boughton Road. Go over the crossroads and M20; Chilston Park is on the left. Price guide: Single £99.50–£140; double/twin £115–£195.

For hotel location, see maps on pages 477-483

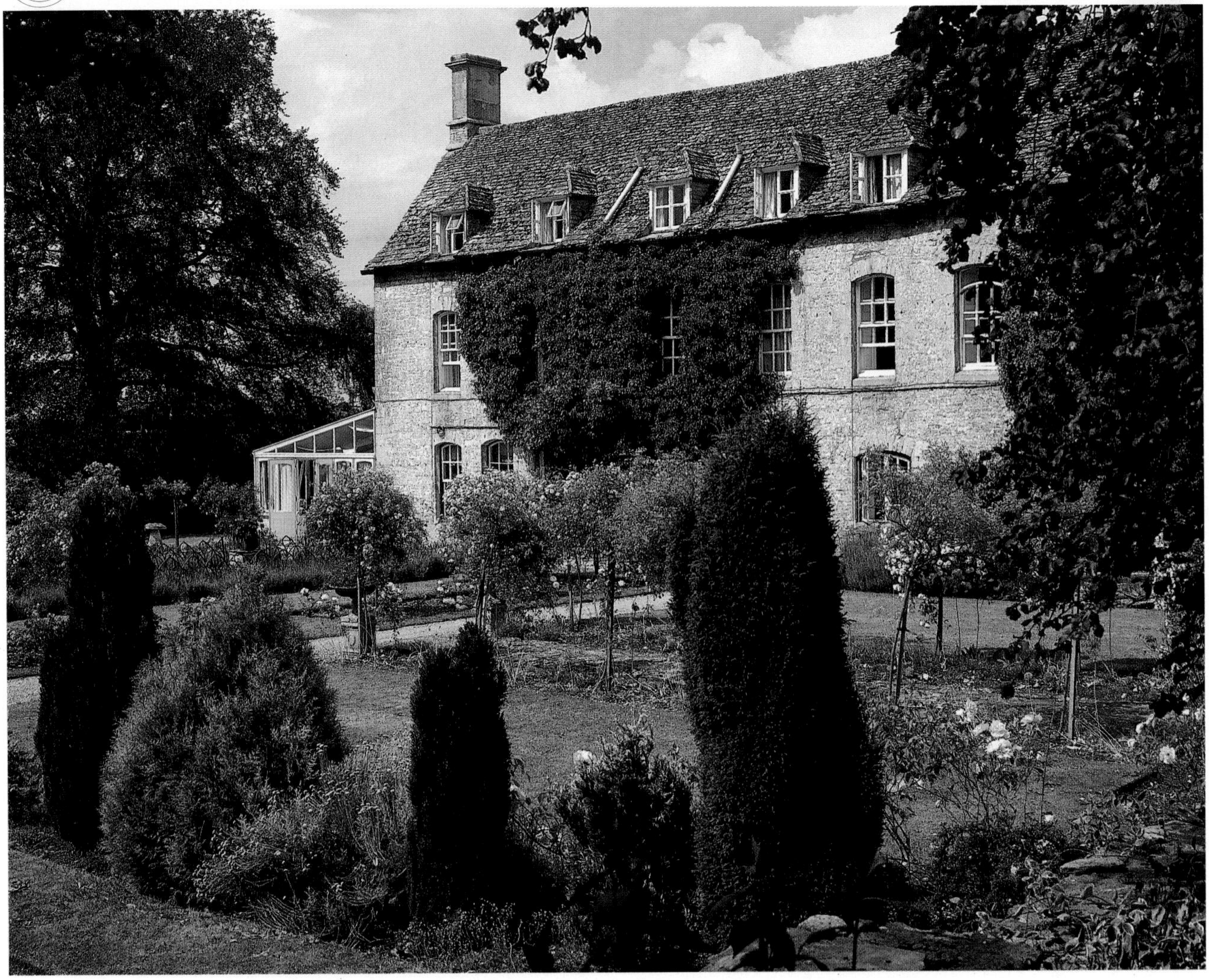

CRUDWELL COURT HOTEL

CRUDWELL, NR MALMESBURY, WILTSHIRE SN16 9EP
TEL: 01666 577194 FAX: 01666 577853

Crudwell Court is a 17th-century rectory, set in three acres of Cotswold walled gardens. The pretty, well-established grounds have lily ponds and a garden gate leading through to the neighbouring Saxon church of All Saints. Completely refurbished in recent years, the old rectory has been decorated with bright, cheery colours. Sunshine yellow in the sitting room, warm apricot in the drawing room and shades of buttercream and blue in the bedrooms lend a fresh feel to this hotel. Visitors enter through a flagstoned hall to discover rooms with comfortable seating and plenty of books to read. In the panelled dining room guests will find a weekly changing menu, which is best described as modern Anglo-French. Cooked to order, the meals are a feast for the eye as well as the palate. The restaurant has recently been extended into a new conservatory, which may also be used for private functions. Malmesbury has a magnificent Norman abbey church and a curious market cross. Nearby are the towns of Tetbury and Cirencester, the picturesque villages of Castle Combe and Lacock and numerous stately homes. **Directions:** Crudwell Court is on the A429. Travelling towards Cirencester, when you reach the village of Crudwell turn right (signposted Oaksey) opposite the Plough Inn, and the hotel is on the left. Price guide: Single £50; double/twin £90.

For hotel location, see maps on pages 477-483

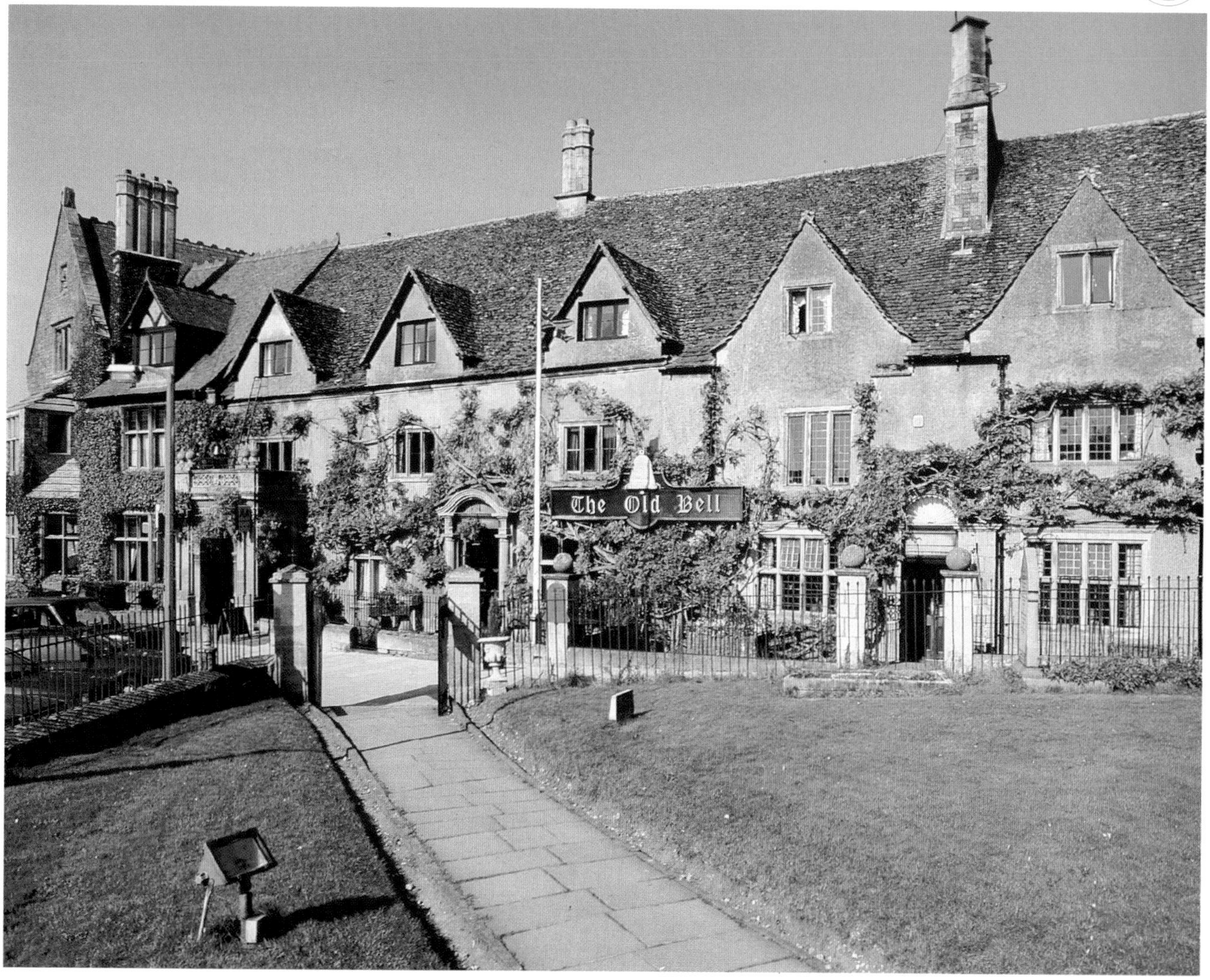

THE OLD BELL

ABBEY ROW, MALMESBURY, WILTSHIRE SN16 0AG
TEL: 01666 822344 FAX: 01666 825145

The Old Bell was established by the Abbot of Malmesbury during the reign of King John as a place to refresh guests who came to consult the Abbey's library. Situated at the edge of the Cotswolds, this Grade I listed building may well be England's most ancient hotel. Inside, the Great Hall boasts a medieval stone fireplace, while each bedroom is decorated and furnished with an individual style and character. A classic and imaginative menu exemplifies the best in English cooking, with meals ranging from four-course dinners complemented by fine wines in the Edwardian dining room, to informal snacks on the terrace. The oak-beamed lounges, which were built in the 16th century for the steward of Malmesbury Abbey, open on to a quiet terrace and traditional English garden complete with gazebo. Families are particularly welcomed at The Old Bell; there is no charge for children sharing parents' rooms and children's menus are available. The 'Den' is equipped with a multitude of toys and open every day. Malmesbury is only 30 minutes from Bath and is close to a number of other beautiful villages such as Castle Combe, Bourton-on-the-Water and Lacock. Outdoor places of interest include the mysterious stone circle at Avebury and the Westonbirt Arboretum. **Directions:** Near the market cross in the centre of Malmesbury. Price guide: Single £60–£70; double/twin £75–£115; suites £125.

For hotel location, see maps on pages 477-483

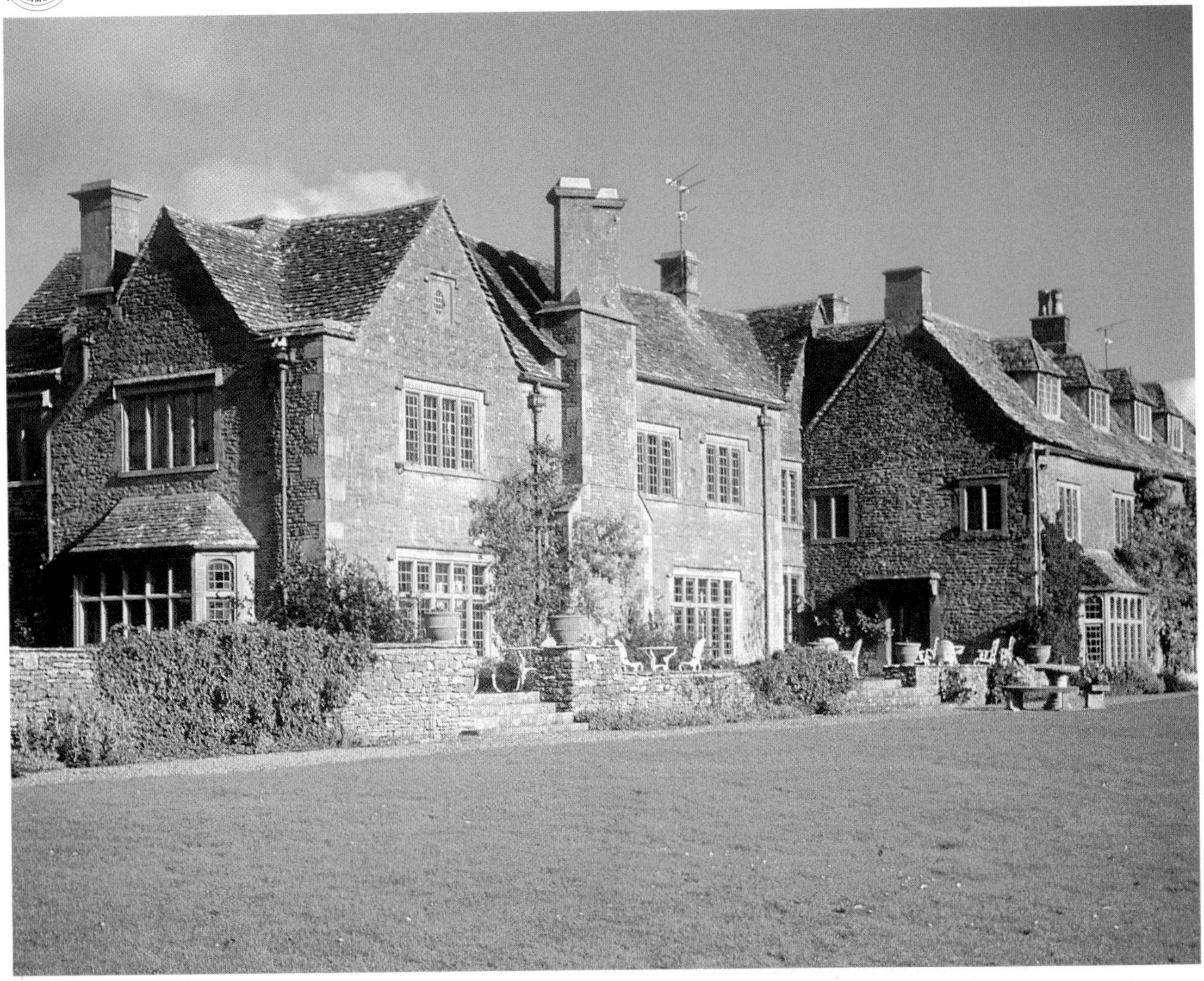

WHATLEY MANOR

NR EASTON GREY, MALMESBURY, WILTSHIRE SN16 0RB
TEL: 01666 822888 FAX: 01666 826120

This Grade II listed manor, set around a central courtyard, stands in 12 acres of grounds running down to a peaceful stretch of the River Avon. Originally built in the 17th century, Whatley Manor was refurbished by a wealthy sportsman in the 1920s and many of the present buildings date from that period. While the hotel's interior is furnished to a high standard, an emphasis has always been placed on maintaining a relaxed, informal atmosphere, enhanced by pine and oak panelling, log fires and the effect of warm colours in the lounge and drawing room. The dining room similarly combines elegance with intimacy and it overlooks the gardens. Ten of the bedrooms are in the 'Courthouse'. Snooker and table-tennis facilities are provided in the original saddle rooms and there is also a sauna, solarium and Jacuzzi. Close for gardening enthusiasts is Hodges Barn at Shipton Moyne. With the Cotswolds, the cities of Bath and Bristol, Tetbury, Cirencester, Westonbirt Arboretum, Longleat, Stourhead Gardens and many places of historic interest nearby, Whatley Manor is the perfect place for long weekend breaks, for which the special terms ensure good value. Two night weekend breaks from £121. **Directions:** The hotel is on the B4040 three miles west of Malmesbury. Price guide: Single £70–£80; double/twin £82–£114.

For hotel location, see maps on pages 477-483

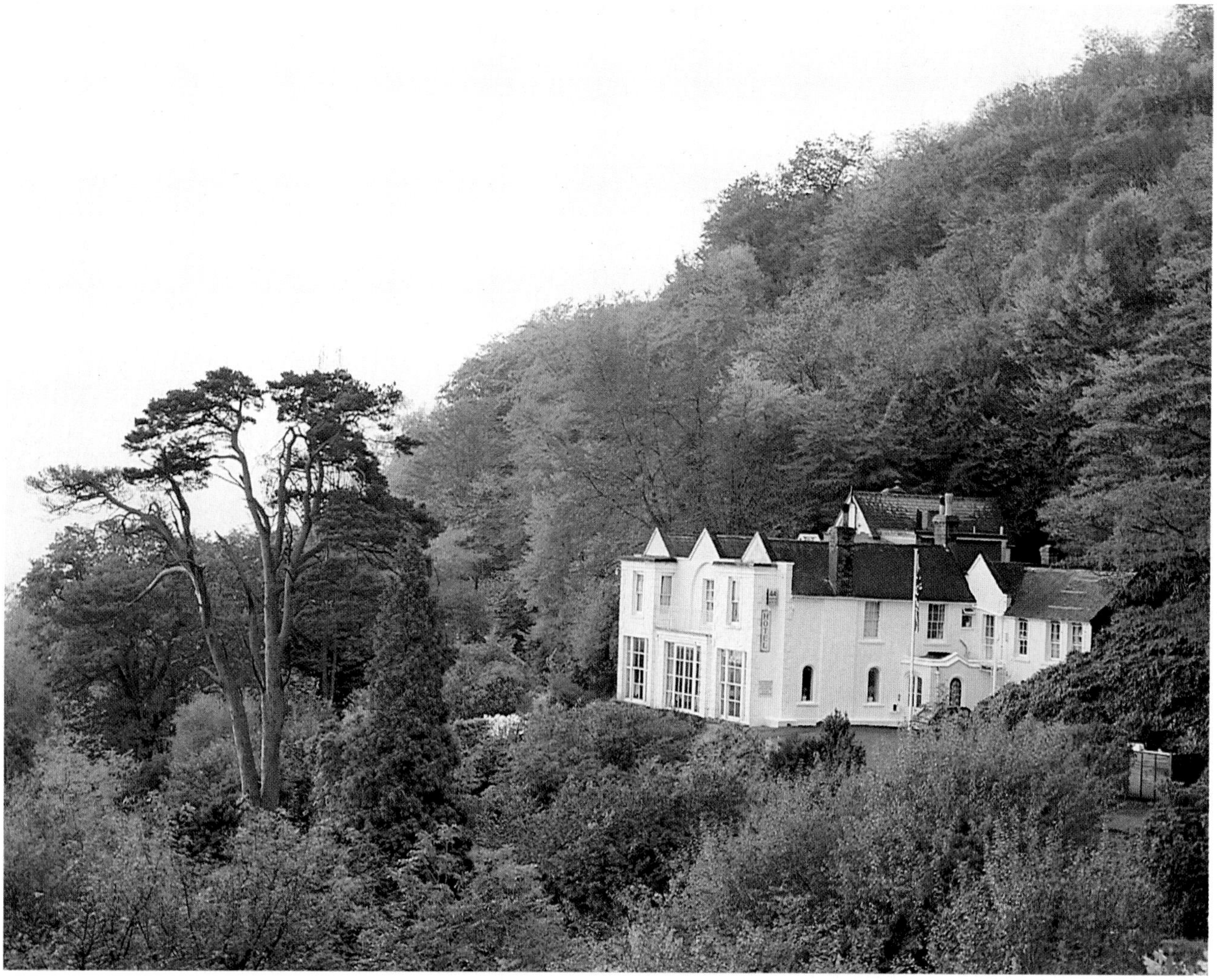

THE COTTAGE IN THE WOOD

HOLYWELL ROAD, MALVERN WELLS, WORCESTERSHIRE WR14 4LG

TEL: 01684 575859 FAX: 01684 560662

The Malvern Hills – the home and inspiration for England's most celebrated composer, Sir Edward Elgar – are the setting for The Cottage in the Wood. The hotel occupies 7 acres of thickly wooded grounds, perched high on the hillside. With its spectacular outlook across the Severn Valley plain, it won acclaim from the *Daily Mail* for 'the best view in England'. Formerly attached to the Blackmore Park seat of Sir Thomas Hornyold, it now comprises three buildings: the Georgian Dower House, Beech Cottage and Coach House. The cottage-style furnishings of all the bedrooms give it an intimate and cosy feel, and the Coach House bedrooms have sun-trap balconies and patios. An essentially English menu is complemented by an extensive wine cellar comprising over 350 bins. To counter any gastronomic indulgence, guests can take an exhilarating trek straight from the hotel grounds to the breezy summits of the Malverns. The Victorian spa town of Great Malvern is nearby, as are the Three Counties Showground and the cathedral cities of Worcester, Gloucester and Hereford. The hotel is personally run by John and Sue Pattin and their family. **Directions:** Three miles south of Great Malvern on A449, turn into Holywell Road opposite Gulf Rover dealer garage. Hotel is 250 yards on right. Price guide: Single £69; double/twin £89–£135. Bargain breaks available.

For hotel location, see maps on pages 477-483

In association with MasterCard

Etrop Grange

THORLEY LANE, MANCHESTER AIRPORT, GREATER MANCHESTER M90 4EG
TEL: 0161 499 0500 FAX: 0161 499 0790

Hidden away near Manchester Airport lies Etrop Grange, a beautiful country house hotel and restaurant. The original house was built in 1780 and more than 200 years on has been lovingly restored. Today, the hotel enjoys a fine reputation for its accommodation, where the luxury, character and sheer elegance of the Georgian era are evident in every feature. The magnificent restaurant offers a well balanced mix of traditional and modern English cuisine, complemented by an extensive selection of fine wines. Attention to detail ensures personal and individual service. In addition to the obvious advantage of having an airport within walking distance, the location of Etrop Grange is ideal in many other ways. With a comprehensive motorway network and InterCity stations minutes away, it is accessible from all parts of the UK. Entertainment for visitors ranges from the shopping, sport and excellent nightlife offered by the city of Manchester to golf, riding, clay pigeon shooting, water sports and outdoor pursuits in the immediate countryside. Cheshire also boasts an abundance of stately homes, museums and historical attractions. **Directions:** Leave M56 at junction 5 towards Manchester Airport. Follow signs for Terminal 2. Go up Ship Road. At roundabout take first exit, take immediate left and hotel is 400yds on the right. Price guide: Single £78–£140; double/twin £90–£145; suites £120–£160.

For hotel location, see maps on pages 477-483

THE IVY HOUSE HOTEL

HIGH STREET, MARLBOROUGH, WILTSHIRE SN8 1HJ

TEL: 01672 515333 FAX: 01672 515338

The Ivy House Hotel is an 18th-century Grade II listed building, overlooking Marlborough High Street. Built in 1707 for the Earl of Aylesbury, it has been refurbished to display the many architectural features of the changing eras. Beyond the reception area, guests may relax in the Churchill Lounge, with its antique furniture. Facing the sun terrace, at the rear of the building, is the elegant Palladian-style Garden Restaurant. The cooking is of a high standard, reflecting both traditional and progressive styles. The purpose-built Beeches Conference and Banqueting Suite provides a venue for business meetings, while the Marlborough Suite is suitable for private dinner parties. The Ivy House is professionally run by owners David Ball and Josephine Scott, who offer guests a comfortable stay which is extremely good value for money. The ancient archaeological sites of Silbury Hill, Stonehenge and Avebury are easily accessible by car, as are the Marlborough Downs and the Savernake Forest. Close by are the stately homes of Bowood House, Corsham Court and Blenheim Palace. **Directions:** The hotel is in Marlborough High Street, just off the A4 from Bath. Price guide: Single £55–£65; double/twin £68–£85.

25 rms MasterCard VISA AMERICAN EXPRESS M 50

For hotel location, see maps on pages 477-483

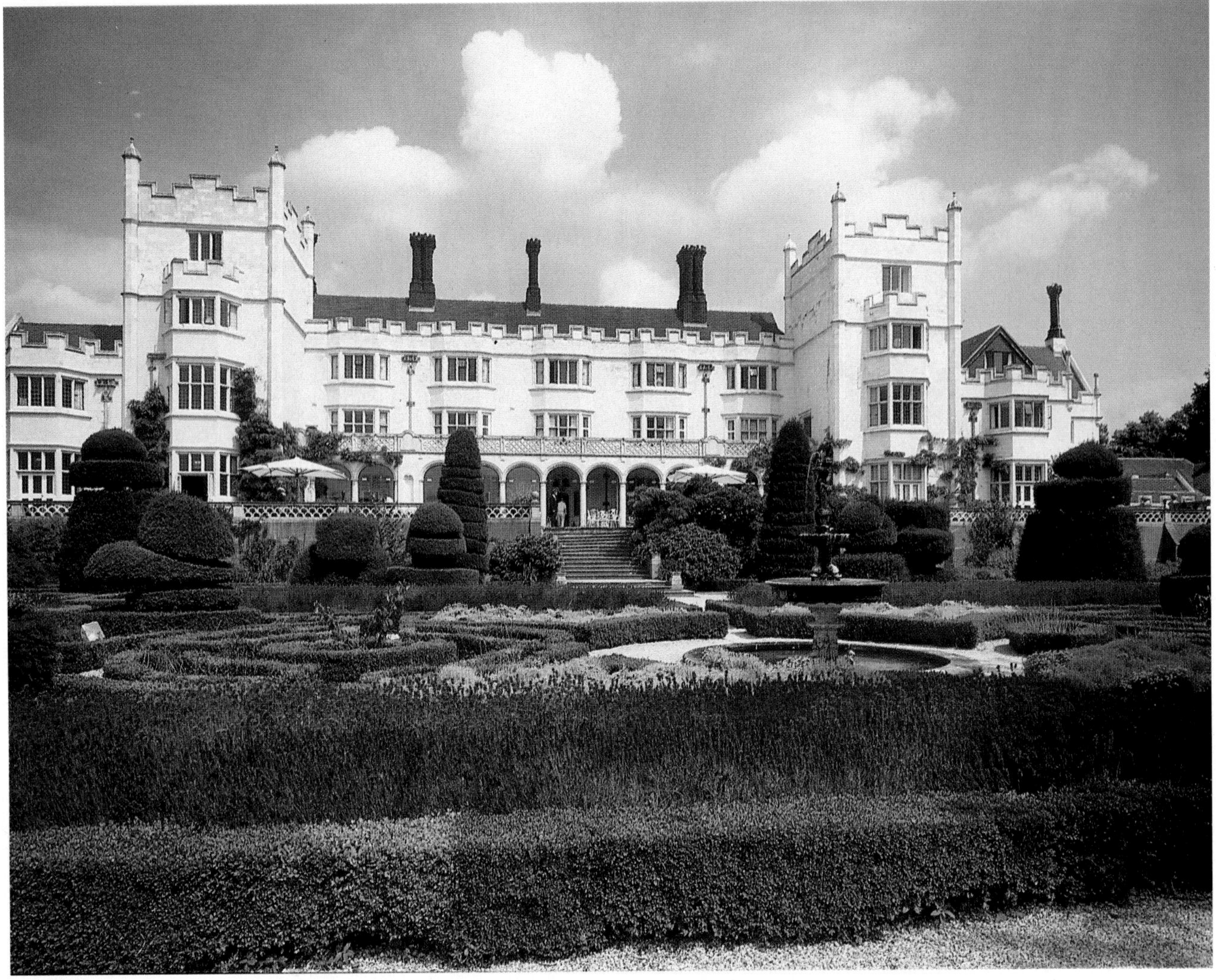

DANESFIELD HOUSE

HENLEY ROAD, MARLOW-ON-THAMES, BUCKINGHAMSHIRE SL7 2EY
TEL: 01628 891010 FAX: 01628 890408

Danesfield House is set in 65 acres of gardens and parkland overlooking the River Thames and offering panoramic views across the Chiltern Hills. It is the third house since 1664 to occupy this lovely setting and it was designed and built in sumptuous style at the end of the 19th century. After years of neglect the house has been fully restored, combining its Victorian splendour with the very best modern hotel facilities. Among the many attractions of its luxury bedrooms, all beautifully decorated and furnished, are the extensive facilities they offer. These include two telephone lines (one may be used for personal fax), satellite TV, mini bar, trouser press, hair dryers, bath robes and toiletries. Guests can relax in the magnificent drawing room with its galleried library or in the sunlit atrium. There is a choice of two restaurants the Oak Room and Loggia Brasserie both of which offer a choice of international cuisine. The hotel also has six private banqueting and conference rooms. Leisure facilities include a squash court, swimming pool, croquet, tennis court and jogging and walking trails. Also within easy reach are Windsor Castle, Disraeli's home at Hughenden Manor, Milton's cottage and the caves of West Wycombe. **Directions:** Between the M4 and M40 on the A4155 between Marlow and Henley-on-Thames. Price guide: Single £130; double/twin £160; suites £195.

For hotel location, see maps on pages 477-483

RIBER HALL

MATLOCK, DERBYSHIRE DE4 5JU
TEL: 01629 582795 FAX: 01629 580475

Enjoy pure tranquillity in the welcoming atmosphere of a bygone age in this historic Derbyshire country house, listed and starred in its class, dating from the 1400's. Recommended by all major hotel and restaurant guides, Riber Hall was recently nominated as one of "The most romantic hotels in Britain". Many original features have been preserved – magnificent oak beams, exposed stone work and period fireplaces. Acknowledged as a restaurant of distinction, English Classical, French Provincial cuisine – game when in season is served on bone china in elegant dining rooms. Superb wines, especially New World, are enjoyed in fine crystal glasses. Quietly located around an attractive courtyard, the bedrooms are appointed to a high standard with antiques throughout, including four poster beds, and many thoughtful extras. The tranquil setting can be appreciated in the secluded old wall garden and orchard which is full of bird life, whilst energetic guests can pit their skills against the tennis trainer ball machine on the all weather tennis court. Conferences, weddings, wedding receptions and small dinner parties are catered for to the highest standard. Nearby are Chatsworth House, Haddon Hall, Hardwick Hall and Calke Abbey; and the Peak National Park. **Directions:** 20 minutes from junction 28 of M1, off A615 at Tansley; 1 mile further to Riber. Price guide: Single £85; double/twin £105.

11 rms MasterCard VISA AMERICAN EXPRESS M 20 10

For hotel location, see maps on pages 477-483

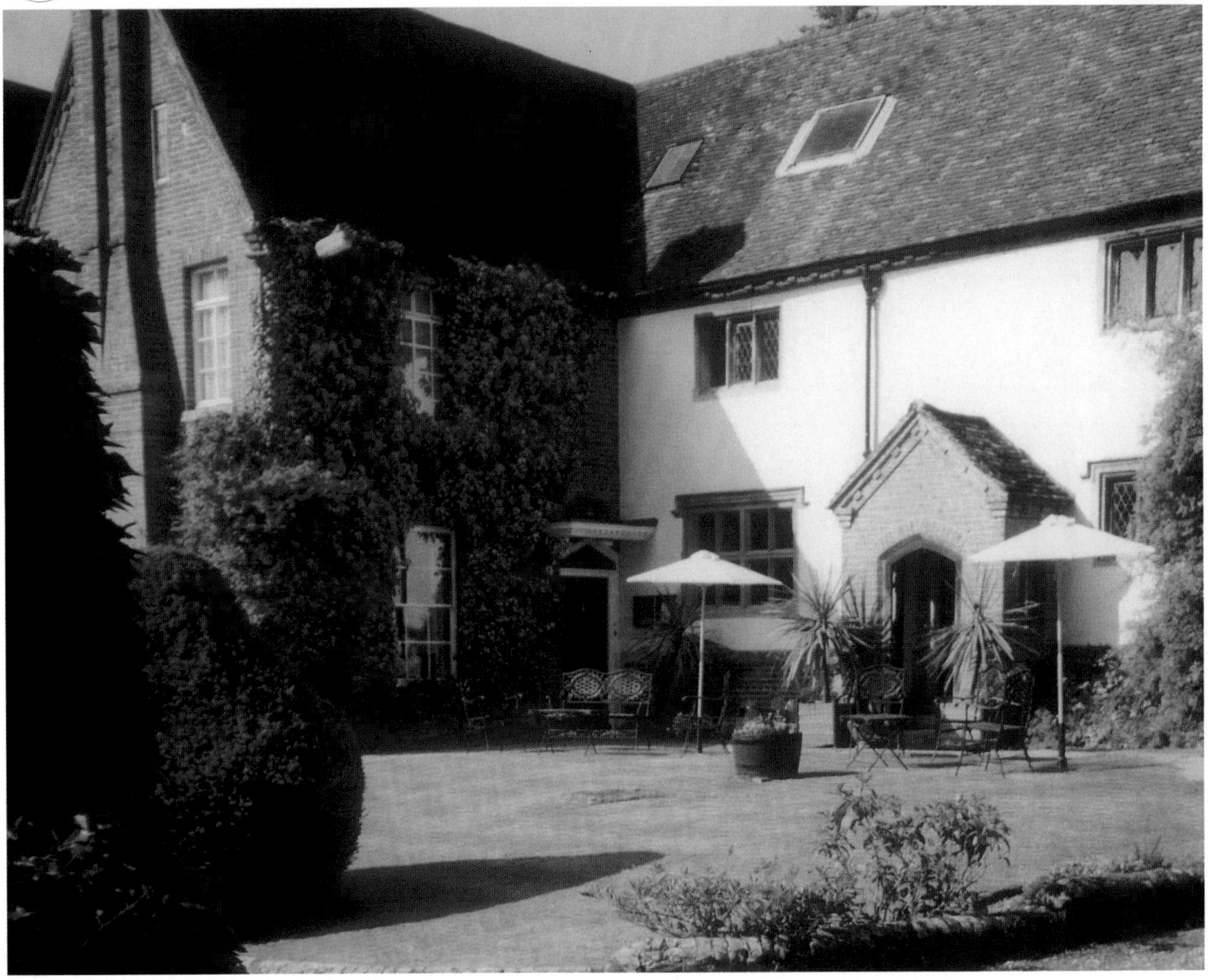

Fifehead Manor

MIDDLE WALLOP, STOCKBRIDGE. HAMPSHIRE SO20 8EG
TEL: 01264 7815665 FAX: 01264 781400

The foundations of this lovely Manor House date from the 11th century when it was owned by the wife of the Saxon Earl of Godwin whose son, King Harold, was killed at the Battle of Hastings. Today, Fifehead Manor offers all the comfort of a country house hotel but, with its barns and stables surrounded by acres of gardens, the historic atmosphere lingers. The beamed dining room with its lead-paned windows and huge open fireplace has a unique atmosphere illuminated by the light of flickering candles and a warmth generated by centuries of hospitality. It is believed to have been the main hall of the mediaeval manor and the remains of the Minstrels' Gallery can still be seen. The hotel's award winning cuisine is outstanding and the restaurant is featured in major guides in England and Europe. Local products are delivered daily whilst the freshest vegetables, fruit and herbs are picked from the kitchen garden. All 15 en-suite bedrooms are individually furnished and have every amenity. Fifehead Manor is ideally situated for visiting Salisbury, Winchester, Stonehenge, Romsey Abbey, Broadlands and Wilton House. Golf, fishing, riding and motor racing at Thruxton are nearby. **Directions:** From M3, exit at junction 8 onto A303 to Andover. Then take A343 south for 6 miles to Middle Wallop. Price guide: Single £60; double/twin £80-£110.

For hotel location, see maps on pages 477-483

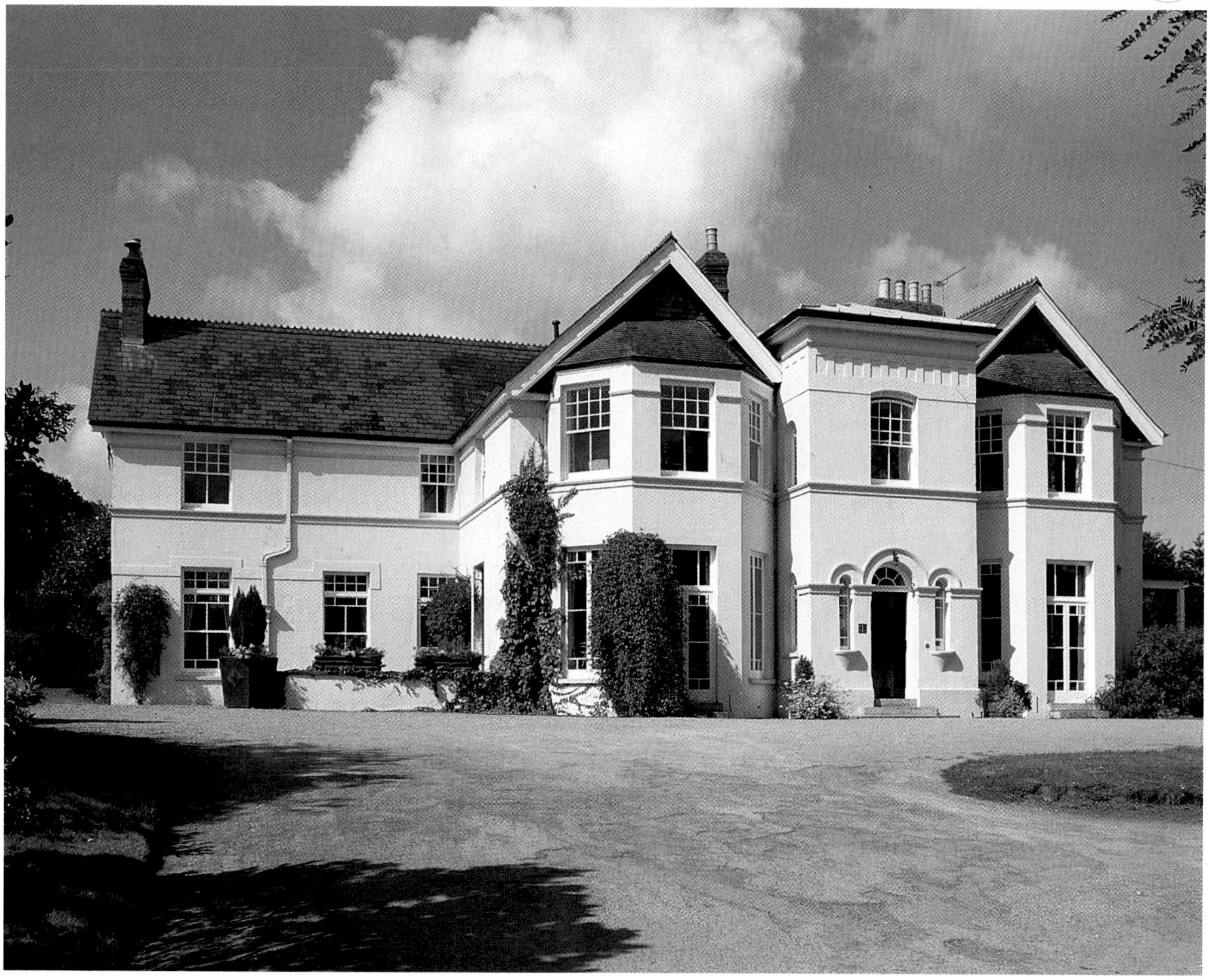

PERITON PARK HOTEL

MIDDLECOMBE, NR MINEHEAD, SOMERSET TA24 8SW
TEL: 01643 706885 FAX: 01643 706885

Bordering on the northern fringe of the Exmoor National Park, the elevated position of this handsome country house gives the visitor magnificent views of the West Somerset hills, with vistas of the Bristol Channel beyond. Through the dawn mists the early riser may be rewarded by the spectacle of a herd of red deer grazing on the moorland below the hotel. Set in 4 acres of woodland, this residence, built in 1875, is now owned by Richard and Angela Hunt whose aim is to run a select hotel in the style of a country gentleman's home. In this they have succeeded – the décor and furnishings in the well-proportioned rooms have been enlivened with warm autumn colours to create a restful impression. The wood-panelled restaurant, with its double aspect views over the grounds, has been completely renovated. Imaginative use of Somerset and West Country produce has earned Periton Park a reputation for gastronomic excellence. The combination of heathered moorland, sheltered combes and rugged coastline makes the hotel an ideal base for walking and field sports, while riding is available from stables close to the hotel. Above the old harbour at Minehead there are quaint cottages to see and an ancient church. **Directions:** Periton Park is situated off the A39 on the left just after Minehead, in the direction of Lynmouth and Porlock. Price guide: Single £65; double/twin £96.

8 rms

For hotel location, see maps on pages 477-483

THE ANGEL HOTEL

NORTH STREET, MIDHURST, WEST SUSSEX GU29 9DN
TEL: 01730 812421 FAX: 01730 815928

The Angel Hotel, is a stylishly restored 16th century coaching inn which has earned widespread praise from national press and guidebooks. Sympathetically renovated to combine contemporary comfort with original character, the Angel bridges the gap between town house bustle and country house calm. To the front, a handsome Georgian façade overlooks the high street,while at the rear, quiet rose gardens lead to the parkland and ruins of historic Cowdray Castle. There are 25 bedrooms, all offering private bathrooms and modern amenities. Individually furnished with antiques, many rooms feature original Tudor beams. The hotel has been widely acclaimed for the quality of its food, which draws on influences as diverse as British, French, Italian and Caribbean cookery, and can be in the informal atmosphere of the brasserie or in the elegant setting of the Cowdray Room restaurant. For business guests the hotel offers two attractive meeting rooms, presentation aids and secretarial services. Racegoers will find it very convenient for Goodwood. The historic market town of Midhurst is well placed for visits to Petworth House, Arundel Castle and the South Downs. **Directions:** From the A272, the hotel is on the left as the town centre is approached from the east. Price guide: Single £65–£95; double/twin £75–£150.

For hotel location, see maps on pages 477-483

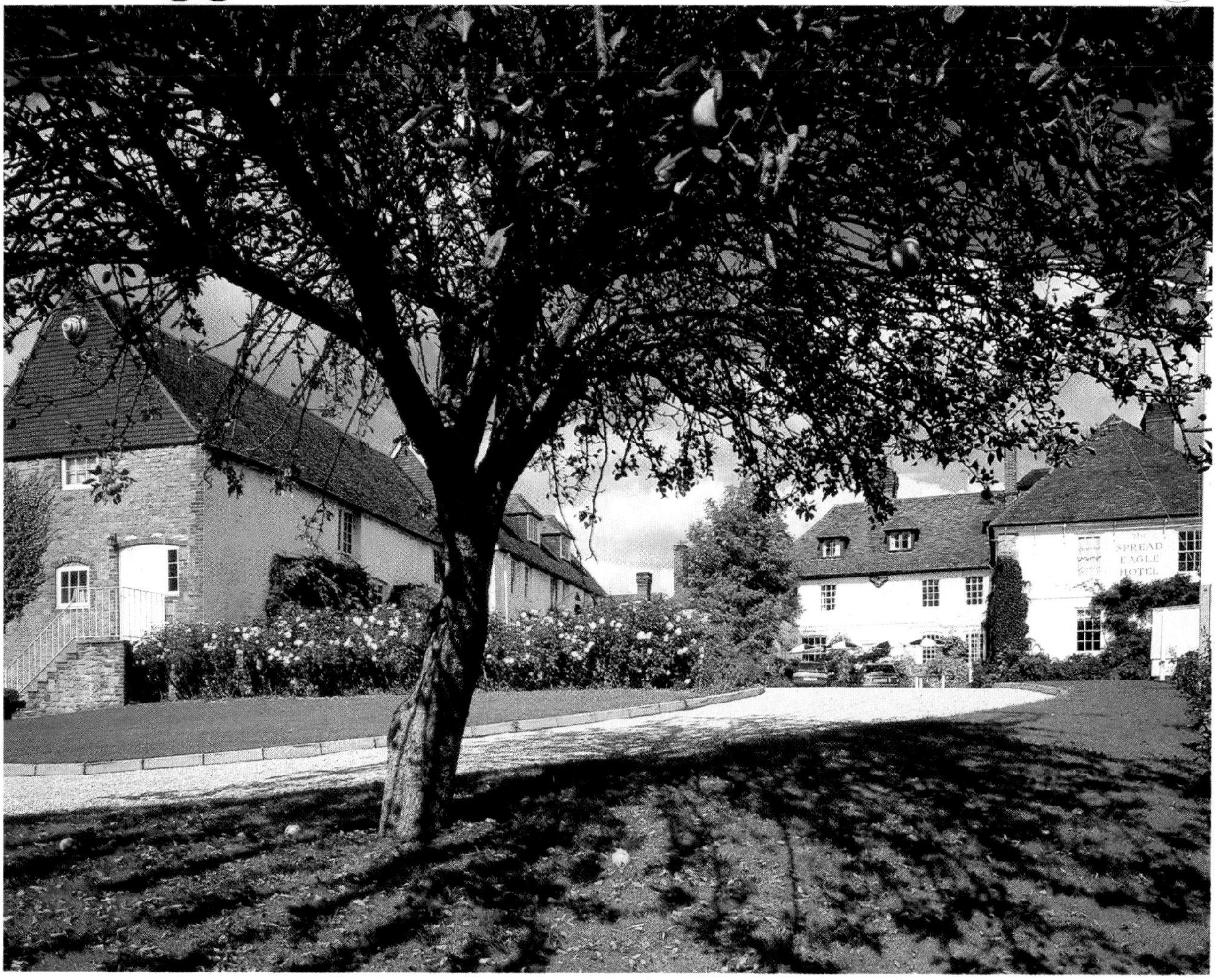

THE SPREAD EAGLE HOTEL

SOUTH STREET, MIDHURST, WEST SUSSEX GU29 9NH
TEL: 01730 816911 FAX: 01730 815668

Dating from 1430, when guests were welcomed to the tavern here, The Spread Eagle with its emblem deriving from the time of the Crusades is one of England's oldest hotels. Throughout the centuries, including its years as a famous coaching inn, the influences of successive eras have been preserved both in the architecture and decorative features of the hotel. Heavy polished timbers, Tudor bread ovens and a series of Flemish stained-glass windows are among the many noteworthy features. Innovative cooking forms the basis of the meals, served in the dining room, with its huge, coppered inglenook fireplace and dark oak beams hung with traditional Sussex Christmas puddings. Colourful, co-ordinated fabrics and antique furnishings make for attractive bedrooms, all fully appointed. The 17th-century Jacobean Hall is an ideal venue for meetings – or perhaps a medieval banquet complete with minstrels! A secluded courtyard garden is flanked, in the summer, by climbing roses and clematis. The stately homes at Petworth, Uppark and Goodwood are all within a short drive, with Chichester Cathedral, the Downland Museum and Fishbourne Roman Palace among the many local attractions. Cowdray Park Polo Club is only 1 mile away. **Directions:** Midhurst is on the A286 between Chichester and Milford. Price guide: Single from £74; double/twin from £89.

For hotel location, see maps on pages 477-483

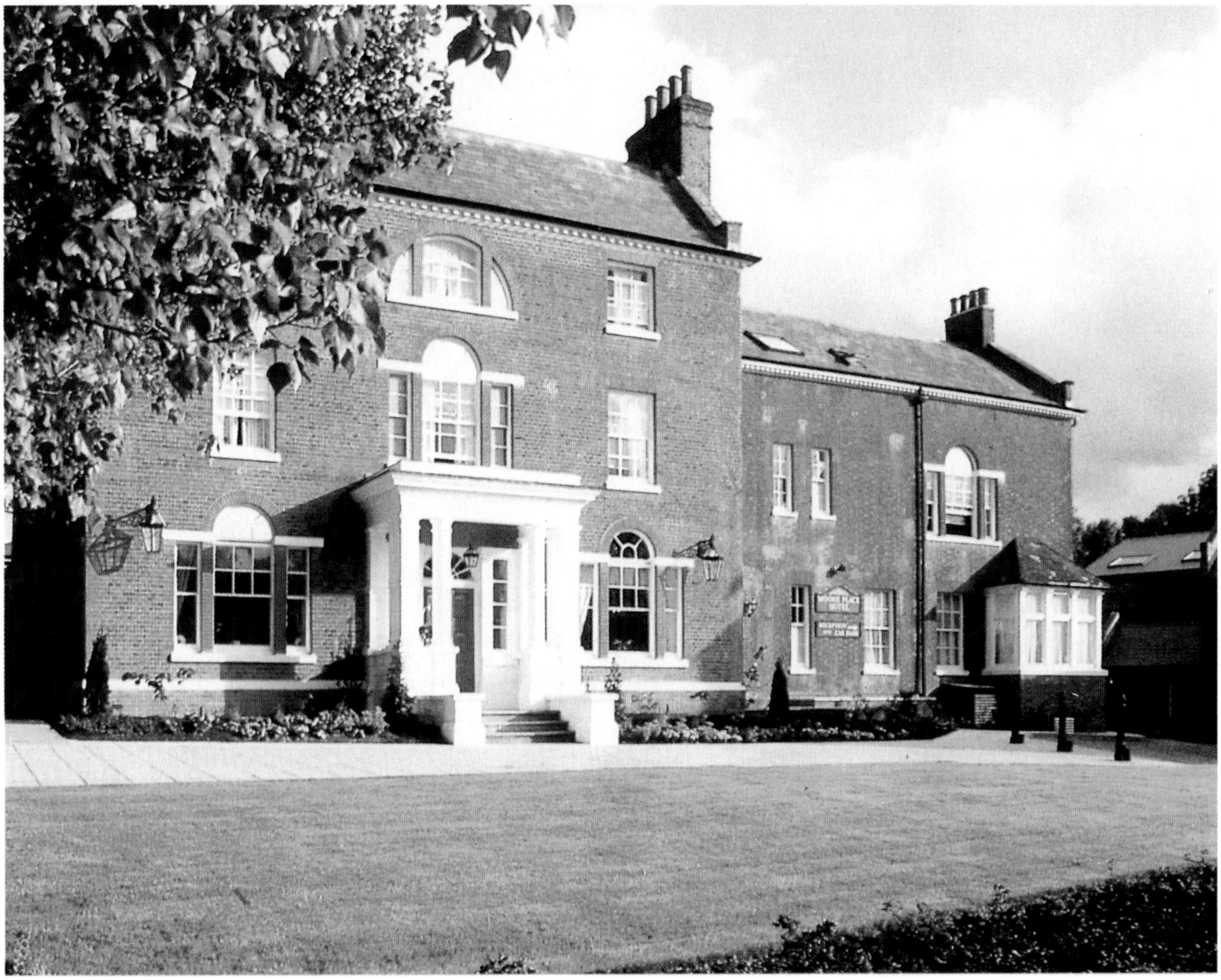

MOORE PLACE HOTEL

THE SQUARE, ASPLEY GUISE, MILTON KEYNES, BEDFORDSHIRE MK17 8DW
TEL: 01908 282000 FAX: 01908 281888

This elegant Georgian mansion was built by Francis Moore in the peaceful Bedfordshire village of Aspley Guise in 1786. The original house, which is set on the village square, has been sympathetically extended to create extra rooms. The additional wing has been built around an attractive courtyard with a rock garden, lily pool and waterfall. The pretty Victorian-style conservatory restaurant, with its floral tented ceiling and festooned drapes, serves food that rates among the best in the area. Vegetarian options can always be found on the menus, which offer dishes prepared in the modern English style and balanced with a selection of fine wines. The 54 bedrooms are well appointed with many amenities, including a trouser press, hairdryer, welcome drinks and large towelling bath robes. Banquets, conferences and dinner parties can be accommodated in five private function rooms: all are decorated in traditional style yet are equipped with the latest audio-visual facilities. The hotel is close to Woburn Abbey, Silverstone, Whipsnade Zoo, Stowe and Milton Keynes. The convenient location and accessibility to the motorway network makes Moore Place Hotel an attractive choice, whether travelling on business or for pleasure. **Directions:** Only two minutes' drive from the M1 junction 13. Price guide: Single £68; double/twin £85–£175; suite £175.

For hotel location, see maps on pages 477-483

THE BEACON COUNTRY HOUSE

BEACON ROAD, MINEHEAD, SOMERSET TA24 5SD
TEL: 01643 703476 FAX: 01643 702668

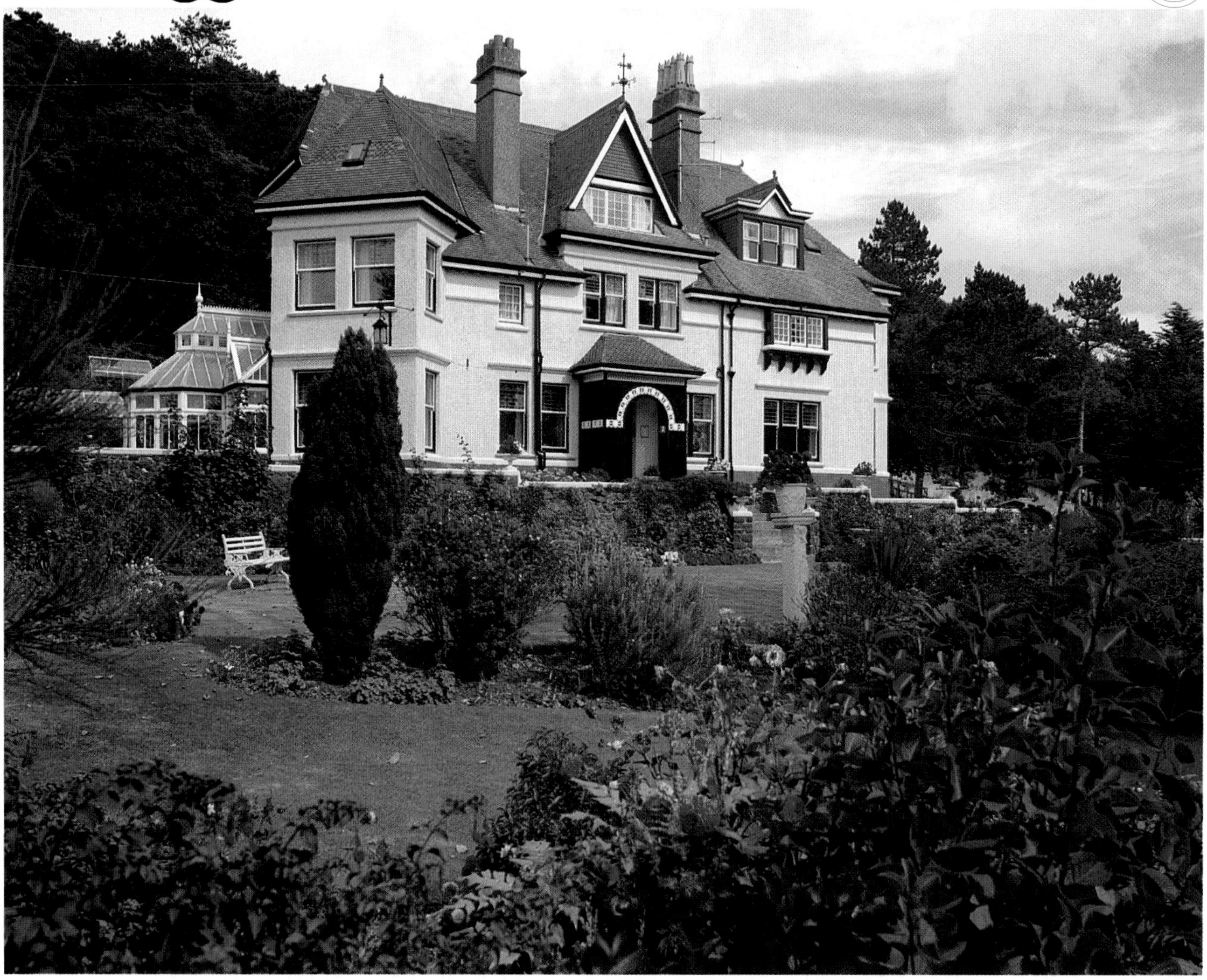

This elegant Edwardian building is surrounded by 20 acres of grounds visited by red deer and home to badgers. From the hotel's woods there is direct access to Exmoor and to a winding coastal path. Although extensively refurbished, the building has maintained the character of a fine country house. All the public rooms are tastefully furnished to create a comfortable and relaxing atmosphere, and a superb, domed, glass conservatory affords views of the gardens and sea beyond. Co-owner and master chef, Pennie Fulcher-Smith, compiles an imaginative menu which places emphasis on fresh local produce, and, although a wide variety of dishes is offered, Pennie is happy to cater for all tastes. There is also an extensive wine list. The individually styled bedrooms are as elegantly furnished as the rest of the hotel and provide every modern facility. Riding or shooting breaks are available by arrangement. The Beacon Country house is an ideal base for those touring the West Country and Exmoor. **Directions:** Leave the M5 at junction 25 to Minehead on the A358. Continue along Townsend Road; right at T-junction, second left at Blenheim Road, first left into Marlett Road. Straight over into Burgundy Road; round hairpin bend, hotel is at end of Beacon Road on the right. Special breaks available on request. Price guide: Single £55; double/twin £75–£85.

For hotel location, see maps on pages 477-483

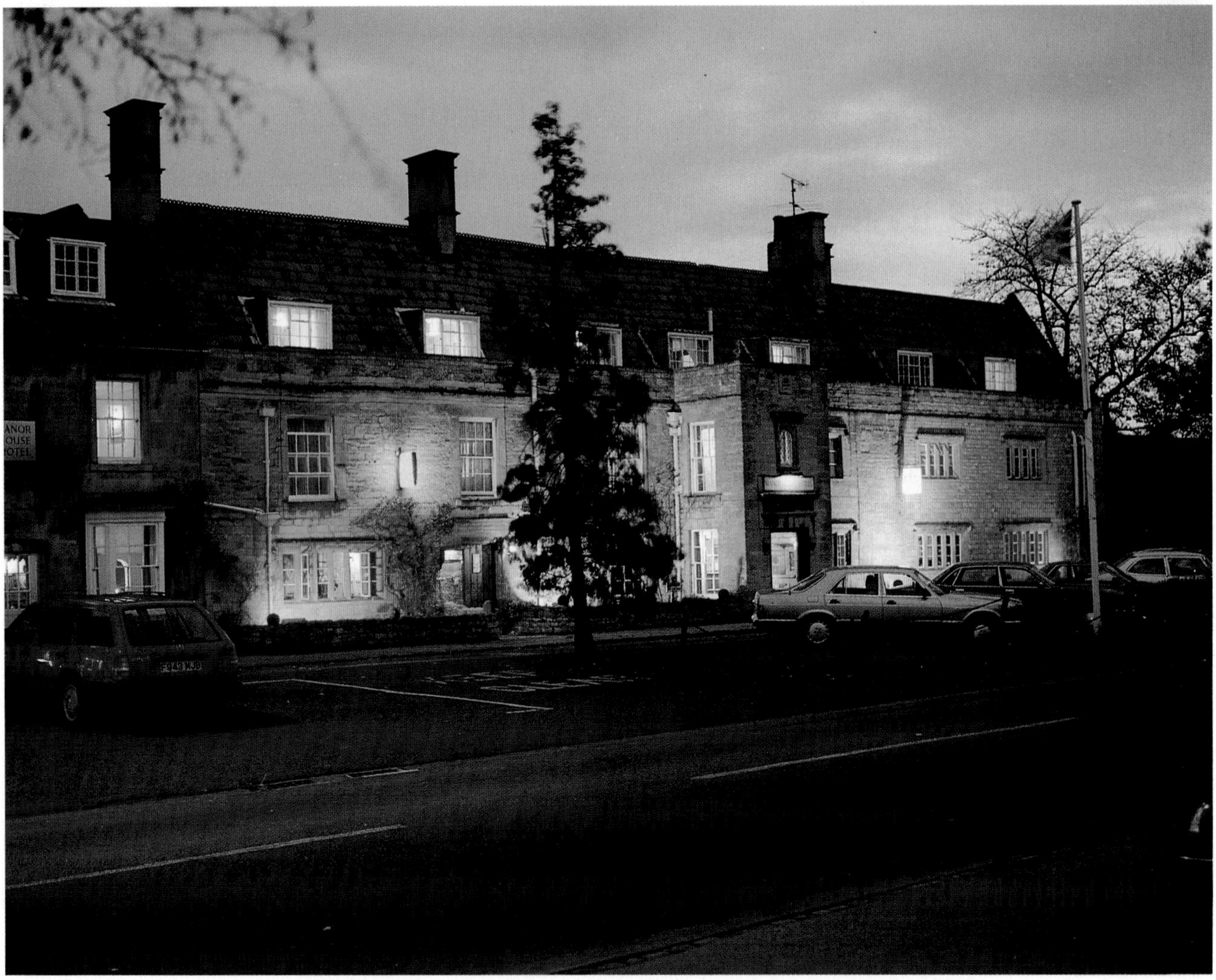

THE MANOR HOUSE HOTEL

MORETON-IN-MARSH, GLOUCESTERSHIRE GL56 0LJ
TEL: 01608 650501 FAX: 01608 651481

This former 16th-century manor house and coaching inn is set in beautiful gardens in the Cotswold village of Moreton-in-Marsh. The Manor House Hotel has been tastefully extended and restored, yet retains many of its historic features, among them a priest's hole and secret passages. The 39 well-appointed bedrooms have been individually decorated and furnished. The restaurant offers imaginative and traditional English dishes using only the freshest ingredients, accompanied by an expertly selected wine list. For the guest seeking relaxation, leisure facilities include an indoor heated swimming pool, spa bath and sauna. Sports enthusiasts will also find that tennis, golf, riding and squash can be arranged locally. The spacious conference facilities are set apart from the rest of the hotel. Modern business facilities, combined with the peaceful location, make this an excellent venue for executive meetings. It is also an ideal base for touring, with many attractions nearby, including Stratford-upon-Avon, Warwick and the fashionable centres of Cheltenham, Oxford and Bath. **Directions:** The Manor House Hotel is on the A429 Fosse Way near the junction of the A44 and A429 north of Stow, on the Broadway side of the intersection. Price guide: Single £55; double/twin £85–£125.

For hotel location, see maps on pages 477-483

ROOKERY HALL

WORLESTON, NANTWICH, NR CHESTER, CHESHIRE CW5 6DQ
TEL: 01270 610016 FAX: 01270 626027

Rookery Hall enjoys a classic location situated within its own 200 acre estate in the heart of Cheshire, yet most convenient for both road/rail and air networks. Within the original house you will find several elegant reception rooms all furnished with antiques and the mahogany and walnut panelled dining room, which is renowned for food prepared by David Alton and his team, who have been awarded 3 AA Rosettes. Other accolades received by the hotel include entry into The Good Hotel Guide, RAC Blue Ribbon award, Egon Ronay rating of 80% and most recently 3 AA Red Stars. All forty five bedrooms are individually designed with spacious marbled bathrooms and fine views over the manicured gardens of the estate where activities can be organised. With meetings in mind a number of suites are available including the self contained stable block. The wine cellar is now open for dinners by candle light, or to study the 300 wines on offer. Over a period of three months Jeremy Rata – General Manager, visited wine merchants throughout the UK while putting the wine list together. The final thirty six wines were chosen from a blind tasting back at the hall. In addition over 20 of these wines can be taken by the glass. **Directions:** From M6 junction 16 take the A500 to Nantwich, then the B5074 to Worleston. Price guide: Single £102.50–£150; double/twin £180–£230; suite £230–£280.

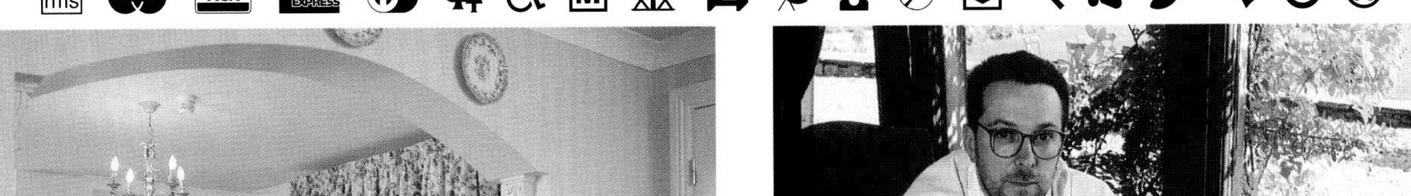

For hotel location, see maps on pages 477-483

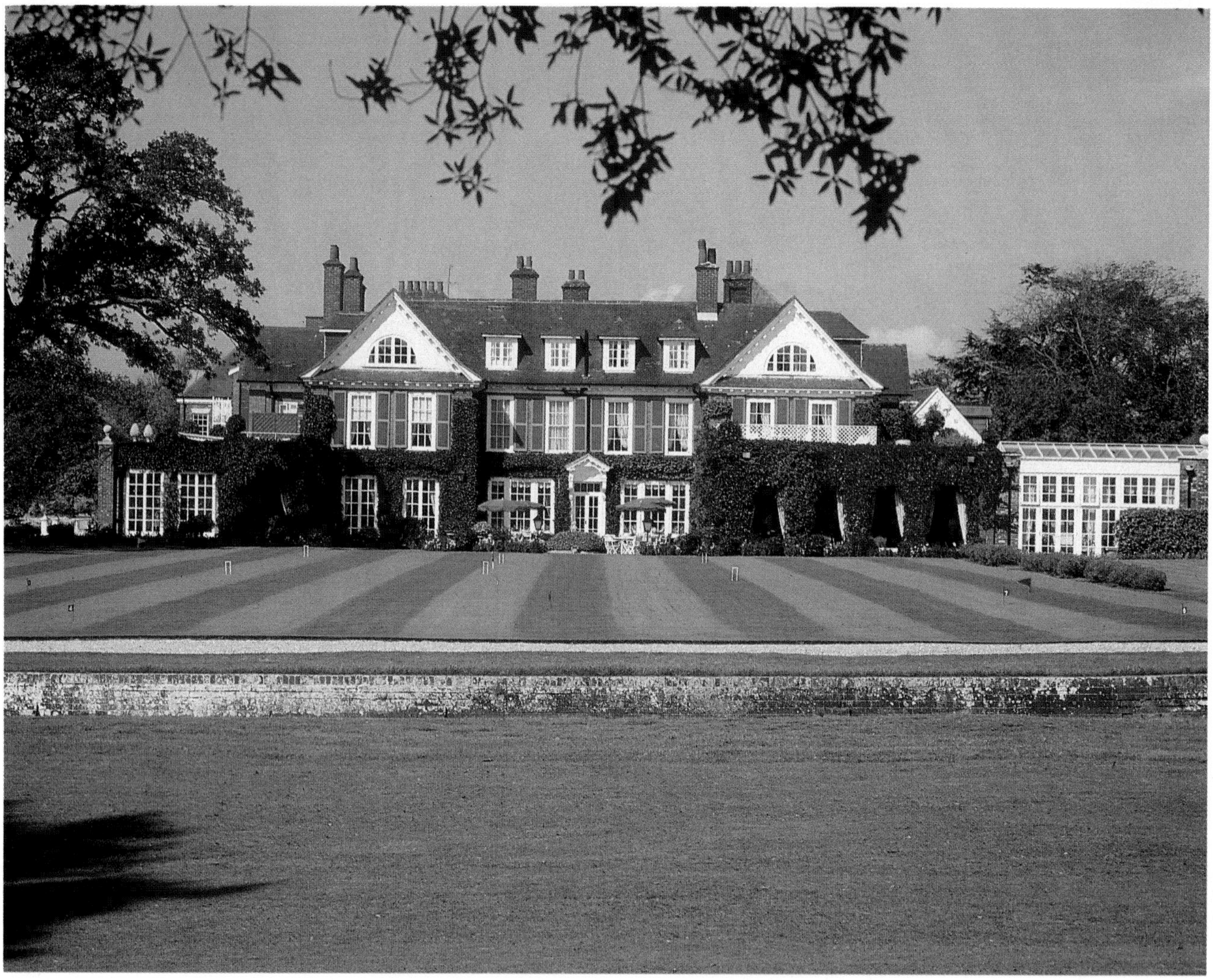

CHEWTON GLEN

CHEWTON GLEN, NEW MILTON, HAMPSHIRE BH25 6QS
TEL: 01425 275341 FAX: 01425 272310

Chewton Glen, a shrine that merits many a pilgrimage, has a setting of lovely gardens, woodland and lawns. The original mansion was built in the short-lived Palladian style of the early 18th century and despite renovations it essentially retains the unique character of an English country house. There are antiques, paintings, memorabilia of the famous author, Captain Marryat, who lived there and wrote *Children of the New Forest* and *Mr Midshipman Easy*, and arrays of fresh flowers. Many bedrooms have balconies that give guests the chance to enjoy beautiful views of the surrounding parkland scenery. The menu in the Marryat Restaurant is a delicious harmony of the classical and the modern, gastronomically accompanied by a list of over 400 wines. The hotel has a health club with a magnificent swimming pool, spa, steam room, saunas and gym. There are excellent conference facilities. Among the other pursuits on hand are golf, tennis, snooker, shooting and riding. Places of interest nearby include Beaulieu, Broadlands, Exbury Gardens, The Solent, Kingston Lacy and Stonehenge. **Directions:** A35 from Lyndhurst to Bournemouth.Turn left at Walkford (approx 10 miles after Lyndhurst). Turn left before roundabout, hotel is on the right. Price guide: Single from £185; double/twin from £195; suites from £300.

For hotel location, see maps on pages 477-483

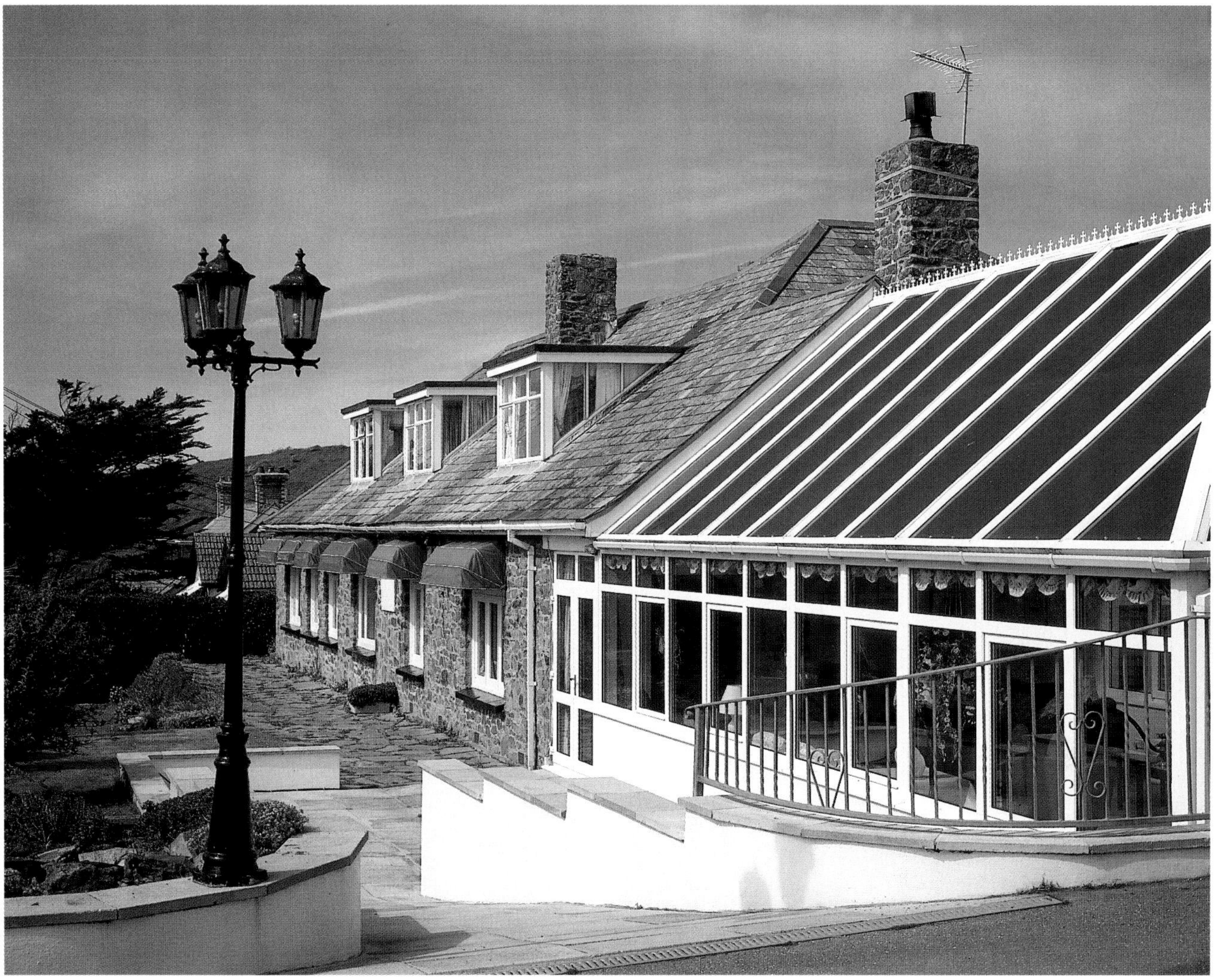

THE CORNISH COTTAGE HOTEL

NEW POLZEATH, NORTH CORNWALL PL27 6US
TEL: 01208 862213 FAX: 01208 862259

The Cornish Cottage Hotel and Gourmet Restaurant is set amid the spectacular scenery of the Cornish coast. The hotel is small, cosy and peaceful, owned and managed by Clive and Christine Mason. The Gourmet cuisine is well renowned and the importance of fresh produce together with the wonderful talents of Tim Rogers the head chef and his team provides the very best in English cuisine. Tim has worked with a number of top international chefs both in Germany and London and he now brings his skills , originality and imagination along with his own recipes to The Gourmet Restaurant. Holder of AA Rosette's and entries in the leading food guides has made The Gourmet Restaurant the focal point of the hotel. All en-suite bedrooms are different in style with traditional cottage furnishings, offering a level of comfort that more than justifies the hotels AA two star status. The bar is a cosy meeting place for pre dinner aperitifs and the conservatory lounge an ideal place in which to relax. Walking, golfing, sailing and surfing are well catered for an many magnificent houses and gardens are within easy reach. Gourmet, seasonal, CHristmas and New Year breaks are available. **Directions:** From Launceston by-pass, follow the North Cornwall sign to Camelford then head towards Port Isaac and follow signs for New Polzeath. Price guide: Single £47–£67; double/twin £94–£118. Closed January

For hotel location, see maps on pages 477-483

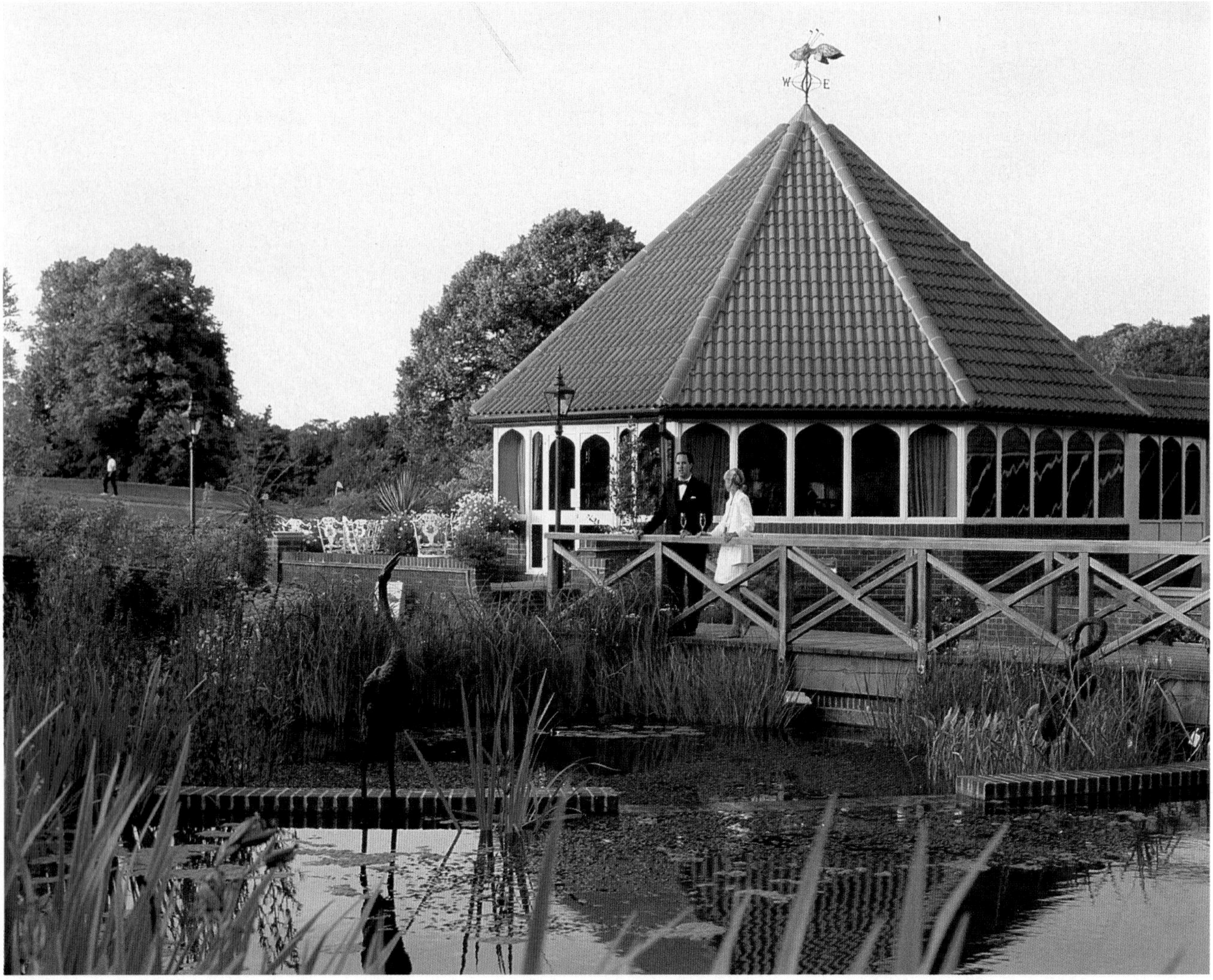

DONNINGTON VALLEY HOTEL & GOLF COURSE

OLD OXFORD ROAD, DONNINGTON, NEWBURY, BERKSHIRE RG14 3AG
TEL: 01635 551199 FAX: 01635 551123 E-MAIL: 101317.506@compuserve.com

Uncompromising quality is the hallmark of this hotel built in contrasting styles in 1991 with its own golf course. The grandeur of the Edwardian era has been captured by the interior of the hotel's reception area with its splendid wood-panelled ceilings and impressive overhanging gallery. Each individually designed bedroom has been thoughtfully equipped to guarantee comfort and peace of mind. In addition to the standard guest rooms Donnington Valley offers a number of non-smoking rooms, family rooms, superior executive rooms and luxury suites. With its open log fire and elegant surroundings, the Piano Bar is an ideal place to meet friends or enjoy the relaxed ambience of the Golf Bar. Guests may dine in the Gallery Restaurant which offers fine international cuisine complemented by an extensive choice of wines and liqueurs. The golf course is the perfect place for a relaxing weekend or mixing business with pleasure. Special corporate golfing packages are offered and tournaments can be arranged. Purpose-built conference suites provide the flexibility to meet the demands of today's executive meeting. Donnington Castle, despite a two-year siege during the Civil War, still survives for sight-seeing. **Directions:** Leave the M4 at junction 13, go south towards Newbury on A34, then follow signs for Donnington Castle. Price guide: Single from £65; double/twin from £90; suite from £115.

For hotel location, see maps on pages 477-483

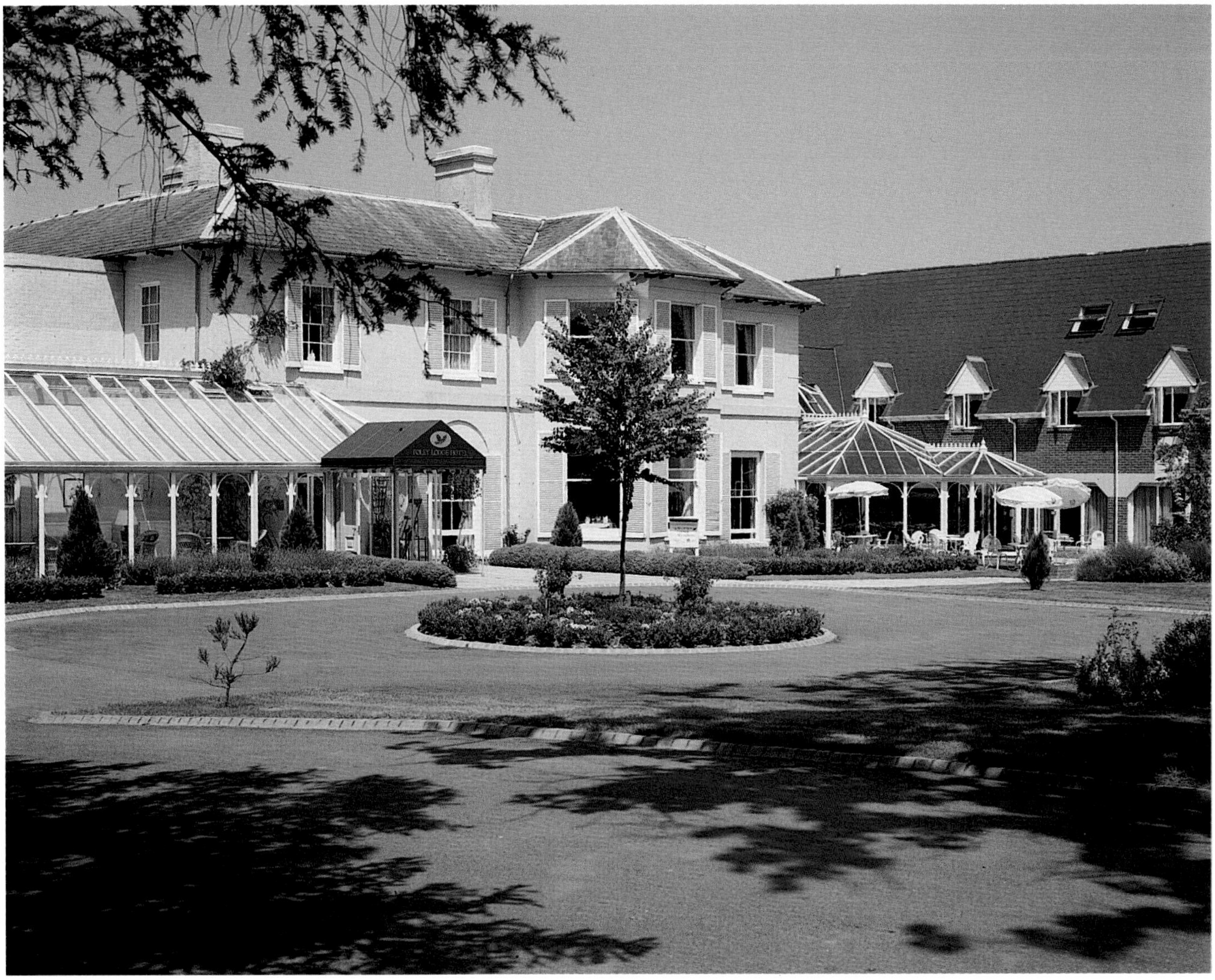

FOLEY LODGE HOTEL

STOCKCROSS, NEWBURY, BERKSHIRE RG20 8JU
TEL: 01635 528770 FAX: 01635 528398

This former Victorian hunting lodge has been developed into a luxury Country House Hotel with extensive conference, banqueting and leisure facilities. Individually designed and attractively furnished bedrooms and suites overlook the landscaped gardens and open countryside. The elegant Victorian décor in the award-winning à la carte restaurant reflects the superb quality of the hotel's fine French and traditional English cuisine. Alternatively, Le Jardin Bistro is a light and airy brasserie with adjoining cocktail bar and conservatory in which to enjoy a relaxing apéritif. The versatile range of conference and banqueting suites provides the idea venue for meetings and events for between 6 and 240 delegates. To complement this superb working environment the hotel boasts a swirling indoor heated pool set in a Victorian styled glass pagoda, with terraced restaurant and bar. For the golf enthusiast, a 9-hole golf course is adjacent and championship 18-hole courses are nearby. **Directions:** Foley Lodge is in the village of Stockcross on the B4000, 1 mile west of Newbury and close to the M4, A4 and A34. Price guide: Single £55–£105; double/twin £80–£120; suite supplement £20 pp.

For hotel location, see maps on pages 477-483

HOLLINGTON HOUSE HOTEL

WOOLTON HILL, NR NEWBURY, BERKSHIRE RG20 9XA
TEL: 01635 255100 FAX: 01635 255075

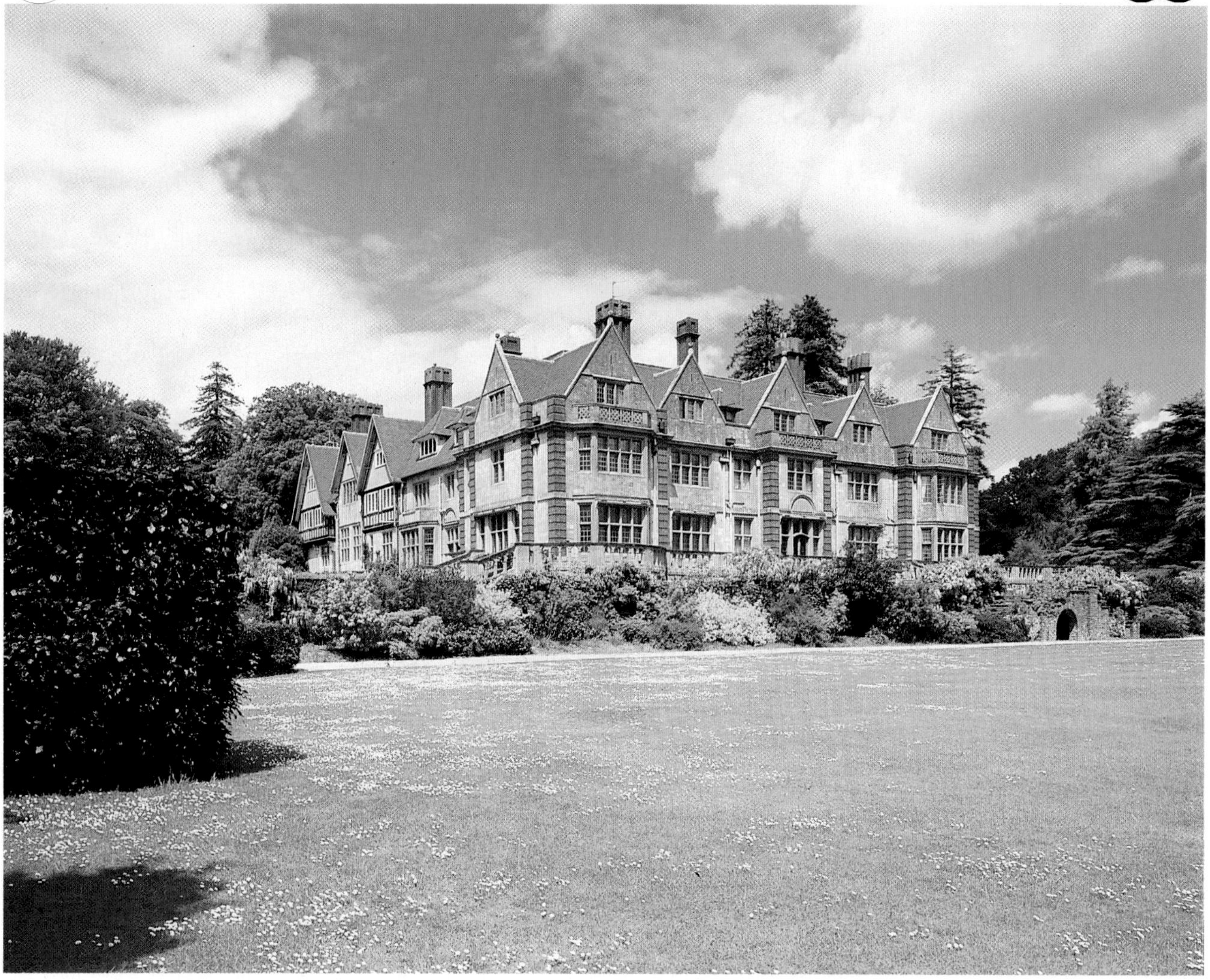

Hollington House Hotel, one of England's foremost luxury country house hotels, opened in July 1992. The Elizabethan-style house, built in 1904, is set in 25 acres of mature Gertrude Jekyll woodland gardens, adjacent to 250 acres of private parkland. Prior to returning to the UK after an absence of 32 years, John and Penny Guy created and owned Burnham Beeches Hotel, near Melbourne, which became Australia's first Relais et Châteaux hotel. No expense has been spared in their endeavours to achieve similar standards of excellence here. The 20 individually designed bedrooms are furnished with antiques and paintings and have sumptuous bathrooms. Elegant reception rooms, an oak-panelled, galleried hall and private boardroom are among the many splendid features of the house. The Chef serves a modern style of cooking with flair and innovation, based on traditional English and French cuisine. Indoors there is a swimming pool and a full-size snooker table, outdoors a solar-heated swimming pool, a tennis court and a croquet lawn. The surrounding countryside offers opportunities for walking, shooting, hunting and horse-racing. Conference, wedding and weekend packages available. **Directions:** From M4 junction13 south of Newbury leave A343 Andover road, follow signs for Hollington Herb Garden. Price guide: Single from £95; deluxe double/twin from £135; junior suite from £195.

For hotel location, see maps on pages 477-483

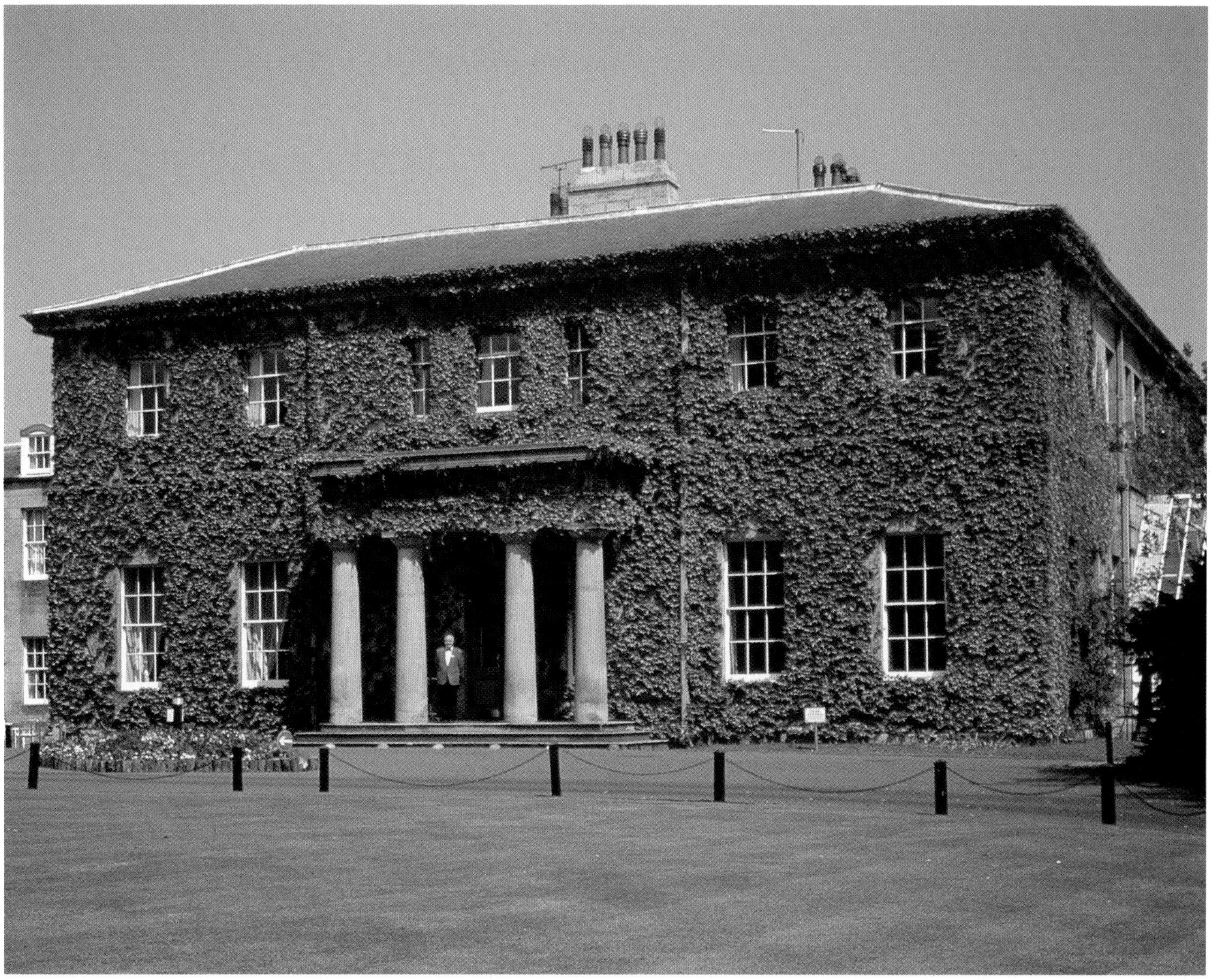

Linden Hall Hotel and Health Spa

LONGHORSLEY, MORPETH, NORTHUMBERLAND NE65 8XF
TEL: 01670 516611 FAX: 01670 788544

Ivy-clad, hidden away among 450 acres of fine park and woodland in mid-Northumberland, Linden Hall is a superb Georgian country house within easy reach of Newcastle-upon-Tyne. An impressive mile-long drive sweeps up to its main door where, upon entering, the visitor will discover a relaxed, dignified atmosphere enhanced by gracious marble hearths, antiques and period pieces. Those wishing to escape the urban stress will be delighted to find every fitness and relaxation requirement catered for at the health and beauty spa: beauty therapy treatments, fitness and steam room, swimming pool, sun terrace and solarium are all available on the premises. The 50 bedrooms are individually and elegantly furnished. Some rooms have four-poster beds; each has its own private bathroom, supplied with thoughtful extras. The Linden Pub serves informal drinks and the Dobson Restaurant, with panoramic views of the Northumberland coastline, serves delicious food, imaginatively prepared. Wedding receptions, banquets, dinner parties and business conferences can be held in comfort in any one of Linden Hall's conference and banqueting suites. 18 hole par 72 golf course opening spring 1997. **Directions:** From Newcastle take A1 north for 15 miles, then A697 toward Coldstream and Wooler. The hotel is one mile north of Longhorsley. Price guide: Single £97–£105; double/twin £125–£185; suite: £195.

For hotel location, see maps on pages 477-483

Slaley Hall

SLALEY, HEXHAM, NR NEWCASTLE-UPON-TYNE, NORTHUMBERLAND NE47 0BY
TEL: 01434 673350 FAX: 01434 673962

Slaley Hall was built as a private residence by the Hunting family in the true splendour of the Edwardian age. Now a hotel with an 18 hole international championship golf course, it is set in 1,000 acres of grounds which include woods, parks, moorland and the rarest Japanese gardens in Britain. Guests have a choice of restaurants, all of which serve superb food. The 142 bedrooms and suites are exquisitely designed with comfort in mind, while the furnished public rooms offer an ideal environment in which to relax and enjoy the wonderful surroundings. Elegant conference and banqueting suites have been designed to accommodate the most prestigious corporate and private events for up to 400 guests. Sporting challenges such as clay pigeon shooting, off-road driving, riding and archery are available at Slaley Hall. There is also a fully-equipped gymnasium, sauna, steam, beauty treatment rooms and a 23 metre indoor swimming pool in landscaped surroundings. Major golfing events include the PGA European Tour Tournament, The Slaley Hall Northumberland Challenge. It is close to Newcastle's international airport and the famous Metro Centre. **Directions:** From Newcastle take A69 towards Carlisle and then the A68 south. Slaley Hall is signposted from the road. Price guide: Single £115–£140; double/twin £145–£170; suites £275–£600

For hotel location, see maps on pages 477-483

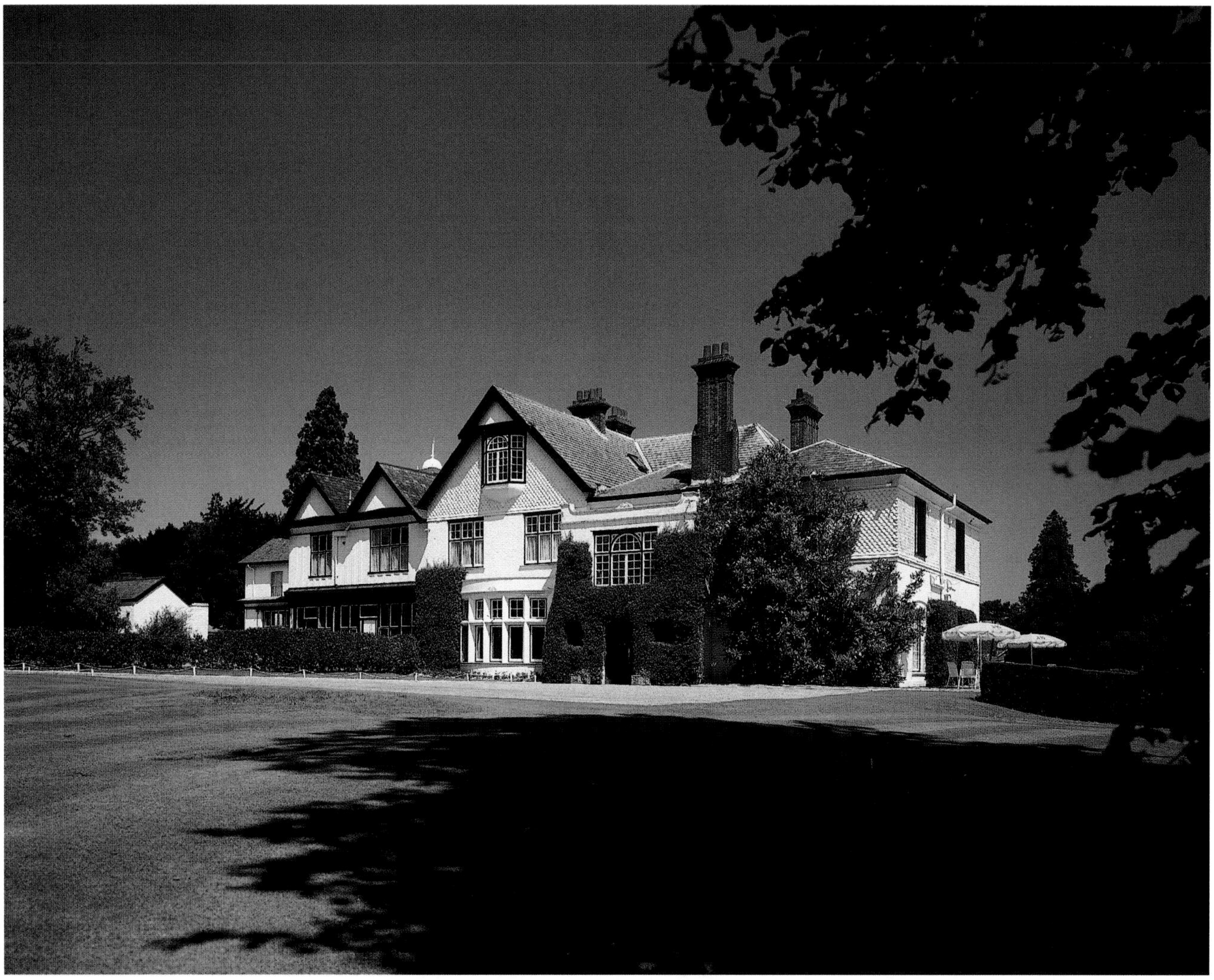

SWYNFORD PADDOCKS HOTEL AND RESTAURANT

SIX MILE BOTTOM, NR NEWMARKET, SUFFOLK
TEL: 01638 570234 FAX: 01638 570283

This graceful, classical white mansion standing in glorious gardens and idyllic countryside with racehorses grazing its pastures has a romantic history. In 1813 it was the scene of a passionate affair between Lord Byron and the wife of owner Colonel George Leigh. Byron was a frequent visitor to the house and wrote many of his poems in the grounds. Swynford was converted into a luxury hotel 20 years ago. It has a country house atmosphere with antique furniture, four-poster beds, open fires and attention to detail of times gone by. Each individually decorated, en suite bedroom has colour television, clock radio alarm, telephone, mini-bar, trouser press, hair dryer and tea and coffee making facilities. The lounge bar overlooks the gardens and the dining room offers an imaginative menu which is changed regularly to take advantage of the season's fresh produce. There is a conference room for up to 20 delegates and a luxury marquee for private and special functions. Tennis, putting and croquet are within the grounds and arrangements can be made for guided tours of Newmarket with a behind the scenes look at the horseracing world. **Directions:** From M11, exit at junction 9 and take A11 towards Newmarket. After 10 miles join A1304 signposted Newmarket. Swynford Paddocks is on the left after 3/4 of a mile. Price guide: Single £80; double/twin £117–£138.

For hotel location, see maps on pages 477-483

PASSAGE HOUSE HOTEL

KINGSTEIGNTON, NEWTON ABBOT, DEVON TQ12 3QH
TEL: 01626 55515 FAX: 01626 63336

Overlooking the Teign Estuary, the Passage House Hotel has been designed to take advantage of the clear and panoramic views. Drawing inspiration from the natural beauty of the surrounding landscapes, the interior colour schemes are soft, muted shades of grey, blue and pink. The bedrooms provide every comfort, while the Penthouse rooms have a private terrace. The relaxing theme is continued in the reception rooms, with natural pale wood and mirrors enhancing the sense of space and light. Five-course table d'hôte and à la carte menus offer imaginatively prepared Devon recipes, using the freshest local fare, including Teign salmon and game. Throughout the hotel the service is extremely friendly and efficient. For active guests, there is a fully equipped leisure club, comprising indoor pool, hydro-spa, steam room, sauna, solarium and gymnasium. Sailing, water-skiing and golf are available locally. Racing fans should note that the hotel is located adjacent to Newton Abbot racecourse. The Devon heartland is rich in history – William of Orange was proclaimed King here on Guy Fawkes Day 1688. The rugged scenery of Dartmoor is only minutes from the hotel. Special rate breaks available. **Directions:** Turn off A380 onto A381, follow signs to racecourse. Turn left at mini-roundabout; hotel is first left. Price guide: Single £59; double/twin £75–£85; suite £125.

For hotel location, see maps on pages 477-483

REDWORTH HALL HOTEL & COUNTRY CLUB

REDWORTH, NR NEWTON AYCLIFFE, COUNTY DURHAM DL5 6NL
TEL: 01388 772442 FAX: 01388 775112 CONFERENCE OFFICE FAX: 01388 775660

Redworth Hall, a Grand Heritage Hotel, is a 17th-century, tastefully converted manor house situated in 25 acres of woodland. There are 100 en suite bedrooms, several of which are suitable for guests with disabilities. The furnishings throughout range from antique to fine reproduction. The hotel's health club includes a heated indoor swimming pool, with a hoist for guests with disabilities, a spa bath, sunbeds, steam bath, squash courts, sauna, snooker tables, all-weather tennis courts and a fully equipped gymnasium. There is an indoor play area and an outdoor adventure playground for children. There are 16 function rooms which can accommodate from 3 to 300 guests, making the hotel ideal for conferences, training courses and weddings. In addition, Medieval Banquets are held in the Great Hall at various times throughout the year. Guests may choose between two restaurants: the elegant Blue Room offering innovative cuisine or the airy Conservatory which features a table d'hôte and contemporary à la carte menu. The hotel has 4 stars AA, RAC, 5 Crowns Highly Commended ETB and 2 AA Rosettes for food and service. **Directions:** A1(M) exit 58, A68 to Corbridge, then A6072 to Bishop Auckland; hotel two miles on left. Price guide: Single £105–£115; double/twin £125–£160; four-poster £160.

For hotel location, see maps on pages 477-483

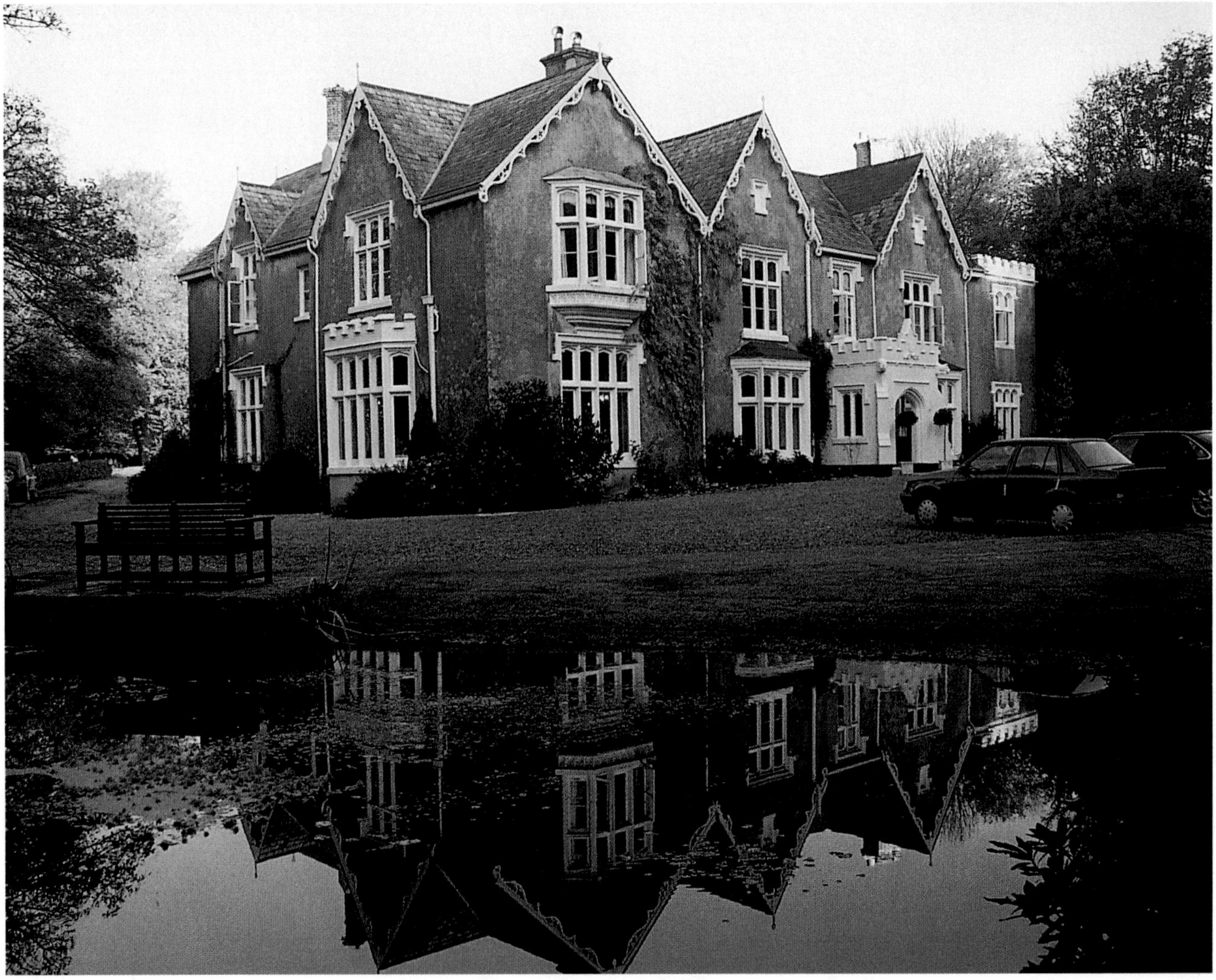

Brookdale House Restaurant and Hotel

NORTH HUISH, SOUTH BRENT, DEVON TQ10 9NR
TEL: 01548 821661 FAX: 01548 821606

This Grade II listed Tudor Gothic mansion is hidden away in a sequestered valley with four acres of picturesque gardens, lawns and woodland. It was originally built in the mid 19th century as a rectory and recently has been sensitively restored and renovated to its former glory. Fine examples of moulded ceilings, Gothic windows and beautiful marble fireplaces have been retained. The hotel's bedrooms, tastefully decorated and furnished with antiques, offer every modern comfort and convenience. The restaurant is at the heart of Brookdale House and the à la carte menu enjoys an excellent reputation locally. The proprietors have concentrated on providing high quality food using local produce: additive free meat and fresh organically grown vegetables. The hotel, which prides itself on providing excellent and personal service, offers good facilities for small conferences of up to 40 people. Places of interest nearby include Dartmoor, Plymouth and Exeter, while leisure activities include riding, lawn tennis, hunting, fishing and walking. Dartington Hall is a short drive away, also Totnes and the Elizabethan Museum. **Directions:** Exit A38 at South Brent and follow signs to Avonwick. At Avon Inn turn right, then next left to North Huish. Price guide: Single from £85; double/twin from £95.

For hotel location, see maps on pages 477-483

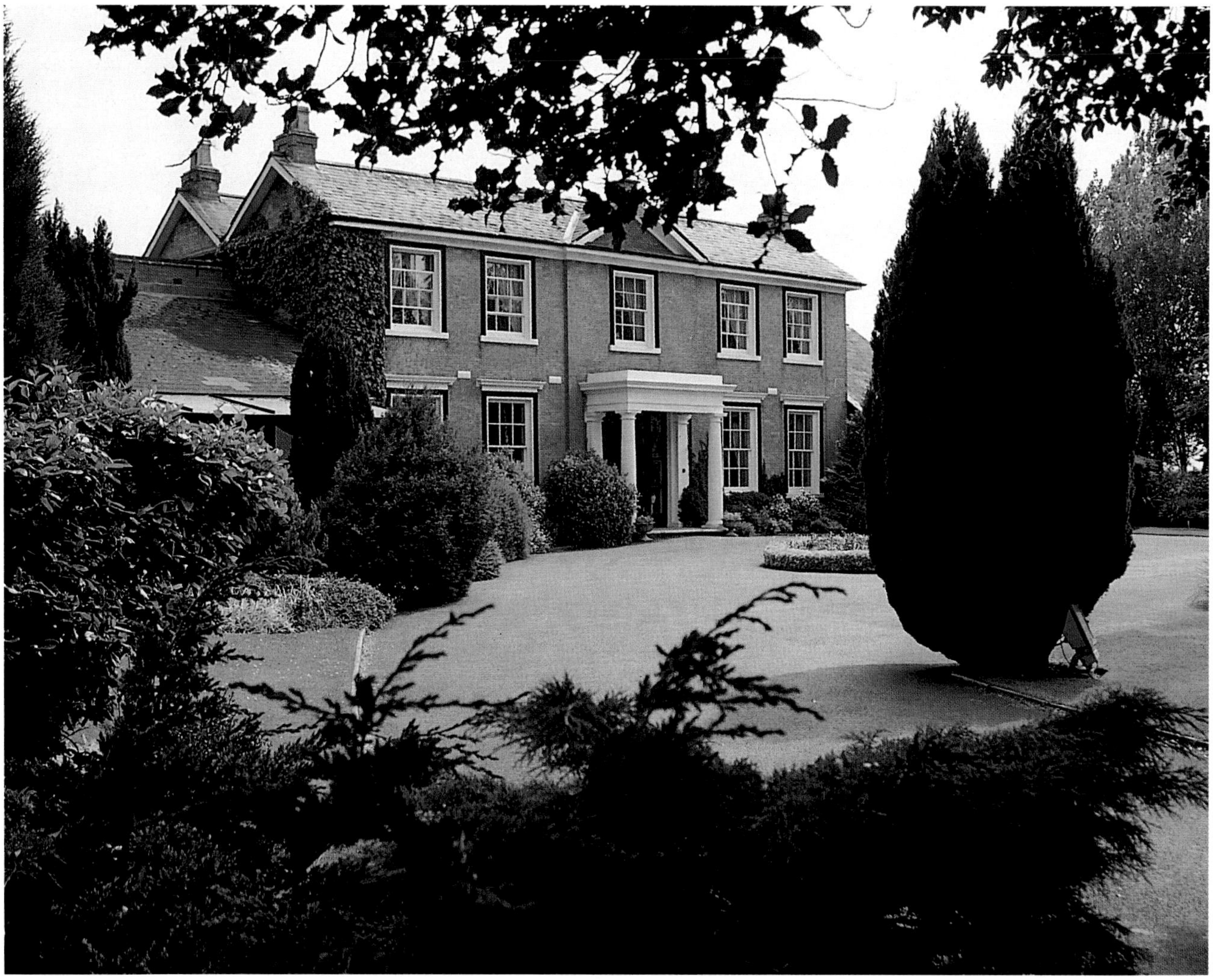

PARK FARM COUNTRY HOTEL & LEISURE

HETHERSETT, NORWICH, NORFOLK NR9 3DL
TEL: 01603 810264 FAX: 01603 812104

Park Farm Hotel occupies a tranquil and secluded location in beautifully landscaped grounds south of Norwich, once the second greatest city in England. There are executive rooms for additional comforts, with four poster beds and Jacuzzi baths. Additional bedrooms have been sympathetically converted from traditional and new buildings to reflect the style of the six rooms available in the main house. A superb leisure complex to suit all ages has been carefully incorporated alongside the original Georgian house to include, heated swimming pool, sauna, steam room, solarium, spa bath, gymnasium and aerobics studio. The croquet lawn, putting green and hard tennis court are situated in the grounds. Associated with the hotel is a superb golf course. The delightful Georgian restaurant is renowned for high standards of cuisine and service, with a wide selection of dishes and fine choice of wines. Conference facilities cater for up to 120 candidates, (24 hour and daily delegate rates available). The Norfolk broads, the coast, Norwich open market, Castle museum and Cathedral are nearby. **Directions:** By road, just off A11 on B1172, Norwich Airport eight miles, Norwich rail station six miles and Norwich bus station five miles. A light aircraft landing strip and helipad are in the grounds. Price guide: Single £60–£100; double/twin £90–£115; suite £120.

37 rms 160

For hotel location, see maps on pages 477-483

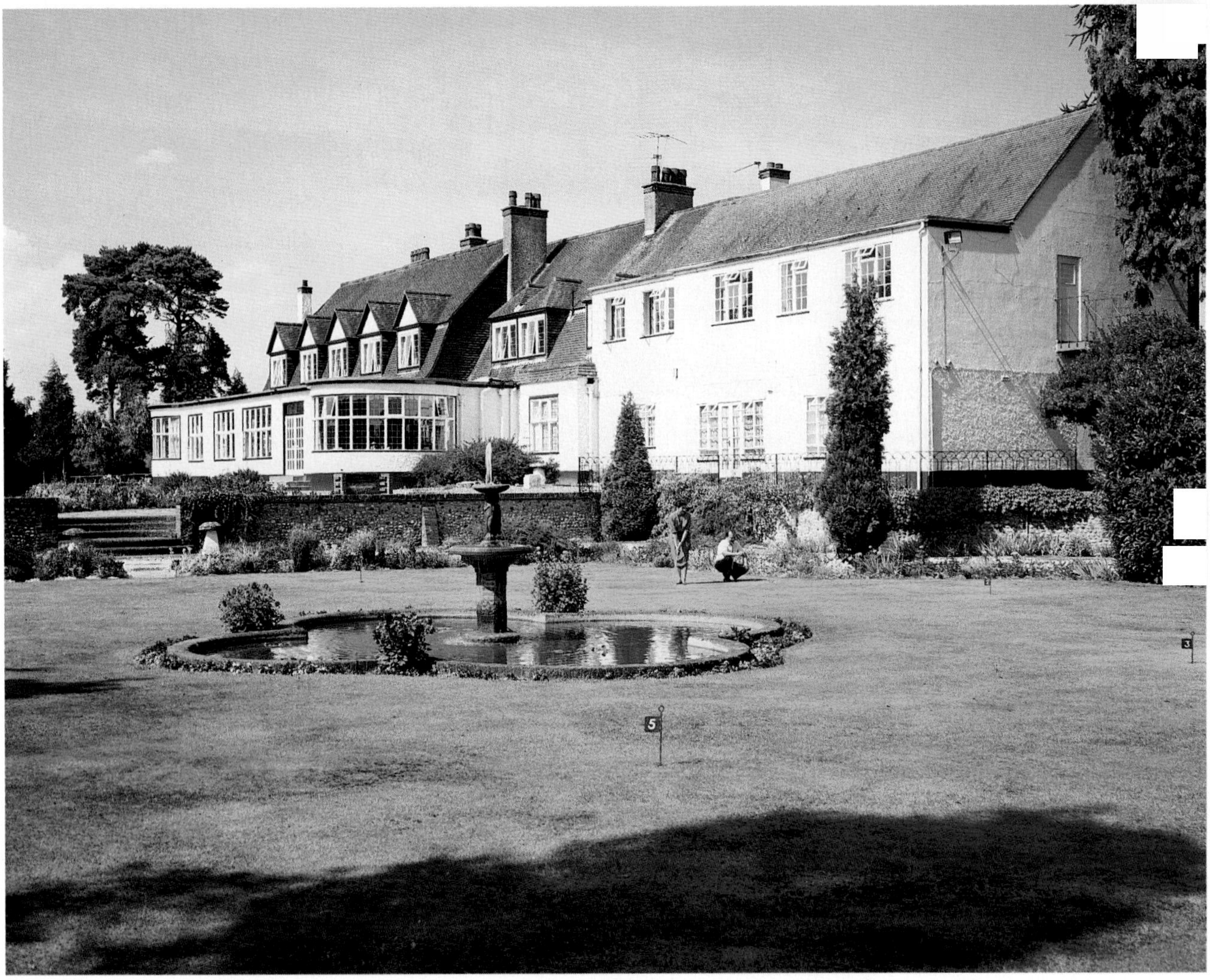

PETERSFIELD HOUSE HOTEL

LOWER STREET, HORNING, NR NORWICH, NORFOLK NR12 8PF
TEL: 01692 630741 FAX: 01692 630745

Petersfield House Hotel is set back from one of the most attractive reaches of the River Bure in the area known as the Norfolk Broads. The original mansion was built in the twenties on a prime site as a large private residence in two acres of gardens with its own moorings on a grassy bank of the river. Today it is a secluded family run hotel whose reputation is based on traditional comfort and hospitality. Guests can be sure of receiving personal attention at all times. The bedrooms, many recently refurbished, are bright and welcoming – most rooms overlook the well-kept landscaped gardens which feature an ornamental pond, a putting green and a flintstone moon gate that leads to a woodland glade. Varied fixed-price and extensive à la carte menus are served in the restaurant where a list of over 60 wines provides an ideal accompaniment. Regular Saturday night dinner-dances are held. Sailing is the popular local pastime and open regattas are held in summer. Golf is within driving range. Other local attractions include Norwich with its famous art gallery and "Ten Ancient Monuments" and Blickling Hall with its interesting furniture and gardens. **Directions:** From Norwich ring road, take A1151 to Wroxham. Cross bridge, turn right at Hoveton on A1062 to Horning; hotel is beyond centre of the village. Price guide: Single £60; double £75.

18 rms · MasterCard · VISA · AMERICAN EXPRESS · M 100

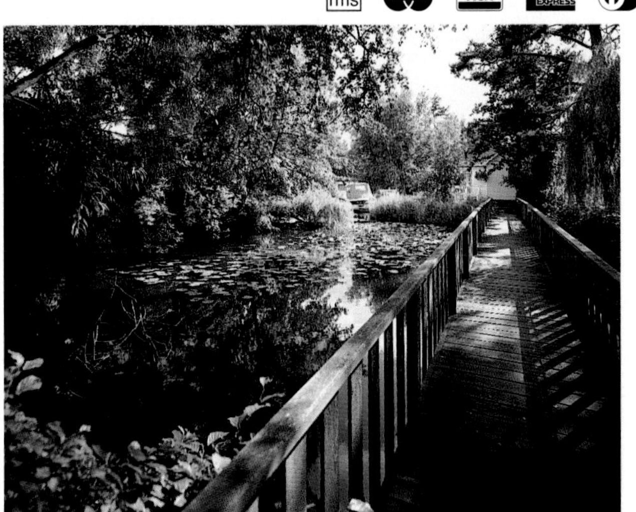

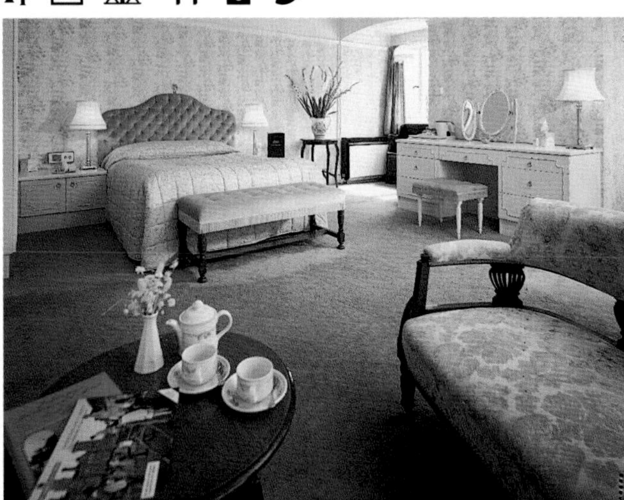

For hotel location, see maps on pages 477-483

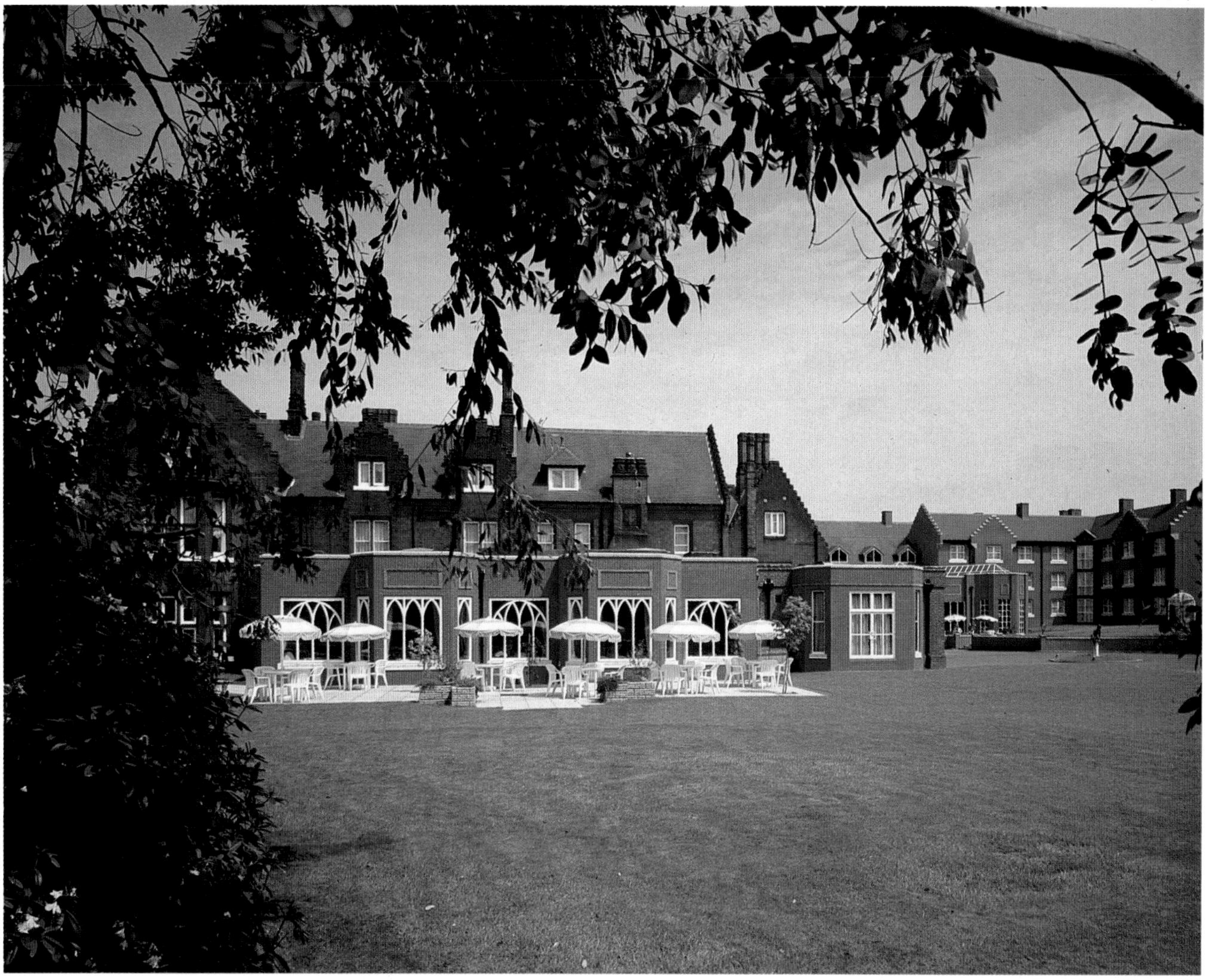

Sprowston Manor Hotel

SPROWSTON PARK, WROXHAM ROAD, NORWICH, NORFOLK NR7 8RP
TEL: 01603 410871 FAX: 01603 423911

This imposing country house, built originally in 1559 and then largely rebuilt in the 19th century, stands at the end of an oak-lined driveway in 10 acres of grounds, just 3 miles from Norwich. The bedrooms, all en suite and some with four-posters, have views over the hotel's parkland setting and are spacious and comfortable. The hotel has two restaurants. In The Orangery lavishly draped Gothic arched windows provide the perfect atmosphere in which to enjoy the finest table d'hôte cuisine. The more traditional Manor Restaurant has been restored to classic splendour with mahogany columns, oil paintings and crystal chandeliers. The à la carte menu offers a good choice of dishes. The large health spa with indoor swimming pool and leisure club, with spa bath, pool bar, fitness studio, steam rooms and sauna, are open to hotel residents free of charge. Solarium and beauty salon are charged as taken. With its well-equipped conference rooms, the hotel is an excellent venue for social and business functions. Adjoining the hotel is the 18-hole Sprowston Park Golf Club, with floodlit driving range. The city of Norwich rich with art and history, Sandringham, the Norfolk Broads and the Norfolk coast are all within easy reach. **Directions:** From Norwich, take the Wroxham Road (A1151) and follow signs to Sprowston Park. Price guide: Single £83–£115; double/twin £89–£105.

For hotel location, see maps on pages 477-483

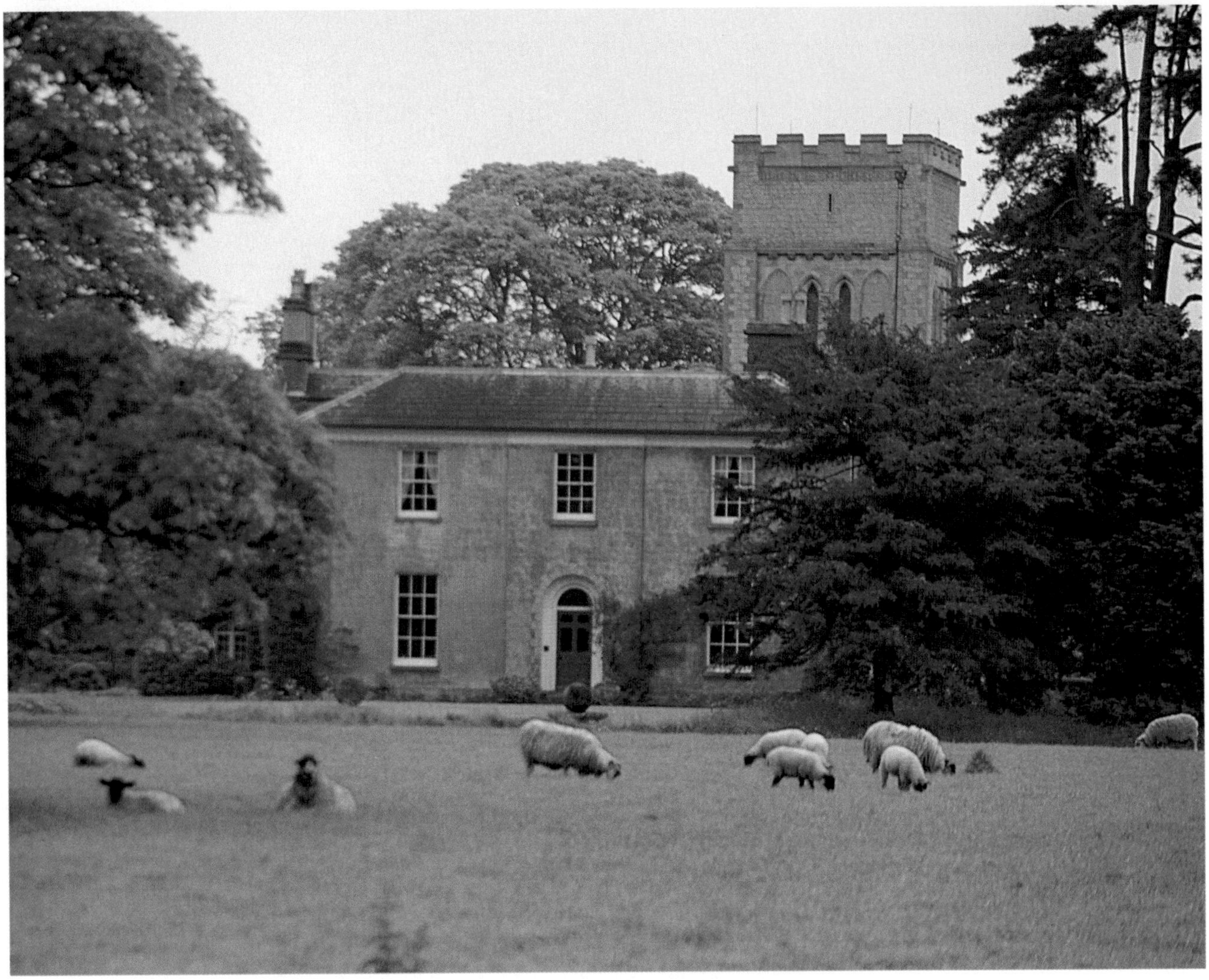

LANGAR HALL

LANGAR, NOTTINGHAMSHIRE NG13 9HG
TEL: 01949 860559 FAX: 01949 861045

Set in the Vale of Belvoir, mid-way between Nottingham and Grantham, Langar Hall is the family home of Imogen Skirving. Epitomising "excellence and diversity" it combines the standards of good hotel-keeping with the hospitality and style of country house living. Having received a warm welcome, guests can enjoy the atmosphere of a private home that is much loved and cared for. The en suite bedrooms are individually designed and comfortably appointed. The public rooms feature fine furnishings and most rooms afford beautiful views of the garden, park and moat. Imogen and her kitchen team collaborate to produce an excellent, varied menu of modern British food. For the perfect start to the weekend it is worth booking early for a special Friday night break which sometimes combines a leisurely dinner with an entertaining in-house opera or theatre performance. Lanagr Hall is an ideal venue for small boardroom meetings. It is also an ideal base from which to visit Belvoir Castle, to see cricket at Trent Bridge, to visit students at Nottingham University and to see Robin Hood's Sherwood Forest. Dogs can be accommodated by arrangement. **Directions:** Langar is accessible via Bingham on the A52, or via Cropwell Bishop from the A46 (both signposted). The house adjoins the church and is hidden behind it. Price guide: Single £50–£85; double/twin £75–£135.

For hotel location, see maps on pages 477-483

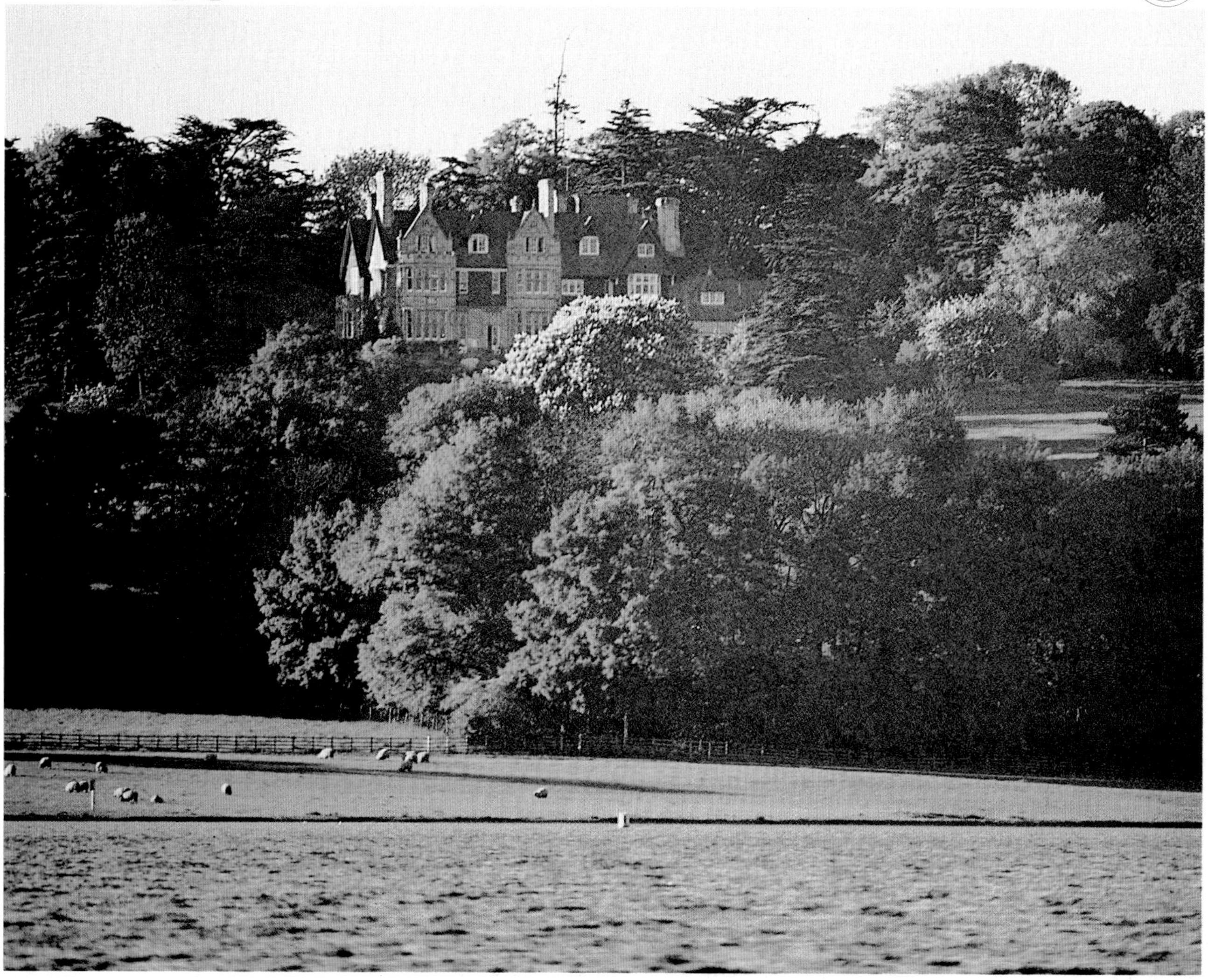

HAMBLETON HALL

HAMBLETON, OAKHAM, RUTLAND, LEICESTERSHIRE LE15 8TH
TEL: 01572 756991 FAX: 01572 724721

Winner of Johansens Most Excellent Country House Hotel 1996, hambleton Hall, originally a Victorian mansion, became a hotel in 1979. Since then its renown has continually grown. It enjoys a spectacular lakeside setting in a charming and unspoilt area of Rutland. The hotel's tasteful interiors have been designed to create elegance and comfort, retaining individuality by avoiding a catalogue approach to furnishing. Delightful displays of flowers, an artful blend of ingredients from local hedgerows and the London flower markets colour the bedrooms. In the restaurant, the chef and his enthusiastic team offer a menu which is strongly seasonal. Grouse, Scottish ceps and chanterelles, partridge and woodcock are all available at just the right time of year, accompanied by the best vegetables, herbs and salads from the Hall's garden. The dishes are beautifully presented and supported by a list of interesting wines at reasonable prices. For the energetic there are lovely walks around the lake and opportunities for tennis and swimming, golf, riding, bicycling, trout fishing, and sailing. Burghley House and Belton are nearby, as are the antique shops of Oakham, Uppingham and Stamford. Hambleton Hall is a Relais et Châteaux member. **Directions:** In the village of Hambleton, signposted from the A606, 1 mile east of Oakham. Price guide: Single £125; double/twin £125–£275.

For hotel location, see maps on pages 477-483

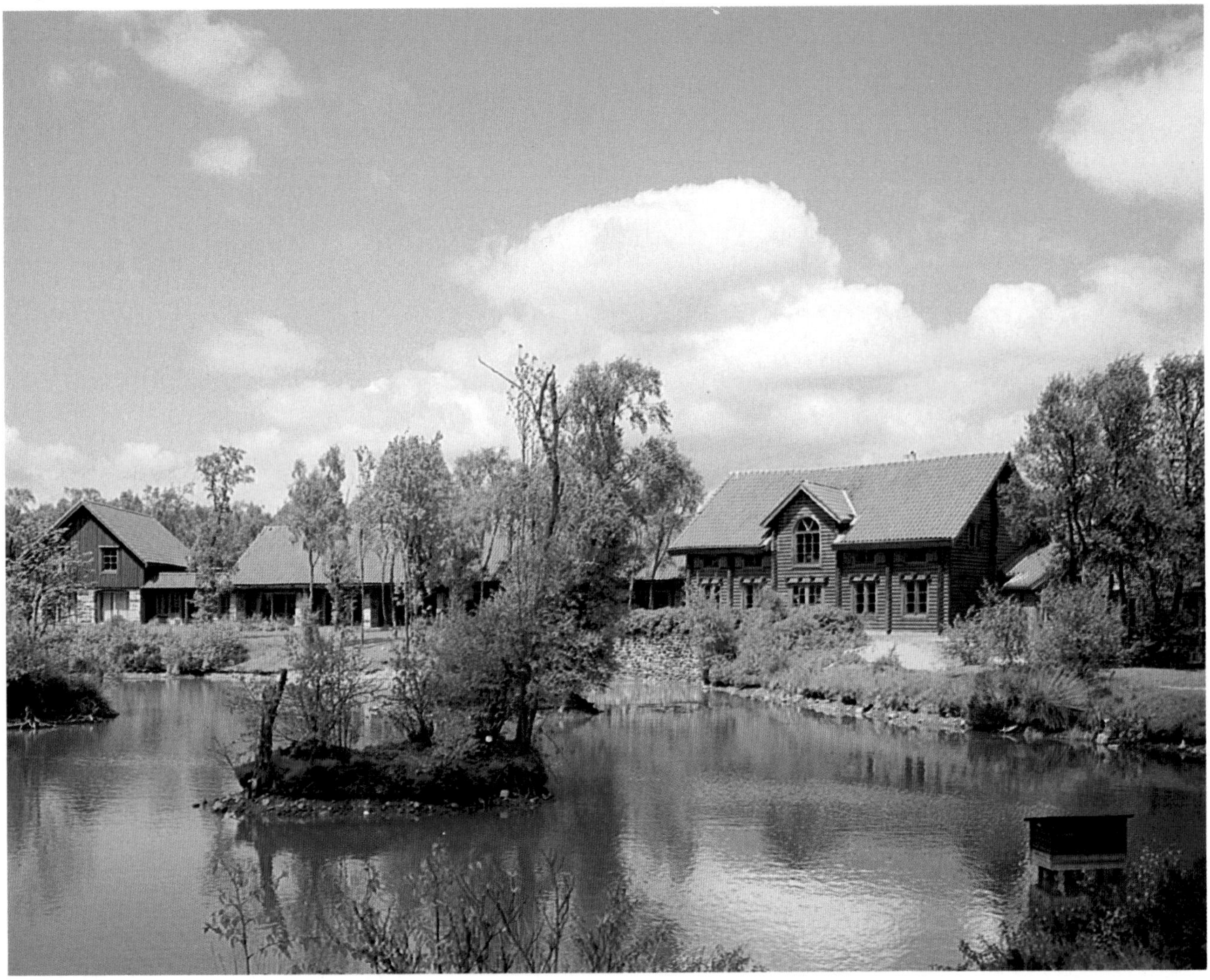

CHEVIN LODGE COUNTRY PARK HOTEL

YORKGATE, OTLEY, WEST YORKSHIRE LS21 3NU

TEL: 01943 467818 FAX: 01943 850335 FREEPHONE RESERVATIONS 0500 340560

A quite unique hotel – you would probably need to travel to Scandinavia to discover a similar complex to Chevin Lodge. Built entirely of Finnish logs and surrounded by birch trees, it is set in 50 acres of lake and woodland in the beauty spot of Chevin Forest Park. The spacious, carefully designed bedrooms are furnished with pine and wicker and some have patio doors leading to the lakeside gardens. In addition, there are several luxury lodges tucked away in the woods, some with their own kitchen, which provide alternative accommodation to the hotel bedrooms. Imaginative and appetising meals are served in the beautiful balconied restaurant, which overlooks the lake. Chevin Lodge offers conference facilities in the Woodlands Suite which is fully equipped for all business requirements. There is a new Club with swimming pool, spa bath, sauna, solarium and gym. There is also a games room, all weather tennis court and jogging and cycling trails that wind through the woods. Leeds, Bradford and Harrogate are within 20 minutes' drive. Special weekend breaks are available. **Directions:** From A658 between Bradford and Harrogate, take the Chevin Forest Park road, then left into Yorkgate for Chevin Lodge. Price guide: Single £92–£100; double/twin £100–£120.

For hotel location, see maps on pages 477-483

LE MANOIR AUX QUAT' SAISONS

GREAT MILTON, OXFORDSHIRE OX44 7PD
TEL: 01844 278881 FAX: 01844 278847

Situated in secluded grounds a few miles south of the historic city of Oxford in rural Cotswold countryside, the restaurant and the country house hotel of Le Manoir aux Quat' Saisons are among the finest in Europe. Le Manoir is the inspired creation of Raymond Blanc whose extraordinary cooking has received the highest tributes from all international guides to culinary excellence. The Times uniquely gives Blanc's cooking 10 out of 10 and rates it 'the best in Britain'. The atmosphere throughout is one of understated elegance while all nineteen bedrooms and suites offer guests the highest standards of comfort and luxury. Every need is anticipated, for service is a way of life here, never intrusive but always present.

For dedicated 'foodies', Le Petit Blanc, Raymond Blanc's highly successful cookery school, is a must. Five-day courses are run from October to April and participation is restricted to eight guests to ensure the highest level of personal tuition. Participants stay at Le Manoir and their partners are welcome to stay free of charge although their meals and drinks are charged separately. **Directions:** From London, M40 and turn off at junction 7 (A329 to Wallingford). From the North, leave M40 at junction 8 and follow signs to Wallingford (A329). After $1^1/_2$ miles, take second turning on right, Great Milton Manor. Price guide: Double/twin £185–£285; suites £345–£395.

For hotel location, see maps on pages 477-483

STUDLEY PRIORY

HORTON-CUM-STUDLEY, OXFORD, OXFORDSHIRE OX33 1AZ

TEL: 01865 351203 FAX: 01865 351613 USA/CANADA TOLL FREE: 800 437 2687

Studley Priory, its exterior little altered since Elizabethan days, is conveniently located only 7 miles from both the main London–Oxford road and the dreaming spires of Oxford. There is a sense of timeless seclusion in the setting of 13 acres of wooded grounds with their fine views of the Cotswolds, the Chilterns and the Vale of Aylesbury. The bedrooms range from single rooms to the Elizabethan Suite, which has a half-tester bed dating from around 1700. Cots are available for young children. The restaurant, offering the best of English and French cuisine, provides a seasonally changing menu created from fresh local produce and complemented by an extensive and well-balanced wine list. Good conference facilities are available, and wedding parties and banquets can be accommodated. Studley Priory is ideally placed for visits to Blenheim Palace, the Manors of Waddesdon and Milton, Broughton Castle, the Great Western Museum of Railways and also horse-racing at Ascot, Newbury and Cheltenham. Clay pigeon shooting and many other activities can be arranged at the hotel and there are riding facilities nearby. The Studley Wood 18 hole golf course is now complete. **Directions:** Leave M40 at junction 8. The hotel is situated at the top of the hill in the village of Horton-cum-Studley. Price guide: Single £95–£108; double/twin £105–£165; suite £175–£225.

For hotel location, see maps on pages 477-483

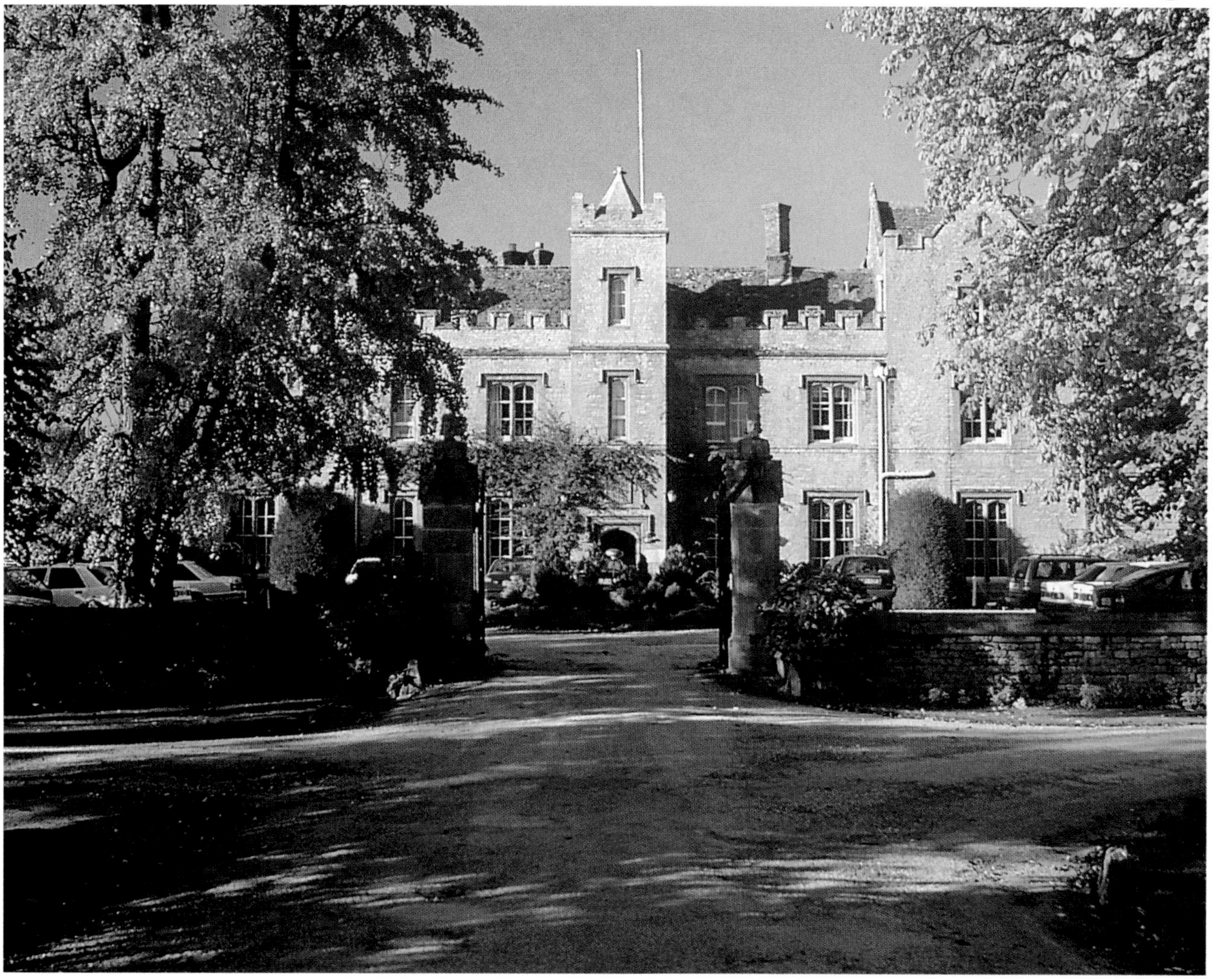

WESTON MANOR

WESTON-ON-THE-GREEN, OXFORDSHIRE OX6 8QL

TEL: 01869 350621 FAX: 01869 350901

Imposing wrought-iron gates flanked by sculptured busts surmounting tall grey stone pillars lead into the impressive entrance to this delightful old manor house, the showpiece of the lovely village of Weston-on-the Green since the 11th century. The ancestral home of the Earls of Abingdon and Berkshire, and once the property of Henry VIII, Weston Manor stands regally in 13 acres of colourful gardens restored as a unique country house hotel of character. A peaceful retreat for visitors wishing to discover the delights of the surrounding Cotswold countryside and of Oxford, Woodstock, Blenheim Palace and Broughton Castle. Many of the Manor's 34 charming bedroom, including four in a cottage and 14 in the old coachhouse, retain antique furniture and all have garden views, private bathrooms and elegant suroundings. There is a squash court, croquet lawn and a secluded, heated outdoor swimming pool. Golf and riding are nearby. At the heart of the Manor is the restaurant, a magnificent vaulted and oak panelled Baronial Hall where delectable cuisine is served. Dining in such splendour is very much the focus of a memorable stay. Directions: From the M40, exit at junction 9 onto the A34 towards Oxford. After approximately one mile turn right onto the B340. Weston Manor is on the left. Price guide: Single £97.50; double/twin £115; suite £155.

For hotel location, see maps on pages 477-483

TREGLOS HOTEL

CONSTANTINE BAY, NR PADSTOW, CORNWALL PL28 8JH
TEL: 01841 520727 FAX: 01841 521163

The atmosphere of a large country house pervades Treglos Hotel, which enjoys a superb position overlooking the spectacular North Cornish coastline. Most of the hotel's bedrooms and suites enjoy magnificent views over Constantine Bay and Trevose Head. All are equipped to a very high standard and a daily laundry service, room service and night porter are all available. Spacious lounges, warmed on chilly days by roaring log fires, are the perfect place to relax, and in warmer weather guests may enjoy the tranquillity of the beautifully landscaped gardens. The restaurant enjoys a good reputation and offers an extensive menu catering for every need. Specialities include fresh local seafood, traditional roasts and vegetables from the kitchen garden. A lovely heated swimming pool and Jacuzzi open onto the lawns and gardens and the patio, overlooking the bay, is a favoured place to enjoy delicious cream teas and early evening drinks. Nearby, the picturesque harbour at Padstow provides fishing from mackerel to shark, along with boat trips. Several National Trust properties are within easy reach. Trevose golf links and sandy beaches are just a short stroll from the hotel. **Directions:** Constantine Bay and Treglos are signposted from St Merryn (B3276 from Padstow. Newquay Airport is eight miles away. Price guide: Single £48–£70; double/twin £96–£140; suites £134–£186. Including dinner.

For hotel location, see maps on pages 477-483

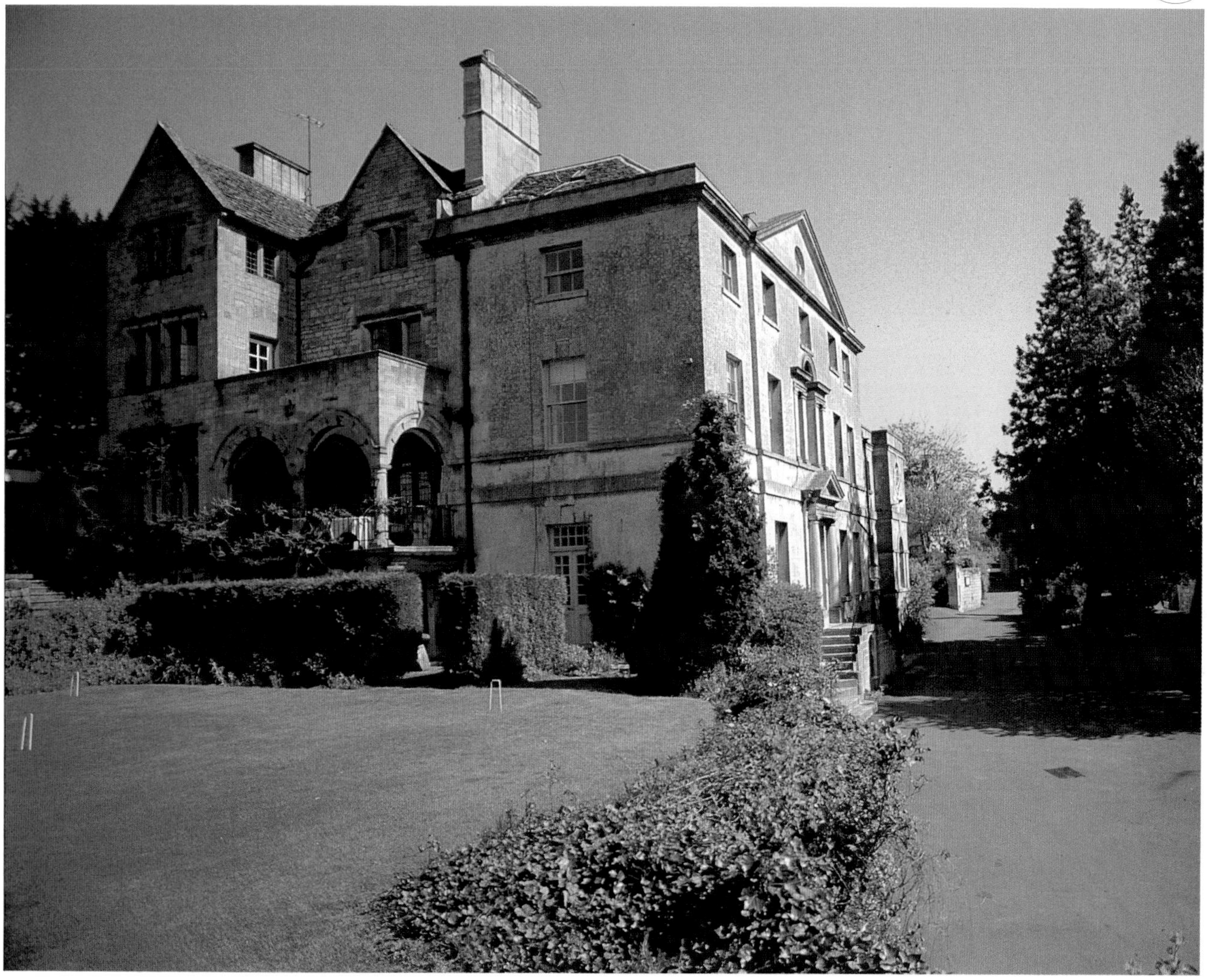

THE PAINSWICK HOTEL

KEMPS LANE, PAINSWICK, GLOUCESTERSHIRE GL6 6YB
TEL: 01452 812160 FAX: 01452 814059 TELEX: 43605

Painswick stands high on a hill overlooking the beautiful rolling Cotswolds valleys – an old wool community of greystone buildings dating back to the 14th century. Medieval cottages mingle with elegant Georgian merchants' houses. There is one of the finest church's in the west and an ancient churchyard graced by 99 large clipped yew trees planted in 1792. Situated majestically in the centre of this architectural gem is the Palladian-style Painswick Hotel, built in 1790 and formerly the home of wealthy village rectors. The hotel's 20 en suite bedrooms have all modern amenities, fine fabrics, soft furnishings, antiques and objets d'art. Combined with the luxury toiletries, baskets of fruit, books and magazines provided for guests there is a distinct impression of staying in a comfortable private house. Delicious and tempting cuisine is served in the stylish dining room with Chef Nick Benson making much use of locally reared Cotswold meat, wild Severn salmon, game, Vale of Evesham vegetables and fresh shellfish from a seawater tank. Quiet meals, wedding occasions and business meetings can be enjoyed in the private dining rooms. Resident dogs – visiting dogs by arrangement. Directions: Exit M5 at junction 13 onto A419 and then left onto the A46 Stroud to Cheltenham road. Painswick is just north of Stroud and the hotel stands behind the church. Price guide: Single from £68; double/twin from £98.

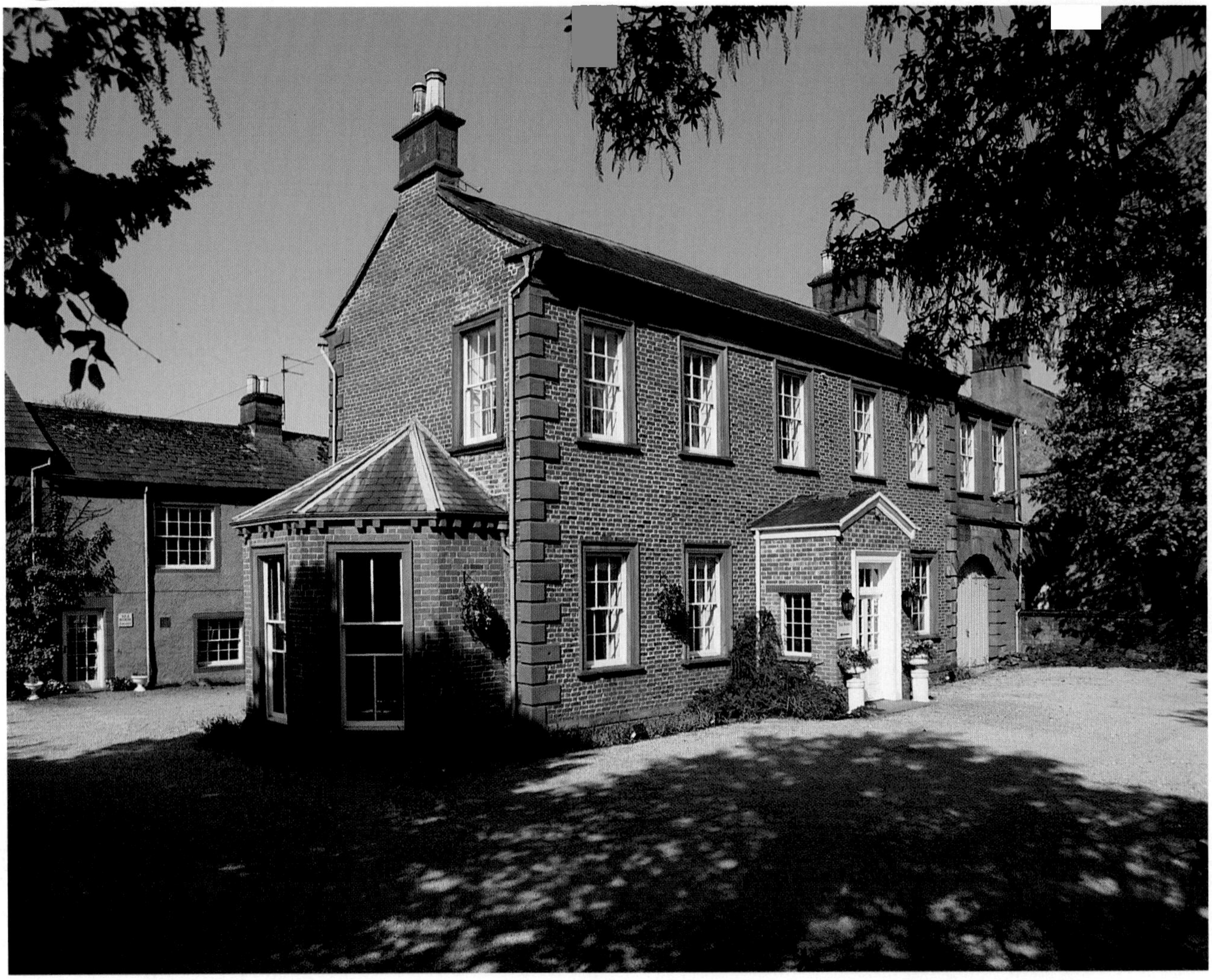

TEMPLE SOWERBY HOUSE HOTEL

TEMPLE SOWERBY, PENRITH, CUMBRIA CA10 1RZ
TEL: 017683 61578 FAX: 017683 61958

Temple Sowerby House looks over at Cross Fell, the highest peak in the Pennines, noted for its spectacular ridge walk. This old Cumbrian farmhouse is set in two acres of gardens and guests are assured of peace and quiet. Geoffrey and Cecile Temple offer a warm, hospitable and friendly family service upon which the hotel prides itself. There are two dining rooms – the panelled room with its cosy atmosphere and the Rose Room which overlooks the garden. Delicious, home-cooked dishes might include a starter of a pithivier of creamed wild mushrooms served with crisp salad leaves in a truffle and olive oil dressing, followed by tuna fillet served on a puré of spiced rhubarb wirh poppy seed vinegar, rounded off with iced chocolate parfait served with a white chocolate sauce. Individually furnished bedrooms all have private bathrooms. Four of the rooms are situated in the Coach House, just yards from the main house. During the winter, apéritifs are taken by the fireside, while in the summer, guests can sip drinks on the terrace and enjoy views across the fells. Lakes Ullswater and Derwentwater, the Borders, Scottish Lowlands, Hadrian's Wall and Yorkshire Dales are within easy reach by car. **Directions:** Temple Sowerby lies on the A66, seven miles from exit 40 of the M6, between Penrith and Appleby. Price guide: Single £55–£60; double/twin £78–£88.

12 rms

For hotel location, see maps on pages 477-483

THE HAYCOCK

WANSFORD-IN-ENGLAND, PETERBOROUGH, CAMBRIDGESHIRE PE8 6JA
TEL: 01780 782223 FAX: 01780 783031

The Haycock is a handsome old coaching inn of great charm, character and historic interest. It was host to Mary Queen of Scots in 1586 and Princess Alexandra Victoria, later Queen Victoria, in 1835. Overlooking the historic bridge that spans the River Nene, the hotel is set in a delightful village of unspoilt cottages. All the bedrooms are individually designed, equipped to the highest standards, and graced by Italian hand-painted furniture. The Tapestry Restaurant is renowned for the quality of its traditional English cooking, with dishes utilising the freshest possible ingredients. It is also famed for its outstanding wine list. A purpose-built ballroom, with lovely oak beams and its own private garden, is a popular venue for a wide range of events, from May Balls, wedding receptions and Christmas parties to the East Anglian Wine Festival. The Business Centre has also made its mark; it is well equipped with every facility required and offers the flexibility to cater for meetings, car launches, product seminars and conferences. Places of interest nearby include Burghley House, Nene Valley Railway, Elton Hall, Rutland Water and Peterborough Cathedral. **Directions:** Clearly signposted on A1 a few miles south of Stamford, on A1/A47 intersection west of Peterborough. Price guide: Single £72-£85; double/twin room £95-£115.

50 rms · 200

For hotel location, see maps on pages 477-483

KITLEY

THE KITLEY ESTATE, YEALMPTON, PLYMOUTH, DEVON PL8 2NW
TEL: 01752 881555 FAX: 01752 881667

This imposing Grade I listed country house hotel, built of silver grey Devonshire "marble", is situated in 300 acres of richly timbered parkland at the head of one of Yealm estuary's wooded creeks a few miles south-east of Plymouth. It is one of the earliest Tudor revival houses in England and has been splendidly restored to its former glory. Approached by a mile long drive through a magnificent private estate, Kitley is an oasis of quiet luxury, providing the highest standards in comfort, cuisine and personal service. A sweeping staircase leads to 19 spacious bedrooms and suites. Each has panoramic views over the estate and is richly appointed with furnishings designed to reflect the traditional elegance of the house whilst incorporating all modern facilities. The lounge area, with its huge open fireplace, and bar are stylish and relaxing. The restaurant is sumptuously decorated in burgundy and gold and provides the perfect atmosphere in which to enjoy the finest of cuisine – whatever the occasion. Guests can enjoy fishing in the private lake and golf, shooting and riding are nearby. **Directions:** A38, exit at the sign for the National Shire Horse Centre (A3121). Then turn right onto the A379. The hotel entrance is on the left after Yealmpton village. Price guide: Single from £75; double/twin from £110; suite from £130.

For hotel location, see maps on pages 477-483

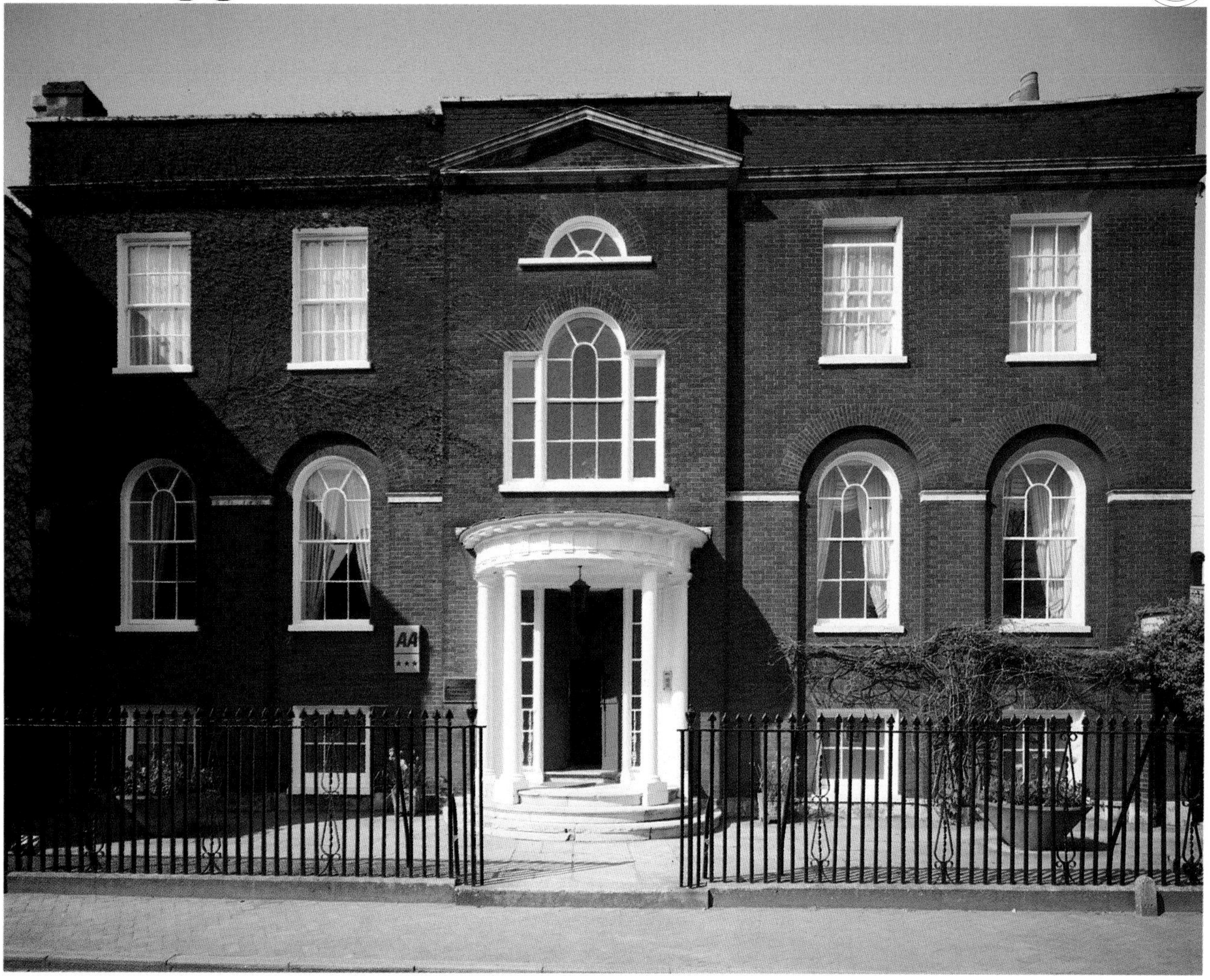

THE MANSION HOUSE

THAMES STREET, POOLE, DORSET BH15 1JN
TEL: 01202 685666 FAX: 01202 665709

A sophisticated Georgian town residence, The Mansion House Hotel is set in a prime location just off Poole's busy quayside, in a quiet cul-de-sac adjacent to St James's Church – offering its visitors a calm retreat. Restored by its owners, The Mansion House provides every modern luxury. From the entrance hall a splendid staircase sweeps up to an elegant hallway featuring statuesque marble pillars. Pretty bedrooms demonstrate the personal touch; all are distinctively styled and named after a famous Georgian or Victorian character. A drink and a crudité in the Canadian Redwood Cocktail Bar – a popular haunt of local business people – is the ideal prelude to a fine meal. Good, English gourmet cooking is served in the panelled Dining Club restaurant. Lunches and lighter meals are also offered downstairs in the less formal Bistro, where stone walls and stripped oak furniture create a rustic atmosphere. Two conference rooms provide good private meeting facilities. For the sports enthusiast, all manner of water activities are available, while local places of interest include the harbour, sandy beaches, the Isle of Purbeck and Corfe Castle. **Directions:** Poole is reached from the M3 via the M27, A31, A349 and A350. Thames Street runs between The Quay and West Street by Poole Bridge. Price guide: Single £77–£82; double/twin £112–£122; suite £155.

For hotel location, see maps on pages 477-483

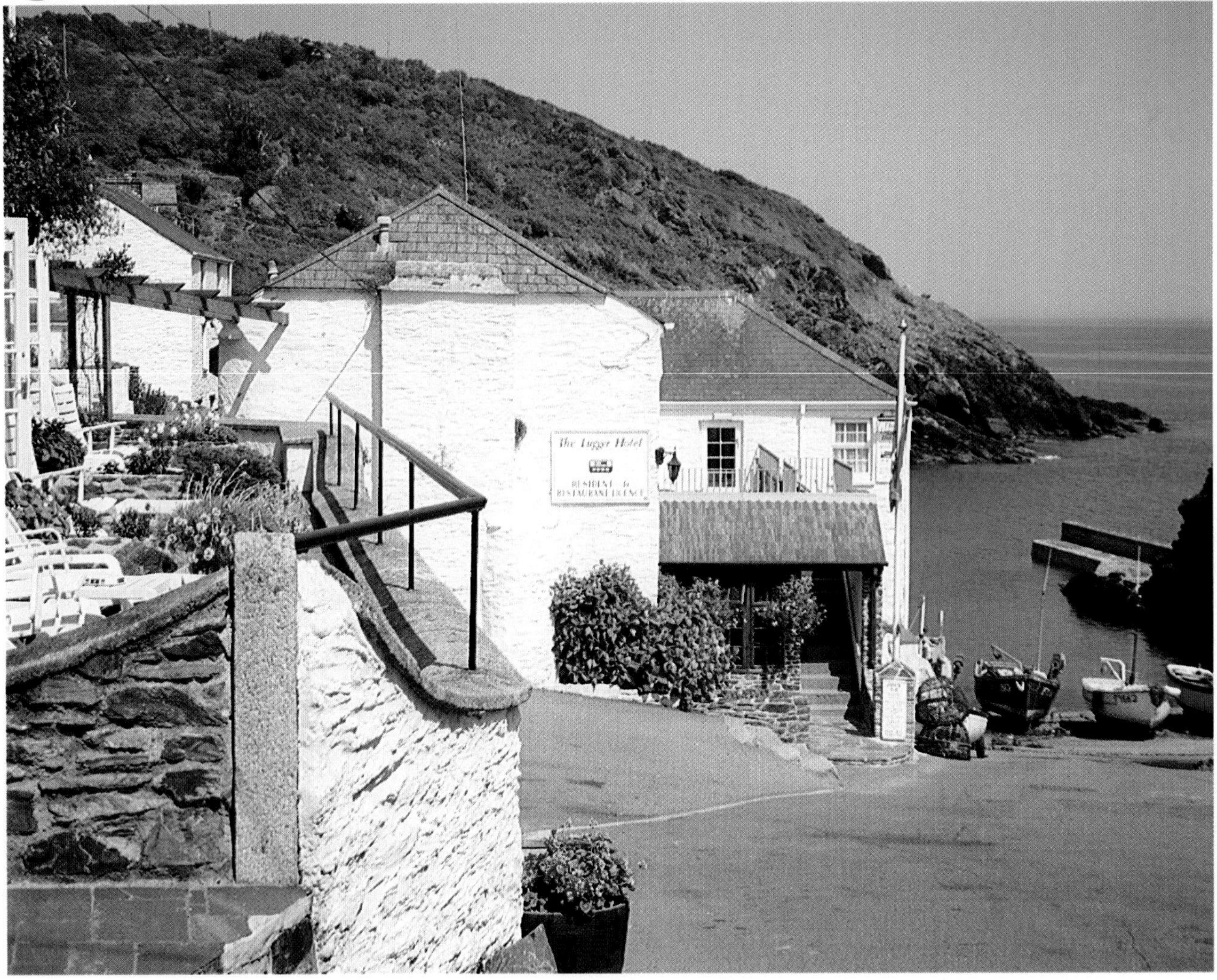

THE LUGGER HOTEL

PORTLOE, NR TRURO, CORNWALL TR2 5RD
TEL: 01872 501322 FAX: 01872 501691

A 17th century inn by the sea – and reputed to have been the haunt of smugglers, it sits at the very water's edge in the picturesque fishing village of Portloe. Situated in a conservation area in the heart of the beautiful Roseland Peninsula, this internationally renowned hotel is like a solid rock in a changing world. The Lugger has been in the Powell family for three generations during which, much thought and care have been taken to preserve its welcoming intimate atmosphere. There are 19 tastefully furnished bedrooms, all with en suite facilities as well as personal safes and refrigerators. A skilled team of chefs offers varied and exciting menus of English and Continental dishes in the attractive restaurant overlooking the cove. Local seafood is a speciality, with crab and lobster being particular favourites. The freshly made desserts on the sweet trolley, topped with clotted cream, are a delight to both the eye and the palate, whilst there is a wide choice of wines including Cornish wine from just a mile away. English Tourist Board 4 Crowns Highly Commended. Closed early November until late February. **Directions:** A390 from Plymouth, B3287 from St Austell to Tregony, then A3078 to Portloe. Price guide (including dinner): Single £70–£80; double/twin £140–£160.

For hotel location, see maps on pages 477-483

THE BRIDGE HOTEL

PRESTBURY, CHESHIRE SK10 4DQ
TEL: 01625 829326 FAX: 01625 827557

The Bridge Hotel is situated in the centre of the village of Prestbury, one of the prettiest villages in the North West of England. Originally dating from 1626, The Bridge today combines the old world charm of an ancient and historic building with the comfort and facilities of a modern hotel, yet within easy reach of Manchester Airport and major motorways. The public rooms have retained much of the former inn's original character, with oak panelling and beams in the bar and reception area. The bedrooms, many of which overlook the River Bollin, are decorated to the highest standard, with 5 rooms in the old building and a further 18 in a recently added wing. In the attractive galleried dining room, table d'hôte and à la carte menus offer traditional English cuisine. There is an extensive selection of wines to accompany your meal. Conference and banqueting facilities are available. Places to visit nearby include the Peak District National Park, Chatsworth, Tatton Park and Liverpool's Albert Dock. While enjoying a quiet location, the hotel is convenient for Manchester, just 30 minutes away, Liverpool, and the medieval city of Chester, which is under 40 minutes' drive. **Directions:** In the centre of the village next to the church. Prestbury is on the A538 from Wilmslow to Macclesfield. Price guide: Single £79; double/twin £93–£110; suites £115. Special weekend rates available.

23 rms MasterCard VISA AMERICAN EXPRESS M 100

For hotel location, see maps on pages 477-483

THE GIBBON BRIDGE HOTEL

NR CHIPPING, FOREST OF BOWLAND, LANCASHIRE PR3 2TQ
TEL: 01995 61456 FAX: 01995 61277

Set in award-winning grounds abound with trees, wildlife and a tarn. The Gibbon Bridge overlooking the Longridge fells in the heart of Lancashires Forest of Bowland, provides a welcoming and peaceful retreat. Created in by 1982 resident proprietor Janet Simpson and her late mother Margaret, the hotel buildings combine traditional architecture with interesting gothic masonry, to create a distinctive and unique atmosphere. Individually designed, furnished and equipped to the highest standard, the eight bedrooms and twenty two suites include four poster, half tester and gothic brass beds and jacuzzi spa baths. The restaurant overlooks the garden and is renowned for traditional and imaginative dishes incorporating home-grown vegetables and herbs. The splendid garden bandstand is perfect for any musical repertoire or civil wedding ceremony, also elegant, unobtrusive private rooms and lounges are available for dinner parties, receptions and executive meetings. Leisure facilities include a beauty salon, gymnasium, solarium, steam room, and all weather tennis court. Numerous sporting activities can be arranged locally. **Directions:** M6 exit 32, A6 to Broughton, B5269 to Longridge, follow signs for Chipping. Turn right at 'T' junction in village. Price guide: Single £70; double/twin £90; suite £120–£180.

30 rms MasterCard VISA AMERICAN EXPRESS M 120

For hotel location, see maps on pages 477-483

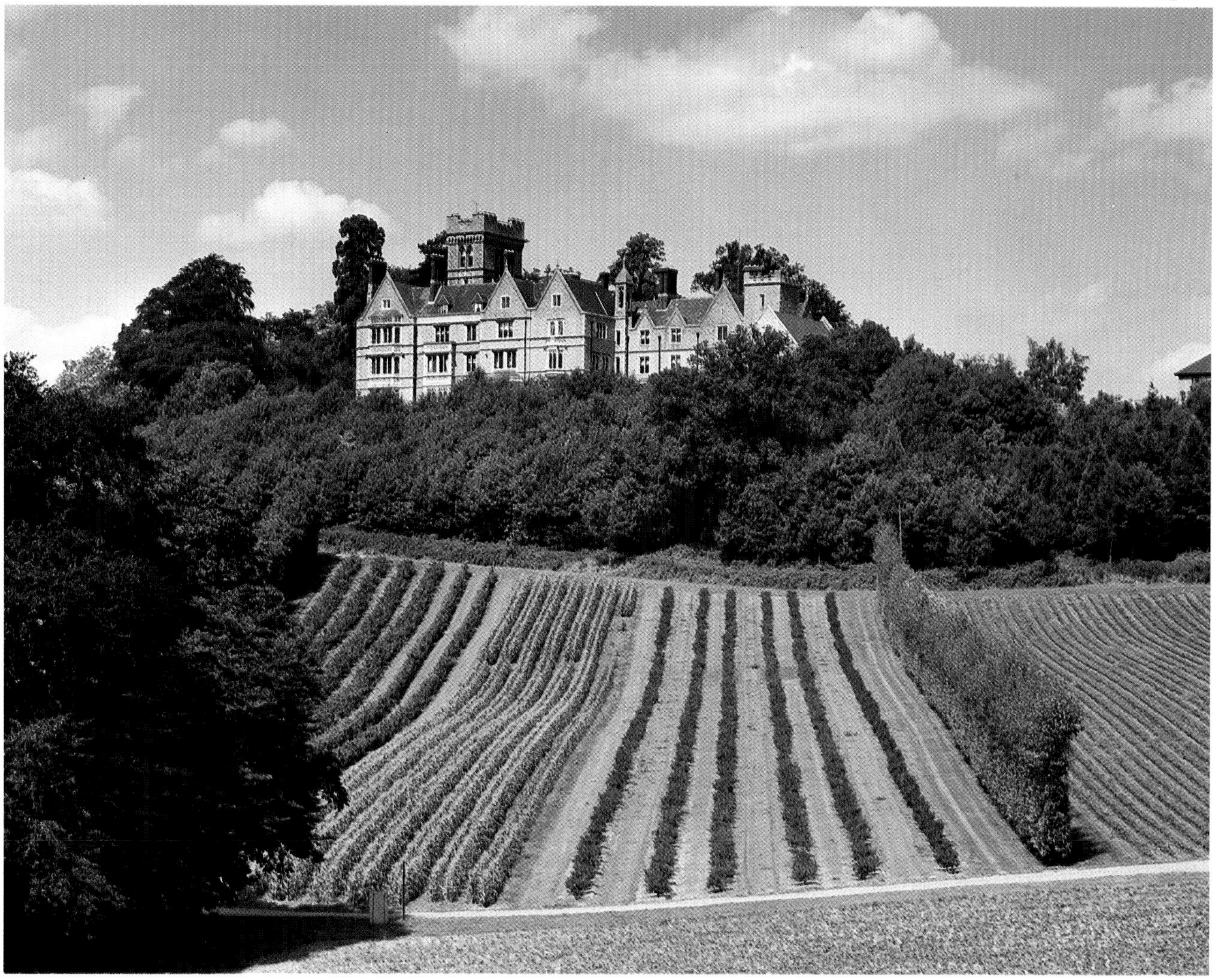

NUTFIELD PRIORY

NUTFIELD, REDHILL, SURREY RH1 4EN
TEL: 01737 822066 FAX: 01737 823321

Built in 1872 by the millionaire MP, Joshua Fielden, Nutfield Priory is an extravagant folly embellished with towers, elaborate carvings, intricate stonework, cloisters and stained glass, all superbly restored to create an unusual country-house hotel. Set high on Nutfield Ridge, the priory has far-reaching views over the Surrey and Sussex countryside, while being within easy reach of London and also Gatwick Airport. The elegant lounges and library have ornately carved ceilings and antique furnishings. Unusually spacious bedrooms – some with beams – enjoy views over the surrounding countryside. Fresh fruit is a thoughtful extra. The cloistered restaurant provides a unique environment in which to enjoy the high standard of cuisine, complemented by an extensive wine list. Conferences and private functions can be accommodated in the splendid setting of one of the hotel's 10 conference rooms. The Priory sports and leisure club, adjacent to the hotel, provides all the facilities for exercise and relaxation that one could wish for, including a swimming pool, sauna, spa, solarium, gym, steam room, beauty & hairdressing and billiard room. **Directions:** Nutfield is on the A25 between Redhill and Godstone and can be reached easily from junctions 6 and 8 of the M25. From Godstone, the Priory is on the left just after the village. Price guide: Single £105–£112.50; double/twin £125–£155; suite £200.

60 rms

For hotel location, see maps on pages 477-483

THE RICHMOND GATE HOTEL AND RESTAURANT

RICHMOND HILL, RICHMOND-UPON-THAMES, SURREY TW10 6RP
TEL: 0181 940 0061 FAX: 0181 332 0354 – FROM USA TOLL FREE: 1-800 544 9993

This former Georgian country house stands on the crest of Richmond Hill close to the Royal Park and Richmond Terrace with its commanding views over the River Thames. The 66 stylishly furnished en suite bedrooms combine every comfort of the present with the elegance of the past and include several luxury four-poster rooms and suites. Exceptional and imaginative cuisine, complemented by prize-winning English country wines, is on offer in the sophisticated surroundings of 'Gates On The Park Restaurant'. Through the week a less formal alternative is available in the Bistro in the Victorian conservatory, overlooking the hotel's beautiful walled garden. Weddings, business meetings and private dining events can be arranged in a variety of rooms. A superb new leisure club includes a 20 metre swimming pool and extensive facilities for relaxation and recreation. Richmond is a unique town, close to central London and the West End yet in a country setting. The Borough offers a wealth of visitor attractions, including Hampton Court Palace, Syon House and Park and the Royal Botanic Gardens at Kew. Weekend breaks are inclusive of entry into one of the local attractions and are available from £120. **Directions:** Opposite the Star & Garter Home at the top of Richmond Hill. Price guide: Single £85–£113; double/twin £110–£133.

66 rms MasterCard VISA AMERICAN EXPRESS M 50

For hotel location, see maps on pages 477-483

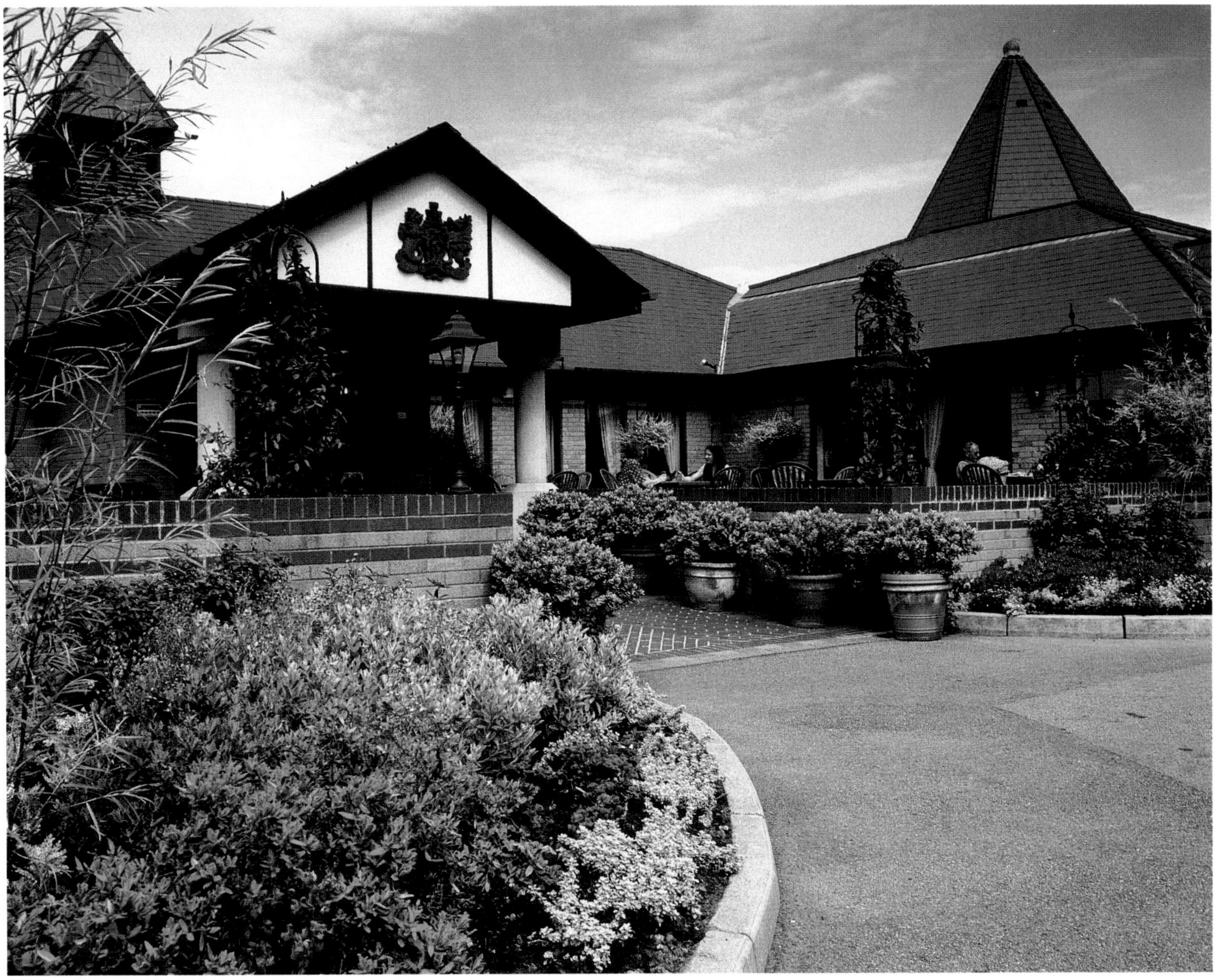

BRIDGEWOOD MANOR HOTEL

BRIDGEWOOD ROUNDABOUT, MAIDSTONE ROAD, ROCHESTER KENT ME5 9AX
TEL: 01634 201333 FAX: 01634 201330

This spacious, purpose-built hotel situated on the edge of the historic city of Rochester has every modern facility that guests could wish for. Strategically placed near Ashford International between London and the Kent Channel Ports, Bridgewood has outstanding conference facilities, also a reputation that has earned it the award of four stars by the AA and RAC. Service is friendly and attentive and fine cuisine is served in the restaurant and in the Terrace Bar, complemented by a wide range of excellent wines. All the bedrooms are comfortable and equipped with colour satellite television, direct-dial telephone and hospitality tray. The leisure facilities include a large indoor swimming pool, a spa bath, sauna and steam room, a gymnasium, solarium, beauty treatment room and full-size snooker table. Outside there is an all-weather tennis court and a putting green. Shooting and riding can be arranged. A short distance away are Rochester and Canterbury, Chatham Dockyard, Leeds Castle and Chartwell and the Tyland Wildlife Centre. **Directions:** From the M2, exit at junction 3 and take the A229 towards Rochester, Chatham and Walderslade. At Bridgewood Roundabout follow sign to Walderslade and Lordswood. The hotel entrance is 50 yards on the left along Walderslade Road. From M20, exit at junction 6 onto A229. Price guide: Single £90; double/twin £110.

For hotel location, see maps on pages 477-483

THE CHASE HOTEL

GLOUCESTER ROAD, ROSS-ON-WYE, HEREFORDSHIRE HR9 5LH
TEL: 01989 763161 FAX: 01989 768330

The Chase Hotel, just a few minutes' walk from the centre of Ross-on-Wye, is a handsome Regency country house standing in pleasant grounds. Careful restoration of the interiors has recaptured the elegance and craftsmanship of the past. After an apéritif in the Chase Bar, guests are ushered into the dining room where the tall windows and voluminous drapes make a striking impression. Chef Ken Tait favours a modern British approach to cooking, with a distinct continental influence. He uses fine local produce, such as Herefordshire beef, game and fresh vegetables in combination, to create dishes that give an unexpected subtlety to traditional ingredients. When the bedrooms were renovated, great care was taken to preserve their original Georgian character: the effect was then softened with comfortable furniture and appealing fabrics. Unobtrusive, up-to-the-minute amenities have been provided in each room and en suite bathroom. The function suites can accommodate a host of events. The surrounding area offers an infinite variety of places to visit, including Hereford Cathedral, Symonds Yat, Monmouth and the Forest of Dean. **Directions:** From M50 exit 4 turn left at roundabout signposted Gloucester and right at first roundabout signposted 'Town Centre'. Hotel is 1/2 mile on left-hand side. Price guide: Single £65; double/twin £80; suite £110.

39 rms · 300

For hotel location, see maps on pages 477-483

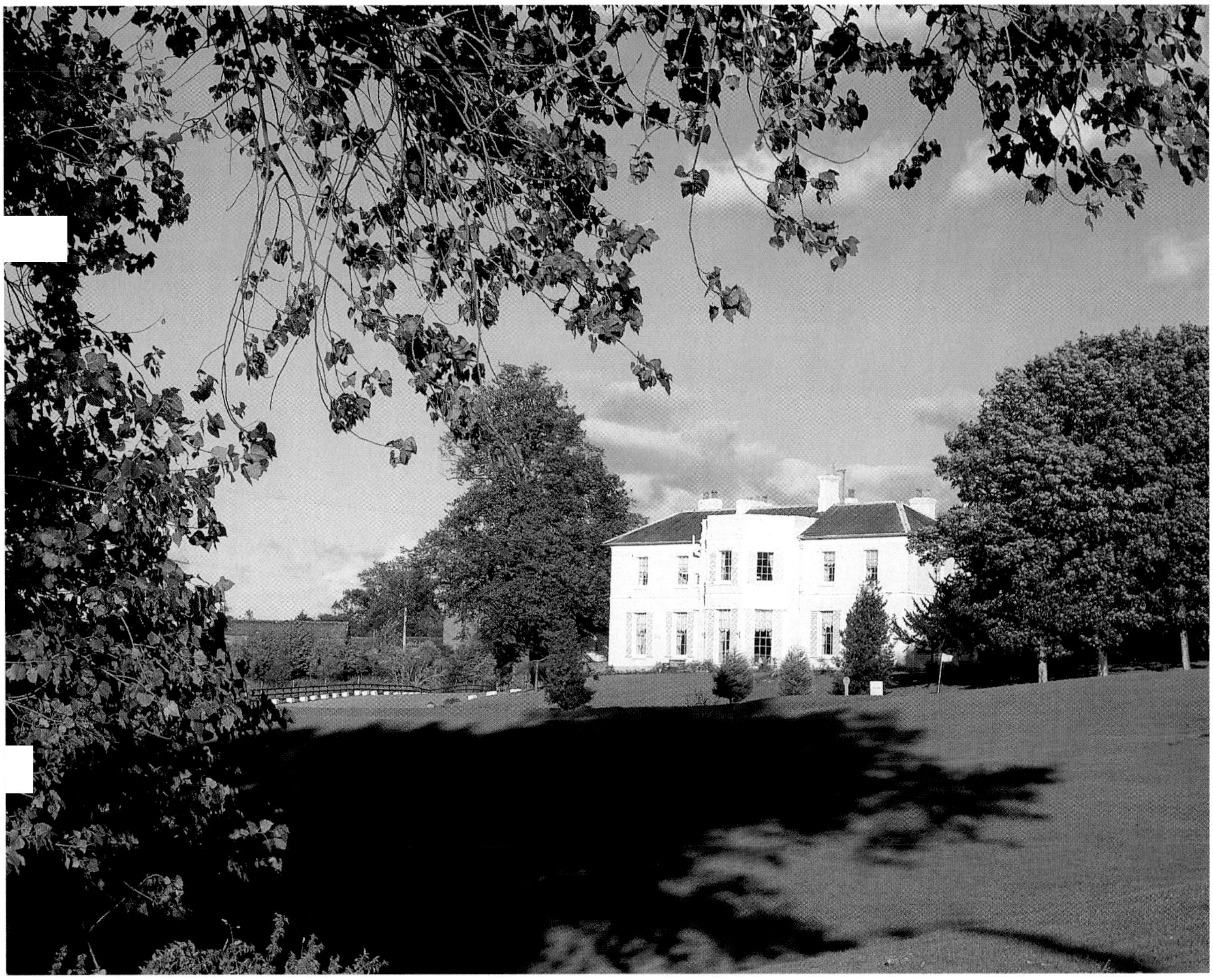

PENGETHLEY MANOR

NR ROSS-ON-WYE, HEREFORDSHIRE HR9 6LL
TEL: 01989 730211 FAX: 01989 730238

The first Baron Chandos, a favourite of Mary I Queen of England is reputed to have acquired Pengethley Estate in 1544, and here he built the original Tudor house. Although much of the building was ravaged by fire in the early 19th century, some parts survived – notably the oak panelling in the entrance hall – and it was rebuilt as a Georgian manor house in 1820. The en suite bedrooms reflect the traditional character of a former nobleman's country home. Drawing on the best produce that rural Herefordshire can offer, the menu includes Wye salmon, prime Hereford beef and tender Welsh lamb. Fresh herbs and the manor's own vineyard flourish within the boundaries of the estate. A complete vegetarian menu is available. Throughout their stay at Pengethley, guests will find the service always attentive, but never intrusive. Chandos House is a purpose-built conference suite which can cater for business and social events. For leisure, there is a snooker room, a well-stocked trout lake, a 9-hole golf improvement course and an outdoor heated pool. Riding and hot-air ballooning can be arranged. The Wye Valley and Welsh border are not very far away and the Malvern Hills are nearby. **Directions:** 4 miles from Ross-on-Wye, 10 miles from Hereford on the A49. Price guide: Single £70–£115; double/twin £100–£160.

For hotel location, see maps on pages 477-483

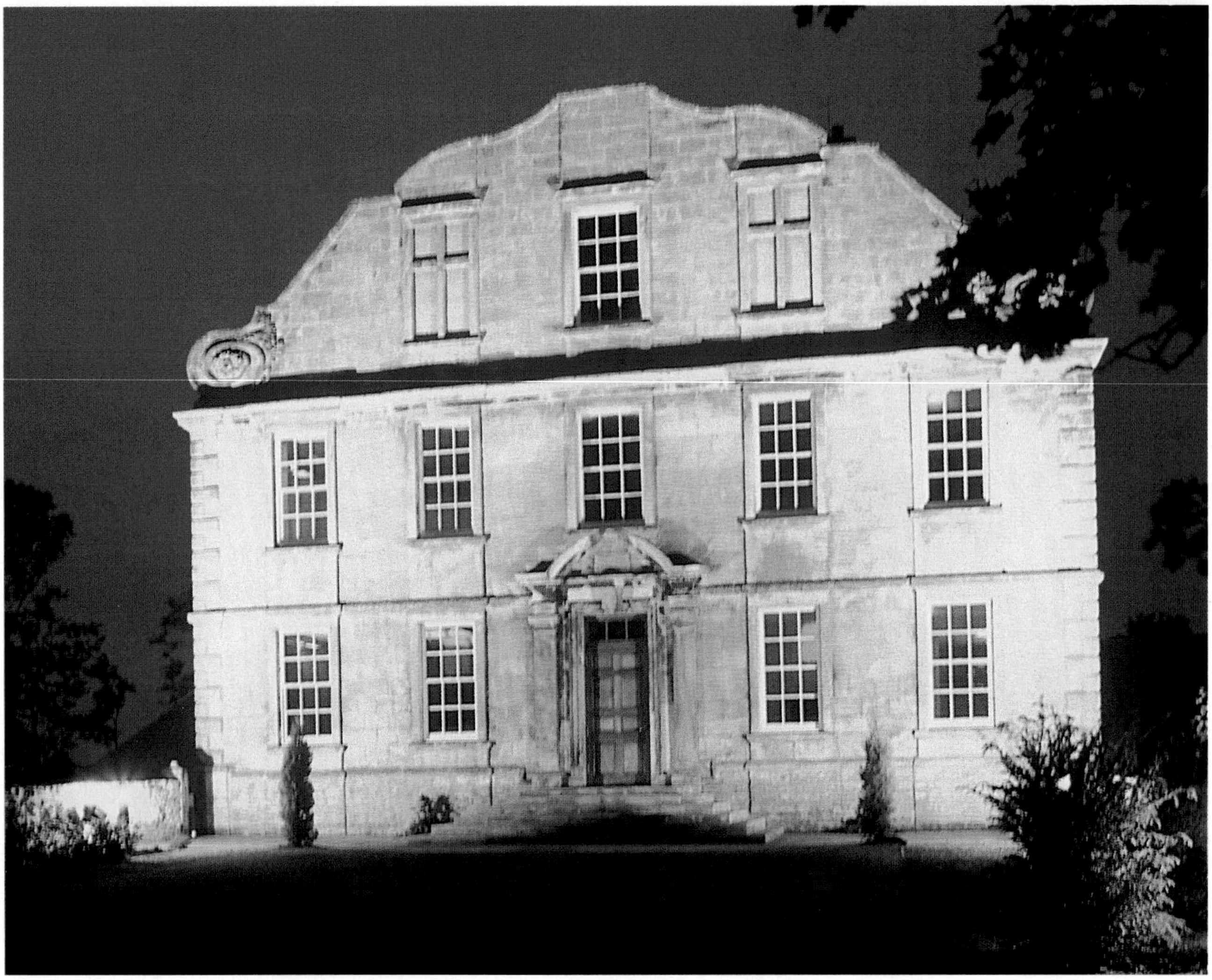

HELLABY HALL HOTEL

OLD HELLABY LANE, HELLABY, NR ROTHERHAM, SOUTH YORKSHIRE S66 8SN
TEL: 01709 702701 FAX: 01709 700979

Hellaby Hall has been welcoming guests since 1692 when it was built by Ralph Fretwell on his return from Barbados. Set in private walled gardens, the hall has been carefully restored to reflect a Dutch Colonial influence. There are 52 en suite bedrooms, three in the original hall, all with modern facilities including satellite television, radio, telephone, trouser press, hair dryer, hospitality tray and with some of the largest beds in Yorkshire. A number of bedrooms are designated for non-smokers and disabled guests. A quiet corner can always be found in the library or drawing room while the oak panelled bar overlooks the gardens where guests can enjoy putting or croquet. The Attic Restaurant with its wall of mirrors and vibrant colours provides an innovative back drop for varied menus and an extensive wine list. The adjoining Missing Scroll dining room can accommodate up to 16 diners. There are excellent conference facilities with a range of meeting and function rooms. Nearby is the city of Sheffield with its concert halls, theatres and night life. Hellaby Hall is conveniently located for the Peak District National Park, Meadowhall shopping and leisure complex and Doncaster Racecourse. **Directions:** From the M18, exit at junction 1 and take the A631 towards Bawtry. The hotel is 1/2 mile on the left. Price guide: Single £50-£88; double/twin £70-£118; suite £138.

For hotel location, see maps on pages 477-483

BROOMHILL LODGE

RYE FOREIGN, RYE, EAST SUSSEX TN31 7UN
TEL: 01797 280421 FAX: 01797 280402

Imposing and ivy-bedecked, Broomhill is a dramatic mock-Jacobean construction towering above three green acres and dating back to the 1820s, when it was commissioned by a prominent local banker. Giving pleasing views over rolling East Sussex terrain, the hotel has been renovated with care by its new owners to offer a standard of accommodation as impressive as the architecture. Relaxed, informal, yet unerringly professional, the management and staff have quickly established an elegant, comfortable and warm place to stay. All 12 rooms are equipped with en suite bath or shower rooms and all modern conveniences. Four-poster bedrooms are available. A splendid new conservatory-style restaurant serves innovative cuisine expertly prepared. A fixed-price menu offers a wide choice (three-course lunch £14.50, dinner £18.50) and a typical menu might include calamares, then venison with cranberries followed by chocolate torte. Special tariffs apply for bookings of two or more nights. Sports available locally include windsurfing, sailing, angling, clay-pigeon shooting and golf on the famous links nearby. Hastings, Winchelsea, Rye itself, Romney Marsh and Battle Abbey are not far away and worth visiting. **Directions:** $1\frac{1}{2}$ miles north of Rye on A268. Price guide: Single £52; double/twin £104.

For hotel location, see maps on pages 477-483

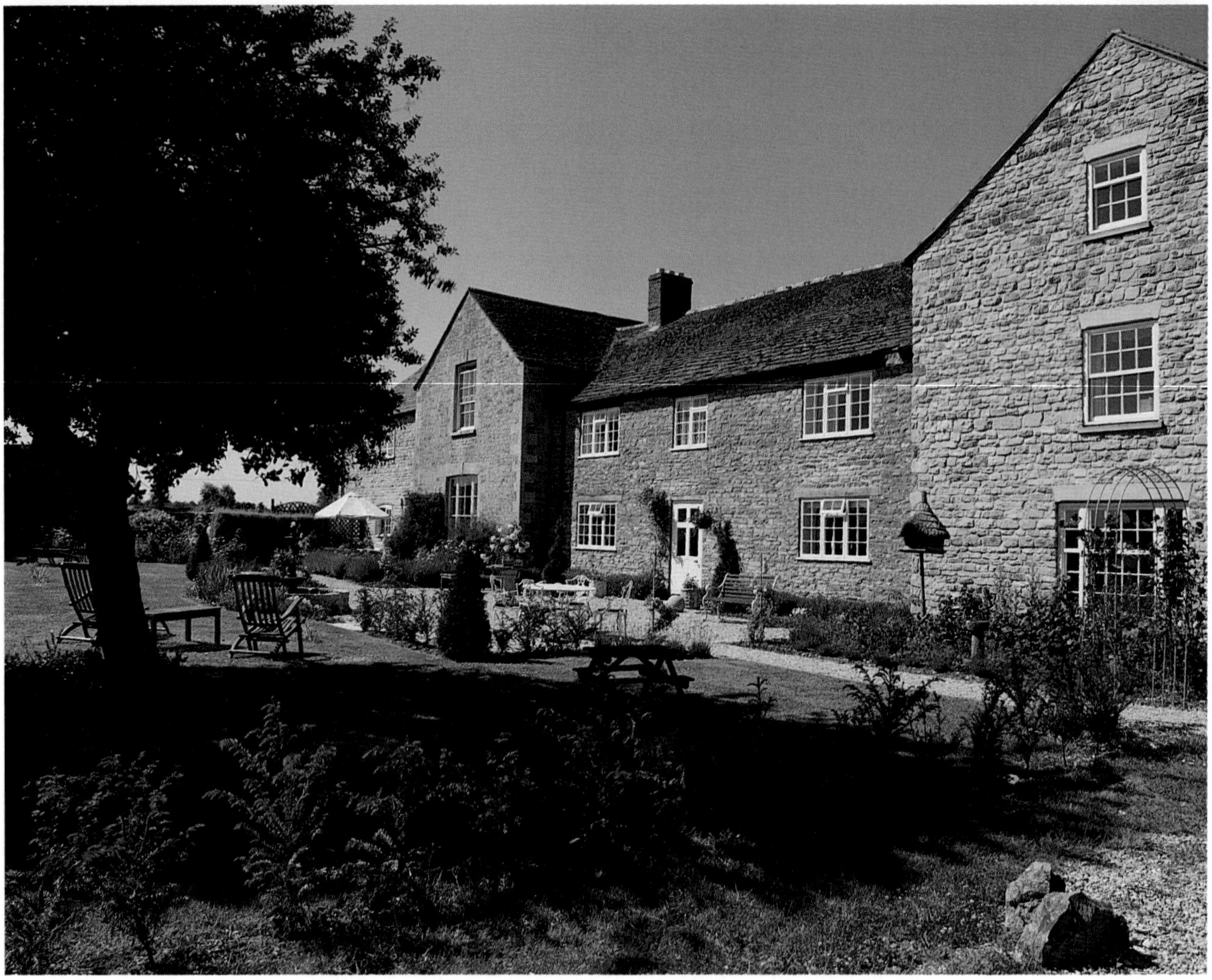

Barnsdale Lodge

THE AVENUE, RUTLAND WATER, NR OAKHAM, RUTLAND, LEICESTERSHIRE LE15 8AH
TEL: 01572 724678 FAX: 01572 724961

Situated in the heart of the ancient county of Rutland, amid unspoiled countryside, Barnsdale Lodge overlooks the rippling expanse of Rutland Water. Guests are invited to enjoy the hospitality offered by hosts The Hon. Thomas Noel and Robert Reid (who is also host at his sister hotel, Normanton Park). A restored 17th-century farmhouse, the atmosphere and style are distinctively Edwardian. This theme pervades throughout, from the courteous service to the furnishings – including chaises-longues and plump, upholstered chairs. The 29 en suite bedrooms, many of which are on the ground floor, including two superb rooms specifically designed for disabled guests, evoke a mood of relaxing comfort. A further 11 to be added for April 97 are to include beauty/aromatherapy. Traditional English cooking and fine wines are served. The chef makes all pastries and cakes as well as preserves. Elevenses, buttery lunches, afternoon teas and suppers may be enjoyed in the garden conservatory or courtyard. There are three conference rooms and facilities for wedding receptions and parties. A baby-listening service and safe play area are provided for children. Belvoir and Rockingham Castles and Burghley House are nearby. Rutland Water offers a wide range of water sports, as well as being of interest to nature lovers, including an Aquatic and Butterfly Centre. **Directions:** Barnsdale Lodge is on the A606 Oakham–Stamford road. Price guide: Single £55; double/twin £75; suite £85.

For hotel location, see maps on pages 477-483

NORMANTON PARK HOTEL

NORMANTON PARK, RUTLAND WATER SOUTH SHORE, RUTLAND, LEICESTERSHIRE LE15 8RP
TEL: 01780 720315 FAX: 01780 721086

Situated alongside the famous 'submerged' church overlooking England's largest man-made reservoir, Normanton Park Hotel has been meticulously restored from its origins as the coach house to Normanton Park Hall. The Grade II listed hotel is set in four acres of grounds, which were landscaped in the 18th century and have one of the country's oldest Cedar of Lebanon trees. Many of the bedrooms overlook the lake, which provides fly and coarse fishing, boat hire, wind-surfing, kite-flying, cycling, walking and birdwatching. The Sailing Bar offers a warm welcome, and a good variety of meals, snacks and drinks is served throughout the day. Designed on an orangery theme, the delightful restaurant offers a gourmet's choice of both à la carte and reasonably priced Sunday lunch table d'hôte menus. The cocktail bar, decorated with ancient bellows and a blazing log fire in cooler months, makes a relaxing lounge area for guests. Many stately homes and National Trust properties are nearby and the A1 is easily accessible. Helicopters may be landed at Barnsdale Lodge, sister hotel to Normanton Park, and guests transeferred from there. **Directions:** From the A1, take A606 at Stamford towards Oakham; turn along the south shore road towards Edith Weston. Price guide: Single £49.50; double/twin £69.50; suite/lake view £79.50.

For hotel location, see maps on pages 477-483

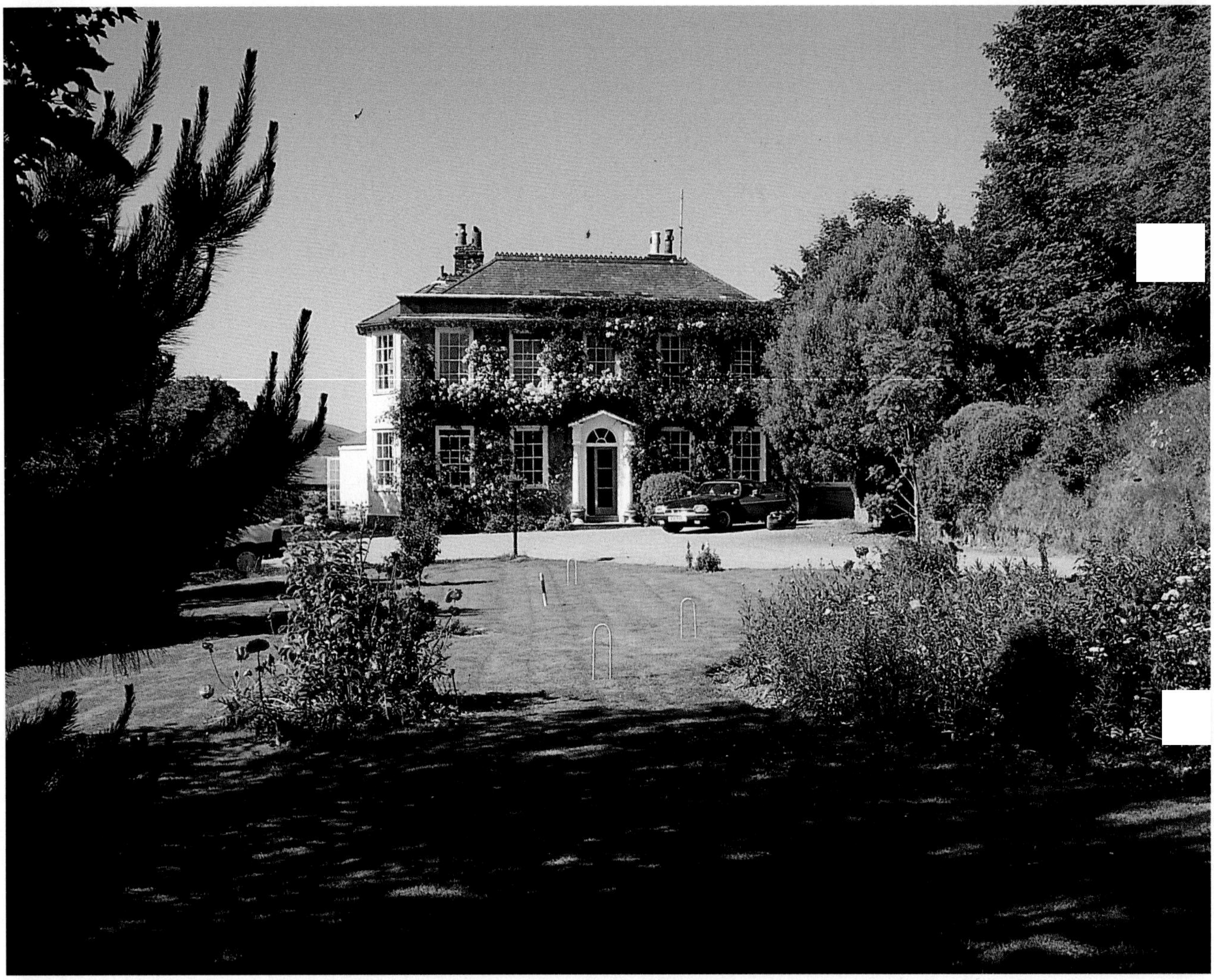

ROSE-IN-VALE COUNTRY HOUSE HOTEL

MITHIAN, ST AGNES, CORNWALL TR5 0QD
TEL: 01872 552202 FAX: 01872 552700

In recent years this 18th century Cornish manor house has been carefully upgraded, extended and refurbished and the sympathetic design of the extensions has successfully blended the old with the new. The decor throughout the bedrooms and the elegant public rooms reflects a restrained floral theme contrasting with dark mahogany, while a new extension offers superior rooms with lovely views across the valley gardens. The new dining room is named after John Opie, the 18th century portrait painter born in the valley. Table d'hôte and à la carte menus are offered and Cornish seafood dishes are a speciality. The wine list represents a variety of countries and a Director's Bin of fine wines is also kept.

The hotel hides away in a glorious secluded setting of 11 acres in a wooded valley of great natural beauty and there is a pervading atmosphere of peace and relaxation. The gardens feature ponds with a collection of waterfowl, a landscape of woodland and pasture, with a stream running through. A heated swimming pool is located in the flower gardens. The magnificent Cornish coast, numerous gardens and National Trust properties, horseriding, watersports, walking, golf and flying are closeby. **Directions:** A30 through Cornwall. Two miles after Zelah turn right onto B3284. Cross A3075. Take third left to Rose in Vale. Price guide: Single £45–£59; double/twin £96–£120; suites £135.

For hotel location, see maps on pages 477-483

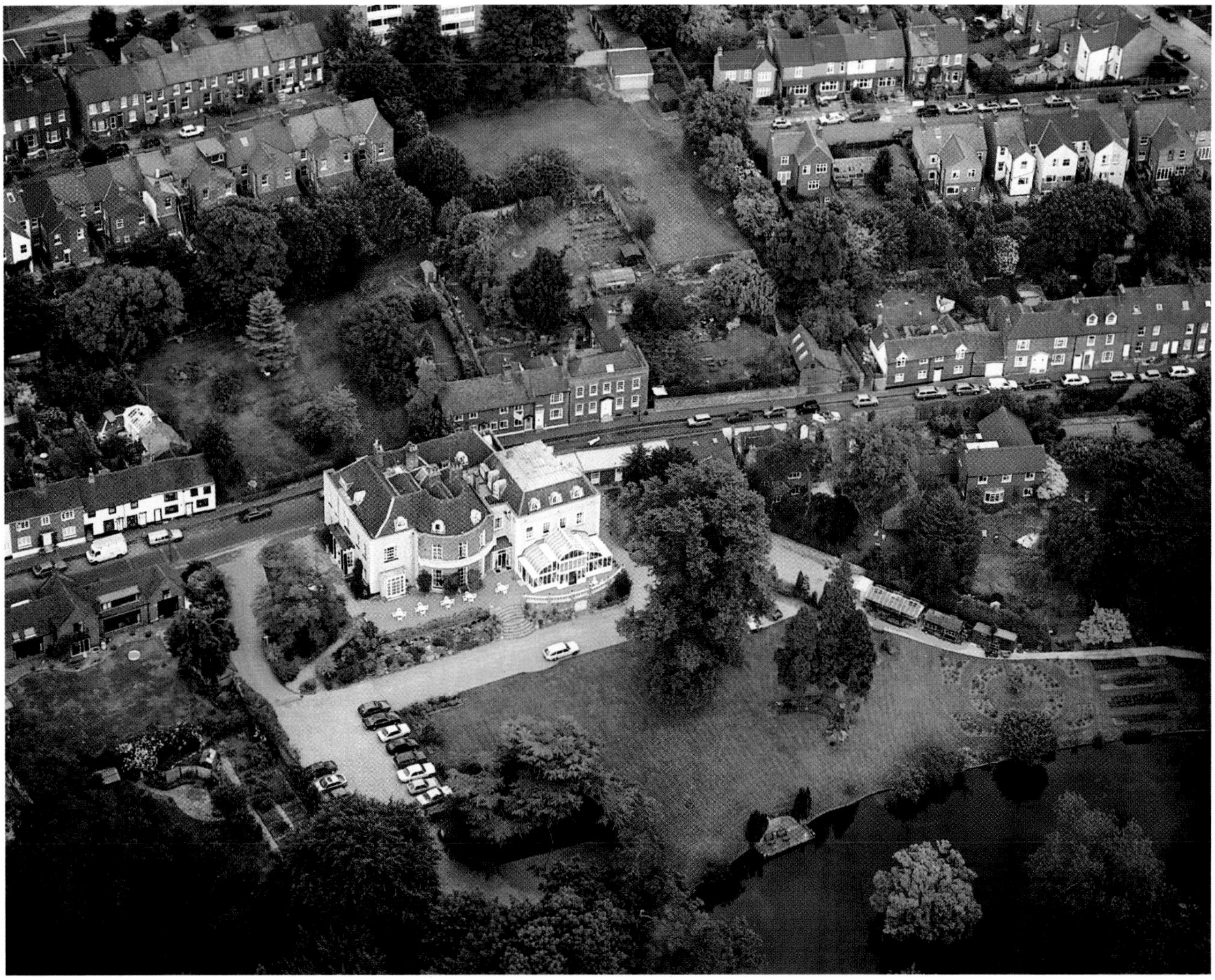

THE MANOR

ST MICHAEL'S VILLAGE, FISHPOOL STREET, ST ALBANS, HERTFORDSHIRE AL3 4RY
TEL: 01727 864444 FAX: 01727 848909

St Michael's Manor Hotel is a happy blending of different architectural styles spanning four centuries, Fishpool Street is one of the oldest city streets in England with over 70 listed properties. The Hotel is located within 5 acres of lakeside gardens, and has been privately owned by the Newling Ward Family since 1965. The 23 individual designed bedrooms have been completely refurbished to a superior standard and now offer every conceivable personal touch from fresh fruit and extensive hospitality tray to luxurious toiletries and bathrobes. The award winning Terrace Room Restaurant and the Victorian Conservatory, which overlooks the carp filled lake, offers the very best in traditional English cooking using only the finest produce. There are lighter informal meals on the Terrace Menu and 24 hour room service. A unique feature of the Manor is its collection of over 70 malt whiskies and 50 bottled beers. Service is highly professional but unobtrusive. Excellent golf courses are within easy reach and Roman St Albans with its magnificent Abbey is a 5 minute walk away. Excellent road and rail communication to all major airports and 15 minutes service throughout the day to London. **Directions:** Fishpool St runs from the High St in George St and continues into Fishpool St. Price guide: Single £95; double/twin from £120; suites £165.

23 rms MasterCard VISA AMERICAN EXPRESS 20

For hotel location, see maps on pages 477-483

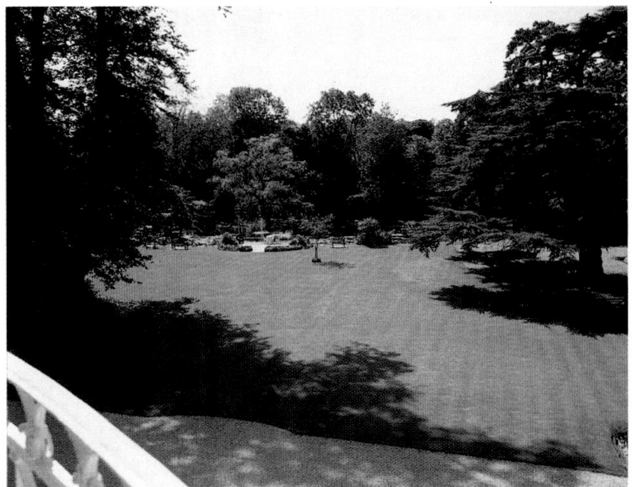

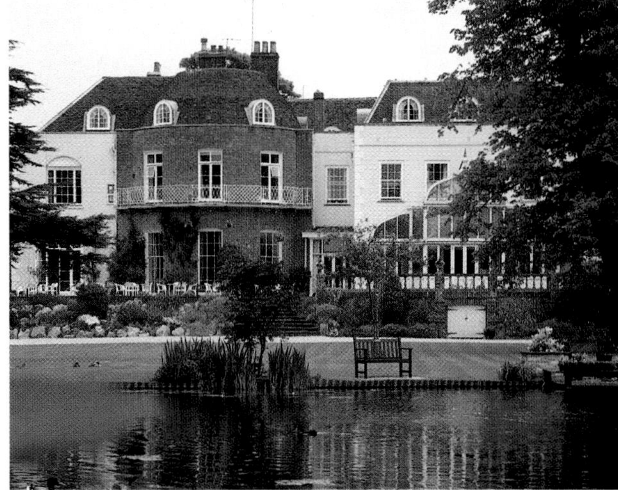

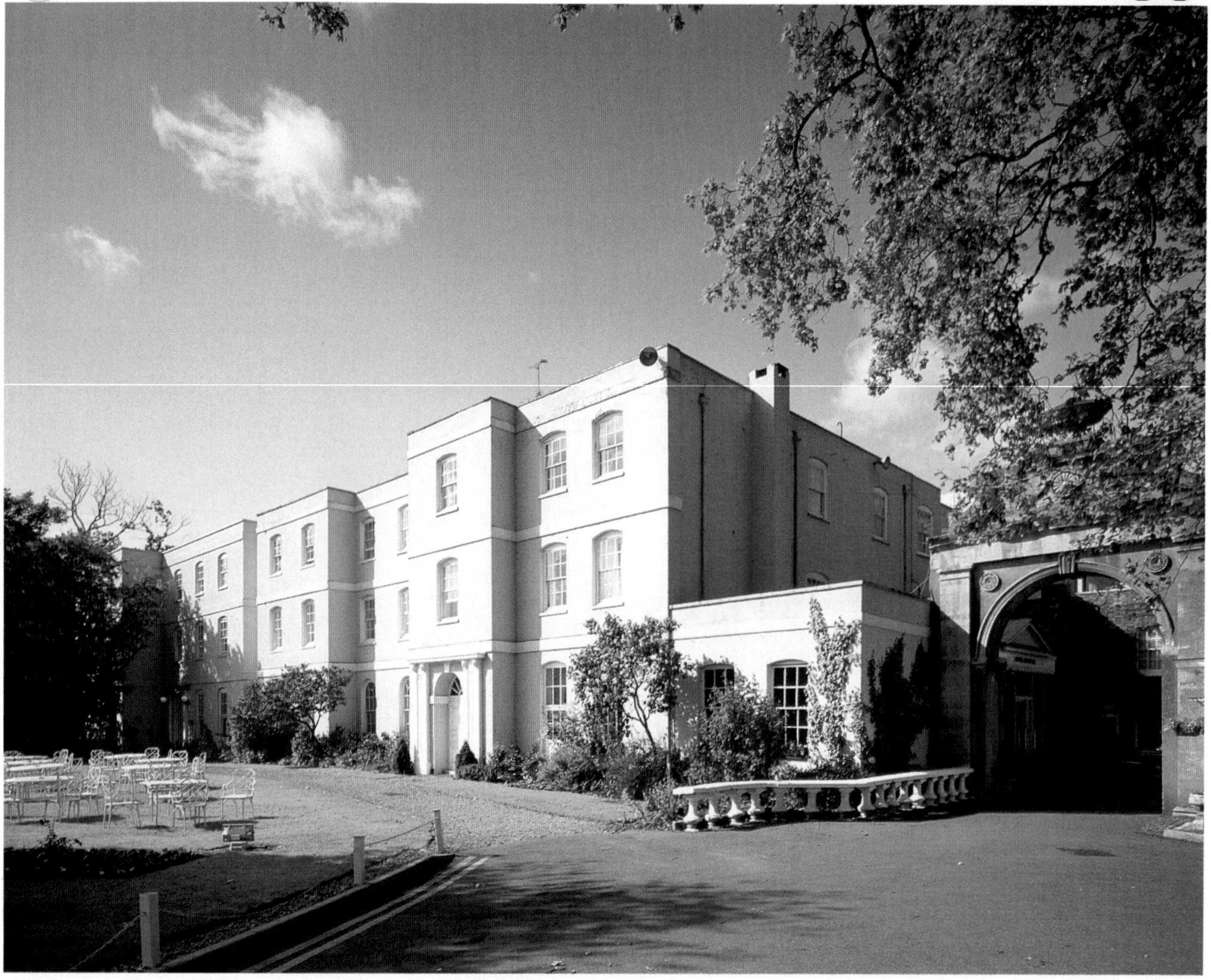

SOPWELL HOUSE HOTEL & COUNTRY CLUB

COTTONMILL LANE, SOPWELL, ST ALBANS, HERTFORDSHIRE AL1 2HQ
TEL: 01727 864477 FAX: 01727 844741/845636

Once the country home of Lord Mountbatten, and surrounded by a peaceful and verdant 11 acre estate, Sopwell House is an oasis just minutes away from the motorway and quickly reached by train from London. The classical reception rooms of the hotel reflect its illustrious past, and the grand panelled ballroom opens out onto the splendid terraces and gardens. The comfortable bedrooms, many with four-posters, are charming and well-equipped with all modern amenities. Dining is enchanting at Sopwell House, guests being seated in the Magnolia Conservatory Restaurant amidst the lovely trees after which it is named. Here they enjoy superb English cooking and appreciate the fine wine list. More informal meals are served in Bejerano's Brasserie in the Country Club. Fifteen purpose-built meeting rooms form the business complex and delegates appreciate the recent addition of the extensive conservatory lounge and bar, overlooking a new ornamental statue and water terrace. Sopwell House is particularly proud of its Country Club & Spa, dedicated to health and relaxation. It has a fabulous pool, a full range of fitness facilities and a team of highly qualified beauty therapists. **Directions:** It is 5 minutes from St Albans Station, close to the M1, M10 and M11, and just 22 miles from Heathrow. Price guide: Single from £99.75; double/twin from £129.75.

For hotel location, see maps on pages 477-483

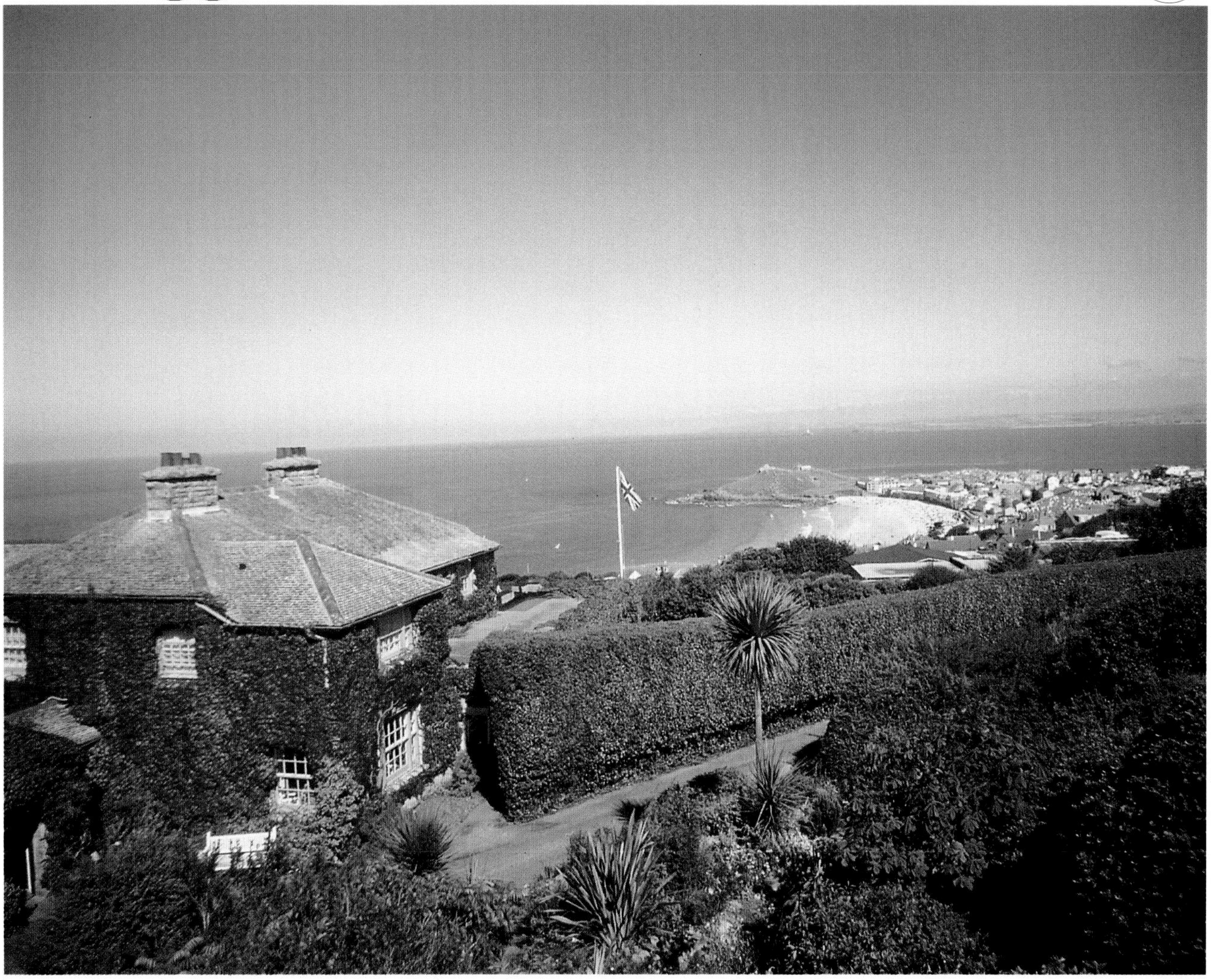

THE GARRACK HOTEL

BURTHALLAN LANE, ST IVES, CORNWALL TR26 3AA

TEL: 01736 796199 FAX: 01736 798955 FREEPONE: 0500 011 325

This family-run hotel, secluded and full of character, ideal for a family holiday, is set in two acres of gardens with fabulous sea views over Porthmeor Beach, the St Ives Tate Gallery and the old town of St Ives. The bedrooms in the original house are in keeping with the style of the building. The additional rooms are modern in design. All rooms have private bathrooms and baby-listening facilities. Superior rooms have either four-poster beds or whirlpool baths. A ground-floor room has been fitted for guests with disabilities. Visitors return year after year to enjoy informal yet professional service, good food and hospitality. The restaurant specialises in seafood especially fresh lobsters. The wine list includes over 70 labels from ten regions. The lounges have books, magazines and board games for all, and open fires. The small attractive leisure centre contains a small swimming pool with integral spa, sauna, solarium and fitness area. The hotel has its own car park. Porthmeor Beach, just below the hotel, is renowned for surfing. Riding, golf, bowls, sea-fishing and other activites can be enjoyed locally. St Ives, with its harbour, is famous for artists and for the new St Ives Tate Gallery. Dogs by prior arrangement. **Directions:** A30–A3074–B3311–B3306. Go 1/2 mile, turn left at mini-roundabout, hotel signs are on the left as the road starts down hill. Price guide: Single £61–£64; double/twin £88–£128.

For hotel location, see maps on pages 477-483

THE WELL HOUSE

ST KEYNE, LISKEARD, CORNWALL PL14 4RN
TEL: 01579 342001 FAX: 01579 343891

The West Country is one corner of England where hospitality and friendliness are at their most spontaneous, and nowhere more so than at The Well House, just beyond the River Tamar. New arrivals are entranced by their first view of this lovely Victorian country manor. Its façade wrapped in rambling wisteria and jasmine trailers is just one of a continuous series of delights including top-quality service, modern luxury and impeccable standards of comfort and cooking. The hotel is professionally managed by proprietor Nick Wainford, whose attention to every smallest detail has earned his hotel numerous awards, among them the AA 2 Red Stars. From the tastefully appointed bedrooms there are fine rural views, and each private bathroom offers luxurious bath linen, soaps and gels by Bronnley. Continental breakfast is served in bed – or a traditional English breakfast may be taken in the dining room. Chef Wayne Pearson selects fresh, seasonal produce to create his superbly balanced and presented cuisine. Tennis, swimming and croquet are on site, and the Cornish coastline offers matchless scenery and walking territory. **Directions:** Leave A38 at Liskeard, take A390 to town centre, then take B3254 south to St Keyne Well and hotel. Price guide: Single from £60; double/twin £75–£125; family suite £140

For hotel location, see maps on pages 477-483

Bolt Head Hotel

SOUTH SANDS, SALCOMBE, SOUTH DEVON TQ8 8LL
TEL: 01548 843751 FAX: 01548 843060

Bolt Head Hotel occupies a spectacular position overlooking Salcombe Estuary, where the mild climate ensures a lengthy holiday season. New improvements have ensured that guests can enjoy a fine range of modern comforts during their stay. The bedrooms are furnished to a high standard, all with good en suite bathrooms, and there are family suites available complete with a baby-listening service. The light and sunny lounge is ideal for relaxation, or guests may sit on the adjoining sun terrace with sweeping views of the sea. In the air-conditioned restaurant special care is taken to cater for all tastes. Both English and French cuisine are prepared, with freshly caught fish, lobster and crab delivered daily, as well as wholesome farm produce and local cheeses. Palm trees surround the heated outdoor swimming pool on the sunny terrace. There is a good golf course within a few miles. Riding, sailing and wind-surfing can be arranged. Sea fishing trips can be organised and private moorings are available. The hotel is adjacent to miles of magnificent National Trust cliff land at Bolt Head, including Overbecks, an unusual house and garden with rare plants. Dogs by arrangement. Closed mid-November to mid-March. **Directions:** Contact the hotel for directions. Price guide (including dinner): Single from £64; double/twin from £128; superior rooms available, as illustrated.

For hotel location, see maps on pages 477-483

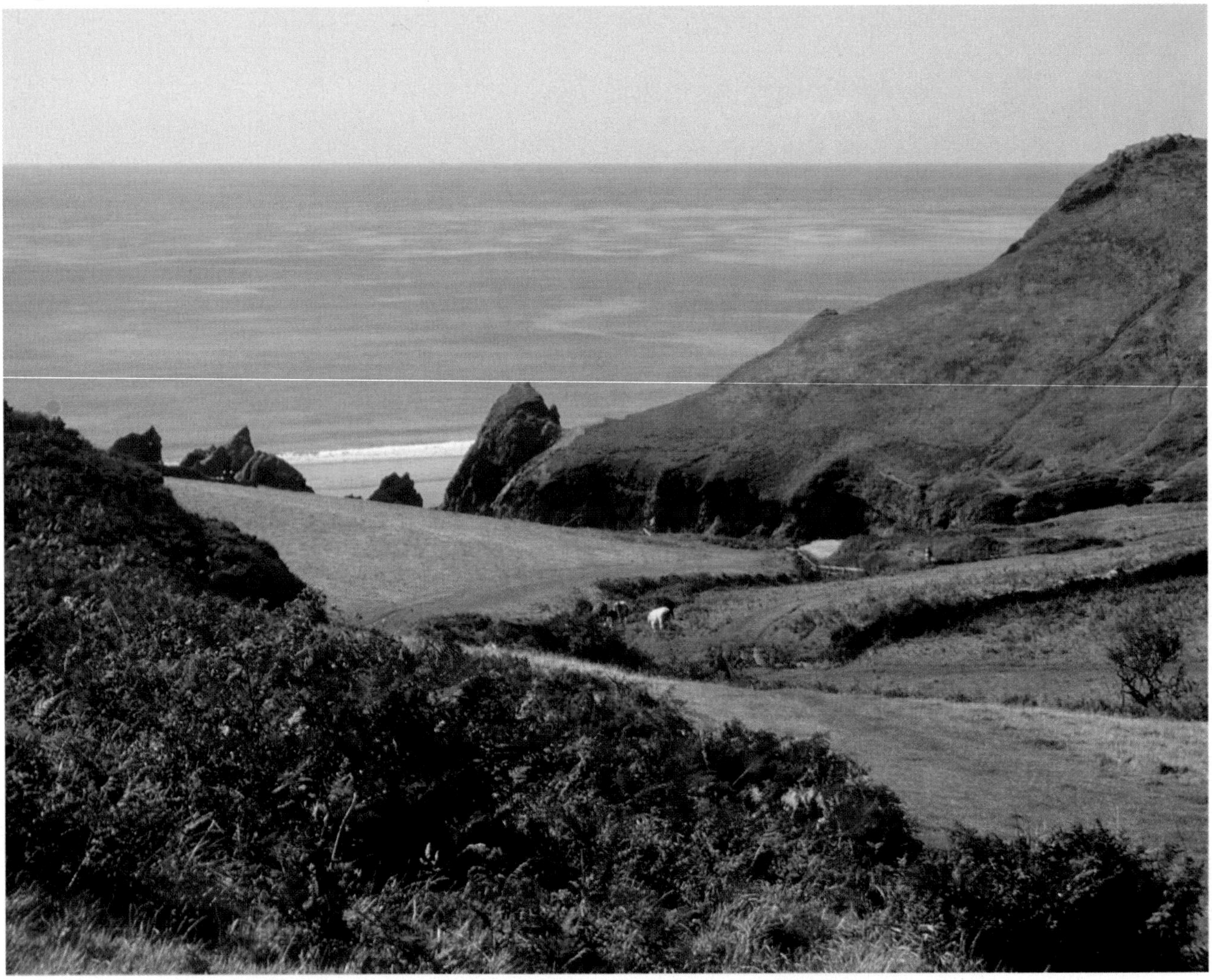

SOAR MILL COVE HOTEL

SOAR MILL COVE, SALCOMBE, SOUTH DEVON TQ7 3DS
TEL: 01548 561566 FAX: 01548 561223

Soar Mill Cove Hotel is owned and loved by the Makepeace family who, with their dedicated staff, provide a special blend of friendly yet professional service. The hotel's spectacular setting is a flower-filled combe, facing its own sheltered sandy bay and entirely surrounded by hundreds of acres of dramatic National Trust coastland. While it is perhaps one of the last truly unspoiled corners of South Devon, Soar Mill Cove is only 15 miles from the motorway system (A38). All the bedrooms are at ground level, each with a private patio opening onto the gardens. Private guests will not find any conferences here. In winter, crackling log fires and efficient double glazing keep the cold weather at bay. Both the indoor and outdoor pools are spring-water fed, the former being maintained all year at a constant 88°F. This is the home of Keith Stephen Makepeace's award winning cuisine, imaginative and innovative, reflecting the very best of the west of England; fresh crabs and lobster caught in the bay are a speciality. Soar Mill Cove is situated on the South Devon Heritage Coast midway between Plymouth and Torquay and close to the old ports of Salcombe and Dartmouth. Dogs by prior arrangement. Closed 1 November to 9 February. **Directions:** A384 to Totnes, then A381 to Soar Mill Cove. Price guide: Single £60–£90; double/twin £100–£160.

For hotel location, see maps on pages 477-483

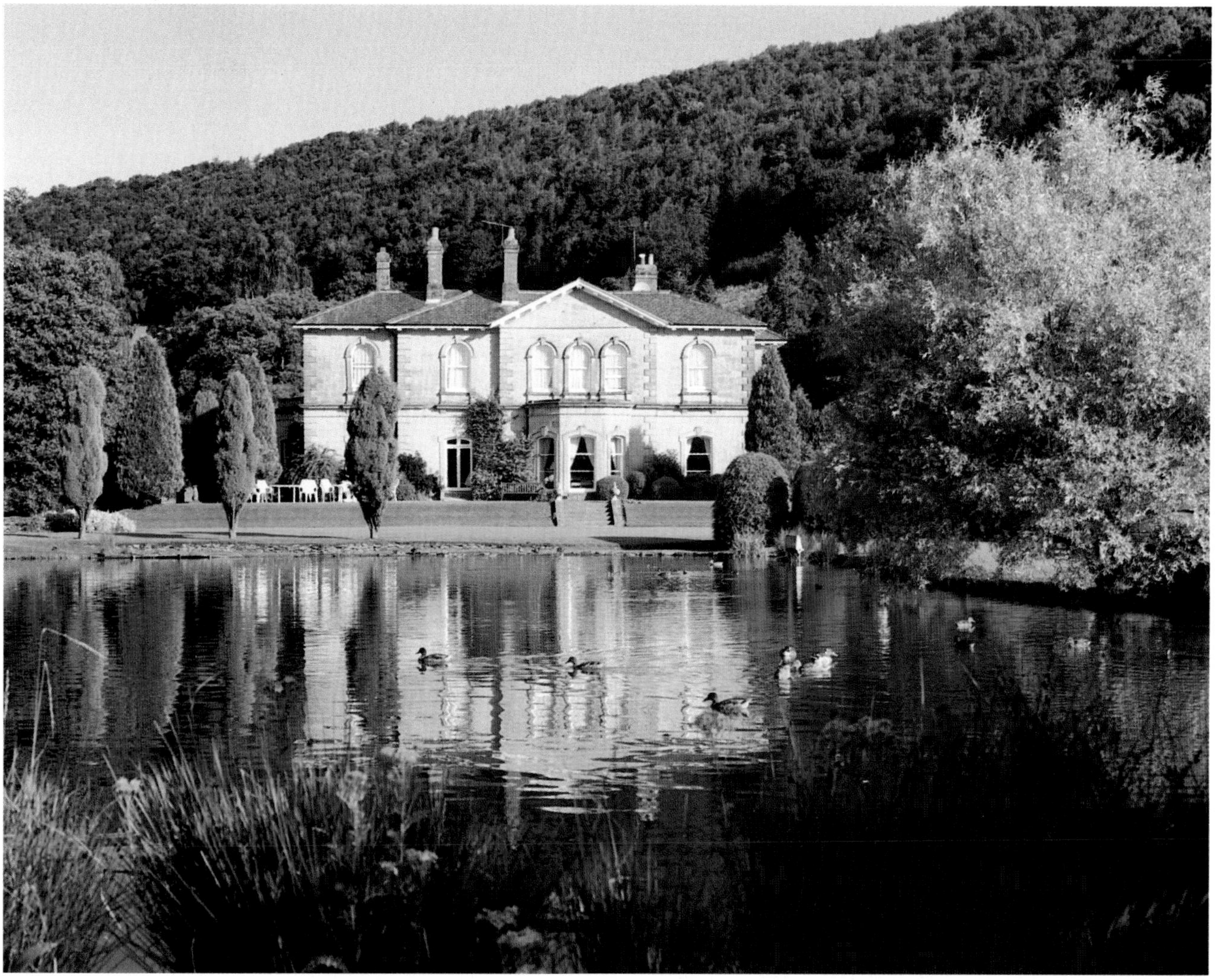

HACKNESS GRANGE

NORTH YORK MOORS NATIONAL PARK, SCARBOROUGH, NORTH YORKSHIRE YO13 0JW
TEL: 01723 882345 FAX: 01723 882391

The attractive Georgian Hackness Grange country house lies at the heart of the dramatic North York Moors National Park – miles of glorious countryside with rolling moorland and forests. Set in acres of private grounds, overlooking a tranquil lake, home to many species of wildlife, Hackness Grange is a haven of peace and quiet for guests. There are charming bedrooms in the elegant courtyard which have enjoyed a delightful refurbishment last year, together with de luxe rooms in the main house. For leisure activites, guests can enjoy 9-hole pitch 'n' putt golf, tennis, private fishing on the River Derwent and an indoor heated swimming pool. Hackness Grange is an ideal meeting location for companies wishing to have exclusive use of the hotel for VIP gatherings. The attractive Derwent Restaurant with its quality décor and paintings, is the setting for lunch and dinner and you will enjoy creatively prepared delicious cuisine, which is partnered by a wide choice of international wines. When you choose to stay at Hackness Grange you will find you have chosen well – a peaceful and relaxing location with so much to see and do: for example, visst Great Ayton, birthplace of Captain Cook. **Directions:** Take A64 York road until left turn to Seamer on to B1261, through to East Ayton. and Hackness. Price guide: Single £80–£85; double/twin £120–£165; suite £185.

28 rms

For hotel location, see maps on pages 477-483

WREA HEAD COUNTRY HOTEL

SCALBY, NR SCARBOROUGH, NORTH YORKSHIRE YO13 0PB
TEL: 01723 378211 FAX: 01723 371780

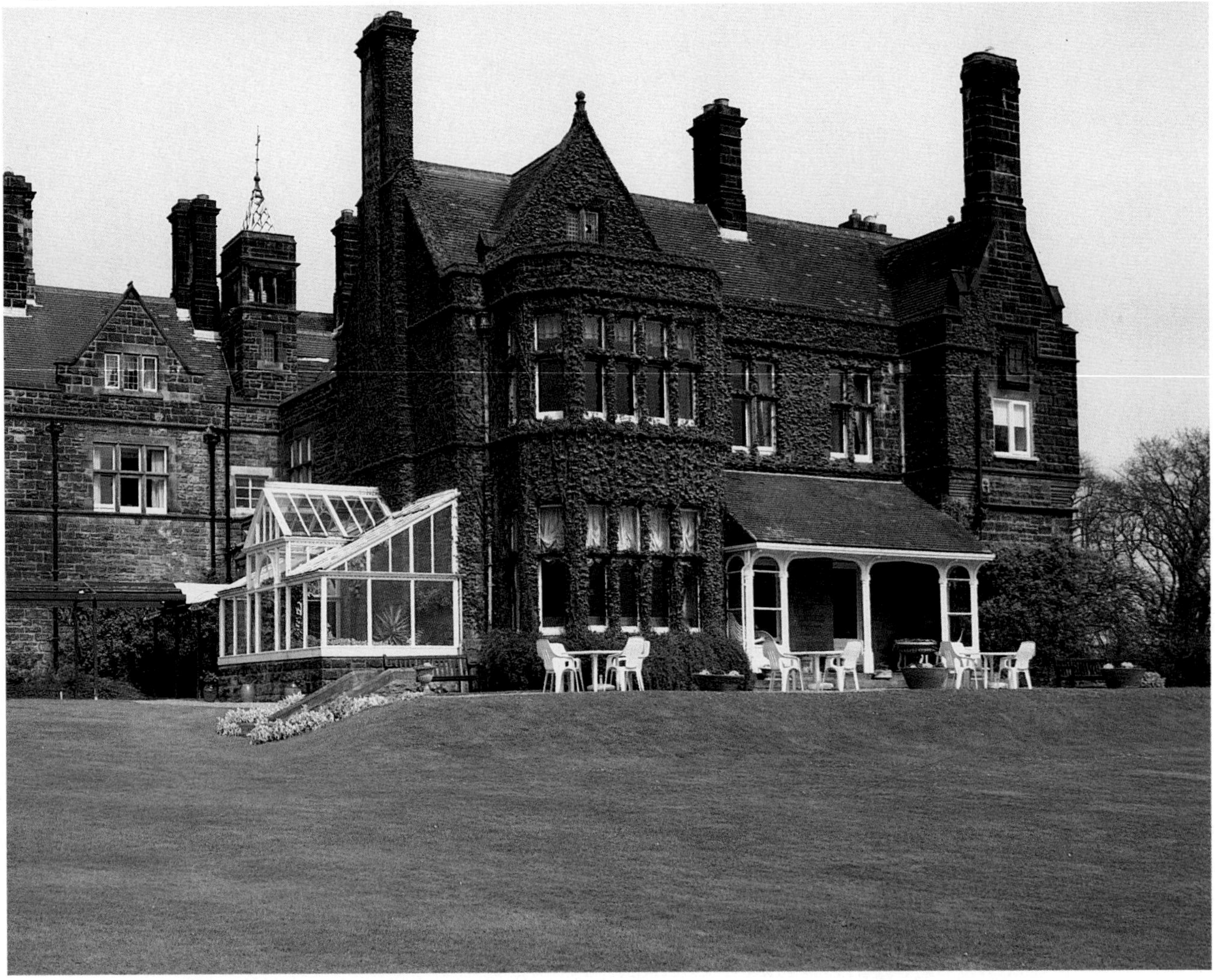

Wrea Head Country Hotel is an elegant, beautifully refurbished Victorian country house built in 1881 and situated in 14 acres of wooded and landscaped grounds on the edge of the North York Moors National Park just three miles from Scarborough. The house is furnished with antiques and paintings, and the oak-panelled front hall with its inglenook fireplace with blazing log fires in the winter, is very welcoming. All the bedrooms are individually decorated to the highest standards, with most having delightful views of the gardens. The elegant Four Seasons Restaurant is renowned for serving the best traditional English fare using fresh local produce and has an AA Rosette for outstanding cuisine. There are attractive meeting rooms, each with natural daylight, ideal for private board meetings and training courses requiring privacy and seclusion. Scarborough is renowned for its cricket, music and theatre. Wrea Head is a perfect location from which to explore the glorious North Yorkshire coast and country, and you can take advantage of special English Rose breaks throughout the year. **Directions:** Follow the A171 north from Scarborough, past the Scalby Village, until the hotel is signposted. Follow the road past the duck pond, and then turn left up the drive. Price guide: Single from £57.50–£75; double/twin from £95–£145; suite £165.

For hotel location, see maps on pages 477-483

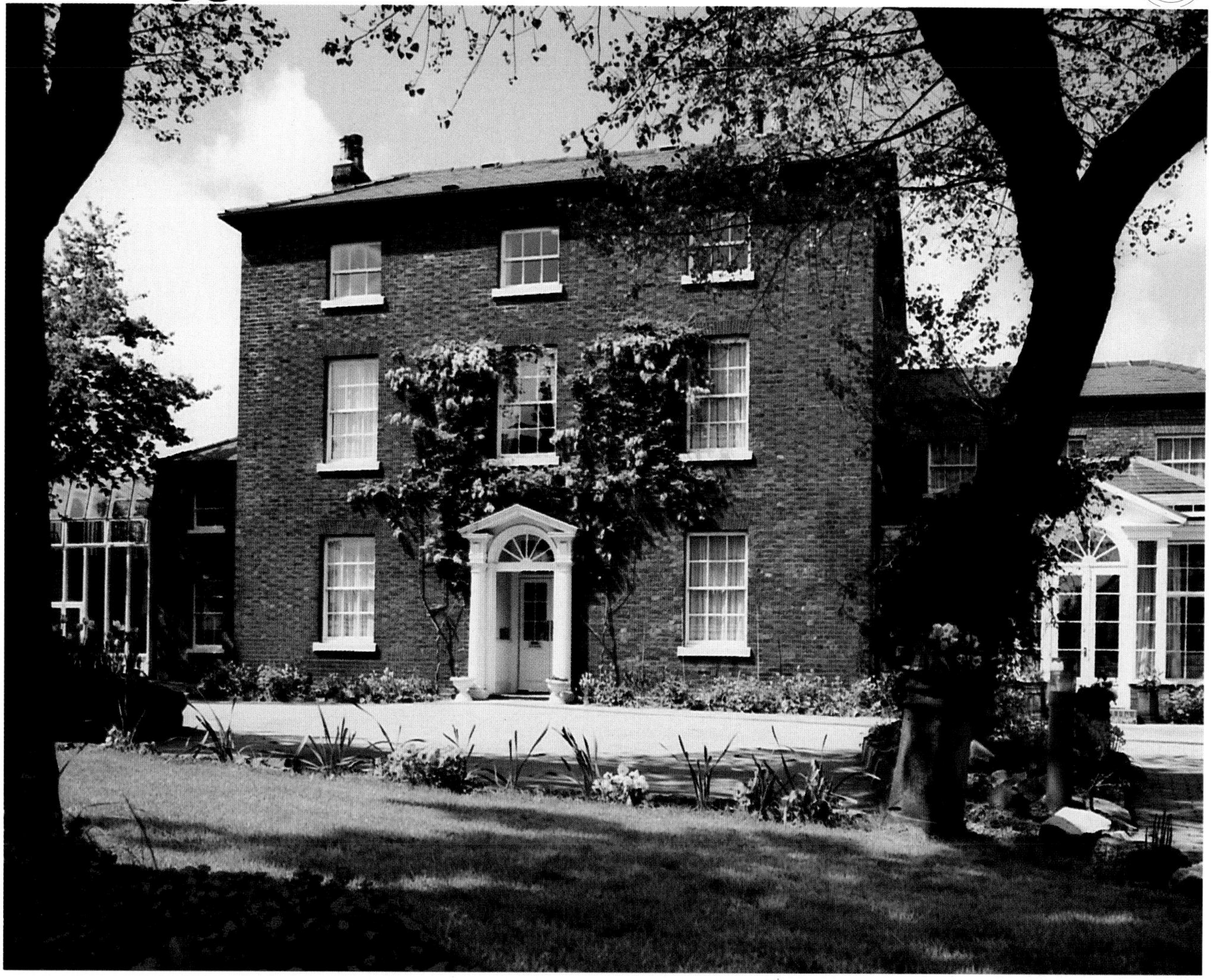

Charnwood Hotel

10 SHARROW LANE, SHEFFIELD, SOUTH YORKSHIRE S11 8AA

TEL: 0114 258 9411 FAX: 0114 255 5107

The Charnwood Hotel is a listed Georgian mansion dating from 1780. Originally owned by John Henfrey, a Sheffield Master Cutler, it was later acquired by William Wilson of the Sharrow Snuff Mill. Restored in 1985, this elegant 'country house in town' is tastefully furnished, with colourful flower arrangements set against attractive décor. The bedrooms are decorated in a country style, with the Woodford suite designed specifically to meet the requirements of a family. Two dining rooms are available for experiencing the gourmet skills of the chef and his brigade. Dignified and formal, Henfrey's Restaurant offers cuisine to match the surroundings, while traditional English/French fare is the order of the day at Brasserie Leo. The Library is ideal for private dining or small meetings and larger functions are catered for in the Georgian Room and Coach House. While approximately a mile from Sheffield city centre, with its concert hall, theatre and hectic night-life, Charnwood Hotel is also convenient for the Peak District National Park. Meadowhall shopping centre and Sheffield Arena are nearby. **Directions:** Sharrow Lane is near the junction of London Road and Abbeydale Road, 1½ miles from city centre. Junction 33 from the M1. Price guide: Single £45–£75; double/twin £60–£90.

22 rms

For hotel location, see maps on pages 477-483

WHITLEY HALL HOTEL

ELLIOTT LANE, GRENOSIDE, SHEFFIELD, SOUTH YORKSHIRE S30 3NR
TEL: 0114 245 4444 FAX: 0114 245 5414

Carved into the keystone above one of the doors is the date 1584, denoting the start of Whitley Hall's lengthy country house tradition. In the bar is a priest hole, which may explain the local belief that a tunnel links the house with the nearby 11th-century church. In the 18th century the house was a prestigious boarding school, with Gothic pointed arches and ornamentation added later by the Victorians. Attractively refurbished, Whitley Hall is now a fine hotel with all the amenities required by today's visitors. Stone walls and oak panelling combine with richly carpeted floors and handsome decoration. A sweeping split staircase leads to the bedrooms, all of which have en suite bathrooms. Varied yet unpretentious cooking is served in generous portions and complemented by a wide choice from the wine cellar, including many clarets and ports. Peacocks strut around the 30-acre grounds, which encompass rolling lawns, mature woodland and two ornamental lakes. Banquets and private functions can be held in the conference suite. **Directions:** Leave M1 at junction 35, following signs for Chapeltown (A629), go down hill and turn left into Nether Lane. Go right at traffic lights, then left opposite Arundel pub, into Whitley Lane. At fork turn right into Elliott Lane; hotel is on left. Price guide: Single £60–£78; double/twin £80–£98; suite £150

18 rms MasterCard VISA AMERICAN EXPRESS M 70

For hotel location, see maps on pages 477-483

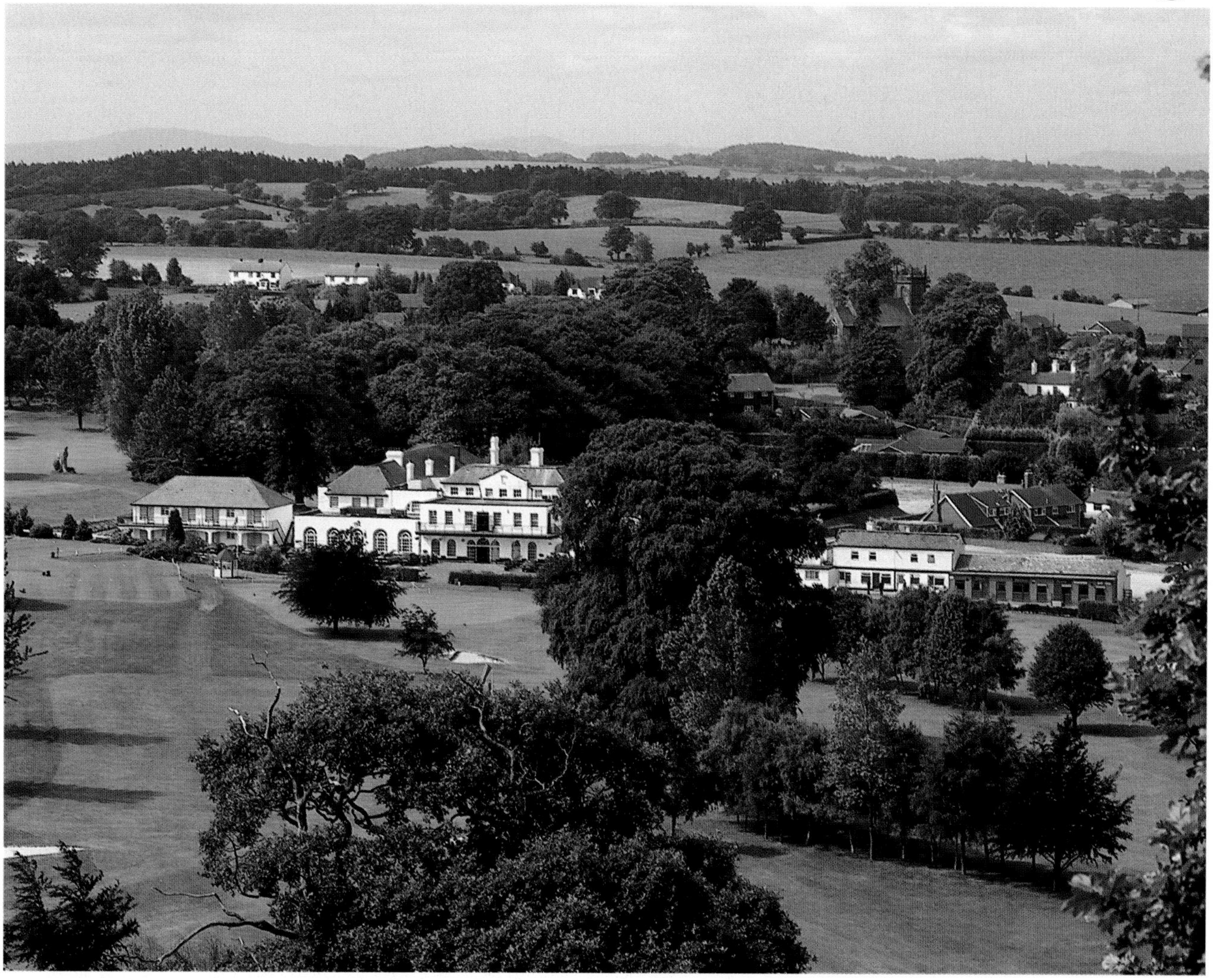

HAWKSTONE PARK HOTEL

WESTON-UNDER-REDCASTLE, SHREWSBURY, SHROPSHIRE
TEL: 01939 200611 FAX: 01939 200311

Hawkstone Park is a golfer's paradise. Set in 400 acres of idyllic Shropshire parkland the hotel is bounded on all sides by two contrasting 18-hole championship courses, on one of which British golfing star Sandy Lyle first learned the game. Supporting these courses is a 6-hole par 3 Academy Course, a driving range, practice area, and a purpose built Golf Centre. The top floor Terrace Room offers all-day bar and restaurant facilities with wonderful, panoramic views over the courses. The hotel's 65 en suite bedrooms, all newly refurbished rooms have tea and coffee making facilities, radio and satellite television, trouser press, iron and hairdryer. In the elegant restaurant which overlooks the landscaped gardens chef John Robinson offers a high standard of traditional British and classical French cuisine. There is a large, comfortable snooker room with two tables, a card room and private bar and a variety of comprehensively equipped meeting and conference rooms. Hawkstone Historic Park and Follies compliments the Hotel and Golf courses situated on 400 acres of English Heritage designated Grade I landscape. Places of interest nearby include Shewsbury Castle, ironbridge, Chester and Nantwich. Clay shooting, archery, croquet and hot-air ballooning are available. Directions: From M54, join A5 and then A49 north towards Whitchurch. Weston is signposted after approximately 11 miles. Price guide: Single/double/twin £74.50

For hotel location, see maps on pages 477-483

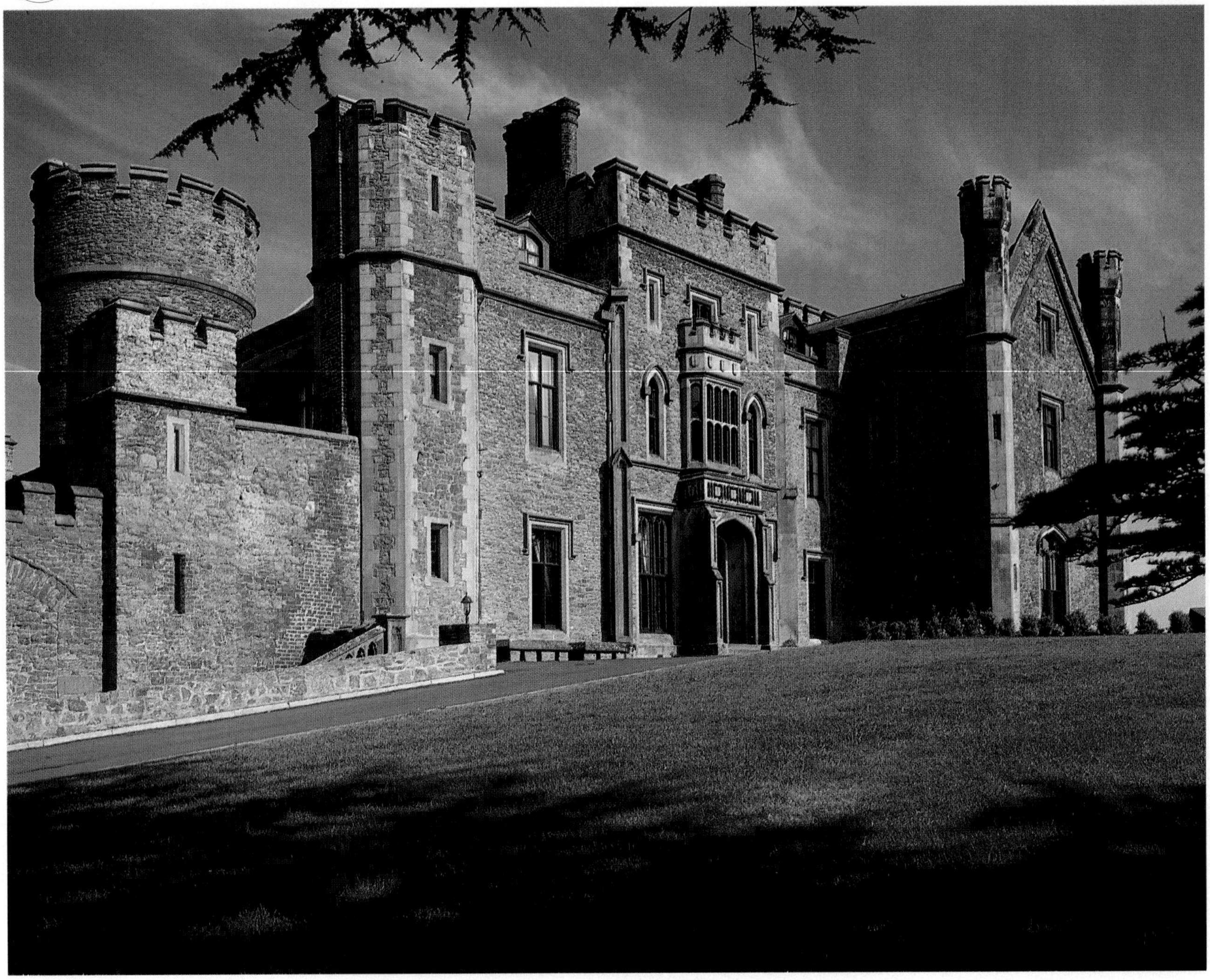

Rowton Castle

SHREWSBURY, SHROPSHIRE SY5 9EP
TEL: 01743 884044 FAX: 01743 884949

Rowton Castle is mentioned in the Domesday Book and stands on the site of a Roman fort. Part of its large tower is reputed to date from the original castle. Residential parts date from 1696, with additions made in the early 19th century. Today it is a sympathetically restored and picturesque hotel set in 17 acres of formal gardens and grounds. From an armchair in the lounge guests are afforded wonderful views of the Welsh mountains through a spectacular avenue of lime trees. Each of the hotel's bedrooms has a unique charm and character and provides a full range of modern conveniences. The oak-panelled restaurant, centred on a 17th century carved oak fireplace, offers table d'hote and à la carte menus in a setting which is ideal for important business entertaining, celebrations and intimate dinners. The Cardeston Suite can accommodate 150 delegates and has a separate reception room and bar. Privately owned leisure complex in grounds adjacent to hotel with extensive leisure facilities available to hotel guests. Places of interest nearby include Shrewsbury Castle, Ironbridge and Llangollen. Golf, shooting. fishing and croquet are available. Shrewsbury, Shropshire's thriving historic market town, is within 10 minutes' drive. **Directions:** Five miles from Shrewsbury on the A458 Welshpool road. Price guide: Single £55; double/twin £69.50; suites £135.

19 rms · 120

For hotel location, see maps on pages 477-483

HOTEL RIVIERA

THE ESPLANADE, SIDMOUTH, DEVON EX10 8AY
TEL: 01395 515201 FAX: 01395 577775

The Hotel Riviera is splendidly positioned at the centre of Sidmouth's esplanade, overlooking Lyme Bay. With its mild climate and the beach just on the doorstep, the setting mirrors the south of France and is the choice for the discerning visitor in search of relaxation and quieter pleasures. Behind the hotel's fine Regency façade lies an alluring blend of old-fashioned service and present-day comforts with a style and ambience that justly reflects its AA and RAC four-star rating. Glorious sea views can be enjoyed from the recently redesigned and refurbished en suite bedrooms, all of which are fully appointed and have many thoughtful extras like hairdryers, fresh flowers, bathrobes and complimentary toiletries. In the elegant bay-view dining room, guests are offered a fine choice of dishes from the extensive menus, prepared by French and Swiss trained chefs, with local seafood being a particular speciality. Arrangements can be made for guests to play golf, while bowls, croquet, tennis, putting, sailing and fishing are available nearby. Explore the many delightful villages of East Devon's rolling countryside and coastline, or just enjoy pottering around Sidmouth, with its enduring architectural charm. **Directions:** The hotel is situated at the centre of the esplanade. Price guide (including dinner): Single £71–£94; double/twin £126–£172; suite £170–£190.

For hotel location, see maps on pages 477-483

THE FRENCH HORN

SONNING-ON-THAMES, BERKSHIRE RG4 OTN
TEL: 01734 692204 FAX: 01734 442210

For over 150 years The French Horn has provided a charming riverside retreat from the busy outside world. Today, although busier on this stretch of the river, it continues that fine tradition of comfortable accommodation and outstanding cuisine in a beautiful setting. The hotel nestles beside the Thames near the historic village of Sonning. The well appointed bedrooms and suites are fully equipped with modern amenities and many have river views. The old pannelled bar provides an intimate setting for pre-dinner drinks and the restaurant speciality, locally reared duck, is spit roasted here over an open fire. By day the sunny restaurant is a lovely setting for lunch, while by night diners can enjoy the floodlit view of the graceful weeping willows which fringe the river. Dinner is served by candlelight and the cuisine is a mixture of French and English cooking using the freshest ingredients. The French Horn's wine list is reputed to be amongst the finest in Europe. Places of interest include Henley, Stratfield Saye, Oxford, Blenheim Palace and Mapledurham. There are numerous golf courses and equestrian centres in the area. **Directions:** Leave the M4 at junction 8/9 and follow the A404 to Reading and then signs for Sonning. The hotel is beside the bridge on the north side of the river. Price guide: Single £85–£120; double/twin £85–£140.

15 rms MasterCard VISA AMERICAN EXPRESS

For hotel location, see maps on pages 477-483

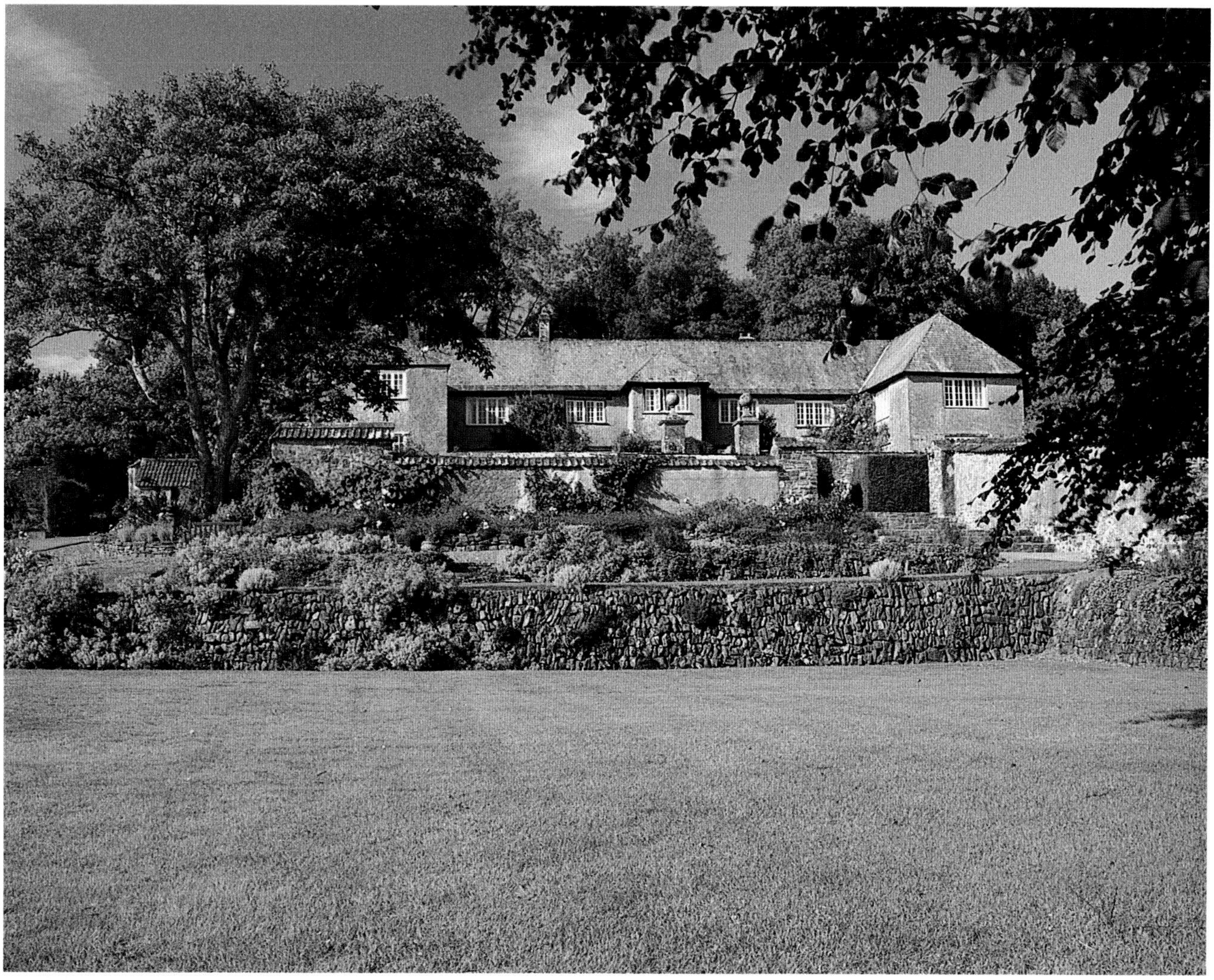

WHITECHAPEL MANOR

NR SOUTH MOLTON, NORTH DEVON EX36 3EG
TEL: 01769 573377 FAX: 01769 573797

Built in 1575 by Robert de Bassett, pretender to the English throne, Whitechapel Manor a Grade I listed building is a vision of the past with terraced and walled gardens of lawns, roses and clipped yew hedges. The entrance hall has a perfect Jacobean carved oak screen. Elsewhere, William & Mary plasterwork and panelling along with painted overmantles have been preserved. The large bedrooms at the front overlooking the gardens and the smaller, cosy rooms which overlook the woodlands are thoughtfully appointed for comfort. The grounds teem with wildlife including numerous varieties of birds and the native Red Deer which are unique to Exmoor. The restaurant combines the essence of modern French and English cuisine and is recognised as one of the best in the West Country. All around is tranquil, unspoilt countryside rising up to Exmoor National Park and the most dramatic coastline in England. Whitechapel is the ideal base from which to explore the moors, coast, ancient woodland valleys, Exmoor's villages and its wildlife. Also nearby are the RHS Gardens at Rosemoor, Dartington Crystal and many National Trust properties. **Directions:** Leave M5 at junction 27. Follow signs to Barnstaple. After 30 minutes turn right at roundabout to Whitechapel. Price guide: Single £70–£155; double/twin £110–£170. Special breaks and events all year round.

For hotel location, see maps on pages 477-483

THE SWAN HOTEL

MARKET PLACE, SOUTHWOLD, SUFFOLK IP18 6EG
TEL: 01502 722186 FAX: 01502 724800

Rebuilt in 1659, following the disastrous fire which destroyed most of the town, The Swan was remodelled in the 1820s, with further additions in 1938. The hotel provides all modern services while retaining its classical dignity and elegance. Many of the antique-furnished bedrooms in the main hotel offer a glimpse of the sea, while the garden rooms – decorated in a more contemporary style – are clustered around the old bowling green. The Drawing Room has the traditional character of an English country house and the Reading Room upstairs is perfect for quiet relaxation or as the venue for a private party. The daily menu offers dishes ranging from simple, traditional fare through the English classics to the chef's personal specialities. An exciting selection of wines is offered. Almost an island, Southwold is bounded on three sides by creeks, marshes and the River Blyth – making it a paradise for birdwatchers and nature lovers. Hardly changed for a century, the town, built around a series of greens, has a fine church, lighthouse and golf course. Music lovers flock to nearby Snape Maltings for the Aldeburgh Festival. Winner of Country Living Gold Award for the Best Hotel 1993/94. **Directions:** Southwold is off the A12 Ipswich–Lowestoft road. The Swan Hotel is in the town centre. Price guide: Single £50–£68; double/twin £84–£118; suite £150.

For hotel location, see maps on pages 477-483

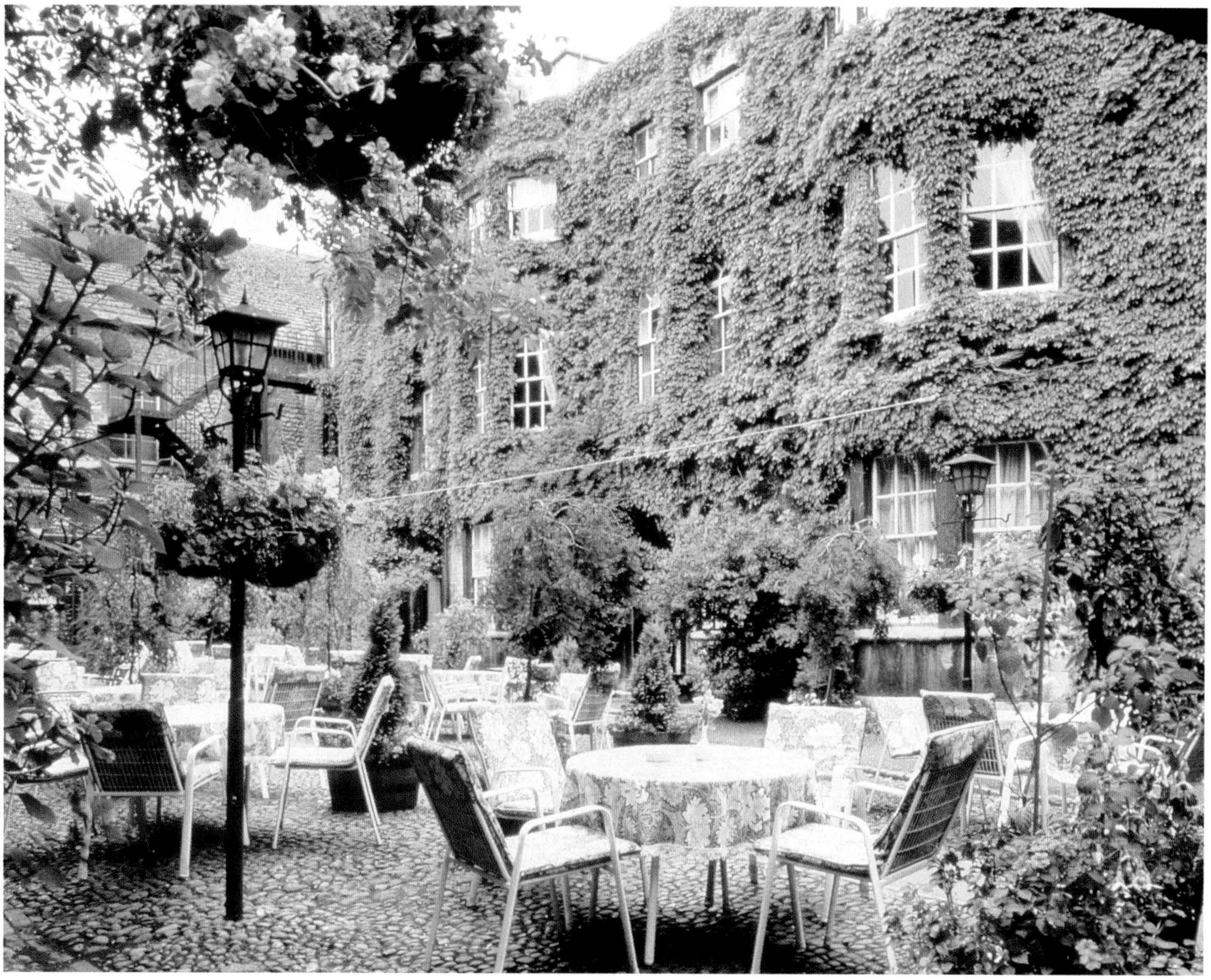

THE GEORGE OF STAMFORD

ST MARTINS, STAMFORD, LINCOLNSHIRE PE9 2LB
TEL: 01780 55171 FAX: 01780 57070

The George, a beautiful, 16th century coaching inn, retains the charm of its long history, as guests will sense on entering the reception hall with its oak travelling chests and famous oil portrait of Daniel Lambert. Over the years, The George has welcomed a diverse clientèle, ranging from highwaymen to kings – Charles I and William III were both visitors. At the heart of the hotel is the lounge, its natural stone walls, deep easy chairs and softly lit alcoves imparting a cosy, relaxed atmosphere, while the blazing log fire is sometimes used to toast muffins for tea! The flair of Julia Vannocci's interior design is evident in all the expertly styled, fully appointed bedrooms. Exotic plants, orchids, orange trees and coconut palms feature in the Garden Lounge, where a choice of hot dishes and an extensive cold buffet are offered. Guests may also dine alfresco in the courtyard garden. The more formal, oak-panelled restaurant serves imaginative but traditional English dishes and an award-winning list of wines. Superb facilities are incorporated in the Business Centre, converted from the former livery stables. Special weekend breaks available. **Directions:** Stamford is 1 mile from the A1 on the B1081. The George is in the town centre opposite the gallows sign. Car parking is behind the hotel. Price guide: Single from £72–£85; double/twin from £95–£115; suite £125–£160.

For hotel location, see maps on pages 477-483

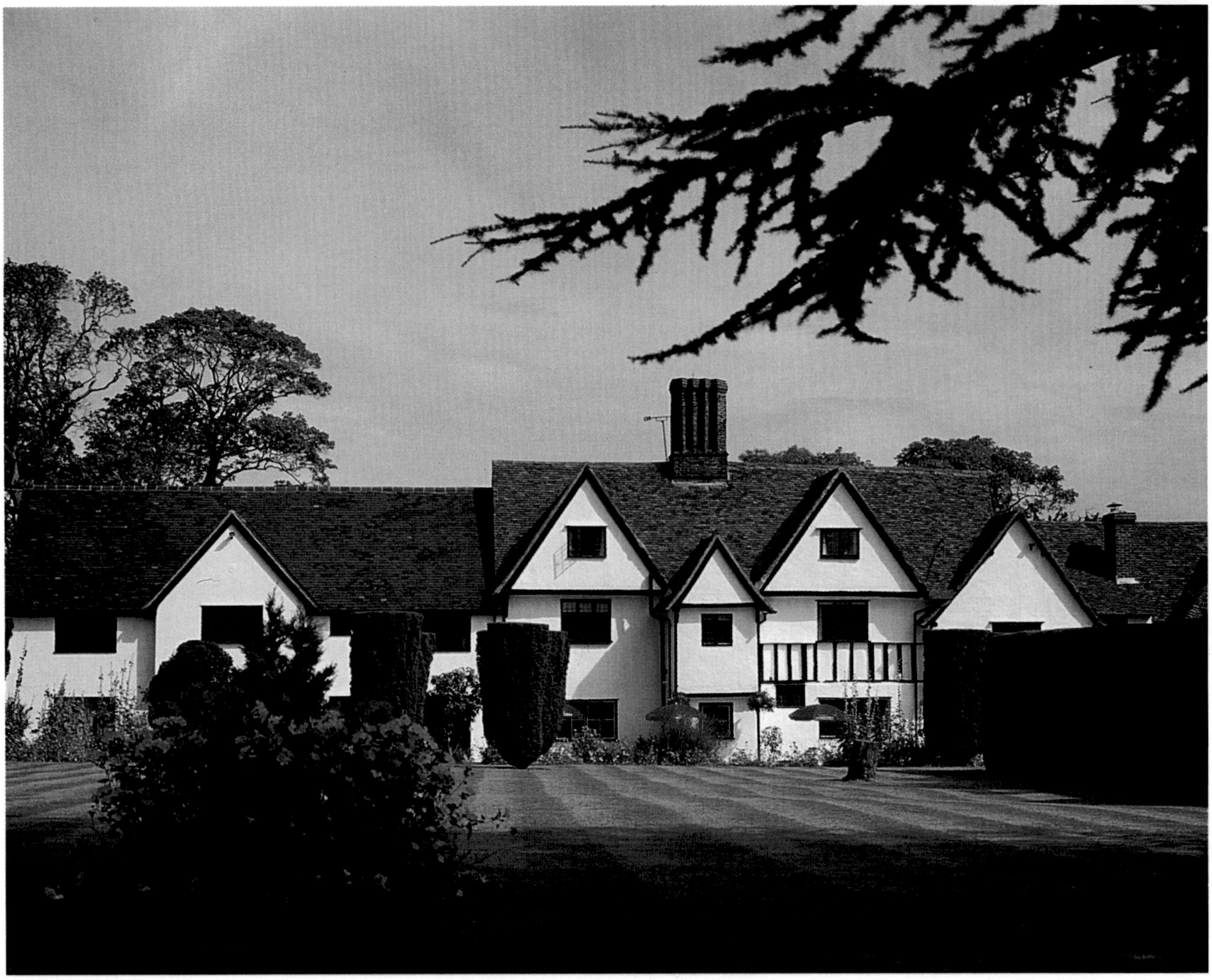

WHITEHALL

CHURCH END, BROXTED, ESSEX CM6 2BZ
TEL: 01279 850603 FAX: 01279 850385

Set on a hillside overlooking the delightful rolling countryside of north-west Essex is Whitehall, one of East Anglia's leading country hotels. While its origins can be traced back to 1151, the manor house is ostensibly Elizabethan in style, with recent additions tastefully incorporated. Traditional features such as beams, wide fireplaces and log fires blend well with the contemporary, fresh pastel shades and subtle-hued fabrics. A spectacular vaulted ceiling makes the dining room an impressive setting for dinner, with an à la carte or six-course set menu offering many a delicious bonne-bouche. For large private functions, the timbered Barn House is an ideal venue, where guests can enjoy the same high standards of cuisine found in the restaurant. Overlooked by the old village church is the attractive Elizabethan walled garden. Whitehall is only a short drive from London's most modern international airport at Stansted opened in 1989 and easily accessible from the M11 motorway, while Cambridge and Newmarket are only 30 minutes' drive away. **Directions:** Take junction 8 from the M11, follow Stansted Airport signs to new terminal building and then signs for Broxted. Price guide: Single £80; double/twin £110–£140.

For hotel location, see maps on pages 477-483

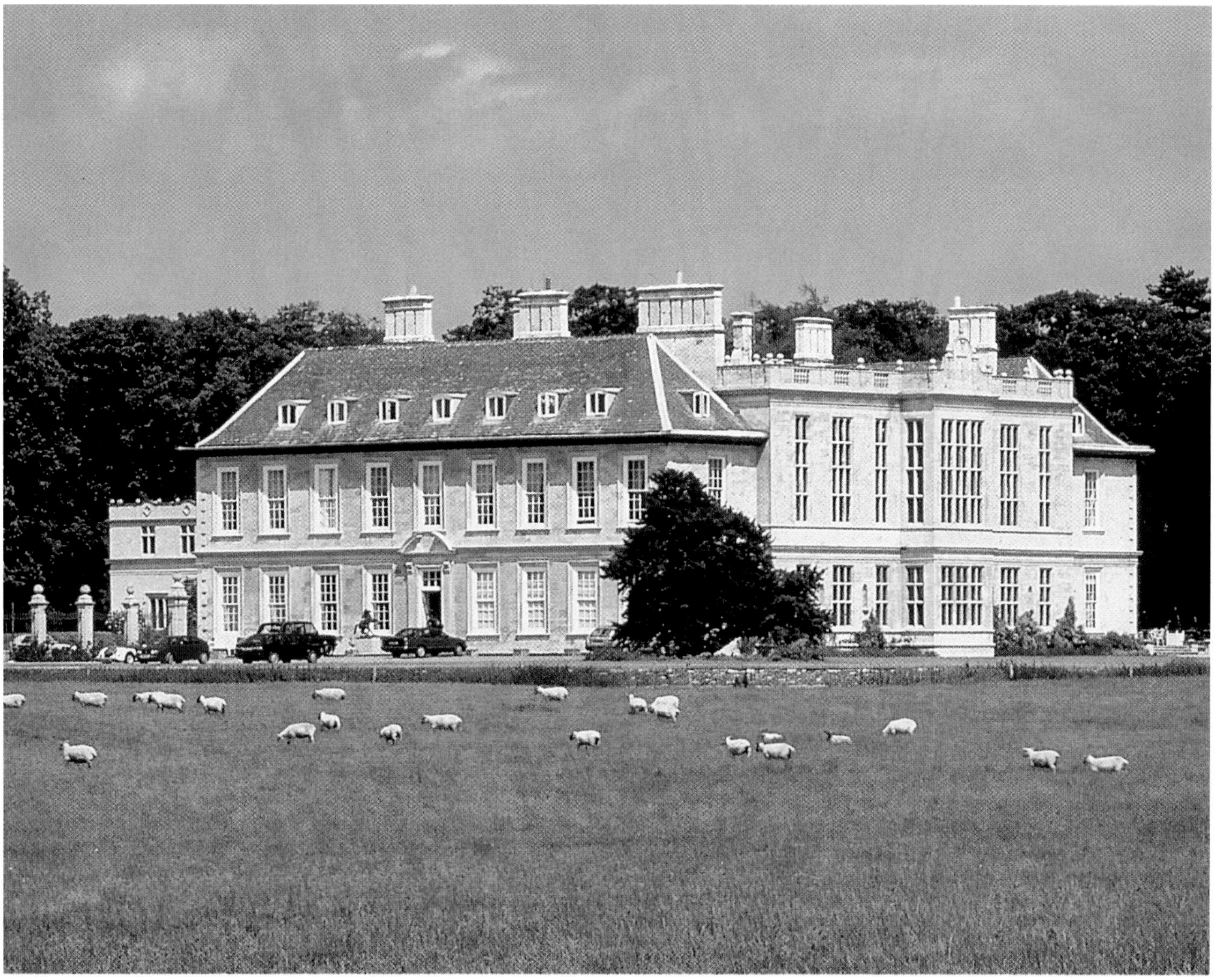

STAPLEFORD PARK

NR MELTON MOWBRAY, LEICESTERSHIRE LE14 2EF

TEL: 01572 787 522 FAX: 01572 787 651

A Stately Home and Sporting Estate for House Guests. Casual luxury is the byword in this pre-eminent 16th century house, which was opened as a hotel in 1988. It was once coveted by Edward, The Prince of Wales, but his mother Queen Victoria forbade him to buy it for fear that his morals would be corrupted by the Leicestershire hunting society! Today, Stapleford Park offers discerning guests supremely elegant surroundings and beautiful views over 500 acres of parkland. Described as "The Best Country House Hotel in the World" in Andrew Harper's Hideaway Report, it has received innumerable awards for its unique style and hospitality. The individually designed bedrooms have been created by famous names such as Tiffany, Wedgwood, Crabtree & Evelyn and Range Rover. An exclusive cottage with four themed bedrooms is also available. Excellent cuisine,is carefully prepared to the highest standards. The wine list is presented by flavour and texture, an original approach which has met with universal approval. There are a host of sporting pursuits including falconry, clay and game shooting, golf, riding, tennis and fishing. Convenient for Burghley Horse Trials. There are facilities for private dinners, weddings, receptions and conferences. An English Outpost of the Carnegie Club. **Directions:** Stapleford Park is only 1½ hours north of London, situated between the A1 and M1. Price guide: Double/twin £145-£215; suites from £230.

51 rms

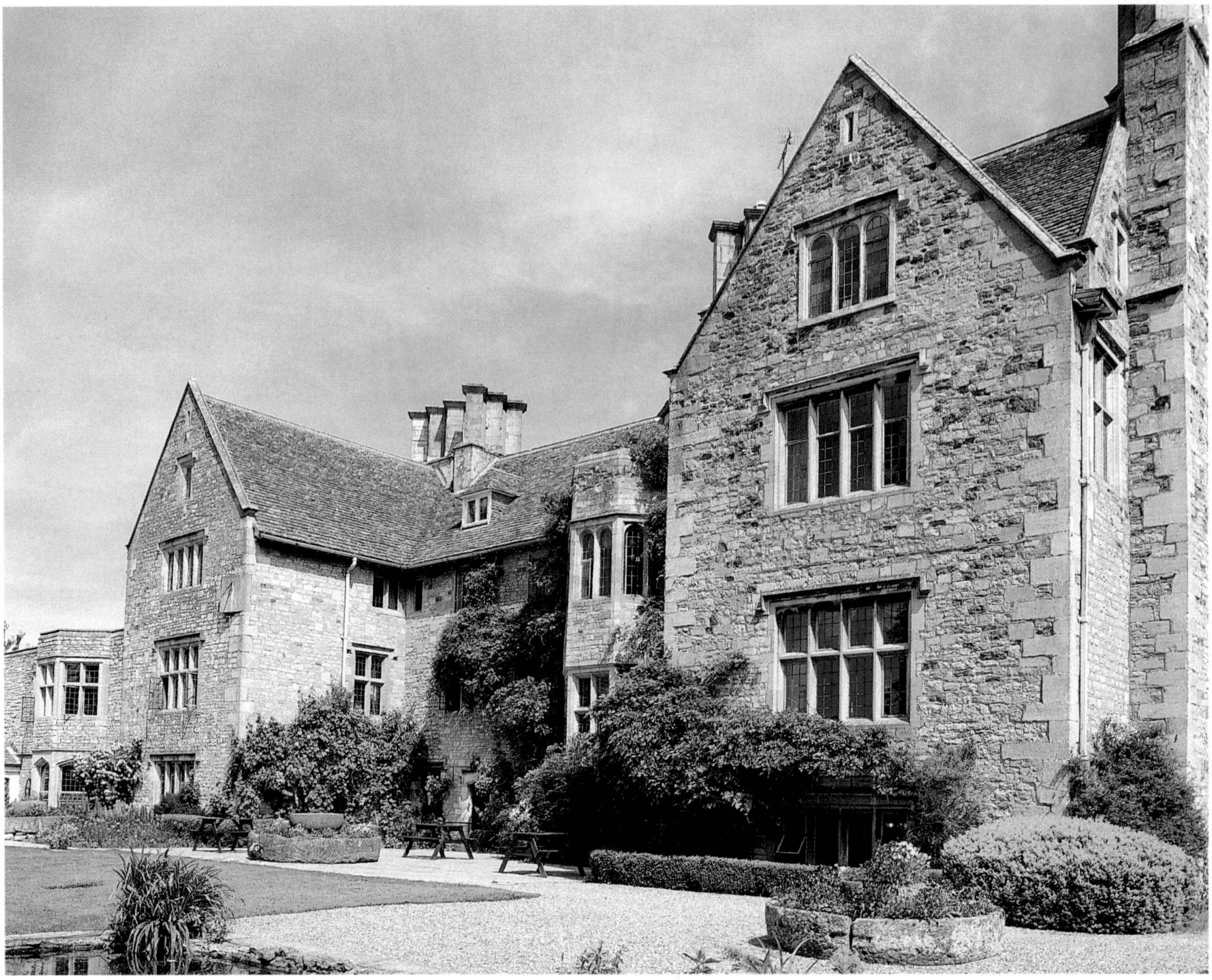

STONEHOUSE COURT

STONEHOUSE, GLOUCESTERSHIRE GL10 3RA
TEL: 01453 825155 FAX: 01453 824611

This outstanding Grade II listed old manor house is set in six acres of mature gardens in lovely countryside on the edge of the South Cotswolds. All the bedrooms are individually decorated and many in the main house feature original fireplaces and mullion windows. The John Henry Restaurant provides the perfect setting to enjoy a relaxed candlelit dinner or informal lunch and the traditional English cuisine is complemented by fine wines. Outdoor pursuits include golf at Minchinhampton golf club, while activity days within the grounds can include laser shooting, archery, quad biking and team building exercises. The conference facilities at Stonehouse Court are designed for all styles of meetings, from informal to boardroom. The self-contained Caroline Suite is well suited to holding product launches, training courses and conferences and the oak-panelled Crellin Room provides an appropriate atmosphere for small meetings or private dining. Among the numerous places of interest nearby are Cheltenham, Berkeley Castle and Slimbridge Wildfowl Trust and guests also have the chance to visit Cheltenham Races, polo at Cirencester or the Badminton horse trials. **Directions:** From junction 13 of the M5 Stonehouse Court is two miles on the A419 towards Stroud. Price guide: Single from £65; double/twin from £90; suites from £105.

For hotel location, see maps on pages 477-483

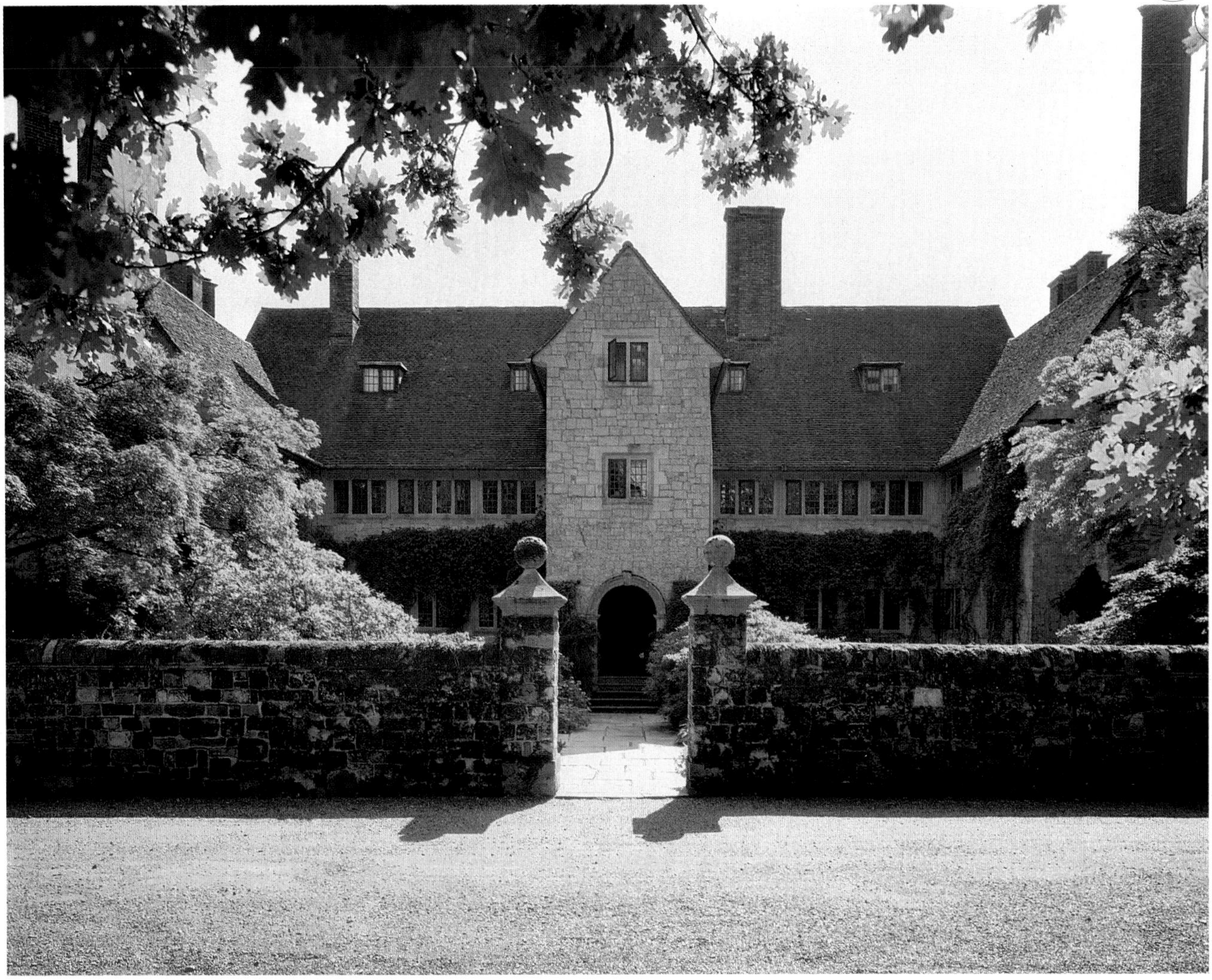

LITTLE THAKEHAM

MERRYWOOD LANE, STORRINGTON, WEST SUSSEX RH20 3HE
TEL: 01903 744416 FAX: 01903 745022

One of the finest examples of a Lutyens Manor house, Little Thakeham is the home of Tim and Pauline Ractliff who have carefully preserved the feeling of a family home. Antiques, open log fires and a minstrel gallery all serve to enhance the authentic atmosphere of gracious living. There are two suites and seven bedrooms all furnished in character with the house. The restaurant, also open to non-residents, serves traditional English food based on local produce such as Southdown lamb and shellfish from the South Coast. The set menu changes daily and there is an excellent cellar. The Surrounding gardens were created in the style of Gertude Jekyll and recently have been the subject of restoration. There is a heated swimming pool in the grounds. The famous country houses of Goodwood, Petworth and Arundel Castle are nearby, racing enthusiasts are well served with Goodwood, Fontwell Park and Plumpton. Antique collectors will not be disappointed, there are shops in Arundel, Petworth and Chichester. **Directions:** From Storrington, take B2139 to Thakeham. After about one mile turn right into Merrywood Lane. Hotel is 400 yards on left. Price guide: Single £95; double/twin £150; suite £240.

For hotel location, see maps on pages 477-483

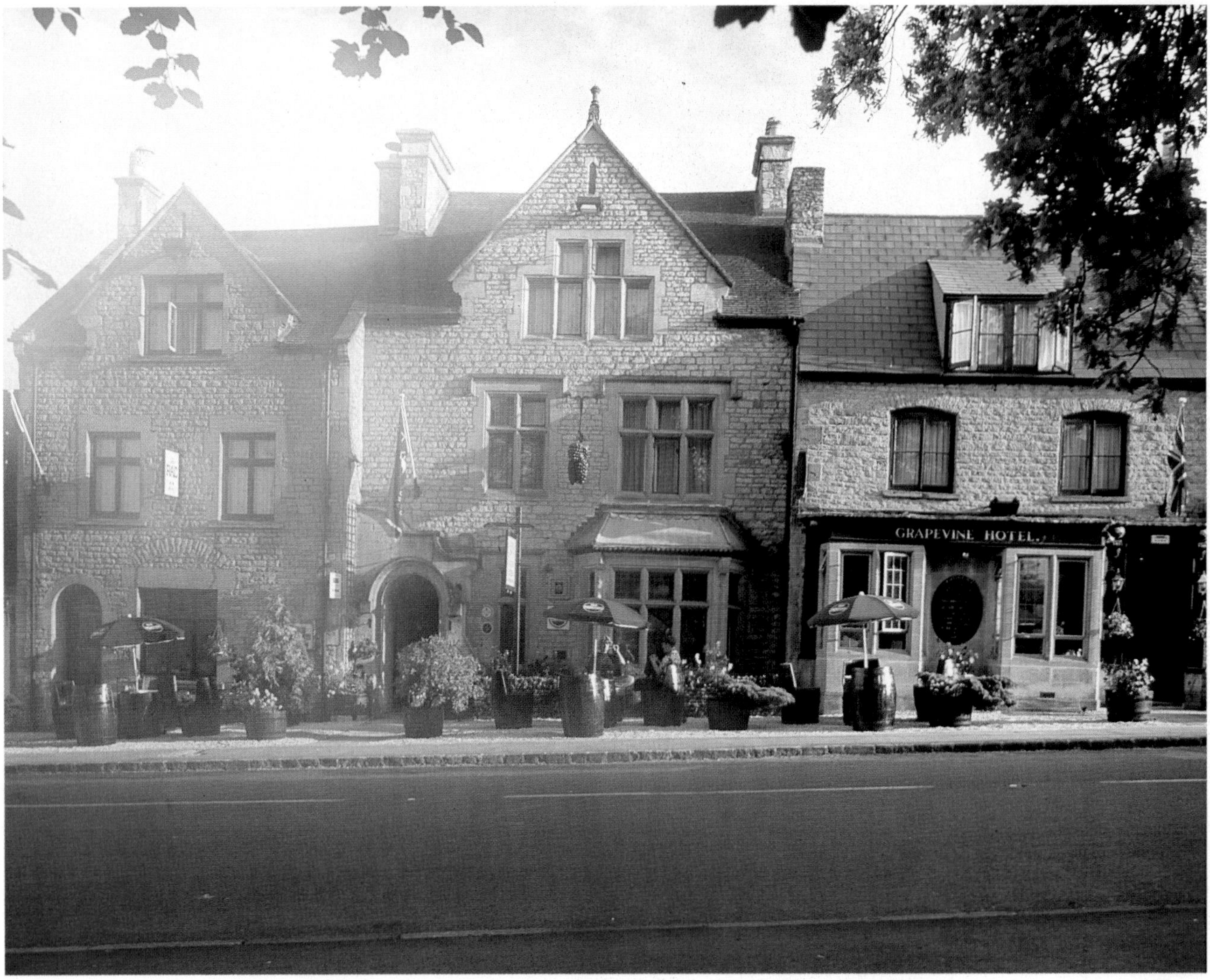

THE GRAPEVINE HOTEL

SHEEP STREET, STOW-ON-THE-WOLD, GLOUCESTERSHIRE GL54 1AU
TEL: 01451 830344 FAX: 01451 832278

Set in the pretty town of Stow-on-the-Wold, regarded by many as the jewel of the Cotswolds, The Grapevine Hotel has an atmosphere which makes visitors feel welcome and at ease. The outstanding personal service provided by a loyal team of staff is perhaps the secret of the hotel's success – nothing is too much trouble for them. This, along with the exceptionally high standard of overall comfort and hospitality, earned The Grapevine the 1991 *Johansens Hotel Award for Excellence* – a well-deserved accolade. Beautifully furnished bedrooms, including six superb garden rooms across the courtyard, offer every facility. Visitors can linger over imaginative cuisine in the relaxed and informal atmosphere of the conservatory restaurant, with its unusual canopy of trailing vines. AA Rosette awarded for food. Whether travelling on business or for pleasure, The Grapevine is a hotel that guests will wish to return to again and again. The local landscape offers unlimited scope for exploration, whether to the numerous picturesque villages tucked away in the Cotswolds or to the nearby towns of Oxford, Cirencester and Stratford-upon-Avon. Champagne breaks available from £55 per person d, b&b. Open over Christmas/New Year. **Directions:** Sheep Street is part of the A436 in the centre of Stow-on-the-Wold. Price guide: Single from £60; double/twin from £120.

For hotel location, see maps on pages 477-483

WYCK HILL HOUSE

WYCK HILL, STOW-ON-THE WOLD, GLOUCESTERSHIRE GL54 1HY
TEL: 01451 831936 FAX: 01451 832243

Wyck Hill House is a magnificent Cotswold mansion built in the early 1700s, reputedly on the site of an early Roman settlement. It is set in 100 acres of wooded and landscaped gardens, overlooking the beautiful Windrush Valley. The hotel has been elegantly restored and the bedrooms individually furnished to combine superb antiques with modern comforts. There is a suite with a large, antique four-poster bed, which is perfect for a honeymoon or for other special occasions. The cedar-panelled library is an ideal room in which to read, if you wish, and to relax with morning coffee or afternoon tea. The award-winning restaurant provides the highest standards of modern British cuisine from the freshest seasonally available local produce. The menus are complemented by a superb wine list. Wyck Hill House hosts several special events, including opera, travel talks, cultural weekends and a variety of theme activities. The hotel is an ideal base from which to tour the university city of Oxford and the Georgian city of Bath. Cheltenham, Blenheim Palace and Stratford-upon-Avon are just a short drive away. Special price 2-night breaks are available. **Directions:** One-and-a-half miles south of Stow-on-the-Wold on the A424 Stow–Burford road. Price guide: Single from £80; double/twin from £130; suite from £180.

31 rms MasterCard VISA AMERICAN EXPRESS M 30

For hotel location, see maps on pages 477-483

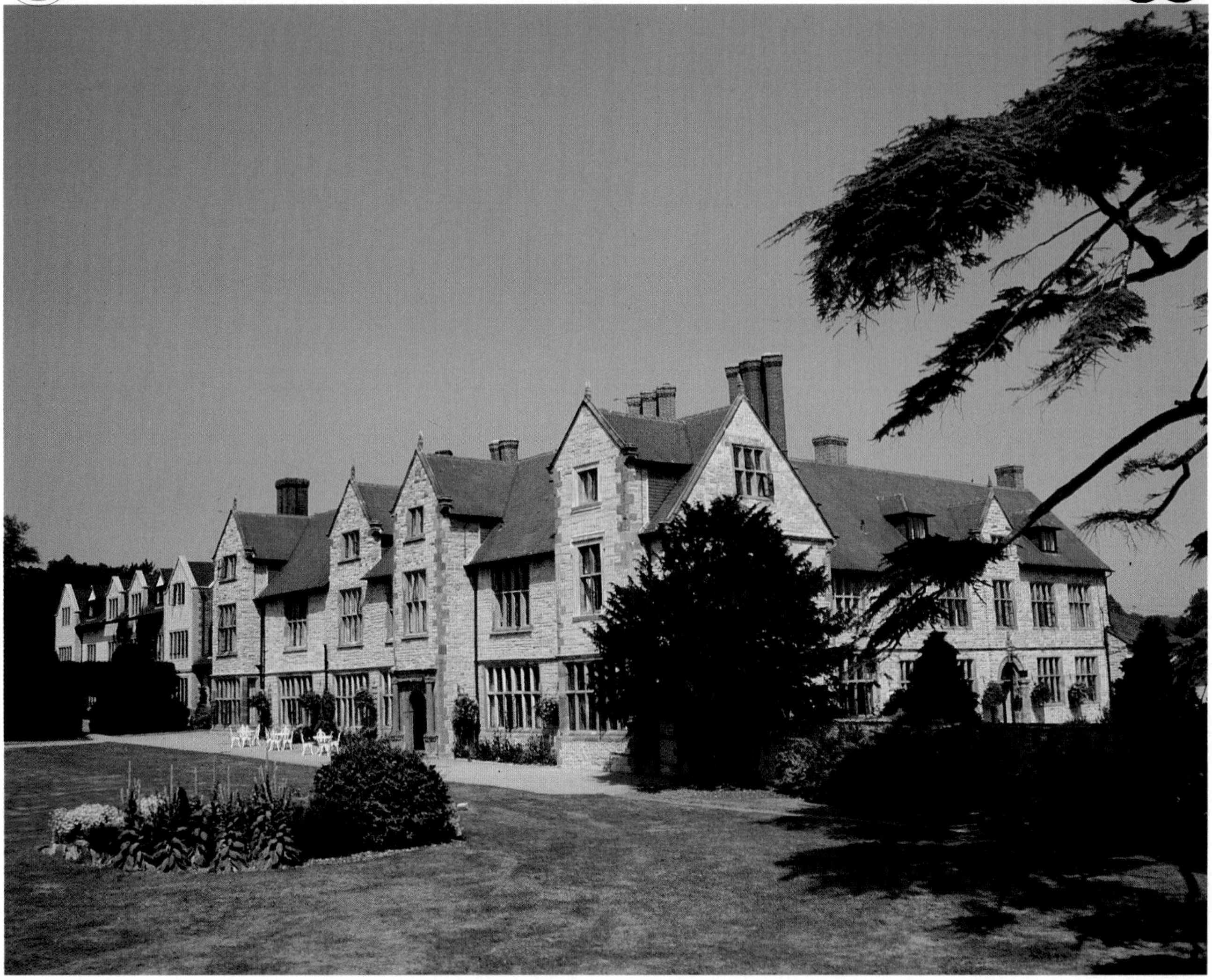

BILLESLEY MANOR

BILLESLEY, ALCESTER, NR STRATFORD-UPON-AVON, WARWICKSHIRE B49 6NF
TEL: 01789 279955 FAX: 01789 764145

Three miles from Stratford-upon-Avon, Billesley Manor is set in 11 acres of delightful grounds with a typically English topiary garden and ornamental pond. Ten centuries of history and tradition welcome guests to this magnificent house in the heart of Shakespeare country. Billesley Manor has been extensively refurbished in recent years, blending old and new to create a hotel that is impressive, spacious and comfortable. Guests may stay in a suite, an oak-panelled four-poster room or one of the well-appointed modern rooms – all have a large bathroom and a good range of facilities. The panelled Tudor and Stuart Restaurants have won awards for their fine food and service, including 2 AA Rosettes. Billesley Manor is particularly suitable for residential conferences and meetings, offering self-contained amenities and seclusion. In addition to the many on-site leisure activities, like the attractive sun patio, pool, mini-golf and tennis courts, weekend breaks can include hot-air ballooning, shooting and riding. The hotel is ideal for visiting the Royal Shakespeare Theatre, Warwick Castle, Ragley Hall and the Cotswolds. **Directions:** From M40 (exit 15) follow A46 towards Evesham and Alcester. Three miles beyond Stratford-upon-Avon turn right to Billesley. Price guide: Single £105; double/twin £155; suite £215.

For hotel location, see maps on pages 477-483

ETTINGTON PARK

ALDERMINSTER, STRATFORD-UPON-AVON, WARWICKSHIRE CV37 8BS
TEL: 01789 450123 FAX: 01789 450472

The foundations of Ettington Park date back at least 1000 years. Mentioned in the *Domesday Book*, Ettington Park rises majestically over 40 acres of Warwickshire parkland, surrounded by terraced gardens and carefully tended lawns, where guests can wander at will to admire the pastoral views. The interiors are beautiful, their striking opulence enhanced by flowers, beautiful antiques and original paintings. Amid these elegant surroundings guests can relax totally, pampered with every luxury. On an appropriately grand scale, the 48 bedrooms and superb leisure complex, comprising an indoor heated swimming pool, spa bath, solarium and sauna, make this a perfect choice for the sybarite. The menu reflects the best of English and French cuisine, served with panache in the dining room, with its elegant 18th century rococo ceiling and 19th century carved family crests. The *bon viveur* will relish the fine wine list. Splendid conference facilities are available: the panelled Long Gallery and 14th century chapel are both unique venues. Riding is a speciality, while clay pigeon shooting, archery and fishing can also be arranged on the premises. **Directions:** From M40 junction 15 (Warwick) take A46 signposted Stratford, then left-hand turn onto A3400. Ettington is five miles south of Stratford-upon-Avon off the A3400. Price guide: Single £115; double/twin from £165; suites from £210.

48 rms MasterCard VISA AMERICAN EXPRESS M 65

For hotel location, see maps on pages 477-483

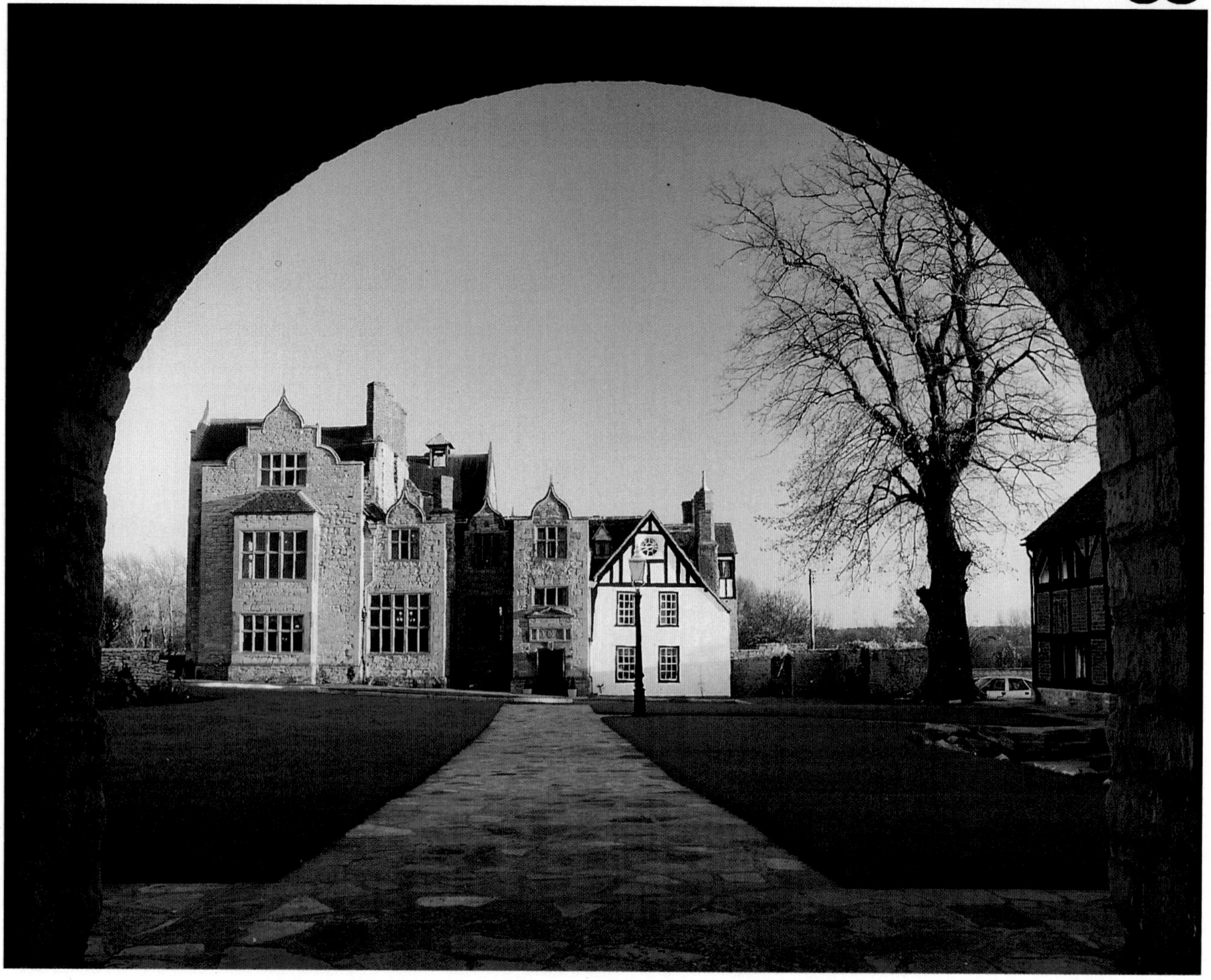

SALFORD HALL HOTEL

ABBOT'S SALFORD, NR EVESHAM, WORCESTERSHIRE WR11 5UT
TEL: 01386 871300 FAX: 01386 871301

Between Shakespeare's Stratford-upon-Avon, the rolling Cotswolds and the Vale of Evesham is the Roman village of Abbot's Salford. Steeped in history, Salford Hall is a romantic Grade I listed manor house. It was built in the late 15th century as a retreat for the monks of Evesham Abbey and the imposing stone wing was added in the 17th century. Essentially unchanged, stained glass, a priest hole, exposed beams, oak panelling and original decorative murals are examples of the well-preserved features of the interior. The period charm is doubly appealing when combined with modern comforts, gracious furnishings, delicious food and an extensive selection of fine wines. Reflecting the past associations of the hall, the bedrooms are named after historical figures, and all are individually appointed with oak furniture and luxury fittings. Guests may relax in the Hawkesbury lounge, formerly a medieval kitchen, the conservatory lounge or on the sunny terrace within the walled flower garden. Facilities include snooker, a sauna and a solarium. Special weekends are arranged for hot-air ballooning, horse-racing, touring the Cotswolds, discovering Shakespeare and murder mysteries. Closed for Christmas. **Directions:** Abbot's Salford is 8 miles west of Stratford-upon-Avon on B439 towards The Vale of Evesham. Price guide: Single £75; double/twin £105–£140.

For hotel location, see maps on pages 477-483

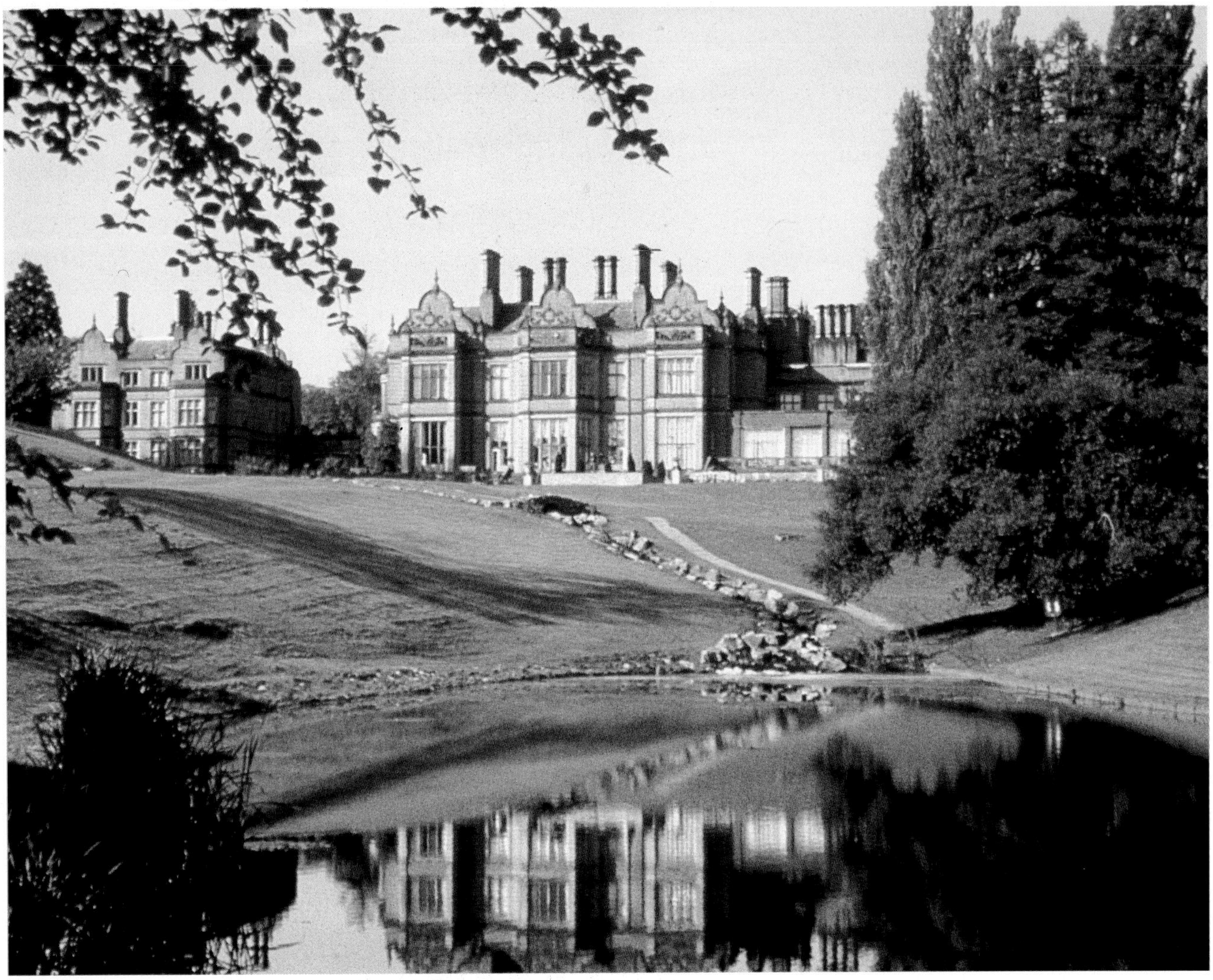

WELCOMBE HOTEL AND GOLF COURSE

WARWICK ROAD, STRATFORD-UPON-AVON, WARWICKSHIRE CV37 0NR
TEL: 01789 295252 FAX: 01789 414666 TELEX: 31347

A splendid Jacobean-style mansion dating from 1869, the aptly named Welcombe Hotel stands in 157 acres of rolling parkland, much of which was owned by Shakespeare. One of the foremost hotels in the heart of England, it is also renowned for its fully equipped 18-hole golf course and resident golf pro Nigel Sears. The magnificent lounge, with its striking black marble fireplace, ornate floor-to-ceiling oak panelling, deep armchairs and bright flower arrangements, typifies the immaculate style of the hotel's interior. Exquisitely decorated, the restaurant is light, airy and spacious – an elegant setting overlooking the extensive formal gardens. The finest English and French cuisine is impeccably prepared, with particular emphasis on delicate sauces and presentation. A well-balanced wine list includes a wide selection of half bottles. Whether staying in one of the suites or bedrooms, guests will find the accommodation appointed to the highest standards. For small meetings or large-scale conferences, the Welcombe Hotel can offer every amenity to support the event. The centre of Stratford-upon-Avon is only 1 mile away. **Directions:** Five miles from exit 15 of M40, on A439. 1 mile from Stratford-upon-Avon. Price guide: Single £110; double/twin £150–£225; suite £275–£500.

For hotel location, see maps on pages 477-483

THE SWAN DIPLOMAT

STREATLEY-ON-THAMES, BERKSHIRE RG8 9HR
TEL: 01491 873737 FAX: 01491 872554

In a beautiful setting on the bank of the River Thames, this hotel offers visitors comfortable accommodation. All of the 46 bedrooms, many of which have balconies overlooking the river, are appointed to high standards with individual décor and furnishings. The elegant Riverside Restaurant, with its relaxing waterside views, serves fine food complemented by a good choice of wines. Guests may also choose to dine in the informal Duck Room Brasserie. Moored alongside the restaurant is the Magdalen College Barge, which is a stylish venue for meetings and cocktail parties. Business guests are well catered for – the hotel has six attractive conference suites. Reflexions Leisure Club is superbly equipped for fitness programmes and beauty treatments, with facilities that include a heated 'fit' pool; rowing boats and bicycles may be hired. Squash, riding and clay pigeon shooting can all be arranged. Special theme weekends are offered, such as bridge weekends. Events in the locality include Henley Regatta, Ascot and Newbury races, while Windsor Castle, Blenheim Palace, Oxford and London's airports are easily accessible. **Directions:** The hotel lies just off the A329 in Streatley village. Price guide: Single £55–£104; double/twin £80–£133.

For hotel location, see maps on pages 477-483

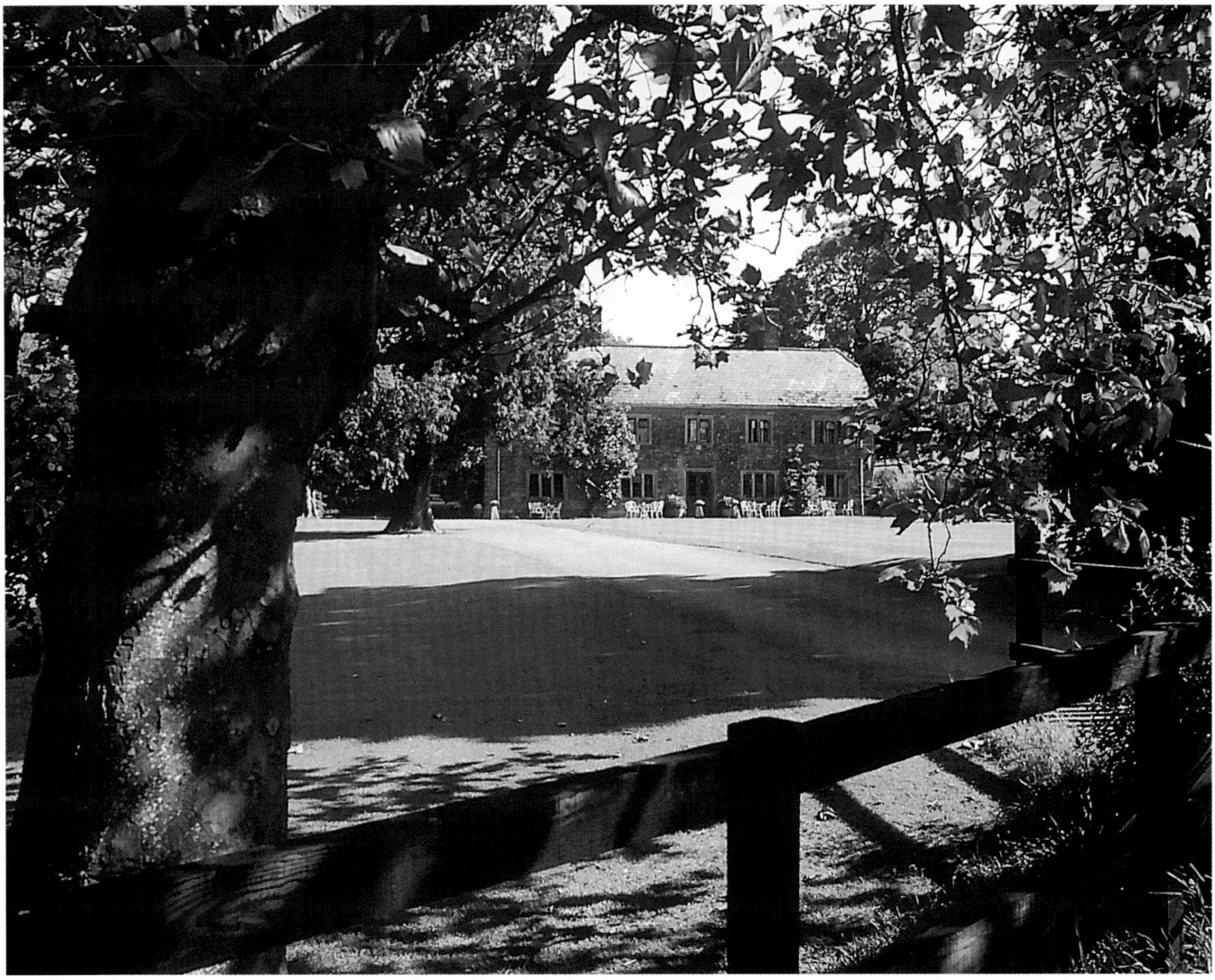

PLUMBER MANOR

STURMINSTER NEWTON, DORSET DT10 2AF
TEL: 01258 472507 FAX: 01258 473370

An imposing Jacobean building of local stone, occupying extensive gardens in the heart of Hardy's Dorset, Plumber Manor has been the home of the Prideaux-Brune family since the early 17th century. Leading off a charming gallery hung with family portraits are six very comfortable bedrooms. The conversion of a natural stone barn lying within the grounds, as well as the courtyard building, has added a further ten spacious bedrooms, some of which have window seats overlooking the garden and the Develish stream. Three interconnecting dining rooms comprise the restaurant, where a good choice of imaginative, well-prepared dishes is presented, supported by a wide-ranging wine list. Chef Brian Prideaux-Brune's culinary prowess has been recognised by all the major food guides. Open for dinner every evening and Sunday lunch. The Dorset landscape, with its picture-postcard villages such as Milton Abbas and Cerne Abbas, is close at hand, while Corfe Castle, Lulworth Cove, Kingston Lacy and Poole Harbour are not far away. Riding can be arranged locally: however, if guests wish to bring their own horse to hack or hunt with local packs, the hotel provides free stabling on a do-it-yourself basis. Closed during February. **Directions:** Plumber Manor is two miles south west of Sturminster Newton on the Hazelbury Bryan road, off the A357. Price guide: Single £65–£80; double/twin £90–£120.

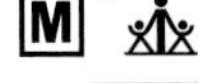

For hotel location, see maps on pages 477-483

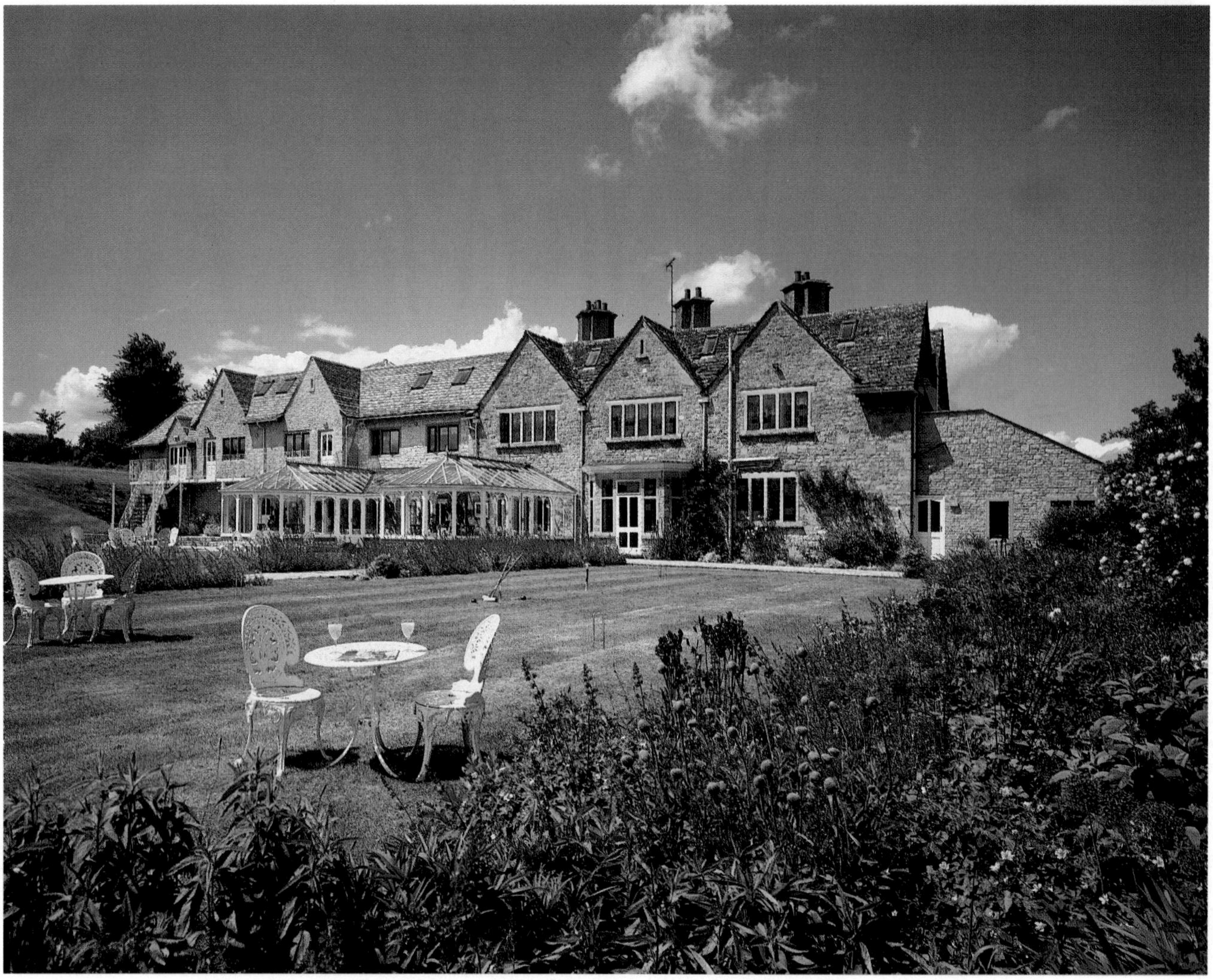

THE PEAR TREE AT PURTON

CHURCH END, PURTON, SWINDON, WILTSHIRE SN5 9ED
TEL: 01793 772100 FAX: 01793 772369

Dedication to service is the hallmark of this excellent honey-coloured stone hotel nestling in the Vale of the White Horse between the Cotswolds and Marlborough Downs. Owners Francis and Anne Young are justly proud of its recognition by the award of the RAC's Blue Ribbon for excellence. Surrounded by rolling Wiltshire farmland, The Pear Tree sits majestically in seven-and-a-half acres of tranquil grounds on the fringe of the Saxon village of Purton, famed for its unique twin towered Parish Church and the ancient hill fort of Ringsbury Camp. Each of the 18 individually and tastefully decorated bedrooms and suites is named after a character associated with the village, such as Anne Hyde, mother of Queen Mary and Queen Anne. All are fitted to a high standard and have satellite television, hairdryer, trouser press and a host of other luxuries. The award-winning conservatory restaurant overlooks colourful gardens and is the perfect setting in which to enjoy good English cuisine prepared with style and flair by Chef Catherine Berry. Cirencester, Bath, Oxford, Avebury, Blenheim Palace, Sudeley Castle and the Cotswolds are all within easy reach. **Directions:** From M4 exit 16 follow signs to Purton and go through the village until reaching a triangle with Spar Grocers opposite. Turn right up the hill and the Pear Tree is on the left after the Tithe Barn. Price Guide: Single/double/twin £80; suite £100.

For hotel location, see maps on pages 477-483

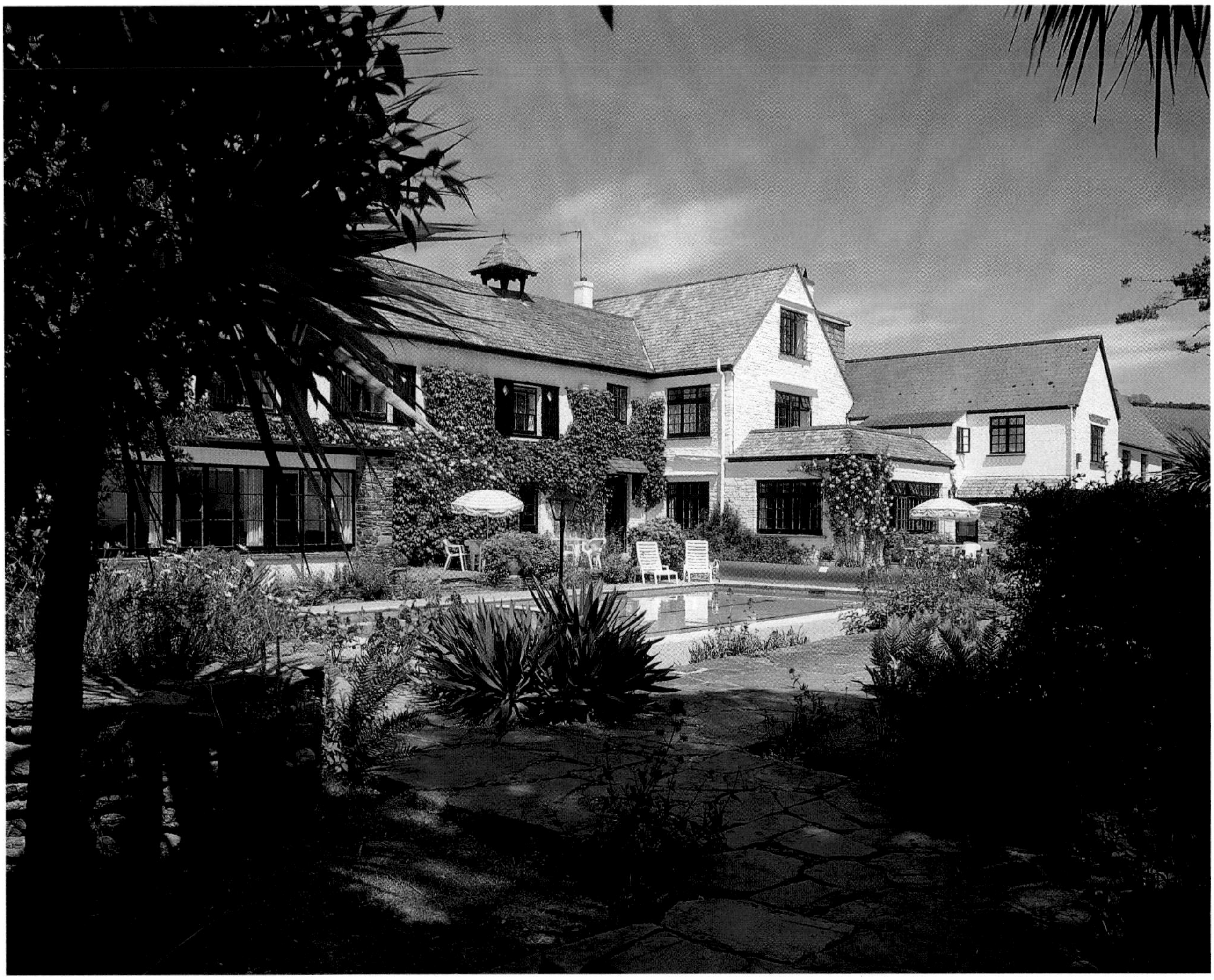

TALLAND BAY HOTEL

TALLAND-BY-LOOE, CORNWALL PL13 2JB
TEL: 01503 272667 FAX: 01503 272940

This lovely old Cornish manor house, parts of which date back to the 16th century, enjoys a completely rural and unspoilt setting. The hotel is surrounded by over 2 acres of beautiful gardens with glorious views over the two dramatic headlands of Talland Bay itself. Bedrooms are individually furnished to a high standard, some having lovely sea views. Sitting rooms open to the south-facing terrace by a heated outdoor swimming pool. Dinner menus are imaginative and incorporate seafood from Looe, Cornish lamb and West Country cheeses. A choice of à la carte supplements changes with the seasons. Meals are complemented by a list of about 100 carefully selected wines. Leisure pursuits at the hotel include: swimming, putting, croquet, table tennis, sauna, painting courses and other special interest holidays. Talland Bay is a magically peaceful spot from which to explore this part of Cornwall – there are breathtaking cliff coastal walks at the hotel's doorstep, and many National Trust houses and gardens to visit locally – but most people come here just to relax and enjoy the view. This hotel provides old fashioned comfort in beautiful surroundings at exceptionally moderate prices. Resident owners: Barry and Annie Rosier. Closed January. **Directions:** The hotel is signposted from the A387 Looe–Polperro road. Price guide: Single £39–£74; double/twin £78–£148.

For hotel location, see maps on pages 477-483

THE CASTLE AT TAUNTON

CASTLE GREEN, TAUNTON, SOMERSET TA1 1NF
TEL: 01823 272671 FAX: 01823 336066 INTERNET: http://www.the–castle–hotel.com/

The Castle at Taunton is steeped in the drama and romance of English history. Once a Norman fortress, it has been welcoming travellers to the town since the 12th century. In 1685, the Duke of Monmouth's officers were heard "roystering at the Castle Inn" before their defeat by the forces of King James II at Sedgemoor. Shortly after, Judge Jeffreys held his Bloody Assize in the Great Hall of the Castle. Today the Castle lives at peace with its turbulent past but preserves the atmosphere of its ancient tradition. The Chapman family have been running the hotel for 46 years and in that time it has acquired a worldwide reputation for the warmth of its hospitality. Laurels in Michelin, Egon Ronay and the AA also testify to the excellence of the Castle's kitchen and cellar. Located in the heart of England's beautiful West Country, the Castle is the ideal base for exploring a region rich in history. This is the land of King Arthur, King Alfred, Lorna Doone's Exmoor and the monastic foundations of Glastonbury and Wells. Roman and Regency Bath, Longleat House and the majestic gardens of Stourhead. All this and much more can be discovered within easy driving distance of Taunton. **Directions:** Exit M5 junction 25 and follow signs for town centre. Alternatively from the south go by A303 and A358. Price guide: Single from £75; double/twin from £115; suites £185.

For hotel location, see maps on pages 477-483

MOUNT SOMERSET COUNTRY HOUSE HOTEL

HENLADE, TAUNTON, SOMERSET TA3 5NB
TEL: 01823 442500 FAX: 01823 442900

This elegant Regency residence stands high on the slopes of the Blackdown Hills, overlooking miles of lovely Somerset countryside. The hotel is rich in intricate craftmanship and displays fine original features. Its owners have committed themselves to creating an atmosphere in which guests can relax and unwind, confident that all needs will be catered for. The bedrooms are sumptuously furnished and many offer excellent views over the Quantock Hills. Most of the luxurious en suite bathrooms have spa baths. Tea, coffee and home-made cakes can be enjoyed in the beautifully furnished drawing room, while in the evening the finest food and wines are served in the dining room. A team of chefs work together to create dishes to meet the expectations of the most discerning gourmet. The President's Health Club is close by and its swimming pool and equipment can be used by hotel guests by arrangement. Somerset is a centre for traditional crafts and exhibitions of basket making, sculpture, wood turning and pottery abound. Places of interest nearby include Glastonbury Abbey and Wells Cathedral. **Directions:** At M5 exit at Junction 25 and join A358 towards Ilminster. Just past Henlade turn right at sign for Stoke St Mary. At T junction turn left, the hotel drive is 150 yards on the right. Price guide: Single from £64; double/twin from £90; suites from £120; 3 Course Luncheon from £15.95 and 4 Course Dinner from £22.95

23 rms MasterCard VISA AMERICAN EXPRESS M 100

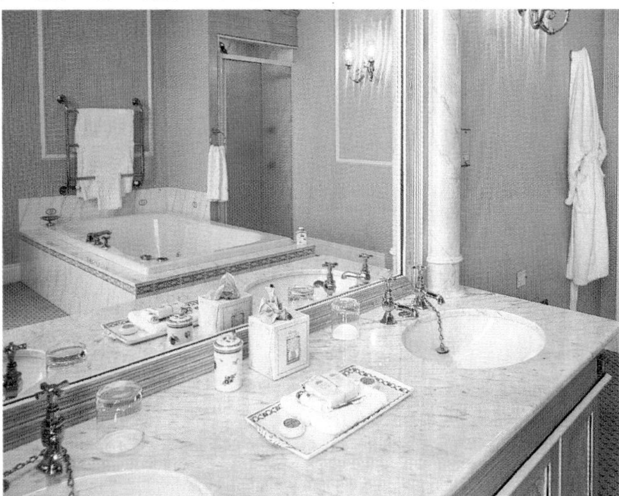

For hotel location, see maps on pages 477-483

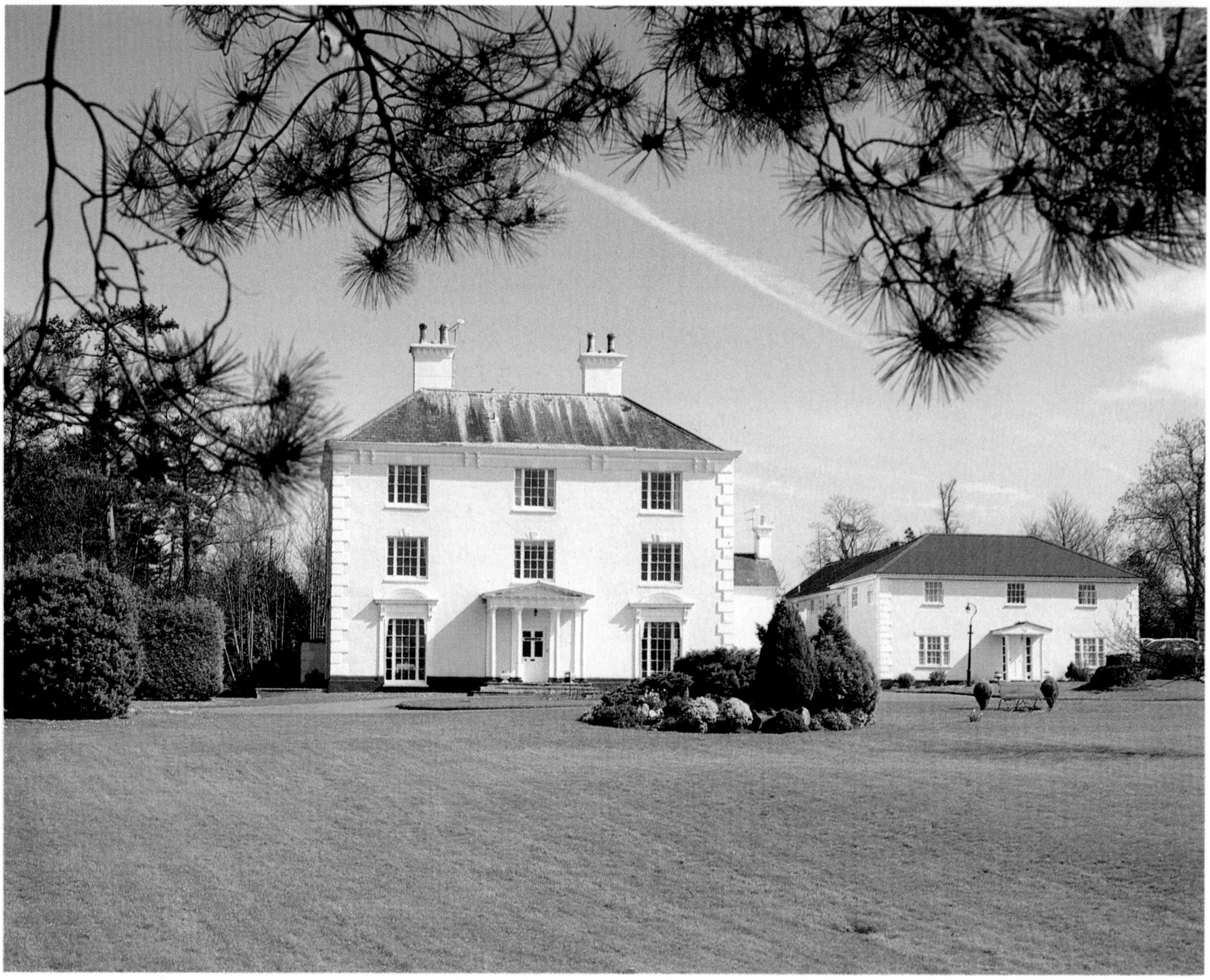

RUMWELL MANOR HOTEL

RUMWELL, TAUNTON, SOMERSET TA4 1EL
TEL: 01823 461902 FAX: 01823 254861

Rumwell Manor Hotel, a magnificent Georgian Manor House, was built in 1805 by William Cadbury of Wellington. Standing in five acres of grounds, it looks south west across the peaceful Somerset countryside to the distant Blackdown Hills. The hotel's bedrooms are divided between the main house and the courtyard. All are individually decorated and furnished, although the main house bedrooms are superior in terms of their spaciousness and their spectacular views across the countryside. A full range of modern amenities is available in every bedroom. The beautifully proportioned public rooms provide an ideal environment in which to relax. The candlelit restaurant boasts an excellent range of imaginative dishes and there is a choice between table d'hôte and à la carte menus. An extensive wine list adds to the dining experience. The well stocked bar is the ideal place to sit. Guests of Rumwell Manor are given a warm and sincere welcome and an atmosphere of friendliness prevails throughout. Cheddar Gorge, the cathedrals of Exeter and Wells, the historic city of Bath, Exmoor, Glastonbury Abbey and Tor are just a few of the outings than can be enjoyed using Rumwell Manor as a base. **Directions:** Exit M5 junction 26. At next roundabout turn right onto A38 towards Taunton. The hotel drive is around three miles along on the right. Price guide: Single: £52–£62; double/twin £78–£110.

For hotel location, see maps on pages 477-483

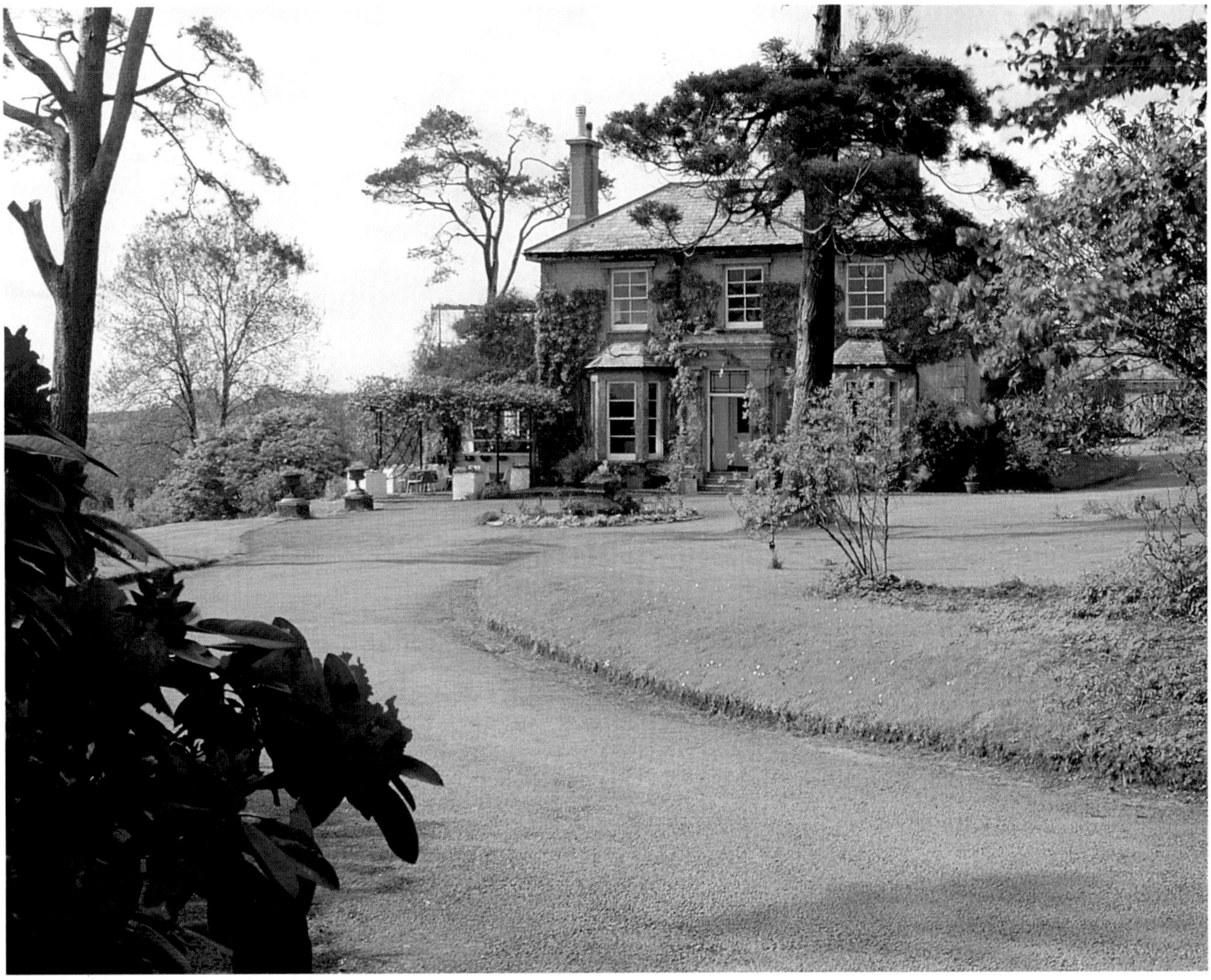

THE HORN OF PLENTY

GULWORTHY, TAVISTOCK, DEVON PL19 8JD
TEL: 01822 832528 FAX: 01822 832528

Nestling in the foothills of Dartmoor and overlooking the Tamar Valley is The Horn of Plenty. Built by the Duke of Bedford, Marquess of Tavistock, nearly 200 years ago, this charming house exudes warmth and welcome. Its four acres of gardens are ablaze with camellias, azaleas and rhododendrons from early spring. Inside, the furnishings are designed for comfort rather than fashion. Throughout the hotel, the smell of fresh flowers competes with the tang of wood smoke from the log fires that burn in the colder winter months. The Coach House has been converted into six lovely en suite bedrooms, all of which are well equipped and have balconies overlooking the walled garden. The heart of The Horn of Plenty is the kitchen, where great thought is put into the taste, texture, contrast and harmony of the food prepared there, whilst the eating experience is enhanced by the surroundings of the restaurant with its beautiful view of the Tamar Valley. Places of interest nearby include Cotehele House and the old market town of Tavistock. The hotel is an ideal base for those interested in active pursuits such as golf, riding on Dartmoor, fishing, walking, sailing and canoeing. Breaks are available. **Directions:** At Tavistock take the A390 and after three miles turn right at Gulworthy Cross and follow the signs to the hotel. Price guide: Single £58–£78; double/twin £78–£98.

For hotel location, see maps on pages 477-483

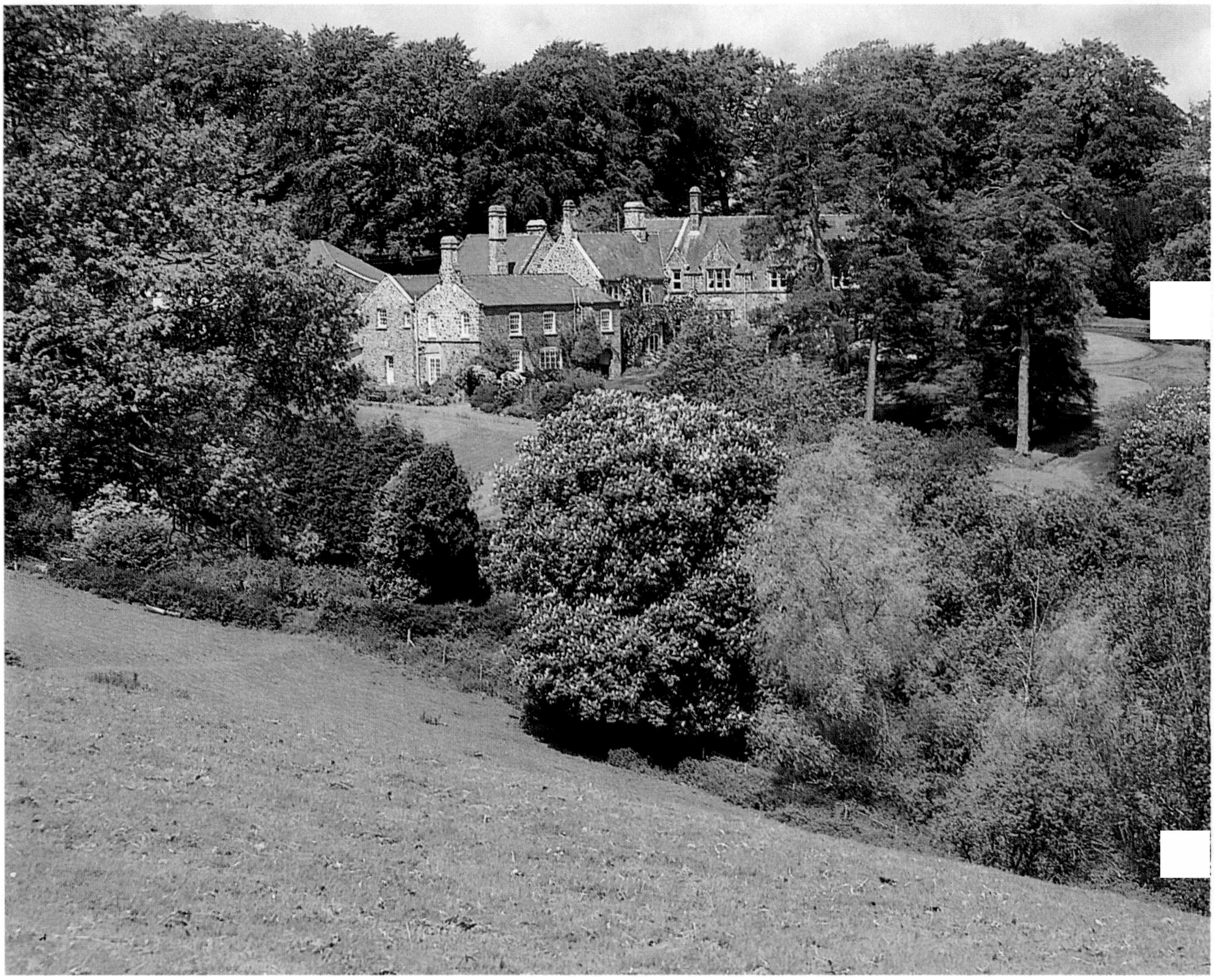

NORTHCOTE MANOR

BURRINGTON AT PORTSMOUTH ARMS, TAW RIVER VALLEY, NORTH DEVON EX37 9LZ
TEL: 01769 560501 FAX: 01769 560770

Northcote Manor is beautifully situated in superb Devon countryside, midway between Exmoor and Dartmoor and the north and south Devon coasts. For nearly 300 years the home of local squires, this 17th century building is set in the seclusion of 20 acres of sweeping lawns, landscaped gardens and lush woodland. It offers a peaceful and relaxed environment, combining today's comfort with an atmosphere of a past era. The luxurious bedrooms are equipped with every modern amenity and the public rooms are both spacious and elegant. The manor's new owners place great emphasis on providing an excellent service which caters for the most individual requirements. Creative first class cuisine relies mainly on home-grown and local produce for which the county is famous. Horses can be taken out from nearby stables and a number of leisure facilities, including a tennis court and an area to practise golf. The 18-hole Libbaton golf course is just round the corner, and arrangements for salmon and sea trout fishing in the nearby River Taw can be made in season. The Manor is ideally placed for touring the whole of Devon, the Cornish coasts, Somerset and beyond. **Directions:** About 25 miles from Exeter on the A377 at Portsmouth Arms turn into private drive. Do not enter Burrington Village. Price guide: Single £79–£129; double/twin £109–£129; suites £169.

For hotel location, see maps on pages 477-483

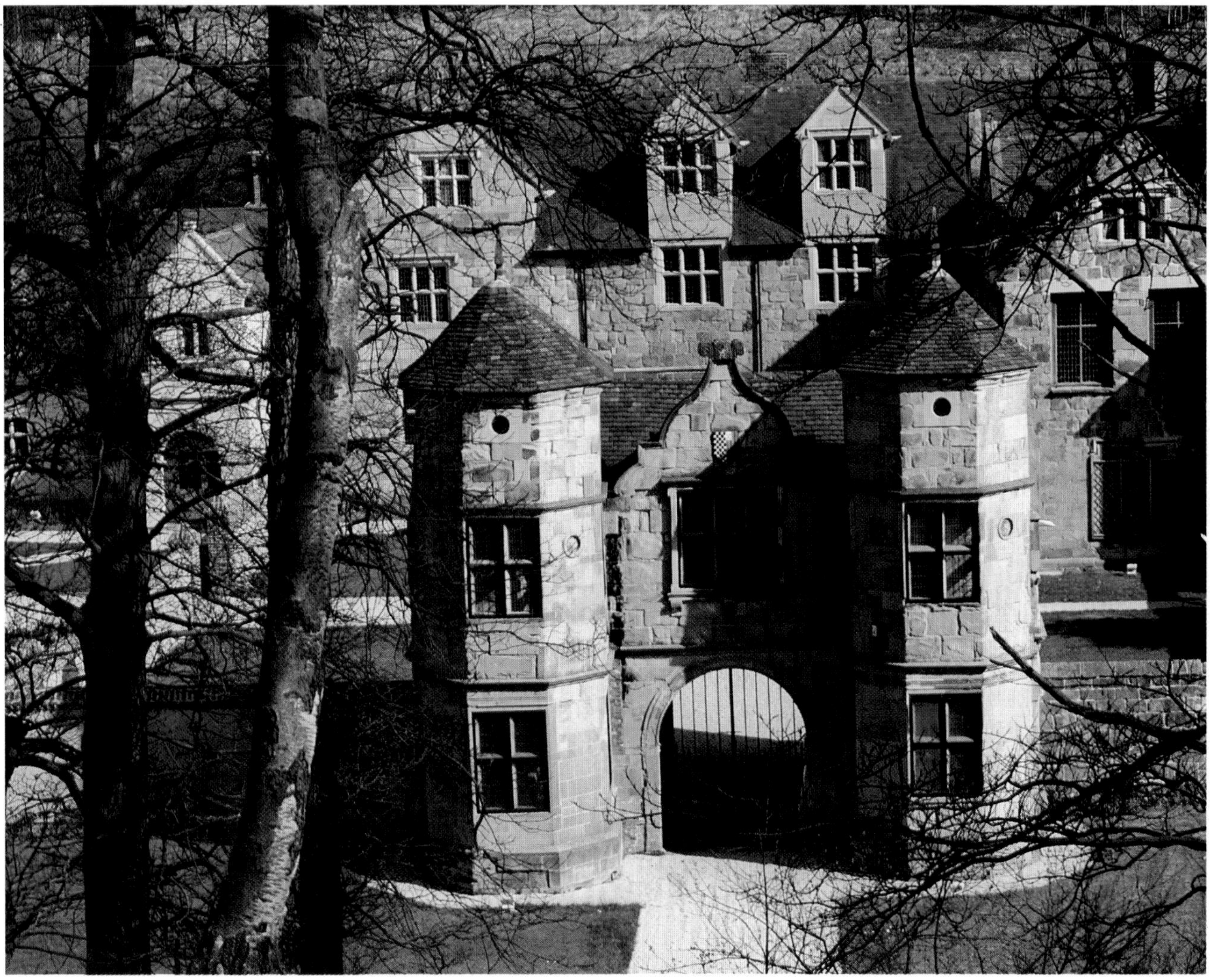

MADELEY COURT

TELFORD, SHROPSHIRE TF7 5DW
TEL: 01952 680068 FAX: 01952 684275

Madeley is a veritable gem of a residence. Its characteristic manor-house façade stands virtually unaltered since the 16th century when it was mainly built, while its interior has been recently expertly rejuvenated – with respect for its history – to provide accommodation suitable for all who stay there whether for pleasure or on business. Furnishings have been judiciously selected to enrich Madeley's period appeal: scatterings of fine fabrics, handsome antique pieces and elaborate fittings all accentuate the historic atmosphere, and ensure that every guest leaves with an indelible impression. Bedrooms, whether located in the old part of the Court or in the newer wing, are quiet and full of character; some offer whirlpool baths and views over the lake, all are en suite. At the heart of Madeley is the original 13th century hall, where the restaurant, awarded 2 coveted AA Rosettes is now located, serving inventive food of the highest standard, with a wine list to match. The Brasserie offers a more informal setting. Business meetings and private functions are happily catered for in the three rooms available. Places of interest nearby include: Ironbridge Gorge, Shrewsbury, Powys Castle and Weston Park. Directions: Four miles from junction 4 of M54; follow A442 then B4373. Signposted Dawley then Madeley. Price guide: Single £85; double/twin £95; historic £110.

For hotel location, see maps on pages 477-483

CALCOT MANOR

NR TETBURY, GLOUCESTERSHIRE GL8 8YJ
TEL: 01666 890391 FAX: 01666 890394

This delightful old manor house, built of Cotswold stone, offers guests tranquillity amidst acres of rolling countryside. Calcot Manor is situated in the southern Cotswolds close to the historic town of Tetbury. The building dates back to the 15th century and was a farmhouse until 1983. Its beautiful stone barns and stables include one of the oldest tithe barns in England, built in 1300 by the Cistercian monks from Kingswood Abbey. These buildings form a quadrangle and the stone glistening in the dawn or glowing in the dusk is quite a spectacle. Calcot achieves the rare combination of professional service and cheerful hospitality without any hint of over formality. The atmosphere is one of peaceful relaxation. All the cottage style rooms are beautifully appointed as are the public rooms. Recent additions are a discreet conference facility and a charming cottage providing four family suites with the sitting areas convertible into children's bedrooms equipped with toys, baby listening system and a safe outdoor play area. At the heart of Calcot Manor is its restaurant, dinner is very much the focus of a memorable stay. There is also the congenial Gumstool Bistro and bar offering a range of simpler traditional food and local ales. **Directions:** From Tetbury, take the A4135 signposted Dursley; Calcot is on the right after 3½ miles. Price guide: Single £75–£100; double/twin £97–£135; family suites £135.

20 rms MasterCard VISA AMERICAN EXPRESS M 60

For hotel location, see maps on pages 477-483

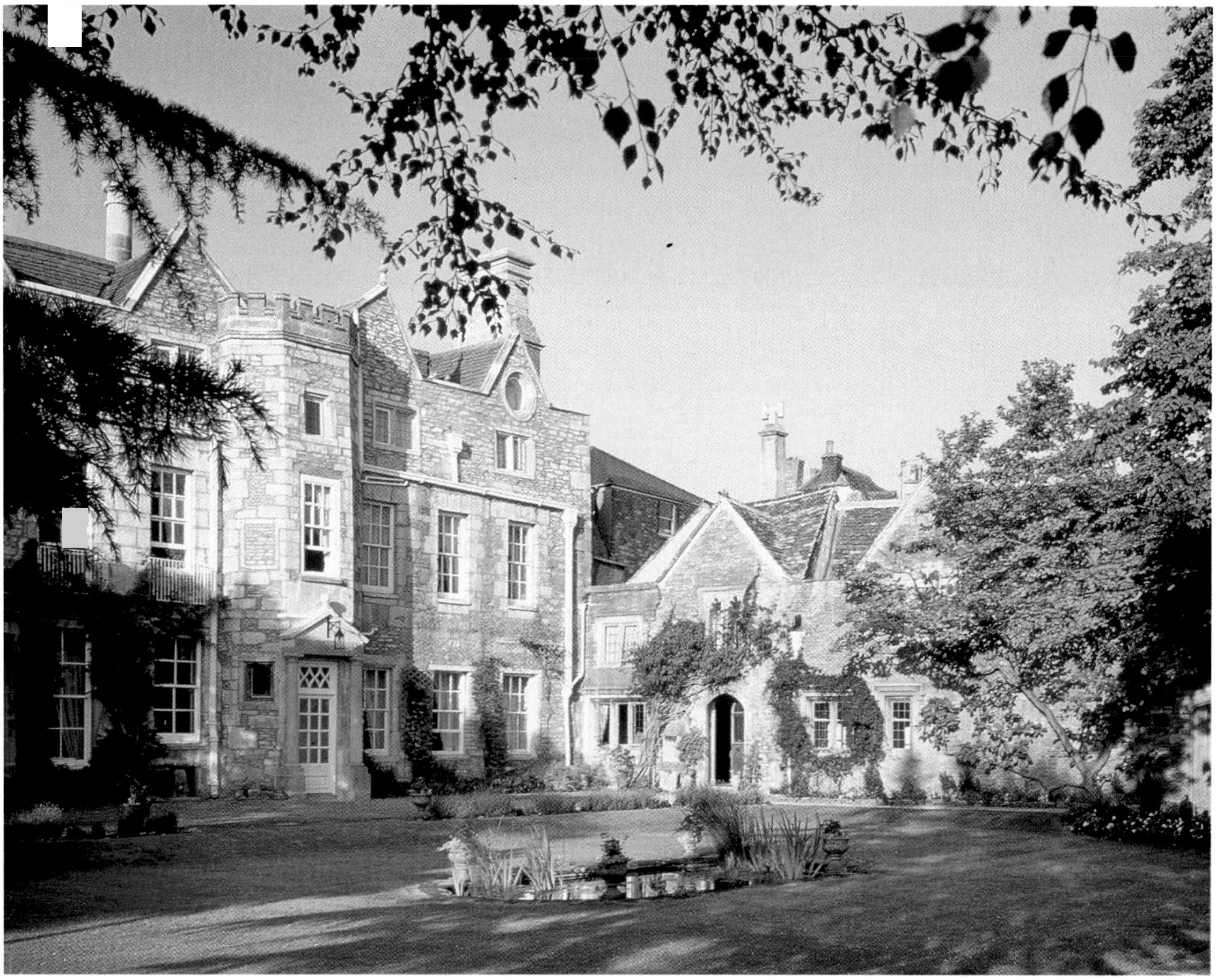

THE CLOSE HOTEL

LONG STREET, TETBURY, GLOUCESTERSHIRE GL8 8AQ
TEL: 01666 502272 FAX: 01666 504401

This distinguished Cotswold town house hotel, built over 400 years ago by a successful wool merchant, has been refurbished to the highest standard. The hotel is renowned for its luxury accommodation, and the individually styled bedrooms are truly elegant. All have superb hand-painted decorated bathrooms. The cuisine, served in the charming Adam dining room, is delicious and imaginative and there is an exceptional choice of wines from an extensive cellar. The restaurant overlooks a walled garden, and you can enjoy a quiet drink on the terrace. The hotel now has a purpose-built suite, The Cloisters, for top-level management meetings and corporate entertainment for up to 24 people boardroom style. Many first-class sporting facilities are within easy reach, including racing at Cheltenham, motor racing at Castle Combe, golf, riding and hot-air ballooning. The Close can be booked for "Exclusive Use" and can hold small wedding services and receptions. It is also the ideal base for exploring the Cotswolds. **Directions:** The Close is on the main street of Tetbury, called Long Street. Tetbury is on the A433, 20 minutes from Bath. Private car park in Close Gardens at rear of the hotel. Price guide: Single £90; double/twin £100.

For hotel location, see maps on pages 477-483

THE SNOOTY FOX

MARKET PLACE, TETBURY, GLOUCESTERSHIRE GL8 8DD
TEL: 01666 502436 FAX: 01666 503479

This old coaching inn dating back to the 16th century is situated right in the heart of the quaint old market town of Tetbury. Built of mellow-hued stone, The Snooty Fox dominates the historic market place in the town centre. The hotel has been imaginatively refurbished by the owners, who have carefully maintained its considerable period character. There are 12 individual and charming en suite bedrooms which are decorated to convey the warm and homely atmosphere of a bygone age. All are well appointed and comfortable. The public areas and restaurant are steeped in history and are full of antiques and fine oil paintings. The prints that decorate the walls depict the hotel's long association with the famous Beaufort Hunt. The Snooty Fox is still a favourite meeting place for the local community of this famous royal town. Guests can choose either to dine in the elegant restaurant or to enjoy the splendid food from the bar menu. Facilities for executive meetings can be arranged and the hotel is the perfect destination for business and short breaks throughout the year. A member of Hatton Hotels. **Directions:** The Snooty Fox is situated in the centre of Tetbury facing the market square. Price guide: Single from £65; double/twin from £85.

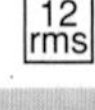

For hotel location, see maps on pages 477-483

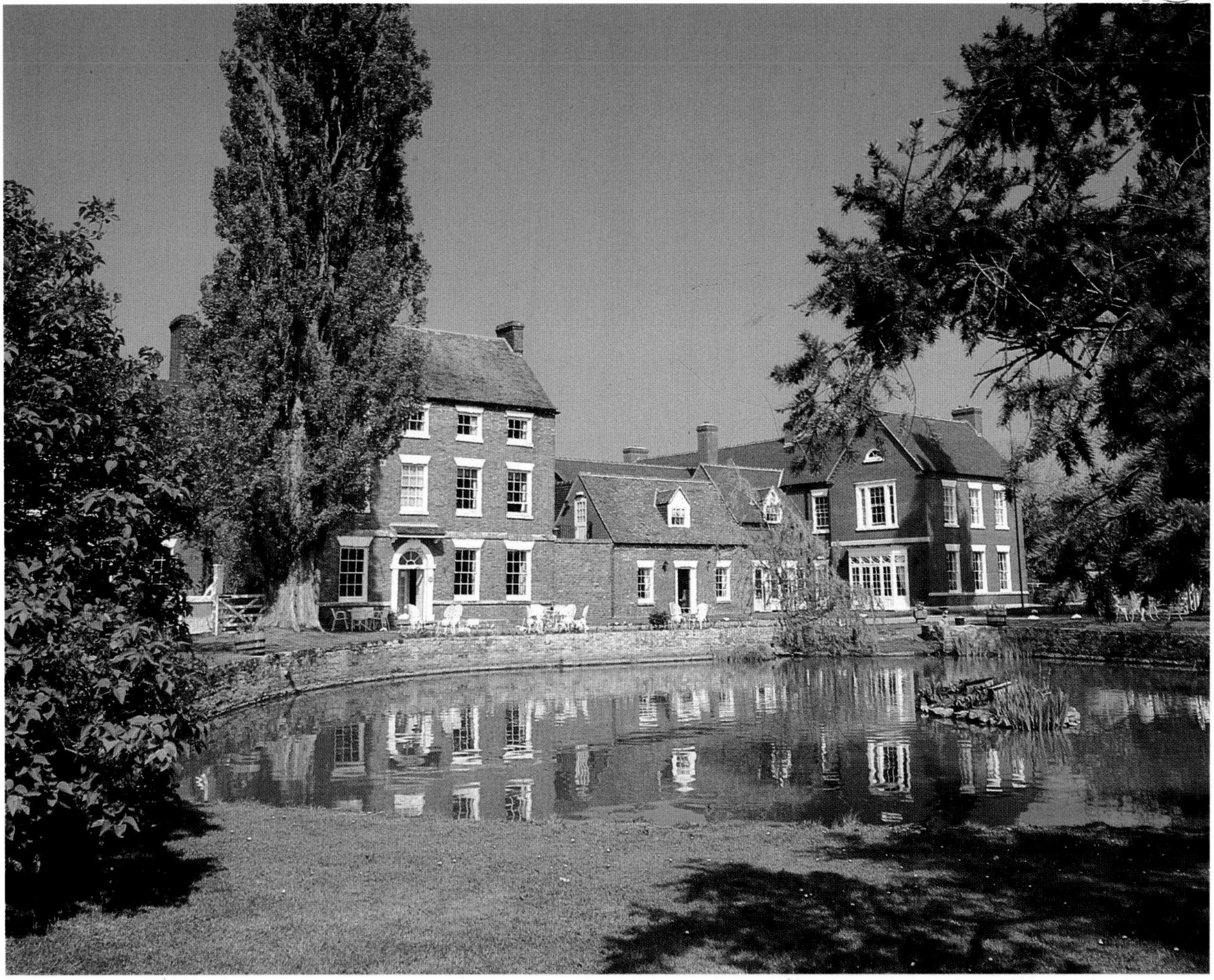

CORSE LAWN HOUSE HOTEL

CORSE LAWN, NR TEWKESBURY, GLOUCESTERSHIRE GL19 4LZ

TEL: 01452 780479/771 FAX: 01452 780840

Though only 6 miles from the M5 and M50, Corse Lawn is a completely unspoiled, typically English hamlet in a peaceful Gloucestershire backwater. The hotel, an elegant Queen Anne listed building set back from the village green, stands in 12 acres of gardens and grounds, and still displays the charm of its historic pedigree. Visitors can be assured of the highest standards of service and cooking: Baba Hine is famous for the dishes she produces, while Denis Hine, of the Hine Cognac family, is in charge of the wine cellar. The service here, now in the hands of son Giles, is faultlessly efficient, friendly and personal. As well as the renowned restaurant, there are three comfortable drawing rooms, a large lounge bar, a private dining-cum-conference room for up to 45 persons, and a similar, smaller room for up to 20. A tennis court, heated swimming pool and croquet lawn adjoin the hotel, and most sports and leisure activities can be arranged. Corse Lawn is ideal for exploring the Cotswolds, Malverns and Forest of Dean. **Directions:** Corse Lawn House is situated on the B4211 between the A417 (Gloucester–Ledbury road) and the A438 (Tewkesbury–Ledbury road). Price guide: Single £70; double/twin £90; four-poster £110; suites £125.

For hotel location, see maps on pages 477-483

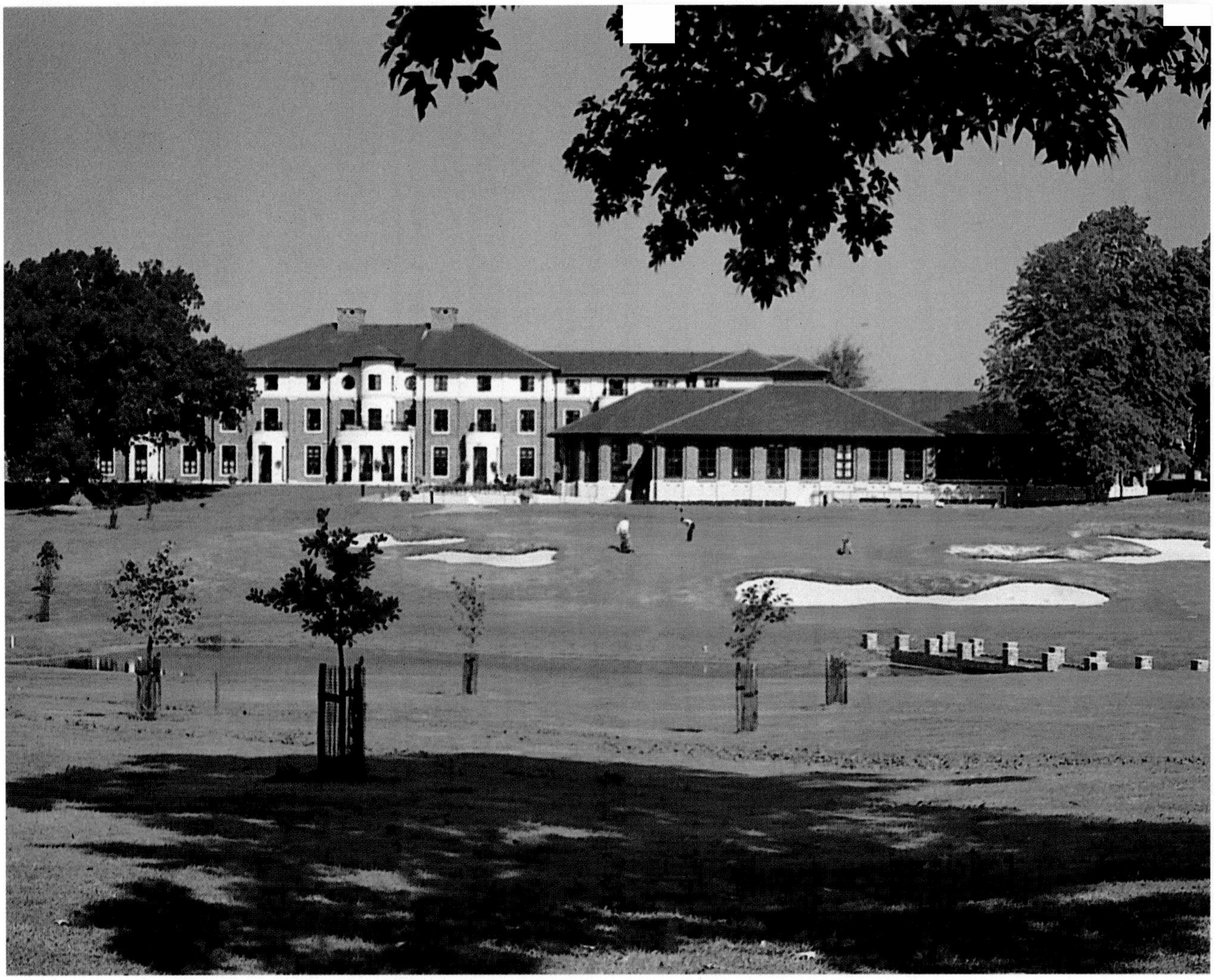

PUCKRUP HALL

PUCKRUP, TEWKESBURY, GLOUCESTERSHIRE GL20 6EL
TEL: 01684 296200 FAX: 01684 850788

Lying between the Cotswolds and the Malvern Hills, set in 140 acres of parkland, Puckrup Hall Hotel and Golf Club is the country house hotel of the future. The original Regency manor house, built in the 19th century has been tastefully extended to combine the most up-to-date hotel and leisure facilities with a taste of England's past. A superb 18 hole championship golf course complements the extensive hotel amenities and leisure complex, which includes aerobics studio, swimming pool, spa bath, solarium, steam room and gymnasium all supported by a beauty treatment centre and crèche. Each of the 84 luxury en suite bedrooms and suites is furnished to the highest standard with all the facilities expected of a country house hotel. The 11 conference and private dining rooms can accommodate between 10 and 200 people for a meeting, presentation or dinner dance. An extensive range of cuisine is available from fine dining in the à la carte restaurant, a varied and exciting choice of menu in "Balharries Brasserie" or a light snack in the coffee shop. A refreshing drink in the "Limes" bar makes a welcome finish to a game of golf and as somewhere to relax. **Directions:** Puckrup Hall is 2 miles north of Tewkesbury on the A38, and only a few minutes from junction 8 of the M5, via junction 1 of the M50. Price guide: Single/double/ twin from £75.50; suite from £110.

For hotel location, see maps on pages 477-483

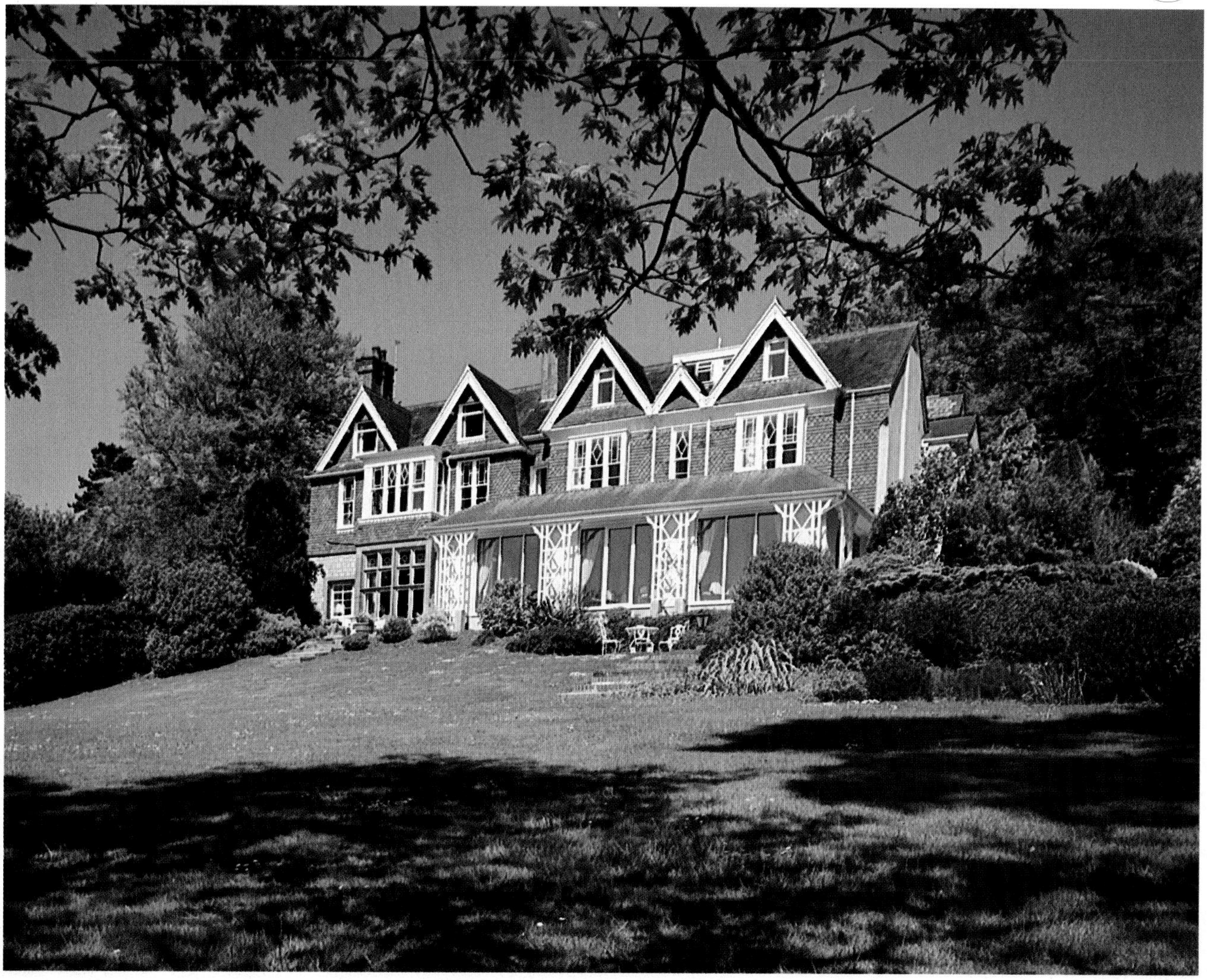

ORESTONE MANOR HOTEL & RESTAURANT

ROCKHOUSE LANE, MAIDENCOMBE, TORQUAY, DEVON TQ1 4SX
TEL: 01803 328098 FAX: 01803 328336

Orestone Manor is an elegant Georgian building set in two acres of secluded gardens in an area of outstanding natural beauty overlooking Lyme Bay. Run by resident proprietors, the atmosphere is welcoming and relaxed. The Manor has been substantially extended since it was built in the early-19th century. The main lounge has a unique pitch-pine ceiling and some bedrooms feature gables. Each en suite bedroom has a colour TV, direct-dial telephone and tea and coffee making facilities. All are individually furnished to a high standard, many with splendid sea views. Not only has Orestone Manor been ranked amoungst the top few in Torbay by the AA (1995), it is only one of two hotels there to be awarded two AA Rosettes (1995) for cuisine. An imaginative menu changed daily always includes a vegetarian option. To enhance its growing reputation for fine food, the restaurant is non-smoking. There are five golf courses within seven miles, as well as sailing, horse-riding, tennis, squash and sailboarding. Dartmoor and many National Trust properties are nearby. Phone for details of special low-season breaks and Christmas and New Year packages. **Directions:** About three miles north of Torquay on B3199 (formerly A379) coast road towards Teignmouth. Price guide: Single £50–£75; double/twin £80–£130.

For hotel location, see maps on pages 477-483

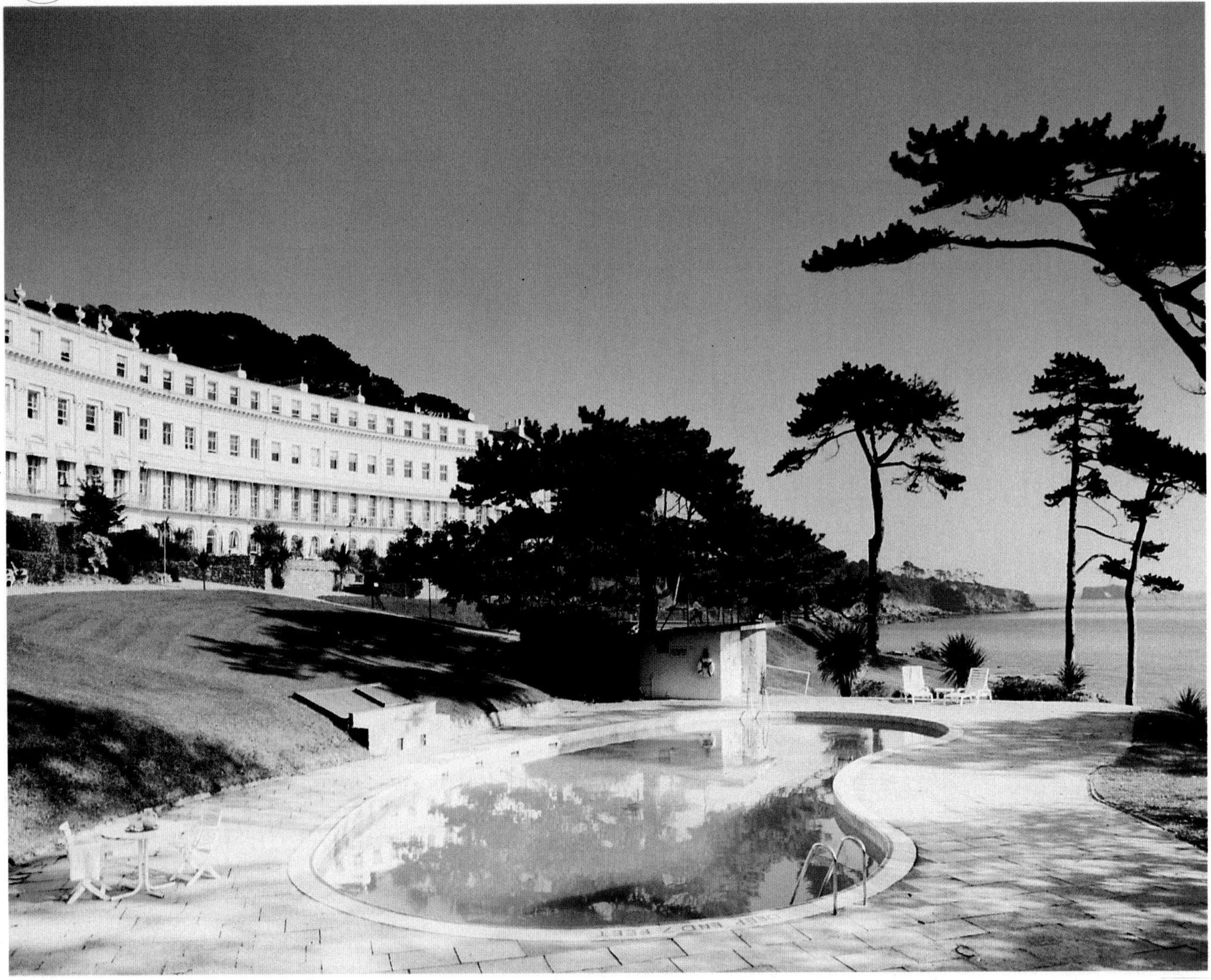

THE OSBORNE HOTEL & LANGTRY'S RESTAURANT

MEADFOOT BEACH, TORQUAY, DEVON TQ1 2LL
TEL: 01803 213311 FAX: 01803 296788

The combination of Mediterranean chic and the much-loved Devon landscape has a special appeal which is reflected at The Osborne. The hotel is the centrepiece of an elegant Regency crescent in Meadfoot, a quiet location within easy reach of the centre of Torquay. Known as a 'country house by the sea', the hotel offers the friendly ambience of a country home complemented by the superior standards of service and comfort expected of a hotel on the English Riviera. Most of the 23 bedrooms have magnificent views and are decorated in pastel shades. Overlooking the sea, Langtry's acclaimed award winning restaurant provides fine English cooking and tempting regional specialities, while the Brasserie has a menu available throughout the day. Guests may relax in the attractive 5-acre gardens and make use of indoor and outdoor swimming pools, tennis court and putting green – all without leaving the grounds. Sailing, archery, clay pigeon shooting and golf can be arranged. Devon is a county of infinite variety, with its fine coastline, bustling harbours, tranquil lanes, sleepy villages and the wilds of Dartmoor. The Osborne is ideally placed to enjoy all these attractions. **Directions:** The hotel is in Meadfoot, to the east of Torquay. Price guide: Single £55–£89; double/twin £78–£128; suite £98–£138.

23 rms         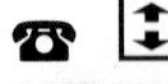   

For hotel location, see maps on pages 477-483

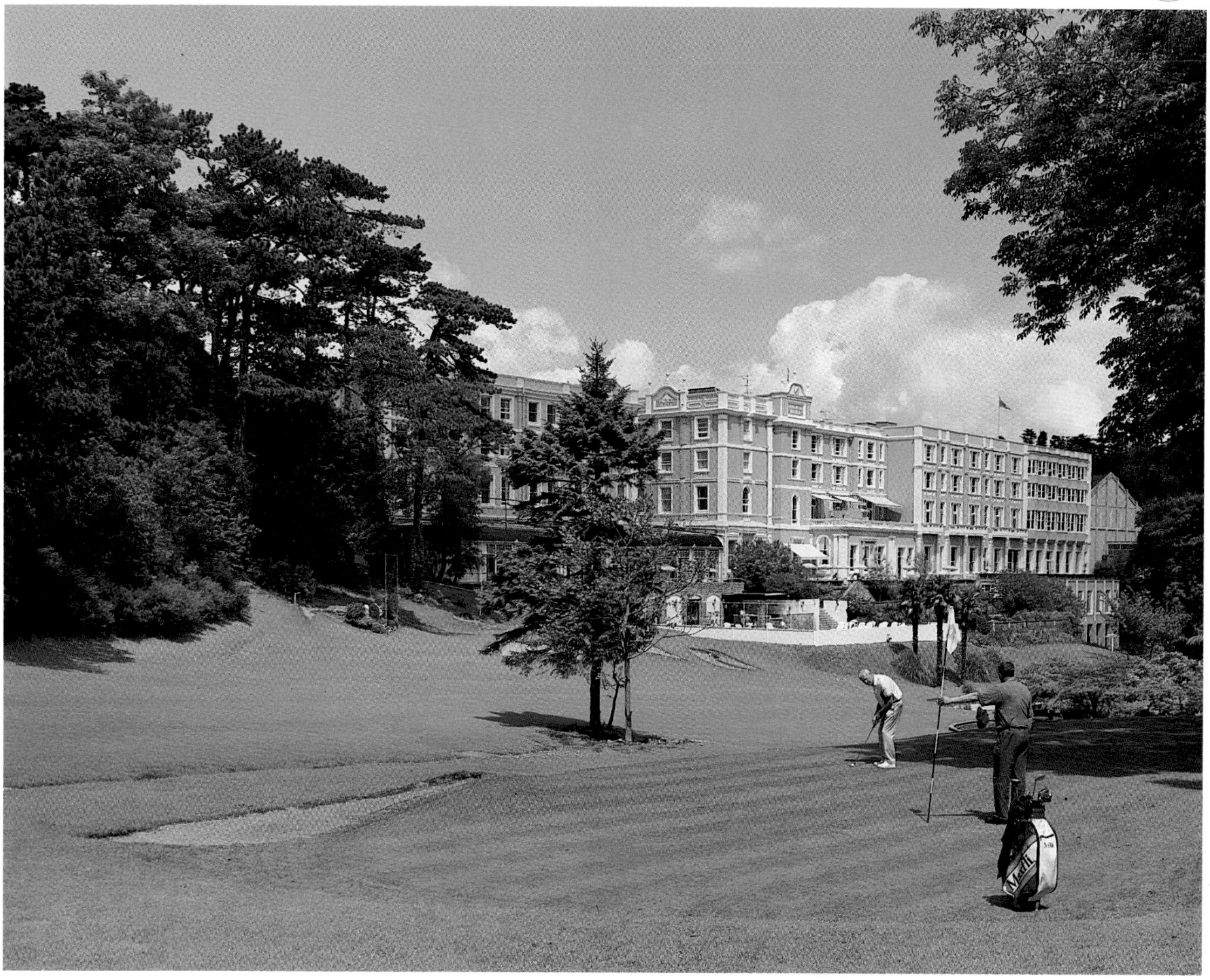

THE PALACE HOTEL

BABBACOMBE ROAD, TORQUAY, DEVON TQ1 3TG
TEL: 01803 200200 FAX: 01803 299899

Once the residence of the Bishop of Exeter, the privately owned Palace Hotel is a gracious Victorian building set in 25 acres of beautifully landscaped gardens and woodlands. The comfortable bedrooms are equipped with every modern amenity and there are also elegant, spacious suites available. Most rooms overlook the hotel's magnificent grounds. The main restaurant provides a high standard of traditional English cooking, making full use of fresh, local produce, as well as offering a good variety of international dishes. The cuisine is complemented by a wide selection of popular and fine wines. Light meals are also available from the lounge and, during the summer months, a barbecue and buffet are served on the terrace. A host of sporting facilities has made this hotel famous. These include a 9-hole championship golf course, indoor and outdoor swimming pools, two indoor and four outdoor tennis courts, two squash courts, saunas and snooker room. A children's nanny is available to give guests extra freedom to enjoy themselves. Places of interest nearby include Dartmoor, South Hams and Exeter. Paignton Zoo, Bygone's Museum and Kent's Cavern are among the local attractions. **Directions:** From seafront follow signs for Babbacombe. Hotel entrance is on the right. Price guide: Single £55–£65; double/twin £110–£130; suites £180–£220. Special breaks available.

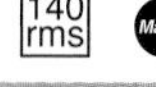

For hotel location, see maps on pages 473–479

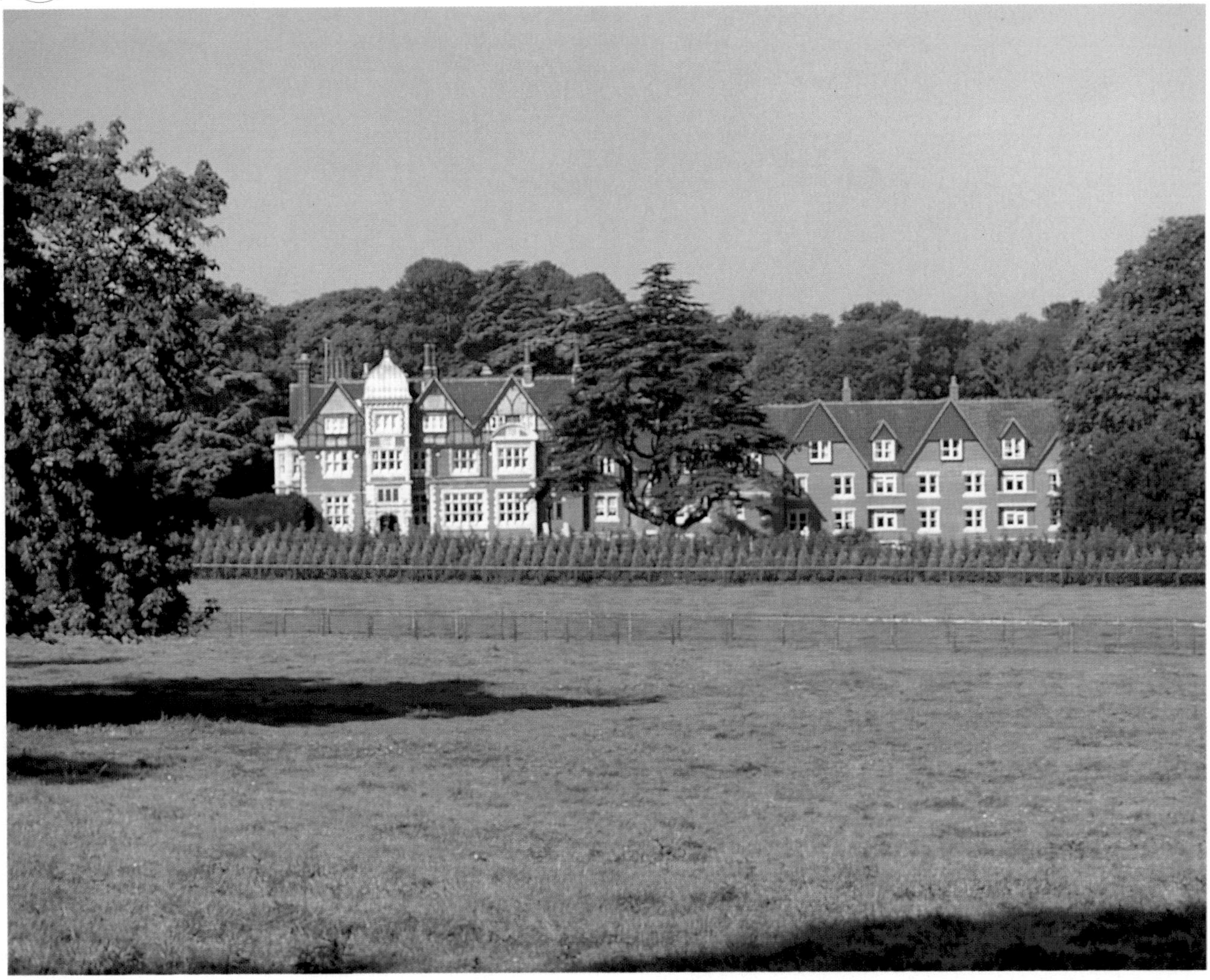

Pendley Manor Hotel & Conference Centre

COW LANE, TRING, HERTFORDSHIRE HP23 5QY
TEL: 01442 891891 FAX: 01442 890687

The Pendley Manor was commissioned by Joseph Grout Williams in 1872. His instructions to architect John Lion were to build it in the Tudor style, reflecting the owner's interest in flora and fauna in the carved woodwork and stained glass panels. It stayed in the Williams family for three generations, but in 1987 the Manor was purchased by an independent hotel company, Craydawn Ltd. A refurbishment programme transformed it to its former glory and today's guests can once again enjoy the elegance and beauty of the Victorian era. The bedrooms are attractively furnished and well equipped, while the cuisine is appealing and well presented. Pendley Manor offers flexible conference facilities for up to 200 people. For indoor recreation a snooker room with a full size table has been added to the amenities. On its estate, which lies at the foot of the Chiltern Hills, sporting facilities include tennis courts, gymnasium, snooker room with full size table, games rooms, buggy riding, laser shooting, archery and hot air balloon rides. Places of interest nearby include Woburn, Winslow Hall, Chenies Manor, Tring Zoological Museum and Dunstable Downs. **Directions:** Take Tring exit from new A41 and from roundabout take road marked Berkhamsted and London. Then take first turn on left. Price guide: Single £85; double/twin £95–£125; suites £130.

For hotel location, see maps on pages 477-483

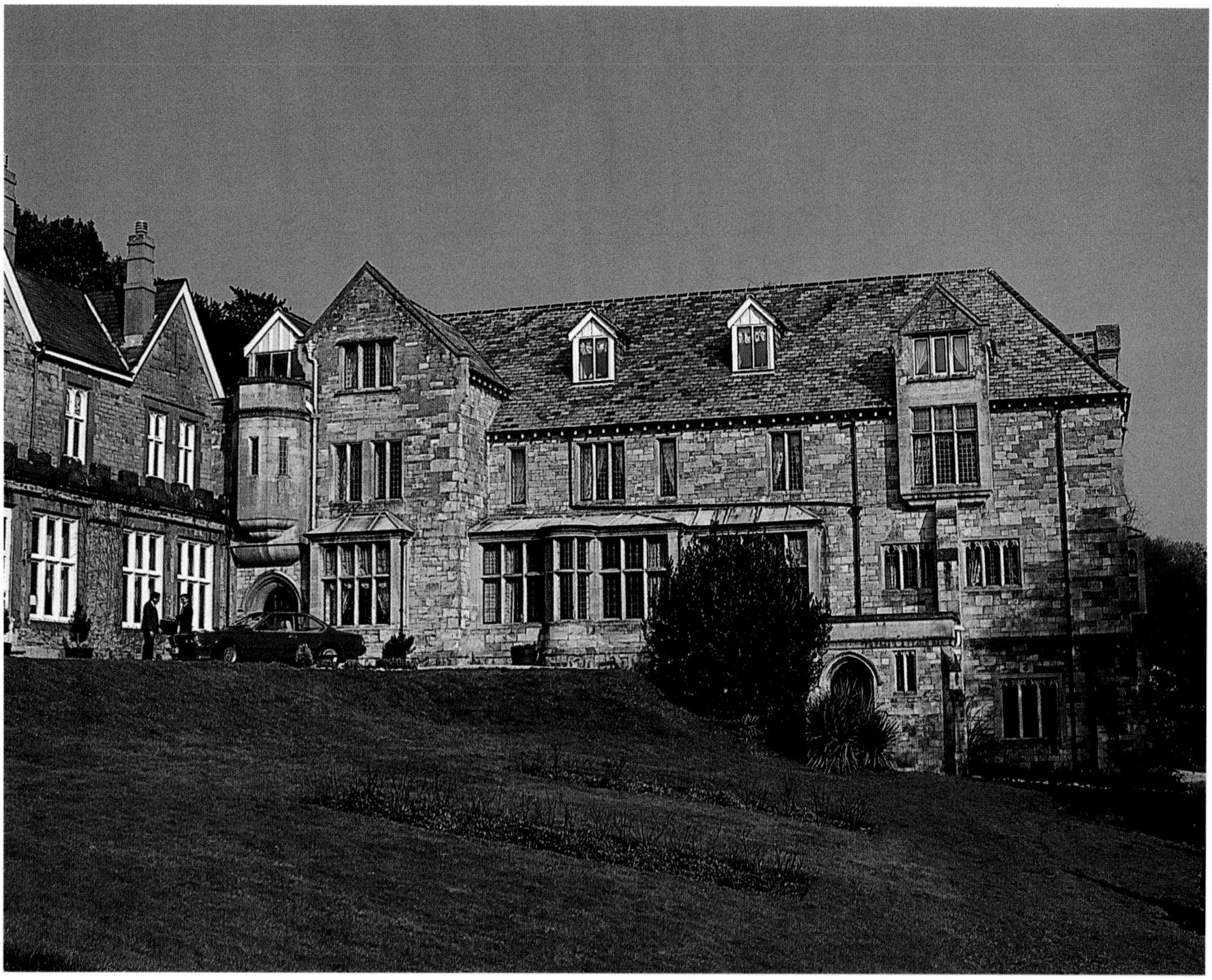

ALVERTON MANOR

TREGOLLS ROAD, TRURO, CORNWALL TR1 1XQ
TEL: 01872 76633 FAX: 01872 222989

Alverton Manor is situated on an eminence in the cathedral city of Truro. It was built over 150 years ago. In recent years it has been beautifully renovated as a modern hotel. It is an impressive sight on its hillside setting with fine period sandstone walls, attractive mullioned windows and original Cornish Delabole slate roof proudly defending its claim to a Grade II listed building of special historical interest. It is outstandingly comfortable in a discreet, elegant way. Each bedroom has been individually designed to provide a special and unique ambience from the intimate to the grand and all are furnished with the amenities visitors expect from a modern, luxury hotel. The spacious dining room is renowned for the excellent modern style English cuisine served and has been recognised by Egon Ronay and awarded two AA Rosettes. Numerous places of interest nearby include Falmouth, the Seal Sanctuary at Gweek, several heritage sites and many magnificent gardens and properties of the National Trust. There are opportunities for playing golf, shooting, riding fishing, gliding, sailing and surfing. Dogs by arrangement. Special weekend breaks available. **Directions:** From St Austell, continue on A390 and the hotel is on the right as you approach the first major roundabout on entering Truro. Price guide: Single £63; double/twin £99-£109; suite £130.

For hotel location, see maps on pages 477-483

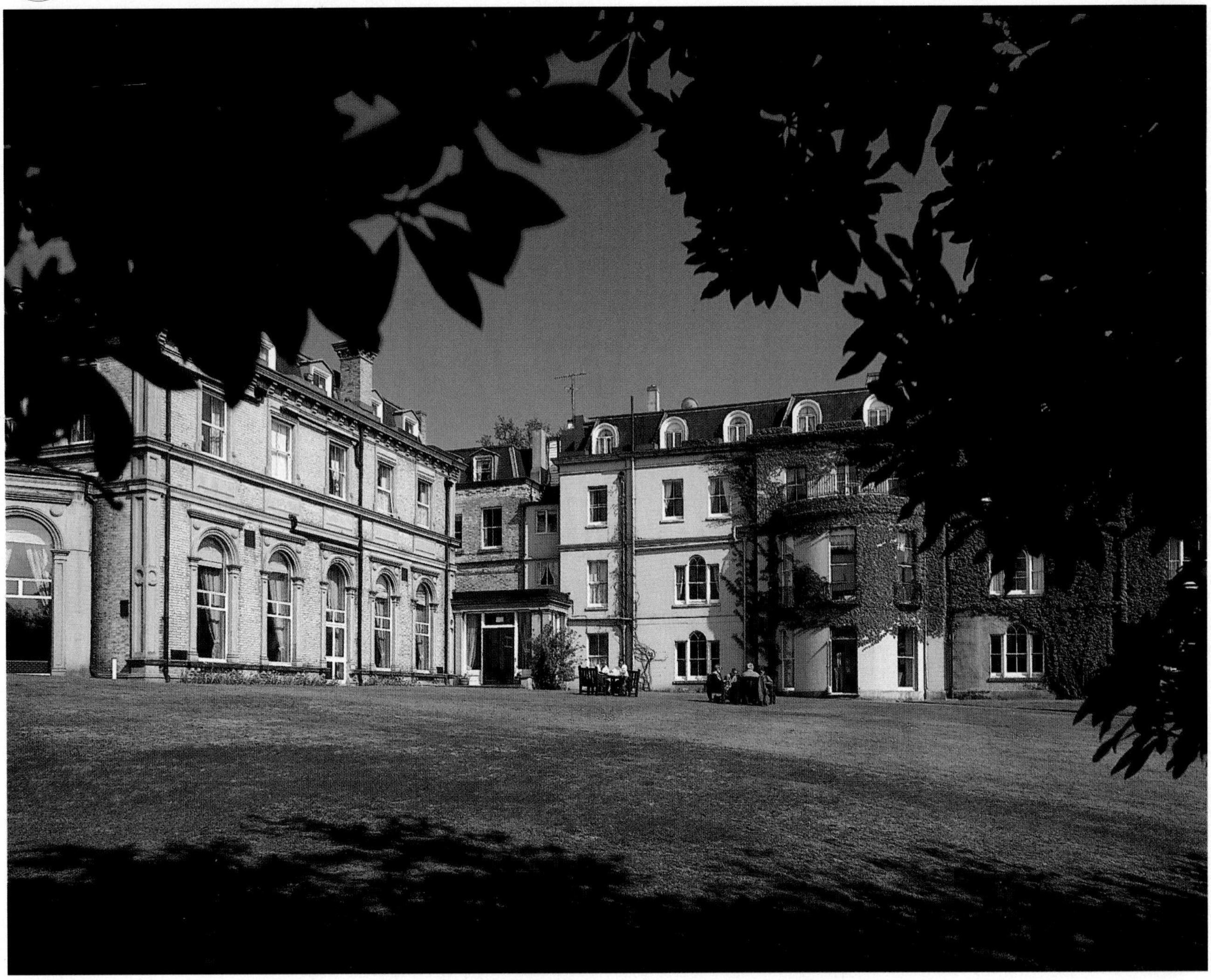

THE SPA HOTEL

MOUNT EPHRAIM, ROYAL TUNBRIDGE WELLS, KENT TN4 8XJ
TEL: 01892 520331 FAX: 01892 510575

The Spa was originally built in 1766 as a country mansion, with its own parkland, landscaped gardens and two beautiful lakes. A hotel for over a century now, it retains standards of service reminiscent of life in Georgian and Regency England. All the bedrooms are individually furnished and many offer spectacular views. Above all else, The Spa Hotel prides itself on the excellence of its cuisine. The grand, Regency-style restaurant features the freshest produce from Kentish farms and London markets, complemented by a carefully selected wine list. Within the hotel is Sparkling Health, a magnificent health and leisure centre which is equipped to the highest standards. Leisure facilities include an indoor heated swimming pool, a fully equipped state-of-the-art gymnasium, cardiovascular gymnasium, aerobics dance studio, steam room, saunas, sunbeds, beauty clinic, hairdressing salon, flood-lit hard tennis court and 1/2 mile jogging track. The hotel is perfectly positioned for exploring of the castles, houses and gardens of Kent and Sussex. Special weekend bargain breaks are offered, with rates from £59.50 per person per night – full details available on request. **Directions:** Facing the common on the A264 in Tunbridge Wells. Price guide (excluding breakfast): Single £69–£74; double/twin £84–£105; suites £95– £130.

For hotel location, see maps on pages 473–479

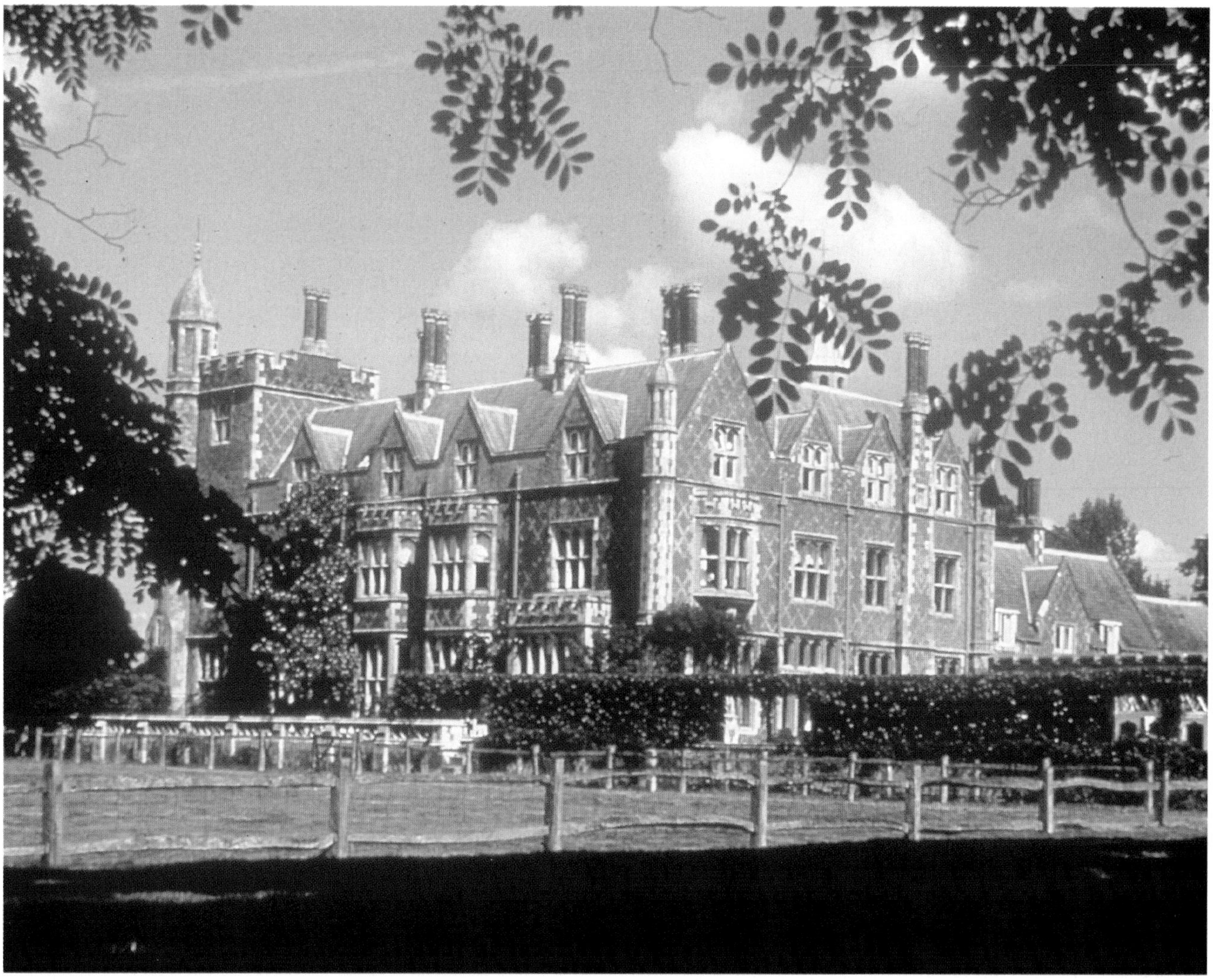

HORSTED PLACE SPORTING ESTATE AND HOTEL

LITTLE HORSTED, NR UCKFIELD, EAST SUSSEX TN22 5TS

TEL: 01825 750581 FAX: 01825 750240

Horsted Place enjoys a splendid location amid the peace of the Sussex Downs. This magnificent Victorian Gothic Mansion, which was built in 1851, overlooks the East Sussex National golf course and boasts an interior predominantly styled by the celebrated Victorian architect, Augustus Pugin. In former years the Queen and Prince Philip were frequent visitors. Guests today are invited to enjoy the unobtrusive but excellent service offered by a committed staff. The bedrooms in this lovely hotel are luxuriously decorated and furnished and offer every modern day comfort. Dining at Horsted is guaranteed to be a memorable experience. Chef Allan Garth offers a number of fixed priced and seasonally changing menus with his eclectic style of cooking. The Horsted Management Centre is a suite of air-conditioned rooms which have been specially designed to accommodate theatre-style presentations and training seminars or top level board meetings. Places of interest nearby include Royal Tunbridge Wells, Lewes and Glyndebourne. For golfing enthusiasts there is the added attraction of the East Sussex National Golf Club, one of the finest golf complexes in the world. **Directions:** The hotel entrance is on the A26 just short of the junction with the A22, two miles south of Uckfield and signposted towards Lewes. Price guide: Double/twin £90; suites from £200.

For hotel location, see maps on pages 477-483

LORDS OF THE MANOR HOTEL

UPPER SLAUGHTER, NR BOURTON-ON-THE-WATER, CHELTENHAM, GLOUCESTERSHIRE GL54 2JD
TEL: 01451 820243 FAX: 01451 820696

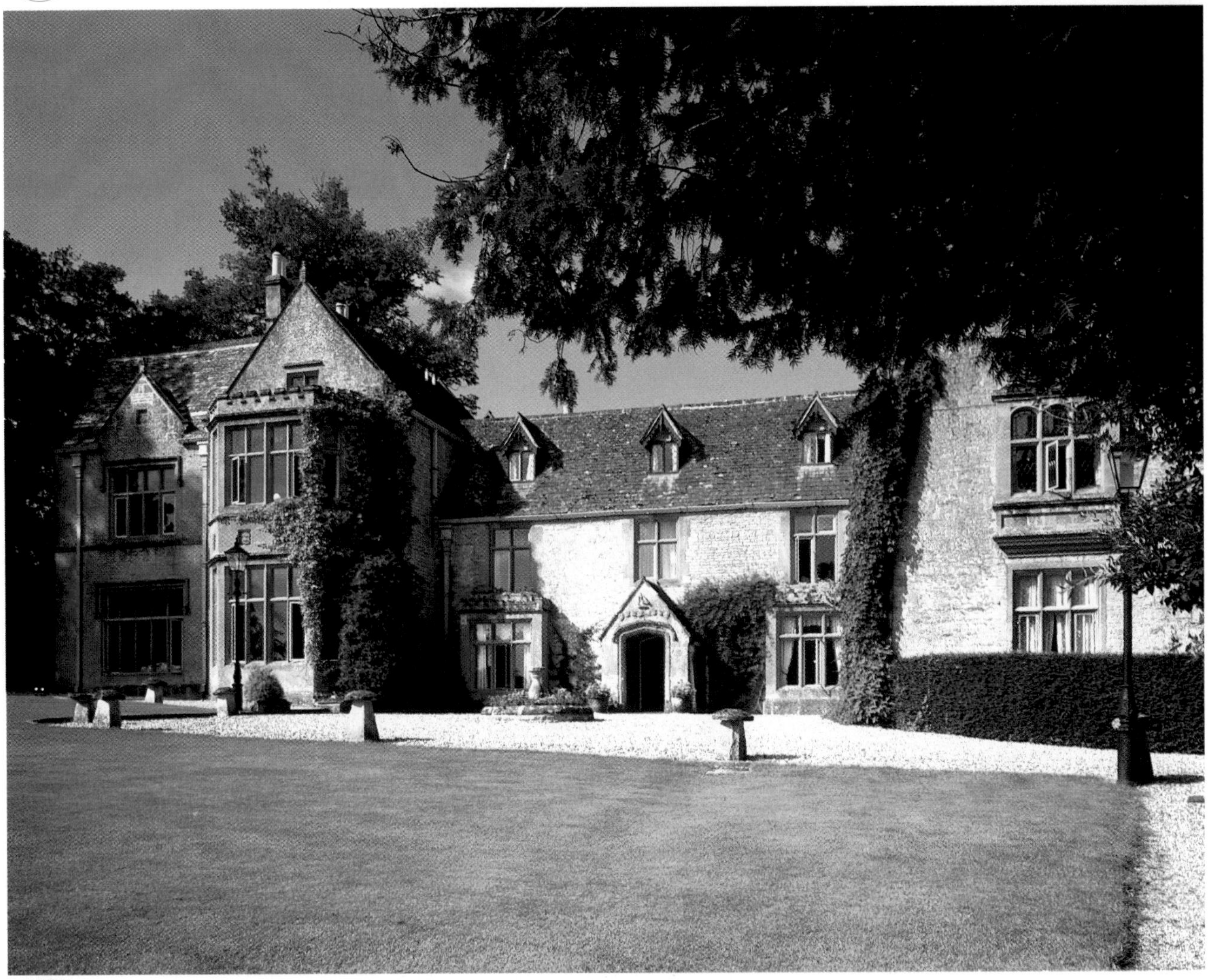

Situated in the heart of the Cotswolds, on the outskirts of one of England's most unspoiled and picturesque villages, stands the Lords of the Manor Hotel. Built in the 17th century of honeyed Cotswold stone, the house enjoys splendid views over the surrounding meadows, stream and parkland. For generations the house was the home of the Witts family, who historically had been rectors of the parish. It is from these origins that the hotel derives its distinctive name. Charming, walled gardens provide a secluded retreat at the rear of the house. Each bedroom bears the maiden name of one of the ladies who married into the Witts family: each room is individually and imaginatively decorated with traditional chintz and period furniture. The reception rooms are magnificently furnished with fine antiques, paintings, traditional fabrics and masses of fresh flowers. Log fires blaze in cold weather. The heart of this English country house is its dining room, where truly memorable dishes are created from the best local ingredients. Nearby are Blenheim Palace, Warwick Castle, the Roman antiquities at Bath and Shakespeare country. **Directions:** Upper Slaughter is 2 miles west of the A429 between Stow-on-the-Wold and Bourton-on-the-Water. Price guide: Single from £90; double/twin £120–£225.

For hotel location, see maps on pages 477-483

THE LAKE ISLE

16 HIGH STREET EAST, UPPINGHAM, RUTLAND, LEICESTERSHIRE LE15 9PZ
TEL: 01572 822951 FAX: 01572 822951

This small personally run restaurant and town house hotel is situated in this pretty market town of Uppingham, dominated by the famous Uppingham School and close to Rutland Water. The entrance to the building, which dates back to the 18th century is via a quiet courtyard where a wonderful display of flowering tubs and hanging baskets greets you. In winter sit in the bar where a log fire burns or relax in the upstairs lounge which overlooks the High Street. In the bedrooms, each named after a wine growing region in France, and all of which are en suite, guests will find fresh fruit, home-made biscuits and a decanter of sherry. Those in the courtyard are cottage-style suites. Under the personal direction of chef-patron David Whitfield the restaurant offers small weekly changing menus using fresh ingredients from far afield. There is an extensive wine list of more than 300 wines ranging from regional labels to old clarets. Special 'Wine Dinners' are held throughout the year, enabling guests to appreciate this unique cellar. Burghley House, Rockingham and Belvoir Castles are within a short drive. **Directions:** Uppingham is near the intersection of A47 and A6003. The hotel is on the High Street and is reached on foot via Reeves Yard and by car via Queen Street. Price guide: Single £45–£50; double/twin £60–£70; suite £70–£80.

12 rms MasterCard VISA AMERICAN EXPRESS M 10

For hotel location, see maps on pages 477-483

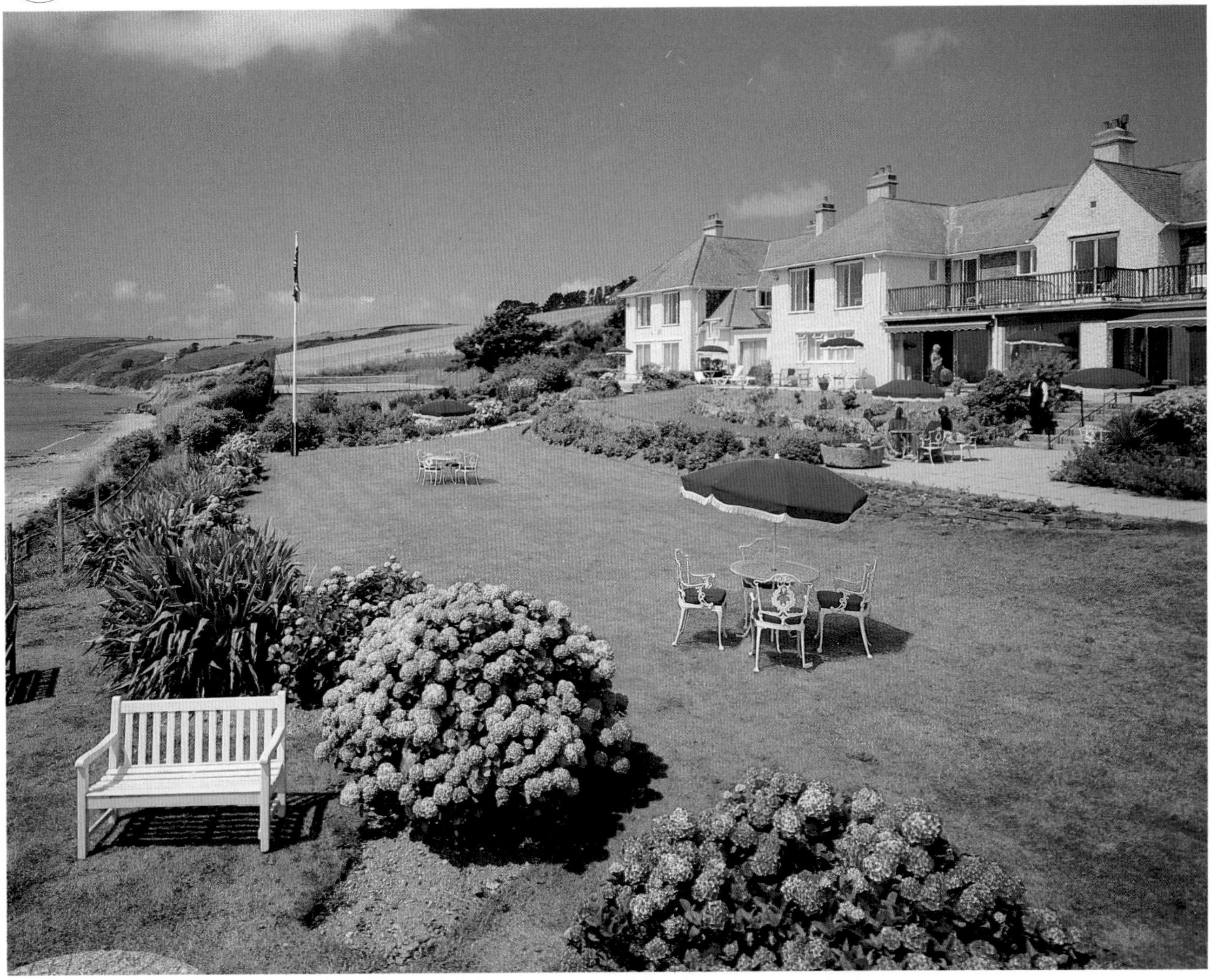

The Nare Hotel

CARNE BEACH, VERYAN-IN-ROSELAND, TRURO TR2 5PF
TEL: 01872 501279 FAX: 01872 501856

The Nare Hotel overlooks the fine sandy beach of Gerrans Bay, facing south, and is sheltered by The Nare and St Mawes headlands. In recent years extensive refurbishments have ensured comfort and elegance without detracting from the country house charm of this friendly hotel. All the bedrooms are within 100 yards of the sea, many with patios or balconies to take advantage of the outlook. While dining in the restaurant, with its colour scheme of soft yellow and green, guests can enjoy the sea views from three sides of the room. Local seafoods such as lobster, and delicious home-made puddings, served with Cornish cream, are specialities, complemented by an interesting range of wines. The Nare is the highest rated AA 4 Star hotel in the South West with a rosette for its food. Surrounded by sub-tropical gardens and National Trust land, the peaceful seclusion of The Nare is ideal for lazing or for exploring the coastline and villages of the glorious Roseland Peninsula where Henry VIII honeymooned with Anne Boleyn and is also central for many of Cornwall's beautiful houses and gardens including the famous Heligan. Guests arriving by train can be met by prior arrangement at Truro. Helipad within the grounds. **Directions:** Follow road to St Mawes; 3 miles after Tregony Bridge turn left for Veryan. The hotel is 1 mile from Veryan. Price guide: Single £53–£124; double/twin £106–£218.

For hotel location, see maps on pages 477-483

THE SPRINGS HOTEL

NORTH STOKE, WALLINGFORD, OXFORDSHIRE OX10 6BE
TEL: 01491 836687 FAX: 01491 836877

The Springs is a grand old country house which dates from 1874 and is set deep in the heart of the beautiful Thames valley. One of the first houses in England to be built in the Mock Tudor style, it stands in six acres of grounds. The hotel's large south windows overlook a spring fed lake from which it takes its name. Many of the luxurious bedrooms and suites offer beautiful views over the lake and lawns, while others overlook the quiet woodland that surrounds the hotel. Private balconies provide patios for summer relaxation. The Lakeside restaurant has an intimate, romantic atmosphere inspired by its gentle décor and the lovely view of the lake. The restaurant's menu is changed regularly to take advantage of fresh local produce and seasonal tastes. A well stocked cellar of carefully selected international wines provides the perfect accompaniment to a splendid meal. Leisure facilities include the swimming pool, a putting green, sauna and touring bicycles. Oxford, Blenheim Palace and Windsor are nearby and the hotel is convenient for sporting events, racing at Newbury and Ascot and the Royal Henley Regatta. Directions: From the M40, take exit 6 onto the B4009, through Watlington to Benson; turn left onto A4074 towards Reading. After 1/2 mile go right onto B4009. The hotel is 1/2 mile further, on the right-hand side. Price guide: Single from £82; double/twin £115–£150; suite from £150.

36 rms · MasterCard · VISA · AMERICAN EXPRESS · M 50

For hotel location, see maps on pages 477-483

HANBURY MANOR

WARE, HERTFORDSHIRE SG12 0SD

TEL: 01920 487722 FAX: 01920 487692

An outstanding hotel, Hanbury Manor combines palatial grandeur with the most up-to-date amenities. Designed in 1890 in a Jacobean style, the many impressive features include elaborately moulded ceilings, carved wood panelling, leaded windows, chandeliers, portraits and huge tapestries. These create an elegant and comfortable environment. The three dining rooms vary in style from the formal Zodiac Restaurant to the informal Vardon Restaurant. All the cuisine is under the inspired guidance of Executive Chef Rory Kennedy. The health club includes an indoor swimming pool, Jacuzzi, fully equipped gymnasium, crèche, sauna and steam baths. Professional treatments include herbal wraps, aromatherapy, mineral baths and massage, while specialists can advise on a personal fitness programme. There is an 18-hole golf course *par excellence* designed by Jack Nicklaus II. Outdoor pursuits include shooting, archery, horse-riding and hot-air ballooning. Ideal for conferences, ten rooms offer versatile business meetings facilities, including fax, photocopying, secretarial services and full professional support. Stansted Airport is 16 miles away. **Directions:** On the A10 25 miles north of London and 32 miles south of Cambridge. Price guide: Single/double/twin from £160; suites £260–£460.

For hotel location, see maps on pages 477-483

THE PRIORY HOTEL

CHURCH GREEN, WAREHAM, DORSET BH20 4ND

TEL: 01929 551666 FAX: 01929 554519

Dating from the early 16th century, the one-time Lady St Mary Priory has for hundreds of years offered sanctuary to travellers. In Hardy's Dorset, 'far from the madding crowd', it placidly stands on the bank of the River Frome in four acres of immaculate gardens. Steeped in history, The Priory has undergone a sympathetic conversion to a hotel which is charming yet unpretentious. Each bedroom is distictively styled, with family antiques lending character and many rooms have views of the Purbeck Hills. A 16th century clay barn has been transformed into the Boathouse, consisting of two spacious luxury suites at the river's edge. Tastefully furnished, the drawing room, residents' lounge and intimate bar together create a convivial atmosphere. The Greenwood Dining Room is open for breakfast and lunch, while splendid dinners are served in the vaulted stone cellars. There are moorings for guests arriving by boat. Dating back to the 9th century, the market town of Wareham has more than 200 listed buildings. Corfe Castle, Lulworth Cove, Poole and Swanage are all close by with superb walks and beaches. **Directions:** Wareham is on the A351 to the west of Bournemouth and Poole. The hotel is beside the River Frome at the southern end of the town near the parish church. Price guide: Single £60–£105; double/twin £85–£195; suite £195.

19 rms MasterCard VISA AMERICAN EXPRESS M 20

For hotel location, see maps on pages 477-483

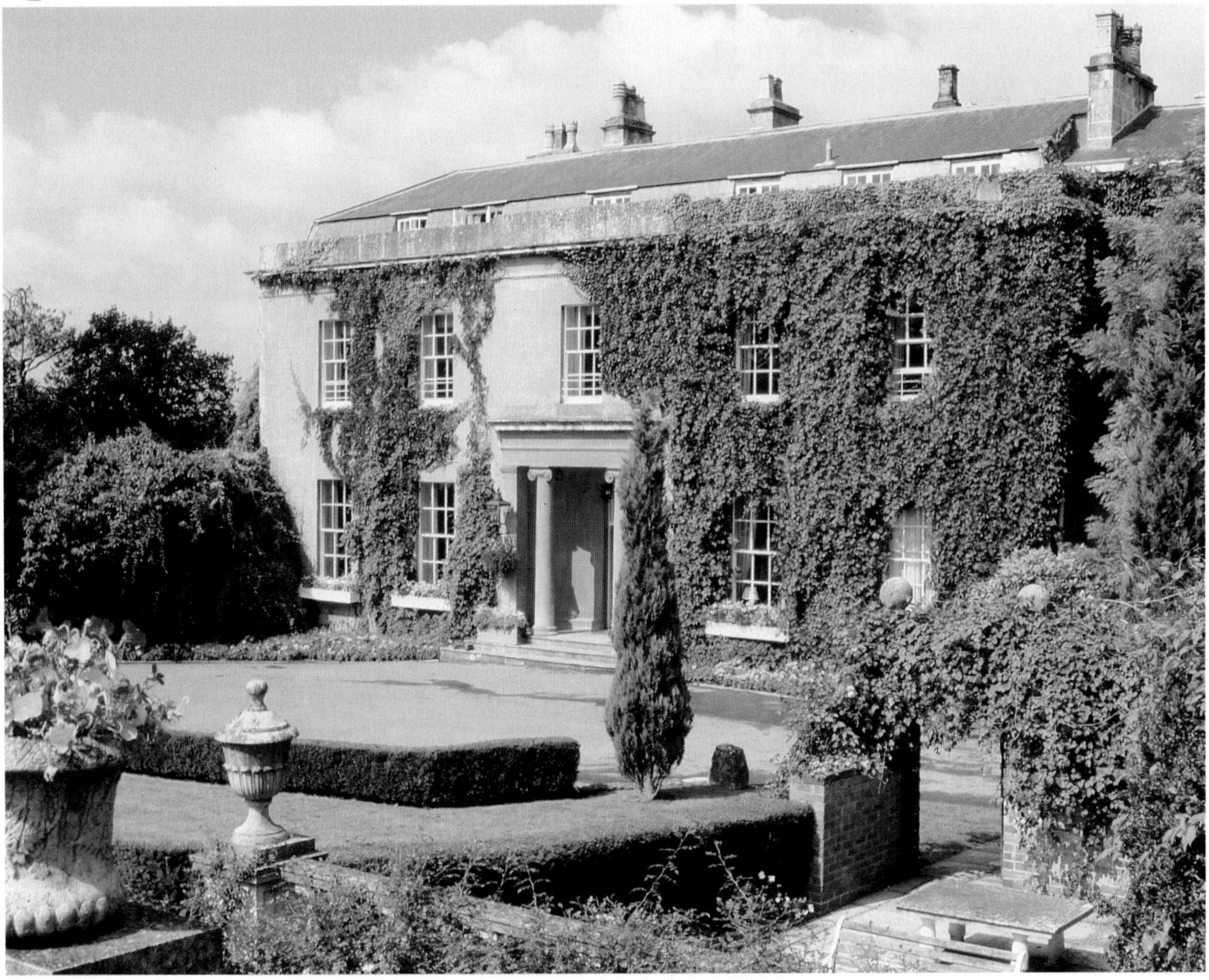

Bishopstrow House

WARMINSTER, WILTSHIRE BA12 9HH
TEL: 01985 212312 FAX: 01985 216769

Bishopstrow House is the quintessential Georgian mansion. It combines, the intimacy of a grand country hotel retreat with all the benefits of modern facilities and the luxury of the new Ragdale spa, offering a superb range of beauty, fitness and relaxation therapies in addition to Michaeljohn's world class hair styling. A Grade II listed building, Bishopstrow House was built in 1817 and has been sympathetically extended to include indoor and outdoor heated swimming pools, a high-tech gymnasium and a sauna. The attention to detail is uppermost in the Library, Drawing Room and Conservatory with their beautiful antiques and Victorian oil paintings. Grandly furnished furnished bedrooms are festooned with fresh orchids and some have opulent marble bathrooms and whirlpool baths. Two restaurants serve skilfully prepared modern British food, with lighter meals available in the Mulberry Bar and the Conservatory which overlooks 27 acres of gardens. There is fly–fishing on the hotel's private stretch of the River Wylye, golf at four nearby courses, riding, game and clay-pigeon shooting. Longleat House, Wilton House, Stourhead, Stonehenge, Bath, Salisbury and Warminster are within easy reach. **Directions:** Bishopstrow House is south–east of Warminster on the B3414 from London via the M3. Price guide: Single from £75; double/twin from £110–£215.

For hotel location, see maps on pages 477-483

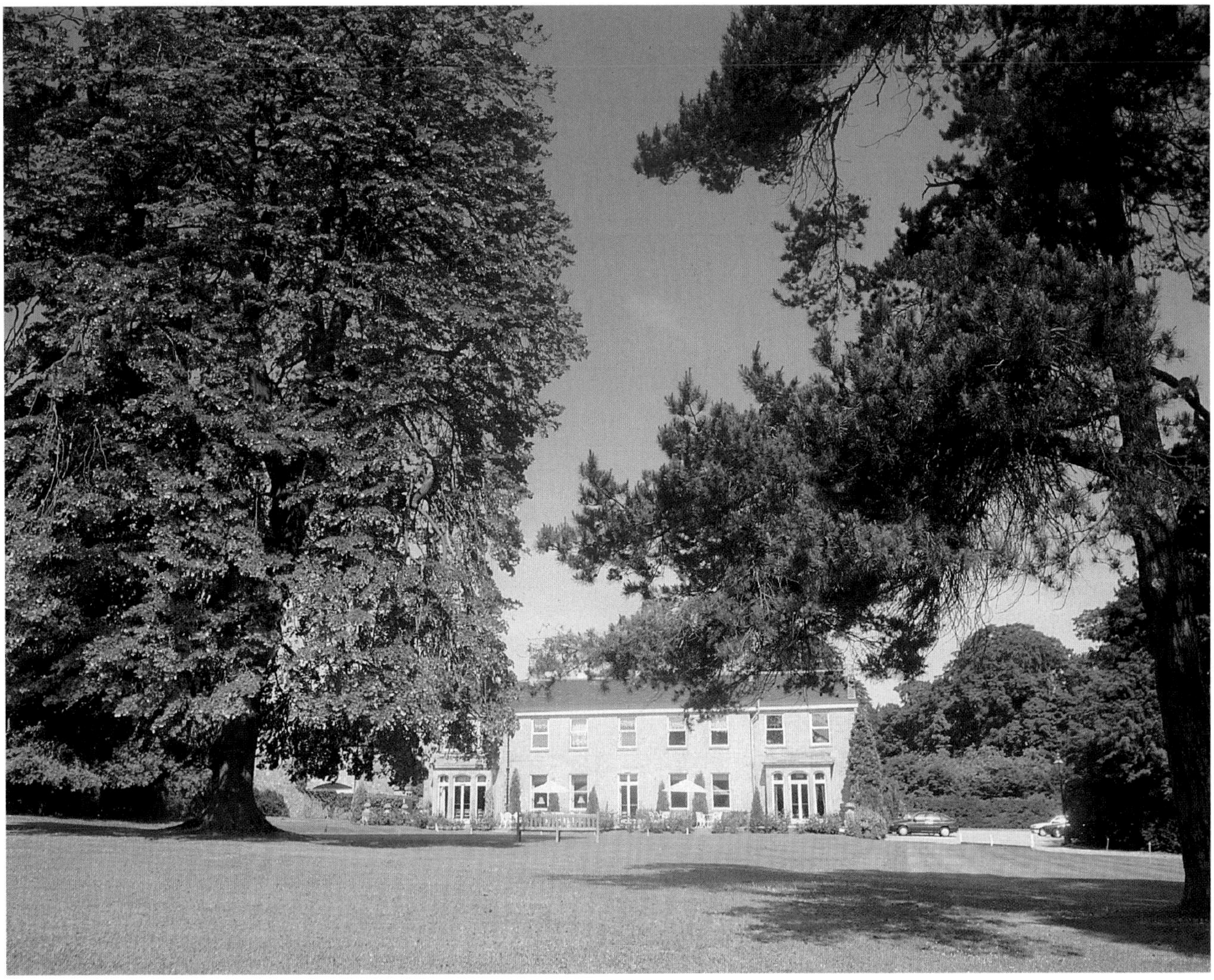

LINTON SPRINGS

SICKLINGHALL ROAD, WETHERBY, WEST YORKSHIRE LS22 4AF
TEL: 01937 585353 FAX: 01937 587579

Set in 14 acres of beautiful parkland, Linton Springs is an elegant country house hotel which successfully combines the grace of an English period mansion with modern day comforts. The house was built in the late 1700s as a shooting lodge for the nearby Harewood Estate. It has undergone extensive restoration work in recent times and boasts tasteful décor and furnishings throughout. The attractive and spacious bedrooms all feature oak panelling and are equipped with every modern amenity to ensure the highest level of comfort and convenience. Meals are served in the Gun Room Restaurant and excellent traditional English cuisine is complemented by a fine wine list. The menu features "special" dishes which are changed daily. The Linton Suite is an ideal setting for special occasions, while The Terrace Room and Boardroom provide privacy for business meetings and private dining. For sporting guests, there is a 250 yard golf driving range and all weather tennis court within the grounds. There are also eight golf courses within a 20 minute drive. Nearby attractions include Leeds, York with its famous minster and the spa town of Harrogate. **Directions:** From A1 go through Wetherby towards Harrogate on the A661. After quarter of a mile turn left to Sicklinghall and the hotel is one mile on the left. Price guide: Single: £65; double/twin £85; suites £105.

For hotel location, see maps on pages 477-483

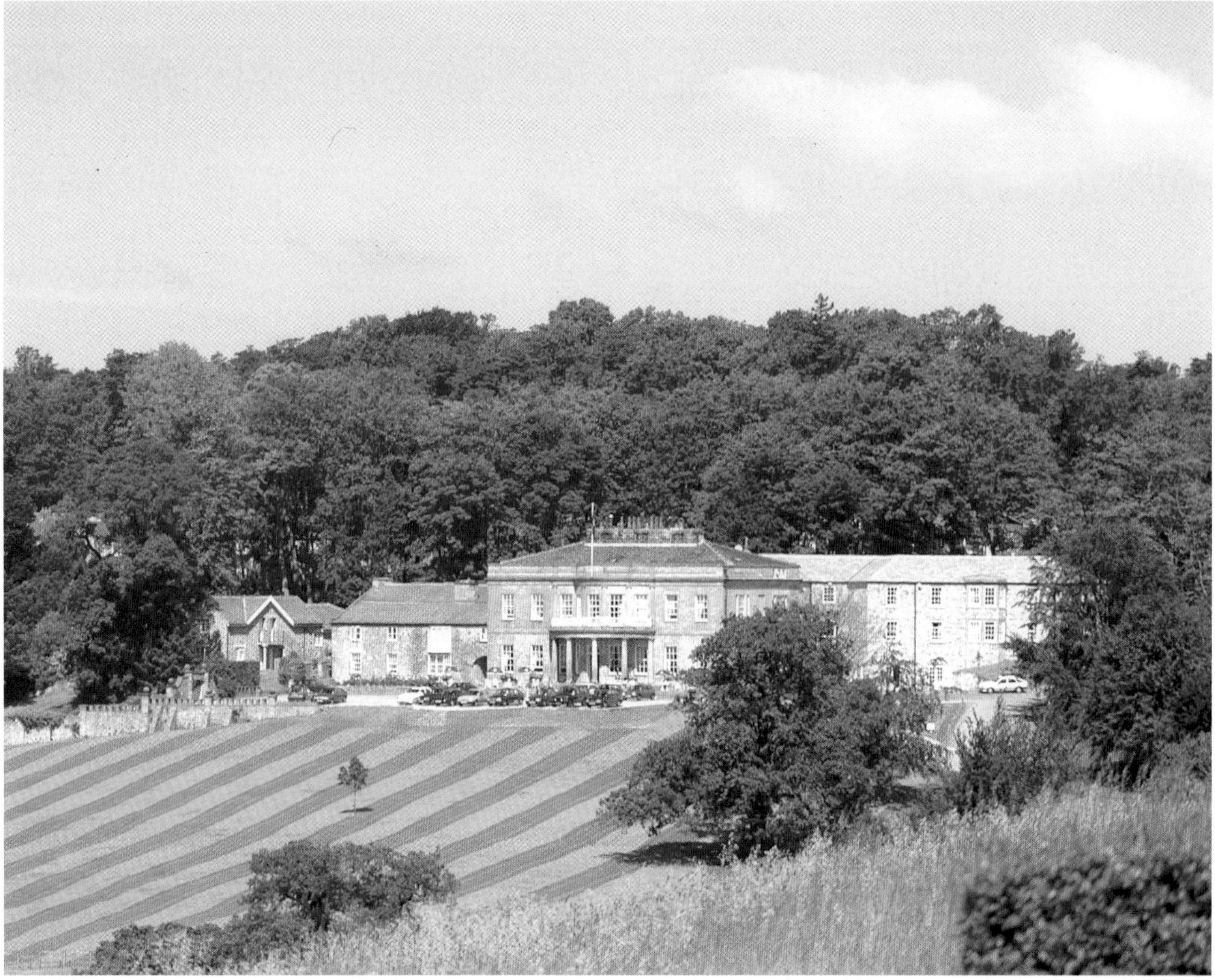

WOOD HALL

TRIP LANE, LINTON, NR WETHERBY, WEST YORKSHIRE LS22 4JA
TEL: 01937 587271 FAX: 01937 584353

Off the A1 about 15 miles due west of York, built of stone from the estate, Wood Hall is an elegant Georgian house overlooking the River Wharfe. Its grounds, over 100 acres in all, are approached along a private drive that winds through a sweep of parkland. The sumptuously furnished drawing room and the oak-panelled bar, with its gentlemen's club atmosphere, lead off the grand entrance hall. Superb floral displays, gleaming chandeliers and immaculately designed interiors hint at the careful attention that has been lavished on Wood Hall. Gastronomes will relish the excellent à la carte menu, which combines contemporary Anglo-French style with attractive presentation. The mile-long private stretch of the Wharfe offers up trout and barbel to the keen angler, while miles of walks and jogging paths encompass the estate. There is a leisure club including a swimming pool, spa bath, steam room, gymnasium, solarium and treatment salon. Near to the National Hunt Race-course at Wetherby, York, Harrogate, Leeds, the Dales and Harewood House are only a short distance away. **Directions:** From Wetherby, take the A661 towards Harrogate. Take turning for Sicklinghall and Linton, then left for Linton and Wood Hall. Turn right opposite the Windmill public house; hotel is 1½ miles further on. Price guide: Single £99–£145; double/twin £109–£155; suite £280.

For hotel location, see maps on pages 477-483

OATLANDS PARK HOTEL

146 OATLANDS DRIVE, WEYBRIDGE, SURREY KT13 9HB
TEL: 01932 847242 FAX: 01932 842252

Records of the Oatlands estate show that Elizabeth I and the Stuart kings spent time in residence in the original buildings. The present mansion dates from the late-18th century and became a hotel in 1856: famous guests included Émile Zola, Anthony Trollope and Edward Lear. The hotel stands in acres of parkland overlooking Broadwater Lake, with easy access to Heathrow, Gatwick and central London. Although it caters for the modern traveller, the hotel's historic character is evident throughout. The accommodation ranges from superior rooms to large de luxe rooms and suites. The elegant, high-ceilinged Broadwater Restaurant is the setting for creative à la carte menus with dishes to suit all tastes. A traditional roast is served every Sunday lunchtime. The professional conference team, six meeting rooms and up-to-date facilities make Oatlands Park a popular function venue. Theme evenings, such as Henry VIII banquets, are a speciality. Many sporting and leisure activities can be arranged, including golf, archery and shooting. There is a new fitness room. **Directions:** From M25 junction 11, follow signs to Weybridge. Follow A317 through High Street into Monument Hill to mini-roundabout. Turn left into Oatlands Drive; hotel is 50 yards on left. Price guide: Single £100–£110; double/twin £130–£145; suite £120–£150. Special Break rate: Single £47.50; double/twin £75–£85.

123 rms MasterCard VISA AMERICAN EXPRESS M 200

For hotel location, see maps on pages 477-483

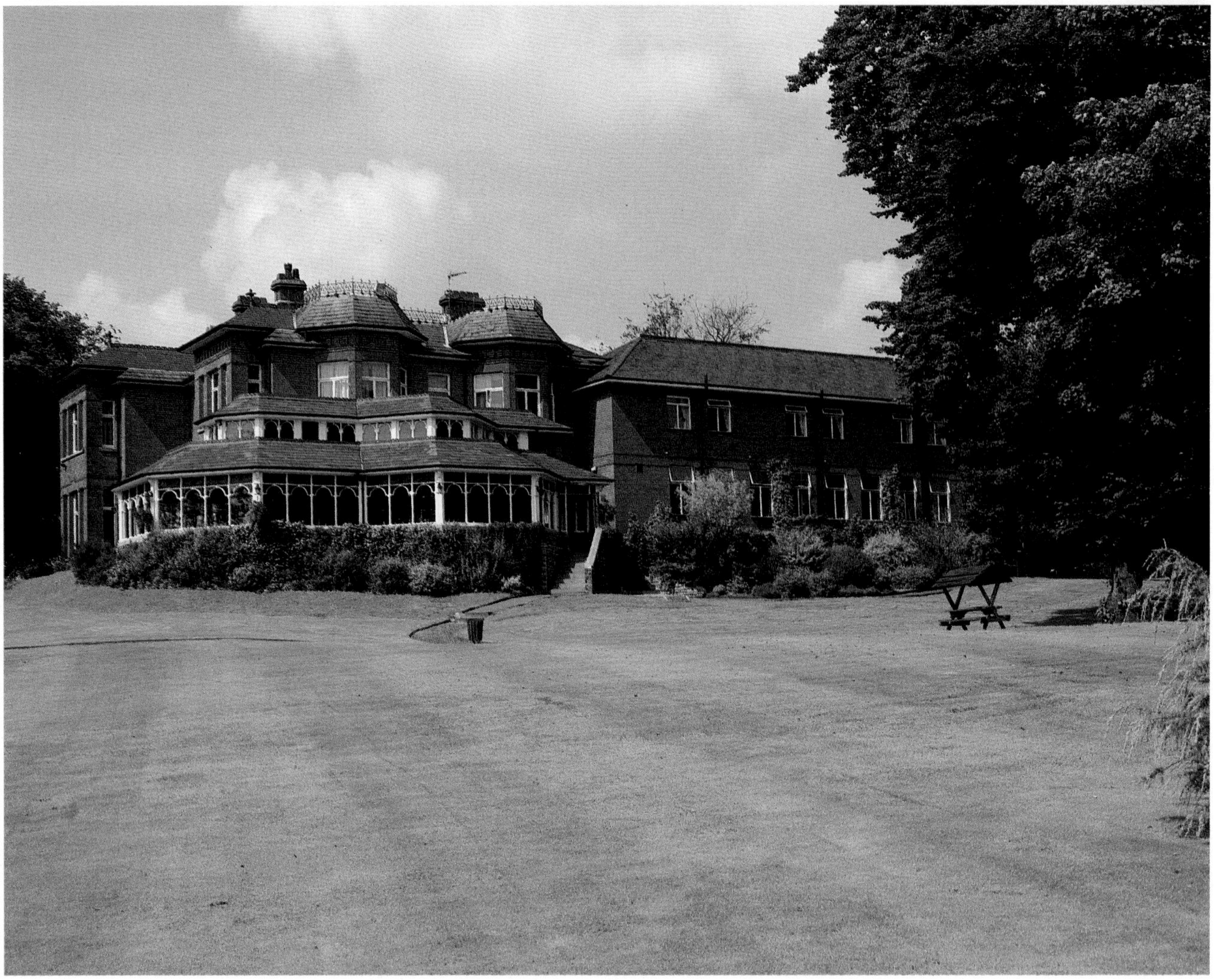

KILHEY COURT

CHORLEY ROAD, STANDISH, WIGAN, LANCASHIRE WN1 2XN
TEL: 01257 472100 FAX: 01257 422401

Kilhey Court, a Virgin Hotel, has a wealth of Victorian features and offers a delightful environment for guests seeking high standards of comfort. The bedrooms provide a full range of facilities, while four luxurious suites complete with spa bath have been recently elegantly refurbished. The Laureate Restaurant, with its idyllic garden room setting and splendid Victorian conservatory, overlooks ten acres of carefully tended lawns and the picturesque Worthington lakes. It has been awarded two coveted Red Rosettes by the AA and its imaginative culinary dishes are carefully prepared using only the finest ingredients. An alternative dining experience is offered in the new Italian Pizza Oven Bistro. Guests seeking either a strenuous workout or some relaxation are invited to take advantage of the leisure centre, which offers guests a range of facilities including air-conditioned aerobics studio, high tech gym, indoor swimming pool, sauna, steam room and solarium. The impressive conference and seminar facilities at Kilhey Court are backed by a full range of support and technical services. The hotel owns the 18-hole Standish Court Golf Course which is just half a mile away. **Directions:** M6 exit 27 go into Standish, through traffic lights to T-junction, turn left and hotel is half a mile on right. Price guide: Single £80–£115; double/twin £95–£120; suites £110–£130.

For hotel location, see maps on pages 477-483

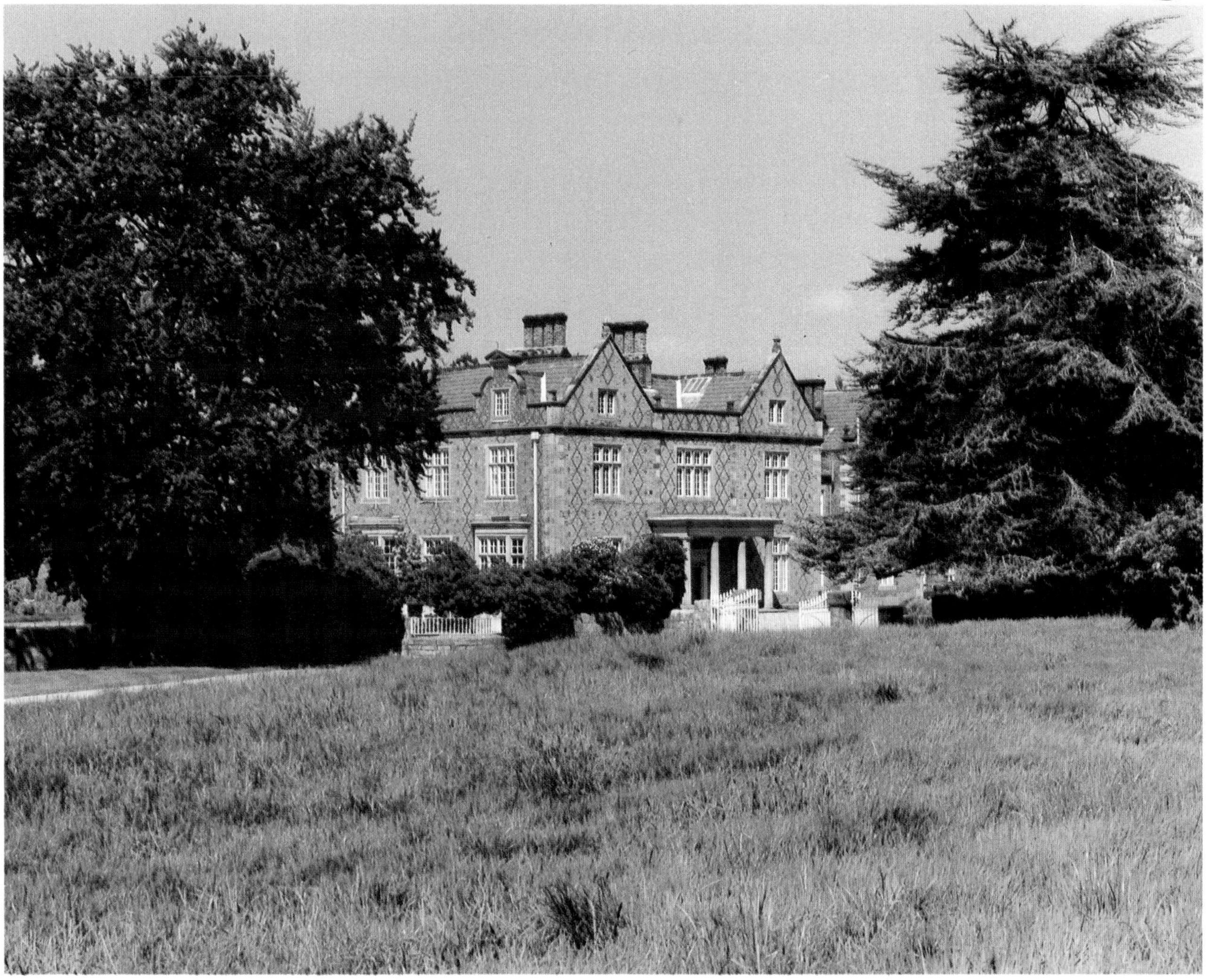

Willington Hall Hotel

WILLINGTON, NEAR TARPORLEY, CHESHIRE CW6 0NB
TEL: 01829 752321 FAX: 01829 752596

Built by Cheshire landowner Charles Tomkinson, Willington Hall was converted into a hotel by one of his descendants in 1977. Set in 17 acres of woods and parkland, the hotel affords wonderful views across the Cheshire countryside towards the Welsh mountains. There are both formally landscaped and 'wild' gardens, which create a beautiful backdrop for the handsome architectural proportions of the house. The hotel is a comfortable and friendly retreat for those seeking peace and seclusion. Under the personal supervision of Ross Pigot, Willington Hall has acquired a good reputation with local people for its extensive bar meals and à la carte restaurant, along with friendly and attentive service. The menus offer traditional English cooking, with dishes such as roast duckling with black cherry sauce. It is an ideal location for visiting the Roman city of Chester, Tatton Park, Beeston Castle and Oulton Park racetrack. North Wales is easily accessible from Willington Hall. The hotel is closed on Christmas Day. **Directions:** Take the A51 from Tarporley to Chester and turn right at the Bull's Head public house at Clotton. Willington Hall Hotel is one mile ahead on the left. Price guide: Single £44–£54; double/twin £80.

THE STANNEYLANDS HOTEL

STANNEYLANDS ROAD, WILMSLOW, CHESHIRE SK9 4EY
TEL: 01625 525225 FAX: 01625 537282

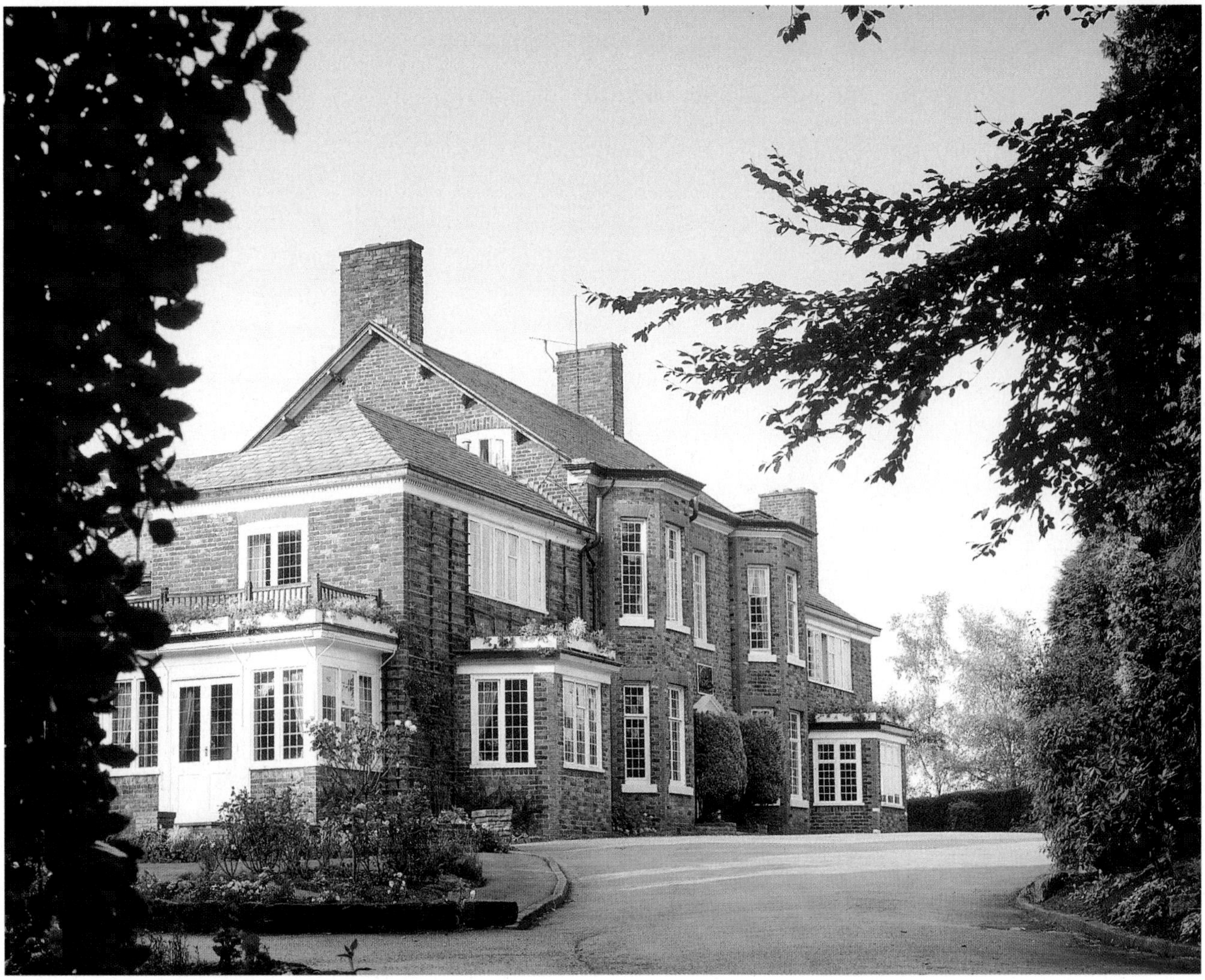

Privately owned and managed by Gordon Beech, Stanneylands is a handsome country house set in several acres of impressive gardens with an unusual collection of trees and shrubs. Some of the bedrooms offer lovely views over the gardens while others overlook the undulating Cheshire countryside. A sense of quiet luxury prevails in the reception rooms, where classical décor and comfortable furnishings create a relaxing ambience. In the restaurant, contemporary English cooking is prepared to a very high standard both in terms of composition and presentation, while live occasional music adds to the atmosphere. For meetings and parties, a private oak-panelled dining room can accommodate up to 50 people, while a larger suite is available for conferences and larger personal celebrations. The Stanneylands Hotel is conveniently located for tours of the rolling Cheshire plain or the more rugged Peak District, as well as the bustling market towns and notable industrial heritage of the area. Special corporate and weekend rates are available. **Directions:** Three miles from Manchester International Airport, Stanneylands is on a minor road which runs from the B5166 at Styal to the B5358 between Wilmslow and Handforth. Bear right on this road to find the hotel just after crossing the River Dean. Price guide: Single £89; double/twin £90–£125; suite £125.

For hotel location, see maps on pages 477-483

HOTEL DU VIN & BISTRO

SOUTHGATE STREET, WINCHESTER, HAMPSHIRE SO23 9EF
TEL: 01962 841414 FAX: 01962 842458

Relaxed, charming and unpretentious are words which aptly describe the stylish and intimate Hotel du Vin & Bistro. This elegant hotel is housed in one of Winchester's most important Georgian buildings, dating back to 1715. It is jointly run by Gerard Basset, perhaps the UK's most famous sommelier, and Robin Hutson, whose career includes time with some of the country's finest hotels. The 19 individually decorated bedrooms feature superb beds made up with crisp, Egyptian cotton and offer every modern amenity, including telephone, trouser press, mini bar and tea and coffee making facilities. Each bedroom is sponsored by a wine house whose vineyard features in its decorations. Bathrooms boasting power showers, oversized baths and fluffy towels add to guests' sense of luxury and comfort. Quality food cooked simply with fresh local ingredients is the philosophy behind the Bistro, where an excellent and reasonably priced wine list is available. There is also a conference room available for special occasions. A welcoming and enthusiastic staff cater for every need. The hotel is a perfect base for exploring England's ancient capital, famous for its Cathedral and antique shops. The New Forest is a short drive away. **Directions:** M3 to Winchester. Southgate Street leads from the City centre to St. Cross. Price guide: Single/double/twin: £75–£105.

19 rms 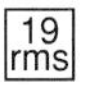      30  

For hotel location, see maps on pages 477-483

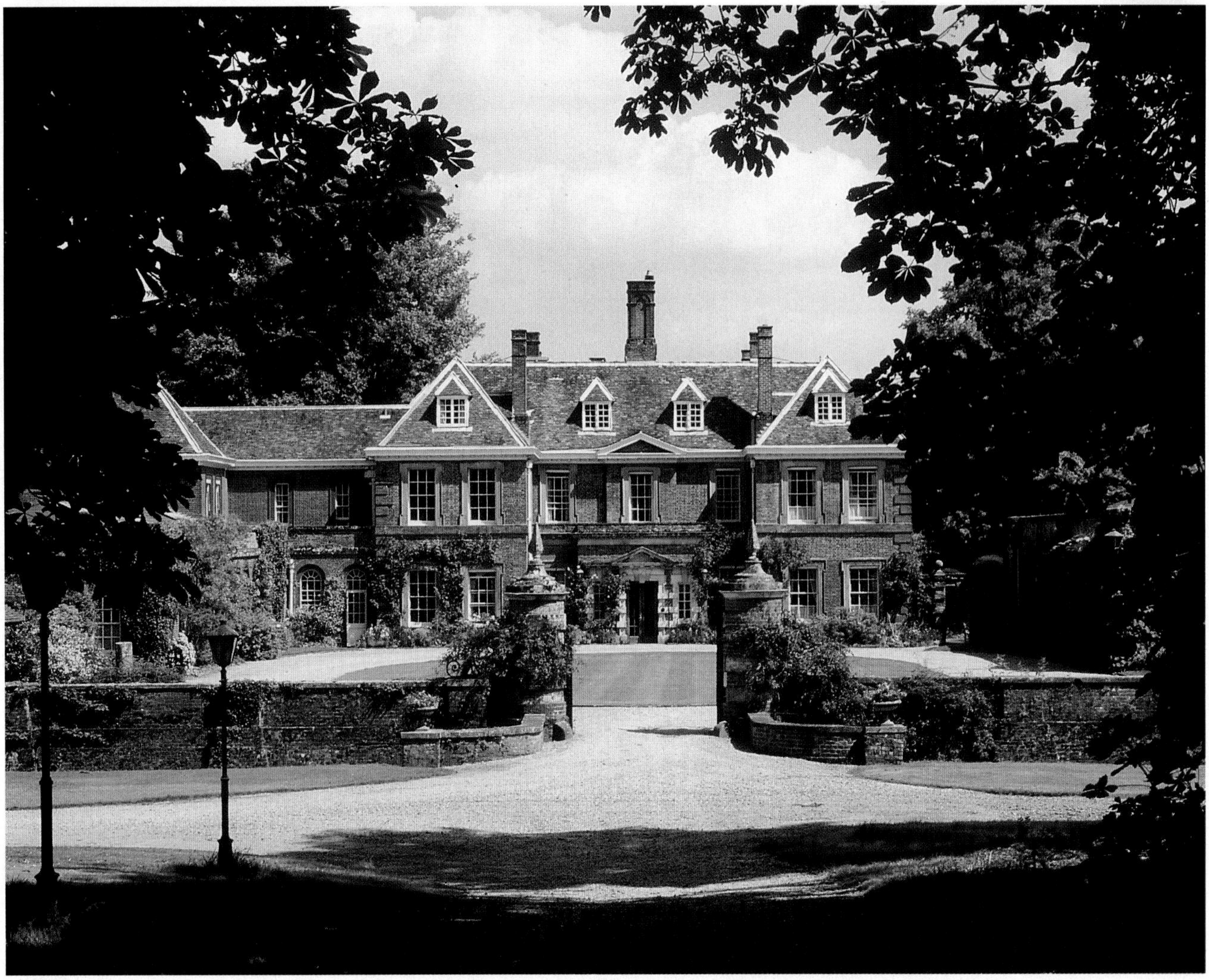

LAINSTON HOUSE HOTEL

SPARSHOLT, WINCHESTER, HAMPSHIRE SO21 2LT
TEL: 01962 863588 FAX: 01962 776672

The fascinating history of Lainston House is well documented, some of its land having been recorded in the *Domesday Book* of 1087. Set in 63 acres of superb downland countryside, this graceful William and Mary country house has been sympathetically restored to create a beautiful hotel. From the individually designed bedrooms to the main reception rooms, elegant and comfortable furnishings are the hallmark of Lainston House. Freshly prepared food, attentive service and views over the lawn make the restaurant one of the most popular in Hampshire. Facilities are available for small meetings in the Mountbatten Room or larger functions in the recently converted 17th century Dawley Barn. The charming grounds hold many surprises – an ancient chapel, reputedly haunted by the legendary Elizabeth Chudleigh, an 18th century herb garden and a dovecote. Historic Winchester is only 2½ miles south, while Romsey Abbey, Salisbury and the New Forest are a short drive away. Other local activities include riding, country walking and good trout fishing on the River Test at nearby Stockbridge. **Directions:** Lainston House is well signposted off the B3049 Winchester–Stockbridge road, at Sparsholt 2½ miles from Winchester. Price guide: Single from £95; double/twin £125–£225; suite from £245.

For hotel location, see maps on pages 477-483

Gilpin Lodge

CROOK ROAD, NR WINDERMERE, CUMBRIA LA23 3NE
TEL: 015394 88818 FREEPHONE: 0800 269460 FAX: 015394 88058

Set in 20 acres of woodlands, moors and country gardens, surrounded by lakeland fells, Gilpin Lodge exudes tranquillity. Yet, only 12 miles from the M6 and two miles from Lake Winderemere, the area provides scope for a profusion of activities and sightseeing: walking and climbing, water sports, fishing, riding, golf (the golf course is almost opposite), historic houses, gardens and castles, and memorabilia of Beatrix Potter, Wordsworth and Ruskin. Guests have free use of a nearby private leisure club. This elegant yet relaxing hotel, a turn of the century Victorian house tastefully extended 90 years later, and modernised to incorporate every comfort, is replete with antiques, flowers, picture lined walls, real fires in winter, comfortable lounges, sumptuous en suite bedrooms (some with four-poster beds and all with sitting areas), and the warmest of welcomes from proprietors Christine and John Cunliffe. Service is attentive but unpretentious. The food, awarded two rosettes by the AA, is a pleasant obsession. Dinner menus offer a wide choice of imaginative dishes. There is an extensive and varied wine list. Gilpin Lodge is graded 4 Crowns De Luxe, AA 81% and is highly acclaimed in most guides. Open throughout the year. 3 night break rates available. **Directions:** M6 exit 36. A591 Kendal bypass then B5284 to Crook. Price guide: Single £65–£85; double/twin £80–£140. Dinner inclusive rates available.

For hotel location, see maps on pages 477-483

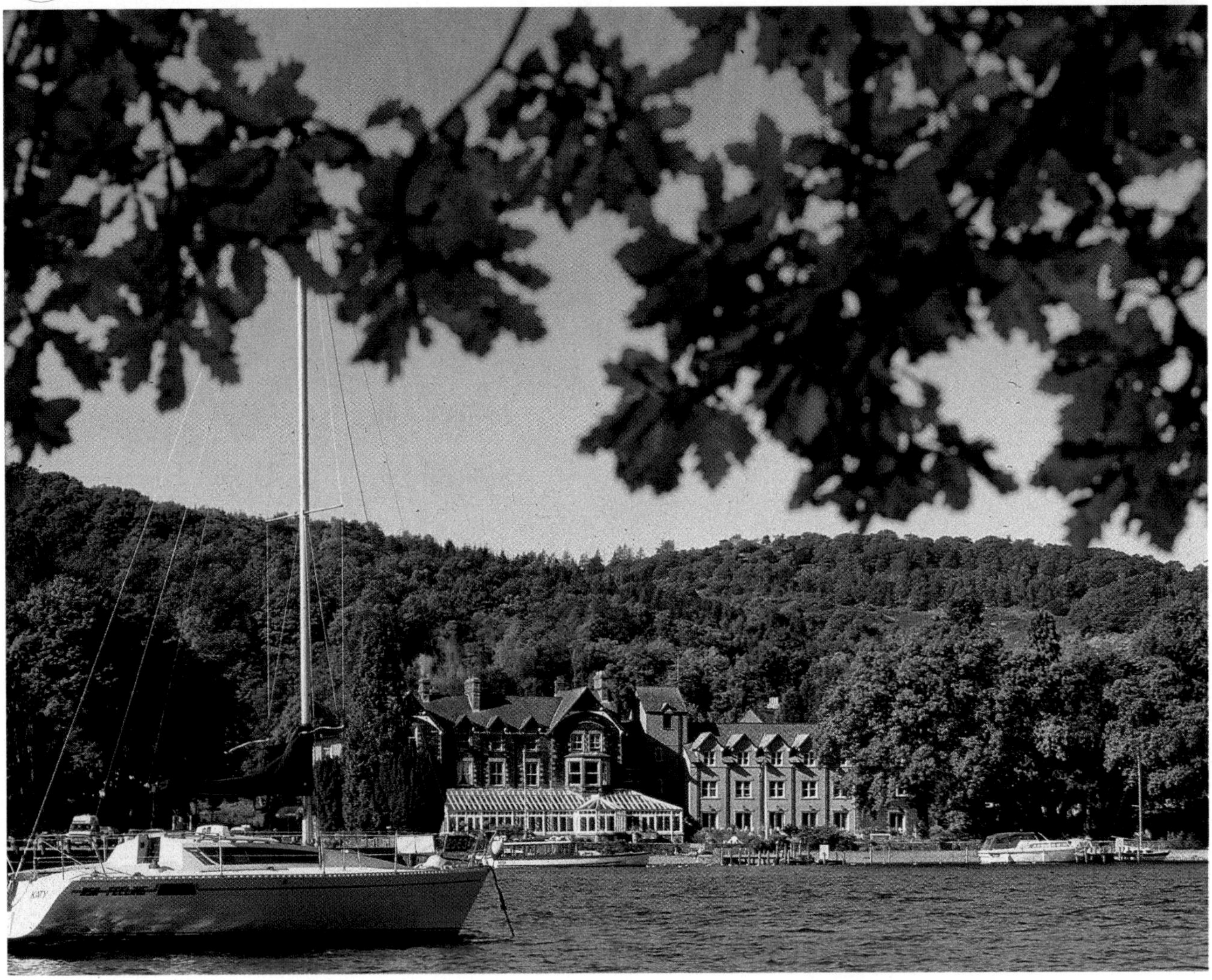

LAKESIDE HOTEL ON LAKE WINDERMERE

LAKESIDE, NEWBY BRIDGE, CUMBRIA LA12 8AT
TEL: 015395 31207 FAX: 015395 31699

Lakeside Hotel offers you a unique location on the water's edge of Lake Windermere. It is a classic, traditional lakeland hotel offering four star facilities and service. All the bedrooms are en suite and enjoy individually designed fabrics and colours, many of the rooms offer superlative views of the lake. Guests may dine in either the award-winning Lakeview Restaurant or Ruskin's Brasserie, where extensive menus offer a wide selection of dishes including Cumbrian specialities. The Lakeside Conservatory serves drinks and light meals throughout the day – once there you are sure to fall under the spell of this peaceful location. Berthed next to the hotel you have cruisers which will enable you to explore the lake from the water and there is also a water ski school. Guests are given free use of the Cascades Leisure Club at Newby Bridge. The hotel offers a fully equipped conference centre and many syndicate suites allowing plenty of scope and flexibility. Most of all you are assured of a stay in an unrivalled setting of genuine character. The original panelling and beams of the old coaching inn create an excellent ambience, whilst you are certain to enjoy the quality and friendly service. **Directions:** From M6 junction 36 join A590 to Newby Bridge, turn right over bridge towards Hawkshead; hotel is one mile on right. Price guide: Single £55–£105; double/twin £120–£145; suites £150–£170.

72 rms

For hotel location, see maps on pages 477-483

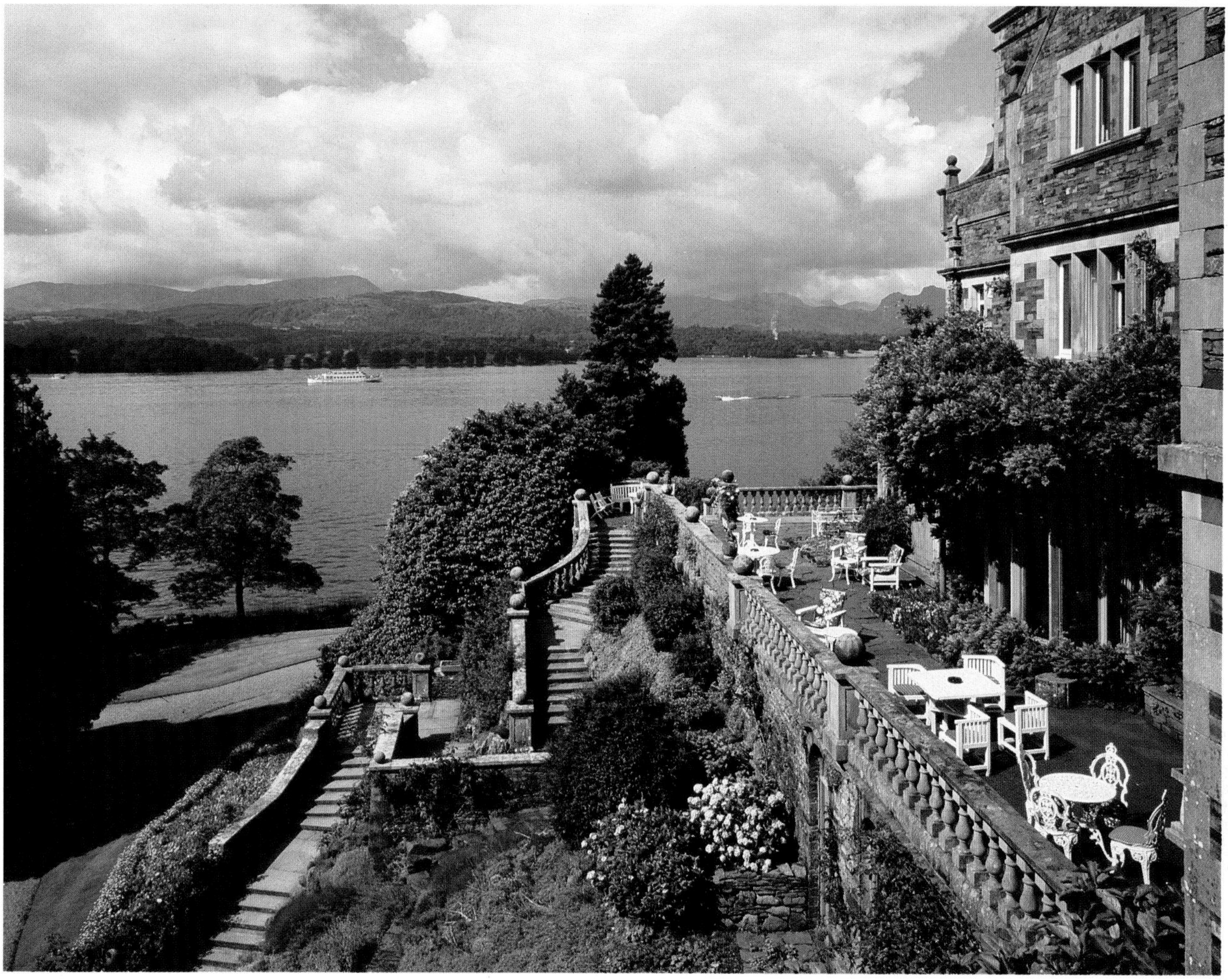

LANGDALE CHASE

WINDERMERE, CUMBRIA LA23 1LW
TEL: 015394 32201 FAX: 015394 32604

Langdale Chase stands in five acres of landscaped gardens on the shores of Lake Windermere, with panoramic views over England's largest lake to the Langdale Pikes beyond. Visitors will receive warm-hearted hospitality in this well-run country home, which is splendidly decorated with oak panelling, fine oil paintings and ornate, carved fireplaces. A magnificent staircase leads to the well-appointed bedrooms, many overlooking the lake. One unique bedroom is sited over the lakeside boathouse, where the traveller may be lulled to sleep by the gently lapping waters below. For the energetic, there is a choice of water-skiing, swimming or sailing from the hotel jetty. Guests can stroll through the gardens along the lake shore, in May the gardens are spectacular when the rhododendrons and azalias are in bloom. Being pampered by attentive staff will be one of the many highlights of your stay at Langdale Chase. The variety of food and wine is sure to delight the most discerning diner. Combine this with a panoramic tableau across England's largest and loveliest of lakes and you have a truly unforgettable dining experience. **Directions:** Situated on the A591, three miles north of Windermere, two miles south of Ambleside. Price guide: Single from £40–£72; double/twin from £75–£110; suite £116–£150.

For hotel location, see maps on pages 477-483

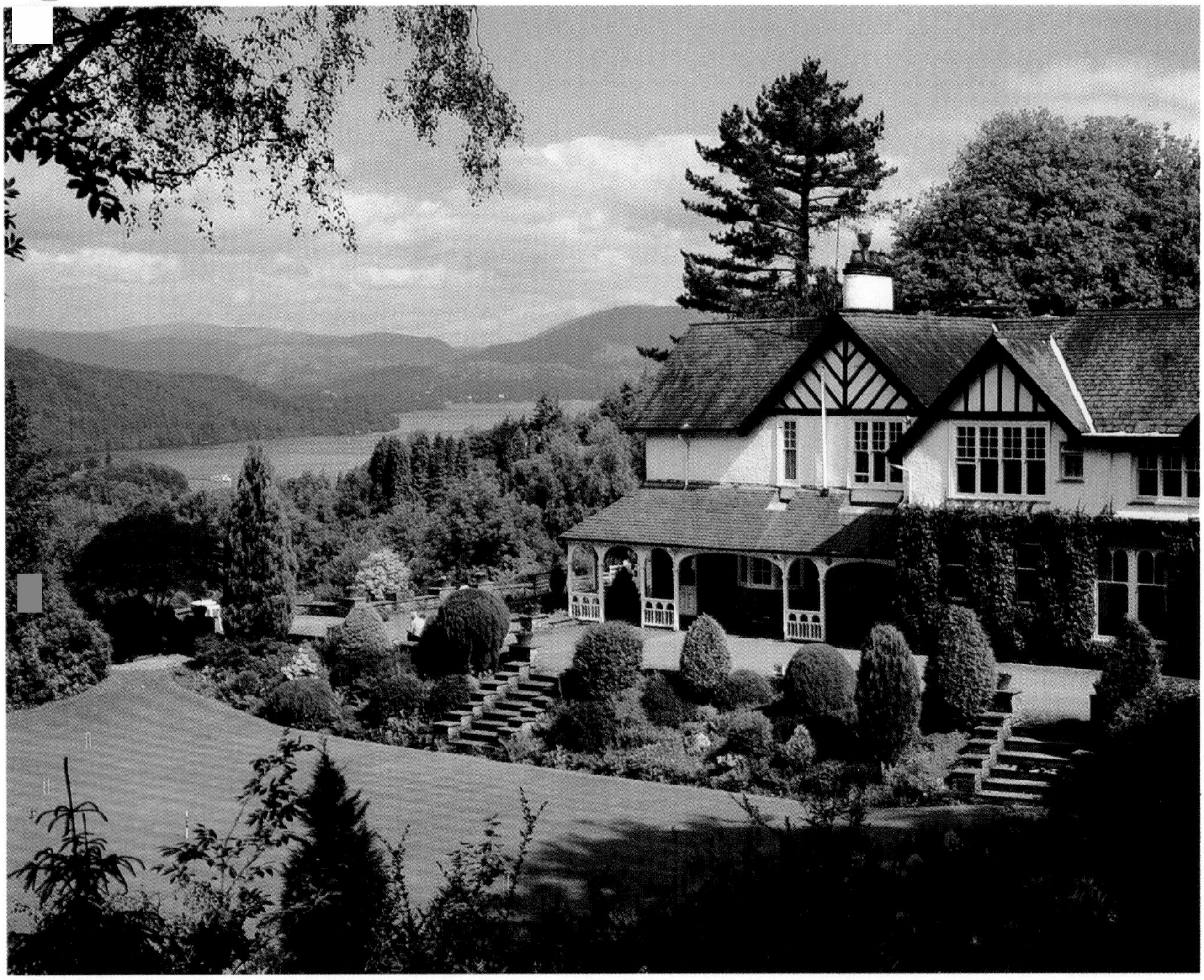

LINTHWAITE HOUSE HOTEL

CROOK ROAD, BOWNESS-ON-WINDERMERE, CUMBRIA LA23 3JA
TEL: 015394 88600 FAX: 015394 88601

Situated in 14 acres of gardens and woods in the heart of the Lake Distict, Linthwaite House overlooks Lake Windermere and Belle Island, with Claiffe Heights and Coniston Old Man beyond. Here, guests will find themselves amid spectacular scenery, yet only a short drive from the motorway network. The hotel combines stylish originality with the best of traditional English hospitality. The superbly decorated bedrooms, all en suite, offer glorious views. The comfortable lounge is the perfect place to unwind and there is a fire on winter evenings. In the restaurant, excellent cuisine features the best of fresh, local produce, accompanied by a fine selection of wines. Within the hotel grounds, there is a 9-hole putting green and a par 3 practice hole. Fly fishermen can fish for brown trout in the hotel tarn. Guests have complimentary use of a private swimming pool and lesiure club nearby, while fell walks begin at the hotel's front door. The area around Linthwaite abounds with places of interest: this is Beatrix Potter and Wordsworth country, and there is much to interest the visitor. **Directions:** From the M6 junction 36 follow Kendal by-pass (A590) for 8 miles. Take B5284 Crook Road for 6 miles. 1 mile beyond Windermere Golf Club, Linthwaite House is signposted on left. Price guide: Single £75–£105; double/twin £110–£160; suite £180.

For hotel location, see maps on pages 477-483

OAKLEY COURT

WINDSOR ROAD, WATER OAKLEY, NR WINDSOR, BERKSHIRE SL4 5UR
TEL: 01753 609988 FAX: 01628 37011

The turreted towers of Oakley Court rise majestically over the banks of the Thames, where this handsome mansion has stood since 1859. The waterside location enables the hotel to offer a unique range of boating facilities, from a champagne picnic hamper for two on a chauffeured punt to a gastronomic feast for a hundred on a steamboat. The hotel's grandeur is quite awe-inspiring. Restored to their original splendour, the entrance hall, library and drawing room feature elaborate plasterwork, fresh flowers and elegant furnishings. An antique billiard table in the games room is kept in pristine condition. All of the bedrooms have views over the river or the 35-acre gardens. Gourmet cuisine is prepared by a skilled team, under Chef Murdo Macsween, and is served with finesse in the candle-lit Le Boulestin Restaurant, or in Boaters for lighter, less formal dining. Private dining can be arranged in the superbly equipped conference and banqueting suites. Activities organised for corporate parties include archery, laser clay pigeon shooting and falconry. There is a 9-hole par 3 golf course on site and the hotel has its own gym, sauna, solarium and new for 1997 an indoor swimming pool. Windsor Castle, Eton and Ascot are nearby, and Heathrow is 20 minutes' drive. **Directions:** Situated just off the A308, between Windsor and Maidenhead. Price guide: Single £120–£150; double/twin £120–£175; suites £275–£395.

113 rms MasterCard VISA AMERICAN EXPRESS M 150

For hotel location, see maps on pages 477-483

THE OLD VICARAGE COUNTRY HOUSE HOTEL

CHURCH ROAD, WITHERSLACK, NR GRANGE-OVER- SANDS, CUMBRIA LA11 6RS
TEL: 015395 52381 FAX: 015395 52373 E-MAIL: hotel@old–vic.demon.co.uk

Near to the lakes...far from the crowds, this lovely old, family-run historic house offers the tranquil timeless atmosphere that reflects the calm and beauty of the surrounding countryside. The delightful, mature garden is stocked with many interesting plants and part of it is left natural for wild flowers, unusual orchids, butterflies, dragonflies and birds. An all-weather tennis court in a delightful setting is for guests use. In the old house, each of the comfortable bedrooms has its own particular character yet with all the modern facilities. The Orchard House, close by, is set beside an ancient damson orchard and has particularly well-equipped, spacious rooms each with its own woodland terrace. With top culinary awards, the well-planned menus include interesting, good quality locally-produced specialities. Diets can, of course, easily be catered for. Lake District National Park, Winderemere, Wordsworth Heritage, Sizergh Castle (National Trust), world famous topiary gardens at Levens Hall. **Directions:** From M6 junction 36, follow A590 to Barrow. After 6 miles turn right into Witherslack, then first left after the telephone box. Price guide: Single £59–£82; double £98–£158. Bargain Breaks all year.

14 rms

For hotel location, see maps on pages 477-483

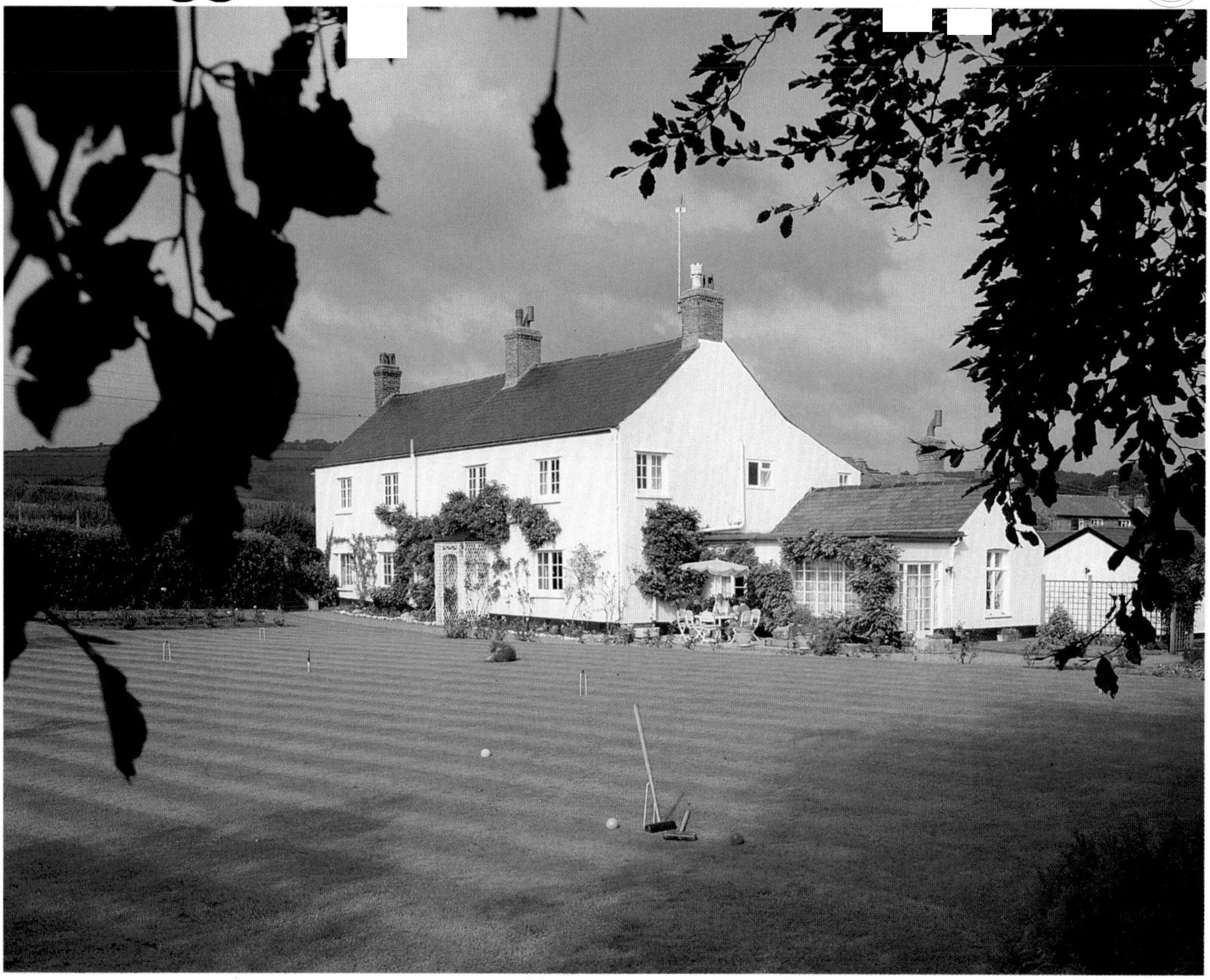

LANGLEY HOUSE HOTEL

LANGLEY MARSH, WIVELISCOMBE, SOMERSET TA4 2UF
TEL: 01984 623318 FAX: 01984 624573

Conveniently located not far from the M5 junction 26, Langley House is a 16th century retreat set in four acres of beautifully kept gardens on the edge of the pretty Somerset town of Wiveliscombe. Modifications in Georgian times have invested this small, cosy hotel with a unique period charm, which explains its enduring popularity. Owners Peter and Anne Wilson have excelled in making Langley House a relaxed and comfortable place to stay. The eight bedrooms, all en suite, are individually decorated, with direct-dial telephone, TV and radio. Most have peaceful garden views and personal touches throughout including fresh flowers and mineral water, books and hot-water bottles. Discreet good taste has been exercised in furnishing the public rooms with pastel sofas, traditional rugs, china and glass, antiques and paintings. (Langley House won the Wedgwood/British Tourist Authority Interior Design Award). In the beamed restaurant, Peter Wilson serves critically acclaimed cuisine and has been awarded a Michelin Red M. The wine list carries over 200 wines. Places of interest nearby include Exmoor, and famous gardens Knightshayes, Stourhead and Hestercombe. **Directions:** Wiveliscombe is 10 miles from Taunton on B3227. Langley House is half a mile north, signposted Langley Marsh. Price guide: Single £64.50–£70; double/twin £89–£115.

For hotel location, see maps on pages 477-483

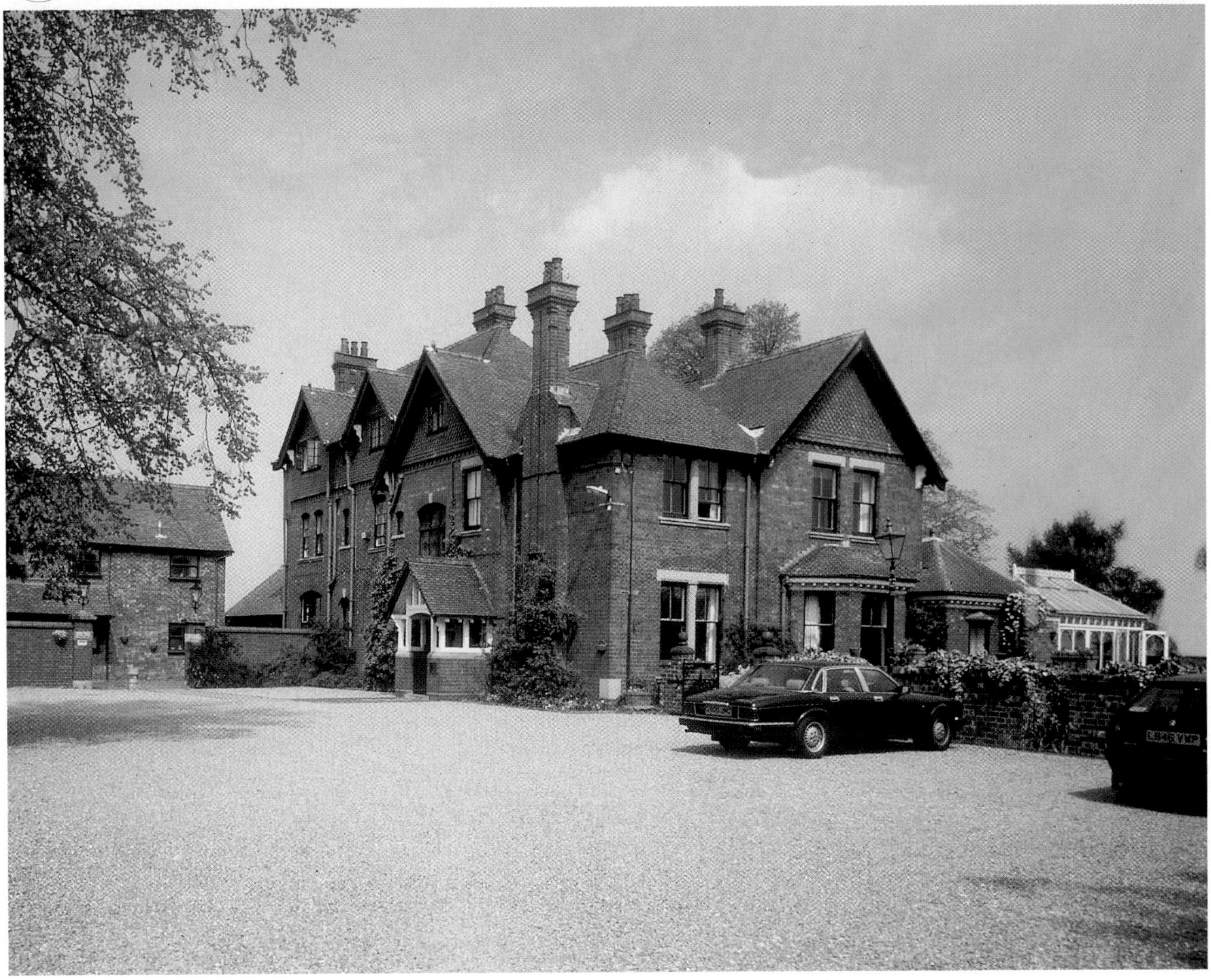

The Old Vicarage Hotel

WORFIELD, BRIDGNORTH, SHROPSHIRE WV15 5JZ
TEL: 01746 716497 FAX: 01746 716552

Standing in 2 acres of mature grounds, this Edwardian parsonage has been lovingly transformed into a delightful country house hotel. Awards abound – Michelin Red M for food, 3 AA Rosettes for food – English Tourist Board De Luxe Hotel and RAC 3 Merit Awards. The Old Vicarage offers guests an opportunity to enjoy a peaceful retreat in countryside of outstanding beauty. The spacious bedrooms are sensitively furnished in Victorian and Edwardian styles to complement the period features of the house. Four Coach House rooms offer complete luxury and comfort – and the Leighton suite has been specially designed with the disabled guest in mind. The daily changing menu features the best of local produce and the award-winning cheeseboard and wine cellar will complete a wonderful evening. Local attractions include the world famous Ironbridge Gorge Museum complex, the Severn Valley preserved steam railway and the splendour of the border towns and villages. Half price golf is available at Worfield Golf Club. Two-day breaks available from £69.50 per person per day, which includes free Passport Tickets to Ironbridge Gorge. **Directions:** Eight miles west of Wolverhampton, one mile off A454, eight miles south of junction 4 of M54. Price guide: Single £68.50–£89.50; double/twin £97–£135.

For hotel location, see maps on pages 477-483

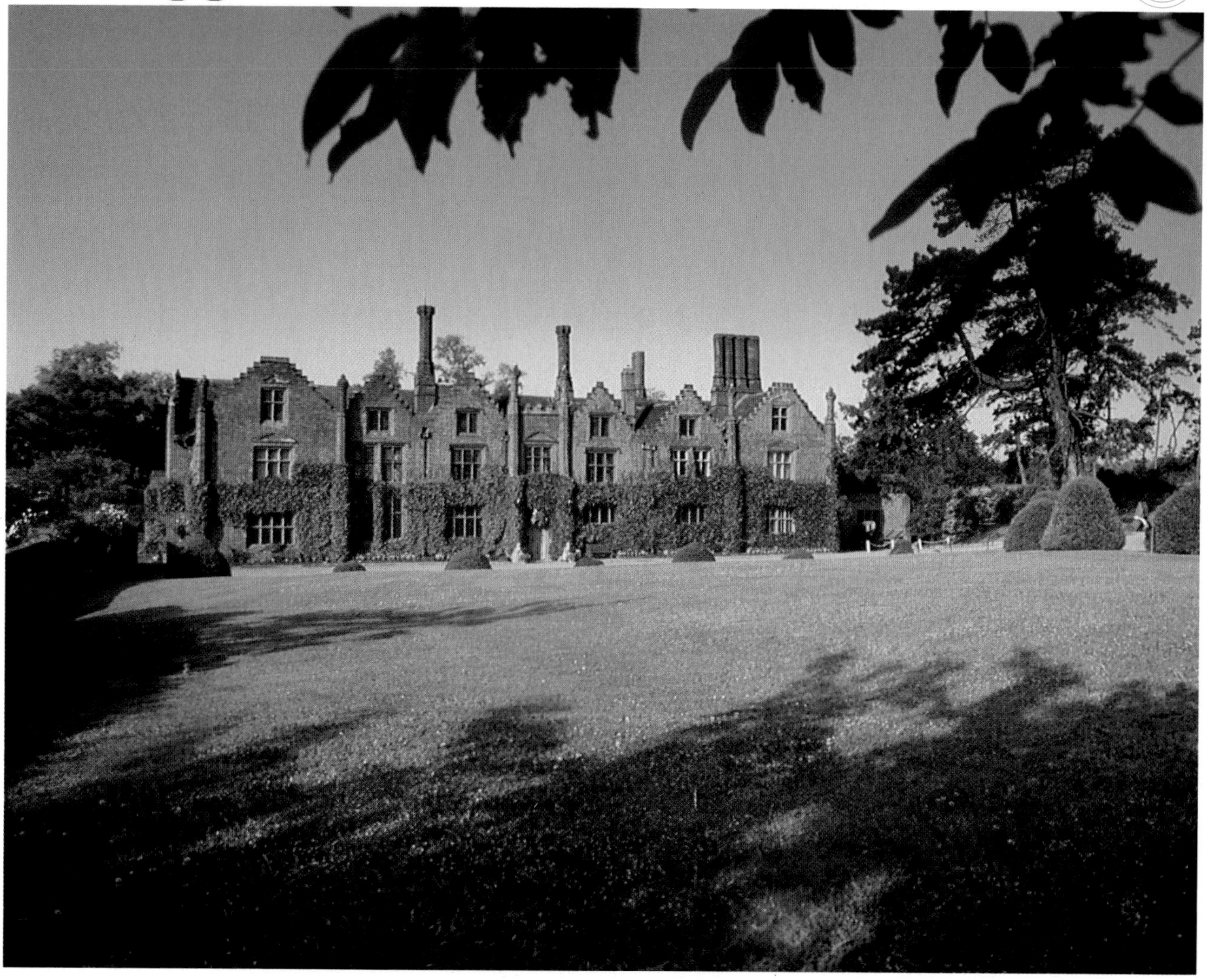

SECKFORD HALL

WOODBRIDGE, SUFFOLK IP13 6NU
TEL: 01394 385678 FAX: 01394 380610

Seckford Hall dates from 1530 and it is said that Elizabeth I once held court there. The hall has lost none of its Tudor grandeur. Furnished as a private house with many fine period pieces, the panelled rooms, beamed ceilings, carved doors and great stone fireplaces are displayed against the splendour of English oak. Local delicacies such as the house speciality, lobster, feature on the à la carte menu. The original minstrels gallery can be viewed in the banqueting hall, which is now a conference and function suite designed in keeping with the general style. The Courtyard area was converted from a giant Tudor tithe barn, dairy and coach house. It now incorporates ten charming cottage-style suites and a modern leisure complex, which includes a heated swimming pool, exercise machines, solarium and spa bath. The hotel is set in 34 acres of tranquil parkland with sweeping lawns and a willow-fringed lake, and guests may stroll about the grounds or simply relax in the attractive terrace garden. There is a 18-hole golf course, where equipment can be hired. A walk along the riverside to picturesque Woodbridge, with its tide mill, antiques shops, yacht harbours and the rose-planted grave of Edward Fitzgerald. Constable country and the Suffolk coast are nearby. **Directions:** Remain on the A12 Woodbridge bypass until the blue-and-white hotel sign. Price guide: Single £79–£99; double/twin £105–@120; suite £120–£148.

For hotel location, see maps on pages 477-483

The Feathers Hotel

MARKET STREET, WOODSTOCK, OXFORDSHIRE OX20 1SX
TEL: 01993 812291 FAX: 01993 813158

The Feathers is a privately owned and run country house hotel, situated in the centre of Woodstock, a few miles from Oxford. Woodstock is one England's most attractive country towns, constructed mostly from Cotswold stone and with buildings dating from the 12th century. The hotel, built in the 17th century, was originally four separate houses. Antiques, log fires and traditional English furnishings lend character and charm. There are only 16 bedrooms, all of which have private bathrooms and showers. Public rooms, including the drawing room and study, are intimate and comfortable. The small garden is a delightful setting for a light lunch or afternoon tea and guests can enjoy a drink in the cosy courtyard bar, which has an open fire in winter. The antique-panelled restaurant is internationally renowned for its fine cuisine, complemented by a high standard of service. The menu changes daily and offers a wide variety of dishes, using the finest local ingredients. Blenheim Palace, seat of the Duke of Marlborough and birthplace of Sir Winston Churchill, is just around the corner. The Cotswolds and the dreaming spires of Oxford are a short distance away. **Directions:** From London leave M40 at junction 8; from Birmingham leave at junction 9. Take A44 and follow signs to Woodstock. The hotel is on the left. Price guide: Single £78; double/twin £99–£150; suite £185–£225.

For hotel location, see maps on pages 477-483

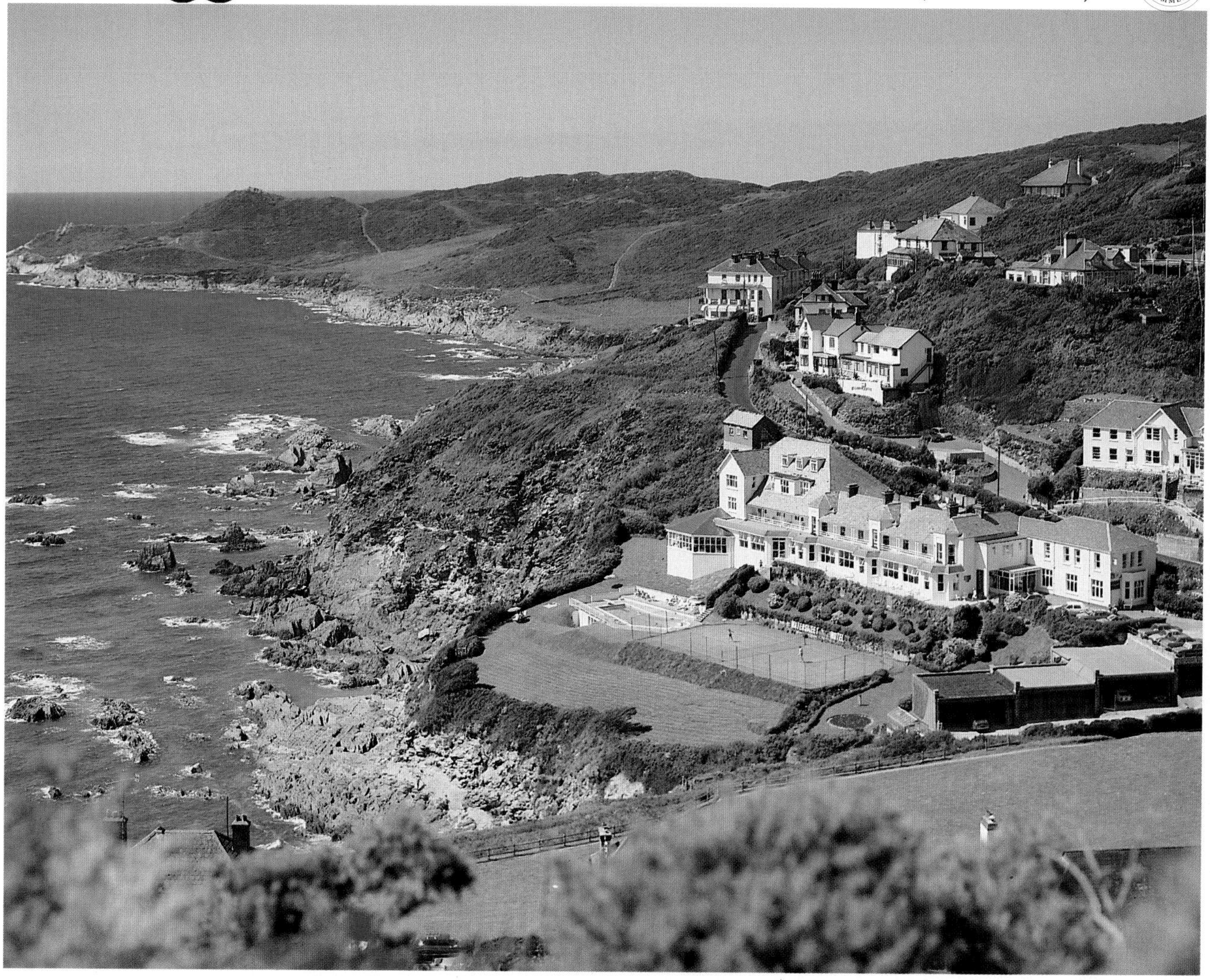

WATERSMEET HOTEL

MORTEHOE, WOOLACOMBE, DEVON EX34 7EB
TEL: 01271 870333 FAX: 01271 870890

Watersmeet Hotel exudes the comfortable luxury of a country house. Majestically situated on the National Trust's rugged North Atlantic coastline the hotel commands dramatic views across the waters of Woolacoombe Bay past Hartland Point to Lundy Island. The gardens reach down to the sea and private steps lead directly to the beach. Attractive decor, combined with soft coloured fabrics, creates a summery impression all year. The main bedrooms look out to sea and guests can drift off to sleep to the sound of lapping waves or rolling surf. Morning coffee, lunch or afternoon tea can be enjoyed in the relaxing comfort of the lounge, on the terrace or by the heated swimming pool. Tempting English and continental dishes are served in the award-winning Pavilion Restaurant where each evening candles flicker as diners absorb a view of the sun dipping below the horizon. The hotel has been awarded two AA Rosettes for cuisine and three RAC Merit awards for excellent hospitality, restaurant and comfort. There is a full-size grass tennis court and locally surfing, riding, clay pigeon shooting and bracing walks along coastal paths. Open February to December. **Directions:** From M5, junction 27, follow A361 towards Ilfracombe, turn left at roundabout and take signs to Mortehoe. Price guide (including dinner): Single £55–£90; double/twin £90–190.

For hotel location, see maps on pages 477-483

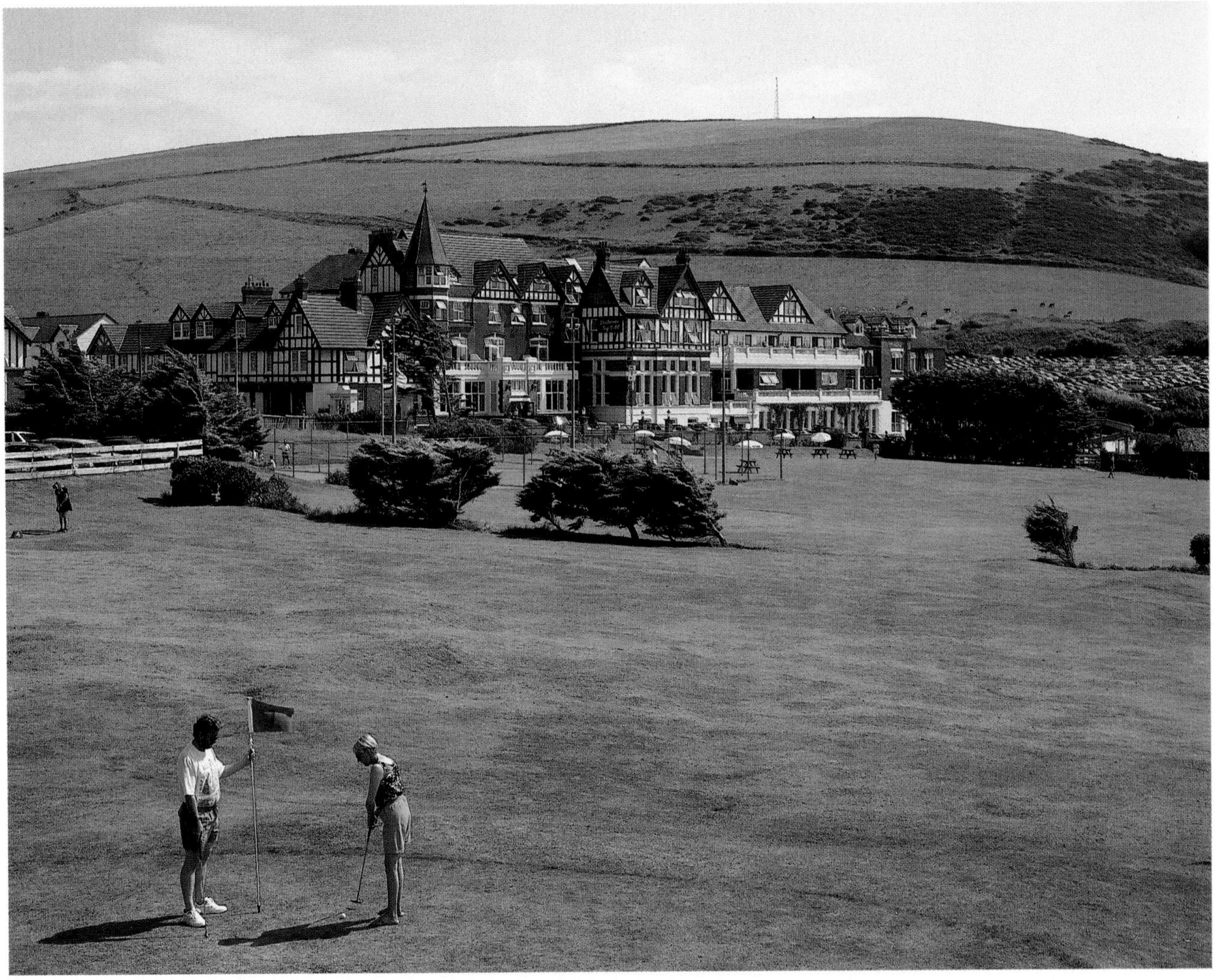

WOOLACOMBE BAY HOTEL

SOUTH STREET, WOOLACOMBE, DEVON EX34 7BN
TEL: 01271 870388 FAX: 01271 870613

Woolacombe Bay Hotel stands in 6 acres of grounds, leading to three miles of golden sand. Built by the Victorians, the hotel has an air of luxury, style and comfort. All rooms are en suite with satellite TV, baby listening, ironing centre, some with a spa bath or balcony. Traditional English and French dishes are offered in the dining room. Superb recreational amenities on site include unlimited free access to tennis, squash, indoor and outdoor pools, billiards, bowls, croquet, dancing and films, a health suite with steam room, sauna, spa bath with heated benches and high impulse shower. Power-boating, shooting and riding can be arranged, and preferential rates are offered for golf at the Saunton Golf Club. New "Hot House" aerobics studio, cardio vascular weights room, solariums, massage and beautician. However, being energetic is not a requirement for enjoying the qualities of Woolacombe Bay. Many of its regulars choose simply to relax in the grand public rooms and in the grounds, which extend to the rolling surf of the magnificent bay. A drive along the coastal route in either direction will guarantee splendid views. Exmoor's beautiful Doone Valley is an hour away by car. ETB 5 Crowns Highly Commended. Closed January. **Directions:** At centre of village, off main Barnstaple–Ilfracombe road. Price guide (including dinner): Single £58–£95; double/twin £116–£166.

For hotel location, see maps on pages 477-483

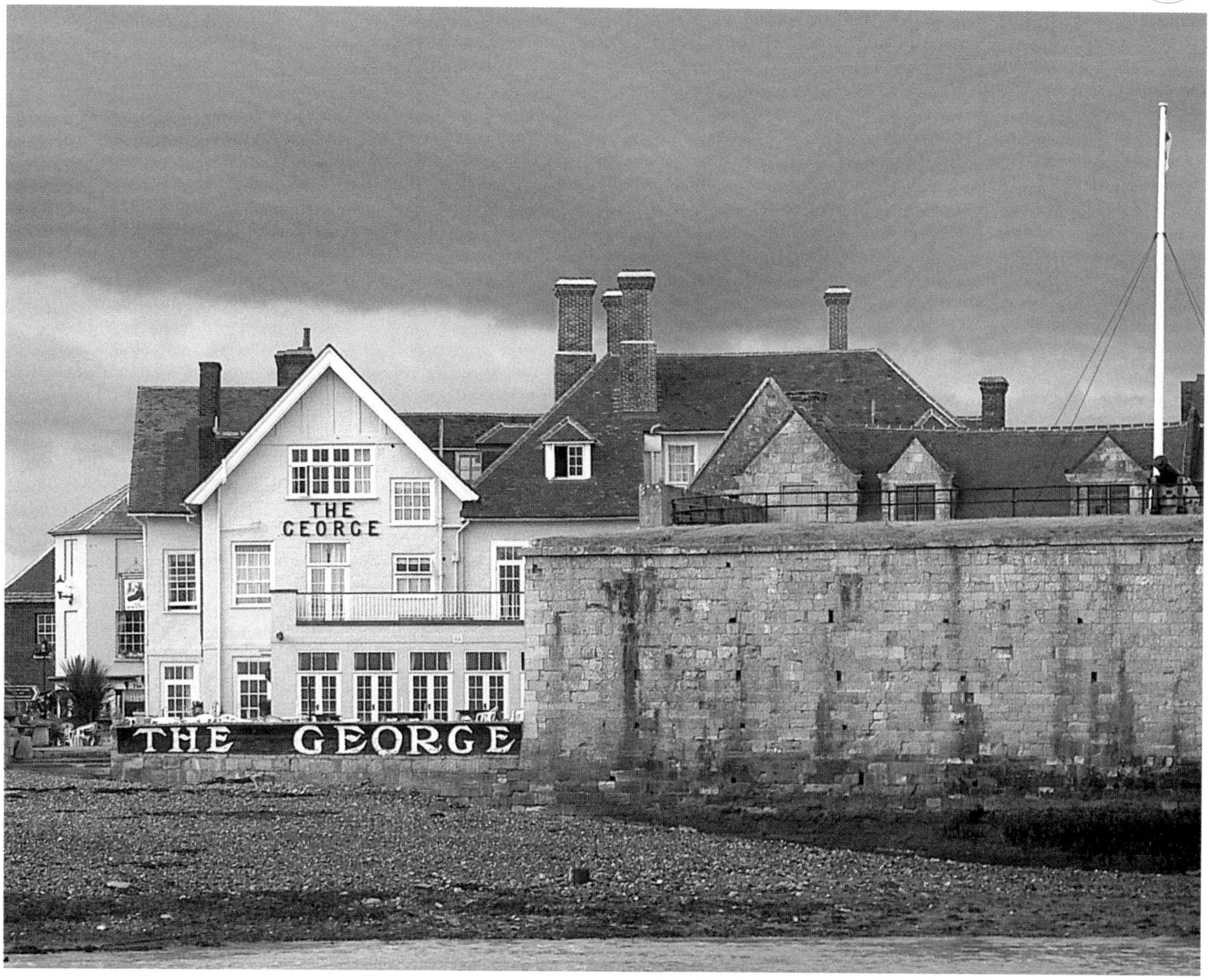

THE GEORGE HOTEL

QUAY STREET, YARMOUTH, ISLE OF WIGHT PO41 0PE
TEL: 01983 760331 FAX: 01983 760425

This splendid 17th century hotel near the Quay at Yarmouth and six miles west of Cowes, was built for Admiral Sir Robert Holmes, a governor of the island. All the rich panelling and the huge, four-abreast staircase remain, but modern standards have demanded a bathroom for all bedrooms, these include an executive suite and inter-connecting family rooms. The Restaurant has been awarded 3 AA Rosettes for its food and there are also several other public rooms: the Brasserie, a private dining room, the quiet of a traditionally decorated sitting room, the bustle of the Solent Bar – popular with visiting yachtsmen and locals – and a well equipped meeting room, The George has the variety of modern facilities more commonly found in far larger hotels. Chef Kevin Mangeolles' cuisine is renowned. The George has its own private beach. Nearby is the great stretch of Compton Beach and an 18-hole golf course. Inland are Carisbrook Castle and Osborne House. There are numerous walks and rides through the surrounding listed areas of outstanding natural beauty, world class sailing on the Solent and all the attractions of the Isle of Wight. **Directions:** From the M3, exit at junction 1 and take the A337 to Lymington and then the ferry to Yarmouth. Alternatively, ferry services run regularly from Southampton and Portsmouth. The A3054 leads direct to Yarmouth. Price guide: Single £90; double/twin £140.

For hotel location, see maps on pages 477-483

The Grange Hotel

CLIFTON, YORK, NORTH YORKSHIRE YO3 6AA
TEL: 01904 644744 FAX: 01904 612453

Set near the ancient city walls, 4 minutes' walk from the famous Minster, this sophisticated Regency town house has been carefully restored and its spacious rooms richly decorated. Beautiful stone-flagged floors in the corridors of The Grange lead to the classically styled reception rooms. The flower-filled Morning Room is welcoming, with its blazing log fire and deep sofas, and double doors between the panelled library and drawing room can be opened up to create a dignified venue for parties, wedding receptions or business entertaining. Prints, flowers and English chintz in the bedrooms reflect the proprietor's careful attention to detail. The Ivy Restaurant has an established reputation for first-class gastronomy, incorporating the best in French and country house cooking. The new Dom Ruimart Seafood bar has two murals depicting racing secenes. The Brasserie is open for lunch and dinner until after the theatre closes in the evening. For conferences, a computer, fax and telex are available as well as secretarial services. Brimming with history, York's list of attractions includes the National Railway Museum, the Jorvik Viking Centre and the medieval Shambles. **Directions:** The Grange Hotel is on the A19 York–Thirsk road, 1/2 mile from the centre on the left. Price guide: Single £95; double/twin £105–£155; suites £185.

30 rms · 50

For hotel location, see maps on pages 477-483

MIDDLETHORPE HALL

BISHOPTHORPE ROAD, YORK YO2 1QB
TEL: 01904 641241 FAX: 01904 620176

Middlethorpe Hall is a delightful William III house, built in 1699 for Thomas Barlow, a wealthy merchant, and was for a time the home of Lady Mary Wortley Montagu, the 18th-century writer of letters. The house has been immaculately restored by Historic House Hotels who have decorated and furnished it in its original elegance and style. There are beautifully designed bedrooms and suites in the main house and in the adjacent classical courtyard. The restaurant offers the best in contemporary English cooking with an imaginative menu and a carefully chosen wine list. Middlethorpe stands in 26 acres of parkland where guests can wander and enjoy the walled garden, the white garden, the lake and the original ha ha's. The hotel overlooks York Racecourse – known as the 'Ascot of the North' – and the medieval city of York with its fascinating museums, restored streets and world-famous Minster is only 2 miles away. From Middlethorpe you can visit Yorkshire's famous country houses, like Castle Howard, Beningbrough and Harewood, the ruined Abbeys of Fountains and Rievaulx and explore the magnificent Yorkshire Moors. Helmsley, Whitby and Scarborough are nearby. **Directions:** Take A64 (T) off A1 (T) near Tadcaster, follow signs to York West, then smaller signs to Bishopthorpe. Price guide: Single £89–£112; double/twin £125–£195; suite from £175–£205.

30 rms MasterCard VISA AMERICAN EXPRESS M 65 8

For hotel location, see maps on pages 477-483

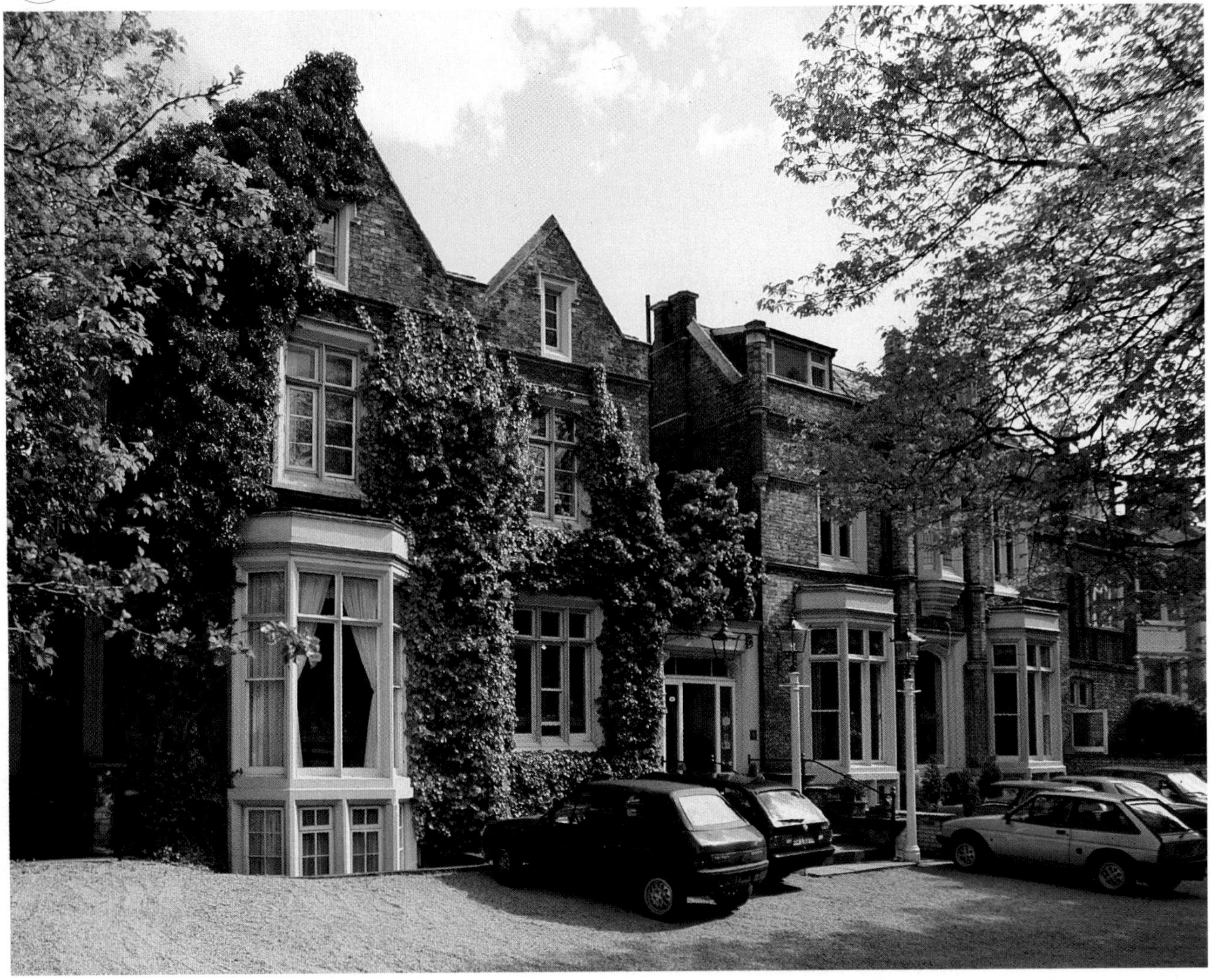

MOUNT ROYALE HOTEL

THE MOUNT, YORK, NORTH YORKSHIRE YO2 2DA
TEL: 01904 628856 FAX: 01904 611171

Two elegant William IV houses have been restored to their former glory to create the Mount Royale Hotel, which is personally run by the Oxtoby family. Comfortable bedrooms are furnished with imagination, all in an individual style. Each of the garden rooms opens onto the garden and has its own verandah. Downstairs, the public rooms are filled with interesting items of antique furniture, *objets d'art* and gilt-framed paintings. To the rear of the building, overlooking the gardens, is the restaurant, where guests can enjoy the best of traditional English cooking and French cuisine. Amenities include a snooker room with a full-sized table, steam room, sauna, solarium and Phytomer treatment centre. With a delightful English garden and heated outdoor pool, the one acre grounds are a peaceful haven just minutes from York's centre. York is a historic and well-preserved city, famous for its Minster and medieval streets. Also within walking distance is York racecourse, where the flat-racing season runs from May to October. Lovers of the great outdoors will find the Yorkshire Dales and North York Moors a 45-minute drive away. Only small dogs by arrangement. **Directions:** From A64, turn onto the A1036 signposted York. Go past racecourse; hotel is on right before traffic lights. Price guide: Single £70–£90; double/twin £90–£120; suites £120.

For hotel location, see maps on pages 477-483

YORK PAVILION HOTEL

45 MAIN STREET, FULFORD, YORK, NORTH YORKSHIRE YO1 4PJ
TEL: 01904 622099 FAX: 01904 626939

Originally a Georgian farm house, the York Pavilion has been extended and converted into a gracious and charming country house hotel. Open fireplaces, deep armchairs and sofas invite visitors to relax. Much of the ground floor is flagged in York Stone. The 34 bedrooms are individually styled and combine traditional furnishings with modern comfort. Each room has a private bathroom, writing desk, satellite television with teletext, radio, direct-dial telephone, hairdryer and tea and coffee making facilities. Some have four-poster beds. The attractive restaurant overlooks mature gardens and chef David Spencer has gained an enviable reputation for fine cuisine. His weekly changing House menus are complemented with an extensive selection of wines. There are conference facilities for up to 150 delegates. A large marquee is available for additional conference use or for wedding or private functions. York Pavilion is 2 miles from the city centre with its many attractions. Fulford championship golf course and York racecourse are a five minute drive away. Shooting, fishing and riding can be arranged. Directions: From the A1 follow A64 outer ring road and turn onto A39 at the York/Selby junction. The hotel is 1/4 mile on the right heading towards York. Price guide: Single £84-£94; double/twin £106-£120.

For hotel location, see maps on pages 477-483

Johansens Recommended Hotels in Wales

Magnificent scenery, a rich variety of natural, cultural and modern leisure attractions, and the very best accommodation awaits the Johansens visitor to Wales.

Every year, millions of visitors visit Wales and discover how much the country has to offer. A high proportion of these come back year after year - a sure sign of their approval.

The opening of the Second Severn Crossing in the summer of 1996 - a tourist attraction in itself - has made South Wales even more accessible for day and staying visitors whilst improved links into North Wales by road, sea and air make the region equally accessible for short breaks and days out.

With some of the most fabulous scenery imaginable, and much to see and do, Wales boasts three national parks, covering nearly 1,600 square miles, as well as five areas designated as being of Outstanding Natural Beauty.

There are a number of major country parks, nature reserves, Sites of Special Scientific Interest and more than 700 miles of breathtakingly beautiful coastline to discover, plus delightful off-shore islands which are home to colonies of seals and rare birds. Pembrokeshire, in particular, is a must for all nature lovers.

Apart from the country's unspoilt natural beauty and endless scenic variety, Wales also has a wealth of interesting and unusual attractions to enjoy.

Visitors will not be short of variety. 1997 marks the Bi-Centenary of the Last Invasion of Britain by 1200 French Troops and several Irish officers under the command of an American colonel, William Tate. Pembrokeshire local heroine, Jemima Nicholas, saved the day back in 1797 and events will be held in the town of Fishguard to celebrate this historic occasion throughout the year. There will be a re-enactment of the invasion attempt on August 31, 1997 and the International Waterway Regatta will be held there in June.

Modern day thrills have taken on a new dimension at Pembrokeshire's Oakwood Leisure Park. Visitors can experience the ride of a lifetime on Europe's biggest wooden rollercoaster, aptly named Megafobia. With 80 ft drops and a top speed of 55 miles an hour.

For a more sedate ride, with time to take in some of Europe's most breathtaking scenery and a haute cuisine meal, visitors are invited to step aboard the Ffestiniog Railway and combine a unique experience in fine dining with a gentle journey by narrow gauge steam train through some of the most spectacular scenery in the country.

Many of the attractions are unique such as the Centre for Alternative Technology, the Green village of the future at Machynlleth in Mid Wales or Port Meirion, the dreamlike Italianate village in North Wales.

Visitors can take a ride on a narrow gauge steam railway, take a trip on a horse-drawn canal boat, go to the summit of the Great Orme in the only cable hauled tramway in Britain, travel across Aberaeron harbour by the Aeron Express Ariel Ferry or journey to the summit of Abersytwyth's Constitution Hill by cliff railway, one of the most spectacular in Britain.

The industrial heritage of the past now provides fascinating visitor attractions like Big Pit in Blaenafon, where ex-miners act as underground guides, or the ever-expanding Rhondda Heritage Park. In North Wales, there are vast slate caverns and copper mines to explore, several narrow gauge steam railways to enjoy. While in Mid Wales, visitors can tour a real gold-mine, try their hand at panning and mining for gold - and keep anything they find!

In the Museum of Welsh Life at St Fagans, near Cardiff, buildings from all over Wales have been carefully re-erected and there are museums covering the maritime, motoring, industrial and aviation history of Wales, as well as those dedicated to the memory of famous Welsh personalities like David Lloyd George and Dylan Thomas.

Wales also has its share of exceptional stately homes with priceless art treasures and antiques, world class gardens like Bodnant or Dyffryn, exciting new attractions like the allegedly haunted Llancaiach Fawr Manor in Rhymney Valley - a living history museum with guides dressed in costume, as well as vast medieval fortresses, castles and cromlechs.

Thanks to successful Millennium bids, Wales will soon boast a Botanical Garden at Middleton Hall near Carmarthen in West Wales and a new National Stadium in Cardiff in time for the 1999 Rugby World Cup.

If you feel bored after all that you could always while away the hours shopping in Europe's fastest growing capital city.

In fact, you could say that Wales truly has something for everyone.

Centre for Alternative Technology
Machynlleth
Powys SY20 9AZ
Tel: 01654 702400

Great Little Trains of Wales
c/o The Station
Llanfair Caereinion
Powys SY21 OSF
Tel: 01938 810441

Big Pit
Blaenafon
Gwent NP4 9XP
Tel: 01495 790311

Llancaiach Fawr Manor
Gelligaer Road
Nelson
Mid Glamorgan CF46 6ER
Tel: 01443 412248

For more information about Wales, please contact:-

Wales Tourist Board
Brunel House
2 Fitzalan Road
Cardiff CF2 1UY
Tel: 01222 499909

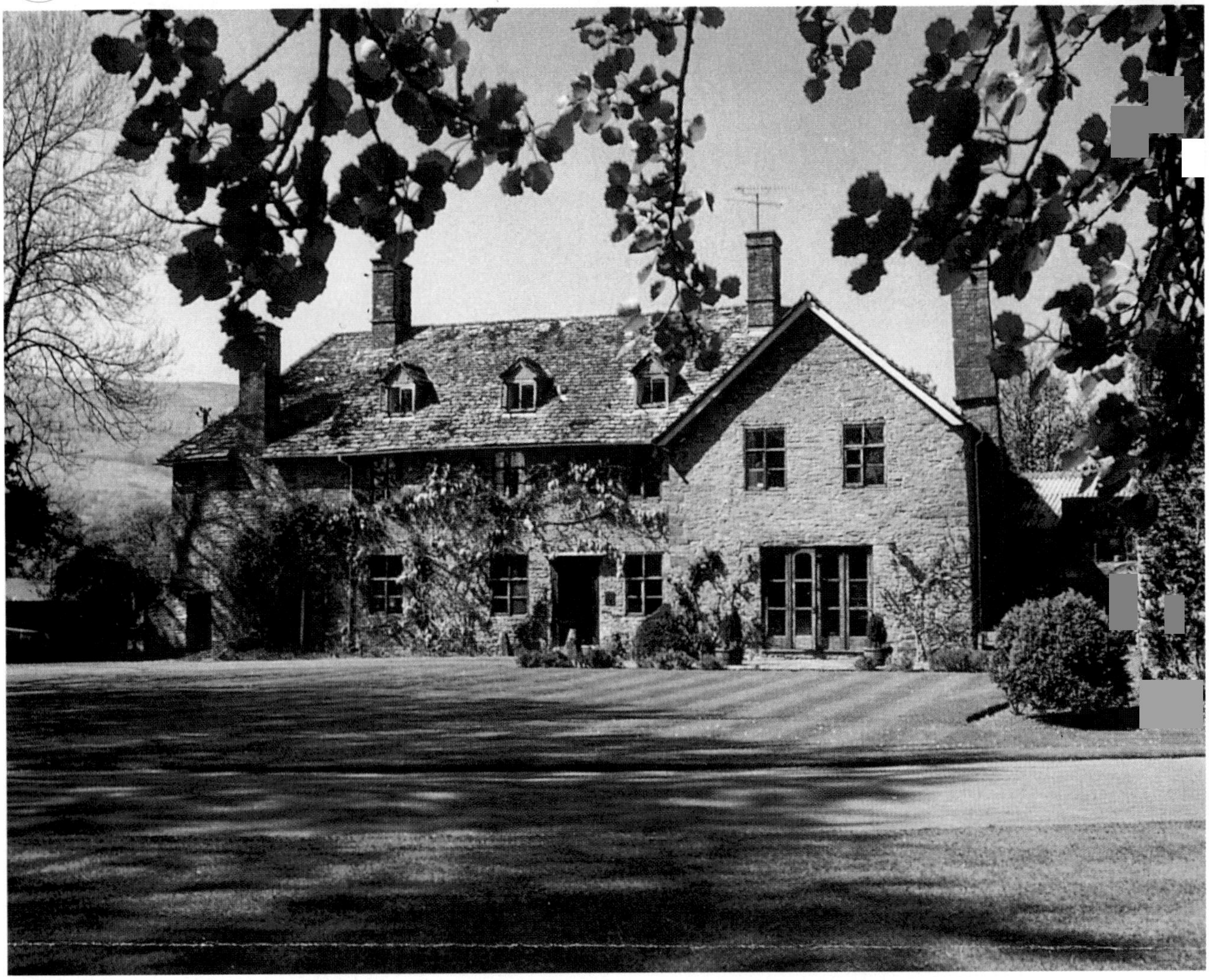

ALLT-YR-YNYS HOTEL

WALTERSTONE, HEREFORDSHIRE HR2 0DU
TEL: 01873 890307 FAX: 01873 890539

Allt-yr-Ynys straddles the border that runs between England and Wales – with rural Herefordshire on one side and the Black Mountains on the other. The original manor house on this site belonged to the estate of Robert Cecil, a Knight of the Court during the reign of King Henry II; however, the buildings that comprise today's hotel date from 1550. Many of the authentic features have been preserved, typically the moulded ceilings, oak panelling and massive oak beams. The bedrooms, some of which are situated in the converted outbuildings, have been beautifully appointed to complement their period character. Delicious British cooking features on the menu, and the chef can also prepare 'special dishes for special occasions' to cater for private functions of up to 60 people. In the bar, adjacent to the Jacuzzi and indoor heated pool, there is an ancient, horse-powered cider press. An undercover clay pigeon range is in the grounds, with all equipment – shotguns, cartridges and tuition. There are four golf courses within the vicinity. **Directions:** Midway between Abergavenny and Hereford, turn off A465 by Pandy Inn. Turn right at Green Park Barn crossroads as signposted to Walterstone. Price guide: Single £55; double/twin £70–£95.

For hotel location, see maps on pages 477-483

Porth Tocyn Country House Hotel

ABERSOCH, PWLLHELI, GWYNEDD LL53 7BU
TEL: 01758 713303 FAX: 01758 713538

Porth Tocyn is a friendly, family-owned hotel offering country charm and good food in a beautiful location. Situated in 25 acres of gardens and pasture, the house enjoys glorious views across Cardigan Bay to Snowdonia. In the 49 years that the Fletcher-Brewer family have owned the hotel, they have concentrated their efforts into creating a comfortable, attractive hotel without the stuffiness associated with some establishments. Children of all ages are welcomed: there are family bedrooms, a small children's sitting room, and high tea is provided for the younger ones every evening. However, this is very much a place where adults can relax. First-class home cooking has long been the cornerstone of Porth Tocyn's reputation. Focusing on the quality of each dish, dinner is a short-choice, five-course affair followed by coffee and home-made petits fours. The menu is changed completely each day. A dinner-party atmosphere brings a sense of occasion to the evening. Lunch is more informal and may be taken in the garden or by the pool. A variety of water sports and riding can be arranged locally, while the heritage coastline makes for ideal clifftop walks. Closed November to Easter. **Directions:** From Abersoch go 2½ miles, through Sarn Bach and Bwlchtocyn. 'Gwesty/Hotel' signs lead to Porth Tocyn. Price guide: Single £43.50; double/twin £67–£104.

For hotel location, see maps on pages 477-483

CONRAH COUNTRY HOUSE HOTEL

RHYDGALED, CHANCERY, ABERYSTWYTH, DYFED SY23 4DF
TEL: 01970 617941 FAX: 01970 624546

One of Wales' much-loved country house hotels, the Conrah is tucked away at the end of a rhododendron-lined drive, only minutes from the spectacular rocky cliffs and sandy bays of the Cambrian coast. Set in 22 acres of rolling grounds, the Conrah's magnificent position gives views as far north as the Cader Idris mountain range. Afternoon tea and Welsh cakes or pre-dinner drinks can be taken at leisure in the quiet writing room or one of the comfortable lounges, where antiques and fresh flowers add to the relaxed country style. The acclaimed restaurant uses fresh local produce, together with herbs and vegetables from the Conrah kitchen garden, to provide the best of both classical and modern dishes. The hotel is owned and run by the Heading family who extend a warm invitation to guests to come for a real 'taste of Wales', combined with old-fashioned, high standards of service. For recreation, guests may enjoy a game of table-tennis in the summer house, croquet on the lawn or a walk around the landscaped gardens. The heated swimming pool and sauna are open all year round. Golf, Pony-trekking and sea fishing are all available locally, while the university town of Aberystwyth is only 3 miles away. Closed Christmas. **Directions:** The Conrah lies 3 miles south of Aberystwyth on the A487. Price guide: Single £59–£69; double/twin £88–£110.

For hotel location, see maps on pages 477-483

HENLLYS HALL

BEAUMARIS, ISLE OF ANGLESEY, NORTH WALES LL58 8HU
TEL: 01248 810412 FAX: 01248 811511

Henllys Hall is in one of the most beautiful parts of Wales, close to Snowdonia and the Menai Straits. First built in 1237, Edward I appointed the Hampton family custodians in 1294. Despite numerous uprisings and fires, the family remained linked with the Hall until 1950. Today, following extensive refurbishment, it is an excellent and comfortable hotel. A magnificent carved staircase is the focal point of the reception area. Big traditional leather furniture is much in evidence, and the drawing room has a splendid log fire in winter months. The bedrooms are charming with the occasional four–poster bed, pretty upholstery, and lovely views over the countryside. (Many are designated non–smoking). The bar is ideal for meeting fellow guests before enjoying the delicious table d'hôte menu or feasting on the à la carte selection and sampling some of the 80 bins in the wine list. In summer salads are served by the pool. Exploring Anglesey is exciting – famous castles, prehistoric sites, old buildings – while across the Menai Straits is the Snowdonia National Park. Active guests will appreciate the golf course in the grounds, the outdoor pool, tennis, croquet, or take the various graded walks which are carefully waymarked. **Directions:** From the centre of Beaumaris take the road to Pentraeth, watching for the sign for the hotel one mile on. Price Guide: Single £55–£65; double £80.

23 rms 100

For hotel location, see maps on pages 473–479

TREARDDUR BAY HOTEL

LON ISALLT, TREARDDUR BAY, NR HOLYHEAD, ANGLESEY LL65 2UN
TEL: 01407 860301 FAX: 01407 861181

This seaside hotel enjoys a magnificent location on the Anglesey coast, overlooking Trearddur Bay and close to a medieval chapel dedicated to the nun St Brigid. An extensive refurbishment programme in recent years has given the hotel a completely new look. Many of the spacious bedrooms, all of which are en suite, have panoramic views over the bay. All are furnished to a high standard. There are also nine studio suites, including one with four-poster bed. The comfortable lounge is the perfect place to relax and read the papers over morning coffee or afternoon tea. Before dinner, enjoy an apéritif in one of the hotel bars. Superb views apart, the hotel restaurant enjoys a reputation for excellent food – including locally caught fish and seafood – complemented by fine wines. Table d'hôte and à la carte menus offer a good choice of dishes. For those who find the Irish Sea too bracing, the hotel has an indoor pool. The beach is just a short walk away and there is an 18-hole golf course nearby. Anglesey is a haven for watersports enthusiasts and birdwatchers. Places of interest include Beaumaris Castle and the Celtic burial mound at Bryn Celli Ddu. Snowdonia is a little further afield. **Directions:** From Bangor, take A5 to Valley crossroads. Turn left onto B4545 for 3 miles, then turn left at garage. Hotel is 350 yards on right. Price guide: Single £70; double/twin £100–£110; studio suite £120–£140.

30 rms MasterCard VISA AMERICAN EXPRESS M 120

For hotel location, see maps on pages 477-483

PALÉ HALL

PALÉ, LLANDDERFEL, BALA, GWYNEDD LL23 7PS
TEL: 01678 530285 FAX: 01678 530220

Palé Hall, a privately owned Victorian mansion, is nestled amongst 150 acres of parkland on the edge of the Snowdonia National Park. The house was built in 1870 for Mr Henry Robertson (a Scottish gentleman) who instructed his architects to spare no expense. Undoubtedly one of the most impressive buildings in Wales, notable guests included Queen Victoria, who described the house as enchanting and stayed. Other guests included Winston Churchill and many other famous people. The house contains stunning interiors and exquisite features of a magnificent entrance hall with its galleried staircase, plus the boudoir with its hand-painted ceiling, marble fireplaces and bar. The comfortable lounges (including a non-smoking lounge) enable quiet relaxation and contemplation. Each of the 17 suites are individually decorated and contain en suite bathrooms, TV, hospitality tray and luxury toiletries, plus a magnificent view of the surrounding scenery. The restaurant offers fine dishes and is complemented by an extensive cellar. Facilities for the pursuit of a number of outdoor activities are available; walking, riding, fishing, shooting, golf or white-water rafting. **Directions:** Palé Hall is situated off the B4401 Corwen to Bala road, four miles from Llandrillo. Price guide: Single £85–£95; double/twin £120–£175. (All prices include breakfast & dinner).

17 rms

For hotel location, see maps on pages 477-483

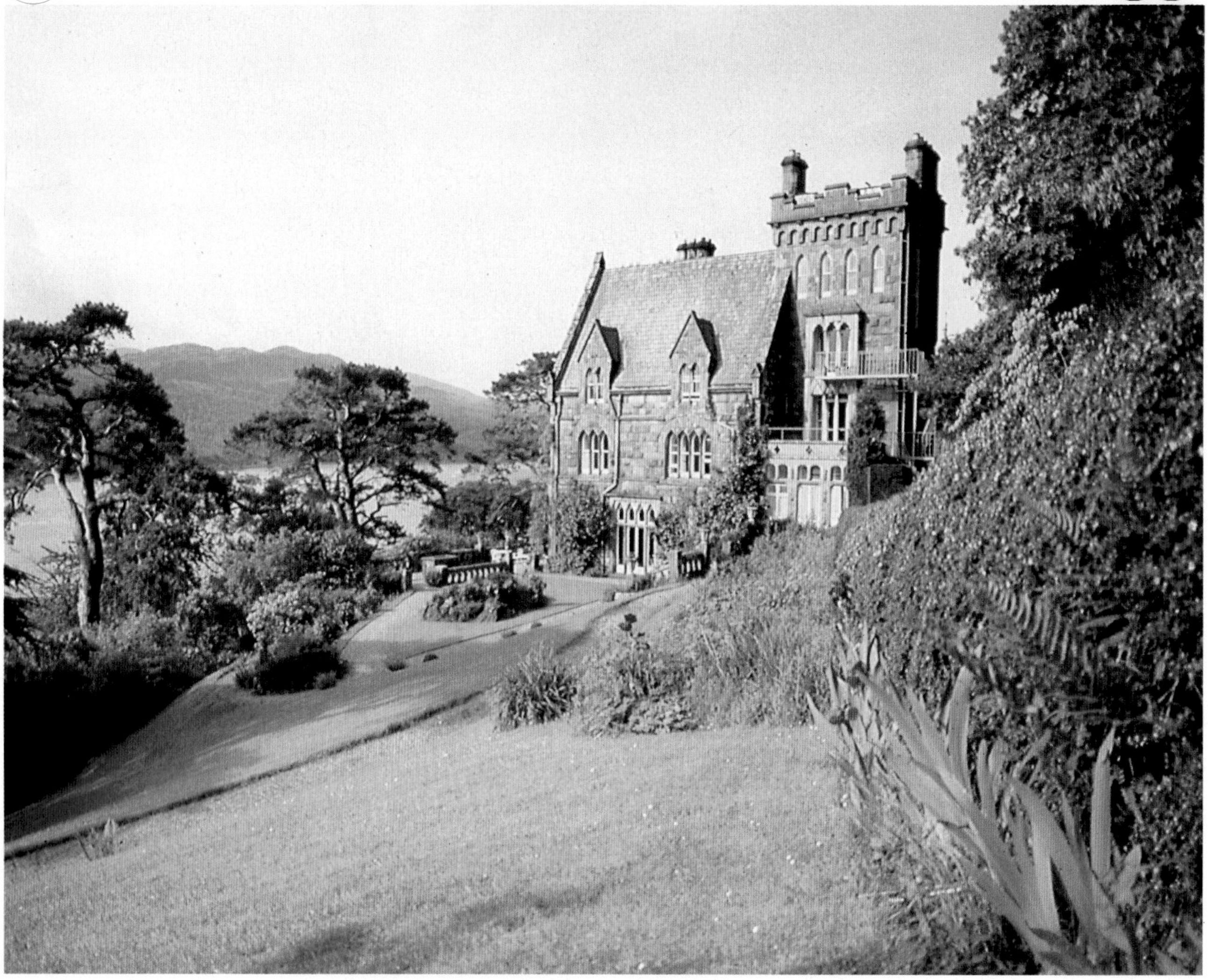

BONTDDU HALL

BONTDDU, NR BARMOUTH, GWYNEDD LL40 2SU
TEL: 01341 430661 FAX: 01341 430284

Set in 14 acres of landscaped gardens with mixed woodland and a rhododendron forest, Gothic-styled Bontddu Hall commands a lofty position overlooking the Mawddach Estuary in Snowdonia National Park. Built in 1873 as a country mansion for the aunt of Neville Chamberlain, the hotel is reminiscent of the Victorian era and was frequented by several Prime Ministers during the days of the British Empire. The reception rooms are richly decorated in a fashion that complements the grandeur of the high, corniced ceilings and ornate, marble fireplaces. As well as the comfortable bedrooms in the main building, a number of suites are available in the Lodge, each with a private balcony facing the mountains. Regional and classical cuisine are served in the Garden Restaurant. Lunch and afternoon teas can be taken on the sun terrace. Hill walking, climbing, pony-trekking, surfing, sail-boarding, skin-diving and bowling are available in the locality. The walks from Dolgellau are famous. Bontddu also has a gold mine. A tour of the area could include a trip on the famous narrow-gauge railways, or a visit to one of the many interesting castles, such as Harlech or Penrhyn. Closed November to Easter. A Virgin hotel. **Directions:** Situated midway between Dolgellau and Barmouth on the A496. Price guide: Single £62.50; double/twin £90–£115; suite £150.

20 rms MasterCard VISA AMERICAN EXPRESS M 40

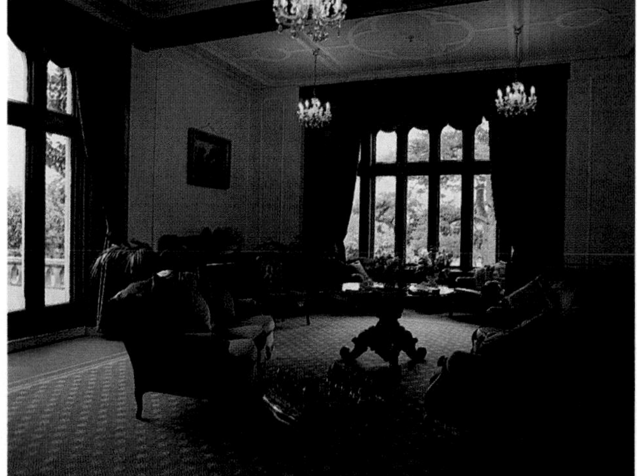

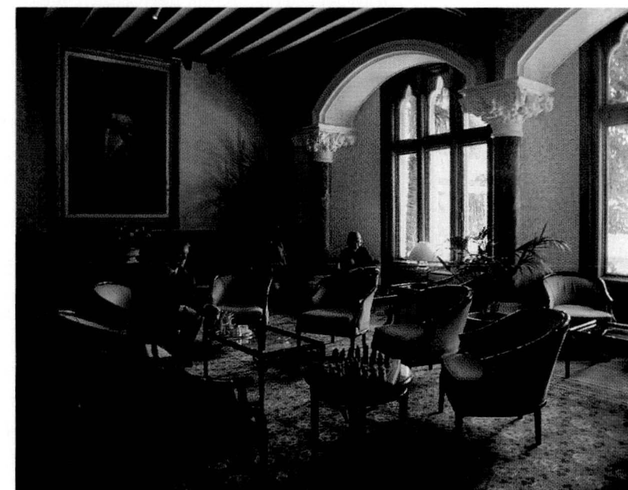

For hotel location, see maps on pages 477-483

LLANGOED HALL

LLYSWEN, BRECON, POWYS, WALES LD3 0YP
TEL: 01874 754525 FAX: 01874 754545

The history of Llangoed Hall dates back to 560 AD when it is thought to have been the site of the first Welsh Parliament. Inspired by this legend, the architect Sir Clough Williams-Ellis, transformed the Jacobean mansion he found here in 1914 into an Edwardian country house. Situated deep in a valley of the River Wye, surrounded by a walled garden, the hotel commands magnificent views of the Black Mountains and Brecon Beacons beyond. The rooms are warm and welcoming, furnished with antiques and oriental rugs and, on the walls, an outstanding collection of paintings acquired by the owner, Sir Bernard Ashley. Head Chef Ben Davies makes eating at Llangoed one of the principal reasons for going there. Classic but light, his Michelin starred menus represent the very best of modern cuisine, complemented by a cellar of more than 300 wines. Tennis and croquet are available on site, and nearby there is golf, fishing, riding, shooting, and some of the best mountain walking and gliding in Britain. For expeditions, there are the Wye Valley, Hay-on-Wye and its bookshops, the border castles, Hereford and Leominster. Children over 8 are welcome. The hotel is a member of Welsh Rarebits and Small Luxury Hotels of the World. **Directions:** The hotel is 9 miles west of Hay, 11 miles north of Brecon on the A470. Price guide: Single £95; double/twin £155–£195; suite £195–£285.

For hotel location, see maps on pages 477-483

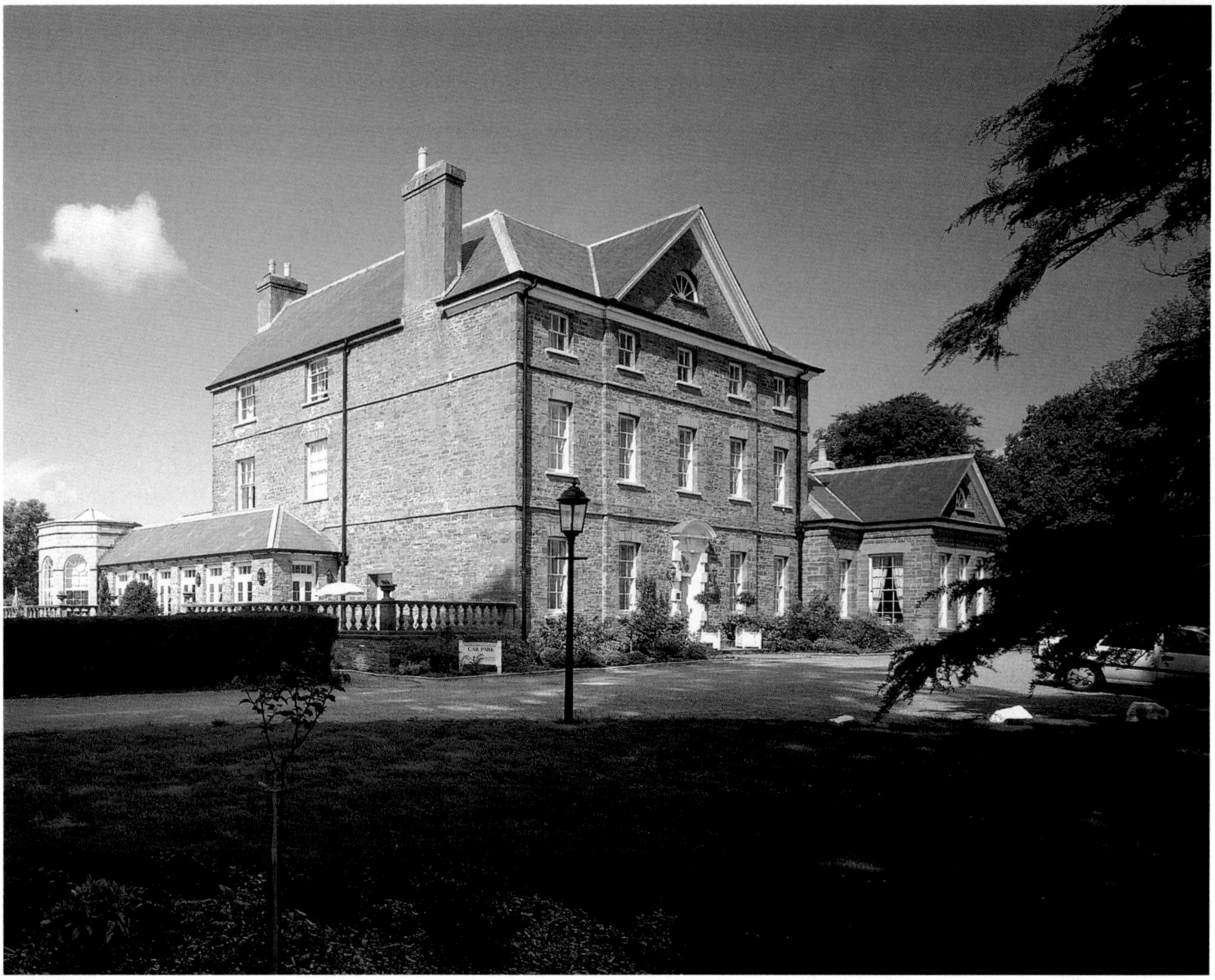

PETERSTONE COURT

LLANHAMLACH, BRECON, POWYS LD3 7YB
TEL: 01874 665387 FAX: 01874 665376

Set in a tiny village on the eastern edge of the mysterious Brecon Beacons National Park, Peterstone is a carefully restored Georgian manor, swathed in history which can be traced back to the time of William the Conqueror. It was voted the best new hotel in Wales by the AA in 1992 and amongst a string of awards the hotel collected merits from the RAC and the Welsh Tourist Board. There are just 12 guest bedrooms at the court, eight beautifully proportioned period style rooms in the main house, and four split level rooms in the former stable that have all the things you expect and many you don't, such as tape players, video players and a welcoming decanter of sherry. Intimate parties and special occasions can be accommodated in one of the two small private rooms. The surrounding countryside has an abundance of walks, one of which starts at the end of the hotel drive and goes along the river and the canal back into Brecon. Alternatively, or perhaps even after all the walking, there is in the hotel basement a fully equipped health club, with gymnasium, sauna, solarium and Jacuzzi. In the grounds are an outdoor heated pool, croquet and putting. **Directions:** Peterstone Court is located in the village of Llanhamlach, on the A40, three miles east of Brecon. Price guide: Single £79.50; double/twin £95–£130. Short breaks available all year round.

For hotel location, see maps on pages 477-483

Coed-y-Mwstwr Hotel

COYCHURCH, NEAR BRIDGEND, MID GLAMORGAN CF35 6AF
TEL: 01656 860621 FAX: 01656 863122

Coed-y-Mwstwr is a country mansion of Victorian origin set in 17 acres of mature woodland, which is also home to an abundance of wildlife – kestrels, woodpeckers and buzzards all nest here, with foxes, rabbits and badgers never far away. Much thought has gone into ensuring that the décor and furnishings are in keeping with the style of the house. High ceilings, chandeliers and large fireplaces feature in the elegant public rooms. The 23 luxurious bedrooms all have en suite facilities and wonderful views. The elegant oak-panelled restaurant enjoys a good reputation locally and offers a blend of traditional and modern cuisine, with both table d'hôte and à la carte menus with 1 AA Rosette. The wine list has more than 80 wines. Private functions for up to 130 people may be held in the Hendre Suite. In addition, there are two private dining rooms. A heated outdoor swimming pool and all-weather tennis court are available for guests' use. For golfers, Royal Porthcawl and Southerndown courses are 10 minutes' drive from the hotel. The beautiful Gower and Pembrokeshire coastline and Brecon Beacons National Park are within easy reach. Open all year. **Directions:** Leave M4 at junction 35, take A473 towards Bridgend for 1 mile, turn right into Coychurch. At filling station turn right and follow signs uphill. Price guide: Single £85; double/twin £125; suite £140.

23 rms MasterCard VISA AMERICAN EXPRESS M 140

For hotel location, see maps on pages 477-483

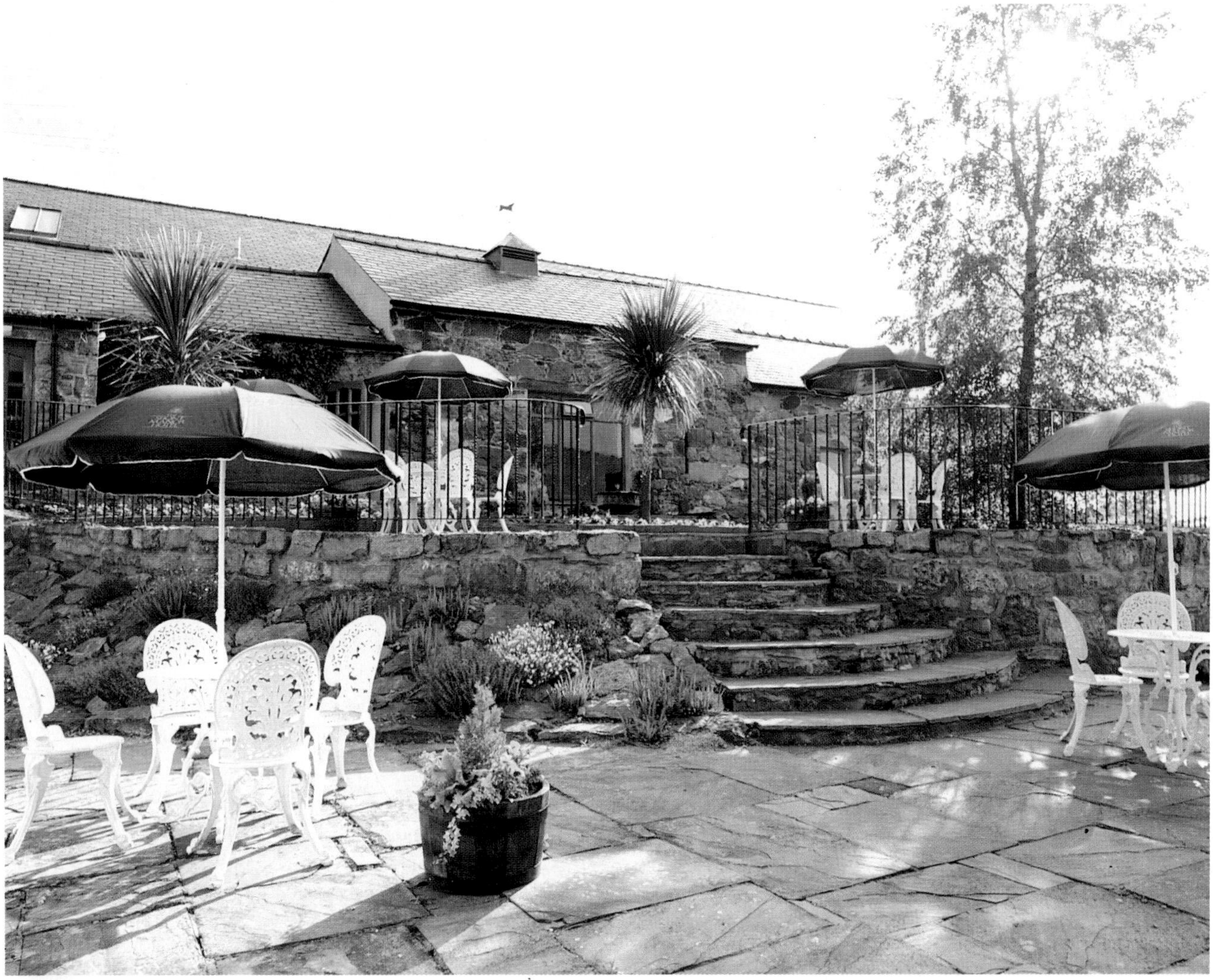

GWESTY SEIONT MANOR HOTEL

LLANRUG, CAERNARFON, GWYNEDD LL55 2AQ
TEL: 01286 673366 FAX: 01286 672840

Set in 150 acres of parkland amid the majestic scenery of Snowdonia, Seiont Manor has been stylishly remodelled from original rustic buildings to create a unique luxury hotel offering guests every comfort. The oak-panelled bar and library, with its collection of leather-bound volumes, provide the perfect environment for relaxing with a drink before dinner. For lovers of good food, the excellent restaurant, overlooking the hotel's lake and grounds, serves classic French cuisine as well as superb local dishes, all prepared from the best ingredients. Each of the 28 bedrooms, with furnishings from around the world, is comfortable and spacious and has en suite facilities. The hotel is an ideal venue for conferences, functions, weddings and meetings of up to 100 people. A heated pool housed in the Victorian-style 'chapel' takes pride of place among the leisure facilities, which also include a sauna, solarium, multi-gym, aromatherapy and reflexology treatments. Mountain bikes and a jogging track are available for guests' use and there is fishing for salmon and trout in the river. Caernarfon golf course, with its stunning views over the Menai Straits, is nearby, as are the Snowdonia Mountain Range, Ffestiniog Mountain Railway and Caernarson Castle. **Directions:** 3 miles from Caernarfon on the A4086. Price guide: Single £79; double/twin £125–£160.

For hotel location, see maps on pages 477-483

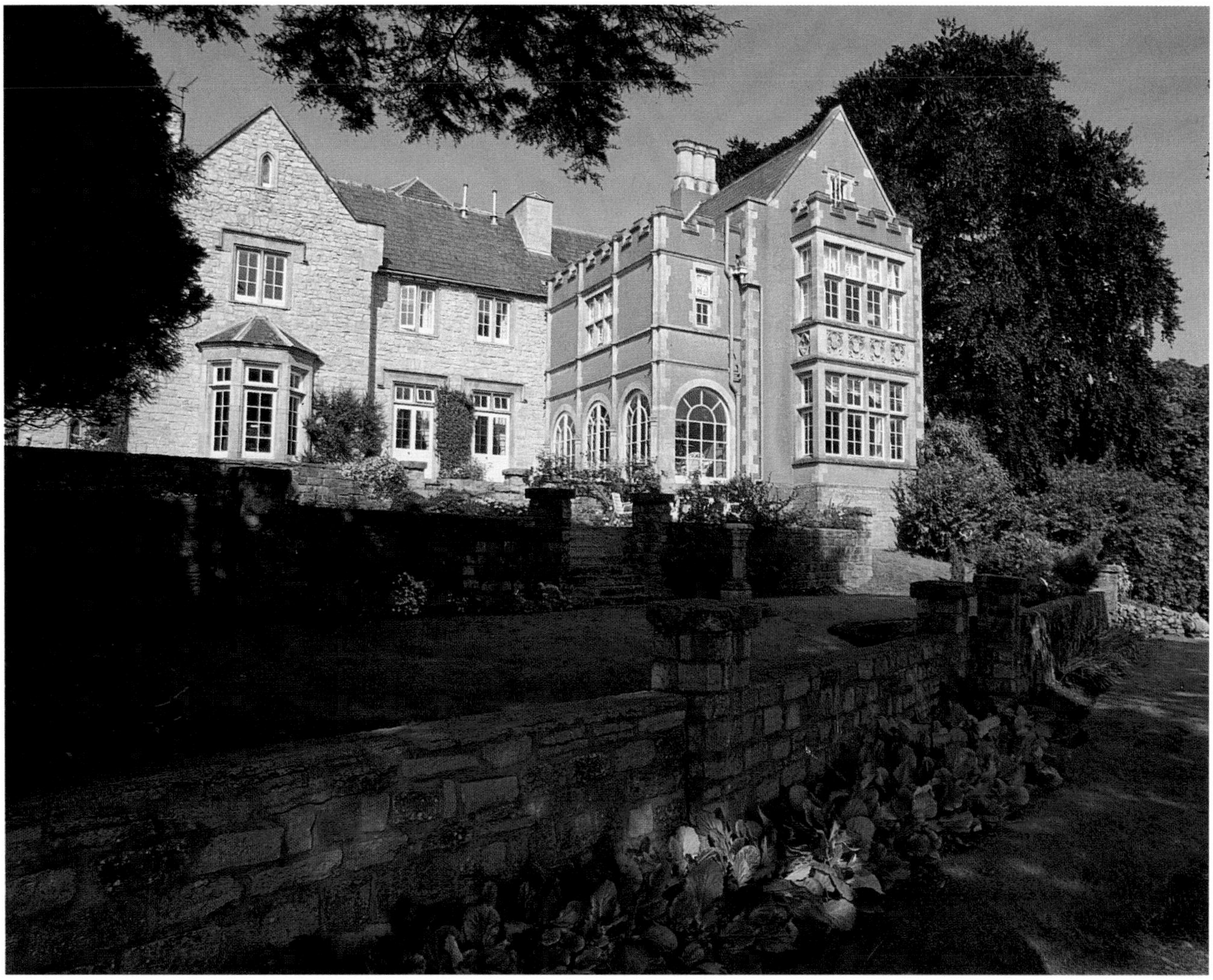

EGERTON GREY COUNTRY HOUSE HOTEL

PORTHKERRY, NR CARDIFF, SOUTH GLAMORGAN CF62 3BZ
TEL: 01446 711666 FAX: 01446 711690
Internet no: http://www.openworld.co.uk/britain/pages/E/EGE69BZa.html

A distinguished former rectory dating from the early-19th century, Egerton Grey is tucked away in seven acres of gardens in a secluded, wooded valley in the Vale of Glamorgan. Visitors can enjoy glorious views towards Porthkerry Park and the sea beyond. The interior design complements the architectural features of the house. The Edwardian drawing room has intricate plaster mouldings, chandeliers, an open fireplace and oil paintings. A quiet library overlooks the garden. All of the immaculately presented bedrooms are extremely comfortable, and several have Victorian baths and brasswork. Original Cuban mahogany panelling and candle-lit tables create an air of intimacy in the main restaurant. High-quality cuisine is presented with finesse on bone china, and wine is served in Welsh Royal Crystal glasses. Riding and sailing can be arranged and there is a pitch-and-putt course a short stroll away by the sea. The Welsh Folk Museum, Castle Coch and Cardiff Castle are nearby. **Directions:** From M4 junction 33, take A4050; follow airport signs for 10 miles. Take A4226 towards Porthkerry; after 400 yards turn into lane between two thatched cottages, hotel is at end of lane. Price guide: Single £55–£95; double/twin £85–£120.

For hotel location, see maps on pages 477-483

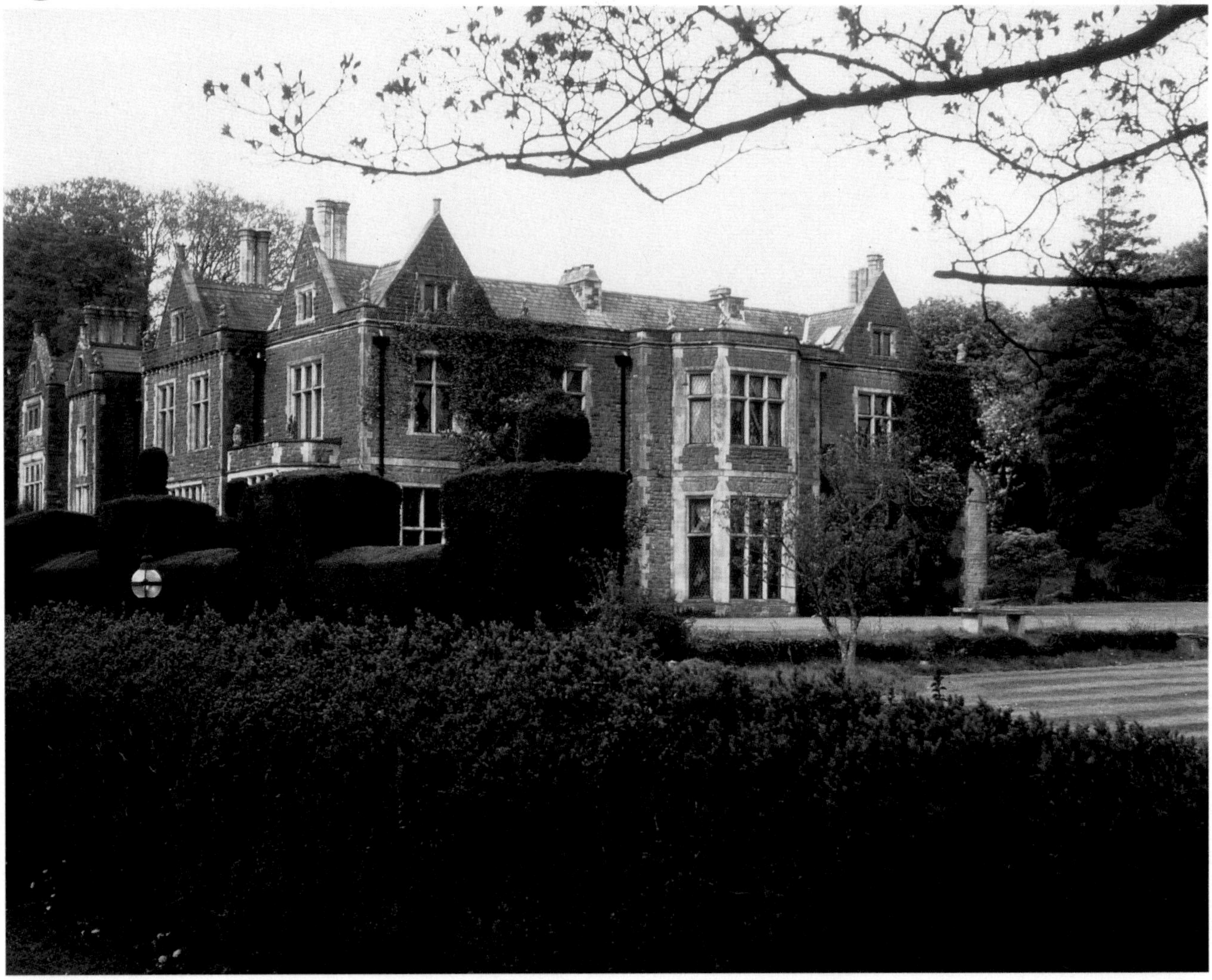

MISKIN MANOR COUNTRY HOUSE HOTEL

MISKIN, MID-GLAMORGAN CF72 8ND
TEL: 01443 224204 FAX: 01443 237606

Although its history dates back to the 11th century, Miskin Manor first became a hotel only in 1986, following extensive restoration and refurbishment. Set amid 20 acres of undisturbed parkland, criss-crossed with streams, peace and seclusion are guaranteed. The uncommonly spacious reception rooms have fine fireplaces, panelled walls and elaborate plasterwork ceilings, all enhanced by rich drapery and comfortable furniture. All of the bedrooms have en suite bathrooms and full facilities. In the 1920s, one of the de luxe suites was occupied by the Prince of Wales (later King Edward VII), a room which is now aptly named the Prince of Wales suite. First-class Welsh cuisine is served in the AA Red Rosette awarded restaurant and complemented by a comprehensive wine list. Within the grounds is the popular sports and leisure club, Frederick's, which guests can use. It comprises three squash courts, badminton court, indoor heated swimming pool, gymnasium, snooker, spa, sauna, solarium, beautician, bistro and crèche. Celebrations, conferences and all manner of functions can be catered for at Miskin Manor, with reliable, professional support assured. Corporate activites can be held on site. **Directions:** From junction 34 of the M4, follow hotel signs, Drive is one mile from the motorway roundabout. Price guide: Single from £80; double/twin £100; suite £175.

For hotel location, see maps on pages 477-483

SOUGHTON HALL COUNTRY HOUSE HOTEL

NORTHOP, NR MOLD, CLWYD CH7 6AB
TEL: 01352 840811 FAX: 01352 840382

Built as a Bishops Palace in 1714, Grade I Soughton Hall set in beautiful landscaped gardens amidst 150 acres of parkland is approached via a spectacular half mile avenue of limes. Beautiful antique furniture adorns a house of unique history and architecture. With just 14 authentic bedrooms and the personal welcome of the Rodenhurst family, a memorable stay is assured. The hotel is also ideal for business use with a boardroom that is second to none. 1997 features the opening of a country inn within the old coach house and stables, a listed building of immense historical and architectural interest also. It will feature a beer parlour specialising in serving many real ales from local breweries and an informal wine and steak bar within the original haylofts. Special three day packages are available to include dinner in either the hotel restaurant (past awards include Welsh Restaurant of the Year) or the inn. Within the surrounding parkland is an 18-hole championship golf course. Golfing holidays are available. From the hotel, excursions can be made into North Wales and historic Chester. An exclusive, full-colour guide to selected holiday drives in the area is provided. **Directions:** From the M56 take the A55 towards North Wales, then the A5119 to Northop. Cross the traffic lights; the hall is one mile along the road on the left. Price guide: Single £70; double/twin £80–£119.

For hotel location, see maps on pages 477-483

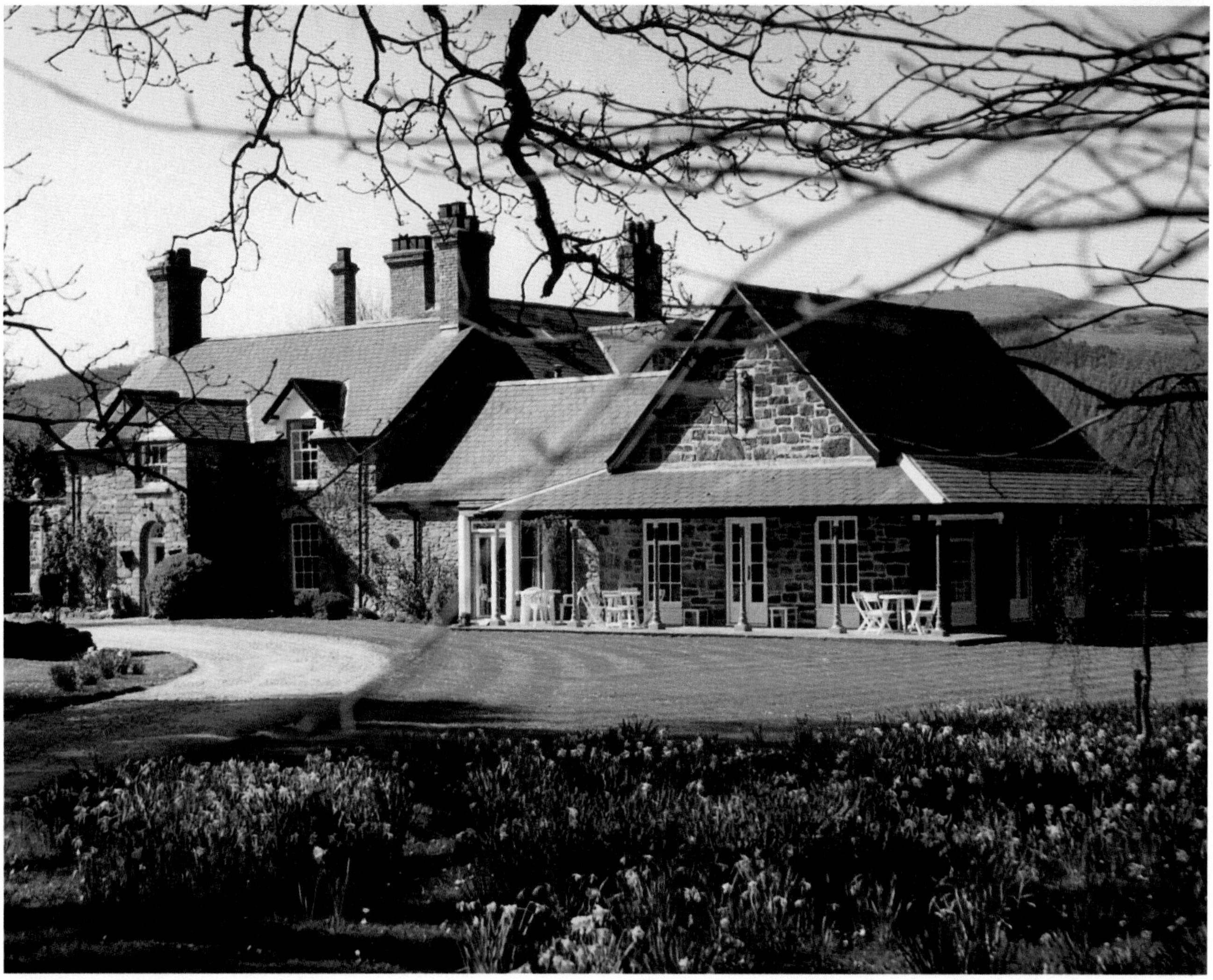

TYDDYN LLAN COUNTRY HOUSE HOTEL

LLANDRILLO, NR CORWEN, DENBIGHSHIRE LL21 0ST

TEL: 01490 440264 FAX: 01490 440414

Tyddyn Llan is an elegant Georgian country house situated amid breathtaking scenery in the Vale of Edeyrnion. Owned and run by Peter and Bridget Kindred, the hotel is a quiet oasis in an area of outstanding natural beauty at the foot of the Berwyn Mountains. There are 10 bedrooms, all individual in style and elegantly furnished with antiques and period furniture. Each enjoys views of the gardens and the mountains beyond and has a bathroom en suite. The hotel is proud of the reputation it has established for the quality of the food served in the restaurant. Inventive and frequently changing menus feature dishes using fresh local ingredients and herbs from the kitchen garden. A carefully selected wine list complements the cuisine. In the gardens, guests may enjoy a game of croquet and tea is served on fine days. The hotel has rights to four miles of fly-fishing on the River Dee. Keen walkers can trace the ancient Roman road, Ffordd Gam Elin, which traverses the Berwyn Mountains. Here naturalists will find many different species of birds and wild flowers. Tyddyn Llan is well placed for exploring nearby Snowdonia, and the Roman city of Chester is only 35 miles away. **Directions:** Llandrillo is midway between Corwen and Bala on the B4401, four miles from the A5 at Corwen. Price guide (including dinner): Single £80–£91; double/twin £145–£155.

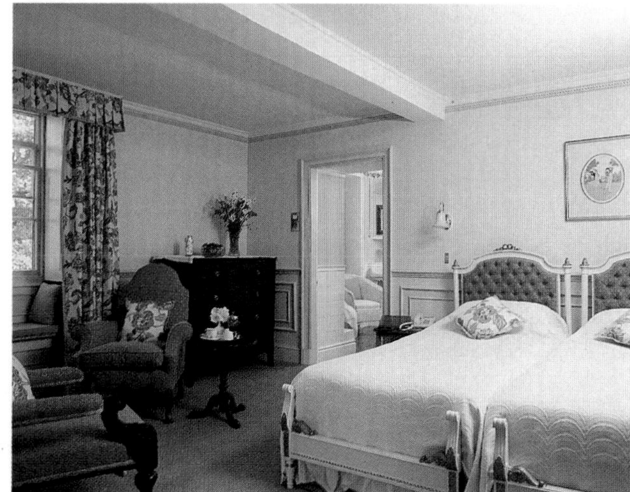

For hotel location, see maps on pages 477-483

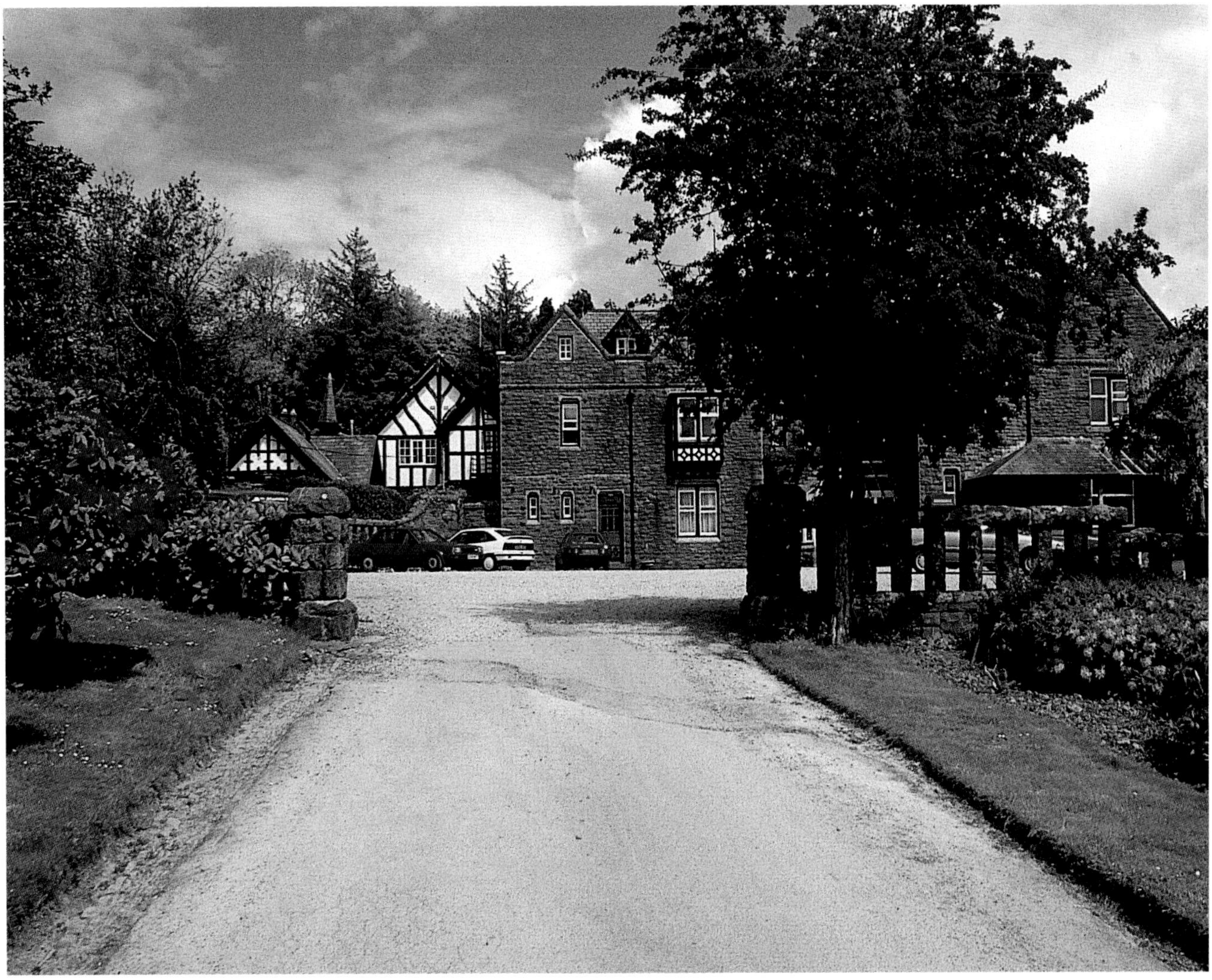

Bron Eifion Country House Hotel

CRICCIETH, GWYNEDD LL52 0SA
TEL: 01766 522385 FAX: 01766 522003

This magnificent baronial mansion stands within five acres of glorious gardens and woodlands, yet only minutes from the sea. It was built by the millionaire slate owner John Greaves whose master craftsmen carved the spectacular pitch and Oregon pine panelled hallway, minstrels gallery and vaulted ceiling. The Conservatory Restaurant, which overlooks the floodlit gardens serves innovative cuisine, complemented by a superb selection of wines. All 19 bedrooms are en suite and are individually decorated, offering king-sized and four-poster beds, or you could choose a standard or de luxe room. The gardens provide interesting walks, from the stone walled terraces to the secluded herb garden. Perhaps you would like to laze on the verandah overlooking the lawns which abound in a variety of wildlife. Golf, shooting, riding and fishing are all nearby. A short car drive will take you to the pretty villages of Criccieth, Porthmadog or the Italiante village of Portmeirion. The rugged beauty of the mountains of Snowdonia, together with castles, stately homes, Lloyd George's Museum and Ffestiniog Railway are all closeby. **Directions:** The hotel is on the A497 on the outskirts of Criccieth and stands at the top of a tree-lined drive, nestled in Woodland. Price guide: Single £57–£67; double/twin £84–£110. De luxe supplement £15 per room per night.

For hotel location, see maps on pages 477-483

GLIFFAES COUNTRY HOUSE HOTEL

CRICKHOWELL, POWYS NP8 1RH
TEL: 01874 730371 FAX: 01874 730463

Visitors may be surprised to discover a hotel featuring distinctive Italianate architecture midway between the Brecon Beacons and the Black Mountains. Gliffaes Country House Hotel is poised 150 feet above the River Usk and commands glorious views of the surroundings hills and valley. The elegantly furnished, Regency style drawing room is an ideal place to relax and leads to a large sun room and on to the terrace, from which guests may enjoy the magnificent scenery. In addition to a panelled lounge, there is a billiard room with a full-size table. An informal atmosphere prevails in the dining room, a wide choice from an imaginative menu covering the best of National dishes and Mediterranean specialities created by a talented team led by Head Chef, Mark Coulton. The Gliffaes fishery includes every type of water, from slow-flowing flats to fast-running rapids, on 2½ miles of the River Usk renowned for its wild brown trout and salmon fishing. The 33 acre hotel grounds have rare trees and shrubs as well as lawns for putting and croquet. Riding can be arranged nearby. Now open throughout the year. **Directions:** Gliffaes is signposted from the A40, 2½ miles west of Crickhowell. Price guide: Single £34.50–£44; double/twin £68–£102.

22 rms

For hotel location, see maps on pages 477-483

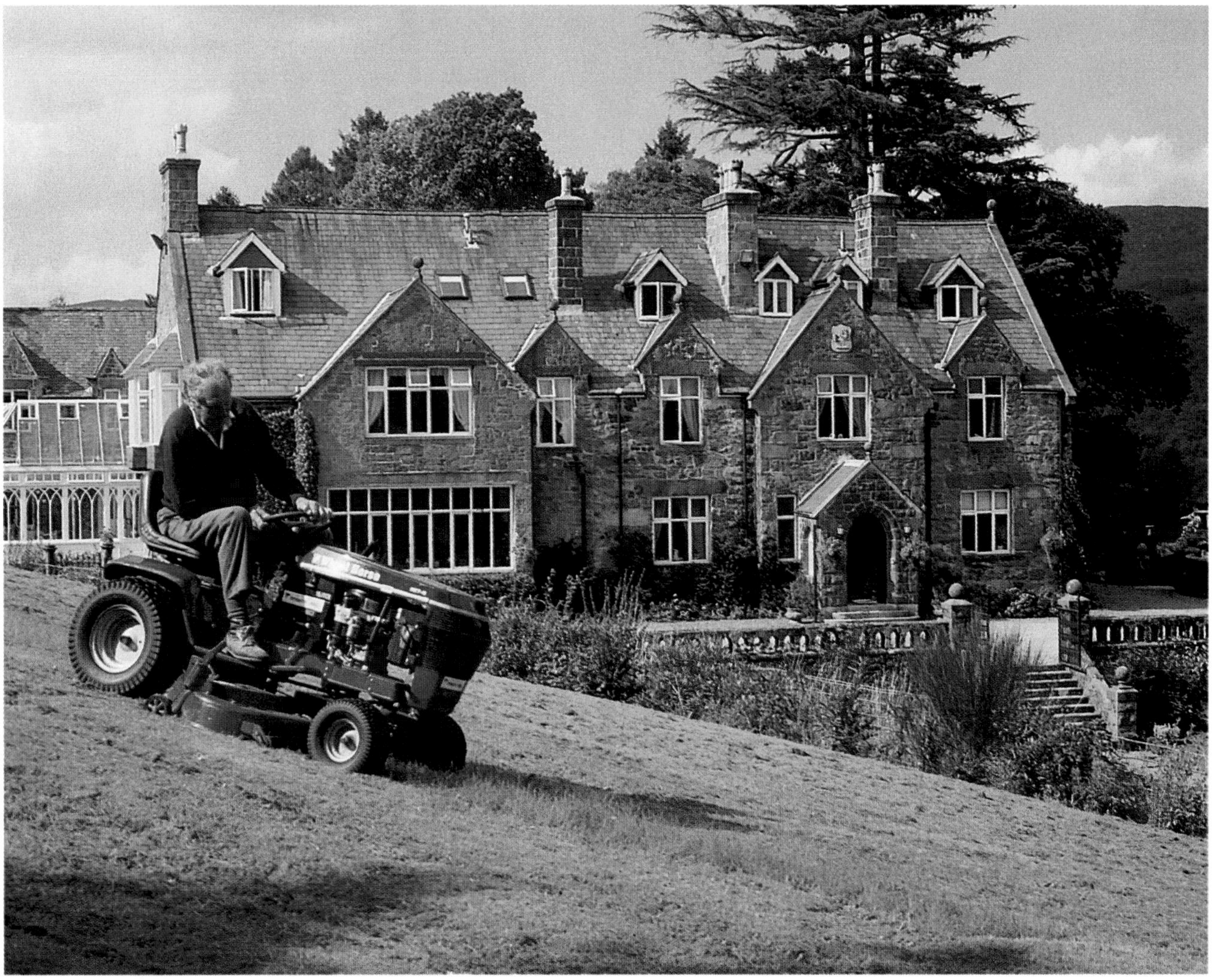

PENMAENUCHAF HALL

PENMAENPOOL, DOLGELLAU, GWYNEDD LL40 1YB
TEL: 01341 422129 FAX: 01341 422129

The splendour of Cader Idris and the Mawddach Estuary forms the backdrop for this handsome Victorian mansion which is an exceptional retreat. Set within the Snowdonia National Park, the 21-acre grounds encompass lawns, a formal sunken rose garden, a water garden and woodland. The beautiful interiors feature oak and mahogany panelling, stained-glass windows, log fires in winter, polished Welsh slate floors and freshly cut flowers. There are 12 luxurious bedrooms, some with four-poster and half-tester beds, and all with interesting views. In the Gothic-style conservatory restaurant, guests can choose from an imaginative menu prepared with the best seasonal produce and complemented by an extensive list of wines. An elegant panelled dining room can be used for private dinners or meetings. Penmaenuchaf Hall is perfect for a totally relaxed holiday. For recreation, guests can fish for trout and salmon along ten miles of the Mawddach River, or take part in a range of water sports. They can also enjoy scenic walks, visit sandy beaches and historic castles and take trips on narrow-gauge railways. **Directions:** The hotel is off the A493 Dolgellau–Tywyn road, about two miles from Dolgellau. Price guide: Single £50–£95; double/twin £95–£150.

For hotel location, see maps on pages 477-483

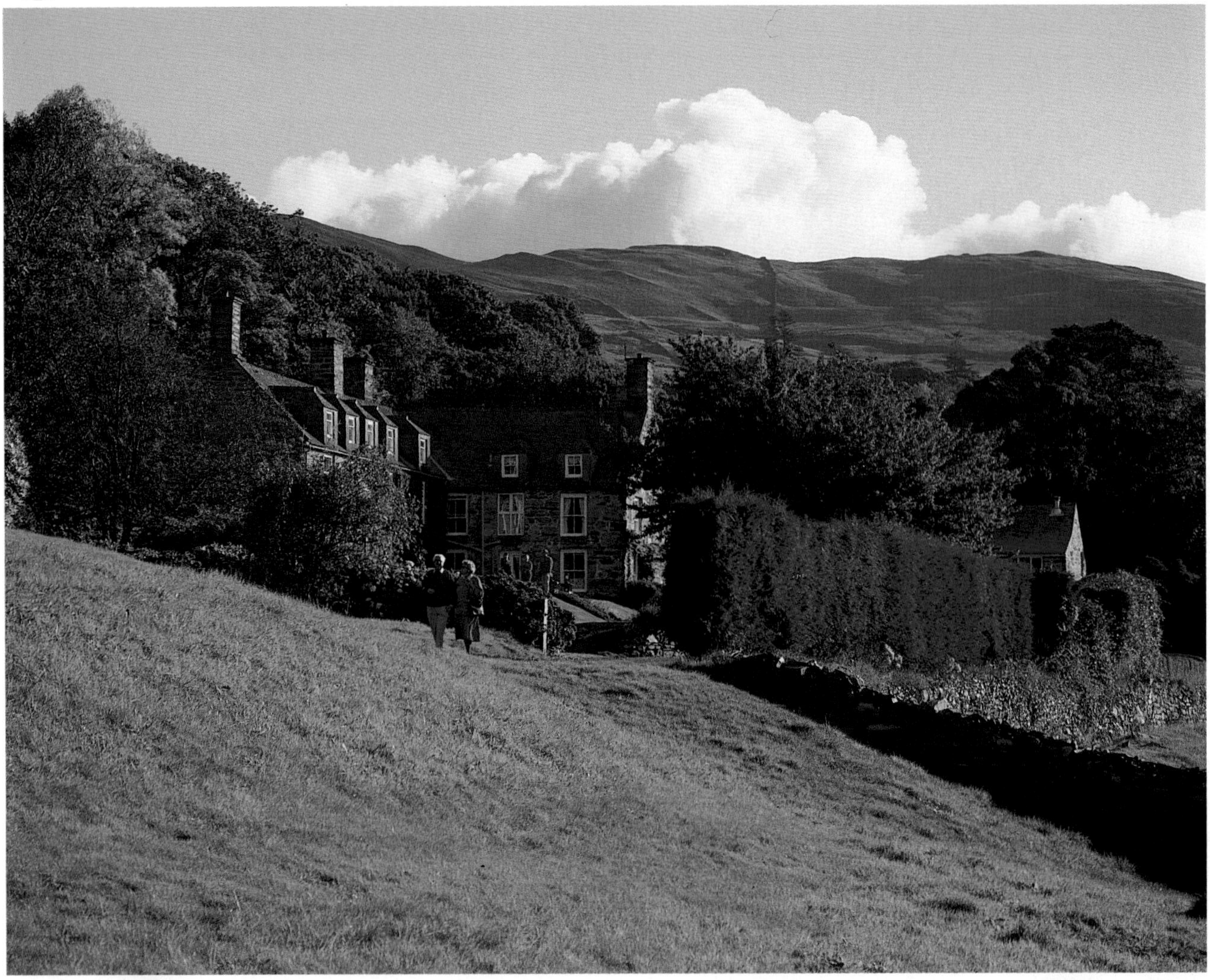

HOTEL MAES-Y-NEUADD

TALSARNAU, NR HARLECH, GWYNEDD LL47 6YA
TEL: 01766 780200 FAX: 01766 780211

This part-14th century house, built of granite and slate, is cradled by eight acres of landscaped mountainside. As a much-loved hotel it has been run by the Horsfall and Slatter families since 1981. Peace and tranquillity are all-pervasive, whether relaxing in the pretty, beamed lounge or reclining in a leather Chesterfield in the bar while enjoying an apéritif. Talented chefs create delicious English and Welsh dishes using fresh produce such as lamb, fish and a variety of Welsh farmhouse cheeses, along with vegetables and herbs from the kitchen garden. As an alternative dining venue for special occasions and parties, dinner can be provided on the world famous Ffestiniog railway. The hotel produces its own oils and vinegars which are stylishly presented for sale. Spring and autumn breaks are available. The bedrooms vary in style, from early beams and dormers to later Georgian elegance with full-length windows. For golfers, the Royal St David's Golf Course is located three miles away. Nearby attractions include the Italianate village of Portmeirion, slate caverns, beautiful beaches, Snowdonia, Edward I's castle at Harlech and the Ffestiniog railway. USA toll-free reservations: 1-800 635 3602. **Directions:** Hotel is 3½ miles north of Harlech, off the B4573, signposted at the end of the lane. Price guide: Single £72; double/twin £147–£198. (Including dinner)

For hotel location, see maps on pages 477-483

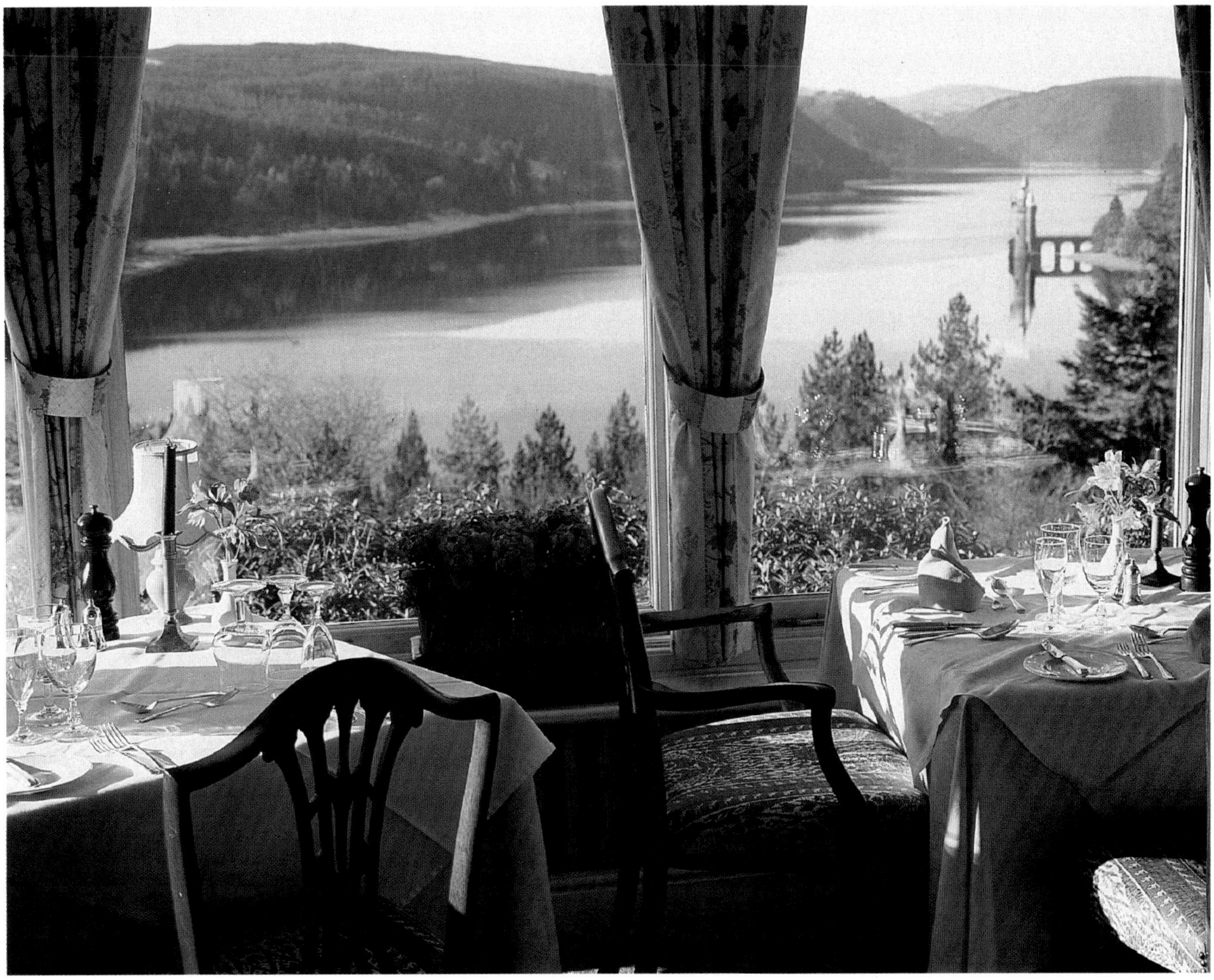

LAKE VYRNWY HOTEL

LAKE VYRNWY, LLANWDDYN, MONTGOMERYSHIRE SY10 OLY
TEL: 01691 870 692 FAX: 01691 870 259

Situated high on the hillside within the 24,000 acre Vyrnwy Estate the hotel commands breathtaking views of mountains, lakes and moorland. It is also surrounded by lawns, an abundance of rhododendrons, woods and meadowlands. Built in 1860 its heritage has been maintained for well over a hundred years as a retreat for all lovers of nature and fine dining. There are 37 bedrooms all individually furnished and decorated, many with antiques and some with special features such as Jacuzzis, balconies, four-posters or suites. There are also dedicated meeting and private dining facilities. The award-winning candle-lit restaurant has a menu which changes 365 days of the year. Everything from the marmalade to the *petits fours* at dinner are created in the Vyrnwy kitchens. Its own market garden provides many of the seasonal herbs, fruits, vegetables and flowers. The hotel owns some of Wales' best fishing together with some 24,000 acres of sporting rights. Other pursuits include sailing, cycling, tennis, quad trekking and some beautiful walking trails. Also an RSPB sanctuary, the estate provides a wealth of wildlife and represents true peace and tranquillity. **Directions:** From Shrewsbury take the A458 to Welshpool, then turn right onto B4393 just after Ford (signposted to Lake Vyrnwy 28 miles). Price guide: Single £63.80; double/twin from £81.80; suite £132.80.

For hotel location, see maps on pages 477-483

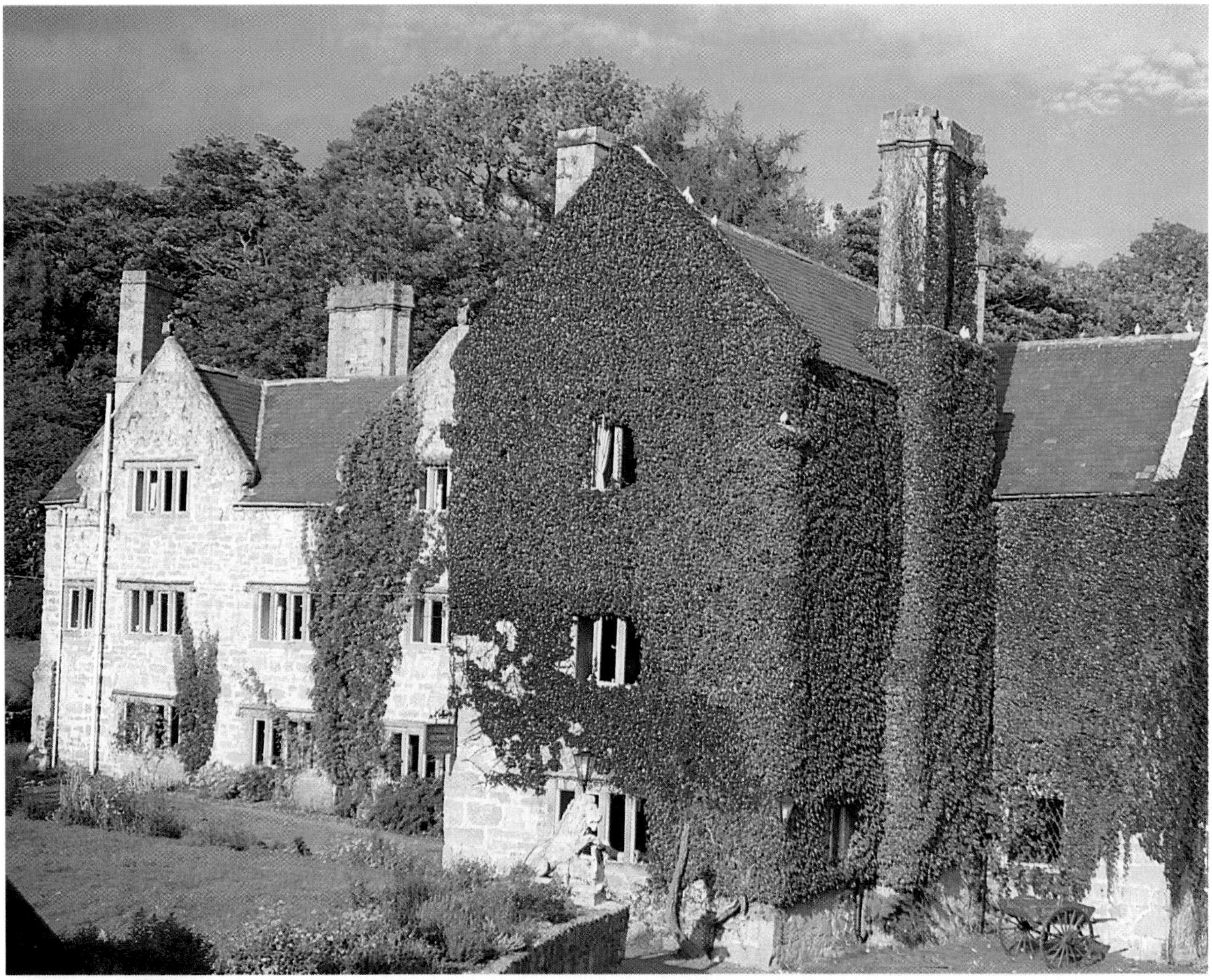

Bodidris Hall

LLANDEGLA, WREXHAM, DENBIGHSHIRE LL 11 3AL
TEL: 01978 790434 FAX: 01978 790335

Ivy-clad Bodidris Hall, amid the wild hills, forests and moorlands of North Wales, is steeped in history and legend. A fortified building has stood on the site since two Crusaders were granted the estate by their Prince, Gryffydd ap Madoc, as a reward for valour. It later became the Tudor hunting lodge of Lord Robert Dudley, controversial favourite of Elizabeth I. The Hall still harbours many historical features inside its thick, grey-stone walls, including a former prison cell, a priest hole and a narrow staircase on which duels were fought. Spacious bedrooms, some with four-poster beds, are individually designed with magnificent views over 50 acres of rugged countryside, landscaped lawns and the Hall's own trout filled pond that is a haven for wildfowl. The heavily beamed bar with its mullion windows is welcoming with nooks that beckon you to relax and unwind, and the intimate restaurant with its excellent British and Continental cuisine features a huge open fireplace built to roast a whole lamb. The Hall is excellent value for money and an ideal base for exploring North Wales, or enjoying walks on nearby Offa's Dyke. Riding, cycling, pony trekking, trout fishing, archery, clay pigeon and driven shooting are available. Directions: Bodidris Hall is 1/2 mile off the main A5104 Chester-Corwen road, 2 miles west of the junction with the A525. Price guide: Single £55-£80; double/twin £70-£105; suite £90-£125.

For hotel location, see maps on pages 477-483

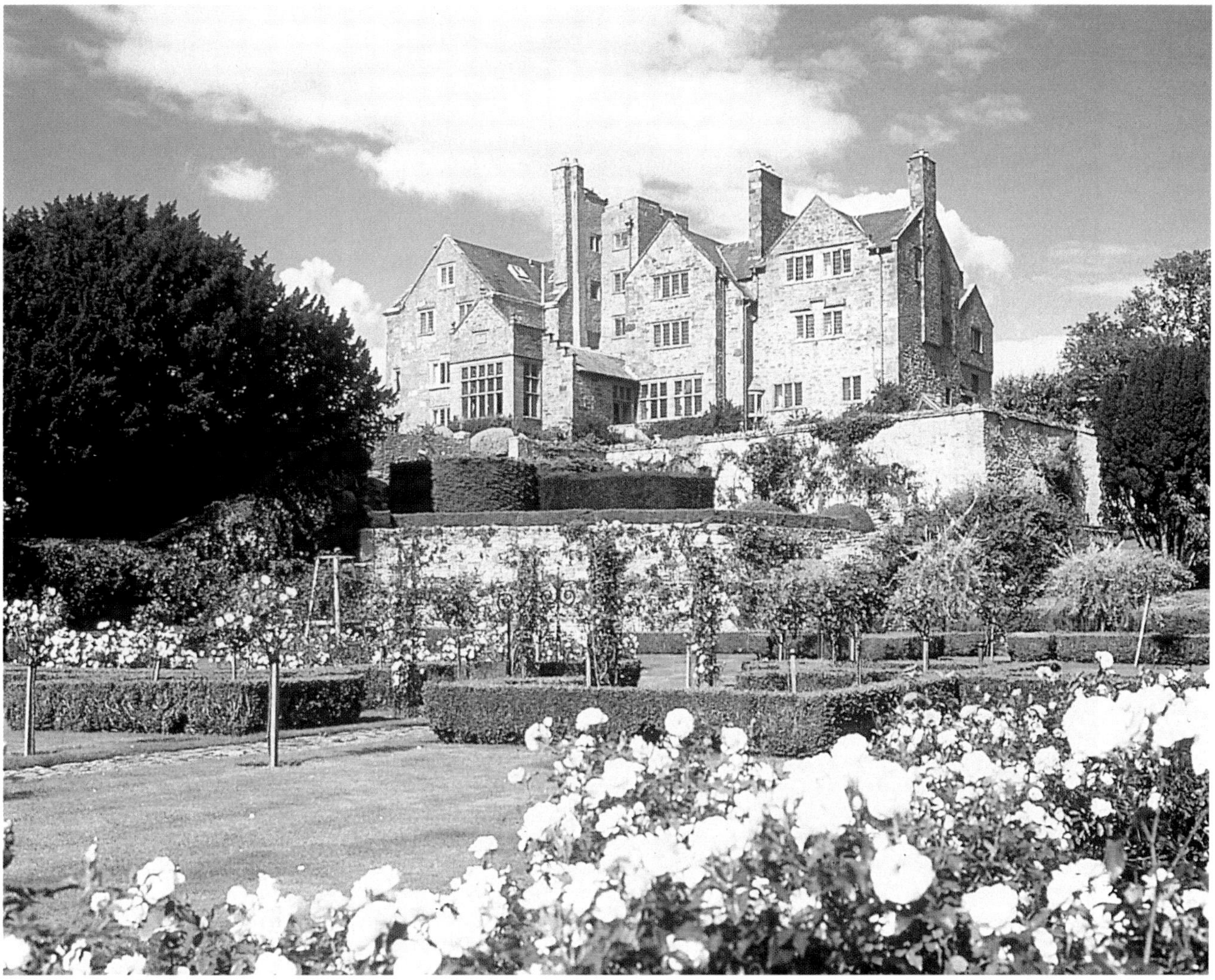

BODYSGALLEN HALL

LLANDUDNO, GWYNEDD LL30 1RS
TEL: 01492 584466 FAX: 01492 582519

Bodysgallen Hall, owned and restored by Historic House Hotels, lies at the end of a winding drive in 200 acres of wooded parkland and beautiful formal gardens. Magnificent views encompass the sweep of the Snowdonia range of mountains, and the hotel looks down on the imposing medieval castle at Conwy. This Grade I listed house was built mainly in the 17th century, but the earliest feature is a 13th century tower, reached by a narrow winding staircase, once used as a lookout for soldiers serving the English kings of Conwy and now a safe place from which to admire the fabulous views. The hotel has 19 spacious bedrooms in the house and 16 delightful cottage suites in the grounds. Two of the finest rooms in the house are the large oak-panelled entrance hall and the first floor drawing room, both with splendid fireplaces and mullioned windows. Head chef is Michael Penny, who produces superb dishes using fresh local ingredients. The Bodysgallen Spa comprises a spacious swimmng pool, steam room, sauna, solaria, gym, beauty salons, restaurant and bar. The hotel is ideally placed for visiting the many historic castles and stately homes in North Wales. Famous golf courses adorn the coastline. **Directions:** On the A470 one mile from the intersection with the A55. Llandudno is a mile further on the A470. Price guide: Single £79–£98; double/twin £115–£170; suite £135–£150.

For hotel location, see maps on pages 477-483

St Tudno Hotel

PROMENADE, LLANDUDNO, GWYNEDD LL30 2LP
TEL: 01492 874411 FAX: 01492 860407

Undoubtedly one of the most delightful small hotels to be found on the coast of Britain, St Tudno Hotel, a former winner of the *Johansens Hotel of the Year Award for Excellence*, certainly offers a very special experience. The hotel, which has been elegantly and lovingly furnished with meticulous attention to detail, offers a particularly warm welcome from owners, Martin and Janette Bland, and their caring and friendly staff. Each beautifully co-ordinated bedroom has been individually designed with many thoughtful extras provided to ensure guests' comfort. The bar lounge and sitting room, which overlook the sea, have an air of Victorian charm. Regarded as one of Wales' leading restaurants, the air-conditioned Garden Room has won three AA Rosettes for its excellent cuisine. This AA Red Star hotel has won a host of other awards, including *Best Seaside Resort Hotel in Great Britain*, *Welsh Hotel of the Year*, national winner of the AA's *Warmest Welcome Award* and even an accolade for having the *Best Hotel Loos in Britain*! St Tudno is ideally situated for visits to Snowdonia, Conwy and Caernarfon Castles, Bodnant Gardens and Anglesey. Golf, riding, swimming and dry-slope skiing and tobogganing can be enjoyed locally. **Directions:** On the promenade opposite the pier entrance and gardens. Price guide: Single £72.50; double/twin £85–£145.

For hotel location, see maps on pages 477-483

THE LAKE COUNTRY HOUSE

LLANGAMMARCH WELLS, POWYS LD4 4BS
TEL: 01591 620202 FAX: 01591 620457

A welcoming Welsh Country house set in its own 50 acres with rhododendron lined pathways, riverside walks and a large well stocked trout lake. Within the hotel, airy rooms filled with fine antiques, paintings and fresh flowers make this the perfect place to relax. Delicious homemade teas are served everyday beside log fires. From the windows ducks and geese can be glimpsed wandering in the gardens which cascade down to the river. In the award winning restaurant, fresh produce and herbs from the gardens are used for seasonal Country House menus, complemented by one of the finest wine lists in Wales. Each of the supremely comfortable bedrooms or suites with beautifully appointed sitting rooms are furnished with the thoughtful attention to details seen throughout the hotel. Guests can fish for trout or salmon on the four miles of river which runs through the grounds, and the 3 acre lake regularly yields trout of five pounds and over. The grounds are a haven for wildlife: herons, dippers and kingfishers skim over the river, there are badgers in the woods and swans and waterfowl abound. There is a large billiard room in the hotel and a 9 hole par three golf course, tennis court, croquet lawn and putting green. AA 3 Red star – RAC Blue Ribbon. **Directions:** From the A483, follow signs to Llangammarch Wells and then to the hotel. Price guide: Single £80; double/twin £120; suite £165.

For hotel location, see maps on pages 477-483

Bryn Howel Hotel and Restaurant

LLANGOLLEN, DENBIGHSHIRE LL20 7UW
TEL: 01978 860331 FAX: 01978 860119

Bryn Howel, set in the magnificent Vale of Llangollen, was built in 1896. Although the hotel has been extended and regularly refurbished over the years, great care has been taken to preserve the original character and unique features of the building and its red brickwork, mullioned windows, oak panelling and intricate plaster mouldings still remain. The hotel is run by a brother and sister team, members of the Lloyd family who have owned the hotel for 30 years. They pride themselves on providing the highest standards of both comfort and service. Well appointed bedrooms, with a full range of modern amenities, offer splendid views of the surrounding countryside. Delicious food, featuring Dee salmon, Welsh lamb and local game and poultry, is served in the Cedar Tree Restaurant, winner of many awards for its tempting cuisine. Alternatively, guests may dine in the intimacy of the Oak Room. The hotel's leisure facilities include a sauna and solarium. Reduced fees for the nearby golf club are available to residents, who may also enjoy free game fishing on a five mile stretch of the River Dee. Places of interest nearby include the historic city of Chester and town of Shrewsbury. Bryn Howel is closed at Christmas. **Directions:** On the A539 (three miles from Llangollen) between Llangollen and the A483. Price guide: Single £39.90–£73; double/twin £79.80–£121; suite £120–£145.

For hotel location, see maps on pages 477-483

YNYSHIR HALL

EGLWYSFACH, MACHYNLLETH, POWYS SY20 8TA
TEL: 01654 781209 FAX: 01654 781366

Once owned by Queen Victoria, Ynyshir Hall is a captivating Georgian manor house that perfectly blends modern comfort and old-world elegance. Its 12 acres of picturesque, landscaped gardens are set alongside the Dovey Estuary, one of Wales' most outstanding areas of natural beauty and the hotel is surrounded by the Ynyshir Bird Reserve. Hosts Rob and Joan Reen offer guests a warm welcome and ensure a personal service, the hallmark of a good family-run hotel. Period furniture and opulent fabrics enhance the eight charming bedrooms. The suites are particularly luxurious and, along with a four-poster room and ground floor room, are popular with many guests. The interiors are exquisitely furnished throughout with comfortable sofas, antiques, contemporary colour schemes, oriental rugs and many original paintings. These works of art are the creation of Rob, an established and acclaimed artist. Local seafood, game, and vegetables from the kitchen garden are used to create superb English, French and Welsh dishes. Dogs by prior arrangement. In 1402 in Machynlleth the patriot Owen Glendower was crowned Prince of Wales. Another local landmark is Cader Idris, Wales' second most popular mountain. **Directions:** Off the main road between Aberystwyth and Machynlleth. Price guide: Single £85–£105; double/twin £100–£130; suite £150.

8 rms        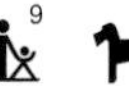   

For hotel location, see maps on pages 477-483

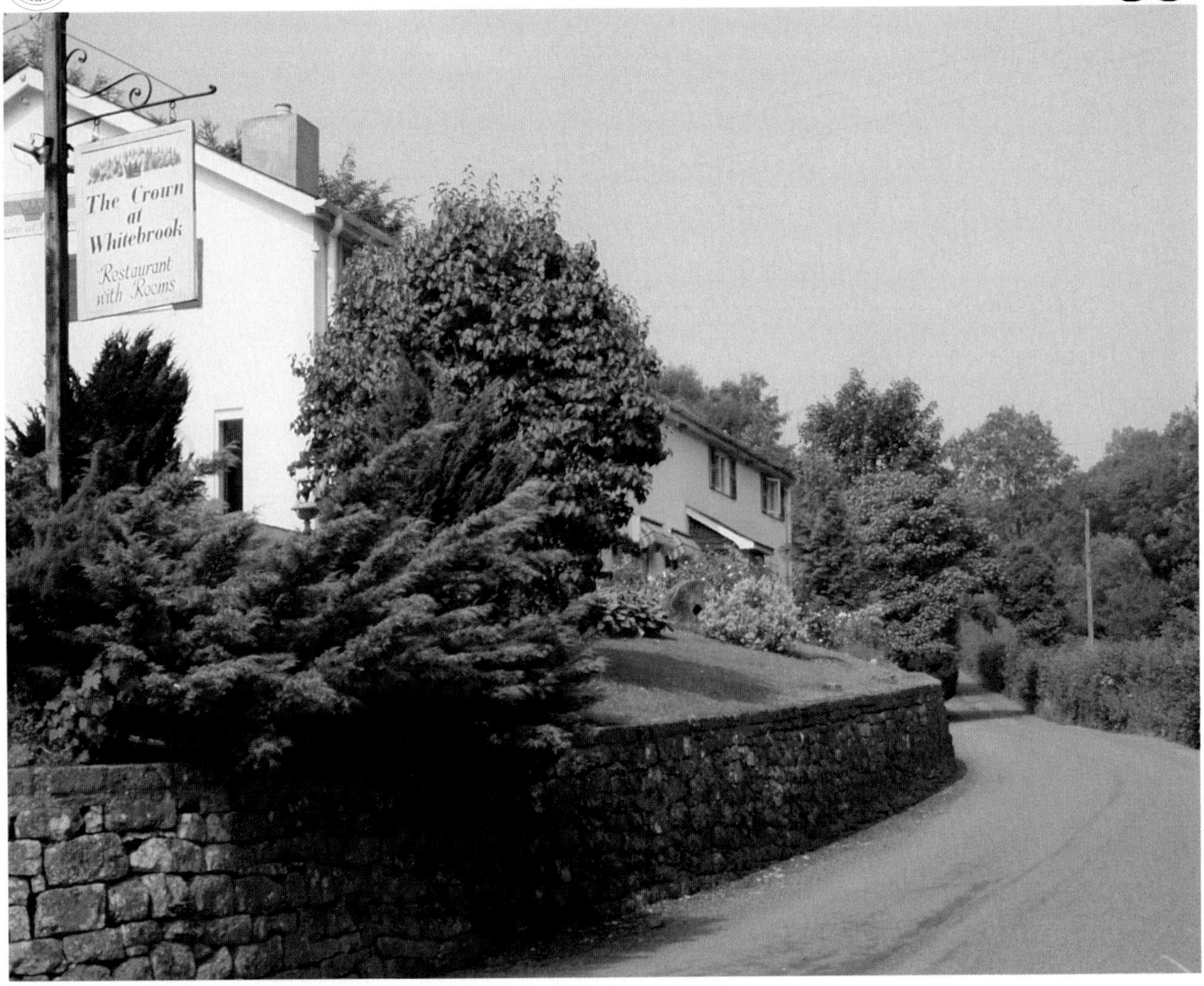

The Crown At Whitebrook

WHITEBROOK, MONMOUTH, GWENT NP5 4TX
TEL: 01600 860254 FAX: 01600 860607

A romantic auberge nestling deep in the Wye Valley, a designated area of outstanding natural beauty, The Crown is ideally situated for those seeking peace and tranquillity. Located in the wooded Whitebrook Valley on the fringe of Tintern Forest and only one mile from the River Wye, this is a place where guests can enjoy spectacular scenery. Roger and Sandra Bates offer their visitors a genuinely friendly welcome. Guests can relax in the cosy lounge and bar areas or in the Manor Room, with its ash furniture, hand-made locally. Sandra Bates' cooking has earned the Restaurant several awards, as well as recommendations from other guides. Dishes include local Welsh lamb and Wye salmon cooked with a classical French influence, followed by a choice of delicious home-made puddings and a selection of British farm cheeses. Most dietary requirements can be catered for as all food is freshly cooked to order. There is an extensive wine list. Tintern Abbey, Chepstow Castle and the Brecon Beacons National Park are nearby. **Directions:** Whitebrook is situated between the A466 and the B4293 approximately five miles south of Monmouth. Price guide: Single £39.50–£50; double/twin £53–£81.

12 rms

For hotel location, see maps on pages 473–479

THE CELTIC MANOR HOTEL & GOLF CLUB

COLDRA WOODS, NEWPORT, GWENT NP6 2YA
TEL: 01633 413000 FAX: 01633 412910/410284

Consistently acknowledged as one of the finest hotels in Wales, this refurbished Victorian manor house is set on the edge of over one thousand acres of rolling Welsh hills. Spacious bedrooms are elegantly furnished with comfort in mind. Sports enthusiasts will enjoy a choice of excellent leisure facilities. The golf complex comprises two 18-hole championship courses designed by Robert Trent-Jones Snr, American style clubhouse, Ian Woosnam Golf Academy and two tier driving range. Two exclusive health and fitness clubs with the very latest cardio-vascular exercise equipment, aerobics, swimming, sauna, steam room, Jacuzzi, beauty treatments and solarium. Three fine restaurants: Dining Terrace, overlooking the 18th green; The Patio Brasserie in the picturesque conservatory and Hedleys, benefit from the culinary skills of twice winner of the title, Welsh Chef of the Year, Trefor Jones and his team. An ancient woodland walk winds through Coldra Woods, with its rare flora and fauna. Activity weekends can be arranged for parties, including murder mysteries and hot-air ballooning. Nearby are Tintern Abbey, the Wye Valley and the castles at Chepstow, Caerphilly and Cardiff. **Directions:** Leave M4 at junction 24; hotel is 400 yards along the A48 towards Newport on the right-hand side. Price guide: Single £85-£100; double/twin £99-£150; suite £150-£165.

For hotel location, see maps on pages 477-483

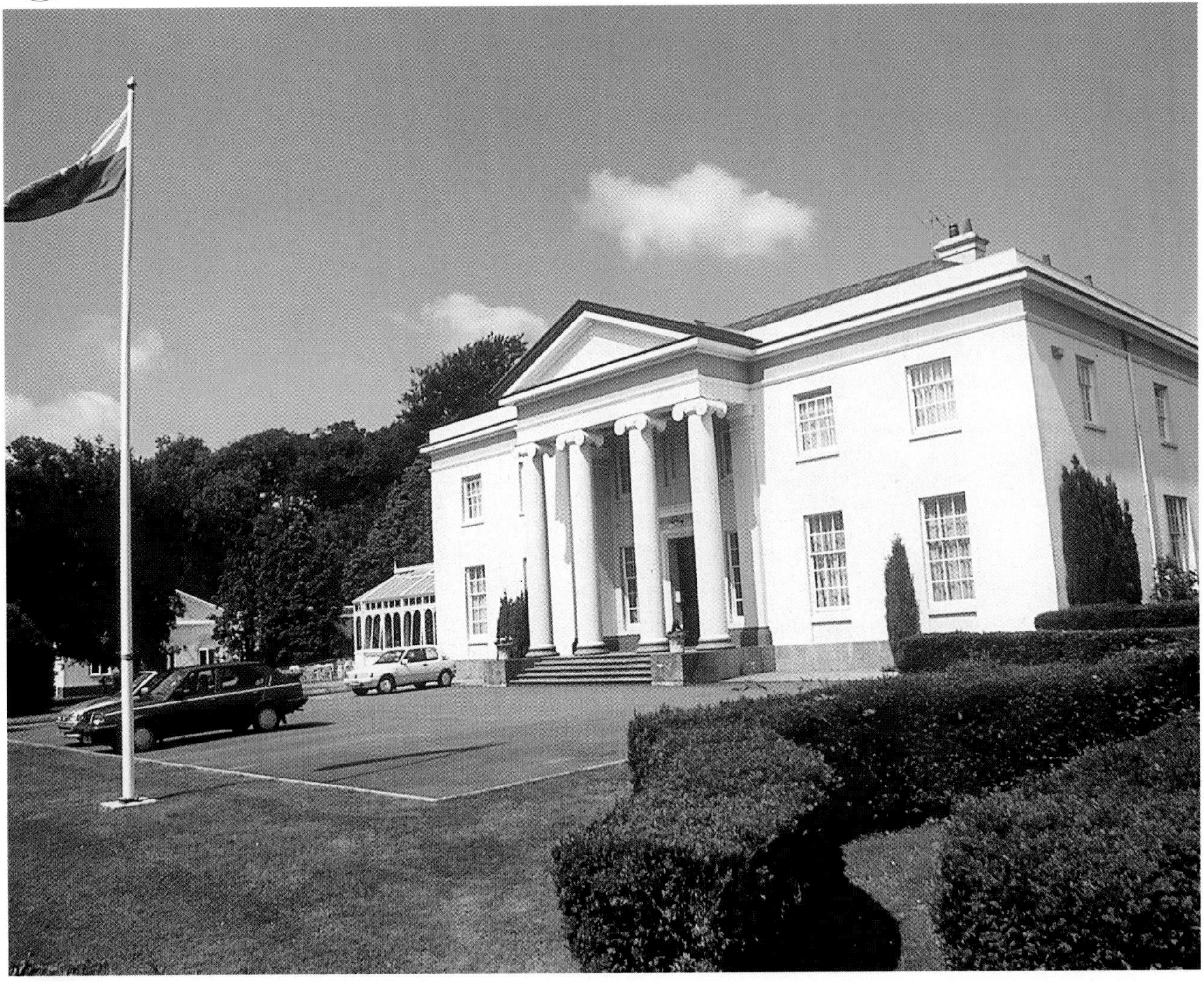

THE COURT HOTEL AND RESTAURANT

LAMPHEY, NR TENBY, PEMBROKESHIRE SA71 5NT
TEL: 01646 672273 FAX: 01646 672480

This magnificent Georgian mansion, with its classical Ionic colonade and splendid portico entrance, is idyllically situated in acres of grounds bordered by the beautiful Pembrokeshire National Park and just one mile from some of Britain's finest coastal scenery and beaches. Warm, friendly and efficient service is enriched by comfortable furnishings and decor. All bedrooms are en suite and have every convenience. The purpose-built Westminster studios situated in the courtyard provide the extra space required by families or visiting business executives. The Court Hotel's restaurant has a prestigious AA Rosette. Traditional flavours and local produce, includes such pleasures as Teifi salmon and Freshwater Bay lobster. Lighter meals and snacks can be taken in the elegant conservatory. The wide range of facilities in the leisure centre includes an indoor heated swimming pool, Jacuzzi, sauna, solarium and a gymnasium. Golf, sailing and fishing are nearby and the hotel's private yacht is available for charter. Well worth a visit is picturesque Tenby, the cliffside chapel of St Govan's, the Bishops Palace at Lamphey and Pembroke's impressive castle. Directions: From M4, exit at junction 49 onto the A48 to Carmarthen. Then follow the A477 and turn left at Milton Village for Lamphey. Price guide: Single £59-£72; double/twin £75-£125; suite £85–£125. Special rates available for short breaks.

For hotel location, see maps on pages 477-483

THE HOTEL PORTMEIRION

PORTMEIRION, GWYNEDD LL48 6ET
TEL: 01766 770228 FAX: 01766 771331

Portmeirion is a magical, private Italianate village, designed by the renowned architect Sir Clough Williams-Ellis. The unique avant-garde complex was started in 1925 and completed in the 1970s. It enjoyed a celebrated clientèle from the start – writers such as George Bernard Shaw, H G Wells, Bertrand Russell and Noel Coward were habitués. It is set in 120 acres of beautiful gardens and woodland, including two miles of tranquil sandy beaches, and provides accommodation for visitors either in the village or in the main hotel. The Hotel Portmeirion, originally a mansion house, has been sensitively restored, retaining striking features from the past, such as the Victorian Mirror Room. The bedrooms are furnished to the highest standards, 14 rooms being in the hotel and 23 rooms and suites in the village. The restaurant offers the best French and Welsh cooking, the seasonal menu relying on fresh, locally produced ingredients. AA Hotel of the Year Wales 1996. Swimming and tennis are available within the grounds as well as golf at Porthmadog (with complimentary green fees), and sailing is close at hand. The Ffestiniog and Snowdon mountain railways, slate caverns and Bodnant Gardens are nearby. Conference facilities can accommodate up to 100 people. Closed 5th January to 7th February. **Directions:** Portmeirion lies off the A487 between Penrhyndeudrath and Porthmadog. Price guide: Single £57–£102; double/twin £67–£112; suite £96–£146.

37 rms · MasterCard · VISA · AMERICAN EXPRESS · M 100

For hotel location, see maps on pages 477-483

WARPOOL COURT HOTEL

ST DAVID'S, PEMBROKESHIRE SA62 6BN

TEL: 01437 720300 FAX: 01437 720676

Originally built as St David's Cathedral Choir School in the 1860s, Warpool Court enjoys spectacular scenery at the heart of the Pembrokeshire National Park, with views over the coast and St Bride's Bay to the islands beyond. First converted to a hotel 40 years ago, the Court has undergone extensive refurbishments over the last two years. All 25 comfortably furnished bedrooms have en suite facilities and some have glorious sea views. The hotel restaurant enjoys a splendid reputation. Imaginative menus, including vegetarian, offer a wide selection of modern and traditional dishes. Local produce, including Welsh lamb and beef, is used whenever possible, with crab, lobster, sewin and sea bass caught just off the coast. Salmon and mackerel are smoked on the premises and a variety of herbs are grown. The hotel gardens are ideal for a peaceful stroll or an after-dinner drink on a summer's evening. There is a covered heated swimming pool (open April to end of October) and all-weather tennis court in the grounds. A path from the hotel leads straight on to the Pembrokeshire Coastal Path, with its rich variety of wildlife and spectacular scenery. Boating and watersports are available locally. St David's Peninsula offers a wealth of history and natural beauty and has inspired many famous artists. **Directions:** The hotel is signposted from St David's town centre. Price guide: Single £65–£80; double/twin £98–£150.

For hotel location, see maps on pages 477-483

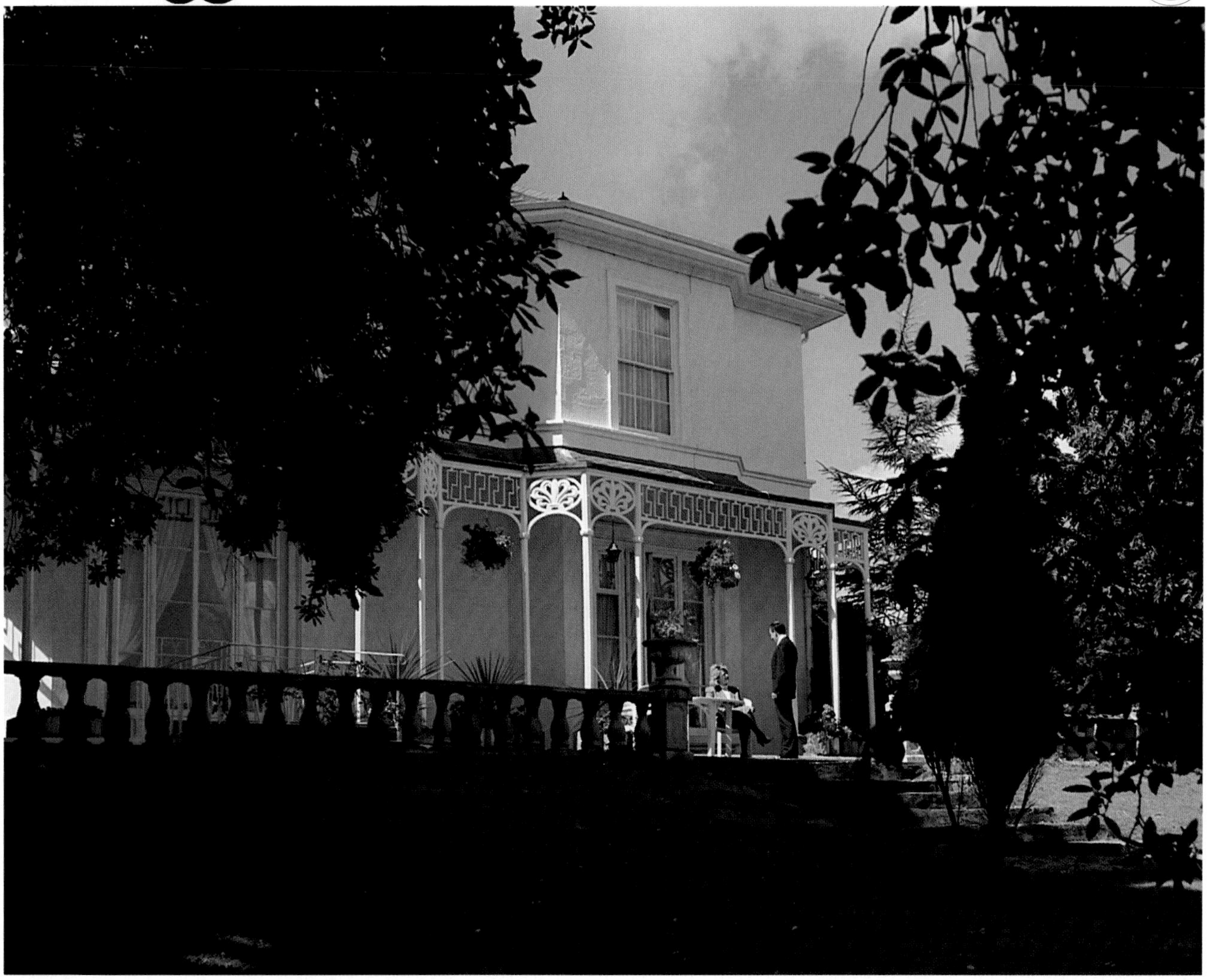

NORTON HOUSE HOTEL AND RESTAURANT

NORTON ROAD, MUMBLES, SWANSEA SA3 5TQ
TEL: 01792 404891 FAX: 01792 403210

This elegant Georgian hotel, set in gardens near the shore of Swansea Bay, provides a comfortable and peaceful base from which to explore the countryside of South Wales. Resident proprietors Jan and John Power have earned a reputation for offering attentive, friendly service. The bedrooms all have private amenities, four of the more spacious rooms have four-poster beds, the majority are smaller rooms in a newer wing. The restaurant overlooks the terrace and gardens. The emphasis is on local produce and traditional flavours with starters such as 'bara lawr' – mushrooms filled with laverbread, cockles and bacon followed by main courses which include 'cig oen mewn pasteiod' – best end of Welsh lamb coated in a duxelle of mushrooms, cooked in puff pastry and served with a minted gravy. Golf and riding can be arranged. The hotel has conference facilities for up to 20 people. The unspoiled Gower Peninsula is nearby, with its sandy bays and rugged cliffs. Mumbles village is a short walk away, while the city of Swansea is alive with galleries, theatres, a good shopping centre, its famous market and the maritime quarter. **Directions:** Leave the M4 at junction 42, take A483 to Swansea, then A4067 alongside Swansea Bay. A mile beyond the Mumbles sign, the hotel is signposted on the right-hand side. Price guide: Single £60–£65; double/twin £80.

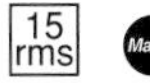

For hotel location, see maps on pages 477-483

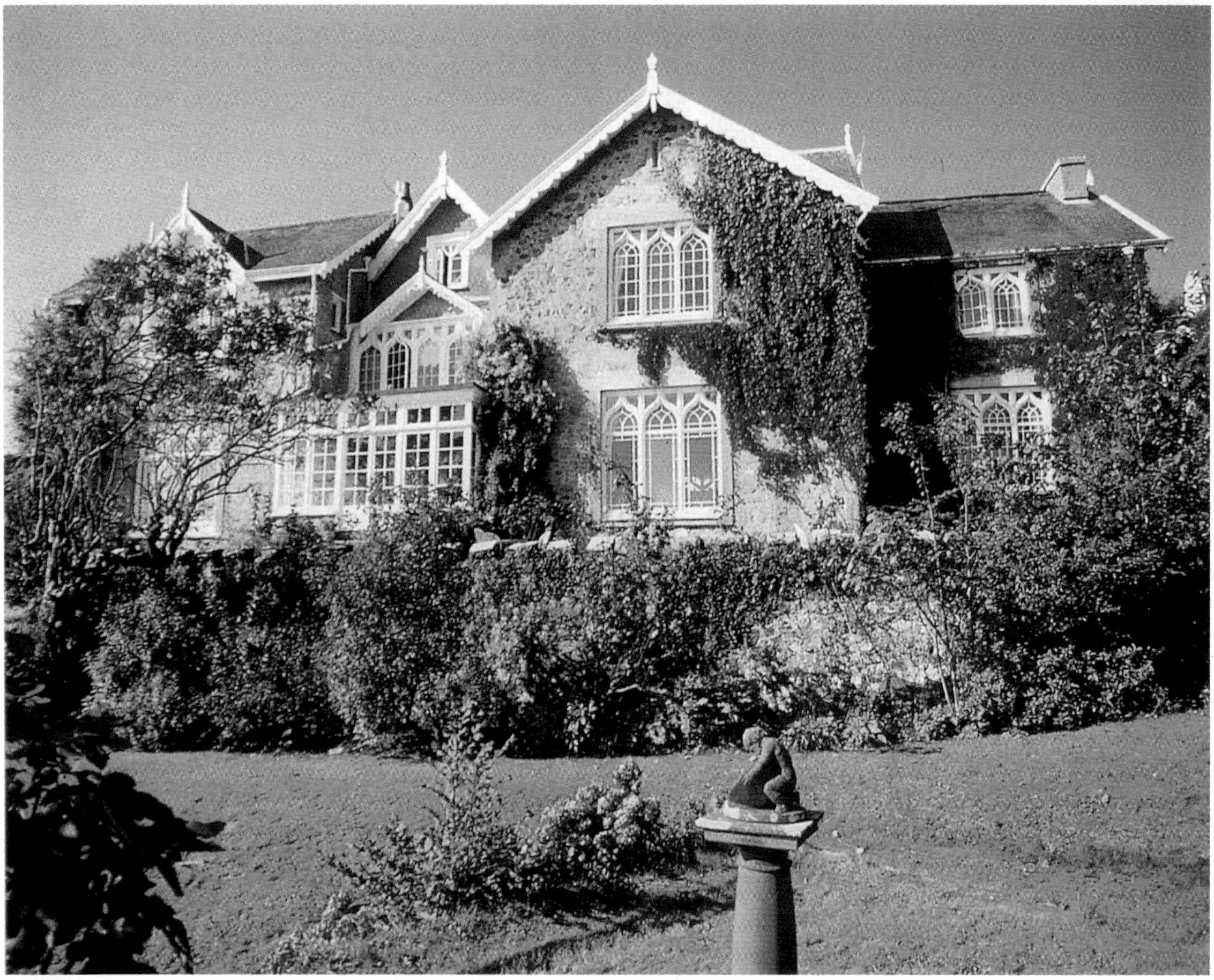

PENALLY ABBEY

PENALLY, TENBY, PEMBROKESHIRE SA70 7PY
TEL: 01834 843033 FAX: 01834 844714

Penally Abbey, a beautiful listed Gothic-style mansion, offers comfort and hospitality in a secluded setting by the sea. Standing in five acres of gardens and woodland on the edge of Pembrokeshire National Park, the hotel overlooks Carmarthen Bay and Caldey Island. The bedrooms in the main building and in the adjoining coach house are well furnished, many with four-poster beds. The emphasis is on relaxation – enjoy a late breakfast and dine at leisure. Fresh seasonal delicacies are offered in the candle-lit restaurant, with its chandeliers and colonnades. Guests can enjoy a game in the snooker room or relax in the elegant sunlit lounge, overlooking the terrace and gardens. In the grounds there is a wishing well and a ruined chapel – the last surviving link with the hotel's monastic past. Water-skiing, surfing, sailing, riding and parascending are available nearby. Sandy bays and rugged cliffs are features of this coastline, making it ideal for exhilarating walks or simply building sandcastles on the beach. As the rates include the cost of dinner, this friendly hotel offers splendid value for money. **Directions:** Penally Abbey is situated adjacent to the church on Penally village green. Price guide (including dinner): Single £86; double/twin £140–£156.

For hotel location, see maps on pages 477-483

TYNYCORNEL HOTEL

TAL-Y-LLYN, TYWYN, GWYNEDD LL36 9AJ
TEL: 01654 782282 FAX: 01654 782679

Situated in the magnificent Snowdonia National Park, Tynycornel Hotel overlooks its own 222-acre lake, whose waters reflect the grandeur of Cader Idris. Originally constructed as a farmhouse in the 16th century, the hotel has been extensively and sensitively refurbished so that none of the original ambience has been lost. The spacious lounge has views over the lake, with comfortable furniture, fine antiques, original prints and a blazing fire in winter. The 17 pretty bedrooms, all with bathrooms including two luxury suites, enjoy lakeside or garden views. The restaurant offers a high standard of cuisine and the set-price menu changes daily. Within the grounds there is a sauna and solarium. Tynycornel is an angler's paradise – wild brown trout, salmon and sea trout fishing are readily available – and the hotel is equipped with 10 petrol-powered boats and provides tackle hire, freezing facilities and a drying room. The stunning landscape offers many opportunities for those interested in birdwatching, walking and photography. Snowdonia and mid-Wales are steeped in history and a wide variety of leisure pursuits can be enjoyed, including scenic golf at Dolgellau. **Directions:** Tal-y-llyn is signposted from the main A487 Machynlleth-Dolgellau road. The hotel is on the lake shore. Price guide: Single £46.50; double/twin £93; suite £125.

17 rms MasterCard VISA AMERICAN EXPRESS M 30

For hotel location, see maps on pages 477-483

THE CWRT BLEDDYN HOTEL

LLANGYBI, NEAR USK, GWENT, SOUTH WALES NP5 1PG
TEL: 01633 450521 FAX: 01633 450220

Set in 17 acres of wooded grounds, this 14th century manor house, not far from the Roman town of Caerleon, is the perfect location from which to explore the Wye Valley and Forest of Dean. The hotel is a fine example of the traditional and the modern under one roof. Carved panelling and huge fireplaces in the lounge lend an air of classic country-house comfort. The 36 en suite bedrooms are spacious and offer guests every amenity, and most have wonderful views over the surrounding countryside. Cwrt Bleddyn's restaurant is renowned for its French-influenced cuisine, with both à la carte and table d'hôte menus. There is a good choice of vegetarian dishes. Light meals are also served in the hotel's country club. Here, extensive leisure facilities include an indoor heated swimming pool, sauna, solarium, steam room and beauty salon. Alternatively, guests may just wish to stroll and relax in the grounds. Nearby is the local beauty spot of Llandegfedd, with its 434-acre reservoir. The hotel is open all year round. Private dining/function rooms are available. **Directions:** From Cardiff/Bristol, leave M4 at junction 25. Hotel is 3 miles north of Caerleon on the road to Usk. From the Midlands, take M5, then A40 to Monmouth. Turn off A449, through Usk, over stone bridge, then left towards Caerleon for 4 miles. Price guide: Single £85; double/twin £105.

36 rms MasterCard VISA AMERICAN EXPRESS M 200

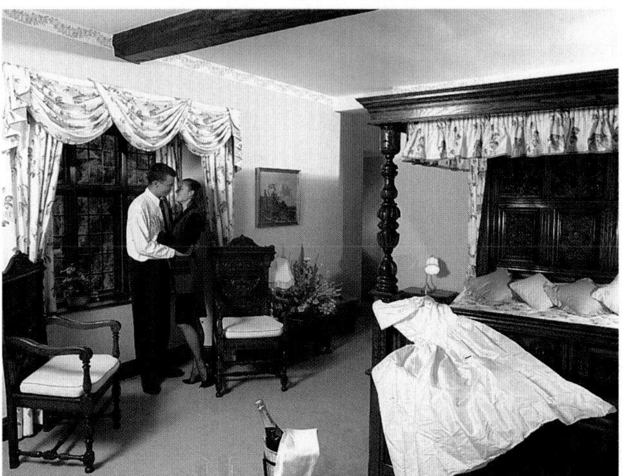

For hotel location, see maps on pages 477-483

Johansens Recommended Hotels in Scotland

Scotland offers the Johansens visitor a fine choice of recommendations amid breathtaking scenery. An abundance of outdoor pursuits will challenge the adventurous, blended with the warmth and charm of traditional hospitality.

The open air assets of spectacular scenery, a veritable paradise for outdoor sport and recreation, highlight Scotland as a breathing space for the visitor seeking a contrast from work and routine.

Nature's generosity has been consolidated by the Scots with their diligence in establishing an attractive choice of formal gardens in all parts, many attached to historic properties, for instance, Balmoral Castle where the gardens are open to the public during summer when the Royal family are not in residence. Scotland created one of the world's first botanic gardens - in Edinburgh - where the most recent attraction is the exciting Chinese garden with waterfall, pond and a limitless collection of rare and exotic flowers, shrubs and trees. A new entrant to the garden trail is the Glen Grant garden at the distillery of the same name in Rothes, Moray. Careful research has restored the oriental aspects of the Victorian layout combined with woodland walks. Enthusiasts will also welcome the inclusion of the original "dram hut", the retreat of the distillery and garden owner, Major Grant. A new visitor centre has opened at one of the most delightfully situated distilleries, Glenkinchie, near Edinburgh, in East Lothian. Set in an unspoiled village, the distillery's old malting barns have been converted to house a display of the whisky industry.

Scotland's turbulent history is not only conserved in its famous castles, abbeys and battlefields, but also in a splendid range of regimental museums including the Royal Scots, the oldest in the British army which is based at Edinburgh castle. One of the few regiments not yet amalgamated, the King's Own Scottish Borderers, has its museum in the first purpose-built barracks in Britain at Berwick upon Tweed. An audio visual display and tableaux provide a compelling insight to military life and ceremonial. The Gordon Highlanders museum in Aberdeen reveals its long association with the north east. Ten of the 19 Victoria Crosses awarded to the regiment are on show.

There has always been a traditional link with Scotland's armed services and religion and several churches display regimental flag honours. All the more apt that churches, cathedrals and abbeys have combined in a more formal way to allow access to visitors. More than 200 locations are featured in a programme similar to the well established Scotland's Garden Scheme.

Scotland's history is the core of Highland Mysteryworld where the folklore and legend of the Celtic and Viking legacies are presented through technology to dramatise the ancient Highland way of life. An indoor attraction located in the atmospheric Glencoe, scene of the massacre of the Macdonalds and a well known hillwalking and ski region.

Stirling, centre of Sir William Wallace's Braveheart country, dips into an aspect of history which would have been familiar to the great Scots patriot who was incarcerated for a while in the Tower of London, before execution. The old town jail, Royal Stirling, stages episodes from prison life 150 years ago including an escape. A lift travels from the dungeons to a viewing platform providing panoramic sweeps of the Stirlingshire countryside.

The time before recorded history is the subject of a major attraction at Oyne, 25 miles out of Aberdeen on the road to Inverness. Archaeolink Pre-History Park explores the ancient mysteries of the stone and iron ages in a specially designed glass dome within the shadow of the slopes of Bennachie.

Cultural attractions of which there are many in Scotland are enhanced by the new Gallery of Modern Art in Glasgow. Housed in a Georgian building in the city centre it has a collection of post war art and design and works acquired by the city since it was European City of Culture in 1990. Artists include David Hockney, Beryl Cook and Peter Howson.

Balmoral Castle
Crathie
Near Ballater
Tel: 013397 42334

Royal Botanic Garden
Inverleith Row
Edinburgh
Tel: 0131 552 7171

Glenkinchie Distillery
Pencaitland
East Lothian
Tel: 01875 340 451

King's Own Scottish Borderers
The Barracks
Berwick Upon Tweed
Tel: 01289 307 426

Scotland's Churches Scheme
Gifford Cottage, Main Street
Gifford, East Lothian
Tel: 01620 810 301

Highland Mysteryworld
Glencoe
Tel: 0185 582 1582

Archaeolink
Inverurie
Aberdeenshire
Tel: 01467 620 981

Gallery of Modern Art
Queen Street
Glasgow
Tel: 0141 229 1996

For more information on Scotland, please contact:

Scottish Tourist Board
23 Ravelston Terrace
Edinburgh EH4 3EU
Tel: 0131 332 2433

Farleyer House Hotel

ABERFELDY, PERTHSHIRE PH15 2JE

TEL: 01887 820332 FAX: 01887 829430 E-MAIL: 100127@compuserve.com

Farleyer House, whose pedigree dates from the 16th century, stands amid mature woodland overlooking the Tay Valley. The hotel has won the *Good Food Guide* Tayside Restaurant of the Year 1990 & 1996 award for its wonderful cuisine, and is highly praised in the most prestigious food guides. The six-course dinner is always delicious with wines to match. A more relaxed and informal meal may be enjoyed in the new Scottish Bistro where the blackboard menu offers an outstanding choice. The house has a lengthy history, dating back to the 16th century. It has a warm luxurious feel with soft-pile carpets, full-bodied drapes, clusters of paintings and scattered '*objets d'art*'. Deer-stalking, fishing, riding, sailing and water sports can be arranged and there is a 6-hole practice golf course in the grounds. The nearby Kenmore Club with its indoor pool and leisure facilities is available for guests. The central location makes this hotel a perfect base for touring the countryside and historic towns of Scotland. Dogs are accommodated separately from the main house and strictly by prior arrangement. **Directions:** Drive through Weem on the B846 past Castle Menzies and Farleyer is on the Kinloch–Rannoch road. Price guide: Single £75–£105; double/twin £150–£195.

For hotel location, see maps on pages 477-483

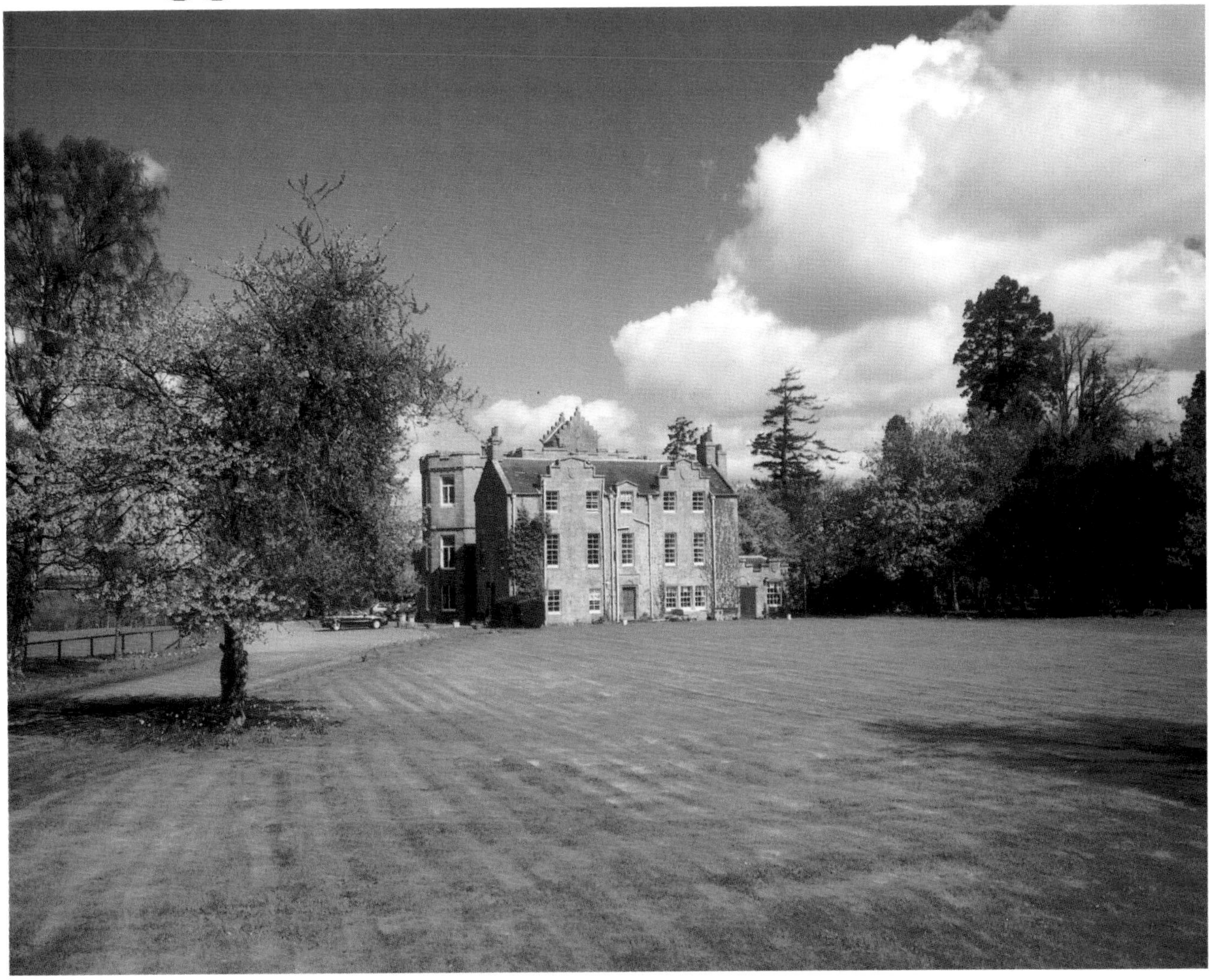

SHIELDHILL HOUSE

QUOTHQUAN, BIGGAR, LANARKSHIRE ML12 6NA
TEL: 01899 220035 FAX: 01899 221092

Set amongst the rolling hills and farmlands of the Upper Clyde Valley lies Shieldhill House. This castle style country house hotel, parts of which date back to 1199, was the ancestral home of the Chancellor family for more than 700 years. It was transformed into a luxurious small hotel in 1959. The 'old keep', the turreted roof and the secret staircase all conjure up bygone days, while open fires and deep soft furnishings ensure modern day comfort. The 11 individually designed, spacious bedrooms all have king, queen, twin or four poster beds and en suite facilities. The hotel's luxurious oak panelled lounge is the perfect place to relax, while in its spacious dining room exquisite cuisine can be guaranteed. An extensive and interesting wine list complements the delicious dishes on offer. For the energetic, the surrounding area provides plenty of opportunity to enjoy walks in the country or golf on a different course every day. Clay pigeon shooting or trout fishing can also be arranged. The three cities of Glasgow, Edinburgh and Carlisle are all easily reached by car. **Directions:** From Biggar take B7016 (signposted Carnwath), after two miles turn left into Sheildhill Road. The hotel is one and a half miles down on the right. Price guide: Single: £68–£89; double/twin: £104–£152.

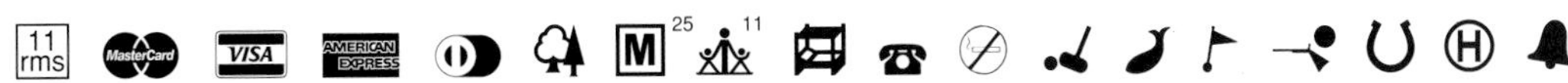

For hotel location, see maps on pages 477-483

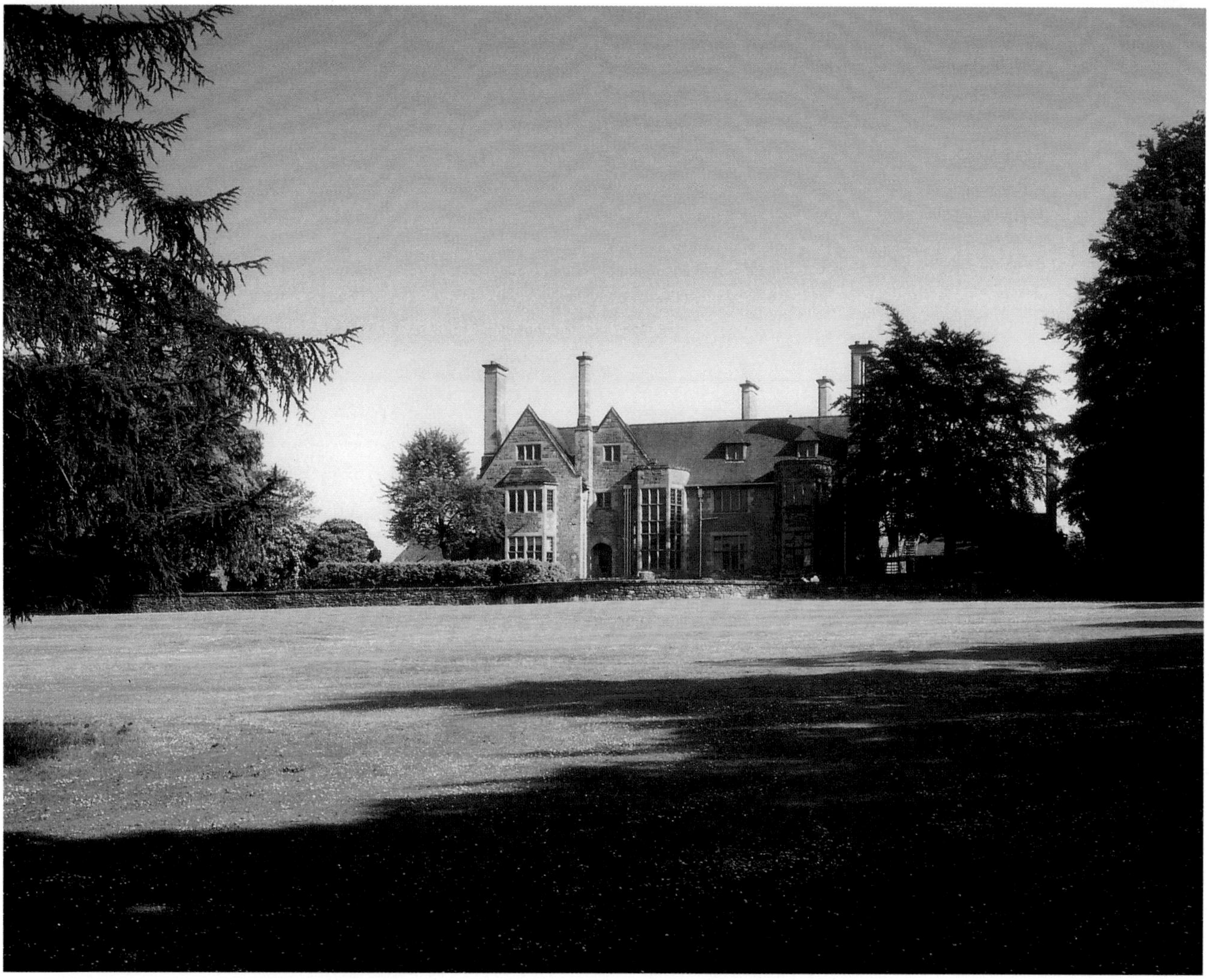

THE GEAN HOUSE

GEAN PARK, ALLOA, NR STIRLING FK10 2HS
TEL: 01259 219275 FAX: 01259 213827

The Gean House was commissioned in 1910 by Alexander Forrester-Paton, a leading industrialist, as a wedding present for his eldest son. Fully restored and beautifully furnished, this architecturally significant house is surrounded by parkland. The elegant reception hall has a minstrels gallery, an inglenook fireplace and fine views of the nearby Ochil Hills. In the south-facing, walnut-panelled dining room – a non-smoking room overlooking the rose garden – guests enjoy the recognised gourmet cuisine. A splendid breakfast menu is also offered and room service is available. With its wide doors and absence of steps on the ground floor, the hotel is particularly suitable for guests with disabilities. Facilities for business meetings and conferences are also available. Only ten minutes drive from Stirling town centre, there is much to enjoy locally – walks in the Ochils, fishing, boating, golf – St Andrews and Gleneagles are forty minutes drive away. Shopping for hand-knits, fine woollens and cashmeres is a popular past-time. **Directions:** Alloa via Kincardine Bridge and A907 from east, or via same road west from Stirling; park entrance is on the B9096 Tullibody Road. Price guide: Single £80; double/twin £120–£140.

For hotel location, see maps on pages 477-483

INVERCRERAN COUNTRY HOUSE HOTEL

GLEN CRERAN, APPIN, ARGYLL PA38 4BJ
TEL: 01631 730 414 FAX: 01631 730 532

The outstanding setting of Invercreran House is one of the many reasons for its popularity. Surrounded by mountains, it stands in 25 secluded acres of shrub gardens and woodland, overlooking the mature trees and meadows of Glen Creran. Guests can stroll through the grounds towards the River Creran which flows through the glen. Viewed from the outside, it is surprising to discover that the hotel has only nine guest bedrooms. The interiors, reception rooms and bedrooms alike are spacious. In the large lounge there is a free-standing fireplace where logs burn beneath a copper canopy. The Kersley family are involved in all aspects of the day-to-day running of the house. Their son Tony, the master chef, prepares delicious dishes that emphasise the full flavour of fresh Scottish game, fish, vegetables and soft fruits. Meals are served in the semi-circular, marble-floored dining room. Invercreran House is well positioned for touring the Western Highlands, offering easy access to Oban, Fort William and Glencoe. Closed November to early March. **Directions:** Hotel is off the A828 Oban–Fort William road, 14 miles north of Connel Bridge, 18 miles south of Ballachulish Bridge. Travelling to Invercreran at the head of Loch Creran, stay on the minor road going north east into Glen Creran; hotel is 3/4 mile on left. Price guide: Single £64; double/twin £94–£130; suite £150.

For hotel location, see maps on pages 477-483

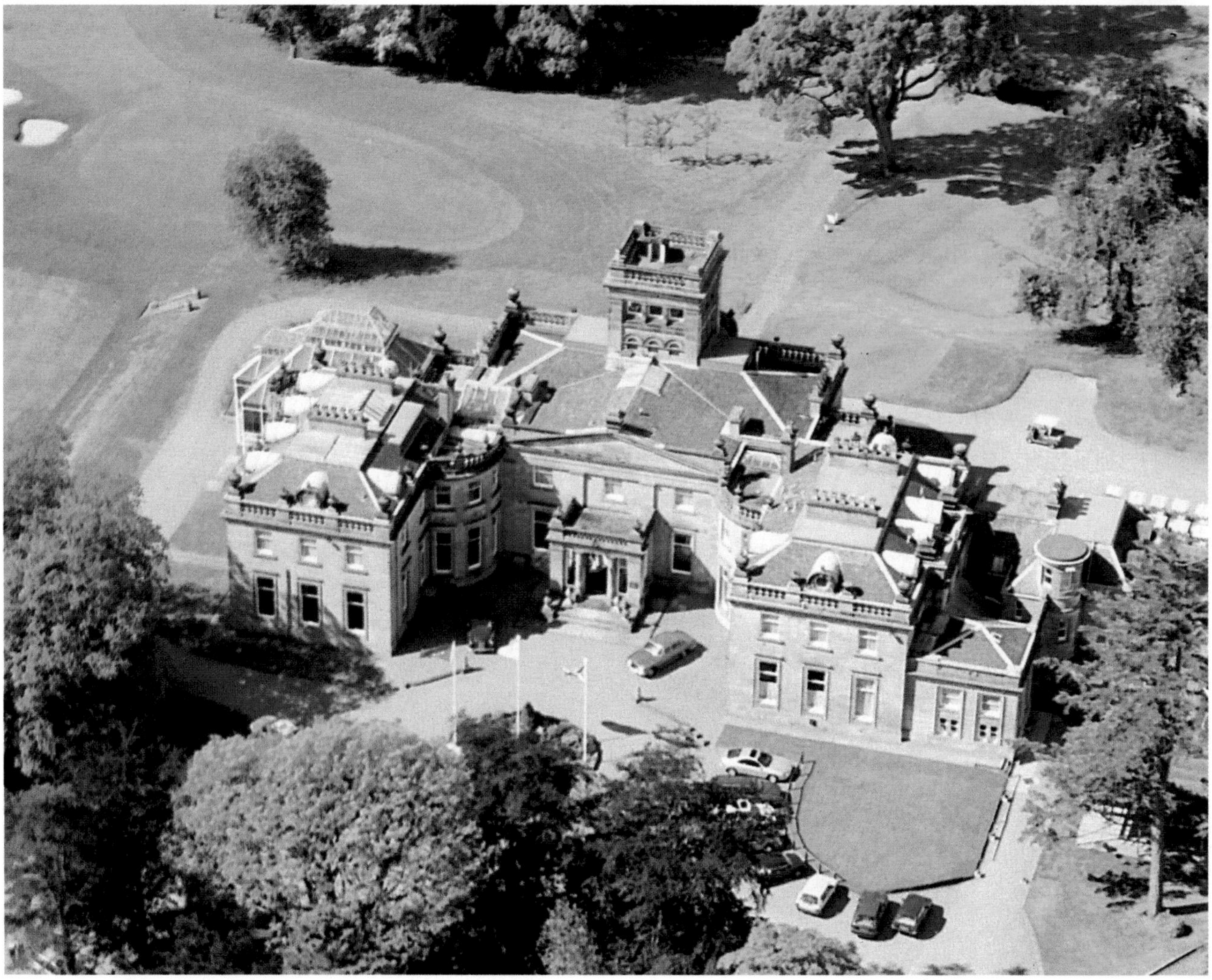

LETHAM GRANGE HOTEL AND GOLF COURSES

COLLISTON, ANGUS DD11 4RL
TEL: 01241 890373 FAX: 01241 890414

Letham Grange is a beautifully renovated Victorian mansion with its original sculptured ceilings, panelling, antique staircase, fireplaces and period paintings faithfully restored to their former splendour. With its splendid scenery, it is a perfect country retreat for either a sporting or leisure break. The sumptuous luxury of country house living that the hotel provides is enhanced by two excellent golf courses and a four-lane curling rink. The bedrooms are individually designed and spacious, with charming decor which reflects the original character of this lovely building. Dining in the restful Rosehaugh Restaurant is a gourmet experience. The finest fresh local foods are selected to create table d'hôte and à la carte menus of international standard. Even the most seasoned golfers will enjoy meeting the demands of the 18-hole championship standard Old Course, which surrounds the hotel. The New Course offers a more relaxing game. The curling rink is overlooked by the spacious Sweep 'n' Swing lounge where drinks are served. Some of Scotland's most majestic scenery lies within easy reach of the hotel. **Directions:** From Dundee take A92 and on the outskirts of Arbroath follow A933 to Colliston village. Turn right, signposted Letham Grange, and at T-junction turn right and follow sign for half a mile. Price guide: Single £79; double/twin £125; suites £145.

39 rms MasterCard VISA AMERICAN EXPRESS M 150

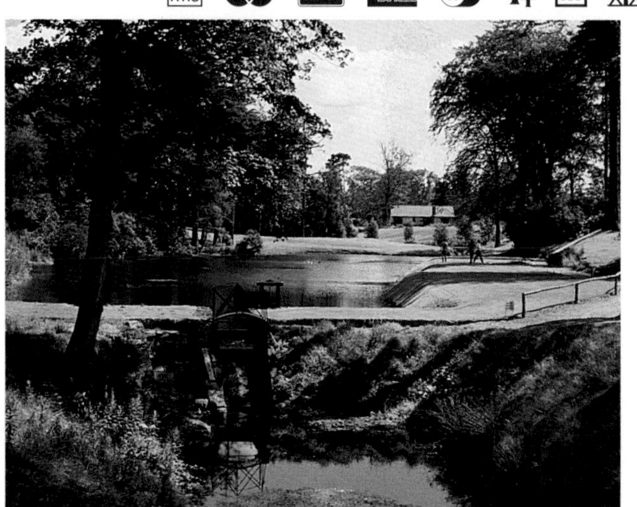

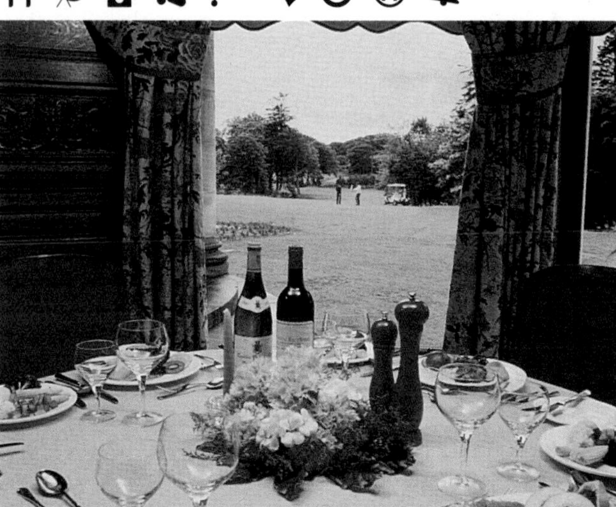

For hotel location, see maps on pages 477-483

Balcary Bay Hotel

AUCHENCAIRN, NR CASTLE DOUGLAS, DUMFRIES & GALLOWAY DG7 1QZ
TEL: 01556 640217 FAX: 01556 640272

The hotel takes its name from the bay on which it stands, in an area of Galloway that is romantic in its isolation and which was once full of intrigue. Heston Isle, the hide-out of 17th century smugglers, fronts the hotel's view across the Solway coast and the Cumbrian Hills beyond. Originally owned by a shipping firm, the hotel was known to harbour illegal loot in its secret underground passages. Nowadays, Scottish hospitality at Balcary Bay includes the provision of modern facilities with a traditional atmosphere. It offers local delicacies such as lobsters, prawns and salmon imaginitavely prepared, plus the reasurring intimacy of a family-run hotel. Despite its northerly aspect, Galloway benefits from the Gulf Stream and enjoys a mild and long holiday season. The area has great coastal and woodland walks. Closed from mid November to early March. Nearby are several 9 and 18 hole golf courses at Colvend, Kirkcudbright, Castle Douglas, Southerness and Dumfries. There are also salmon rivers and trout lochs, sailing, shooting, riding and bridwatching facilities. The area abounds with National Trust historic properties and gardens. **Directions:** Located off the A711 Dumfries–Kirkcudbright road, two miles out of Auchencairn on the Shore Road. Price guide: Single £52; double/twin £92–£104. Seasonal short breaks and reduced inclusive rates for 3 and 7 nights.

For hotel location, see maps on pages 477-483

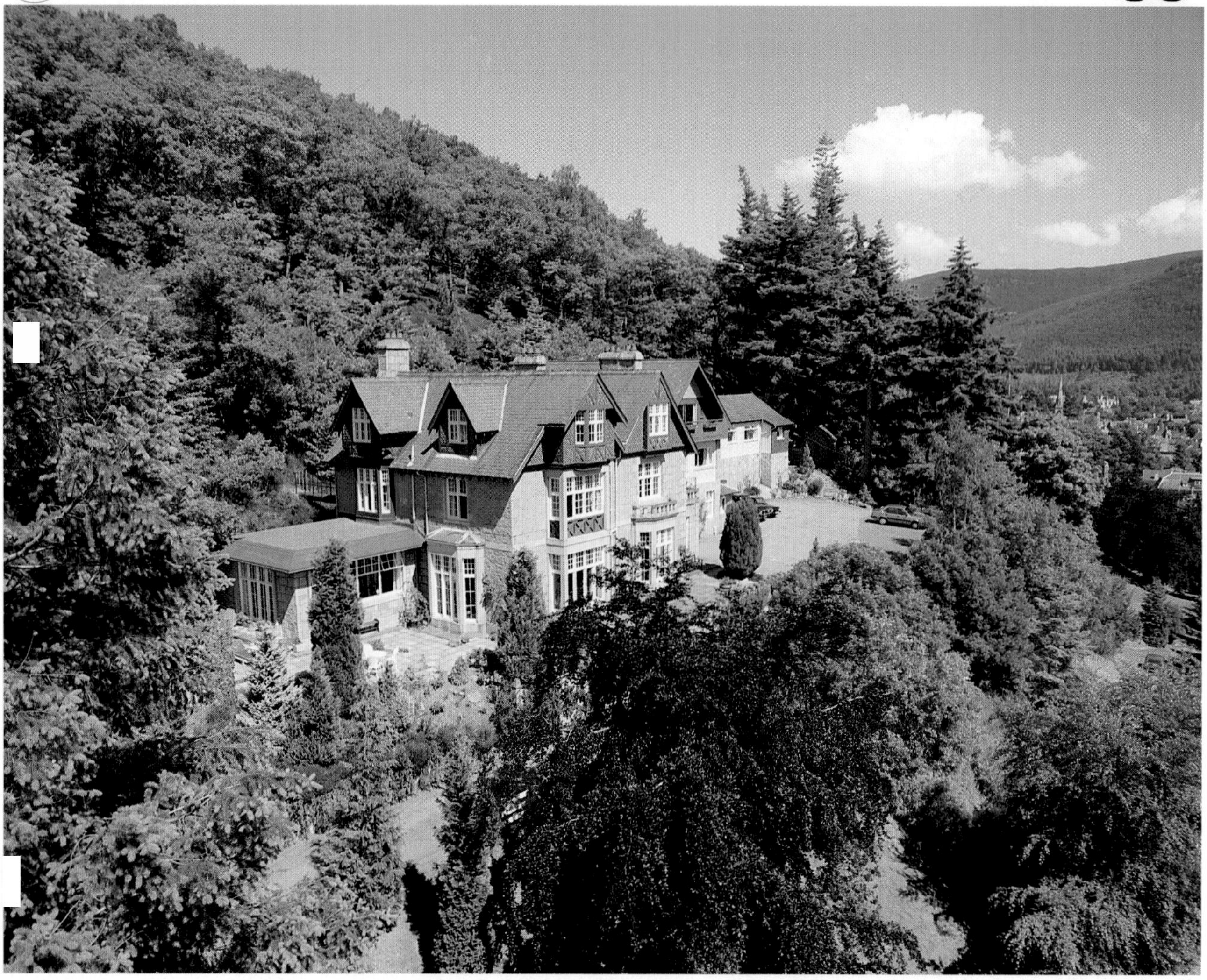

DARROCH LEARG HOTEL

BRAEMAR ROAD, BALLATER, ABERDEENSHIRE AB35 5UX
TEL: 013397 55443 FAX: 013397 55252

Four acres of leafy grounds surround Darroch Learg, sited on the side of the rocky hill which dominates Ballater. The hotel, which was built in 1888 as a fashionable country residence, offers panoramic views over the golf course, River Dee and Balmoral Estate to the fine peaks of the Grampian Mountains. Oakhall, an adjacent mansion built in Scottish baronial style and adorned with turrets, contains five of the 18 bedrooms ideal for private groups. All are individually furnished and decorated, providing every modern amentity. The reception rooms in Darroch Learg are similarly elegant and welcoming, a comfortable venue in which to enjoy a relaxing drink. Log fires create a particularly cosy atmosphere on chilly nights. The beautifully presented food has been awarded 2AA Rosettes. A wide choice of wines complements the cuisine, which is best described as modern and Scottish in style. To perfect the setting, there is a wonderful outlook south towards the hills of Glen Muick. The wealth of outdoor activities on offer include walking, riding, mountain-biking, loch and river fishing, gliding and ski-ing. Ballater itself is interesting with an old ruined Kirk and ancient Celtic stones.A few miles away stands Balmoral Castle, the Highland residence of the British sovereign. **Directions:** At the western edge of Ballater on the A93. Price guide: Single £45; double/twin £75–£110.

For hotel location, see maps on pages 477-483

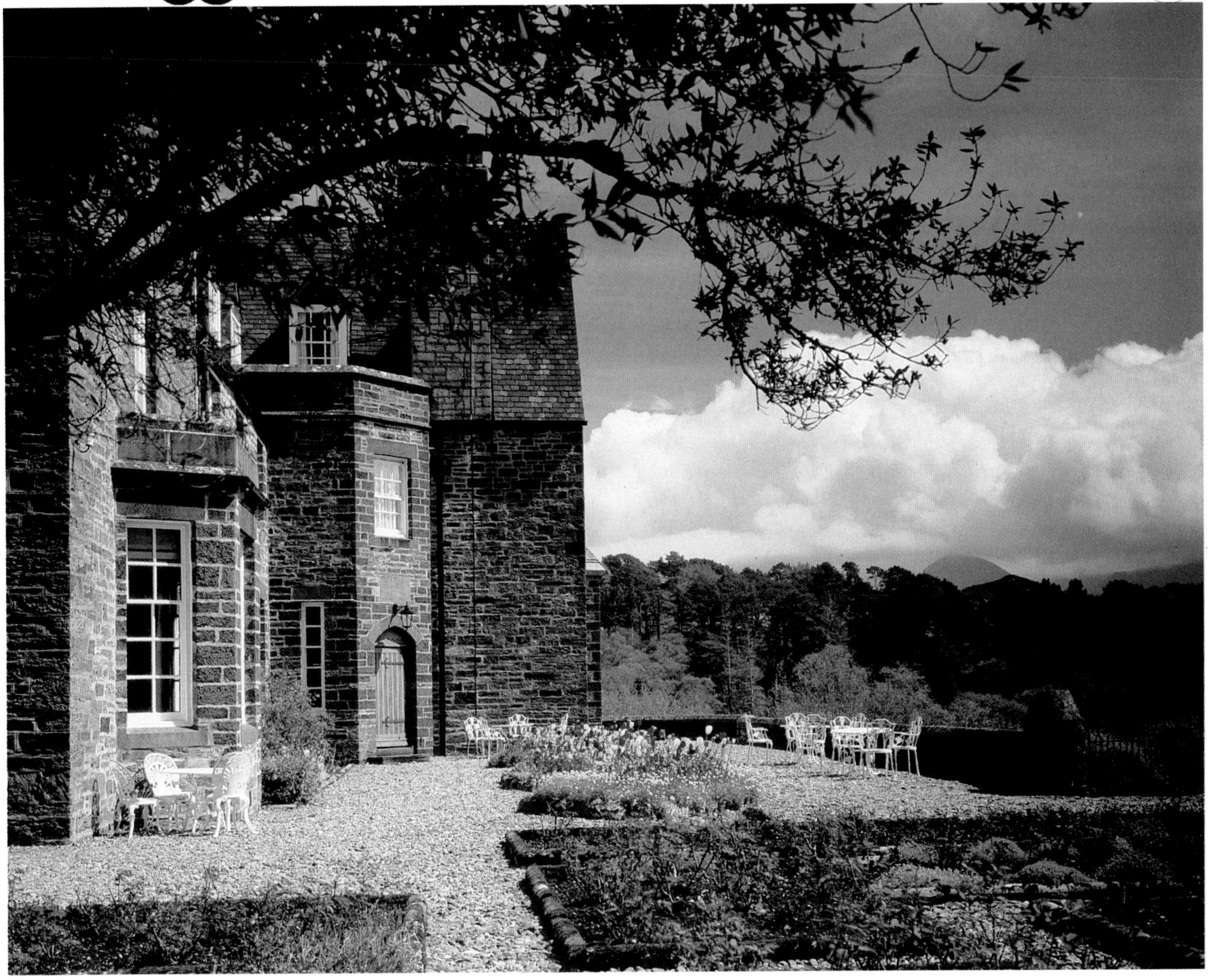

ARISAIG HOUSE

BEASDALE, BY ARISAIG, INVERNESS-SHIRE PH39 4NR
TEL: 01687 450622 FAX: 01687 450626

Princely redwoods rising above the sudden abundance of Arisaig's oak and rhododendron declare your journey done: now it is time to relax and enjoy the hospitality offered by your hosts, the Smither family. Natural light floods into the house, streaming through tall windows into the inner hall to warm the oak staircase and cast a gleam across polished furniture. The chef's epicurean offerings – supported by a lineage of fine château bottlings – give promise of the restoration of body and soul. Comprising game in season, crisp local vegetables, fruits de mer and pâtisserie baked daily, the cuisine is always a gastronomic delight. High above the ponticum and crinodendrons, the 14 spacious bedrooms afford a magnificent vista of mountains, sea and ever-changing sky. On some days, the clink of billiard balls or the clunk of croquet from the beautiful grounds are the only sounds to thread their way across the rustle of a turning page. On other days guests are hard to find, taking trips on ferries to Skye and the Inner Hebrides or discovering the landscape that has barely changed since Bonnie Prince Charlie's passage through these parts many years ago. Closed early November to mid-March. Arisaig House is a Relais et Châteaux member. **Directions:** Three miles from Arisaig village on the A830 Mallaig road. Price guide : Single £78.50; double/twin £160–£250.

For hotel location, see maps on pages 477-483

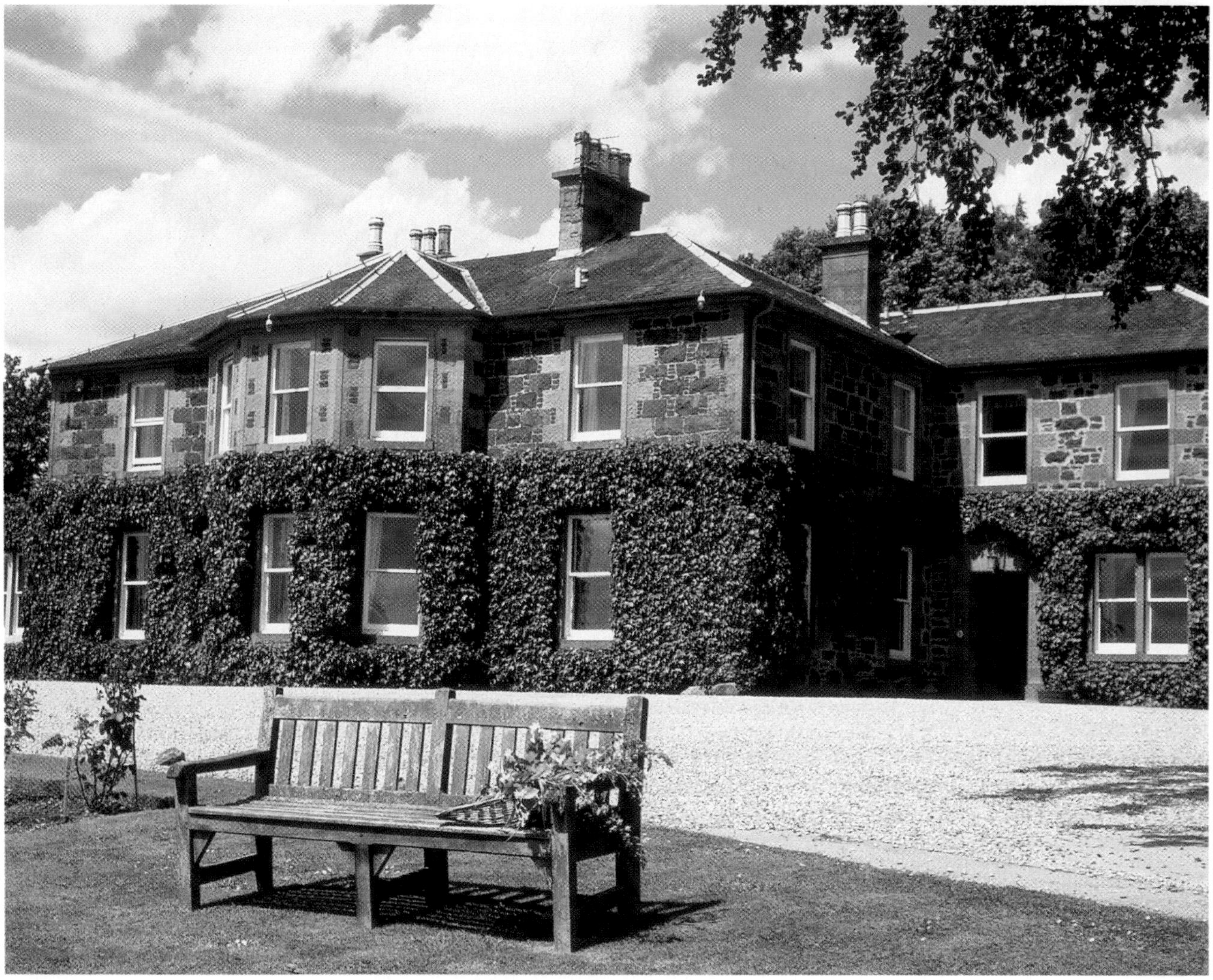

KINLOCH HOUSE HOTEL

BY BLAIRGOWRIE, PERTHSHIRE PH10 6SG
TEL: 01250 884237 FAX: 01250 884333

Winner of the 1994 Johansens Country Hotel Award, Kinloch House is an elegant example of a Scottish country home built in 1840. Set in 25 acres of wooded parkland grazed by Highland cattle, it offers panoramic views to the south over Marlee Loch to the Sidlaw Hills beyond. It has a grand galleried hall with an ornate glass ceiling and fine paintings and antiques in the reception rooms. A carefully incorporated extension echoes the original style, with oak panelling and ornate friezes. Chef Bill McNicoll has built a reputation for good Scottish fare – lamb, fish, shellfish, wildfowl and game are all available in season. Choices from the menu such as sautéed breast of woodcock or roast partridge are complemented by an extensive wine list. The cocktail bar, which stocks over 140 malt whiskies, is adjacent to the conservatory and is a focal point of the hotel. David and Sarah Shentall offer a warm personal welcome to all their guests, whether they come simply to enjoy the beauty of the area, or to take advantage of the local pursuits of golf, hill walking, fishing and shooting. For the sightseer, Glamis Castle, Scone Palace and Blair Castle are among the area's attractions. 3 AA Rosettes and 3 AA Red Stars. Closed at Christmas. **Directions:** The hotel is 3 miles west of Blairgowrie, off the A923 Dunkeld road. Price guide (including dinner): Single £83; double/twin £166–£205.

For hotel location, see maps on pages 477-483

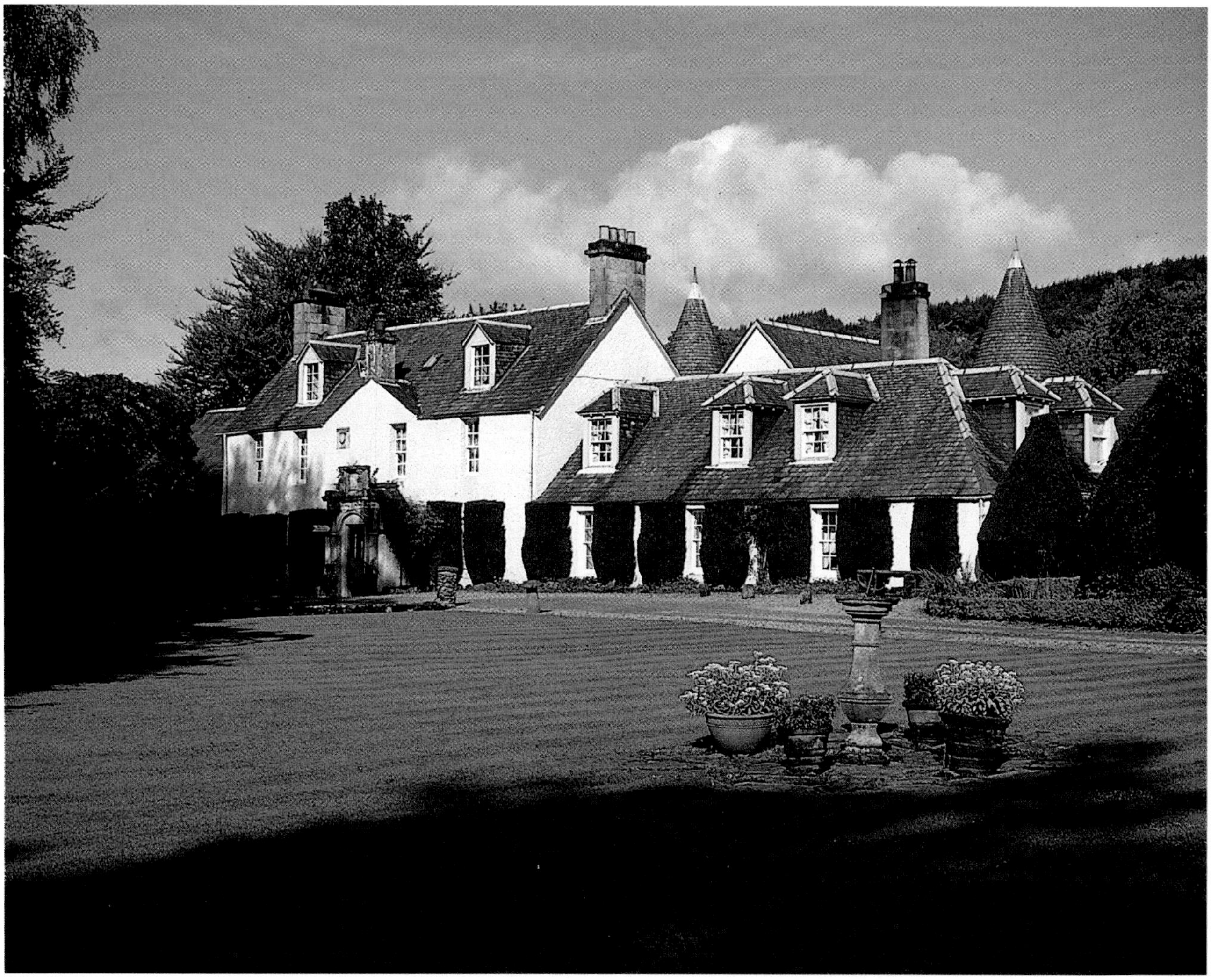

ROMAN CAMP HOTEL

CALLANDER, PERTHSHIRE FK17 8BG
TEL: 01877 330003 FAX: 01877 331533

Roman Camp Hotel, originally built in 1625 as a hunting lodge for the Dukes of Perth, takes its name from a nearby Roman encampment. Reminiscent of a French château, the hotel's turrets house a myriad of period features, including a tiny chapel, linenfold wood panelling and ornate moulded ceilings. Set on the banks of the River Teith, the hotel is surrounded by 20 acres of superb grounds including a listed walled garden where herbs and flowers are grown for the hotel. The public rooms, drawing room, sun lounge and library are characterised by grand proportions, antique furnishings and fine views over the river and gardens. The bedrooms are individually and most becomingly furnished. A richly painted ceiling, depicting traditional Scottish designs, is a unique feature of the restaurant, where the thoughtfully compiled menu is accompanied by a long and tempting wine list. Guests are welcome to fish free of charge on the private stretch of the river, while all around there are plenty of interesting walks. Callander is an ideal tourist centre for Central Scotland. Within easy reach are the Trossachs, Doune Motor Museum and Aberfoyle. Dogs are welcome by prior arrangement. **Directions:** Approaching Callander on the A84, the entrance to the hotel is between two cottages in Callander's main street. Price guide: Single £59–£89; double/twin from £85–£139; suite £115–£159.

For hotel location, see maps on pages 477-483

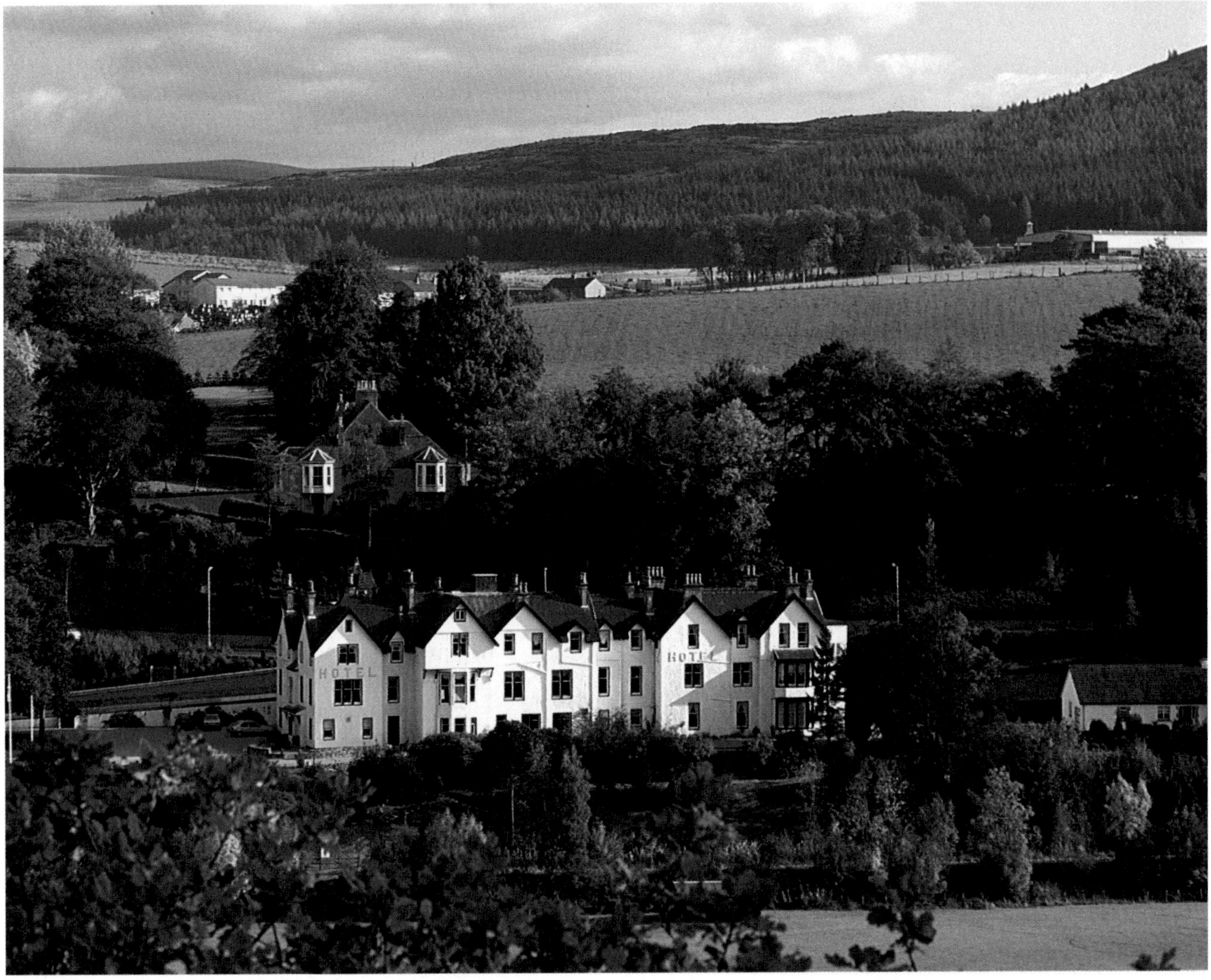

CRAIGELLACHIE HOTEL

CRAIGELLACHIE, BANFFSHIRE AB38 9SR
TEL: 01340 881204 FAX: 01340 881253

Overlooking the River Spey, with direct access to the Speyside Walk, Craigellachie Hotel is located in the centre of Scotland's famous Malt Whisky and Castle Trails, in one of the most picturesque villages in Moray. This Victorian hotel opened in 1893 and has recently undergone a meticulous restoration to incorporate all the amenities of a first-class hotel while retaining the charm and elegance of a Scottish country house. Many of the 30 individually designed bedrooms overlook the River Spey and several have a view of the local landmark, Thomas Telford's slender iron bridge. The Ben Aigan and Rib Room have firmly established a good reputation for their innovative treatment of traditional Scottish recipes. Only fresh local produce is used in the preparation of dishes, which are always beautifully presented and accompanied by an extensive wine list. After dinner, guests can choose from a wide selection of 300 malt whiskies. Craigellachie specialises in personalised packages including traditional Scottish Christmas and New year events. Sporting holidays can include golf with private tuition, salmon and trout fishing, deer stalking, game shooting, falconry and pony-trekking. There is also a sauna & solarium and an old-fashioned games room. **Directions:** Just off A95 between Grantown-on-Spey (24 miles) and Elgin (12 miles). Price guide: Single £52–£89; double/twin £104–£131.

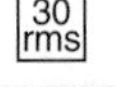

For hotel location, see maps on pages 477-483

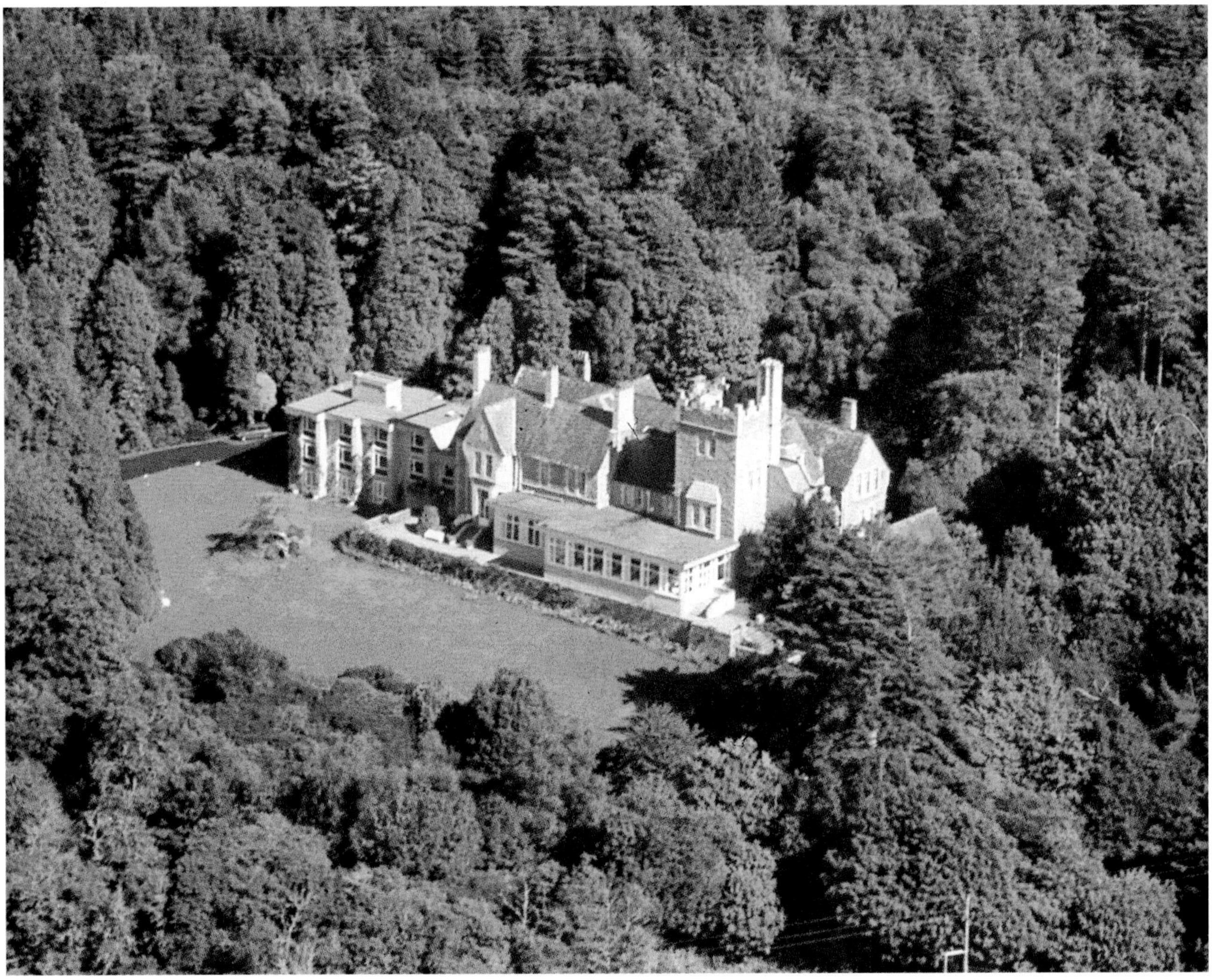

BARON'S CRAIG HOTEL

ROCKCLIFFE BY DALBEATTIE, KIRKCUDBRIGHTSHIRE DG5 4QF

TEL: 01556 630225 FAX: 01556 630328

Baron's Craig Hotel stands in wooded country overlooking Solway and Rough Firth, a tidal inlet biting deep into tree-covered and heathered hills. Thanks to the mild climate, the 12-acre grounds are ablaze with colour throughout much of the holiday season, especially in May, when masses of rhododendrons are in bloom. An imposing granite edifice, Baron's Craig was built in 1880 and harmoniously extended more recently. The 22 bedrooms have en suite facilities, both bath and shower; all have colour TV, radio, direct-dial telephone and baby-listening service. Tea and coffee making facilities are in all rooms for the convenience of guests but room service is available too. The original character of the building has been retained, with furnishings chosen to complement the period style. Excellent international cooking is augmented by a comprehensive wine list. Only three minutes from the hotel is a safe beach for swimming, while there is abundant scope for golf, fishing, boating, sailing and walking nearby. Among the local attractions are Castle Douglas, New Abbey, Glen Trool and Kirkcudbright. The new owner, Alberto Capaccioli, offers a warm welcome to all guests. Closed from November to Easter. **Directions:** Rockcliffe is a small village just off the A710 south of Dalbeattie. Price guide: (including breakfast) Single £104–£118; double/twin £43–£51 (per person). Reductions for stays of three days or more.

For hotel location, see maps on pages 477-483

THE CARNEGIE OUTPOST AT SKIBO CASTLE

DORNOCH, SUTHERLAND IV25 3RQ
TEL: 01862 894600 FAX: 01862 894601 E-MAIL:carnegie_skibo@cali.co.uk

Castles do not come more impressive, more handsome, more grand or more sumptuously accommodating than Skibo. Secluded in the scenic Highlands, Skibo was once the retreat of Scottish born American multi-millionaire industrialist and philanthropist Andrew Carnegie. Now it is the home of The Carnegie Club, an international private members residential club. Surrounded by 7,500 acres of rolling parkland, deer forests, immaculate gardens and with its own 18-hole championship links golf course Skibo offers total privacy and enjoyment. A grand staircase sweeps up to luxurious, individually designed bedrooms which overlook the wild landscape. Most have comfortable feather beds, antique armoires and spacious, old-fashioned baths. Hot water bottle are tucked into beds on winter evenings. The dining hall is baronial with products for the delicious cuisine supplied from the estate's farms, tidal inlets and grouse moors. Guests who do not play golf will delight in the nostalgic indoor swimming pavilion with its original heated marble pool, spa and gymnasium. Sailing, fishing, riding, tennis, shooting are available. Directions: From Inverness, take A9 towards Wick. After Dornoch Firth Bridge turn left onto A949 signposted Bonar Bridge and Lairg and after 500 yards, in the centre of the village of Clashmore, turn left into Skibo Castle. Price guide (fully inclusive): Single £425 plus VAT; double £550 plus VAT.

41 rms

For hotel location, see maps on pages 477-483

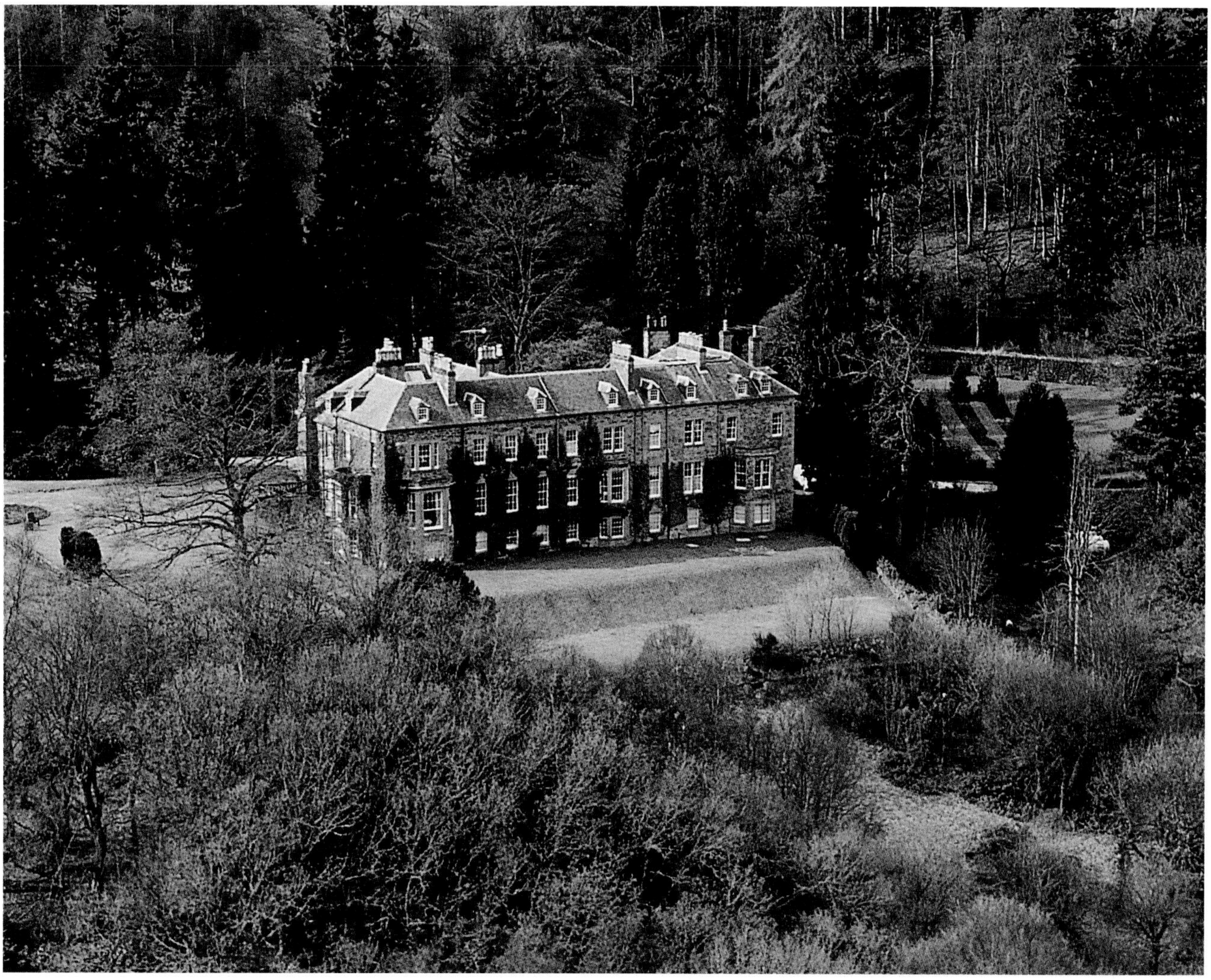

KINNAIRD

KINNAIRD ESTATE, BY DUNKELD, PERTHSHIRE PH8 0LB
TEL: 01796 482440 FAX: 01796 482289

Kinnaird is surrounded by a beautiful estate of 9,000 acres and offers breathtaking views of the moors and the Tay valley. Built in 1770, the house has been privately owned by the Ward family since 1927 and was completely renovated in 1990 by Mrs Constance Ward. Its friendly atmosphere has survived the centuries. The bedrooms are individually decorated with lovely fabrics and furnishings and each has a gas log fire and every modern convenience. The house is furnished almost entirely with fine and rare pieces of antique furniture, china and pictures, and decorated with fresh flowers. The dining rooms enjoy magnificent views and provide a stunning setting for a menu of carefully chosen and beautifully presented dishes. Kinnaird's cuisine has already won acclaim from local and international food critics. The original wine cellars are stocked with an extensive array of fine wines, liqueurs and malt whiskies. The estate also has several cottages to let. A wide variety of sporting facilities is available from salmon and trout fishing to shooting of pheasant, grouse, duck and partridge. The estate offers excellent walking, bird watching and a new all-weather tennis court. **Directions:** Two miles north of Dunkeld on A9, take B898 for four and a half miles. Price guide: Single £140–£220; double/twin £220–£240; suite £275. Special winter rates on application

For hotel location, see maps on pages 477-483

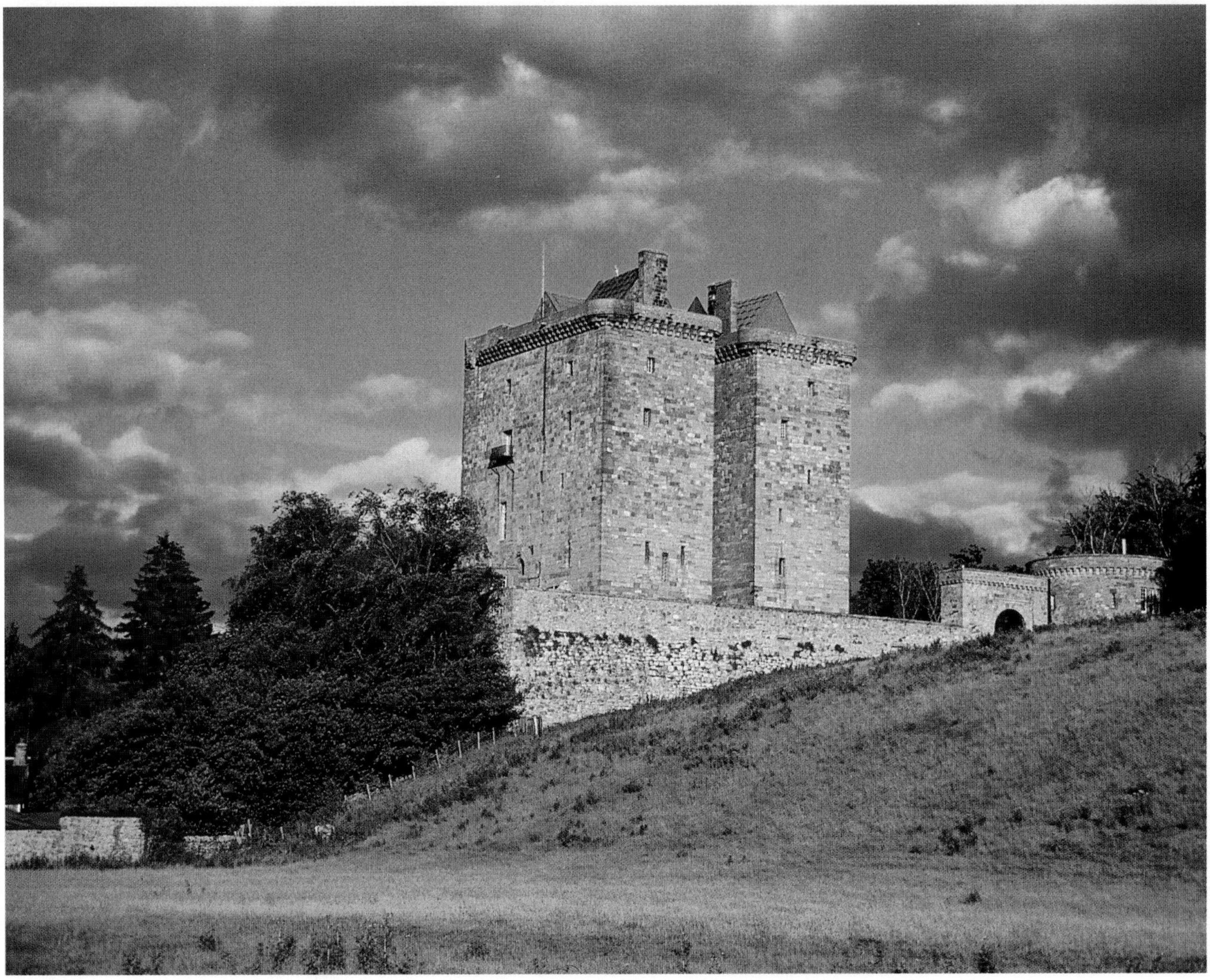

Borthwick Castle

BORTHWICK, NORTH MIDDLETON, MIDLOTHIAN EH23 4QY
TEL: 01875 820514 FAX: 01875 821702

To the south of Edinburgh, off the A7, stands historic Borthwick Castle Hotel, a twenty minute drive from Scotland's capital. Built in 1430 by the Borthwick family, this ancient stronghold has witnessed many of the great events of Scotland's history at first hand. Notably, the safe keeping of Mary Queen of Scots following her wedding to the Earl of Bothwell and a forceful visitation by Oliver Cromwell in 1650. At Borthwick Castle there are 10 bedchambers, each with en suite facilities and four with four-poster beds. In the evening, guests dine in the magnificent setting of the candle-lit Great Hall where a four-course set menu is prepared by the chef. The cooking is traditional Scottish, serving fresh local produce. A comprehensive wine list is complemented by a fine selection of malt whiskies. While the castle caters for banquets of up to 50 guests, it especially welcomes those in search of that intimate dinner for two. In either case, the experience is unforgettable. Open from March to January 2nd. **Directions:** 12 miles south of Edinburgh on the A7. At North Middleton, follow signs for Borthwick. A private road then leads to the castle. Price guide: Single £80–£165; double/twin £95–£180.

For hotel location, see maps on pages 477-483

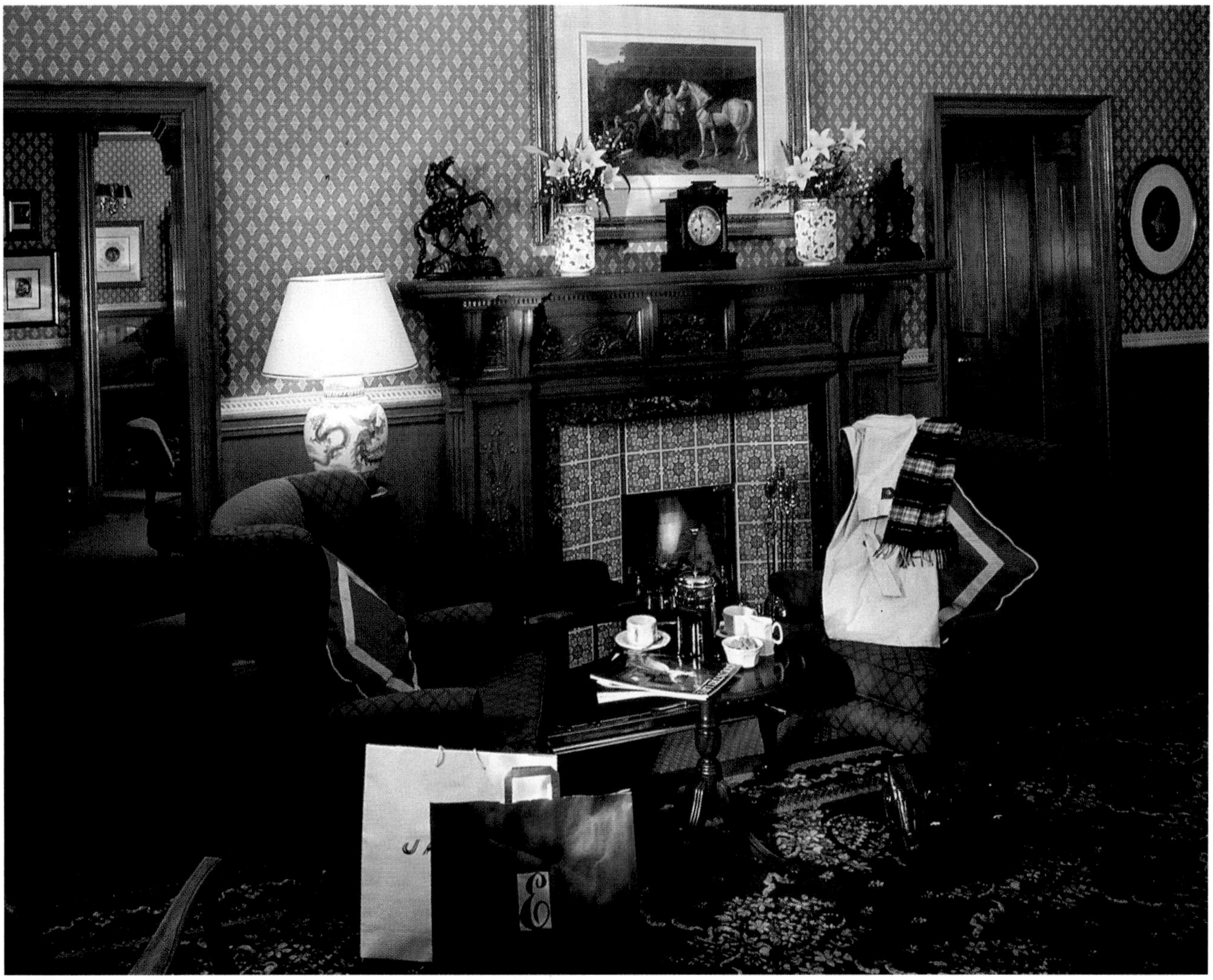

CHANNINGS

SOUTH LEARMONTH GARDENS, EDINBURGH EH4 1EZ
TEL: 0131 315 2226 FAX: 0131 332 9631

Channings is located on a quiet cobbled street only 10 minutes' walk from the centre of Edinburgh, with easy access to the host of shops on Princes Street and the timeless grandeur of Edinburgh Castle. Formerly five Edwardian town houses, the original features have been restored with flair and consideration and the atmosphere is like that of an exclusive country club. Guests can relax in one of the lounges with coffee or afternoon tea. For those who like to browse, the hotel has an interesting collection of antique prints, furniture, *objets d'art*, periodicals and books. The Brasserie (AA Rosette) offers varied menus from a light lunch to full evening meals. Five ground floor suites provide versatile accommodation for corporate requirements, small seminars and presentations, while both the Kingsleigh Suite and oak-panelled library make an ideal venue for cocktail parties and private dinners. At the rear of the hotel is a terraced, patio garden. Special weekend breaks are available throughout the year and offer good value. Closed for Christmas. **Directions:** Go north-west from Queensferry Street, over Dean Bridge on to Queensferry Road. Take third turning on right down South Learmonth Avenue, turn right at end into South Learmonth Gardens. Price guide: Single £90–£102; double/twin £120–£150.

48 rms

For hotel location, see maps on pages 477-483

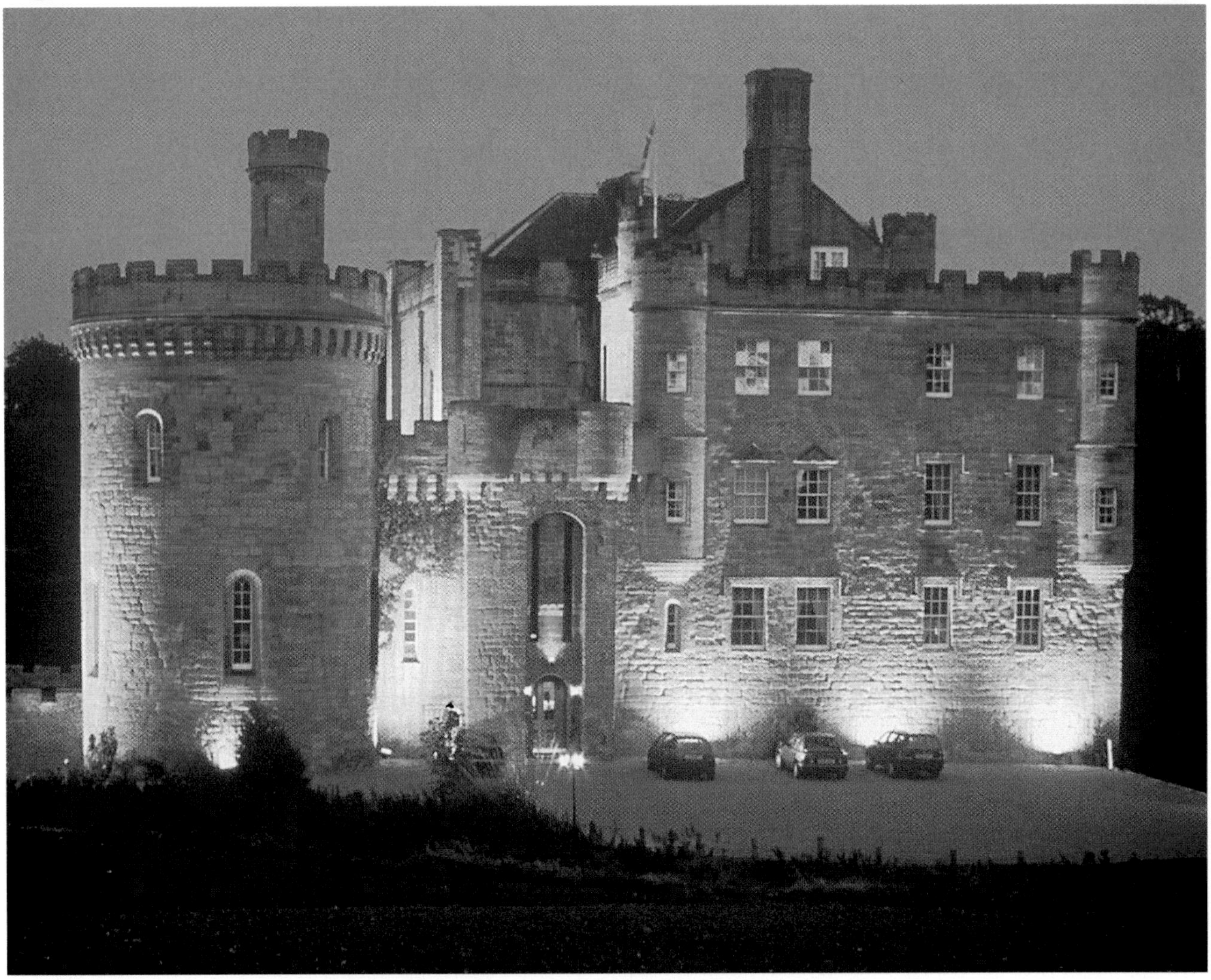

DALHOUSIE CASTLE

EDINBURGH, BONNYRIGG EH19 3JB
TEL: 01875 820153 FAX: 01875 821936

The Dalhousie Castle nestles in acres of forest, river, pasture and parkland overlooking the South Esk River. For 800 years it has been host to numerous famous figures, including Edward I, Oliver Cromwell, Sir Walter Scott and Queen Victoria. Today, following sympathetic restoration, the family seat of the Ramsays of Dalhousie, it is a 29 bedroom, luxurious hotel which retains many fine features. Historically themed bedrooms comprise Robert the Bruce, Queen Victoria and others. Ornate plasterwork, fine panelling, stone walls and rich drapes adorn the public rooms, whilst the ancient barrel-vaulted dungeons offer a unique setting for candlelit dining. Both French and Scottish cuisine is served in the restaurant, complemented by attentive and personal service. Game and clay shooting, salmon and trout fishing, 'dry' skiing and golf at St Andrews, North Berwick and locally at Broomieknowe are all within easy reach. Archery and falconry can be arranged in the hotel's grounds. Five carefully renovated banqueting and conference suites provide an excellent setting for conferences, meetings, banquets and weddings. The Castle is only 20 minutes drive from Edinburgh. STB 4 Crowns Highly Commended – Taste of Scotland Approved. **Directions:** From Edinburgh A7 south, through Lasswade and Newtongrange. Turn right at junction onto the B704 and the hotel is within 1/4 mile. Price guide: Single £80–£110; double £100–£175.

For hotel location, see maps on pages 477-483

THE HOWARD

32-36 GREAT KING STREET, EDINBURGH EH3 6QH
TEL: 0131-557 3500 FAX: 0131-557 6515

Since its conversion from private residence to hotel, The Howard has been sumptuously appointed throughout and offers a service to match the surroundings. The original character of this Georgian town house still prevails. The 16 bedrooms, including two suites, are beautifully furnished with antiques, while the drawing room centres on an elaborate crystal chandelier. The Oval and Cumberland suite offers quiet and elegant surroundings for either meetings or private dining, accommodating 12–30 guests. The Howard is an integral part of the largest classified historical monument in Britain: Edinburgh's New Town. Having a private car park to the rear, The Howard is a superb city centre base from which to explore Edinburgh's cultural heritage, being in close proximity to such monuments as Edinburgh Castle, the Palace of Holyrood and the Royal Mile. Equally it is just minutes from much of the citys business community. **Directions:** Travelling east on Princes Street, take the third left into Frederick Street and turn right into George Street. Take the next left into Hanover Street, go through three sets of lights then turn right into Great King Street. Hotel is on the left. Price guide: Single £110; double £195; suite £275.

16 rms MasterCard VISA AMERICAN EXPRESS M 45

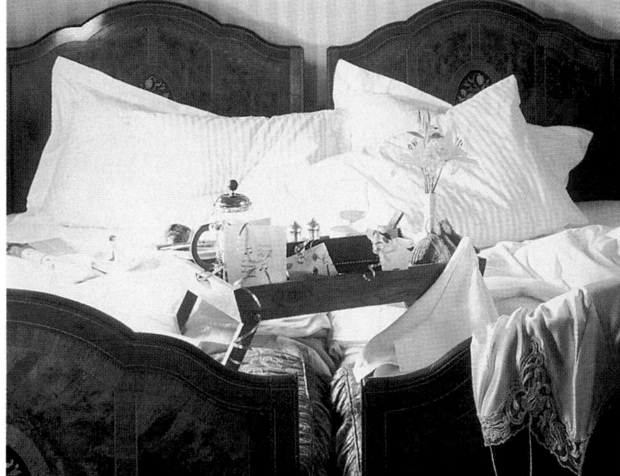

For hotel location, see maps on pages 477-483

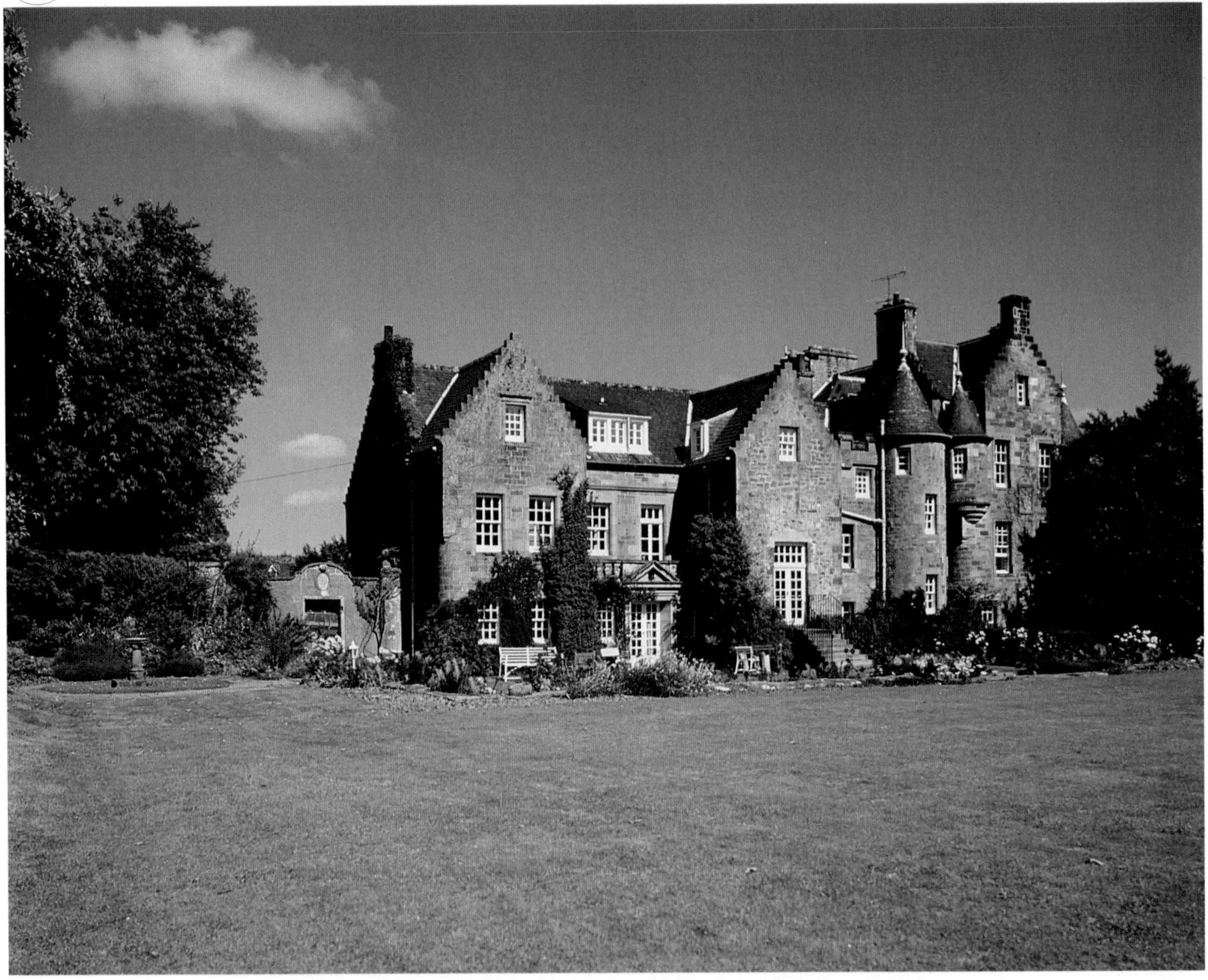

JOHNSTOUNBURN HOUSE

HUMBIE, NR EDINBURGH, EAST LOTHIAN EH36 5PL
TEL: 01875 833696 FAX: 01875 833626

Dating from 1625, Johnstounburn House stands at the foot of the Lammermuir Hills, only 15 miles south of Edinburgh. Today it is a superb country house hotel. Set amid lawns and parklands in a private estate, its grounds feature imposing yew hedges, an orchard, a patio rose garden and a herbaceons walled garden. Upon entering the house, guests will sense the depth of Scottish heritage preserved here. Refurbishments have enhanced the historical features while enabling guests to enjoy modern comforts. Of the 20 well-appointed bedrooms, 11 are in the house and nine in the tastefully converted coach house. There is a spacious cedar-panelled lounge where an open fire will warm you on chilly days. In the 18th-century, pine-panelled dining room, chef Bryan Thom prepares sumptuous fare from the finest Scottish produce. In the grounds, guests can enjoy clay pigeon shooting, off-road and all terrain vehicle driving and fishing in a trout-filled pond. There is also a "fairway course" where the golfer can practise. Muirfield and Gullane are among 15 golf courses nearby. Tantallon Castle, Abbotsford and Traquair House are a short drive away. **Directions:** From Edinburgh take A68 through Dalkeith and Pathhead to Fala. Turn left through Fala 1½ miles to T-junction; the hotel is on your right. Price guide: Single £99; double/twin £135–£185; suite £185.

For hotel location, see maps on pages 477-483

THE NORTON HOUSE HOTEL

INGLISTON, EDINBURGH EH28 8LX
TEL: 0131 333 1275 FAX: 0131 333 5305

This Victorian mansion, dating back to 1861, is a part of the Virgin Group. Situated in 55 acres of mature parkland, Norton House combines modern comforts with elegance. The 47 en suite bedrooms are bright and spacious, with many facilities, including a video channel and satellite TV. Influenced by the best Scottish and French traditions, the menu offers a balanced choice. Moments away, through leafy woodlands, a former stable block has been converted into The Gathering Bistro and Bar, where drinks and snacks are available to family and friends. Set in a walled garden, it is an ideal venue for the barbecues which are a regular feature in the summer months. The Patio, Veranda and Usher Room lend a sense of occasion to small gatherings, while the Linlithgow Suite can cater for large-scale events such as banquets, weddings and conferences. Norton House is 1 mile from Edinburgh Airport and 6 miles from the city centre, making it a convenient base from which to explore the Trossachs, Borders and Lothians. Dogs accommodated by request. **Directions:** From Edinburgh take A8 past airport and hotel is 1/2 mile on left. From Glasgow, follow M8 to junction 2, take the first exit off the roundabout following signs for Ratho, take the first exit off the roundabout, following signs for Ratho, then turn left at the top of the hill. Price guide: Single £99–£115; double/twin £120–£145; suite £165.

For hotel location, see maps on pages 477-483

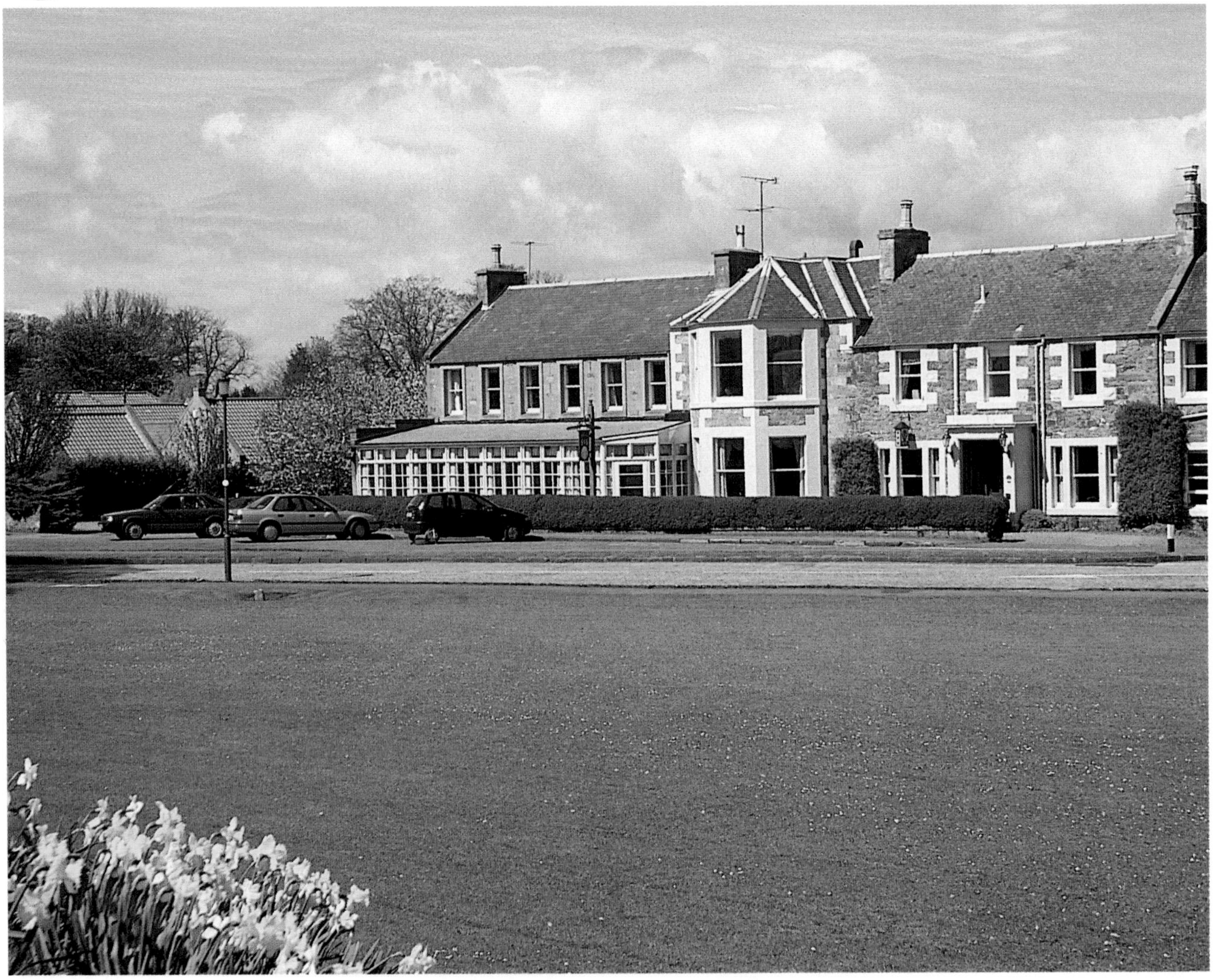

THE OPEN ARMS

DIRLETON (NR EDINBURGH), EAST LOTHIAN EH39 5EG
TEL: 01620 850241 FAX: 01620 850570

Perfectly positioned at the end of the village green, overlooking a 13th century castle, this enchanting hotel, built in the local stone in the 17th century and surrounded by its own extensive gardens, is in one of the prettiest villages in Scotland. The Open Arms is an apt name, for it has a great ambience enhanced by the traditional log fires, comfortable lounges and warm welcome from the hosts, Tom and Emma Hill, deservedly recognised by awards from The Scottish Tourist Board. The bedrooms are delightful, with harmonious colour schemes and all the extra details expected by today's traveller. Guests mingle with the locals in the friendly, well stocked bar before feasting in the restaurant (AA accolades) which has founder membership of "Taste of Scotland", the menu listing local fish, shellfish, beef and produce as well as game from nearby estates presented with great flair by the talented chef – all accompanied by carefully selected wines. This is a golfer's paradise, with nineteen excellent courses nearby including the Open championship course, Muirfield. Others enjoy the coast or nature reserves, explore Edinburgh 20 minutes drive away, and visit castles and stately homes, absorbing the evocative atmosphere of the area. **Directions:** On the A198 from Edinburgh (city bypass), which links with the M8, M9 and M90. Price guide: Single £57–£110.

For hotel location, see maps on pages 477-483

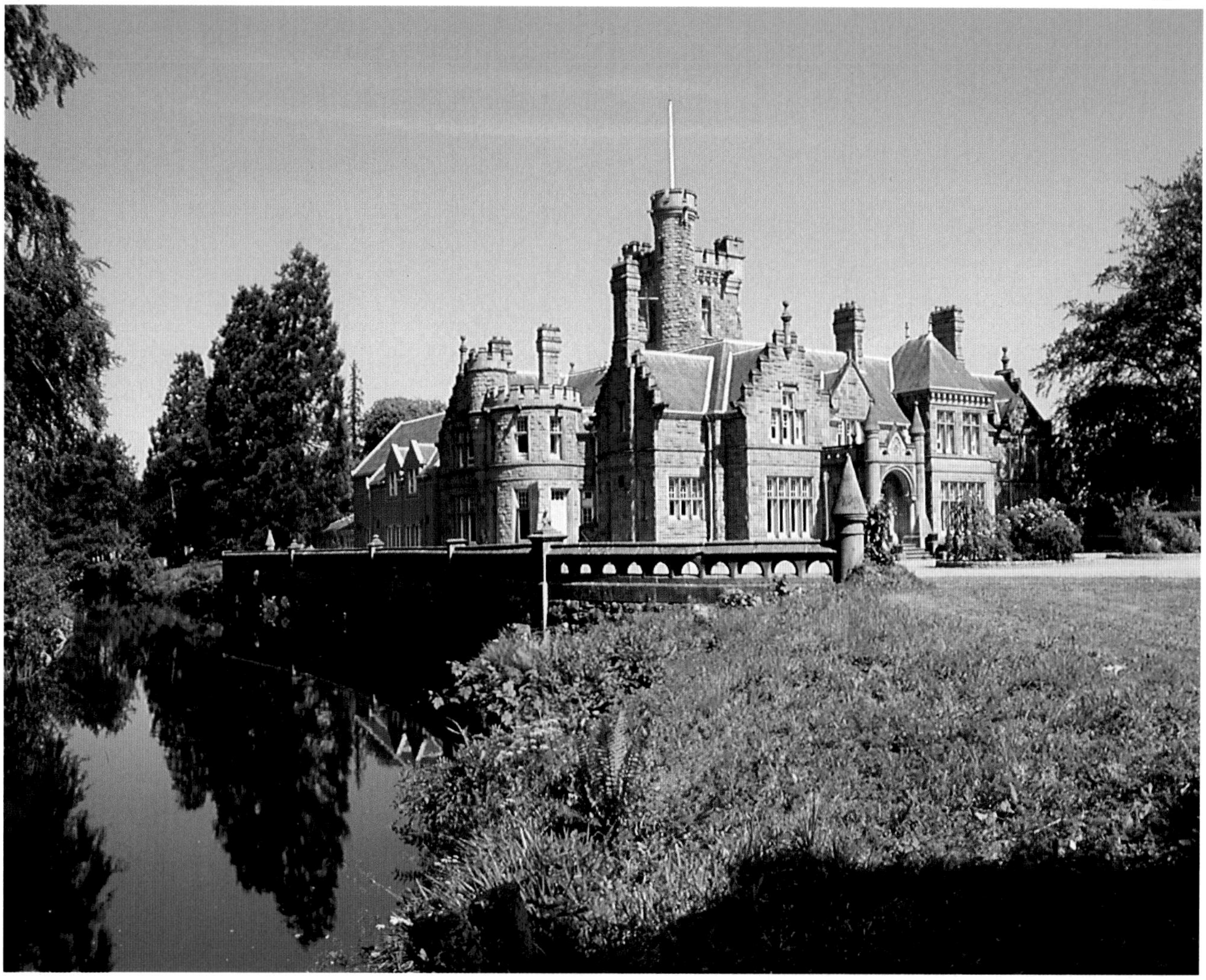

Mansion House Hotel

THE HAUGH, ELGIN, MORAY IV30 1AW
TEL: 01343 548811 FAX: 01343 547916

Set within private woodland and overlooking the River Lossie stands the grand Mansion House Hotel. This former baronial mansion is only a minute's walk from the centre of the ancient city of Elgin. A welcoming entrance hall boasts oak-panelled walls, fresh flowers and many antique curiosities. Its majestic staircase leads to the well appointed bedrooms, featuring four-poster beds and containing a welcoming glass of sherry. The Piano Lounge is an ideal place to relax before entering the elegant restaurant. Here the cuisine is creative, delicious and beautifully presented. The "Wee Bar" is in the centre of the house, well placed next to the Snooker Room, while a unique collection of whiskies gives the name to the Still Room. A purpose built function room, called the Haugh Room, has its own entrance, bar, toilets, and dance area. Guests at the hotel are invited to use the Country Club facilities which include a swimming pool, gymnasium, spa, steam room, sauna and sun bed. Complementing this is the Beauty Spot, which provides a multitude of unisex services. There is a choice of ten golf courses within ten miles, the opportunity to fish on the Spey and unlimited water sports in Findhorn Bay. **Directions:** In Elgin, turn off the main A96 road into Haugh Road. The hotel is at the end of this road by the river. Price guide: Single £75–£95;

For hotel location, see maps on pages 477-483

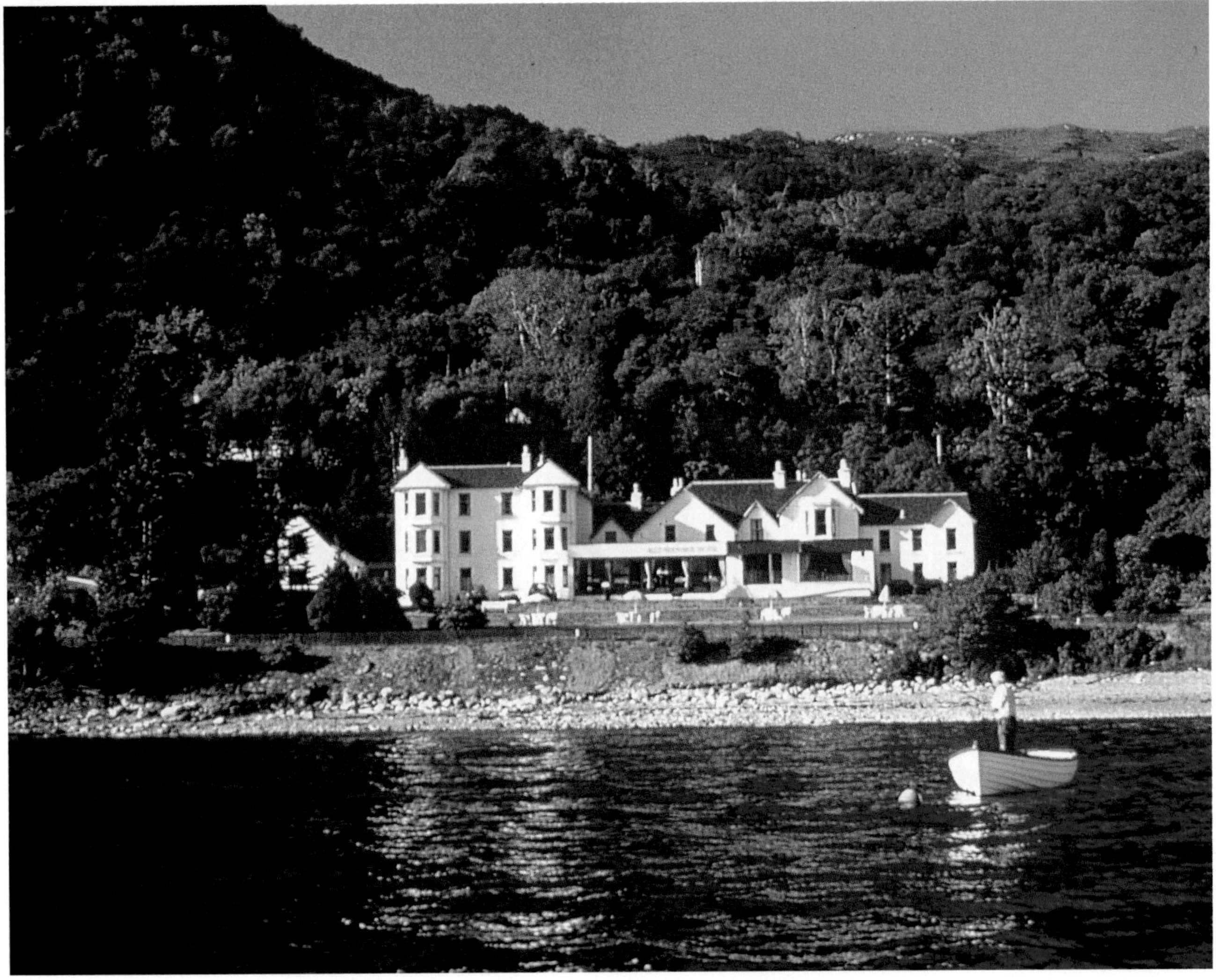

ALLT-NAN-ROS HOTEL

ONICH, FORT WILLIAM, INVERNESS-SHIRE PH33 6RY
TEL: 01855 821210 FAX: 01855 821462

Situated on the north shore of Loch Linnhe, Allt-nan-Ros Hotel (Gaelic for 'Burn of the Roses') was originally built as a Victorian shooting lodge. It has been tastefully upgraded by its resident proprietors, the MacLeod family, and it offers both a high standard of comfort and exceptional views of the surrounding mountains and lochs. The design of the hotel takes advantage of its southerly aspect and all bedrooms and public rooms overlook the loch. Quality furnishings and a full range of amenities are provided in all the bedrooms, while the superior rooms available each incorporate a bay window. In the traditionally furnished lounges, dining room and bar a country house atmosphere prevails and guests are invited to relax and enjoy the lovely views. The cuisine served in the splendid restaurant is influenced by modern and French styles, but also adapts traditional Scottish recipes to today's tastes. A comprehensive and reasonably priced wine list incorporates wines from all around the world. Lying midway between Ben Nevis and Glencoe, the hotel is located in an area of unsurpassed scenery and history. Among the many local activities are climbing, walking, touring the towns and islands, sailing, fishing or taking a trip on the steam trains. **Directions:** Ten miles south of Fort William on the main A82. Price guide: Single £35–£55; double/twin £70–£110; suites £76–£130.

For hotel location, see maps on pages 477-483

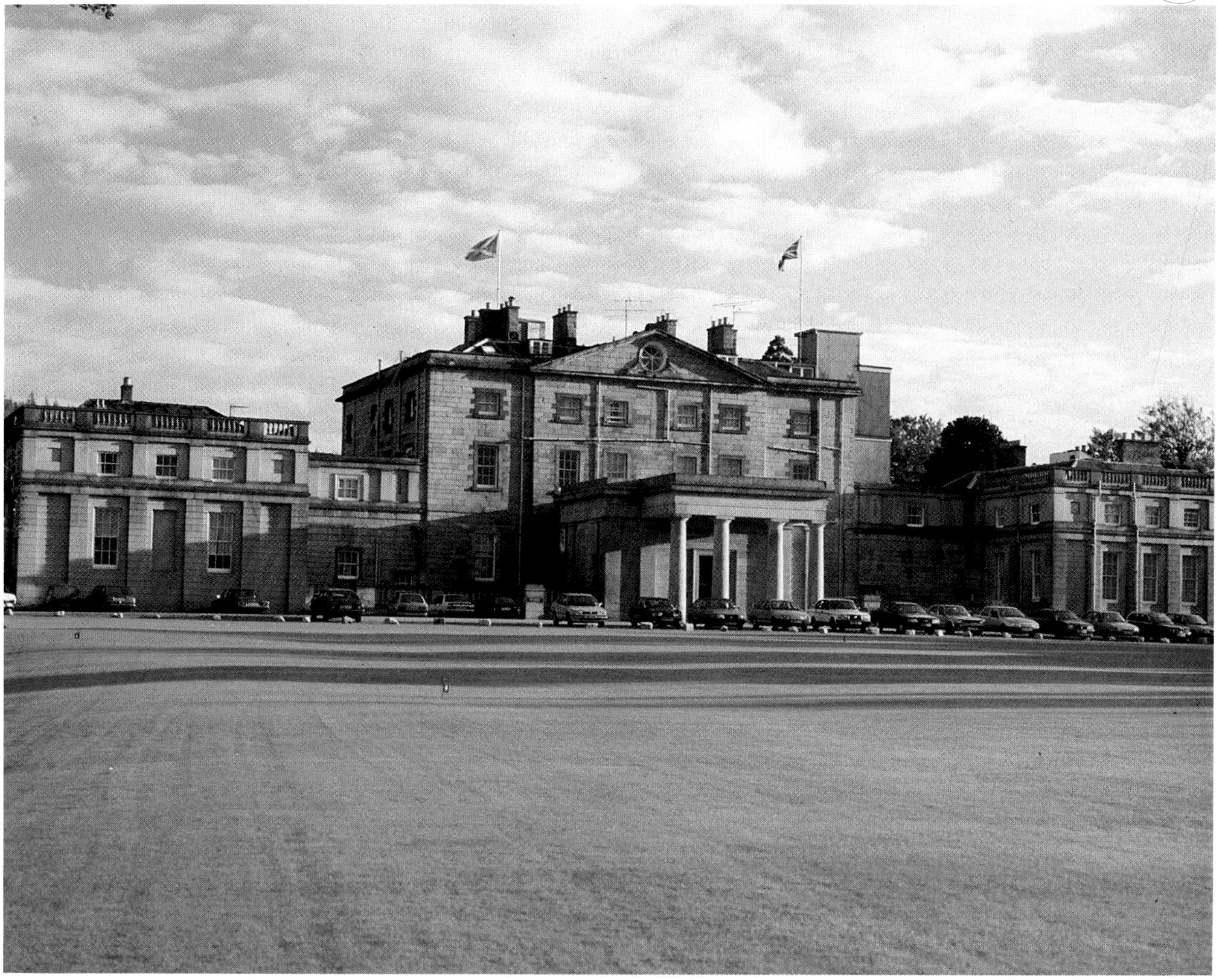

CALLY PALACE HOTEL

GATEHOUSE OF FLEET, DUMFRIES & GALLOWAY DG7 2DL

TEL: 01557 814341 FAX: 01557 814522

Set in over 100 acres of forest and parkland, on the edge of Robert Burns country, this 18th-century country house has been restored to its former glory by the McMillan family, the proprietors since 1981. On entering the hotel, guests will initially be impressed by the grand scale of the interior. Two huge marble pillars support the original moulded ceiling of the entrance hall. All the public rooms have ornate ceilings, original marble fireplaces and fine reproduction furniture. Combine these with grand, traditional Scottish cooking and you have a hotel *par excellence*. The 56 en suite bedrooms have been individually decorated. Some are suites with a separate sitting room; others are large enough to accommodate a sitting area. An indoor leisure complex, completed in the style of the marble entrance hall, includes heated swimming pool, Jacuzzi, saunas and solarium. The hotel has an all-weather tennis court, a putting green, croquet, and a lake for private fishing or boating. Also, for exclusive use of hotel guests is an 18-hole golf course, par 70, length 5,500 yards set around the lake in the 150 acre grounds. Special weekend and over-60s breaks are available out of season. Closed January and February. **Directions:** Sixty miles west of Carlisle, 1-1½ miles from Gatehouse of Fleet junction on the main A75 road. Price guide: (including dinner): Single £70; double/twin £114–£140.

For hotel location, see maps on pages 477-483

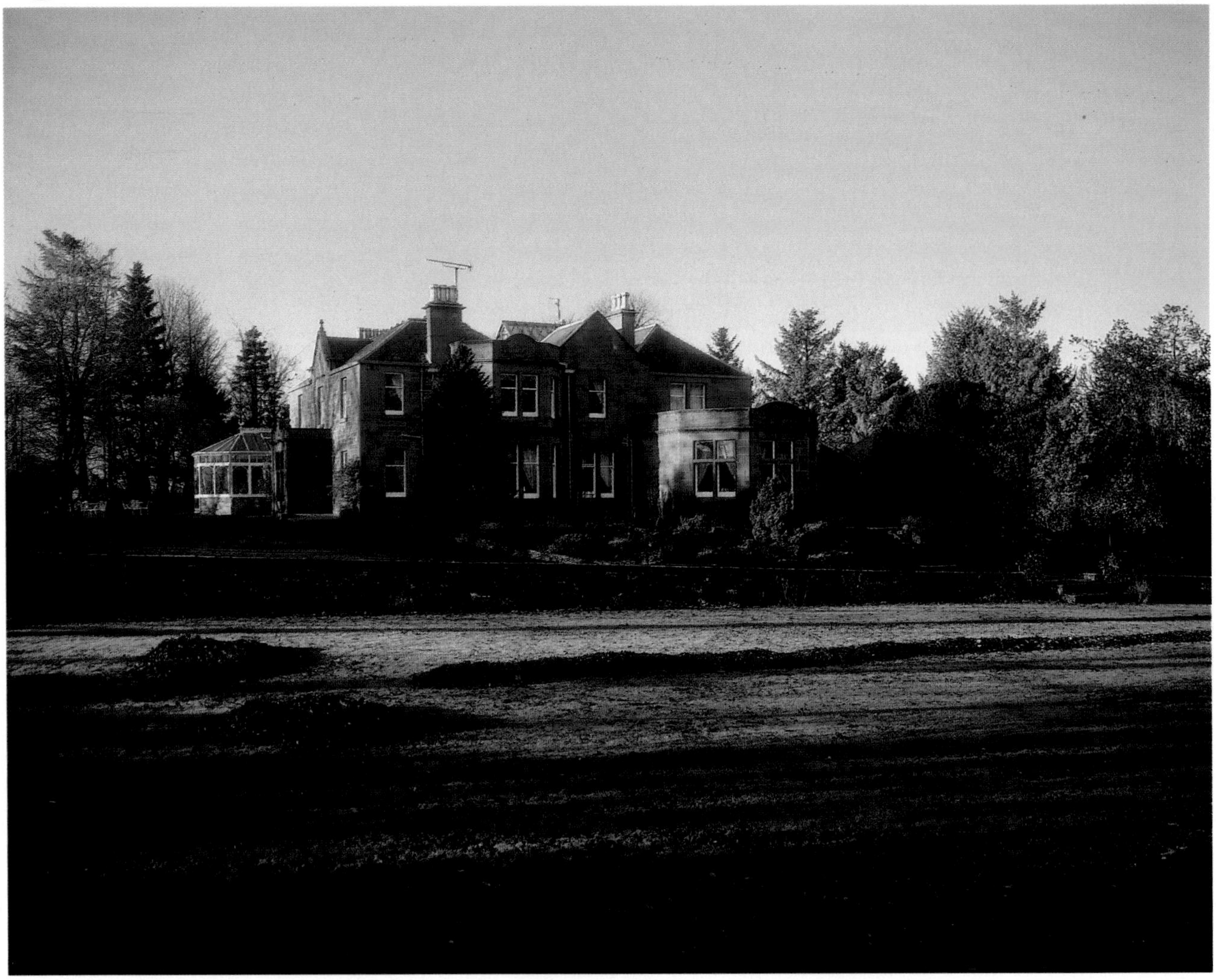

CASTLETON HOUSE HOTEL

GLAMIS, BY FORFAR, ANGUS DD8 1SJ
TEL: 01307 840340 FAX: 01307 840506

Castleton House stands on the site of an old fort and is set in extensive grounds. Its proprietors pride themselves on offering guests excellent accommodation and outstanding cuisine in an informal and refreshing country atmosphere. Each of the bedrooms has been furnished to the highest standards and includes a full range of modern amenities. Castleton House is at the heart of Scotland's larder with abundant, highly-prized local supplies of fresh fruit, vegetables, meat, poultry, game and fish. The hotel enjoys a reputation for fine cuisine, which is served both in the dining room and conservatory and its cellars are stocked with an outstanding selection of wines. There is no shortage of activities for sporting enthusiasts. Golf at St Andrews, Gleneagles, Carnoustie and Rosemount are all within a short distance, while game shooting and stalking can be arranged on a nearby estate. The Grampians offer hill walking and rock climbing and Britain's largest ski area is only a 40 minute drive away. The surrounding area is rich in history and there are numerous standing stones, ancient houses, castles and forts to remind visitors of the past. Tayside offers many delights from the wild expanse of Rannoch Moor to the grandeur of the Grampians and the golden sands of Lunan Bay. **Directions:** Off A94, three miles from Glamis. Price guide: Single £70; double/twin £100.

6 rms 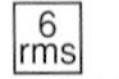      140  

For hotel location, see maps on pages 477-483

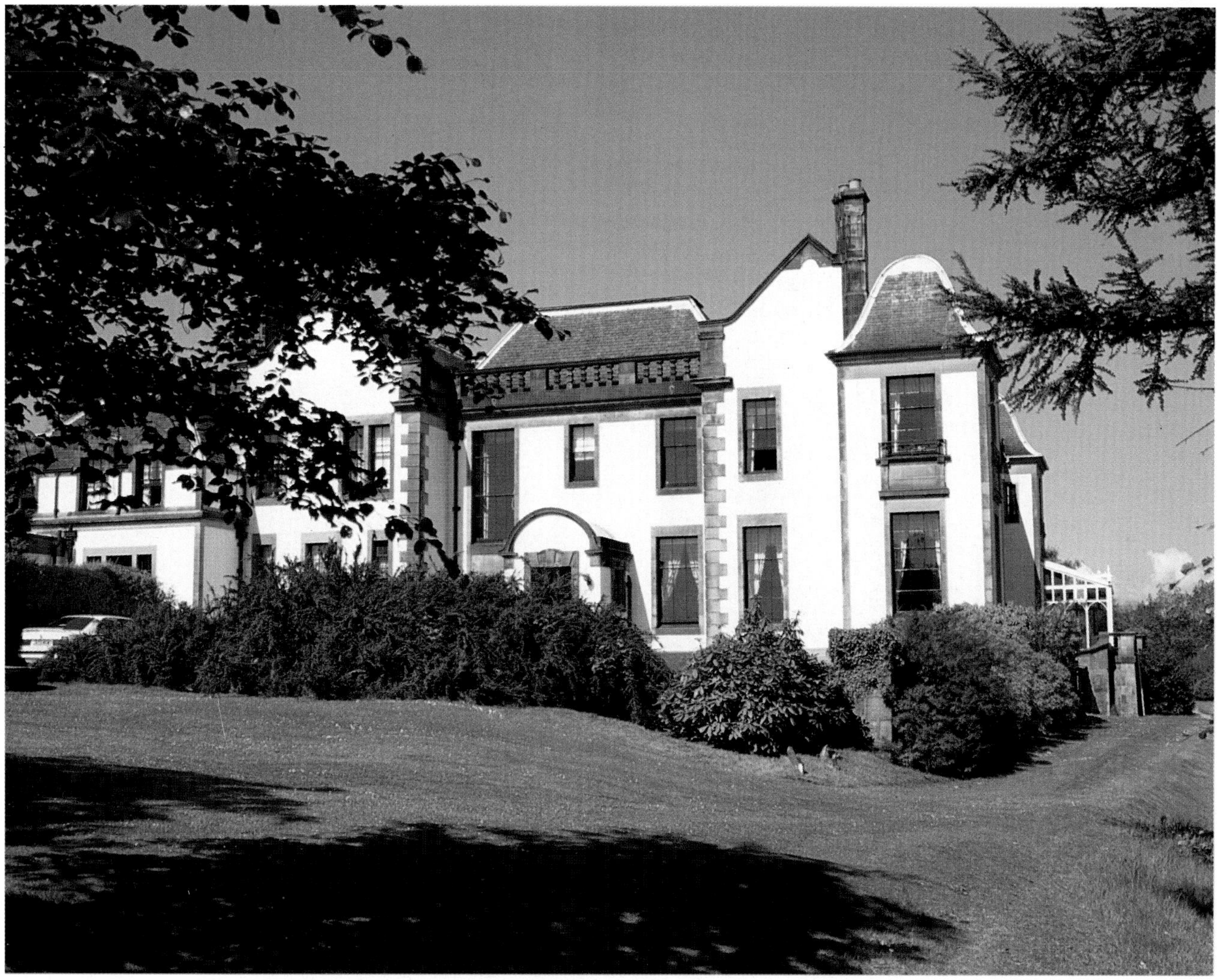

GLEDDOCH HOUSE

LANGBANK, RENFREWSHIRE PA14 6YE

TEL: 01475 540711 FAX: 01475 540201

Once the home of a Glasgow shipping baron, Gleddoch House stands in 360 acres, with dramatic views across the River Clyde to Ben Lomond and the hills beyond. The individually appointed bedrooms all have en suite facilities and some have four-poster beds. Executive rooms and suites and family rooms are also available. There are also self-catering lodges on the estate. Other amenities include a range of meeting rooms to cater for up to 120 delegates theatre style. The Restaurant is renowned for its award-winning modern Scottish cuisine and is complemented by a comprehensive wine list. On the estate a series of activities are available such as golf, clay pigeon shooting, archery and off-road driving, making Gleddoch an ideal venue to host corporate events. Additionally the equestrian centre caters for all levels, from trekking to pony rides and individual tuition. Gleddoch's location offers an experience of a bygone era yet amid the sophistication that today's traveller requires. A range of short breaks, golfing packages and gourmet events are available throughout the year. Glasgow Airport is only 10 minutes drive away and the City Centre 20 minutes. **Directions:** M8 towards Greenock; take B789 Langbank/ Houston exit. Follow signs to left and then right after 1/2 mile; hotel is on left. Price guide: Single £95; double/twin £140; suite £175.

For hotel location, see maps on pages 477-483

MALMAISON

278 WEST GEORGE STREET, GLASGOW G2 4LL
TEL: 0141 221 6400 FAX: 0141 221 6411

In 1799, Josephine de Beauharnais, along with her husband, Emperor Napoleon I, bought a house near the Palace of Versailles just outside Paris. The house was called Malmaison and it soon became widely regarded as an example of the new chic contemporary style of its era. The Malmaison in Glasgow is today's equivalent of that independent style. A small contemporary hotel with spacious, stylish bedrooms, individually designed, complete with CD players and satellite televisions. With an art nouveau Brasserie and Café Bar serving traditional French cooking with an ever changing menu and an interesting list of wines by the glass, pot and bottle. Malmaison is situated in the heart of Glasgow, within easy walking distance of theatres, shopping, railway stations and only 20 minutes by road from the Airport. **Directions:** From south and east (Edinburgh) leave M8 at junction 17. Turn left at traffic lights into Sauchiehall Street and assume the right hand lane of the one way system. Take the third right, Pitt Street, and follow that road across three blocks until it turns round onto West George Street at the Strathclyde Police Headquarters. Malmaison is immediately on your left hand side. From the west (Glasgow Airport) leave M8 at junction 19. Price guide: Single £75; double/twin £75; suites £105.

21 rms MasterCard VISA AMERICAN EXPRESS

For hotel location, see maps on pages 477-483

ONE DEVONSHIRE GARDENS

GLASGOW G12 0UX
TEL: 0141 339 2001 FAX: 0141 337 1663

Situated just ten minutes from the city centre, One Devonshire Gardens is set in the heart of a tree-lined Victorian terrace once the homes of the wealthy merchants and shipowners of Glasgow. This luxurious hotel prides itself of providing a caring, friendly service in relaxing surroundings. The bedrooms are superbly decorated and furnished and offer the ultimate in comfort and convenience. Fine cuisine, beautifully prepared and presented, is served in the elegant dining room. Try fillet of Angus beef with mushrooms, smoked bacon, roasted onions in a red wine jus, or fricassee of lobster, scallops and langoustines with baby summer vegetables in a ginger and cardamon nage. These culinary delights are complemented by an extensive and interesting cellar. In the warmer months, afternoon teas may be enjoyed on the colourful terrace. There is plenty to do and see in Glasgow. Visit the cathedral the only complete medieval cathedral on the Scottish mainland or some of the fine museums such as Pollok House, which contains one of the best collections of Spanish paintings in Britain. **Directions:** From M8 junction 17 follow A82 (Great Western Road) for $1^1/_2$ miles, turn left at traffic lights into Hyndland Road. Take first right into Hughenden Road, right at mini-roundabout then right again at end of road. Keep going – car park in front of hotel. Price guide: Single £135; double/twin £160; suites £180.

For hotel location, see maps on pages 477-483

Dalmunzie House

SPITTAL O'GLENSHEE, BLAIRGOWRIE, PERTHSHIRE PH10 7QG
TEL: 01250 885224 FAX: 01250 885225

Dalmunzie House is beautifully tucked away high in the Scottish Highlands, 18 miles north of Blairgowrie and 15 miles south of Braemar. Standing in its own mountainous 6,000-acre sporting estate, it is run by Simon and Alexandra Winton. Guests come to enjoy the relaxed family atmosphere which, together with unobtrusive service and attention, ensures a comfortable stay. The bedrooms are individual in character, some with antiques, others romantically set in the turrets of the house, all tastefully decorated. Delicately cooked traditional Scottish fare is created from local ingredients fresh from the hills and lochs. The menu changes daily and meals are served in the dining room, accompanied by wines from the well-stocked cellar. Among the sporting activities available on site are golf (the 9-hole course is the highest in Britain) and shooting for grouse, ptarmigan and black game. Other country pursuits include river and loch fishing and stalking for red deer. Pony-trekking can be organised locally. Glenshee Ski Centre is 6 miles away: it offers cross-country and downhill skiing. Closer to home, the hotel games room provides more sedate pastimes for all the family. Closed early November to 28 December. Special winter/Skiing Rates. **Directions:** Dalmunzie is on the A93 at the Spittal O'Glenshee, south of Braemar. Price guide: Single £48–£54; double/twin £75–£90.

For hotel location, see maps on pages 477-483

GREYWALLS

MUIRFIELD, GULLANE, EAST LOTHIAN EH31 2EG
TEL: 01620 842144 FAX: 01620 842241

Greywalls, neighbouring Muirfield golf course, the home of the Honourable Company of Edinburgh Golfers, was designed by Sir Edwin Lutyens. King Edward VII was a frequent visitor. The hotel is a beautiful crescent shaped building made of warm, honey coloured stone from the local quarry. A delightful garden, believed to be the work of Gertrude Jekyll, provides secret enclaves where guests can escape to enjoy a good book and savour the delightful scents of roses and lavender. The hotel's bedrooms, all of varying size and design, are individually furnished and include many fine antiques. Downstairs is the peaceful panelled library, Edwardian tea room and small bar stocked with a selection of excellent brandies and whiskies. Hearty breakfasts of porridge, kippers from Achiltibuie, tasty sausages and freshly made croissants make an ideal start to the day while dinner is an outstanding feast provided by dedicated chefs. East Lothian has excellent golf courses, including Muirfield, where The Open is held regularly. Beautiful sandy beaches are within easy reach, along with nature reserves, ruined castles, villages, market towns and stately homes. The hotel is closed from November through to March. **Directions:** On A198 from city bypass which links to the M8, M9 and M90. Price guide: Single £95; double/twin £155–£175.

For hotel location, see maps on pages 477-483

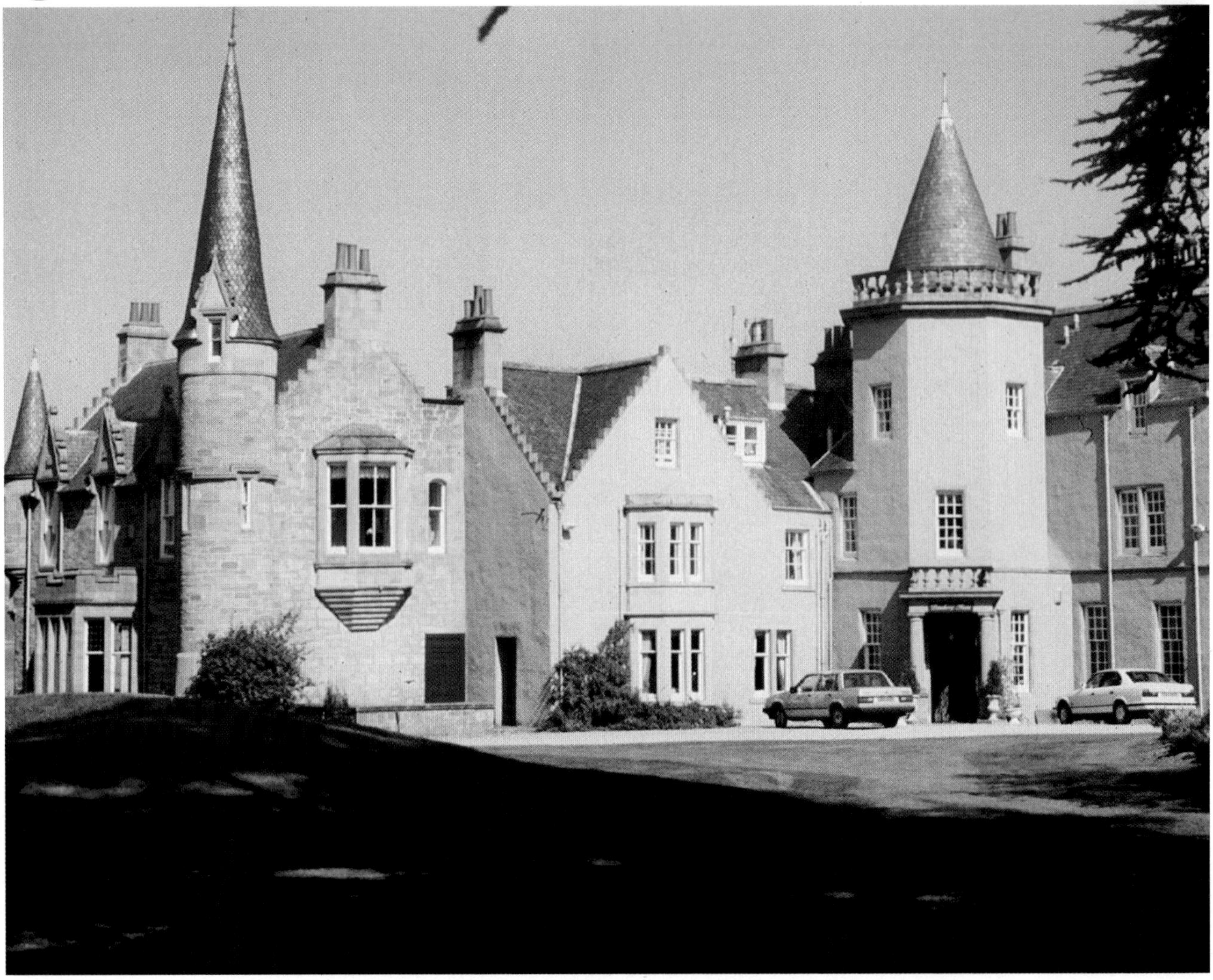

BUNCHREW HOUSE HOTEL

INVERNESS, SCOTLAND IV3 6TA
TEL: 01463 234917 FAX: 01463 710620

This splendid 17th century Scottish mansion, owned by Stewart and Lesley Dykes, is set amidst 20 acres of landscaped gardens and woodlands on the shores of Beauly Firth. Guests can enjoy breathtaking views of Ben Wyvis and the Black Isle, while just yards from the house the sea laps at the garden walls. Bunchrew has been carefully restored to preserve its heritage, while still giving its guests the highest standards of comfort and convenience. A further schedule of refurbishment began in 1995. The luxury suites are beautifully furnished and decorated to enhance their natural features. The elegant panelled drawing room is the ideal place to relax at any time, while during the winter log fires lend it an added appeal. In the candle-lit restaurant the traditional cuisine includes prime Scottish beef, fresh lobster and langoustines, locally caught game and venison and freshly grown vegetables. A carefully chosen wine list complements the menu. Local places of interest include Cawdor Castle, Loch Ness, Castle Urquhart and a number of beautiful glens. For those who enjoy sport there is skiing at nearby Aviemore, sailing, cruising and golf. **Directions:** From Inverness follow signs to Beauly, Dingwall on the A862. One mile from the outskirts of Inverness the entrance to Bunchrew House is on the right. Price guide: Single £55–£75; double/twin £75–£100; suites £105–£120.

For hotel location, see maps on pages 477-483

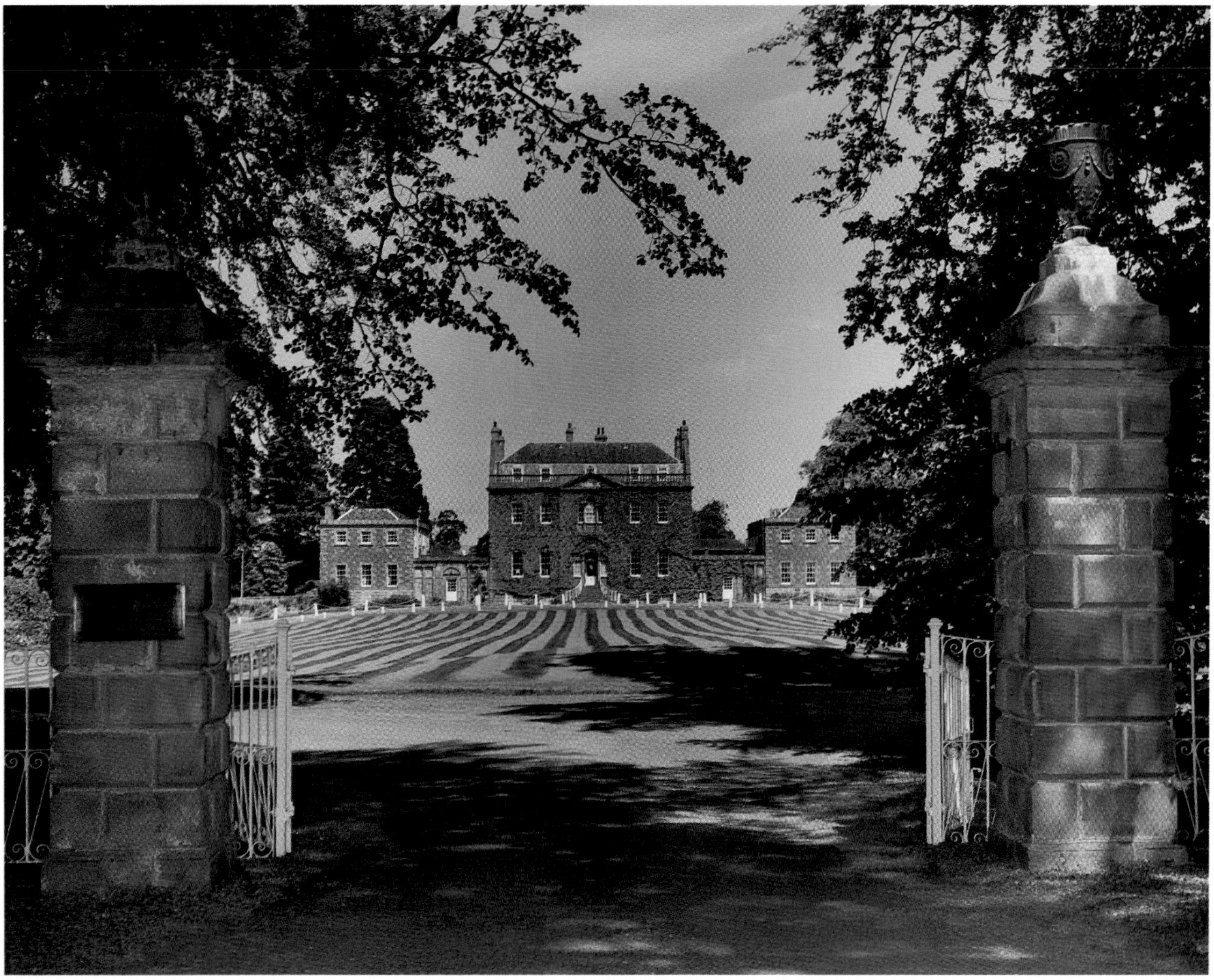

CULLODEN HOUSE HOTEL

INVERNESS, INVERNESS-SHIRE IV1 2NZ

TEL: 01463 790461 FAX: 01463 792181 FROM USA TOLL FREE FAX 1 800 373 7987

Culloden House is a handsome Georgian mansion with a centuries-old tradition of hospitality. Among its famous visitors was Bonnie Prince Charlie, who fought his last battle by the park walls 251 years ago. The house stands in 40 acres of elegant lawns and parkland, where wild deer occasionally roam. High reputation with guests from all over the world. Thorough refurbishments of the décor and furnishings have enhanced the magnificent interiors. A good choice of accommodation is offered – from en suite single rooms to a four-poster double, or room with Jacuzzi – with the assurance that all rooms are appointed to the highest standards. New no-smoking suites are situated near the walled garden. In the Adam Dining Room, guests can savour superb cuisine prepared by acclaimed chef Michael Simpson, who trained at the Gleneagles Hotel and Hamburg Congress Centre. Business lunches, celebrations and functions can be held in the private dining room. Boat trips to Loch Ness can be arranged, while nearby are Cawdor Castle, the Clava Cairns burial ground and Culloden battlefield. Numerous routes lead to lovely glens. **Directions:** Take the A96 road and turn as signed to Culloden. Turn again at Culloden House Avenue. Price guide: Single £125–£175; double/twin £175–£220; suite £220.

23 rms 40 10

For hotel location, see maps on pages 477-483

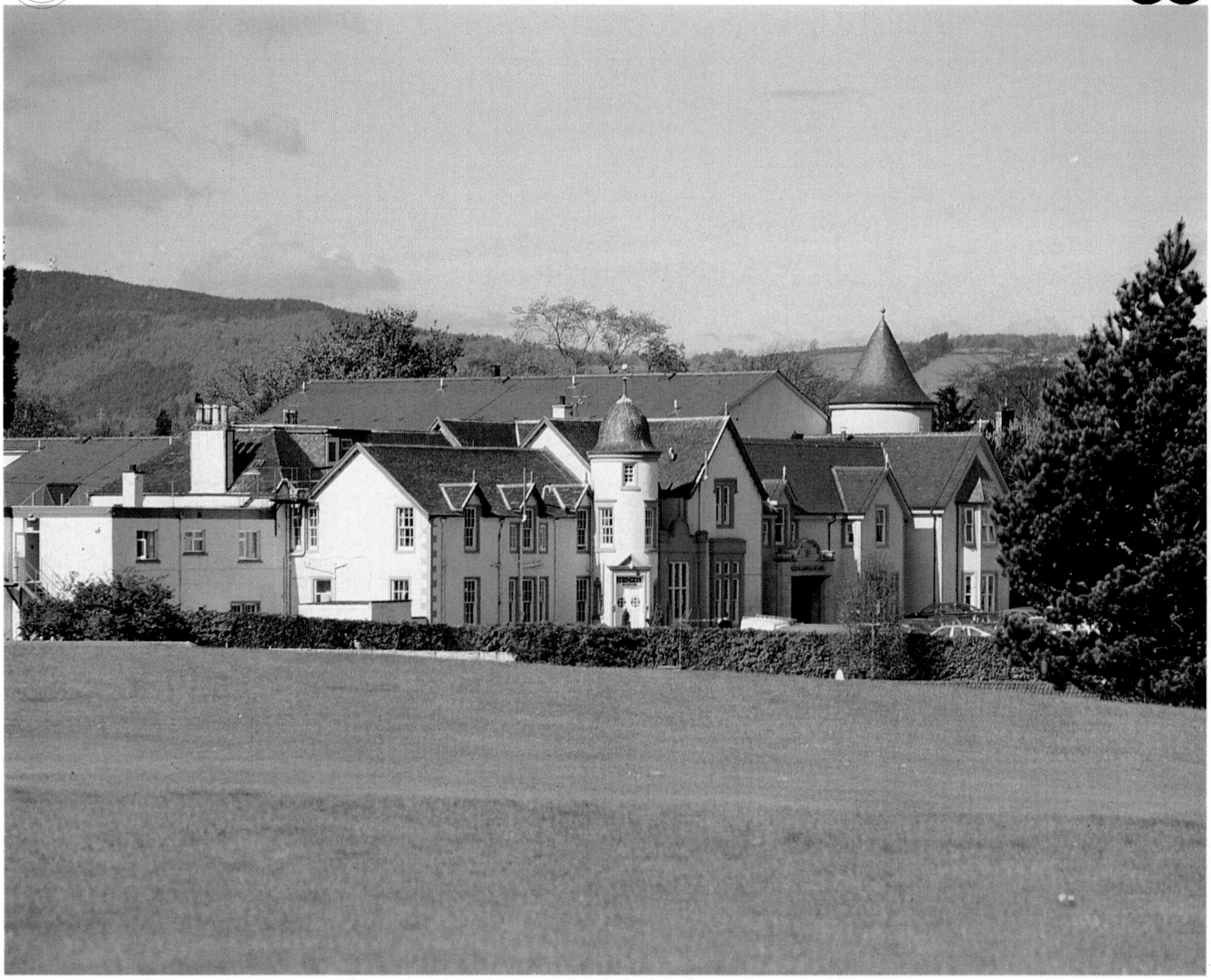

KINGSMILLS HOTEL

CULCABOCK ROAD, INVERNESS, INVERNESS-SHIRE IV2 3LP
TEL: 01463 237166 FAX: 01463 225208

Built in the capital of The Highlands in 1785, this historic hotel has been extended and it offers guests both comfort and elegance. It is only a mile from the town centre, in three acres of gardens, adjacent to Inverness Golf Course. There is a choice of attractively appointed bedrooms, all with modern amenities. In addition to the standard rooms, as pictured below, there are seven beautifully furnished suite-style rooms, also family rooms with bunk beds and six self-catering villas. The Leisure Club incorporates a heated swimming pool, spa bath, steam cabin, sauna, sunbeds, mini-gym and pitch-and-putt. Hairdressing facilities are also provided. Throughout the year exceptionally good value is offered by special breaks which include local seasonal attractions. Golf, fishing, skiing, riding and pony-trekking can all be enjoyed nearby and arranged as part of an activity holiday. Christmas, Easter and New Year packages are also available. The Kingsmills Hotel is well placed for visiting the Highlands, Loch Ness, the Whisky Trail, Culloden battlefield and Cawdor Castle. USA representative – Thomas McFerran, telephone toll free: 1-800-215 443 7990. **Directions:** Turn left off A9 signposted Kingsmills and Culcabock. Turn right at the first roundabout, left at the second and the hotel is on the left just past the golf course. Price guide: Single £100–£135; double/twin £135–£170; suite £145.

For hotel location, see maps on pages 477-483

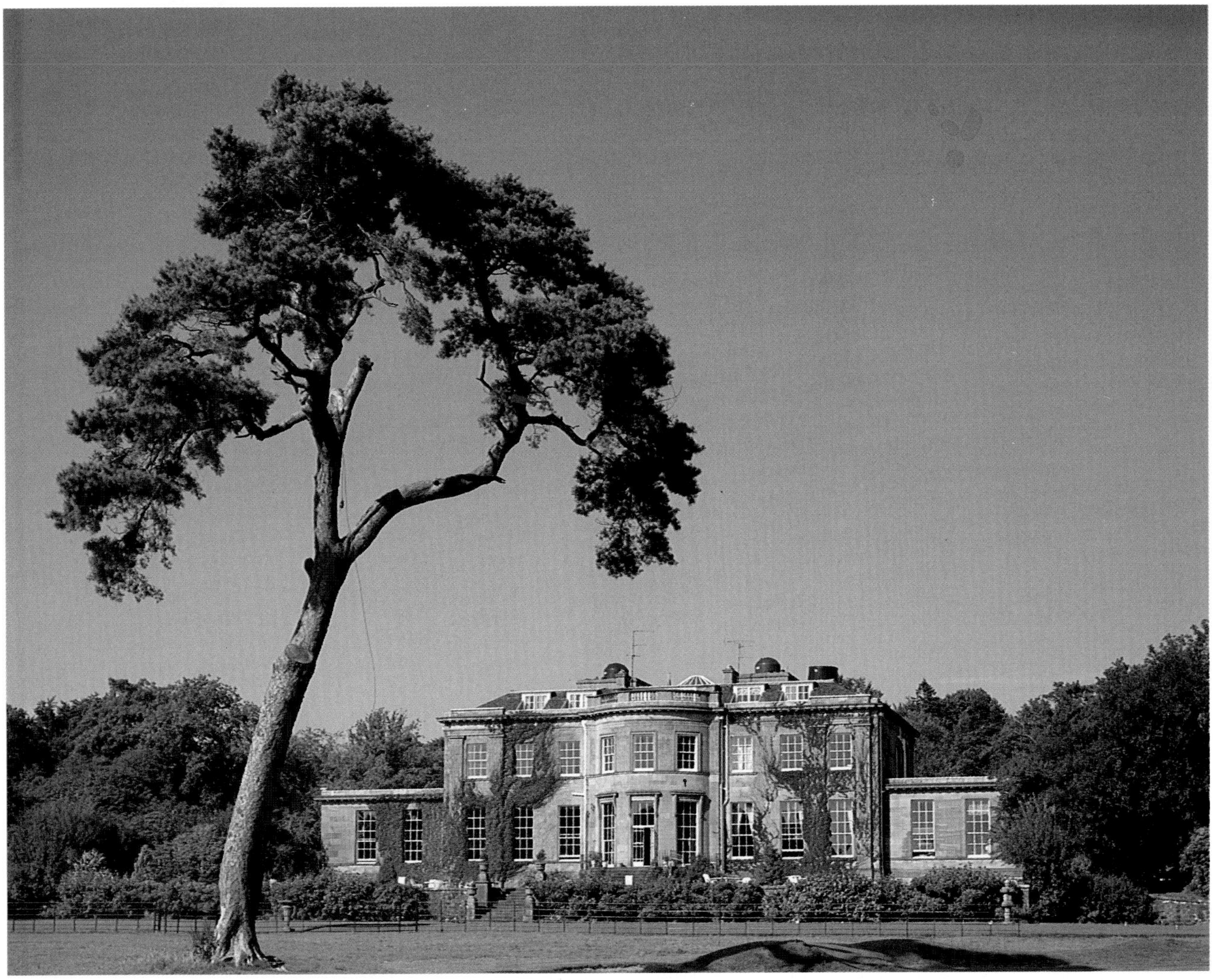

MONTGREENAN MANSION HOUSE HOTEL

MONTGREENAN ESTATE, KILWINNING, AYRSHIRE KA13 7QZ
TEL: 01294 557733 FAX: 01294 850397

Set in 48 acres of wooded gardens, Montgreenan commands views towards Ailsa Craig and the Arran Hills, which make a spectacular sight at sunset. The history of the estate dates back to 1310, and the present mansion house was built in 1817 by Dr Robert Glasgow. The original features, including marble and brass fireplaces, decorative ceilings and plasterwork, have been retained. A family home until 1980, the hotel has a friendly atmosphere. The bedrooms are well appointed with antique and reproduction furniture and one of the bedrooms has a Jacuzzi bath. The elegant dining room, with burgundy-and-gold tapestried chairs, is the setting for dinner. Gourmet cooking features fresh Scottish salmon, lobster, game and Ayrshire beef. To accompany your meal, choose from 200 fine vintages. Whatever the occasion, there are good facilities for conferences and entertaining. In addition to the 5-hole golf course on site, over 30 courses, including those at Royal Troon and Turnberry, are within 45 minutes' drive. Special rates available. **Directions:** Glasgow and Prestwick Airport are only 30 minutes' drive away. 19 miles south of Glasgow, 4 miles north of Irvine. From Irvine take A736 towards Glasgow for 4 miles. Turn left at Torranyard Inn; hotel entrance is 2 minutes from there. Price guide: Single £70; double/twin £100–£146.

For hotel location, see maps on pages 477-483

ISLE OF ERISKA

LEDAIG, BY OBAN, ARGYLL PA37 1SD
TEL: 01631 720371 FAX: 01631 720531

Isle of Eriska was built in 1884, towards the end of the Scots Baronial period. Its imposing exterior of grey granite and red sandstone stands as a living monument to a bygone age. Inside, no two bedrooms are the same in size or outlook and each is named after one of the neighbouring Hebridean islands. With its bay window and chintz covered furniture, the Drawing Room is the perfect place to relax while there can be no better place than the library to enjoy a drink from the selection of malt whiskies. Internationally acclaimed standards of cuisine are meticulously maintained in the dining room, the garden supplying a wide range of herbs, vegetables and soft fruits. For energetic guests there are sports such as water-skiing and windsurfing, tennis on the all-weather court and clay pigeon shooting. Croquet and the golf putting green are available for those who prefer leisurely pursuits. In addition, there is now a 9-hole golf course, fitness suite and indoor swimming pool. Oban is 20 minutes away by car and from here steamers ply to and from the islands. **Directions:** From Edinburgh and Glasgow, drive to Tyndrum, then A85 towards Oban. At Connel proceed on A828 for four miles to north of Benderloch. Thereafter follow signs to Isle of Eriska. Price guide: Single £150; double/twin £185–£215.

For hotel location, see maps on pages 477-483

WESTERN ISLES HOTEL

TOBERMORY, ISLE OF MULL, ARGYLL PA75 6PR
TEL: 01688 302012 FAX: 01688 302297

Poised above Tobermory Harbour, the Western Isles Hotel combines friendly hospitality with breathtaking views over an ever-changing vista of mountain and sea. An appetite sharpened by the fresh sea air is certain to be sated in the elegant restaurant, with its spectacular outlook over the Sound of Mull. Special diets and vegetarians are well catered for with some notice. The lounge has an atmosphere of grace and comfort, while the now rebuilt conservatory, with a bar and magnificent views across the harbour, is delightful on scented summer evenings. The bedrooms are spacious. Off Mull's coast is the holy island of Iona, while Fingal's Cave can be seen on Staffa. Special rates for Easter and New Year. If bringing a dog, please say when booking and bring a basket/bed for it. **Directions:** Travelling to Mull is so pleasurable that it should be considered part of the holiday. On booking, contact ferry operators Caledonian MacBrayne, The Pier, Gourock; or ring 01631 62285 and book the Oban–Craignure ferry (40 minutes). There is an hourly Lochaline–Fishnish ferry. Oban is on the A82/A85 from Glasgow (two hours) or the A85 from Perth. At Craignure, turn right off ferry; Tobermory is 40 minutes' drive. A warm welcome awaits! Price guide: Single £37–£95; double/twin £74–£169.

For hotel location, see maps on pages 477-483

EDNAM HOUSE HOTEL

BRIDGE STREET, KELSO, ROXBURGHSHIRE TD5 7HT
TEL: 01573 224168 FAX: 01573 226319

Overlooking the River Tweed, in 3 acres of gardens, Ednam House is one of the region's finest examples of Georgian architecture. This undulating, pastoral countryside was immortalised by Sir Walter Scott. Ednam House has been owned and managed by the Brooks family for over 65 years, spanning four generations. Although the grandiose splendour may seem formal, the warm, easy-going atmosphere is all-pervasive. The lounges and bars are comfortably furnished and command scenic views of the river and grounds. All 32 bedrooms are en suite, individually decorated and well equipped. In the elegant dining room which overlooks the river, a blend of traditional and creative Scottish cuisine, using fresh local produce, is served. The wine list is very interesting and reasonably priced. Ednam House is extremely popular with fishermen, the Borders being renowned for its salmon and trout. Other field sports such as stalking, hunting and shooting can be arranged as can riding, golfing and cycling. Local landmarks include the abbeys of Kelso, Melrose, Jedburgh and Dryburgh. Closed Christmas and New Year. **Directions:** From the south, reach Kelso via A698; from the north, via A68. Hotel is just off market square by the river. Price guide: Single £48; double/twin £66–£93.

For hotel location, see maps on pages 477-483

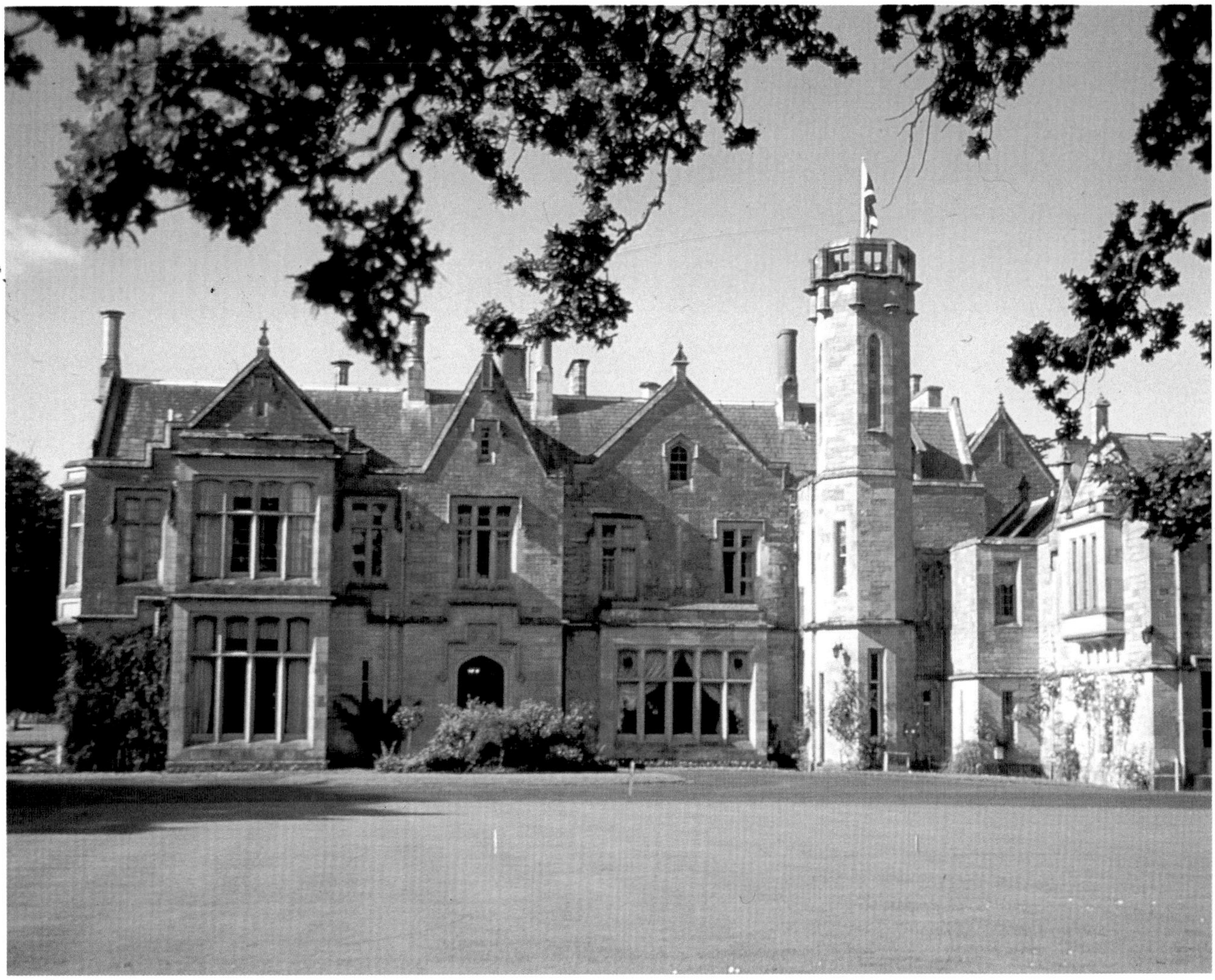

SUNLAWS HOUSE HOTEL & GOLF COURSE

KELSO, ROXBURGHSHIRE TD5 8JZ
TEL: 01573 450331 FAX: 01573 450611

Converted by the owner, the Duke of Roxburghe, into a luxury hotel of character and charm, Sunlaws House is situated in 200 hundred acres of rolling grounds on the bank of the River Teviot. There are 22 bedrooms, including four poster rooms and suites, and like the spacious reception rooms, they are furnished with care and elegance. The menu, which is changed daily, reflects the hotel's position at the source of some of Britain's finest fish, meat and game – salmon and trout from the waters of the Tweed, or grouse, pheasant and venison from the Roxburghe estate – complemented with wines from the Duke's own cellar. Fine whiskies are served in the Library Bar, with its log fire and leather-bound tomes. The new Beauty Clinique *Elixir* brings to guests the régimes of Decleor, Paris. Surrounding the estate is the magnificent Roxburghe Golf Course, designed by Dave Thomas. This parkland course is the only championship standard golf course in the Scottish Borders. A full sporting programme can be arranged, including fly and coarse fishing, and falconry. The shooting school offers tuition in game and clay shooting. Seven great country houses are within easy reach including Floors Castle, the home of the Duke of Roxburghe. **Directions:** The hotel is at Heiton, just off the A698 Kelso–Jedburgh road. Price guide: Single £95; double/twin £140; suite £180–£225.

For hotel location, see maps on pages 477-483

Ardsheal House

KENTALLEN OF APPIN, ARGYLL PA38 4BX
TEL: 01631 740227 FAX: 01631 740342

Ardsheal House is set high on a peninsula, commanding wonderful views of Loch Linnhe and the mountains of Morvern. The house is approached along a private drive that borders the loch and winds through ancient woodland. Set in 900 acres of hills, woods, gardens and shore front, this historic manor, built in 1760, has a charming, country house atmosphere. A friendly welcome is extended to all guests by resident managers Michelle and George Kelso. The interiors are cosy and decorative, with polished oak panelling and open fires on chilly evenings. Antique furniture and bright fabrics are to be found in all the en suite bedrooms. In the conservatory dining room, memorable dishes delight the eye and please the palate. Fresh seafood, prime local meat and game, herbs and fruit from the hotel garden and home-made jellies, preserves and seasoned vinegars form the basis for innovative cooking. Dinner may be accompanied by a selection from the excellent wine list. Ardsheal House is open daily for lunch and dinner: non-residents are welcome. Using the hotel as a base, guests can visit islands, castles, lochs and glens or enjoy splendid walks in every direction. Closed 10 January to 10 February. **Directions:** Hotel is on the A828 five miles south of Ballachulish Bridge on the way to Oban. Price guide (including dinner): Single £85–£100; double/twin £130–£180. Special reduced winter and spring rates. Special Christmas and New Year breaks.

For hotel location, see maps on pages 477-483

ARDANAISEIG

KILCHRENAN BY TAYNUILT, ARGYLL PA35 1HE
TEL: 01866 833333 FAX: 01866 833222

This romantic small luxury hotel, built in 1834, stands alone in a setting of almost surreal natural beauty at the foot of Ben Cruachan. Directly overlooking Loch Awe and surrounded by wild wooded gardens, Ardanaiseig is evocative of the romance and history of the Highlands. Skilful restoration has ensured that this lovely old mansion has changed little since it was built. The elegant drawing room has log fires, bowls of fresh flowers, superb antiques, handsome paintings and marvellous views of the islands in the Loch and of faraway mountains. The traditional library, sharing this outlook, is ideal for post-prandial digestifs. The charming bedrooms are peaceful, appropriate to the era of the house, yet equipped thoughtfully with all comforts. True Scottish hospitality is the philosophy of the Ardanaiseig Restaurant, renowned for its inspired use of fresh produce from the Western Highlands. The wine list is magnificent. Artistic guests enjoy the famous 100 acre Ardanaiseig gardens and nature reserve, filled with exotic shrubs and trees brought back from the Himalayas over the years. Brilliant rhododendrons and azaleas add a riot of colour. The estate also offers fishing, boating, tennis and croquet (snooker in the evenings) and exhilarating hill or lochside walks. **Directions:** Reaching Taynuilt on A85, take B845 to Kilchrenan. Price guide: Single £42–£80; double/twin £84–£160.

14 rms · MasterCard · VISA · AMERICAN EXPRESS · M 28 · 8

For hotel location, see maps on pages 477-483

KILDRUMMY CASTLE HOTEL

KILDRUMMY, BY ALFORD, ABERDEENSHIRE AB33 8RA
TEL: 019755 71288 FAX: 019755 71345

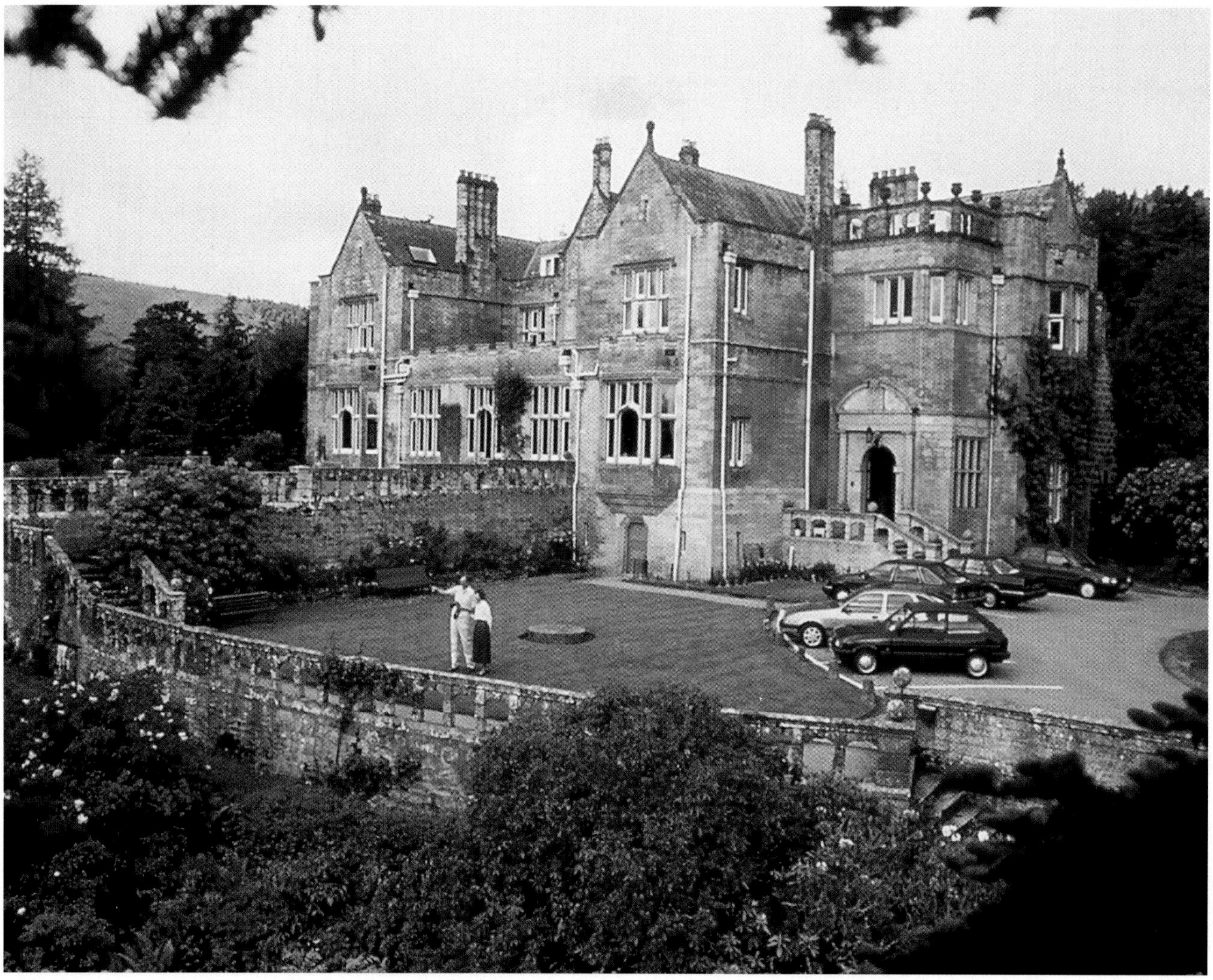

In the heart of Donside near to the renowned Kildrummy Castle Gardens, and overlooking the ruins of the original 13th century castle from which it takes its name, Kildrummy Castle Hotel offers a rare opportunity to enjoy the style and elegance of a bygone era combined with all the modern comforts of a first-class hotel. Recent improvements have not detracted from the turn-of-the century interior, featuring the original wall tapestries and oak-panelled walls and high ceilings. The bedrooms, some with four-poster beds, all have en suite bathrooms. All have been refurbished recently to a high standard. The hotel restaurant was runner-up for Johansens 1996 Restaurant Award. Chef Kenneth White prepares excellent menus using regional produce that includes local game and both fish and shellfish from the Moray Firth. Kildrummy Castle is ideally located for touring Royal Deeside and Balmoral, the Spey Valley, Aberdeen and Inverness, while the surrounding Grampian region has more castles than any other part of Scotland – 8 of the National Trust for Scotland's finest properties are within an hour's drive of the hotel. Also within an hour's drive are more than 20 golf courses. Visitors can discover the 'Scotch Whisky Trail' and enjoy a tour of some of Scotland's most famous distilleries. **Directions:** Off the A97 Ballater/Huntly road, 35 miles west of Aberdeen. Price guide: Single £70; double/twin £115–£145.

For hotel location, see maps on pages 477-483

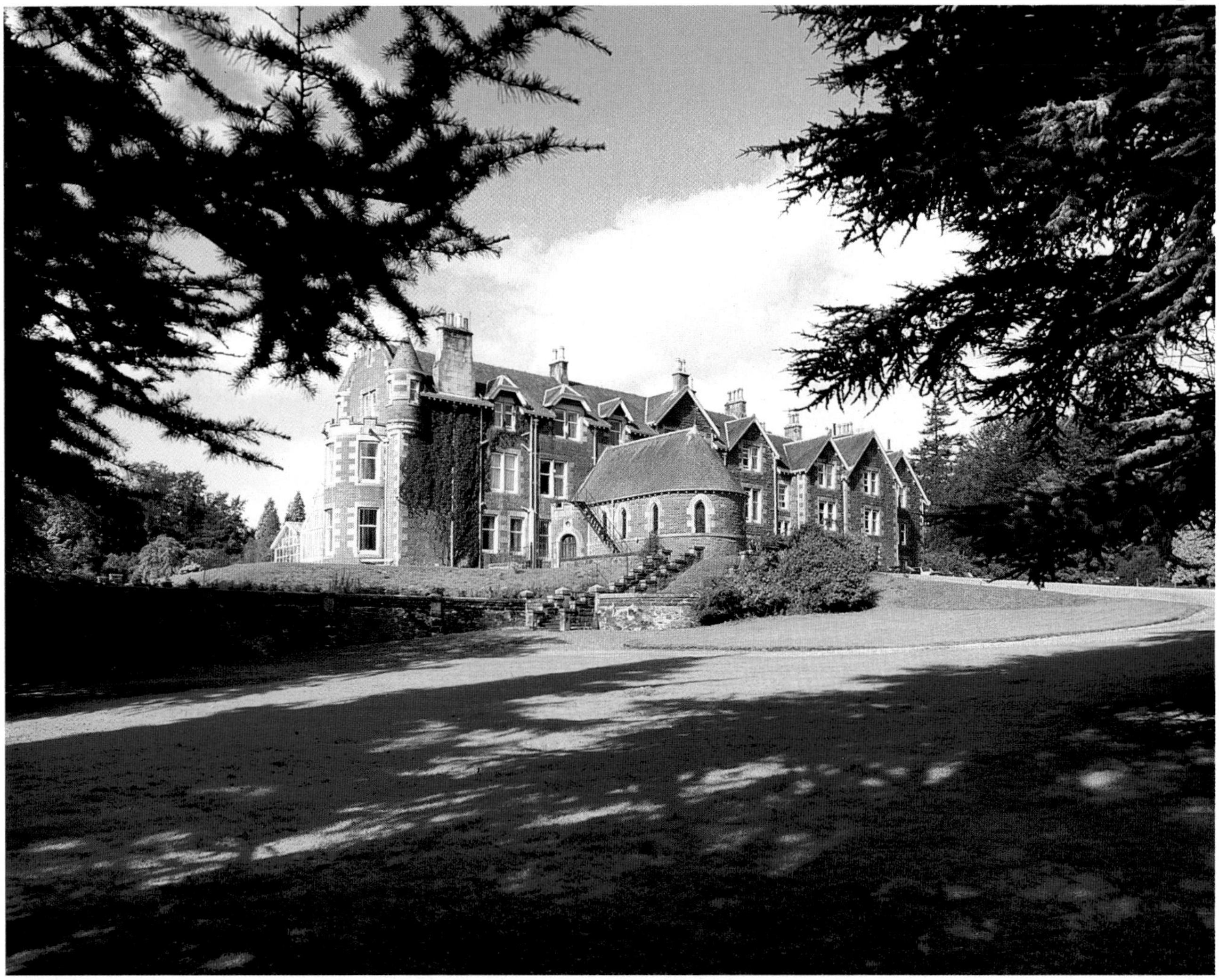

CROMLIX HOUSE

KINBUCK, BY DUNBLANE, PERTHSHIRE FK15 9JT
TEL: 01786 822125 FAX: 01786 825450

The Cromlix estate of some 3,000 acres in the heart of Perthshire is a relaxing retreat. Built as a family home in 1874, much of the house remains unchanged including many fine antiques acquired over the generations. Proprietors David and Ailsa Assenti are proud of their tradition of country house hospitality. The individually designed bedrooms and spacious suites have recently been redecorated with period fabrics to enhance the character and fine furniture whilst retaining the essential feeling of a much loved home. Unpretentious, relaxing and most welcoming, the large public rooms have open fires. In the restaurant, the finest local produce is used, including game from the estate, lamb and locally caught salmon. Cromlix is an ideal venue for small conferences and business meetings, and there is a little chapel – the perfect setting for weddings. Extensive sporting and leisure facilities include trout and salmon fishing and game shooting in season. Challenging golf courses within easy reach include Rosemount, Carnoustie and St Andrews. The location is ideal for touring the Southern Highlands, with Edinburgh and Glasgow only an hour away. **Directions:** Cromlix House lies four miles north of Dunblane, north of Kinbuck on B8033 and four miles south of Braco. Price guide: Single £95–£120; double/twin £140–£170; suite £170–£260.

For hotel location, see maps on pages 477-483

NIVINGSTON HOUSE

CLEISH, KINROSS-SHIRE KY13 7LS
TEL: 01577 850216 FAX: 01577 850238

Peacefully set in 12 acres of landscaped gardens at the foot of the Cleish Hills, this comfortable old country house and its celebrated restaurant offer the warmest of welcomes. Standing more or less half-way between Edinburgh and Perth the original 1725 building has benefited from several architectural additions and it is now further enlarged and refurbished with all the characteristics of an up-to-date hotel. Nivington House is particularly well known for its fine food, prepared from traditional Scottish produce such as Perthshire venison and locally caught salmon. The restaurant has regularly been commended in leading guides and deservedly it has "Taste of Scotland" status. The menus are changed daily. Scones and cream tea are however a permanent temptation. The attractive en suite bedrooms are decorated in soft, subtle colours, with Laura Ashley fabrics and wallpapers. In the grounds there are two croquet lawns and a putting green and practice net for keen golfers. Sporting facilities within easy reach include the famous golf courses at St Andrews, Gleneagles and countless others of lesser renown. Loch Leven is popular for trout fishing and there are boat trips to Loch Leven Castle. **Directions:** From M90 take exit 5 towards Crook of Devon. Cleish is 2 miles from motorway. Price guide: Single £75–£100; double/twin £95–£125.

17 rms · MasterCard · VISA · AMERICAN EXPRESS · M 50

For hotel location, see maps on pages 477-483

CAMERON HOUSE

LOCH LOMOND, DUMBARTONSHIRE G83 8QZ
TEL: 01389 755565 FAX: 01389 759522

The splendour and location of this impressive baronial house has lured many famous visitors, from Dr Johnson and the Empress Eugénie to Sir Winston Churchill. Standing in over 100 acres of green lawns and wooded glades leading down to the shores of Loch Lomond, Cameron House offers luxurious accommodation and superlative recreational amenities. The indoor leisure club includes squash, badminton and aerobic facilities, three beauty treatment rooms, a games room with three full-size snooker tables and a state-of-the-art gymnasium. For children there is a games room, toddlers' pool, crèche and a children's club. Outside, another sporting world unfolds, with professional tennis coaching, 9-hole golf, clay pigeon shooting, archery, off-road driving, sailing, cruising and wind-surfing available. Each of the bedrooms and the five opulent suites is furnished in soft colours that complement the beautiful views from the windows. Guests can dine in the intimate Georgian Room or the Brasserie both overlooking the loch. The conference, banqueting and function facilities are second to none and Glasgow, with its museums, art galleries and theatres, is less than 30 minutes' drive away. **Directions:** Cameron House is on the southern banks of Loch Lomond, via the A82 from Glasgow. Price guide: Single £130–£135; double/twin £165–£175; suite £250–£350.

68 rms 240

For hotel location, see maps on pages 477-483

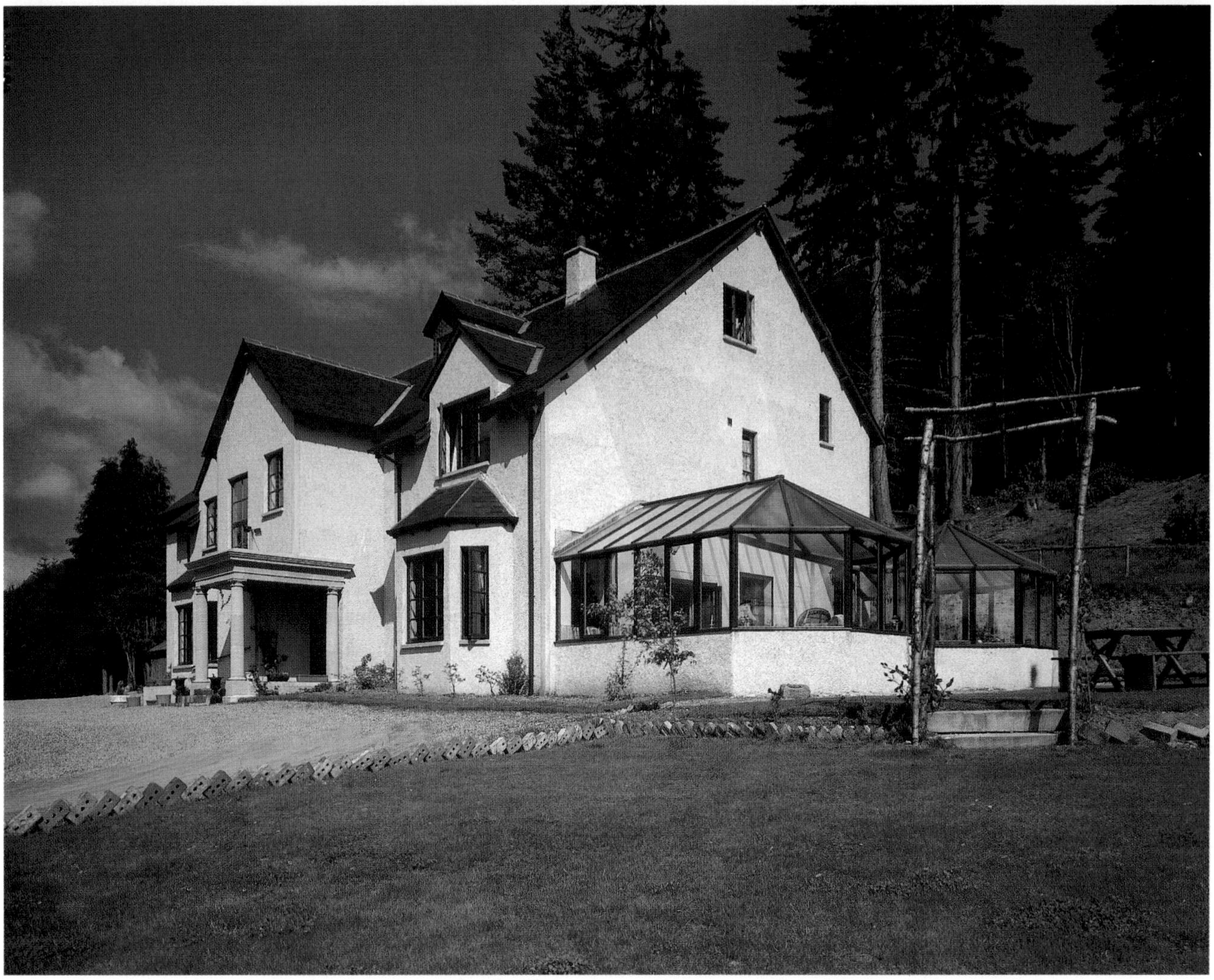

CRAIGDARROCH HOUSE HOTEL

FOYERS, LOCH NESS SIDE, INVERNESS-SHIRE IV1 2XU
TEL: 01456 486 400 FAX: 01456 486 444

Situated in 35 acres of woodland on the southern hillside shore of Loch Ness, Craigdarroch House looks over Loch Ness and the mountainous Highlands beyond. Completely rebuilt after fire devastated the original century-old Mansion House three years ago Craigdarroch incorporates all the facilities expected in a prestigious country hotel. Owners David and Kate Munro have taken great care to recreate an air of history. High ceilings and open log fires combined with traditional soft furnishings help to create the ambience of a 19th century Highland Lodge. Most of the bedrooms, some with four-poster beds, and all the public rooms enjoy panoramic views. There is a family bedroom and also one specially adapted for disabled guests. The lounge bar, aptly named the "Malt Shop", has over 50 malt whiskies and the restaurant offers a wide choice of cuisine expertly prepared from local produce by chef Andrew Munro. Local places of interest include Loch Ness Visitors Centre, Fort Augustus, Inverness, Culloden battlefield and a number of beautiful glens. Golf, fishing, shooting and riding are nearby. Directions: From Inverness take the B862 towards Dores and then the B852 signposted Foyers. From Fort Augustus take the B862 to just beyond the village of Whitebridge and then the B852. Price guide: Single £50-£80; double £100-£120.

For hotel location, see maps on pages 477-483

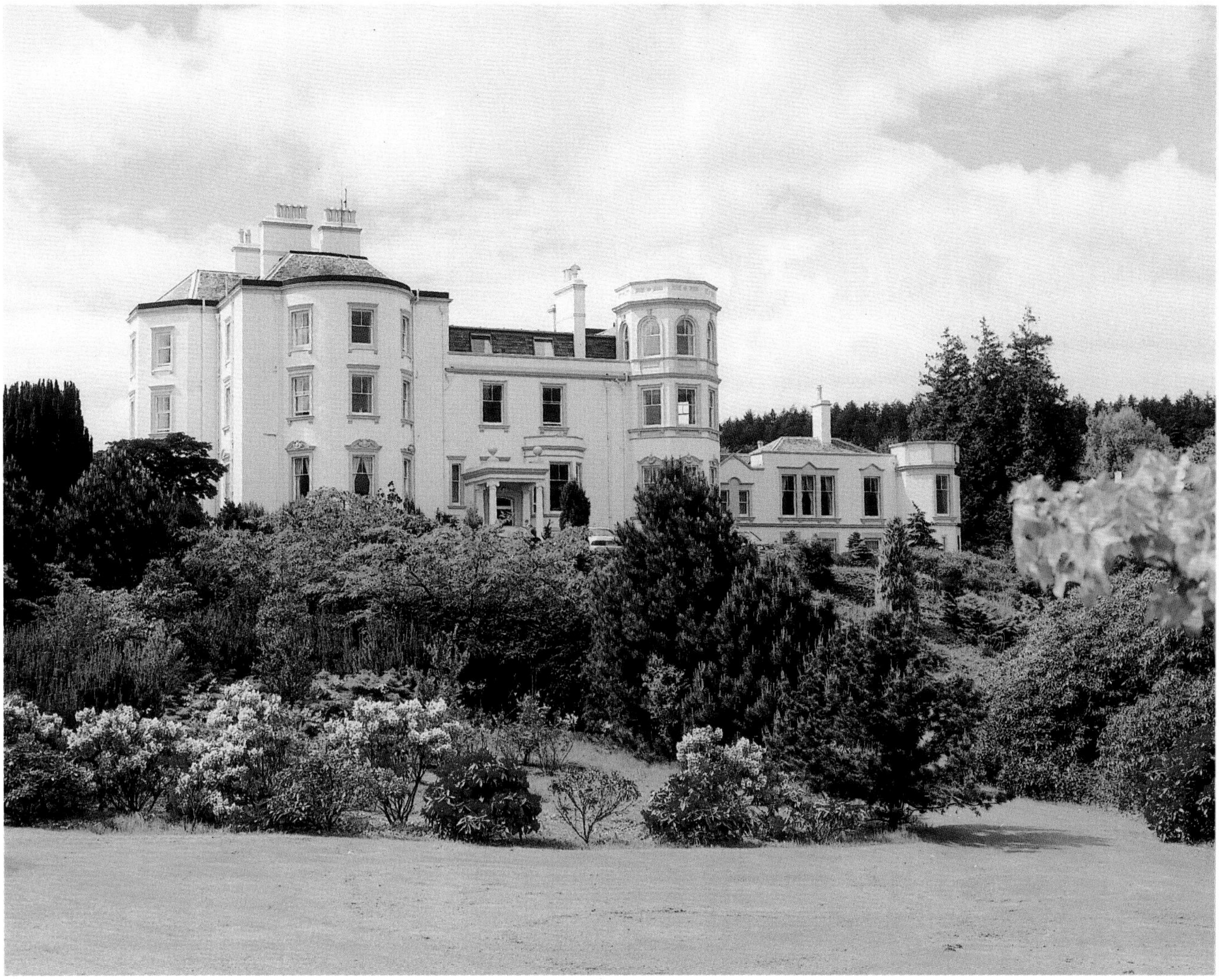

KIRROUGHTREE HOTEL

NEWTON STEWART, WIGTOWNSHIRE DG8 6AN
TEL: 01671 402141 FAX: 01671 402425

Winner of the Johansens Most Excellent Service Award 1996 Kirroughtree Hotel is situated in the foothills of the Cairnsmore of Fleet, on the edge of Galloway Forest Park. The hotel stands in eight acres of landscaped gardens, where guests can relax and linger over the spectacular views. This striking mansion was built by the Heron family in 1719 and the rococo furnishings of the oak-panelled lounge reflect the style of that period. From the lounge rises the original staircase, from which Robert Burns often recited his poems. Each bedroom is well furnished – guests may choose to spend the night in one of the hotel's spacious deluxe bedrooms with spectacular views over the surrounding countryside. Many guests are attracted by Kirroughtree's culinary reputation – only the finest produce is used to create meals of originality and finesse. This is a good venue for small conferences. Pitch-and-putt, lawn tennis and croquet can be enjoyed in the grounds. Residents can play golf on the many local courses and also have use of our sister hotel's new exclusive 18-hole course at Gatehouse of Fleet. Trout and salmon fishing can be arranged nearby, as can rough shooting and deer stalking during the season. Closed 3 January to mid February. **Directions:** The hotel is signposted one mile outside Newton Stewart on the A75. Price guide: Single £72–£95; double/twin £124–£144; suite £170. (Including dinner)

For hotel location, see maps on pages 477-483

KNIPOCH HOTEL

BY OBAN, ARGYLL PA34 4QT
TEL: 01852 316251 FAX: 01852 316249

Six miles south of Oban lies Knipoch, an elegant Georgian building set halfway along the shore of Loch Feochan, an arm of the sea stretching 4 miles inland. Wildlife is abundant in this area – rare birds of prey, deer and otters can often be seen. The hotel is owned and personally run by the Craig family, who go out of their way to ensure that their guests enjoy their stay. All the bedrooms are fully equipped and offer splendid views either of the loch or the surrounding hills. High standards of cooking are proudly maintained here. The daily menu features many Scottish specialities, prepared with imaginative flair. Not only is the choice of wines extensive – there are over 350 labels – but the list is informative too. Guests are given a copy to peruse at leisure rather than to scan hurriedly before ordering. In addition, the bar stocks a wide range of malt whiskies. Sporting activities available locally include fishing, sailing, yachting, golf, tennis, pony-trekking and skiing. A traditional Scottish event, the Oban Highland Games, is particularly renowned for its solo piping competition. The Knipoch Hotel makes a good base from which to visit the Western Isles and explore the spectacular scenery of the area. Closed mid-November to mid-February. **Directions:** On the A816, 6 miles south of Oban. Price guide: Single £40–£75; double/twin £80–£150; suite £195–£250

17 rms

For hotel location, see maps on pages 477-483

Cringletie House Hotel

PEEBLES EH45 8PL
TEL: 01721 730233 FAX: 01721 730244

This distinguished mansion, turreted in the Scottish baronial style, stands in 28 acres of beautifully maintained gardens and woodland. Designed by Scottish architect David Bryce, Cringletie was built in 1861 for the Wolfe Murray family, whose ancestor, Colonel Alexander Murray, accepted the surrender of Quebec after General Wolfe was killed. All of the bedrooms have fine views and many have been redesigned with attractively co-ordinated curtains and furnishings. The splendid panelled lounge has an impressive carved oak and marble fireplace, a painted ceiling and many oil portraits. The imaginative cooking, prepared with flair, attracts consistently good reports. The range and quality of fruit and vegetables grown in the 2-acre walled garden make this the only Scottish garden recommended in Geraldene Holt's *The Gourmet Garden*, which includes some of Britain's most distinguished hotels. On-site facilities include a new hard tennis court, croquet lawn and putting green. Golf can be played at Peebles and fishing is available by permit on the River Tweed. Convenient for visiting Edinburgh, Cringletie is a good base from which to discover the rich historic and cultural heritage of the Borders. Closed 2 January to 7 March. **Directions:** The hotel is on the A703 Peebles–Edinburgh road, 2½ miles from Peebles. Price guide: Single £55; double/twin £100–£110.

For hotel location, see maps on pages 477-483

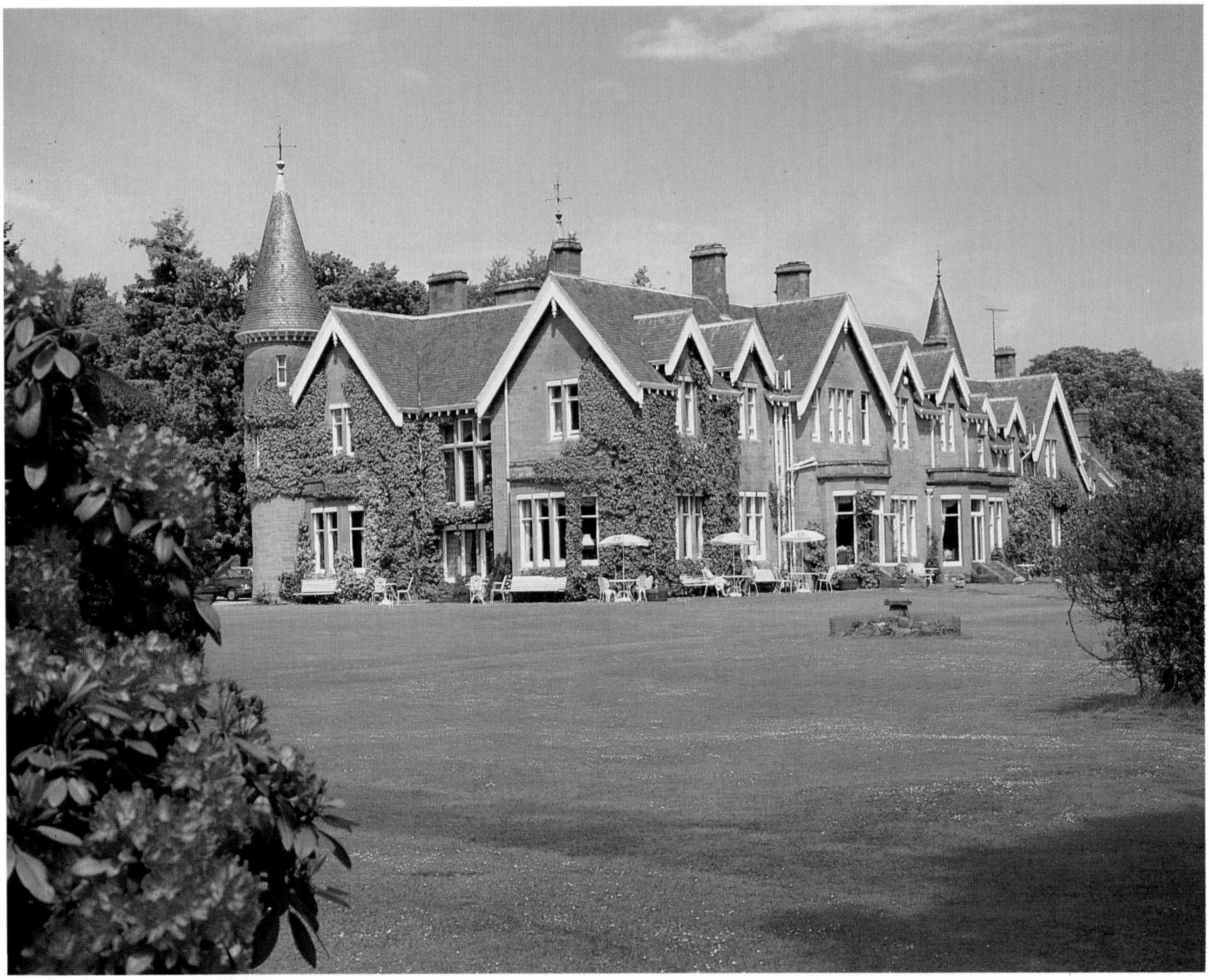

BALLATHIE HOUSE HOTEL

KINCLAVEN BY STANLEY, NR PERTH, PERTHSHIRE PH1 4QN
TEL: 01250 883268 FAX: 01250 883396

Set in an estate overlooking the River Tay, Ballathie House Hotel offers Scottish hospitality in a house of character and distinction. Dating from 1850, this mansion has a French baronial façade and handsome interiors. Overlooking lawns which slope down to the riverside, the drawing room is an ideal place to relax with coffee and the papers, or to enjoy a malt whisky after dinner. The premier bedrooms are large and elegant, while the standard rooms are designed in a cosy, cottage style. On the ground floor there are several bedrooms suitable for guests with disabilities. Local ingredients such as Tay salmon, Scottish beef, seafoods and piquant soft fruits are used by chef Kevin MacGillivray to create menus catering for all tastes. The hotel has two rosettes for fine Scottish cuisine. Activities available on the estate include trout and salmon fishing and clay pigeon shooting. The Sporting Lodge adjacent to the main house is designed to accommodate sporting parties. The area has many good golf courses. Perth, Blairgowrie and Edinburgh are within an hour's drive. STB 4 Crowns De Luxe. Dogs in certain rooms only. **Directions:** From A93 at Beech Hedges, signposted for Kinclaven and Ballathie, or off the A9, 2 miles north of Perth take the Stanley Road. The hotel is 8 miles north of Perth. Price guide: Single £62–£95; double/twin £115–£180; suite £200–£240.

For hotel location, see maps on pages 477-483

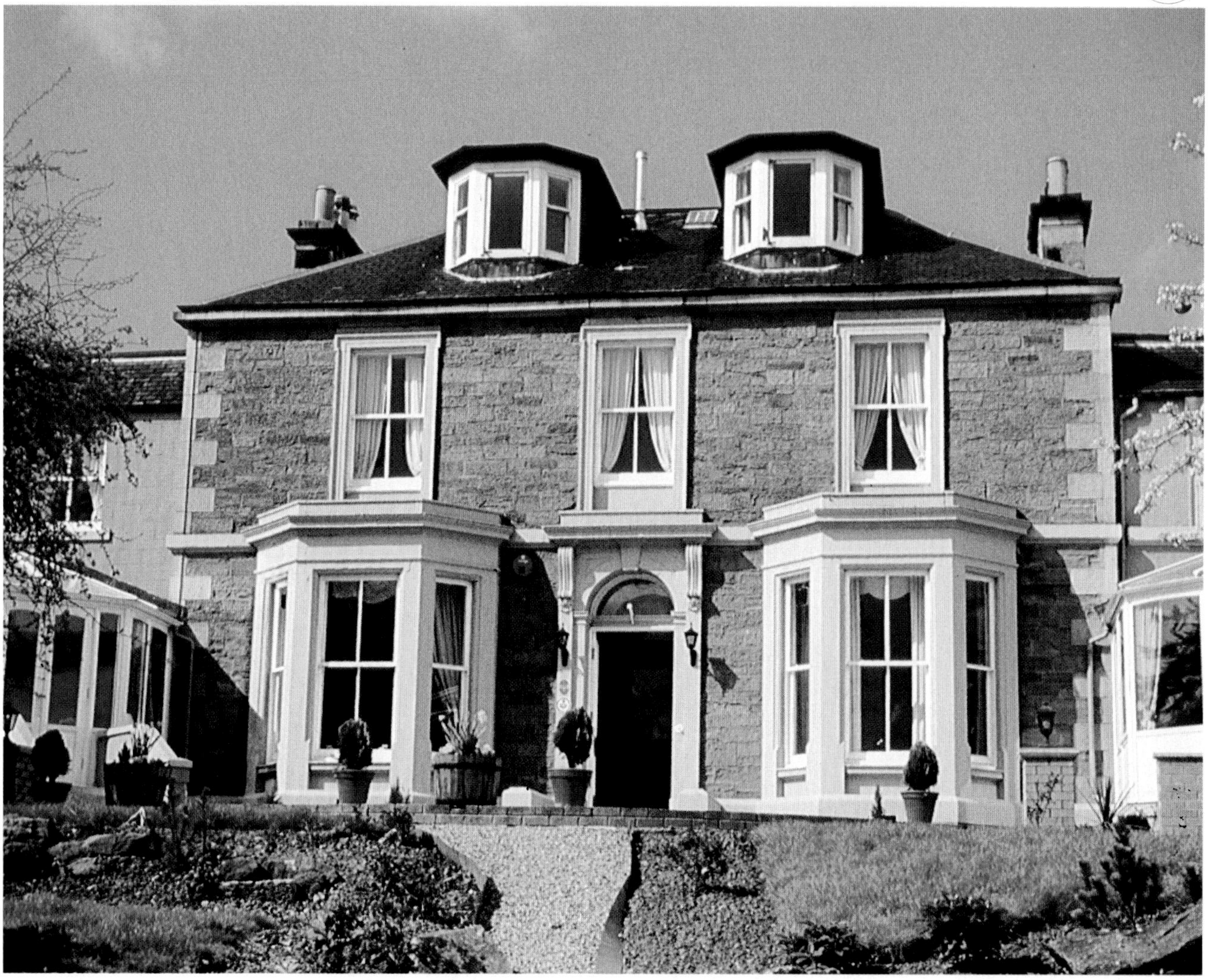

Parklands Hotel & Restaurant

ST LEONARD'S BANK, PERTH, PERTHSHIRE PH2 8EB
TEL: 01738 622451 FAX: 01738 622046

The Parklands Country Hotel and Restaurant, which overlooks Perth's South Inch Park, has benefited from an extensive programme of improvements. The hotel, with its classic lines, was formerly the home of John Pullar, who was Lord Provost of the City of Perth from 1867 to 1873. The 14 bedrooms all have en suite facilities and are immaculate. Each has been individually decorated to high standards under the personal supervision of proprietor Allan Deeson. In the main restaurant the accent is on light, traditional Scottish food. A full choice of à la carte and table d'hôte meals is available at both lunchtime and dinner. The boardroom opens off the hotel's entrance and overlooks the hotel gardens. It is a perfect venue for small private lunches or dinners or for business meetings and seminars, and has a large mahogany table and all the latest audio-visual equipment. Perth is a Royal Burgh of great age on the Tay Estuary, at the entrance to Strath Earn and Strath More, full of historical buildings, rich in story and legend. Interesting places to visit locally include Scone Palace and Blair Castle. **Directions:** From the M90 head towards the station; Parklands is on the left at the end of the park. Price guide: Single £77.50–£107.50; double/twin £100–£140.

For hotel location, see maps on pages 477-483

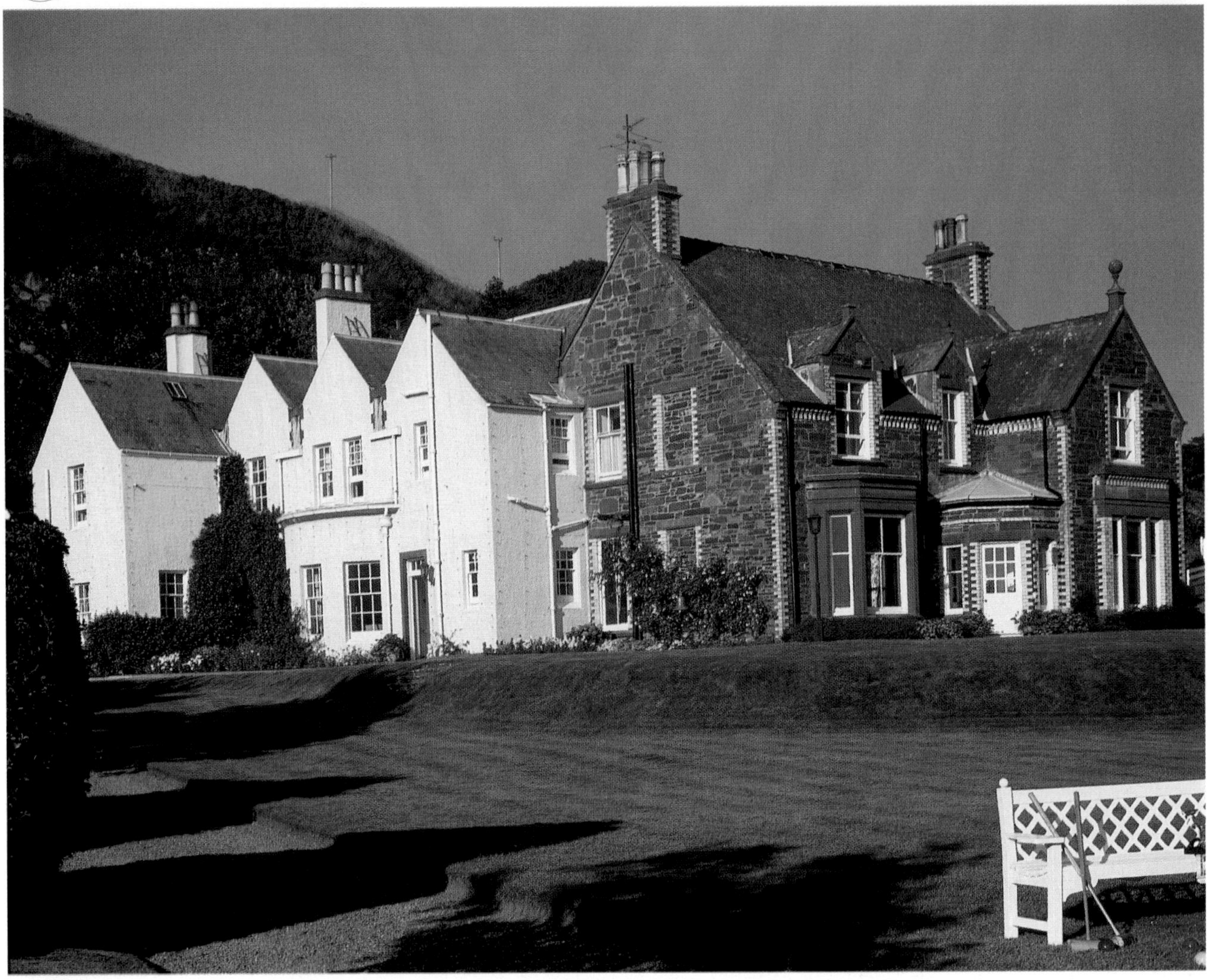

KNOCKINAAM LODGE

PORTPATRICK, WIGTOWNSHIRE DG9 9AD
TEL: 01776 810471 FAX: 01776 810435

On the beautiful West Coast of Scotland, surrounded on three sides by sheltering cliffs, lies Knockinaam. This delightful Lodge is perfectly situated to allow guests to enjoy magnificent views of the distant Irish coastline and to marvel at the stupendous sunsets and the changing moods of the sea and sky. In this atmosphere of timelessness and tranquillity, Sir Winston Churchill held a secret meeting here with General Eisenhower during the Second World War. Cheerful colour schemes and fabrics have been chosen for the comfortable en-suite bedrooms, while the public rooms are warm and cosy and during cooler months residents can relax in front of their lovely open log fires. The AA 3 Rosette restaurant offers a daily changing menu of superb international cuisine, complimented by an extensive wine list of over 400 wines. There are also 101 single malt scotch whiskies for lovers of fine malts. Due to the mild climate there are many famous gardens within easy reach of Knockinaam. There are several excellent golf courses close to the hotel. All inclusive low season rates are available from November until mid-December and from January 5th until Easter. **Directions:** On the A77 to Portpatrick look out for the roadside signpost to the hotel. Price guide (inclusive of dinner and VAT): Single £90–£115; double/twin £73–£115 pp.

For hotel location, see maps on pages 477-483

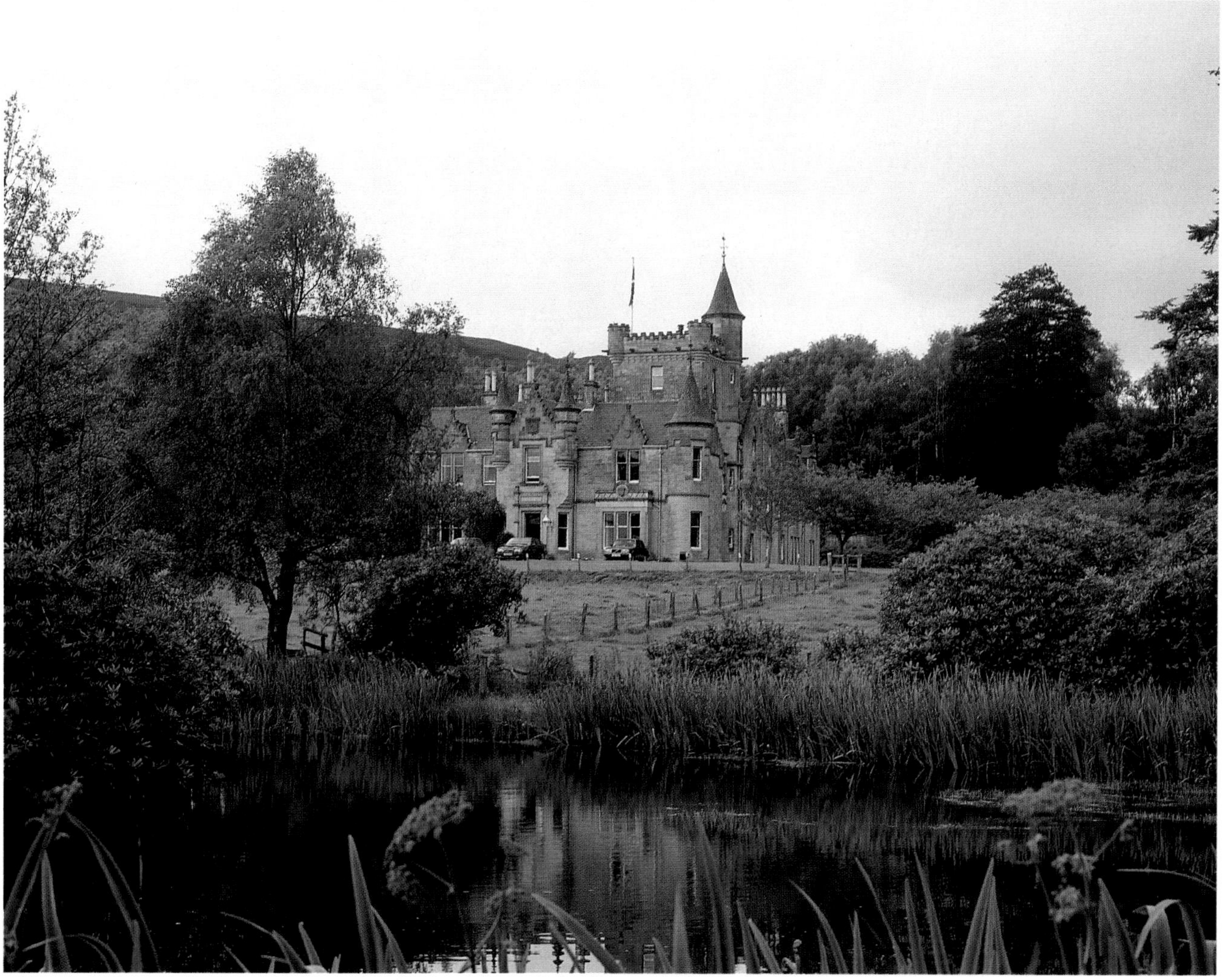

ROTHES GLEN

ROTHES, MORAYSHIRE AB38 7AQ
TEL: 01340 831254 FAX: 01340 831566

Situated at the head of the Glen of Rothes and surrounded by acres of parkland where pedigree Highland cattle graze, this comfortable old country mansion offers the warmest of welcomes. Designed similarly to Balmoral castle in 1893 for the wealthy Dunbar shipping family, Rothes Glen provides spectacular views from every window and turret over the beautiful Spey Valley and distant, heather-clad Banffshire hills. Every bedroom is equipped to the highest standard. Rothes Glen is noted for its fine food. The best of Scottish beef and venison are a feature of the menus, together with freshly caught Spey salmon and fish and shellfish from the Moray Firth. There is an extensive wine list and a good selection of Speyside malts and the Fountain Patio is an idyllic sun spot on which to sit and sample them on a warm summer evening. In the hotel grounds there is a nine-hole putting green, croquet and a quarter acre lochan which is stocked with rainbow trout. Elgin, with its ancient ruined cathedral, and the bustling resort of Lossiemouth, with their challenging golf courses, are only short drives away, as is 13th century Pluscardin Priory, 14th century Balvenie Castle, the many whisky distilleries and the sandy shores and picturesque fishing villages of the Moray Firth. Directions: Rothes Glen is situated on the A941, seven miles south of Elgin.Price guide: Single £65–£90; double/twin £95-£130; suite £105–£140.

For hotel location, see maps on pages 477-483

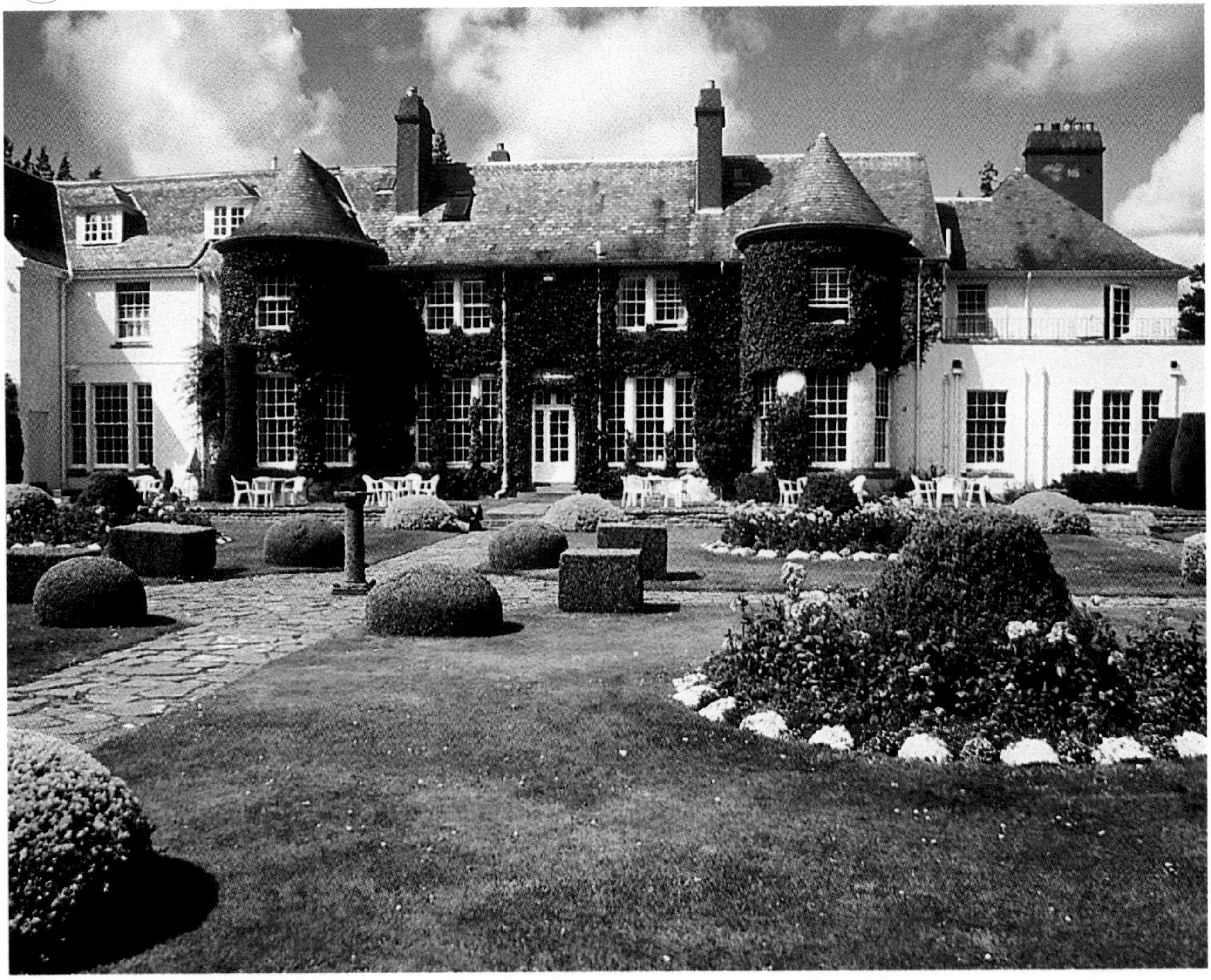

Rufflets Country House and Restaurant

STRATHKINNESS LOW ROAD, ST ANDREWS, FIFE KY16 9TX
TEL: 01334 472594 FAX:01334 478703 E-MAIL: rufflets@standrews.co.uk

One of the oldest country house hotels in Scotland, Rufflets has been privately owned and managed by the same family since 1952 and extends a friendly and personal service to its guests. Over the years the original turreted house, built in 1924, has been tastefully extended and upgraded to the optimum level of luxury and comfort. It faces south and overlooks ten acres of beautifully landscaped gardens. The hotel's 25 en suite bedrooms are individually designed, using a blend of contemporary and antique furnishings. Three of them are located in the charming Rose Cottage within the grounds of Rufflets. A well stocked kitchen garden supplies fresh herbs, vegetables and fruit for the award-winning restaurant. Featured on the menus are the finest quality Scottish beef, lamb, venison and East Neuk seafood. A carefully selected wine list is available to complement the cuisine. St Andrews is famous for its university and its golf courses and among the many places of interest nearby is the British Golf Museum. Other places well worth a visit include Falkland Palace, Kellie Castle and Crail Harbour. **Directions:** Rufflets is situated 1½ miles west of St Andrews. Price guide: Single £48–£85; double/twin £96–£170. Seasonal prices.

For hotel location, see maps on pages 477-483

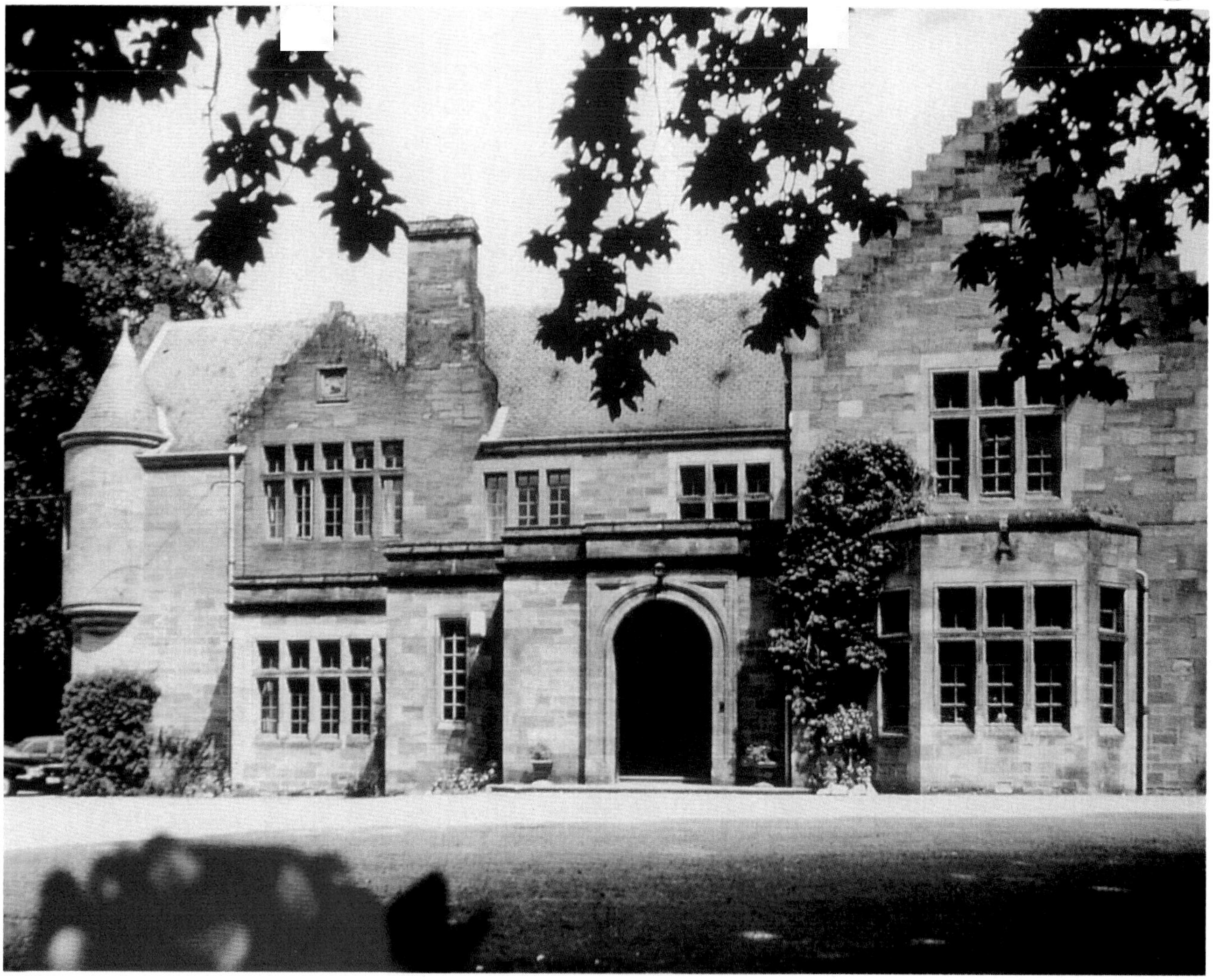

THE MURRAYSHALL COUNTRY HOUSE HOTEL

SCONE, PERTHSHIRE PH2 7PH
TEL: 01738 551171 FAX: 01738 552595

The Murrayshall Country House Hotel is set in 300 acres of undulating parkland and wooded hillside, with views sweeping across to the Grampians. Entering the hotel through the arched front door, visitors are welcomed by a friendly team of staff. The Old Masters' Restaurant, hung with Dutch 16th and 17th century oil paintings, is a visual delight, well suited to complement the artistry of the hotel's chef. Vegetables from the hotel's walled garden, and an abundance of local produce, form the basis of the menus, which have a Scottish flavour and a hint of modern French cuisine. The bedrooms have been designed to suit the varied demands of holiday-makers, honeymooners and fishermen, golfers and business travellers alike. With its own club house and bar, there is an 18-hole golf course adjacent to the hotel, where a golf professional is available to offer tuition. The Murrayshall offers special courses on golf. Guests may play croquet and bowls on the premises or follow one of the published walks that start from the hotel. Dogs by arrangement. Off season rates begin from £50 for dinner, bed and breakfast. **Directions:** Signposted a mile out of Perth on A94. Price guide: Single £50–£95; double/twin £100–£150; suites £130–£180.

For hotel location, see maps on pages 477-483

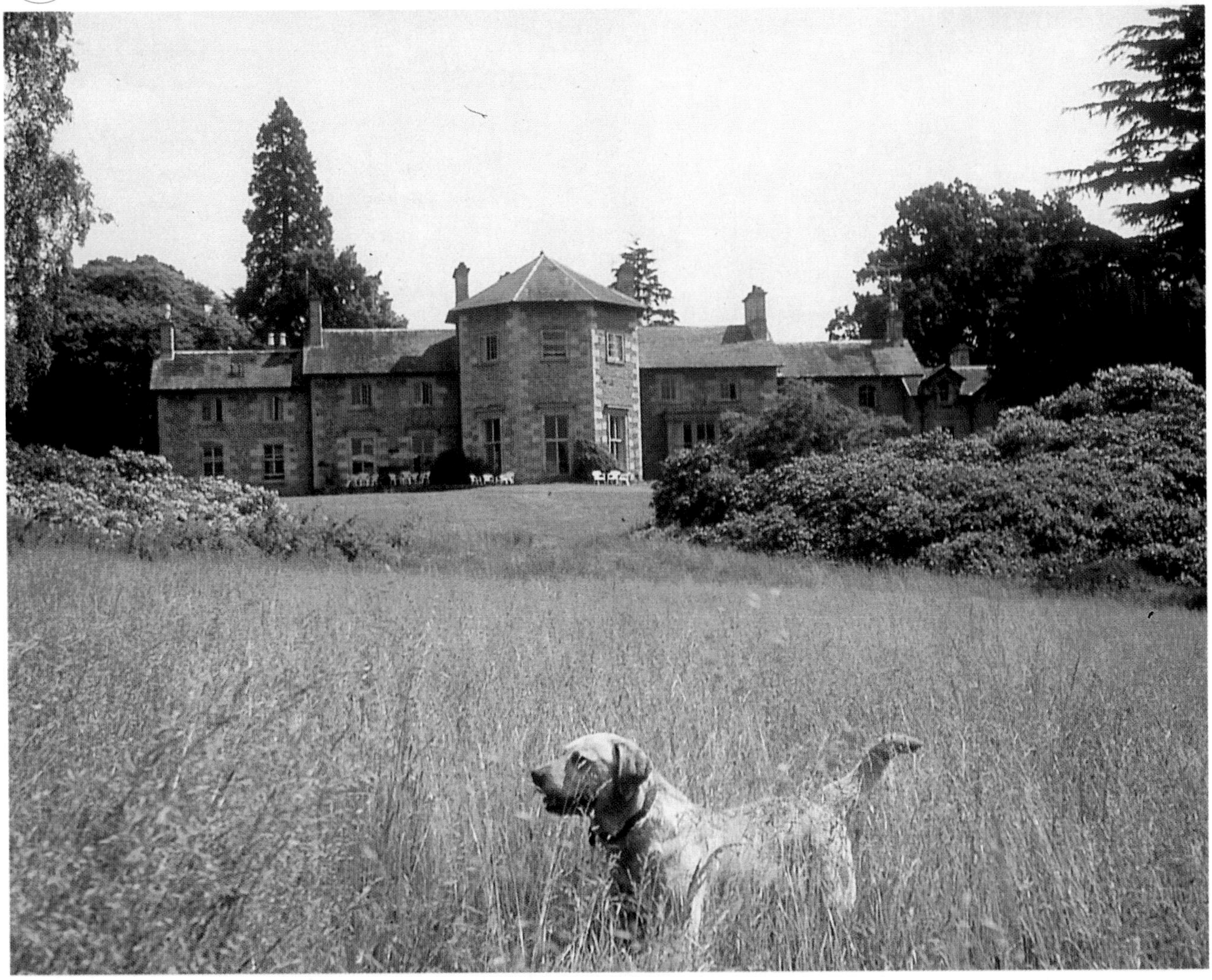

COUL HOUSE HOTEL

CONTIN, BY STRATHPEFFER, ROSS-SHIRE IV14 9EY
TEL: 01997 421487 FAX: 01997 421945

Coul House is a handsome country mansion in secluded grounds with magnificent, uninterrupted views. Owners Martyn and Ann Hill have a reputation for their friendly, personal service and high standards, both of food and accommodation. Thorough refurbishments of the decor and furnishings have enhanced the lovely interiors. All bedrooms are en suite, individually designed and each has a colour television, clock radio, trouser press, hairdryer, iron and hospitality tray. One has a four-poster bed. There are three elegant lounges with log burning fires, a cocktail bar and a Kitchen Bar where there is regular evening entertainment. A piper entertains in the gardens during summer months. In the dining room guests can savour "Taste of Scotland" cuisine such as fresh salmon and venison. Conferences and private functions can be accommodated. A cruise on Loch Ness or a sailing trip to to the Summer Isles can be arranged while nearby are Cawdor Castle, Culloden battlefield, fishing, pony-trekking, shooting and golf. Numerous routes lead to lovely glens. **Directions:** From the south, bypassing Inverness, continue on A9 over the Moray Firth Bridge and after 5 miles take second exit at roundabout onto A835. Follow to Contin. The hotel is 1/2 mile along a private drive to the right. Price guide (including dinner): Single £61.50-£83.50; double/twin £99-£143; suite £129-£183.

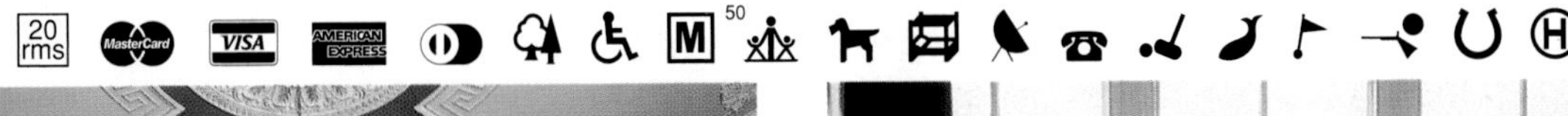

For hotel location, see maps on pages 477-483

Loch Torridon Hotel

TORRIDON, BY ACHNASHEEN, WESTER-ROSS IV22 2EY
TEL: 01445 791242 FAX: 01445 791296

Loch Torridon Hotel is gloriously situated at the foot of wooded mountains beside the loch which gives it its name. The hotel was built as a shooting lodge for the first Earl of Lovelace in 1887. The 58-acre estate contains formal gardens, mature trees and the shores of the loch. David and Geraldine Gregory, formerly of the Kinlochbervie Hotel, acquired the hotel in March 1992. They brought with them an excellent reputation for their brand of Highland hospitality and good cooking. A phased upgrading of the property has been completed to enhance the impact of the interiors and provide every comfort. Chef Nicholas Green, from the Grosvenor, Chester, has brought with him a reputation for inovation and uses only the finest of local ingredients from the lochs and hills. The hotel was chosen as the Best New Three Star Hotel in Scotland by the AA Inspector for 1993 and awarded two Rosettes for its food. Dinner is served between 7.15pm and 8.30pm. A starter of home-made Scotch broth or spinach roulade with prawns and cream could be followed by roast saddle of hare with caramelized onion tart or seafood kebab with tomato sauce and saffron rice. **Directions:** Ten miles from Kinlochewe on the A896. Do not turn off to Torridon village. Price guide: Single £50–£80; double/twin £100–£220; suites £200–£240.

For hotel location, see maps on pages 477-483

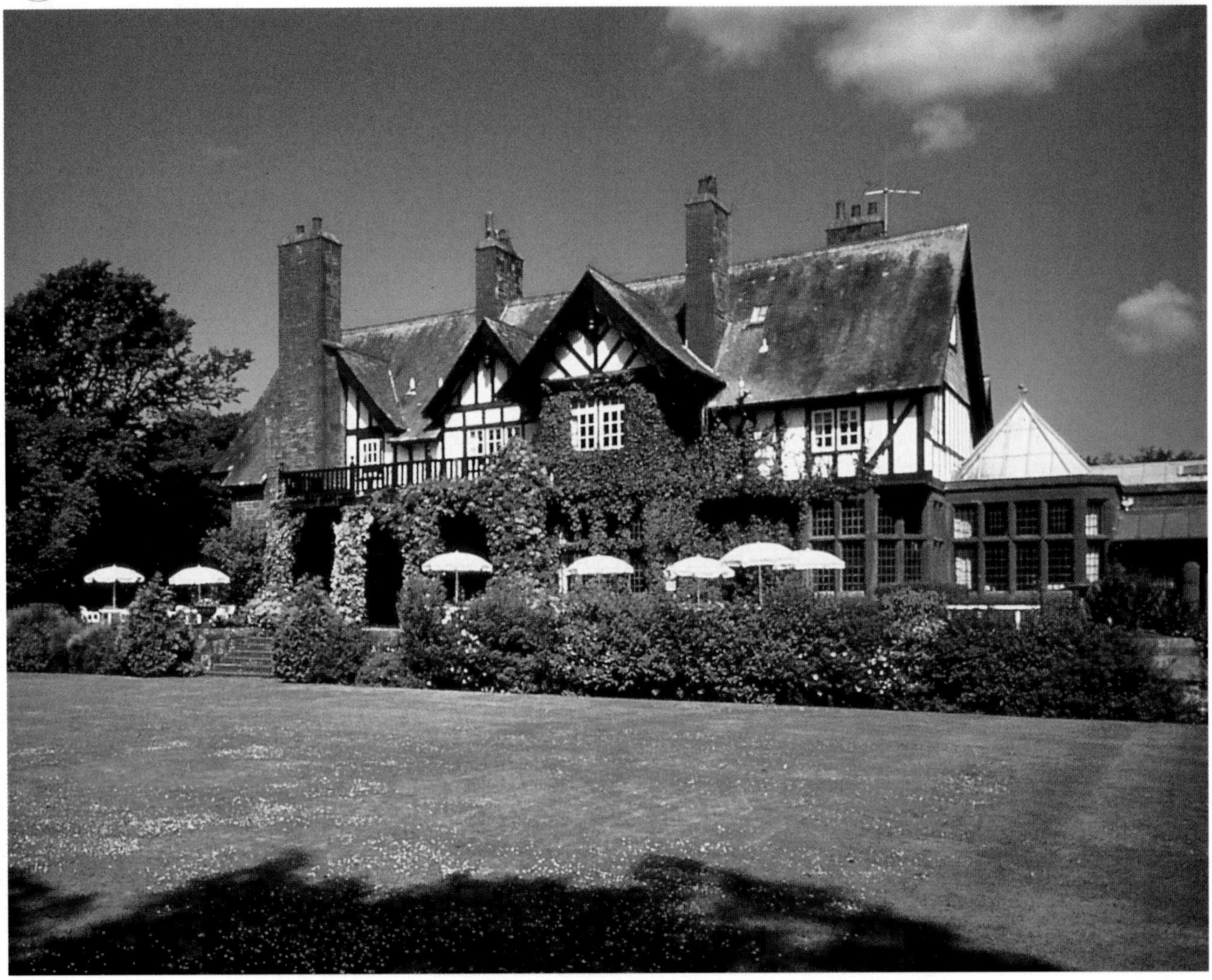

PIERSLAND HOUSE HOTEL

CRAIGEND ROAD, TROON, AYRSHIRE KA10 6HD
TEL: 01292 314747 FAX: 01292 315613

This historic listed house, built for the grandson of Johnnie Walker, founder of the Scottish whisky brand, is as attractive inside as out. All the public rooms are spacious and inviting, with original features such as oak panelling and a frieze of Jacobean embroidery. Retaining their original charm, the bedrooms are formally decorated in a period style with soft colourings. For residents only afternoon cream teas are served on the verandah, an airy sun-lounge opening on to beautiful gardens. The four acre grounds include immaculate lawns, a Japanese water garden and a croquet lawn. Guests can enjoy classically prepared gourmet dishes and continental-style cooking in the warm, intimate atmosphere of the restaurant. The wine list is compiled from labels supplied by one of Scotland's oldest-established wine firms. For golfers, Royal Troon is across the road, and Turnberry and Old Prestwick are nearby. Ayr, the birthplace of Robert Burns, Kilmarnock and Irvine are a short drive and Culzean Castle, the seat of the Kennedy clan, is 19 miles away. Glasgow, Stirling and Edinburgh are easily accessible, as are Loch Lomond, the Trossachs and the isles of the Firth of Clyde. **Directions:** The hotel is on the B749, just beside Royal Troon Golf Club. Price guide: Single £59.50–£77; double/twin £99–£120.

For hotel location, see maps on pages 477-483

Johansens Recommended Hotels in Ireland

Celtic treasures and legends, medieval architecture, racecourses and golf courses, great art collections and a richness of literature are all to be found amongst the green landscapes of Ireland.

Ireland's story is a long one. History and legend are entwined in its green landscapes. Everywhere are memories of the Celts whose character and culture created this country and its people. For thousands of years Ireland was all their own. Successive invaders, the Vikings and Normans struggled to take it from them, and the land echoed with the clamour of battles lost and won. During the pious Middle Ages, the monks ruled. Today's museums guard their intricate manuscripts, and their majestic stonework survives as Ireland's greatest landmarks.

So much of Ireland's history is preserved in the architecture and ancient monuments of many of the towns and villages around the country that an association, Heritage Towns of Ireland, has been formed to assist the visitor in achieving the most comprehensive experience during a visit.

Dublin, in spite of its modest size, is a centre of inifinte interest and variety. Medieval, Georgian and modern architecture provide a backdrop to a bustling but friendly port. The city's cultural heart lies north of the Liffey, where the widest and largest streets, the best Georgian houses and the most magnificent public buildings are to be found.

The National Gallery, The Royal Hospital Kilmainham and the Municipal Art Gallery in Dublin have extensive collections of great quality. The Chester Beatty Library, a gift to the State by an American scholar, has some of the rarest oriental manuscripts in existence. Russborough, a beautiful mansion in Co. Wicklow, has an excellent collection of paintings.

Ireland has three internationally recognised national parks. Killarney National Park is perhaps the best known with Muckross House and Gardens as the centrepiece of this magnificent lakeside park. Connemara National Park in Letterfrack is set amid the wild rugged beauty so typical of the West of Ireland, and Glenveagh National Park in County Donegal has a beautiful castle and gardens.

Northern Ireland is usually referred to as a well-kept secret, but hundreds of thousands of visitors in the past ten years have uncovered its secrets, returning the next year for more.

This small part of the island – six counties in Northern Ireland – there are 26 in the Republic – attracts visitors in search of a different Ireland. English visitors say it reminds them of England 50 years ago with all the hedgerows and empty roads. For European visitors it is a little like entering a beautiful wilderness.

The visitor to Ireland, north and south, usually has adventure at the back of his or her mind and steeped in ancient pre-Celtic history the north's heritage offers the explorer any amount of fascinating finds. Navan Fort in Armagh, the home of Ulster's legends which date back as far as the Greek Ilyad, the statues on the islands in Lough Erne in County Fermanagh and the other myths of the Giant's Causeway are a starting point for the lover of myths and legends.

The biggest fairy thorn in Ireland is County Down for instance, and marks the sacred spot where de danaan or the underground people live. Some, of course, scorn the superstitions and old myths of Ireland and Ulster but these are inescapable in a country where your ability to tell a good story places you very highly on the social scale no matter your economic circumstances.

Northern Ireland people love to talk and what better than having visitors who have never heard their stories before! But if its isolated bliss you are in search of then you will be left well alone. You might like to try part of the 500-mile Ulster Way, or devote your time to a stretch of the River Finn, judged by some English commentators to be among the best salmon rivers in the world.

Or you might prefer to go absent for a few days on a comfortable cruiser on the vast empty waters of Upper and Lower Lough Erne.

The nature of the landscape provides the visitor with a feast of beauty and a superb environment for such activities as fishing, walking, water sports, horse-riding, hire-cruising and golf. Indeed, many come to golf on the famous links courses. The Royal Portrush and Royal County Down repeatedly feature in the top ten in the world lists and green fees are still remarkably reasonable. Other links courses such as Portstewart, Castlerock, Ballycastle and many more give Northern Ireland's northern most coastline the nickname of the Golf Coast.

For those whose interests lie in more leisurely pursuits, a varied cultural life is easily accessible by way of established theatres, museums, visitor and interpretative centres.

Heritage Towns of Ireland
92 Sandymount Road
Sandymount Village
Dublin 4
Tel: 00 353 1 668 9688

The National Art Gallery of Ireland
Merrion Square West
Dublin 2
Tel: 00 353 1 661 5133

Chester Beatty Library
20 Shrewsbury Road
Ballsbridge
Dublin
Tel: 00 353 1 269 2386

For more information about Ireland, please contact:

The Irish Tourist Board
Bord Failte
Baggot Street Bridge
Dublin 2
Tel: 00353 1 676 5871

For more information about Northern Ireland, please contact:

Northern Ireland Tourist Board
St Anne's Court
59 North Street
Belfast BT1 1NB
Tel: 01232 246609

Galgorm Manor

BALLYMENA, CO ANTRIM BT42 1EA
TEL: 01266 881001 FAX: 01266 880080

This converted gentleman's residence is set amidst some of Northern Ireland's most beautiful lush scenery, with the River Maine running less than 100 yards from the main entrance. Most of the comfortable en suite bedrooms offer spectacular views of the surrounding countryside. The Dining Room offers a choice of table d'hôte or à la carte menus with local produce used wherever possible. For lighter eating there is a full bar menu in the Gillies Bar. There are six self-catering cottages available in the grounds which are perfect for weekend breaks or the longer stay. The Manor offers a varied choice of meeting rooms, all with the most modern facilities. Its estate includes 12 stables, a show jumping course and an eventing cross-country practice area, so there is plenty of scope for the equestrian enthusiast. Clay pigeon shooting is also available and there are opportunites to play golf on some of the best links courses in Ireland. Galgorm Manor is perfectly located for touring Northern Ireland. The lovely Antrim Coast, including the Giant's Causeway, is only a short drive away. **Directions:** Follow the A42 towards Ballymena. Shortly after passing Galgorm Castle on the right, turn left at Galgorm towards Cullybackey. Galgorm Manor is halfway between Galgorm and Cullybackey. Price guide: Single £99; double/twin £120; suites £135.

For hotel location, see maps on pages 477-483

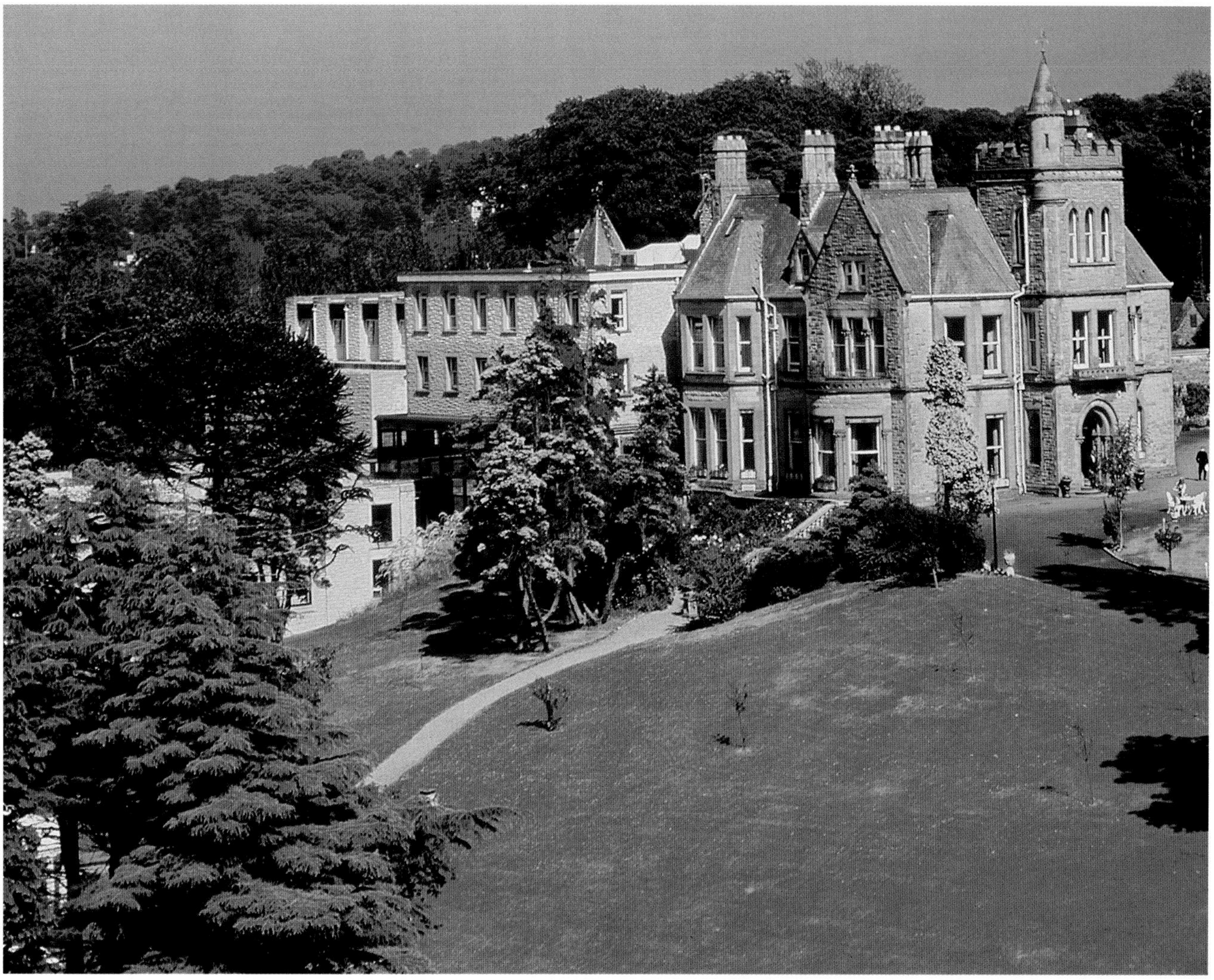

CULLODEN HOTEL

BANGOR ROAD, HOLYWOOD, CO DOWN, N. IRELAND BT18 OEX
TEL: 01232 425223 FAX: 01232 426777

Standing in 12 acres of beautifully secluded gardens on the wooded slopes of Holywood overlooking Belfast Lough and the County Antrim coastline is the magnificent and palatial Culloden Hotel. Once an official palace for the Bishops of Down it is a magnificent example of 19th-century Baronial Architecture and is Northern Ireland's only five star hotel. Antique furniture, valuable paintings, elegant plasterwork ceilings and Louis XV chandeliers give it a unique elegance. All modern amenities have been blended to this background to make the Culloden an excellent hotel. The bedrooms have magnificent views over the gardens and coast, and the sumptuous, 900 square feet "Palace Suite" boasts the finest four-poster bedroom in Ireland. As well as superb cuisine in the award-winning Mitre Restaurant, informal dining is available in the Cultra Inn situated in the grounds. The hotel has a range of leisure facilities and guests have full use of the Elysium private health spa whose state-of-the-art facilities are complemented by a splendid octagonal-shaped ozone pool. There are 10 golf courses nearby, including the Royal Belfast where an exclusive arrangement for tee-off times is available for Culloden guests. Directions: The Culloden Hotel is six miles east of Belfast city centre on the A2 towards Bangor. Price guide: Single £120; double/twin £150; suite £350.

For hotel location, see maps on pages 477-483

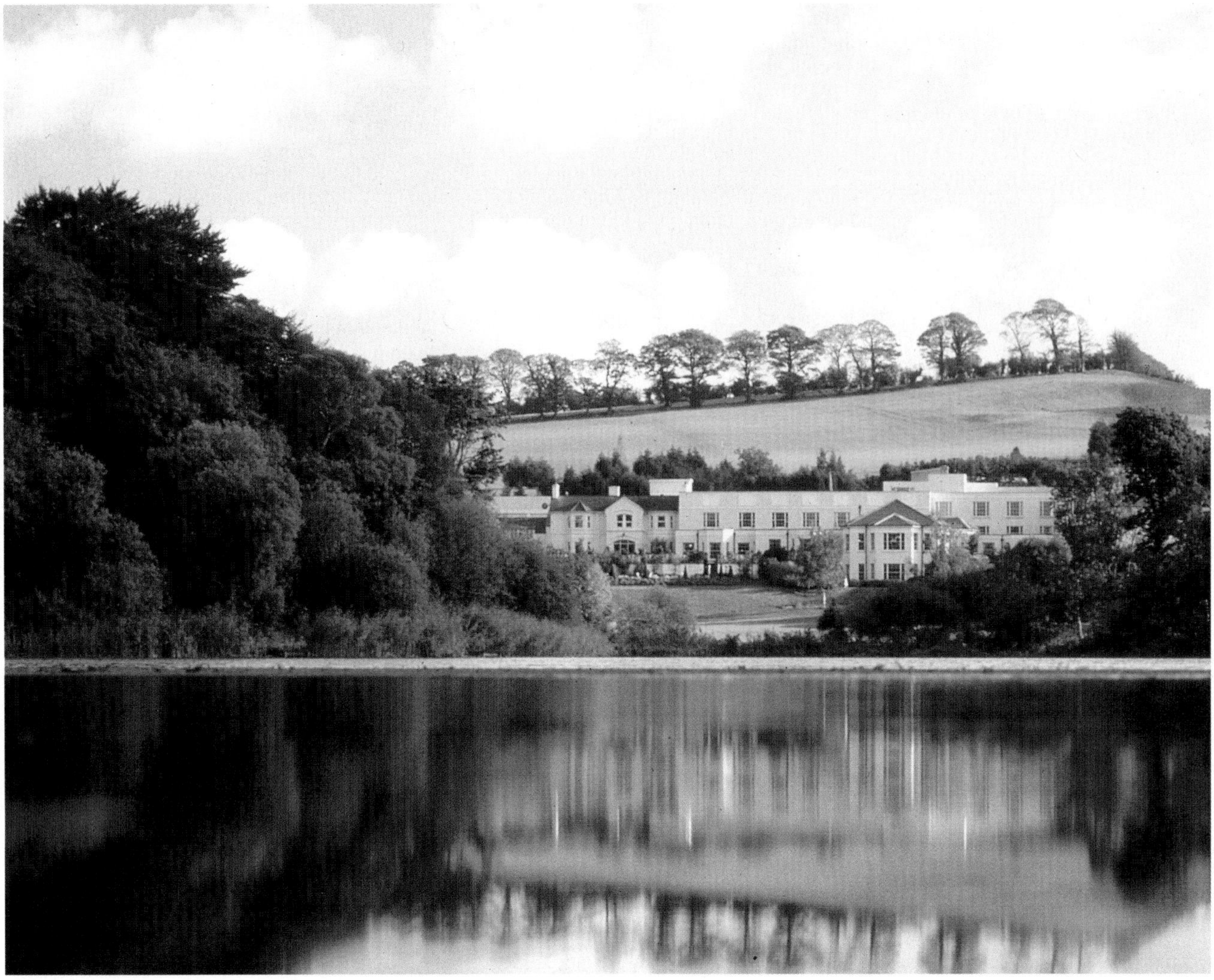

NUREMORE HOTEL

CARRICKMACROSS, CO MONAGHAN, IRELAND
TEL: 042 61438 FAX: 042 61853

Set in 200 acres of glorious countryside on the fringe of Carrickmacross, the Nuremore Hotel has been extensively renovated. It offers guests all-round enjoyment, a vast array of activities and facilities and all that is best in a first-class country hotel. The bedrooms are well appointed and attractively designed to create a generous sense of personal space. Lunch and dinner menus, served in a spacious and elegant dining room, emphasise classic European cooking, with French and Irish dishes featured alongside. For sport, fitness and relaxation, guests are spoiled for choice by the range of amenities. A major feature is the championship-length, par 73, 18-hole golf course designed by Eddie Hackett to present an exciting challenge to beginners and experts alike. Maurice Cassidy has been appointed as resident professional and is on hand to give tuition. Riding nearby in Carrickmacross. The leisure club has a superb indoor pool, modern gymnasium, squash and tennis courts, sauna, steam room and whirlpool bath. Meetings, conferences and seminars held here are guaranteed a professional support service. Dublin is 90 minutes' drive away, while Drogheda and Dundalk are nearby for shopping. From the UK phone 00 353 42 61438. **Directions:** The hotel is on the main N2 road between Dublin and Monaghan. Price guide: Single IR£80–IR£100; double/twin IR£120–IR£140; suite IR150.

For hotel location, see maps on pages 477-483

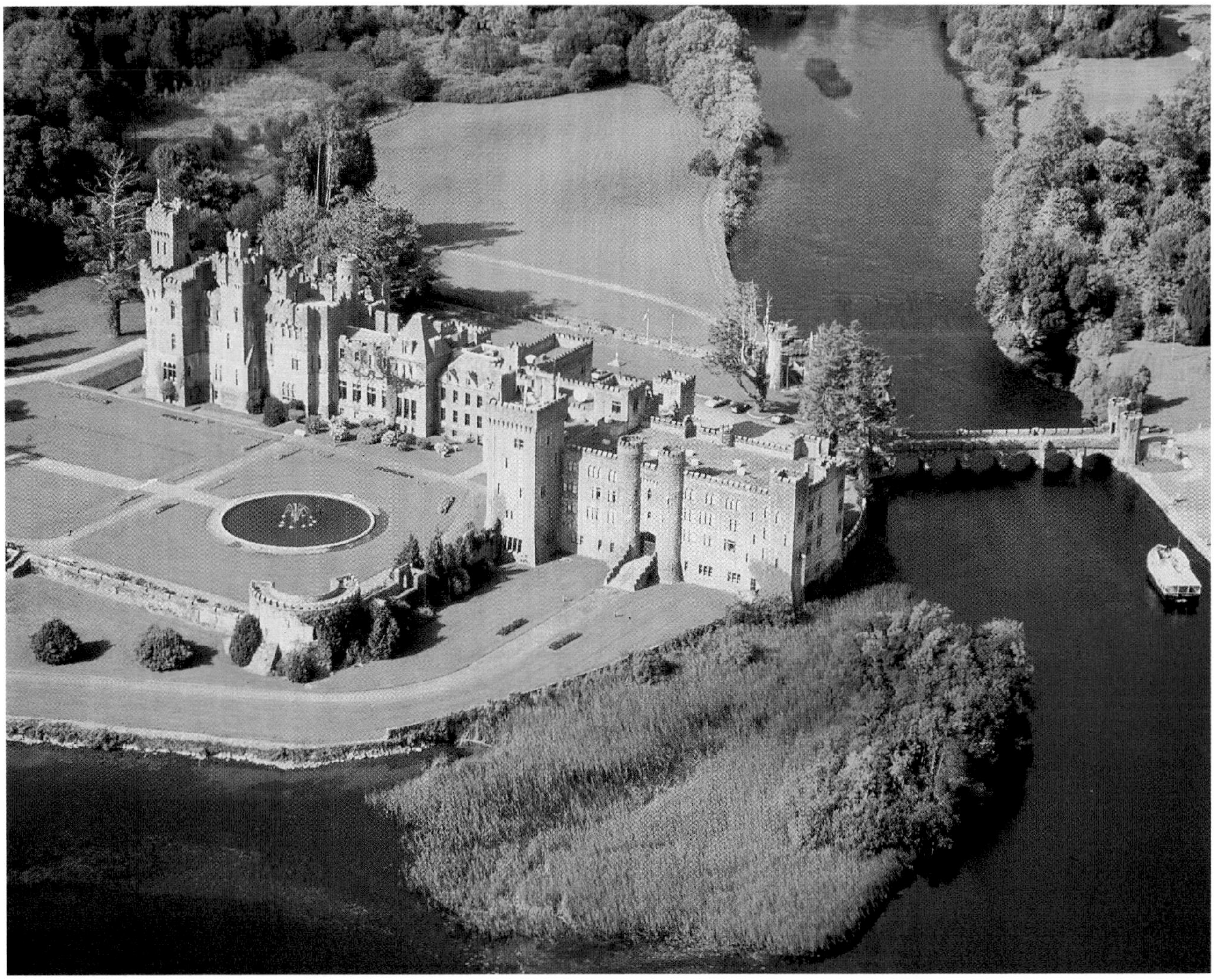

ASHFORD CASTLE

CONG, CO MAYO

TEL: 353 92 46003 FAX: 353 92 46260

Ashford Castle is set on the northern shores of Lough Corrib amidst acres of beautiful gardens and forests. Once the country estate of Lord Ardilaun and the Guinness family, it was transformed into a luxury hotel in 1939. The castle's Great Hall is lavishly decorated with rich panelling, fine period pieces, *objets d'art* and masterpiece paintings. Guest rooms are of the highest standards and many feature high ceilings, enormous bathrooms and delightful lake views. The main dining room offers superb continental and traditional menus, while the gourmet restaurant, The Connaught Room, specialises in excellent French cuisine. Before and after dinner in the Dungeon Bar guests are entertained by a harpist or pianist. Ashford Castle offers a full range of country sports, including fishing on Lough Corrib, clay pigeon shooting, riding and an exclusive 9-hole golf course. The hotel has just added a health centre comprising a whirlpool, sauna, steam room, fully equipped gymnasium and conservatory. Ashford is an ideal base for touring the historic West Ireland, places like Kylemore Abbey and Westport House, Sligo and Drumcliffe Churchyard, the burial place of W.B. Yeats. **Directions:** 30 minutes from Galway on the shore of Lough Corrib, on the left when entering the village of Cong. Price guide: Single/twin/double IR£121–IR£255; suite IR£300–IR£430.

83 rms 110

For hotel location, see maps on pages 477-483

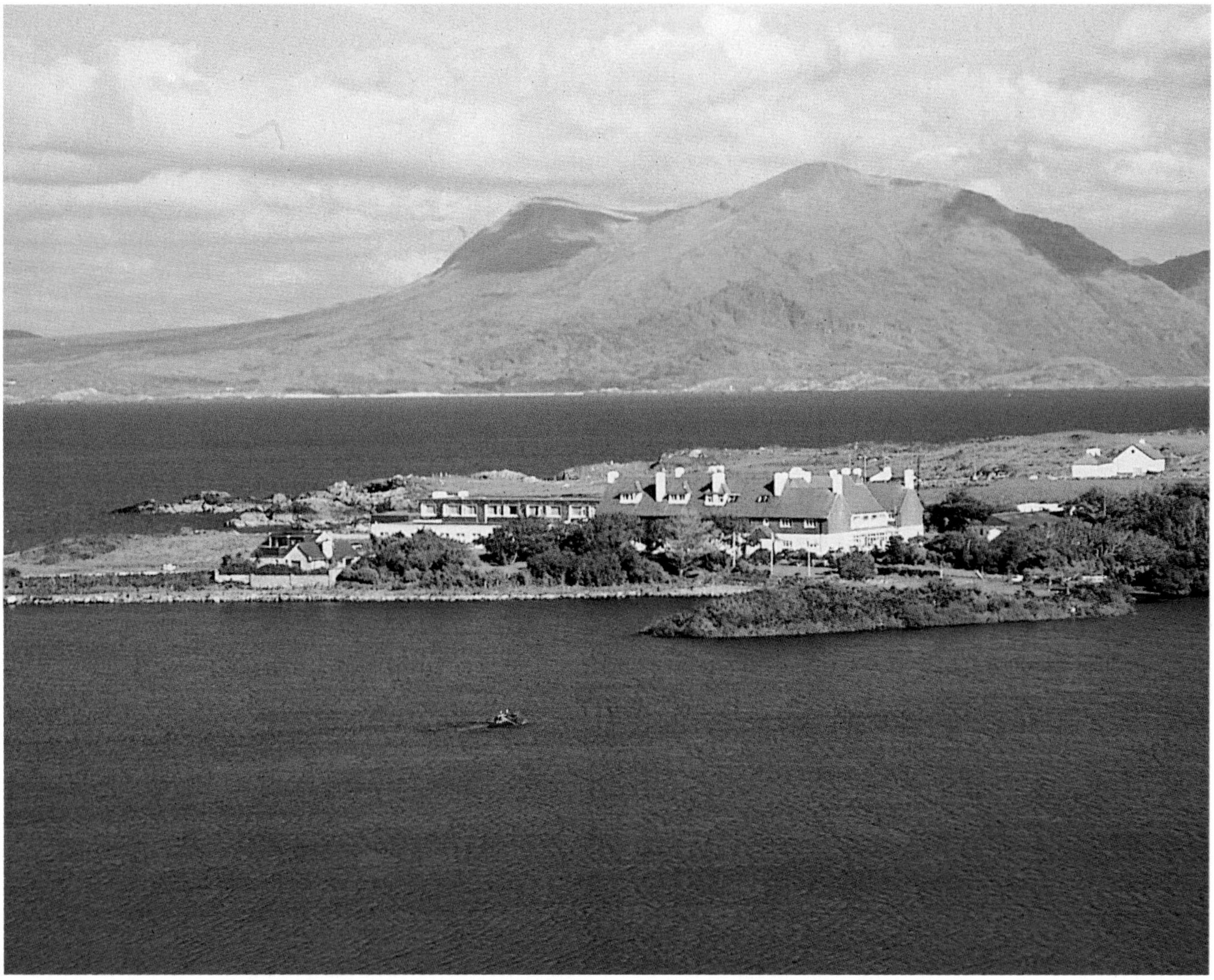

RENVYLE HOUSE HOTEL

CONNEMARA, CO GALWAY
TEL: 353 95 43511 FAX: 353 95 43515

Renvyle House Hotel has occupied its rugged, romantic position on Ireland's west coast for over four centuries. Set between mountains and sea on the unspoilt coast of Connemara, this hardy, beautiful building with its superlative views over the surrounding countryside is just an hour's drive from Galway or Sligo. Originally constructed in 1541, Renvyle has been an established hotel for over 100 years, witnessing in that time a procession of luminaries through its doors – among them Augustus John, Lady Gregory, Yeats and Churchill, drawn no doubt by an atmosphere as warm and convivial then as it is today. Renvyle now welcomes visitors with turf fires glowing in public areas, wood-beamed interiors and comfortable, relaxed furnishings in the easy rooms. The bedrooms are comfortably appointed and all have been refurbished in the past two years. In the dining room, meals from a constantly-changing menu are served with emphasis on local fish and Renvyle lamb. In the grounds activities include tennis, croquet, riding, bowls and golf. Beyond the hotel, there are walks in the heather-clad hills, or swimming and sunbathing on empty beaches. **Directions:** On the N59 from Galway turn right at Recess, take the Letterfrack turning to Tully Cross and Renvyle is signposted. Price guide: Single IR£40–IR£100; double/twin IR£80–IR£160.

For hotel location, see maps on pages 477-483

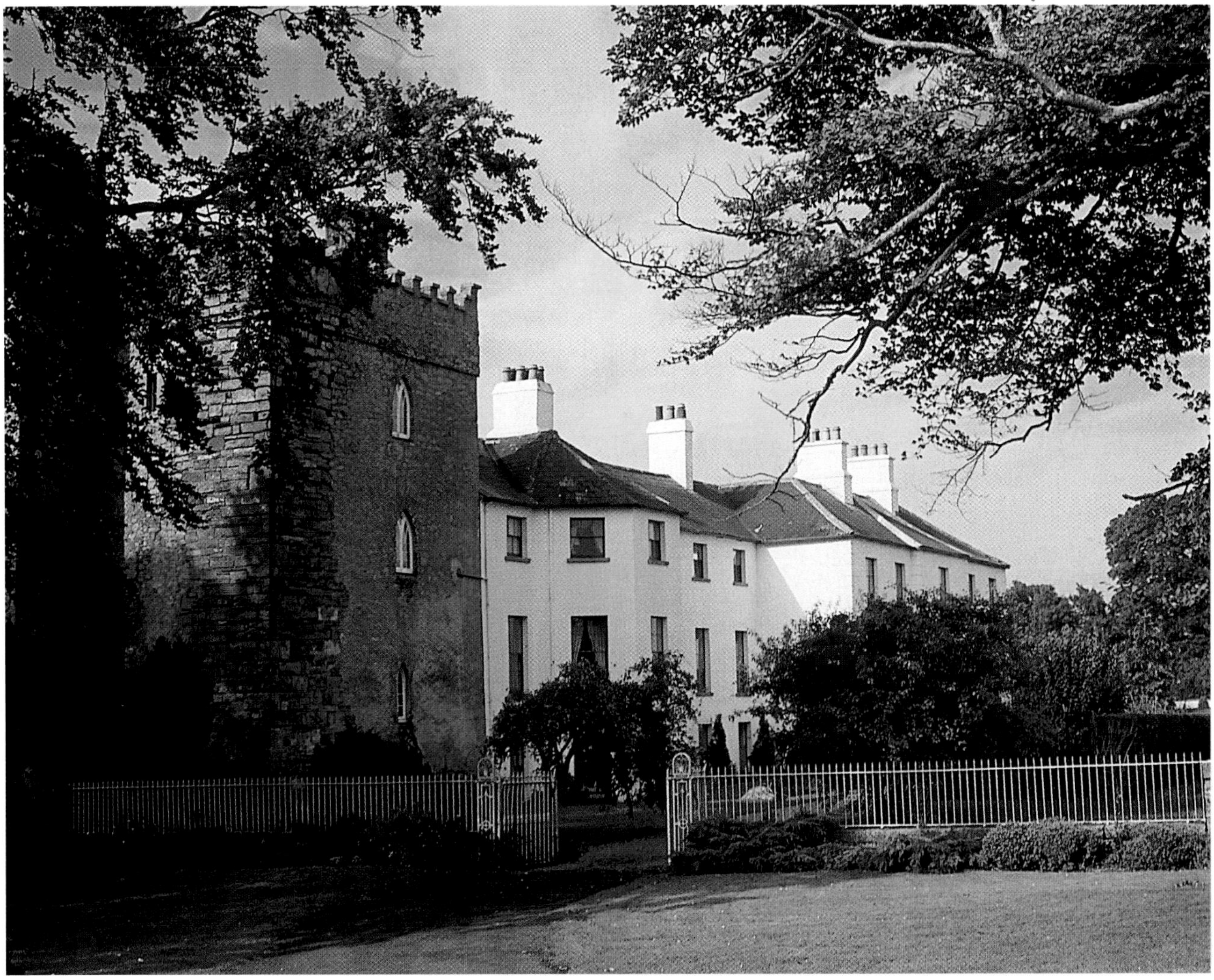

BARBERSTOWN CASTLE

STRAFFAN, CO KILDARE
TEL: 353 1 6288157 FAX: 353 1 6277027

Barberstown Castle was one of the first great Irish country houses to open up its splendour to the outside world. The Castle was built in the early 13th century by Nicholas Barby, a heritage that embraces over 750 years of Irish history. The restaurant at Barberstown is renowned for its creative food and has received the RAC Restaurant Award for 1994/95 and also two Rosettes from the AA for 1994/95. Each of the en suite bedrooms has been decorated in an individual style and dedicated to the ordinary and extraordinary people who have lived within its walls. The Castle received Hospitality and Comfort Awards from the RAC for 1995. Golf can be arranged at The Kildare Country Club and at several other courses nearby. Expert equestrian tuition as well as hunting, racing, tennis, gym, squash and clay pigeon shooting are all available in the area. Coarse, trout and salmon fishing on the River Liffey, ghillies available. For the less active, relax in an atmosphere of pure calm and tranquillity, deep in the heart of County Kildare. **Directions:** Barberstown Castle is 30 minutes drive from Dublin City centre and 30 minutes drive from the airport. It is an ideal first or last stop on your country house tour of Ireland. South on the N7 take the turn for Straffan at Kill. Travelling west on N4 take the turn for Straffan at Maynooth. Price guide: Single IR£65–IR£85; double/twin IR£121–IR£130; suite IR£175.

For hotel location, see maps on pages 477-483

THE HIBERNIAN HOTEL

EASTMORELAND PLACE, BALLSBRIDGE, DUBLIN 4
TEL: (353) 01668 7666 FAX: (353) 01660 2655

Tucked away in bustling downtown Dublin, the Hibernian Hotel is a magnificent architectural feat constructed just before the turn of the century in the commercial heart of the city. Refurbished and reopened in 1993 as a grand townhouse hotel, The Hibernian now prides itself on the elegance, style and warmth of service it can offer visitors to this vibrant metropolis: the hotel has a unique blend of modern ease and bygone atmosphere. David Butt, the general manager, is ably assisted by a professional team who ensure that the needs of both business and holiday guests are met quickly and efficiently. Luxury prevails at The Hibernian in soft furnishings, rich fabrics and deep upholstery; in each of the 40 individually designed bedrooms and suites. En suite bathrooms with a full range of toiletries are standard, as are fax/modem points, drinks facilities, individually controlled thermostats and and hairstyling appliances. In the restaurant, the luncheon and à la carte menus offer the full gamut of gastronomic dishes, from locally caught, artfully interpreted seafood to modern cuisine classics and fine wines to accompany them. The hotel makes an ideal base from which to explore the city. **Directions:** Turn right from Mespil road into Baggot Street Upper, then left into Eastmoreland Place; The Hibernian is on the left. Price guide: Single IR£110; double/twin IR£145; suite IR£180.

For hotel location, see maps on pages 477-483

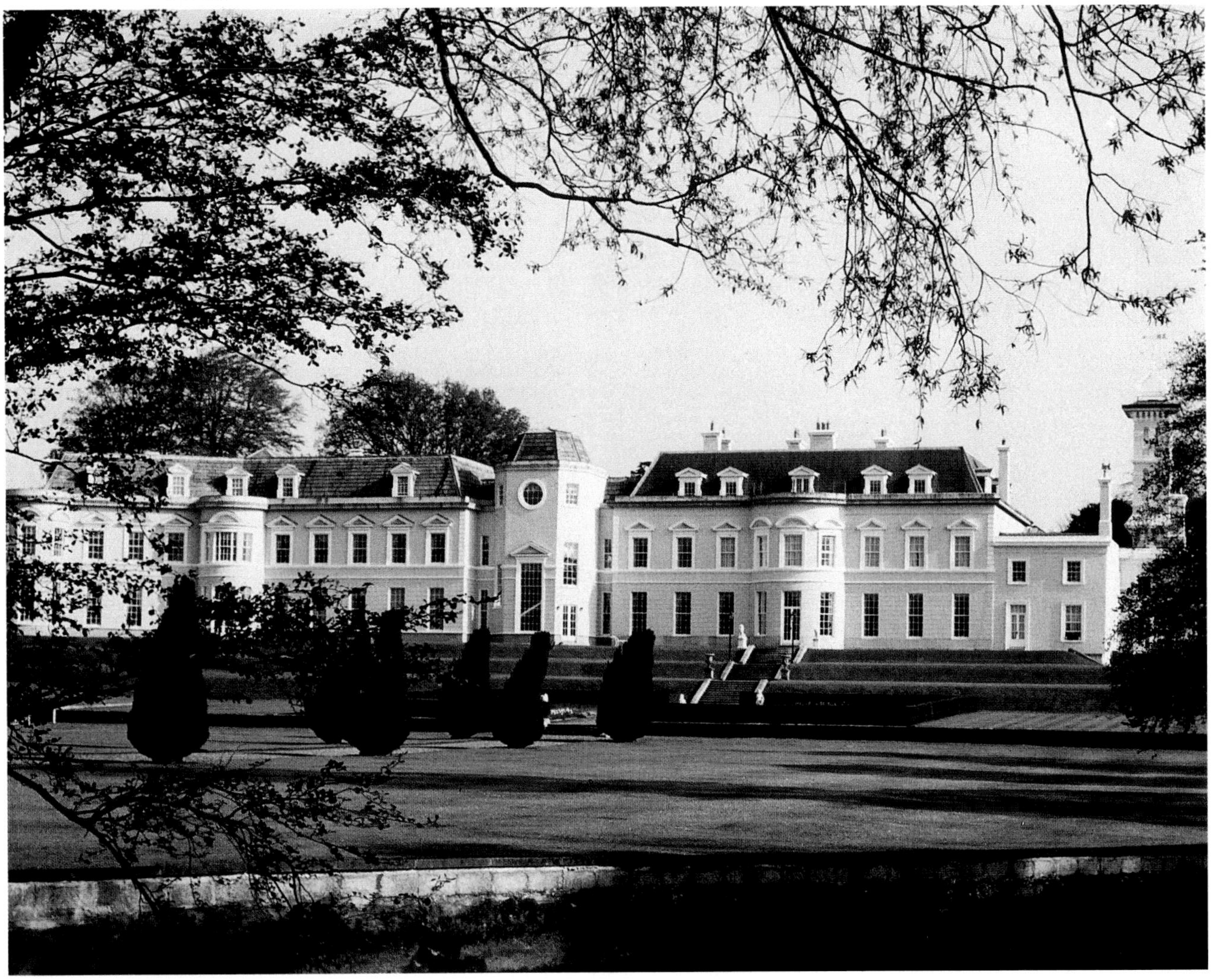

THE KILDARE HOTEL & COUNTRY CLUB

AT STRAFFAN, CO KILDARE

TEL: 353 (1) 627 3333 FAX: 353 (1) 627 3312

Straffan House is one of Ireland's most elegant 19th century manor houses, set in 330 acres of beautiful countryside and overlooking the River Liffey. Just 17 miles from Dublin this is an international world class resort with its graceful reception rooms, totally luxurious bedrooms and palatial en suite bathrooms, also a superb leisure club with a sybaritic indoor pool. The public areas of the hotel are a treasure trove of contemporary paintings and works of art. There are excellent conference areas for business meetings, while corporate entertaining is dominated by facilities which include the Arnold Palmer course which is the venue for The Smurfit European Open, September 1996 and 1997, indoor tennis and squash courts, a gymnasium, clay pigeon shooting, fishing and riding, croquet. Formal entertaining, meeting in the bar followed by a magnificent meal in the prestigious Byerley Turk Restaurant, with table d'hôte and à la carte menus complemented by an extensive wine list, is effortless, The Legend Bar and Restaurant in the Country Club offer less formality. The Arnold Palmer Room is available for gala functions and conferences at the Clubhouse. **Directions:** Leave Dublin on N7 driving south for 17 miles. Straffan is signposted on the left. Price guide: Double/twin IR£260–IR£320; suite IR£470–£1,000. Conference rates on request.

For hotel location, see maps on pages 477-483

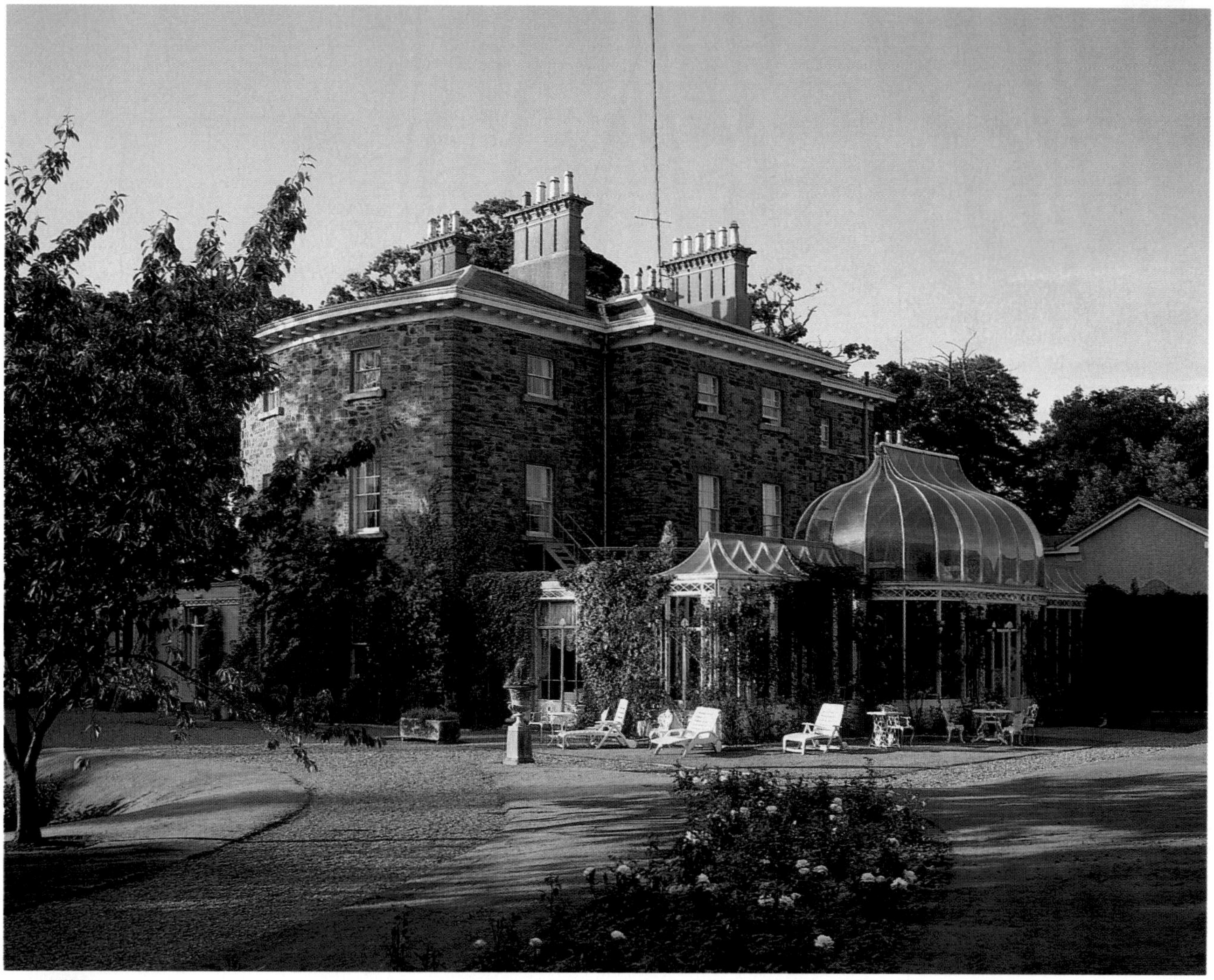

MARLFIELD HOUSE

GOREY, CO WEXFORD
TEL: 055 21124 FAX: 055 21572

Staying at Marlfield House is a memorable experience. Set in 34 acres of woodland and gardens, this former residence of the Earl of Courtown preserves the Regency lifestyle in all its graciousness. Built in 1820 it is recognised as one of the finest country houses in Ireland, and is supervised by its welcoming hosts and proprietors, Raymond and Mary Bowe and their daughter Margaret. The suites have been built in a very grand style and have period fireplaces where open fires burn even in the cooler weather. All of the furniture is antique and the roomy beds are draped with sumptuous fabrics. The bathrooms are made of highly polished marble and have large freestanding bathtubs. There is a grand entrance hall, luxurious drawing room and an impressive curved Richard Turner conservatory. The kitchen's gastronomic delights have earned it numerous awards. Located two miles from fine beaches and Courtown golf club, the house is central to many touring high points: Glendalough, Mount Usher and Powerscourt Gardens and the medieval city of Kilkenny. When phoning from the British mainland dial 00 353 55 21124. Closed mid-December to mid-January. **Directions:** On the Gorey–Courtown road, just over a mile east of Gorey. Price guide: Single from IR£85; double/twin IR£144–IR£160; suites from IR£200–IR£400.

For hotel location, see maps on pages 477-483

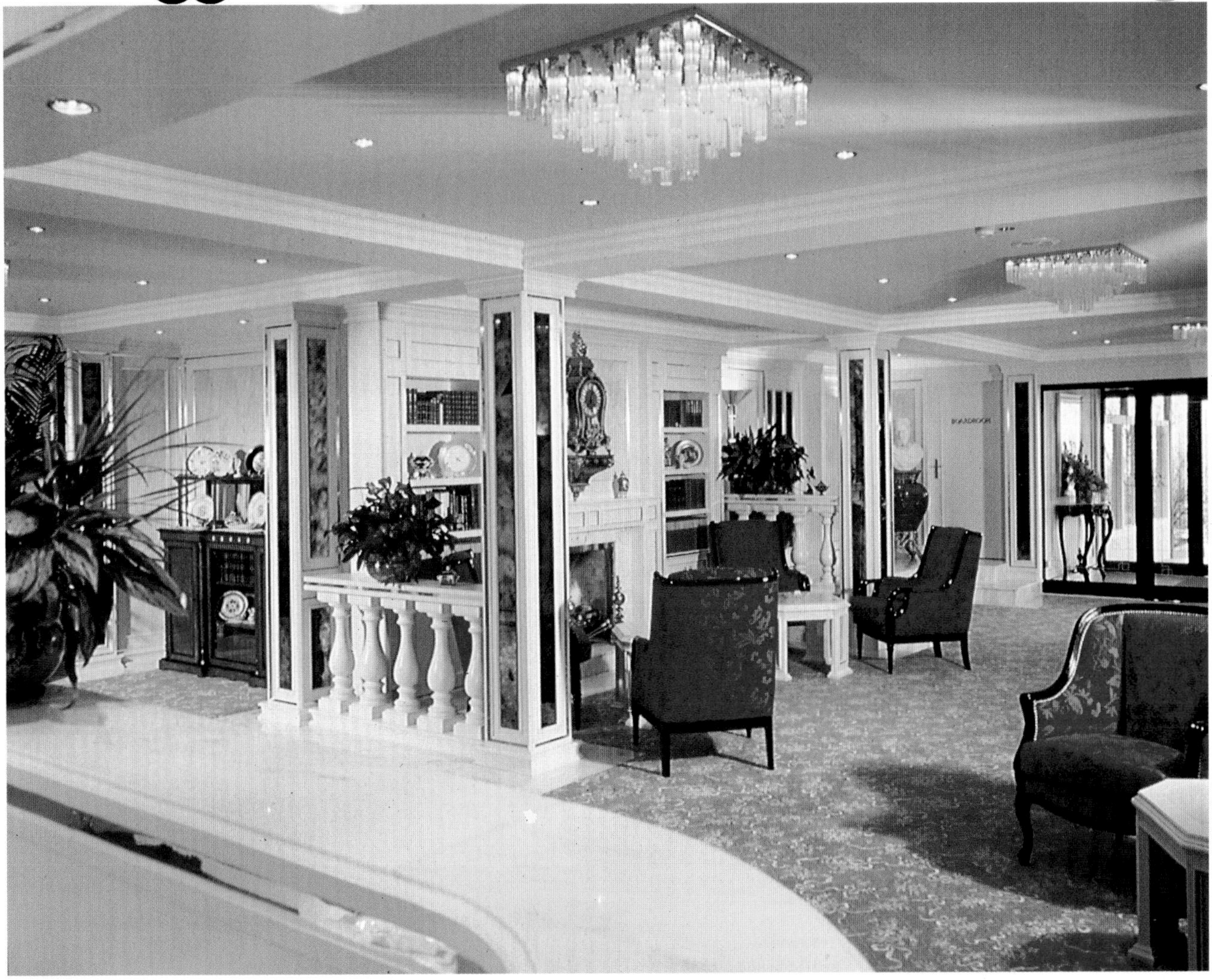

AGHADOE HEIGHTS HOTEL

AGHADOE, KILLARNEY, CO KERRY
TEL: 064 31766 FAX: 064 31345

In the heart of beautiful County Kerry overlooking stunning panoramic views of the lakes and mountains of Killarney, stands the Aghadoe Heights Hotel, sister hotel to Fredrick's of Maidenhead. It reflects owner Fredrick Losel's influence: rich tapestries, crystal chandeliers, paintings and antiques. Much attention has been given to the bedrooms. The furniture is of mahogany, ash or cherry wood, with soft drapes and deep carpets. Excellent cuisine and fine wines are served in the rooftop restaurant. Chef Robin Suter uses the freshest local ingredients to create innovative dishes. Three function rooms offer good conference facilities. A leisure club includes an indoor pool, Jacuzzi, sauna, plunge pool, solarium, fitness room and now by appointment a massage and beauty treatment service in the hotel. Aghadoe Heights is a good departure point for tours of Kerry or for playing south-west Ireland's premier golf courses, such as Killarney, Waterville and Ballybunion. The hotel has its own stretch of river for salmon and trout fishing and there is also a tennis court within the eight acre gardens. Pony-trekking, lake and sea fishing are also offered locally. From the UK phone 00 353 64 31766. **Directions:** The hotel is ten miles south of Kerry Airport, three miles north of Killarney. It is situated off the N22 Tralee road. Price guide: Single IR£85–IR£125; double/twin IR£120–IR£175; suite IR£175–£225.

For hotel location, see maps on pages 477-483

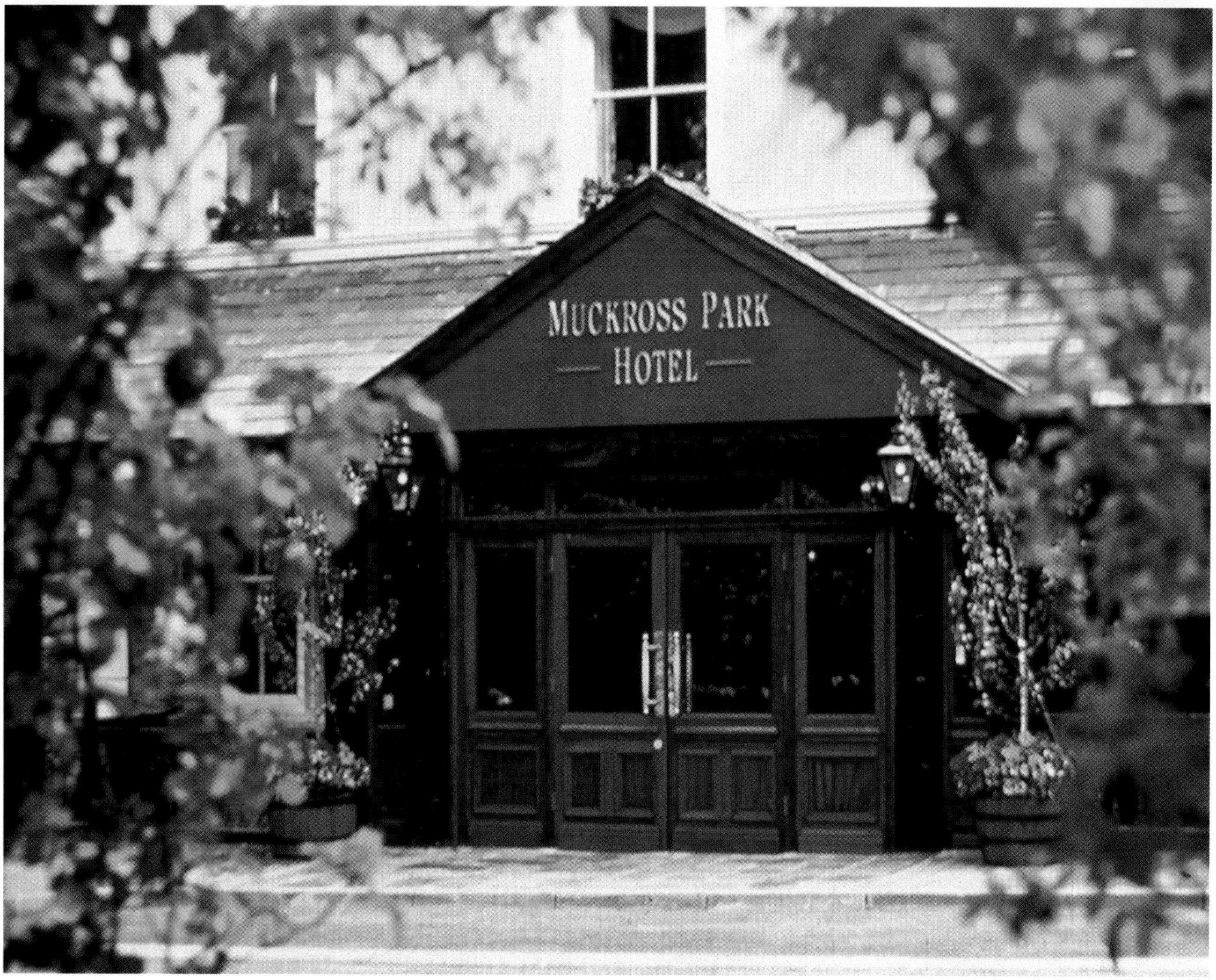

Muckross Park Hotel

MUCKROSS, KILLARNEY, CO KERRY
TEL: 353 64 31938 FAX: 353 64 31965 – FROM USA TOLL FREE 800 223 6510

Muckross Park stands in the heart of beautiful County Kerry surrounded by the 25,000 acre Killarney National Park with its lakes, mountains and peaceful gardens with giant rhododendrons and tropical plants. It is a redevelopment of an 18th century hotel with stone wall interiors, wooden panelling and exposed beams. Fine antiques and paintings, deep carpets and glittering chandeliers combine the luxurious ambience of a traditional country house with the comfort of a modern four star hotel. All the en suite bedrooms are charmingly old-world. Each has satellite television, direct dial telephone, trouser press and hair dryer. Innovative cuisine and fine wines are served in the bright, sunny Blue Pool Restaurant which looks out over two acres of landscaped gardens that lead down to the hotel's river frontage. Adjacent to the hotel is Mollys, a famous, award-winning traditional Irish pub and restaurant, where bare wooden floors, beamed ceilings, open fires and live entertainment recreate the pleasures of bygone days. Muckross Park is a good base from which to tour Kerry, to explore Killarney National Park, or play south west Ireland's premier golf courses. Boating, fishing, tennis, clay pigeon shooting, riding and hill walking can all be arranged. Directions: The hotel is $2^1/2$ miles south of Killarney on N71 towards Kenmare. Price guide: Single IR£80; double/twin IR£120; suite IR£180–IR£250.

For hotel location, see maps on pages 477-483

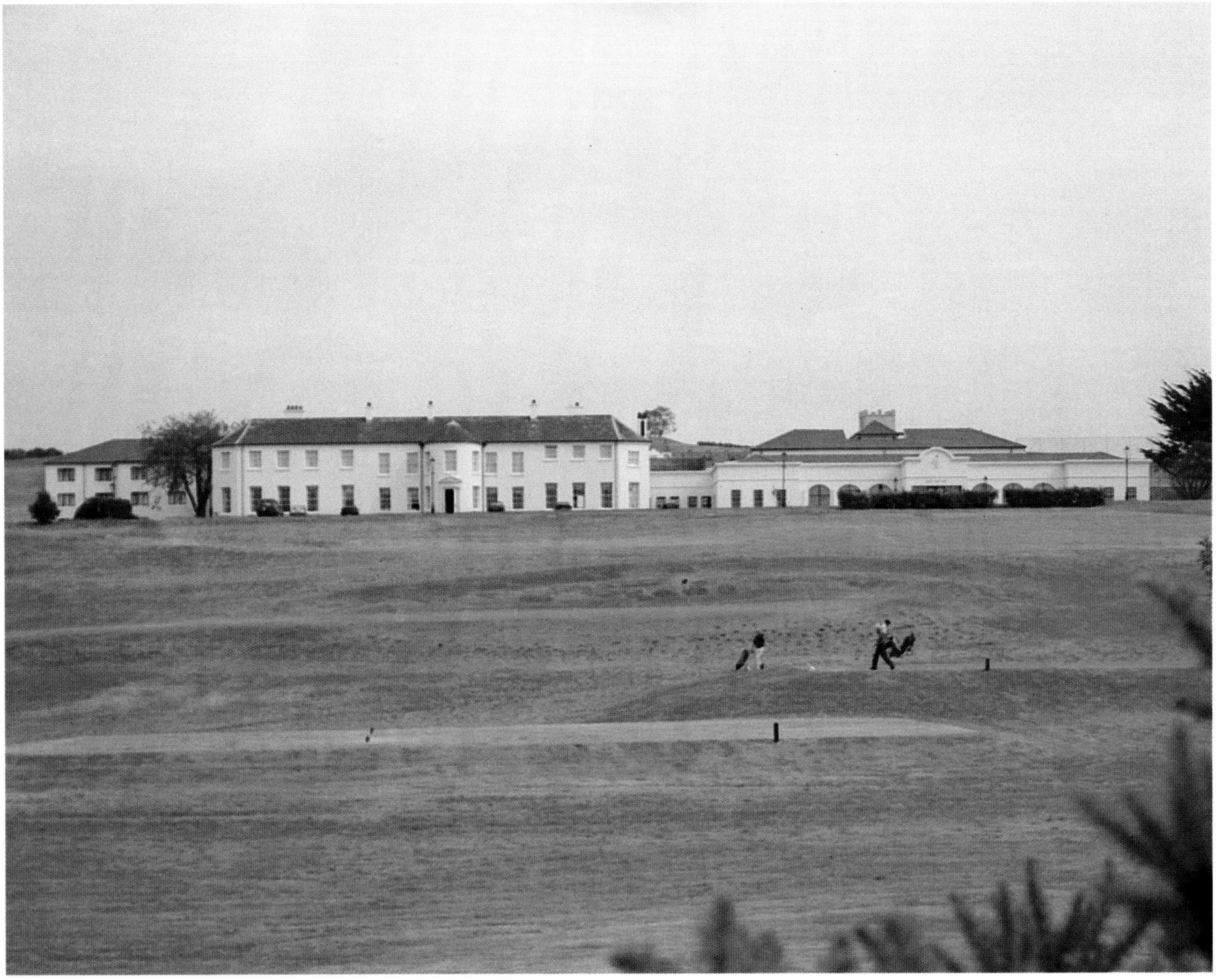

RADISSON ROE PARK HOTEL AND GOLF RESORT

ROE PARK, LIMAVADY, CO LONDONDERRY BT49 9LB
TEL: 015047 22212 FAX: 015047 22313

Situated amidst the beautiful Roe Valley countryside with mountains to the south and Lough Foyle and the sea to the north, Radisson Roe Park Hotel brings together the atmosphere and elegance of the historic Irish country house with the best of today's international hotel facilities. Guests enjoy bedrooms whose furnishings include everything from satellite television and a trouser press to an iron and tea and coffee making facilities. Fresh seafood from Donegal's Atlantic coast, succulent lamb from the hill farms of the Sperrins, the finest game and poultry and tempting deserts are enhanced by outstanding presentation in the Courtyard Restaurant. Golfers can practice on the hotel's driving range and tuition is available from a PGA professional. A fully equipped leisure club has a heated swimming pool and a wide range of health, beauty and fitness facilities. Radisson Roe Park is the ideal base from which to discover some of the best countryside in Ireland. The legendary Giant's Causeway and Glenveagh National Park are short distances away. Benone Strand's award-winning beach is close to the hotel and there is fishing at nearby Roe Valley Country Park. Directions: On the A2 road, 16 miles from Londonderry and one mile from Limavady. **Price guide:** Single £75-£85; double/twin £90-£120; suite £120–£150.

For hotel location, see maps on pages 477-483

Dromoland Castle

NEWMARKET-ON-FERGUS, SHANNON AREA, CO CLARE
TEL: 061 368144 FAX: 061 363355 TELEX: 70654

Dromoland Castle, just 8 miles from Shannon Airport, is one of the most famous baronial castles in Ireland, dating from the 16th century. Dromoland was the ancestral seat of the O'Briens, direct descendants of Irish King Brian Boru. Priceless reminders of its past are everywhere: in the splendid wood and stone carvings, magnificent panelling, oil paintings and romantic gardens. The 73 en suite guest rooms and suites are all beautifully furnished. Stately halls and an elegant dining room are all part of the Dromoland experience. The new Dromoland International Centre is one of Europe's most comprehensive conference venues, hosting groups of up to 450. Classical cuisine is prepared by award-winning chef David McCann. Fishing, 18-hole golf and boating are all available on the estate, while activities nearby include riding, shooting and golf on some of Ireland's other foremost courses. The castle is an ideal base from which to explore this breathtakingly beautiful area. Dromoland Castle is a Relais et Châteaux member. From UK phone 00 353 61 368144. **Directions:** Take the N18 to Newmarket-on-Fergus, go two miles beyond the village and the hotel entrance is on the right-hand side. Price guide: Double/twin IR£121–IR£255; suite IR£300–IR£430.

For hotel location, see maps on pages 477-483

HUNTER'S HOTEL

NEWRATH BRIDGE, RATHNEW, CO WICKLOW
TEL: 0404 40106 FAX: 0404 40338 E-MAIL: hunters@indigo.ie

Hunter's Hotel, one of Ireland's oldest coaching inns, has been established for over 275 years, since the days of post horses and carriages. Run by the same family for five generations, the hotel has built up a strong tradition based on good food, comfortable surroundings and unique, old-world charm. Set in one of Ireland's most beautiful counties, the hotel stands in gardens bordering the River Vartry. All the rooms retain the character of bygone days, with antique furniture, open fires, fresh flowers and polished brass. Most of the 16 attractive bedrooms overlook the gardens. In 1806 John Carr, traveller and author of *The Stranger in Ireland* wrote: 'Here we took a fresh chaise and proceeded to Newrath Bridge where we found an old but comfortable inn. This spot we made our headquarters and strongly recommended them to every future Wicklow wanderer.' When these words were written, John Hunter, a direct ancestor of the present owners – the Gelletlie family – was in charge. Today Hunter's Hotel continues to be recommended by leading international guides, as it upholds the tradition of providing good hospitality for travellers. From the UK phone 00 353 404 40106. **Directions:** Take N11 to Rathnew; turn left just before village on Dublin side. Price guide: Single IR£45–IR£70; double/twin IR£90–IR£120.

For hotel location, see maps on pages 477-483

KELLY'S RESORT HOTEL

ROSSLARE, CO. WEXFORD, IRELAND
TEL: 353 32114 FAX: 353 32222

Situated beside the long, sandy beach at Rosslare, Kelly's is very much a family hotel, now managed by the fourth generation of Kellys. With a firm reputation as one of Ireland's finest hotels, based on a consistently high standard of service, Kelly's extends a warm welcome to its guests, many of whom return year after year. The public rooms are tastefully decorated and feature a collection of carefully selected paintings. The Carmen Bar, with its soft lighting and grand piano, is the perfect venue for pre-dinner drinks. All bedrooms have been refurbished and extended in the last three years and have en suite facilities. The hotel restaurant is highly regarded for its superb cuisine, served with great attention to detail. An extensive wine list includes individual estate wines imported directly from France. Children are catered for with special menus and mealtimes. Ireland's Egon Ronay Hotel of the Year 1995. For exercise and relaxation, guests have the use of the hotel's new Aqua Club, with two swimming pools and a range of water and health facilities including hydro massage, 'swimming lounge', plunge pool and hot tub, also a beauty salon. Golfers have courses at Rosslare and Wexford, which has an excellent shopping centre. Places of interest nearby include the Irish National Heritage Park at Ferrycarrig. **Directions:** Follow signs to Rosslare. Price guide: Single IR£63; double/twin IR£100–IR£120.

99 rms MasterCard VISA AMERICAN EXPRESS M 20

For hotel location, see maps on pages 477-483

TINAKILLY HOUSE HOTEL

RATHNEW, WICKLOW, CO WICKLOW
TEL: 0404 69274 FAX: 0404 67806

Less than an hour's drive from Dublin, romantic hideaway Tinakilly House stands on seven acres of beautifully landscaped gardens overlooking the Irish Sea. Tinakilly was built by Captain Halpin, the man who, as Commander of the *Great Eastern*, laid the transatlantic telegraph cables in the 1860s. Tinakilly is now a luxury country house and restaurant, where owners William and Bee Power create a house-party atmosphere for guests. The bedrooms, including three suites, are a perfect blend of Victorian splendour and modern comfort and most offer breathtaking views. Superb country house cooking is augmented by an excellent wine cellar. Open all year round, Tinakilly offers special short break packages to take advantage of the many wonderful gardens, touring (Ballykissangel), and historic attractions of County Wicklow. Top class golf courses including European Club and Druid's Glen are nearby. Business meetings are welcome. A brochure, suggesting a variety of sporting pursuits and evening entertainment is available. A Small Luxury Hotel of the World, Tinakilly is also an AA Red Star, ITB 4 Star, RAC Blue Ribbon hotel. From the UK phone 00 353 404 69274. **Directions:** Take the N11 from Dublin to Rathnew village. The hotel is 500 metres outside the village. Dublin 29 miles; Dunlaoighaire ferryport 20 miles. Price guide: Single IR£96–IR£104; double/twin IR£116–IR£160; suites IR£180–IR£200.

For hotel location, see maps on pages 477-483

PARTNERS IN WINE
JOHANSENS GUIDES AND THE AOC WINES OF FRANCE
Johansens' guests demand the best things in life; first class travel, luxurious hotels, gourmet menus and the finest wines. Which is why you will find such a vast range of French wines on offer at Johansens' hotels, inns and country houses. Recognised as the best in the world and certainly the most imitated, French wines are the ideal partners for your stay at your favourite Johansens hotel or inn.
With such a huge choice of tastes and flavours, selecting the right wine for each occasion can be daunting. But treat it as a voyage of discovery or great adventure and mulling over the "Carte des Vins" could well become one of the highlights of your stay.
The first thing to look for are the words "Appellation d'Origine Contrôlée" on the label. These signify that the wine has been produced in accordance with a strict set of regulations laid down by the French wine governing bodies. They are your guarantee that the wine in the bottle must be exactly as it is described: the grapes must be cultivated in a strictly defined geographical area, they must be certain allowed varieties, the wine must reach a minimum alcohol level and only a set amount of wine per hectare can be produced. While this guarantee of authenticity doesn't come cheap, you can be sure that you are getting excellent value for the money you spend.
Then, look for the region. In general terms, wines produced further north such as Alsace, Champagne and the Loire are lighter and more suited to delicate dishes. Bordeaux, Languedoc and Rhône in the south of France produce bigger wines, which stand up better to robust foods such as game and casseroles.
Bordeaux and south-west wines, as well as Loire wines, such as Saumur-Champigny and Bourgueil are perfect partners for lamb. Seafood and fish, especially salmon, find their soulmate in Loire whites, such as Muscadet, Vouvray and Touraine. The aromatic spiciness of Alsace wines, particularly Gewurztraminer, Riesling and Pinot Gris is the perfect match for the exotic flavours found in curries, Thai and Chinese dishes.
Beef cries out for red Burgundy while white Burgundy, issue of the Chardonnay grape, is sublime with smoked salmon and rich, sauced fish dishes. Beaujolais, with its heady aromas of fruit and flowers, is the ideal foil for hard cheeses such as cheddar and gruyère as well as roast chicken or pork.
Rhône wines, such as Châteauneuf-du-Pape, Crozes Hermitage and Vacqueyras need strong, meaty flavours to balance them. Game stew, jugged hare, or medallions of venison develop a whole new range of tastes when accompanied by these peppery wines.
Puddings meet their match in France's sweet wines; luscious, rich Muscat de Rivesaltes, fruity, delicate Coteaux du Layon or sumptuous, full Sauternes.
So to find your perfect partner during a visit to Johansens just look for the best, French AOC wines.
VINS de FRANCE

Johansens Recommended Hotels in the Channel Islands

With a wealth of wonderful scenery, magnificent coastlines, historic buildings, natural and man-made attractions plus mouthwatering local produce, the Channel Islands provide a memorable destination that's distinctly different.

Throughout their history, the Channel Islands have been closely linked with France, and, being so far south, claim higher sunshine rates than even the sunniest resorts on the south coast of England.

Both islands offer VAT and duty-free shopping, the official language is English, passports are not required and both islands can be reached by sea from Weymouth or any one of about 30 airports in Britain and Europe.

And don't forget the other islands. Herm has dazzling beaches, Sark lives in a rural timewarp without traffic and Alderney's cobbled streets, pretty cottages and Victorian forts are another world again.

Many of the Johansens Recommended establishments in the Channel Islands are able to make travel arrangements for you.

JERSEY

The most southerly of the Channel Islands, Jersey, is just twelve miles from the French coast and measures only nine miles by five.

With over 50 miles of magnificent coastline ranging from cliffs, which rise above 400 feet in some parts, to wide stretches of golden sand, Jersey is an island of immense variety of landscapes and great beauty.

As both a major international finance centre and a popular holiday destination, one of Jersey's many charms is that although it has an area of just 45 square miles, there are miles of peaceful country lanes in the island's rural interior which are ideal for exploring by foot or bicycle.

The creation of a network of 'green lanes' is an exciting new idea with leisure and the environment in mind. The designated lanes have a speed limit of 15 miles per hour and pedestrians, cyclists and horse-riders take precedence over motorists.

World-wide recognition has been achieved for Jersey's clean bathing water and beaches following the British Airways Tourism for Tomorrow award given to the island's Bellozane treatment plant, which ensures that no untreated sewage is allowed into the sea.

Jersey's sightseeing has much to offer. This small island is home to one of the world's most famous zoos, founded by the late Gerald Durrell, and is also home to one of the world's foremost collection of orchids at the Eric Young Orchid Foundation.

The island is steeped in history with forts, castles and museums to explore. Mont Orgueil Castle overlooking Gorey Harbour, is one of Europe's finest castles, and well worth a visit, as is the German Underground Hospital, a chilling reminder of the island's occupation during World War II.

Islanders celebrated the 50th anniversary of their liberation with a commemorative tapestry which can be seen at the Occupation Tapestry Gallery. The colour tapestry consists of 12 panels, one from each of the island's parishes, depicting island life during the occupation and liberation.

Good food has been one of Jersey's attractions for many years and the island has built up an international reputation for its range of restaurants and cooking styles. The widespread use of fresh local seafood and produce, a friendly welcome and outstanding value all provide a memorable dining experience whether in a gourmet restaurant, country pub, or beach café. The annual Jersey Good Food Festival, held in early summer, is a must for food lovers.

Jersey's reputation as the 'floral island' is celebrated each July with the Jersey Floral Festival. This is an essential event for gardening enthusiasts with opportunities to meet top TV and radio gardening experts, visit private open gardens, watch demonstrations and enjoy floral walks and talks.

GUERNSEY

Guernsey, washed by the last tides of the Gulf stream, is smaller than Jersey, being around twenty-five square miles. 59,000 islanders support a successful and self-sufficient economy that mingles offshore finance with tourism and horticulture. Unemployment and taxes are low while the quality of life is high. Traditional values are respected (the pubs remain closed on Sundays) and there is little crime.

Visitors soon notice signs of Guernsey's independent status; the post boxes are royal blue, the telephone kiosks yellow and you may get a £1 note in your change, but the differences don't end there. The Channel Islands were the only part of the British Isles to be occupied by the Germans in World War II, and the coastline bristles with fortifications now being developed as heritage sites. There are also museums, castles, art galleries and the remarkable house where Victor Hugo lived and wrote 'Les Miserables'.

French style farmhouses in verdant little valleys speckled with cows, fishermen's cottages peeping over the sea wall at sandy beaches and rocky coves, the hillside capital, St Peter Port, commanding spectacular views across the harbour and islands of Sark and Herm. These are the impressions that visitors take away, along with memories of fresh seafood (for gourmets, the island's annual restaurant festival is held in April) and cliff top walks among the wildflowers.

INFORMATION SUPPLIED BY:

Jersey Tourism
Liberation Square
St Helier
Jersey JE1 1BB
Tel: 01534 500700

Guernsey Tourist Board
PO BOX 23
St Peter Port
Guernsey GY1 3AN
Tel: 01481 723552

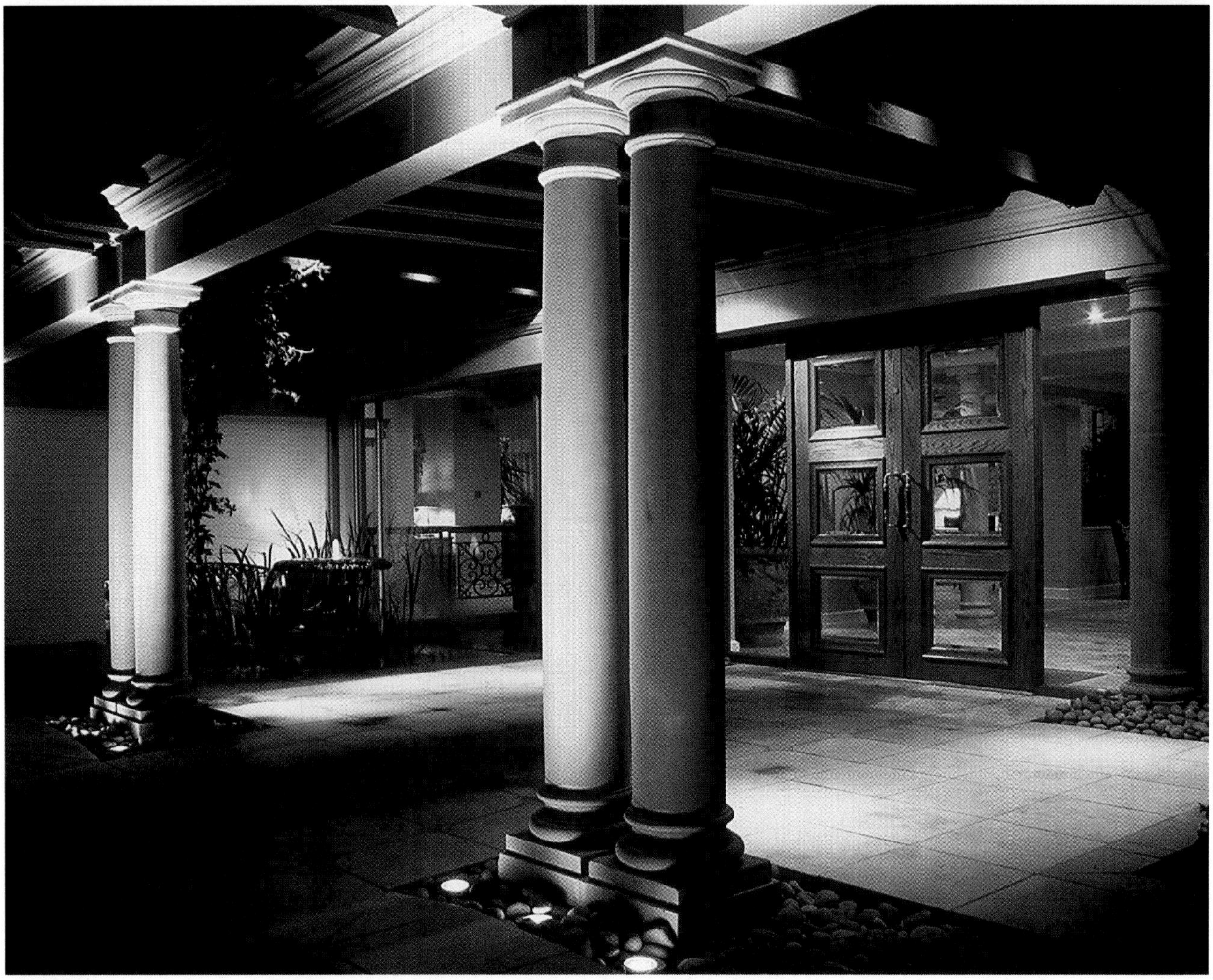

THE ATLANTIC HOTEL

LA MOYE, ST BRELADE, JERSEY JE3 8HE
TEL: 01534 44101 FAX: 01534 44102

A major refurbishment programme in 1994 has transformed this modern building into one with classical warmth and style internally. Privately owned and supervised, every aspect of the four-star service matches its location overlooking the five-mile sweep of St Ouen's Bay. Situated in three acres of private grounds alongside La Moye Golf Course, there is something here for everyone. General Manager, Simon Dufty and his team provide the highest standards of welcome and service. The 50 bedrooms are furnished in the style of the 18th century and like the public rooms, all have co-ordinated colours and fabrics. All have picture windows with views of the sea or the golf course. There are luxury suites and garden studios within the hotel as well. The award-winning restaurant, beautifully situated overlooking the open air pool and terrace, specialises in modern British cooking created by Head Chef, Tom Sleigh. For the more energetic guest, or those wishing to lose excess calories, The Atlantic has extensive indoor health and leisure facilities in The Palm Club including an indoor ozone treated pool. The hotel is an ideal spot from which to walk on the beach or coast paths, to play golf, go riding or just relax. There are comprehensive meeting facilities. **Directions:** Off a private drive off the A13 at La Pulente, two miles from the airport. Price guide: Single £75; double/twin £110; suite £175.

For hotel location, see maps on pages 477-483

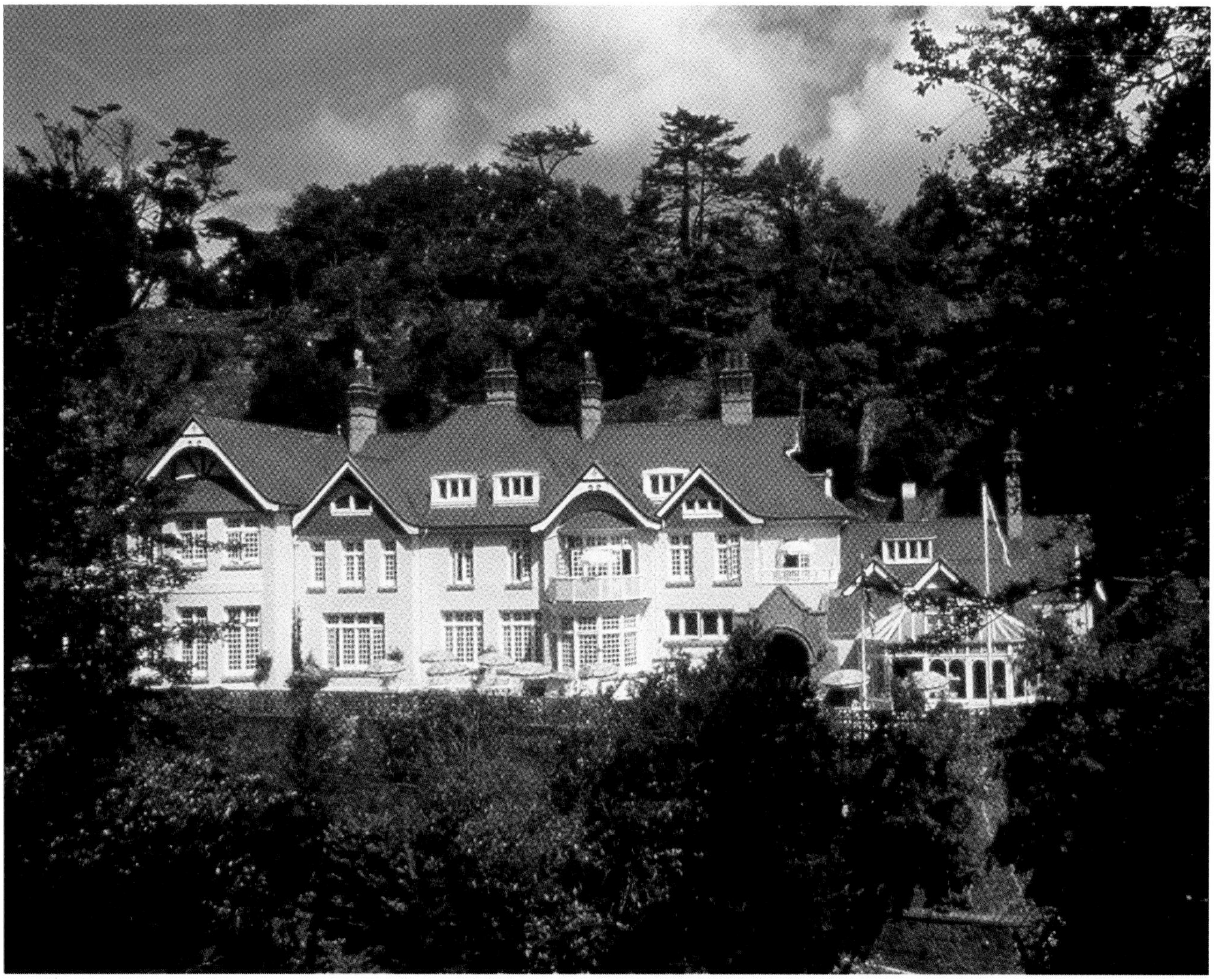

CHATEAU LA CHAIRE

ROZEL BAY, JERSEY JE3 6AJ
TEL: 01534 863354 FAX: 01534 865137

Nestling on the Rozel Valley's sunny slopes is Chateau La Chaire, an elegantly proportioned Victorian house surrounded by terraced gardens. Built in 1843, the Chateau has been enhanced and transformed into a luxurious hotel providing its guests with a superb blend of superior comfort, service and cuisine. Each of the bedrooms has been furnished to the highest standards and offers an impressive array of personal comforts many en suite bathrooms feature Jacuzzis. The same attention to detail is evident in the public rooms, such as the splendid rococo lounge. The atmophere throughout the hotel is enhanced by the exceptional personal service that its residents receive. Both adventurous and traditional dishes can be enjoyed in the oak panelled setting of La Chaire restaurant. Seafood is a speciality, but there is plenty of choice to cater for all tastes. Awarded 3AA Red Stars and 2 AA Rosettes. A few minutes from the hotel is the picturesque Rozel Bay, a bustling fishing harbour with safe beaches close by. The island's capital, St Helier, is just six miles away. Local tours, golf, fishing and riding are among the many leisure activities that the hotel's staff will be happy to arrange for guests. **Directions:** The hotel is signposted off the main coastal road to Rozel Bay, six miles north east of St Helier. Price guide: Single from £59 ; double/twin from £85; suites from £155.

For hotel location, see maps on pages 477-483

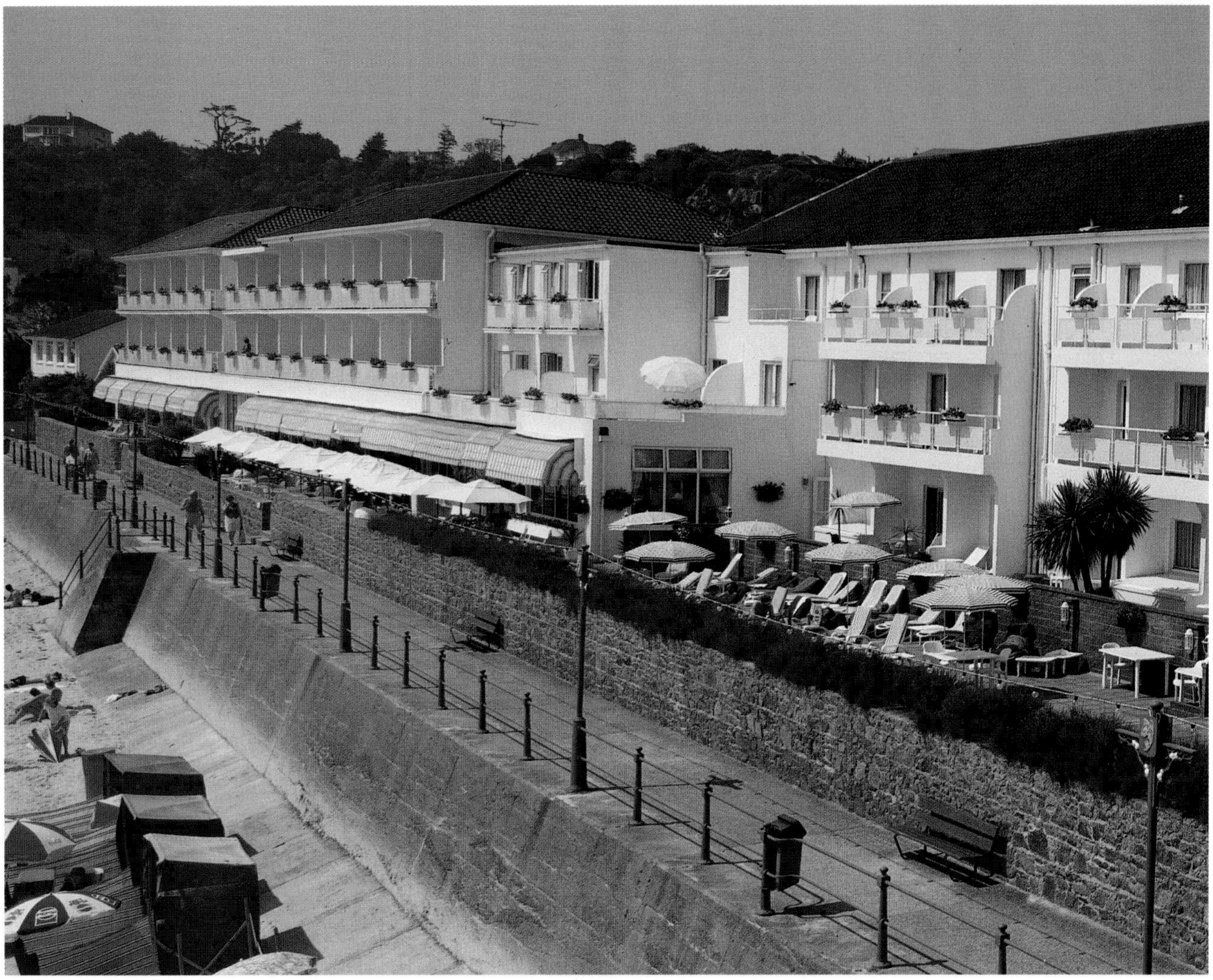

HOTEL L'HORIZON

ST BRELADE'S BAY, JERSEY, CHANNEL ISLANDS

TEL: 01534 43101 FAX: 01534 46269

A premier hotel in the Channel Islands, L'Horizon is situated on Jersey's lovely St Brelade's Bay. Its south facing position ensures that the hotel enjoys many hours of sunshine. A variety of reception areas provides guests with a choice of environments in which to sit and relax. Comfortable and spacious bedrooms provide every modern amenity and many enjoy a wonderful view across the bay. All sea facing bedrooms have balconies. There are three restaurants, each noted for its individual style, the informal Brasserie, the traditional and elegant Crystal Room and the intimate Grill Room. L'Horizon has won many international accolades and its menus are compiled from the best fresh Jersey produce and from speciality ingredients from the world's top markets.In summer, relax and sip your favourite cocktails enjoying the panoramic views from the terrace. Guests are invited to take advantage of the superb facilities of the Club L'Horizon, which include a mini gym, large swimming pool, steam room, sauna and hairdressing salon. Activities available nearby are swimming, walking, and golf. There are two 18-hole golf courses on the island. Seafarers can go on boat trips round the island or across to Guernsey, Alderney, Herm, Sark, even France **Directions:** In the heart of St Brelade's Bay, ten minutes from the airport. Price guide: Single from £100; double/twin from £150. Special breaks available.

For hotel location, see maps on pages 477-483

HOTEL LA PLACE

ROUTE DU COIN, LA HAULE, ST BRELADE, JERSEY JE3 8BF
TEL: 01534 44261 FAX: 01534 45164

Originally an ancient farmhouse first mentioned in the King's Rentes of 1640, Hotel La Place embodies all the charm that derives from pink granite lintels and corner stones, large fireplaces and wood beams. A stone in the south facing courtyard is carved with the initials of François de la Place, who owned the building in the 19th century and lends his name to the hotel. The bedrooms have been recently upgraded and offer pleasant decor and comfortable furnishings. All ground floor rooms have direct access to the swimming pool patio. The Knights Restaurant enjoys a good reputation for its high culinary standards and although the style of the hotel is largely informal, gentlemen are requested to wear a jacket and tie at dinner. Hotel La Place provides a choice of extensive menus – table d'hôte and à la carte. Personal requests are welcomed. The hotel is well placed to allow guests to enjoy the delights of Jersey which include an exceptional variety of land and seascapes, superb beaches, craggy cliffs and bays, valleys and wood. **Directions:** Contact the hotel direct for advice on air and sea travel. Hotel La Place is five minutes from the airport and 20 minutes from St Helier. Price guide: Single £55–£75; double/twin £70–£100; suites £110–£160.

For hotel location, see maps on pages 477-483

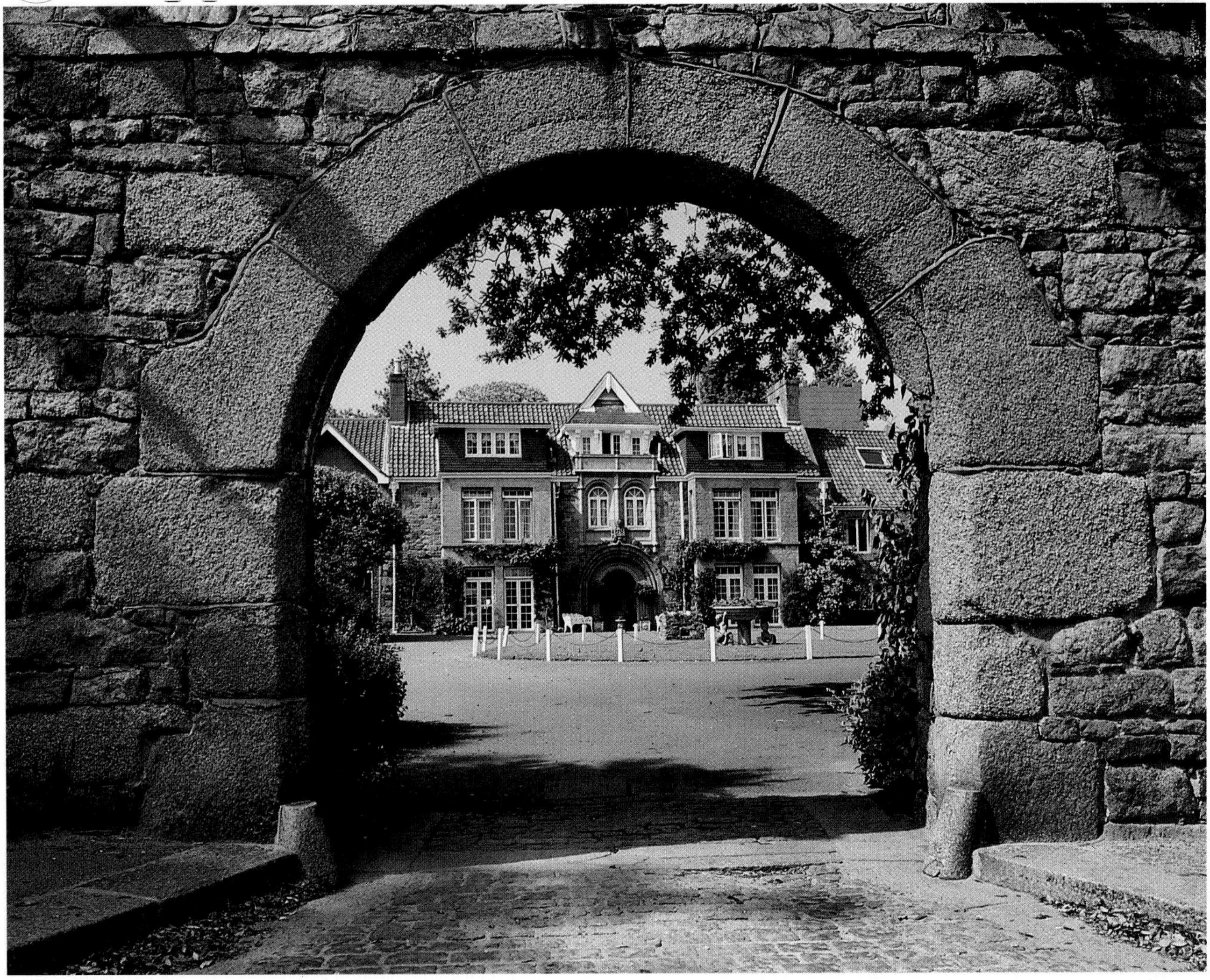

LONGUEVILLE MANOR

ST SAVIOUR, JERSEY JE2 7WF

TEL: 01534 25501 FAX: 01534 31613 E-MAIL: longman@itl.net

Three generations of the Lewis family have welcomed guests to Longueville Manor for more than forty years. For their endeavours, Longueville was deservedly named the 1991 Egon Ronay Hotel of the Year. Set in 15 acres at the foot of its private wooded valley, the manor has stood here since the 13th century. Nowadays, in the comfort of exquisitely decorated rooms and surrounded by beautiful floral displays, fine antique furnishings and elegant fabrics, guests are pampered by attentive staff. The ancient, oak-panelled dining room sports an array of silver trophies awarded for excellent cuisine. Many of the fruits, vegetables, herbs and flowers are grown in the walled kitchen gardens, which include hothouses to provide fresh produce that would otherwise be out of season. Wines from all over the world are stocked in the expertly managed cellars. Each bedroom is individually decorated with flair and imagination – separate sitting areas have books, magazines, flowers and fresh fruit. By the heated swimming pool, a bar and service area offer a special alfresco menu in the summer months. Beyond this, a stream trickles down a hillside into a lake, with black swans and mandarin ducks completing the picture. Longueville Manor is a Relais et Châteaux hotel. **Directions:** On the A3, one mile from St Helier. Price guide: Single from £115; double/twin £150; suite £275.

For hotel location, see maps on pages 477-483

Johansens Recommended Inns With Restaurants in Great Britain

ENGLAND

Amberley,Near Arundel – The Boathouse Brasserie, Houghton Bridge, Amberley, West Sussex, BN18 9LR. 01798 831059

Ambleside (Great Langdale) – New Dungeon Ghyll Hotel, Great Langdale, Ambleside, Cumbria, LA22 9JY. 015394 37213

Appleby-In-Westmorland – Royal Oak Inn, Bongate, Appleby-In-Westmorland, Cumbria, CA16 6UN. 017683 51463

Ashbourne (Waterhouses) – Old Beams Restaurant with Rooms, Waterhouses, Staffordshire, ST10 3HW. 01538 308254

Askrigg (Wensleydale) – Kings Arms Hotel And Restaurant, Market Place, Askrigg-In-Wensleydale, Askrigg-In-Wensleydale, North Yorkshire, DL8 3HQ. 01969 650258

Badby Nr Daventry – Windmill At Badby, Main Street, Badby, Northamptonshire, NN11 6AN. 01327 702363

Barnard Castle (Greta Bridge) – Morritt Arms Hotel, Greta Bridge, County Durham, DL12 9SE. 01833 627232

Beckington Nr Bath – Woolpack Inn, Beckington, B & NE Somerset, BA3 6SP. 01373 831244

Belbroughton – Freshmans Restaurant, Church Hill, Belbroughton, Worcestershire, DY9 0DT. 01562 730467

Belford – Blue Bell Hotel, Market Place, Belford, Northumberland, NE70 7NE. 01668 213543

Blakeney – White Horse Hotel, 4 High Street, Blakeney, Holt, Norwich, NR25 7AL. 01263 740574

Boroughbridge – Crown Hotel, Horsefair, Boroughbridge, North Yorkshire, YO5 9LB. 01423 322328.

Bourton-On-The-Water – Old Manse, Victoria Street, Bourton-On-The-Water, Gloucestershire, GL54 2BX. 01451 820082

Bridport (West Bexington) – Manor Hotel, West Bexington, Dorchester, Dorset, DT2 9DF. 01308 897616

Broadway – Broadway Hotel, The Green, Broadway, Worcestershire, WR12 7AA. 01386 852401

Burford – Lamb Inn, Sheep Street, Burford, Oxfordshire, OX18 4LR. 01993 823155

Burford – Cotswold Gateway Hotel, Cheltenham Road, Burford, Oxfordshire, OX18 4HX. 01993 822695

Burnham Market – Hoste Arms Hotel, The Green, Burnham Market, Norfolk, PE31 8HD. 01328 738777

Burnley (Fence) – Fence Gate Inn, Wheatley Lane Road, Fence, Lancashire, BB12 9EE. 01282 618101

Burnsall (Skipton) – Red Lion, By the bridge at Burnsall, North Yorkshire, BD23 6BU. 01756 720204

Burton Upon Trent (Branston) – Old Vicarage Restaurant, Main Street, Branston, Burton Upon Trent, Staffordshire, DE14 3EX. 01283 533222

Burton Upon Trent (Sudbury) – Boar's Head Hotel, Lichfield Road, Sudbury, Derbyshire, DE6 5GX. 01283 820344

Calver,Nr Bakewell – Chequers Inn, Froggatt Edge, Derbyshire, S30 1ZB. 01433 630231

Camborne – Tyacks Hotel, 27 Commercial Street, Camborne, Cornwall, TR14 8LD. 01209 612424

Cambridge – Panos Hotel & Restaurant, 154-156 Hills Road, Cambridge, Cambridgeshire, CB2 2PB. 01223 212958

Carlisle (Talkin Tarn) – Tarn End House Hotel, Talkin Tarn, Brampton, Cumbria, CA8 1LS. 01677 2340

Castle Ashby – Falcon Hotel, Castle Ashby, Northampton, Northamptonshire, NN7 1LF. 01604 696200

Castle Cary – George Hotel, Market Place, Castle Cary, Somerset, BA7 7AH. 01963 350761

Castle Combe – Castle Inn, Castle Combe, Wiltshire, SN14 7HN. 01249 783030

Castleton – Ye Olde Nags Head Hotel, Cross Street, Castleton, Derbyshire, S30 2WH. 01433 620248

Cheltenham (Birdlip) – Kingshead House Restaurant, Birdlip, Gloucestershire, GL4 8JH. 01452 862299

Chester (Higher Burwardsley) – Pheasant Inn, Higher Burwardsley, Tattenhall, Chester, Cheshire, CH3 9PF. 01829 770434

Chester (Tarporley) – Wild Boar Hotel & Restaurant, Whitchurch Road, Near Beeston, Tarporley, CW6 9NW. 01829 260309

Chipping Campden (Broad Campden) – Noel Arms, High Street, Chipping Campden, Gloucestershire, GL55 6AT. 01386 840317

Cirencester (Colne St-Aldwyns) – New Inn, Colne St-Aldwyns, Gloucestershire, GL7 5AN. 01285 750651

Cirencester (Meysey Hampton) – Masons Arms, Meysey Hampton, Gloucestershire, gl7 5jT. 01285 850164

Clavering (Stansted) – Cricketers, Clavering, Essex, CB11 4QT. 01799 550442

Cleobury Mortimer – Crown At Hopton, Hopton Wafers, Cleobury Mortimer, Worcestershire, DY14 0NB. 01299 270372

Cleobury Mortimer – Redfern Hotel, Cleobury Mortimer, Shropshire, DY14 8AA. 01299 270 395

Clovelly – New Inn Hotel, High Street, Clovelly, Devon, EX39 5TQ. 01237 431303

Cockermouth – Trout Hotel, Crown Street, Cockermouth, Cumbria, CA13 0EY. 01900 823591

Colchester – Red Lion, High Street, Colchester, Essex CO1 1DJ. 01206 577986

Dorchester-On-Thames – George Hotel, High Street, Dorchester-On-Thames, Oxford, OX9 8HH. 01865 340404

Dronfield – Manor House Hotel & Restaurant, High Street, Old Dronfield, Derbyshire, SY18 6PY. 01246 413971

Dulverton (Exbridge) – Anchor Country Inn & Hotel, Exbridge, Somerset, TA22 9AZ. 01398 323433

Easington (Long Crendon) – Mole & Chicken, The Terrace, Long Crendon, Aylesbury, Buckinghamshire, HP18 9EY. 01844 208387

East Witton – Blue Lion, East Witton, North Yorkshire, DL8 4SN. 01969 624273

Egton – Wheatsheaf Inn, Egton, North Yorkshire, YO21 1TZ. 01947 895271

Evesham (Offenham) – Riverside Restaurant And Hotel, The Parks, Offenham Road, Worcestershire, WR11 5JP. 01386 446200

Exlade Street (Checkendon) – Highwayman, Exlade Street, Checkendon, Berkshire, RG8 0UA. 01491 682020

Exmoor – Royal Oak Inn, Winsford, Exmoor National Park, Somerset, TA24 7JE. 01643 851455

Falmouth (Constantine) – Trengilly Wartha Country Inn & Restaurant, Nancenoy, Constantine, Falmouth, Cornwall, TR11 5RP. 01326 40332

Ford, Nr Bath – White Hart, Ford, Chippenham, Wiltshire, SN14 8RP. 01249 782213

Fordingbridge (New Forest) – Woodfalls Inn, The Ridge, Woodfalls, Fordingbridge, Hampshire, SP5 2LN. 01725 513222

Fulbeck (Lincoln) – Hare & Hounds, The Green, Fulbeck, Lincolnshire, NG32 3SS. 01400 272090

Goathland – Mallyan Spout Hotel, Goathland, North Yorkshire, YO22 5AN. 01947 896486

Godalming – The Inn On The Lake, Ockford Road, Godalming, Surrey, GU7 1RH. 01483 415575

Goring-On-Thames – Leatherne Bottel Riverside Inn & Restaurant, The Bridleway, Goring-On-Thames, Berkshire, RG8 0HS. 01491 872667

Great Yeldham – White Hart, Great Yeldham, Halstead, Essex, CO9 4HJ. 01787 237250

Grimsthorpe (Bourne) – Black Horse Inn, Grimsthorpe, Bourne, Lincolnshire, PE10 0LY. 01778 591247

Grindleford – Maynard Arms, Main Road, Grindleford, Derbyshire, S30 1HP. 01433 630321

Halifax/Huddersfield – Rock Inn Hotel, Holywell Green, Halifax, West Yorkshire, HX4 9Bs. 01422 379721

Handcross (Slaugham) – Chequers At Slaugham, Slaugham, West Sussex, RH17 6AQ. 01444 400239/400996

Hathersage – Plough Inn, Leadmill Bridge, Hathersage, Derbyshire, S30 1BA. 01433 650319

Hawkshead – Red Lion Inn, Hawkshead, Ambleside, Cumbria, LA22 0MV. 015394 36213

Haworth – Old White Lion Hotel, Haworth, Keighley, West Yorkshire, BD22 8DU. 01535 642313

Hayfield (Birch Vale) – The Waltzing Weasel, New Mills Road, Birch Vale, Hayfield, Derbyshire, SK12 5BT. 01663 743402

Helmsley – Feversham Arms Hotel, Helmsley, North Yorkshire, YO6 5AG. 01439 770766

Henley (Ibstone) – Fox Country Hotel, Ibstone, Buckinghamshire, HP14 3GG. 01491 638289

Hinkley (Nr Leicester) – Barnacles Restaurant, Watlins Street, Leicestershire, LE10 3JA. 01455 633220

Honiton (Wilmington) – Home Farm Hotel, Wilmington, Devon, EX14 9JQ. 01404 831278

Horndon-on-the-Hill – Bell Inn and Hill House, High Road, Horndon-on-the-Hill, Essex, SS17 8LD. 01375 642463

Kingsbury (Sutton Coldfield) – Marston Farm Hotel, Bodymoor Heath, Sutton Coldfield, Warwickshire, B76 9JD. 01827 872133

Kirkby Lonsdale (Casterton) – Pheasant Inn, Casterton, Kirkby Lonsdale, Cumbria, LA26 2RX. 015242 71230

Kirkby Lonsdale – The Snooty Fox, Main Street, Kirkby Lonsdale, Cumbria, LA6 2AH. 015242 71308

Kirkby Lonsdale – Whoop Hall Inn, Burrow-With-Burrow, Kirkby Lonsdale, Cumbria, LA6 2HP. 015242 71284

Knutsford – Longview Hotel And Restaurant, 51/55 Manchester Road, Knutsford, Cheshire, WA16 0LX. 01565 632119

Ledbury – Feathers Hotel, High Street, Ledbury, Herefordshire, HR8 1DS. 01531 635266

Leek (Blackshaw Moor) – Three Horseshoes Inn & Restaurant, Buxton Road, Blackshaw Moor, Staffordshire, ST13 8TW. 01538 300296

Leominster (Stoke Prior) – Wheelbarrow Castle, Stoke Prior, Leominster, Herefordshire, HR6 0NB. 01568 612219

Long Melford – Countrymen, The Green, Long Melford, Suffolk, CO10 9DN. 01787 312356

Lynmouth – Rising Sun, Harbourside, Lynmouth, Devon, EX35 6EQ. 01598 753223

Maidenhead – Boulters Lock Hotel, Boulters Island, Maidenhead, Berkshire, SL6 8PE. 01628 21291

Maidstone (Ringlestone) – Ringlestone Inn, 'Twixt' Harrietsham and Wormshill, Kent, ME17 1NX. 01622 859900

Maidstone (Warren Street) – Harrow At Warren Street, Warren Street, Kent, ME17 2ED. 01622 858727

Malmesbury – Horse And Groom Inn, Charlton, Wiltshire, SN16 9DL. 01666 823904

Malton – Green Man, 15 Market Street, Malton, North Yorkshire, YO17 0LY. 01653 600370

Malton – Talbot Hotel, Yorkesgate, Malton, Malton, North Yorkshire, YO17 0AA. 01653 694031

Minchinhampton (Hyde) – Ragged Cot, Hyde, Minchinhampton, Gloucestershire, GL6 8PE. 01453 884643/731333

Montacute – King's Arms Inn & Restaurant, Montacute, Somerset, TA16 6UU. 01935 822513

Nailsworth – Egypt Mill, Gloucestershire, Gl6 0AE. 01453 833449

Newbury (Kingsclere) – Swan Hotel, Swan Street, Kingsclere, Berkshire, RG20 5PP. 01635 298314

Newby Bridge – Swan Hotel, Newby Bridge, Cumbria, LA12 8NB. 015395 31681

Norwich (Rackheath) – Garden House Hotel, Salhouse Road, Rackheath, Norwich, Norfolk, NR13 6AA. 01603 720007

Nottingham – Hotel Des Clos, Old Lenton Lane, Nottingham, Nottinghamshire, NG7 2SA. 0115 9866566

Oakham – Whipper-in-Hotel, Market Square, Oakham, Rutland, Leicestershire, LE15 6DT. 01572 756971.

Onneley – Wheatsheaf Inn At Onneley And La Puerta Del Sol Restaurante Espanol, Barhill Road, Onneley, Staffordshire, CW3 9QF. 01782 751581

Oxford (Banbury) – Holcombe Hotel, High Street, Deddington, Oxfordshire, OX15 0SL. 01869 338274

Oxford (Middleton Stoney) – Jersey Arms, Middleton Stoney, Oxfordshire, OX6 8SE. 01869 343234

Oxford (Minster Lovell) – Mill & Old Swan, Minster Lovell, Oxfordshire, OX8 5RN. 01993 774441

Oxford (Stanton-St-John) – Talkhouse, Wheatley Road, Stanton-St-John, Oxfordshire, OX33 1EX. 01865 351648

Padstow – Old Custom House Hotel, South Quay, Padstow, Cornwall, PL28 8ED. 01841 532359

Pelynt, Nr Looe – Jubilee Inn, Pelynt, Cornwall, PL13 2JZ. 01503 220312

Peterborough (Eye) – Ristorante I Toscanini, 2 Peterborough Road, Eye, Cambridgeshire, PE6 7YB. 01733 223221

Petworth (Sutton) – White Horse Inn, Sutton, West Sussex, RH20 1PS. 01798 869 221

Pickering – White Swan, The Market Place, Pickering, North Yorkshire, YO18 7AA. 01751 472288

Port Gaverne – Port Gaverne Hotel, North Cornwall, PL29 3SQ. 01208 880244

Porthleven (Nr Helston) – Harbour Inn, Commercial Road, Porthleven, Cornwall, TR13 9JD. 01326 573876

Preston (Goosnargh) – Ye Horn's Inn, Horn's Lane, Goosnargh, Lancashire, PR3 2FJ. 01772 865230

Ringwood (Ashley Heath) – Struan Country Inn and Restaurant, Horton Road, Ashley Heath, Nr Ringwood, Hampshire, BH24 2EG. 01425 473553 / 473029

Rosedale Abbey – Milburn Arms Hotel, Rosedale Abbey, Pickering, North Yokshire, YO18 8RA. 01751 417312

Rugby (Easenhall) – Golden Lion Inn of Easenall, Easenall, Warwickshire, CV23 0JA. 01788 832265

Rye – Mermaid Inn, Mermaid Street, Rye, East Sussex, TN31 7EU. 01797 223065

Saddleworth (Delph) – Old Bell Inn Hotel, Huddersfield Road, Delph, Saddleworth, Lancashire, OL3 5EG. 01457 870130

Salisbury – Milford Hall Hotel And Restaurant, 206 Castle Street, Salisbury, Wiltshire, SP1 3TE. 01722 417411

Scarborough (East Ayton) – East Ayton Lodge Country Hotel & Restaurant, Moor Lane, Forge Valley, East Ayton, Scarborough, North Yorkshire, YO13 9EW. 01723 864227

Sevenoaks – Royal Oak, High Street, Sevenoaks, Kent, TN14 5PG. 01732 451109

Sherborne (West Camel) – Walnut Tree, West Camel, Somerset, BA22 7QW. 01935 851292

Shipton Under Wychwood – Shaven Crown Hotel, High Street, Shipton Under Wychwood, Oxfordshire, OX7 6BA. 01993 830330

Southport (Formby) – Tree Tops Country House Restaurant & Hotel, Southport Old Road, Formby, Mersyside, L37 0AB. 01704 879651

St Austell – White Hart Hotel, Church Street, St Austell, Cornwall, PL25 4AT. 01726 72100

St Mawes – Rising Sun, The Square, St Mawes, Cornwall, TR2 5DJ. 01326 270233

Stow-On-The-Wold – Royalist Hotel, Digbeth Street, Stow-On-The-Wold, Gloucestershire, GL54 1BN. 01451 830670

Stow-On-The-Wold (Bledington) – Kings Head Inn & Restaurant, The Green, Bledington, Oxfordshire, OX7 6HD. 01608 658365

Stow-on-the-Wold (Oddington) – Horse and Groom, Upper Oddington, Moreton-in-Marsh, Gloucestershire, GL56 0XH. 01451 830584

Tavistock (Peter Tavy) – Peter Tavy Inn, Peter Tavy, Tavistock, Devon, PL19 9NN. 01822 810348

Telford (Norton) – Hundred House Hotel, Bridgnorth Road,Norton, Nr Shifnal, Telford, Shropshire, TF11 9EE. 01952 730353

Tewkesbury – Bell Hotel, Church Street, Tewkesbury, Gloucestershire, GL20 5SA. 01684 293293

Thame – Thatchers Inn, 29-30 Lower High Street, Thame, Oxfordshire, OX9 2AA. 0184421 2146

Thelbridge – Thelbridge Cross Inn, Thelbridge, Devon, EX17 4SQ. 01884 860316

Thornham – Lifeboat Inn, Ship Lane, Thornham, Norfolk, PE36 6LT. 01485 512236

Thorpe Market – Green Farm Restaurant And Hotel, North Walsham Road, Thorpe Market, Norfolk, NR11 8TH. 01263 833602

Tintagel (Trebarwith Strand) – Port William, Trebarwith Strand, PL34 0HB. 01840 770230

Torbryan Nr Totnes – Old Church House Inn, Torbryan, Ippleden, Devon TQ12 5UR. 01803 812372

Torquay (Kingskerswell) – Barn Owl Inn, Aller Mills, Kingskerswell, Devon, TQ12 5AN. 01830 872130

Totnes (Staverton) – Sea Trout Inn, Staverton, Devon, TQ9 6PA. 01803 762274

Troutbeck (Near Windermere) – Mortal Man Hotel, Troutbeck, Cumbria, LA23 1PL. 015394 33193

Tunbridge Wells – Royal Wells Inn, Mount Ephraim, Tunbridge Wells, Kent, TN4 8BE. 01892 511188

Upton-Upon-Severn, Nr Malvern – White Lion Hotel, High Street, Upton-Upon-Severn, Worcestershire, WR8 0HJ. 01684 592551

Walberswick – Anchor, Walberswick, Suffolk, IP18 6UA. 01502 722112

Wells – City Arms, High Street, Wells, Somerset, BA5 2AG. 01749 673916

Weobley – Ye Olde Salutation Inn, Market Pitch, Weobley, Herefordshire, HR4 8SJ. 01544 318443

West Witton (Wensleydale) – Wensleydale Heifer Inn, West Witton, Wensleydale, North Yorkshire, DL8 4LS. 01969 622322

Whitewell – Inn At Whitewell, Forest Of Bowland, Clitheroe, Lancashire, BB7 3AT. 01200 448222

Withypool (Exmoor) – Royal Oak Inn, Withypool, Exmoor National Park, Somerset, TA24 7QP. 01643 831506

Johansens Recommended Inns With Restaurants in Great Britain continued

Woodbridge – Bull Inn, Market Hill, Woodbridge, Suffolk, IP12 4LR. 01394 382089

Worthing (Bramber) – Old Tollgate Restaurant And Hotel, The Street, Bramber, Steyning, West Sussex, BN44 3WE. 01903 879494

Wroxham – Barton Angler Country Inn, Irstead Road, Neatishead, Norfolk, NR12 8XP. 01692 630740

Yattendon – Royal Oak Hotel, Yattendon, Newbury, Berkshire, RG18 0UG. 01635 201325

York (Easingwold) – George at Easingwold, Market Place, Easingwold, York, North Yorkshire, YO6 3AD. 01347 821698

WALES

Chepstow – Castle View Hotel, 16 Bridge Street, Chepstow, Gwent, NP6 5EZ. 01291 620349

Dolgellau (Penmaenpool) – George III Hotel, Penmaenpool, Dolgellau, Gwynedd, LL40 1YD. 01341 422525

Llanarmon Dyffryn Ceiriog – West Arms Hotel, Llanarmon D C, Denbighshire, LL20 7LD. 0169600 665

Llandeilo (Rhosmaen) – Plough Inn, Rhosmaen, Llandeilo, Carmarthenshire, SA19 6NP. 01558 823431

Welshpool (Berriew) – Lion Hotel And Restaurant, Berriew, Montgomeryshire, SY21 8PQ. 01686 640452

SCOTLAND

Banchory (Royal Deeside) – Potarch Hotel, By Banchory, Royal Deeside, Kincardineshire, AB31 4BD. 013398 84339

Blairgowrie (Glenisla) – Glenisla Hotel, Kirkton of Glenisla, By Alyth, Perthshire, PH11 8PH. 01575 582223

Isle Of Skye (Eilean Iarmain) – Hotel Eilean Iarmain or Isle Ornsay Hotel, Eilean Iarmain, Sleat, Isle Of Skye, IV43 8QR. 01471 833332

Isle Of Skye (Uig) – Uig Hotel, Uig, Isle Of Skye, Isle Of Skye, IV51 9YE. 01470 542205

Lochgilphead – Cairnbaan Hotel, By Lochgilphead, Argyll, PA31 8SJ. 01546 603668

Powmill (Nr Kinross) – Whinsmuir Country Inn, Powmill, By Dollar, FK14 7NW. 01577 840595

CHANNEL ISLANDS

Jersey (Gorey) – Moorings Hotel, Gorey Pier, Jersey, JE3 6EW. 01534 853633

Jersey (St Brelade) – Sea Crest Hotel And Restaurant, Petit Port, St Brelade, JE3 8HH. 01534 46353

Johansens Recommended Country Houses & Small Hotels in Great Britain & Ireland

ENGLAND

Alcester – Arrow Mill Hotel And Restaurant, Arrow, Warwickshire, B49 5NL. 01789 762419

Ambleside – Laurel Villa, Lake Road, Ambleside, Cumbria, LA22 0DB. 015394 33240

Ambleside (Clappersgate) – Nanny Brow Hotel, Clappersgate, Ambleside, Cumbria, LA22 9NF. 015394 32036

Appleton-Le-Moors – Appleton Hall, Appleton-Le-Moors, North Yorkshire, YO6 6TF. 01751 417227

Arundel (Burpham) – Burpham Country Hotel, Old Down, Burpham, West Sussex, BN18 9RV. 01903 882160

Ashbourne – Beeches Farmhouse, Waldley, Doveridge, Derbyshire, DE6 5LR. 01889 590288

Ashwater – Blagdon Manor Country Hotel, Ashwater, Devon, EX21 5DF. 01409 211224

Atherstone – Chapel House, Friars' Gate, Atherstone, Warwickshire, CV9 1EY. 01827 718949

Badminton – Petty France, Dunkirk, Badminton, South Gloucestershire, GL9 1AF. 01454 238361

Bakewell (Rowsley) – East Lodge Country House Hotel, Rowsley, Matlock, Derbyshire, DE4 2EF. 01629 734474

Bakewell (Rowsley) – Peacock Hotel at Rowsley, Rowsley, Derbyshire, DE4 2EB. 01629 733518

Bamburgh – Waren House Hotel, Waren Mill, Bamburgh, Northumberland, NE70 7EE. 01668 214581

Banbury (Charlton) – Home Farm House, Charlton, Oxfordshire, OX17 3DR. 01295 811683

Bath – Bloomfield House, 146 Bloomfield Road, Bath, B & NE Somerset, BA2 2AS. 01225 420105

Bath – Apsley House, 141 Newbridge Hill Road, Bath, B & NE Somerset, BA1 3PT. 01225 336966

Bath – Eagle House, Church Street, Bathford, B & NE Somerset, BA1 7RS. 01225 859946

Bath – Paradise House, Holloway, Bath, B & NE Somerset, BA2 4PX. 01225 317723

Bath – Newbridge House Hotel, Kelston Road, Bath, B & NE Somerset, BA1 3QH. 01225 446676

Bath (Bradford-On-Avon) – Widbrook Grange, Trowbridge Road, Bradford-On-Avon, Wiltshire, BA15 1UH. 01225 864750 / 863173

Bath (Norton St Philip) – Bath Lodge Hotel, Norton St Philip, Bath, B & NE Somerset, BA3 6NH. 01225 723040

Beaminster – The Lodge, Beaminster, Dorset, DT8 3BL. 01308 863468

Bedford (Barton-Le-Clay) – Fielden Farm Country House, Lower Gravehurst, Bedfordshire, MK 4HJ. 01525 861386

Beer – Bovey House, Beer, Seaton, Devon, EX12 3AD. 01297 680 241

Belper (Shottle) – Dannah Farm Country Guest House, Bowman's Lane, Shottle, Derbyshire, DE56 2DR. 01773 550273 / 630

Bibury – Bibury Court, Bibury, Gloucestershire, GL7 5NT. 01285 740337

Biggin-By-Hartington – Biggin Hall, Biggin-By-Hartington, Buxton, Derbyshire, SK17 0DH. 01298 84451

Blackpool (Singleton) – Mains Hall, Mains Lane, Little Singleton, Lancashire, FY6 7LE. 01253 885130

Blockley (Chipping Campden) – Lower Brook House, Blockley, Gloucestershire, GL56 9DS. 01386 700286

Bolton (Edgworth) – Quarton Manor Farm, Plantation Road, Turton, Bolton, Lancashire, BL7 0DD. 01204 852277

Bonchurch (Isle of Wight) – Peacock Vane Hotel, Bonchurch, Isle of Wight, PO38 1RU. 01983 852019

Bourton-On-The-Water – Dial House Hotel, The Chestnuts, High Street, Bourton-On-The-Water, Gloucestershire, GL54 2AN. 01451 822244

Bridgnorth – Cross Lane House Hotel, Astley Abbots, Bridgnorth, Shropshire, WV16 4SJ. 01746 764887

Broadway – Collin House Hotel, Collin Lane, Broadway, Worcestershire, WR12 7PB. 01386 858354/852544

Broadway (Willersey) – Old Rectory, Church Street, Willersey, Gloucestershire, WR12 7PN. 01386 853729

Brockenhurst – Thatched Cottage Hotel, 16 Brookley Road, Brockenhurst, Hampshire, SO42 7RR. 01590 623090

Brockenhurst – Whitley Ridge & Country House Hotel, Beaulieu Road, Brockenhurst, Hampshire, SO42 7QL. 01590 622354

Bury St Edmunds – Bradfield House Restaurant And Hotel, Bradfield Combust, Bury St Edmunds, Suffolk, IP30 0LR. 01284 386301

Cambridge (Melbourn) – Melbourn Bury, Melbourn, Cambridgeshire, Cambridgeshire, SG8 6DE. 01763 261151

Canterbury (Boughton under Blean) – Garden Hotel, 167-169 The Street, Boughton under Blean, Faversham, ME13 9BH. 01227 751411

Carlisle – Number Thirty One, 31 Howard Place, Carlisle, Cumbria, CA1 1HR. 01228 597080.

Carlisle (Crosby-On-Eden) – Crosby Lodge Country House Hotel, High Crosby, Crosby-On-Eden, Carlisle, Cumbria, CA6 4QZ. 01228 573618

Cartmel – Aynsome Manor Hotel, Cartmel, Grange-Over-Sands, Cumbria, LA11 6HH. 015395 36653

Castleton (Hope) – Underleigh House, Off Edale Road, Hope, Derbyshire, s30 2rf. 01433 621372

Chagford – Easton Court Hotel, Easton Cross, Chagford, Devon, TQ13 8JL. 01647 433469

Cheltenham (Charlton Kings) – Charlton Kings Hotel, Charlton Kings, Cheltenham, Gloucestershire, Gl52 6UU. 01242 231061

Cheltenham (Withington) – Halewell, Halewell Close, Withington, Gloucestershire, GL54 4BN. 01242 890238

Chester (Broxton) – Frogg Manor, Nantwich Road,Fullers Moor, Broxton, Chester, Cheshire, CH3 9JH. 01829 782629

Chipping Campden (Broad Campden) – Malt House, Broad Campden, Gloucestershire, GL55 6UU. 01386 840295

Clearwell – Tudor Farmhouse Hotel & Restaurant, High Street, Clearwell, Gloucestershire, GL16 8JS. 01594 833046

Clovelly (Horns Cross) – Foxdown Manor, Horns Cross, Devon North, EX39 5PJ. 01237 451325

Coalville (Greenhill) – Abbots Oak, Greenhill, Coalville, Leicestershire, LE67 4UY. 01530 832 328

Colchester (Frating) – Hockley Place, Frating, Colchester, Essex, CO7 7HF. 01206 251703

Coltishall (Norwich) – Norfolk Mead Hotel, Coltishall, Norwich, Norfolk, NR12 7DN. 01603 737531

Combe Martin (East Down) – Ashelford, Ashelford, East Down, Devon North, EX31 4LU. 01271 850469

Corbridge (Stocksbridge) – Glenview, 6 Meadowfield Road, Stocksfield, Northumberland, NE43 7QX. 01661 843674

Cornhill-On-Tweed – Wark Farm House, Wark, Cornhill-On-Tweed, Northumberland, TD12 4RE. 01890 883570

Dartmoor (Nr Two Bridges) – Prince Hall Hotel, Two Bridges, Dartmoor, PL20 6SA. 01822 890403

Diss – Salisbury House, Victoria Road, Diss, Norfolk, IP22 3JG. 01379 644738

Dorchester (Lower Bockhampton) – Yalbury Cottage Hotel, Lower Bockhampton, Dorchester, Dorset, DT2 8PZ. 01305 262382

Dover (Temple Ewell) – Woodville Hall, Temple Ewell, Dover, Kent, CT16 1DJ. 01304 825256

Dover (West Cliffe) – Wallett's Court, West Cliffe, St. Margaret's-at-Cliffe, Kent, CT15 6EW. 01304 852424

Dulverton – Ashwick Country House Hotel, Dulverton, Somerset, TA22 9QD. 01398 323868

Evesham (Harvington) – Mill At Harvington, Anchor Lane, Harvington, Evesham, Worcestershire, WR11 5NR. 01386 870688

Exeter (Dunchideock) – Lord Haldon Hotel, Dunchideock, Devon, EX6 7YF. 01392 832483

Exford (Exmoor) – Crown Hotel, Exford, Exmoor National Park, Somerset, TA24 7PP. 01643 831554/5

Fakenham – Vere Lodge, South Raynham, Fakenham, Norfolk, NR21 7HE. 01328 838261

Falmouth (Mawnan Smith) – Trelawne Hotel, Mawnan Smith, Cornwall, TR11 5HS. 01326 250226

Fenny Drayton (Leicestershire) – White Wings, Quaker Close, Fenny Drayton, Leicestershire, CV13 6BS. 01827 716100

Fressingfield (Diss) – Chippenhall Hall, Fressingfield, Eye, Suffolk, IP21 5TD. 01379 588180 / 586733

Gatwick (Charlwood) – Stanhill Court Hotel, Stanhill, Charlwood, Surrey, RH6 0EP. 01293 862166

Gillan – Tregildry Hotel and Herra Restaurant, Gillan Manaccan, Helston, Cornwall, TR12 6HG. 01326 231378

Glossop – Wind In The Willows, Derbyshire Level, Glossop, Derbyshire, SK13 9PT. 01457 868001

Golant by Fowey – Cormorant Hotel, Golant, Fowey, Cornwall, PL23 1LL. 01726 833426

Grasmere (Rydal Water) – White Moss House, Rydal Water, Grasmere, Cumbria, LA22 9SE. 015394 35295

Great Snoring – Old Rectory, Great Snoring, Fakenham, Norfolk, NR21 0HP. 01328 820597

Grindon – Porch Farmhouse, Grindon, Staffordshire, ST13 7TP. 01538 304545

Hamsterley Forest (Near Durham) – Grove House, Hamsterley Forest, Co.Durham, DL13 3NL. 01388 488203

Harrogate – White House, 10 Park Parade, Harrogate, North Yorkshire, HG1 5AH. 01423 501388

Harrogate(Pateley Bridge) – Old Smoke House, Bewerley, Pateley Bridge, North Yorkshire, HG3 5JA. 01423 711928

Hawes (Wensleydale) – Rookhurst Georgian Country House Hotel, West End, Gayle, Hawes, North Yorkshire, DL8 3RT. 01969 667454

Haytor Nr Bovey Tracey – Bel Alp House, Haytor, Devon South, TQ13 9XX. 01364 661217

Helston – Nansloe Manor, Meneage Road, Helston, Cornwall, TR13 0SB. 01326 574691

Hereford (Fownhope) – Bowens Country House, Fownhope, Herefordshire, HR1 4PS. 01432 860430.

Hereford (Ullingswick) – Steppes, Ullingswick, Herefordshire, HR1 3JG. 01432 820424

Hethel (Norwich) – Moat House, Rectory Lane, Hethel, Norwich, Norfolk, NR14 8HD. 01508 570149

Keswick (LakeThirlmere) – Dale Head Hall Lakeside Hotel, Thirlmere, Keswick, Cumbria, CA12 4TN. 017687 72478

Keswick (Newlands) – Swinside Lodge Hotel, Grange Road, Newlands, Keswick, Cumbria, CA12 5UE. 017687 72948

Keswick-On-Derwentwater – Grange Country House Hotel, Manor Brow, Keswick-On-Derwentwater, Cumbria, CA12 4BA. 017687 72500

Kingsbridge (Chillington) – White House, Chillington, Kingsbridge, Devon, . 01548 580580

Kirkby Lonsdale – Hipping Hall, Cowan Bridge, Kirkby Lonsdale, Cumbria, LA6 2JJ. 015242 71187

Ledbury – Westhill, Ledbury, Herefordshire, HR8 1JF. 01531 632544.

Ledbury (Bromsberrow Heath) – Grove House, Bromsberrow Heath, Herefordshire, HR8 1PE. 01531 650584

Leominster – Lower Bache, Kimbolton, Herefordshire, HR6 0ER. 01568 750304

Lifton (Sprytown) – Thatched Cottage Country Hotel And Restaurant, Sprytown, Lifton, Devon, PL16 0AY. 01566 784224

Lincoln (Washingborough) – Washingborough Hall, Church Hill, Washingborough, Lincoln, LN4 1BE. 01522 790340

Looe (Talland Bay) – Allhays Country House, Talland Bay, Looe, Cornwall, PL13 2JB. 01503 272434

Looe (Widegates) – Coombe Farm, Widegates, Cornwall, PL13 1QN. 01503 240223

Ludlow (Clee Downton) – Moor Hall, Shropshire. 01584 823209

Ludlow (Diddlebury) – Delbury Hall, Diddlebury, Craven Arms, Shropshire, SY7 9DH. 01584 841267

Ludlow (Downton) – Brakes, Downton, Shropshire, SY8 2LF. 01584 856485

Ludlow (Overton) – Overton Grange Hotel, Overton, Ludlow, Shropshire, SY8 4AD. 01584 873500

Luton (Little Offley) – Little Offley, Hitchin, Hertfordshire, SG5 3BU. 01462 768243

Lydford (Vale Down) – Moor View House, Vale Down, Lydford, Devon, EX20 4BB. 01822 820220

Lyme Regis – Thatch Lodge Hotel, The Street, Charmouth, Dorset, DT6 6PQ. 01297 560407

Lymington (Hordle) – Gordleton Mill Hotel, Silver Street, Hordle, Hampshire, SO41 6DJ. 01590 682219

Lynton – Hewitt's Hotel, North Walk, Lynton, Devon, EX35 6HJ. 01598 752293

Maidstone (Boughton Monchelsea) – Tanyard, Wierton Hill, Boughton Monchelsea, Kent, ME17 4JT. 01622 744705

Malton – Newstead Grange, Norton-On-Derwent, Malton, North Yorkshire, YO17 9PJ. 01653 692502

Market Drayton (Colehurst) – Old Colehurst Manor, Colehurst, Sutton, Market Drayton, Shropshire, TF9 2JB. 01630 638833

Matlock (Dethick) – Manor Farmhouse, Dethick, Matlock, Derbyshire, DE4 5GG. 01609 534246

Middlecombe (Minehead) – Periton Park Hotel, Middlecombe, Somerset, TA24 8SW. 01643 706885

Middleham (Wensleydale) – Millers House Hotel, Middleham, Wensleydale, North Yorkshire, DL8 4NR. 01969 622630

Minchinhampton – Burleigh Court, Minchinhampton, Gloucestershire, GL5 2PF. 01453 883804

Morchard Bishop – Wigham, Morchard Bishop, Devon, EX17 6RJ. 01363 877350

Much Wenlock – Raven Hotel, Much Wenlock, Shropshire, TF13 6EN. 01952 727251

New Romney (Littlestone) – Romney Bay House, Coast Road, Littlestone, New Romney, Kent, TN28 8QY. 01797 364747

Newcastle-upon-Tyne – Hope House, 47 Percy Gardens, Tynemouth, Tyne & Wear, NE30 4HH. 0191 257 1989

North Walsham – Beechwood Hotel, Cromer Road, North Walsham, Norfolk, NR28 0HD. 01692 403231

Norwich – Beeches Hotel & Victorian Gardens, 4-6 Earlham Road, Norwich, Norfolk, NR2 3DB. 01603 621167

Norwich (Drayton) – Stower Grange, School Road, Drayton, Norfolk, NR8 6EF. 01603 860210

Norwich (Old Catton) – Catton Old Hall, Lodge Lane, Catton, Norwich, Norfolk, NR6 7HG. 01603 419379

Norwich (Thorpe St Andrew) – Old Rectory, 103 Yarmouth Road, Thorpe St Andrew, Norwich, Norfolk, NR7 0HF. 01603 700772

Nottingham (Ruddington) – Cottage Country House Hotel, Ruddington, Nottingham, Nottinghamshire, NG11 6LA. 01159 846882

Oulton Broad – Ivy House Farm, Ivy Lane, Oulton Broad, Lowestoft, Suffolk, NR33 8HY. 01502 501353

Owlpen – Owlpen Manor, Gloucestershire, GL11 5BZ. 01453 860261

Oxford (Kingston Bagpuize) – Fallowfields, Kingston Bagpuize With Southmoor, Oxfordshire, OX13 5BH. 01865 820416

Porthleven (Nr Helston) – Tye Rock Hotel, Loe Bar Road, Porthleven, South Cornwall, TR13 9EW. 01326 572695

Pulborough – Chequers Hotel, Church Place, Pulborough, West Sussex, RH20 1AD. 01798 872486

Redditch (Ipsley) – Old Rectory, Ipsley Lane, Redditch, Worcestershire, B98 0AP. 01527 523000

Ross-On-Wye – Peterstow Country House, Peterstow, Ross-On-Wye, Herefordshire, HR9 6LB. 01989 562826

Ross-On-Wye (Glewstone) – Glewstone Court, Herefordshire, HR6 6AW. 01989 770367

Ross-On-Wye (Kilcot) – Orchard House, Aston Ingham Road, Kilcot, Gloucestershire, GL18 1NP. 01989 720417

Rye – White Vine House, High Street, Rye, East Sussex, TN31 7JF. 01797 224748

Seavington St Mary, Nr Ilminster – Pheasant Hotel, Seavington St Mary, Somerset, TA19 0HQ. 01460 240502

Sheffield (Chapeltown) – Staindrop Lodge, Lane End, Chapeltown, Sheffield, South Yorkshire, S30 4HH. 0114 284 6727

Sherborne – Eastbury Hotel, Long Street, Sherborne, Dorset, DT9 3by. 01935 813131

Simonsbath (Exmoor) – Simonsbath House Hotel, Simonsbath, Exmoor, Somerset, TA24 7SH. 01643 831259

South Molton – Marsh Hall Country House Hotel, South Molton, Devon North, EX36 3HQ. 01769 572666

St Ives (Trink) – Countryman At Trink Hotel & Restaurant, Old Coach Road, St Ives, Cornwall, TR26 3JQ. 01736 797571

Stamford (Ketton) – Priory, Church Road, Ketton, Stamford, Lincolnshire, PE9 3RD. 01780 720215

Stamford (Tallington) – Old Mill, Mill Lane, Tallington, Stamford, Lincolnshire, PE9 4RR. 01780 740815

Staverton (Nr Totnes) – Kingston House, Staverton, Totnes, Devon, TQ9 6AR. 01803 762 235

Stonor (Henley-on-Thames) – Stonor Arms, Stonor, Oxfordshire, RG9 6HE. 01491 638345

Stratford (Halford) – Old Manor House, Halford, Shipston on Stour, Warwickshire, CV36 5BT. 01789 740264

Taunton (Fivehead) – Langford Manor, Fivehead, Taunton, Somerset, TA3 6PH. 01460 281674

Taunton (Hatch Beauchamp) – Farthings Hotel & Restaurant, Hatch Beauchamp, Taunton, Somerset, TA3 6SG. 01823 480664

Thetford – Broom Hall, Richmond Road, Saham Toney, Thetford, Norfolk, IP25 7EX. 01953 882125

Tintagel (Trenale) – Trebrea Lodge, Trenale, Tintagel, Cornwall, PL34 0HR. 01840 770410

Tunstead (Broadland) – Old Farm Cottages, Old Farm, Tunstead, Norwich, Norfolk, NR12 8HS. 01692 536612

Uckfield – Hooke Hall, High Street, Uckfield, East Sussex, TN22 1EN. 01825 761578

Wareham (East Stoke) – Kemps Country House Hotel & Restaurant, East Stoke, Wareham, Dorset, BH20 6AL. 01929 462563

Wells – Glencot House, Glencot Lane, Wookey Hole, Somerset, BA5 1BH. 01749 677160

Wells – Beryl, Wells, Somerset, BA5 3JP. 01749 678738

Whitby – Dunsley Hall, Dunsley, Whitby, North Yorkshire, YO21 3TL. 01947 893437

Wimborne Minster – Beechleas, 17 Poole Road, Wimborne Minster, Dorset, BH21 1QA. 01202 841684

Winchelsea – Country House At Winchelsea, Hastings Road, Winchelsea, East Sussex, TN36 4AD. 01797 226669

Windermere – Braemount House Hotel, Sunny Bank Road, Windermere, Cumbria, LA23 2EN. 015394 45967

Windermere (Bowness) – Fayrer Garden House Hotel, Lyth Valley Road, Bowness-On - Windermere, Cumbria, LA23 3JP. 015394 88195

Woodbridge – Wood Hall Hotel & Country Club, Shottisham, Woodbridge, Suffolk, IP12 3EG. 01394 411283

Woolverton (Bath) – Woolverton House, Somerset, BA3 6QS. 01373 830415

York – 4 South Parade, 4 South Parade, York, North Yorkshire, YO2 2BA. 01904 628229

York (Escrick) – Parsonage Country House Hotel, Escrick, York, North Yorkshire, YO4 6LF. 01904 728111

Yoxford – Hope House, High Street, Yoxford, Saxmundham, Suffolk, IP17 3HP. 01728 668281

WALES

Aberdovey – Plas Penhelig Country House Hotel, Aberdovey, Gwynedd. 01654 767676

Abergavenny (Glangrwyney) – Glangrwyney Court, Glangrwyney, Powys, NP8 1ES. 01873 811288

Abergavenny (Govilon) – Llanwenarth House, Govilon, Abergavenny, Gwent, NP7 9SF. 01873 830289

Abergavenny (Llanfihangel Crucorney) – Penyclawdd Court, Llanfihangel Crucorney, Abergavenny, Gwent, NP7 7LB. 01873 890719

Betws-y-Coed – Tan-y-Foel, Capel Garmon, Aberconwy, LL26 0RE. 01690 710507

Brecon (Three Cocks) – Old Gwernyfed Country Manor, Felindre, Three Cocks, Brecon, Powys, LD3 0SU. 01497 847376

Caernarfon – Ty'n Rhos Country House, Llanddeiniolen, Caernarfon, Gwynedd, LL55 3AE. 01248 670489

Cardigan (Cilgeram) – Pembrokeshire Retreat, Rhosygilwen Mansion, Cilgeran, Dyfed, SA43 2TW. 01239 841387

Conwy – Berthlwyd Hall Hotel, Llechwedd, Gwynedd, LL32 8DQ. 01492 592409

Conwy – Old Rectory, Llansanffried Glan Conwy, Nr Conwy, Colwyn Bay, Conwy, LL28 5LF. 01492 580611

Criccieth – Mynydd Ednyfed Country House Hotel, Caernarfon Road, Criccieth, Gwynedd, LL52 0PH. 01766 523269

Dolgellau (Ganllwyd) – Dolmelynllyn Hall, Ganllwyd, Dolgellau, Gwynedd, LL40 2HP. 01341 440273

Tenby (Waterwynch Bay) – Waterwynch House Hotel, Waterwynch Bay, Tenby, Pembrokeshire, SA70 8TJ. 01834 842464

Tintern – Parva Farmhouse and Restaurant, Tintern, Chepstow, Gwent, NP6 6SQ. 01291 689411

SCOTLAND

Ardelve (By Kyle of Lochalsh) – Conchra House, Ardelve, Kyle of Lochalsh, Invernessshire, IV40 8DZ. 01599 555233

Ballater, Royal Deeside – Balgonie Country House, Braemar Place, Royal Deeside, Ballater, Aberdeenshire, AB35 5RQ. 013397 55482

Dingwall – Kinkell House, Easter Kinkell, by Dingwall, Ross-shire, IV7 8HY. 01349 861270

Drumnadrochit (Loch Ness) – Polmaily House Hotel, Drumnadrochit, Loch Ness, Inverness-shire, IV3 6XT. 01456 450343

Dumfries (Thornhill) – Trigony House, Closeburn, Thornhill, Dumfriesshire, DG3 5RZ. 01848 331211

Fernie, By Cupar – Fernie Castle, Fernie, Letham, KY7 7RU. 01337 810381

Fintry (Stirlingshire) – Culcreuch Castle Hotel, Fintry, Loch Lomond, Stirlingshire, G63 0LW. 01360 860228

Forres – Knockomie Hotel, Grantown Road, Forres, Moray, IV36 0SG. 01309 673146

Fort William – Ashburn House, 6 Achintore Road, Fort William, PH33 6RQ. 01397 706000

Inverness – Culduthel Lodge, 14 Culduthel Road, Inverness, Inverness-shire, IV2 4AG. 01463 240089

Isle Of Harris – Ardvourlie Castle, Aird amhulaidh, Isle Of Harris, Western Isles, HS3 3AB. 01859 502307

Isle Of Mull – Killiechronan, Killiechronan, Argyll, PA72 6JU. 01680 300403

Isle of Skye (By Dunvegan) – Harlosh House, By Dunvegan, Isle of Skye, Invernes-shire, IV55 8ZG. 01470 521367

Killiecrankie, By Pitlochry – Killiecrankie Hotel, Killiecrankie, By Pitlochry, Perthshire, PH16 5LG. 01796 473220

Moffat – Well View Hotel, Ballplay Road, Moffat, Dumfriesshire, DG10 9JU. 01683 220184

Oban – Manor House Hotel, Gallanach Road, Oban, Argyllshire, PA34 4LS. 01631 562087

Oban – Dungallen House Hotel, Gallanach Road, Oban, Argyll, PA34 4PD. 01631 563799

Perth – Dupplin Castle, Dupplin Estate, By Perth, Perthshire, PH2 0PY. 01738 623224

Perth (Guildtown) – Newmiln Country House, Newmiln Estate, Guildtown, Perth, PH2 6AE. 01738 552364

Pitlochry – Dunfallandy House, Logierait Road, Pitlochry, Perthshire, PH16 5NA. 01796 472648

Port Of Menteith – Lake Hotel, Port Of Menteith, Perthshire, FK8 3RA. 01877 385258

Strathtummel By Pitlochry – Queens View Hotel, Strathtummel, By Pitlochry, Perthshire, PH16 5NR. 01796 473291

IRELAND

Annalong Co Down – Glassdrumman Lodge, 85 Mill Road, Annalong, Co Down, BT34 4RH. 013967 68451

Bangor Co Down – Cairn Bay Lodge, 278 Seacliffe Road, Bangor, Co Down, BT20 5HS. 01247 467636

Letterkenny (Co Donegal) – Castle Grove Country House, Ramelton Road, Letterkenny, Co Donegal. 00 353 745 1118

Nenagh (Co Tipperary) – St David's Country House & Restaurant, Puckane, Nenagh, Co Tipperary. 00 353 67 24145

Riverstown, Co Sligo – Coopershill House, Riverstown, Co Sligo. 00 353 71 65108

Skibbereen Co.Cork – Liss Ard Lake Lodge, Skibbereen, Co.Cork. 00 353 28 22365

Sligo, Co Sligo – Markree Castle, Colooney, Co Sligo. 00 353 71 67800

Wicklow, Co Wicklow – Old Rectory, Wicklow Town, Co Wicklow. 00 353 404 67048

Craigantlet, Newtownards Northern Ireland – Beech Hill, 23 Ballymoney Road, Craigantlet, Newtownards, Co Down, BT23 4TG. 01232 425892

Portaferry Co Down Northern Ireland – Portaferry Hotel, The Strand, Portaferry, Co Down, Bt22 1PE. 012477 28231

CHANNEL ISLANDS

Guernsey (Castel) – Hotel Hougue Du Pommier, Hougue Du Pommier Road, Castel, Guernsey, GY5 7FQ. 01481 56531

Guernsey (Fermain Bay) – La Favorita Hotel, Fermain Bay, Guernsey, GY4 6SD. 01481 35666

Guernsey (St Martin) – Hotel Bella Luce, La Fosse, St Martin, Guernsey, . 01481 38764

Guernsey (St Martin's) – St Margaret's Lodge Hotel, Forest Road, St Martin's, Guernsey, GY4 6UE. 01481 35757

Jersey (St Helier) – Almorah Hotel, One Almorah Crescent, Lower Kings Cliff, St Helier, Jersey, JE2 3GU. 01534 21648

Johansens Recommended Hotels in Europe

AUSTRIA

Bad Gastein – Thermenhotel Haus Hirt, Kaiserhofstrasse, 14, Bad Gastein. 43 64 34 27 97

Bregenz – Deuring Schlôssle, Ehre-Guta-Platz 4, A-6900, Bregenz. 43 55 74 47800

Dürnstein – Hotel Schloss Dürnstein, 3601, Dürnstein. 43 2711 212

Ebreichsdorf Bri Wein – Domino Suites Hotel, 1 Dominostrasse, 2483 Ebreichsdorf Bri Wein. 43 2254 746 14

Igls – Schlosshotel Igls, Viller Steig 2, A-6080 Igls, Tirol. 43 512 377217

Igls – Sporthotel Igls, Hilberstrasse 17, A-6080 Igls, Tirol. 43 512 377241

Innsbruck – Romantik Hotel Schwarzer Adler, Kaiserjägerstrasse 2, 6020, Innsbruck. 43 512 587109

Kitzbühel – Romantik Hotel Tennerhof, 6370, Kitzbühel, Griesenauweg 26. 43 5356 3181

Klagenfurt – Hotel Palais Porcia, Neuer Platz 13, 9020, Klagenfurt. 43 463 51 1590

Pörtschach am Wörthersee – Hotel Schloss Seefels, Töschling 1, A-9210 Pörtschach am. 43 42 72 23 77

Salzburg – Hotel Schloss Mönchstein, Mönchsberg Park A-5020, 26-Joh A-5020, City Center, Salzburg. 43 662 84 85 55 0

Salzburg – Hotel Auersperg, Auerspergstrasse 61, A-5021, Salzburg. 43 662 88944

Salzburg – Hotel Altstadt Radisson SAS, Rudolfskai 28 / Judengasse 15, 5020, Salzburg. 43 662 8485710

Schwarzenberg im Bregenzerwald – Romantik-Hotel Gasthof Hirschen, Hof 14, 6867, Schwarzenberg. 43 55 12/29 44 0

Seefeld – Hotel Viktoria, Geigenbühelweg 589 A-6100, Seefeld /Tirol. 43 52 12 44 41

Seefeld – Hotel Klosterbräu, 6100, Seefeld/Tirol. 43 5212 26210

Vienna – Hotel im Palais Schwarzenberg, Schwarzenberg 9, 1030, Vienna. 43 1 798 4515

BELGIUM

Bruges – Relais Oud Huis Amsterdam, Spiegelrei 3, 8000, Bruges. 32-50- 34 18 10

Bruges – Hotel Prinsenhof, Ontvangersstraat 9, 8000, Bruges. 32 50 342690

Bruges – Die Swaene, Steenhouwersdijk, 8000, Bruges. 32 50 34 2798

Bruges – Romantik Pandhotel, Pandreitje 16, 8000, Bruges. 32 50 340666

Brussels – L'Amigo, 1-3 Rue L'Amigo, 1000, Brussels. 32 2 547 4747

Genval – Château Du Lac, Avenue Du Lac 87, B-1332, Genval. 32 2 655 71 11

Malmedy – Hostellerie Trôs Marets, Route Des Trôs Marets, B-4960, Malmedy. 32-80- 33 79 17

March-En-Famenne – Château d'Hassonville, Marche-En-Famenne, 6900. 32 84 31 10 25

CYPRUS

Paphos – Annabelle, P.O. Box 401, Paphos. 357 62 38 333

DENMARK

Faaborg – Steensgaard Herregårdspension, Steensgaard, 5642 Millinge, Faaborg. 45 62 61 94 90

Fanø – Sønderho Kro, Kroplasden 11, Sønderho 6720, Fanø. 45 75 164009

Hornbaek – Havreholm Slot, 4 Klosterrisvej, Havreholm, 3100 Hornbaek. 45 4224 8600

Middelfart – Hindsgavl SLot, Hindsgval, Allé 7–5500, Middelfart. 45 64 41 88 11

Nyborg – Hotel Hesselet, Christianslundsvej 119, 5800 Nyborg. 45 65 31 30 29

BRITISH ISLES

Amberley – Amberley Castle, Amberley, West Sussex, BN18 9ND. 01798 831992

Berwick-Upon-Tweed – Tillmouth Park, Cornhill-on-Tweed, Northumberland, TD12 4UU. 01890 882255

Chagford – Gidleigh Park, Chagford, Devon, TQ13 8HH. 01647 432367

Chester – Chester Grosvenor, Eastgate, Chester, Cheshire, CH1 1LT. 0244 324024

Chichester, Bosham – Millstream Hotel, Bosham, West Sussex, PO18 8HL. 01243 573234

Chipping Campden – Charingworth Manor, Gloucestershire, GL55 6NS. 01386 593555

Colchester – Five Lakes Hotel Golf & Country Club, Colchester Road,Whitehouse Hill, Tolleshunt Knights, Maldon, Essex, CM9 8HX. 01621 868888

Coventry, Berkswell – Nailcote Hall, Nailcote Lane, Berkswell, Warwickshire, CV7 7DE. 01203 466174

Dartford, Wilmington – Rowhill Grange, Wilmington, Dartford, Kent, DA2 7QH. 01322 615136

Dublin, Straffan – Kildare Hotel & Country Club, At Straffan, Co Kildare. 00 353 1 627 3333

Flitwick – Flitwick Manor, Church Rd, Flitwick, Bedfordshire MK45 1AE. 01525 712 242

Haslemere – Lythe Hill Hotel, Petworth Road, Haslemere, Surrey, GU27 3BQ. 01428 651251

Isle Of Mull, Tobermory – Western Isles Hotel, Tobermory, Isle Of Mull, Argyll, PA75 6PR. 01688 302012

Jersey, St Brelade – Atlantic Hotel, La Moye, St Brelade, Jersey, JE3 8HE. 01534 44101

Lake Ullswater – Sharrow Bay Country House Hotel, Howtown, Lake Ullswater, Penrith, Cumbria, CA10 2LZ. 017684 86301

London – Ascott Mayfair, 49 Hill Street, London, W1X 7FQ. 0171 499 6868

London – Basil Street Hotel, Basil Street, London, SW3 1AH. 0171 581 3311

London – The Beaufort, 33 Beaufort Gardens, Knightsbridge, London, SW3 1PP. 0171 584 5252

London – Beaufort House Apartments, 45 Beaufort Gardens, London, SW3 1PN. 0171 584 2600

London – Blakes Hotel, 33 Roland Gardens, London, SW7 3PF. 0171 370 6701

London – The Cadogan, Sloane Street, London, SW1X 9SG. 0171 235 7141

London – Cannizaro House, West Side, Wimbledon Common, London, SW19 4UE. 0181 879 1464

London – Cliveden Town House, 26 Cadogan Gardens, London, SW3 2RP. 0171 730 6466

London – The Dorchester, Park Lane, Mayfair, London, WIA 2HJ. 0171 629 8888

London – Draycott House Apartments, 10 Draycott Avenue, Chelsea, London, SW3 3AA. 0171 584 4659

London – The Halcyon, 81 Holland Park, London, W11 3RZ. 0171 727 7288

London – Harrington Hall, 5-25 Harrington Gardens, London, SW7 4JW. 0171 396 9696

London – The Hempel, Hempel Garden Square, 31-35 Craven Hill Gardens, London, W2 3EA. 0171 298 9000

London – The Howard, Temple Place, The Strand, London, WC2R 2PR. 44 171 836 3555

London – The Leonard, 15 Seymour Street, London, W1H 5AA. 0171 935 2010

London – The Milestone, 1-2 Kensington Court, London, W8 5DL. 0171 917 1000

London – Number Sixteen, 16 Sumner Place, London, SW7 3EG. 0171 589 5232

London, – Pembridge Court Hotel, 34 Pembridge Gardens, London, W2 4DX. 0171 229 9977

London – The Ritz, 150 Piccadilly, London, W1V 9DG. 0171 493 8181

Maidenhead – Cliveden, Taplow, Berkshire, SL6 0JF. 01628 668561

Matlock, Riber – Riber Hall, Matlock, Derbyshire, DE4 5JU. 01629 582795

New Milton – Chewton Glen, New Milton, Hampshire, BH25 6QS. 01425 275341

Preston, Chipping – Gibbon Bridge Country House Hotel, Chipping, Preston, Lancashire, PR3 2TQ. 01995 61456

Streatley-On-Thames,Reading – The Swan Diplomat, Streatley-On-Thames, Berkshire, RG8 9HR. 01491 873737

Wallingford, North Stoke – Springs Hotel, North Stoke, Wallingford, Oxfordshire, OX10 6BE. 01491 836687

Winchester, Sparsholt – Lainston House Hotel, Sparsholt, Winchester, Hampshire, SO21 2LT. 01962 863588

Woodbridge – Seckford Hall, Woodbridge, Suffolk, IP13 6NU. 01394 385678

Wales (Llandudno) – St Tudno Hotel, Promenade, Llandudno, Gwynedd, LL30 2LP. 01492 874411

FRANCE

Annecy – Hôtel L'Impérial Palace, 32 Avenue d'Albigny, 74000, Annecy. 33 4 5009 3000

Avignon (Noves) – Auberge De Noves, 13550, Noves. 33 4 90 94 19 21

Avignon-Le Pontet – Auberge de Cassagne, 450 Ave de Cassagne, 84130 Le Pontet, Avignon . 33 4 90 31 04 18

Biarritz – Hôtel Du Palais, 64200 Biarritz, Avenue de L'Impératrice. 33 5 59 41 64 00

Cannes – Hotel L'Horset Savoy, 5 Rue François Einesy, 6400, Cannes. 33 4 92 99 72 00

Cannes – Hôtel Majestic, La Croisette, BP 163, Cannes-Cedex. 331 92 98 77 00

Chambolle-Musigny – Château Hôtel André Ziltener, F-21220 Chambolle-Musigny, Côte D'or. 33 3 80 62 41 62

Chamonix – Hôtel Albert 1er, 119 Impasse du Montenvers, 74402, Chamonix-Mont Blanc. 33 4 50 53 05 09

Champigné – Chateau Des Briottierès, 49330, Champignè. 33 2 41 42 00 02

Chenehutte-Les-Tuffeaux – Le Prieuré, 49350, Chenehutte-Les-Tuffeaux, Saumur. 33 2 41 67 90 14

Collias – Hostellerie Le Castellas, Grand' Rue, 30210, Collias. 33 66 22 88 88

Colmar – Romantik Hostellerie Le Maréchal, 4-6 Places Des Six Montagnes Noires, 68000 Colmar. 33 3 89 41 60 32

Connelles – Le Moulin De Connelles, 39 Route d'Amfreville-Sous-Les-Monts, 27430, Connelles. 33 2 32 59 53 33

Courcelles-sur-Vesle – Château de Courcelles, 2220, Courcelles-sur-Vesle. 33 3 23 74 13 53

Courchevel – Hôtel Des Trois Vallées, BP 22, F-73122, Courchevel, Cedex. 33 4 79 08 00 12

Courchevel – L'Hôtel Des Neiges, Rue de Bellecote, BP 96, Courchevel, 1850 Cedex. 33 4 79 08 03 77

Courchevel – Hôtel Annapurna, 73120, Courchevel, 1850. 33 4 79 08 04 60

Courchevel – Hôtel Le Lana, B.P 95, 73121 Courchevel Cedex, Savoie. 33 4 79 08 01 10

Deauville – Hôtel Royal, Boulevard Cornuché, 14800, Deauville, Calvados. 33 31 98 66 33

Épernay – Hostellerie La Briqueterie, 4 Route de Sézanne, Vinay 51530, Epernay. 33 3 26 59 99 99

Eze Village – Château Eze, Rue De La Pise, 6360, Eze Village. 33 4 93 41 12 24

Faverges de La Tour – Le Château, 38110 Faverges de La Tour, Isere. 33 4 74 97 42 52

Gordes (Joucas) – Hostellerie Le Phébus, Joucas, 84220 Gourdes. 33 4 90 05 78 83

Gressy-en-France – Le Manoir de Gressy, 77410, Gressy-en-France, Seine et Marne. 33 1 60 26 68 00

Luynes – Domaine de Beauvois, Le Pont Clouet, 37230, Luynes. 33 2 4755 5011

Lyon – La Tour Rose, 22 Rue de Boeuf, 69005, Lyon. 33 4 78 37 25 90

Monestier – Château Des Vigiers, 24240 Monestier. 33 5 53 61 50 00

Monetier-Les-Bains – L'Auberge du Choucas, 5220, Monetier-Les-Bains, Serre-Chevalier 1550. 33 4 92 24 42 73

Paris – Hôtel Lancaster, 7 Rue de Berri, Champs Elysées, Paris, 75008. 33 1 4076 4076

Paris – Les Suites Saint Honoré, 13 Rue d'Aguesseau, 75008, Paris. 33 1 44 51 16 35

Paris – Hôtel L'Horset Opera, 18 Rue d'Antin, 75002, Paris. 33 1 44 71 87 00

Paris – Montalembert, 3 Rue de Montalembert, 75007, Paris. 33 01 45 49 68 68

Paris – Hôtel Buci Latin, 34 Rue de Buci, 75006, Paris. 33 1 4329 0720

Paris – Hôtel De L'Arcade, 9 Rue de L'Arcade, 75008, Paris. 331 533 0 60 00

Paris – Hôtel Majestic, 29 Rue Dumont d'Urville, 75116, Paris. 33 1 45 00 83 70

Paris – Hôtel Raphael, 17 Avenue Kléber, 75116, Paris. 33 1 44 28 00 28

Paris – Hôtel Regina, 2 Place des Pyramides, 75001, Paris. 33 1 42 60 31 10

Paris – Hôtel Vernet, 25 Rue Vernet, 75008, Paris. 331 49 31 98 00

Roquebrune Cap-Martin/Monaco – Vista Palace Hotel, Route De La Grande Corniche, F-06190 Roquebrune/Cap-Martin. 33 4 92 10 40 00

Saint-Emilion – Hotel Château Grand Barrail, Route de Libourne, F-33330, Saint-Emilion. 33 57 55 37 00

Saint-Félix – Les Bruyérès, Mercy, 74540 Saint-Félix, Haute-Savoie. 33 4 5060 9653

St Paterne – Château de Saint Paterne, 72610 Saint Paterne. 33 2 3327 5471

St Paul – Mas d'Artigny, Route De La Colle, 6570, Saint-Paul. 33 93 32 84 54

St Rémy – Domaine de Valmouriane, Petite Route des Baux, 13210, Saint Rémy de Provence. 33 4 90 92 44 62

St Rémy-de-Provence – Hostellerie Du Vallon De Valrugues, Chemin Cant Cigalo, 13210, Saint Rémy De Provence. 33 4 90 92 04 40

St-Rémy-de-Provence – Château Des Alpilles, Route Départementale 31, Ancienne Route du Grés, 13210, St-Rémy-de-Provence. 33 4 90 92 03 33

GERMANY

Alt Duvenstedt Nr Rendsburg – Hotel Töpferhaus, Am Bistensee, D-24791, Alt Duvenstedt. 49 43 38 333

Aschau – Residenz Heinz Winkler, Kirchplatz 1, 83229 Aschau im Cheimgau. 49 8052 17990

Bad Herrenbald – Mônchs Posthotel, 76328, Bad Herrenbald. 49 70 83 74 40

Cologne – Hotel im Wasserturm, Kaygasse 2, D-50676. 49 221 20080

Dresden – Bülow Residenz, Rähnitzgasse 19, 1097, Dresden. 49 35 14 40 33

Friedrichsruhe – Wald & Schlosshotel, 74639 Friedrichsruhe/Zweiflingen. 49 7941 60870

Garmisch Partenkirchen – Reindl's Partenkirchner Hof, Bahnhofstasse 15, Garmisch Partenkirchen. 49 8821 58025

Kettwig – Schlosshotel Hugenport, August-Thyssen Strasse-51, 45219, Essen-Kettwig. 49 20 54 12 040

Konstanz – Seehotel Siber, Seestrasse 25, 78464, Konstanz. 49 7531 63044

Munich – Hotel Kônigshof, Karlsplatz 25, 80335, Munich. 49 89 551 360

Murnau – Alpenhof Murnau, Ramsachstasse 8, 82418, Murnau. 49 8841 4910

Niederstotzingen – Schlosshotel Oberstotzingen, Stettener Strasse 35-37, 89168, Niederstotzingen. 49 69 2384 600

Oberwesel/Rhein – Burghotel Auf Schönburg, 55430, Oberwesel/Rhein. 49 67 44 93 93 0

Pegnitz – Pflaums Posthotel Pegnitz, Nürnbergerstrasse 12-16, 91257 Pegnitz, Frankishe Schweiz. 49 92 41 72 50

Rothenburg Ob der Tauber – Hôtel Eisenhut, Herrngasse 3-7, D-91541. 49 9861 70 50

Rüdesheim am Rhein – Jagdschloss Neiderwald, Auf Dem Niederwald 1, 65385 Rüdesheim am Rhein. 49 67 22 1004

Schlangenbad – Parkhotel Schlangenbad, Rheingauer Strasse 47, D-65388, Schlangenbad. 49 61 29 420

Wassenberg – Hotel Burg Wassenberg, Kirchstrasse 17, 41849 Wassenberg. 49 2432 9490

Wertheim-Bettingen – Schweizer Stuben, Geiselbrunnwre, 97877 Wertheim-Bettingen. 49 9342 3070

GREECE

Athens – Andromeda Athens, 22 Timoleontos Vassou Street, GR-115 21, Athens. 30 1 6437302-4

Athens – Hotel Pentelikon, 66 Diligianni Street, G-14562, Athens. 30 1 8080 311 17

Crete – Elounda Beach, 721 00, Aghios Nikolaos, Crete. 30 841 41412 / 41413

Crete – Hotel Elounda Mare, PO Box GR-721 00, Aghios Nikolaos, Crete. 30 841 41102/3

Mykonos – Kivotus Clubhotel, Ornos Bay, 84600 Mykonos. 30 17 24 67 66

HUNGARY

Budapest – Hotel Gellért, Gellért Tér 1, H-1111, Budapest. 36 1 185 2200

ICELAND

Iceland (Reykjavik) – Hotel Borg, Posthusstraeti 11, P.O Box 200, 121 Reykjavik. 354 551 14 40

ITALY

Assisi – Le Silve di Armenzano, I-06081 Loc Armenzano, Assisi. 39 75 801 90 00

Brixen-South Tyrol – Hotel Dominik, Via Terzo Di Sotto 13, 39042 Brixen-Bressanone, South Tyrol.

Cogne – Romantik Hotel Miramonti, Avenue Cavagnet 31, 11012, Cogne. 39 165 74030

Como – Hotel Villa Flori, Via Cernobbio, 12 - 22100, Como. 39 31 573105

Como – Albergo Terminus, Lungo Lario Trieste, 14-22100, Como. 39 31 329111

Ferrara – Ripagrande Hotel, Via Ripagrande 21, 44100, Ferrara. 39 532 765250

Florence – Romantik Hotel J & J, Via Mezzo 20, 50121 Florence. 39 55 2345005

Madonna Di Campiglio – Hotel Lorenzetti, Via Dolomiti Di Campiglio 119, 38084 Madonna Di Campiglio. 39 465 44 1404

Marling/Meran – Romantic Hotel Oberwirt, St Felixweg 2, I-39020, Marling/Meran. 39 473 22 20 20

Messina, Sicily – Museo Albergo Atelier Sul Mare, via Cesare Battisti, Castel di Tusa (Me), Sicily. 39 921 334 295

Milan – Regency Hotel, Via Arimondi 12, 20155 Milan. 39 2 39216021

Mira – Villa Margherita, Via Nazionale 416/417, 30030 Mira, Venezia. 39 41 42 65 800

Naples – Albergo Miramare, Via Nazario Sauro 24, Naples. 39 81 76 47 589

Perugia – Hotel Palazzo Bocci, Via Cavour 17, 06038 Spello, Perugia. 39 742 301021

Porto Ercole – Il Pellicano , Hotel in Porto Ercole, Aeralita Cala Dei Santi, Porto Ercole (GR). 39 564 833801

Positano – Romantik Hotel Poseidon, Via Pasitea 148, I-84017, Positano. 39 89 81 11 11

Ravarotta di Pasiano – Villa Luppis, Via San Martino 34, 33080 Ravarotta. 39 434 626969

Rome – Hotel Farnese, Via Alessandro Farnese, 30 (Anglo Viale Giulio Cesare) 00192, Rome. 39 6 321 25 53

Rome – Hotel Majestic Roma, Via Veneto 50, 187, Rome. 39 6 48 68 41

Rome – Romantik Hotel Barocco, Piazza Barberini, 9 I-00187, Rome. 39 6 4872001

Saturnia – Terme Di Saturnia Hotel, 58050, Saturnia, Grosseto. 39 564 601061

Sestri Leuante – Grand Hotel Villa Balbi, Viale Rimembranza 1, 16039, Sestri Leuante. 39 185 42941

Sicily – Romantic Hotel Villa Ducale, Via Leonardo Da Vinci 60, 98039 Taormina, Sicily. 0 942/28 153

Sinalunga – Locanda dell 'Amorosa, 53048, Sinalunga, Siona. 39 577 679497

Sorrento – Grand Hotel Cocumella, Via Cocumella 7, 80065 Sant-Agnello, Sorrento. 39 81 878 2933

Tyrol (Mauls) – Romantik Hotel Stafler, Mules 10, 39040 Mauls Freienfeld. 39 472 771136

Tyrol (Meran) – Castel Rundegg, Via Scena 2, 39020, Meran. 39 473 234100

Trento – Hotel Accademia, Vicolo Colico 4/6, 38100, Trento. 39 461 233600

Venice – Hotel Londra Palace, Riva Degli Schiavoni, 30122, Venice. 39 41 520 05 33

Venice (Lido) – Albergo Quattro Fontane, 30126, Lido di Venezia. 39-41 5260227

LUXEMBOURG

Berdorf – Parc Hotel, 16 Rue De Grundhof, L-6550, Berdorf. 352 790195

MONACO

Monte Carlo – Hotel Mirabeau, 1 Avenue Princesse Grace, Monte Carlo MC 98007. 00 377 92 166565

Monte Carlo – Hotel Hermitage, Square Beaumarchais BP277, MC 98005. 33 92 16 40 00

NETHERLANDS

Amsterdam – Hotel Ambassade, Herengracht 341, 1016 AZ, Amsterdam. 31 20 626 2333

Ootmarsum – Hotel de Wiemsel, Winhofflaan 2, 7631 HX, Ootmarsum. 31 541 292 155

PORTUGAL

Cascais – Estalagem Senhora.Da Guia, Estrada do Guincho, Cascais. 351 1 486 92 39

Faro – La Réserve, Santa Barbara de Nexe, P-8000 Faro, Algarve. 351 89 90474

Faro – Monte do Casal, Cerro do Lobo, Estoi 8000 Faro, Algarve. 351 89 91503

Lisbon – As Janelas Verdes, Rua das Janelas Verdes 47, 1200, Lisbon. 351 1 39 68 143

Madeira – Reid's Hotel, P-9000 Funchal, Madeira. 351 91 763001

Madeira – Quinta Da Bela Vista, Caminho Do Avista Navios, 4, 9000, Funchal-Madeira. 351 91 764144

RUSSIAN FEDERATION

St Petersburg – Grand Hotel Europe, Mikkhailovskaya Ulitsa 1/7, 191073, St Petersburg. 7 812 329 60 00

SLOVENIA

Bled – Hotel Vila Bled, Cesta Svobode 26, SLO 64260, Bled. 386 64 7915

SPAIN

Barcelona – Hotel Claris, Pau Claris 150, 8009, Barcelona. 34 3 4876262

Girona – Mas de Torrent, 17123 Torrent-Girona, Girona. 34 72 303292

Lloret de Mar – Hotel Santa Marta, Playa de Santa Cristina, 17310 Lloret de Mar, Gerona. 34 72 364904

Loja, Granada – Hotel La Bobadilla, Finca La Bobadilla, Loja 18300, Granada. 34 958 321861

Madrid – Villa Real, Plaza De Las Cortes 10, Madrid 28014. 34 14203767

Mallorca – Hotel Vistamar De Valldemosa, Ctra. Valldemosa, Andratx, Km 2 07170 Valldemosa, Mallorca. 34 71 61 23 00

Mallorca – Read's, Ca'n Moragues, 07320 Santa Maria, Mallorca. 34 71 140 261

Marbella – Hotel Puente Romano, P.O Box 204, 29600, Marbella. 34 5 282 0900

Marbella – Marbella Club Hotel, Boulevard Principe Alfonson von Hohenlohe s/n, 29600, Marbella. 34 5 282 22 11

Salamanca – Residencia Rector, Rector Esparabé, 10-Apartado 399, 37008 Salamanca. 34 23 21 84 82

Seville – Casa De Carmona, Plaza de Lasso, 41410 Carmona, Seville. 34 54 14 33 00

Tenerife – Gran Hotel Bahia Del Duque, Playa Del Duque, Fanabe, Adeje, Tenerife. 34 22 74 69 00

SWEDEN

Åre – Hotell Åregården, Box 6, S-83013, Åre. 46 647 178 00

Aspa Bruk – Aspa Herrgård, S-696 93, Aspa Bruk. 46 583 50210

Borgholm – Halltorps Gästgiveri, S-387 92, Borgholm. 46 485 85000

Eskilstuna – Sundbyholms Slott, S-635 08, Eskilstuna. 46 16 96500

Sôderkôping – Romantik Hotel Sôderkôpings Brunn, Skônbergagatan 35, Box 44 614 21, Sôderkôping. 46 121 109 00

Stockholm – Hotell Diplomat, Strandvägen 7C, Box 14059 S-10440, Stockholm. 46 8 663 58 00

Tällberg – Romantik Hotel Åkerblads, S-793 70, Tällberg. 46 247 50800

Vikbolandet – Mauritzbergs Slott, S-61031, Vikbolandet. 46 125 50100

SWITZERLAND

Chateau d'Oex – Hostellerie Bon Acceuil, 1837, Chateau d'Oex. 41 26 924 6300

Grindelwald – Romantik Hotel Schweizerhof, 3818, Grindelwald. 41 33 853 22 02

Kandersteg – Royal Hotel Bellevue, CH 3718, Kandersteg. 41 33 75 12 12

Lugano – Villa Principe Leopoldo, Via Montalbano, 6900, Lugano. 41 91 985 8855

Saas Fee – Romantik Hotel Beau-Site, 3906, Saas Fee. 41 27 958 1560

Zuoz – Posthotel Engiadina, Via Maistra, Zuoz. 41 82 71021

TURKEY

Alanya – Hotel Grand Kaptan, Oba, Göl, Mevkii, 07400 Alanya. 90 242 514 0101

Kalkan – Hotel Villa Mahal, P.K 4 Kalkan, 7960, Antalya. 90 242 844 3268

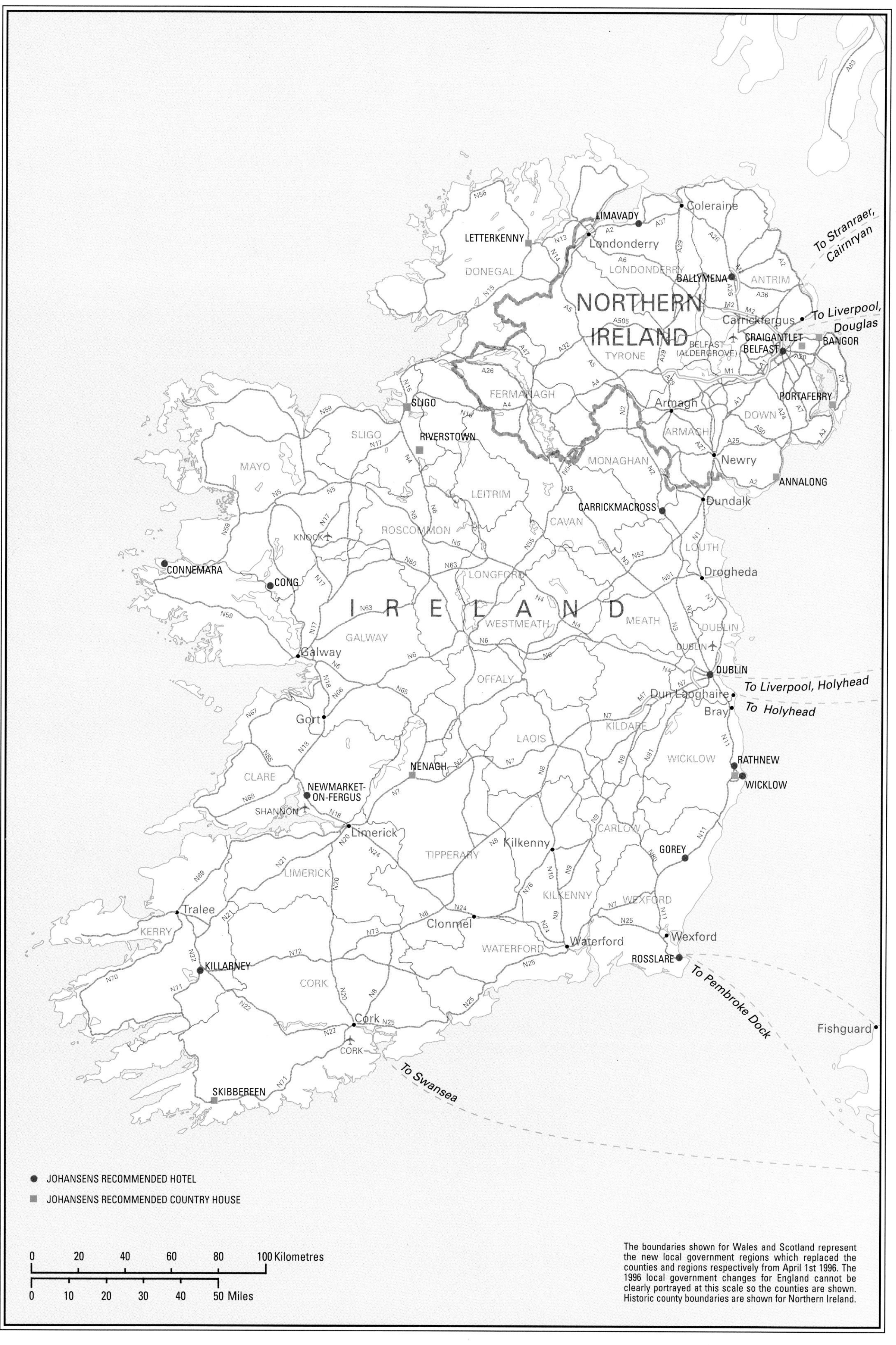

NORTHERN IRELAND
IRELAND
LIMAVADY
Coleraine
LETTERKENNY
Londonderry
DONEGAL
LONDONDERRY
BALLYMENA
ANTRIM
Carrickfergus
CRAIGANTLET
BELFAST
BANGOR
TYRONE
BELFAST (ALDERGROVE)
FERMANAGH
SLIGO
RIVERSTOWN
Armagh
ARMAGH
DOWN
PORTAFERRY
Newry
ANNALONG
MONAGHAN
MAYO
LEITRIM
CARRICKMACROSS
Dundalk
CAVAN
KNOCK
ROSCOMMON
LOUTH
CONNEMARA
CONG
LONGFORD
Drogheda
MEATH
WESTMEATH
GALWAY
DUBLIN
Galway
DUBLIN
OFFALY
Dun Laoghaire
Bray
Gort
KILDARE
LAOIS
WICKLOW
RATHNEW
WICKLOW
CLARE
NENAGH
NEWMARKET-ON-FERGUS
SHANNON
Limerick
CARLOW
Kilkenny
TIPPERARY
GOREY
LIMERICK
KILKENNY
WEXFORD
Tralee
KERRY
Clonmel
Waterford
Wexford
WATERFORD
ROSSLARE
KILLARNEY
CORK
Cork
CORK
SKIBBEREEN
Fishguard
To Stranraer, Cairnryan
To Liverpool, Douglas
To Liverpool, Holyhead
To Holyhead
To Pembroke Dock
To Swansea
JOHANSENS RECOMMENDED HOTEL
JOHANSENS RECOMMENDED COUNTRY HOUSE
0 20 40 60 80 100 Kilometres
0 10 20 30 40 50 Miles
The boundaries shown for Wales and Scotland represent the new local government regions which replaced the counties and regions respectively from April 1st 1996. The 1996 local government changes for England cannot be clearly portrayed at this scale so the counties are shown. Historic county boundaries are shown for Northern Ireland.

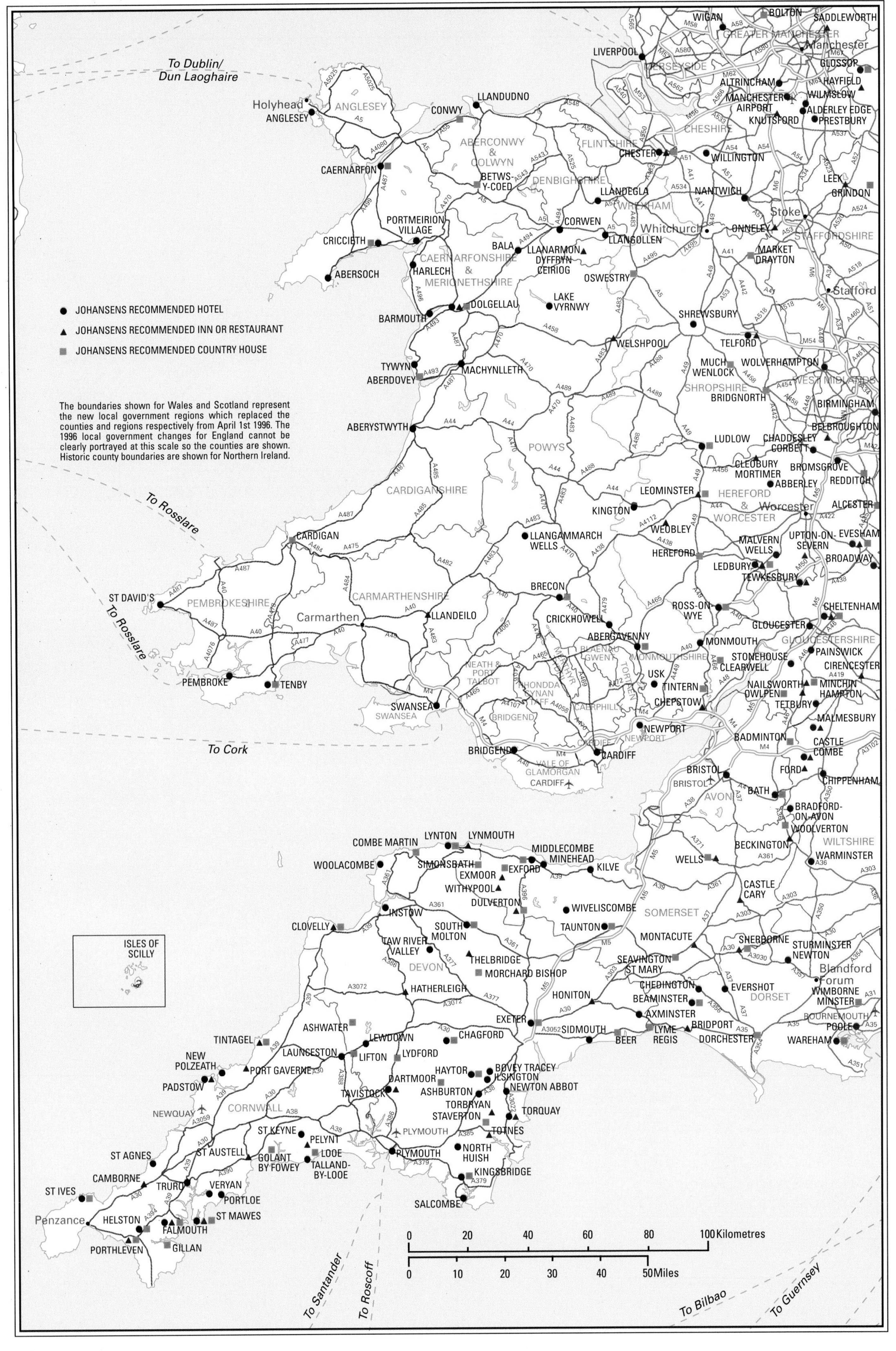

JOHANSENS RECOMMENDED HOTEL
JOHANSENS RECOMMENDED INN OR RESTAURANT
JOHANSENS RECOMMENDED COUNTRY HOUSE
The boundaries shown for Wales and Scotland represent the new local government regions which replaced the counties and regions respectively from April 1st 1996. The 1996 local government changes for England cannot be clearly portrayed at this scale so the counties are shown. Historic county boundaries are shown for Northern Ireland.
To Dublin/ Dun Laoghaire
To Rosslare
To Rosslare
To Cork
To Santander
To Roscoff
To Bilbao
To Guernsey
ISLES OF SCILLY
WIGAN
BOLTON
SADDLEWORTH
GREATER MANCHESTER
Manchester
LIVERPOOL
MERSEYSIDE
GLOSSOP
ALTRINCHAM
HAYFIELD
MANCHESTER AIRPORT
WILMSLOW
KNUTSFORD
ALDERLEY EDGE
PRESTBURY
CHESHIRE
Holyhead
ANGLESEY
ANGLESEY
LLANDUDNO
CONWY
ABERCONWY & COLWYN
FLINTSHIRE
CHESTER
WILLINGTON
CAERNARFON
BETWS-Y-COED
DENBIGHSHIRE
LLANDEGLA
WREXHAM
NANTWICH
LEEK
GRINDON
Stoke
CORWEN
Whitchurch
ONNELEY
STAFFORDSHIRE
PORTMEIRION VILLAGE
CRICCIETH
BALA
LLANARMON DYFFRYN CEIRIOG
LLANGOLLEN
MARKET DRAYTON
CAERNARFONSHIRE & MERIONETHSHIRE
HARLECH
ABERSOCH
OSWESTRY
Stafford
LAKE VYRNWY
DOLGELLAU
BARMOUTH
SHREWSBURY
TELFORD
WELSHPOOL
TYWYN
ABERDOVEY
MACHYNLLETH
MUCH WENLOCK
WOLVERHAMPTON
WEST MIDLANDS
SHROPSHIRE
BRIDGNORTH
BIRMINGHAM
ABERYSTWYTH
POWYS
LUDLOW
CHADDESLEY CORBETT
BELBROUGHTON
CLEOBURY MORTIMER
BROMSGROVE
ABBERLEY
REDDITCH
CARDIGANSHIRE
LEOMINSTER
HEREFORD & WORCESTER
KINGTON
Worcester
ALCESTER
WEOBLEY
CARDIGAN
LLANGAMMARCH WELLS
MALVERN WELLS
UPTON-ON-SEVERN
EVESHAM
HEREFORD
BROADWAY
LEDBURY
TEWKESBURY
ST DAVID'S
PEMBROKESHIRE
CARMARTHENSHIRE
BRECON
Carmarthen
LLANDEILO
CRICKHOWELL
ROSS-ON-WYE
CHELTENHAM
ABERGAVENNY
GLOUCESTER
MONMOUTH
GLOUCESTERSHIRE
BLAENAU GWENT
MONMOUTHSHIRE
PAINSWICK
NEATH & PORT TALBOT
STONEHOUSE
CLEARWELL
CIRENCESTER
PEMBROKE
TENBY
USK
TINTERN
NAILSWORTH
MINCHINHAMPTON
OWLPEN
RHONDDA CYNAN TAFF
CAERPHILLY
CHEPSTOW
TETBURY
SWANSEA
SWANSEA
BRIDGEND
MALMESBURY
NEWPORT
CARDIFF
NEWPORT
BADMINTON
CASTLE COMBE
BRIDGEND
CARDIFF
VALE OF GLAMORGAN
CARDIFF
BRISTOL
BRISTOL
FORD
CHIPPENHAM
AVON
BATH
BRADFORD-ON-AVON
WOOLVERTON
WILTSHIRE
COMBE MARTIN
LYNTON
LYNMOUTH
MIDDLECOMBE
MINEHEAD
BECKINGTON
WARMINSTER
WOOLACOMBE
SIMONSBATH
EXMOOR
EXFORD
KILVE
WELLS
WITHYPOOL
CASTLE CARY
DULVERTON
INSTOW
WIVELISCOMBE
SOMERSET
CLOVELLY
SOUTH MOLTON
TAUNTON
MONTACUTE
TAW RIVER VALLEY
SHERBORNE
STURMINSTER NEWTON
THELBRIDGE
SEAVINGTON ST MARY
DEVON
MORCHARD BISHOP
Blandford Forum
CHEDINGTON
EVERSHOT
HATHERLEIGH
HONITON
BEAMINSTER
DORSET
WIMBORNE MINSTER
EXETER
AXMINSTER
BOURNEMOUTH
ASHWATER
BRIDPORT
POOLE
CHAGFORD
SIDMOUTH
LYME REGIS
TINTAGEL
LEWDOWN
BEER
DORCHESTER
WAREHAM
NEW POLZEATH
LAUNCESTON
LIFTON
LYDFORD
PORT GAVERNE
HAYTOR
BOVEY TRACEY
ILSINGTON
PADSTOW
DARTMOOR
NEWTON ABBOT
TAVISTOCK
ASHBURTON
NEWQUAY
CORNWALL
TORBRYAN
STAVERTON
TORQUAY
ST KEYNE
PLYMOUTH
TOTNES
PELYNT
ST AGNES
ST AUSTELL
LOOE
NORTH HUISH
GOLANT BY FOWEY
TALLAND-BY-LOOE
PLYMOUTH
CAMBORNE
KINGSBRIDGE
TRURO
VERYAN
ST IVES
PORTLOE
SALCOMBE
Penzance
HELSTON
ST MAWES
FALMOUTH
PORTHLEVEN
GILLAN
0 20 40 60 80 100 Kilometres
0 10 20 30 40 50 Miles

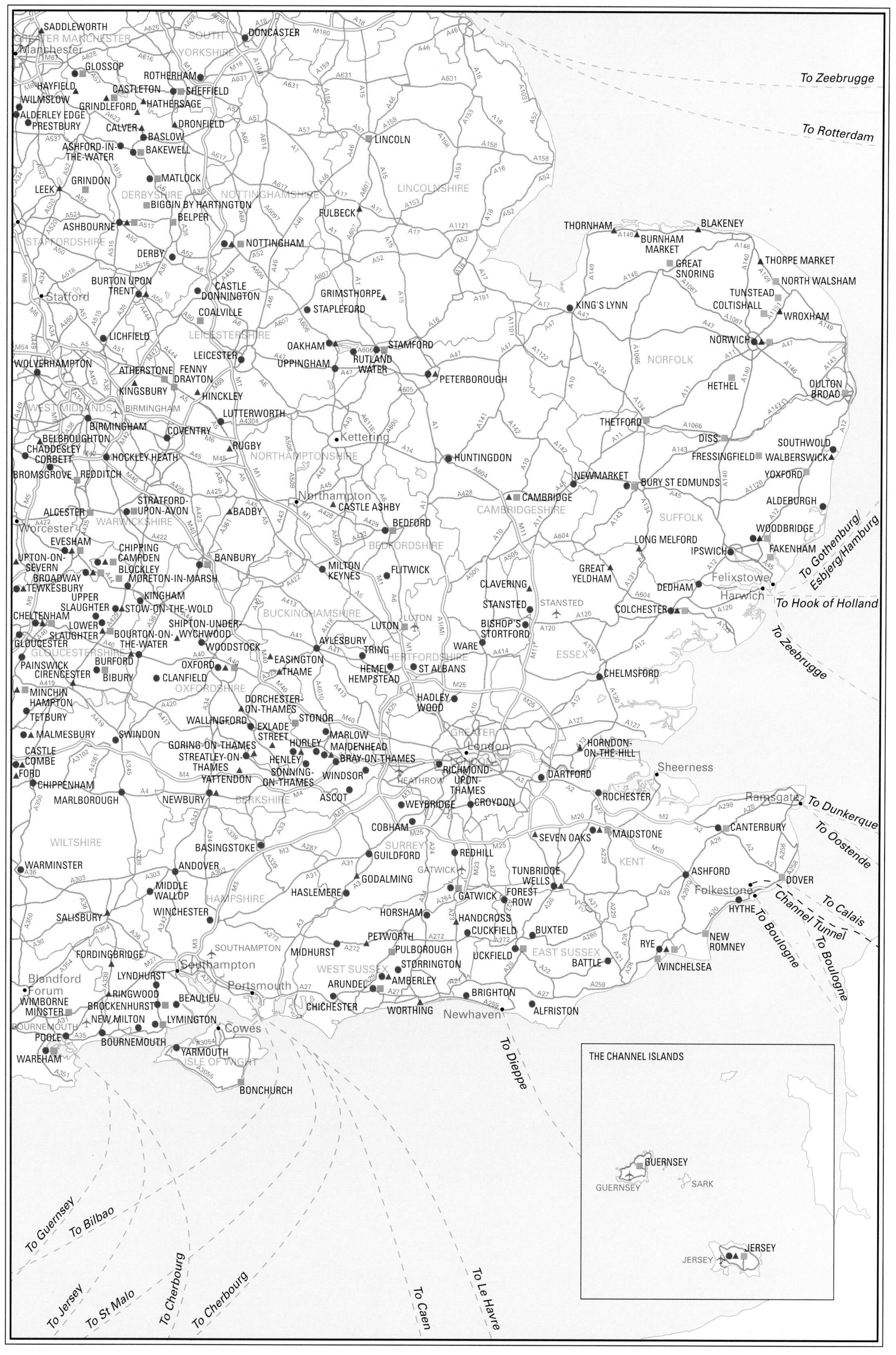

SADDLEWORTH
GREATER MANCHESTER
Manchester
SOUTH YORKSHIRE
DONCASTER
GLOSSOP
ROTHERHAM
HAYFIELD
WILMSLOW
CASTLETON
SHEFFIELD
GRINDLEFORD
HATHERSAGE
ALDERLEY EDGE
PRESTBURY
CALVER
DRONFIELD
BASLOW
ASHFORD-IN-THE-WATER
BAKEWELL
LINCOLN
GRINDON
MATLOCK
LEEK
DERBYSHIRE
NOTTINGHAMSHIRE
LINCOLNSHIRE
BIGGIN BY HARTINGTON
BELPER
FULBECK
ASHBOURNE
STAFFORDSHIRE
NOTTINGHAM
DERBY
BURTON UPON TRENT
CASTLE DONNINGTON
GRIMSTHORPE
Stafford
STAPLEFORD
COALVILLE
LICHFIELD
LEICESTERSHIRE
OAKHAM
STAMFORD
WOLVERHAMPTON
LEICESTER
UPPINGHAM
RUTLAND WATER
ATHERSTONE
FENNY DRAYTON
PETERBOROUGH
KINGSBURY
HINCKLEY
WEST MIDLANDS
BIRMINGHAM
LUTTERWORTH
COVENTRY
BELBROUGHTON
CHADDESLEY CORBETT
RUGBY
Kettering
HOCKLEY HEATH
NORTHAMPTONSHIRE
HUNTINGDON
BROMSGROVE
REDDITCH
STRATFORD-UPON-AVON
Northampton
CASTLE ASHBY
ALCESTER
BADBY
WARWICKSHIRE
Worcester
BEDFORD
BEDFORDSHIRE
EVESHAM
CHIPPING CAMPDEN
UPTON-ON-SEVERN
BLOCKLEY
BANBURY
MILTON KEYNES
FLITWICK
BROADWAY
MORETON-IN-MARSH
TEWKESBURY
UPPER SLAUGHTER
KINGHAM
STOW-ON-THE-WOLD
BUCKINGHAMSHIRE
CHELTENHAM
LOWER SLAUGHTER
SHIPTON-UNDER-WYCHWOOD
BOURTON-ON-THE-WATER
LUTON
GLOUCESTER
GLOUCESTERSHIRE
WOODSTOCK
AYLESBURY
TRING
HERTFORDSHIRE
EASINGTON
PAINSWICK
BURFORD
OXFORD
THAME
HEMEL HEMPSTEAD
ST ALBANS
CIRENCESTER
BIBURY
CLANFIELD
OXFORDSHIRE
MINCHIN HAMPTON
TETBURY
DORCHESTER-ON-THAMES
HADLEY WOOD
WALLINGFORD
STONOR
EXLADE STREET
MALMESBURY
SWINDON
MARLOW
MAIDENHEAD
GREATER London
CASTLE COMBE
GORING-ON-THAMES
HURLEY
HENLEY
BRAY-ON-THAMES
FORD
STREATLEY-ON-THAMES
SONNING-ON-THAMES
WINDSOR
HEATHROW
RICHMOND-UPON-THAMES
CHIPPENHAM
YATTENDON
MARLBOROUGH
NEWBURY
BERKSHIRE
ASCOT
WEYBRIDGE
CROYDON
WILTSHIRE
COBHAM
SURREY
BASINGSTOKE
GUILDFORD
REDHILL
WARMINSTER
ANDOVER
GATWICK
MIDDLE WALLOP
GODALMING
HASLEMERE
HAMPSHIRE
SALISBURY
WINCHESTER
HORSHAM
FORDINGBRIDGE
PETWORTH
SOUTHAMPTON
Southampton
MIDHURST
PULBOROUGH
WEST SUSSEX
STORRINGTON
LYNDHURST
Blandford Forum
RINGWOOD
Portsmouth
ARUNDEL
AMBERLEY
WIMBORNE MINSTER
BROCKENHURST
BEAULIEU
CHICHESTER
WORTHING
BRIGHTON
NEW MILTON
LYMINGTON
BOURNEMOUTH
Cowes
POOLE
BOURNEMOUTH
YARMOUTH
WAREHAM
ISLE OF WIGHT
BONCHURCH
Newhaven
To Dieppe
To Zeebrugge
To Rotterdam
THORNHAM
BLAKENEY
BURNHAM MARKET
GREAT SNORING
THORPE MARKET
NORTH WALSHAM
TUNSTEAD
COLTISHALL
KING'S LYNN
WROXHAM
NORWICH
NORFOLK
HETHEL
OULTON BROAD
THETFORD
DISS
SOUTHWOLD
FRESSINGFIELD
WALBERSWICK
NEWMARKET
BURY ST EDMUNDS
YOXFORD
CAMBRIDGE
CAMBRIDGESHIRE
ALDEBURGH
SUFFOLK
WOODBRIDGE
LONG MELFORD
IPSWICH
FAKENHAM
To Gothenburg/Esbjerg/Hamburg
GREAT YELDHAM
Felixstowe
DEDHAM
Harwich
CLAVERING
To Hook of Holland
STANSTED
STANSTED
COLCHESTER
BISHOP'S STORTFORD
WARE
ESSEX
To Zeebrugge
CHELMSFORD
HORNDON-ON-THE-HILL
Sheerness
DARTFORD
ROCHESTER
Ramsgate
To Dunkerque
CANTERBURY
To Oostende
SEVEN OAKS
MAIDSTONE
KENT
ASHFORD
TUNBRIDGE WELLS
DOVER
FOREST ROW
Folkestone
To Calais
HYTHE
Channel Tunnel
HANDCROSS
CUCKFIELD
BUXTED
NEW ROMNEY
To Boulogne
To Boulogne
UCKFIELD
EAST SUSSEX
RYE
BATTLE
WINCHELSEA
ALFRISTON
THE CHANNEL ISLANDS
GUERNSEY
SARK
GUERNSEY
JERSEY
JERSEY
To Guernsey
To Bilbao
To Jersey
To St Malo
To Cherbourg
To Cherbourg
To Caen
To Le Havre

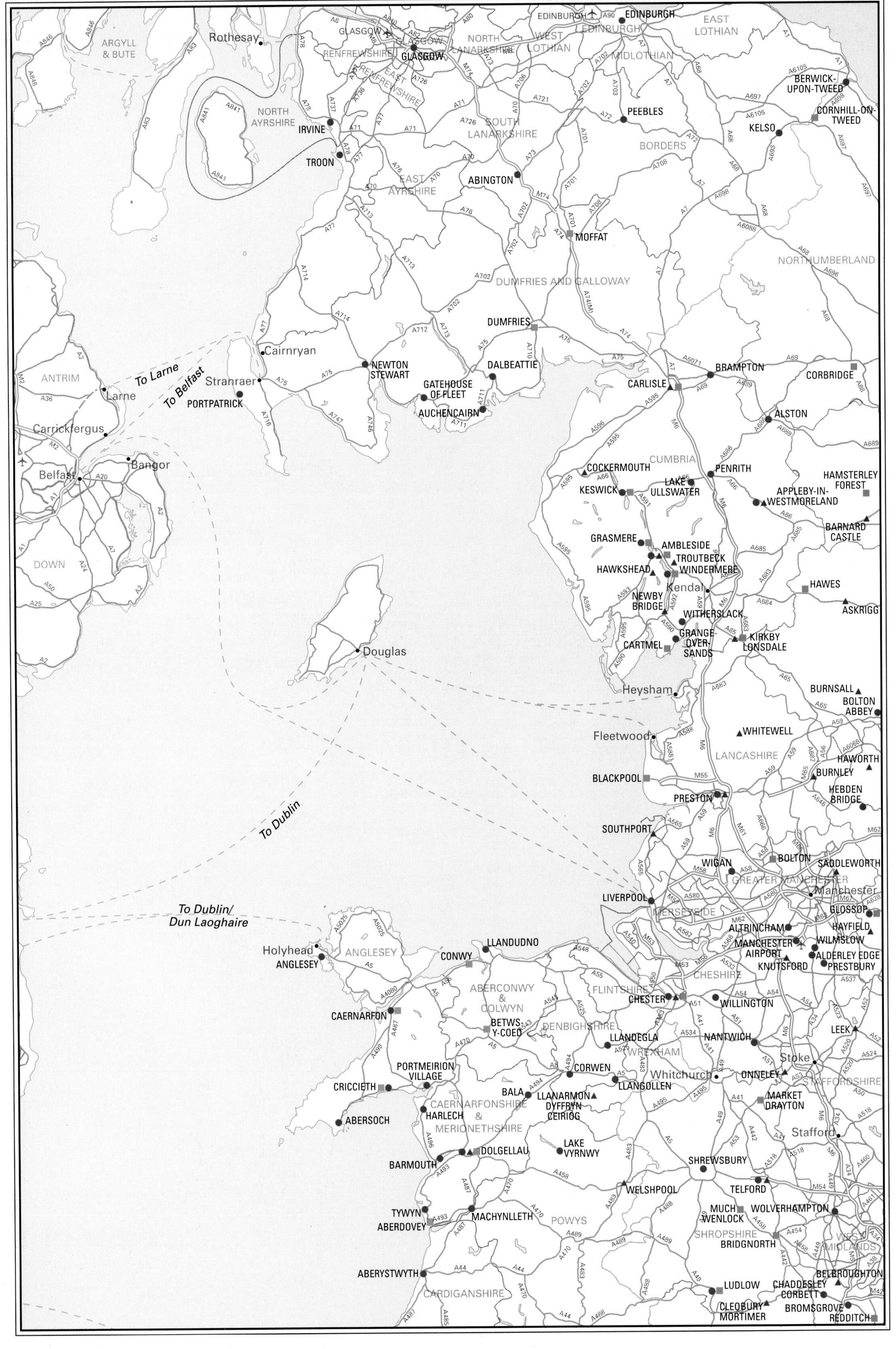

ARGYLL & BUTE
Rothesay
NORTH AYRSHIRE
EDINBURGH
EAST LOTHIAN
WEST LOTHIAN
MIDLOTHIAN
GLASGOW
RENFREWSHIRE
EAST RENFREWSHIRE
NORTH LANARKSHIRE
SOUTH LANARKSHIRE
BERWICK-UPON-TWEED
CORNHILL-ON-TWEED
PEEBLES
KELSO
BORDERS
IRVINE
TROON
EAST AYRSHIRE
ABINGTON
MOFFAT
NORTHUMBERLAND
DUMFRIES AND GALLOWAY
DUMFRIES
Cairnryan
NEWTON STEWART
DALBEATTIE
GATEHOUSE OF FLEET
AUCHENCAIRN
To Larne
To Belfast
Stranraer
PORTPATRICK
ANTRIM
Larne
Carrickfergus
Belfast
Bangor
DOWN
CARLISLE
BRAMPTON
CORBRIDGE
ALSTON
CUMBRIA
COCKERMOUTH
KESWICK
LAKE ULLSWATER
PENRITH
HAMSTERLEY FOREST
APPLEBY-IN-WESTMORELAND
BARNARD CASTLE
GRASMERE
AMBLESIDE
TROUTBECK
HAWKSHEAD
WINDERMERE
Kendal
HAWES
NEWBY BRIDGE
WITHERSLACK
ASKRIGG
CARTMEL
GRANGE-OVER-SANDS
KIRKBY LONSDALE
Douglas
Heysham
BURNSALL
BOLTON ABBEY
Fleetwood
WHITEWELL
LANCASHIRE
HAWORTH
BLACKPOOL
BURNLEY
HEBDEN BRIDGE
PRESTON
To Dublin
SOUTHPORT
BOLTON
SADDLEWORTH
WIGAN
GREATER MANCHESTER
LIVERPOOL
Manchester
MERSEYSIDE
GLOSSOP
To Dublin/ Dun Laoghaire
ALTRINCHAM
HAYFIELD
Holyhead
ANGLESEY
LLANDUDNO
CONWY
MANCHESTER AIRPORT
WILMSLOW
ALDERLEY EDGE
KNUTSFORD
PRESTBURY
CHESHIRE
ABERCONWY & COLWYN
FLINTSHIRE
CHESTER
WILLINGTON
CAERNARFON
BETWS-Y-COED
DENBIGHSHIRE
LLANDEGLA
NANTWICH
LEEK
WREXHAM
Stoke
PORTMEIRION VILLAGE
CORWEN
LLANGOLLEN
Whitchurch
ONNELEY
STAFFORDSHIRE
CRICCIETH
BALA
LLANARMON DYFFRYN CEIRIOG
MARKET DRAYTON
CAERNARFONSHIRE & MERIONETHSHIRE
ABERSOCH
HARLECH
Stafford
DOLGELLAU
LAKE VYRNWY
BARMOUTH
SHREWSBURY
WELSHPOOL
TELFORD
TYWYN
MACHYNLLETH
MUCH WENLOCK
WOLVERHAMPTON
ABERDOVEY
POWYS
SHROPSHIRE
BRIDGNORTH
WEST MIDLANDS
ABERYSTWYTH
BELBROUGHTON
CARDIGANSHIRE
LUDLOW
CHADDESLEY CORBETT
CLEOBURY MORTIMER
BROMSGROVE
REDDITCH

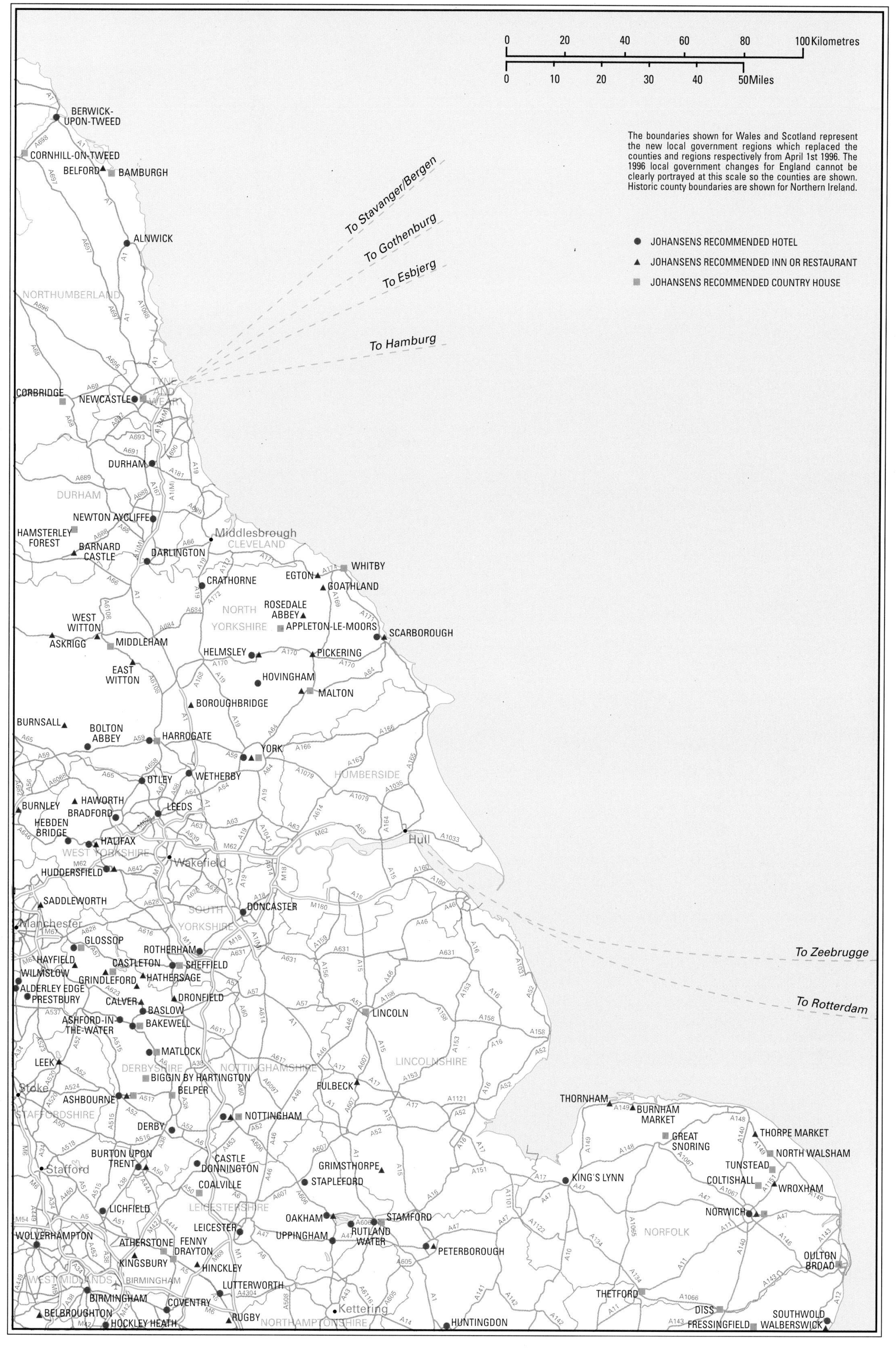
0 20 40 60 80 100 Kilometres
0 10 20 30 40 50 Miles
The boundaries shown for Wales and Scotland represent the new local government regions which replaced the counties and regions respectively from April 1st 1996. The 1996 local government changes for England cannot be clearly portrayed at this scale so the counties are shown. Historic county boundaries are shown for Northern Ireland.
JOHANSENS RECOMMENDED HOTEL
JOHANSENS RECOMMENDED INN OR RESTAURANT
JOHANSENS RECOMMENDED COUNTRY HOUSE
To Stavanger/Bergen
To Gothenburg
To Esbjerg
To Hamburg
To Zeebrugge
To Rotterdam
BERWICK-UPON-TWEED
CORNHILL-ON-TWEED
BELFORD
BAMBURGH
ALNWICK
NORTHUMBERLAND
TYNE AND WEAR
CORBRIDGE
NEWCASTLE
DURHAM
NEWTON AYCLIFFE
HAMSTERLEY FOREST
BARNARD CASTLE
DARLINGTON
Middlesbrough
CLEVELAND
WHITBY
EGTON
GOATHLAND
CRATHORNE
NORTH YORKSHIRE
ROSEDALE ABBEY
APPLETON-LE-MOORS
SCARBOROUGH
WEST WITTON
ASKRIGG
MIDDLEHAM
EAST WITTON
HELMSLEY
PICKERING
HOVINGHAM
MALTON
BOROUGHBRIDGE
BURNSALL
BOLTON ABBEY
HARROGATE
YORK
HUMBERSIDE
OTLEY
WETHERBY
BURNLEY
HAWORTH
BRADFORD
LEEDS
HEBDEN BRIDGE
HALIFAX
Hull
WEST YORKSHIRE
Wakefield
HUDDERSFIELD
SADDLEWORTH
DONCASTER
SOUTH YORKSHIRE
Manchester
GLOSSOP
ROTHERHAM
HAYFIELD
CASTLETON
SHEFFIELD
WILMSLOW
GRINDLEFORD
HATHERSAGE
ALDERLEY EDGE
PRESTBURY
DRONFIELD
CALVER
BASLOW
ASHFORD-IN-THE-WATER
BAKEWELL
LINCOLN
MATLOCK
LEEK
DERBYSHIRE
NOTTINGHAMSHIRE
LINCOLNSHIRE
BIGGIN BY HARTINGTON
FULBECK
Stoke
ASHBOURNE
BELPER
STAFFORDSHIRE
NOTTINGHAM
THORNHAM
BURNHAM MARKET
DERBY
THORPE MARKET
GREAT SNORING
NORTH WALSHAM
BURTON UPON TRENT
CASTLE DONNINGTON
Stafford
GRIMSTHORPE
TUNSTEAD
STAPLEFORD
KING'S LYNN
COLTISHALL
WROXHAM
COALVILLE
LICHFIELD
LEICESTERSHIRE
OAKHAM
STAMFORD
NORWICH
LEICESTER
WOLVERHAMPTON
UPPINGHAM
RUTLAND WATER
NORFOLK
ATHERSTONE
FENNY DRAYTON
PETERBOROUGH
KINGSBURY
HINCKLEY
OULTON BROAD
WEST MIDLANDS
BIRMINGHAM
LUTTERWORTH
THETFORD
COVENTRY
Kettering
BELBROUGHTON
RUGBY
DISS
SOUTHWOLD
HOCKLEY HEATH
NORTHAMPTONSHIRE
HUNTINGDON
FRESSINGFIELD
WALBERSWICK

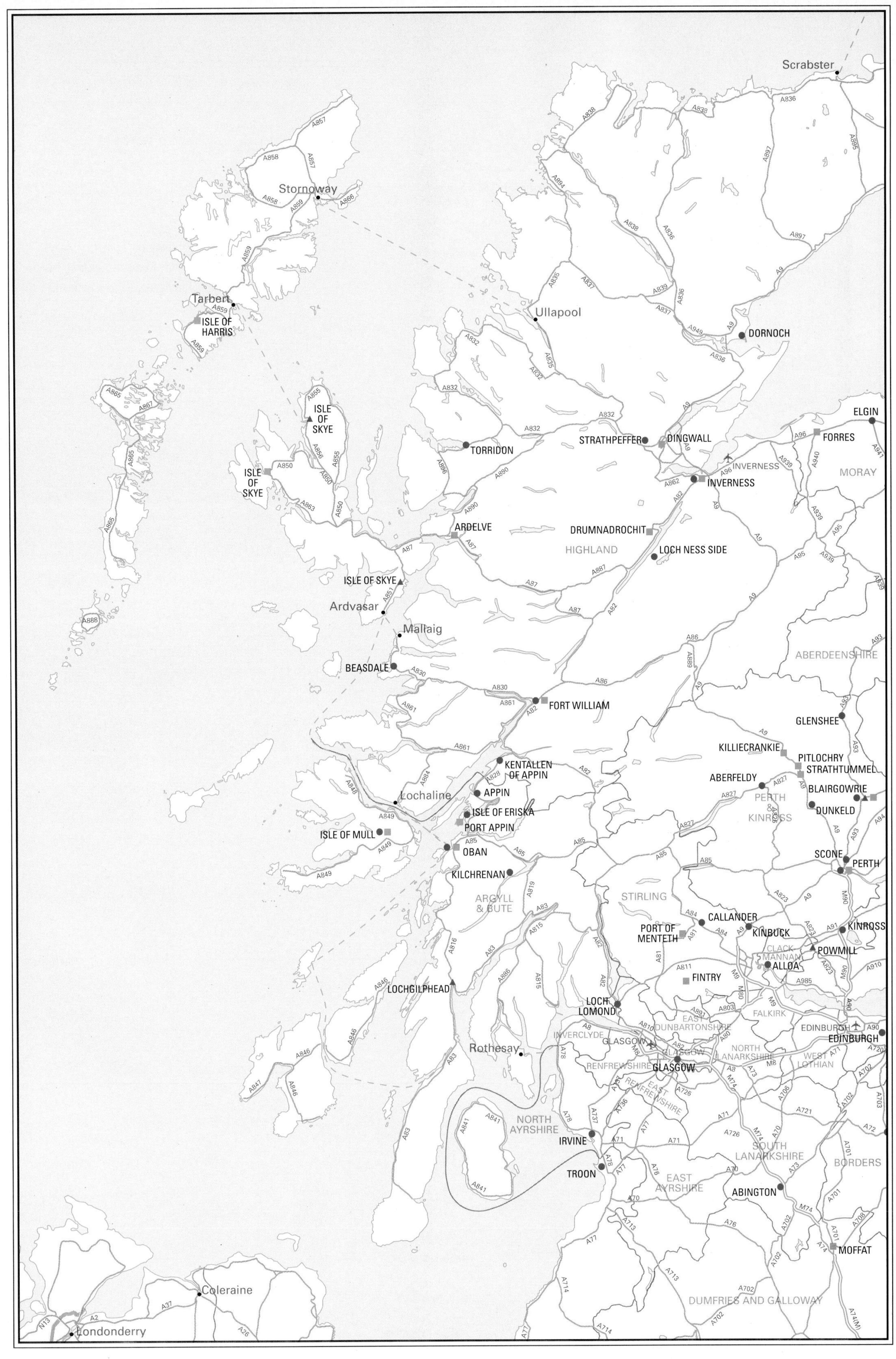
Scrabster
Stornoway
Tarbert
ISLE OF HARRIS
Ullapool
DORNOCH
ISLE OF SKYE
ELGIN
STRATHPEFFER
DINGWALL
FORRES
TORRIDON
INVERNESS
MORAY
ARDELVE
DRUMNADROCHIT
HIGHLAND
LOCH NESS SIDE
Ardvasar
Mallaig
ABERDEENSHIRE
BEASDALE
FORT WILLIAM
GLENSHEE
KILLIECRANKIE
PITLOCHRY
STRATHTUMMEL
KENTALLEN OF APPIN
ABERFELDY
BLAIRGOWRIE
APPIN
Lochaline
PERTH
KINROSS
DUNKELD
ISLE OF ERISKA
PORT APPIN
ISLE OF MULL
OBAN
SCONE
KILCHRENAN
ARGYLL & BUTE
STIRLING
CALLANDER
PORT OF MENTETH
KINBUCK
CLACKMANNAN
POWMILL
ALLOA
FINTRY
LOCHGILPHEAD
LOCH LOMOND
FALKIRK
EAST DUNBARTONSHIRE
EDINBURGH
INVERCLYDE
GLASGOW
NORTH LANARKSHIRE
WEST LOTHIAN
Rothesay
RENFREWSHIRE
EAST RENFREWSHIRE
NORTH AYRSHIRE
IRVINE
SOUTH LANARKSHIRE
BORDERS
TROON
EAST AYRSHIRE
ABINGTON
MOFFAT
Coleraine
DUMFRIES AND GALLOWAY
Londonderry

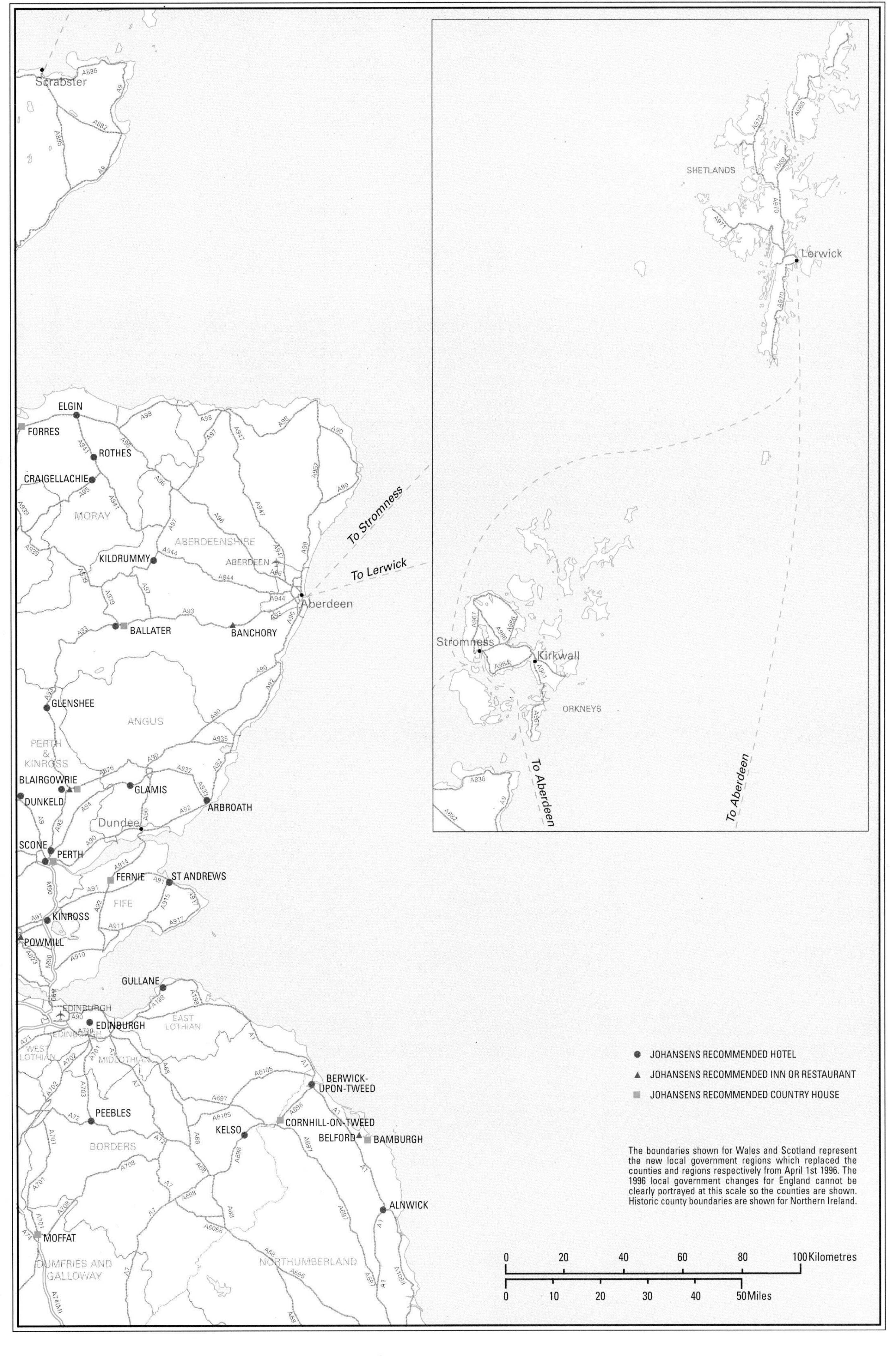

Scrabster
SHETLANDS
Lerwick
ELGIN
FORRES
ROTHES
CRAIGELLACHIE
MORAY
ABERDEENSHIRE
KILDRUMMY
ABERDEEN
Aberdeen
To Stromness
To Lerwick
BALLATER
BANCHORY
Stromness
Kirkwall
ORKNEYS
To Aberdeen
To Aberdeen
GLENSHEE
ANGUS
PERTH & KINROSS
BLAIRGOWRIE
DUNKELD
GLAMIS
ARBROATH
Dundee
SCONE
PERTH
FERNIE
ST ANDREWS
FIFE
KINROSS
POWMILL
GULLANE
EDINBURGH
EDINBURGH
EAST LOTHIAN
WEST LOTHIAN
MIDLOTHIAN
BERWICK-UPON-TWEED
CORNHILL-ON-TWEED
PEEBLES
KELSO
BELFORD
BAMBURGH
BORDERS
ALNWICK
MOFFAT
DUMFRIES AND GALLOWAY
NORTHUMBERLAND
JOHANSENS RECOMMENDED HOTEL
JOHANSENS RECOMMENDED INN OR RESTAURANT
JOHANSENS RECOMMENDED COUNTRY HOUSE
The boundaries shown for Wales and Scotland represent the new local government regions which replaced the counties and regions respectively from April 1st 1996. The 1996 local government changes for England cannot be clearly portrayed at this scale so the counties are shown. Historic county boundaries are shown for Northern Ireland.
0 20 40 60 80 100 Kilometres
0 10 20 30 40 50 Miles

To enable you to use your 1997 Johansens Recommended Hotels Guide more effectively the following pages of indexes contain a wealth of useful information about the hotels featured in the guide. As well as listing the hotels alphabetically by region and by county, the indexes also show at a glance which hotels offer certain specialised facilities.

The indexes are as follows:

- By region
- By county
- With a heated indoor swimming pool
- With a golf course on site
- With shooting arranged
- With salmon or trout fishing on site
- With health/fitness facilities
- With childcare facilities
- With conference facilities for 250 delegates or more
- Relais et Châteaux members
- Small Luxury Hotels of the World members
- Pride of Britain members
- Exclusive Hotels members
- Taste of Wales members
- Welsh Gold Collection members
- Johansens Preferred Partners
- Hotels accepting Johansens Gift Vouchers
- Hotels accepting Johansens Privilege Card

1997 Johansens Recommended Hotels listed by region

LONDON

ENGLAND

WALES

SCOTLAND

IRELAND

CHANNEL ISLANDS

1997 Johansens Recommended Hotels by county

1997 Johansens Recommended Hotels by county continued...

Hotel	Location	Page
Norton House Hotel	Edinburgh	411
Morayshire		
Rothes Glen	Rothes	443
Peebleshire		
Cringletie House Hotel	Peebles	439
Perthshire		
Ballathie House Hotel	Perth	440
Cromlix House	Kinbuck	433
Dalmunzie House	Glenshe	420
Farleyer House Hotel	Aberfeldy	392
Kinloch House Hotel	Blairgowrie	400
Kinnaird	Dunkeld	405
Murrayshall Country House Hotel	Scone	445
Parklands Hotel	Perth	441
Roman Camp Hotel	Callander	401
Renfrewshire		
Gleddoch House	Glasgow	417
Ross-shire		
Coul House	Strathpeffer	446
Roxburghshire		
Ednam House Hotel	Kelso	428
Sunlaws House Hotel	Kelso	429
Stirlingshire		
The Gean House	Alloa	394
Sutherland		
Carnegie Outpost at Skibo Castle	Dornoch	404
Wigtownshire		
Kirroughtree Hotel	Newton Stewart	437
Knockinaam Lodge	Portpatrick	442
IRELAND		
Co Antrim (N.Ireland)		
Galgorm Manor	Ballymena	450
Co Clare		
Dromoland Castle	Newmarket-on-Fergus	462
Co Down (N.Ireland)		
Culloden Hotel	Belfast	451
Co Dublin		
The Hibernian Hotel	Dublin	456
Co Galway		
Renvyle House	Connemara	454
Co Kerry		
Aghadoe Heights Hotel	Killarney	459
Muckross Park	Killarney	460
Co Kildare		
Barberstown Castle	Dublin	455
Kildare Hotel and Country Club	Dublin (Straffan)	457
Co Londonderry (N. Ireland)		
Radisson Row Park Hotel	Limavady	461
Co Mayo		
Ashford Castle	Cong	453
Co Monaghan		
Nuremore Hotel	Carrickmacross	452
Co Wexford		
Kelly's Resort Hotel	Rosslare	464
Marlfield House	Gorey	458
Co Wicklow		
Hunters Hotel	Rathnew	463
Tinakilly House Hotel	Wicklow	465
CHANNEL ISLANDS		
Jersey		
The Atlantic Hotel	Jersey	468
Château La Chaire	Jersey	469
Hotel L'Horizon	Jersey	470
Hotel La Place	Jersey	471
Longueville Manor	Jersey	472

Hotels with a heated indoor swimming pool

Swimming pools at these hotels are open all year round

ENGLAND

Appleby Manor Country House Hotel ... 49
Ashdown Park ... 153
Belstead Brook Manor Hotel ... 184
Billesley Manor ... 296
Bishopstrow House ... 328
Brandshatch Place Hotel ... 137
Bridgewood Manor Hotel ... 265
Budock Vean Golf and Country Club ... 148
Careys Manor ... 98
Carlton Hotel ... 85
Charingworth Manor ... 124
Cheltenham Park ... 114
Chevin Lodge ... 250
Chewton Glen ... 234
Cliveden ... 215
Combe Grove Manor Hotel ... 66
Devonshire Arms Country House Hotel ... 84
Down Hall Hotel ... 83
Ettington Park Hotel ... 297
The Evesham Hotel ... 145
Five Lakes Hotel, Golf and Country Club ... 128
Foley Lodge Hotel ... 237
The Garrack Hotel ... 275
The Glebe at Barford ... 314
Hackness Grange ... 279
Hallgarth Golf & Country Club ... 135
Hanbury Manor ... 326
Hartwell House ... 59
Headlam Hall Hotel ... 136
Hoar Cross Hall Health Spa Resort ... 204
Hollington House Hotel ... 238
Horsted Place ... 321
Hythe Imperial ... 181
Ilsington Hotel ... 182
Kilhey Court ... 332
Linden Hall Hotel ... 239
Lower Slaughter Manor ... 207
Lucknam Park ... 69
The Lygon Arms ... 97
The Manor House Hotel ... 141
Mickleover Court ... 141
Mill House & Lombard Room ... 80
Nailcote Hall ... 131
The Nare Hotel ... 324
Nutfield Prioy ... 263
The Osborne ... 316
Oulton Hall ... 201
The Palace Hotel ... 317
Park Farm Hotel and Leisure ... 245
Passage House Hotel ... 242
Passford House ... 213
Penmere Manor ... 151
The Pheasant ... 171
The Polurrian Hotel ... 172
Pontlands Park Hotel ... 113
The Priory ... 170
Puckrup Hall ... 314
Redworth Hall Hotel and Country Club ... 243
Rhinefield House ... 99
The Richmond Gate Hotel and Restaurant ... 264
Rowhill Grange ... 138
Rowton Castle ... 284
Rowton Hall ... 121
The Royal Berkshire Hotel ... 53
Seckford Hall ... 345
Slaley Hall ... 240
Soar Mill Cove Hotel ... 278
Sopwell House Hotel and Country Club ... 274
The Spa Hotel ... 320
Sprowston Manor ... 247
Stapleford Park ... 291
The Swallow Hotel ... 82
Swallow Royal Hotel ... 93
Treglos Hotel ... 254
Tylney Hall ... 63
Wood Hall ... 330
Woolacombe Bay Hotel ... 348
The Wordsworth Hotel ... 160

WALES

Allt-Yr-Ynys Hotel ... 356
Bodysgallen Hall ... 377
Celtic Manor ... 383
Conrah Country Hotel ... 358
The Court Hotel ... 384
The Cwrt Bleddyn Hotel ... 390
Gwesty Seiont Manor ... 366
Miskin Manor ... 368
Penally Abbey ... 388
St Tudno Hotel ... 378
Trearddur Bay Hotel ... 360
Warpool Court ... 386

SCOTLAND

The Cally Palace Hotel ... 415
Cameron House ... 435
Carnegie Outpost at Skibo Castle ... 404
Isle of Eriska ... 426
Kingsmills Hotel ... 424
Mansion House Hotel, Elgin ... 413

IRELAND

Aghadoe Heights Hotel ... 459
Culloden Hotel ... 451
Kelly's Resort Hotel ... 464
Kildare Hotel and Country Club ... 457
Nuremore Hotel ... 452
Radisson Row Park ... 461

CHANNEL ISLANDS

The Atlantic Hotel ... 468
Hotel L'Horizon ... 470

Hotels with golf

Hotels with golf on site

ENGLAND

Ashdown Park ... 153
Bagden Hall ... 178
Cheddington Court ... 112
Chewton Glen ... 234
Donnington Valley ... 236
Five Lakes Hotel, Golf and Country Club ... 128
Hallgarth Hotel ... 135
Hanbury Manor ... 326
Hawkstone Park ... 283
Hintlesham Hall ... 185
Hythe Imperial Hotel ... 181
The Manor House ... 108
Nailcote Hall ... 131
New Hall ... 81
Oakley Court ... 341
Oulton Hall ... 201
The Palace Hotel ... 317
Pengethley Manor ... 267
Puckrup Hall ... 314
Seckford Hall ... 345
Slaley Hall ... 240
Stocks ... 173
Studley Priory ... 252
Tylney Hall ... 63
Welcombe Hotel ... 299

WALES

Celtic Manor ... 383
Soughton Hall ... 389

SCOTLAND

The Cally Palace Hotel ... 415
Cameron House ... 435
Carnegie Outpost at Skibo Castle ... 404
Dalmunzie House ... 420
Gleddoch House ... 417
Letham Grange ... 396
Murrayshall Country House Hotel ... 445
Sunlaws House ... 429

IRELAND

Ashford Castle ... 453
Dromoland Castle ... 462
Kelly's Resort ... 464
Kildare Hotel and Country Club ... 457
Nuremore Hotel ... 452
Radisson Row Park ... 461
Renvyle House ... 454

Hotels with shooting

Shooting on site, to which guests have access, can be arranged

ENGLAND

Bishopstrow House ... 328
Boars Head Hotel ... 165
Chilston Park ... 217
Cliveden ... 215
Combe Grove Manor Hotel ... 66
Crabwall Manor ... 119
Crathorne Hall ... 132
Danesfield House ... 224
Ettington Park Hotel ... 297
Hawkstone Park ... 283
Headlam Hall Hotel ... 136
Langar Hall ... 248
Linden Hall Hotel ... 239
Nunsmere Hall ... 120
Oakley Court ... 341
Pengethley Manor ... 267
The Priest House ... 109
Puckrup Hall ... 314
Redworth Hall Hotel and Country Club ... 243
Rookery Hall ... 233
Slaley Hall ... 240
Stapleford Park ... 291
Studley Priory ... 252
Tillmouth Park ... 78
Tylney Hall ... 63
Welcombe Hotel ... 299
Whitley Hall ... 282
Wood Hall ... 330
Wood Norton Hall ... 146
Wyck Hill House ... 295

WALES

Allt-Yr-Ynys Hotel ... 356
Bodidris Hall ... 376
Lake Vyrnwy ... 375

SCOTLAND

Cameron House ... 435
Carnegie Outpost at Skibo Castle ... 404
Cromlix House ... 433
Dalmunzie House ... 420
Gleddoch House ... 417
Johnstounburn House Hotel ... 410
Kinnaird ... 405
Sunlaws House Hotel ... 429

Hotels with fishing

Guests may obtain rights to fishing within the hotel grounds

ENGLAND

42 The Calls ... 198
The Arundell Arms ... 195
Bishopstrow House ... 328
The Boars Head Hotel ... 165
Callow Hall ... 54
Chevin Lodge ... 250
Chilston Park ... 217
Coulsdon Manor ... 133
Crathorne Hall Hotel ... 132
Devonshire Arms Country House Hotel ... 84
Ettington Park ... 297
Gibbon Bridge Country House Hotel ... 262
Hackness Grange ... 279
Hambleton Hall ... 249
Hartwell House ... 59
The Haycock ... 257
Headlam Hall Hotel ... 136
Holme Chase Hotel ... 55

Hotels with health/fitness facilities

At the following hotels there are health/fitness facilities available

Hotels with childcare facilities

Comprehensive childcare facilities are available, namely crèche, babysitting and organised activities for children of all ages

Hotels with conference facilities

These hotels can accommodate theatre-style conferences for 250 delegates or over

Relais et Châteaux members

Small Luxury Hotels of the World members

Pride of Britain members

Exclusive Hotels UK members

Taste of Wales members

Welsh Gold Collection members

Johansens Preferred Partners

Hotels Accepting Johansens Gift Vouchers

Terms & Conditions available on request

LONDON

ENGLAND

WALES

SCOTLAND

IRELAND

Hotels Accepting Johansens Privilege Card

Terms & Conditions available on request

LONDON

ENGLAND

WALES

SCOTLAND

IRELAND

CHANNEL ISLANDS

Play the role of Hotel Inspector

At the back of this book you will notice a quantity of Guest Survey Forms. If you have had an enjoyable stay at one of our recommended hotels, or alternatively you have been in some way disappointed, please complete one of these forms and send it to us FREEPOST.

These reports essentially complement the assessments made by our team of professional inspectors, continually monitoring the standards of hospitality in every establishment in our guides. Guest Survey reports also have an important influence on the selection of nominations for our annual awards for excellence.

Guest Survey Report

Your own Johansens 'inspection' gives reliability to our guides and assists in the selection of Award Nominations

Name/location of hotel: ______________________ Page No: ________

Date of visit: ______________________

Name & address of guest: ______________________

______________________ Postcode: ________

Please tick one box in each category below:	*Excellent*	*Good*	*Disappointing*	*Poor*
Bedrooms				
Public Rooms				
Restaurant/Cuisine				
Service				
Welcome/Friendliness				
Value For Money				

PLEASE return your Guest Survey Report form!

Occasionally we may allow other reputable organisations to write with offers which may be of interest.
If you prefer not to here from them, tick this box ☐

To: Johansens, FREEPOST (CB264), 175-179 St John Street, London EC1B 1JQ

Guest Survey Report

Your own Johansens 'inspection' gives reliability to our guides and assists in the selection of Award Nominations

Name/location of hotel: ______________________ Page No: ________

Date of visit: ______________________

Name & address of guest: ______________________

______________________ Postcode: ________

Please tick one box in each category below:	*Excellent*	*Good*	*Disappointing*	*Poor*
Bedrooms				
Public Rooms				
Restaurant/Cuisine				
Service				
Welcome/Friendliness				
Value For Money				

PLEASE return your Guest Survey Report form!

Occasionally we may allow other reputable organisations to write with offers which may be of interest.
If you prefer not to here from them, tick this box ☐

To: Johansens, FREEPOST (CB264), 175-179 St John Street, London EC1B 1JQ

Order Coupon

To order Johansens guides, simply indicate which publications you require by putting the quantity(ies) in the boxes provided. Choose you preferred method of payment and return this coupon (NO STAMP REQUIRED). You may also place your order using FREEPHONE 0800 269397 or by fax on 0171 490 2538.

❑ I enclose a cheque for £______________ payable to Biblios PDS Ltd (Johansens book distributor).

❑ I enclose my order on company letterheading, please invoice me. (UK companies only)

❑ Please debit my credit/charge card account (please tick)

❑ MASTERCARD ❑ VISA ❑ DINERS ❑ AMEX ❑ SWITCH

Switch Issue Number

Card No

Signature ______________ Expiry Date ______________

Name (Mr/Mrs/Miss) ______________

Address ______________

______________ Postcode ______________

(We aim to despatch your order within 10 days, but please allow 28 days for delivery)

Post free to:
JOHANSENS, FREEPOST (CB264), HORSHAM, WEST SUSSEX RH13 8ZA

Occasionally we may allow reputable organisations to write to you with offers which may interest you. If you prefer not to hear from them, tick this box ❑

save £12

	PRICE	QTY	TOTAL
The Complete Collection of 4 Johansens Guides ~~£51.80~~	£39.00		
The Collection in a Presentation Boxed Set ~~£55.80~~	£44.00		
The 2 CD ROMS ~~£49.90~~	£39.00		
Johansens Recommended Hotels in Great Britain & Ireland 1997	£18.95		
Johansens Recommended Country Houses and Small Hotels in GB & Ireland 1997	£9.95		
Johansens Recommended Inns with Restaurants in GB & Ireland 1997	£9.95		
Johansens Recommended Hotels in Europe 1997	£12.95		
CD ROM Hotels, Country Houses & Inns in GB & Ireland 1997	£29.95		
CD ROM Hotels in Europe (incl. Business Meeting Venues)	£19.95		
HISTORIC HOUSES CASTLES & GARDENS, Published March 1997*	£7.99		
Handling & Package	£4.00		£4.00
	TOTAL	£	

CALL THE JOHANSENS CREDIT CARD ORDER SERVICE FREE ☎ **0800 269397**

Outside the UK add £3 for each single guide ordered, or £5 for a set or boxed set to cover additional postage. PRICES VALID UNTIL 31/12/97 J19

Order Coupon

To order Johansens guides, simply indicate which publications you require by putting the quantity(ies) in the boxes provided. Choose you preferred method of payment and return this coupon (NO STAMP REQUIRED). You may also place your order using FREEPHONE 0800 269397 or by fax on 0171 490 2538.

❑ I enclose a cheque for £______________ payable to Biblios PDS Ltd (Johansens book distributor).

❑ I enclose my order on company letterheading, please invoice me. (UK companies only)

❑ Please debit my credit/charge card account (please tick)

❑ MASTERCARD ❑ VISA ❑ DINERS ❑ AMEX ❑ SWITCH

Switch Issue Number

Card No

Signature ______________ Expiry Date ______________

Name (Mr/Mrs/Miss) ______________

Address ______________

______________ Postcode ______________

(We aim to despatch your order within 10 days, but please allow 28 days for delivery)

Post free to:
JOHANSENS, FREEPOST (CB264), HORSHAM, WEST SUSSEX RH13 8ZA

Occasionally we may allow reputable organisations to write to you with offers which may interest you. If you prefer not to hear from them, tick this box ❑

save £12

	PRICE	QTY	TOTAL
The Complete Collection of 4 Johansens Guides ~~£51.80~~	£39.00		
The Collection in a Presentation Boxed Set ~~£55.80~~	£44.00		
The 2 CD ROMS ~~£49.90~~	£39.00		
Johansens Recommended Hotels in Great Britain & Ireland 1997	£18.95		
Johansens Recommended Country Houses and Small Hotels in GB & Ireland 1997	£9.95		
Johansens Recommended Inns with Restaurants in GB & Ireland 1997	£9.95		
Johansens Recommended Hotels in Europe 1997	£12.95		
CD ROM Hotels, Country Houses & Inns in GB & Ireland 1997	£29.95		
CD ROM Hotels in Europe (incl. Business Meeting Venues)	£19.95		
HISTORIC HOUSES CASTLES & GARDENS, Published March 1997*	£7.99		
Handling & Package	£4.00		£4.00
	TOTAL	£	

CALL THE JOHANSENS CREDIT CARD ORDER SERVICE FREE ☎ **0800 269397**

Outside the UK add £3 for each single guide ordered, or £5 for a set or boxed set to cover additional postage. PRICES VALID UNTIL 31/12/97 J19

Guest Survey Report

Your own Johansens 'inspection' gives reliability to our guides and assists in the selection of Award Nominations

Name/location of hotel: ______________________ Page No: __________

Date of visit: ______________________

Name & address of guest: ______________________

______________________ Postcode: __________

Please tick one box in each category below:	*Excellent*	*Good*	*Disappointing*	*Poor*
Bedrooms				
Public Rooms				
Restaurant/Cuisine				
Service				
Welcome/Friendliness				
Value For Money				

PLEASE return your Guest Survey Report form!

Occasionally we may allow other reputable organisations to write with offers which may be of interest.
If you prefer not to here from them, tick this box ☐

To: Johansens, FREEPOST (CB264), 175-179 St John Street, London EC1B 1JQ

Guest Survey Report

Your own Johansens 'inspection' gives reliability to our guides and assists in the selection of Award Nominations

Name/location of hotel: ______________________ Page No: __________

Date of visit: ______________________

Name & address of guest: ______________________

______________________ Postcode: __________

Please tick one box in each category below:	*Excellent*	*Good*	*Disappointing*	*Poor*
Bedrooms				
Public Rooms				
Restaurant/Cuisine				
Service				
Welcome/Friendliness				
Value For Money				

PLEASE return your Guest Survey Report form!

Occasionally we may allow other reputable organisations to write with offers which may be of interest.
If you prefer not to here from them, tick this box ☐

To: Johansens, FREEPOST (CB264), 175-179 St John Street, London EC1B 1JQ

Order Coupon

To order Johansens guides, simply indicate which publications you require by putting the quantity(ies) in the boxes provided. Choose you preferred method of payment and return this coupon (NO STAMP REQUIRED). You may also place your order using FREEPHONE 0800 269397 or by fax on 0171 490 2538.

❑ I enclose a cheque for £______________ payable to Biblios PDS Ltd (Johansens book distributor).

❑ I enclose my order on company letterheading, please invoice me. (UK companies only)

❑ Please debit my credit/charge card account (please tick)

❑ MASTERCARD ❑ VISA ❑ DINERS ❑ AMEX ❑ SWITCH

Switch Issue Number

Card No

Signature ______________________ Expiry Date ________________

Name (Mr/Mrs/Miss) ______________________________

Address ______________________________

______________________ Postcode ________________

(We aim to despatch your order within 10 days, but please allow 28 days for delivery)

Post free to:

JOHANSENS, FREEPOST (CB264), HORSHAM, WEST SUSSEX RH13 8ZA

Occasionally we may allow reputable organisations to write to you with offers which may interest you. If you prefer not to hear from them, tick this box ❑

CALL THE JOHANSENS CREDIT CARD ORDER SERVICE FREE ☎ **0800 269397**

save £12

	PRICE	QTY	TOTAL
The Complete Collection of 4 Johansens Guides ~~£51.80~~	£39.00		
The Collection in a Presentation Boxed Set ~~£55.80~~	£44.00		
The 2 CD ROMS ~~£49.90~~	£39.00		
Johansens Recommended Hotels in Great Britain & Ireland 1997	£18.95		
Johansens Recommended Country Houses and Small Hotels in GB & Ireland 1997	£9.95		
Johansens Recommended Inns with Restaurants in GB & Ireland 1997	£9.95		
Johansens Recommended Hotels in Europe 1997	£12.95		
CD ROM Hotels, Country Houses & Inns in GB & Ireland 1997	£29.95		
CD ROM Hotels in Europe (incl. Business Meeting Venues)	£19.95		
HISTORIC HOUSES CASTLES & GARDENS, Published March 1997*	£7.99		
Handling & Package	£4.00		£4.00
	TOTAL	**£**	

Outside the UK add £3 for each single guide ordered, or £5 for a set or boxed set to cover additional postage. PRICES VALID UNTIL 31/12/97 J19

Order Coupon

To order Johansens guides, simply indicate which publications you require by putting the quantity(ies) in the boxes provided. Choose you preferred method of payment and return this coupon (NO STAMP REQUIRED). You may also place your order using FREEPHONE 0800 269397 or by fax on 0171 490 2538.

❑ I enclose a cheque for £______________ payable to Biblios PDS Ltd (Johansens book distributor).

❑ I enclose my order on company letterheading, please invoice me. (UK companies only)

❑ Please debit my credit/charge card account (please tick)

❑ MASTERCARD ❑ VISA ❑ DINERS ❑ AMEX ❑ SWITCH

Switch Issue Number

Card No

Signature ______________________ Expiry Date ________________

Name (Mr/Mrs/Miss) ______________________________

Address ______________________________

______________________ Postcode ________________

(We aim to despatch your order within 10 days, but please allow 28 days for delivery)

Post free to:

JOHANSENS, FREEPOST (CB264), HORSHAM, WEST SUSSEX RH13 8ZA

Occasionally we may allow reputable organisations to write to you with offers which may interest you. If you prefer not to hear from them, tick this box ❑

CALL THE JOHANSENS CREDIT CARD ORDER SERVICE FREE ☎ **0800 269397**

save £12

	PRICE	QTY	TOTAL
The Complete Collection of 4 Johansens Guides ~~£51.80~~	£39.00		
The Collection in a Presentation Boxed Set ~~£55.80~~	£44.00		
The 2 CD ROMS ~~£49.90~~	£39.00		
Johansens Recommended Hotels in Great Britain & Ireland 1997	£18.95		
Johansens Recommended Country Houses and Small Hotels in GB & Ireland 1997	£9.95		
Johansens Recommended Inns with Restaurants in GB & Ireland 1997	£9.95		
Johansens Recommended Hotels in Europe 1997	£12.95		
CD ROM Hotels, Country Houses & Inns in GB & Ireland 1997	£29.95		
CD ROM Hotels in Europe (incl. Business Meeting Venues)	£19.95		
HISTORIC HOUSES CASTLES & GARDENS, Published March 1997*	£7.99		
Handling & Package	£4.00		£4.00
	TOTAL	**£**	

Outside the UK add £3 for each single guide ordered, or £5 for a set or boxed set to cover additional postage. PRICES VALID UNTIL 31/12/97 J19

Guest Survey Report

Your own Johansens 'inspection' gives reliability to our guides and assists in the selection of Award Nominations

Name/location of hotel: ______________________ Page No: __________

Date of visit: ______________________

Name & address of guest: ______________________

______________________ Postcode: __________

Please tick one box in each category below:	*Excellent*	*Good*	*Disappointing*	*Poor*
Bedrooms				
Public Rooms				
Restaurant/Cuisine				
Service				
Welcome/Friendliness				
Value For Money				

PLEASE return your Guest Survey Report form!

Occasionally we may allow other reputable organisations to write with offers which may be of interest.
If you prefer not to here from them, tick this box ☐

To: Johansens, FREEPOST (CB264), 175-179 St John Street, London EC1B 1JQ

Guest Survey Report

Your own Johansens 'inspection' gives reliability to our guides and assists in the selection of Award Nominations

Name/location of hotel: ______________________ Page No: __________

Date of visit: ______________________

Name & address of guest: ______________________

______________________ Postcode: __________

Please tick one box in each category below:	*Excellent*	*Good*	*Disappointing*	*Poor*
Bedrooms				
Public Rooms				
Restaurant/Cuisine				
Service				
Welcome/Friendliness				
Value For Money				

PLEASE return your Guest Survey Report form!

Occasionally we may allow other reputable organisations to write with offers which may be of interest.
If you prefer not to here from them, tick this box ☐

To: Johansens, FREEPOST (CB264), 175-179 St John Street, London EC1B 1JQ

Order Coupon

To order Johansens guides, simply indicate which publications you require by putting the quantity(ies) in the boxes provided. Choose you preferred method of payment and return this coupon (NO STAMP REQUIRED). You may also place your order using FREEPHONE 0800 269397 or by fax on 0171 490 2538.

❑ I enclose a cheque for £______________ payable to Biblios PDS Ltd (Johansens book distributor).

❑ I enclose my order on company letterheading, please invoice me. (UK companies only)

❑ Please debit my credit/charge card account (please tick)

❑ MASTERCARD ❑ VISA ❑ DINERS ❑ AMEX ❑ SWITCH

Switch Issue Number

Card No

Signature ______________________ Expiry Date ______________

Name (Mr/Mrs/Miss) ______________________

Address ______________________

______________________ Postcode ______________

(We aim to despatch your order within 10 days, but please allow 28 days for delivery)

Post free to:

JOHANSENS, FREEPOST (CB264), HORSHAM, WEST SUSSEX RH13 8ZA

Occasionally we may allow reputable organisations to write to you with offers which may interest you. If you prefer not to hear from them, tick this box ❑

CALL THE JOHANSENS CREDIT CARD ORDER SERVICE FREE ☎ **0800 269397**

save £12

	PRICE	QTY	TOTAL
The Complete Collection of 4 Johansens Guides ~~£51.80~~	£39.00		
The Collection in a Presentation Boxed Set ~~£55.80~~	£44.00		
The 2 CD ROMS ~~£49.90~~	£39.00		
Johansens Recommended Hotels in Great Britain & Ireland 1997	£18.95		
Johansens Recommended Country Houses and Small Hotels in GB & Ireland 1997	£9.95		
Johansens Recommended Inns with Restaurants in GB & Ireland 1997	£9.95		
Johansens Recommended Hotels in Europe 1997	£12.95		
CD ROM Hotels, Country Houses & Inns in GB & Ireland 1997	£29.95		
CD ROM Hotels in Europe (incl. Business Meeting Venues)	£19.95		
HISTORIC HOUSES CASTLES & GARDENS, Published March 1997*	£7.99		
Handling & Package	£4.00		£4.00
	TOTAL	**£**	

Outside the UK add £3 for each single guide ordered, or £5 for a set or boxed set to cover additional postage. PRICES VALID UNTIL 31/12/97 J19

Order Coupon

To order Johansens guides, simply indicate which publications you require by putting the quantity(ies) in the boxes provided. Choose you preferred method of payment and return this coupon (NO STAMP REQUIRED). You may also place your order using FREEPHONE 0800 269397 or by fax on 0171 490 2538.

❑ I enclose a cheque for £______________ payable to Biblios PDS Ltd (Johansens book distributor).

❑ I enclose my order on company letterheading, please invoice me. (UK companies only)

❑ Please debit my credit/charge card account (please tick)

❑ MASTERCARD ❑ VISA ❑ DINERS ❑ AMEX ❑ SWITCH

Switch Issue Number

Card No

Signature ______________________ Expiry Date ______________

Name (Mr/Mrs/Miss) ______________________

Address ______________________

______________________ Postcode ______________

(We aim to despatch your order within 10 days, but please allow 28 days for delivery)

Post free to:

JOHANSENS, FREEPOST (CB264), HORSHAM, WEST SUSSEX RH13 8ZA

Occasionally we may allow reputable organisations to write to you with offers which may interest you. If you prefer not to hear from them, tick this box ❑

CALL THE JOHANSENS CREDIT CARD ORDER SERVICE FREE ☎ **0800 269397**

save £12

	PRICE	QTY	TOTAL
The Complete Collection of 4 Johansens Guides ~~£51.80~~	£39.00		
The Collection in a Presentation Boxed Set ~~£55.80~~	£44.00		
The 2 CD ROMS ~~£49.90~~	£39.00		
Johansens Recommended Hotels in Great Britain & Ireland 1997	£18.95		
Johansens Recommended Country Houses and Small Hotels in GB & Ireland 1997	£9.95		
Johansens Recommended Inns with Restaurants in GB & Ireland 1997	£9.95		
Johansens Recommended Hotels in Europe 1997	£12.95		
CD ROM Hotels, Country Houses & Inns in GB & Ireland 1997	£29.95		
CD ROM Hotels in Europe (incl. Business Meeting Venues)	£19.95		
HISTORIC HOUSES CASTLES & GARDENS, Published March 1997*	£7.99		
Handling & Package	£4.00		£4.00
	TOTAL	**£**	

Outside the UK add £3 for each single guide ordered, or £5 for a set or boxed set to cover additional postage. PRICES VALID UNTIL 31/12/97 J19